Cooking Light

ANNUAL
RECIPES 2009

Oxmoor
House.

Our Year at *Cooking Light*.

Cooking Light Annual Recipes has a beautifully simple premise— to collect between hard covers every recipe the magazine has run in the past year.

That simplicity contrasts with the bustle of producing a year's worth of magazine issues. Yet all those story conferences, taste testings, photo shoots, and line edits are worth the effort: As the magazine enters its 22nd year, 12 million people turn to *Cooking Light* every month for the latest in how to eat smart, be fit, and live well.

Of course, as editor in chief, I know that our signature better-for-you recipes and trademark photography have everything to do with that success. In fact, we tested more than 6,000 recipes in our Test Kitchens last year, and ran more than 800 of them.

▲ The annual walnut harvest is a reason to celebrate for this California family. Their menu commemorates the beginning of another harvest by spotlighting the ingredient in dishes redolent with crisp, toasty flavor (page 294).

Knowing the magazine so well, I want to share some of the highlights that have made 2008 special, both for *Cooking Light* and for this cookbook:

• *Cooking Light* readers crave nutrition news. "Body Boosters" explores the relationship between various nutrients and overall good health. Ten terrific recipes point to tasty ways to nourish every part of your body (page 19).

• Food is an indelible marker of place, and we bring readers authentic recipes from some of America's most distinctive locations. We visited Vermont's Morse Farm Sugar Shack (page 83). The recipes developed by New Englander Barbara Lauterbach—a frequent contributor to the magazine—run the gamut from a piquant salad to a satisfyingly sweet snack cake.

• The magazine's popular "Cooking Class" series focused this year on the fundamental techniques every home chef should master. Among the top topics: Grilling (page 180), Stir-frying (page 289), and Roasting (page 366).

• Our seasonal cookbooks are both perennial reader favorites. "The Summer Cookbook" (page 161) shows how to capitalize on the choicest ingredients, from apricots to baby squash to beefsteak tomatoes. "The Holiday Cookbook" (page 339) offers a selection of great appetizers, entrees, side dishes, and desserts. It even includes all-new recipes for making Christmas gifts from the kitchen.

• Food can evoke powerful associations. In one of our most unforgettable stories ever (page 390), we asked some of our favorite contributors to share their favorite holiday recipes and the memories associated with them.

Looking at this edition of *Cooking Light Annual Recipes* gives me a chance to appreciate the variety of things we've done this year. This year's volume will have pride of place in my pantry, and I hope it does in yours as well.

Mary Kay Culpepper
Editor in Chief

◄ Maple syrup in both the cake and the frosting of Maple-Pecan Snack Cake yield tasty results (page 84).

▼ Make your grill an outdoor kitchen with dishes such as Grilled Vegetable Salad (page 183).

◄ Turn to our "Cooking Class" section on stir-frying (page 289) and master the basics of this versatile fast and fresh way to cook.

3

Our Favorite Recipes

Not all recipes are created equal. At *Cooking Light.*, only those that have passed muster with our Test Kitchens staff and food editors—not an easy crowd to please—make it onto the pages of our magazine. We rigorously test each recipe, often two or three times, to ensure that they're healthy, reliable, and taste as good as they possibly can. So which of our recipes are our favorites? They're the dishes that are the most memorable. They're the ones readers keep calling and writing about, the ones our staff whip up for their own families and friends.

◄ **Cool, Creamy Chocolate Dessert** *(page 156)*
Cream cheese and chocolate pudding are layered over a shortbread crust and chilled to a cool, creamy delight. What's not to love?

▼ **Heirloom Tomato Salad with Herbs and Capers**
(page 224)
The colors of a summer sunset, dressed simply with herbs, tangy feta, and capers, this simple salad of mixed tomatoes shows off all the flavors of the season.

◄**Cherry-Pistachio Wedding Cookies**
(page 278)
The surprise tang of dried cherries and lightly salted pistachios give these melt-in-your-mouth buttery cookies an addictive twist.

▼ **Pecan Sticky Rolls**
(page 306)
Tender spirals of yeast dough loaded with butter, cinnamon, and pecans—no one will ever guess that these decadent rolls are the trim cousins of the diet-busting original recipe. These rolls are an all-time Test Kitchens favorite.

◄**Caramelized Onion and Shiitake Soup with Gruyere-Blue Cheese Toasts** *(page 328)*
Onions cooked to sweet golden brown and a generous amount of sautéed shiitake mushrooms give this soup depth and richness.

Tarte Tatin (*page 331*)
This iconic dessert was allegedly created by
the Tatin sisters of France's Loire Valley. Legend
is that while trying to repair a baking error, they
ended up with this upside-down dessert of flaky
pastry and golden-hued apples bathed in caramel.

Our Favorite Recipes

◄ **Roasted Potatoes with North Indian Spices**
(page 99)
Red jacket potatoes go global with a coating of mustard seeds, chilies, garlic, and garam masala. Roasted until tender, browned, and aromatic, fresh lime and green herbs take the humble potato to new heights.

▼ **Caribbean Shrimp Salad with Lime Vinaigrette**
(page 29)
This easy, no-cook recipe took grand prize in our 2008 *Cooking Light* Ultimate Reader Recipe Contest in the entrée category. It can be prepared in less than 30 minutes.

Our Favorite Recipes

▶ **Potato Chips with Blue Cheese Dip** *(page 94)*
Crispy, hot potato chips with rich, tangy blue cheese for dipping—could it get any better? Not according to our Test Kitchens. This recipe received our highest rating.

▼ **Sliders with Shallot-Dijon Relish** *(page 180)*
Sliders are mini-burgers—and in this recipe, mini-burgers with maximum taste. Grilled sirloin patties start things off right, and dollops of buttery shallot relish and Parker House rolls finish the sandwiches off in fine style.

Red-Cooked Short Ribs *(page 33)*
Redolent with ginger, orange, sherry, and
cinnamon, these ribs are cooked long and low.
The result is meltingly tender beef glazed in
its own aromatic sauce.

Maple Grilled Salmon *(page 202)*
Buttery salmon marinated in zesty orange and sweet maple, chargrilled and juicy—this is the perfect summer dinner. Only six ingredients add up to big flavor.

Our Favorite Recipes

◀ **Butterscotch Pudding**
(page 21)
Creamy spoonfuls of old-fashioned flavor—dark brown sugar, butter, and vanilla meld into a deceptively rich taste. As an added bonus to this yum factor, each serving packs a good dose of calcium.

▼ **Parmesan Flans with Tomatoes and Basil**
(page 207)
Use a variety of colorful tomatoes including red, yellow, orange, and green to make this elegant dish more visually appealing.

Our Favorite Recipes

▶ **Grilled Peaches over Arugula with Goat Cheese and Prosciutto** *(page 162)*
Beautiful and simple, this bountiful salad makes the most of fresh summer peaches. Lightly grilling the fruit caramelizes the natural sugars and heightens their flavors.

▼ **Risotto with Italian Sausage, Caramelized Onions, and Bitter Greens** *(page 51)*
Creamy risotto sets the stage for savory sausage, sweet onions, and the lovely counterbalance of bitter greens.

Blueberry and Blackberry Galette with Cornmeal Crust *(page 192)*
A unanimous favorite in our Test Kitchens, this free-form crust stuffed with ripe summer berries has the additional appeal of looking difficult while being quite easy to make.

Chocolate-Mint Bars *(page 88)*
It's hard to improve on the classic pairing of mint and
chocolate—but we did it. Our dreamy bars start with a layer of
dense chocolate cake, topped with a slather of cool mint, and capped
with dark chocolate. It's enough to make a Girl Scout jealous.

Our Favorite Recipes

◄ **Shrimp Étouffée** (*page 215*)
Deep, rich sauce spiked with garlic and red pepper, onions, celery, and herbs, loaded with plump shrimp—our much-lightened version of the classic drew raves from our Test Kitchens and readers alike.

▼ **Beef Tenderloin Steaks with Shiitake Mushroom Sauce** (*page 100*)
Tenderloin is so good on its own, any topping has to be spectacular—and this simple sauce of shiitakes, butter, and herbs fills the bill. The earthy flavor and silky mouthfeel of the shiitakes pair beautifully with the tender beef.

Our Favorite Recipes

Sweet and Sour Cipollini Onions *(page 31)*
Caramelized onions, raisins, pine nuts, and red wine vinegar make savory harmony in this Venetian-inspired side dish.

Cardamom-Lime Sweet Rolls *(page 40)*
Famous in Danish pastries, cardamom finds a happy home in these tender rolls. A tangy, lime-spiked glaze keeps these treats moist and flavorful.

Crab Cakes with Roasted Vegetables and Tangy Butter Sauce *(page 96)*
Fresh lump crabmeat shines in these toothsome cakes. A touch of parsley and red onion keeps the flavors bright while a crispy coating of panko delivers a satisfying crunch.

Steamed Pork Buns *(page 130)*
These warm, soft buns with savory shredded pork filling are an at-home version of a popular street food in China. We awarded these buns our highest Test Kitchens rating.

Beef Tenderloin with Mustard and Herbs *(page 165)*
Coating grilled tenderloin steaks with chopped herbs and Dijon mustard adds a fresh, new dimension of flavor.

Spiked Peach Limeade Granita *(page 209)*
Fresh summer peaches meet the rum and mint goodness of Mojitos in this cooling treat.

Thai Chicken in Cabbage Leaves *(page 276)*
This piquant dish is all about contrasts: spicy, warm chicken filling with sweet herbs, wrapped in cold, crunchy cabbage leaves.

Peanut Butter and Chocolate Cookies *(page 338)*
Like popcorn and butter or apple and cinnamon, chocolate and peanut butter are an enduringly irresistible combination. Drizzle the icing in whatever patterns you like.

Limoncello *(page 362)*
This homemade Italian liqueur is as tasty as any you will find on the Amalfi coast. Limoncello is good ice cold on its own, in a lemon drop martini, with sparkling wine, or splashed over a bowl of fresh fruit.

New Potatoes with Roasted Garlic Vinaigrette *(page 366)*
While raw garlic is pungent, roasted garlic is sweet and mild with a buttery texture. Serve this warm twist on potato salad as a side dish with steak or roast chicken.

Roasted Butternut Squash and Shallot Soup *(page 369)*
Spicy fresh ginger complements the sweetness of roasted winter squash and shallots in this straightforward recipe.

▼ Classic Crème Caramel *(page 327)*
Great crème caramel is defined by two things: firm yet smooth sweet custard topped with a bittersweet layer of amber caramel. This version does its heritage proud.

contents

©2008 by Oxmoor House, Inc.
Book Division of Southern Progress Corporation
P.O. Box 2262, Birmingham, Alabama 35201-2262

ISBN-13: 978-0-8487-3236-3
ISBN-10: 0-8487-3236-7
ISSN: 1091-3645

Printed in the United States of America
First printing 2008

Be sure to check with your health-care provider before making any changes in your diet.

Oxmoor House, Inc.
Editor in Chief: Nancy Fitzpatrick Wyatt
Executive Editor: Katherine M. Eakin
Art Director: Keith McPherson
Managing Editor: Allison Long Lowery

Cooking Light. Annual Recipes 2009
Editor: Rachel Quinlivan, R.D.
Copy Chief: L. Amanda Owens
Photography Director: Jim Bathie
Director of Production: Laura Lockhart
Senior Production Manager: Greg A. Amason

Contributors:
Designer: Carol Damsky
Copy Editors: Jasmine Hodges, Kathryn G. Stroud
Proofreaders: Adrienne S. Davis, Catherine C. Fowler, Carmine B. Loper
Indexer: Mary Ann Laurens
Interns: Anne-Harris Jones, Shea Staskowski, Lauren Wiygul

To order additional publications, call 1-800-765-6400.
For more books to enrich your life, visit **oxmoorhouse.com**

To search, savor, and share thousands of recipes, visit **myrecipes.com**

Cover: *Crab Cakes with Roasted Vegetables and Tangy Butter Sauce* (page 96)
Page 1: *Spiked Peach Limeade Granita* (page 209)

Cooking Light.

Editor in Chief: Mary Kay Culpepper
Executive Editor: Billy R. Sims
Creative Director: Susan Waldrip Dendy
Managing Editor: Maelynn Cheung
Senior Food Editor: Alison Mann Ashton
Senior Editor: Phillip Rhodes
Projects Editor: Mary Simpson Creel, M.S., R.D.
Food Editor: Ann Taylor Pittman
Associate Food Editors: Timothy Q. Cebula, Kathy Kitchens Downie, R.D., Julianna Grimes
Associate Editors: Cindy Hatcher, Brandy Rushing
Test Kitchens Director: Vanessa Taylor Johnson
Assistant Test Kitchens Director: Tiffany Vickers
Senior Food Stylist: Kellie Gerber Kelley
Food Stylist: M. Kathleen Kanen
Test Kitchens Professionals: Mary Drennen Ankar, SaBrina Bone, Kathryn Conrad, Eunice Mun, Mike Wilson
Art Director: Maya Metz Logue
Associate Art Directors: Fernande Bondarenko, J.Shay McNamee
Senior Designer: Brigette Mayer
Senior Photographer: Randy Mayor
Senior Photo Stylist: Cindy Barr
Photo Stylists: Jan Gautro, Leigh Ann Ross
Studio Assistant: Hayden Patton
Copy Chief: Maria Parker Hopkins
Assistant Copy Chief: Susan Roberts
Copy Editor: Johannah Gilman Paiva
Copy Researcher: Michelle Gibson Daniels
Production Manager: Liz Rhoades
Production Editor: Hazel R. Eddins
Production Assistant: Lauri Short
CookingLight.com Editor: Kim Cross
Administrative Coordinator: Carol D. Johnson
Editorial Assistants: Jason Horn, Rita A. Jackson
Interns: Kelsey Blackwell, Maggie Gordon, MaryAnne Gragg, Holly V. Kapherr, Hallie Marshall, Deb Wise

Body Boosters

How what you eat can improve your health, mind, and appearance

FOR MANY, THE NEW YEAR MEANS revamping exercise regimens, improving appearance, reading more books, taking on a new hobby, and improving dietary habits. Great news is that following good-for-you food goals will help your whole body—from your skin to your brain—so you can tackle those other resolutions with ease. "The best way to have healthy hair, eyes, and skin is to take good overall care of yourself. That means eating well," says David L. Katz, MD, MPH, director of the Yale Prevention Research Center at Yale University. So whether it's your heart, brain, bones, eyes, skin, or hair you seek to nurture, there are foods up to the task.

"The more colors you get into your diet, the better," Katz says. A variety of fruits and vegetables supplies antioxidants and vitamins that are most powerful when working together. Daily servings of whole grains, lean protein, and dairy round out your body's needs. A diet rich in fresh, whole foods, full of colors and rich textures, satisfies with abundant flavor, and nourishes every part of your body.

Spicy Stir-Fried Tofu with Snow Peas, Peanut Butter, and Mushrooms

One serving of this vegetarian entrée gives a boost to skin and hair with all the vitamin C and about 15 percent of a day's worth of folate and vitamin E.

- 1 (14-ounce) package extrafirm tofu, drained and cut into 1-inch cubes
- 2 teaspoons canola oil
- ¾ pound snow peas, trimmed
- 1 cup red bell pepper strips
- ¾ cup water, divided
- ½ cup sliced green onions
- 2 teaspoons minced peeled fresh ginger
- 2 garlic cloves, minced
- 3 cups sliced shiitake mushrooms (about 8 ounces)
- 2 tablespoons reduced-sodium tamari
- 2 tablespoons creamy peanut butter
- 1 teaspoon cornstarch
- 2 teaspoons Sriracha (hot chile sauce)
- ¼ teaspoon salt

❶ Place tofu on several layers of paper towels. Cover with additional paper towels; let stand 5 minutes.
❷ Heat oil in a large nonstick skillet over medium-high heat. Add tofu to pan; cook 7 minutes or until lightly browned, gently turning occasionally. Remove from pan; keep warm. Add snow peas, bell pepper, ¼ cup water, and next 3 ingredients to pan; stir-fry 3 minutes. Add mushrooms; stir-fry 2 minutes.
❸ Combine remaining ½ cup water, tamari, and remaining ingredients in a small bowl; stir well. Add tamari mixture and tofu to pan; cook 1 minute or until thickened, stirring constantly. Yield: 4 servings (serving size: 1½ cups).

CALORIES 212 (37% from fat); FAT 8.7g (sat 1.4g, mono 3.7g, poly 3g); PROTEIN 13.1g; CARB 21.5g; FIBER 4.7g; CHOL 0mg; IRON 3.6mg; SODIUM 639mg; CALC 84mg

QUICK & EASY • MAKE AHEAD
Simple Clam Chowder

The protein in the milk benefits hair and skin, and the vitamin B12 from the clams and B6 from the potatoes nourish hair. Garnish with additional fresh thyme.

- 2 bacon slices
- 2 cups chopped onion
- 1¼ cups chopped celery
- ½ teaspoon salt
- ½ teaspoon dried thyme
- 2 garlic cloves, minced
- 6 (6½-ounce) cans chopped clams, undrained
- 5 cups diced peeled baking potato (about 1 pound)
- 4 (8-ounce) bottles clam juice
- 1 bay leaf
- 3 cups fat-free milk
- ½ cup all-purpose flour (about 2¼ ounces)

❶ Cook bacon in a large Dutch oven over medium heat until crisp. Remove bacon from pan, reserving 1 teaspoon drippings in pan. Crumble bacon; set aside. Add onion and next 4 ingredients to pan; cook 4 minutes or until vegetables are tender.
❷ Drain clams, reserving liquid. Add clam liquid, potato, clam juice, and bay leaf to pan; bring to a boil. Reduce heat, and simmer 15 minutes or until potato is tender. Discard bay leaf.
❸ Combine milk and flour, stirring with a whisk until smooth. Add flour mixture to pan; bring to a boil. Cook 12 minutes or until thick, stirring constantly. Add clams; cook 2 minutes. Sprinkle with bacon. Yield: 12 servings (serving size: 1 cup).

CALORIES 257 (10% from fat); FAT 2.9g (sat 0.6g, mono 0.6g, poly 0.7g); PROTEIN 28.5g; CARB 27.9g; FIBER 2g; CHOL 67mg; IRON 26.6mg; SODIUM 475mg; CALC 242mg

Eating for Your Health

For Silky Skin & Hair

Antioxidants like lycopene and vitamin C, as well as soy protein and omega-3 fatty acids, help keep skin glowing. Antioxidants have long been the rage in topical skin care, but those same nutrients work even better from the inside out. When skin (the body's largest organ) is exposed to the sun's rays, free radicals can develop, Katz explains. "These free radicals attack the skin and impair blood flow to the area, causing premature aging. Antioxidants fight that process."

Vitamin C, found in citrus fruits, facilitates collagen production, a critical component for vibrant skin. Another antioxidant, lycopene, found in foods like canned tomatoes and red grapefruit juice, also promotes skin health. Tofu is a good option since its omega-3 fatty acids help regenerate new skin cells and reduce inflammation, while its soy protein has been shown to boost collagen.

Shiny, healthy hair starts with the vitality of cells in the hair follicle, where hair is manufactured, says Katz. Eat foods high in calcium and quality protein like eggs, dairy, or fish such as in Simple Clam Chowder (page 19) and Spicy Stir-Fried Tofu with Snow Peas, Peanut Butter, and Mushrooms (page 19). Eggs also provide biotin, a structural component of both bone and hair. Vitamins B6, B12, and folate nourish follicle cells, too.

Eat For Your Eyes

According to a study published in the *Archives of Ophthalmology,* people who ate two servings of fish weekly benefited from an almost 50 percent decrease in the risk of age-related macular degeneration (AMD), says Emily Chew, MD, deputy director of the division of epidemiology and clinical research at the National Eye Institute. Eggs, leafy greens, broccoli, winter squash, and Brussels sprouts all contain the antioxidants lutein and zeaxanthin (both associated with eye health), as well as vitamins C and E, zinc, and beta-carotene.

Build Better Bones

Calcium, vitamin D, and phosphorus work together to build strong bones. Even though green leafy and cruciferous vegetables (like spinach and broccoli) contain calcium, the body absorbs it best from dairy products, says Joan Lappe, PhD, RN, a bone health researcher and professor at Creighton University. Dairy products offer a package deal: they are abundant in phosphorous, and vitamin D added to milk and dairy products aids in calcium absorption. Some nondairy foods high in calcium include canned salmon, sardines, and calcium-fortified firm tofu.

Greens are still good bone foods, however. Broccoli, kale, and bok choy may provide little calcium, but they offer plenty of vitamin K. Research is showing promise that vitamin K—or some antioxidant or phytochemical in foods high in the vitamin—boosts bone mineralization.

Heart Helpers

Whole grains, fatty fish, and fresh fruits and vegetables are the keys to keeping your heart in prime condition.

A recent review of seven studies showed that two and a half servings of whole grains per day reduced heart attack and stroke risk by 21 percent, according to lead author Philip Mellen, MD, MS, then an assistant professor at the Wake Forest School of Medicine. Whole grains are rich in antioxidants, especially vitamin E (also found in almonds, peanuts, and green leafy vegetables), which helps maintain healthy blood vessels. And soluble fiber from fruits, vegetables, and nuts helps lower harmful LDL cholesterol and control weight, both of which have a positive impact on heart health.

Further cut your risk of a heart attack by eating fish high in omega-3 polyunsaturated fats like salmon, mackerel, or rainbow trout. Omega-3s make platelets in the blood less sticky, reducing clotting and the likelihood of a heart attack.

Brain Boosters

Omega-3 fatty acids and whole grains are good for your heart—and they're good for your brain and mental health, too. "People who are heart healthy are brain healthy," says Joseph S. Kass, MD, assistant professor of neurology at Baylor College of Medicine.

Kristen E. D'Anci, PhD, a research psychologist in the Nutrition and Neurocognition Laboratory at Tufts University and professor of psychology at Tufts, notes, "Diets rich in vitamins C and E are consistently associated with lower levels of cognitive impairment in aging." Abundant in fruits, vitamin C may also reduce the risk of stroke.

Additionally, vitamins B12, C, E, and folate may play a direct role in keeping your mind sharp. Research shows that B12 (found in lean protein like turkey) and folate (found in many grains fortified with the vitamin) help improve memory and lower the risk of Alzheimer's disease. They may also help people over age 60 with learning, attention, and response speed, according to study results from Tufts University.

Orange-Cranberry Wheat Germ Muffins

These muffins are at their best warm, so reheat briefly if you make ahead. Wheat germ is an excellent source of vitamin E.

- 1½ cups all-purpose flour (about 6¾ ounces)
- ½ cup raw wheat germ
- ½ cup sweetened dried cranberries
- 1 teaspoon baking powder
- ½ teaspoon baking soda
- ½ teaspoon ground cinnamon
- ¼ teaspoon salt
- ⅛ teaspoon ground nutmeg
- ¾ cup packed brown sugar
- ¼ cup canola oil
- 1 teaspoon grated orange rind
- ½ cup fresh orange juice
- 2 large eggs, lightly beaten
- Cooking spray
- 1 tablespoon turbinado sugar

① Preheat oven to 375°.
② Lightly spoon flour into dry measuring cups; level with a knife. Combine flour and next 7 ingredients in a large bowl; stir with a whisk. Make a well in center of mixture.
③ Combine brown sugar and next 4 ingredients; stir with a whisk. Add egg mixture to flour mixture; stir just until combined. Spoon batter into 12 muffin cups coated with cooking spray. Sprinkle with turbinado sugar. Bake at 375° for 17 minutes or until muffins spring back when touched in center. Yield: 1 dozen (serving size: 1 muffin).

CALORIES 197 (26% from fat); FAT 5.8g (sat 0.6g, mono 3.1g, poly 1.6g); PROTEIN 3.4g; CARB 33.8g; FIBER 1.2g; CHOL 35mg; IRON 1.7mg; SODIUM 149mg; CALC 54mg

Butternut Caramel Flan

- Cooking spray
- ⅓ cup sugar
- 3 tablespoons water
- 1 teaspoon light-colored corn syrup
- 4 cups cubed peeled butternut squash
- ½ cup sugar
- ½ cup 2% reduced-fat milk
- ⅓ cup egg substitute
- 1 teaspoon vanilla extract
- ¼ teaspoon ground ginger
- ¼ teaspoon ground cinnamon
- ⅛ teaspoon salt
- 4 large eggs, lightly beaten

① Preheat oven to 325°.
② Coat 6 (6-ounce) custard cups or ramekins with cooking spray; set aside.
③ Combine ⅓ cup sugar, 3 tablespoons water, and syrup in a small, heavy saucepan over medium-high heat; cook until sugar dissolves, stirring gently to dissolve sugar evenly. Continue cooking 11 minutes or until golden (do not stir). Immediately pour sugar mixture into prepared custard cups, tipping quickly to coat bottoms of cups.
④ Place squash in a large saucepan; cover with water. Bring to a boil; cover and cook 12 minutes or until very tender. Drain in a colander over a bowl, reserving 3 tablespoons cooking liquid. Place squash and reserved cooking liquid in a blender or food processor. Remove center piece of blender lid (to allow steam to escape); secure blender lid on blender. Place a clean towel over opening in blender lid (to avoid splatters); blend until smooth, scraping sides of bowl. Place pureed squash, ½ cup sugar, and remaining ingredients in a large bowl; stir with a whisk. Pour mixture evenly into prepared cups. Place cups in a 13 x 9-inch baking pan; add hot water to pan to a depth of 1 inch. Bake at 325° for 1 hour or until a knife inserted in center comes out clean. Remove cups from pan; cool on a wire rack 15 minutes. Lightly cover, and chill 4 hours or overnight.

⑤ Loosen edges of custards with a knife or rubber spatula. Place a dessert plate, upside down, on top of each cup; invert onto plates. Drizzle any remaining caramelized syrup over custards. Yield: 6 servings (serving size: 1 flan).

CALORIES 232 (15% from fat); FAT 3.8g (sat 1.3g, mono 1.4g, poly 0.5g); PROTEIN 7.4g; CARB 44.7g; FIBER 3.9g; CHOL 143mg; IRON 1.7mg; SODIUM 140mg; CALC 105mg

Butterscotch Pudding

Vitamin D aids calcium absorption in dairy foods. One serving of this dish offers about one-fifth of your daily calcium needs.

- 1 cup packed dark brown sugar
- ¼ cup cornstarch
- ½ teaspoon salt
- 3 cups 1% low-fat milk, divided
- 1 large egg, lightly beaten
- 1 large egg yolk, lightly beaten
- 1 tablespoon butter
- 1 teaspoon vanilla
- 6 tablespoons frozen reduced-calorie whipped topping, thawed

① Combine first 3 ingredients in a saucepan. Gradually add 2 cups milk; stir with a whisk until blended. Heat mixture to 180° or until tiny bubbles form around edge (do not boil).
② Combine remaining 1 cup milk, egg, and egg yolk in a bowl; stir with a whisk.
③ Gradually add 1 cup of hot milk mixture to egg mixture, stirring constantly with a whisk. Add egg mixture to saucepan. Bring to a boil; cook 1 minute or until thick, stirring constantly. Remove from heat; stir in butter and vanilla. Place pan in a large ice-filled bowl for 20 minutes or until mixture cools to room temperature; stir occasionally. Cover surface of pudding with plastic wrap. Chill. Serve with whipped topping. Yield: 6 servings (serving size: ⅔ cup pudding and 1 tablespoon topping).

CALORIES 281 (20% from fat); FAT 6.3g (sat 4.1g, mono 1.5g, poly 0.4g); PROTEIN 5.5g; CARB 51.5g; FIBER 0.1g; CHOL 79mg; IRON 1mg; SODIUM 300mg; CALC 190mg

Noteworthy Nutrients

Researchers are digging deeper to discover which foods will take the health spotlight next. Here are a few rising stars that show promise.

Cocoa flavonols for the brain: These antioxidants, also found in tea, red wine, and berries, may boost blood flow to the brain for two to three hours, which could help keep you more alert and fight fatigue, according to recent research from the University of Nottingham in England. Scientists are quick to point out, however, that the level of cocoa flavonols used in the study can't yet be found in supermarkets.

Lutein for the skin: Ten milligrams of the carotenoid lutein daily may help improve skin elasticity and hydration, according to research from a number of Italian hospitals and universities, including the University of Naples, which supplemented the diet of 40 women aged 25 to 50 for 12 weeks. The study used lutein supplements; two cups of fresh spinach provides about 8 milligrams of lutein.

Omega-3 fatty acids for bones: A small study from Pennsylvania State University investigating omega-3 fats from walnuts and flaxseed (and not supplements) found the plant-based fats may help promote bone formation. Researchers say the results merit a further look.

Wild Rice and Barley Salad

In addition to fiber, whole grains like wild and brown rice offer plenty of vitamins B6, E, and folate to maintain heart health.

- 1¾ cups fat-free, less-sodium chicken broth
- ½ cup uncooked brown and wild rice mix
- ½ cup uncooked pearl barley
- ¾ cup rinsed and drained canned chickpeas (garbanzo beans)
- ⅓ cup golden raisins
- ¼ cup sliced green onions
- 2 tablespoons red wine vinegar
- 1½ teaspoons extravirgin olive oil
- 1 teaspoon Dijon mustard
- ¼ teaspoon salt
- ¼ teaspoon freshly ground black pepper
- 2 tablespoons chopped fresh basil
- 2 tablespoons slivered almonds, toasted

① Combine first 3 ingredients in a medium saucepan; bring to a boil. Cover, reduce heat, and simmer 40 minutes or until liquid is absorbed. Remove from heat, and let stand, covered, 5 minutes. Spoon rice mixture into a medium bowl. Add chickpeas, raisins, and green onions. ② Combine vinegar and next 4 ingredients in a small bowl; stir with a whisk. Pour over barley mixture; toss well. Cover; chill 2 hours. Stir in basil and almonds. Yield: 8 servings (serving size: about ⅔ cup).

CALORIES 146 (14% from fat); FAT 2.3g (sat 0.3g, mono 1.3g, poly 0.6g); PROTEIN 5g; CARB 27.6g; FIBER 4.3g; CHOL 0mg; IRON 1.2mg; SODIUM 235mg; CALC 29mg

Bread Salad with Cranberries, Spinach, and Chicken

Chicken, high in vitamin B12, teams up with spinach, nuts, and a little oil to offer a one-dish meal loaded with vitamin E, vitamin C, and folate.

CHICKEN:
- 1 teaspoon ground fennel
- 1 teaspoon ground coriander
- ½ teaspoon kosher salt
- ⅛ teaspoon ground red pepper
- 4 (6-ounce) skinless, boneless chicken breast halves
- 4 teaspoons olive oil

VINAIGRETTE:
- 2 tablespoons thinly sliced shallots
- 5 garlic cloves, thinly sliced
- ¼ cup red wine vinegar
- 1 teaspoon grated orange rind
- 2 tablespoons orange juice
- 2 tablespoons cranberry juice
- 2 tablespoons honey
- ½ teaspoon ground fennel
- ½ teaspoon freshly ground black pepper
- ¼ teaspoon kosher salt

SALAD:
- 6 cups loosely packed spinach (about 6 ounces)
- 2½ cups (½-inch) cubed French bread, toasted (about 4 ounces)
- ½ cup dried sweetened cranberries
- 2 tablespoons pine nuts, toasted
- 2 tablespoons thinly sliced shallots
- 2 tablespoons sliced pitted kalamata olives

① To prepare chicken, combine first 4 ingredients; rub evenly over chicken. Heat oil in a large nonstick skillet over medium heat. Add chicken to pan; cook 5 minutes on each side or until done. Remove chicken from pan. ② To prepare vinaigrette, add 2 tablespoons shallots and garlic to pan; cook 3 minutes or until shallots and garlic begin to brown, stirring occasionally. Stir in vinegar and next 7 ingredients; cook over

medium-high heat until reduced to ¹/₂ cup (about 1 minute). Remove vinaigrette from pan, and cool completely.
❸ To prepare salad, cut chicken into bite-sized pieces. Combine chicken, spinach, and remaining ingredients in a large bowl. Add vinaigrette; toss gently to coat. Serve immediately. Yield: 6 servings (serving size: about 1²/₃ cups).

CALORIES 307 (24% from fat); FAT 8.2g (sat 1.1g, mono 4g, poly 1.7g); PROTEIN 29.5g; CARB 28.9g; FIBER 2.2g; CHOL 66mg; IRON 2.7mg; SODIUM 511mg; CALC 70mg

Broccoli with Two-Cheese Sauce

Not only is broccoli a good source of folate, but it also offers plenty of vitamin K, a bit of vitamin E, and vitamin C to boost brain power.

    1 cup fat-free milk
    ¹/₂ cup sliced onion
    2 garlic cloves, crushed
    Dash of ground nutmeg
    2 tablespoons all-purpose flour
    ¹/₃ cup (about 1¹/₂ ounces) grated fresh Parmigiano-Reggiano cheese
    ¹/₃ cup (about 1¹/₂ ounces) shredded reduced-fat Jarlsberg cheese
    ¹/₄ teaspoon salt
    Dash of ground red pepper
    6 cups broccoli spears

❶ Combine first 4 ingredients in a small, heavy saucepan over medium heat. Heat to 180° or until tiny bubbles form around edge (do not boil). Remove from heat; let stand 15 minutes. Strain milk mixture through a sieve into a bowl, reserving milk. Discard solids. Wipe pan clean with paper towels; add strained milk and flour to pan, stirring with a whisk. Return pan to medium heat; cook 2 minutes or until thick, stirring constantly with a whisk. Remove from heat. Add cheeses, salt, and pepper, stirring with a whisk until smooth. Keep warm.

❷ Cook broccoli in boiling water 3 minutes or until crisp-tender; drain. Top with cheese sauce; serve immediately. Yield: 8 servings (serving size: ³/₄ cup broccoli and about 2¹/₂ tablespoons sauce).

CALORIES 67 (30% from fat); FAT 2.2g (sat 1.3g, mono 0.6g, poly 0.2g); PROTEIN 6.4g; CARB 6.4g; FIBER 1.8g; CHOL 6mg; IRON 0.6mg; SODIUM 215mg; CALC 175mg

Fish Fare Menu
serves 4

The green bean side dish is a quick, fresh take on the flavors of classic green bean casserole. It makes a homey accompaniment for the croquettes.

Lemon-Dill Salmon Croquettes with Horseradish Sauce

Green bean–mushroom sauté
Cook 1 pound trimmed green beans in boiling water 4 minutes or until crisp-tender. Drain and plunge into ice water; drain. Melt 1 tablespoon butter in a large skillet. Add ¹/₄ cup thinly sliced shallot rings; sauté 2 minutes. Add 2 cups quartered cremini mushrooms, ¹/₄ teaspoon salt, and ¹/₄ teaspoon freshly ground black pepper; sauté 4 minutes or until liquid evaporates. Add cooked beans, ¹/₄ teaspoon salt, and ¹/₄ teaspoon freshly ground black pepper to pan; sauté 1 minute or until thoroughly heated.

Long-grain rice with parsley

Lemon-Dill Salmon Croquettes with Horseradish Sauce

Salmon is a great source of omega-3 fatty acids. A serving of croquettes supplies about a day's worth of the fat.

SAUCE:
    2 tablespoons light mayonnaise
    2 tablespoons fat-free sour cream
    1 teaspoon prepared horseradish
    ¹/₈ teaspoon ground red pepper
    ¹/₈ teaspoon black pepper
    Dash of salt
CROQUETTES:
    1 tablespoon all-purpose flour
    1 tablespoon chopped fresh dill
    3 tablespoons light mayonnaise
    ¹/₂ teaspoon grated lemon rind
    ¹/₂ teaspoon black pepper
    1 (15-ounce) can salmon
    1 egg white
    5 tablespoons dry breadcrumbs, divided
    Cooking spray

❶ To prepare sauce, combine first 6 ingredients in a small bowl; stir with a whisk. Cover and refrigerate.
❷ To prepare croquettes, combine flour, next 6 ingredients, and 3 tablespoons breadcrumbs. Divide mixture into 4 equal portions, shaping each into a ¹/₂-inch-thick patty. Refrigerate 1 hour. Place remaining 2 tablespoons breadcrumbs on a plate; dredge patties in breadcrumbs.
❸ Heat a large nonstick skillet over medium-high heat. Coat pan with cooking spray. Add patties to pan; cook 9 minutes on each side or until golden. Serve with sauce. Yield: 4 servings (serving size: 1 croquette and about 1 tablespoon sauce).

CALORIES 193 (48% from fat); FAT 10.3g (sat 1.9g, mono 3.2g, poly 4.4g); PROTEIN 13.6g; CARB 11.1g; FIBER 0.6g; CHOL 30mg; IRON 1.2mg; SODIUM 537mg; CALC 157mg

QUICK & EASY
Quick Kale with Bacon and Onions

One serving of this hearty side offers more than your day's need of vitamin K.

- 2 teaspoons olive oil
- 1 cup chopped onion
- 10 cups chopped kale, divided
- ½ cup fat-free, less-sodium chicken broth, divided
- ¼ teaspoon salt
- ⅛ teaspoon crushed red pepper
- ⅛ teaspoon black pepper
- 2 bacon slices, cooked and crumbled
- 6 lemon wedges

① Heat oil in a Dutch oven over medium-high heat. Add onion to pan; sauté 6 minutes or until onion is tender and begins to brown. Add 5 cups kale, ¼ cup broth, salt, and peppers to pan. Cover, reduce heat, and cook 4 minutes. Add remaining 5 cups kale and remaining ¼ cup broth to pan. Cover and cook 16 minutes or until tender, stirring occasionally. Sprinkle with bacon. Serve with lemon wedges. Yield: 6 servings (serving size: about ¾ cup and 1 lemon wedge).

CALORIES 75 (36% from fat); FAT 3g (sat 0.6g, mono 1.5g, poly 0.5g); PROTEIN 3.8g; CARB 10.2g; FIBER 2.1g; CHOL 2mg; IRON 1.4mg; SODIUM 213mg; CALC 110mg

A World of Soup

Explore our collection of recipes from around the globe. Flavors may vary, but the technique is universal.

A UNIVERSAL PLEASURE, soups are staples in most cuisines around the globe. Many homemade soups are simple to prepare. Actually, most recipes from around the world follow a surprisingly universal technique. Each is based on a flavorful liquid, such as broth or stock. Any additional ingredients contribute specific flavors or textures, or lend visual appeal to the soup. Once you master the technique, it's easy to customize recipes to suit your personal tastes (see "Four Steps to Great Soup," page 28).

Our collection of recipes showcases quintessential soups from nine countries. The flavors are as varied as the cultures themselves, and each dish has a unique place in the food traditions of the country from which it hails.

French Potage

With the first known recipe dating back to medieval cuisine in Northern France, the filling dish known as *potage* is so common throughout the country, the word is often interchangeable with *soupe*. Flavors and ingredients vary, but most recipes yield a thick vegetable-based soup (meat is optional).

Golden Winter Soup
(pictured on page 241)

- 2 tablespoons butter
- 5 cups (½-inch) cubed peeled butternut squash (about 1½ pounds)
- 2 cups (½-inch) cubed peeled russet potato (about 12 ounces)
- 1 teaspoon kosher salt
- ½ teaspoon freshly ground black pepper
- 2 cups sliced leek (about 2 medium)
- 4 cups fat-free, less-sodium chicken broth
- 1 cup half-and-half
- 12 ounces baguette, cut into 16 slices
- ¾ cup (3 ounces) shredded Gruyère cheese
- 3 tablespoons chopped chives
Freshly ground black pepper (optional)

① Preheat broiler.

② Melt butter in a large Dutch oven over medium-high heat. Add squash and next 3 ingredients to pan; sauté 3 minutes. Add leek; sauté 1 minute. Stir in broth; bring to a boil. Reduce heat, and simmer 20 minutes or until potato is tender, stirring occasionally. Place half of potato mixture in a blender. Remove center piece of blender lid (to allow steam to escape); secure blender lid on blender. Place a clean towel over opening in blender lid (to avoid splatters). Blend until smooth. Pour into a large bowl. Repeat procedure with remaining potato mixture. Stir in half-and-half. Cover and keep warm.

③ Arrange bread slices in a single layer on a baking sheet; sprinkle evenly with cheese. Broil bread slices 2 minutes or until golden. Ladle 1 cup soup into each of 8 bowls; top each serving with about 1 teaspoon chives. Serve 2 bread slices with each serving. Garnish with black pepper, if desired. Yield: 8 servings.

CALORIES 329 (30% from fat); FAT 10.9g (sat 6.2g, mono 3g, poly 0.9g); PROTEIN 12.8g; CARB 46.7g; FIBER 4.8g; CHOL 30mg; IRON 3.2mg; SODIUM 813mg; CALC 217mg

Ecuadorian Chupes

Along the Ecuadorian coast, *chupes*, cream-based soups thickened with potato, similar to chowder, are popular. Our version is based on soups served in homes, restaurants, and open-air markets in Ecuador.

Ecuadorian Potato Soup

Cooking spray
½ cup finely chopped onion
1 teaspoon ground cumin
1 teaspoon ground annatto
4 cups fat-free milk, divided
1 large egg yolk
4 cups (3-inch) cubed peeled baking potato (about 1½ pounds)
1½ teaspoons chopped fresh cilantro
½ small jalapeño pepper, chopped
¾ teaspoon kosher salt
¼ teaspoon freshly ground black pepper
3 hard-cooked large eggs
½ cup sliced peeled avocado
¼ cup chopped fresh cilantro
1½ teaspoons chopped seeded jalapeño pepper
Hot pepper sauce (optional)

❶ Heat a large saucepan over medium-high heat. Coat pan with cooking spray. Add onion to pan; sauté 5 minutes. Stir in cumin and annatto; sauté 30 seconds.
❷ Combine 2 tablespoons milk and egg yolk. Chill. Add remaining milk, potato, 1½ teaspoons cilantro, and ½ small jalapeño to pan; bring to a boil. Cover, reduce heat, and simmer 35 minutes, stirring occasionally. Partially mash potato mixture with potato masher.
❸ Stir ¼ cup potato mixture into egg yolk mixture. Return potato mixture to pan; stir in salt and black pepper. Simmer 5 minutes, stirring frequently. Remove yolks from 2 hard-cooked eggs, and discard; coarsely chop whites and whole hard-cooked egg. Ladle about 1 cup soup into each of 6 bowls; top each serving with 2 teaspoons chopped egg mixture, about 1 tablespoon avocado, 2 teaspoons cilantro, and ¼ teaspoon jalapeño. Garnish each serving with hot pepper sauce, if desired. Yield: 6 servings.

CALORIES 252 (22% from fat); FAT 6.1g (sat 2g, mono 2.8g, poly 0.7g); PROTEIN 13.3g; CARB 36.8g; FIBER 3.1g; CHOL 79mg; IRON 1.2mg; SODIUM 368mg; CALC 282mg

Cuban Black Bean Soup

Cuban cooking reflects the influence of Spain and Africa as well as other Caribbean islands. Spicy heat is not as pronounced in Cuban cuisine as in some other Latin fare. In keeping with this tradition, Cuban Black Bean Soup is a balance of earthy flavors from the black beans and cumin, pungent *sofrito* (onion, green bell pepper, garlic, and oregano), and citrus. Finally, Cubans don't usually soak the beans for soup before cooking; they simply cook the beans longer and relish the deep flavor of the cooking liquid.

Cuban Black Bean Soup

2 bay leaves
1 pound dried black beans
12½ cups water, divided
1 tablespoon canola oil
3½ cups chopped green bell pepper (about 3 medium)
2½ cups coarsely chopped onion
⅓ cup chopped shallots (about 2 small)
1 tablespoon ground cumin
2 tablespoons dried oregano
2 tablespoons chopped fresh oregano
1½ tablespoons sugar
2 teaspoons kosher salt
2 cups diced peeled avocado
2 tablespoons fresh lime juice
2 cups thinly sliced red onion
1½ cups chopped 33%-less-sodium smoked, fully cooked ham
1 cup chopped fresh cilantro
1 cup light sour cream
10 teaspoons unsalted pumpkinseed kernels, toasted
⅓ cup finely chopped seeded jalapeño pepper (about 2 medium)
Lime wedges (optional)

❶ Place bay leaves and beans in a Dutch oven. Add 12 cups water to pan; bring to a boil. Reduce heat, and simmer 2½ hours or until tender, stirring occasionally.
❷ Heat oil in a large skillet over medium heat. Add bell pepper, chopped onion, and shallots to pan; cook 10 minutes or until onion is tender, stirring frequently. Stir in cumin, dried oregano, and fresh oregano; cook 2 minutes, stirring frequently. Remove from heat; let stand 10 minutes. Place vegetable mixture in a blender; add remaining ½ cup water. Puree until smooth.
❸ Add vegetable mixture, sugar, and salt to beans; simmer 10 minutes, stirring occasionally. Discard bay leaves. Combine avocado and juice; toss gently. Ladle ¾ cup bean mixture into each of 10 bowls; top each serving with about 3 tablespoons avocado mixture, about 3 tablespoons red onion, 2 tablespoons ham, about 1½ tablespoons cilantro, about 1½ tablespoons sour cream, 1 teaspoon pumpkinseed kernels, and about ½ teaspoon jalapeño pepper. Serve with lime wedges, if desired. Yield: 10 servings.

CALORIES 344 (31% from fat); FAT 12g (sat 3.4g, mono 5.7g, poly 2.3g); PROTEIN 18.6g; CARB 43.9g; FIBER 14.7g; CHOL 14mg; IRON 6.1mg; SODIUM 637mg; CALC 110mg

Soups are a staple in most cuisines around the globe. Steamy bowls offer solace against the cold outside.

Russian Borscht

Borscht, popular in Russia and other former Soviet nations, is a hearty beet-based soup. It's enjoyed year-round and prized for its sweet-sour flavor and adaptability. Beets are almost always the main attraction, and other ingredients vary according to season. Our version is an appetizer soup, but you can add beef or smoked pork to make it an entrée.

Borscht

There are many different versions of this Russian soup. Unlike this interpretation, many are chunky. If you puree the soup as the recipe directs, you don't have to worry about precision when you're chopping. The simplest way to peel celeriac is to remove the rough, knobby skin with a sharp chef's knife.

- 1 tablespoon canola oil
- 1½ cups button mushrooms, thinly sliced
- 1¾ cups chopped onion
- 1¾ cups chopped peeled celeriac (celery root)
- ⅓ cup chopped carrot
- ⅓ cup chopped parsnip
- 1 tablespoon tomato paste
- 7 cups water
- ½ cup light beer
- 2½ cups shredded red cabbage
- 2 cups chopped peeled baking potato
- 2 garlic cloves, crushed
- 12 ounces sliced peeled beets
- 3 tablespoons cider vinegar
- 2 teaspoons sugar
- 1 teaspoon kosher salt
- ¼ teaspoon freshly ground black pepper
- ½ cup sour cream
- 2 tablespoons chopped fresh dill

❶ Heat oil in a large Dutch oven over medium heat. Add mushrooms to pan; cook 5 minutes, stirring frequently. Add onion; cook 6 minutes. Add celeriac, carrot, and parsnip; cook 4 minutes or until onion is tender, stirring occasionally. Stir in tomato paste. Add 7 cups water and beer; stir well. Reduce heat, and simmer 5 minutes. Stir in cabbage and next 3 ingredients; bring to a boil. Reduce heat, and simmer 20 minutes or until vegetables are tender, stirring occasionally. Remove from heat.

❷ Place half of beet mixture in a blender. Remove center piece of blender lid (to allow steam to escape); secure blender lid on blender. Place a clean towel over opening in blender lid (to avoid splatters). Blend until smooth. Pour into a large bowl. Repeat procedure with remaining beet mixture. Stir in vinegar and next 3 ingredients. Ladle 1½ cups soup into each of 8 bowls; top each serving with 1 tablespoon sour cream and ¾ teaspoon dill. Yield: 8 servings.

CALORIES 164 (28% from fat); FAT 5.1g (sat 2.1g, mono 2g, poly 0.8g); PROTEIN 3.7g; CARB 26.5g; FIBER 4.2g; CHOL 6mg; IRON 1.1mg; SODIUM 345mg; CALC 64mg

Chinese Egg Drop Soup

Egg drop soup is popular in China because eggs are prized as symbols of new life and represent the yin and yang—the contrast of light (the white) and dark (the yolk). It's the easiest in our roundup of world soups, basically eggs cooked in seasoned chicken broth and garnished with sliced green onions. Thin soups such as this are often served as a beverage to accompany a meal or as a palate cleanser between courses in China.

QUICK & EASY
Egg Drop Soup

Pour the beaten eggs through a sieve into the simmering broth to create the characteristic ribbons in the soup.

- 4 cups fat-free, less-sodium chicken broth
- 2 large eggs, lightly beaten
- 3 tablespoons chopped green onions
- ¼ teaspoon salt

❶ Place broth in a medium saucepan; bring to a boil. Reduce heat to low; place a wire mesh sieve over saucepan. Strain eggs through sieve into pan. Remove from heat; stir in onions and salt. Yield: 4 servings (serving size: 1 cup).

CALORIES 54 (45% from fat); FAT 2.7g (sat 0.9g, mono 1.1g, poly 0.4g); PROTEIN 5.7g; CARB 1.5g; FIBER 1.1g; CHOL 106mg; IRON 1mg; SODIUM 570mg; CALC 31mg

Greek Lentil Soup

Lentil soup dates back to ancient Greece, and it's still popular for casual meals and special occasions. For example, some Greeks eat lentil soup during Lent because it represents tears of the Virgin Mary. It is also a common lunch staple year-round, served with simple accompaniments, such as vinegar and olives.

Anthos Lentil Soup

Acidic flavor is pronounced in many Greek foods. This recipe calls for sherry vinegar to deglaze the pan, which intensifies the tart taste.

- 2 tablespoons olive oil
- 1½ cups cubed peeled baking potato (about 8 ounces)
- 1 cup finely chopped carrot (about 2 medium)
- 1 cup finely chopped celery
- ¾ cup finely chopped parsnip
- ⅓ cup finely chopped shallots
- 3 tablespoons sherry vinegar
- 6 cups fat-free, less-sodium chicken broth
- ¾ cup brown lentils
- 2 bay leaves
- ½ teaspoon freshly ground black pepper
- ¼ teaspoon kosher salt

❶ Heat oil in a large Dutch oven over medium-high heat. Add potato and next 4 ingredients to pan; sauté 7 minutes or until tender. Add vinegar to pan, scraping pan to loosen browned bits. Add broth, lentils, and bay leaves to pan; bring to a boil. Reduce heat, and simmer 45 minutes or until lentils are tender. Discard bay leaves.

2 Transfer half of lentil mixture to a blender. Remove center piece of blender lid (to allow steam to escape); secure blender lid on blender. Place a clean towel over opening in blender lid (to avoid splatters). Blend until smooth, scraping sides. Return lentil mixture to pan; stir in pepper and salt. Yield: 6 cups (serving size: 1 cup).

CALORIES 203 (23% from fat); FAT 5.2g (sat 0.8g, mono 3.5g, poly 0.7g); PROTEIN 10g; CARB 29.6g; FIBER 10.7g; CHOL 0mg; IRON 2.8mg; SODIUM 501mg; CALC 55mg

---

American Chicken Soup

Like our nation, American cuisine is born of immigrants, so our version resembles that of many other countries. For centuries people around the world have turned to this comfort food when they're sick.

Chicken-Vegetable Soup

Americans of Eastern European heritage add a variety of root vegetables, such as turnips and parsnips, to chicken soup for subtle sweetness and bite. Be sure to cook the egg noodles separately so the starch in the noodles doesn't cloud the clear soup broth.

- 1 (6-pound) roasting chicken
- 8 cups water
- 2½ cups chopped celery (about 4 stalks)
- 2 cups thinly sliced leek (about 2 large)
- 1½ cups (½-inch) cubed parsnip (about 8 ounces)
- 1½ cups (½-inch) cubed carrot (about 8 ounces)
- 1½ cups (½-inch) cubed turnip (about 8 ounces)
- 1 teaspoon kosher salt
- ½ teaspoon freshly ground black pepper
- 1 teaspoon chopped fresh dill (optional)
- 8 ounces egg noodles

1 Remove and discard giblets and neck from chicken. Remove and discard skin; trim excess fat. Split chicken in half lengthwise; place in a Dutch oven. Cover with 8 cups water; bring to a boil. Cook 10 minutes. Skim fat from surface of broth; discard fat. Add celery and next 4 ingredients to pan, stirring well; bring to a boil. Reduce heat, and simmer 30 minutes or until vegetables are almost tender, stirring occasionally. Remove chicken; let stand 10 minutes. Remove chicken from bones; shred chicken with 2 forks to yield 6 cups meat. Discard bones. Simmer vegetable mixture 10 minutes or until tender. Return shredded chicken to pan. Stir in salt, pepper, and dill, if desired.
2 Cook noodles according to package directions, omitting salt and fat. Place ½ cup noodles in each of 8 bowls; top each serving with 1½ cups chicken mixture. Yield: 8 servings.

CALORIES 404 (31% from fat); FAT 14.2g (sat 3.6g, mono 4.7g, poly 3.5g); PROTEIN 36.5g; CARB 31.2g; FIBER 3.6g; CHOL 107mg; IRON 3.4mg; SODIUM 392mg; CALC 76mg

---

Japanese Miso Soup

Miso soup is a staple at the Japanese breakfast table, and it's consumed as a beverage at other meals. It's simple to prepare: tofu, mushrooms, and ginger are simmered in the dashi (kelp broth), and a variety of optional ingredients can be added just before serving. Each ingredient should offer a unique color or appearance, as well as flavor, to the dish. Miso (soybean paste) comes in many different varieties, ranging in color from red to yellow; the darker the miso, the stronger and saltier the flavor.

QUICK & EASY
Miso Soup

The essence of Japanese soup, dashi is a flavorful broth made from simmering *kombu* (kelp, a kind of seaweed) in water. Wipe it with a damp cloth before using, and cut into strips with kitchen shears to extract maximum flavor. *Shiso* is a member of the mint family. Look for both kombu and shiso at Asian specialty markets. If you can't find shiso, use spinach.

DASHI:
- 8⅔ cups water
- 1¾ ounces kombu (kelp), cut into (4-inch) pieces

REMAINING INGREDIENTS:
- 2 tablespoons miso (soybean paste)
- ½ cup straw mushrooms, rinsed and halved
- 4 ounces silken firm tofu, drained and cut into ½-inch cubes
- 1 (½-inch) piece peeled fresh ginger, thinly sliced
- ¼ cup thinly sliced green onions
- 3 ounces thinly sliced shiso

1 To prepare dashi, combine 8⅔ cups water and kombu in a saucepan; bring to a boil. Partially cover, reduce heat, and simmer until reduced to about 4 cups (about 1 hour). Strain dashi through a sieve into a bowl; discard solids.
2 Place ¼ cup dashi in a small bowl; stir in miso. Return dashi mixture to pan; bring to a simmer. Add mushrooms, tofu, and ginger to pan. Simmer 10 minutes; discard ginger. Stir in green onions and shiso. Yield: 4 servings (serving size: about 1½ cups).

CALORIES 63 (21% from fat); FAT 1.5g (sat 0.1g, mono 0.3g, poly 0.8g); PROTEIN 4.7g; CARB 7.7g; FIBER 2.2g; CHOL 0mg; IRON 1.5mg; SODIUM 370mg; CALC 82mg

Spicy Thai Shrimp Soup
(*Tom Yum Goong*)

1½   pounds medium shrimp
9½   cups water, divided
½   cup chopped peeled fresh galangal (about 2 ounces)
½   cup (2-inch) pieces peeled fresh lemongrass (about 4 stalks)
6   fresh or frozen kaffir lime leaves
½   cup canned straw mushrooms, quartered
2   tablespoons roasted red chili paste
1   tablespoon fish sauce
2   Thai chiles
½   cup chopped green onions
½   cup chopped fresh cilantro
1   tablespoon fresh lime juice
6   tablespoons chopped dry-roasted unsalted peanuts
4   lime wedges

① Peel and devein shrimp, reserving shells. Combine shrimp shells and 6 cups water in a Dutch oven; bring to a simmer. Cook 1 hour. Strain broth through a sieve into a bowl; discard solids. Combine broth and remaining 3½ cups water in a large saucepan; bring to a boil. Add galangal, lemongrass, and lime leaves to pan; simmer 10 minutes. Strain broth mixture through a sieve into a bowl; discard solids. Return broth mixture to pan. Add mushrooms and next 3 ingredients; bring to a boil. Stir in shrimp, green onions, and cilantro; cook 3 minutes or until shrimp are done. Discard chiles. Stir in lime juice. Ladle 2 cups soup into each of 4 bowls; sprinkle evenly with peanuts. Serve with lime wedges. Yield: 4 servings.

CALORIES 282 (31% from fat); FAT 10g (sat 1.5g, mono 3.8g, poly 3.4g); PROTEIN 39.2g; CARB 8.7g; FIBER 2.5g; CHOL 259mg; IRON 5.2mg; SODIUM 992mg; CALC 116mg

All About Soup

Four Steps to Great Soup

1 Choose a foundation. A flavorful liquid is the basis for all soups. Stock or broth is most common, but some rich, hearty soups have a milk or cream base or a combination of dairy and broth. (Stock imparts more intensity and richness than broth because it's typically made with bone-in cuts of meat or meat scraps and bones that have been roasted to bring out more flavor. Broth tastes milder since it is typically made from meat off the bone.) Homemade stock or broth is ideal, but making either can be time-consuming. Store-bought broth certainly works, and we tested many of our recipes using it. Choose meat stock or broth for meat-based soups, and shrimp stock or clam juice for seafood soups.

2 Add dimension. Vegetables, herbs, spices, or meats provide a second dimension of flavor in soups. Sauté aromatic vegetables, such as carrot, onion, and celery, in butter or oil before adding liquid, and they will release more flavor into the final dish.

3 Round out the flavor. Some soups need an acidic background note, so the recipe may call to deglaze the pan (adding liquid after sautéing meat or vegetables and scraping the tasty browned bits from the bottom of the pan). Acidic ingredients, such as wine or vinegar, are often used for deglazing, and most of that liquid evaporates as it cooks, concentrating the tart flavor. The stock or broth is added next, and it becomes infused with the flavor of the aromatic vegetables as the soup simmers.

4 Finish it. Some soups are pureed for special occasions for a refined, smooth texture. Others may be only partially pureed to give the soup body and thicken the broth. For an everyday meal, it may not be necessary to puree—chunks in the dish offer a more casual, rustic feel. Choose garnishes depending on the soup's flavor. A creamy garnish, such as cheese or sour cream, soothes a spicy or tart soup and smoothes out the acidic or spicy notes. Chopped fresh herbs or fresh citrus juice brighten other flavors in the dish.

The International Soup Pantry

It's difficult to generalize much about the flavors of any given country because regional preferences and cooking styles may vary. However, some ingredients are common throughout and ultimately define the tastes of a nation. Below we list the key ingredients that turn up repeatedly in soups from each country we feature.

France: *Mirepoix* (onion, carrot, and celery), leeks, mushrooms, wine, broth or stock, beans, seafood, duck, and several different cuts of pork

Russia/Ukraine: Beets, potatoes, cabbage, mushrooms, sour salt or vinegar, highly seasoned meats like sausage, and sour cream

Cuba: Black beans, *sofrito* (onion, green bell pepper, garlic, and often ham or other pork), oregano, cumin, and olive oil, plus starches like plantains, or a root, such as yucca

Japan: Ginger, miso, green onions, shiso, tofu, mushrooms, mirin or rice wine, soy sauce, and noodles (most Japanese soups are based on *dashi*)

Greece: Salty and acidic flavors, such as fresh lemon juice or vinegar, feta cheese, olives, olive oil, garlic, oregano, mint, and lentils

China: Ginger, soy sauce, sesame oil, eggs, rice wine, mushrooms, noodles, meat broths, cornstarch, star anise, and five-spice powder

Ecuador: Potatoes, corn, beans, cilantro, chile peppers, and lemon (more affluent cooks may add lard, chicken, meat, or seafood)

Thailand: Lemongrass, galangal, ginger, shallots, garlic, hot peppers, kaffir lime leaves, coconut milk, tamarind, fish sauce, basil, jasmine rice, noodles, shrimp, and chicken

And the Winners Are...

The third annual *Cooking Light* Ultimate Reader Recipe Contest honors versatility in four original creations.

QUICK & EASY

Caribbean Shrimp Salad with Lime Vinaigrette

Grand Prize Winner
Category Winner—Entrées

"I wanted to create a recipe for a festive meal with local ingredients that could be prepared ahead of time and assembled at the last minute.

—Katherine Hinrichs,
West Boothbay Harbor, Maine

    4 cups chopped cooked shrimp (about
       1½ pounds)
    5 tablespoons seasoned rice vinegar,
       divided
    2 tablespoons chili garlic sauce (such
       as Lee Kum Kee)
 1½ tablespoons olive oil
    1 tablespoon grated lime rind
   ¼ cup fresh lime juice (about 3 large
       limes)
   ½ teaspoon paprika
   ½ teaspoon ground cumin
    2 garlic cloves, minced
Dash of salt
    8 cups fresh baby spinach
    1 cup chopped peeled mango (about
       1 large)
    1 cup julienne-cut radishes
   ¼ cup diced peeled avocado
   ½ cup thinly sliced green onions
    2 tablespoons unsalted pumpkinseed
       kernels

❶ Combine shrimp, 2 tablespoons vinegar, and chili garlic sauce in a large bowl; toss well. Cover and chill 1 hour.
❷ Combine remaining 3 tablespoons vinegar, oil, and next 6 ingredients in a small bowl, stirring with a whisk.
❸ Place 2 cups spinach on each of 4 plates; top each serving with 1 cup shrimp mixture. Arrange ¼ cup mango, ¼ cup radishes, and 1 tablespoon avocado around shrimp on each plate. Top each serving with 2 tablespoons green onions and 1½ teaspoons pumpkinseed kernels. Drizzle each salad with 2 tablespoons vinaigrette. Yield: 4 servings.

CALORIES 281 (32% from fat); FAT 10g (sat 1.7g, mono 5.7g, poly 2.2g); PROTEIN 30.3g; CARB 18.4g; FIBER 3.6g; CHOL 252mg; IRON 6.3mg; SODIUM 879mg; CALC 126mg

MAKE AHEAD

Korean-Spiced Beef and Cabbage Rolls

Category Winner—
Starters and Beverages

"I am originally from Nebraska; one of my favorite places to eat is a small chain of sandwich restaurants called Runza. They are famous for their pillowlike beef and cabbage sandwiches. Since my husband is Korean, I created these pairing the traditional filling ingredients and flavors from his culture. These make a great snack."

—Mollie Lee, San Jose, California

FILLING:
   ½ cup chopped green onions
   ¼ cup low-sodium soy sauce
    1 tablespoon sesame seeds
    1 tablespoon dark sesame oil
    1 tablespoon dry sherry
    2 teaspoons sugar
   ¼ teaspoon freshly ground black
       pepper
   ¼ teaspoon bottled ground fresh
       ginger
   ¼ teaspoon bottled minced garlic
   ⅛ teaspoon ground red pepper
   ½ pound ground sirloin
       Cooking spray
    2 cups thinly sliced green cabbage
DOUGH:
    4 cups all-purpose flour (about 18
       ounces)
    2 tablespoons baking powder
   ½ teaspoon salt
 1⅓ cups water
   ¼ cup honey
    2 tablespoons canola oil
    1 tablespoon water
    1 large egg white, lightly beaten
    1 tablespoon sesame seeds

❶ Preheat oven to 375°.
❷ To prepare filling, combine first 11 ingredients in a large bowl.
❸ Heat a large nonstick skillet over medium-high heat. Coat pan with cooking spray. Add beef mixture to pan; cook 8 minutes or until done, stirring occasionally. Stir in cabbage; cook 4 minutes or until cabbage is tender. Remove from heat; cool completely.
❹ To prepare dough, lightly spoon flour into dry measuring cups; level with a knife. Combine flour, baking powder, and salt in a large bowl, stirring with a whisk. Combine 1⅓ cups water, honey, and canola oil, stirring with a whisk. Add honey mixture to flour mixture; stir until a soft dough forms. Turn dough out onto a lightly floured surface. Knead until smooth and elastic (about 5 minutes); cover and let stand 5 minutes.

Continued

⑤ Roll dough into a 16 x 12–inch rectangle (about ¼-inch-thick) on a lightly floured surface. Cut dough into 12 (4-inch) squares. Working with 1 square at a time (cover remaining dough with a towel to prevent drying), spoon about ¼ cup beef mixture into center of each square. Moisten edges of dough with water; bring 2 opposite corners to center, pinching points to seal. Pinch 4 edges together to seal. Place rolls, seam sides down, on a baking sheet lined with parchment paper. Combine 1 tablespoon water and egg white in a small bowl, stirring with a whisk. Lightly brush tops of dough with egg white mixture; sprinkle evenly with sesame seeds. Bake at 375° for 25 minutes or until rolls are lightly browned. Remove from baking sheet; cool on wire racks. Yield: 12 servings (serving size: 1 roll).

CALORIES 247 (20% from fat); FAT 5.4g (sat 0.8g, mono 2.5g, poly 1.7g); PROTEIN 9.1g; CARB 40.7g; FIBER 1.8g; CHOL 10mg; IRON 2.8mg; SODIUM 564mg; CALC 152mg

MAKE AHEAD

Carrot Cake with Toasted Coconut Cream Cheese Frosting

Category Winner—Desserts
"I grind oats with flour in a food processor to make this cake more nutritious, and use only ¼ cup canola oil and pureed baby food carrots to make it moist."
—Christine Dohlmar, Valrico, Florida

CAKE:
- ¾ cup all-purpose flour (about 3⅓ ounces)
- ¼ cup quick-cooking oats
- 1½ teaspoons ground cinnamon
- 1 teaspoon baking powder
- ½ teaspoon baking soda
- ¼ teaspoon salt
- 1 cup granulated sugar
- ¼ cup canola oil
- 1 (2½-ounce) jar carrot baby food
- 2 large eggs, lightly beaten
- 1¼ cups finely grated carrot
- ½ cup golden raisins
  Cooking spray

FROSTING:
- ⅓ cup (3 ounces) ⅓-less-fat cream cheese, softened
- 1 tablespoon butter, softened
- 1¼ cups powdered sugar, sifted
- ½ teaspoon vanilla extract
- ¼ cup flaked sweetened coconut, toasted

① Preheat oven to 325°.
② To prepare cake, lightly spoon flour into dry measuring cups; level with a knife. Combine flour and next 5 ingredients in a food processor; pulse 6 times or until well blended. Place flour mixture in a large bowl. Combine granulated sugar and next 3 ingredients; stir with a whisk. Add to flour mixture; stir just until moist. Stir in carrot and raisins. Spoon batter into an 8-inch square baking pan coated with cooking spray.
③ Bake at 325° for 40 minutes or until a wooden pick inserted in center comes out clean. Cool in pan on a wire rack.
④ To prepare frosting, combine cheese and butter in a large bowl. Beat with a mixer at high speed until creamy. Gradually add powdered sugar and vanilla, beating at low speed until smooth (do not overbeat). Spread over cake; sprinkle with coconut. Cover and chill. Yield: 12 servings (serving size: 1 piece).

CALORIES 262 (30% from fat); FAT 8.8g (sat 2.7g, mono 3.6g, poly 1.6g); PROTEIN 3.2g; CARB 44.1g; FIBER 1.2g; CHOL 44mg; IRON 0.9mg; SODIUM 201mg; CALC 47mg

MAKE AHEAD

Oatmeal Knots

Category Winner—Sides and Salads
"I am continually looking for ways to incorporate more omega-3s and whole wheat into my diet. Making yeast breads has always been a tradition in my family, and I enjoy working with more nutrient-rich ingredients for this part of our meal."
—Melissa Hinrichs, Omaha, Nebraska

- 1 cup regular oats
- ½ cup honey
- 2 tablespoons butter
- 1½ teaspoons salt
- 2 cups boiling water
- 1 package dry yeast (about 2¼ teaspoons)
- ⅓ cup warm water (100° to 110°)
- ¼ cup flaxseed meal
- 3 cups whole wheat flour (about 14¼ ounces)
- 1½ cups all-purpose flour (about 6¾ ounces), divided
  Cooking spray
- 1 teaspoon water
- 1 large egg, lightly beaten
- 1 tablespoon regular oats
- 1 tablespoon poppy seeds
- 1 tablespoons sesame seeds

① Combine first 4 ingredients in a large bowl, and add 2 cups boiling water, stirring until well blended. Cool to room temperature.
② Dissolve yeast in ⅓ cup warm water in a small bowl; let stand 5 minutes. Add yeast mixture to oats mixture; stir well. Stir in flaxseed meal.
③ Lightly spoon flours into dry measuring cups; level with a knife. Gradually add whole wheat flour and 1 cup all-purpose flour to oats mixture; stir until a soft dough forms. Turn dough out onto a lightly floured surface. Knead until smooth and elastic (about 8 minutes); add enough of remaining all-purpose flour, 1 tablespoon at a time, to prevent dough from sticking to hands (dough will feel tacky).

④ Place dough in a large bowl coated with cooking spray, turning to coat top. Cover and let rise in a warm place (85°), free from drafts, 1 hour or until doubled in size. (Press two fingers into dough. If indentation remains, dough has risen enough.) Punch dough down, and let rest 5 minutes.

⑤ Divide dough in half; cut each half into 12 equal portions. Working with one portion at a time (cover remaining dough to prevent from drying), shape each portion into an 8-inch rope. Tie each rope into a single knot; tuck top end of rope under bottom edge of roll. Place rolls on a baking sheet coated with cooking spray. Cover with plastic wrap coated with cooking spray; let rise in a warm place (85°), free from drafts, 30 minutes or until doubled in size.

⑥ Preheat oven to 400°.

⑦ Combine 1 teaspoon water and egg in a small bowl; brush egg mixture over rolls. Combine 1 tablespoon oats, poppy seeds, and sesame seeds; sprinkle evenly over rolls. Bake at 400° for 15 minutes or until golden. Cool on wire racks. Yield: 24 servings (serving size: 1 roll).

CALORIES 138 (18% from fat); FAT 2.7g (sat 0.9g, mono 0.7g, poly 0.9g); PROTEIN 4.3g; CARB 25.6g; FIBER 2.9g; CHOL 13mg; IRON 1.4mg; SODIUM 160mg; CALC 22mg

INSPIRED VEGETARIAN
The Delicious Veneto

The cuisine of this Northern Italian province boasts abundant vegetables and cheeses paired with polenta and rice for hearty fare.

The Veneto region of northeastern Italy is a portion of what was once the 1,000-year Venetian Republic, birthplace of some of the West's greatest art, music, and architecture. It also offers extraordinary culinary treasures, such as risotto, polenta, sumptuous cheeses, and perhaps Italy's most sublime olive oil.

Every city in the Veneto has a square where fruit and vegetable vendors set up their stands each morning and locals shop for whatever is in season. Locally grown produce is always most prized, and vendors will highlight it with signs that proclaim *nostrani*, meaning "ours." Here are some of the dishes you might find if you were to visit this region.

QUICK & EASY
Sweet and Sour Cipollini Onions

Pearl onions or boiling onions also work well in this application. After the onions are blanched to make peeling easier, this assertive side dish easily comes together.

- ¼ cup raisins
- ½ cup hot water
- 2 pounds cipollini onions
- 1 tablespoon butter
- 3 tablespoons water
- 2 tablespoons red wine vinegar
- 1 tablespoon sugar
- ¼ teaspoon salt
- ¼ teaspoon freshly ground black pepper
- 2 tablespoons pine nuts

① Place raisins in a bowl; cover with ½ cup hot water. Let stand 30 minutes or until plump. Drain.

② Trim top and root end of onions. Cook onions in boiling water 2 minutes. Drain. Cool and peel.

③ Melt butter in a large nonstick skillet over medium-high heat. Add onions to pan, stirring well to coat. Stir in 3 tablespoons water and next 4 ingredients. Cover, reduce heat, and cook 40 minutes, stirring every 10 minutes. Add raisins and pine nuts to pan. Increase heat to medium, and cook, uncovered, 10 minutes or until lightly browned and liquid almost evaporates, stirring occasionally. Yield: 6 servings (serving size: ½ cup).

CALORIES 116 (30% from fat); FAT 3.9g (sat 1.3g, mono 1g, poly 1g); PROTEIN 2.4g; CARB 19.8g; FIBER 3.9g; CHOL 5mg; IRON 0.3mg; SODIUM 113mg; CALC 4mg

Polenta with Tomato-Braised Beans

If you can find canned cranberry beans, use those for a more traditional Veneto preparation of this dish. You can substitute either red or white (cannellini) kidney beans.

- 2 tablespoons extravirgin olive oil
- 1 tablespoon finely chopped fresh flat-leaf parsley
- 2 garlic cloves, minced
- 1 teaspoon chopped fresh sage
- 1 (14.5-ounce) can diced tomatoes, undrained
- ¼ teaspoon freshly ground black pepper
- ⅛ teaspoon salt
- 1 (19-ounce) can cannellini beans, rinsed and drained
- 4 cups water
- ½ teaspoon salt
- 1 cup coarse yellow dry polenta

① Heat oil in a large saucepan over medium-high heat. Add parsley and garlic to pan; sauté 1 minute. Add sage and tomatoes; cook 12 minutes or until liquid almost evaporates. Add pepper, ⅛ teaspoon salt, and beans to pan. Cover, reduce heat, and cook 10 minutes, stirring occasionally.

② Bring 4 cups water and ½ teaspoon salt to a boil in a large saucepan. Add polenta in a thin stream, stirring constantly. Cook 2 minutes, stirring constantly. Cover and cook 10 minutes. Uncover and cook 2 minutes, stirring constantly. Cover and cook 5 minutes. Uncover and cook 2 minutes, stirring constantly. Cover and cook 5 minutes. Uncover and cook 2 minutes, stirring constantly. Serve polenta with bean mixture. Yield: 4 servings (serving size: ⅔ cup polenta and ¾ cup bean mixture).

CALORIES 249 (30% from fat); FAT 8.2g (sat 1.1g, mono 5.2g, poly 1.5g); PROTEIN 6.2g; CARB 39.1g; FIBER 6.7g; CHOL 0mg; IRON 2.5mg; SODIUM 666mg; CALC 55mg

Ingredients from the Veneto

Here's a roundup of produce and pantry staples to look for in your grocery store.

Asiago: Named for the town at the foot of the Dolomites, this cheese is available both young, when it is tender and almost creamy, and as a firm aged cheese with a pronounced flavor.

Celery root: The celery of Verona is not actually the head of celery but celery root, which is used raw in salads, cooked in soups, and as a filling for ravioli.

Cranberry beans: The *borlotti* (cranberry beans) of Lamon are rich and creamy, and used in the classic *pasta e fagioli,* as well as on their own in side dishes. From late summer to December they are available fresh, but canned and dried beans are available year-round.

Dried porcini mushrooms: These mushrooms offer comforting earthy flavor and meaty textures.

Monte Veronese: This rich, full-flavored cow's milk cheese is prized as a table cheese and used in pasta and risotto dishes.

Olive oil: The Veneto is one of the northernmost olive tree growing regions in Europe and produces a delicate olive oil that is suitable for a variety of dishes. Extravirgin olive oil is commonly used in all manner of cooking in Italy, from salad dressings to baked goods to sautéing.

Peas: In May and June, the sweet fresh peas of Peseggia, north of Venice, are in season, and the locals make *risi e bisi* (rice and peas) and freeze whatever is left to use in other dishes they prepare throughout the year.

Pumpkin: A pumpkin known by the name *zucca barucca* is used in risottos and as a filling for ravioli. Its flavor is quite different from that of American pumpkin, so substitute butternut squash, which more closely resembles this variety.

Radicchio: The Veneto produces many varieties of the vegetable. *Chioggia,* the round radicchio, is the best known in the United States. The long, romaine-shaped *Treviso* radicchio is distinguished by its curled-in tops, and the variegated radicchio of *Castelfranco* is used raw in salads.

Taleggio: From Treviso, the eastern part of Veneto, this creamy, rich Brie-like cheese is often used in pastas and risottos.

QUICK & EASY
Radicchio, Endive, and Carrot Salad

Sweet carrot balances the bitter notes from radicchio and Belgian endive. If you want to slightly reduce the bitterness of radicchio, soak the torn leaves for 10 minutes; drain well.

  2   cups torn radicchio
1½   cups sliced Belgian endive
  1   cup grated peeled carrot
  2   tablespoons extravirgin olive oil
  1   tablespoon red wine vinegar
  ¼   teaspoon salt
  ¼   teaspoon freshly ground black pepper

❶ Combine first 3 ingredients in a medium bowl. Add oil and remaining ingredients; toss well. Serve immediately. Yield: 6 servings (serving size: ³/₄ cup).

CALORIES 56 (74% from fat); FAT 4.6g (sat 0.7g, mono 3.3g, poly 0.5g); PROTEIN 0.7g; CARB 3.5g; FIBER 1.4g; CHOL 0mg; IRON 0.4mg; SODIUM 121mg; CALC 21mg

WINE NOTE: Here's a great vegetarian risotto that's perfect with red wine because of all the mushrooms. Try the northern Italian red Barbera called "Le Orme" from Michele Chiarlo. The 2005, with earthy, dried cherry flavors, is $13.

Rice and Peas (*Risi e Bisi*)

This version of the Italian classic rice and pea dish is almost like a thick soup, though it can also be prepared as a risotto.

  2   tablespoons butter
  ½   cup finely chopped yellow onion
  1   cup Arborio rice or other short-grain rice
2½   cups organic vegetable broth (such as Swanson Certified Organic)
  2   cups water
  ¼   teaspoon salt
  ¼   teaspoon freshly ground black pepper
  ½   cup (2 ounces) freshly grated Parmigiano-Reggiano cheese
  2   tablespoons finely chopped fresh flat-leaf parsley
  1   (16-ounce) package frozen green peas, thawed

❶ Melt butter in a large saucepan over medium-high heat. Add onion to pan; sauté 5 minutes or until golden. Add rice to pan; sauté 1 minute. Add broth and next 3 ingredients to pan; bring to a boil. Cover, reduce heat, and cook 20 minutes, stirring occasionally. Stir in cheese, parsley, and peas; cook 2 minutes. Yield: 6 servings (serving size: 1 cup).

CALORIES 257 (25% from fat); FAT 7.1g (sat 3.8g, mono 1.8g, poly 0.3g); PROTEIN 10.8g; CARB 38.3g; FIBER 4.8g; CHOL 17mg; IRON 1.4mg; SODIUM 615mg; CALC 156mg

Foods of the Veneto come from a region known not only for exquisite art and music but also for exceptional produce.

Risotto with Mushrooms

- 2 cups hot water
- 1 ounce dried porcini mushrooms
- 4½ cups organic vegetable broth (such as Swanson Certified Organic)
- 3 tablespoons butter, divided
- ½ cup finely chopped yellow onion
- 3 cups coarsely chopped cremini mushrooms (about 8 ounces)
- 1½ cups sliced shiitake mushrooms (about 3½ ounces)
- 1¾ cups Arborio rice or other short-grain rice
- ¾ teaspoon chopped fresh sage
- ½ teaspoon salt
- ¼ teaspoon freshly ground black pepper
- ½ cup (2 ounces) freshly grated Parmigiano-Reggiano cheese

① Combine 2 cups hot water and porcini mushrooms in a bowl; cover and let stand 15 minutes. Drain mushrooms in a colander over a bowl, reserving soaking liquid. Coarsely chop porcinis.
② Bring soaking liquid and broth to a simmer in a medium saucepan (do not boil). Keep warm over low heat.
③ Melt 2 tablespoons butter in a large saucepan over medium-high heat. Add onion to pan; sauté 5 minutes. Add porcini, cremini, and shiitake mushrooms; cook 8 minutes or until tender. Add rice; sauté 1 minute. Stir in sage, salt, and pepper. Stir in 1 cup broth mixture; cook 5 minutes or until liquid is nearly absorbed; stirring constantly. Add remaining broth mixture, ½ cup at a time, stirring constantly until each portion is absorbed before adding the next (about 25 minutes total). Remove from heat. Add remaining 1 tablespoon butter and cheese, stirring until cheese melts. Yield: 7 servings (serving size: 1 cup).

CALORIES 291 (24% from fat); FAT 7.7g (sat 4.2g, mono 1.9g, poly 0.2g); PROTEIN 9.8g; CARB 45.4g; FIBER 3.6g; CHOL 19mg; IRON 1.3mg; SODIUM 718mg; CALC 124mg

Braising

Use this slow-cooking method to deliver rich taste and tender meats.

FRUGAL-MINDED COOKS find braising a godsend. The method involves slowly simmering food, usually meat, in a moderate amount of liquid in a covered pot. It works wonders with inexpensive, tough cuts, such as bottom round, pork shoulder, and short ribs—meat that would be tough without a long, slow simmer in aromatic broth. It's also a forgiving technique. If you use a little more onion, a little less carrot, that's OK. After an hour or more of cooking, the flavors meld, and no one will know the difference.

Braising is sometimes confused with stewing. In a stew, the ingredients are submerged—as in soup. In a braise, the meat and vegetables are partially submerged (the liquid shouldn't reach more than halfway up the sides of the meat) so that they are cooked both in steam and liquid, a combination yielding richer results and more profound layering of the flavors.

We'll explore this easy technique and explain how, why, and when it works.

Red-Cooked Short Ribs

Red cooking refers to a Chinese technique of braising meat in a soy sauce and sherry mixture.

- Cooking spray
- 2 pounds boneless beef short ribs, trimmed and cut into 8 equal pieces
- 2 tablespoons minced peeled fresh ginger
- 1 tablespoon grated orange rind
- 4 garlic cloves, minced
- ½ cup dry sherry
- 2 cups sliced shiitake mushroom caps (about 3½ ounces)
- ¾ cup fat-free, less-sodium beef broth
- 6 tablespoons low-sodium soy sauce
- 1 tablespoon honey
- ¼ teaspoon crushed red pepper
- 1 (8-ounce) can sliced bamboo shoots, drained
- 1 (4-inch) cinnamon stick
- 1 (8-ounce) can diced water chestnuts, drained
- 4 cups hot cooked short-grain rice
- 1 cup (1-inch) slices green onions

① Heat a large Dutch oven over medium-high heat. Coat pan with cooking spray. Add half of beef to pan; cook 3 minutes, browning on all sides. Remove beef from pan. Repeat procedure with cooking spray and remaining beef.
② Add ginger, rind, and garlic to pan; sauté 30 seconds or until fragrant. Stir in sherry, scraping pan to loosen browned bits. Add mushrooms; cook 3 minutes or until tender, stirring frequently. Add beef, broth, and next 5 ingredients; bring to a simmer. Cover, reduce heat, and simmer 2½ hours or until beef is very tender. Stir in water chestnuts; cook 5 minutes. Discard cinnamon. Serve over rice; sprinkle with onions. Yield: 8 servings (serving size: ½ cup rice, 1 rib piece, ⅓ cup mushroom mixture, and 2 tablespoons onions).

CALORIES 331 (26% from fat); FAT 9.4g (sat 3.9g, mono 4g, poly 0.4g); PROTEIN 19.8g; CARB 40.1g; FIBER 2.7g; CHOL 46mg; IRON 3.8mg; SODIUM 370mg; CALC 26mg

All About Braising

Best Braising Choices

Typically, braising is best employed with tough cuts of meat—meat with lots of collagen, which slowly melts into the broth and infuses it with flavor. (Small, tender steaks and pork chops fare poorly in a braise; lacking the necessary connective tissue, they simply dry out.) Hard, fibrous vegetables are also good in braises, which is why you'll often see hearty root vegetables in the cooking liquid.

Equipment

A braise should be cooked in a tightly closed pot—a Dutch oven is ideal. The pot should be deep enough to hold ample liquid to partially submerge the meat and vegetables so they benefit from cooking in the broth, as well as steaming in the aromatic flavors. The pan should also be wide enough to contain a large mix of ingredients—a whole roast and lots of vegetables, for example. Be sure to choose a heavy pan, too, because it needs to maintain an even temperature. We tested the recipes in a variety of pans—aluminum, stainless steel, enamel-coated cast iron, and nonstick—and as long as the pans had a heavy bottom, they performed well.

The only other necessary component is a tight-fitting lid to seal in flavor, create internal condensation so the broth doesn't evaporate and reduce too far, and keep the food evenly heated. If your pan's lid doesn't fit snugly (or if you don't have a lid), place a sheet of aluminum foil over the pan (as a liner), and cover with the lid, a large skillet, or a baking sheet.

Browning

Browning caramelizes the natural protein, sugars, and fat on the outside of the meat. As the meat browns, some of those proteins, fats, and sugars also stick to the pot's bottom. Those browned bits are then dissolved by the cooking liquid, enriching the broth, coloring it deeply, and contributing a great deal of flavor.

Cooking Liquid

Braising is about layering flavors, starting with the caramelized meat and building up to a last touch of perhaps vinegar, honey, or fresh herbs. To further enhance the taste, braise in a broth enriched with other liquid: wine, fortified wine such as dry sherry or vermouth, fruit juices, liqueurs like brandy, or vinegar. Braising in broth alone may result in a finished dish without much depth. But enhanced broth provides a rich base with notes of sweet or sour, herby or floral, which will balance the flavor and texture of the meat and vegetables.

Flavorings

Braising is an application where dried herbs shine. When they are added at the beginning and simmer for the duration, they have plenty of time to soften and release their woodsy, hearty essence; crush them to release more flavor and aroma before adding them to the pot. Fresh herbs, on the other hand, should be added at the end to brighten the taste and offer color.

Most of our recipes also include flavorings such as onions and carrots, which cook with the meat the entire time and enrich both the meat and the broth. For a more refined presentation, these ingredients would be strained out to give way to a smooth sauce. For our homey, more casual recipes, we keep these vegetables. Onions actually melt over time; carrots provide sweet tidbits of color.

Simmering

Brown the meat on medium to medium-high, but braise on low, just so a few bubbles surface every few seconds. (Boiling will cook the meat too quickly and make it tough.) Once the broth comes to a simmer, cover the pot and turn the heat down. The meat's collagen melts when it reaches a temperature of about 160°. The trick is to bring the temperature up slowly so the sauce thickens as the meat cooks—and then hold the meat at about that temperature for the juiciest results.

Side Dish Braises

Braising is most often used with meats. But sturdy vegetables—such as sliced or quartered fennel bulbs, halved leeks, chopped kale, and cubed winter squash—can also be braised with flavorful results.

You can brown the vegetables first, or skip that step; it's not as crucial as it is for meat braises. The vegetables shouldn't be submerged; rather, some pieces should sit above and some below the liquid line. Give them a gentle stir occasionally so those in the liquid do not become too soft. Most braised vegetables are enhanced by a little acid at the end of cooking. Try a squeeze of lemon juice or a splash of vinegar. Then transfer the vegetables to a plate, and reduce the broth to a tasty glaze that can be spooned over top.

The Bottom Line

These are the most important things to remember about braising.

1 Brown the meat for more flavor.
2 Don't completely submerge the meat in liquid.
3 Cover the pan, and simmer over low heat.

Lamb Shanks with Lemon and White Beans

This is an excellent example of the way braising benefits tough cuts—lamb shanks are slowly simmered in a flavorful liquid until the meat starts to fall off the bones. Mashed beans help thicken the sauce.

Cooking spray
4   (12-ounce) lamb shanks, trimmed
2   cups chopped yellow onion
2   cups (1-inch) cubed carrot
1   cup dry white wine
1   tablespoon grated lemon rind
1   teaspoon dried sage
¾   teaspoon salt
½   teaspoon celery seeds
½   teaspoon freshly ground black pepper
1   cup fat-free, less-sodium chicken broth
2   tablespoons fresh lemon juice
1   (16-ounce) can cannellini beans or other white beans, rinsed, drained, and divided
Chopped fresh parsley (optional)

① Heat a large Dutch oven over medium heat. Coat pan with cooking spray. Add half of lamb to pan, and cook 9 minutes, browning on all sides. Remove lamb from pan. Repeat procedure with cooking spray and remaining lamb.
② Add onion and carrot to pan; cook 4 minutes, stirring frequently. Increase heat to medium-high. Stir in wine, scraping pan to loosen browned bits. Add rind and next 4 ingredients; cook 5 minutes. Add lamb and broth; bring to a simmer. Cover, reduce heat, and simmer 2½ hours or until lamb is very tender.
③ Remove lamb and vegetables from pan with a slotted spoon; place in a large bowl. Place a large zip-top plastic bag inside an 8-cup glass measure or bowl. Pour broth mixture into bag; let stand 10 minutes (fat will rise to the top). Seal bag, and carefully snip off 1 bottom corner of bag. Drain drippings into pan, stopping before fat layer reaches opening; discard fat.
④ Combine juice and 1 cup beans in a small bowl; mash with a fork until paste-like. Add juice mixture and remaining beans to pan; stir well to combine. Add lamb mixture; cook 5 minutes or until thoroughly heated. Garnish with parsley, if desired. Yield: 4 servings (serving size: 1 shank and about 1½ cups vegetable mixture).

CALORIES 399 (35% from fat); FAT 15.6g (sat 6.4g, mono 6.5g, poly 1.4g); PROTEIN 37g; CARB 25.7g; FIBER 6g; CHOL 119mg; IRON 4.1mg; SODIUM 757mg; CALC 95mg

Southwestern Pork and Sweet Potatoes

Sweet potatoes mitigate this braise's spicy heat, brought on by the combination of a pickled jalapeño's sour spiciness and the more complex heat of ancho chile powder.

2   tablespoons ancho chile powder
1   teaspoon salt
1   teaspoon ground cumin
2   garlic cloves
1   small onion, peeled and quartered (about 7 ounces)
1   pickled jalapeño pepper, stemmed
Cooking spray
2½ pounds boneless pork shoulder (Boston butt), trimmed
1   (12-ounce) dark Mexican beer (such as Dos Equis Ambar)
1   (4-inch) cinnamon stick
3   cups (1-inch) cubed peeled sweet potato (about 1 pound)
Chopped fresh cilantro (optional)

① Place first 6 ingredients in a food processor; process 1 minute or until a thick paste forms.
② Heat a large Dutch oven over medium-high heat. Coat pan with cooking spray. Add pork to pan; cook 4 minutes, browning on all sides. Remove pork from pan.
③ Add chile mixture to pan; cook 2 minutes or until fragrant, stirring occasionally. Stir in beer, scraping pan to loosen browned bits. Add pork and cinnamon; bring to a simmer. Cover, reduce heat, and simmer 2 hours or until pork is tender.
④ Remove pork from pan; shred into large pieces with 2 forks. Stir shredded pork and sweet potato into pan; cover and simmer 20 minutes or until potato is tender. Discard cinnamon stick. Garnish with cilantro, if desired. Yield: 8 servings (serving size: about ¾ cup).

CALORIES 243 (30% from fat); FAT 8g (sat 2.7g, mono 3.6g, poly 0.9g); PROTEIN 26.4g; CARB 13.6g; FIBER 2g; CHOL 83mg; IRON 2mg; SODIUM 499mg; CALC 32mg

Moroccan Chicken Thighs

Inspired by North African tagines, this aromatic dish uses skinless, boneless chicken thighs and is ready in a little over an hour. This braise tastes best with dried California apricots; they're brighter and slightly more sour than Turkish ones. Serve over couscous, and garnish with a cilantro sprig for color.

½   teaspoon olive oil
2   pounds skinless, boneless chicken thighs
2   cups thinly sliced yellow onion
1   tablespoon minced peeled fresh ginger
1   teaspoon ground cumin
½   teaspoon salt
½   teaspoon ground coriander
½   teaspoon ground cinnamon
½   teaspoon freshly ground black pepper
4   garlic cloves, minced
1½ cups fat-free, less-sodium chicken broth
1   (15½-ounce) can chickpeas (garbanzo beans), rinsed and drained
1   (7-ounce) package dried apricots (about 1⅓ cups), halved

① Heat oil in a large Dutch oven over medium-high heat. Add half of chicken to pan; cook 5 minutes, browning on all sides. Remove chicken from pan. Repeat procedure with remaining chicken.

Continued

2 Add onion to pan; sauté 3 minutes or until tender. Add ginger and next 6 ingredients; sauté 30 seconds or until fragrant. Stir in broth, scraping pan to loosen browned bits. Return chicken to pan; bring to a simmer. Cover, reduce heat, and simmer 1 hour or until chicken is tender.

3 Remove chicken from pan with a slotted spoon; cool slightly. Cut chicken into bite-sized pieces. Add chicken, chickpeas, and apricots to pan. Cover and simmer 10 minutes or until thoroughly heated. Yield: 8 servings (serving size: about ³/₄ cup).

CALORIES 301 (29% from fat); FAT 9.7g (sat 2.5g, mono 3.8g, poly 2.2g); PROTEIN 24.5g; CARB 28.2g; FIBER 5.2g; CHOL 76mg; IRON 2.7mg; SODIUM 397mg; CALC 53mg

Cuban Table Menu
serves 8

To prevent the avocado from browning, prepare the salad at the last minute.

Ropa Vieja

Grapefruit-avocado salad
Combine 4 cups pink grapefruit sections, 1 cup diced peeled avocado, and ½ cup thinly vertically sliced red onion in a large bowl. Combine 2 tablespoons chopped fresh cilantro, 2 tablespoons fresh lime juice, 1 tablespoon canola oil, ½ teaspoon sugar, ¼ teaspoon salt, and ¼ teaspoon ground red pepper, stirring with a whisk. Drizzle dressing over salad; toss gently to coat.

Warm tortillas

Ropa Vieja

This Cuban stew is made by braising beef until it can be shredded—thus the name (translated as "old clothes").

Cooking spray
2   (1-pound) flank steaks, trimmed
3   cups thinly vertically sliced red onion
2   cups red bell pepper strips (about 2 peppers)
2   cups green bell pepper strips (about 2 peppers)
4   garlic cloves, minced
6   tablespoons thinly sliced pitted green olives
1   teaspoon salt
1   teaspoon dried oregano
1   teaspoon ground cumin
½   teaspoon dried rosemary, crushed
½   teaspoon freshly ground black pepper
6   tablespoons sherry vinegar
3   cups fat-free, less-sodium beef broth
1   tablespoon no-salt-added tomato paste
2   bay leaves
½   cup chopped fresh cilantro

1 Heat a large Dutch oven over medium-high heat. Coat pan with cooking spray. Add 1 steak to pan; cook 2½ minutes on each side or until browned. Remove steak from pan. Repeat procedure with cooking spray and remaining steak.

2 Reduce heat to medium. Add onion, bell peppers, and garlic to pan; cook 7 minutes or until tender, stirring frequently. Stir in olives and next 5 ingredients; cook 30 seconds or until fragrant. Stir in vinegar, scraping pan to loosen browned bits; cook 2 minutes or until liquid almost evaporates. Stir in broth, tomato paste, and bay leaves. Add steaks; bring to a simmer. Cover, reduce heat, and cook 1½ hours or until steaks are very tender. Discard bay leaves.

3 Remove steaks from pan; shred with two forks. Stir shredded beef and cilantro into pan. Yield: 8 servings (serving size: about ³/₄ cup).

CALORIES 229 (36% from fat); FAT 9.1g (sat 3.4g, mono 3.9g, poly 0.6g); PROTEIN 26g; CARB 9.6g; FIBER 2g; CHOL 40mg; IRON 2.4mg; SODIUM 614mg; CALC 53mg

WINE NOTE: A savory beef dish such as this needs a rich red wine, but preferably one that won't break the bank since this is a humble meal. A good choice is Reds, a blend of several varietals, with zinfandel predominating. And the 2005 is $9.

Spanish Daube
(pictured on page 243)

A daube is a classic aromatic beef braise from the South of France, but here it's crossed with Spanish flavors for a twist.

Cooking spray
3   pounds bottom round roast, trimmed
2   cups thinly vertically sliced yellow onion
³/₄   cup thinly sliced bottled roasted red bell pepper
4   garlic cloves, minced
1   teaspoon salt
1   teaspoon dried thyme
½   teaspoon Spanish smoked paprika
½   teaspoon fennel seeds
½   teaspoon freshly ground black pepper
¼   teaspoon saffron threads
1   cup dry sherry
¼   teaspoon hot pepper sauce
2   cups fat-free, less-sodium beef broth
1½   cups frozen green peas, thawed
¼   cup chopped fresh parsley
1   tablespoon sherry vinegar
1   tablespoon cornstarch
1   tablespoon water

1 Heat a large Dutch oven over medium-high heat. Coat pan with cooking spray. Add beef to pan; cook 5 minutes, browning on all sides. Remove beef from pan.

2 Recoat pan with cooking spray. Add onion to pan; sauté 4 minutes or until tender. Add bell pepper and garlic; cook 1 minute, stirring constantly. Add salt and next 5 ingredients; cook 30 seconds or until fragrant, stirring constantly. Stir in sherry and hot pepper sauce, scraping pan to loosen browned bits; cook 4 minutes or until liquid is reduced by about half. Add beef and broth to pan; bring to a simmer. Cover, reduce heat, and simmer 2 hours or until beef is tender.

❸ Remove beef from pan; cool slightly. Cut beef across grain into thin slices; cover and keep warm.

❹ Add peas, parsley, and vinegar to pan; cook 5 minutes. Combine cornstarch and 1 tablespoon water in a small bowl; stir cornstarch mixture into broth mixture. Bring to a boil; cook 1 minute. Add sliced beef; cook 1 minute or until thoroughly heated. Yield: 8 servings (serving size: about 3 ounces beef and about 1/2 cup vegetable mixture).

CALORIES 291 (28% from fat); FAT 9g (sat 3.2g, mono 3.8g, poly 0.4g); PROTEIN 36.3g; CARB 10.8g; FIBER 2.2g; CHOL 98mg; IRON 3.6mg; SODIUM 561mg; CALC 36mg

Coq au Vin

Although traditionally made with an older bird, this French braise is great with supermarket chicken.

- 2   cups red wine
- 1   cup chopped yellow onion
- 1   cup chopped carrot
- 1   teaspoon salt
- 1   teaspoon dried thyme
- 1/2 teaspoon dried rosemary, crushed
- 1/2 teaspoon freshly ground black pepper
- 2   (8-ounce) chicken breast halves, skinned
- 2   (4-ounce) chicken thighs, skinned
- 2   (4-ounce) chicken drumsticks, skinned
- 1/2 cup all-purpose flour (about 2 1/4 ounces)
- 3   bacon slices, chopped
- 1/2 cup pitted dried plums, quartered
- 2   bay leaves
  Chopped fresh parsley (optional)

❶ Combine first 10 ingredients in a large bowl; cover and marinate in refrigerator at least 4 hours or up to 24 hours.

❷ Remove chicken from marinade, reserving marinade, and pat chicken dry. Place flour in a shallow dish. Dredge chicken in flour; set aside.

❸ Cook bacon in a large Dutch oven over medium-high heat until crisp. Remove bacon from pan, reserving drippings in pan; set bacon aside. Add half of chicken to pan; cook 4 minutes, browning on all sides. Remove chicken from pan. Repeat procedure with remaining chicken.

❹ Remove onion and carrot from marinade with a slotted spoon, reserving marinade. Add onion and carrot to pan; sauté 5 minutes or until softened. Stir in marinade, scraping pan to loosen browned bits. Add chicken, bacon, plums, and bay leaves; bring to a simmer. Cover, reduce heat, and simmer 1 hour and 20 minutes or until chicken is tender. Discard bay leaves. Garnish with parsley, if desired. Yield: 4 servings (serving size: about 3/4 cup sauce and 1 breast half or 1 thigh and 1 drumstick).

CALORIES 353 (29% from fat); FAT 11.2g (sat 3.5g, mono 4.4g, poly 1.7g); PROTEIN 34.2g; CARB 28.7g; FIBER 3.7g; CHOL 106mg; IRON 2.8mg; SODIUM 869mg; CALC 62mg

> ## Braised dishes are hearty and satifying, making them ideal cold-weather fare.

Fresh Fruits To Try

Exotic and unusual produce is cropping up in grocery stores, and it's a cinch to incorporate them into your diet.

Thanks to growing demand for fresh, seasonal produce and better availability of once-exotic ingredients, larger grocery stores now offer intriguing fruits from around the globe. The USDA recommends that we each consume two cups of fruit per day, and that we enjoy a variety of fruits for maximum nutrition. With so many options, you can easily expand your culinary repertoire and your palate.

We chose three widely available "new" fruits—cherimoya, horned melon, and Uniq fruit—to showcase the taste and texture of each one in familiar recipes.

Romaine Salad with Edamame and Creamy Horned Melon Dressing

DRESSING:
- 1   horned melon, halved lengthwise
- 1/3 cup nonfat buttermilk
- 1/4 cup reduced-fat mayonnaise
- 1   tablespoon fresh lemon juice
- 1/4 teaspoon salt
- 1/4 teaspoon freshly ground black pepper

REMAINING INGREDIENTS:
- 1   cup frozen shelled edamame (green soybeans)
- 1   cup thinly sliced Braeburn apple (about 1/2 apple)
- 1/2 cup thinly sliced red onion
- 7   cups torn romaine lettuce (about 14 ounces)

❶ To prepare dressing, squeeze horned melon into a fine mesh strainer over a bowl; press with back of a spoon to extract juice. Discard solids. Add buttermilk and next 4 ingredients to bowl; stir with a whisk. Cover and chill.

Continued

❷ Cook edamame according to package directions, omitting salt. Drain. Rinse with cold water; drain well.

❸ Combine edamame and remaining ingredients in a large bowl; pour dressing over, and toss gently to combine. Serve immediately. Yield: 6 servings (serving size: about 1½ cups).

CALORIES 83 (27% from fat); FAT 2.5g (sat 0.4g, mono 0.5g, poly 1.4g); PROTEIN 4.2g; CARB 11.4g; FIBER 3.3g; CHOL 0mg; IRON 1.4mg; SODIUM 214mg; CALC 61mg

Fiery Chicken Pita Sandwiches with Horned Melon Raita

RAITA:

- 1 horned melon, halved lengthwise
- 1 teaspoon fresh lemon juice
- ¼ teaspoon salt
- ¼ teaspoon ground cumin
- 1 (7-ounce) container whole plain yogurt

REMAINING INGREDIENTS:

- 3 (6-ounce) skinless, boneless chicken breast halves
- ¼ teaspoon salt
- ¼ to ½ teaspoon ground red pepper
- 2 teaspoons minced fresh garlic
- 1 teaspoon olive oil, divided
  Cooking spray
- 4 (6-inch) whole wheat pitas, warmed and cut in half

❶ Squeeze horned melon into a fine mesh strainer over a bowl; press with back of a spoon to extract juice. Discard solids. Add horned melon juice, lemon juice, and next 3 ingredients to bowl; stir with a whisk. Cover and chill.

❷ Place chicken breast halves between 2 sheets of heavy-duty plastic wrap; pound each to ½-inch thickness using a meat mallet or small heavy skillet. Sprinkle both sides of chicken with ¼ teaspoon salt and pepper; rub with garlic.

❸ Heat ½ teaspoon oil in a nonstick grill pan coated with cooking spray over medium-high heat. Add 2 breast halves to pan; cook 4 minutes on each side or until done. Remove from heat, and keep warm. Repeat procedure with remaining ½ teaspoon oil and chicken. Transfer chicken to cutting board, and cool slightly. Cut chicken into thin strips. Fill each pita half with about ½ cup chicken, and top with 2 tablespoons raita. Yield: 4 servings (serving size: 2 stuffed pita halves).

CALORIES 408 (15% from fat); FAT 6.6g (sat 2g, mono 2g, poly 1.3g); PROTEIN 47.7g; CARB 39.1g; FIBER 5g; CHOL 105mg; IRON 3.6mg; SODIUM 769mg; CALC 97mg

Horned Melon

These oblong, bright orange and yellow fruits have tough, inedible shells studded with pointed, slightly sharp horns. The interior has a lime-green, gelatin-like pulp filled with small, edible seeds. You can easily squeeze flesh and seeds from the fibrous shell. The flavor is subtle, similar to cucumber with a grassy, slightly lemony taste. Horned melons don't become very sweet, even when ripe, or have the firm flesh typical of most melons.

Selection and Storage:
Horned melons are usually ripe by the time they reach the supermarket, and the more orange the exterior, the riper the fruit. Look for fruit with a smooth skin, firm horns, and no bruising. Store at room temperature for up to two to three weeks.

Culinary Uses:
Because of its subtle, clean flavor and gelatinous texture, the fruit has broad applications in savory and sweet dishes. Strain out the seeds, and use the pulp in salad dressings, soups, sauces, or sorbet.

Test Kitchens Tip:
Hold the sliced fruit half with a dish towel to avoid pricking your fingers with the horns.

Spicy Pork Tenderloins with Uniq Fruit Salsa

The spice mixture easily doubles; use it to season chicken for a quick entrée.

PORK:

- 1 tablespoon salt-free Mexican seasoning blend
- 1 teaspoon ground cinnamon
- 1 teaspoon ground cumin
- ¾ teaspoon kosher salt
- ¼ teaspoon ground red pepper
- ⅛ teaspoon ground nutmeg
- 2 teaspoons minced garlic
- 2 (1-pound) pork tenderloins, trimmed
  Cooking spray

SALSA:

- 2 cups chopped peeled Uniq fruit (about 1)
- ½ cup diced red onion
- ½ cup diced red bell pepper
- ½ cup diced avocado
- ¼ cup chopped fresh cilantro
- 1 tablespoon honey
- 1 tablespoon fresh lime juice
- ¼ teaspoon kosher salt

❶ To prepare pork, combine first 6 ingredients in a small bowl. Rub garlic over pork. Rub spice mixture over pork. Cover and chill 1 hour.

❷ Preheat oven to 400°.

❸ Heat a cast-iron or ovenproof grill pan over medium-high heat. Coat pan with cooking spray. Add pork to pan; cook 4 minutes or until lightly browned on all sides. Transfer pork to oven. Bake at 400° for 20 minutes or until a thermometer registers 160° (slightly pink). Let pork stand 10 minutes before cutting into ¼-inch-thick slices.

❹ To prepare salsa, combine Uniq fruit and remaining ingredients in a bowl. Cover and chill until ready to serve. Serve pork with salsa. Yield: 8 servings (serving size: 3 ounces pork and ⅓ cup salsa).

CALORIES 211 (30% from fat); FAT 7g (sat 2.2g, mono 3.1g, poly 0.7g); PROTEIN 26.8g; CARB 9.9g; FIBER 1.7g; CHOL 80mg; IRON 1.7mg; SODIUM 323mg; CALC 23mg

Uniq Fruit and Cream Cheese Tart

Draining the fruit on paper towels prevents excess moisture from seeping into the filling and causing a soggy crust. Substitute orange marmalade if you don't have the mild Uniq fruit version on hand.

- 9 low-fat graham cracker cookie sheets
- ¼ cup sugar, divided
- 2 tablespoons butter, melted
- 1 large egg white
- Cooking spray
- ½ cup (4 ounces) ⅓-less-fat cream cheese, softened
- ½ cup (4 ounces) fat-free cream cheese, softened
- 5 tablespoons Uniq Fruit and Lemon Marmalade (at right), divided
- ⅛ teaspoon salt
- 3 cups Uniq fruit sections (about 2)

1 Preheat oven to 350°.

2 Place crackers in a food processor; process until finely ground and crumbs measure about 1⅓ cups. Add 2 tablespoons sugar and butter; pulse 6 times or just until mixture resembles coarse meal. Add egg white; pulse 10 times or just until blended (do not allow mixture to form a ball). Press into bottom and up sides of a 9-inch tart pan coated with cooking spray. Bake at 350° for 10 minutes; cool on a wire rack.

3 Combine cream cheeses, remaining 2 tablespoons sugar, 3 tablespoons Uniq Fruit and Lemon Marmalade, and salt in a medium bowl. Beat with a mixer at high speed until smooth. Spoon cream cheese mixture into prepared crust; cover and chill 1 hour.

4 Just before serving, place fruit sections onto several layers of heavy-duty paper towels; pat gently with additional paper towels to dry (do not press down). Place remaining 2 tablespoons Uniq Fruit and Lemon Marmalade in a small microwave-safe bowl. Microwave at MEDIUM-HIGH (70% power) 10 seconds or until melted. Arrange fruit sections over cream cheese filling, and brush with melted marmalade. Cut into 10 wedges. Yield: 10 servings (serving size: 1 wedge).

CALORIES 217 (29% from fat); FAT 6.9g (sat 4.2g, mono 1.7g, poly 0.1g); PROTEIN 5.7g; CARB 34.7g; FIBER 1.7g; CHOL 19mg; IRON 0.7mg; SODIUM 314mg; CALC 51mg

Uniq Fruit and Lemon Marmalade

A food processor makes quick work of this mild marmalade.

- 2 large Uniq fruit
- 1 lemon
- 2 cups sugar
- 2 cups water
- ⅛ teaspoon salt

1 Carefully remove rind from Uniq fruit and lemon using a vegetable peeler, making sure to avoid white pithy part of the rind. Cut Uniq rind into julienne strips to measure ¼ cup. Cut lemon rind into julienne strips to measure about 2 tablespoons. Peel and section Uniq fruit, discarding pithy white part of rind; set aside 4 cups Uniq fruit sections. Peel and section lemon, discarding pithy white part of rind.

2 Place Uniq fruit and lemon in food processor; pulse 8 times or until coarsely chopped.

3 Combine Uniq fruit mixture, Uniq fruit rind, lemon rind, sugar, 2 cups water, and salt in a large saucepan; bring to a boil. Reduce heat to medium, and cook 1 hour or until thick, stirring occasionally. Cool. (Mixture will continue to thicken as it cools.) Yield: 2½ cups (serving size: 2 tablespoons).

NOTE: Store in airtight container in refrigerator up to two weeks.

CALORIES 94 (1% from fat); FAT 0.1g (sat 0g, mono 0g, poly 0g); PROTEIN 0.3g; CARB 24.4g; FIBER 0.7g; CHOL 0mg; IRON 0.1mg; SODIUM 16mg; CALC 10mg

Uniq Fruit

Uniq citrus fruit originally grew in Jamaica. The thick, spotted, yellow-green skin that fits slackly over the segmented interior has also earned it the moniker Ugli fruit. Often seedless, the interior is like a cross between a grapefruit and a mandarin orange, with juicy flesh but without the acidity and slight bitter aftertaste of grapefruit. Uniq fruit range from the size of a navel orange to that of a large grapefruit. Look for them in the citrus section of your market from November through spring.

Selection and Storage:
Uniq fruit are sold ripe so you can enjoy them immediately. They range in color from yellow to pale orange with patches of green to almost completely green; the color does not affect the fruit's sweetness. Choose fruit that feels heavy for its size. Store at room temperature for up to five days, or refrigerate in the crisper for up to two weeks.

Culinary Uses:
Uniq fruit's easy-to-peel skin makes it ideal for snacking, while its sweet juiciness is perfect for fruit salads or mixed fresh greens. Add Uniq fruit segments at the end of cooking to shrimp or chicken stir-fries, or use them to make a chutney or relish. The juice is also good as a glaze for meats, simple syrup for desserts, zesty vinaigrette, or to flavor cooked couscous or rice.

Test Kitchens Tip:
Peel and segment the fruit as you would an orange.

Cherimoya and Lemon Frozen Daiquiris

The cherimoya's texture adds to the creaminess of this cocktail, while the fruit's delicate flavor balances the zing of the lemon and rum. Lemonade concentrate comes in 12-ounce cans, so use the extra for a sweet presentation. Dip the rims of the glasses in the remaining concentrate, then in coarse sugar.

    3   cherimoyas, peeled and halved
        lengthwise
    4   cups ice cubes
    ¾   cup white rum
    9   ounces frozen lemonade
        concentrate, thawed and undiluted
        (about 1 cup)
        Lemon wedges (optional)

1 Cut each cherimoya half into 2 wedges. Remove seeds from cherimoya pulp; discard seeds. Place pulp in a blender. Add ice, rum, and concentrate to blender. Puree until smooth. Divide cherimoya mixture evenly among 8 glasses; garnish with lemon wedges, if desired. Serve immediately. Yield: 8 servings (serving size: about ³/₄ cup).

CALORIES 192 (2% from fat); FAT 0.5g (sat 0g, mono 0g, poly 0g); PROTEIN 1.6g; CARB 43.1g; FIBER 2.9g; CHOL 0mg; IRON 0.8mg; SODIUM 5mg; CALC 29mg

Cherimoya

Native to Ecuador and Colombia, the cherimoya (chair-uh-MOY-yuh), also known as custard apple or sherbet fruit, is a green, round fruit with rough, scale-like skin. The cherimoya's creamy flesh (similar to that of a banana) holds inedible black seeds. Its flavor is tropical, a fragrant fusion of pineapple and banana with berry undertones. Cherimoyas are available in most large supermarkets from December through June or online year-round.

Selection and Storage:
Since cherimoyas bruise easily, they're usually sold unripe in a protective mesh covering. Allow the fruit to ripen at room temperature for a day or two or until they yield to gentle pressure. As they soften, cherimoyas often turn brown, which doesn't affect the flavor. Wrap ripe cherimoyas in paper towels, and refrigerate; use ripe fruit within two days since it quickly loses its flavor and texture.

Culinary Uses:
Cherimoya's creamy, custardy texture makes it a natural base for smoothies, ice cream, or even sauces for cakes. We like fresh, chilled cherimoyas best since the fruit has a mild, bitter finish that is more pronounced once cooked.

Test Kitchens Tip:
The skin of a ripe cherimoya should yield like that of an avocado. Cut fruit in half lengthwise, and scoop out flesh with a spoon, removing the hard seeds as you go.

Cardamom-Lime Sweet Rolls

Each day at *Cooking Light* taste testing, we sample from five to 20 dishes. We take small portions of each, just enough for two or three bites so that we can discuss the recipe. At the end of our gathering, we always go back for more of our favorite dish so that the most pleasant tastes of the day linger with us. It's the concept that sparked the idea for this new column: End on a high note with a satisfying dish that, more often than not, fulfills a seasonal craving. All of our recipes must meet high standards in order to be published. But to make it into this column, a recipe must be memorable and compelling—in short, sublime—good enough to lure you back for one more taste.

Cardamom-Lime Sweet Rolls
(pictured on page 242)

DOUGH:
    1   package dry yeast (about
        2¼ teaspoons)
    ¼   cup warm water (100° to 110°)
    ½   cup reduced-fat sour cream
    ⅓   cup granulated sugar
    ¼   cup butter, melted
    1   teaspoon vanilla extract
    ¾   teaspoon salt
    1   large egg, lightly beaten
    2⅓ cups all-purpose flour (about
        10½ ounces), divided
        Cooking spray
FILLING:
    ½   cup packed brown sugar
    1   tablespoon grated lime rind
    ½   to ¾ teaspoon ground cardamom
    2   tablespoons butter, melted, divided
GLAZE:
    1   cup powdered sugar
    3   tablespoons fresh lime juice

① To prepare dough, dissolve yeast in warm water in a small bowl; let stand 5 minutes.
② Combine sour cream and next 5 ingredients in a large bowl, stirring until well blended. Gradually stir yeast mixture into sour cream mixture. Lightly spoon flour into dry measuring cups; level wth a knife. Add 2 cups flour to sour cream mixture, stirring to form a soft dough.
③ Turn dough out onto a lightly floured surface. Knead until smooth and elastic (about 8 minutes); add enough of remaining flour, 1 tablespoon at a time, to prevent dough from sticking to hands (dough will feel slightly tacky).
④ Place dough in a large bowl coated with cooking spray, turning to coat top. Cover and let rise in a warm place (85°), free from drafts, 1 hour or until doubled in size. (Gently press two fingers into dough. If indention remains, dough has risen enough.)
⑤ To prepare filling, combine brown sugar, rind, and cardamom. Divide dough into two equal portions. Working with 1 portion at a time, roll dough into a 12 x 10–inch rectangle; brush with 1 tablespoon butter. Sprinkle half of filling over dough. Beginning with a long side, roll up jelly-roll fashion; pinch seam to seal (do not seal ends of roll). Repeat procedure with remaining dough, 1 tablespoon butter, and filling. Cut each roll into 12 (1-inch) slices. Place slices, cut sides up, in a 13 x 9–inch baking pan coated with cooking spray. Cover and let rise 30 minutes or until doubled in size.
⑥ Preheat oven to 350°.
⑦ Uncover dough. Bake at 350° for 25 minutes or until lightly browned. Cool in pan 5 minutes on a wire rack.
⑧ To prepare glaze, combine powdered sugar and juice, stirring until smooth. Drizzle glaze over warm rolls. Yield: 24 rolls (serving size: 1 roll).

CALORIES 130 (26% from fat); FAT 3.8g (sat 2.3g, mono 0.8g, poly 0.2g); PROTEIN 1.9g; CARB 22.2g; FIBER 0.5g; CHOL 19mg; IRON 0.8mg; SODIUM 102mg; CALC 17mg

Dinner Day

On this annual January holiday, Pennsylvania encourages neighbors to meet and forge bonds over supper.

"GOOD FENCES MAKE GOOD NEIGHBORS," one neighbor reminds another in a famous poem by Robert Frost. But on the second Saturday of January an official Pennsylvania holiday encourages us to turn that wisdom on its head. Invite a Neighbor to Dinner Day celebrates the slogan "build bridges, not fences" and urges everyone, Pennsylvania resident or not, to strengthen their communities through the simple act of inviting a neighbor over for dinner.

DINNER DAY MENU
(Serves 6)

Edamole with crudités

Winter Minestrone

Bitter Greens Salad

Lemon Chicken with Ginger and Pine Nuts
or
Chile-Brined Roasted Pork Loin

Baked Pommes Frites
or
Turnip-Gruyère Gratin

Chardonnay

Apple Upside-Down Cake
or
Butter Rum Pound Cake

Coffee and tea

QUICK & EASY • MAKE AHEAD
Edamole

This dip looks like traditional guacamole, but edamame lends it a pleasing green color. Combine the ingredients, and chill up to one day ahead. Serve with cut-up veggies to get the party rolling.

¾ cup frozen shelled edamame, thawed
3 tablespoons water
2 tablespoons avocado or extravirgin olive oil
1 tablespoon fresh lemon juice
¼ teaspoon kosher salt
¼ teaspoon hot pepper sauce
1 garlic clove, halved

① Combine all ingredients in a food processor; process until smooth. Cover and chill. Yield: 6 servings (serving size: about 2½ tablespoons).

CALORIES 68 (73% from fat); FAT 5.5g (sat 0.5g, mono 3.3g, poly 0.6g); PROTEIN 2.5g; CARB 2.1g; FIBER 1g; CHOL 0mg; IRON 0.7mg; SODIUM 85mg; CALC 11mg

"You can change the fabric of your neighborhood ... just by stopping neighbors in the street and inviting them to dinner." —Jeffrey Smith, founder of Dinner Day

Winter Minestrone

Prep all the vegetables a day ahead, and this soup will come together quickly just before guests arrive.

- 2 teaspoons olive oil
- ½ cup chopped onion
- ½ teaspoon dried basil
- ½ teaspoon dried oregano
- 2 garlic cloves, minced
- 1¼ cups cubed peeled acorn or butternut squash (about 1 medium)
- ¾ cup diced zucchini
- ½ cup chopped carrot
- ½ cup diced fennel
- 1 cup water
- 1 (14-ounce) can fat-free, less-sodium chicken broth
- 5 tablespoons no-salt-added tomato paste
- ¼ cup uncooked ditalini (very short tube-shaped pasta)
- 2½ cups chopped Swiss chard
- ½ cup rinsed and drained canned Great Northern beans
- ½ teaspoon freshly ground black pepper
- 2 tablespoons grated Asiago cheese

① Heat oil in a Dutch oven over medium-high heat. Add onion and next 3 ingredients to pan; sauté 5 minutes or until onion is tender. Add squash and next 3 ingredients; sauté 5 minutes. Stir in 1 cup water, broth, and tomato paste; bring to a boil. Reduce heat, and simmer 10 minutes or until vegetables are crisp-tender. Stir in pasta; cook 8 minutes, stirring occasionally. Add chard; cook 3 minutes. Add beans; cook 2 minutes or until thoroughly heated. Stir in pepper. Serve with cheese. Yield: 6 servings (serving size: about 1 cup minestrone and 1 teaspoon cheese).

CALORIES 102 (22% from fat); FAT 2.5g (sat 0.7g, mono 1.4g, poly 0.2g); PROTEIN 4.5g; CARB 16.7g; FIBER 3.6g; CHOL 2mg; IRON 1.6mg; SODIUM 263mg; CALC 71mg

Bitter Greens Salad

To prepare this salad ahead, whisk together the dressing ingredients, then refrigerate. Combine the greens, and refrigerate separately; toss with the dressing and garnish with cheese right before serving.

DRESSING:
- 1 tablespoon cider vinegar
- 1½ teaspoons sugar
- 1 teaspoon chopped fresh thyme
- 1½ teaspoons extravirgin olive oil
- 1 teaspoon Dijon mustard
- ¼ teaspoon salt
- ¼ teaspoon freshly ground black pepper

REMAINING INGREDIENTS:
- 4 cups torn Boston lettuce
- 2 cups torn radicchio
- 1 cup torn Belgian endive
- ¼ cup (1 ounce) shaved Parmigiano-Reggiano cheese

① To prepare dressing, combine first 7 ingredients in a large bowl, stirring with a whisk. Add lettuce, radicchio, and endive; toss to coat. Arrange on a platter; top with cheese. Yield: 6 servings (serving size: about ¾ cup salad and about 1½ teaspoons cheese).

CALORIES 45 (50% from fat); FAT 2.5g (sat 1g, mono 1.2g, poly 0.2g); PROTEIN 2.6g; CARB 3.5g; FIBER 1.1g; CHOL 3mg; IRON 0.7mg; SODIUM 193mg; CALC 77mg

Lemon Chicken with Ginger and Pine Nuts

- 2 tablespoons pine nuts
- 2 tablespoons minced fresh parsley
- ⅛ teaspoon saffron threads, crushed
- 1 garlic clove, minced
- ¾ teaspoon kosher salt, divided
- 6 (6-ounce) skinless, boneless chicken breast halves
- 2 tablespoons olive oil
- 1½ cups finely chopped onion (about 1 medium)
- 2 tablespoons finely chopped prosciutto (about 1 ounce)
- ⅛ teaspoon crushed red pepper
- ⅓ cup fat-free less-sodium chicken broth
- ⅓ cup dry white wine
- 2 tablespoons fresh lemon juice
- 1½ teaspoons chopped fresh thyme
- ½ teaspoon grated peeled fresh ginger
- ⅛ teaspoon freshly ground black pepper
- 1 bay leaf

① Combine first 4 ingredients in a mini food chopper; add ¼ teaspoon salt. Process until mixture forms a paste. Sprinkle remaining ½ teaspoon salt evenly over chicken.

② Heat oil in a large nonstick skillet over medium-high heat. Add chicken; cook 3 minutes on each side or until browned. Remove chicken from pan; keep warm. Add onion, prosciutto, and red pepper to pan; sauté 2 minutes or until onion is tender. Stir in broth and remaining ingredients; bring to a boil. Cover, reduce heat, and simmer 20 minutes. Return chicken to pan. Stir in pine nut mixture; cook 10 minutes or until chicken is done. Discard bay leaf. Yield: 6 servings (serving size: 1 chicken breast half and about 2 tablespoons pine nut mixture).

CALORIES 280 (30% from fat); FAT 9.2g (sat 1.5g, mono 4.4g, poly 1.9g); PROTEIN 41.6g; CARB 3.9g; FIBER 0.9g; CHOL 103mg; IRON 1.8mg; SODIUM 461mg; CALC 36mg

Chile-Brined Roasted Pork Loin

An entire can of chipotle chiles may sound like a lot, but because it is in the brine, the heat in the pork is subtle. Mexican oregano is stronger and not as sweet as the more typical Greek oregano, though that's an acceptable substitute. Leftover pork also freezes well for up to two months.

- 1 cup water
- 2 tablespoons cumin seeds
- 2 tablespoons grated lime rind
- 1 tablespoon Mexican dried oregano
- 6 garlic cloves, minced
- 6 cups water
- ½ cup kosher salt
- ½ cup sugar
- 1 (7-ounce) can chipotle chiles in adobo sauce, chopped
- 2 cups ice cubes
- 1 (3-pound) boneless pork loin, trimmed
- ¼ cup fresh lime juice
- 2 teaspoons freshly ground black pepper
- 1 teaspoon Mexican dried oregano
- 2 garlic cloves, minced
  Cooking spray

❶ Combine first 5 ingredients in a small saucepan. Bring to a boil; remove from heat. Pour into a large bowl; cool to room temperature. Add 6 cups water, salt, and sugar, stirring until salt and sugar dissolve. Stir in chiles. Pour salt mixture into a 2-gallon zip-top plastic bag. Add ice and pork; seal. Marinate in refrigerator 24 hours, turning occasionally.
❷ Preheat oven to 450°.
❸ Remove pork from bag; discard brine. Pat pork dry with paper towels. Combine juice and next 3 ingredients. Place pork in a roasting pan coated with cooking spray. Brush juice mixture over pork. Bake at 450° for 15 minutes. Reduce oven temperature to 325° (do not remove pork from oven); bake an additional 45 minutes or until thermometer inserted in thickest portion of pork registers 155°. Place pork on a platter. Cover with foil; let stand 15 minutes. Cut into thin slices. Yield: 12 servings (serving size: about 3 ounces).

CALORIES 154 (44% from fat); FAT 7.5g (sat 2.7g, mono 3.5g, poly 0.5g); PROTEIN 18.9g; CARB 1.5g; FIBER 0.3g; CHOL 51mg; IRON 0.7mg; SODIUM 225mg; CALC 10mg

Baked Pommes Frites

These "fries" are easy to assemble and can bake in the oven while the chicken cooks on the stovetop.

- 3 potatoes (about 2 pounds), each cut into 8 wedges
- 1½ tablespoons olive oil
  Cooking spray
- ¾ teaspoon minced fresh thyme
- ½ teaspoon salt
- ½ teaspoon freshly ground black pepper

❶ Preheat oven to 425°.
❷ Combine potatoes and oil in a large bowl; toss well to coat. Arrange potatoes in a single layer on a baking sheet coated with cooking spray. Bake at 425° for 35 minutes or until golden brown, turning 2 times.
❸ Combine thyme, salt, and pepper in a small bowl. Sprinkle potatoes evenly with thyme mixture; toss to coat. Yield: 6 servings (serving size: 4 wedges).

CALORIES 195 (16% from fat); FAT 3.5g (sat 0.5g, mono 2.5g, poly 0.4g); PROTEIN 3.5g; CARB 38.3g; FIBER 3.7g; CHOL 0mg; IRON 2.1mg; SODIUM 209mg; CALC 16mg

Turnip-Gruyère Gratin

This rich gratin is a satisfying accompaniment for roasts.

- 1 pound turnips, peeled and cut into ¼-inch-thick slices
- 1 pound baking potatoes, peeled and cut into ¼-inch-thick slices
- ½ teaspoon salt, divided
  Cooking spray
- 1 cup fat-free milk, divided
- 2 tablespoons all-purpose flour
- ¼ teaspoon dried thyme
- ¼ teaspoon freshly ground black pepper
- 6 tablespoons (1½ ounces) shredded Gruyère cheese
- 3 tablespoons seasoned breadcrumbs
- 1 tablespoon butter, melted

❶ Preheat oven to 425°.
❷ Place turnips in a large saucepan, and cover with water. Bring to a boil. Reduce heat, and simmer 5 minutes. Add potatoes to pan, and simmer 8 minutes or until potatoes are almost tender. Drain. Sprinkle turnips and potatoes evenly with ¼ teaspoon salt, and arrange slices in an 11 x 7–inch baking dish coated with cooking spray.
❸ Combine ¼ cup milk, flour, and thyme in a medium saucepan, and stir with a whisk until well blended. Gradually add remaining ¾ cup milk, stirring with a whisk until smooth. Stir in remaining ¼ teaspoon salt and black pepper. Cook over medium heat 7 minutes or until thick, stirring frequently. Remove from heat, and add cheese, stirring until smooth. Pour cheese mixture over turnip and potato slices, and toss gently.
❹ Combine breadcrumbs and butter; sprinkle over turnip mixture. Bake at 425° for 15 minutes or until thoroughly heated. Serve immediately. Yield: 6 servings.

CALORIES 166 (24% from fat); FAT 4.5g (sat 2.6g, mono 1.2g, poly 0.4g); PROTEIN 6.1g; CARB 25.8g; FIBER 2.9g; CHOL 13mg; IRON 0.8mg; SODIUM 372mg; CALC 189mg

Apple Upside-Down Cake

Flaxseed meal is sold in supermarkets, or you can make your own by grinding ⅓ cup flaxseed in a blender. If you don't have a 10-inch cast-iron skillet, bake the cake in a 9-inch square cake pan.

    1 tablespoon dark corn syrup
    2 teaspoons butter
    Cooking spray
    ½ cup packed brown sugar
    2 tablespoons chopped pecans
    3 cups thinly sliced peeled Braeburn
       apple (about 1¼ pounds)
    ⅔ cup cake flour
    ½ cup flaxseed meal
    1 teaspoon baking powder
    ¼ teaspoon salt
    ⅔ cup packed brown sugar, divided
    2 teaspoons grated orange rind
    1 teaspoon vanilla extract
    2 large eggs, lightly beaten
    2 large egg whites
    ½ cup whipped cream
    Ground cinnamon (optional)

1 Preheat oven to 375°.
2 Melt syrup and butter in a 10-inch cast-iron skillet coated with cooking spray over medium-high heat; remove from heat. Sprinkle with ½ cup sugar and pecans; arrange apple slices spokelike over sugar mixture, working from center of skillet to edge.
3 Lightly spoon flour into dry measuring cups; level with a knife. Combine flour and next 3 ingredients, stirring with a whisk.
4 Combine ⅓ cup sugar, rind, vanilla, and eggs, stirring with a whisk. Beat egg whites with a mixer at high speed until soft peaks form. Add remaining ⅓ cup sugar, 1 tablespoon at a time, beating until stiff peaks form. Add vanilla mixture to flour mixture; stir just until moist. Gently fold in egg white mixture.
5 Spoon batter over apples. Bake at 375° for 30 minutes or until a wooden pick inserted in center comes out clean. Cool in pan 5 minutes on a wire rack. Loosen cake from sides of pan with a knife. Place a plate upside down on top of cake. Invert cake onto plate. Cut into wedges. Serve with whipped cream. Garnish with cinnamon, if desired. Yield: 8 servings (serving size: 1 wedge).

CALORIES 306 (29% from fat); FAT 9.8g (sat 3.1g, mono 2.9g, poly 3.1g); PROTEIN 5.4g; CARB 51.1g; FIBER 3.2g; CHOL 58mg; IRON 2.3mg; SODIUM 178mg; CALC 109mg

MAKE AHEAD
Butter Rum Pound Cake

Butter, a classic ingredient in pound cake, contributes to the flavor and tender texture of this dense, rich dessert. Slices of leftover cake are good toasted and garnished with fresh fruit.

CAKE:
    Cooking spray
    2 tablespoons all-purpose flour
    1½ cups all-purpose flour (about
       6¾ ounces)
    ¼ teaspoon baking powder
    ¼ teaspoon baking soda
    ¼ teaspoon salt
    1 cup granulated sugar
    ½ cup butter, softened
    2 large eggs
    ½ cup spiced rum (such as Captain
       Morgan's)
GLAZE:
    1 cup powdered sugar
    1½ tablespoons spiced rum (such as
       Captain Morgan's)

1 Preheat oven to 350°.
2 To prepare cake, coat an 8 x 4–inch loaf pan with cooking spray; dust with 2 tablespoons flour.
3 Lightly spoon 1½ cups flour into dry measuring cups; level with a knife. Combine 1½ cups flour and next 3 ingredients, stirring with a whisk until blended.
4 Place granulated sugar and butter in a large bowl; beat with a mixer at medium speed until well blended (about 5 minutes). Add eggs, 1 at a time, beating well after each addition. Add flour mixture and ½ cup rum alternately to sugar mixture, beginning and ending with flour mixture. Spoon batter into prepared pan. Bake at 350° for 50 minutes or until a wooden pick inserted in center comes out clean. Cool in pan 10 minutes on a wire rack. Run a knife around edges of pan; remove cake from pan. Cool completely on wire rack.
5 To prepare glaze, combine powdered sugar and 1½ tablespoons rum, stirring until smooth. Drizzle glaze over cake. Yield: 12 servings (serving size: 1 slice).

CALORIES 261 (30% from fat); FAT 8.6g (sat 5.1g, mono 2.3g, poly 0.5g); PROTEIN 2.9g; CARB 39.6g; FIBER 0.5g; CHOL 55mg; IRON 1mg; SODIUM 150mg; CALC 14mg

MENU OF THE MONTH
Table for Two

Take a make-ahead approach to cook a memorable Valentine's Day feast for your sweetheart.

VALENTINE'S DINNER MENU
(Serves 2)

Onion Soup with Cheese Crostini

Spicy Grilled Shrimp over Shaved Fennel Slaw

Fennel and Rosemary–Crusted Roasted Rack of Lamb

Spicy-Sweet Pepper Medley

Truffled Polenta

Cinnamon-Orange Crème Brûlée

Onion Soup with Cheese Crostini

Prepare the recipe, through step one, up to two days ahead and refrigerate. The flavor intensifies with time. Gently reheat on the stovetop, and then broil with the crostini.

SOUP:

- 1 teaspoon butter
- 2 cups thinly sliced onion (about 2 medium)
- ¼ teaspoon sugar
- ⅛ teaspoon freshly ground black pepper
- ¼ cup dry red wine
- 1½ cups fat-free, less-sodium chicken broth
- 1½ cups water
- ⅛ teaspoon dried thyme

REMAINING INGREDIENTS:

- 2 (½-inch-thick) slices diagonally cut French bread baguette, toasted
- 2 tablespoons grated Gruyère cheese

1 To prepare soup, melt butter in a medium saucepan over medium heat. Add onion, sugar, and pepper to pan. Cook 15 minutes or until golden brown, stirring occasionally. Stir in wine; cook 2 minutes or until wine almost evaporates. Add broth, 1½ cups water, and thyme; bring to a boil. Cook until reduced to 2½ cups (about 15 minutes).
2 Preheat broiler.
3 Place 1¼ cups soup into each of 2 oven-proof soup bowls. Place bowls on a baking sheet. Top each serving with 1 slice baguette. Sprinkle 1 tablespoon cheese over each serving. Broil 3 minutes or until cheese melts. Serve immediately. Yield: 2 servings.

CALORIES 172 (24% from fat); FAT 4.6g (sat 2.6g, mono 1.4g, poly 0.3g); PROTEIN 6.6g; CARB 20.6g; FIBER 2g; CHOL 12mg; IRON 0.7mg; SODIUM 464mg; CALC 106mg

Spicy Grilled Shrimp over Shaved Fennel Slaw

The colorful slaw also makes a fresh, crunchy side to roasted poultry or pork.

SLAW:

- 1 cup thinly sliced fennel bulb (about 1 small)
- ½ cup thinly sliced red bell pepper
- ¼ cup vertically sliced red onion
- 2 teaspoons coarse-grain Dijon mustard
- 2 teaspoons extravirgin olive oil
- 2 teaspoons fresh lime juice
- ¼ teaspoon freshly ground black pepper
- ⅛ teaspoon salt
- ⅛ teaspoon sugar

SHRIMP:

- 6 peeled and deveined jumbo shrimp (about ¾ pound)
- 1 teaspoon olive oil
- ⅛ teaspoon salt
- ⅛ teaspoon ground red pepper
- 1 tablespoon thinly sliced fresh mint
- 1 teaspoon grated lime rind

1 To prepare slaw, combine first 9 ingredients in a small bowl. Cover and chill up to 2 hours.
2 To prepare shrimp, combine shrimp and next 3 ingredients. Heat a grill pan over medium-high heat. Add shrimp to pan; cook 2 minutes on each side or until done. Place shrimp in a small bowl. Add mint and rind; toss well. Serve warm shrimp over slaw. Yield: 2 servings (serving size: ¾ cup slaw and 3 shrimp).

CALORIES 143 (48% from fat); FAT 7.7g (sat 1.1g, mono 5.5g, poly 0.8g); PROTEIN 7.2g; CARB 13.7g; FIBER 4.5g; CHOL 32mg; IRON 1.5mg; SODIUM 508mg; CALC 77mg

Fennel and Rosemary–Crusted Roasted Rack of Lamb

- 1 tablespoon fennel seeds, crushed
- 1 tablespoon chopped fresh rosemary
- 1 teaspoon freshly ground black pepper
- ¼ teaspoon salt
- 6 garlic cloves, minced
- 1 (12-ounce) French-cut rack of lamb, trimmed (6 ribs)
- Cooking spray
- Rosemary sprigs (optional)

1 Preheat oven to 475°.
2 Combine first 5 ingredients in a small bowl. Rub lamb evenly with garlic mixture; place on a broiler pan coated with cooking spray. Bake at 475° for 15 minutes or until a thermometer registers 145° (medium-rare) to 160° (medium). Garnish with rosemary sprigs, if desired. Yield: 2 servings (serving size: 3 ribs).

CALORIES 227 (49% from fat); FAT 12.3g (sat 5.5g, mono 5g, poly 0.5g); PROTEIN 23.1g; CARB 5.2g; FIBER 1.6g; CHOL 72mg; IRON 2.8mg; SODIUM 354mg; CALC 68mg

Spicy-Sweet Pepper Medley

If you chop and prepare ingredients for this dish the night before, this sauté will come together easily and quickly on Valentine's evening.

- 1 teaspoon olive oil
- ¾ cup (1-inch) pieces yellow bell pepper
- ¾ cup (1-inch) pieces orange bell pepper
- ¾ cup (1-inch) pieces red onion
- ¼ teaspoon crushed red pepper
- 2 garlic cloves, minced
- ¼ cup chopped seeded plum tomato (about 2)
- ⅛ teaspoon salt
- 1 teaspoon red wine vinegar
- 2 tablespoons chopped basil

Continued

1 Heat oil in a medium saucepan over medium heat. Add bell peppers and next 3 ingredients. Cook 15 minutes or until peppers are tender, stirring occasionally. Stir in tomato and salt. Cover, reduce heat, and cook 30 minutes, stirring occasionally. Stir in vinegar. Increase heat, and cook, uncovered, 5 minutes or until liquid almost evaporates. Sprinkle with basil. Yield: 2 servings (serving size: about 1 cup).

CALORIES 60 (41% from fat); FAT 2.7g (sat 0.4g, mono 1.7g, poly 0.4g); PROTEIN 1.5g; CARB 9g; FIBER 2.2g; CHOL 0mg; IRON 0.7mg; SODIUM 156mg; CALC 21mg

QUICK & EASY
Truffled Polenta

A two-ounce bottle of truffle oil costs about $12, but a little goes a long way to add an earthy and seductive fragrance to this easy side dish. Look for small bottles of the oil in gourmet grocery stores or online. It's also delicious drizzled over mashed potatoes or risotto.

- 1 cup fat-free milk
- ⅓ cup fat-free, less-sodium chicken broth
- ⅛ teaspoon salt
- ⅓ cup dry instant polenta
- ¼ cup (1 ounce) grated fresh Parmesan cheese
- 1½ teaspoons white truffle oil

1 Combine first 3 ingredients in a small saucepan; bring to a boil. Gradually add polenta, stirring constantly with a whisk. Cook 1 minute or until thick over medium heat, stirring constantly. Remove from heat; stir in cheese. Drizzle with oil. Serve immediately. Yield: 2 servings (serving size: ¾ cup polenta and ¾ teaspoon oil).

CALORIES 237 (28% from fat); FAT 7.4g (sat 3g, mono 3.8g, poly 0.4g); PROTEIN 12.3g; CARB 30.3g; FIBER 2.6g; CHOL 13mg; IRON 0.7mg; SODIUM 514mg; CALC 331mg

MAKE AHEAD
Cinnamon-Orange Crème Brûlée

Bake and refrigerate this dessert the night before, so all you need to do is caramelize the sugar topping before serving dinner.

- 1 cup 2% reduced-fat milk
- 6 tablespoons nonfat dry milk
- Dash of salt
- 1 (1-inch) orange rind strip
- 1 (1-inch) piece cinnamon stick
- ¼ teaspoon vanilla extract
- ¼ cup granulated sugar, divided
- 2 large egg yolks, lightly beaten

1 Preheat oven to 300°.
2 Combine first 3 ingredients in a small saucepan over medium heat. Heat to 180° or until tiny bubbles form around edge (do not boil), stirring occasionally. Remove from heat; stir in rind and cinnamon stick. Cover and let steep 10 minutes. Strain milk mixture through a sieve into a bowl; discard solids. Stir in vanilla.
3 Combine 2 tablespoons sugar and egg yolks in a medium bowl; stir well with a whisk to combine.
4 Gradually add milk mixture to egg mixture, stirring constantly with a whisk. Divide milk mixture evenly between 2 shallow (6-ounce) dishes. Place dishes in a 13 x 9–inch baking pan; add hot water to pan to a depth of 1 inch. Bake at 300° for 40 minutes or until center barely moves when dish is touched. Remove dishes from pan; cool completely on a wire rack. Cover and chill at least 4 hours or overnight.
5 Sift remaining 2 tablespoons sugar evenly over top of brûlées. Holding a kitchen blowtorch about 2 inches from top of each custard, heat sugar, moving torch back and forth, until sugar is completely melted and caramelized (about 1 minute). Serve within 1 hour. Yield: 2 servings (serving size: 1 brûlée).

CALORIES 301 (21% from fat); FAT 7g (sat 3.2g, mono 2.7g, poly 0.8g); PROTEIN 15.6g; CARB 44.1g; FIBER 0g; CHOL 219mg; IRON 0.6mg; SODIUM 273mg; CALC 479mg

LIGHTEN UP
Party-Worthy Dip

An Alabama reader has a cheesy bean dip revamped for get-togethers and football parties.

Jennifer Valenti of Alabaster, Alabama, is an avid entertainer and has a playbook of tasty party recipes that she calls on for quick and easy crowd-pleasers. Party Bean Dip with Baked Tortilla Chips, which uses several canned or bottled items and preshredded cheese, has been a long-time favorite. But since Valenti has a history of diabetes in her family and works to maintain a healthful weight, it's become more important for her to prepare good-for-you foods. Valenti turned to *Cooking Light* for help with her high-fat predicament.

To reinvent this dip, our first step was to trade heavy corn chips for healthier homemade flour tortilla chips. This cut almost nine grams of fat and 87 calories per serving and allowed us to keep regular cheese in the recipe. To further reduce fat, we switched from regular sour cream to light, trimming another gram of fat per serving. We also slightly reduced the amount of sour cream and cheese to keep calories and fat in check. Changing sliced olives to chopped allowed for better distribution of a slightly smaller amount and shaved 25 milligrams of sodium per serving. Using organic refried beans and salsa also helped manage sodium levels, dropping 141 milligrams per serving. A little fresh lime juice and ground cumin perked up the flavor of the beans without adding extra calories.

serving size: ½ cup dip and 4 tortilla wedges	before	after
CALORIES PER SERVING	293	162
FAT	18.2g	5.6g
PERCENT OF TOTAL CALORIES	56%	31%

Party Bean Dip with Baked Tortilla Chips

Using organic salsa and organic refried beans helps keep sodium in check. This dip comes together quickly for parties or as an appetizer course.

- 6 (8-inch) flour tortillas
- Cooking spray
- ½ teaspoon paprika
- 2 teaspoons fresh lime juice
- ½ teaspoon ground cumin
- 1 (16-ounce) can organic refried beans (such as Amy's or Eden Organic)
- 1 cup organic bottled salsa (such as Muir Glen)
- ⅔ cup frozen whole-kernel corn, thawed
- ¼ cup chopped green onions
- 2 tablespoons chopped black olives
- ¾ cup (3 ounces) preshredded 4-cheese Mexican blend cheese
- ¾ cup (6 ounces) light sour cream
- 2 tablespoons chopped fresh cilantro

① Preheat oven to 350°.
② Cut each tortilla into 8 wedges, and arrange wedges in single layers on 2 baking sheets. Lightly coat wedges with cooking spray; sprinkle with paprika. Bake at 350° for 15 minutes or until lightly browned and crisp. Cool.
③ Combine juice, cumin, and beans in a medium bowl, stirring until well combined. Spread mixture evenly into an 11 x 7-inch baking dish coated with cooking spray. Spread salsa evenly over beans. Combine corn, onions, and olives; spoon corn mixture evenly over salsa. Sprinkle cheese over corn mixture. Bake at 350° for 20 minutes or until bubbly. Let stand 10 minutes. Top with sour cream; sprinkle with cilantro. Serve with tortilla chips. Yield: 12 servings (serving size: ½ cup dip and 4 tortilla wedges).

CALORIES 162 (31% from fat); FAT 5.6g (sat 2.4g, mono 1.9g, poly 0.4g); PROTEIN 6.8g; CARB 23.2g; FIBER 2.8g; CHOL 13mg; IRON 1.3mg; SODIUM 331mg; CALC 143mg

20 Minute Dishes

From steak to shrimp, chicken to chili, here are simple, fresh, and easy meals you can make superfast.

Pork Medallions with Apricot-Orange Sauce

Serve with steamed green beans topped with toasted sliced almonds.

- 1 tablespoon olive oil, divided
- 1 (1-pound) pork tenderloin, cut into 8 (1-inch-thick) slices
- ½ teaspoon salt
- ¼ teaspoon black pepper
- 1 cup thinly sliced onion
- ½ cup dried apricots, sliced
- ½ cup fat-free, less-sodium chicken broth
- 2 tablespoons fresh orange juice
- 2 teaspoons bottled minced garlic
- ⅛ teaspoon black pepper
- 1 tablespoon chopped fresh flat-leaf parsley

① Heat 2 teaspoons oil in a large nonstick skillet over medium-high heat. Sprinkle pork evenly with salt and ¼ teaspoon pepper. Add pork to pan; cook 3 minutes on each side or until browned. Remove from pan; keep warm.
② Heat remaining 1 teaspoon oil in pan. Add onion to pan; sauté 3 minutes or until tender. Stir in apricots and next 4 ingredients; bring to a boil. Cook 2 minutes or until slightly thickened. Remove from heat; stir in parsley. Serve sauce with pork. Yield: 4 servings (serving size: 2 pork slices and ¼ cup sauce).

CALORIES 236 (29% from fat); FAT 7.6g (sat 1.8g, mono 4g, poly 0.7g); PROTEIN 23.8g; CARB 15.8g; FIBER 1.6g; CHOL 63mg; IRON 2.2mg; SODIUM 390mg; CALC 23mg

Chipotle Barbecue Burgers with Slaw

The cool sour cream dressing in the slaw balances the spiciness of chiles in the burger. Toast the buns while the patties cook. Serve with baked sweet potato chips.

- ½ cup dry breadcrumbs
- 2 tablespoons barbecue sauce
- 1 tablespoon chopped chipotle chiles, canned in adobo sauce
- 1 teaspoon bottled minced garlic
- 1 pound lean ground beef
- 1 large egg, lightly beaten
- Cooking spray
- 2 cups cabbage-and-carrot coleslaw
- 1 tablespoon reduced-fat mayonnaise
- 1 tablespoon reduced-fat sour cream
- 1 teaspoon sugar
- 1 teaspoon cider vinegar
- ⅛ teaspoon salt
- ⅛ teaspoon black pepper
- 4 (1½-ounce) hamburger buns

① Combine first 6 ingredients. Divide mixture into 4 equal portions, shaping each into a ½-inch-thick patty.
② Heat a large nonstick skillet over medium-high heat. Coat pan with cooking spray. Add patties to pan; cook 4 minutes on each side or until a meat thermometer registers 160°.
③ Combine coleslaw and next 6 ingredients in a large bowl; toss well. Place 1 patty on bottom half of each bun; top each serving with ½ cup coleslaw mixture and top half of bun. Yield: 4 servings (serving size: 1 burger).

CALORIES 358 (23% from fat); FAT 9.1g (sat 3g, mono 2.7g, poly 1.9g); PROTEIN 32.1g; CARB 36.3g; FIBER 2.6g; CHOL 115mg; IRON 4.3mg; SODIUM 609mg; CALC 112mg

Shrimp and Broccoli Stir-Fry

¼ cup fat-free, less-sodium chicken broth
2 tablespoons rice vinegar
2 tablespoons low-sodium soy sauce
2 teaspoons cornstarch
½ teaspoon dark sesame oil
¼ teaspoon crushed red pepper
1 tablespoon canola oil, divided
1 tablespoon minced peeled fresh ginger
1 tablespoon bottled minced garlic
1 pound peeled and deveined large shrimp
¼ teaspoon salt
4 cups small broccoli florets
1 cup vertically sliced onion

❶ Combine first 6 ingredients in a small bowl, stirring with a whisk.
❷ Heat 2 teaspoons canola oil in a large nonstick skillet over medium-high heat. Add ginger and garlic to pan; stir-fry 30 seconds. Sprinkle shrimp with salt. Add shrimp to pan, and stir-fry 3 minutes or until done. Remove shrimp mixture from pan.
❸ Add remaining 1 teaspoon canola oil to pan. Add broccoli and onion to pan; stir-fry 4 minutes or until broccoli is crisp-tender. Add shrimp mixture and broth mixture to pan; cook 1 minute or until thickened, stirring constantly. Yield: 4 servings (serving size: 1 cup).

CALORIES 220 (27% from fat); FAT 6.7g (sat 0.8g, mono 2.4g, poly 1.9g); PROTEIN 26.2g; CARB 11.8g; FIBER 2.8g; CHOL 172mg; IRON 3.6mg; SODIUM 577mg; CALC 105mg

Broiled Flank Steak with Warm Tomato Topping

1¼ teaspoons ground cumin, divided
¾ teaspoon salt, divided
⅛ teaspoon ground red pepper
1 (1-pound) flank steak, trimmed
Cooking spray
1 teaspoon olive oil
1 teaspoon bottled minced garlic
1 jalapeño pepper, seeded and minced (about 1 tablespoon)
2 cups grape or cherry tomatoes, halved
¼ cup chopped fresh cilantro

❶ Preheat broiler.
❷ Combine 1 teaspoon cumin, ½ teaspoon salt, and red pepper; sprinkle evenly over steak. Place steak on a broiler pan coated with cooking spray; broil 10 minutes or until desired degree of doneness, turning once. Cut steak diagonally across grain into thin slices.
❸ Heat oil in a large nonstick skillet over medium heat. Add garlic and jalapeño to pan; cook 1 minute. Add remaining ¼ teaspoon cumin, remaining ¼ teaspoon salt, and tomatoes to pan; cook 3 minutes or until tomatoes begin to soften. Remove from heat; stir in cilantro. Serve tomato topping with steak. Yield: 4 servings (serving size: 3 ounces meat and about ⅓ cup topping).

CALORIES 194 (37% from fat); FAT 7.9g (sat 2.5g, mono 3.1g, poly 0.5g); PROTEIN 25.3g; CARB 4.3g; FIBER 1.2g; CHOL 37mg; IRON 2.4mg; SODIUM 514mg; CALC 38mg

Moroccan Chicken with Fruit and Olive Topping

The pairing of dried fruit and olives is also characteristic of other North African cuisines, such as Tunisian and Algerian. Serve over Israeli couscous, a pearl-like pasta; sprinkle with chopped green onions.

1 tablespoon olive oil, divided
½ teaspoon salt
¼ teaspoon black pepper
¼ teaspoon dried thyme
4 (6-ounce) skinless, boneless chicken breasts
½ cup prechopped onion
2 teaspoons bottled minced garlic
¾ cup dried mixed fruit
½ cup dry white wine
½ cup fat-free, less-sodium chicken broth
¼ cup chopped pitted green olives
⅛ teaspoon salt
⅛ teaspoon black pepper

❶ Heat 2 teaspoons oil in a large nonstick skillet over medium-high heat. Sprinkle ½ teaspoon salt, ¼ teaspoon pepper, and thyme evenly over chicken. Add chicken to pan; cook 4 minutes on each side or until done. Remove from pan; cover and keep warm.
❷ Heat remaining 1 teaspoon oil in pan. Add onion to pan; sauté 2 minutes or until tender. Add garlic to pan; sauté 30 seconds. Add fruit and remaining ingredients to pan; cook 5 minutes or until liquid almost evaporates. Yield: 4 servings (serving size: 1 chicken breast half and about ⅓ cup fruit mixture).

CALORIES 346 (20% from fat); FAT 7.5g (sat 1g, mono 4.3g, poly 1.3g); PROTEIN 40.6g; CARB 26g; FIBER 2.1g; CHOL 99mg; IRON 2.4mg; SODIUM 591mg; CALC 45mg

Three-Bean Chili

- 2   teaspoons olive oil
- 1   cup prechopped onion
- ½   cup prechopped green bell pepper
- 2   teaspoons bottled minced garlic
- ¾   cup water
- 2   tablespoons tomato paste
- 2   teaspoons chili powder
- 2   teaspoons ground cumin
- ¼   teaspoon black pepper
- 1   (15½-ounce) can garbanzo beans, rinsed and drained
- 1   (15½-ounce) can red kidney beans, rinsed and drained
- 1   (15½-ounce) can black beans, rinsed and drained
- 1   (14½-ounce) can organic vegetable broth (such as Swanson Certified Organic)
- 1   (14½-ounce) can no-salt-added diced tomatoes, undrained
- 1   tablespoon yellow cornmeal
- ¼   cup chopped fresh cilantro
- 6   tablespoons reduced-fat sour cream

1 Heat oil in a large saucepan over medium-high heat. Add onion, bell pepper, and garlic to pan; sauté 3 minutes. Stir in ³/₄ cup water and next 9 ingredients; bring to a boil. Reduce heat, and simmer 8 minutes. Stir in cornmeal; cook 2 minutes. Remove from heat; stir in cilantro. Serve with sour cream. Yield: 6 servings (serving size: 1¹/₃ cups chili and 1 tablespoon sour cream).

CALORIES 180 (25% from fat); FAT 4.9g (sat 1.5g, mono 1.7g, poly 0.3g); PROTEIN 8.4g; CARB 29.5g; FIBER 8.6g; CHOL 5mg; IRON 2.3mg; SODIUM 714mg; CALC 86mg

Tasty Tilapia

This mild fish is widely available, quick to cook, and flourishes with a variety of ingredients.

Tilapia Menu 1
serves 4

Grilled Tilapia with Smoked Paprika and Parmesan Polenta

Sautéed broccoli rabe

Heat 1 tablespoon olive oil in a medium nonstick skillet over medium-high heat. Add 2 minced garlic cloves to pan; sauté 30 seconds, stirring constantly. Add 1 pound trimmed broccoli rabe, ½ teaspoon salt, and ¼ teaspoon crushed red pepper; sauté 3 minutes or until broccoli rabe is crisp-tender, tossing frequently.

Orange sections

Game Plan

1 While milk comes to a boil:
- Season fish.

2 Prepare polenta.

3 While fish cooks:
- Prepare broccoli rabe.

QUICK & EASY
Grilled Tilapia with Smoked Paprika and Parmesan Polenta

Total time: 30 minutes

POLENTA:
- 4   cups fat-free milk
- 1   cup quick-cooking polenta
- ¼   teaspoon salt
- ⅓   cup grated Parmesan cheese

FISH:
- 1½   tablespoons olive oil
- 1   teaspoon smoked paprika
- ½   teaspoon garlic powder
- ½   teaspoon salt
- ¼   teaspoon black pepper
- 4   (6-ounce) tilapia fillets
- Cooking spray

1 To prepare polenta, bring milk to a boil in a medium saucepan; gradually add polenta, stirring constantly with a whisk. Reduce heat, and cook 5 minutes or until thick, stirring constantly; stir in ¼ teaspoon salt. Remove from heat. Stir in cheese; cover and keep warm.

2 To prepare fish, heat a large nonstick grill pan over medium-high heat. Combine oil and next 4 ingredients in a bowl, stirring well. Rub fish evenly with oil mixture. Coat pan with cooking spray. Add fish to pan; cook 4 minutes on each side or until fish flakes easily when tested with a fork or until desired degree of doneness. Yield: 4 servings (serving size: 1 fillet and 1 cup polenta).

CALORIES 422 (21% from fat); FAT 9.7g (sat 3g, mono 5.1g, poly 1.1g); PROTEIN 39.9g; CARB 34.2g; FIBER 4.1g; CHOL 73mg; IRON 1mg; SODIUM 751mg; CALC 414mg

Tilapia Menu 2
serves 4

Roasted Tilapia with Tomatoes and Olives

Arugula salad

Combine 6 cups trimmed arugula, ¼ cup (1 ounce) shaved fresh pecorino Romano cheese, and 2 tablespoons toasted chopped slivered almonds. Combine 2 tablespoons sherry vinegar and 2 teaspoons extravirgin olive oil. Drizzle vinegar mixture over arugula mixture, and toss gently.

Brown rice

Game Plan

1 While rice cooks:
- Prepare fish.

2 While fish roasts:
- Prepare salad.

Quick Tip

Boil-in-bag brown rice cooks in about half the time required for cooking regular white rice.

Continued

Roasted Tilapia with Tomatoes and Olives

Total time: 42 minutes

- 4 (6-ounce) tilapia fillets
- ¼ teaspoon salt
- ¼ teaspoon freshly ground black pepper
- Cooking spray
- 1 cup cherry tomatoes, halved
- ¾ cup pitted green olives, coarsely chopped
- 3 tablespoons chopped fresh flat-leaf parsley
- 3 garlic cloves, minced

1 Preheat oven to 375°.

2 Sprinkle fish with salt and pepper. Arrange fish in a single layer in a jelly-roll pan lightly coated with cooking spray. Combine tomatoes and remaining ingredients; toss gently. Arrange tomato mixture around fish.

3 Bake at 375° for 20 minutes or until fish flakes easily when tested with a fork or until desired degree of doneness. Place 1 fillet on each of 4 plates; top each serving with about ¼ cup tomato mixture. Yield: 4 servings.

CALORIES 207 (27% from fat); FAT 6.3g (sat 1.4g, mono 3.3g, poly 1g); PROTEIN 34.9g; CARB 3.6g; FIBER 1.3g; CHOL 85mg; IRON 1.5mg; SODIUM 572mg; CALC 38mg

Tilapia Menu 3

serves 4

Pan-Seared Tilapia with Citrus Vinaigrette

Couscous pilaf

Bring 1½ cups fat-free, less-sodium chicken broth to a boil in a medium saucepan over medium-high heat. Add 1 cup uncooked couscous to pan. Cover and remove from heat. Let couscous stand 5 minutes. Uncover and fluff with a fork. Stir in ⅓ cup dried cherries, ¼ cup toasted slivered almonds, 3 tablespoons chopped fresh flat-leaf parsley, 1 tablespoon extravirgin olive oil, ½ teaspoon grated fresh lemon rind, ¼ teaspoon salt, and ¼ teaspoon freshly ground black pepper; stir well.

Roasted Brussels sprouts

Game Plan

1 While oven preheats:
- Trim Brussels sprouts.

2 While Brussels sprouts roast:
- Hydrate couscous.

3 While couscous stands:
- Prepare fish.

4 Finish couscous.

Quick Tip

Cut Brussels sprouts into halves so they will cook quickly and evenly.

Pan-Seared Tilapia with Citrus Vinaigrette

Total time: 36 minutes

- Cooking spray
- 4 (6-ounce) tilapia fillets
- ½ teaspoon salt, divided
- ½ teaspoon freshly ground black pepper, divided
- ½ cup white wine
- 2 tablespoons finely chopped shallots
- 2 tablespoons fresh lemon juice
- 2 tablespoons fresh orange juice
- 4 teaspoons extravirgin olive oil
- 2 teaspoons sherry vinegar

1 Heat a large nonstick skillet over medium-high heat. Coat pan with cooking spray. Sprinkle fish evenly with ¼ teaspoon salt and ¼ teaspoon pepper. Add 2 fillets to pan; cook 4 minutes on each side or until fish flakes easily when tested with a fork or until desired degree of doneness. Remove from pan; keep warm. Repeat procedure with remaining fillets.

2 Add wine to pan; cook 30 seconds or until liquid almost evaporates. Combine shallots and remaining ingredients, stirring well with a whisk; stir in remaining ¼ teaspoon salt and remaining ¼ teaspoon pepper. Add shallot mixture to pan; sauté 1 minute or until thoroughly heated, stirring frequently. Place 1 fillet on each of 4 plates; top each serving with about 3 tablespoons sauce. Yield: 4 servings.

CALORIES 215 (31% from fat); FAT 7.4g (sat 1.6g, mono 4.1g, poly 1.1g); PROTEIN 34.5g; CARB 2.9g; FIBER 0.2g; CHOL 85mg; IRON 1.2mg; SODIUM 357mg; CALC 24mg

On Balance

Bring out the best in your cooking by harmonizing sweet, sour, salty, bitter, and savory tastes.

BALANCE IS THE JUDICIOUS combination of the four basic tastes: sweet, sour, salty, and bitter, as well as the so-called fifth taste, *umami*, best described as savoriness (see "Umami," page 52). How much of each is determined by what you're making. A vinaigrette, for instance, should obviously be on the acidic (sour) side. But you can slightly temper the sourness from the acid with a little sugar—brown sugar, the sugar naturally present in an onion, or even the sugar in an onion that's made more complex through roasting.

"You need that balance with sugar and acid to make up for the minimal use of fat when you're cooking healthfully," says John Besh, chef and owner of August and other restaurants in Louisiana. "While a classic vinaigrette may have a four-to-one oil-to-vinegar ratio, lightened vinaigrettes often contain less oil than vinegar. A sweet element helps counter the pronounced acid."

Michael Pardus, a professor at the Culinary Institute of America, advises to first become acquainted with basic elements. "Taste salt," he said, "and pay attention to the effect of it on your tongue. White table sugar is almost pure sweet—taste it. Distilled white vinegar is flavorless acid—taste it.

"Then, when you taste a recipe in process, if you think, 'It needs something, but I'm not sure what,' go back to those basics. If I add salt, will it be better? If I add something sweet, will it be better? And so on. You're not trying to make the dish taste salty or sour or sweet. The biggest news to my students is that vinegar can be used as a seasoning almost subliminally."

QUICK & EASY
Radicchio, Haricots Verts, and Sweet Lettuce Salad

2 cups (2-inch) cut haricots verts
1 tablespoon walnut oil
1 tablespoon balsamic vinegar
2 teaspoons honey
½ teaspoon salt
½ teaspoon grated orange rind
½ teaspoon Dijon mustard
4 cups torn Boston lettuce
2 cups (1-inch) cubed sourdough bread (about 4 ounces), toasted
1 cup shredded radicchio
¾ cup chopped prosciutto (about 2 ounces)
½ cup orange sections

① Cook haricots verts in boiling water 2 minutes or until crisp-tender. Drain and rinse with cold water; drain.
② Combine oil and next 5 ingredients in a large bowl; stir well with a whisk. Add haricots verts, lettuce, and remaining ingredients; toss gently to coat. Yield: 6 servings (serving size: about 1⅓ cups).

CALORIES 122 (26% from fat); FAT 3.5g (sat 0.5g, mono 1g, poly 1.6g); PROTEIN 5.5g; CARB 17.7g; FIBER 2.5g; CHOL 6mg; IRON 1.6mg; SODIUM 449mg; CALC 35mg

STAFF FAVORITE
Risotto with Italian Sausage, Caramelized Onions, and Bitter Greens

4 cups fat-free, less-sodium chicken broth
½ cup water
2 teaspoons olive oil
2 cups chopped onion (about 1 large)
2 teaspoons sugar
8 ounces sweet turkey Italian sausage
¼ cup chopped shallots
1 cup Arborio rice or other medium-grain rice
⅓ cup dry white wine
2 cups arugula leaves
3 tablespoons freshly grated pecorino Romano cheese
1 teaspoon grated lemon rind

① Bring broth and ½ cup water to a simmer in a medium saucepan (do not boil). Keep warm over low heat.
② Heat oil in a large saucepan over medium-high heat. Add onion and sugar; sauté 7 minutes or until onion is golden. Place onion mixture in a small bowl; set aside.
③ Remove casings from sausage. Add sausage to pan; sauté 4 minutes or until browned, stirring to crumble. Add shallots; sauté 2 minutes. Add rice; sauté 30 seconds. Stir in wine; cook 45 seconds or until liquid is nearly absorbed, stirring constantly. Stir in 1 cup broth; cook 2 minutes or until liquid is nearly absorbed, stirring constantly. Add remaining broth, ½ cup at a time, stirring constantly until each portion is absorbed before adding the next (about 20 minutes total). Remove from heat; stir in onion, arugula, cheese, and rind. Yield: 4 servings (serving size: 1 cup).

CALORIES 390 (24% from fat); FAT 10.3g (sat 3.6g, mono 3.6g, poly 1.4g); PROTEIN 21.1g; CARB 53.1g; FIBER 4.4g; CHOL 54mg; IRON 2.4mg; SODIUM 900mg; CALC 104mg

Balanced Flavors

The Four Classic Tastes

To make a dish harmonious, it helps to be familiar with ingredients that possess predominant tastes. The following chart lists items known for their particular taste characteristics. Sometimes taste combinations are found within the same ingredient, as with sweet-tart Granny Smith apples and pineapples. For this reason, some items are listed below in multiple categories.

Sour

- Buttermilk
- Cranberries
- Lemon and lime juice
- Lemongrass
- Mustard
- Pickles
- Rhubarb
- Sour cream
- Tamarind
- Vinegar
- Wine
- Yogurt

Bitter

- Freshly ground black pepper
- Broccoli rabe
- Brussels sprouts
- Cabbage
- Campari
- Dark chocolate
- Coffee
- Endive
- Grapefruit
- Kale
- Mustard greens
- Radicchio
- Walnuts
- Watercress

Sweet

- Roasted bell peppers
- Chocolate
- Many fruits
- Fruit juice
- Hoisin sauce
- Honey
- Ketchup
- Maple syrup
- Molasses
- Caramelized onions
- Sugar

Salty

- Anchovies
- Capers
- Brined or aged cheese such as feta or Parmesan
- Fish sauce
- Cured meats, such as bacon, pancetta, or prosciutto
- Mustard
- Olives
- Soy sauce

Umami

In addition to sweet, sour, salty, and bitter, our tongues are capable of detecting a fifth taste known as umami. First identified in the early 20th century by a Tokyo chemistry professor, umami (loosely translated as "delicious essence") is often described as a savory or meaty taste. In 2000, researchers at the University of Miami found that we are equipped with a taste bud designed to recognize umami, lending credence to its status as a basic taste. These foods are rich in umami:

- Aged cheeses such as Parmigiano-Reggiano
- Vine-ripened tomatoes
- Mushrooms, particularly portobellos, shiitakes, porcini, and morels
- Corn
- Cured pork such as prosciutto or serrano ham
- Smoked or cured fish
- Shellfish
- Asian fish sauce
- Soy sauce
- Miso

Tip the Scales

Balancing the tastes of a dish is a nuanced skill, but it's not difficult. Sour likes sweet. Salt is a constant. Bitter tastes should not dominate and can be balanced with salt and fat. Consider these strategies:

- **Too sour?** Add sugar, honey, or another sweet ingredient. The filling in a rhubarb pie, for example, may need an extra teaspoon or two of sugar to temper the tartness of the rhubarb.
- **Too sweet?** Try a dash of vinegar, lemon juice, or another sour ingredient.

Salt will also tone down sweetness.
- **Too bitter?** Add salt, if possible. Fats can also take the edge off bitter ingredients. Olive oil and salt will make broccoli rabe less bitter, while milk and sugar mellow both coffee and bitter dark chocolate.

- **Too bland?** Start with salt, if your diet allows. Used judiciously, salt enhances the flavor of all ingredients in a dish without making them taste salty. A touch of an acidic ingredient such as vinegar or citrus juice also brightens flat flavors. Depending on

the dish—a tomato sauce, a stew—even a pinch of sugar might help round out the taste.
- **Be careful with salt.** An oversalted dish is usually beyond repair. Start by adding a little salt to the dish. You can always add more, if needed.

Seared Scallops over Bacon and Spinach Salad with Cider Vinaigrette

Savory umami tastes from the scallops and bacon lay the foundation for this dish, which delivers apple flavor in three layers.

- 1   cup apple cider
- 2   teaspoons sugar
- 4   slices center-cut bacon
- ¼   cup chopped shallots
- 1   tablespoon cider vinegar
- ¾   teaspoon salt, divided
- ¼   teaspoon freshly ground black pepper
- 1½ cups thinly sliced Granny Smith apple (about 1)
- ⅓   cup thinly sliced red onion
- 1   (6-ounce) package fresh baby spinach
- ¼   teaspoon curry powder
- ⅛   teaspoon ground red pepper
- 20 sea scallops (about 1½ pounds)
- 2   teaspoons olive oil

① Combine cider and sugar in a small saucepan over medium-high heat. Bring to a boil; cook until reduced to ¼ cup (about 9 minutes). Remove from heat.
② Cook bacon in a small nonstick skillet over medium-high heat until crisp. Remove bacon from pan, reserving 1 teaspoon drippings in pan; set bacon aside. Add shallots to drippings in pan; sauté 1 minute. Remove pan from heat; stir in

cider mixture, vinegar, ¼ teaspoon salt, and black pepper.
③ Crumble reserved bacon. Combine bacon, apple, onion, and spinach in a large bowl.
④ Combine remaining ½ teaspoon salt, curry powder, and red pepper in a small bowl. Sprinkle salt mixture evenly over both sides of scallops. Heat oil in a large nonstick skillet over medium-high heat. Add scallops to pan; cook 3 minutes on each side or until done.
⑤ Drizzle cider mixture over spinach mixture; toss gently to coat. Place about 2½ cups salad mixture on each of 4 plates; top each serving with 5 scallops. Yield: 4 servings.

CALORIES 298 (21% from fat); FAT 7g (sat 1.7g, mono 3.3g, poly 1.1g); PROTEIN 32.1g; CARB 26.7g; FIBER 3.3g; CHOL 63mg; IRON 2.2mg; SODIUM 921mg; CALC 81mg

Inspired by Italy Menu
serves 4

You can prepare the *agrodolce*, an Italian sweet and sour sauce combining sugar and vinegar, a day ahead and reheat just before serving; any leftover sauce would also be good on a goat cheese–topped pizza.

Fennel-Rubbed Pork Tenderloin with Shallot-Onion Agrodolce

Pecorino polenta

Combine 2 cups water, ¾ cup 1% low-fat milk, and ½ teaspoon salt in a medium saucepan; bring to a boil. Gradually add ¾ cup instant dry polenta, stirring constantly with a whisk; reduce heat, and cook 2 minutes or until thick, stirring constantly. Remove from heat. Add 1 tablespoon butter and ½ cup grated fresh pecorino Romano cheese, stirring until butter and cheese melt .

Sautéed Broccolini

Fennel-Rubbed Pork Tenderloin with Shallot-Onion Agrodolce

AGRODOLCE:
- 1   tablespoon olive oil
- 3   cups vertically sliced onion
- 1   cup sliced shallots
- 1   tablespoon sugar
- ¾   cup dry white wine
- ⅓   cup golden raisins
- ¼   cup red wine vinegar
- ¼   teaspoon salt
- ⅛   teaspoon freshly ground black pepper

PORK TENDERLOIN:
- 2   teaspoons fennel seeds, crushed
- ½   teaspoon salt
- ½   teaspoon ground coriander
- ½   teaspoon ground cumin
- ¼   teaspoon freshly ground black pepper
- 1   (1-pound) pork tenderloin, trimmed

Cooking spray

① To prepare agrodolce, heat oil in a large nonstick skillet over medium-high heat. Add onion, shallots, and sugar; sauté 12 minutes or until golden. Stir in wine, raisins, and vinegar; bring to a boil. Reduce heat, and simmer 9 minutes or until liquid almost evaporates. Remove from heat; stir in ¼ teaspoon salt and ⅛ teaspoon pepper.
② Prepare grill.
③ To prepare pork tenderloin, combine fennel seeds and next 4 ingredients in a small bowl. Sprinkle pork with fennel seed mixture. Place pork on grill rack coated with cooking spray; grill 20 minutes or until a thermometer registers 155° (slightly pink), turning pork occasionally. Let stand 10 minutes. Cut into ¼-inch-thick slices. Serve with agrodolce. Yield: 4 servings (serving size: 3 ounces pork and about ½ cup agrodolce).

CALORIES 281 (24% from fat); FAT 7.6g (sat 1.9g, mono 4.1g, poly 0.8g); PROTEIN 25.2g; CARB 28.9g; FIBER 2.8g; CHOL 63mg; IRON 2.6mg; SODIUM 502mg; CALC 64mg

Apricot, Plum, and Chicken Tagine with Olives

In this dish, briny olives counter the sweetness of dried fruit and sautéed onions. Sautéing the spices draws out their essences and makes them more potent.

- 1 teaspoon olive oil
- 1 pound skinless, boneless chicken thighs, halved
- 1 cup chopped onion (about 1 medium)
- 1 tablespoon grated peeled fresh ginger
- 3 garlic cloves, minced
- 1 teaspoon ground turmeric
- 1 teaspoon ground cumin
- ¼ teaspoon fennel seeds
- ¼ teaspoon ground cinnamon
- ½ cup dried apricots, halved
- ½ cup pitted dried plums, halved
- ½ teaspoon salt
- 20 pitted kalamata olives, halved
- 1 (14-ounce) can fat-free, less-sodium chicken broth
- 3 tablespoons chopped fresh cilantro
- ½ teaspoon grated lemon rind
- 3 cups hot cooked couscous

1 Heat oil in a large Dutch oven over medium-high heat. Add chicken to pan; cook 3 minutes on each side or until browned. Place chicken on a plate, and keep warm.

2 Add onion to pan; sauté 4 minutes or until golden. Add ginger and garlic; sauté 30 seconds. Stir in turmeric and next 3 ingredients; sauté 15 seconds, stirring constantly. Return chicken to pan. Add apricots and next 4 ingredients; bring to a boil. Cover, reduce heat, and simmer 30 minutes or until chicken is tender. Remove from heat; stir in cilantro and rind. Serve over couscous. Yield: 6 servings (serving size: ⅔ cup chicken mixture and ½ cup couscous).

CALORIES 334 (27% from fat); FAT 10.1g (sat 2.2g, mono 5.3g, poly 1.8g); PROTEIN 18.8g; CARB 40.5g; FIBER 3.7g; CHOL 50mg; IRON 2.4mg; SODIUM 568mg; CALC 45mg

WINE NOTE: This dish tantalizes your tongue with its lush fruit textures and the balance between sweet and savory flavors. It needs a wine that is equally rich and complex, as well as one that can really hold up to the sweetness of the dried fruit. A ripe German riesling is an ideal partner, because it mirrors both the fruitiness and the voluptuous textures of the tagine. A gorgeous example is the Dr. Loosen Ürziger Würzgarten Riesling Spätlese 2006, about $35.

QUICK & EASY
Spicy Coconut Shrimp Soup

Southeast Asian cuisine is known for balanced tastes. Adding the green onions, basil, and lime juice just before serving brightens the overall taste of the soup. For a spicier finish, stir in an additional ¼ teaspoon red curry paste.

- 3½ cups fat-free, less-sodium chicken broth
- 1 cup sliced mushrooms
- ¼ cup finely chopped red bell pepper
- 1 tablespoon light brown sugar
- 1 tablespoon fish sauce
- ½ teaspoon grated peeled fresh ginger
- ¼ teaspoon red curry paste
- 1 cup light coconut milk
- 1 pound large shrimp, peeled and deveined
- ¼ cup thinly sliced green onions
- 2 tablespoons thinly sliced fresh basil
- 2 tablespoons fresh lime juice

1 Combine first 7 ingredients in a large saucepan over medium-high heat; bring to a boil. Cover, reduce heat, and simmer 10 minutes. Stir in coconut milk; cook 2 minutes or until hot. Add shrimp; cook 3 minutes or until shrimp are done. Remove pan from heat; stir in onions, basil, and juice. Yield: 4 servings (serving size: about 1½ cups).

CALORIES 194 (25% from fat); FAT 5.3g (sat 3.3g, mono 0.4g, poly 0.9g); PROTEIN 26.9g; CARB 9.9g; FIBER 1.4g; CHOL 172mg; IRON 3.8mg; SODIUM 878mg; CALC 85mg

Pork Chops with Hoisin-Molasses Barbecue Sauce

Sugar, hoisin sauce, and molasses provide deep, sweet notes in the sauce, rounded out by tartness and saltiness from rice vinegar, soy sauce, and mustard.

- 3 tablespoons sugar
- 1 tablespoon molasses
- 3 tablespoons hoisin sauce
- 1 tablespoon rice vinegar
- 1 tablespoon low-sodium soy sauce
- 2 garlic cloves, minced
- 2 teaspoons Chinese hot mustard (such as Ty Ling brand)
- Cooking spray
- ½ teaspoon salt, divided
- ¼ teaspoon freshly ground black pepper
- 6 (4-ounce) boneless center-cut loin pork chops (about ½ inch thick)
- 4 green onions
- 3 cups hot cooked white rice

1 Combine sugar and molasses in a small heavy saucepan over medium heat. Cook 3 minutes or until sugar melts, stirring occasionally. Stir in hoisin and next 3 ingredients; bring to a boil. Cook 5 minutes or until slightly thickened, stirring frequently. Remove from heat; stir in mustard. Keep warm.

2 Heat a grill pan over medium-high heat. Coat pan with cooking spray. Sprinkle ¼ teaspoon salt and pepper over pork. Add pork to pan; cook 2 minutes on each side or until done. Add pork to hoisin mixture, turning to coat. Keep warm.

3 Add onions to grill pan; cook 2 minutes or until wilted. Remove onions from pan; chop. Combine onions, remaining ¼ teaspoon salt, and rice; serve with pork. Yield: 6 servings (serving size: 1 pork chop and ½ cup rice).

CALORIES 317 (22% from fat); FAT 7.7g (sat 2.7g, mono 3.4g, poly 0.7g); PROTEIN 23.9g; CARB 35.8g; FIBER 0.8g; CHOL 58mg; IRON 2mg; SODIUM 478mg; CALC 49mg

Blackened Shrimp with Tropical Pico de Gallo Salad

Sweet-tart pico de gallo complements the shrimp. We recommend seeding the serrano chile so its heat doesn't overpower the relish.

PICO DE GALLO:

1½ cups diced pineapple
1½ cups diced peeled ripe mango
½ cup finely chopped red onion
½ cup chopped red bell pepper
2 tablespoons chopped fresh cilantro
2 tablespoons fresh lime juice
1 teaspoon finely chopped seeded serrano chile
¼ teaspoon salt

SHRIMP:

1 tablespoon paprika
1 teaspoon sugar
1 teaspoon ground cumin
1 teaspoon dried oregano
¾ teaspoon garlic powder
½ teaspoon dried thyme
¼ teaspoon salt
¼ teaspoon ground chipotle chile powder
24 jumbo shrimp, peeled and deveined (about 1½ pounds)
4 teaspoons canola oil, divided

1 To prepare pico de gallo, combine first 8 ingredients; toss well.

2 To prepare shrimp, combine paprika and next 7 ingredients in a shallow dish. Dredge shrimp in paprika mixture. Heat 2 teaspoons oil in a large nonstick skillet over medium-high heat. Add half of shrimp to pan; cook 2 minutes on each side or until shrimp are done. Repeat procedure with remaining 2 teaspoons oil and remaining shrimp. Serve shrimp over pico de gallo. Yield: 4 servings (serving size: 6 shrimp and 1 cup pico de gallo).

CALORIES 319 (24% from fat); FAT 8.3g (sat 1g, mono 3.3g, poly 2.7g); PROTEIN 36.1g; CARB 26g; FIBER 3.8g; CHOL 259mg; IRON 5.4mg; SODIUM 557mg; CALC 125mg

---

INSPIRED VEGETARIAN

Asian Fusion

Influenced by Indian, Thai, and Chinese cuisines, Malaysian fare is a multiethnic blend that can be adapted to suit your liking.

Malaysia's position in the trade routes between Europe, the Mediterranean, and the Spice Islands in what is now Indonesia has been its destiny. The country straddles the South China Sea, with the west region occupying a peninsula it shares with Thailand and Singapore, and the east portion on the island of Borneo, which it shares with Indonesia and Brunei. As a result, Malaysian cooks fashioned a cuisine of Chinese, Indonesian, Thai, and Indian influences, which blend naturally in the curries, steamed rice, noodle stir-fries, and fresh salads that now characterize Malaysian dishes.

One cornerstone of Malaysian cooking is the spice paste, a blend of Indian-influenced dry spice mixtures with Thai and Indonesian roots, leaves, and fresh herbs that enriches a wide array of vegetable dishes. A southern-style spice paste may start with sautéing pungent ginger, heady garlic, Thai chiles, and perfumy galangal; dried spices like coriander, cinnamon, and turmeric add earthy undertones. A sauce is then made with the addition of sweet-nutty coconut milk. Vegetables, tempeh, or tofu complete the dish and soak up the flavorful sauce.

Malaysian food has adapted over the centuries based on local ingredients, cooks' preferences, and inspiration from other cultures. Take a cue from Malaysian cooks, and adapt these flavors to your liking. Use a few more unseeded chiles in spice paste if you prefer extra heat, or add other seasonal vegetables of your choosing to a stir-fry for a crunchy texture. There are no right or wrongs in this flexible cuisine.

Bright Fruit and Vegetable Salad (*Rojak*)

This dish combines vibrant fruits and crunchy vegetables. We used fried tofu slices (*inari* in Japanese), available at Asian grocery stores, in place of fried dough. Omit the tofu, if you like.

¼ cup sugar
¼ cup fresh lime juice
¼ cup natural-style chunky peanut butter
1 tablespoon minced seeded red Thai chiles (about 2 chiles)
½ teaspoon salt
½ cup green beans, trimmed and halved crosswise
1½ cups diced pineapple
1¼ cups julienne-cut peeled jicama
½ cup diced peeled mango
½ cup fresh bean sprouts
1½ ounces fried tofu, cut into ½-inch strips
½ English cucumber, halved lengthwise and cut into ¼-inch-thick slices (about 1½ cups)

1 Combine sugar and juice in a small bowl, stirring with a whisk. Add peanut butter, chiles, and salt; stir with a whisk until well combined.

2 Cook green beans in boiling water 4 minutes or until crisp-tender. Drain and plunge beans into ice water; drain. Combine beans, pineapple, and remaining ingredients in a large bowl. Drizzle with dressing. Yield: 8 servings (serving size: ³⁄₄ cup).

CALORIES 153 (31% from fat); FAT 5.3g (sat 0.7g, mono 2.3g, poly 1.9g); PROTEIN 4.1g; CARB 24.1g; FIBER 5.8g; CHOL 0mg; IRON 1.2mg; SODIUM 184mg; CALC 43mg

Stir-Fried Water Spinach (*Kangkung*)

Common in Southeast Asia, water spinach has a pleasingly mild flavor. All but the bottom half of the stems are used in cooking. Wash in several changes of cold water to remove sand or soil. If you can't find water spinach in your local Asian grocery store, use regular spinach and cook two minutes.

- 1 tablespoon roasted peanut oil
- 1 large garlic clove, minced
- ½ teaspoon sugar
- 2 pounds water spinach, trimmed and cut into 2-inch pieces (about 16 cups)
- 2 tablespoons low-sodium soy sauce
- ¼ teaspoon black pepper

1 Heat oil in a large nonstick skillet over medium-high heat. Add garlic to pan; stir-fry 30 seconds or until golden. Add sugar and spinach to pan; stir-fry 3 minutes or until spinach wilts. Add soy sauce; stir-fry 1 minute. Remove from heat; stir in pepper. Yield: 6 servings (serving size: about ⅓ cup).

CALORIES 54 (43% from fat); FAT 2.6g (sat 0.4g, mono 1.1g, poly 0.9g); PROTEIN 4.3g; CARB 5.8g; FIBER 3.3g; CHOL 0mg; IRON 2.7mg; SODIUM 349mg; CALC 119mg

Coconut Rice with Spicy Tomato Sauce (*Nasi Lemak with Sambal Tomat*)

Coconut rice is popular throughout Southeast Asia. *Sambal* means "sauce" in Malay, and this spicy tomato condiment is great with rich, sweet rice.

RICE:
- 3 cups light coconut milk
- 2 cups uncooked long-grain white rice
- 2 bay leaves
- ½ teaspoon kosher salt

SAMBAL:
- 8 red Thai chiles
- 1 tablespoon peanut oil
- 1 cup peeled and quartered shallots (about 4 large)
- 2 teaspoons minced garlic
- 1 tablespoon brown sugar
- 1 teaspoon grated lime rind
- 2 tablespoons fresh lime juice
- 1 (14.5-ounce) can whole plum tomatoes, undrained, seeded, and chopped
- ¼ teaspoon kosher salt

1 To prepare rice, combine first 3 ingredients in a medium saucepan; bring to a boil. Cover, reduce heat, and simmer 20 minutes or until liquid is absorbed. Let stand 5 minutes; discard bay leaves. Fluff rice with a fork. Stir in ½ teaspoon salt.

2 To prepare sambal, seed 7 chiles; leave seeds in 1 chile. Mince chiles. Heat oil in a large saucepan over medium-high heat. Add shallots and garlic to pan; sauté 3 minutes or until lightly browned.

The Malaysian Pantry

Most of these ingredients can be found at local Asian grocery stores or specialty produce markets. These products are worth seeking out for the most authentic taste.

Noodles: Fresh **round egg noodles** resemble spaghetti. Soak or parboil **dried** varieties before cooking, following the package directions. **Broad rice noodles** are chewy and may be sold in sheets of pasta, which you will need to cut into flat noodles.

Thai chiles: Also referred to as Thai bird peppers, these very hot, small, thin pods measure about one to one-and-a-half inches in length. In a pinch, substitute one-fourth of a Scotch bonnet, which is much hotter, for one whole Thai chile.

Tamarind concentrate: This dark, sour paste is used in Indonesia, India, and Mexico to flavor drinks, curries, and chutneys.

Galangal: Resembles ginger in appearance, but differs in flavor with a distinct peppery, citrus aroma. Fresh or frozen galangal is sold in Asian supermarkets.

Water spinach: Wash these leafy greens thoroughly. With its delicate flavor, water spinach works well in sautés or stir-fries.

Lemongrass: As its name suggests, lemongrass is a grass with a strong citrus note. Always discard the bruised outer leaf and root end.

Pandan, or screwpine, leaves: Available fresh or dried, these leaves are about four inches long and are used to add piney flavor to all sorts of savory or sweet dishes.

Kaffir lime leaves: Though more popular in Thailand than Malaysia, these fragrant leaves offer floral and citrus aromas to stir-fries. Look for fresh or frozen options.

Soy sauces: A dark soy sauce (may be labeled "black" or "thick") has a sweet backnote and is used mostly for color in our Stir-Fried Noodles with Green Onions and Eggs (page 57). It's more pungent and less salty than regular soy and is used sparingly. It is typically paired with common, thin soy sauce, which has a salty edge. Additionally, *kecap manis*, the Indonesian sweet soy sauce, is used in a variety of dishes. Palm sugar adds the sweet element to this. The variety of soy sauces adds complexity that stands in for shrimp paste, a common ingredient in Malaysian dishes.

Tempeh: A cake made of whole or chopped fermented soybeans, tempeh is ideal for stir-frying. Plus, its crunchy, dense texture is a welcome addition to stews and curries.

Tofu and fried tofu slices: Firmer tofu holds up best in stir-fries. Fried tofu slices, which may be labeled as "pockets" or "inari," make an excellent substitute for fried dough called for in some Malaysian salad recipes.

Add chiles and sugar to pan; sauté 1 minute or until fragrant. Add rind, juice, and tomatoes to pan; cover, reduce heat, and simmer 20 minutes or until thickened. Stir in ¼ teaspoon salt. Serve sambal over rice. Yield: 6 servings (serving size: 1 cup rice and about ¼ cup sambal).

CALORIES 399 (21% from fat); FAT 9.3g (sat 6.3g, mono 1.6g, poly 1.1g); PROTEIN 9g; CARB 72.8g; FIBER 2.6g; CHOL 0mg; IRON 4.5mg; SODIUM 375mg; CALC 62mg

Stir-Fried Egg Noodles with Mushrooms, Tomatoes, and Bean Sprouts (*Bakmie Goreng*)

Bakmie or *mi goreng* means stir-fried egg noodles, which are added to a variety of vegetables for breakfast or a snack. We like this entrée as a simple supper. Sweet soy sauce is sugary compared to the thin and thick versions of soy sauce; it balances the saltiness of regular soy in this dish.

      3   tablespoons peanut oil, divided
      3   Thai chiles, seeded and minced
      2   large shallots, cut into thin wedges
      1   large garlic clove, minced
   1¾   cups thinly sliced cremini
            mushrooms (about 4 ounces)
      1   cup thinly sliced leek
      2   cups fresh bean sprouts
    14   ounces fresh Chinese egg noodles
      3   tablespoons sweet soy sauce
            (such as ABC brand)
      2   tablespoons low-sodium soy sauce
      2   cups tomato wedges (about 2)
      8   Thai basil leaves, torn
      6   lime wedges

❶ Heat 1 tablespoon oil in a large nonstick skillet over medium-high heat. Add chiles, shallots, and garlic to pan; stir-fry 1½ minutes or until shallots and garlic begin to brown. Stir in mushrooms and leek; stir-fry 3 minutes or until leek is tender. Remove from pan; keep warm. ❷ Return pan to heat; add remaining 2 tablespoons oil to pan. Add sprouts and noodles to pan; stir-fry 2 minutes or until thoroughly heated. Return mushroom mixture to pan; stir in soy sauces, tossing to coat noodles. Place 1 cup noodle mixture in each of 6 bowls; top each serving with ⅓ cup tomato wedges and Thai basil. Serve with lime wedges. Yield: 6 servings.

CALORIES 327 (23% from fat); FAT 8.2g (sat 1.6g, mono 3.4g, poly 2.5g); PROTEIN 14.2g; CARB 51.5g; FIBER 3.6g; CHOL 0mg; IRON 2.2mg; SODIUM 624mg; CALC 54mg

Stir-Fried Noodles with Green Onions and Eggs (*Char Kway Teow*)

Fresh broad rice noodles are sometimes sold in sheets in Asian supermarkets; just cut the dough into about ½-inch-wide strips (or use flat rice stick noodles and prepare them following package directions).

      1   pound fresh broad rice noodles
            (*shah fen* or *banh canh*)
            Cooking spray
      4   large eggs, lightly beaten
      2   teaspoons peanut oil
      2   cups fresh bean sprouts
      ½   cup (1-inch) pieces green onions
      ¼   cup low-sodium soy sauce
      2   teaspoons dark (or black or thick)
            soy sauce

❶ Place noodles in boiling water for 2 seconds; drain. ❷ Heat a large nonstick skillet over medium-high heat. Coat pan with cooking spray. Add eggs to pan; cook 3 minutes or until done. Remove eggs from pan; cut into 1-inch pieces. Wipe pan clean with paper towels. ❸ Heat oil in pan over medium-high heat. Add noodles to pan; sauté 5 minutes or until thoroughly heated. Add bean sprouts and remaining ingredients to pan; sauté 1 minute. Return eggs to pan; cook 30 seconds or until thoroughly heated. Yield: 4 servings (serving size: 1 cup).

CALORIES 352 (19% from fat); FAT 7.6g (sat 2g, mono 3g, poly 1.5g); PROTEIN 12.1g; CARB 57.7g; FIBER 1.9g; CHOL 212mg; IRON 4.5mg; SODIUM 634mg; CALC 58mg

Tempeh Rendang

Probably the most well-known Malaysian dish, rendang is a curried stew that cooks down, concentrating the sauce's flavors. The pan should be nearly dry at the end of cooking; this distinguishes a rendang dish from a saucy curry. Serve with rice and steamed carrots.

      6   red Thai chiles
            Cooking spray
      1   cup minced shallots (about 6)
   1½   tablespoons grated peeled fresh
            galangal
      1   tablespoon grated peeled fresh
            ginger
      1   tablespoon finely chopped peeled
            fresh lemongrass (about 1 stalk)
      ¼   teaspoon ground turmeric
      1   cup light coconut milk
      ½   cup water
      5   tablespoons shredded unsweetened
            coconut, toasted and divided
      1   teaspoon kosher salt
      2   kaffir lime leaves
   1½   pounds tempeh, cut into ½-inch
            cubes
      2   tablespoons chopped fresh cilantro

❶ Seed 5 chiles; leave seeds in 1 chile. Thinly slice chiles. ❷ Heat a large nonstick skillet over medium heat. Coat pan with cooking spray. Add chiles, shallots, and next 4 ingredients to pan; cook 5 minutes or until fragrant, stirring frequently. Add coconut milk, ½ cup water, 3 tablespoons coconut, salt, lime leaves, and tempeh to pan. Cover, reduce heat, and simmer 20 minutes or until sauce thickens. Discard lime leaves. Sprinkle with remaining 2 tablespoons coconut and cilantro. Yield: 6 servings (serving size: 1 cup tempeh, 1 teaspoon coconut, and 1 teaspoon cilantro).

CALORIES 353 (35% from fat); FAT 13.9g (sat 5.8g, mono 3.1g, poly 2.2g); PROTEIN 28.4g; CARB 36.5g; FIBER 10.7g; CHOL 0mg; IRON 4.8mg; SODIUM 332mg; CALC 47mg

Mixed Vegetable Curry (*Sayur Kari*)

This curry's distinctly Malaysian taste comes from the addition of galangal to build fragrant, balanced flavor.

Cooking spray
½ cup minced shallots (about 2 large)
2 teaspoons minced garlic
2 tablespoons chopped peeled fresh lemongrass (about 2 stalks)
2 tablespoons minced seeded red Thai chiles (about 2 chiles)
2 teaspoons grated peeled fresh ginger
2 teaspoons grated peeled fresh galangal
½ teaspoon curry powder
1½ cups light coconut milk
1 cup (2-inch) cut green beans
1 cup organic vegetable broth
¾ cup (½-inch-thick) diagonally cut slices carrot
1 tablespoon brown sugar
3 tablespoons tamarind concentrate
¾ teaspoon kosher salt
18 fresh or frozen okra pods (about 8 ounces)
12 fresh shiitake mushrooms, stemmed and halved (about 4 ounces)
2 kaffir lime leaves, lightly crushed

❶ Heat a large Dutch oven over medium heat. Coat pan with cooking spray. Add shallots and garlic to pan; cook 3 minutes or until fragrant, stirring frequently. Add lemongrass and next 3 ingredients; cook 3 minutes, stirring frequently. Add curry powder; cook 2 minutes, stirring frequently. Add coconut milk and remaining ingredients to pan; bring to a boil. Partially cover, reduce heat, and simmer 20 minutes. Uncover and simmer 10 minutes or until vegetables are tender. Discard lime leaves. Yield: 4 servings (serving size: 1 cup).

CALORIES 154 (29% from fat); FAT 4.9g (sat 4.3g, mono 0.2g, poly 0.1g); PROTEIN 4.7g; CARB 26.7g; FIBER 4.8g; CHOL 0mg; IRON 2.5mg; SODIUM 557mg; CALC 89mg

Fad-Free Nutrition Advice

These five simple dietary recommendations bring food and health back to the basics.

SOMETIMES NUTRITION NEWS may seem arbitrary about what to eat for optimal health. But if you read between headlines, you'll see that good nutrition is built around basic, no-fuss tenets—information that's grounded in landmark studies or thoroughly researched recommendations. We've identified five smart strategies to help you get back to the basics.

Mango and Black Bean Salad

(pictured on page 245)

Canned beans are a great option for working protein and fiber into dishes. We tested this recipe with organic, no-salt-added beans to keep sodium in check. The sweet mango brightens the earthiness of the beans and wild rice. Garnish with fresh cilantro. Serve with spicy pork tenderloins.

1½ cups chopped peeled ripe mango
1 cup thinly sliced green onions
½ cup cooked wild or brown rice
3 tablespoons finely chopped fresh cilantro
2 tablespoons roasted tomatillo or fresh salsa
2 tablespoons fresh lime juice
2 tablespoons extravirgin olive oil
¾ teaspoon salt
¼ teaspoon freshly ground black pepper
1 (15-ounce) can organic no-salt-added black beans, rinsed and drained

❶ Combine all ingredients in a large bowl. Toss gently to mix. Yield: 6 servings (serving size: ²/₃ cup).

CALORIES 167 (29% from fat); FAT 5.4g (sat 0.7g, mono 3.4g, poly 0.8g); PROTEIN 5.2g; CARB 25.5g; FIBER 5.5g; CHOL 0mg; IRON 1.1mg; SODIUM 226mg; CALC 41mg

Mustard Seed–Chive Vinaigrette

We like this vinaigrette drizzled over gourmet salad greens, but it would also pair well with salmon. Olives—and their oil—offer heart-healthy monounsaturated fat.

2 tablespoons sherry vinegar
1 tablespoon water
1 teaspoon country-style Dijon mustard
1 teaspoon honey
1 tablespoon extravirgin olive oil
2 tablespoons chopped fresh chives
½ teaspoon kosher salt
½ teaspoon mustard seeds
½ teaspoon freshly ground black pepper

❶ Combine first 4 ingredients in a small bowl; stir with a whisk. Slowly add oil, stirring constantly with a whisk until well blended. Stir in chives and remaining ingredients. Yield: ⅓ cup (serving size: about 1 tablespoon).

CALORIES 32 (81% from fat); FAT 2.8g (sat 0.4g, mono 2g, poly 0.3g); PROTEIN 0.2g; CARB 1.7g; FIBER 0.1g; CHOL 0mg; IRON 0.1mg; SODIUM 212mg; CALC 4mg

Five Dietary Recommendations

❶ Slash Sodium

For most people, the more sodium you consume, the higher your blood pressure will be. And as blood pressure jumps, so does the risk for heart disease and stroke. The American Heart Association and the revised Dietary Guidelines for Americans suggest limiting sodium to less than 2,300 milligrams a day (the amount in one teaspoon of salt).

Cooking with fresh ingredients makes it easy to control added sodium, says Kathleen Cappellano, MS, RD, instructor at the Friedman School of Nutrition Science and Policy at Tufts University in Boston.

It's also important to read labels. Look for brands of packaged convenience foods with the lowest levels of sodium. "Any switch you can make is going to be a step in the right direction," says Cappellano.

Indeed, huge clinical studies like DASH (Dietary Approaches to Stopping Hypertension) continue to document that as people eat less sodium—as part of a diet emphasizing whole grains, fruits, vegetables, lean proteins, and unsaturated fats—their blood pressure drops dramatically.

❷ Go Fish

The American Heart Association (AHA) recommends at least six ounces of (cooked) fish weekly as part of a healthful diet that can help lower risks of coronary heart disease. Fish is high in protein, like meat, but doesn't carry high levels of saturated fat. And certain types of fatty fish like salmon and trout offer beneficial omega-3 fatty acids. This type of fat is linked with lowering triglycerides, likely reducing blood clot risks and preventing abnormal heart rhythms, and possibly slowing plaque buildup on artery walls, according to a 2002 paper published in the AHA's journal *Circulation*.

And don't let news about possible marine contaminants scare you away from this lean protein. "The average person doesn't need to worry," says researcher

William E. Connor, MD, of Oregon Health and Science University. "The benefits of eating fish far outweigh the tiny amounts of any contaminants that may be present." The only exceptions are pregnant women and children, who should avoid fish that can contain higher levels of mercury, such as shark, tilefish, swordfish, and king mackerel.

❸ Eat Your Beans and Legumes

Longtime nutrition researcher Gerald Combs, PhD, director of the USDA Grand Forks Human Nutrition Research Center, thinks beans don't earn nearly enough attention for all their nutritional merits. "Beans and legumes are low in fat and calories, and good sources of protein, folate, fiber, and antioxidants," says Combs. In fact, these vegetables are so important, the USDA Dietary Guidelines recommend consuming three cups of cooked beans weekly. A cup of cooked black beans provides about one-third of daily protein needs, more than 60 percent of the recommended amount of folate, one-fifth of iron needs, a good dose of potassium, and 15 grams of fiber in a complex carbohydrate package. Beans and legumes may also help maintain a healthy body weight, manage and prevent type 2 diabetes, promote cardiac health, and reduce risk of some digestive tract cancers, Combs adds.

❹ Be Wise About Fat

In a 2006 report from Harvard called *Healthy Eating: A Guide to the New Nutrition*, Frank Sacks, MD, professor of cardiovascular disease prevention at the Harvard School of Public Health, sums up the latest research findings to illustrate that it's the *type* of fat you eat, and not so much the amount, that has the biggest effect on health. For example, in the landmark 2005 OmniHeart Trial, Sacks and his colleagues found that diets rich in unsaturated fats could help lower cholesterol levels and blood pressure. Unsatu-

rated fats include monounsaturated fats (olive oil, canola, avocado, and most tree nuts) and polyunsaturated fats (corn and safflower oils, sunflower seeds, and the oils found in fatty fish).

But saturated and trans fats—the solid-at-room-temperature kinds—may increase artery-clogging LDL cholesterol levels. The American Heart Association advises consuming no more than seven percent of calories from saturated fats like beef, butter, or cheese. That amounts to about 16 grams (which easily adds up with a day's menu that includes three ounces of roasted beef tenderloin, one cup of whole milk, one ounce of cheddar cheese, and one teaspoon of butter) for the average 2,000-calorie-a-day diet. Keep commercial bakery products, fried foods, and snacks that harbor trans fats (including partially hydrogenated oils) to a minimum.

❺ Go for Whole Grains

Eating just two-and-a-half servings of whole grains per day is enough to lower risk for cardiovascular disease 21 percent, according to a 2007 study from Wake Forest University School of Medicine. (One serving equals a slice of bread or one-third cup of cooked brown rice.) Lead researcher Philip Mellen, MD, says there is evidence whole grains do more than protect the heart. "Greater whole-grain intake is associated with less obesity, diabetes, high blood pressure, and high cholesterol," says Mellen. Indeed, a study published in the *American Journal of Clinical Nutrition*, following almost 500,000 men and women between age 50 and 71, investigated the effect of fiber and whole grain on digestive tract cancers. The result: Whole-grain (and not just fiber) intake was linked to a slightly reduced risk of colorectal cancer. And a study published in 2003 conducted by a team at Harvard's School of Public Health found that women with higher whole-grain intakes weighed less than those who did not consume as many whole grains.

Crispy Tilapia Sandwiches

Made with a whole wheat hoagie bun and lots of fresh veggie toppings, this sandwich is an easy way to obtain one of your two weekly fish servings.

- 2 tablespoons light sour cream
- 2 tablespoons creamy mustard blend (such as Dijonnaise)
- 15 fat-free saltine crackers
- 2 tablespoons all-purpose flour
- ¼ cup egg substitute
- 4 (5-ounce) tilapia fillets
- ⅛ teaspoon salt
- ⅛ teaspoon freshly ground black pepper
- 2 tablespoons canola oil
- 4 (3-ounce) whole wheat hoagie rolls, toasted
- 8 (¼-inch-thick) slices tomato
- 12 thin slices red onion
- 4 romaine leaves

❶ Combine sour cream and mustard blend in a small bowl.
❷ Place crackers in a food processor; process until fine crumbs measure 1 cup. Place crumbs in a shallow dish. Place flour in another shallow dish, and egg substitute in another. Sprinkle fish with salt and pepper. Dredge 1 fillet in flour. Dip in egg substitute; dredge in crumbs. Repeat procedure with remaining fillets, flour, egg substitute, and crumbs.
❸ Heat oil in a large nonstick skillet over medium-high heat. Add fish to pan; cook 4 minutes on each side or until fish flakes easily when tested with a fork or until desired degree of doneness.
❹ Spread 1½ teaspoons sour cream mixture on each roll half. Place 1 fillet on bottom half of each roll. Top each serving with 2 tomato slices, 3 onion slices, 1 romaine leaf, and top half of roll. Yield: 4 servings (serving size: 1 sandwich).

CALORIES 494 (25% from fat); FAT 13.8g (sat 2.3g, mono 5.9g, poly 4.5g); PROTEIN 36.2g; CARB 58.5g; FIBER 7.1g; CHOL 66mg; IRON 3.8mg; SODIUM 768mg; CALC 128mg

---

MAKE AHEAD
Seeded Cornmeal Biscuits

Measure the cornmeal as you would flour, lightly spooning into a measuring cup, to prevent a dry, tough biscuit. The cornmeal and whole wheat flour added to these hearty biscuits contribute to your daily whole-grain intake. We achieved the best results baking one sheet of biscuits at a time. Skip the seed topping for a simpler breakfast biscuit.

- 2 cups all-purpose flour (about 9 ounces)
- 2 cups whole wheat flour (about 9½ ounces)
- 1 cup stone-ground whole-grain cornmeal (about 5 ounces)
- ¼ cup sugar
- 1 tablespoon baking soda
- 1 teaspoon baking powder
- ½ teaspoon salt
- 7 tablespoons chilled butter, cut into small pieces
- 2 cups low-fat buttermilk
- Cooking spray
- 1 egg white, lightly beaten
- 2 teaspoons poppy seeds
- 2 teaspoons sesame seeds

❶ Preheat oven to 450°.
❷ Lightly spoon flours and cornmeal into dry measuring cups; level with a knife. Combine flours, cornmeal and next 4 ingredients in a large bowl; stir with a whisk. Cut in butter with a pastry blender or 2 knives until mixture resembles coarse meal. Add buttermilk; stir just until moist.
❸ Turn dough out onto a lightly floured surface. Roll dough to a ³/₄-inch thickness; cut with a 2½-inch biscuit cutter into 18 biscuits. Gather remaining dough. Roll to a ³/₄-inch thickness, and cut with a 2½-inch biscuit cutter into 6 biscuits. Place 12 biscuits on a baking sheet coated with cooking spray. Brush tops of biscuits with half of egg white. Combine poppy seeds and sesame seeds in a small bowl, and sprinkle half of seed mixture evenly over biscuit tops. Bake at 450° for 10 minutes or until biscuits are golden; place on a wire rack. Repeat with remaining 12 biscuits, egg white, and seed mixture. Yield: 24 servings (serving size: 1 biscuit).

CALORIES 139 (27% from fat); FAT 4.2g (sat 2.3g, mono 1g, poly 0.3g); PROTEIN 3.7g; CARB 22.3g; FIBER 2.4g; CHOL 10mg; IRON 1.5mg; SODIUM 276mg; CALC 46mg

---

Whole-Grain Guide

Substituting a little whole wheat flour for some all-purpose white flour is now a familiar practice for many cooks. Enhance the nutrients and flavor of your cooking by trying other whole grains.

- **Rye**, **amaranth**, and **spelt** work well in homemade breads as a supplement to wheat flour. Toast a tablespoonful or two in a hot, dry skillet to add to breakfast cereal.
- Look for pearled **barley** kernels or berries to add a new starchy side to your recipe repertoire. The cereal's chewy texture enhances soups, pilafs, and salads. Its hearty flavor pairs well with mushrooms, beef, herbs, and tomatoes.
- Even though **buckwheat** isn't technically wheat, or even a grain at all, its nutrition profile is similar. Soba noodles are made from buckwheat, and you can also try roasted buckwheat grains, or kasha, for a hot cereal, a filling side dish, or as the base for vegetable stuffing.
- With its nutty flavor and chewy texture, **bulgur wheat** is especially tasty as a salad with fresh herbs and vegetables or as a binder for burgers.
- Versatility is the virtue of **millet**. You can use it toasted in cookies, or simmer and serve it with Parmesan and herbs as a side dish similar to couscous.

Classic Marinara and Pizza Sauce

This tomato sauce compensates for moderate sodium with vibrant taste. If you have an immersion blender, use it instead of the countertop blender to make a smooth sauce. Freeze leftovers to have on hand for pasta or pizza.

- 1 large red bell pepper
- 2 large garlic cloves, peeled
- Cooking spray
- ½ cup chopped onion
- 1 teaspoon dried basil
- ½ teaspoon dried oregano
- ½ cup dry red wine
- ¼ cup tomato paste with Italian herbs
- ¾ teaspoon kosher salt, divided
- 1 (14.5-ounce) can no-salt-added diced tomatoes, undrained
- 1 (14.5-ounce) can diced tomatoes, undrained
- 3 tablespoons chopped fresh parsley
- 2 tablespoons red wine vinegar
- 1 tablespoon extravirgin olive oil

1 Preheat broiler.

2 Cut bell pepper in half lengthwise; discard seeds and membranes. Place garlic cloves and pepper halves, skin sides up, on a foil-lined baking sheet; flatten pepper halves with hand. Broil 12 minutes or until blackened. Place pepper in a zip-top plastic bag; seal. Let stand 15 minutes. Peel pepper; chop pepper and garlic.

3 Heat a large nonstick skillet over medium-high heat. Coat pan with cooking spray. Add onion to pan; cook 5 minutes or until tender, stirring frequently. Add basil and oregano; cook 1 minute. Stir in pepper, garlic, wine, tomato paste, ½ teaspoon salt, and tomatoes; bring to a boil. Reduce heat, and simmer 20 minutes, stirring occasionally. Place half of tomato mixture in a blender. Remove center piece of blender lid (to allow steam to escape); secure blender lid on blender. Place a clean towel over opening in blender lid (to avoid splatters). Process until smooth. Pour into a large bowl. Repeat procedure with remaining tomato mixture. Stir in parsley, vinegar, oil, and remaining ¼ teaspoon salt. Yield: 8 servings (serving size: ½ cup).

CALORIES 57 (30% from fat); FAT 1.9g (sat 0.3g, mono 1.2g, poly 0.2g); PROTEIN 1.5g; CARB 9.5g; FIBER 2.6g; CHOL 0mg; IRON 0.9mg; SODIUM 338mg; CALC 29mg

---

Flavor Sans Salt

Here are quick, easy ways to accent dishes without adding extra sodium. For more tips on how to use these and other ingredients to create harmonious flavor, see "On Balance" (page 51).

Herbs: Dried herbs work well in sauces and soups with long cooking times (like chili or the marinara sauce at left). Always crush dried herbs to release their flavorful aromatic oils. (Rub herbs between two fingers to add a pinch, or just pound in a mortar and pestle if you are using a large amount.) Stir in **fresh** herbs just before serving to enliven a dish.

Spices: Freshly ground spices add zest to roasted vegetables or meats and seafood. Basic vegetable dishes take on an ethnic flair with a blend of spices like cardamom, cumin, ginger, and freshly ground black pepper. Infuse liquids with whole spices for milder spice notes.

Acid: A drizzle of an acidic component, like fresh lime juice or vinegar, perks up flavor and is an alternative to high-sodium bottled dressings and condiments.

Citrus rind: Roasted pork or flank steak benefits from a rub of grated citrus peel, minced garlic, and cracked black pepper.

Chicken with Green Peppercorn Sauce

Crush peppercorns in a plastic bag with a small heavy skillet. Reducing wine and low-sodium chicken broth builds flavor and keeps added sodium at a minimum. Finishing the sauce with butter adds richness. Serve with roasted baby carrots and mashed potatoes. For pretty presentation, slice breast halves crosswise before spooning on the sauce.

- ¼ cup all-purpose flour
- ½ teaspoon paprika
- 4 (6-ounce) skinless, boneless chicken breast halves
- ½ teaspoon salt
- 1 tablespoon olive oil
- ¼ cup finely chopped shallots
- ⅔ cup dry white wine
- ½ cup fat-free, less-sodium chicken broth
- 1 tablespoon green peppercorns, crushed
- 1 tablespoon butter

1 Combine flour and paprika in a shallow dish. Sprinkle chicken with salt. Dredge chicken in flour mixture.

2 Heat oil in a large nonstick skillet over medium heat. Add chicken to pan; cook 5 minutes on each side or until done. Remove chicken from pan; keep warm.

3 Increase heat to medium-high. Add shallots to pan; sauté 1 minute. Stir in wine, broth, and peppercorns; bring to a boil. Cook until reduced to ¼ cup (about 7 minutes). Remove from heat; stir in butter. Yield: 4 servings (serving size: 1 chicken breast half and about 1 tablespoon sauce).

CALORIES 263 (29% from fat); FAT 8.5g (sat 2.8g, mono 3.7g, poly 1g); PROTEIN 40.2g; CARB 4.3g; FIBER 0.5g; CHOL 106mg; IRON 1.7mg; SODIUM 530mg; CALC 33mg

Fontina and Parmesan Mushroom Bread Pudding

- 6 cups (1-inch) cubed sturdy 100% whole wheat bread (about 12 ounces)
- Cooking spray
- 1 teaspoon olive oil
- ⅓ cup chopped shallots
- 2 (8-ounce) packages presliced cremini mushrooms
- 2 tablespoons chopped fresh parsley
- 1 tablespoon chopped fresh thyme
- ¼ teaspoon salt
- ¼ teaspoon freshly ground black pepper
- 1 cup (4 ounces) shredded fontina cheese, divided
- 2 tablespoons grated fresh Parmesan cheese, divided
- 1½ cups 1% low-fat milk
- ½ cup fat-free, less-sodium chicken broth
- 3 large eggs, lightly beaten

1 Preheat oven to 350°.

2 Place bread cubes on a jelly-roll pan; coat with cooking spray. Bake at 350° for 20 minutes or until lightly toasted, turning twice. Remove from oven; cool.

3 Heat oil in a large nonstick skillet over medium-high heat. Add shallots and mushrooms; sauté 12 minutes or until lightly browned and moisture evaporates. Remove from heat; stir in parsley and next 3 ingredients.

4 Place half of bread cubes in bottom of an 11 x 7–inch baking dish coated with cooking spray. Arrange mushroom mixture evenly over bread cubes; sprinkle with ½ cup fontina and 1 tablespoon Parmesan. Top with remaining bread cubes. Combine milk, broth, and eggs, stirring with a whisk; pour over bread mixture. Gently press with back of a spoon; let stand 30 minutes. Top with remaining ½ cup fontina and remaining 1 tablespoon Parmesan.

5 Bake at 350° for 45 minutes or until set. Let stand 10 minutes before serving. Cut into 6 squares. Yield: 6 servings.

CALORIES 316 (34% from fat); FAT 12.1g (sat 5.1g, mono 3.4g, poly 0.8g); PROTEIN 18.9g; CARB 36.7g; FIBER 4.8g; CHOL 131mg; IRON 2.6mg; SODIUM 696mg; CALC 228mg

MAKE AHEAD

Spicy Orange Noodles

- 1 (8-ounce) package soba (buckwheat noodles)
- 2½ tablespoons Orange and Pepper–Infused Oil
- 1 cup thinly sliced green onions
- ½ cup chopped fresh cilantro
- 1 tablespoon low-sodium soy sauce
- 1 tablespoon rice vinegar
- ¼ teaspoon salt

1 Cook noodles according to package directions, omitting salt and fat; drain. Rinse with cold water; drain.

2 Combine Orange and Pepper–Infused Oil and noodles in a large bowl. Add onions and remaining ingredients; toss gently to combine. Yield: 8 servings (serving size: ¾ cup).

CALORIES 137 (28% from fat); FAT 4.2g (sat 0.4g, mono 1.9g, poly 1g); PROTEIN 4.2g; CARB 22.4g; FIBER 0.6g; CHOL 0mg; IRON 1mg; SODIUM 353mg; CALC 21mg

MAKE AHEAD

ORANGE AND PEPPER–INFUSED OIL:

- ½ cup canola oil
- 2 tablespoons dark sesame oil
- 1½ teaspoons finely grated orange rind
- 1½ teaspoons crushed red pepper
- 1 garlic clove, crushed

1 Combine all ingredients in a small, heavy saucepan over medium-low heat. Cook 10 minutes, stirring occasionally. Remove from heat; cool 10 minutes. Store in an airtight container in refrigerator up to 1 month. Yield: about ⅔ cup (serving size: 1 tablespoon).

CALORIES 113 (100% from fat); FAT 12.5g (sat 1.1g, mono 6.9g, poly 4g); PROTEIN 0.1g; CARB 0.3g; FIBER 0.1g; CHOL 0mg; IRON 0mg; SODIUM 0mg; CALC 1mg

QUICK & EASY

Cornmeal and Spice–Crusted Scallops

A pinch of salt in a spice rub brings robust flavor to meats, poultry, and seafood. Serve the scallops over your favorite pasta or a gourmet green salad mix.

- 1 tablespoon yellow cornmeal
- 2 teaspoons ground coriander
- ½ teaspoon garlic powder
- ½ teaspoon onion powder
- ⅛ teaspoon salt
- ⅛ teaspoon freshly ground black pepper
- 1½ pounds large sea scallops
- 1 tablespoon olive oil
- 2 teaspoons butter

1 Combine first 6 ingredients in a shallow dish. Dredge both sides of scallops in cornmeal mixture.

2 Heat oil and butter in a large skillet over medium-high heat. Add scallops to pan, and cook 3 minutes. Carefully turn over; cook 1 minute or until done. Yield: 4 servings (serving size: about 3 scallops).

CALORIES 208 (29% from fat); FAT 6.6g (sat 1.8g, mono 3g, poly 0.9g); PROTEIN 28.8g; CARB 6.5g; FIBER 0.1g; CHOL 61mg; IRON 0.6mg; SODIUM 362mg; CALC 43mg

Tasteful Innovations

Here are four more outstanding finalist recipes from the *Cooking Light* Ultimate Reader Recipe Contest.

In the January/February chapter, we presented the category winners from the third annual *Cooking Light* Ultimate Reader Recipe Contest. Here, we introduce four finalists and their dishes from each of the four categories—sides and salads, entrées, starters and beverages, and desserts. Versatile and inspiring, these recipes represent the finalists' familiarity with light, tasteful dishes and easy-to-follow, thorough cooking techniques.

QUICK & EASY
Asian Green Bean Salad

Category Finalist—Sides and Salads
"I created this make-ahead dish to have after a long day at work. Snow peas can be substituted for the beans. Garnish with a cilantro sprig."

—Linda Dalton,
Stoughton, Massachusetts

SALAD:
- 3 ounces uncooked linguine
- 1 pound green beans, trimmed
- 2 cups diagonally sliced celery
- 1 cup thinly sliced red bell pepper
- ½ cup (½-inch) slices green onions
- ⅓ cup chopped fresh cilantro

DRESSING:
- ¼ cup rice wine vinegar
- ¼ cup low-sodium soy sauce
- 2 tablespoons dark sesame oil
- 2 teaspoons grated peeled fresh ginger
- ½ teaspoon sugar
- ¼ teaspoon freshly ground black pepper
- 3 garlic cloves, minced
- 1 red jalapeño pepper, seeded and finely chopped (about 1 tablespoon)

1 To prepare salad, break linguine in half. Cook pasta according to package directions, omitting salt and fat; add beans during last 3 minutes of cooking. Drain and rinse with cold water; drain. Place mixture in a large bowl. Stir in celery and next 3 ingredients.

2 To prepare dressing, combine vinegar and remaining ingredients in a small bowl; stir with a whisk until blended. Add to salad; toss well. Cover and chill. Yield: 8 servings (serving size: 1 cup).

CALORIES 101 (34% from fat); FAT 3.8g (sat 0.5g, mono 1.5g, poly 1.6g); PROTEIN 3g; CARB 14.9g; FIBER 3.1g; CHOL 0mg; IRON 0.8mg; SODIUM 282mg; CALC 42mg

MAKE AHEAD • FREEZABLE
Roasted Tomato–Beef Goulash with Caraway

Category Finalist—Entrées
"Hungarian goulash was a family favorite when I was growing up. I've updated my mom's recipe with fresh vegetables. Replacing plain tomato sauce with roasted diced tomatoes improved the taste and texture of the gravy."

—Sheryl Chomak,
Beaverton, Oregon

- 2 pounds bottom round roast, trimmed and cut into 1-inch pieces
- 1 teaspoon kosher salt, divided
- ½ teaspoon freshly ground black pepper
- 2 teaspoons canola oil
- 2 tablespoons paprika, divided
- 1 to 2 teaspoons caraway seeds
- 1¼ cups coarsely chopped onion (about 1 large)
- ½ cup finely chopped celery
- ½ cup finely chopped carrot
- 1 tablespoon minced garlic
- 1 (14.5-ounce) can fire-roasted diced tomatoes, undrained (such as Muir Glen)
- 4 cups cooked medium egg noodles (about 2½ cups uncooked pasta)

1 Sprinkle beef with ½ teaspoon salt and pepper.

2 Heat oil in a large Dutch oven over medium-high heat. Add beef to pan; cook 3 minutes or until browned on all sides. Add 1 tablespoon paprika and caraway seeds. Reduce heat to medium, and cook 2 minutes, stirring constantly. Stir in remaining ½ teaspoon salt, remaining 1 tablespoon paprika, onion, celery, carrot, and garlic; cook 5 minutes, stirring occasionally. Add tomatoes; bring to a boil. Cover, reduce heat, and simmer 1½ hours or until beef is tender. Serve over noodles. Yield: 8 servings (serving size: ½ cup goulash and ½ cup noodles).

CALORIES 299 (26% from fat); FAT 8.5g (sat 2.3g, mono 3.6g, poly 1.2g); PROTEIN 27.2g; CARB 27.6g; FIBER 2.9g; CHOL 91mg; IRON 4.5mg; SODIUM 403mg; CALC 41mg

Ginger-Shrimp Pot Stickers with Spicy Peanut Dipping Sauce
(pictured on page 244)

Category Finalist—
Starters and Beverages
"I love the huge flavor packed into these tiny packages, especially when they're dipped in the peanut sauce. These are best served immediately, but they can be made in advance, refrigerated, and then served at room temperature."

—Lindsay Weiss,
Overland Park, Kansas

POT STICKERS:
- ¾ cup shredded green cabbage
- ⅓ cup chopped green onions
- ¼ cup matchstick-cut carrots
- 2 tablespoons chopped fresh cilantro
- 1 tablespoon low-sodium soy sauce
- 2 teaspoons minced peeled fresh ginger
- 1 teaspoon dark sesame oil
- ½ teaspoon salt
- ½ pound cooked peeled small shrimp
- Dash of hot sauce
- 24 wonton wrappers
- 2 tablespoons cornstarch
- 1 tablespoon canola oil, divided
- 1 cup water, divided

Continued

SAUCE:

- ¼ cup water
- ¼ cup peanut butter
- 2 tablespoons low-sodium soy sauce
- 1½ tablespoons seasoned rice vinegar
- 1½ tablespoons chile paste with garlic (such as sambal oelek)
- ½ teaspoon sugar

REMAINING INGREDIENT:

Chopped green onions (optional)

❶ To prepare pot stickers, combine first 10 ingredients in a food processor; pulse 4 times or until coarsely chopped. Working with 1 wonton wrapper at a time (cover remaining wrappers with a damp towel to prevent drying), spoon about 1½ teaspoons shrimp mixture into center of each wrapper. Moisten edges of dough with water; bring 2 opposite corners to center, pinching points to seal. Bring remaining 2 corners to center, pinching points to seal. Pinch 4 edges together to seal. Place pot stickers on a large baking sheet sprinkled with cornstarch.

❷ Heat 1½ teaspoons canola oil in a large nonstick skillet over medium-high heat. Add 12 pot stickers to pan; cook 2 minutes or until bottoms are golden brown. Slowly add ½ cup water to pan; cover and cook 4 minutes. Uncover and cook 3 minutes or until liquid evaporates. Repeat procedure with remaining 1½ teaspoons canola oil, remaining pot stickers, and ½ cup water.

❸ To prepare sauce, combine ¼ cup water and next 5 ingredients in a small bowl, stirring with a whisk. Serve sauce with pot stickers. Garnish with chopped green onions, if desired. Yield: 12 servings (serving size: 2 pot stickers and 1 tablespoon sauce).

CALORIES 125 (35% from fat); FAT 4.9g (sat 0.8g, mono 2.2g, poly 1.5g); PROTEIN 7.1g; CARB 13.6g; FIBER 0.9g; CHOL 30mg; IRON 1.1mg; SODIUM 484mg; CALC 25mg

Decadent Double-Chocolate Bundt Cake

Category Finalist—Desserts
"The cake has a delicate chocolate flavor, so it's not overpowering. I enjoy the special glaze the most. Although I wrote the recipe to say "cool completely," the cake tastes delicious served slightly warm about a half-hour after you have inverted it from the pan."

—Barb Combs, Fort Collins, Colorado

GLAZE:

- ⅔ cup granulated sugar
- ¼ cup water
- ¼ cup chocolate-flavored liqueur
- 2 tablespoons butter

CAKE:

- 1½ teaspoons canola oil
- 2 tablespoons all-purpose flour
- Cooking spray
- 1½ cups granulated sugar
- 6 tablespoons butter, softened
- 2 large eggs
- 2 large egg whites
- 2 teaspoons vanilla extract
- 3 cups all-purpose flour (about 13½ ounces)
- ½ cup unsweetened cocoa
- 1 teaspoon baking powder
- ½ teaspoon baking soda
- ½ teaspoon salt
- 1½ cups 1% low-fat milk
- ⅔ cup semisweet chocolate minichips
- 2 tablespoons powdered sugar

❶ To prepare glaze, combine first 4 ingredients in a small saucepan. Bring to a boil over medium-high heat, stirring constantly. Cool completely.

❷ Preheat oven to 350°.

❸ To prepare cake, drizzle oil into a 12-cup Bundt pan; coat pan thoroughly with a pastry brush. Sprinkle with 2 tablespoons flour, shaking out excess. Coat prepared pan with cooking spray.

❹ Place 1½ cups granulated sugar and 6 tablespoons butter in a large bowl; beat with a mixer at medium speed until well blended (about 5 minutes). Add eggs and egg whites, 1 at a time, beating well after each addition. Beat in vanilla.

❺ Lightly spoon 3 cups flour into dry measuring cups; level with a knife. Combine 3 cups flour and next 4 ingredients, stirring with a whisk. Add flour mixture and milk alternately to sugar mixture, beginning and ending with flour mixture; mix after each addition. Beat 2 minutes. Fold in chips. Spoon batter into prepared pan. Swirl batter using a knife.

❻ Bake at 350° for 45 minutes or until a wooden pick inserted in center comes out clean. Immediately pour glaze over cake. Cool cake in pan on a wire rack 30 minutes. Invert cake onto a serving plate; cool completely. Sprinkle with 2 tablespoons powdered sugar. Yield: 16 servings (serving size: 1 slice).

CALORIES 326 (28% from fat); FAT 10.3g (sat 5.8g, mono 2.7g, poly 0.5g); PROTEIN 5.5g; CARB 54.8g; FIBER 2g; CHOL 43mg; IRON 1.9mg; SODIUM 211mg; CALC 59mg

These finalists integrated global ingredients and flavors in their dishes with pleasing results.

Simmering & Boiling

Although they're variations of the same process, these methods are essentially distinct. Here's why it's good to know the difference.

WHILE NEITHER SIMMERING nor boiling is difficult, both are essential techniques used to prepare everything from pasta to green vegetables to stewed meats. They're really degrees of the same thing, but the effect each has on food is profoundly different. These two basic cooking methods are used in most kitchens every day and require little more than a heavy-bottomed pot or saucepan to evenly distribute the heat.

Unlike the French, who are gifted with a vocabulary that describes the stages of a liquid about to boil (such as *fremir*, which means to tremble or shake), we have no equivalent words to describe variations in simmering. But for most purposes, a simmer is the stage when the water is in motion but almost no bubbles break the surface; they're trying to, but the water's surface tension holds them in place. Boiling, though, refers to liquid that's in full motion, with bubbles rapidly rising to the surface. The following recipes and tips will distinguish between the two and illustrate when each works best.

MAKE AHEAD ▪ FREEZABLE
Brown Chicken Stock

Roasting the chicken and vegetables imbues the stock with deep color and flavor. This recipe employs both boiling and simmering to different effect. Boiling water helps release the fond, or browned bits that stick to the bottom of the roasting pan; this process, called deglazing, enriches the stock. The secret to keeping the stock clear is to simmer very gently so that none of the fat or insoluble specks of protein emulsify into the liquid but instead float to the top where they're easily skimmed off. The long cooking time depletes the chicken of most of its flavor and texture, so the meat is best discarded or offered to pets (discard bones). Refrigerate stock up to one week, or freeze in one-cup increments for up to three months.

5 pounds chicken drumsticks, skinned
2 large carrots, halved lengthwise and cut into 2-inch pieces
1 large onion, quartered
Cooking spray
16 cups cold water, divided
7 thyme sprigs
1 bunch parsley stems
1 bay leaf

❶ Preheat oven to 450°.
❷ Arrange chicken, carrots, and onion in a single layer in the bottom of 2 broiler pans or roasting pans coated with cooking spray. Bake at 450° for 30 minutes. Turn chicken over, and rotate pans on oven racks. Bake an additional 30 minutes or until browned.
❸ Transfer chicken and vegetables to a 6-quart stockpot. Carefully discard drippings from broiler pans, leaving browned bits. Place 1 broiler pan on stovetop; add 2 cups water to pan. Bring to a boil over medium-high heat. Reduce heat; simmer 2 minutes, scraping pan to loosen browned bits. Carefully pour contents of broiler pan into stockpot. Repeat procedure with remaining broiler pan and 2 cups water.
❹ Add remaining 12 cups water, thyme, parsley, and bay leaf to stockpot; bring to a simmer over medium-high heat. Reduce heat to low, and simmer gently 2 hours, skimming foam and fat from the surface occasionally. Strain stock through a fine sieve into a large bowl. Discard solids. Cover and chill stock 8 hours or overnight. Skim solidified fat from surface of stock; discard fat. Yield: 8 cups (serving size: 1 cup).

CALORIES 22 (29% from fat); FAT 0.7g (sat 0.2g, mono 0.2g, poly 0.2g); PROTEIN 3.4g; CARB 0.4g; FIBER 0.1g; CHOL 11mg; IRON 0.2mg; SODIUM 13mg; CALC 3mg

QUICK & EASY
Chicken Noodle Soup

This is the classic soup at its most basic, yet the flavorful stock makes it satisfying and surprisingly memorable. Add leftover roast chicken for a heartier version.

5 cups Brown Chicken Stock (at left)
¼ pound uncooked vermicelli, broken into 1-inch pieces
¾ teaspoon salt
¼ teaspoon freshly ground black pepper

❶ Bring Brown Chicken Stock to a simmer in a medium saucepan. Add pasta; cook 8 minutes or until al dente. Stir in salt and pepper. Yield: 4 servings (serving size: about 1¼ cups).

CALORIES 131 (8% from fat); FAT 1.2g (sat 0.3g, mono 0.3g, poly 0.2g); PROTEIN 8.1g; CARB 21.8g; FIBER 1.1g; CHOL 14mg; IRON 1.2mg; SODIUM 460mg; CALC 10mg

All About Simmering & Boiling

Simmering

A cooking method gentler than boiling, simmering refers to cooking food in liquid (or cooking just the liquid itself) at a temperature slightly below the boiling point—around 180° to 190°. It requires careful regulation of the temperature so the surface of the liquid shimmers with a bubble coming up every few seconds.

What Simmering Does

Simmering cooks food gently and slowly. Delicate foods such as fish are poached at or below a simmer to prevent them from breaking apart. Meats that are simmered remain moist and fork-tender, while boiled meats are often dry and tough because the heat of boiling liquid can cause their proteins to toughen. Stocks are simmered so the fat and proteins released by any cooking meat or bones float to the top, where they can be skimmed off instead of being churned back in, which can make the stock cloudy and greasy.

Best Bets for Simmering

This technique is more versatile than boiling and lends itself to a variety of foods. Simmering is used to cook proteins (fish, poultry, and meats), often in the form of poaching (cooking in enough liquid to cover the food) and braising (cooking in a small amount of liquid). It's also essential when making broth or stock. While boiling works well for tender green vegetables, tough, fibrous root vegetables (such as potatoes, turnips, and beets) are best simmered so they cook evenly throughout.

Simmering Liquid

Food is usually simmered in flavored liquid, such as broth/stock or wine, but sometimes water is used. As a general rule, add meat to cold liquid, and bring it up to a simmer. If you add uncooked meat to already-simmering broth, the meat immediately releases proteins that cloud the broth. When you start the meat in cold liquid, these proteins are released more gradually and become entangled with one another in a frothy mass that's easy to skim off the surface. Fish are an exception. If you start poaching small

pieces of fish in cold liquid, by the time it comes to a simmer, the fish will be overcooked.

Maintaining a Simmer

A constant simmer isn't always easy to regulate, especially on a gas stovetop. Even at the lowest setting, the heat may be too intense and cause the liquid to boil. Turning the flame too low may cause it to extinguish, or the self-lighting mechanism may click incessantly. To avoid this, put the pot to one side of the flame, or use a device called a flame tamer or heat diffuser (or sometimes called a simmer ring) to absorb some of the stove's heat.

Boiling

This technique cooks food at a relatively high temperature—212° is the boiling point for water at sea level. When liquids boil, bubbles break through and pop on the surface while the whole batch of liquid churns vigorously. Bubbles are caused by water vapor, a gas, rushing to the surface.

What Boiling Does

In the case of pasta, churning, boiling water keeps the food in motion, prevents sticking, and cooks quickly so the pasta doesn't get soggy. Green vegetables are tossed into boiling water to cook as quickly as possible so they retain their flavor and bright color in a process called blanching; if they were to simmer gently in a covered pot, their color would dull, and they would lose much of their texture. Boiling causes speedy evaporation, a useful effect for reducing sauces, where the volume of the liquid decreases and flavors are concentrated.

Boiling Liquid

When ingredients are boiled, they are done so in water, sometimes containing salt and oil or butter for flavor and texture. The food is usually added to the liquid once it reaches a boil.

Best Bets for Boiling

This intense cooking method is well suited for pasta, some grains, and green vegetables. Boiling is also useful for reducing sauces.

Creamy Fettuccine with Porcini Mushrooms

Pasta needs to cook at a full boil to ensure an even al dente texture. The sauce, made of cream, porcini, and porcini soaking liquid, simmers and reduces for a short time to thicken it enough to cling to the pasta.

- ½ cup boiling water
- ¼ cup dried porcini mushrooms (about ¼ ounce)
- 12 ounces uncooked fettuccine
- ½ cup whipping cream
- ¾ teaspoon salt
- ¼ teaspoon freshly ground black pepper
- 6 tablespoons grated Parmigiano-Reggiano cheese
- 2 tablespoons (1-inch) cut fresh chives

❶ Combine ½ cup boiling water and mushrooms in a small bowl; cover and let stand 30 minutes or until soft. Drain through a sieve over a bowl, reserving soaking liquid. Finely chop mushrooms.
❷ Cook pasta according to package directions, omitting salt and fat. Drain in a colander over a bowl, reserving ¼ cup pasta water.
❸ Combine mushrooms and cream in a medium saucepan over medium heat; bring to a simmer. Stir in salt, pepper, and reserved mushroom soaking liquid; simmer 5 minutes or until slightly thickened. Add pasta and reserved ¼ cup pasta water to pan; toss well to coat. Sprinkle with cheese and chives. Serve immediately. Yield: 6 servings (serving size: 1 cup pasta mixture, 1 tablespoon cheese, and 1 teaspoon chives).

CALORIES 329 (29% from fat); FAT 10.6g (sat 5.6g, mono 2.2g, poly 0.4g); PROTEIN 12.3g; CARB 44.4g; FIBER 2g; CHOL 32mg; IRON 2mg; SODIUM 430mg; CALC 116mg

Ginger-Sesame Broccoli Rabe

Broccoli rabe is first boiled to eliminate some of its bitterness, then it's stir-fried with an aromatic combination of ginger, garlic, and sesame oil. Serve hot or at room temperature atop an Asian noodle salad or alongside steaks or roast chicken.

- 1½ pounds broccoli rabe (rapini), cut into 2-inch pieces
- 1 tablespoon canola oil
- 1 teaspoon minced peeled fresh ginger
- 1 garlic clove, minced
- 1½ teaspoons dark sesame oil
- ½ teaspoon salt
- ¼ teaspoon crushed red pepper

❶ Cook broccoli rabe in boiling water 3 minutes or until crisp-tender. Drain and plunge into ice water; drain well.
❷ Heat canola oil in a large skillet over medium-high heat. Add broccoli rabe, ginger, and garlic; stir-fry 2 minutes or until thoroughly heated. Remove from heat; stir in sesame oil, salt, and pepper. Yield: 6 servings (serving size: ²/₃ cup).

CALORIES 65 (48% from fat); FAT 3.5g (sat 0.3g, mono 1.9g, poly 1.2g); PROTEIN 4.1g; CARB 5.6g; FIBER 0g; CHOL 0mg; IRON 1mg; SODIUM 230mg; CALC 54mg

Simple Poached Pears

Many recipes for this delicate dessert are made with assertive spices that may overwhelm the delicate taste of the fruit. This approach calls for simmering the pears in an unspiced syrup that is reduced to concentrate the fruity flavor. It's worth it to seek out Poire Williams (a pear-flavored eau-de-vie) to finish the dish, but you can also use brandy.

- 6 cups water
- 1 cup sugar
- 6 firm Anjou pears, peeled, cored, and halved
- 1 (2-inch) lemon rind strip
- 3 tablespoons Poire Williams or other pear liqueur
- 6 (2-inch) lemon rind strips (optional)

❶ Combine first 3 ingredients in a large saucepan; bring to a simmer. Add 1 rind strip. Reduce heat, and simmer 25 minutes or until tender. Remove pears from pan with a slotted spoon; cover and chill.
❷ Bring cooking liquid to a boil over high heat; cook until syrupy and reduced to 1 cup (about 20 minutes). Strain through a sieve into a bowl, discarding solids; cover and chill. Stir in liqueur. Arrange 2 pear halves in each of 6 shallow bowls; top each serving with about 3 tablespoons sauce and 1 rind strip, if desired. Yield: 6 servings.

CALORIES 277 (1% from fat); FAT 0.3g (sat 0g, mono 0.1g, poly 0.1g); PROTEIN 0.8g; CARB 68.1g; FIBER 2.1g; CHOL 0mg; IRON 0.4mg; SODIUM 2mg; CALC 19mg

New England Boiled Dinner

This meal-in-a-pot is actually simmered, not boiled, which produces fork-tender results. Warm pumpernickel bread, whole-grain mustard, and pickled beets make fine accompaniments.

- 7 thyme sprigs
- 1 bunch fresh parsley stems
- 1 bay leaf
- 1 (3-pound) cured corned beef brisket, trimmed
- 2 quarts water
- 18 small boiling onions, peeled
- 3 carrots, cut crosswise into 2-inch pieces
- 1 (2-pound) green cabbage, cored and cut into 8 wedges
- 1 pound fingerling potatoes, halved crosswise
- Grated fresh horseradish (optional)

❶ Place first 3 ingredients on a double layer of cheesecloth. Gather edges of cheesecloth together; tie securely.
❷ Place brisket in an 8-quart stockpot; cover with 2 quarts water. Bring to a simmer; cover, reduce heat, and simmer 1 hour. Add onions, carrots, and cheesecloth bag; cover and simmer 30 minutes. Add cabbage and potatoes; cover and cook 30 minutes or until vegetables are tender. Remove vegetables and brisket from pan; cut brisket across grain into thin slices. Discard cheesecloth bag and half of cooking liquid. Serve with horseradish, if desired. Yield: 8 servings (serving size: about 2 ounces brisket, 1 cabbage wedge, about ²/₃ cup vegetables, and about ¹/₃ cup cooking liquid).

CALORIES 238 (42% from fat); FAT 11g (sat 3.7g, mono 5.3g, poly 0.5g); PROTEIN 13.5g; CARB 21.6g; FIBER 4.2g; CHOL 56mg; IRON 2.1mg; SODIUM 982mg; CALC 57mg

Green Bean Salad Amandine

Boiling water cooks the beans quickly so they retain their vibrant color. Haricots verts are slender French green beans; if you substitute regular green beans, cook an additional 30 seconds to one minute. The almonds are toasted for the most robust flavor.

- 1 pound haricots verts, trimmed
- 1 tablespoon sherry vinegar
- 1½ teaspoons extravirgin olive oil
- 1 teaspoon Dijon mustard
- ¼ teaspoon salt
- ¼ teaspoon freshly ground black pepper
- 1 tablespoon sliced almonds, toasted

1 Cook beans in boiling water 4 minutes or until crisp-tender. Drain and plunge beans into ice water; drain well. Pat beans dry with paper towels.
2 Combine vinegar and next 4 ingredients, stirring with a whisk until well blended. Add beans to vinegar mixture; toss well to coat. Sprinkle with almonds. Yield: 4 servings (serving size: 1 cup).

CALORIES 62 (41% from fat); FAT 2.8g (sat 0.3g, mono 1.8g, poly 0.5g); PROTEIN 2.5g; CARB 8.7g; FIBER 4.1g; CHOL 0mg; IRON 1.3mg; SODIUM 186mg; CALC 48mg

White Veal Stock

This is a special-occasion recipe based on classic techniques. Since the meat is not browned, it's referred to as a white stock. Reserve a Saturday or Sunday for this recipe, as it needs to simmer 12 hours; the time lends complexity only found in homemade broth. We use the stock in Pot-au-Feu (at right), but it can also work in sauces or refined soups. Although it's still something of an investment, veal breast is the most economical cut for this recipe. Blanching the meat in boiling water before simmering rids it of albumin, ensuring a clear stock. The 12-hour simmer will render the meat exhausted, so it's best to discard it.

- 10 pounds bone-in veal breast, trimmed
- 12 quarts cold water, divided
- 1 large carrot, halved lengthwise and cut into 2-inch pieces
- 1 small onion, quartered
- 7 thyme sprigs
- 1 bunch fresh parsley stems
- 1 bay leaf

1 Cut veal between bones to separate meat. Add veal to a 12-quart stockpot, and cover with 6 quarts water. Bring to a boil, and cook 5 minutes. Drain. Rinse veal with cold water; drain. Rinse pan, and wipe pan dry with paper towels. Add veal, carrot, and onion to pan.
2 Add remaining 6 quarts water, thyme, parsley, and bay leaf to pan; bring to a simmer. Reduce heat to low, and simmer gently 12 hours, skimming foam and fat from the surface occasionally. Strain stock through a fine sieve into a large bowl; discard solids. Cover and chill stock 8 hours or overnight. Skim solidified fat from surface of stock; discard fat. Yield: 10 cups (serving size: 1 cup).

CALORIES 100 (41% from fat); FAT 4.5g (sat 1.7g, mono 2.1g, poly 0.4g); PROTEIN 13.8g; CARB 0.2g; FIBER 0.1g; CHOL 53mg; IRON 0.5mg; SODIUM 32mg; CALC 6mg

Pot-au-Feu

French for "pot on fire," pot-au-feu is made by simmering an assortment of meats in water or broth. We have chosen to cook in our White Veal Stock (at left), but you can use commercial low-sodium beef broth, if you prefer. Because the dish simmers uncovered the entire time, the stock reduces, concentrating the flavors. We recommend tying the leek halves with twine so they don't fall apart. Dijon mustard rounds out the flavors of the finished dish, and the cornichons (small pickles) are a traditional accompaniment.

- 1 large onion, halved
- 2 whole cloves
- 7 thyme sprigs
- 1 bunch fresh parsley stems
- 1 bay leaf
- 10 cups White Veal Stock (at left) or beef broth
- 8 cups cold water
- 4 pounds beef shank, trimmed
- 2 pounds beef short ribs, trimmed
- 1 (2-pound) boneless chuck roast, trimmed
- 6 leeks, trimmed and halved lengthwise
- 4 carrots, halved lengthwise and cut into 2-inch pieces
- 2 large turnips, peeled and each cut into 6 wedges (about 1 pound)
- 1 teaspoon kosher salt
- ¼ cup Dijon mustard
- 12 cornichons

1 Stud onion halves with cloves.
2 Place thyme, parsley, and bay leaf on a double layer of cheesecloth. Gather edges of cheesecloth together; tie securely.
3 Place onion halves, cheesecloth bag, White Veal Stock, and next 4 ingredients in an 8-quart stockpot; bring to a boil. Reduce heat, and simmer, uncovered, 3½ hours.
4 Tie twine around leek halves to secure. Add leek halves, carrots, and turnips to pan; simmer 1½ hours or until vegetables

and meat are tender. Strain mixture through a cheesecloth-lined colander into a large bowl; transfer meat, leeks, carrots, and turnips to a bowl. Remove twine from leeks. Discard twine, onion, and cheesecloth bag. Place 2 large zip-top plastic bags inside 2 large bowls. Carefully pour stock mixture into bags; let stand 10 minutes (fat will rise to top). Seal bags. Working with 1 bag at a time, carefully snip off 1 bottom corner of each bag. Drain stock mixture into pan, stopping before fat layer reaches opening; discard fat. Stir in salt.

⑤ Shred roast with 2 forks. Remove meat from shank and rib bones; discard bones, fat, and gristle. Add meat to stock mixture. Serve with mustard and cornichons. Yield: 12 servings (serving size: about 3/4 cup stock mixture, about 3 1/2 ounces meat, about 3 carrot pieces, 1 leek half, 1 turnip wedge, 1 teaspoon mustard, and 1 cornichon).

CALORIES 385 (40% from fat); FAT 17g (sat 6.6g, mono 7.4g, poly 0.9g); PROTEIN 43.2g; CARB 12.8g; FIBER 2g; CHOL 123mg; IRON 4.8mg; SODIUM 852mg; CALC 71mg

WINE NOTE: Although Pot-au-Feu is chock-full of meat, this version is not as heavy as others. Therefore, serve a lighter-style cabernet, one that's medium bodied rather than full bodied but still has exquisite flavors. The elegant cabernets of Australia's Margaret River region fill the bill nicely. One of the best—and a wine that will certainly elevate this dish to entertaining status—is Leeuwin Estate 2002 Art Series Cabernet Sauvignon, about $45.

Chicken with Red Wine Broth

This recipe starts with the process used for Brown Chicken Stock (page 65), but wine is used in place of water. Its tannins and acids yield soft but profound flavors. Serve over mashed potatoes.

BROTH:

- 4 pounds chicken drumsticks, skinned
- 2 large carrots, halved lengthwise and cut into 2-inch pieces
- 1 large onion, quartered
- Cooking spray
- 2 (750-milliliter) bottles zinfandel or other full-bodied red wine, divided
- 7 thyme sprigs
- 1 bunch parsley stems
- 1 bay leaf

CHICKEN:

- 1 (3 1/2-pound) whole chicken, quartered and skinned
- 3 1/2 cups quartered cremini mushrooms (about 10 ounces)
- 1 tablespoon all-purpose flour
- 1 tablespoon butter, softened
- 3/4 teaspoon salt
- 1/2 teaspoon freshly ground black pepper
- 2 tablespoons chopped fresh parsley

① Preheat oven to 450°.

② To prepare broth, arrange first 3 ingredients in a single layer in the bottom of 2 broiler pans or roasting pans coated with cooking spray. Bake at 450° for 30 minutes. Turn chicken over; rotate pans on oven racks. Bake 30 minutes or until browned.

③ Transfer chicken and vegetables to a 6-quart stockpot. Carefully discard drippings from broiler pans, leaving browned bits. Place 1 broiler pan on stovetop; add 2 cups wine to pan. Bring to a boil over medium-high heat. Reduce heat; simmer 2 minutes, scraping pan to loosen browned bits. Carefully pour contents of broiler pan into stockpot. Repeat procedure with remaining broiler pan and 2 cups wine.

④ Add remaining wine, thyme, parsley, and bay leaf to stockpot; bring to a simmer over medium-high heat. Reduce heat to low, and simmer gently 2 hours, skimming foam and fat from the surface occasionally. Strain broth through a fine sieve into a large bowl. Discard solids. Cover and chill broth for 8 hours or overnight. Skim solidified fat from surface of broth; discard fat.

⑤ To prepare chicken, heat a large saucepan over medium-high heat. Coat pan with cooking spray. Add chicken quarters to pan; cook 5 minutes on each side or until browned. Remove chicken from pan. Wipe drippings from pan with paper towels. Add chicken quarters, mushrooms, and broth to pan; bring to a boil. Cover, reduce heat, and simmer 10 minutes or until chicken is done. Remove chicken from pan; cover and keep warm.

⑥ Simmer broth mixture until liquid is reduced to about 1 1/2 cups (about 25 minutes). Combine flour and butter, stirring with a fork until a paste forms. Add flour mixture to pan, stirring with a whisk; simmer 4 minutes or until slightly thickened. Stir in salt and pepper. Spoon sauce over chicken; sprinkle with parsley. Yield: 4 servings (serving size: 1 chicken quarter and about 1/3 cup sauce).

CALORIES 335 (26% from fat); FAT 9.5g (sat 3.5g, mono 2.8g, poly 1.8g); PROTEIN 49.3g; CARB 10.9g; FIBER 0.8g; CHOL 156mg; IRON 4.6mg; SODIUM 669mg; CALC 73mg

Leeks

Enjoy the delicate qualities of this slender green allium.

With large, glossy green leaves and slender white bulbs, leeks look like overgrown green onions. But their flavor is milder and sweeter than that of other alliums, such as onions and garlic.

Cooks have prized their subtle quality for millennia. The Bible mentions leeks as an Egyptian crop, and the freed Israelites craved them while wandering in the desert. Upper-class Romans considered them a delicacy. The Roman emperor Nero reportedly ate copious amounts of leeks to improve his singing voice, earning him the nickname "Porrophagus" (leek eater). Folklore holds that sixth-century Welsh warriors pinned the vegetable to their battle headgear as a means of identification, and eventually bestowed on leeks mythical properties of fortitude and strength. To this day, on March 1—St. David's Day, a holiday that honors the patron saint of Wales—the Welsh wear leeks on their lapels and feast on *cawl cennin*, or leek broth.

Still popular throughout Europe, leeks are a common ingredient in soups, including Scottish cock-a-leekie, a hearty mixture of leeks, chicken, and herbs often thickened with potatoes, rice, or barley, and French vichyssoise, a classic chilled leek and potato soup. The French serve leeks in a variety of other preparations, such as leeks vinaigrette, a classic side dish of braised leeks.

Leeks are delicious raw or cooked. You can add chopped, uncooked leeks to salads, sandwich spreads, dips, or salsas. Cooking leeks intensifies their natural sweetness, and they yield a supple, silky texture.

Braised Leeks with Warm Pancetta Dressing

Cook the vegetables slowly in a flavorful liquid for our interpretation of leeks vinaigrette. The leek halves will slightly overlap in the pan. Pancetta is Italian cured pork. If you can't find it, substitute your favorite cured bacon.

LEEKS:

- 4 leeks, trimmed and halved lengthwise
- ¼ teaspoon kosher salt
- ¼ teaspoon freshly ground black pepper
- 1½ cups fat-free, less-sodium chicken broth
- 1 large carrot, cut into 3-inch pieces
- 1 garlic clove, crushed
- 1 thyme sprig
- Cooking spray

DRESSING:

- 1 teaspoon olive oil
- ⅓ cup finely chopped pancetta (about 1 ounce)
- 2 tablespoons finely chopped leek
- 2 tablespoons light brown sugar
- ¼ cup red wine vinegar
- ⅛ teaspoon freshly ground black pepper
- Dash of kosher salt

REMAINING INGREDIENT:

Thyme sprigs (optional)

① Preheat oven to 325°.

② To prepare leeks, arrange leek halves in an 8-inch baking dish; sprinkle evenly with ¼ teaspoon salt and ¼ teaspoon pepper. Add broth and next 3 ingredients. Cut 1 (8-inch) square of parchment paper; lightly coat with cooking spray. Place parchment over leek mixture, coated side down. Bake at 325° for 50 minutes or until leeks are tender. Let stand 5 minutes; drain cooking liquid through a sieve over a bowl, reserving solids.

③ Place cooking liquid in a small, heavy saucepan; bring to a boil. Cook until reduced to ¼ cup (about 8 minutes). Chop cooked carrot; set aside. Coarsely chop cooked garlic; set aside.

④ To prepare dressing, heat oil in a small skillet over medium-high heat. Add pancetta to pan; sauté 5 minutes or until crisp. Stir in garlic and chopped leek; sauté 2 minutes, stirring occasionally. Sprinkle with sugar; sauté 1 minute or until sugar dissolves. Stir in vinegar; simmer 2 minutes. Add braising liquid, ⅛ teaspoon pepper, and dash of salt; simmer 2 minutes or until slightly thick. Remove from heat. Arrange leek halves in a serving dish; sprinkle with carrot. Drizzle pancetta mixture over leek halves. Garnish with thyme sprigs, if desired. Yield: 4 servings (serving size: 2 leek halves and 2 tablespoons dressing).

CALORIES 133 (26% from fat); FAT 3.8g (sat 1.2g, mono 2g, poly 0.6g); PROTEIN 3.6g; CARB 22.2g; FIBER 2.6g; CHOL 5mg; IRON 2.3mg; SODIUM 391mg; CALC 74mg

Selection and Storage

Although increasingly available year-round, leeks are abundant in fall through early spring. Because they're a cool-weather crop, late-winter and spring leeks offer a milder flavor and delicate texture.

Choose slender, straight-sided, and dry leeks, free of blemishes and cracks; bulbous leeks or those that are thicker than one inch may be old and tough. Look for a bright white bulb and dark green, fresh-looking tops (trimmed leaves are often a sign of age). The longer the white and light green part, the better—that's the edible section.

Store leeks wrapped in damp paper towels in a plastic bag in the refrigerator's crisper drawer for up to six days. Wash, trim, and chop leeks just before use.

Artichoke, Leek, and Goat Cheese Dip with Garlic Pita Chips

A small amount of raw leek rounds out the dip's flavor, imparting a mild onion taste without bite.

DIP:

- ½ cup plain fat-free yogurt
- 3 ounces goat cheese, softened
- ¼ cup sliced leek
- 1 (14-ounce) can artichoke hearts, rinsed and drained
- ½ cup (2 ounces) grated fresh pecorino Romano cheese
- 2 teaspoons fresh lemon juice
- ¼ teaspoon freshly ground black pepper
- Dash of kosher salt
- Fresh chives (optional)

CHIPS:

- 6 (6-inch) whole wheat pitas
- Cooking spray
- ½ teaspoon kosher salt
- ½ teaspoon garlic powder

1 To prepare dip, combine yogurt and goat cheese in a food processor; process until smooth. Add leek and artichoke; process until finely chopped, scraping sides. Add pecorino Romano and next 3 ingredients; pulse until blended. Cover and chill 2 hours. Garnish with chives, if desired.

2 Preheat oven to 350°.

3 To prepare chips, cut each pita into 8 wedges. Arrange pita wedges in a single layer on a baking sheet; lightly coat with cooking spray. Sprinkle evenly with ½ teaspoon salt and garlic powder. Bake at 350° for 14 minutes or until toasted. Cool completely. Serve with dip. Yield: 12 servings (serving size: 4 chips and about 2½ tablespoons dip).

CALORIES 118 (29% from fat); FAT 3.8g (sat 2.3g, mono 0.9g, poly 0.3g); PROTEIN 6.2g; CARB 16.1g; FIBER 2.4g; CHOL 10mg; IRON 0.8mg; SODIUM 420mg; CALC 83mg

Farfalle with Turkey Sausage, Leeks, and Broccoli Rabe

Slightly sweet, mild leeks and turkey sausage balance the characteristic bitter flavor of broccoli rabe. Blanch the rabe as the recipe directs to leach out some of its bitterness, or substitute Broccolini, if you prefer.

- ¾ pound broccoli rabe (rapini), cut into 4-inch pieces (about 1 bunch)
- 8 ounces uncooked farfalle (bow tie pasta)
- 1 tablespoon olive oil
- 2 cups thinly sliced leek (about 2 large)
- ½ teaspoon crushed red pepper
- 2 garlic cloves, thinly sliced
- 1 pound turkey Italian sausage
- ½ teaspoon grated lemon rind
- ½ cup fat-free ricotta cheese
- ¼ cup (1 ounce) grated fresh Parmigiano-Reggiano cheese
- ¼ teaspoon kosher salt

1 Cook broccoli rabe in boiling water in a large Dutch oven 2 minutes or until wilted. Remove broccoli rabe with a slotted spoon. Rinse with cold water; drain. Reserve ¾ cup cooking liquid.

2 Cook pasta according to package directions, omitting salt and fat. Drain.

3 Heat oil in a large nonstick skillet over medium heat. Add leek to pan; cook 2 minutes or until wilted, stirring occasionally. Stir in pepper and garlic; cook 2 minutes, stirring occasionally. Increase heat to medium-high. Remove casings from sausage. Add sausage to pan; sauté 4 minutes, stirring to crumble. Add ½ cup reserved cooking liquid; cook 5 minutes or until sausage is done. Add remaining ¼ cup reserved cooking liquid, broccoli rabe, pasta, and rind to pan; toss to combine. Cook 5 minutes or until thoroughly heated. Remove from heat; stir in cheeses and salt. Yield: 8 servings (serving size: 1¼ cups).

CALORIES 285 (29% from fat); FAT 9.1g (sat 2.5g, mono 3.2g, poly 1.4g); PROTEIN 20.4g; CARB 29.2g; FIBER 1.4g; CHOL 54mg; IRON 3mg; SODIUM 604mg; CALC 115mg

---

Rinse Leeks Thoroughly

Notorious for hiding dirt within their concentric layers, leeks require thorough washing. **(A)** To clean, trim the roots with a sharp knife. Then remove the dark green leaves at the opposite end of the leek, cutting at the point where the color changes from light to dark. **(B)** Halve it lengthwise. Hold leek halves with the white tops pointing up, and gently fan the layers under running water. This technique allows the grit to wash away with the water.

If a recipe calls for sliced or chopped leeks, cut them first and place pieces in a bowl of cold water; agitate gently, allowing any debris to fall to the bottom. Use a strainer to carefully remove leeks from the bowl. Repeat as necessary, then rinse in a colander.

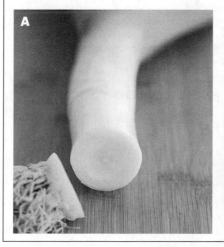
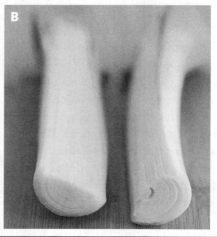

Beef and Leek Potpie with Chive Crust

This recipe calls for regular table salt in the crust and kosher salt in the filling. Fine iodized salt will dissolve easily in the crust, giving it a nice texture. Kosher salt has the purest flavor and most presense in the filling since it's used to finish the dish. We tested this recipe with trans-fat-free shortening with satisfactory results.

CRUST:

- 1¼ cups all-purpose flour (about 5½ ounces)
- 2 tablespoons chopped fresh chives
- ¼ teaspoon salt
- ¼ cup vegetable shortening
- ¼ cup ice water

FILLING:

- Cooking spray
- 1½ pounds boneless chuck roast, trimmed and cut into (1-inch) cubes
- 4 cups thinly sliced leek (about 4)
- 1½ cups chopped carrot, divided
- 1 cup finely chopped celery, divided
- 1 teaspoon minced fresh garlic
- 1 teaspoon chopped fresh rosemary
- 1 teaspoon chopped fresh thyme
- ½ cup dry red wine
- 2¼ cups fat-free, less-sodium beef broth, divided
- 3 tablespoons all-purpose flour
- 1½ cups (½-inch) cubed peeled baking potato
- 1 cup frozen peas, thawed
- ¾ teaspoon kosher salt
- ¼ teaspoon freshly ground black pepper

❶ To prepare crust, lightly spoon 1¼ cups flour into dry measuring cups; level with a knife. Combine 1¼ cups flour, chives, and ¼ teaspoon salt in a medium bowl, stirring with a whisk. Cut in shortening with a pastry blender or 2 knives until mixture resembles coarse meal. Sprinkle ice water over flour mixture, 1 tablespoon at a time; toss with a fork until moist and crumbly. Press mixture gently into a disk, and wrap tightly with plastic wrap. Chill dough 30 minutes.

❷ To prepare filling, heat a Dutch oven over medium-high heat. Coat pan with cooking spray. Add beef to pan; sauté 8 minutes, turning to brown on all sides. Remove beef with a slotted spoon; set aside. Add leek to pan; sauté 4 minutes, stirring occasionally. Add ¾ cup carrot, ½ cup celery, and garlic; sauté 2 minutes, stirring frequently.

❸ Return beef to pan; add rosemary and thyme. Sauté 1 minute. Stir in wine; cook 30 seconds, stirring frequently. Stir in 1½ cups beef broth; bring to a boil. Cover, reduce heat, and simmer 1 hour or until beef is tender, stirring occasionally. Combine remaining ¾ cup broth and 3 tablespoons flour, stirring until smooth; set aside.

❹ Preheat oven to 400°.

❺ Stir in remaining ¾ cup carrot, remaining ½ cup celery, and potato. Cook, covered, 10 minutes. Stir in peas. Add flour mixture, kosher salt, and pepper to beef mixture; bring to a boil. Cook 1 minute, stirring constantly. Transfer mixture to an 11 x 7–inch baking dish coated with cooking spray.

❻ Roll dough into an 8 x 12–inch rectangle. Place dough over beef mixture, pressing edges to seal. Cut 5 slits in top of crust to allow steam to escape. Bake at 400° for 20 minutes or until crust is browned. Yield: 6 servings (serving size: 1⅓ cups).

CALORIES 493 (38% from fat); FAT 20.8g (sat 7.2g, mono 8.1g, poly 2.3g); PROTEIN 28.3g; CARB 46.3g; FIBER 4.9g; CHOL 70mg; IRON 5.1mg; SODIUM 587mg; CALC 77mg

---

Substitution Savvy

Use mild-flavored leeks in any dish that calls for onions, especially if you want to impart a more nuanced flavor. The opposite isn't always true, however. Pungent onions may not be a suitable substitute for leeks, especially if you use them in recipes that call for them to be raw.

Caramelized Leeks with Roasted Salmon Fillets

When leeks cook slowly, they take on a supple, silky texture. The results complement fish, as well as pork or chicken.

- 2 leeks
- 1½ teaspoons butter
- 1 teaspoon light brown sugar
- ½ teaspoon kosher salt, divided
- ½ teaspoon fresh lemon juice
- 4 (6-ounce) salmon fillets
- Cooking spray
- ¼ teaspoon freshly ground black pepper
- ⅛ teaspoon ground red pepper

❶ Preheat oven to 400°.

❷ Remove roots, outer leaves, and tops from leeks. Cut leeks in half lengthwise. Rinse thoroughly with cold water, and cut each half into 3-inch julienne strips.

❸ Melt butter in a large nonstick skillet over medium heat. Add leeks to pan; cook 4 minutes or until slightly wilted, stirring occasionally. Stir in brown sugar and ¼ teaspoon salt; cook 20 minutes or until edges are browned, stirring occasionally. Remove from heat; stir in juice. Keep warm.

❹ Place salmon on a baking sheet coated with cooking spray; sprinkle salmon with remaining ¼ teaspoon salt, black pepper, and red pepper. Bake salmon at 400° for 8 minutes or until fish flakes easily when tested with a fork or until desired degree of doneness. Place 1 fillet on each of 4 plates; top each with 2 tablespoons leek mixture. Yield: 4 servings.

CALORIES 320 (39% from fat); FAT 13.9g (sat 2.8g, mono 4.5g, poly 5.1g); PROTEIN 39.2g; CARB 7.6g; FIBER 0.9g; CHOL 111mg; IRON 2.5mg; SODIUM 339mg; CALC 51mg

WINE NOTE: Salmon pairs comfortably with red or white wine. But the natural sweetness of the leeks can be a challenge for very dry or tannic wines, making them seem hollow or bitter. Try a Washington State Riesling like Hayman and Hill Reserve Selection ($15).

Leek and Garlic Soup

1 whole garlic head
6 parsley sprigs
4 thyme sprigs
2 (4-inch) green leek leaves
1 bay leaf
1 tablespoon olive oil
3 cups thinly sliced leek (about 3 large)
2 cups (1-inch) cubed crusty bread (about 2 ounces)
1 tablespoon chopped fresh garlic
4 cups organic vegetable broth
¼ teaspoon coarsely ground black pepper
¼ cup finely chopped fresh chives

1 Preheat oven to 350°.
2 Remove white papery skin from garlic head (do not peel or separate cloves). Wrap head in foil. Bake at 350° for 45 minutes; cool 10 minutes. Separate cloves; squeeze to extract garlic pulp. Discard skins.
3 Place parsley and next 3 ingredients on a double layer of cheesecloth. Gather edges together; tie securely.
4 Heat oil in a Dutch oven over medium heat. Add sliced leek to pan; cook 7 minutes or until wilted, stirring occasionally. Stir in bread and chopped garlic; cook 2 minutes. Add herb bundle, broth, and pepper; bring to a boil. Reduce heat, and simmer 10 minutes, stirring occasionally; discard herb bundle.
5 Place half of leek mixture and half of roasted garlic pulp in a blender. Remove center piece of blender lid (to allow steam to escape); secure blender lid on blender. Place a clean towel over opening in blender lid (to avoid splatters). Process until smooth. Pour into a large bowl. Repeat procedure with remaining leek mixture and roasted garlic pulp. Ladle about ²/₃ cup soup into each of 6 bowls; sprinkle each serving with 2 teaspoons chives. Yield: 6 servings.

CALORIES 96 (25% from fat); FAT 2.7g (sat 0.3g, mono 1.7g, poly 0.3g); PROTEIN 2g; CARB 16.1g; FIBER 1.4g; CHOL 0mg; IRON 1.5mg; SODIUM 451mg; CALC 49mg

Easter Buffet

From appetizer to dessert, this menu features the first hints of spring.

THIS MENU FEATURES TRADITIONAL recipes inspired by world cuisines from Ireland to Spain, and several dishes highlight spring flavors. Fresh herbs add definition to classics like Smoked Salmon Dip, Basil-Lime Fruit Salad, and Garlic-Studded Rosemary Roast Rack of Lamb. And our "Prep Plan" (page 74) will help you do much of the work ahead of time so you can welcome guests with ease. You might even recruit young helpers to decorate Easter Egg Cookies or assist in frosting the Ginger Angel Food Cake. And if you can entice Dad, with a glass of White Sangria, to carve the roast, everyone can play a role in assembling the feast.

EASTER BRUNCH BUFFET MENU

(Serves 12)

White Sangria

Smoked Salmon Dip

Basil-Lime Fruit Salad

Brown Sugar and Spice-Crusted Ham
or
Garlic-Studded Rosemary Roast Rack of Lamb

Lemon-Chive Roasted Vegetables

Spotted Puppies

Easter Egg Cookies
or
Ginger Angel Food Cake with Coconut Frosting

Coffee or tea

QUICK & EASY • MAKE AHEAD
White Sangria

Prepare this Spanish libation the day before for best flavor and add the chilled sparkling water just before serving. We use white Rioja wine, but any dry white wine will work.

⅓ cup brandy
⅓ cup peach schnapps
1½ tablespoons sugar
2 (750-milliliter) bottles white Rioja wine, chilled
1 lemon, thinly sliced
1 small navel orange, quartered and sliced
1 green apple, cored and sliced
1 ripe peach, peeled and sliced
1 (12-ounce) bottle sparkling water, chilled

1 Combine first 3 ingredients in a large pitcher; stir to dissolve sugar. Stir in wine and next 4 ingredients. Chill at least 2 hours or until cold.
2 Stir in sparkling water. Yield 12 servings (serving size: about 1 cup).

CALORIES 163 (0% from fat); FAT 0g; PROTEIN 0.1g; CARB 10.8g; FIBER 0.2g; CHOL 0mg; IRON 0.5mg; SODIUM 7mg; CALC 11mg

Prep Plan

Up to 2 days ahead:
- Bake and decorate Easter Egg Cookies; store in an airtight container. (Or bake the cookies ahead and let the kids decorate them on the big day.)

Up to 1 day ahead:
- Prepare White Sangria through step one; refrigerate.
- Make syrup and cut up fruit for Basil-Lime Fruit Salad; refrigerate separately.
- Bake Ginger Angel Food Cake with Coconut Frosting.

The night before:
- Marinate Garlic-Studded Rosemary Roast Rack of Lamb.
- Prepare Smoked Salmon Dip, and refrigerate.

2 hours ahead:
- Put Brown Sugar and Spice-Crusted Ham in the oven.

30 minutes ahead:
- Place Garlic-Studded Rosemary Roast Rack of Lamb in the oven.
- Toss the fruit and syrup for Basil-Lime Fruit Salad.

As guests arrive:
- Add sparkling water to White Sangria.
- Set out Smoked Salmon Dip and crackers.

The key to a relaxed Easter celebration: Do as much of the work ahead as you can.

QUICK & EASY • MAKE AHEAD

Smoked Salmon Dip

1 (8-ounce) tub light cream cheese
2 tablespoons chopped fresh dill
1 tablespoon fresh lemon juice
4 ounces smoked salmon, chopped, divided
Dill sprigs (optional)

1 Combine first 3 ingredients in a food processor. Add half of salmon; process until smooth. Fold in remaining half of salmon. Garnish with dill sprigs, if desired. Yield: 12 servings (serving size: 2 tablespoons).

CALORIES 56 (56% from fat); FAT 3.5g (sat 2.1g, mono 0g, poly 0g); PROTEIN 4g; CARB 1.4g; FIBER 0g; CHOL 9mg; IRON 0.2mg; SODIUM 89mg; CALC 30mg

MAKE AHEAD

Basil-Lime Fruit Salad

½ cup sugar
½ cup water
½ cup packed basil leaves
1 tablespoon grated lime rind
4 cups cubed pineapple (about 1 medium)
3 cups quartered strawberries (about 1 pound)
2 cups cubed peeled mango (about 2 large)
4 kiwifruit, peeled, halved lengthwise, and sliced (about 1½ cups)

1 Combine sugar and ½ cup water in a saucepan; bring to a boil. Cook 1 minute or until sugar dissolves. Remove from heat; stir in basil and rind. Cool. Strain sugar mixture through a fine mesh sieve into a bowl; discard solids.
2 Combine pineapple and remaining ingredients in a large bowl. Drizzle with sugar mixture; toss gently. Yield: 12 servings (serving size: about ¾ cup).

CALORIES 92 (3% from fat); FAT 0.3g (sat 0g, mono 0.1g, poly 0.1g); PROTEIN 0.8g; CARB 23.8g; FIBER 2.2g; CHOL 0mg; IRON 0.4mg; SODIUM 2mg; CALC 20mg

Brown Sugar and Spice-Crusted Ham

2 tablespoons brown sugar
1 teaspoon ground coriander
1 teaspoon ground cinnamon
¾ teaspoon ground cumin
½ teaspoon freshly ground black pepper
¼ teaspoon ground allspice
1 (5-pound) bone-in 33%-less-sodium smoked, fully cooked ham half
Cooking spray
¼ cup honey
1 tablespoon fresh orange juice

1 Preheat oven to 350°.
2 Combine first 6 ingredients. Trim fat and rind from ham. Rub ham evenly with sugar mixture. Place ham on a broiler pan coated with cooking spray. Cover loosely with foil. Bake at 350° for 1 hour and 15 minutes.
3 Combine honey and juice in a small bowl, stirring with a whisk. Remove foil from ham; brush honey mixture over ham. Bake, uncovered, 30 minutes or until a thermometer registers 140°. Transfer ham to a platter; let stand 15 minutes before cutting into slices. Yield: 22 servings (serving size: about 3 ounces).

CALORIES 169 (39% from fat); FAT 7.3g (sat 2.4g, mono 3.5g, poly 0.9g); PROTEIN 19.6g; CARB 4.9g; FIBER 0.1g; CHOL 51mg; IRON 1.3mg; SODIUM 850mg; CALC 11mg

Garlic-Studded Rosemary Roast Rack of Lamb

- 3 (1½-pound) French-cut racks of lamb (8 ribs each)
- Cooking spray
- 6 garlic cloves, thinly sliced (48 slices)
- ¾ teaspoon freshly ground black pepper
- ¼ cup chopped fresh rosemary
- 1 teaspoon kosher salt

1 Place lamb, meat side down, on a broiler pan coated with cooking spray. Cut a 1-inch-deep slit between ribs on underside of each rack; stuff 2 garlic slices into each slit. Turn lamb, meat side up; coat with cooking spray. Sprinkle with pepper and rosemary, pressing gently to adhere. Cover and marinate in refrigerator 8 hours or overnight.

2 Preheat oven to 450°.

3 Sprinkle lamb evenly with salt. Bake at 450° for 20 minutes or until a thermometer registers 145° (medium-rare) to 160° (medium). Cover with foil; let stand 10 minutes before cutting each rack into 8 pieces. Yield: 12 servings (serving size: 2 chops).

CALORIES 178 (49% from fat); FAT 9.7g (sat 4.2g, mono 3.7g, poly 0.4g); PROTEIN 20.6g; CARB 0.7g; FIBER 0.2g; CHOL 66mg; IRON 1.6mg; SODIUM 225mg; CALC 18mg

Lemon-Chive Roasted Vegetables

- 1½ pounds small red potatoes, halved
- 1½ pounds small fingerling potatoes, halved
- 1 pound baby carrots
- 2 Vidalia or other sweet onions, each cut into 8 wedges
- 1 tablespoon olive oil
- Cooking spray
- 2 tablespoons chopped fresh chives
- 1½ teaspoons grated lemon rind
- 2 tablespoons fresh lemon juice
- ½ teaspoon salt
- ¼ teaspoon black pepper

1 Preheat oven to 425°.

2 Combine first 5 ingredients in a large bowl; toss well to coat. Arrange vegetables in a single layer on 2 jelly-roll pans coated with cooking spray. Bake at 425° for 30 minutes or until tender and lightly browned, turning after 15 minutes.

3 Combine vegetables, chives, and remaining ingredients in a large bowl; toss gently to coat. Yield: 12 servings (serving size: 1 cup).

CALORIES 129 (9% from fat); FAT 1.3g (sat 0.2g, mono 0.8g, poly 0.2g); PROTEIN 3.1g; CARB 26.3g; FIBER 3.2g; CHOL 0mg; IRON 1.3mg; SODIUM 139mg; CALC 23mg

Choice Ingredient: Chives

Learn: Chives are the smallest members of the onion family and have hollow, tube-like leaves that resemble blades of grass. Similar to scallions and leeks, chives' slim leaves hold the plant's mild, onionlike flavor. Chives are classified as an herb, and because they grow in clumps, they are referred to in the plural sense. Bonus: Their sulfur content makes them natural insect repellents; plant them in your garden for pest control.

Purchase: Fresh chives are available year-round. Look for long, slender, vivid green stems that aren't wilted or brown.

Store: Wrap in a paper towel, and transfer to a zip-top plastic bag. Store in the refrigerator for up to a week.

Use: Rinse in cool water when ready to use, gently pat dry, then snip into your favorite dish using a pair of kitchen shears. A teaspoon of chopped chives can provide a beautiful garnish on anything from fish to soup. Used in higher quantity, they can become an integral element of your dish, as with the Lemon-Chive Roasted Vegetables (at left).

MAKE AHEAD
Spotted Puppies

The trick to making Spotted Puppies is not to overmix the dough. Mix and knead it as quickly and gently as possible so the rolls turn out light.

- 3½ cups all-purpose flour (15¾ ounces)
- 1 teaspoon baking soda
- ¼ teaspoon salt
- ½ cup golden raisins
- 2 teaspoons sugar
- 1⅔ cups buttermilk
- 1 large egg, lightly beaten

1 Preheat oven to 425°.

2 Lightly spoon flour into dry measuring cups; level with a knife. Sift together flour, baking soda, and salt into a large bowl; stir in raisins and sugar. Combine buttermilk and egg; add to flour mixture, stirring until dough forms. Turn dough out onto a lightly floured surface; knead lightly 4 times with floured hands (dough will be sticky). Divide dough into 12 equal portions. Shape each portion into a ball (cover remaining dough to prevent drying). Arrange rolls on a lightly floured baking sheet. Bake at 425° for 10 minutes. Reduce oven temperature to 400° (do not remove rolls from oven); bake an additional 8 minutes or until rolls sound hollow when tapped. Yield: 12 servings (serving size: 1 roll).

CALORIES 186 (9% from fat); FAT 1.9g (sat 0.9g, mono 0.2g, poly 0.2g); PROTEIN 5.7g; CARB 36.3g; FIBER 1.3g; CHOL 22mg; IRON 1.9mg; SODIUM 202mg; CALC 11mg

Easter Egg Cookies

These festive cookies are loosely based on the Greek Easter specialty *koulourakia*. Use egg-shaped cookie cutters to create these Easter "eggs." Tint the frosting any color you like (or use several colors). Spread it onto the cookies, or spoon the frosting into a zip-top plastic bag, snip a small hole in one corner of the bag, and pipe the frosting in designs of your choice. The kids can help with the fun.

COOKIES:

- 1½ cups all-purpose flour (about 6½ ounces)
- ½ teaspoon baking powder
- ½ teaspoon baking soda
- ¼ teaspoon salt
- ½ cup granulated sugar
- ¼ cup butter, softened
- 1 teaspoon vanilla extract
- 1 large egg

ICING:

- 2 cups powdered sugar
- 3 tablespoons fat-free milk
- ¼ teaspoon vanilla extract
- Food coloring (optional)

❶ To prepare cookies, spoon flour into dry measuring cups; level with a knife. Combine flour and next 3 ingredients, stirring with a whisk.

❷ Place granulated sugar and butter in a large bowl; beat with a mixer at medium speed until well blended (about 5 minutes). Beat in 1 teaspoon vanilla and egg. Add flour mixture, beating at low speed until blended.

❸ Place dough between two sheets of plastic wrap. Roll dough to a ¼-inch thickness. Chill 1 hour.

❹ Preheat oven to 375°.

❺ Cut dough with a 2¼-inch egg-shaped cutter. Place cookies on a baking sheet lined with parchment paper. Bake at 375° for 8 minutes or until edges of cookies are browned. Cool cookies 1 minute on pan. Remove cookies from parchment; cool completely on a wire rack.

❻ To prepare icing, combine powdered sugar, milk, and ¼ teaspoon vanilla; stir until smooth. Add food coloring, if desired. Stir well. Spread or pipe icing onto cookies. Yield: 28 cookies (serving size: 1 cookie).

CALORIES 90 (19% from fat); FAT 1.9g (sat 1.1g, mono 0.5g, poly 0.1g); PROTEIN 1g; CARB 17.5g; FIBER 0.2g; CHOL 12mg; IRON 0.4mg; SODIUM 67mg; CALC 9mg

Ginger Angel Food Cake with Coconut Frosting

CAKE:

- 1 cup sifted cake flour (4 ounces)
- ½ cup cornstarch
- 12 large egg whites
- 1½ teaspoons cream of tartar
- ¼ teaspoon salt
- 1½ cups sugar
- 1 teaspoon vanilla extract
- ½ teaspoon ground ginger

FROSTING:

- 1 cup sugar
- ¼ cup water
- ¼ teaspoon cream of tartar
- 3 large egg whites
- 1 teaspoon vanilla extract
- ¼ teaspoon coconut extract
- ¾ cup flaked sweetened coconut, toasted

❶ Preheat oven to 350°.

❷ To prepare cake, combine flour and cornstarch, stirring with a whisk.

❸ Place 12 egg whites in a large bowl; beat with a mixer at high speed until foamy. Add 1½ teaspoons cream of tartar and salt; beat until soft peaks form. Add 1½ cups sugar, 2 tablespoons at a time, beating until stiff peaks form. Beat in 1 teaspoon vanilla and ginger. Sift ¼ cup flour mixture over egg white mixture; fold in. Repeat with remaining flour mixture, ¼ cup at a time.

❹ Spoon batter into an ungreased 10-inch tube pan, spreading evenly. Break air pockets by cutting through batter with a knife. Bake at 350° for 35 minutes or until cake springs back when lightly touched. Invert pan; cool completely. Loosen cake from sides of pan using a narrow metal spatula. Invert cake onto a plate.

❺ To prepare frosting, combine 1 cup sugar, ¼ cup water, ¼ teaspoon cream of tartar, and 3 egg whites in top of a double boiler. Beat at low speed of a mixer 30 seconds or until blended. Place over boiling water; beat constantly at high speed until stiff peaks form and a thermometer registers 160°, about 7 minutes. Remove from heat; beat in 1 teaspoon vanilla and coconut extract.

❻ Spread frosting evenly over cake. Sprinkle cake with coconut. Yield: 12 servings (serving size: 1 wedge).

CALORIES 261 (5% from fat); FAT 1.5g (sat 1.2g, mono 0.1g, poly 0.1g); PROTEIN 5.5g; CARB 56.7g; FIBER 0.7g; CHOL 0mg; IRON 0.8mg; SODIUM 133mg; CALC 5mg

Good Eggs

Decorating eggs is a big part of the Easter fun. You can do it a day ahead, or set out eggs and decorating supplies for guests to decorate when they arrive. Either way, hide them for a lively egg hunt.

To decorate eggs:

- Hard boil and refrigerate a carton of eggs earlier in the week.
- Whip up easy egg dyes by dissolving six to eight drops of liquid food coloring in one cup hot water. Stir in ¼ cup distilled white vinegar.
- Use the empty egg carton as a handy egg-drying rack. Just be sure to blot up excess dye from egg bottoms when you lift them from the rack.

Designer eggs: Dye an egg in a base color. Use crayon or masking tape to apply designs to the egg. Re-dye the egg. Remove tape when the egg is dry to reveal a subtle pattern.

Banded eggs: Wrap rubber bands of assorted sizes around an egg and dye it. Remove rubber bands when egg is dry.

Marbled eggs: Stir one to three teaspoons canola oil into the dye and dip an egg in the dye several times. The oil will repel the dye in spots, creating a marbled effect. Wipe off excess oil when the egg is dry.

Taking Sides

Problem: A California reader grows bored with the same companion dishes. Strategy: Break free with new ingredients and innovative combinations of vegetables and starches.

Surrounded by lush farmland in Reedley, California, Susan Warkentin is never at a loss for fresh produce, including what she and her husband, Darrell, grow in their garden. But she says she's often unsure how to fix those vegetables and other side dishes that complement the main course. So the same sides tend to show up at every meal.

Like Warkentin, many cooks turn to the same few side dishes out of habit. But it's easy enough to break out of the routine once you implement a few strategies. First, there is nothing wrong with repeating favorite veggies or starches. The trick is to pair new flavors with familiar ingredients. It also helps to try new vegetables or grains. With a little resourcefulness, Warkentin can depart from the ordinary with interesting, original sides.

Middle Eastern Carrot Salad

Serve this colorful side salad at room temperature with roasted or grilled meats.

    2   cups coarsely chopped carrot
        (about 4 medium)
    1   cup uncooked Israeli couscous
    2¼ cups water
    1   (3-inch) cinnamon stick
    3   tablespoons finely chopped fresh
        cilantro
    2   tablespoons finely chopped fresh
        parsley
    2½ tablespoons extravirgin olive oil
    ¼   teaspoon grated lemon rind
    1   tablespoon fresh lemon juice
    ¾   teaspoon salt
    ½   teaspoon ground cumin
    1   garlic clove, minced

❶ Combine first 4 ingredients in a large saucepan; bring to a boil. Cook 10 minutes or until carrot and couscous are tender. Drain; discard cinnamon stick. Combine couscous mixture, cilantro, and remaining ingredients in a large bowl; toss gently to coat. Yield: 8 servings (serving size: ½ cup).

CALORIES 160 (27% from fat); FAT 4.8g (sat 0.7g, mono 3.1g, poly 0.5g); PROTEIN 4.3g; CARB 25.6g; FIBER 2.2g; CHOL 0mg; IRON 1.2mg; SODIUM 253mg; CALC 23mg

Wild Rice with Cremini Mushrooms

Elevate plain rice to something a little more special with the help of just a few ingredients. If you don't have a wild rice blend, or are short on time, substitute three cups of cooked instant rice. Serve with pork loin, beef tenderloin, duck, or chicken.

    1   cup uncooked long-grain and
        wild rice mix
    2   tablespoons sherry
    ¾   teaspoon salt
    1   tablespoon butter
    1   tablespoon olive oil
    ½   cup finely chopped shallots
    4   cups chopped cremini mushrooms
        (about ½ pound)
    ¼   cup finely chopped fresh parsley
    ¼   teaspoon freshly ground black
        pepper

❶ Cook rice according to package directions, omitting salt and fat. Stir in sherry and salt; cover and keep warm.
❷ Heat butter and oil in a large nonstick skillet over medium-high heat. Add shallots to pan; sauté 2 minutes. Add mushrooms; sauté 4 minutes. Stir in rice mixture, parsley, and pepper. Yield: 6 servings (serving size: about ¾ cup).

CALORIES 164 (25% from fat); FAT 4.5g (sat 1.6g, mono 2.2g, poly 0.4g); PROTEIN 4g; CARB 26.2g; FIBER 1.4g; CHOL 5mg; IRON 1.4mg; SODIUM 315mg; CALC 22mg

Curry-Spiced Sweet Potatoes

Enliven a familiar side dish with exotic flavors. Curry powder, cumin, and cinnamon combine with a hint of heat from ground red pepper to make these Indian-inspired sweet potatoes stand out in a meal. Use leftovers to top a shepherd's pie, or thin them out with milk and broth to make curried sweet potato soup that you can sprinkle with chopped cilantro. This highly seasoned dish pairs well with chicken, pork, and turkey.

    6½ cups (1-inch) cubed peeled sweet
        potato (about 2 pounds)
    1   tablespoon butter
    ¼   cup finely chopped shallots
    1   tablespoon brown sugar
    ½   teaspoon salt
    ½   teaspoon curry powder
    ½   teaspoon ground cumin
    ¼   teaspoon ground cinnamon
    ⅛   teaspoon ground red pepper
    ⅓   cup half-and-half
    1   tablespoon fresh lemon juice

❶ Place potato in a medium saucepan; cover with water. Bring to a boil. Reduce heat, and simmer 15 minutes or until tender. Drain well. Keep warm.
❷ Melt butter in a small nonstick skillet over medium heat. Add shallots to pan; cook 6 minutes or until tender, stirring occasionally. Stir in sugar and next 5 ingredients; cook 1 minute, stirring constantly. Add shallot mixture, half-and-half, and lemon juice to potato. Mash with a potato masher to desired consistency. Yield: 6 servings (serving size: about ⅔ cup).

CALORIES 183 (18% from fat); FAT 3.7g (sat 2.2g, mono 1g, poly 0.2g); PROTEIN 3.7g; CARB 35g; FIBER 5.2g; CHOL 10mg; IRON 1.3mg; SODIUM 272mg; CALC 79mg

Side Sense

- **Combine vegetables and starches in one side dish.** Double-duty side dishes like Dijon Vegetable Roast (page 79) pair both in a simple preparation. The combination makes the dish more interesting and allows one side dish to do the work of two at mealtime. Add chopped chicken, pork, or beef to leftovers for a one-dish meal another night.
- **Double or triple vegetables.** Combining two or three vegetables in a dish like Spring Vegetable Gratin (at right), which uses asparagus and peas, adds appeal. Mix vegetables like peppers, onions, and spinach in a simple sauté, or roast a few with chopped herbs, shallots, and garlic. Vary the shape, color, taste, and texture of ingredients to boost interest.
- **Try new ingredients.** Using peppercorn-sized pearls of Israeli couscous instead of the fine-grained and more expected North African couscous gives the Middle Eastern Carrot Salad (page 77) a fresh look and texture. If black-eyed peas, red lentils, kohlrabi, or rutabagas are unfamiliar to you, try them. Experiment with one new ingredient a week. Each new food you enjoy broadens your options.
- **Use familiar vegetables and starches in different ways.** Even your favorite side dishes may begin to pall if prepared in the same way time after time, but applying new flavors or cooking techniques keeps them interesting. Curry-Spiced Sweet Potatoes (page 77) puts an Indian twist on a standard root vegetable. Or rather than soft polenta, try serving baked or grilled polenta cakes—spread soft polenta evenly on a jelly-roll pan, chill until firm, cut into squares, and bake or grill until thoroughly heated.
- **Sauce it.** Veggies and grains can change personality with the addition of vinaigrettes or ethnic condiments. Toss Dijon Vegetable Roast with pesto or white balsamic vinaigrette instead of the mustard mixture. Spice up potato or rice sides with a tablespoon or two of chutney.

Spring Vegetable Gratin

For variety, switch vegetable combinations depending on the season. Try chopped eggplant and zucchini in summer, and quartered Brussels sprouts and cubed butternut squash in the fall.

- 1 (6-ounce) package original recipe long-grain and wild rice
- ⅓ cup all-purpose flour (about 1½ ounces)
- 3 cups 1% low-fat milk
- 1 cup (4 ounces) shredded fontina cheese, divided
- 1 cup (4 ounces) grated fresh Parmesan cheese, divided
- 1 tablespoon chopped fresh thyme
- ½ teaspoon salt
- ½ teaspoon freshly ground black pepper
- 2⅓ cups (2-inch) slices asparagus (about ¾ pound)
- 2 cups frozen green peas, thawed
- 1½ cups thinly sliced green onions
- Cooking spray

① Cook rice according to package directions, omitting salt, fat, and seasoning packet.

② Preheat oven to 400°.

③ Lightly spoon flour into a dry measuring cup; level with a knife. Place flour in a medium saucepan. Gradually add milk, stirring constantly with a whisk until blended. Cook over medium heat until thick (about 8 minutes), stirring constantly. Remove from heat. Add ¾ cup fontina, ¾ cup Parmesan, and next 3 ingredients; stir until cheese melts. Stir in rice, asparagus, peas, and onions. Spoon rice mixture into a 13 x 9–inch baking dish coated with cooking spray. Sprinkle evenly with remaining ¼ cup fontina and remaining ¼ cup Parmesan. Bake at 400° for 18 minutes or until bubbly. Yield: 12 servings (serving size: about ½ cup).

CALORIES 197 (29% from fat); FAT 6.4g (sat 3.5g, mono 1.7g, poly 0.4g); PROTEIN 12g; CARB 22.5g; FIBER 2.9g; CHOL 20mg; IRON 1.9mg; SODIUM 375mg; CALC 286mg

Honey-Roasted Acorn Squash Rings

Honey boosts the natural sweetness of acorn squash. Serve this simple side with roasted chicken or pork tenderloin.

- 2 acorn squash (about 3 pounds)
- 2 tablespoons honey
- 4 teaspoons olive oil
- ½ teaspoon freshly ground black pepper
- ¼ teaspoon salt
- Cooking spray

① Preheat the oven to 375°.

② Cut ¼ inch from stem end and bottom of each squash, and discard. Cut each squash in half crosswise. Discard seeds and membrane. Cut each squash half crosswise into 2 (1-inch-thick) slices. Combine honey and next 3 ingredients in a large bowl. Add squash, and toss to coat. Place squash on a jelly-roll pan coated with cooking spray. Bake at 375° for 30 minutes or until tender. Yield: 4 servings (serving size: 2 squash slices).

CALORIES 186 (23% from fat); FAT 4.8g (sat 0.7g, mono 3.3g, poly 0.6g); PROTEIN 2.3g; CARB 38.4g; FIBER 4.3g; CHOL 0mg; IRON 2.1mg; SODIUM 157mg; CALC 95mg

> Successful sides are versatile enough to accompany a variety of main dishes, yet unique enough to make an impression.

Dijon Vegetable Roast

Dijon mustard and olives bring bold flavor to this side. Serve with lightly seasoned roast chicken, beef tenderloin, salmon, or tuna steaks.

    1   (1-ounce) slice white bread
    5½ teaspoons olive oil, divided
    5   teaspoons country-style Dijon
        mustard
    ¼   teaspoon salt
    ¼   teaspoon freshly ground black
        pepper
    ¼   teaspoon grated lemon rind
    1½ pounds small red potatoes,
        quartered
    1   onion, cut into ¼-inch-thick wedges
        (about 8 ounces)
        Cooking spray
    2   cups cherry tomatoes, halved
    12 pitted ripe olives, drained and
        halved (about ⅓ cup)

❶ Preheat oven to 350°.
❷ Place bread in a food processor; pulse 10 times or until coarse crumbs measure ½ cup. Spread crumbs on a baking sheet. Bake at 350° for 5 minutes or until golden.
❸ Increase oven temperature to 450°.
❹ Combine 4 teaspoons oil, mustard, and next 3 ingredients; stir well with a whisk.
❺ Combine potatoes, onion, and remaining 1½ teaspoons oil in a large bowl; toss well to coat. Place potato mixture on a foil-lined jelly-roll pan coated with cooking spray. Bake at 450° for 20 minutes. Add tomatoes and olives to pan. Bake an additional 10 minutes or until potatoes are tender. Add potato mixture to mustard mixture; toss gently to coat. Sprinkle with breadcrumbs. Yield: 6 servings (serving size: 1 cup).

CALORIES 175 (28% from fat); FAT 5.4g (sat 0.8g, mono 3.8g, poly 0.7g); PROTEIN 3.7g; CARB 27.9g; FIBER 2.6g; CHOL 0mg; IRON 1.7mg; SODIUM 319mg; CALC 22mg

SUPERFAST
20 Minute Dishes

From chicken to chops, steak to sandwiches, here are simple, fresh, and easy meals you can make superfast.

QUICK & EASY
Peanut-Crusted Chicken with Pineapple Salsa
(pictured on page 243)

Pick up a container of fresh pineapple chunks in the produce section of the supermarket; chop into half-inch pieces for the salsa. Serve with steamed broccoli and warm rolls to complete the dinner.

    1   cup chopped fresh pineapple
    2   tablespoons chopped fresh cilantro
    1   tablespoon finely chopped red onion
    ⅓   cup unsalted, dry-roasted peanuts
    1   (1-ounce) slice white bread
    ½   teaspoon salt
    ⅛   teaspoon black pepper
    4   (4-ounce) chicken cutlets
    1½ teaspoons canola oil
        Cooking spray
        Cilantro sprigs (optional)

❶ Combine first 3 ingredients in a small bowl, tossing well.
❷ Combine peanuts and bread in a food processor; process until finely chopped. Sprinkle salt and pepper evenly over chicken. Dredge chicken in the breadcrumb mixture.
❸ Heat oil in a large nonstick skillet coated with cooking spray over medium-high heat. Add chicken to pan; cook 2 minutes on each side or until done. Serve chicken with pineapple mixture. Garnish with cilantro sprigs, if desired. Yield: 4 servings (serving size: 1 cutlet and ¼ cup salsa).

CALORIES 219 (30% from fat); FAT 7.4g (sat 1.1g, mono 3.4g, poly 2.1g); PROTEIN 28.9g; CARB 9.1g; FIBER 1.3g; CHOL 66mg; IRON 1.2mg; SODIUM 398mg; CALC 27mg

QUICK & EASY
Flounder Piccata with Spinach

You can substitute any flaky white fish, such as tilapia and sole.

    1   (3½-ounce) bag boil-in-bag
        long-grain rice
    ½   teaspoon salt, divided
    ¼   teaspoon black pepper, divided
    4   (6-ounce) flounder fillets
    2   tablespoons all-purpose flour
    2   teaspoons olive oil
    ⅓   cup dry white wine
    2   tablespoons fresh lemon juice
    1   tablespoon drained capers,
        chopped
    2   tablespoons butter
    4   cups fresh baby spinach

❶ Cook rice according to package directions, omitting salt and fat. Place rice in a medium bowl; stir in ¼ teaspoon salt and ⅛ teaspoon pepper.
❷ Sprinkle fish with remaining ¼ teaspoon salt and remaining ⅛ teaspoon pepper. Dredge fish in flour.
❸ Heat oil in a large nonstick skillet over medium-high heat. Add fish to pan; cook 1½ minutes on each side or until fish flakes easily when tested with a fork or until desired degree of doneness.
❹ Add wine, juice, and capers to pan; cook 1 minute. Add butter to pan, stirring until butter melts. Remove fish and sauce from pan; keep warm. Wipe pan clean with a paper towel. Add spinach to pan; sauté 1 minute or until wilted. Place ½ cup rice onto each of 4 plates. Top each serving with about ⅓ cup spinach, 1 fillet, and 1 tablespoon sauce. Yield: 4 servings.

CALORIES 332 (28% from fat); FAT 10.2g (sat 4.4g, mono 3.5g, poly 1.2g); PROTEIN 31.3g; CARB 27.4g; FIBER 1.9g; CHOL 95mg; IRON 3mg; SODIUM 713mg; CALC 51mg

Filet Mignon with Port and Mustard Sauce

Port, a fortified dessert wine, has a distinctively smooth sweetness. If you don't have port, substitute red wine. Serve with sour cream and chive mashed potatoes and fresh green beans.

Cooking spray
4 (4-ounce) filet mignon steaks, trimmed
¼ teaspoon salt
¼ teaspoon black pepper
½ cup port or other sweet red wine
3 tablespoons chopped shallots
½ cup fat-free, less-sodium beef broth
1 tablespoon Dijon mustard

❶ Heat a large nonstick skillet over medium-high heat. Coat pan with cooking spray. Sprinkle both sides of steaks with salt and pepper. Add steaks to pan; cook 3½ minutes on each side or until desired degree of doneness. Remove steaks from pan; cover and keep warm.
❷ Add port and shallots to pan. Cook 1 minute or until liquid almost evaporates, scraping pan to loosen browned bits. Stir in broth; cook until reduced to ⅓ cup (about 1 minute). Remove from heat; stir in mustard. Serve steaks with sauce. Yield: 4 servings (serving size: 1 steak and about 1½ tablespoons sauce).

CALORIES 217 (39% from fat); FAT 9.3g (sat 3.4g, mono 3.6g, poly 0.5g); PROTEIN 24.3g; CARB 3.8g; FIBER 0.1g; CHOL 70mg; IRON 3.4mg; SODIUM 361mg; CALC 17mg

Steak and Cheese Sandwiches with Mushrooms

Add baked potato chips and coleslaw for a quick and casual supper.

1 teaspoon olive oil
2 cups presliced onion
2 cups green bell pepper strips
2 teaspoons bottled minced garlic
1 cup presliced mushrooms
¾ pound top round steak, trimmed and cut into thin strips
¼ teaspoon salt
⅛ teaspoon black pepper
2 teaspoons Worcestershire sauce
4 (0.6-ounce) slices reduced-fat provolone cheese, cut in half
4 (2½-ounce) hoagie rolls with sesame seeds

❶ Heat oil in a large nonstick skillet over medium-high heat. Add onion, bell pepper, and garlic to pan; sauté 3 minutes. Add mushrooms to pan; sauté 4 minutes. Sprinkle beef with salt and black pepper. Add beef to pan; sauté 3 minutes or until browned, stirring occasionally. Stir in Worcestershire sauce; cook 1 minute.
❷ Place 1 cheese slice half on bottom half of each roll, and top each serving with one-fourth of beef mixture. Top each with 1 cheese slice half and a roll top. Yield: 4 servings (serving size: 1 sandwich).

CALORIES 384 (23% from fat); FAT 9.8g (sat 4.1g, mono 2.9g, poly 0.4g); PROTEIN 32.9g; CARB 44.9g; FIBER 4.1g; CHOL 43mg; IRON 4.7mg; SODIUM 580mg; CALC 231mg

Pork Chops with Bourbon-Peach Sauce

Serve steamed asparagus with this Southern-style entrée.

4 (4-ounce) boneless center-cut loin pork chops (about ¼ inch thick)
¾ teaspoon salt
¼ teaspoon black pepper
¼ teaspoon ground red pepper
Cooking spray
1 tablespoon minced shallots
1 teaspoon minced bottled garlic
1½ cups frozen sliced peaches
½ cup fat-free, less-sodium chicken broth
2 teaspoons brown sugar
2 thyme sprigs
2 tablespoons bourbon
2 teaspoons butter

❶ Sprinkle pork with salt and peppers. Heat a large skillet over medium-high heat. Coat pan with cooking spray. Add pork to pan; cook 2½ minutes on each side or until browned. Remove pork from pan; keep warm.
❷ Add shallots and garlic to pan; sauté 30 seconds. Add peaches and broth; sauté 2 minutes. Add sugar and thyme; cook 1 minute. Add bourbon and butter; cook 4½ minutes or until butter melts and sauce is slightly thickened. Discard thyme sprigs. Serve with pork. Yield: 4 servings (serving size: 1 chop and ¼ cup sauce).

CALORIES 233 (32% from fat); FAT 8.4g (sat 3.6g, mono 3.4g, poly 0.5g); PROTEIN 24.7g; CARB 8.6g; FIBER 0.9g; CHOL 70mg; IRON 0.8mg; SODIUM 560mg; CALC 30mg

Greek-Style Scampi

Add a spinach-mushroom salad to round out your menu.

6 ounces uncooked angel hair pasta
1 teaspoon olive oil
½ cup chopped green bell pepper
2 teaspoons bottled minced garlic
1 (14.5-ounce) can diced tomatoes with basil, garlic, and oregano, undrained
⅛ teaspoon black pepper
1 pound peeled and deveined medium shrimp
⅛ teaspoon ground red pepper
6 tablespoons (about 1½ ounces) crumbled feta cheese

❶ Cook pasta according to package directions, omitting salt and fat. Drain and keep warm.
❷ Heat oil in a large nonstick skillet over medium-high heat. Add bell pepper to pan; sauté 1 minute. Add garlic and tomatoes; cook 1 minute. Add black pepper and shrimp; cover and cook 3 minutes or until shrimp are done. Stir in red pepper; remove from heat. Place 1 cup pasta on each of 4 plates. Top each serving with 1 cup shrimp mixture and 1½ tablespoons cheese. Yield: 4 servings.

CALORIES 379 (20% from fat); FAT 8.5g (sat 3g, mono 2.8g, poly 1.7g); PROTEIN 31.7g; CARB 43.3g; FIBER 2.6g; CHOL 185mg; IRON 4.1mg; SODIUM 139mg; CALC 656mg

Creative Casseroles

Put a modern slant on a few old-fashioned favorites.

Casserole Menu 1
serves 8

Ham and Cheese Macaroni Bake with Peas

Spinach salad with poppy seed dressing

Combine ¼ cup low-fat evaporated milk, 3 tablespoons sugar, 1½ tablespoons poppy seeds, 2 tablespoons light sour cream, and 2 tablespoons white vinegar, stirring until smooth. Combine 1½ cups quartered strawberries, ¼ cup thinly sliced red onion, and 1 (6-ounce) package baby spinach; toss gently. Drizzle dressing mixture over spinach mixture; toss gently. Serve immediately.

Orange sections over low-fat vanilla ice cream

Game plan
1 Preheat oven.
2 While water comes to a boil:
  • Prepare ingredients for casserole.
3 While pasta cooks:
  • Prepare salad dressing; chill.
  • Prepare orange sections; chill.
4 While casserole bakes:
  • Prepare salad.

Quick tip
Look for preshredded cheese in the dairy section of the supermarket.

Ham and Cheese Macaroni Bake with Peas

Total time: 43 minutes

1 pound uncooked medium elbow macaroni
1½ cups chopped lean ham
1½ cups frozen peas
  Cooking spray
½ cup finely chopped onion
3 cups 2% reduced-fat milk
1 cup (4 ounces) shredded reduced-fat extrasharp Cheddar cheese
1 cup (4 ounces) shredded Swiss cheese
¾ teaspoon salt
¼ teaspoon freshly ground black pepper
⅛ teaspoon ground red pepper
2 (1-ounce) slices white bread
2 tablespoons butter, melted

❶ Preheat oven to 400°.
❷ Cook pasta in boiling water 6 minutes. Drain and rinse with cold water; drain. Combine pasta, ham, and peas in a large bowl.
❸ Heat a medium saucepan over medium heat. Coat pan with cooking spray. Add onion to pan; cook 4 minutes, stirring frequently. Add milk; bring to simmer. Remove from heat; stir in cheeses, salt, and peppers. Pour cheese mixture over pasta mixture; stir to coat. Spoon pasta mixture into a 13 x 9-inch baking dish coated with cooking spray.
❹ Place bread in a food processor; pulse 10 times or until coarse crumbs measure 1¼ cups. Combine breadcrumbs and butter in a bowl. Arrange breadcrumb mixture evenly over pasta mixture. Bake at 400° for 20 minutes or until lightly browned. Yield: 8 servings (serving size: 1¼ cups).

CALORIES 470 (29% from fat); FAT 15.1g (sat 8.5g, mono 4.4g, poly 1.1g); PROTEIN 27g; CARB 56.1g; FIBER 3.1g; CHOL 54mg; IRON 2.8mg; SODIUM 771mg; CALC 393mg

Casserole Menu 2

serves 4

Parmesan Chicken and Rice Casserole

Green beans with warm bacon dressing

Cook 1 pound trimmed fresh green beans in boiling water 3 minutes or until crisp-tender; drain. Cook 2 strips bacon in a skillet over medium heat until crisp. Remove bacon; crumble. Add ¼ cup chopped shallots to drippings in pan; cook 3 minutes, stirring frequently. Add 2 tablespoons white wine vinegar; cook 1 minute, stirring constantly. Add green beans; toss to coat. Sprinkle with bacon.

Broiled plum tomatoes

Game plan

1 While oven preheats:
- Prepare ingredients for casserole.
- Prepare ingredients for green beans.
- Halve tomatoes; sprinkle with salt and pepper.
2 While casserole bakes:
- Cook green beans.
3 Broil tomatoes.

Parmesan Chicken and Rice Casserole

Total time: 37 minutes

Cooking spray
1 cup chopped onion
2 garlic cloves, minced
2 (3½-ounce) bags boil-in-bag brown rice
⅓ cup dry white wine
8 skinless, boneless chicken thighs (about 1¾ pounds)
1½ teaspoons chopped fresh thyme
½ teaspoon salt
2 cups fat-free, less-sodium chicken broth
3 tablespoons whipping cream
⅓ cup (1½ ounces) shredded Parmesan cheese

1 Preheat oven to 450°.
2 Heat a large nonstick skillet over medium-high heat. Coat pan with cooking spray. Add onion to pan; sauté 2 minutes. Add garlic; sauté 30 seconds. Remove rice from bags; add to pan. Sauté 30 seconds. Stir in wine; cook 30 seconds or until liquid almost evaporates. Spoon rice mixture in an even layer into a 13 x 9–inch baking dish coated with cooking spray.
3 Arrange chicken in a single layer over rice mixture; sprinkle evenly with thyme and salt. Combine broth and cream, stirring well; pour over chicken and rice mixture.
4 Bake at 450° for 15 minutes. Sprinkle with cheese. Bake an additional 5 minutes or until chicken is done. Yield: 4 servings (serving size: 2 chicken thighs and 1 cup rice).

CALORIES 498 (35% from fat); FAT 19.1g (sat 7.5g, mono 6.7g, poly 3.1g); PROTEIN 38.2g; CARB 43.8g; FIBER 5.6g; CHOL 122mg; IRON 3mg; SODIUM 765mg; CALC 198mg

Casserole Menu 3

serves 6

Shrimp and Grits Casserole

Cherry tomato salad

Combine 3 cups halved cherry tomatoes, ½ cup thinly sliced green onion, and ¼ cup chopped fresh flat-leaf parsley. Sprinkle with ½ teaspoon salt and ¼ teaspoon freshly ground black pepper. Combine 3 tablespoons red wine vinegar, 1½ tablespoons extravirgin olive oil, and 1 tablespoon Dijon mustard, stirring well. Drizzle vinegar mixture over tomato mixture; toss gently.

Lima beans

Game plan

1 Preheat oven.
2 While milk mixture comes to a boil:
- Prepare ingredients for casserole.
3 While casserole bakes:
- Prepare salad.
- Cook lima beans.

Shrimp and Grits Casserole

Total time: 43 minutes

2 cups 2% reduced-fat milk
¾ cup fat-free, less-sodium chicken broth
1 cup uncooked quick-cooking grits
¼ teaspoon salt
½ cup (2 ounces) shredded Parmesan cheese
2 tablespoons butter
1 (3-ounce) package ⅓-less-fat cream cheese
3 tablespoons chopped fresh flat-leaf parsley
1 tablespoon chopped fresh chives
1 tablespoon fresh lemon juice
2 large egg whites, lightly beaten
1 pound peeled and deveined medium shrimp, coarsely chopped
Cooking spray
Hot pepper sauce (optional)

1 Preheat oven to 375°.
2 Combine milk and broth in a medium heavy saucepan; bring to a boil. Gradually add grits and salt to pan, stirring constantly with a whisk. Cook 5 minutes or until thick, stirring constantly. Remove from heat. Stir in Parmesan, butter, and cream cheese. Stir in parsley and next 4 ingredients. Spoon mixture into an 11 x 7–inch baking dish coated with cooking spray. Bake at 375° for 25 minutes or until set. Serve with hot pepper sauce, if desired. Yield: 6 servings (serving size: about 1 cup).

CALORIES 341 (34% from fat); FAT 13g (sat 7.5g, mono 3.5g, poly 1g); PROTEIN 27.5g; CARB 27.2g; FIBER 0.6g; CHOL 149mg; IRON 3.2mg; SODIUM 571mg; CALC 293mg

Sweet Season

When the sap runs from the maple trees, it's a busy time in Vermont's sugar shacks. The syrup that pours forth lends rich flavor to all manner of dishes.

ONE OF OUR COUNTRY'S most beloved (and certainly sweetest) native products is produced in Burr Morse's 75-year-old sugar shack, which looks much as it did when his grandfather was in charge. As Burr, representing the seventh generation of maple sugarers in his family, explains the process, visitors wander into the shack, which is just outside the town of Montpelier. He invites them up on the riser to look down into where the sap enters from a tank and flows through a maze of pans. As the syrup travels toward the final point, Burr says, "It just gets sweeter, like my wife, Betsy."

The flavor nuances of maple syrup are a matter of personal choice. Some people prefer a thicker, darker syrup with a heavier maple taste on their pancakes; others opt for a lighter, thinner syrup to fill the holes on their waffles. Maple syrup lends richness to both sweet and savory dishes, and works well whenever a sweetener is called for—in salad dressings, barbecue sauce, baked beans, and baked goods. Whatever type you choose, know that you're enjoying the pure taste of a national treasure.

Roasted Root Vegetables with Maple Glaze

Cubed butternut squash or sweet potatoes would also work well in this mixture.

- 1½ cups (½-inch) slices carrot
- 1½ cups (½-inch) slices parsnip
- 1½ cups (½-inch) cubed peeled turnip
- 4 teaspoons olive oil
- ½ teaspoon kosher salt
- ¼ teaspoon freshly ground black pepper
- Cooking spray
- 2 tablespoons maple syrup

❶ Preheat oven to 450°.
❷ Combine first 6 ingredients in a 13 x 9-inch baking dish coated with cooking spray, tossing well to coat. Bake at 450° for 10 minutes. Stir in syrup. Bake an additional 20 minutes or until tender and golden, stirring after 10 minutes. Yield: 4 servings (serving size: about ½ cup).

CALORIES 150 (30% from fat); FAT 4.9g (sat 0.7g, mono 3.3g, poly 0.6g); PROTEIN 1.7g; CARB 26.1g; FIBER 3.8g; CHOL 0mg; IRON 0.8mg; SODIUM 379mg; CALC 63mg

QUICK & EASY
Spinach Salad with Maple-Dijon Vinaigrette

Syrup provides body and a rich, sweet base to the dressing. Using a lighter syrup grade creates a more delicate vinaigrette. For even more maple punch, seek out maple-cured bacon.

- ¼ cup maple syrup
- 3 tablespoons minced shallots (about 1 medium)
- 2 tablespoons red wine vinegar
- 1 tablespoon canola oil
- 1 tablespoon country-style Dijon mustard
- ¼ teaspoon salt
- ¼ teaspoon freshly ground black pepper
- 1 garlic clove, minced
- 1 cup sliced mushrooms
- ½ cup vertically sliced red onion
- ½ cup chopped Braeburn apple
- 4 bacon slices, cooked and crumbled
- 1 (10-ounce) package fresh spinach

❶ Combine first 8 ingredients in a large bowl, stirring with a whisk. Add mushrooms and remaining ingredients; toss well to coat. Yield: 8 servings (serving size: about 1½ cups).

CALORIES 80 (37% from fat); FAT 3.3g (sat 0.6g, mono 1.6g, poly 0.7g); PROTEIN 2.6g; CARB 11.1g; FIBER 1.2g; CHOL 3mg; IRON 1.2mg; SODIUM 219mg; CALC 43mg

QUICK & EASY
Maple Corn Bread

A preheated cast-iron skillet is essential to create a crisp crust and moist interior.

- 1⅓ cups all-purpose flour (about 6 ounces)
- ⅔ cup stone-ground cornmeal
- 2 teaspoons baking powder
- ¾ teaspoon salt
- 1 cup plain low-fat yogurt
- ⅓ cup maple syrup
- ¼ cup butter, melted
- 2 large eggs, lightly beaten
- Cooking spray

❶ Preheat oven to 425°.
❷ Place an 8-inch cast-iron skillet in preheated oven for 10 minutes.
❸ Lightly spoon flour into dry measuring cups; level with a knife. Combine flour, cornmeal, baking powder, and salt in a large bowl, stirring with a whisk. Combine yogurt and next 3 ingredients, stirring with a whisk. Add yogurt mixture to flour mixture; stir just until moist (batter will be thick).
❹ Remove pan from oven; coat pan with cooking spray. Spoon batter into preheated pan, smoothing top with a spatula. Bake at 425° for 20 minutes or until a wooden pick inserted in center comes out clean. Remove from oven; cool in pan on a wire rack 10 minutes. Yield: 10 servings (serving size: 1 wedge).

CALORIES 187 (30% from fat); FAT 6.3g (sat 3.4g, mono 1.7g, poly 0.4g); PROTEIN 4.8g; CARB 27.9g; FIBER 1.8g; CHOL 56mg; IRON 1.5mg; SODIUM 341mg; CALC 115mg

Spiced Pork Tenderloin with Maple-Chipotle Sauce
(pictured on page 244)

PORK:
- ½ teaspoon salt
- ½ teaspoon dried thyme
- ¼ teaspoon ground nutmeg
- ¼ teaspoon ground cinnamon
- ¼ teaspoon freshly ground black pepper
- ⅛ teaspoon ground allspice
- 2 (1-pound) pork tenderloins, trimmed
- 2 teaspoons olive oil

SAUCE:
- 1 (7-ounce) can chipotle chiles, canned in adobo sauce
- ½ cup maple syrup
- 3 tablespoons fat-free, less-sodium chicken broth
- 1½ tablespoons cider vinegar

1 To prepare pork, combine first 6 ingredients; sprinkle evenly over pork. Place in a large zip-top plastic bag; seal and refrigerate 3 hours.

2 Preheat oven to 375°.

3 Remove pork from bag. Place pork in a roasting pan; drizzle with oil. Bake at 375° for 30 minutes or until a thermometer inserted in center of pork registers 155°. Remove pork from pan; cover and let stand 10 minutes.

4 To prepare sauce, remove 2 teaspoons adobo sauce from can of chiles; reserve remaining chiles and sauce for another use. Add 2 teaspoons adobo sauce, syrup, broth, and vinegar to roasting pan, scraping pan to loosen browned bits. Cook over medium heat 5 minutes, stirring constantly. Remove from heat. Place pork in pan, turning to coat. Remove pork from pan, reserving sauce in pan. Cut pork into ½-inch-thick slices. Strain sauce through a fine sieve into a bowl; serve with pork. Yield: 8 servings (serving size: 3 ounces pork and about 1 tablespoon sauce).

CALORIES 201 (23% from fat); FAT 5.1g (sat 1.5g, mono 2.6g, poly 0.6g); PROTEIN 23.9g; CARB 13.8g; FIBER 0.3g; CHOL 74mg; IRON 1.8mg; SODIUM 229mg; CALC 23mg

---

MAKE AHEAD
Maple-Pecan Snack Cake

Syrup in the cake batter and the frosting yields tasty results in this moist cake. Walnuts would also play up with maple's distinctive taste.

CAKE:
- 1 cup maple syrup
- 1 cup reduced-fat sour cream
- ¼ cup butter, melted
- 1 teaspoon vanilla extract
- 1 large egg, lightly beaten
- 2½ cups all-purpose flour (about 11¼ ounces)
- 1 teaspoon baking soda
- ¼ cup chopped pecans, toasted
- ½ teaspoon salt
- Cooking spray

FROSTING:
- 1½ cups powdered sugar
- 2½ tablespoons maple syrup
- 1 tablespoon whipping cream
- ⅛ teaspoon salt
- ¼ cup chopped pecans, toasted

1 Preheat oven to 350°.

2 To prepare cake, combine first 5 ingredients, stirring well with a whisk.

3 Lightly spoon flour into dry measuring cups; level with a knife. Combine flour, baking soda, ¼ cup pecans, and ½ teaspoon salt in a large bowl, stirring with a whisk. Add syrup mixture to flour mixture; stir until well blended. Pour batter into a 9-inch square baking pan coated with cooking spray. Bake at 350° for 30 minutes or until a wooden pick inserted in center comes out clean. Cool completely on a wire rack.

4 To prepare frosting, combine sugar and next 3 ingredients. Beat with a mixer at medium speed until smooth. Spread frosting evenly over cooled cake; sprinkle with ¼ cup pecans. Yield: 16 servings (serving size: 1 piece).

CALORIES 261 (29% from fat); FAT 8.4g (sat 3.6g, mono 3.1g, poly 1.2g); PROTEIN 3.8g; CARB 43.2g; FIBER 0.9g; CHOL 27mg; IRON 1.4mg; SODIUM 208mg; CALC 44mg

---

Bacon Maple Waffles

Bacon and maple are a natural match— maybe why many people dip bacon into their pancake syrup. In this recipe, crumbled bacon is cooked into maple-sweetened waffles, so every bite contains that classic pairing. If you're using a Belgian waffle maker, spread about ½ cup batter per waffle onto the waffle iron, and you'll get about 8 waffles.

- 2 cups all-purpose flour (about 9 ounces)
- 1 tablespoon baking powder
- ½ teaspoon salt
- 1¼ cups 2% reduced-fat milk
- 3 tablespoons maple syrup
- 2 tablespoons butter, melted
- 4 bacon slices, cooked and crumbled
- 3 large eggs, lightly beaten
- Cooking spray
- ⅓ cup maple syrup

1 Lightly spoon flour into dry measuring cups; level with a knife. Place flour, baking powder, and salt in a bowl; stir with a whisk. Make a well in center of mixture. Combine milk and next 4 ingredients, stirring with a whisk. Add milk mixture to flour mixture; stir just until moist.

2 Preheat a waffle iron. Coat iron with cooking spray. Spoon about ⅓ cup batter per waffle onto hot waffle iron, spreading batter to edges. Cook 4 to 5 minutes or until steaming stops; repeat procedure with remaining batter. Serve waffles with ⅓ cup syrup. Yield: 5 servings (serving size: 2 waffles and about 1 tablespoon syrup).

CALORIES 411 (25% from fat); FAT 11.4g (sat 5.3g, mono 3.7g, poly 1.1g); PROTEIN 12.9g; CARB 64.5g; FIBER 1.4g; CHOL 149mg; IRON 3.7mg; SODIUM 754mg; CALC 284mg

Maple Kettle Corn

Intensely sweet maple sugar flavors this version of the classic sweet-salty snack. To prevent the sugar from burning, shake the pan as the popcorn cooks.

- 2 tablespoons canola oil
- ½ cup unpopped popcorn kernels
- ¼ cup maple sugar
- ½ teaspoon kosher salt

1 Heat oil in a 3-quart saucepan over medium-high heat. Add popcorn, sugar, and salt to pan; cover and cook 3 minutes or until kernels begin to pop, shaking pan frequently. Continue cooking 2 minutes, shaking pan constantly to prevent burning. When popping slows down, remove pan from heat. Let stand, covered, until all popping stops. Yield: 8 servings (serving size: 1½ cups).

CALORIES 89 (40% from fat); FAT 4g (sat 0.3g, mono 2.1g, poly 1g); PROTEIN 1.3g; CARB 12.3g; FIBER 1.8g; CHOL 0mg; IRON 0.3mg; SODIUM 118mg; CALC 4mg

Cinnamon-Maple Applesauce

Use any apple variety or a combination of them. We enjoyed a mixture of Granny Smith for tartness and Rome for sweetness. Serve with roast pork or chicken, or atop French toast or waffles.

- 1 cup maple syrup
- ½ cup water
- 8 cups chopped peeled apple (about 8 medium apples)
- ½ teaspoon ground cinnamon
- ⅛ teaspoon ground nutmeg

1 Combine syrup and ½ cup water in a Dutch oven; bring to a boil. Add apple, cinnamon, and nutmeg; cover and cook over medium-low heat 25 minutes or until tender. Mash apples with a potato masher. Cook, uncovered, 20 minutes or until most of liquid evaporates. Serve warm or chilled. Yield: 8 servings (serving size: ½ cup).

CALORIES 166 (2% from fat); FAT 0.3g (sat 0g, mono 0g, poly 0.1g); PROTEIN 0.4g; CARB 43.3g; FIBER 1.8g; CHOL 0mg; IRON 0.6mg; SODIUM 4mg; CALC 35mg

Maple Syrup Grades

The U. S. Department of Agriculture has set the standard by which maple syrup is graded. Grading is based on the color of the syrup, not the flavor—though color is a general indication of flavor (the lighter the color, the more delicate the taste). Each bottle of syrup is labeled with one of four grades. All of our recipes work well with any grade of syrup, but we recommend specific grades for a few of the dishes.

• **U.S. Grade A Light Amber** is the lightest in color—transparent gold—and flavor. Although it can be used at the table for pancakes and waffles, it's often poured on ice cream or used to make maple candy.

• **U.S. Grade A Medium Amber** is darker than Grade A Light and has a slightly more intense maple flavor. It is the most popular grade of table syrup.

• **U.S. Grade A Dark Amber** has an even stronger flavor, is somewhat thicker, and is often used in cooking. The darker syrup (including Grade B syrup) is preferred for cooking because, as Burr Morse says, "the flavor goes through," meaning that the assertive taste is apparent even after being combined with other ingredients and cooked.

• **U.S. Grade B** is sometimes called "cooking syrup" and is preferred by many chefs for baking and cooking because of its deep maple flavor and caramel undertones.

Maple-Glazed French Toast

A hint of syrup in the egg wash subtly infuses the bread with maple notes. Top with additional maple syrup or our Cinnamon-Maple Applesauce (at left).

- ¾ cup 2% reduced-fat milk
- ¼ cup maple syrup
- ¼ teaspoon salt
- ¼ teaspoon ground cinnamon
- 3 large eggs, lightly beaten
- Cooking spray
- 12 (1-ounce) slices day-old white bread (such as Pepperidge Farm sandwich bread)
- 1 tablespoon powdered sugar

1 Combine first 5 ingredients in a shallow dish.
2 Heat a large nonstick skillet over medium heat. Coat pan with cooking spray. Working with 4 bread slices at a time, place bread slices in milk mixture, quickly turning to coat both sides. Remove bread slices from milk mixture. Add bread slices to pan; cook 2 minutes on each side or until lightly browned. Remove toast from pan. Repeat procedure with cooking spray, remaining 8 bread slices, and remaining milk mixture. Sprinkle powdered sugar evenly over toast. Yield: 6 servings (serving size: 2 toast pieces).

CALORIES 231 (20% from fat); FAT 5.1g (sat 1.1g, mono 1.8g, poly 0.6g); PROTEIN 8.2g; CARB 39.9g; FIBER 1.1g; CHOL 108mg; IRON 2.1mg; SODIUM 420mg; CALC 140mg

Vermont Baked Beans

Use a darker grade of syrup for the most richness and intensity. A small portion of the syrup is stirred in at the end so the flavor is more pronounced.

    1   pound dried navy beans (about
        2 cups)
        Cooking spray
1½ cups chopped yellow onion
 ½ cup diced salt pork (about 4 ounces)
5½ cups water
 ¾ cup maple syrup, divided
1½ tablespoons Dijon mustard
    1   teaspoon salt
 ¼ teaspoon hot pepper sauce (such as
        Tabasco)

1 Sort and wash beans; place in a large bowl. Cover with water to 2 inches above beans; cover and let stand 8 hours or overnight. Drain beans.

2 Preheat oven to 325°.

3 Heat a Dutch oven over medium-high heat. Coat pan with cooking spray. Add onion and pork to pan; sauté 5 minutes. Add beans, 5½ cups water, ½ cup syrup, mustard, salt, and pepper sauce; bring to a boil. Cover and bake at 325° for 2½ hours or until beans are tender, stirring occasionally. Uncover and bake an additional 30 minutes or until mixture begins to thicken. Stir in remaining ¼ cup syrup. Yield: 12 servings (serving size: ½ cup).

CALORIES 254 (29% from fat); FAT 8.2g (sat 2.9g, mono 3.7g, poly 1.3g); PROTEIN 7.8g; CARB 38.2g; FIBER 9.4g; CHOL 8mg; IRON 2.4mg; SODIUM 379mg; CALC 78mg

A Sweet History

Native Americans of the Northeast woodlands first used hollowed-out logs to collect liquid trickling from maple trees. White-hot stones were dropped in the liquid, and as it evaporated, the liquid condensed into syrup, which crystallized into sugar.

Maple sugar was durable and could be carried in pouches more easily than syrup; the sugar was traded with the colonists, and eventually production know-how was passed on to them. According to Burr Morse, this made Americans self-sufficient in sugar production and less dependent on imported sugar. But as transportation improved and the railroads made the cheaper cane sugar from the South available, sugar makers diverted their production efforts toward a market for syrup.

Maple Sugar

Maple sugar is twice as sweet as granulated sugar and can be used in many recipes calling for sugar, but in lesser quantity. It's available in many specialty shops and through online sources. Be sure to look for pure maple sugar and avoid maple-flavored sugar (which tends to consist of granulated sugar with artificial maple flavoring).

Maple syrup lends richness to both sweet and savory dishes, and works well whenever a sweetener is called for.

Cabernet-Braised Beef Short Ribs

Conventional wisdom says March comes in roaring and goes out bleating. The transition to spring means that March, for many of us, offers a last chance to prepare hearty, slow-cooked comfort food. We can't think of a better choice than these delectable short ribs, which earned our Test Kitchens' highest rating. Beef short ribs and aromatics braise for three-and-a-half hours in cabernet sauvignon, which yields a rich, velvety sauce that coats the fork-tender meat.

Admittedly, this dish is indulgent. Short ribs are inherently fatty, which renders them tender when slow cooked. But the comparatively lean calories from the egg noodles balance the dish. Prepare it on a weekend, and you can savor the aroma that fills the kitchen as it cooks.

STAFF FAVORITE
Cabernet-Braised Beef Short Ribs

    Cooking spray
  2 pounds beef short ribs, trimmed
  ½ teaspoon salt
  ½ teaspoon freshly ground black
    pepper
1½ cups fat-free, less-sodium beef
    broth
  1 cup cabernet sauvignon or other dry
    red wine
  2 tablespoons tomato paste
1½ cups (1-inch) slices celery (about
    2 stalks)
  1 cup (1-inch) slices carrot (about
    2 medium)
  6 garlic cloves, sliced
  2 (6-inch) rosemary sprigs
  1 onion, cut into 8 wedges
  1 tablespoon all-purpose flour
  4 cups hot cooked wide egg noodles
    Chopped parsley (optional)

1 Preheat oven to 300°.

2 Heat a large skillet over medium-high heat. Coat pan with cooking spray. Sprinkle ribs with salt and pepper. Add ribs to pan; cook 8 minutes, browning on all sides. Remove from pan. Add broth to pan, scraping pan to loosen browned bits.

3 Combine broth, wine, and tomato paste in a medium bowl; stir with a whisk. Place ribs, celery, and next 4 ingredients in a 13 x 9-inch baking dish coated with cooking spray. Pour broth mixture over rib mixture. Cover with foil; bake at 300° for 3½ hours or until ribs are very tender.

4 Uncover dish; strain beef mixture through a sieve over a bowl, reserving liquid. Reserve ribs; discard remaining solids. Place a zip-top plastic bag inside a 2-cup glass measure. Pour reserved liquid into bag; let stand 10 minutes (fat will rise to top). Seal bag; carefully snip off 1 bottom corner of bag. Drain liquid into a small saucepan, stopping before fat layer reaches opening; discard fat.

5 Add flour to pan, stirring well with a whisk. Place pan over medium heat; bring to a boil, stirring constantly with a whisk. Reduce heat, and simmer 3 minutes or until thick, stirring constantly with a whisk. Serve sauce with ribs and noodles. Garnish with chopped parsley, if desired. Yield: 6 servings (serving size: 2 short ribs, ²/₃ cup noodles, and about 2½ tablespoons sauce).

CALORIES 499 (41% from fat); FAT 22.8g (sat 9.2g, mono 9.7g, poly 1.2g); PROTEIN 40.8g; CARB 30.1g; FIBER 1.7g; CHOL 136mg; IRON 5.8mg; SODIUM 427mg; CALC 33mg

Choice Ingredient: Rosemary

Learn: A member of the mint family, rosemary is an evergreen herb with needlelike leaves. It has a strong, fragrant pine scent with a lemony flavor. Although rosemary is native to the Mediterranean, it is easy to grow in almost any garden. In spring, plant in full sunlight and well-drained, sandy soil.

Purchase: Look for fresh rosemary that is sage green in color and free of yellowing or browning sprigs. Leaves should appear succulent, not brittle. Buy dried rosemary in a sealed container.

Store: Rinse fresh rosemary in cold water, shake to dry, then wrap in paper towels, place in a zip-top bag, and refrigerate for up to two weeks. Dried rosemary can be kept for about six months when stored in an airtight container and kept from light, heat, and moisture.

Use: Rosemary pairs nicely with savory meats and vegetables. Rosemary also can add depth of flavor to sweet dishes. To substitute fresh for dried, use one tablespoon of fresh rosemary leaves per one teaspoon of dried.

Mint Condition Treats

Our trimmed-down Chocolate-Mint Bars surpass their former rich reputation.

Chocolate-Mint Bars have a reputation to preserve. Since Imogene Reppe of Two Harbors, Minnesota, received the recipe many years ago from her daughter, Becky, Reppe has made these bars often, especially for church functions. The fudgy brownie layer is iced twice: first with a thin, sweet, and minty topping, and then with a rich chocolate glaze. The bars have become acclaimed enough to earn their own heart-shaped serving platter for church gatherings. In fact, when Reppe attempts to make another dessert, the church kitchen staff teases, "Sorry, but we can't use these. Only your Chocolate-Mint Bars will do." But all the chocolate and butter in the recipe concerned Reppe, who wanted to serve a more healthful treat while preserving its velvety, rich appeal.

Reppe's Chocolate-Mint Bars are decadently divine for a reason: Her recipe employs nearly a half cup of butter in each layer of this three-tiered dessert. Factor in four eggs and plenty of chocolate chips along with all that butter, and one serving of Reppe's bars contains about 17 total grams of fat, including 10 grams of saturated fat. According to the American Heart Association, one bar supplies two-thirds of the daily saturated fat allotment for someone on a 2,000-calorie-per-day diet. We started by halving the butter in each layer, shaving six grams of fat (including nearly four grams of saturated fat) and 55 calories per serving. We combined two whole eggs with one-half cup of egg substitute to offer enough liquid and structure to the brownie layer. Changing the number of eggs, along with reducing the butter,

dropped about 40 milligrams of cholesterol per serving. And reducing the semisweet chocolate chips from one cup to three-quarters cup trimmed a few more calories per portion.

Chocolate-Mint Bars

The dense base layer is like a rich, fudgy brownie, so don't overcook it or the dessert bars will be dry. Refrigerating the mint bars allows the chocolaty top layer to set properly. You can make the dessert up to one day ahead.

BOTTOM LAYER:

- 1 cup all-purpose flour (about 4½ ounces)
- ½ teaspoon salt
- 1 cup granulated sugar
- ½ cup egg substitute
- ¼ cup butter, melted
- 2 tablespoons water
- 1 teaspoon vanilla extract
- 2 large eggs, lightly beaten
- 1 (16-ounce) can chocolate syrup (about 1⅓ cups)
- Cooking spray

MINT LAYER:

- 2 cups powdered sugar
- ¼ cup butter, melted
- 2 tablespoons fat-free milk
- ½ teaspoon peppermint extract
- 2 drops green food coloring

GLAZE:

- ¾ cup semisweet chocolate chips
- 3 tablespoons butter

❶ Preheat oven to 350°.
❷ To prepare bottom layer, lightly spoon flour into a dry measuring cup; level with a knife. Combine flour and salt; stir with a whisk. Combine granulated sugar and next 6 ingredients in a medium bowl; stir until smooth. Add flour mixture to chocolate mixture, stirring until blended. Pour batter into a 13 x 9–inch baking pan coated with cooking spray. Bake at 350° for 28 minutes or until a wooden pick inserted in center comes out

almost clean. Cool completely in pan on a wire rack.
❸ To prepare mint layer, combine powdered sugar and next 4 ingredients in a medium bowl; beat with a mixer until smooth. Spread mint mixture over cooled cake.
❹ To prepare glaze, combine chocolate chips and 3 tablespoons butter in a medium microwave-safe bowl. Microwave at HIGH 1 minute or until melted, stirring after 30 seconds. Let stand 2 minutes. Spread chocolate mixture evenly over mint layer. Cover and refrigerate until ready to serve. Cut into 20 pieces. Yield: 20 servings (serving size: 1 piece).

CALORIES 264 (30% from fat); FAT 8.7g (sat 5.2g, mono 2.5g, poly 0.4g); PROTEIN 2.8g; CARB 45g; FIBER 0.5g; CHOL 38mg; IRON 0.9mg; SODIUM 139mg; CALC 12mg

serving size: 1 piece		
	before	after
CALORIES PER SERVING	339	264
FAT	16.7g	8.7g
PERCENT OF TOTAL CALORIES	44%	30%

The Facts On Fats

What you need to know about fats and how they fit into your diet

DIETARY FATS CONTINUE TO MAKE NEWS, and the latest findings could be a surprise: Lower-fat diets may not be as healthful as once believed.

We now know fats are necessary components of our diet: They deliver essential fatty acids the body cannot manufacture, such as omega-3 fatty acids, which bolster heart health. Additionally, certain vitamins are fat-soluble, meaning they are digested and absorbed or transported in the body with fat. These include vitamins A, D, E, and K.

While the revised Dietary Guidelines from 2005 took a more liberal approach to how much fat is healthful, the American Heart Association recently tightened its recommendations about saturated fat for healthy Americans.

What does it mean? All fats are high in calories, so you should enjoy them in moderation. And once you understand a little of the science behind the four types of fats in foods, it's easy to strike a balance between flavorful cooking and good health.

MAKE AHEAD • FREEZABLE
Tropical Muffins with Coconut-Macadamia Topping

Most of the monounsaturated fat in each serving comes from mild-flavored canola oil and rich macadamia nuts.

MUFFINS:

1⅓ cups all-purpose flour (about 6 ounces)
1 cup regular oats
1 teaspoon baking powder
½ teaspoon baking soda
½ teaspoon salt
1 cup mashed ripe banana (about 2)
1 cup low-fat buttermilk
½ cup packed brown sugar
2 tablespoons canola oil
1 teaspoon vanilla extract
1 large egg, lightly beaten
½ cup canned crushed pineapple in juice, drained
⅓ cup flaked sweetened coconut
3 tablespoons finely chopped macadamia nuts, toasted
Cooking spray

TOPPING:

2 tablespoons flaked sweetened coconut
1 tablespoon finely chopped macadamia nuts
1 tablespoon granulated sugar
1 tablespoon regular oats

1 Preheat oven to 400°.
2 To prepare muffins, lightly spoon flour into dry measuring cups; level with a knife. Combine flour and next 4 ingredients in a large bowl. Make a well in center of flour mixture. Combine banana and next 5 ingredients in a medium bowl; add to flour mixture, stirring just until moist. Stir in pineapple, ⅓ cup coconut, and 3 tablespoons nuts. Spoon batter into 12 muffin cups coated with cooking spray.
3 To prepare topping, combine 2 tablespoons coconut and remaining ingredients in a small bowl.
4 Sprinkle about 1 teaspoon topping over each muffin. Bake at 400° for 18 minutes or until muffins spring back when touched lightly in center. Remove muffins from pans immediately; place on a wire rack. Yield: 1 dozen (serving size: 1 muffin).

CALORIES 205 (29% from fat); FAT 6.7g (sat 1.7g, mono 3.4g, poly 1g); PROTEIN 4.3g; CARB 33.3g; FIBER 2g; CHOL 19mg; IRON 1.5mg; SODIUM 215mg; CALC 69mg

MAKE AHEAD • FREEZABLE
Manchego, Herb, and Sun-Dried Tomato Scones

Since cheeses contain saturated fat, use flavorful ones in small amounts.

2 cups all-purpose flour (about 9 ounces)
1½ teaspoons baking powder
¼ teaspoon salt
3 tablespoons chilled butter, cut into small pieces
½ cup (2 ounces) shredded Manchego cheese
½ cup chopped sun-dried tomatoes
2 tablespoons chopped fresh basil
¾ cup low-fat buttermilk
2 large egg whites, lightly beaten
Cooking spray

1 Preheat oven to 425°.
2 Lightly spoon flour into dry measuring cups; level with a knife. Combine flour, baking powder, and salt in a large bowl, stirring with a whisk. Cut in butter with a pastry blender or 2 knives until mixture resembles coarse meal. Stir in cheese, tomatoes, and basil. Add buttermilk and egg whites, stirring just until moist.
3 Turn dough out onto a lightly floured surface; knead lightly 4 times with floured hands. Pat dough into an 8-inch circle on a baking sheet coated with cooking spray. Cut dough into 8 wedges, cutting into but not through dough. Coat top of dough lightly with cooking spray. Bake at 425° for 15 minutes or until scones are golden. Yield: 8 servings.

CALORIES 197 (29% from fat); FAT 6.4g (sat 3.8g, mono 1.6g, poly 0.4g); PROTEIN 7.4g; CARB 27.5g; FIBER 1.3g; CHOL 17mg; IRON 1.9mg; SODIUM 382mg; CALC 141mg

All About Fats

Monounsaturated Fats

Liquid at room temperature, these plant-based fats can lower cholesterol when used in place of saturated fat in the diet. **Sources:** Canola, olive, and peanut oils, as well as peanuts, pecans, and avocados. **What you need to know:** Studies show that healthful fats like olive oil and peanuts, in particular, are good for the heart, weight loss, and health in general, possibly because they are rich and satisfying even in small amounts. **Cooking strategies:** While olive oil attracts the most attention, other liquid oils are healthful and versatile, too. Canola and peanut oils are both good sources of monounsaturated fat with high smoke points (the temperature where oil begins to burn); canola has a mild flavor great for baking or sautéing, while peanut oil delivers nutty flavor to stir-fries or Asian-inspired vinaigrettes. There's no reason to use a single type of oil exclusively, but use these healthful oils sparingly. The idea is to enjoy moderate amounts and to use unsaturated fats most often.

Polyunsaturated Fats

Liquid at room temperature, these plant- and fish-derived fats can lower cholesterol when they replace saturated fat in the diet. **Sources:** Vegetable oils like safflower, sunflower, soybean, corn, and sesame oils. Sunflower seeds; soybeans; fatty fish like tuna, mackerel, and salmon; and most nuts are also rich in these fats. **What you need to know:** Unsaturated fats garner the most attention when it comes to heart health, and the polyunsaturated type is a good replacement for saturated fat in the diet, says Julia Zumpano, RD, of the Cleveland Clinic's department of preventive cardiology. She also points out that fatty fish like salmon and tuna contain their own special variety of

polyunsaturated fats called omega-3 fatty acids. These specific fats appear to keep the heart healthy, even when consumed in small amounts. What's more, certain nuts, oils, and greens offer another type of omega-3 fats. **Cooking strategies:** Use small amounts of nuts and their oils in cooking, says Harvard cardiologist Dariush Mozaffarian, MD, DrPH. Toast nuts and seeds to intensify flavor, and sprinkle them on top of a salad or dish to get the most textural and flavorful impact. And eat more fish. "If you eat only one fatty fish meal per week, that's enough to reap much of the benefits of omega-3s."

Saturated Fats

Found mostly in animal products, these solid fats raise harmful LDL cholesterol and increase cardiovascular disease risk. **Sources:** Beef, lamb, pork, bacon, cheese, full-fat yogurt, butter, and whole milk. Snack chips and bakery items made with tropical oils like coconut, palm, and palm kernel also contain these fats, which are solid at room temperature. **What you need to know:** The American Heart Association advises limiting saturated fat to less than seven percent of total calories, about 15 grams for the average person on a 2,000-calorie-a-day diet. If you're counting, a teaspoon of butter contains nearly three grams of saturated fat, and one three-ounce filet mignon has about 10 grams. However, saturated fats do fit into a heart-healthy eating plan if you manage the portions of meats, choose lower-fat dairy products, and use cheeses, butter, and cream in moderation. **Cooking strategies:** The key with saturated fats, says Nelson, is to choose wisely and then use them judiciously. "A high-quality, imported fresh Parmesan cheese, in small amounts, can add a lot of flavor." In comparison, a similar amount of a processed cheese carries the same

amount of fat but less vibrancy. Another tactic: Use meats as an accent in a dish rather than the main attraction. If you eat red meat as a main course, Nelson notes that a recommended serving amounts to three ounces cooked—about the size of a deck of cards. For dairy products, choosing one percent or fat-free options helps limit the amount of saturated fat in your diet.

Trans Fats

Produced when liquid oils are processed into solid shortenings, trans fats (also known as partially hydrogenated oils) raise LDL, or "bad," cholesterol and lower HDL, or "good," cholesterol. **Sources:** Foods can harbor trans fats if they're made with partially hydrogenated oils. Since January 2006, the Food and Drug Administration has required all food manufacturers to indicate the amount of trans fat in a serving of food. (Food with less than one-half gram of trans fat per serving can be labeled "trans fat–free.") Some meat and dairy products contain trace amounts of naturally occurring trans fats. It's unknown whether these fats have the same harmful effects to your health as manufactured trans fats. **What you need to know:** Harvard's landmark 2005 Nurses' Health study, which followed nearly 79,000 women, was one of the first to find that trans fats raise LDL cholesterol, lower HDL cholesterol, and increase heart disease risk. Now a 2007 Harvard report confirms that the more trans fats you consume, the greater your risk. **Cooking strategies:** Since even small amounts of trans fats are harmful to your health, Mozaffarian thinks it's best to avoid eating foods made with partially hydrogenated oil. Focus instead on whole foods—fresh produce, fish, liquid vegetable oils, and whole grains—all of which are naturally trans fat–free.

Skordalia

This dip's olive oil—with its beneficial monounsaturated fats—tame the heady garlic. Serve with crudités.

- 1 pound peeled red potatoes, cut into 1-inch pieces
- 10 garlic cloves, peeled
- 1/3 cup olive oil
- 2 tablespoons fresh lemon juice
- 3/4 teaspoon kosher salt
- 4 teaspoons chopped fresh chives

1 Place potatoes in a large saucepan; cover with water. Bring to a boil. Reduce heat, and simmer 14 minutes. Add garlic to pan; cook 1 minute. Drain potato mixture in a colander over a bowl, reserving 1/2 cup cooking liquid. Place potato mixture and reserved liquid in a food processor; add oil, juice, and salt. Pulse until smooth. Spoon into a medium bowl. Cover and chill overnight. Sprinkle with chives before serving. Yield: 2 1/3 cups (serving size: about 1 1/2 tablespoons).

CALORIES 38 (67% from fat); FAT 2.9g (sat 0.4g, mono 2.1g, poly 0.3g); PROTEIN 0.5g; CARB 2.7g; FIBER 0.4g; CHOL 0mg; IRON 0.1mg; SODIUM 57mg; CALC 3mg

Spicy South Asian Roasted Fish

Even though salmon gets the most attention for omega-3 fats, one serving of this halibut entrée has about 0.6 grams omega-3 fats, about half the amount of one's daily intake goal.

- 1/2 cup light coconut milk
- 2 tablespoons minced peeled fresh lemongrass
- 1 tablespoon minced peeled fresh ginger
- 2 tablespoons chili sauce
- 1 1/2 tablespoons fish sauce
- 1 tablespoon fresh lime juice
- 2 garlic cloves, minced
- 4 (6-ounce) skinless halibut fillets

1 Preheat oven to 425°.
2 Combine first 7 ingredients in a food processor or blender; pulse 30 seconds or until well combined.
3 Arrange fillets in a single layer in a 13 x 9–inch baking dish. Pour lemongrass mixture over fish; turn fillets to coat evenly. Bake at 425° for 13 minutes or until fish flakes easily when tested with a fork or until desired degree of doneness. Serve sauce with fish. Yield: 4 servings (serving size: 1 fillet and about 1 tablespoon sauce).

CALORIES 213 (22% from fat); FAT 5.3g (sat 2g, mono 1.3g, poly 1.2g); PROTEIN 35g; CARB 5g; FIBER 0.1g; CHOL 52mg; IRON 1.8mg; SODIUM 710mg; CALC 84mg

Chicken Roulade with Olives and Simple Preserved Lemons

The tasty olives and olive oil boost the monounsaturated fats. Skinless chicken breasts keep the saturated fat low.

CHICKEN:
- 1/3 cup dry breadcrumbs
- 6 tablespoons capers, rinsed, drained, and divided
- 1 tablespoon chopped Simple Preserved Lemons
- 12 pitted ripe olives, drained and divided
- 2 garlic cloves, minced
- 4 (6-ounce) skinless, boneless chicken breast halves
- 2 teaspoons olive oil
- 2 cups chopped onion (about 1 medium)
- 1/2 cup dry white wine
- 1 cup water
- 1 cup fat-free, less-sodium chicken broth
- 2 tablespoons fresh lemon juice
- 1/2 cup golden raisins
- 1/4 teaspoon ground turmeric

1 Combine breadcrumbs, 1/4 cup capers, Simple Preserved Lemons, 6 olives, and garlic in a food processor or blender, and pulse 10 times or until mixture is coarsely chopped.

2 Place each breast half between 2 sheets of heavy-duty plastic wrap; pound to 1/4-inch thickness using a meat mallet or small heavy skillet. Divide breadcrumb mixture into 4 equal portions; spread 1 portion on each breast half, leaving 1/4-inch borders around edges. Roll up each breast half, jelly-roll fashion, starting with short side. Secure with wooden picks or twine.
3 Heat oil in a large nonstick skillet over medium-high heat. Add chicken to pan; cook 6 minutes, browning on all sides. Remove chicken from pan; keep warm. Add onion to pan; sauté 2 minutes or until browned. Add wine; cook until reduced to 1/4 cup (about 1 minute), stirring frequently. Add remaining 2 tablespoons capers, 1 cup water, and next 4 ingredients. Quarter remaining 6 olives. Add to pan; bring to a boil. Add chicken to pan; cover, reduce heat, and simmer 20 minutes, turning chicken after 10 minutes. Serve chicken with sauce. Yield: 4 servings (serving size: 1 roulade and 1/4 cup sauce).

CALORIES 371 (22% from fat); FAT 9.1g (sat 1.9g, mono 4.5g, poly 1.5g); PROTEIN 43.2g; CARB 29.4g; FIBER 3.1g; CHOL 108mg; IRON 3.3mg; SODIUM 825mg; CALC 80mg

SIMPLE PRESERVED LEMONS:

Use the preserved lemon liquid in vinaigrettes or to enliven dips or spreads. Add lemon pieces to tagines or lamb stews for a salty-sour twist.

- 4 lemons, quartered
- 2 teaspoons kosher salt

1 Squeeze lemon quarters in a sieve over a bowl, reserving juice and rinds; discard seeds. Place rinds in a large zip-top plastic bag; add salt. Shake well to coat. Add reserved juice; seal bag. Store in refrigerator 2 weeks, turning bag daily. Yield: about 1 cup (serving size: about 1 tablespoon).

CALORIES 5 (18% from fat); FAT 0.1g (sat 0g, mono 0g, poly 0g); PROTEIN 0.3g; CARB 2.9g; FIBER 1.3g; CHOL 0mg; IRON 0.2mg; SODIUM 241mg; CALC 16mg

Grilled Rack of Lamb with Saffron Rice

A rich, succulent cut of lamb with an earthy spice rub and rice maintain a good nutrition profile. The spices add flavor to the lamb with no additional fat and negligible sodium, while the three-ounce serving size of meat keeps fat in check.

Cooking spray
1 cup diced onion
2 garlic cloves, minced
1 cup uncooked basmati rice
2 cups fat-free, less-sodium chicken broth
¼ teaspoon saffron threads, crushed
1 bay leaf
¾ teaspoon kosher salt
½ teaspoon ground cumin
½ teaspoon ground cinnamon
½ teaspoon paprika
⅛ teaspoon ground coriander
⅛ teaspoon ground cardamom
⅛ teaspoon ground red pepper
1 (1½-pound) French-cut rack of lamb (8 ribs)
1 teaspoon olive oil

1 Heat a medium saucepan over medium heat. Coat pan with cooking spray. Add onion and garlic to pan; cook 5 minutes or until golden brown, stirring frequently. Add rice and next 3 ingredients; bring to a boil. Cover, reduce heat, and simmer 20 minutes. Discard bay leaf. Keep warm.
2 Prepare grill.
3 Combine salt and next 6 ingredients. Brush lamb with oil, and rub with salt mixture. Place lamb on grill rack coated with cooking spray; grill 10 minutes, turning once, or until a thermometer registers 145° (medium-rare) to 160° (medium). Let stand 5 minutes before cutting into chops. Serve lamb with rice. Yield: 4 servings (serving size: 2 lamb chops and ¾ cup rice).

CALORIES 294 (35% from fat); FAT 11.3g (sat 4.5g, mono 4.7g, poly 0.5g); PROTEIN 24.1g; CARB 22.6g; FIBER 1.9g; CHOL 68mg; IRON 2.4mg; SODIUM 618mg; CALC 40mg

Herb-Crusted Salmon with Mixed Greens Salad

Chopped fresh herbs dress up salmon fillets, which are a great source of heart-healthy omega-3 fatty acids.

SALMON:
½ cup dry breadcrumbs
2 teaspoons chopped fresh oregano
2 teaspoons chopped fresh rosemary
2 teaspoons chopped fresh flat-leaf parsley
1½ teaspoons grated lemon rind
½ teaspoon black pepper
2 garlic cloves, minced
4 (6-ounce) salmon fillets (about 1 inch thick), skinned
Cooking spray
¼ teaspoon kosher salt

SALAD:
1 tablespoon fresh lemon juice
1 tablespoon extravirgin olive oil
1 teaspoon Dijon mustard
¼ teaspoon kosher salt
¼ teaspoon black pepper
4 cups mixed salad greens

1 To prepare salmon, combine first 7 ingredients in a shallow dish or pie plate. Lightly coat both sides of fillets with cooking spray, and sprinkle evenly with ¼ teaspoon salt. Dredge fillets in breadcrumb mixture.
2 Heat a large nonstick skillet over medium-high heat. Coat pan with cooking spray. Add fillets to pan; cook 3 minutes. Reduce heat to medium; carefully turn fillets over. Cook 4 minutes or until fish flakes easily when tested with a fork or until desired degree of doneness.
3 To prepare salad, combine juice and next 4 ingredients in a large bowl. Add mixed greens; toss gently to coat. Place ⅔ cup salad on each of 4 plates; top each serving with 1 fillet. Yield: 4 servings.

CALORIES 256 (33% from fat); FAT 9.5g (sat 2g, mono 4.6g, poly 2.2g); PROTEIN 32.1g; CARB 9g; FIBER 1.8g; CHOL 70mg; IRON 2mg; SODIUM 399mg; CALC 110mg

QUICK & EASY • MAKE AHEAD
Green Olive and Artichoke Tapenade

This tangy spread is delicious with crackers, such as Kashi or Whole Foods 365 Everyday Value Golden Stoneground Wheat Things.

3 tablespoons capers, drained
1 tablespoon chopped fresh parsley
1 tablespoon fresh lemon juice
1 teaspoon Dijon mustard
½ teaspoon black pepper
10 large pitted green olives
2 garlic cloves, minced
1 (14-ounce) can artichoke hearts, drained

1 Combine all ingredients a food processor. Pulse to desired smoothness. Yield: 1½ cups (serving size: 1½ tablespoons).

CALORIES 16 (34% from fat); FAT 0.6g (sat 0g, mono 0.5g, poly 0.1g); PROTEIN 0.6g; CARB 2.3g; FIBER 0.6g; CHOL 0mg; IRON 0.1mg; SODIUM 211mg; CALC 2mg

Meal Makeover

The biggest strides in cutting saturated fat come from halving average red meat portions and switching from full-fat dairy to the reduced-fat variety. Our *before* menu is modeled on government surveys of the average American diet. The *after* menu shows how trimming saturated fat allows you to double up on fruits and include more food overall. Both daily intakes average around 2,000 calories.

AVERAGE AMERICAN MENU

	Calories	Fat (grams)	Saturated fat (grams)
BREAKFAST			
Oatmeal raisin granola bar (1 ounce)	110	2	0.5
8 ounces whole milk	156	8.9	5.6
5 ounces black coffee or tea	3	0	0
LUNCH			
Ham and Swiss sandwich (3 ounces ham, 1 ounce Swiss cheese, 2 slices rye bread)	382	13.4	6.3
1 ounce potato chips	150	10	3
1 apple	72	0.2	0
12 ounces cherry cola	141	0	0
SNACK			
1 ounce pretzels	108	0.8	0.1
½ cup grapes	55	0.1	0
SUPPER			
5 ounces broiled rib-eye steak (trimmed)	350	20.9	8.1
1 medium baked potato, 1 teaspoon butter	196	4.1	2.4
2½ cups mixed green salad, 2 tablespoons bottled vinaigrette dressing	173	14.5	2.1
1 cup green beans	27	0	0
½ cup chocolate ice cream	180	9	5
TOTALS:	**2,103** (36% fat)	**84**	**33**

REMODELED MENU

	Calories	Fat (grams)	Saturated fat (grams)
1 cup cooked oatmeal with one tablespoon brown sugar	**182**	**2.8**	**0.5**
2 tablespoons almonds	**102**	**8.6**	**0.6**
½ cup fresh blueberries	42	0.2	0
½ cup 1% low-fat milk and 5 ounces black coffee or tea	**52**	**1.3**	**0.8**
Ham and Swiss sandwich (2 ounces ham, 1 ounce light Jarlsberg cheese, 2 slices rye bread)	**326**	**11.4**	**5.2**
1 ounce baked potato chips	**110**	**1.5**	**0**
1 apple and banana	182	0.2	0
Unsweetened iced tea	0	0	0
1 ounce roasted peanuts	**170**	**14.9**	**2.5**
2 medium tangerines	89	0.5	0.1
Steak stir-fry: 2½ ounces cooked lean sirloin strips, 1 cup stir-fried vegetables, 1 cup cut green beans	**178**	**4.1**	**1.6**
1 cup steamed brown rice	**218**	**1.6**	**0.3**
3 cups salad, 1 tablespoon homemade vinaigrette	**132**	**9.5**	**1.3**
1½ cups sliced strawberries	80	0.8	0
TOTALS:	**1,863** (28% fat)	**57**	**13**

Parsley and Walnut Pesto

Pair with rich fish like salmon or trout (good sources of healthful omega-3 fatty acids), white-meat poultry (low in saturated fat), pasta, or steamed rice. Hearty walnuts add polyunsaturated omega-3 fatty acids, while olive oil is a good source of monounsaturated fats.

- 3 cups fresh flat-leaf parsley leaves (about 2½ ounces)
- ½ cup chopped walnuts, toasted
- 3 tablespoons olive oil
- 1 tablespoon fresh lemon juice
- ½ teaspoon salt
- ½ teaspoon ground black pepper
- 3 garlic cloves, chopped

1 Combine all ingredients in a food processor; process until smooth. Yield: ¾ cup (serving size: 1 tablespoon).

CALORIES 69 (87% from fat); FAT 6.7g (sat 0.8g, mono 2.9g, poly 2.7g); PROTEIN 1.3g; CARB 2g; FIBER 0.9g; CHOL 0mg; IRON 1.1mg; SODIUM 156mg; CALC 27mg

Asian Steak Dinner Menu

serves 4

Flank Steak with Hot Peanut Sauce

Glazed baby bok choy

Bring ⅓ cup water to a boil in a large skillet over medium-high heat. Add 1 pound halved baby bok choy; cover and cook 4 minutes. Remove bok choy from pan. Wipe pan clean with paper towels. Heat 2 teaspoons dark sesame oil in pan over medium heat. Add ½ teaspoon minced peeled fresh ginger and 1 minced garlic clove; cook 30 seconds, stirring constantly. Stir in 1½ tablespoons rice vinegar, 1 tablespoon hoisin sauce, and 1 tablespoon low-sodium soy sauce; cook 1 minute. Return bok choy to pan; toss to coat.

Steamed short-grain rice

Flank Steak with Hot Peanut Sauce

By keeping the meat serving to a sensible three-ounce cooked portion and using the low-fat but flavorful flank cut, this entrée limits saturated fat while offering plenty of iron and protein. Prepare steamed rice and sautéed baby bok choy while the meat marinates.

- ⅓ cup chopped green onions
- ⅓ cup low-sodium soy sauce
- 1 tablespoon brown sugar
- 1 tablespoon minced peeled fresh ginger
- 1 tablespoon fresh lime juice
- 2 teaspoons sesame oil
- 1 teaspoon crushed red pepper
- 2 garlic cloves, minced
- 1 (1-pound) flank steak, trimmed and cut diagonally into thin slices
- ½ cup water
- 1 tablespoon crunchy peanut butter
- 1 teaspoon cornstarch

1 Combine first 8 ingredients in a small bowl, stirring with a whisk. Place steak and ¼ cup onion mixture in a large zip-top plastic bag; seal. Marinate in refrigerator at least 2 hours or overnight, turning bag occasionally.
2 Combine remaining ¼ cup marinade, ½ cup water, peanut butter, and cornstarch in a small saucepan. Bring to a simmer; cook 1 minute, stirring frequently. Remove from heat; keep warm.
3 Remove steak from bag, discarding marinade. Heat a large nonstick skillet over medium-high heat. Add beef to pan; cook 2 minutes on each side or until desired degree of doneness. Serve with sauce. Yield: 4 servings (serving size: 3 ounces steak and about ¼ cup sauce).

CALORIES 212 (38% from fat); FAT 9g (sat 2.9g, mono 3.7g, poly 1.4g); PROTEIN 25.8g; CARB 6.4g; FIBER 0.7g; CHOL 37mg; IRON 2mg; SODIUM 549mg; CALC 29mg

Fry No More

Use the oven and stovetop to achieve authentic fried texture with a fraction of the fat.

Americans love fried food. Fried chicken, French fries, potato chips, fried fish, and onion rings are all hugely popular. Since fried ingredients vary so widely—from vegetables and meats to sweets—it seems our fondness stems from the crisp, crunchy coating and the way frying locks in the flavor and moistness of whatever lies below the surface. Yet those seductive qualities come at a high nutritional price; deep-fried foods are notoriously high in calories and fat.

At *Cooking Light*, we've found ways to replicate the great flavor and texture associated with deep frying—without the extra fat and calories. Some of these dishes call for oven-baking to mimic deep-fried results, while others are pan-fried. Armed with a few key strategies (see "Crunch Time," page 96), you'll easily master the methods for achieving deep-fried results without the fryer.

Potato Chips with Blue Cheese Dip

For the best results, use a mandoline to cut the potato; hand-cutting is less likely to produce sufficiently thin and uniform slices. Store any leftover chips in an airtight container for up to a week, and bake for 2 minutes at 450° to recrisp them.

- ⅓ cup (1½ ounces) finely crumbled blue cheese
- ⅓ cup fat-free sour cream
- 2 tablespoons light mayonnaise
- 2 tablespoons skim milk
- ¼ teaspoon Worcestershire sauce
- 1 pound russet potato, thinly sliced and divided (about 1 large)
- Cooking spray
- ½ teaspoon salt, divided

① Preheat oven to 400°. Place baking sheet in oven.

② Combine first 5 ingredients in a small bowl, stirring well. Cover and chill.

③ Place potato slices on paper towels; pat dry. Arrange half of potato slices in a single layer on preheated baking sheet coated with cooking spray. Sprinkle with ¼ teaspoon salt. Bake at 400° for 10 minutes. Turn potato slices over; bake an additional 5 minutes or until golden. Repeat procedure with remaining potatoes and remaining ¼ teaspoon salt. Serve immediately with blue cheese mixture. Yield: 6 servings (serving size: about ½ cup chips and about 2 tablespoons dip).

CALORIES 117 (29% from fat); FAT 3.7g (sat 1.6g, mono 0.6g, poly 0.1g); PROTEIN 4.2g; CARB 16.8g; FIBER 1g; CHOL 9mg; IRON 0.7mg; SODIUM 352mg; CALC 80mg

Oven-Fried Catfish Sandwiches

Serve with Garlic and Cumin-Seasoned Fries with Chipotle Ketchup (page 96). You can substitute tilapia for the catfish, if desired, though check for doneness a few minutes earlier because tilapia fillets are usually thinner.

- ¼ cup light mayonnaise
- 1 tablespoon sweet pickle relish
- 2 teaspoons capers, chopped
- ⅜ teaspoon salt, divided
- ¼ teaspoon hot pepper sauce (such as Tabasco)
- 2 tablespoons all-purpose flour
- 1 teaspoon paprika
- ¾ teaspoon garlic powder, divided
- ¼ teaspoon black pepper
- 2 large egg whites, lightly beaten
- ⅔ cup yellow cornmeal
- 4 (4-ounce) catfish fillets
  Cooking spray
- 4 (2-ounce) hoagie rolls, toasted
- 1 cup shredded romaine lettuce
- 8 (¼-inch-thick) slices tomato
- 4 (¼-inch-thick) slices red onion

① Preheat oven to 450°. Place baking sheet in oven.

② Combine mayonnaise, relish, capers, ⅛ teaspoon salt, and pepper sauce in a small bowl, stirring well. Set aside.

③ Combine flour, paprika, ½ teaspoon garlic powder, ⅛ teaspoon salt, and pepper in a shallow dish. Place egg whites in a shallow bowl. Combine cornmeal, remaining ⅛ teaspoon salt, and remaining ¼ teaspoon garlic powder in a shallow dish. Working with 1 fillet at a time, dredge in flour mixture. Dip in egg whites; dredge in cornmeal mixture. Place fillet on a plate; repeat procedure with remaining fillets, flour mixture, egg whites, and cornmeal mixture.

④ Transfer fillets to preheated baking sheet coated with cooking spray. Lightly coat fillets with cooking spray. Bake at 450° for 6 minutes. Turn fillets, and coat with cooking spray; bake an additional 6 minutes or until fish flakes easily when tested with a fork or until desired degree of doneness.

⑤ Place 1 bottom half of roll on each of 4 plates. Top each serving with ¼ cup lettuce, 1 fillet, 2 tomato slices, and 1 onion slice. Spread 4 teaspoons mayonnaise mixture on cut side of each roll top; place on top of sandwiches. Serve immediately. Yield: 4 servings (serving size: 1 sandwich).

CALORIES 431 (34% from fat); FAT 16.2g (sat 3.5g, mono 5.5g, poly 5.6g); PROTEIN 25.4g; CARB 45.2g; FIBER 4.8g; CHOL 60mg; IRON 2.9mg; SODIUM 785mg; CALC 91mg

BEER NOTE: Long before the term "pilsner" was appropriated by American megabrewers, it described a lager with floral aromatics and a clean, dry finish. Stoudt's Pils ($8/6 pack) from Pennsylvania revives that tradition, making this beer ideal with lighter fare like these sandwiches. This pilsner is crisp, yet flavorful, with a frothy white head, bready aromas, and satisfying hop bitterness that cuts through the creamy mayonnaise.

Crunchy Buttermilk-Coconut Chicken Fingers

These crispy chicken fingers appeal to kids, so serve them with ketchup for dipping. Grown-ups will enjoy them atop a salad.

- 1 pound skinless, boneless chicken breasts
- 1½ cups fat-free buttermilk
- ½ cup all-purpose flour (about 2¼ ounces)
- 1 large egg, lightly beaten
- 1 large egg white, lightly beaten
- ¾ cup crushed cornflakes
- ¾ cup flaked sweetened coconut, chopped
- 1 teaspoon garlic powder
- ¾ teaspoon salt
- ½ teaspoon curry powder
- ¼ teaspoon ground red pepper
  Cooking spray

① Cut chicken into 20 (¼-inch-thick) strips. Combine chicken and buttermilk in a shallow dish; cover and chill 1 hour. Drain chicken, discarding liquid. Combine chicken and flour in a medium bowl, tossing to coat.

② Preheat oven to 475°. Place baking sheet in oven.

③ Combine egg and egg white in a small bowl. Combine cornflakes and next 5 ingredients in a shallow dish.

④ Dip 1 chicken strip into egg mixture; dredge in cornflake mixture. Repeat procedure with remaining chicken, egg mixture, and cornflake mixture. Arrange chicken in a single layer on preheated baking sheet coated with cooking spray. Lightly coat chicken with cooking spray. Bake at 475° for 6 minutes or until done. Serve immediately. Yield: 4 servings (serving size: 5 chicken fingers).

CALORIES 346 (19% from fat); FAT 7.4g (sat 4.8g, mono 1g, poly 0.6g); PROTEIN 35g; CARB 33.8g; FIBER 1.7g; CHOL 120mg; IRON 4.2mg; SODIUM 767mg; CALC 139mg

Crab Cakes with Roasted Vegetables and Tangy Butter Sauce

(pictured on page 246)

Panko gives these crab cakes an irresistibly crisp coating. Chilling the crab cake mixture helps them hold their shape as they cook.

CRAB CAKES:

- ¼ cup finely chopped red onion
- 2 tablespoons chopped fresh parsley
- 3 tablespoons light mayonnaise
- 2 teaspoons Dijon mustard
- ¾ teaspoon Old Bay seasoning
- ½ teaspoon Worcestershire sauce
- 2 egg whites, lightly beaten
- 1 pound lump crabmeat, drained and shell pieces removed
- 1½ cups panko (Japanese breadcrumbs), divided
- 1 tablespoon olive oil, divided
  Cooking spray

VEGETABLES:

- 21 baby carrots (about 12 ounces)
- 5 small red potatoes, quartered (about 8 ounces)
- 4 shallots, halved lengthwise
- ⅛ teaspoon salt
- 8 ounces haricots verts, trimmed

SAUCE:

- ⅔ cup fat-free, less-sodium chicken broth
- 3 tablespoons chopped shallots
- 2 tablespoons white wine vinegar
- 2½ tablespoons butter

❶ To prepare crab cakes, combine first 7 ingredients in a medium bowl. Gently fold in crabmeat. Gently stir in ¾ cup panko. Cover and chill 30 minutes.
❷ Divide crab mixture into 8 equal portions (about ½ cup each); shape each into a ¾-inch-thick patty. Place remaining ¾ cup panko in a shallow dish. Dredge 1 patty in panko. Repeat procedure with remaining patties and panko.
❸ Heat 1½ teaspoons oil in a medium nonstick skillet over medium heat. Coat both sides of crab cakes with cooking spray. Add 4 crab cakes to pan; cook 7 minutes. Carefully turn cakes over; cook 7 minutes or until golden. Repeat procedure with remaining 1½ teaspoons oil, cooking spray, and remaining 4 crab cakes.
❹ Preheat oven to 450°.
❺ To prepare vegetables, leave root and 1 inch stem on carrots; scrub with a brush. Combine carrots, potatoes, and halved shallots in a small roasting pan. Coat vegetables with cooking spray; sprinkle with ⅛ teaspoon salt. Toss. Bake at 450° for 20 minutes, turning once. Coat haricots verts with cooking spray. Add haricots verts to vegetable mixture; toss. Bake an additional 10 minutes or until vegetables are tender.
❻ To prepare sauce, combine broth, chopped shallots, and vinegar in a small saucepan; bring to a boil. Cook until reduced to ¼ cup (about 4 minutes); remove from heat. Stir in butter. Serve with crab cakes and vegetables. Yield: 4 servings (serving size: 2 crab cakes, about 1 cup vegetables, and about 1½ tablespoons sauce).

CALORIES 443 (34% from fat); FAT 16.7g (sat 5.6g, mono 5.2g, poly 2.9g); PROTEIN 32.8g; CARB 42g; FIBER 7g; CHOL 103mg; IRON 2mg; SODIUM 969mg; CALC 163mg

Garlic and Cumin–Seasoned Fries with Chipotle Ketchup

In this recipe, strips of potatoes are tossed with dried spices and baked to a crunch. The ketchup on the side delivers an extra punch of flavor.

- ½ cup ketchup
- 1 teaspoon sugar
- 1 teaspoon fresh lime juice
- ¼ teaspoon ground chipotle chile powder
- ½ teaspoon ground cumin
- ¼ teaspoon salt
- ¼ teaspoon garlic powder
- 2 pounds peeled Yukon gold potatoes, cut into ¼-inch strips
- 1 tablespoon extravirgin olive oil
  Cooking spray

❶ Combine first 4 ingredients in a small bowl. Combine cumin, salt, and garlic powder in a large bowl.
❷ Preheat oven to 450°. Place baking sheet in oven.
❸ Toss potatoes with oil. Arrange potatoes in a single layer on preheated baking sheet coated with cooking spray. Bake at 450° for 10 minutes. Turn potatoes; bake an additional 5 minutes or until golden and crisp. Add potatoes to cumin mixture; toss gently to coat. Serve immediately with ketchup mixture. Yield: 6 servings (serving size: 1 cup fries and about 1 tablespoon ketchup mixture).

CALORIES 143 (16% from fat); FAT 2.5g (sat 0.3g, mono 1.7g, poly 0.3g); PROTEIN 3.9g; CARB 26.1g; FIBER 2.7g; CHOL 0mg; IRON 1.1mg; SODIUM 329mg; CALC 13mg

---

Crunch Time

Follow these tips to ensure crisp, golden, deep-fried texture.

- **Slice thin.** When you use small measures of oil, keep food thin—as with potato chips—to expose maximum surface area and improve crisping and browning.
- **Give it room.** Leave ample space between items on a baking sheet or in a skillet. If food is crowded, it will steam, not crisp.
- **Keep food dry.** Drain or blot any moisture on the food—such as potatoes—before cooking. Excess moisture evaporates during cooking and creates steam, resulting in a soggy crust.
- **Use high heat.** Set the oven temperature between 400° and 475° to sear the food and crisp its surface.
- **Try crunchy coatings.** Ingredients such as nuts, crushed cornflakes, and cornmeal lend an appealing texture to oven- and pan-fried foods. We prefer panko (Japanese breadcrumbs) to regular dry breadcrumbs because they don't absorb oil as readily and resist sogginess.
- **Preheat the baking sheet.** Achieve better results for oven-fried foods like chicken fingers or French fries by placing them on a preheated baking sheet, which helps the undersides stay crisp.

Barbecue-Flavored Onion Rings

Regular yellow onions will work in this recipe, but sweet onions have a milder flavor. Coating the onion rings with breadcrumbs in batches keeps the crumbs dry for maximum crispness. Rotate pans during cooking for even browning.

- 3 tablespoons all-purpose flour
- 1 tablespoon sugar
- 1 teaspoon chili powder
- 1 teaspoon ground cumin
- ½ teaspoon salt
- ½ teaspoon paprika
- ¼ teaspoon ground allspice
- 2 large eggs, lightly beaten
- 1 pound Vidalia or other sweet onions, cut into ¼-inch-thick slices and separated into rings (about 2 large)
- 1½ cups dry breadcrumbs, divided
  Cooking spray

❶ Preheat oven to 450°.
❷ Combine first 8 ingredients in a large bowl. Dip onion rings in flour mixture. Place half of onion rings in a zip-top plastic bag; add ¾ cup breadcrumbs, shaking bag to coat onion rings. Repeat procedure with remaining onion rings and remaining ¾ cup breadcrumbs.
❸ Arrange onion rings in a single layer on 2 baking sheets coated with cooking spray. Lightly coat onion rings with cooking spray. Bake at 450° for 5 minutes. Rotate pans on racks; bake 5 minutes. Turn onion rings over; lightly coat with cooking spray and bake 5 minutes. Rotate pans and bake 5 minutes or until crisp. Serve immediately. Yield: 6 servings (serving size: about ½ cup).

CALORIES 188 (16% from fat); FAT 3.3g (sat 0.9g, mono 0.9g, poly 0.8g); PROTEIN 6.9g; CARB 32.6g; FIBER 2.6g; CHOL 71mg; IRON 2.1mg; SODIUM 431mg; CALC 79mg

---

INSPIRED VEGETARIAN

Vegetarian Delhi

A chef from the cuisine capital of India shares his hometown's sometimes subtle, often spicy, and sumptuous meatless fare.

Of all the cities in India, New Delhi, where Suvir Saran grew up as a Hindu as well as a vegetarian, offers the most exciting and varied vegetarian options. (Hinduism entreats believers to eat delicious, easily digestible foods. For many Hindus, vegetarian foods are the easiest and most fitting options.) New Delhi is not only the primary political hub of the nation but also where the foods and flavors of the country's 28 states converge.

Indian food is best known for heady spices, bold seasonings, and hot dishes, yet ingredients work together to offer contrasts. At meals, spicy balances cool, creamy pairs with crunchy, and warm offsets cold.

And this balance of textures and flavors has been a part of Indian culture for centuries. We aim to balance protein (like lentils or beans) with starch (from naan flatbreads to potatoes), and to enrich dishes with vegetables. For example, instead of using flour to thicken soup, we use lentils and potatoes. Yogurt, rich in calcium, is part of nearly every meal, in a raita or *lassi* (a yogurt-based drink). Spices, aromatics, herbs, pickles, and fruit-based chutneys add excitement to even the most humble potato dish.

Eating as a vegetarian in India is not about substitutions and replacements; it is about cooking and eating with passion, with a nod to nutrition, and with a great appetite. Vegetables are the life and soul of Indian cuisine.

Roasted Manchurian Cauliflower

This side dish has origins in Chinese cooking (hence the name) and is typically fried. This version roasts the cauliflower instead to intensify the flavor, and the spicy tomato-based sauce reduces with the vegetables. Serve with a simple cooked spinach side, a mild curry with potatoes and peas, and plenty of flatbread (naan) to scoop up the sweet-salty sauce.

- 5½ cups cauliflower florets (about 1 large head)
- 2 tablespoons Garam Masala (page 99)
- ¼ teaspoon kosher salt
- 2 teaspoons canola oil, divided
  Cooking spray
- ½ teaspoon black pepper
- 8 garlic cloves, minced
- ¾ cup ketchup
- ½ teaspoon ground red pepper

❶ Preheat oven to 425°.
❷ Combine first 3 ingredients and 1 teaspoon oil in a large bowl; toss well. Place cauliflower mixture in an 11 x 7-inch baking dish coated with cooking spray. Bake at 425° for 20 minutes.
❸ Heat remaining 1 teaspoon oil in a medium nonstick skillet over medium-high heat. Add black pepper to pan, and sauté 1 minute. Add garlic; sauté 30 seconds. Stir in ketchup; cook 2 minutes, stirring occasionally. Stir in red pepper; reduce heat, and simmer 3 minutes or until thick.
❹ Remove cauliflower mixture from oven. Stir in ketchup mixture. Bake at 425° for an additional 20 minutes or until cauliflower is tender, stirring after 10 minutes. Yield: 9 servings (serving size: about ⅓ cup).

CALORIES 67 (20% from fat); FAT 1.5g (sat 0.1g, mono 0.8g, poly 0.5g); PROTEIN 3g; CARB 12.9g; FIBER 3.4g; CHOL 0mg; IRON 1.2mg; SODIUM 311mg; CALC 43mg

Spicy Stir-Fried Mushroom Bruschetta

A component of some curry powders, fenugreek adds an earthy, subtly bitter essence to Indian dishes. Omit if you can't find it. Even though the jalapeños are seeded in this appetizer, the dried chiles and ground red pepper deliver plenty of spicy heat. This dish is inspired by flavors from the northern mountainous region of India (Kashmir), whose people brought their love of mushrooms with them when they settled in Delhi. Garnish with fresh cilantro leaves.

1 tablespoon canola oil
½ teaspoon cumin seeds
1 whole dried red chile
1½ teaspoons grated peeled fresh ginger
1 cup finely chopped red onion
2 tablespoons dried fenugreek leaves (*kasoori methi*)
¼ teaspoon salt
1 minced seeded jalapeño pepper
1½ teaspoons ground coriander
⅛ teaspoon ground red pepper
2 garlic cloves, minced
2 cups quartered mushrooms
1 cup (½-inch) cubed tomato
7 tablespoons no-salt-added tomato sauce
3 tablespoons chopped fresh cilantro, divided
⅛ teaspoon Garam Masala (page 99)
8 (1-ounce) slices country bread, toasted

① Heat first 3 ingredients in a large skillet over medium-high heat; sauté 1 minute or until cumin begins to darken. Add ginger to pan; sauté 30 seconds. Add onion and fenugreek; sauté 2 minutes or until onion is tender. Add salt and jalapeño; sauté 2 minutes or until onion softens and begins to brown. Add coriander, pepper, and garlic; sauté 30 seconds. Add mushrooms; cook 7 minutes or until liquid evaporates. Stir in tomato, tomato sauce, 2 tablespoons cilantro, and Garam Masala; bring to a simmer. Cook 15 minutes or until sauce thickens. Sprinkle with the remaining 1 tablespoon cilantro. Serve with country bread. Yield: 8 servings (serving size: 3½ tablespoons mushroom mixture and 1 bread slice).

CALORIES 110 (18% from fat); FAT 2.2g (sat 0.2g, mono 1.1g, poly 0.7g); PROTEIN 4.2g; CARB 19.1g; FIBER 1.9g; CHOL 0mg; IRON 1.8mg; SODIUM 238mg; CALC 23mg

QUICK & EASY
Vegetable Burgers

These tender vegetable patties are meant to be soft. Prepare through step two the day before since the mixture is easier to work with once its has been refrigerated overnight and the flavors have had time to marry. Amchur (or amchoor) powder is a tart green mango-based seasoning. Omit if you can't find it. Serve with Fiery Tomato Chutney (at right).

1 cup canned chickpeas (garbanzo beans), rinsed and drained
1 cup chopped fresh cilantro
½ cup coarsely chopped carrot
1¼ teaspoons kosher salt
1 teaspoon Garam Masala (page 99)
1 teaspoon amchur powder
½ teaspoon freshly ground black pepper
¼ teaspoon ground red pepper
1 jalapeño, seeded and quartered
2 pounds peeled red potatoes, cut into 2-inch pieces
¼ cup coarsely chopped red onion
1 cup dry breadcrumbs
2 tablespoons extravirgin olive oil, divided
2⅔ cups spinach
4 (6-inch) whole-grain pitas, cut in half
8 red onion slices

① Combine first 9 ingredients in a food processor; process until finely chopped.
② Place potatoes in a large saucepan; cover with water. Bring to a boil; cook 13 minutes. Add onion, and cook 2 minutes or until potatoes are tender. Drain; cool 10 minutes. Place potato mixture in a large bowl; mash with a potato masher or fork. Stir in chickpea mixture and breadcrumbs; cover and chill 8 hours or overnight.
③ Divide potato mixture into 8 equal portions, shaping each portion into a ½-inch-thick patty (about ⅔ cup mixture). Heat 1 tablespoon oil in a large skillet over medium heat. Add 4 patties to pan; cook 5 minutes on each side or until browned and heated through. Repeat procedure with remaining 1 tablespoon oil and remaining 4 patties. Place ⅓ cup spinach and 1 patty in each pita half. Top each serving with 1 onion slice. Yield: 8 servings (serving size: 1 stuffed pita half).

CALORIES 292 (18% from fat); FAT 5.7g (sat 0.8g, mono 2.9g, poly 1.3g); PROTEIN 9.7g; CARB 51.8g; FIBER 7.1g; CHOL 0mg; IRON 3.1mg; SODIUM 675mg; CALC 58mg

MAKE AHEAD • FREEZABLE
Fiery Tomato Chutney

Chutneys can range from thick to chunky, hot to mild, and typically contain fruit cooked with a variety of spices. This piquant condiment is great as a sandwich spread or as a flavor booster for stir-fried vegetables. Store in the refrigerator for up to one week, or freeze leftovers for up to two months.

1 tablespoon canola oil
1 teaspoon black mustard seeds
1 teaspoon cumin seeds
4 small dried red chiles
¼ teaspoon ground turmeric
4 cups chopped cored tomatoes
1 tablespoon sugar
2 tablespoons tomato paste
¾ teaspoon kosher salt
¼ teaspoon curry powder
⅛ teaspoon ground red pepper

① Heat oil in a saucepan over medium-high heat. Add mustard seeds, cumin seeds, and chiles to pan; cook 1 minute. Stir in turmeric; cook 30 seconds. Add tomatoes and remaining ingredients;

bring to a boil. Reduce heat, and simmer until reduced to 2 cups (about 50 minutes). Spoon into a bowl; cover and chill. Yield: 2 cups (serving size: 2 tablespoons).

CALORIES 36 (38% from fat); FAT 1.5g (sat 0.1g, mono 0.6g, poly 0.5g); PROTEIN 1.2g; CARB 5.8g; FIBER 1.8g; CHOL 0mg; IRON 0.8mg; SODIUM 109mg; CALC 12mg

Roasted Potatoes with North Indian Spices

Potatoes are a staple throughout India. While Northern Indian cuisine is not known for hot and spicy dishes (unlike the southern part of the country), you can finish these deliciously zesty potatoes with ¼ teaspoon ground red pepper for extra spiciness, if you like.

3½ tablespoons canola oil, divided
3 pounds small red potatoes, halved (about 8 cups)
1¾ teaspoons black mustard seeds
6 dried red chiles
2 teaspoons minced peeled fresh ginger
3 garlic cloves, minced
½ jalapeño, seeded and minced
1½ teaspoons kosher salt
1 teaspoon ground turmeric
½ teaspoon Garam Masala (at right)
Cooking spray
½ cup chopped fresh cilantro
½ cup chopped fresh mint
1 tablespoon fresh lime juice
8 lime wedges

1 Preheat oven to 400°.
2 Combine 1 tablespoon oil and potatoes, tossing to coat. Set aside.
3 Heat remaining 2½ tablespoons oil, mustard seeds, and chiles in a large skillet over medium-high heat; cook 1½ minutes or until seeds begin to pop. Reduce heat to medium-low. Add ginger, garlic, and jalapeño to pan; cook 1 minute, stirring constantly. Stir in salt, turmeric, and Garam Masala; cook 1 minute, stirring constantly. Add spice mixture to potatoes, tossing to coat. Arrange potato

mixture in a single layer in a 13 x 9-inch baking dish coated with cooking spray.
4 Bake at 400° for 40 minutes or until potatoes are tender and browned, stirring every 10 minutes. Stir in cilantro, mint, and juice. Serve with lime wedges. Yield: 8 servings (serving size: about ¾ cup potato mixture and 1 lime wedge).

CALORIES 241 (28% from fat); FAT 7.4g (sat 0.6g, mono 3.7g, poly 2.4g); PROTEIN 5.9g; CARB 38.9g; FIBER 5.5g; CHOL 0mg; IRON 3.2mg; SODIUM 370mg; CALC 19mg

Garam Masala

This North Indian spice mixture can be stored in an airtight container for up to six months. Spicy heat from black pepper, cinnamon, and chile is underscored by smoky cumin, fragrant cardamom, warm cloves, and nutmeg. This blend boosts flavor when stirred into a finished dish or mellows while cooking.

⅓ cup coriander seeds
¼ cup cumin seeds
1 tablespoon green cardamom pods
1 tablespoon black peppercorns
2 teaspoons whole cloves
2 bay leaves
1 (1-inch) cinnamon stick, broken
1 dried red chile
¼ teaspoon grated whole nutmeg
⅛ teaspoon ground mace

1 Combine first 8 ingredients in a medium skillet over medium-high heat; cook 2½ minutes or until cumin seeds begin to brown, stirring constantly. Combine cumin seed mixture, nutmeg, and mace in a spice or coffee grinder; process until finely ground. Yield: ¾ cup (serving size: 1 teaspoon).

CALORIES 7 (51% from fat); FAT 0.4g (sat 0g, mono 0.2g, poly 0.1g); PROTEIN 0.3g; CARB 1.2g; FIBER 0.6g; CHOL 0mg; IRON 0.7mg; SODIUM 2mg; CALC 14mg

Spicy Cabbage Slaw with Peanuts

Find *chaat masala* in Indian grocery stores.

½ teaspoon ground cumin
1½ tablespoons sugar
1 tablespoon fresh lime juice
1½ teaspoons white wine vinegar
1 teaspoon kosher salt
1 teaspoon grated peeled fresh ginger
¾ teaspoon chaat masala
¼ teaspoon Garam Masala (at left)
¼ teaspoon black pepper
Dash of ground red pepper
¾ cup thinly sliced green onions
½ cup finely chopped fresh cilantro
1 tablespoon minced fresh mint
1 minced seeded serrano chile
1 pint grape tomatoes, halved
4 cups thinly sliced green cabbage
4 cups thinly sliced red cabbage
⅓ cup chopped dry-roasted peanuts

1 Heat cumin in a small skillet over medium heat; cook 2 minutes or until dark golden, stirring constantly. Combine cumin and next 9 ingredients in a large bowl. Add onions and next 4 ingredients; toss to combine. Add cabbages, tossing gently to combine. Cover and chill 4 hours. Sprinkle with peanuts. Yield: 8 servings (serving size: 1¼ cups salad and 2 teaspoons peanuts).

CALORIES 78 (33% from fat); FAT 2.9g (sat 0.4g, mono 1.3g, poly 0.9g); PROTEIN 3g; CARB 11.1g; FIBER 3g; CHOL 0mg; IRON 1mg; SODIUM 300mg; CALC 54mg

Sauté Away

Use this quick and easy technique with tender seasonal produce to create speedy meals.

SAUTÉING IS A BASIC cooking technique essential to many recipes. Soups and stews, for example, almost always begin with sautéed aromatics; sautéing browns the vegetables, which enhances the flavor of the soup. But it's also used to fully cook whole dishes—and do so quickly. Sautéed chicken breasts with a simple pan sauce, for example, may be ready in as little as 20 minutes, which is helpful on busy weeknights.

Because it cooks food fast, sautéing keeps the flavors vivid. This is especially welcome with seasonal ingredients such as tender asparagus. Just as hearty winter root vegetables benefit from long, slow braising, the delicate produce of spring favors a light touch. With a few tips, this technique is easy to master.

Patatas Bravas

Spanish for "fierce potatoes," *patatas bravas* are a common tapas offering of crisp potato cubes served with a spicy sauce. If you like fiery food, use ¼ to ½ teaspoon ground red pepper in the sauce. For the crispest potatoes, stir only every 2 or 3 minutes; frequent stirring can damage them.

POTATOES:

- 4 cups (1-inch) cubed peeled baking potato (about 1½ pounds)
- 1 tablespoon butter
- 2 teaspoons olive oil
- ¼ teaspoon salt
- ⅛ teaspoon ground red pepper
- 2 garlic cloves, minced

SAUCE:

- 1 teaspoon olive oil
- 1 cup diced onion
- 1 cup diced green bell pepper
- ¼ teaspoon salt
- ⅛ teaspoon ground red pepper
- 1 (8-ounce) can tomato sauce
- Parsley sprigs (optional)

❶ To prepare potatoes, place potato in a medium saucepan; cover with water. Bring to a boil. Cook 1 minute or until crisp-tender; drain well.

❷ Heat a large nonstick skillet over medium-high heat. Add butter and 2 teaspoons oil to pan, swirling to coat bottom of pan; heat 30 seconds or until foam subsides. Add potato to pan; sauté 8 minutes or until browned, stirring twice. Stir in ¼ teaspoon salt, ⅛ teaspoon red pepper, and garlic; sauté 1 minute. Remove potato mixture from pan; keep warm.

❸ To prepare sauce, heat pan over medium-high heat. Add 1 teaspoon oil to pan, swirling to coat; heat 15 seconds. Add onion and bell pepper; sauté 5 minutes or until tender, stirring frequently. Add ¼ teaspoon salt, ⅛ teaspoon red pepper, and tomato sauce; bring to a simmer. Cook 1 minute. Pour onion mixture into a blender. Remove center piece of blender lid (to allow steam to escape); secure blender lid on blender. Place a clean towel over opening in blender lid (to avoid splatters). Blend until smooth. Serve sauce with potato mixture. Garnish with parsley sprigs, if desired. Yield: 6 servings (⅔ cup potato mixture and ¼ cup sauce).

CALORIES 153 (26% from fat); FAT 4.4g (sat 1.6g, mono 2.2g, poly 0.4g); PROTEIN 3.5g; CARB 26.5g; FIBER 2.9g; CHOL 5mg; IRON 1.5mg; SODIUM 416mg; CALC 31mg

Beef Tenderloin Steaks with Shiitake Mushroom Sauce

The steaks are sautéed in cooking spray to create a crust, while the mushrooms are sautéed in butter for flavor. Serve with mashed potatoes and Broccolini.

- 4 (4-ounce) beef tenderloin steaks, trimmed (1 inch thick)
- ½ teaspoon salt, divided
- ¼ teaspoon freshly ground black pepper, divided
- Cooking spray
- 2 teaspoons butter
- 2 garlic cloves, minced
- 4 cups thinly sliced shiitake mushroom caps (about 8 ounces)
- ½ teaspoon chopped fresh thyme
- 2 tablespoons balsamic vinegar
- 1 tablespoon water
- 1 teaspoon low-sodium soy sauce
- 1 tablespoon fresh thyme leaves

❶ Sprinkle steaks with ¼ teaspoon salt and ⅛ teaspoon pepper. Heat a large nonstick skillet over medium-high heat. Coat pan with cooking spray. Add steaks to pan; sauté 3 minutes on each side or until desired degree of doneness. Transfer steaks to a serving platter.

❷ Heat pan over medium-high heat. Add butter to pan, swirling to coat; cook 15 seconds or until foam subsides. Add garlic to pan; sauté 30 seconds, stirring constantly. Add mushrooms, chopped thyme, remaining ¼ teaspoon salt, and remaining ⅛ teaspoon pepper to pan; sauté 3 minutes or until mushrooms are tender, stirring frequently. Stir in vinegar, 1 tablespoon water, and soy sauce; cook 1 minute or until liquid almost evaporates. Spoon mushroom mixture over steaks. Sprinkle with thyme leaves. Yield: 4 servings (serving size: 1 steak, ¼ cup mushroom mixture, and ¾ teaspoon thyme leaves).

CALORIES 326 (31% from fat); FAT 11.2g (sat 4.7g, mono 4.2g, poly 0.5g); PROTEIN 34.9g; CARB 22.9g; FIBER 3.2g; CHOL 95mg; IRON 2.9mg; SODIUM 428mg; CALC 34mg

All About Sautéing

Sautéing, Defined

To sauté is to cook food quickly in a minimal amount of fat over relatively high heat. The word comes from the French verb *sauter*, which means "to jump," and describes not only how food reacts when placed in a hot pan but also the method of tossing the food in the pan. The term also refers to cooking tender cuts of meat in a small amount of fat over moderately high heat without frequent stirring—just flipping it over when one side is browned.

What Sautéing Does

The browning achieved by sautéing lends richness to meats and produce. And because the food is cooked quickly, the integrity of the flavor and texture remains intact; asparagus, for example, retains its slightly grassy punch, as well as a pleasing crisp-tender bite.

Best Foods to Sauté

Whether it's meat or vegetables, time in the pan is brief, so the food should be naturally tender. Cuts such as beef tenderloin, fish fillets, and chicken breasts are good candidates; tougher cuts like brisket or pork shoulder are better for long cooking over low heat. The same principle holds for produce. Asparagus tips will be more successfully sautéed than beets. Many other tender vegetables, including baby artichokes, sugar snap peas, mushrooms, and bell peppers, lend themselves to this technique. Denser, tougher vegetables can be sautéed—they just may need to be blanched (briefly cooked in boiling water) first to get a head start on cooking.

Equipment

Use either a skillet (a wide pan with sloped sides) or sauté pan (a wide pan with straight sides) for this technique. Both have a large surface area, so food is less likely to become overcrowded.

Choose a pan with a dense bottom that evenly distributes heat. Nonstick, anodized aluminum, and stainless steel options work well.

Size Matters

Cutting food to a uniform thickness and size ensures that it will cook evenly. Vegetables should be bite-sized, meat no larger than portion-sized. Meat that is too thick or vegetables that are too large run the risk of burning or forming a tough, overly browned outer crust in the time that it takes to completely cook them.

Heat the Pan

Be sure to warm the pan over medium-high heat for a few minutes. It needs to be quite hot in order to cook the food properly. If the heat is too low, the food will end up releasing liquid and steaming rather than sautéing.

Add Fat

Fats such as butter, oil, or bacon fat are used to coat the food and prevent it from sticking to the pan, aid in browning, and add flavor. Once the pan is hot, add the fat, and swirl to coat the bottom of the pan. (Heating the fat with the pan may cause food to stick.) Heat the fat for 10 to 30 seconds—until oil shimmers or butter's foam subsides—and then add the food.

In general, use fats that have a high smoke point—peanut oil, regular olive oil, canola oil, or rendered pork fat. Once the fat begins to smoke, the flavor changes and can affect the food's taste. Butter adds great flavor, but it may burn, so you will either need to clarify it to remove the milk solids (which are prone to burning) or combine it with oil so there's less chance of burning. Oils that have low smoke points, like extravirgin olive oil and many nut and infused oils, lose their char-

acteristic taste when heated to sautéing's high temperatures. It's OK to sauté with these oils—just remember that their flavor will not be as pungent.

Don't Overcrowd

It's crucial that only one layer of food cooks in the pan at a time. When sautéing cuts of meat, there should be at least a half-inch between pieces. Food releases steam when cooking. If that steam doesn't have enough room to escape, it stays in the pan, and the food ends up steaming rather than sautéing, and won't brown.

Toss and Turn

When sautéing vegetables and bite-sized pieces of meat, stir frequently (but not constantly) to promote even browning and cooking. Dense vegetables such as cubed potatoes, though, should be stirred once every few minutes so that they don't fall apart as they grow tender. Portion-sized cuts of meat (chicken breasts, steaks, or pork medallions, for example) should only be turned once so they have enough time to form a nice crust, which will also keep the meat from sticking to the pan.

Stir-Fry vs. Sauté

Stir-frying and sautéing are techniques that share some similarities. Both methods cook food quickly in a small amount of fat. Stir-frying calls for intensely high heat and constant stirring. Sautéing involves only moderately high heat, and the food is not in continuous motion.

The Bottom Line

These are the three most important things to know about sautéing.
1 Heat the pan (and then the fat) adequately before adding food.
2 Don't overcrowd the pan.
3 Stir frequently but not constantly.

QUICK & EASY

Sautéed Chard with Pancetta

The pancetta (Italian unsmoked bacon) renders a small amount of fat, which is then used to sauté the chard. Serve this robust side with steaks, roast chicken, or roast pork.

- 2 bunches Swiss chard (about ¾ pound)
- 1 ounce pancetta, diced (about ¼ cup)
- 2 garlic cloves, minced
- ¼ teaspoon crushed red pepper
- 2 tablespoons grated fresh Parmigiano-Reggiano cheese

1 Rinse and drain chard; pat dry with paper towels. Trim stalks from chard leaves, reserving stalks and leaves. Coarsely chop stalks to equal 1 cup; discard remaining stalks. Chop leaves.
2 Heat a large nonstick skillet over medium-high heat. Add pancetta to pan; sauté 2 minutes or until lightly browned, stirring frequently. Add garlic and chard stalks to pan; sauté 2 minutes or until tender, stirring frequently. Add half of chard leaves to pan; sauté 1 minute or until leaves wilt, stirring frequently. Add remaining chard leaves and pepper to pan; sauté 1 minute or until leaves wilt, stirring frequently. Sprinkle with cheese. Yield: 6 servings (serving size: ½ cup chard mixture and 1 teaspoon cheese).

CALORIES 37 (51% from fat); FAT 2.1g (sat 1g, mono 0.9g, poly 0.2g); PROTEIN 2.4g; CARB 2.6g; FIBER 1g; CHOL 5mg; IRON 1.1mg; SODIUM 224mg; CALC 49mg

QUICK & EASY

Sautéed Asparagus and Shrimp with Gremolata

Sauté the two main ingredients separately to avoid overcrowding the pan. A fresh lemon-herb topping rounds out the flavors in this entrée. You could also try this recipe with chicken and broccoli.

GREMOLATA:
- ¼ cup finely chopped fresh flat-leaf parsley
- 2 teaspoons grated lemon rind
- ⅛ teaspoon salt
- ⅛ teaspoon freshly ground black pepper
- 3 garlic cloves, minced

SHRIMP:
- 4 teaspoons olive oil, divided
- 3 cups (1½-inch) slices asparagus (about ½ pound)
- 1½ pounds peeled and deveined medium shrimp
- ⅛ teaspoon salt
- ⅛ teaspoon freshly ground black pepper

1 To prepare gremolata, combine first 5 ingredients; set aside.
2 To prepare shrimp, heat a large nonstick skillet over medium-high heat. Add 2 teaspoons oil to pan, swirling to coat; heat 20 seconds. Add asparagus to pan; sauté 3 minutes, stirring frequently. Remove asparagus from pan; keep warm.
3 Add remaining 2 teaspoons oil to pan, swirling to coat; heat 20 seconds. Add shrimp; sauté 3 minutes or until done, stirring occasionally. Add asparagus, ⅛ teaspoon salt, and ⅛ teaspoon pepper to pan; sauté 1 minute or until thoroughly heated. Sprinkle evenly with gremolata. Yield: 4 servings (serving size: 1½ cups).

CALORIES 240 (29% from fat); FAT 7.6g (sat 1.2g, mono 3.7g, poly 1.7g); PROTEIN 36.1g; CARB 5.2g; FIBER 1.6g; CHOL 259mg; IRON 5.6mg; SODIUM 403mg; CALC 115mg

MAKE AHEAD

Thai Noodle Salad with Sautéed Tofu

This colorful salad is a zesty one-dish meal. Leftovers are great chilled or at room temperature. Draining tofu under a weight expels moisture, making the sautéed tofu crisp; see page 103 for pictures of this process. For a pronounced nutty flavor, use roasted peanut oil.

TOFU:
- ¾ pound firm water-packed tofu, drained
- 2 tablespoons fresh lime juice
- 1 tablespoon low-sodium soy sauce
- 1 tablespoon chili garlic sauce (such as Lee Kum Kee)
- 1 teaspoon sugar
- 2 teaspoons grated peeled fresh ginger
- ½ teaspoon crushed red pepper
- 2 garlic cloves, minced
- 1 tablespoon peanut oil

NOODLES:
- ¾ pound uncooked rice vermicelli

DRESSING:
- ¼ cup fresh lime juice
- 3 tablespoons chili garlic sauce (such as Lee Kum Kee)
- 2 tablespoons low-sodium soy sauce
- 2 tablespoons peanut oil
- 1 tablespoon Thai fish sauce (such as Three Crabs)
- 2 teaspoons sugar
- 2 teaspoons grated peeled fresh ginger
- ¼ teaspoon salt
- ¼ teaspoon crushed red pepper

REMAINING INGREDIENTS:

- 2 cups thinly sliced romaine lettuce
- 1 cup shredded carrot
- ½ cup chopped fresh cilantro
- ¼ teaspoon salt

1 To prepare tofu, cut tofu into ³/₄-inch-thick slices. Arrange tofu slices in a single layer on several layers of paper towels. Top with several more layers of paper towels; top with a cast-iron skillet or other heavy pan. Let stand 30 minutes. Remove tofu from paper towels; cut into ³/₄-inch cubes. Combine tofu, 2 tablespoons juice, and next 6 ingredients in a zip-top plastic bag. Seal and marinate at room temperature 2 hours, turning bag occasionally.

2 Heat a large nonstick skillet over medium-high heat. Add 1 tablespoon oil to pan, swirling to coat; heat 30 seconds. Remove tofu from bag; discard marinade. Add tofu to pan; sauté 5 minutes or until crisp, carefully turning to brown all sides. Remove from heat.

3 To prepare noodles, while tofu marinates, place vermicelli in a large bowl. Cover with boiling water. Let stand 20 minutes or until tender. Drain and rinse with cold water; drain well. Set noodles aside.

4 To prepare dressing, combine ¼ cup juice and next 8 ingredients, stirring with a whisk.

5 Combine vermicelli, lettuce, and remaining ingredients in a large bowl. Add dressing; toss well to combine. Top with tofu. Yield: 6 servings (serving size: about 2 cups).

CALORIES 336 (26% from fat); FAT 9.8g (sat 1.5g, mono 5g, poly 2.8g); PROTEIN 10.3g; CARB 57.2g; FIBER 2.4g; CHOL 0mg; IRON 2.5mg; SODIUM 794mg; CALC 132mg

How to Press Tofu

Tofu is the Japanese word for soybean curd. It's made from soymilk, similar to the way cheddar cheese is made from cow's milk, for example, then shaped into spongelike blocks. Tofu comes in five varieties—silken, soft, medium, firm, and extrafirm—and most are packaged in water to keep the product fresh. It's best to remove some of that water from the medium to extrafirm varieties before sautéing or stir-frying. That way, the tofu will brown more easily and won't release excess water into the pan.

1 Remove tofu from package, and cut into slices for easier draining.

2 Lay each slice flat on a few absorbent heavy-duty paper towels.

3 Top with another layer of towels; place a heavy pan on top.

4 Let sit for 30 minutes, pressing occasionally to release excess water.

Sautéing is a quick technique that helps you get dinner on the table fast.

Sautéed Baby Squash with Basil and Feta

This simple preparation yields delicious results in a versatile side dish. If baby pattypan squash are not available, substitute four cups of thinly sliced zucchini or yellow squash.

- 1 tablespoon olive oil
- 4 cups baby pattypan squash, halved (about 18 ounces)
- 2 cups sliced leek (about 2)
- ½ teaspoon salt
- ⅛ teaspoon freshly ground black pepper
- 3 tablespoons crumbled reduced-fat feta cheese
- 2 tablespoons finely chopped fresh basil

❶ Heat a large nonstick skillet over medium-high heat. Add oil to pan, swirling to coat; heat 20 seconds. Add squash and leek to pan; sauté 5 minutes or until tender, stirring frequently. Stir in salt and pepper. Transfer squash mixture to a serving platter. Sprinkle with cheese and basil. Yield: 6 servings (serving size: ⅔ cup).

CALORIES 61 (43% from fat); FAT 2.9g (sat 0.6g, mono 1.6g, poly 0.3g); PROTEIN 2.3g; CARB 7.5g; FIBER 1.7g; CHOL 1mg; IRON 0.7mg; SODIUM 253mg; CALC 30mg

Baby Artichoke Sauté with Basil-Asiago Breadcrumbs

Because they are small and tender, baby artichokes are great sauté candidates. A combination of butter and oil offers layered flavor with less risk of the butter burning. Panko, however, is sautéed in butter alone because the breadcrumbs immediately soak up the fat, which makes burning less likely. If you don't have panko, use fresh breadcrumbs made from leftover bread, and sauté an additional minute or two.

- 1½ teaspoons butter, divided
- ¼ cup panko (Japanese breadcrumbs)
- 1 garlic clove, minced
- 2 tablespoons grated fresh Asiago cheese
- 1 tablespoon finely chopped fresh basil
- ⅛ teaspoon freshly ground black pepper
- 2 tablespoons reduced-fat mayonnaise
- 2 tablespoons fat-free sour cream
- 2 teaspoons fresh lemon juice
- 6 cups water
- 1 tablespoon fresh lemon juice
- 1½ pounds baby artichokes (about 12)
- 1½ teaspoons olive oil
- ⅛ teaspoon salt
- Lemon wedges (optional)

❶ Heat a large nonstick skillet over medium-high heat. Add 1 teaspoon butter to pan, swirling to coat; heat 10 seconds or until foam subsides. Add panko and garlic to pan; sauté 1 minute or until panko is lightly browned, stirring frequently. Place panko mixture in a small bowl; cool slightly. Stir in cheese, basil, and pepper.

❷ Combine mayonnaise, sour cream, and 2 teaspoons juice; set aside.

❸ Combine 6 cups water and 1 tablespoon juice. Working with 1 artichoke at a time, cut off stem of artichoke to within 1 inch of base; peel stem. Remove bottom leaves and tough outer leaves from artichoke, leaving tender heart and bottom. Trim about 1 inch from top of artichoke. Cut artichoke in quarters. Place artichoke quarters in lemon water. Repeat procedure with remaining artichokes.

❹ Heat pan over medium-high heat. Drain artichokes, and pat dry. Add remaining ½ teaspoon butter and oil to pan, swirling to coat bottom of pan; heat 15 seconds or until foam subsides. Add artichokes to pan; sauté 7 minutes or until tender, stirring frequently. Stir in salt. Sprinkle panko mixture over artichokes; toss gently to combine. Serve with sauce and lemon wedges, if desired. Yield: 4 servings (serving size: ½ cup artichoke mixture and 1 tablespoon sauce).

CALORIES 153 (32% from fat); FAT 5.4g (sat 1.8g, mono 1.9g, poly 0.9g); PROTEIN 7.6g; CARB 23.3g; FIBER 9.4g; CHOL 8mg; IRON 2.2mg; SODIUM 335mg; CALC 126mg

Browned Butter Bananas with Orange-Brandy Sauce

Browned butter gives the dessert a rich, caramelized, almost nutty flavor. Choose firm bananas with no spots; they'll hold up better when cooked.

- 4 bananas
- 1½ tablespoons butter
- 3 tablespoons brown sugar, divided
- 2 tablespoons thawed orange juice concentrate
- 1 tablespoon brandy
- 1 tablespoon water
- ⅛ teaspoon salt
- 2 cups vanilla low-fat ice cream
- Mint sprigs (optional)

❶ Peel and cut bananas in half lengthwise. Cut each half crosswise into 2 pieces.

❷ Heat a large nonstick skillet over medium-high heat. Add butter to pan, swirling to coat. Cook butter 1 minute or until lightly browned. Add bananas; sauté 1 minute or until browned and tender, turning once. Add 1 tablespoon sugar, stirring gently until sugar dissolves. Place bananas in a medium bowl.

❸ Combine remaining 2 tablespoons sugar, juice concentrate, and next 3 ingredients in pan. Bring to a simmer; cook 1 minute. Drizzle sauce over bananas. Serve immediately over ice cream. Garnish with mint sprigs, if desired. Yield: 4 servings (serving size: 4 banana pieces, 1 tablespoon sauce, and ½ cup ice cream).

CALORIES 293 (18% from fat); FAT 5.8g (sat 3.7g, mono 1.1g, poly 0.2g); PROTEIN 4.2g; CARB 62.1g; FIBER 3g; CHOL 16mg; IRON 0.6mg; SODIUM 164mg; CALC 112mg

On A Roll

Lidia Bastianich shows how to make pasta the way she first learned—no special equipment needed.

IT ISN'T DIFFICULT TO MAKE FRESH PASTA. In fact, Lidia Bastianich often makes it at home, a process that requires no special equipment. She kneads the dough by hand to make it smooth like satin, resilient like silk, and then rolls it out with a wooden pin. The process takes about half an hour (not counting the time the dough needs to rest). The experience of this process is very satisfying, and the final result is extraordinarily sensuous and delicious.

Make the Dough

Measure the flour carefully by lightly spooning it into dry measuring cups, then leveling with a knife. If you are making a mixed-flour pasta, whisk flours together to blend them.

To make the dough, combine all dry ingredients in the food processor. Combine the wet ingredients separately, stirring well with a whisk. Slowly pour the wet ingredients through the food chute with the motor running. Process just until the dough begins to form a ball.

Turn the dough out onto a lightly floured work surface and knead a few minutes, until the dough is smooth and shiny on the outside, soft throughout (no lumps), and stretchy.

Form the dough into a disk, wrap it tightly in plastic wrap, and let it rest at room temperature 30 minutes. You can store it tightly wrapped with plastic wrap in the refrigerator for one day, or freeze it for up to six weeks. Defrost frozen dough in the refrigerator, and let it stand at room temperature about 15 minutes before rolling. Previously frozen dough will need a bit more flour to keep the dough from sticking to the rolling pin.

Roll the Dough

Try rolling your pasta by hand on a wooden table or board with a wooden rolling pin. It is a satisfying skill to master and a speedy way to roll out pasta in large pieces. Most important, you'll get pasta with a quality that a stainless steel machine can't produce. When you roll on a wooden board, with a wooden pin, the sheet of pasta, and any shapes you cut, are imprinted with the irregular textures of the wood surfaces.

This roughness, though not apparent to the eye, gives the pasta a more pleasing texture in the mouth and better ability to carry sauce.

Bring the dough to room temperature for rolling. Cut it into equal pieces, and work with one piece at a time, keeping the others covered so they don't dry out.

Have flour close at hand for sprinkling when needed.

Lightly flour the work surface and rolling pin. Press the first piece of dough flat, and begin rolling it into a rectangle. Working from the center of the dough, roll up and down, then left and right. Occasionally flip the dough over and lightly dust the surface with flour, if necessary. Use just enough to prevent the dough from sticking—too much flour makes it difficult to roll. Periodically turn the dough 90 degrees. If the dough springs back as you roll it, cover and let it rest 10 to 15 minutes. Start rolling another piece of dough, and return to the first one once it has rested. Separate resting pasta sheets with kitchen towels, waiting at least 15 minutes before cutting them.

Master Steps for Making Homemade Pasta

Making homemade pasta is simple. Most doughs start with three basic steps.

Combine any dry ingredients in a food processor, and slowly add wet ingredients through the food chute with the motor running.

Turn the dough out onto a lightly floured work surface; knead it until it's satiny smooth, stretchy, and shiny.

Flatten each portion of dough into a narrow rectangle before rolling it out. As you roll, pull one short end of dough toward you to help lengthen and flatten the pasta sheet.

Makaruni Pasta with Morel Mushroom Sauce

"I refer to the dough for this rustic hand-shaped pasta as 'Rich Man's Golden Pasta,' because in Italy it's a luxury to use precious egg yolks to moisten and enrich pasta dough. *Makaruni*, common in my birthplace of Istria, is a pasta my grandmother used to make when there was no time to roll, cut, and shape other pastas. Use this rich dough to prepare pappardelle when time allows."

PASTA:

- 2 cups all-purpose flour (about 9 ounces)
- Dash of salt
- 6 tablespoons water
- 1½ tablespoons extravirgin olive oil
- 5 large egg yolks, lightly beaten
- 6 quarts water

SAUCE:

- 2¼ cups fat-free, less-sodium chicken broth
- 2 ounces dried morel mushrooms
- 1½ teaspoons olive oil
- 1 cup thinly sliced onion
- 2 garlic cloves, minced
- 1 teaspoon kosher salt
- 2 teaspoons finely chopped fresh thyme
- ½ teaspoon freshly ground black pepper
- 1½ pounds cremini mushrooms, sliced
- ¼ cup no-salt-added tomato paste
- 2 tablespoons chopped fresh flat-leaf parsley
- 1 tablespoon truffle oil
- ¼ cup (1 ounce) grated fresh Parmigiano-Reggiano cheese

1 To prepare pasta, lightly spoon flour into dry measuring cups; level with a knife. Combine flour and dash of salt in a food processor. Combine 6 tablespoons water, 1½ tablespoons extravirgin olive oil, and egg yolks in a bowl, stirring well with a whisk. (A) With processor on, slowly pour egg mixture through food chute, processing just until dough forms a ball. (B) Turn dough out onto a lightly floured surface; knead lightly 5 times. Shape dough into a disk. Dust dough lightly with flour; wrap in plastic wrap. Let stand 30 minutes.

2 Pat dough into a 3 x 8–inch rectangle 1-inch thick. Divide dough into 8 equal portions. Working with 1 portion at a time (cover remaining dough to prevent drying), divide dough portion into 14 equal pieces. (C) Roll each piece between your palms back and forth, into a strand about 2 inches long. Place strands on a well-floured jelly-roll pan. Repeat procedure with remaining dough portions to form 112 strands.

3 Bring 6 quarts water to a boil in a large Dutch oven. (D) Place pasta in a sieve, and shake off excess flour. Add pasta to pan. Cook 1½ minutes or until done; drain.

4 To prepare sauce, bring broth to a boil in a medium saucepan. Add morel mushrooms to pan. Remove from heat. Cover and let stand 40 minutes. Drain morel mushrooms through a colander over a bowl, reserving morel mushrooms and liquid. Halve morel mushrooms lengthwise; set aside.

5 Heat 1½ teaspoons olive oil in a large nonstick skillet over medium-high heat. Add onion to pan, and sauté 3 minutes, stirring frequently. Clear a spot in bottom of pan. Add garlic to clear spot in pan, and sauté 30 seconds. Add salt, thyme, and pepper; sauté 30 seconds, stirring frequently. Add reserved morel mushrooms and cremini mushrooms to pan. Cover, reduce heat, and cook 4 minutes. Uncover, increase heat to medium-high, and cook 2 minutes or until liquid almost evaporates, stirring frequently. Clear a spot in bottom of pan. Add tomato paste to clear spot; cook 1 minute. Stir tomato paste into mushroom mixture.

6 Stir in 1 cup reserved mushroom liquid. Cook 8 minutes or until very thick, stirring occasionally. Stir in remaining mushroom liquid; cook 4 minutes or until slightly thick, stirring occasionally. Add pasta and parsley to

Master Steps

+

How to Make Makaruni

sauce mixture; toss well. Stir in truffle oil. Serve with cheese. Yield: 4 servings (serving size: 1²/₃ cups pasta mixture and 1 tablespoon cheese).

CALORIES 525 (31% from fat); FAT 18.3g (sat 4.8g, mono 10.6g, poly 2.4g); PROTEIN 22.4g; CARB 64.4g; FIBER 4.5g; CHOL 263mg; IRON 7.8mg; SODIUM 882mg; CALC 165mg

All About Pasta

How to Store Cut Pasta

If you don't plan to cook fresh pasta within a day, lay it out on trays. Lightly flour the pasta, and separate it so it doesn't stick together. Pasta that has air-dried will take a bit longer to cook.

To freeze, place the pasta on trays that fit into your freezer, and freeze just until it's set. After it's set, pack it in small air-tight plastic bags or containers. This makes it easy to portion pasta. Don't defrost before you cook it; simply drop the frozen pieces into boiling water. When you cook frozen pasta, always use an additional quart of water so the boiling point does not drop when the pasta is added. When the water temperature drops and it takes too long to return to a boil, the pasta will stick together in the pot.

Cook Fresh Pasta

1 You can cook fresh pasta as soon as it's shaped (or follow directions above for freezing). Shake excess flour from pasta before dropping it into the cooking water.
2 Drop the pasta into the boiling water in several batches, stirring with each addition to separate the pieces.
3 Keep the heat high while the pasta cooks, but don't cover the pot. Let the water return to a boil, stirring occasionally. Start timing when the boil resumes.
4 Cook until the pasta rises to the top; at that point many pastas are done, though some are not. Remove and taste a bit of

pasta when it surfaces. Cooking times will vary with the composition of the dough, the shape and thinness of the pasta, and the degree to which it dried before cooking.
5 Fresh pastas are not cooked to al dente like dried pastas. Instead, cook until they are tender all the way through. Taste is the best test to determine doneness. Tender white flour pastas will cook the quickest. Some mixed-flour pastas like flaxseed and potato pasta also cook quite fast. Heavier whole-grain pastas take longer.

Shape the Pasta

Makaruni is the easiest shape to master. You don't even have to roll the dough. After it rests, simply divide the dough into 8 equal portions; divide each portion into 14 equal subportions. Roll each subportion between the palms of your hands to form plump, short strands. Toss noodles onto a floured baking sheet, and roll them around in the flour so they don't stick together.

Long, flat shapes like **tagliolini, tagliatelle** (fettuccine), or **pappardelle** are the quickest to cut and cook.

Lay one pasta sheet flat, and dust it lightly with flour. Fold in the ends so they meet in the middle. (When folding dough for these shapes, make sure any surfaces that will touch are sprinkled with flour so they don't stick together.) Then fold the sheet in the middle, like closing a book; fold in half again. (You'll have a narrow

rectangle with eight layers of pasta.) Slice this rectangle crosswise into strips, which will unfold as long, flat noodles.
• For *pappardelle,* cut strips 1½ inches wide.
• For *tagliatelle,* cut strips ½ inch wide.
• For *tagliolini,* cut strips ¼ inch wide.
Now unfurl the layered noodles by shaking them open (unfold carefully if they're stuck). Sprinkle lightly with flour. Then toss them with a bit more flour so they don't stick together, and pile gently in a little nest on a floured baking sheet. Fold, slice, and unfurl the rest of the dough sheets in the same way.

Ravioli grande is traditionally about three or four inches square, and the flavor and texture of the pasta are equally as important as the filling. Be sure to cook the pasta in batches in plenty of salted water so the ravioli don't stick together. Serve them on large plates so the pasta doesn't overlap.

When you roll the dough for ravioli, make sure your pasta sheets are three inches wide and 18 inches long. Place a mound of filling 1½ inches in from the left edge of the sheet. Then continue placing filling at 3-inch intervals along the pasta sheet. Brush around the edges and between portions with water; place a second pasta sheet over the first, pressing to seal. Use a sharp long-handled knife or pastry-cutting wheel to cut dough into squares and trim edges so they're uniform. Be sure to store ravioli between layers of kitchen towels, arranging them so they don't overlap. You can freeze filled ravioli, if you like.

"The experience of making pasta by hand is very satisfying, and the final result is extraordinarily sensuous and delicious." —Lidia Matticchio Bastianich

Chickpea Ravioli with Basil Pesto and Hazelnuts

PASTA:

- 1⅓ cups plus 10 tablespoons all-purpose flour (about 9 ounces)
- ⅔ cup chickpea (garbanzo bean) flour (about 2¾ ounces)
- ½ teaspoon salt
- 5 tablespoons water
- 1 tablespoon extravirgin olive oil
- 2 large eggs, lightly beaten
- 2 cups drained and rinsed canned chickpeas (garbanzo beans)
- 2 tablespoons chopped fresh chives
- 2 tablespoons mascarpone cheese
- ½ teaspoon grated lemon rind
- ¼ teaspoon salt
- ⅛ teaspoon grated whole nutmeg
- 1 small garlic clove
- 6 quarts water
- 1 tablespoon kosher salt

PESTO:

- 2 cups packed basil leaves
- ⅔ cup fat-free, less-sodium chicken broth
- ¼ cup (1 ounce) grated fresh Parmigiano-Reggiano cheese
- ½ teaspoon kosher salt
- ½ teaspoon crushed red pepper
- 1 garlic clove, crushed
- 1½ tablespoons extravirgin olive oil

REMAINING INGREDIENT:

- 3 tablespoons chopped hazelnuts, toasted

① To prepare pasta, lightly spoon flours into dry measuring cups; level with a knife. Combine flours and ½ teaspoon salt in a food processor; process 30 seconds. Combine 5 tablespoons water, 1 tablespoon oil, and eggs, stirring well. (A) With processor running, slowly pour egg mixture through food chute, processing just until dough forms a ball. (B) Turn dough out onto a lightly floured surface; knead 6 times. Shape dough into a disk. Dust dough lightly with flour; wrap in plastic wrap. Let stand 30 minutes.

② Divide dough into 14 equal portions. Working with 2 portions at a time (cover remaining dough to prevent drying), press dough flat. (C) Roll 2 dough portions into 18 x 3–inch rectangles (turning dough over occasionally and dusting surface lightly with flour). Lay pasta sheets flat; cover.

③ Combine chickpeas and next 6 ingredients in a food processor; process until smooth. Place 1 pasta sheet on a lightly floured work surface. (D) Spoon about 1½ teaspoons chickpea mixture 1½ inches from left edge of sheet; spoon 1½ teaspoons filling mixture at 3-inch intervals along length of sheet. (E) Moisten edges and in between filling portions with water; place remaining pasta sheet on top, pressing to seal. Cut filled pasta into 6 (3 x 3–inch) ravioli, trimming edges with a sharp knife or pastry wheel. Brush excess flour from ravioli; (F) press gently to flatten tops. Place ravioli on a lightly floured baking sheet (cover with a damp towel to prevent drying). Repeat procedure with remaining dough portions and filling mixture to form 42 ravioli.

④ Bring 6 quarts water and 1 tablespoon kosher salt to a boil in a large Dutch oven. Add 6 ravioli to pan; cook 1½ minutes or until no longer translucent. Remove ravioli from water with a slotted spoon. Place ravioli on a tray, making sure they do not overlap; cover and keep warm. Repeat procedure with remaining ravioli.

⑤ To prepare pesto, combine basil and next 5 ingredients in a food processor; process until smooth. With processor on, slowly pour 1½ tablespoons oil through food chute; process until well blended. Serve with ravioli. Sprinkle with hazelnuts. Yield: 7 servings (serving size: 6 ravioli, about 1½ tablespoons pesto, and about 1 teaspoon hazelnuts).

CALORIES 510 (31% from fat); FAT 17.5g (sat 4.3g, mono 6.9g, poly 2.8g); PROTEIN 21.8g; CARB 68g; FIBER 13.7g; CHOL 64mg; IRON 6.8mg; SODIUM 635mg; CALC 175mg

Master Steps

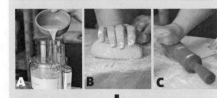

+

How to Make Ravioli

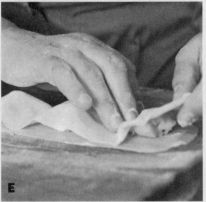

Whole Wheat Tagliolini with Fresh Cherry Tomato Sauce
(pictured on page 247)

The nutty, slightly sweet flavor of whole wheat flour is a tasty addition to a basic pasta recipe. Look for the smallest sweet tomatoes you can find for this simple sauce.

PASTA:

1 cup all-purpose flour (about 4½ ounces)
1 cup whole wheat flour (about 4¾ ounces)
¼ teaspoon salt
5 tablespoons water
2 tablespoons extravirgin olive oil
2 large eggs, lightly beaten
6 quarts water
1 tablespoon salt

SAUCE:

2 tablespoons olive oil
2 garlic cloves, minced
5 cups quartered cherry tomatoes
½ cup thinly sliced fresh basil
3 tablespoons drained capers
1 teaspoon grated lemon rind
¼ teaspoon crushed red pepper

❶ To prepare pasta, lightly spoon flours into dry measuring cups; level with a knife. Combine flours and ¼ teaspoon salt in a food processor; process 30 seconds. Combine 5 tablespoons water, extravirgin olive oil, and eggs in a bowl, stirring well with a whisk. (A) With processor running, pour egg mixture through food chute, processing just until dough forms a ball. (B) Turn dough out onto a lightly floured surface; knead 5 or 6 times. Shape dough into a disk. Dust dough lightly with flour; wrap in plastic wrap. Let stand 30 minutes.
❷ Divide dough into 3 equal portions. Working with 1 portion at a time (cover remaining dough to prevent drying), press dough into a rectangle. (C) Roll dough into a 14–inch square, dusting with flour, if necessary (turning dough over occasionally and dusting surface with flour as needed). (D) Lay dough sheet flat; fold ends so they meet in the middle. (E) Fold in half like closing a book. Fold in half again to form 8 layers of pasta. (F) Using a sharp knife, cut pasta crosswise into ¼-inch-wide noodles. Separate noodles, and dust with flour. Place noodles on a jelly-roll pan dusted with flour. Repeat procedure with remaining dough portions.
❸ Bring 6 quarts water and 1 tablespoon salt to a boil in a large Dutch oven. Place noodles in a sieve; shake off excess flour. Add noodles to pan. Cook 1½ minutes or until done; drain.
❹ To prepare sauce, heat 2 tablespoons oil in a large nonstick skillet over medium-low heat. Add garlic to pan; cook 3 minutes, stirring frequently (do not brown). Remove from heat. Stir in tomatoes and remaining ingredients. Toss with noodles. Yield: 4 servings (serving size: 1¼ cups).

CALORIES 408 (38% from fat); FAT 17.1g (sat 2.8g, mono 11.2g, poly 2.6g); PROTEIN 12.7g; CARB 53.5g; FIBER 7.3g; CHOL 93mg; IRON 4mg; SODIUM 565mg; CALC 58mg

Matchmaking

When matching pasta to sauce, there are really two considerations: the flavor of the pasta and the shape. For example, Chickpea Ravioli with Basil Pesto and Hazelnuts (page 108) gains a flavor boost from the chickpea flour in the pasta dough, and it's combined with a complex-flavored filling. A simple sauce, such as broth, butter, herbs, or herb pesto, makes a good match for the ravioli.

On the other hand, a neutral-flavored pasta, such as semolina pasta (used in Semolina Lasagna with Spicy Amatriciana, page 110), should be paired with a more assertive sauce. Otherwise, let the shape of the pasta determine the appropriate sauce. With long, flat ribbons, such as tagliolini or pappardelle, sauce them simply with cheese sauces, marinara, or long-cooking meat sauces. Sauce short pastas with chopped vegetable sauces or shredded meats.

Master Steps

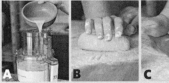

+

How to Make Tagliolini

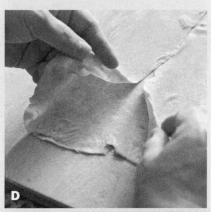

Semolina Lasagna with Spicy Amatriciana

Named for the town from which it hails (Amatrice in central Italy), this sauce typically combines pancetta with tomatoes. Imported San Marzano tomatoes were used to test this recipe. Use cured bacon to allow the tomatoes and heat to star, or add a smoky note with smoked bacon. It's best to cook pasta sheets one at a time. Then build the individual lasagna portions, and bake them all together.

PASTA:
- 1 cup all-purpose flour (about 4½ ounces)
- 1 cup semolina flour (about 6¼ ounces)
- ⅓ cup water
- 2 tablespoons extravirgin olive oil
- 2 large eggs, lightly beaten

SAUCE:
- 2 bacon slices, cut crosswise into ½-inch pieces
- 4 cups thinly sliced onion
- 1 tablespoon extravirgin olive oil
- 4 garlic cloves, crushed
- ½ cup water
- 1 (28-ounce) can diced tomatoes, undrained (such as San Marzano)
- ½ teaspoon sea salt
- ½ teaspoon crushed red pepper

REMAINING INGREDIENTS:
- 6 quarts water
- 1 tablespoon salt
- Cooking spray
- ½ cup (2 ounces) finely chopped fresh mozzarella cheese
- 6 tablespoons (1½ ounces) shredded Parmigiano-Reggiano cheese

1 To prepare pasta, lightly spoon flours into dry measuring cups; level with a knife. Combine flours in a food processor; process 30 seconds. Combine ⅓ cup water, 2 tablespoons oil, and eggs in a bowl, stirring well with a whisk. (A) With processor running, slowly pour egg mixture through food chute, processing just until dough forms a ball. (B) Turn dough out onto a lightly floured surface; knead lightly 5 times. Shape dough into a disk. Dust dough lightly with flour; wrap in plastic wrap. Let stand 30 minutes.
2 Divide dough into 6 equal portions. Working with 1 portion at a time (cover remaining dough to prevent drying), press dough portion into a flat narrow rectangle. (C) Roll dough into a 20 x 4–inch rectangle, dusting with flour, if necessary (turning dough over occasionally and dusting surface with flour). Lay pasta sheet flat; cover. Repeat procedure with remaining dough portions to form 6 sheets.
3 To prepare sauce, cook bacon in a large nonstick skillet over medium heat until crisp. Add onion, 1 tablespoon oil, and garlic to drippings in pan; sauté 5 minutes or until browned, stirring frequently. Add ½ cup water and tomatoes; bring to a boil. Stir in sea salt and pepper. Reduce heat, and simmer 20 minutes or until slightly thick, stirring occasionally.
4 Bring 6 quarts water and 1 tablespoon salt to a boil. Slowly lower 1 pasta sheet into boiling water; cook 1½ minutes or until done. Carefully remove pasta from water with a slotted spoon; lay pasta flat on a jelly-roll pan covered with a damp towel; cover. Repeat procedure with remaining pasta sheets.
5 Preheat oven to 350°.
6 (D) Place 1 pasta sheet on each of 6 individual baking dishes lightly coated with cooking spray; (E) spoon 1 tablespoon sauce over each serving. Fold noodles over sauce. Repeat procedure 5 times, ending with sauce. (F) Top each serving with 4 teaspoons mozzarella and 1 tablespoon Parmigiano-Reggiano. Cover each baking dish with foil coated with cooking spray. Bake at 350° for 10 minutes or until cheese melts and pasta is thoroughly heated. Yield: 6 servings (serving size: 1 lasagna).

CALORIES 342 (31% from fat); FAT 11.9g (sat 3.5g, mono 5.3g, poly 1.3g); PROTEIN 13.3g; CARB 44.8g; FIBER 4.9g; CHOL 63mg; IRON 2.2mg; SODIUM 819mg; CALC 173mg

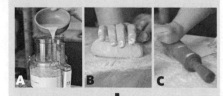

Master Steps

+

How to Make Lasagna

Multicultural Seder

Serve a Passover supper that draws on a world of culinary traditions.

THERE ARE MANY DIVERSE Passover tables. There is a richness to this ancient springtime holiday during which Jews relive the story of the Exodus, of the Israelites escaping from slavery in Egypt to freedom in the land of Canaan. They teach this story to their children through the reading of the Haggadah, passing the legend from generation to generation. But each culture celebrates with its own customs that reflect its adaptation to life in different countries all over the world. These customs enrich our understanding and appreciation of the holiday, and they point to the diversity of age-old Jewish traditions that evolved from the cultures in which they were nurtured.

GLOBAL SEDER MENU

(Serves 8)

Choose one entrée, or offer guests a selection of two or three to represent more cultures.

Chicken Soup with Matzo Balls

French Honey-Baked Chicken with Preserved Lemons
or
Brisket with Olives and Preserved Lemons
or
Persian Pomegranate-Walnut Chicken

Moroccan Tri-Color Pepper Salad

Quinoa Salad with Asparagus, Dates, and Orange

Sauvignon blanc (with chicken)

Rioja (with brisket)

Lemon-Almond Cake with Lemon Curd Filling
or
Chocolate-Pecan Macaroons

Coffee, tea

MAKE AHEAD
Chicken Soup with Matzo Balls

This is a must-have dish at many American seders. Prepare the broth a day ahead so it's easier to skim the fat. You can assemble the matzo balls up to a day ahead, too.

BROTH:

- 1 quart fat-free, less-sodium chicken broth
- 1 quart water
- 6 chicken leg quarters (about 5¼ pounds)
- 2 tablespoons chopped fresh parsley
- 1 tablespoon chopped fresh dill
- 2 celery stalks, halved lengthwise
- 2 carrots, halved lengthwise
- 1 large onion, peeled and quartered
- 1 parsnip, halved lengthwise

MATZO BALLS:

- 1½ cups matzo meal
- 1¼ cups egg substitute
- 1 tablespoon chopped fresh parsley
- 1 tablespoon chopped fresh dill
- 3 tablespoons canola oil
- ½ teaspoon salt
- ½ teaspoon ground ginger
- ⅛ teaspoon freshly grated nutmeg

REMAINING INGREDIENTS:

- 4 cups finely chopped zucchini (about 1 pound)
- ½ teaspoon salt
- ½ teaspoon freshly ground black pepper
- 1 tablespoon chopped fresh dill

1 To prepare broth, combine first 3 ingredients in a large stockpot; bring to a boil. Reduce heat, and simmer 2 hours. Add 2 tablespoons parsley and next 5 ingredients to pan; simmer 1 hour. Strain broth through a sieve into a large bowl. Reserve 2 carrot halves; thinly slice, and set aside. Discard remaining solids. Cover and chill broth overnight. Skim solidified fat from surface; discard.
2 To prepare matzo balls, combine matzo meal and next 7 ingredients in a large bowl; cover and chill 4 hours or overnight. Lightly coat hands with water. Divide matzo mixture into 16 equal portions; roll each portion into a ball. Gently drop balls into a large pot of simmering water, and cook 20 minutes or until done (matzo balls will rise to surface). Remove from water with a slotted spoon.
3 Transfer broth to a large Dutch oven. Add zucchini, ½ teaspoon salt, pepper, and reserved carrot to pan; bring to a boil. Reduce heat, and simmer until reduced to 8 cups (about 5 minutes). Add cooked matzo balls to pan; cook 2 minutes or until thoroughly heated. Remove from heat; sprinkle with 1 tablespoon dill. Yield: 8 servings (serving size: 1 cup soup and 2 matzo balls).

CALORIES 153 (38% from fat); FAT 6.5g (sat 0.7g, mono 3.5g, poly 1.8g); PROTEIN 9.1g; CARB 15.7g; FIBER 1.6g; CHOL 9mg; IRON 1.7mg; SODIUM 597mg; CALC 31mg

French Honey-Baked Chicken with Preserved Lemons

Using bone-in chicken and leaving the skin on during cooking yields succulent results.

- ½ cup honey, divided
- 3 cups dry white wine
- ⅓ cup Preserved Lemons (at right)
- 1½ teaspoons olive oil
- 2 onions, sliced and separated into rings
- Cooking spray
- 4 (8-ounce) chicken breast halves
- 4 (4-ounce) chicken thighs
- 4 (4-ounce) chicken drumsticks
- 1¼ teaspoons kosher salt
- ¾ teaspoon freshly ground black pepper
- 2½ tablespoons matzo meal

❶ Combine 6 tablespoons honey and wine in a small saucepan; bring to a boil. Cook until reduced to 1½ cups (about 20 minutes); stir in Preserved Lemons.
❷ Preheat oven to 375°.
❸ Heat oil in a large nonstick skillet over medium-high heat. Add onions to pan; sauté 5 minutes or until slightly tender. Transfer to a roasting pan coated with cooking spray.
❹ Place chicken, meaty sides up, on onions. Combine remaining 2 tablespoons honey, salt, and pepper in a small bowl. Rub honey mixture under chicken skin. Pour wine mixture over chicken.
❺ Bake at 375° for 50 minutes or until chicken is done. Remove chicken from pan, reserving wine mixture. Let chicken stand 10 minutes. Remove skin from chicken; discard.
❻ Place a zip-top plastic bag inside a 2-cup glass measure. Strain wine mixture from pan through a fine sieve into bag; discard solids. Let stand 10 minutes (fat will rise to top). Seal bag; carefully snip off 1 bottom corner of bag. Drain drippings into a small saucepan, stopping before fat layer reaches opening; discard fat. Add matzo meal to pan, stirring with a whisk. Bring to a boil; cook 1 minute or until thickened. Serve with chicken. Yield: 8 servings (serving size: 1 breast or 1 thigh and 1 drumstick and ¼ cup gravy).

CALORIES 266 (23% from fat); FAT 6.9g (sat 1.8g, mono 2.8g, poly 1.5g); PROTEIN 30.1g; CARB 20.5g; FIBER 0.4g; CHOL 91mg; IRON 1.8mg; SODIUM 511mg; CALC 26mg

Brisket with Olives and Preserved Lemons

Look for oil-cured olives in the deli section of a gourmet grocery. With Preserved Lemons, they add a pleasant briny, bitter finish to the dish.

- 1 (2½-pound) beef brisket, trimmed
- 5 garlic cloves
- 1 teaspoon kosher salt
- ½ teaspoon freshly ground black pepper
- Cooking spray
- 8 cups chopped onion (about 4 large)
- ½ cup water
- ⅓ cup diced celery
- 2 teaspoons grated peeled fresh ginger
- ½ teaspoon ground turmeric
- ⅛ teaspoon white pepper
- 1 (14.5-ounce) can stewed tomatoes, undrained
- 2 bay leaves
- ¼ cup coarsely chopped fresh parsley, divided
- ¼ cup coarsely chopped fresh cilantro, divided
- ¼ cup finely chopped Preserved Lemons (at right)
- ⅓ cup oil-cured olives, pitted and thinly sliced

❶ Preheat oven to 350°.
❷ Make 5 (½-inch-deep) slits in brisket; place 1 garlic clove in each slit. Sprinkle brisket evenly with salt and black pepper.
❸ Heat a large nonstick skillet over medium-high heat. Coat pan with cooking spray. Add brisket to pan; cook 5 minutes, browning on all sides. Remove from pan.
❹ Recoat pan with cooking spray. Add onion to pan; sauté 10 minutes or until tender. Add ½ cup water and next 6 ingredients to pan; cook 2 minutes or until thoroughly heated.
❺ Place brisket in a 13 x 9–inch baking dish coated with cooking spray; top with onion mixture. Cover dish with foil. Bake at 350° for 3 hours or until brisket is very tender. Remove brisket from dish, reserving onion mixture. Discard bay leaves. Stir 2 tablespoons parsley and 2 tablespoons cilantro into onion mixture.
❻ Cut brisket diagonally across grain into thin slices. Arrange brisket and onion mixture on a serving platter; sprinkle with remaining 2 tablespoons parsley and remaining 2 tablespoons cilantro. Serve with Preserved Lemons and olives. Yield: 8 servings (serving size: about 3 ounces brisket, ½ cup onion mixture, 1½ teaspoons Preserved Lemons, and about 2½ teaspoons olives).

CALORIES 396 (29% from fat); FAT 12.9g (sat 4.4g, mono 5.8g, poly 0.7g); PROTEIN 48.7g; CARB 20.2g; FIBER 3.4g; CHOL 113mg; IRON 4.8mg; SODIUM 749mg; CALC 88mg

MAKE AHEAD
Preserved Lemons

No other condiment adds quite the same salty-citrusy note as this Moroccan favorite. This homemade version has a clean flavor that sharpens a variety of savory dishes. A jar of these makes a great hostess gift.

- 8 lemons (about 1½ pounds)
- ½ cup kosher salt, divided
- ½ cup fresh lemon juice (about 4 lemons)
- ¼ cup water
- 2 tablespoons extravirgin olive oil

❶ Cut a small slice from 1 end of each lemon; stand lemons upright. Cut each lemon lengthwise into quarters, cutting to, but not through, opposite end. Sprinkle 1 teaspoon salt into each lemon. Place lemons in a medium bowl; sprinkle with remaining salt, juice, ¼ cup water, and oil. Let stand, partially covered, at room temperature 2 days, stirring occasionally and pressing lemons to extract juice. Cover and refrigerate 3 weeks, stirring occasionally and pressing to extract juice from lemons.

2 Rinse lemons. Remove flesh, seeds, and white pith; discard. Chop peel, and place in a small bowl. Cover and refrigerate up to 6 months. Yield: 1¹⁄₂ cups (serving size: 1 tablespoon).

CALORIES 5 (36% from fat); FAT 0.2g (sat 0g, mono 0.2g, poly 0g); PROTEIN 0.1g; CARB 1.1g; FIBER 0.6g; CHOL 0mg; IRON 0.1mg; SODIUM 377mg; CALC 8mg

Persian Pomegranate-Walnut Chicken

    1   cup walnuts, toasted
    8   (6-ounce) skinless, boneless chicken breast halves
 1³⁄₄   teaspoons kosher salt, divided
  ¹⁄₂   teaspoon freshly ground black pepper, divided
        Cooking spray
  ¹⁄₂   cup finely chopped onion
    2   garlic cloves, minced
    1   cup fat-free, less-sodium chicken broth
    1   cup pomegranate juice
    1   tablespoon tomato paste
    2   teaspoons sugar
  ¹⁄₈   teaspoon saffron threads, crushed
        Dash of ground cinnamon
        Cilantro sprigs (optional)

1 Place walnuts in a food processor; process until finely ground. Set aside.
2 Sprinkle chicken with 1 teaspoon salt and ¹⁄₄ teaspoon pepper. Heat a large nonstick skillet over medium-high heat. Coat pan with cooking spray. Add half of chicken to pan; cook 4 minutes on each side. Remove from pan. Repeat procedure with remaining chicken.
3 Recoat pan with cooking spray. Add onion and garlic to pan; sauté 3 minutes. Add remaining ³⁄₄ teaspoon salt, remaining ¹⁄₄ teaspoon pepper, ground walnuts, broth, and next 5 ingredients, stirring with a whisk until smooth. Bring to a

boil; reduce heat, and simmer until reduced to 1¹⁄₂ cups (about 15 minutes), stirring occasionally. Return chicken to pan; cover and simmer 10 minutes or until thoroughly heated. Garnish with cilantro sprigs, if desired. Yield: 8 servings (serving size: 1 chicken breast half and about 3 tablespoons sauce).

CALORIES 299 (31% from fat); FAT 10.3g (sat 1.3g, mono 1.6g, poly 6.4g); PROTEIN 41.7g; CARB 9g; FIBER 1.2g; CHOL 99mg; IRON 1.7mg; SODIUM 585mg; CALC 41mg

MAKE AHEAD
Moroccan Tri-Color Pepper Salad

You can use one or two colors of bell peppers for this make-ahead side dish, if you prefer.

    3   yellow bell peppers
    3   red bell peppers
    2   orange bell peppers
    2   tablespoons fresh lemon juice
 1¹⁄₂   tablespoons extravirgin olive oil
  ¹⁄₂   teaspoon kosher salt
  ¹⁄₄   teaspoon freshly ground black pepper
  ¹⁄₄   teaspoon ground coriander
    3   garlic cloves, minced
  ¹⁄₄   cup chopped fresh cilantro

1 Preheat broiler.
2 Cut bell peppers in half lengthwise; discard seeds and membranes. Place pepper halves, skin sides up, on a foil-lined baking sheet; flatten with hand. Broil 20 minutes or until blackened. Place in a large zip-top plastic bag; seal. Let stand 20 minutes. Peel and cut into ¹⁄₄-inch-wide strips.
3 Combine juice and next 5 ingredients in a medium bowl, stirring well with a whisk. Add peppers to bowl; toss gently to combine. Cover and chill overnight. Sprinkle with cilantro before serving. Yield: 8 servings (serving size: about ¹⁄₃ cup).

CALORIES 72 (38% from fat); FAT 3g (sat 0.4g, mono 1.9g, poly 0.4g); PROTEIN 1.9g; CARB 11.8g; FIBER 2.6g; CHOL 0mg; IRON 0.9mg; SODIUM 122mg; CALC 20mg

Quinoa Salad with Asparagus, Dates, and Orange

SALAD:
    1   teaspoon olive oil
  ¹⁄₂   cup finely chopped white onion
    1   cup uncooked quinoa
    2   cups water
  ¹⁄₂   teaspoon kosher salt
    1   cup fresh orange sections (about 1 large orange)
  ¹⁄₄   cup chopped pecans, toasted
    2   tablespoons minced red onion
    5   dates, pitted and chopped
  ¹⁄₂   pound (2-inch) slices asparagus, steamed and chilled
  ¹⁄₂   jalapeño pepper, diced
DRESSING:
    2   tablespoons fresh lemon juice
    1   tablespoon extravirgin olive oil
  ¹⁄₄   teaspoon kosher salt
  ¹⁄₄   teaspoon freshly ground black pepper
    1   garlic clove, minced
    2   tablespoons chopped fresh mint
        Mint sprigs (optional)

1 To prepare salad, heat 1 teaspoon oil in a large nonstick skillet over medium-high heat. Add white onion to pan; sauté 2 minutes. Add quinoa to pan; sauté 5 minutes. Add 2 cups water and ¹⁄₂ teaspoon salt to pan; bring to a boil. Cover, reduce heat, and simmer 15 minutes. Remove from heat; let stand 15 minutes or until water is absorbed. Transfer quinoa mixture to a large bowl. Add orange and next 5 ingredients; toss gently to combine.
2 To prepare dressing, combine juice and next 4 ingredients in a small bowl, stirring with a whisk. Pour dressing over salad; toss gently to coat. Sprinkle with chopped mint. Garnish with mint sprigs, if desired. Serve at room temperature. Yield: 8 servings (serving size: ³⁄₄ cup).

CALORIES 164 (35% from fat); FAT 6.3g (sat 0.7g, mono 3.5g, poly 1.7g); PROTEIN 4.3g; CARB 24.7g; FIBER 3.4g; CHOL 0mg; IRON 2.5mg; SODIUM 186mg; CALC 38mg

Lemon-Almond Cake with Lemon Curd Filling

Citrus and almond is a quintessential Mediterranean flavor combination, while the lemon curd filling is a traditional British dessert topping. And as with many Passover desserts, this cake gets its structure from beaten egg whites instead of chemical leaveners. Prepare the curd a day or two ahead of time. You can bake the cake earlier in the day and let it cool on a wire rack, but decorate with the curd and berries just before serving.

Cooking spray
2 teaspoons matzo cake meal
4 large egg yolks
1 cup sugar
¼ cup matzo cake meal
1½ teaspoons water
½ teaspoon grated lemon rind
1 teaspoon fresh lemon juice
¼ teaspoon salt
¼ cup blanched almonds, ground
4 large egg whites
1 cup Lemon Curd
2 cups fresh raspberries

❶ Preheat oven to 350°.
❷ Coat a 9-inch springform pan with cooking spray. Dust pan with 2 teaspoons matzo cake meal.
❸ Place egg yolks in a large bowl, and beat with a mixer at high speed 2 minutes. Gradually add sugar, beating until thick and pale (about 1 minute). Add ¼ cup matzo cake meal and next 4 ingredients; beat just until blended. Fold in almonds.
❹ Place egg whites in a large bowl. Using clean, dry beaters, beat egg whites with a mixer at high speed until stiff peaks form. Gently stir one-fourth of egg whites into egg yolk mixture; gently fold in remaining egg whites. Spoon batter into prepared pan.
❺ Bake at 350° for 35 minutes or until golden brown and set. Cool 10 minutes in pan on a wire rack. Run a knife around edge of cake. Remove cake from pan. Cool completely on a wire rack. (Cake will sink in center as it cools.) Spread 1 cup Lemon Curd in center of cake; top with raspberries. Cut cake into wedges using a serrated knife. Serve immediately. Yield: 8 servings (serving size: 1 wedge).

CALORIES 238 (25% from fat); FAT 6.6g (sat 2.1g, mono 2.7g, poly 1g); PROTEIN 5.9g; CARB 41.4g; FIBER 2.7g; CHOL 149mg; IRON 1.1mg; SODIUM 123mg; CALC 36mg

LEMON CURD:

½ cup sugar
3 large eggs
2 tablespoons grated lemon rind
¾ cup fresh lemon juice
2 tablespoons unsalted butter

❶ Place sugar and eggs in a medium bowl; beat with a mixer at medium speed until blended. Gradually beat in rind and juice. Spoon mixture into a heavy-duty saucepan over medium heat. Add butter to pan; cook 5 minutes or until thick, stirring constantly (do not boil). Spoon mixture into a bowl. Cover surface with plastic wrap. Chill thoroughly. Yield: 2 cups (serving size: 1 tablespoon).

CALORIES 27 (40% from fat); FAT 1.2g (sat 0.6g, mono 0.4g, poly 0.1g); PROTEIN 0.6g; CARB 3.7g; FIBER 0.1g; CHOL 22mg; IRON 0.1mg; SODIUM 7mg; CALC 4mg

Chocolate-Pecan Macaroons

Macaroons are a European confection especially popular at Passover. Here, the use of pecans adds a taste of the American South.

2¼ cups kosher-for-Passover powdered sugar, sifted
½ cup unsweetened cocoa
2 tablespoons matzo meal
⅛ teaspoon salt
3 large egg whites
1 teaspoon vanilla extract
¾ cup chopped pecans, toasted
Cooking spray

❶ Preheat oven to 325°.
❷ Combine first 4 ingredients in a large bowl; stir with a whisk. Add egg whites, 1 at a time, beating with a mixer at medium speed until combined; scrape bowl occasionally. Add vanilla, and beat well. Fold in pecans. Drop batter by level tablespoons 2 inches apart onto baking sheets coated with cooking spray.
❸ Bake at 325° for 15 minutes or until dry on surface and centers are soft. Remove from oven; cool on wire racks 15 minutes or until cookies can be easily removed with a spatula. Cool completely on wire racks. Yield: 26 cookies (serving size: 1 cookie).

CALORIES 73 (33% from fat); FAT 2.7g (sat 0.4g, mono 1.5g, poly 0.8g); PROTEIN 1.1g; CARB 12.3g; FIBER 0.9g; CHOL 0mg; IRON 0.3mg; SODIUM 18mg; CALC 5mg

Foods on the Seder Table

Food symbolism plays a large role in Passover seders.

• **Salt water** symbolizes the tears shed during the years of slavery and the water needed in the spring to make things grow.

• **Bitter herbs,** grated horseradish, or romaine lettuce are reminders of the bitterness of slavery.

• **A roasted shank bone** symbolizes the ancient sacrificial lamb of the Passover service.

• **Haroset,** a fruit and nut mixture that usually includes a combination of apples, walnuts, cinnamon, and wine, represents the mortar used by the Hebrew slaves to build buildings for the pharaohs.

• **Parsley,** or other available greens, recalls the verdant spring and the renewal of faith and hope.

• **An egg,** roasted in its shell, represents life and the continuity of existence, as well as the special festival offering in the Temple of Jerusalem.

Great Catch

Halibut's universal appeal and mild quality make it a good companion for a host of ingredients.

Among the flounder family, the halibut is king. The fish can live up to 40 years and grow as large as 700 pounds, though 50 pounds is the average. Halibut troll the chilly waters of the Atlantic and north Pacific, but most commercial halibut fishing takes place along the West Coast of the United States and Canada. This firm, white-fleshed fish is widely available fresh and at its best from spring through mid-fall. Regardless of its point of origin, halibut is a good source of lean protein, high in B vitamins, magnesium, and omega-3 fatty acids.

Poached Halibut with Warm Bacon Vinaigrette

This recipe uses *court-bouillon,* a flavorful broth often used to poach fish and seafood.

- 3 cups chopped leek
- 2 cups water
- 1 cup chopped carrot
- 1 cup chopped celery
- 1 cup white wine
- 1 cup low-sodium, fat-free chicken broth
- 6 garlic cloves, peeled
- 1 bay leaf
- 4 (6-ounce) halibut fillets, skinned
- 2 slices center-cut bacon
- 3 tablespoons finely chopped shallots
- 3 tablespoons red wine vinegar, divided
- 2 teaspoons Dijon mustard
- 2 teaspoons maple syrup
- 1½ teaspoons extravirgin olive oil
- ¼ teaspoon salt
- ⅛ teaspoon freshly ground black pepper
- 4 (½-ounce) slices French bread, toasted
Parsley sprigs (optional)

❶ Combine first 8 ingredients in a large Dutch oven over medium-high heat; bring to a boil. Cover, reduce heat, and simmer 30 minutes. Strain mixture through a colander into a bowl, reserving broth and vegetable mixture. Return broth to pan; bring to a simmer. Add fish to pan. Cook 8 minutes or until fish flakes easily when tested with a fork or until desired degree of doneness. Remove fish from cooking liquid using a slotted spoon; reserve 1 cup plus 2 tablespoons cooking liquid. Discard remaining cooking liquid.
❷ Cook bacon in a large nonstick skillet over medium heat until crisp. Remove bacon from pan; crumble. Add shallots to drippings in pan; sauté 1 minute or until tender, stirring constantly. Stir in 2 tablespoons vinegar and mustard; cook 1 minute, stirring occasionally. Stir in 2 tablespoons reserved cooking liquid, remaining 1 tablespoon vinegar, syrup, and next 3 ingredients; cook 30 seconds, stirring occasionally. Stir in bacon.
❸ Place about ³/₄ cup vegetable mixture in each of 4 shallow bowls; top each with ¼ cup remaining cooking liquid. Place 1 bread slice and 1 fish fillet in each serving. Drizzle each serving with about 1 tablespoon bacon mixture. Garnish with parsley sprigs, if desired. Yield: 4 servings.

CALORIES 387 (27% from fat); FAT 11.5g (sat 2.7g, mono 4.9g, poly 2.4g); PROTEIN 41.3g; CARB 28.4g; FIBER 3.4g; CHOL 62mg; IRON 4.2mg; SODIUM 631mg; CALC 171mg

Source Check

From Northern California to Alaska's Bering Sea coast, fishermen hauled in some 65 million pounds of halibut in 2007, according to the International Pacific Halibut Commission.

There is a comparably small commercial catch—about 100,000 pounds per year—along the U.S. Northeast coast. Having been heavily overfished in the 19th century, Atlantic Halibut is listed as a "species of concern" by the National Oceanic and Atmospheric Administration.

Mediterranean Fish Stew

Firm-textured halibut stands up to quick simmering and still holds its shape. Serve with crusty French bread and a salad.

- 1 tablespoon olive oil
- ½ cup finely chopped onion
- 2 garlic cloves, minced
- 2 cups (1-inch) cut green beans (about ½ pound)
- ⅓ cup thinly sliced carrot
- 2 (14-ounce) cans fat-free, less-sodium chicken broth
- 1 (15-ounce) can cannellini beans or other white beans, rinsed and drained
- 1 (14.5-ounce) can no-salt-added diced tomatoes, undrained
- 1 cup uncooked medium seashell pasta
- 2 tablespoons finely chopped fresh basil
- 1 tablespoon finely chopped fresh oregano
- 2 tablespoons tomato paste
- ¼ teaspoon freshly ground black pepper
- ¾ pound skinless halibut fillets, cut into 1-inch pieces
- ¼ cup (1 ounce) shaved Parmesan cheese

❶ Heat oil in a Dutch oven over medium-high heat. Add onion and garlic to pan; sauté 5 minutes or until tender. Add green beans and next 4 ingredients; bring to a boil. Add pasta. Cover, reduce heat, and simmer 12 minutes or until pasta is tender.
❷ Stir in basil, and next 3 ingredients. Gently stir in fish; cook 3 minutes or until fish flakes easily when tested with a fork or until desired degree of doneness. Sprinkle with Parmesan cheese. Yield: 4 servings (serving size: 2 cups stew and 1 tablespoon cheese).

CALORIES 385 (19% from fat); FAT 8.3g (sat 2.1g, mono 4g, poly 1.3g); PROTEIN 31.4g; CARB 45.9g; FIBER 7.9g; CHOL 32mg; IRON 4.2mg; SODIUM 698mg; CALC 218mg

Continued

WINE NOTE: In southern France, dry rosé wine is the classic match with the summery flavors of fish stew. The fresh white fruit and subtle berry flavors of a rosé like Château d'Aqueria Tavel Rosé 2006 ($17) are delicate enough for firm fish, while the generous acidity can handle tomato paste and basil. These dry wines are best when fresh, so watch for new releases.

QUICK & EASY

Halibut Sandwiches with Tartar Sauce

The sandwich spread, inspired by traditional tartar sauce, is brightened with the addition of fresh shallots and briny capers.

- ⅓ cup light mayonnaise
- 1½ tablespoons chopped capers
- 1 tablespoon finely chopped shallots
- 1 tablespoon sweet pickle relish
- 4 (6-ounce) halibut fillets
- ½ teaspoon salt
- ¼ teaspoon freshly ground black pepper
  Cooking spray
- 4 (1½-ounce) hamburger buns, toasted
- 2 halved romaine lettuce leaves
- 4 (¼-inch-thick) slices tomato

❶ Combine first 4 ingredients in a small bowl, stirring well.

❷ Sprinkle fish evenly with salt and pepper. Heat a large nonstick grill pan over medium-high heat. Coat pan with cooking spray. Add fish to pan; sauté 4 minutes on each side or until fish flakes easily when tested with a fork or until desired degree of doneness.

❸ Spread 1 tablespoon mayonnaise mixture over cut side of each bun half. Line bottom half of each bun with 1 lettuce leaf half and 1 tomato slice. Top each serving with 1 fillet. Place top halves of buns on sandwiches. Yield: 4 servings (serving size: 1 sandwich).

CALORIES 378 (29% from fat); FAT 12.3g (sat 2g, mono 3.4g, poly 5.9g); PROTEIN 38.7g; CARB 26g; FIBER 1.4g; CHOL 59mg; IRON 3mg; SODIUM 875mg; CALC 144mg

Pan-Seared Fennel-Scented Halibut with Puttanesca

Tomato-based sauces, such as this, are a zesty match for halibut.

ORZO:
- 6 ounces orzo
- 1 teaspoon grated lemon rind
- 1 tablespoon fresh lemon juice
- 2 teaspoons butter
- ¼ teaspoon salt
- ⅛ teaspoon freshly ground black pepper

FISH:
- 2 teaspoons fennel seeds, crushed
- ½ teaspoon salt, divided
- ⅛ teaspoon freshly ground black pepper
- 4 (6-ounce) halibut fillets
- 4 teaspoons extravirgin olive oil, divided
- ½ cup chopped onion
- ⅛ teaspoon crushed red pepper
- 3 garlic cloves, minced
- 2 cups cherry tomatoes, halved
- 1 tablespoon drained capers
- ¼ cup sliced fresh basil

❶ To prepare orzo, cook pasta according to package directions, omitting salt and fat; drain. Place pasta in a bowl; stir in rind and next 4 ingredients. Toss to combine.

❷ To prepare fish, combine fennel seeds, ¼ teaspoon salt, and ⅛ teaspoon black pepper; stir well. Sprinkle both sides of fish with fennel seed mixture. Heat 2 teaspoons oil in a large nonstick skillet over medium-high heat. Add fish to pan; sauté 5 minutes on each side or until fish flakes easily when tested with a fork or until desired degree of doneness. Transfer to a plate, and keep warm.

❸ Heat remaining 2 teaspoons oil over medium-high heat. Add onion and red pepper to pan; sauté 1 minute. Add garlic; sauté 15 seconds. Stir in tomatoes and capers; cook 2 minutes. Remove from heat; stir in basil and remaining

¼ teaspoon salt. Divide pasta evenly among 4 plates; top each with 1 fillet. Spoon ⅓ cup tomato mixture over each serving. Yield: 4 servings.

CALORIES 435 (24% from fat); FAT 11.6g (sat 2.6g, mono 5.8g, poly 2.2g); PROTEIN 42.1g; CARB 38.7g; FIBER 3.5g; CHOL 59mg; IRON 2mg; SODIUM 604mg; CALC 115mg

QUICK & EASY

Blackened Halibut with Remoulade

SAUCE:
- ⅓ cup low-fat mayonnaise
- 2 tablespoons chopped fresh flat-leaf parsley
- 1 tablespoon chopped fresh chives
- 1 tablespoon finely chopped cornichon
- 1 tablespoon whole-grain Dijon mustard
- 1 teaspoon fresh lemon juice
- ⅛ teaspoon salt
- 1 garlic clove, minced

FISH:
- 2 teaspoons paprika
- 1 teaspoon ground cumin
- ½ teaspoon salt
- ½ teaspoon sugar
- ½ teaspoon garlic powder
- ½ teaspoon dried oregano
- ¼ teaspoon dried thyme
- ¼ teaspoon ground red pepper
- 4 (6-ounce) halibut fillets
- 2 teaspoons canola oil

❶ To prepare sauce, combine first 8 ingredients in a bowl. Cover and chill.

❷ To prepare fish, combine paprika and next 7 ingredients. Sprinkle fish evenly with seasoning mixture. Heat oil in a large nonstick skillet over medium-high heat. Add fish to pan; sauté 4 minutes on each side or until fish flakes easily when tested with a fork or until desired degree of doneness. Serve with sauce. Yield: 4 servings (serving size: 1 fillet and 2 tablespoons sauce).

CALORIES 245 (33% from fat); FAT 9.1g (sat 0.7g, mono 2.6g, poly 3.3g); PROTEIN 34.8g; CARB 5.9g; FIBER 1.4g; CHOL 52mg; IRON 2.2mg; SODIUM 719mg; CALC 97mg

Halibut Souvlaki

Be sure to use thick, whole-milk Greek-style yogurt for this sauce. Its flavor and texture are essential.

- 1 tablespoon fresh lemon juice
- 1 teaspoon dried oregano
- 2 teaspoons extravirgin olive oil
- 5/8 teaspoon salt, divided
- 1/4 teaspoon freshly ground black pepper
- 4 (6-ounce) halibut fillets
- Cooking spray
- 1/3 cup Greek-style yogurt (such as Fage Total Classic)
- 1/4 cup finely chopped cucumber
- 1 1/2 teaspoons chopped fresh dill
- 1/4 teaspoon minced fresh garlic
- 4 pita wraps
- 2 cups chopped romaine lettuce
- 1/2 cup thinly sliced red onion
- 8 plum tomato slices

1 Preheat broiler.
2 Combine first 3 ingredients in a shallow dish; stir in 1/2 teaspoon salt and pepper. Add fillets, turning to coat; let stand 15 minutes. Arrange fillets on rack of a broiler pan coated with cooking spray; place rack in pan. Broil 8 minutes or until fish flakes easily when tested with a fork or until desired degree of doneness.
3 Combine remaining 1/8 teaspoon salt, yogurt, and next 3 ingredients in a bowl, stirring well. Spread 1 1/2 tablespoons yogurt mixture in center of each pita wrap; top each with 1 fillet, 1/2 cup lettuce, 2 tablespoons onion, and 2 tomato slices. Roll up. Yield: 4 servings (serving size: 1 wrap).

CALORIES 405 (18% from fat); FAT 8.1g (sat 2.3g, mono 3.2g, poly 1.6g); PROTEIN 43.3g; CARB 38.5g; FIBER 2.6g; CHOL 55mg; IRON 4.7mg; SODIUM 627mg; CALC 156mg

Steamed Halibut with Sesame-Lime Sauce and Coconut Rice

Steamed halibut has a clean, mild flavor that complements this pungent sauce. We used a bamboo steamer set over simmering water to steam the fish. It's helpful to lightly coat the bamboo with cooking spray before adding the fish.

- 1/4 cup finely chopped green onions
- 2 tablespoons finely chopped fresh mint
- 2 tablespoons fresh lime juice
- 1 tablespoon rice vinegar
- 1 1/2 teaspoons sugar
- 1 1/2 teaspoons fish sauce
- 1 1/2 teaspoons dark sesame oil
- 1/4 teaspoon red curry paste
- 1 cup water
- 3/4 cup basmati rice
- 3/4 cup light coconut milk
- 1/2 teaspoon salt, divided
- 3 tablespoons chopped fresh cilantro
- 4 (6-ounce) halibut fillets
- 1/4 teaspoon freshly ground black pepper
- 4 lime wedges

1 Combine first 8 ingredients in a small bowl, stirring with a whisk. Set aside.
2 Combine 1 cup water, rice, coconut milk, and 1/4 teaspoon salt in a medium saucepan; bring to a boil. Cover, reduce heat, and simmer 15 minutes or until liquid is absorbed. Remove from heat; let stand 5 minutes. Stir in cilantro.
3 Sprinkle fish evenly with remaining 1/4 teaspoon salt and pepper. Steam fish, covered, 8 minutes or until fish flakes easily when tested with a fork or until desired degree of doneness. Place 1/2 cup rice on each of 4 plates; top each with 1 fillet. Drizzle each serving with 2 tablespoons sauce. Serve with lime wedges. Yield: 4 servings.

CALORIES 293 (24% from fat); FAT 7.8g (sat 2.9g, mono 1.9g, poly 1.9g); PROTEIN 36.1g; CARB 18.7g; FIBER 0.6g; CHOL 52mg; IRON 1.9mg; SODIUM 576mg; CALC 87mg

Malaysian Barbecue-Glazed Halibut

These fillets simultaneously taste sweet, salty, and slightly spicy from the Asian inspired sauce that's brushed on them. Serve with long-grain rice, such as basmati or jasmine.

- 4 (6-ounce) halibut fillets
- 1/4 teaspoon salt
- Cooking spray
- 1 tablespoon fresh lemon juice
- 1 tablespoon orange juice
- 1 tablespoon honey
- 1 1/2 teaspoons rice vinegar
- 1 1/2 teaspoons hoisin sauce
- 1 teaspoon fish sauce
- 1/2 teaspoon chile paste with garlic (such as sambal oelek)
- 1/4 teaspoon cornstarch
- Lemon wedges (optional)

1 Sprinkle fish evenly with salt. Heat a nonstick skillet over medium-high heat. Coat pan with cooking spray. Add fish to pan; sauté 5 minutes on each side or until fish flakes easily when tested with a fork or until desired degree of doneness.
2 Combine lemon juice and next 7 ingredients in a small saucepan over medium-high heat, stirring well; bring to a boil. Cook 20 seconds, stirring constantly. Remove from heat. Brush about 1 tablespoon sauce over each fillet. Serve with lemon wedges, if desired. Yield: 4 servings (serving size: 1 fillet).

CALORIES 205 (17% from fat); FAT 3.9g (sat 0.6g, mono 1.3g, poly 1.2g); PROTEIN 34.3g; CARB 6.9g; FIBER 0.3g; CHOL 52mg; IRON 1.5mg; SODIUM 387mg; CALC 81mg

Four Finalists

First course to last, here are more entries from the 2007 *Cooking Light* Ultimate Reader Recipe Contest.

Shrimp Toast Puffs with Two Sauces

Category Finalist—Starters and Drinks

"The combination of the shrimp puffs served with two sauces makes this a perfect party appetizer."

—Julie DeMatteo, Clementon, New Jersey

PUFFS:

- 1 pound peeled and deveined medium shrimp
- 2 bacon slices, diced
- 1/3 cup finely chopped green onions
- 1 1/2 teaspoons bottled ground fresh ginger (such as Spice World)
- 1 cup all-purpose flour (about 4 1/2 ounces)
- 1 cup water
- 3 tablespoons butter
- 1/2 teaspoon sugar
- 2 large egg whites
- 1 large egg
- Cooking spray

SOY-GARLIC SAUCE:

- 1/4 cup low-sodium soy sauce
- 2 tablespoons finely chopped green onion tops
- 2 tablespoons seasoned rice vinegar
- 1 teaspoon hot chili sauce with garlic
- 1/2 teaspoon dark sesame oil

SWEET CHILI SAUCE:

- 6 tablespoons sweet chili garlic sauce (such as Taste of Asia)
- 4 teaspoons seasoned rice vinegar

① Preheat oven to 425°.
② To prepare puffs, place shrimp in a food processor; pulse until finely chopped.
③ Cook bacon in a large nonstick skillet over medium-high heat until crisp. Remove bacon from pan, reserving 2 teaspoons drippings in pan (reserve bacon for another use). Add shrimp to reserved drippings in pan, and sauté 3 minutes. Add 1/3 cup green onions to pan; sauté 1 minute. Stir in ginger.
④ Lightly spoon flour into a dry measuring cup; level with a knife. Combine 1 cup water, butter, and sugar in a large heavy saucepan; bring to a boil, stirring occasionally with a wooden spoon. Reduce heat to low; add flour, stirring well until mixture is smooth and pulls away from sides of pan. Remove from heat. Add egg whites and egg, 1 at a time; beat with a mixer at medium speed until smooth. Gently stir in shrimp mixture.
⑤ Drop dough by level tablespoons 2 inches apart onto baking sheets coated with cooking spray. Bake at 425° for 10 minutes. Reduce oven temperature to 350° (do not remove puffs from oven); bake an additional 10 minutes or until browned and crisp.
⑥ To prepare soy-garlic sauce, combine soy sauce and next 4 ingredients in a small bowl, stirring with a whisk.
⑦ To prepare sweet chili sauce, combine chili garlic sauce and 4 teaspoons vinegar in a small bowl, stirring with a whisk. Serve sauces with shrimp puffs. Yield: 12 servings (serving size: 3 puffs and 2 teaspoons of each sauce).

CALORIES 141 (31% from fat); FAT 4.9g (sat 2.4g, mono 1.3g, poly 0.5g); PROTEIN 10.4g; CARB 12.9g; FIBER 0.5g; CHOL 83mg; IRON 1.6mg; SODIUM 628mg; CALC 30mg

Seoul-ful Chicken with Minted Cucumbers

Category Finalist—Entrées

"My family loves Asian food. This is my spin on Korean grilled chicken with a speedy kimchi-type accompaniment. I prefer using chicken thighs for this dish because they are juicier and tastier than boneless breasts."

—Janice Elder, Charlotte, North Carolina

CUCUMBERS:

- 1 English cucumber, peeled, halved lengthwise, and thinly sliced (about 2 1/2 cups)
- 1/4 teaspoon salt
- 1/4 cup minced shallots
- 2 tablespoons chopped fresh mint
- 1 tablespoon seasoned rice vinegar
- 1 tablespoon honey
- 1 teaspoon dark sesame oil
- 1/4 teaspoon ground red pepper
- 1 serrano chile, seeded and minced

CHICKEN:

- 8 skinless, boneless chicken thighs (about 1 1/4 pounds)
- 1/4 cup soy sauce
- 2 tablespoons dark sesame oil
- 1 tablespoon minced peeled fresh ginger
- 1 tablespoon honey
- 1/2 teaspoon freshly ground black pepper
- 3 garlic cloves, thinly sliced
- Cooking spray
- 1/4 cup thinly sliced green onions
- 4 teaspoons sesame seeds, toasted

① To prepare cucumbers, place cucumber slices in a colander; sprinkle with salt, tossing well. Drain 1 hour. Place cucumber slices on several layers of paper towels; cover with additional paper towels. Let stand 5 minutes, pressing down occasionally. Combine cucumber, shallots, and next 6 ingredients in a large bowl; toss gently. Cover and set aside.
② To prepare chicken, place each chicken thigh between 2 sheets of heavy-duty plastic wrap; pound to 1/2-inch thickness using a meat mallet or small heavy skillet. Combine soy sauce and next 5 ingredients in a large zip-top plastic bag. Add chicken to bag; seal. Marinate in refrigerator 30 minutes, turning bag occasionally.
③ Heat a grill pan over medium-high heat. Coat pan with cooking spray. Remove chicken from bag; discard marinade. Place 4 thighs in pan; cook 6 minutes on each side or until done. Repeat procedure with remaining 4 thighs.

Place 2 thighs and ¹/₂ cup cucumbers on each of 4 plates; sprinkle each serving with 1 tablespoon green onions and 1 teaspoon sesame seeds. Yield: 4 servings.

CALORIES 262 (31% from fat); FAT 8.9g (sat 1.9g, mono 3g, poly 2.8g); PROTEIN 29.9g; CARB 14.9g; FIBER 1.5g; CHOL 115mg; IRON 2.7mg; SODIUM 502mg; CALC 40mg

WINE NOTE: Serve an herbaceous sauvignon blanc to echo the crisp freshness of the dish's cucumber and mint. Chilean versions, like Veramonte Sauvignon Blanc Reserva 2007 ($11), strike a balance between the crisp, green flavors of the New Zealand–style wine and the juicy tropical fruit and melon of California versions in an affordable package.

MAKE AHEAD
Light and Fresh Potato Salad
(pictured on page 246)

Category Finalist—Sides and Salads
"My husband doesn't like mayonnaise, so I created a potato salad with a vinaigrette. I experimented and realized how little oil I need. Add the dressing while the potatoes are still hot. It really helps the vinegar permeate the potatoes."

—Elsie Gonto,
Savannah, Georgia

DRESSING:
¼ cup seasoned rice vinegar
2 tablespoons canola oil
¼ teaspoon salt
⅛ teaspoon freshly ground black pepper
SALAD:
5 cups cubed red potato (about 2 pounds)
½ teaspoon salt
1 cup chopped peeled cucumber
¾ cup sliced grape or cherry tomatoes
¾ cup chopped green bell pepper
½ cup chopped orange bell pepper
¼ cup chopped green onions
1 (2¼-ounce) can sliced ripe olives, drained

① To prepare dressing, combine first 4 ingredients in a large bowl; stir with a whisk.
② To prepare salad, place potato and ¹/₂ teaspoon salt in a medium saucepan. Cover with water to 2 inches above potato; bring to a boil. Reduce heat, and simmer 8 minutes or until tender; drain.
③ Add potato to dressing in bowl, tossing gently to coat; let stand 15 minutes. Stir in cucumber and remaining ingredients; toss well. Cover and chill. Yield: 12 servings (serving size: ³/₄ cup).

CALORIES 90 (28% from fat); FAT 2.8g (sat 0.2g, mono 1.6g, poly 0.8g); PROTEIN 1.8g; CARB 14.9g; FIBER 2g; CHOL 0mg; IRON 0.9mg; SODIUM 295mg; CALC 19mg

MAKE AHEAD
Old-Fashioned Oatmeal Honey Apple Cake

Category Finalist—Desserts
"I've been making oatmeal cake for my family for more than 45 years. Several years ago I revised the recipe, eliminating vegetable oil and using applesauce for added moistness. The original frosting called for coconut, but I chose almonds, a more healthful option."

—Barbara Estabrook,
Rhinelander, Wisconsin

CAKE:
1 cup quick-cooking oats
1 cup hot water
1½ cups all-purpose flour (about 6¾ ounces)
2 teaspoons ground cinnamon
1 teaspoon baking soda
½ teaspoon salt
1⅓ cups packed light brown sugar
¾ cup chunky applesauce
⅓ cup honey
2 large eggs
Cooking spray
FROSTING:
¼ cup butter
⅓ cup packed light brown sugar
¼ cup honey
½ cup coarsely chopped almonds, toasted

REMAINING INGREDIENTS:
1 cup frozen fat-free whipped topping, thawed
Ground cinnamon (optional)

① Preheat oven to 350°.
② To prepare cake, combine oats and 1 cup hot water in a small bowl; set aside.
③ Lightly spoon flour into dry measuring cups; level with a knife. Combine flour and next 3 ingredients. Combine 1⅓ cups sugar and next 3 ingredients in a large bowl; beat with a mixer at high speed 1 minute. Add oat mixture; beat at low speed until well blended. Add half of flour mixture to sugar mixture; beat well. Add remaining flour mixture; beat well. Spoon batter into an 11 x 7-inch baking dish coated with cooking spray. Bake at 350° for 48 minutes or until a wooden pick inserted in center comes out clean. Place dish on a wire rack.
④ To prepare frosting, melt butter in a small heavy saucepan over medium heat. Add ¹/₃ cup sugar and ¹/₄ cup honey; cook 2 minutes or until bubbly, stirring constantly. Stir in almonds. Quickly pour frosting over cake; spread evenly using a rubber spatula.
⑤ Preheat broiler.
⑥ Broil cake 1 minute or until frosting is bubbly and golden. Cool completely on a wire rack. Serve with whipped topping; sprinkle with ground cinnamon, if desired. Yield: 16 servings (serving size: 1 cake piece and 1 tablespoon topping).

CALORIES 255 (19% from fat); FAT 5.4g (sat 2.1g, mono 1.7g, poly 0.5g); PROTEIN 3.4g; CARB 48.9g; FIBER 1.5g; CHOL 34mg; IRON 1.8mg; SODIUM 193mg; CALC 40mg

Novel Gnocchi

These small Italian potato dumplings inspire entrées with outsized satisfaction.

Gnocchi Menu 1
serves 4

Gnocchi with Broccoli Rabe, Caramelized Garlic, and Parmesan

Sliced oranges and red onions

Combine 1 tablespoon white wine vinegar, 1 tablespoon extravirgin olive oil, 2 teaspoons chopped fresh rosemary, 2 teaspoons honey, ¼ teaspoon salt, and ⅛ teaspoon freshly ground black pepper in a small bowl; stir with a whisk. Peel and slice 4 large navel oranges. Peel and thinly slice 1 small red onion. Arrange orange slices evenly on 4 salad plates; top evenly with onion. Drizzle with white wine vinegar mixture.

Angel food cake with raspberries

Game Plan
1 Preheat oven.
2 While water comes to a boil:
  • Trim broccoli rabe.
  • Slice oranges and onion for salad.
  • Combine dressing for salad.
3 While broccoli rabe and gnocchi cook:
  • Cook garlic.
  • Assemble salad.

Taste Tip
Broccoli rabe can be a bit pungent; substitute milder Broccolini, if you prefer.

Gnocchi with Broccoli Rabe, Caramelized Garlic, and Parmesan

Keep an eye on the garlic to be sure it browns but doesn't burn, which can make it unpleasantly bitter. Blanching the broccoli rabe helps tame its bitterness.
Total time: 25 minutes

  ¾ **pound broccoli rabe (rapini), trimmed**
  1 **(16-ounce) box vacuum-packed gnocchi (such as Vigo)**
  2 **tablespoons olive oil**
  4 **garlic cloves, thinly sliced**
  ¼ **teaspoon salt**
  ¼ **teaspoon crushed red pepper**
  ¼ **cup (1 ounce) shredded Parmesan cheese**

❶ Cook broccoli rabe in boiling water 4 minutes. Remove broccoli rabe with a slotted spoon, and place in a colander; drain. Add gnocchi to pan; cook 3 minutes or until done. Drain gnocchi in a colander over a bowl, reserving ¼ cup cooking liquid.

❷ Heat oil in a large nonstick skillet over medium heat. Add garlic to pan; cook 3 minutes or until lightly browned, stirring frequently. Add broccoli rabe, gnocchi, and reserved cooking liquid to pan; cook 2 minutes. Stir in salt and pepper. Place 1¼ cups gnocchi mixture in each of 4 shallow bowls; top each serving with 1 tablespoon cheese. Yield: 4 servings.

CALORIES 281 (28% from fat); FAT 8.7g (sat 2.2g, mono 5.6g, poly 0.8g); PROTEIN 9.9g; CARB 41.8g; FIBER 0.1g; CHOL 5mg; IRON 0.9mg; SODIUM 806mg; CALC 134mg

Gnocchi Menu 2
serves 4

Gnocchi with Asparagus and Pancetta

Mesclun salad with Dijon dressing

Combine 1 tablespoon Dijon mustard, 1 tablespoon red wine vinegar, 1 tablespoon extravirgin olive oil, ⅛ teaspoon salt, and ⅛ teaspoon black pepper in a large bowl; stir with a whisk. Add 6 cups mesclun greens, ¼ cup thinly sliced red onion, and 2 plum tomatoes, quartered; toss.

Low-fat coffee ice cream with chocolate sauce

Game Plan
1 While water comes to a boil:
  • Prepare salad ingredients.
  • Prepare ingredients for gnocchi.
2 While gnocchi cooks:
  • Sauté pancetta, asparagus, and shallots.
3 Toss salad.

Gnocchi with Asparagus and Pancetta

Pancetta is cured unsmoked Italian bacon available at the grocery deli counter.
Total time: 30 minutes

  1 **(16-ounce) package vacuum-packed gnocchi (such as Vigo)**
  2 **ounces pancetta, cut into thin strips (about ½ cup)**
  ¼ **cup thinly sliced shallots**
  1 **pound asparagus, trimmed and cut into 1½-inch pieces**
  2 **garlic cloves, minced**
  1 **tablespoon fresh lemon juice**
  ⅛ **teaspoon salt**
  ⅛ **teaspoon black pepper**
  ¼ **cup (1 ounce) shaved Parmesan cheese**

❶ Cook gnocchi according to package directions, omitting salt and fat. Drain in a colander over a bowl, reserving ¼ cup cooking liquid. Keep gnocchi warm.
❷ Heat a large nonstick skillet over medium-high heat. Add pancetta; sauté 3 minutes or until lightly browned. Transfer to a paper towel–lined plate.
❸ Add shallots and asparagus to pan; sauté 5 minutes or until tender. Stir in garlic; sauté 1 minute. Add gnocchi, pancetta, reserved cooking liquid, juice, salt, and pepper to pan; cook 1 minute. Serve with cheese. Yield: 4 servings (serving size: 1½ cups gnocchi mixture and 1 tablespoon cheese).

CALORIES 277 (21% from fat); FAT 6.5g (sat 3.1g, mono 2.5g, poly 0.1g); PROTEIN 11.2g; CARB 43.7g; FIBER 2.6g; CHOL 15mg; IRON 2.6mg; SODIUM 932mg; CALC 110mg

Gnocchi Menu 3
serves 4

Gnocchi with Chicken Sausage, Bell Pepper, and Fennel

Creamy tomato soup

Combine 1 (14½-ounce) can diced tomatoes (undrained); ½ cup fat-free, less sodium chicken broth; ¼ teaspoon salt; and ¼ teaspoon black pepper in a small saucepan; bring to a simmer. Cook 10 minutes or until heated through. Transfer tomato mixture to a blender. Remove center piece of blender lid (to allow steam to escape); secure blender lid on blender. Place a clean towel over opening in blender lid (to avoid splatters). Blend until smooth. Pour into a medium bowl. Stir in 2 tablespoons heavy cream. Garnish with basil.

Chocolate sorbet

Game Plan

1 Prepare soup; keep warm.
2 While water comes to a boil:
 • Prepare ingredients for gnocchi.
3 While gnocchi cooks:
 • Sauté sausage, fennel, bell pepper and onion.

Gnocchi with Chicken Sausage, Bell Pepper, and Fennel

Vary the flavor by using a different cheese, such as pecorino Romano.
Total time: 33 minutes

 1 (16-ounce) package vacuum-packed gnocchi (such as Vigo)
 2 teaspoons olive oil, divided
 6 ounces basil, pine nut, and chicken sausage (such as Gerhard's), casing removed and sliced
 1 cup thinly sliced fennel
 1 cup thinly sliced red bell pepper
 1 cup thinly sliced onion
 ½ cup (2 ounces) freshly grated Asiago cheese
 ⅛ teaspoon freshly ground black pepper
 2 tablespoons chopped fresh flat-leaf parsley

❶ Cook gnocchi according to package directions, omitting salt and fat. Drain in a colander over a bowl, reserving ¼ cup cooking liquid. Keep gnocchi warm.
❷ Heat 1 teaspoon oil in large nonstick skillet over medium-high heat. Add sausage to pan; sauté 3 minutes or until lightly browned, stirring frequently. Remove sausage from skillet using a slotted spoon.
❸ Heat remaining 1 teaspoon oil in pan. Add fennel, bell pepper, and onion to pan; cook 13 minutes or until tender, stirring occasionally. Add sausage, gnocchi, cheese, black pepper, and reserved cooking liquid to pan; cook 1 minute or until cheese melts, stirring constantly. Remove from heat; stir in parsley. Yield: 4 servings (serving size: 1½ cups).

CALORIES 342 (30% from fat); FAT 11.5g (sat 4.3g, mono 4.7g, poly 1.6g); PROTEIN 15.9g; CARB 45.4g; FIBER 2.9g; CHOL 50mg; IRON 1.1mg; SODIUM 829mg; CALC 155mg

20 Minute Dishes

From chicken salad to shrimp, pork to tuna, here are six simple, fresh, and easy meals you can make superfast.

Pork Medallions with Red Currant Sauce

Red currant jelly renders the sauce a vibrant crimson, though you can use any variety of fruit jelly.

 ½ teaspoon dried thyme
 ½ teaspoon salt
 ¼ teaspoon smoked paprika
 ¼ teaspoon dried rubbed sage
 ⅛ teaspoon black pepper
 1 (1-pound) pork tenderloin, trimmed
 Cooking spray
 ⅓ cup red currant jelly
 3 tablespoons cider vinegar
 2 tablespoons chopped fresh chives

❶ Combine first 5 ingredients in a small bowl. Cut pork crosswise into 8 (1-inch-thick) pieces. Place each piece between 2 pieces of heavy-duty plastic wrap, and pound to ½-inch thickness using a meat mallet or small heavy skillet. Rub pork with spice mixture.
❷ Heat a large nonstick skillet over medium-high heat. Coat pan with cooking spray. Add pork to pan, and cook 3 minutes on each side. Remove pork from pan; keep warm.
❸ Add jelly to pan; cook 30 seconds, scraping pan to loosen browned bits. Remove from heat; stir in vinegar. Serve sauce with pork; sprinkle with chives. Yield: 4 servings (serving size: 2 medallions, 1 tablespoon sauce, and 1½ teaspoons chives).

CALORIES 202 (17% from fat); FAT 3.9g (sat 1.3g, mono 1.6g, poly 0.3g); PROTEIN 22.6g; CARB 17.8g; FIBER 0.3g; CHOL 63mg; IRON 1.4mg; SODIUM 341mg; CALC 10mg

Asian Beef and Noodle-Filled Lettuce Cups

Rice vermicelli is similar to angel hair and sometimes sticks together after it is cooked. Use a pair of kitchen shears to snip through the noodles a few times to make them easier to toss with the remaining ingredients.

  3 ounces uncooked rice vermicelli
 12 ounces ground sirloin
  2 teaspoons bottled minced garlic
 ½ cup matchstick-cut carrots
 ½ cup chopped cucumber
 ⅓ cup chopped red bell pepper
 ⅓ cup prechopped onion
  3 tablespoons chopped fresh mint
 ¼ cup fresh lime juice
  2 teaspoons sugar
  2 teaspoons low-sodium soy sauce
  4 Boston lettuce leaves
 ¼ cup chopped dry-roasted peanuts

❶ Cook pasta according to package directions, omitting salt and fat. Drain and rinse with cold water; drain.
❷ Heat a large nonstick skillet over medium-high heat. Add beef to pan, and cook 3 minutes, stirring to crumble. Stir in garlic, and cook 2 minutes or until browned. Stir in noodles, carrots, and next 4 ingredients. Combine juice, sugar, and soy sauce in a small bowl, stirring until sugar dissolves. Add juice mixture to beef mixture; tossing gently to coat. Arrange 1 lettuce leaf on each of 4 plates; spoon 1¼ cups beef mixture into each leaf. Top each serving with 1 tablespoon peanuts. Yield: 4 servings (serving size: 1 stuffed lettuce leaf).

CALORIES 270 (29% from fat); FAT 8.6g (sat 2.2g, mono 3.7g, poly 1.9g); PROTEIN 21.2g; CARB 27.8g; FIBER 2.6g; CHOL 45mg; IRON 2.8mg; SODIUM 234mg; CALC 37mg

Chicken-Orzo Salad with Goat Cheese

(pictured on page 248)

Leftover salad is also good the next day for lunch; stir in a handful of arugula to add a fresh touch, if you have extra on hand. Serve with pita wedges.

 1¼ cups uncooked orzo (rice-shaped pasta)
  3 cups chopped grilled chicken breast strips (such as Tyson)
 1½ cups trimmed arugula
  1 cup grape tomatoes, halved
 ½ cup chopped red bell pepper
 ¼ cup prechopped red onion
  2 tablespoons chopped fresh basil
  1 teaspoon chopped fresh oregano
  2 tablespoons red wine vinegar
  1 tablespoon extravirgin olive oil
 ⅛ teaspoon salt
 ⅛ teaspoon black pepper
  6 tablespoons (1½ ounces) crumbled goat cheese

❶ Cook pasta according to package directions, omitting salt and fat; drain well.
❷ Combine pasta, chicken, and next 6 ingredients in a large bowl; toss well.
❸ Combine vinegar and next 3 ingredients in a small bowl, stirring with a whisk. Drizzle vinegar mixture over pasta mixture; toss well to coat. Sprinkle with cheese. Yield: 6 servings (serving size: 1⅓ cups salad and 1 tablespoon cheese).

CALORIES 295 (23% from fat); FAT 7.7g (sat 2.9.g, mono 2.8g, poly 1.1g); PROTEIN 24.4g; CARB 32.1g; FIBER 2g; CHOL 55mg; IRON 2.4mg; SODIUM 788mg; CALC 40mg

Coriander-Crusted Tuna with Black Bean Salsa

Serve with warm flour tortillas, and garnish with sliced avocado.

  1 tablespoon ground coriander
  1 teaspoon ground cumin
 ¾ teaspoon kosher salt, divided
 ¼ teaspoon black pepper
  4 (6-ounce) tuna steaks (about 1 inch thick)
  1 tablespoon olive oil
  1 cup diced plum tomato (about 3 tomatoes)
 ½ cup chopped yellow bell pepper
 ¼ cup sliced green onions
  3 tablespoons chopped fresh cilantro
  2 tablespoons fresh lime juice
  1 (15-ounce) can no-salt-added black beans, rinsed and drained
 Cilantro sprigs (optional)

❶ Combine coriander, cumin, ½ teaspoon salt, and black pepper in a small bowl. Rub spice mixture evenly over both sides of fish.
❷ Heat oil in a large nonstick skillet over medium-high heat. Add fish to pan; cook 2 minutes on each side or until desired degree of doneness. Remove from heat.
❸ Combine tomato and next 5 ingredients in a medium bowl. Stir in remaining ¼ teaspoon salt, and toss well. Serve salsa with fish. Garnish with cilantro sprigs, if desired. Yield: 4 servings (serving size: 1 tuna steak and about ¾ cup salsa).

CALORIES 356 (31% from fat); FAT 12.3g (sat 2.6g, mono 5.2g, poly 2.9g); PROTEIN 43.9g; CARB 15.4g; FIBER 4.9g; CHOL 65mg; IRON 3.1mg; SODIUM 501mg; CALC 64mg

Chile-Garlic Shrimp

This meal is inspired by the lemony, bright flavors of Spain.

- 1 (3½-ounce) bag boil-in-bag brown rice
- ½ teaspoon salt
- ⅛ teaspoon black pepper
- 1½ pounds peeled and deveined large shrimp (about 32)
- 1½ tablespoons olive oil
- ¼ teaspoon crushed red pepper
- 3 large garlic cloves, sliced
- 1 bay leaf
- ½ cup dry white wine
- 4 (¼-inch-thick) lemon slices
- 2 tablespoons chopped fresh parsley
- 1 tablespoon butter
- Lemon wedges (optional)

① Cook rice according to package directions, omitting salt and fat.
② Sprinkle salt and black pepper evenly over shrimp. Heat oil in a large skillet over medium heat. Add shrimp, red pepper, garlic, and bay leaf to pan; cook 3 minutes, stirring frequently. Add wine and lemon slices to pan. Increase heat to medium-high, and bring to a simmer; cook until liquid is reduced to ¼ cup (about 3 minutes). Remove from heat. Discard bay leaf and lemon. Add parsley and butter, stirring until butter melts. Serve shrimp and sauce over rice. Serve with lemon wedges, if desired. Yield: 4 servings (serving size: about 8 shrimp, ½ cup rice, and 2 tablespoons sauce).

CALORIES 344 (29% from fat); FAT 11.4g (sat 3.1g, mono 4.9g, poly 1.8g); PROTEIN 36.9g; CARB 21.9g; FIBER 1.5g; CHOL 266mg; IRON 4.8mg; SODIUM 581mg; CALC 99mg

Brandy and Mustard–Glazed Tenderloin Steaks

Serve with mashed potatoes drizzled with olive oil. Place fresh broccoli florets in a bowl with a small amount of water. Microwave three minutes or until crisp-tender; garnish with grated lemon rind, if desired.

- 4 (4-ounce) beef tenderloin steaks
- ¼ teaspoon salt
- ⅛ teaspoon black pepper
- 2 teaspoons butter
- ¼ cup minced shallots
- ½ cup fat-free, less-sodium beef broth
- 1 tablespoon Dijon mustard
- 2 tablespoons brandy

① Heat a large nonstick skillet over medium heat. Sprinkle both sides of steaks evenly with salt and pepper. Add steaks to pan; cook 3 minutes on each side or until browned. Remove steaks from pan; keep warm.
② Melt butter in pan. Add shallots to pan; cook 2 minutes, stirring occasionally. Add broth and mustard to pan; cook 1 minute or until sauce thickens, stirring occasionally. Stir in brandy. Return steaks to pan, and cook 1 minute on each side or until desired degree of doneness. Serve sauce with steaks. Yield: 4 servings (serving size: 1 steak and 4 teaspoons sauce).

CALORIES 218 (38% from fat); FAT 9.3g (sat 3.9g, mono 3.5g, poly 0.4g); PROTEIN 25.7g; CARB 2.7g; FIBER 0.2g; CHOL 81mg; IRON 2.1mg; SODIUM 371mg; CALC 34mg

LIGHTEN UP
A Hearty Start

A Connecticut teacher begins busy days with a serving of this revamped sausage and egg casserole.

Lisanne Kaplan of Lyme, Connecticut, flipped through a favorite cookbook years ago to find an impressive breakfast she could make ahead for a family gathering. Her savory Sausage and Cheese Breakfast Casserole was a smashing success and soon became a family tradition. But with her schedule, Kaplan needs a make-ahead meal that will be a more healthful, energizing start to the day.

We use 12 ounces of flavorful breakfast turkey sausage instead of 1½ pounds pork sausage. This eliminates three grams of saturated fat, 187 milligrams of sodium, and 20 milligrams of cholesterol per serving. Instead of using nine large eggs, we combine three eggs with two cups egg substitute to offer a fluffy egg texture and taste without missing another two and a half grams of fat (one gram saturated) and 115 milligrams of cholesterol in each portion. The swap from whole milk to one percent low-fat milk trims another gram of fat. The last big change involves using a bit less cheese, and finely shredding reduced-fat extrasharp Cheddar to better distribute the smaller amount and perk up the flavor. This cuts another two and a half grams of fat per serving. Since we halved the original amount of salt, a bit of ground red pepper adds a little spiciness and zest to the casserole while shaving some sodium.

serving size: about 1 cup	before	after
CALORIES PER SERVING	346	184
FAT	25.8g	6.8g
PERCENT OF TOTAL CALORIES	67%	33%

Continued

Sausage and Cheese Breakfast Casserole

Prep this the night before for an easy breakfast or brunch.

     Cooking spray
12   ounces turkey breakfast sausage
 2   cups 1% low-fat milk
 2   cups egg substitute
 1   teaspoon dry mustard
¾   teaspoon salt
½   teaspoon freshly ground black pepper
¼   teaspoon ground red pepper
 3   large eggs, lightly beaten
16   (1-ounce) slices white bread
 1   cup (4 ounces) finely shredded reduced-fat extrasharp Cheddar cheese
¼   teaspoon paprika

1 Heat a large nonstick skillet over medium-high heat. Coat pan with cooking spray. Add sausage to pan; cook 5 minutes or until browned, stirring and breaking sausage to crumble. Remove from heat; cool.
2 Combine milk and next 6 ingredients in a large bowl, stirring with a whisk.
3 Trim crusts from bread. Cut bread into 1-inch cubes. Add bread cubes, sausage, and cheese to milk mixture, stirring to combine. Pour bread mixture into a 13 x 9–inch baking or 3-quart casserole dish coated with cooking spray, spreading evenly. Cover and refrigerate 8 hours or overnight.
4 Preheat oven to 350°.
5 Remove casserole from refrigerator; let stand 30 minutes. Sprinkle casserole evenly with paprika. Bake at 350° for 45 minutes or until set and lightly browned. Let stand 10 minutes. Yield: 12 servings (serving size: about 1 cup).

CALORIES 184 (33% from fat); FAT 6.8g (sat 3.2g, mono 1.5g, poly 0.8g); PROTEIN 15.9g; CARB 14g; FIBER 0.6g; CHOL 76mg; IRON 2.2mg; SODIUM 636mg; CALC 181mg

Risotto with Spring Vegetables and Smoked Ham

In its simplest form—little more than rice simmered in broth and finished with cheese—risotto is wholly satisfying. Yet it offers many opportunities for variation and serves as a rich backdrop to highlight fresh, seasonal ingredients.

This luscious risotto showcases spring's bounty. Fava beans, asparagus, and peas provide garden-fresh counterpoints to the savory ham and rich, creamy rice. This comforting dinner is well worth a trip to the farmers' market.

Risotto with Spring Vegetables and Smoked Ham

¾   cup shelled fava beans (about 1½ pounds unshelled)
 2   cups water
 2   cups (1-inch) slices asparagus (about ½ pound)
 4   cups fat-free, less-sodium chicken broth
 2   tablespoons extravirgin olive oil
 1   cup finely chopped onion (about 1 small)
½   cup finely chopped smoked ham (about 3 ounces)
1½   cups Arborio rice or other medium-grain rice
 1   cup dry white wine
 1   cup shelled green peas (about 1 pound unshelled)
¾   cup (3 ounces) grated Parmigiano-Reggiano cheese, divided
¼   cup whipping cream
 1   tablespoon butter
½   teaspoon salt
¼   teaspoon freshly ground black pepper

1 Cook beans in boiling water 1 minute; drain. Plunge beans into ice water; drain. Remove tough outer skins from beans; discard skins. Set aside.
2 Bring 2 cups water to a boil in a medium saucepan. Add asparagus to pan; cook 4 minutes or until crisp-tender. Remove asparagus from pan with a slotted spoon; rinse with cold water. Set aside. Add broth to boiling water; reduce heat. Keep warm over low heat.
3 Heat oil in a large saucepan over medium heat. Add onion and ham to pan; cook 10 minutes or until onion is tender, stirring occasionally. Add rice; cook 2 minutes, stirring frequently. Increase heat to medium-high. Stir in wine, and cook 2 minutes or until liquid is nearly absorbed, stirring constantly. Set aside ¾ cup broth mixture; keep warm. Add remaining broth mixture, ½ cup at a time, stirring constantly until each portion of broth is absorbed before adding the next (about 25 minutes total).
4 Stir in peas, reserved beans, and reserved asparagus. Add reserved ¾ cup broth mixture, stirring until liquid is absorbed (about 4 minutes). Remove from heat; stir in ½ cup cheese, cream, and next 3 ingredients. Place about 1 cup risotto into each of 6 shallow bowls; sprinkle each serving with 2 teaspoons remaining cheese. Yield: 6 servings.

CALORIES 439 (30% from fat); FAT 14.4g (sat 6.1g, mono 6g, poly 1.1g); PROTEIN 19.7g; CARB 59.4g; FIBER 9.8g; CHOL 31.5mg; IRON 3.3mg; SODIUM 758mg; CALC 173mg

Build A Smarter Salad

Mix and match ingredients to bring an array of nutrients, fresh tastes, and new textures to your plate.

WHILE THE QUINTESSENTIAL PAIRING of ripe tomatoes and lettuce is certainly enjoyable, a good salad can be so much more. Adding fruits, nuts, and other well-chosen ingredients offers a welcome change. More importantly, incorporating a few more nutritious ingredients is an easy way to serve a more healthful dish.

Sautéed Tuna and Green Onion Stalks on Romaine

(pictured on page 250)

Carrot contributes beta-carotene, while bok choy, a unique and hearty choice for a salad, is rich in potential cancer-fighting indoles. And tuna is a good source of heart-healthy omega-3 fats.

  1   large carrot
  1   tablespoon rice vinegar
  1   tablespoon fresh orange juice
  1   teaspoon salt, divided
  ½   teaspoon chili garlic sauce (such as Lee Kum Kee)
  ½   teaspoon Dijon mustard
  1   tablespoon dark sesame oil, divided
  1   tablespoon canola oil, divided
  4   (6-ounce) yellowfin tuna steaks
  ¼   teaspoon freshly ground black pepper
 16   green onions, cut into 5-inch pieces (about 2 bunches)
  4   cups torn romaine lettuce
  2   cups shredded bok choy
  2   cups grape tomatoes, halved
  1   tablespoon toasted sesame seeds

1 Cut carrot lengthwise into ribbons using a vegetable peeler. Curl ribbons around fingers, and place carrot curls in a bowl of ice water.

2 Combine vinegar, juice, ³/₄ teaspoon salt, chili garlic sauce, and mustard. Add 1½ teaspoons sesame oil and 1½ teaspoons canola oil, stirring with a whisk.
3 Heat 1 teaspoon sesame oil and 1 teaspoon canola oil in a large nonstick skillet over medium-high heat. Sprinkle fish evenly with remaining ¼ teaspoon salt and pepper. Add fish to pan; cook 5 minutes on each side or until desired degree of doneness. Remove fish from pan.
4 Heat remaining ½ teaspoon sesame oil and remaining ½ teaspoon canola oil in pan over medium-high heat. Add onions to pan; sauté 5 minutes or until lightly browned, turning occasionally.
5 Combine lettuce, bok choy, and tomatoes in a large bowl. Drain carrot curls; add carrot curls to lettuce mixture. Drizzle vinegar mixture over lettuce mixture; toss gently to coat. Arrange 1½ cups lettuce mixture on each of 4 plates. Cut each tuna steak into thin slices. Arrange 1 tuna steak and 4 onions on each serving; sprinkle each serving with ³/₄ teaspoon sesame seeds. Yield: 4 servings.

CALORIES 314 (29% from fat); FAT 10.1g (sat 1.4g, mono 4.2g, poly 3.6g); PROTEIN 43.3g; CARB 12.9g; FIBER 4.9g; CHOL 77mg; IRON 3.4mg; SODIUM 731mg; CALC 143mg

Summer's Best Garden Salad

Adding five vegetables and one fruit rounds out the nutrition in this side dish.

  3   tablespoons fresh lime juice
  2   teaspoons honey
  ½   teaspoon Dijon mustard
  ¼   teaspoon salt
  ¼   teaspoon freshly ground black pepper
  2   teaspoons extravirgin olive oil
  4   cups shredded romaine lettuce
  1   cup yellow pear tomatoes, halved
  1   cup chopped peeled cucumber
  ½   cup finely chopped orange bell pepper
  ½   cup thinly sliced radishes
  2   tablespoons chopped fresh chives
  1   small yellow squash, halved lengthwise and thinly sliced (about 1 cup)
  ½   cup chopped avocado

1 Combine first 5 ingredients in a small bowl. Gradually add oil, stirring with a whisk.
2 Combine lettuce and next 6 ingredients in a large bowl. Drizzle dressing over lettuce mixture, and toss gently to coat. Top with avocado. Yield: 6 servings (serving size: about 1 cup salad and 4 teaspoons avocado).

CALORIES 64 (52% from fat); FAT 3.7g (sat 0.6g, mono 2.3g, poly 0.5g); PROTEIN 1.6g; CARB 7.8g; FIBER 2.4g; CHOL 0mg; IRON 0.9mg; SODIUM 123mg; CALC 28mg

Sesame Shrimp Salad

More adventurous greens, such as napa cabbage and watercress, add crunch. Shrimp boosts levels of lean, low-saturated-fat protein and omega-3s, while sesame seeds offer the minerals iron, magnesium, and zinc.

    1   tablespoon sugar
    3   tablespoons fresh lime juice,
        divided
    1   tablespoon water
    1   garlic clove, minced
    2   teaspoons chili garlic sauce
        (such as Lee Kum Kee), divided
  1½   teaspoons fish sauce
    ½   teaspoon salt, divided
    1   tablespoon orange marmalade
    2   teaspoons dark sesame oil,
        divided
   24   large shrimp, peeled and deveined
        (about 1 pound)
    5   cups shredded napa (Chinese)
        cabbage
  1½   cups trimmed watercress leaves
  1½   cups shredded carrot
    ⅓   cup chopped fresh cilantro
    ⅓   cup chopped fresh mint
    2   tablespoons toasted sesame
        seeds

① Combine sugar, 2 tablespoons juice, 1 tablespoon water, and garlic in a small microwave-safe bowl; cover with plastic wrap. Microwave at HIGH 40 seconds or until sugar dissolves. Cool. Stir in 1 teaspoon chili garlic sauce, fish sauce, and ¼ teaspoon salt. Set aside.

② Combine remaining 1 tablespoon juice, remaining 1 teaspoon chili garlic sauce, remaining ¼ teaspoon salt, marmalade, and 1 teaspoon oil in a large bowl, stirring with a whisk. Add shrimp to bowl; toss to coat. Marinate shrimp in refrigerator 15 minutes, tossing occasionally. Remove shrimp from bowl, reserving marinade. Thread 3 shrimp onto each of 8 (8-inch) wooden skewers.

③ Heat remaining 1 teaspoon oil in a large nonstick skillet over medium-high

heat. Add shrimp skewers and reserved marinade to pan; cook 3½ minutes or until shrimp is done and glazed, turning once.

④ Combine cabbage and remaining ingredients in a large bowl. Drizzle fish sauce mixture over cabbage mixture; toss well to coat. Arrange 2 cups cabbage mixture on each of 4 plates; top each serving with 2 skewers. Yield: 4 servings.

CALORIES 239 (27% from fat); FAT 7.3g (sat 1.2g, mono 2.4g, poly 3g); PROTEIN 26.3g; CARB 17.9g; FIBER 3.4g; CHOL 172mg; IRON 3.4mg; SODIUM 726mg; CALC 179mg

Mesclun with Berries and Sweet Spiced Almonds

Raspberries add several good-for-you nutrients like fiber, antioxidants, and vitamin C. Almonds are a good source of vitamin E and monounsaturated fats.

    5   cups gourmet salad greens
  1¾   cups raspberries (about 1 [6-ounce]
        container)
    ¼   cup chopped fresh chives
    3   tablespoons champagne vinegar or
        white wine vinegar
    2   teaspoons honey
    ½   teaspoon country-style Dijon
        mustard
    ¼   teaspoon salt
    ⅛   teaspoon freshly ground black
        pepper
    1   tablespoon canola oil
    6   tablespoons Sweet Spiced Almonds

① Combine first 3 ingredients in a large bowl. Combine vinegar and next 4 ingredients in a small bowl. Gradually add oil, stirring with a whisk. Drizzle vinegar mixture over lettuce mixture; toss gently to coat. Arrange 1 cup salad on each of 6 plates; top each serving with 1 tablespoon Sweet Spiced Almonds. Yield: 6 servings.

CALORIES 84 (45% from fat); FAT 4.2g (sat 0.3g, mono 2.4g, poly 1.3g); PROTEIN 2g; CARB 11.2g; FIBER 3.8g; CHOL 0mg; IRON 1.1mg; SODIUM 123mg; CALC 47mg

MAKE AHEAD
SWEET SPICED ALMONDS:

    1   cup sliced almonds
    ⅓   cup packed brown sugar
    1   teaspoon ground cinnamon
    ½   teaspoon ground coriander
    ½   teaspoon ground cumin
    1   large egg white, lightly beaten
        Cooking spray

① Preheat oven to 325°.
② Combine first 5 ingredients in a small bowl. Stir in egg white. Spread mixture evenly onto a foil-lined baking sheet coated with cooking spray. Bake at 325° for 10 minutes. Stir mixture; bake an additional 15 minutes or until crisp. Transfer foil to a wire rack; cool almond mixture. Break almond mixture into small pieces. Yield: 2 cups (serving size: 1 tablespoon).

NOTE: Store at room temperature in an airtight container for up to one week.

CALORIES 27 (50% from fat); FAT 1.5g (sat 0.1g, mono 1g, poly 0.4g); PROTEIN 0.8g; CARB 2.9g; FIBER 0.4g; CHOL 0mg; IRON 0.2mg; SODIUM 3mg; CALC 11mg

Adding fruits, nuts, and other well-chosen ingredients to salads offer a welcome change.

Salad Building Blocks

Greens

What they add: Most leafy greens contribute folate, the B vitamin critical to red blood cell health and the reduction of neural tube birth defects like spina bifida. Also, they provide generous amounts of vitamin A and the antioxidants lutein and zeaxanthin, which may help protect against macular degeneration.

Good to know: Lutein is better absorbed when combined with a splash of oil, particularly olive oil, according to a 2007 preliminary study with animals from the *Journal of Agriculture and Food Chemistry*. So a classic vinaigrette not only tastes great on your salad, but it may also help you absorb more nutrients.

Tomatoes

What they add: With plenty of vitamin C, some blood pressure–lowering potassium, and folate, tomatoes also impart the plant chemicals flavonoids (potential cancer fighters) and phytosterols (which may help lower cholesterol).

Good to know: Lycopene, an antioxidant in tomatoes, is under question as a cancer fighter. The 2006 Prostate, Lung, Colorectal, and Ovarian Cancer Trial found no protective benefits from a greater lycopene intake. Harvard researcher Edward Giovannucci, MD, still thinks there's plenty of evidence to tag this favorite salad fruit as a "probable" cancer fighter and suggests tomatoes may have other beneficial ingredients "and, conceivably, complex interactions among multiple components may contribute to the anticancer properties."

Fruits

What they add: All fruit provides abundant good nutrients (vitamin C and potassium, in particular) and a laundry list of disease-fighting chemicals in a package that's naturally low in fat, sodium, and calories. Blueberries contain polyphenol (a phytochemical linked to heart disease and cancer prevention) compounds called anthocyanins and proanthocyanins that may play a role in preserving memory. Grapes also offer polyphenols.

Good to know: The fiber in fruits can help lower blood cholesterol levels and reduce risk of heart disease. For example, one cup of blueberries has nearly four grams of fiber, and one medium apple yields five.

Vegetable Oils

What they add: Liquid vegetable oils are rich in vitamin E and unsaturated fats (monounsaturated and polyunsaturated), which don't clog arteries. Olive oil is particularly rich in phenol antioxidants.

Good to know: Look for virgin or extravirgin varieties of olive oils, states an August 2007 report in *Mayo Clinic Women's HealthSource*. The freshest oils (check to verify that the bottling date is less than a year old) and virgin or extravirgin olive oils tend to be richest in antioxidants.

Nuts and Seeds

What they add: One-fourth cup of nuts or seeds adds nearly five grams of high-quality protein, as well as generous amounts of vitamin E, fiber, minerals, and arginine, a compound that helps blood vessels to function. Nuts are high in fat, the healthful unsaturated kind.

Good to know: A report in *Harvard Men's Health Watch* suggests that as little as two ounces of nuts per week might lower your risk of heart disease. "Adding nuts to a balanced, healthful diet can take you one step away from heart disease," says editor Harvey B. Simon, MD, an associate professor of medicine at Harvard Medical School.

Onions

What they add: Onions are plentiful sources of disease-fighting phenols and flavonoids, both potential cancer fighters and weapons against some chronic diseases. The richer its phenolic and flavonoid content, the better an onion's protective effect, according to Rui Hai Liu, MD, PhD, an associate professor of food science at Cornell University.

Good to know: In a 2004 study, Liu looked at 10 varieties of onions and found shallots have six times the phenolic content of sweet Vidalia onions, the lowest on the scale. Pungent yellow onions and red onions also measured high.

Seafood and Other Proteins

What they add: Fatty fish like salmon or tuna offer omega-3 fats, which help lower the risk for heart disease. The American Heart Association suggests eating at least two three-ounce cooked servings of fish per week.

Good to know: Fish, skinless chicken, or small amounts of cheese can also help boost the protein content of salads. According to a 2007 study from Purdue University, increased protein improves satiety at meals.

Arugula, Grape, and Sunflower Seed Salad

Grapes add polyphenol antioxidants, while the seeds and oil deliver vitamin E.

   3   tablespoons red wine vinegar
   1   teaspoon honey
   1   teaspoon maple syrup
   ½   teaspoon stone-ground mustard
   2   teaspoons grapeseed oil
   7   cups loosely packed baby arugula
   2   cups red grapes, halved
   2   tablespoons toasted sunflower seed
       kernels
   1   teaspoon chopped fresh thyme
   ¼   teaspoon salt
   ¼   teaspoon freshly ground black
       pepper

❶ Combine first 4 ingredients in a small bowl. Gradually add oil, stirring with a whisk.
❷ Combine arugula and next 3 ingredients in a large bowl. Drizzle vinegar mixture over arugula; sprinkle with salt and pepper. Toss gently to coat. Yield: 6 servings (serving size: about 1 cup).

CALORIES 81 (34% from fat); FAT 3.1g (sat 0.3g, mono 0.5g, poly 2g); PROTEIN 1.6g; CARB 13.1g; FIBER 1.2g; CHOL 0mg; IRON 0.7mg; SODIUM 124mg; CALC 47mg

Watercress Salad with Pan-Seared Mahimahi

Tomatoes boost vitamin C and deliver lycopene. Shallots are particularly high in phenols, a compound that may protect against cancer. Rounding out the dish with a lean fish delivers heart-healthy protein and fat.

   2½ teaspoons extravirgin olive oil,
       divided
   2   (6-ounce) mahimahi fillets
   ¼   teaspoon salt, divided
   ¼   teaspoon freshly ground black
       pepper, divided
   2   cups watercress
   2   cups torn Bibb lettuce
   ½   cup chopped yellow tomato
   ½   cup chopped red tomato
   ¼   cup thinly sliced shallots
   1   tablespoon red wine vinegar
   1   tablespoon balsamic vinegar
   2   teaspoons honey
   ½   teaspoon Dijon mustard

❶ Heat 1 teaspoon oil in a large nonstick skillet over medium-high heat. Sprinkle fish evenly with ⅛ teaspoon salt and ⅛ teaspoon pepper. Add fish to pan; cook 4 minutes or until browned. Carefully turn fish over; cook 3 minutes or until fish flakes easily when tested with a fork or until desired degree of doneness. Remove fish from pan; keep warm.
❷ Combine watercress and next 4 ingredients in a large bowl. Combine vinegars, honey, mustard, remaining ⅛ teaspoon salt, and remaining ⅛ teaspoon pepper in a small bowl; gradually add remaining 1½ teaspoons oil, stirring with a whisk. Pour vinaigrette over lettuce mixture; toss gently to coat. Arrange 2½ cups lettuce mixture on each of 2 plates; top each serving with 1 fillet. Yield: 2 servings.

CALORIES 220 (28% from fat); FAT 6.9g (sat 1.1g, mono 4.3g, poly 1g); PROTEIN 26.1g; CARB 13.4g; FIBER 1.9g; CHOL 93mg; IRON 2.7mg; SODIUM 468mg; CALC 95mg

Southwest Salmon Caesar

Adding grilled salmon to this salad elevates it to a main dish rich in omega-3s.

DRESSING:
   ¼   cup fat-free mayonnaise
   ¼   cup (1 ounce) grated fresh Parmesan
       cheese
   2   tablespoons fat-free buttermilk
   2   tablespoons fresh lemon juice
   1   tablespoon water
   ½   teaspoon freshly ground black
       pepper
   ½   teaspoon Dijon mustard
   2   garlic cloves, minced
   2   canned anchovy fillets, drained and
       chopped

SALAD:
   ½   teaspoon salt
   ½   teaspoon paprika
   ½   teaspoon Spanish smoked paprika
       Dash of ground red pepper
   4   (6-ounce) salmon fillets, skinned
       Cooking spray
   8   cups torn romaine lettuce
   1   cup fresh corn kernels
   1   cup garlic-flavored croutons

❶ To prepare dressing, combine first 9 ingredients in a mini chopper or blender; pulse until well blended. Cover and chill 1 hour.
❷ To prepare salad, combine salt and next 3 ingredients; sprinkle evenly over fish.
❸ Heat a large nonstick skillet over medium-high heat. Coat pan with cooking spray. Add fish, spiced sides down, to pan; cook 4 minutes or until browned. Carefully turn fish over, and cook 4 minutes or until fish flakes easily when tested with a fork or until desired degree of doneness.
❹ Combine lettuce, corn, and croutons in a large bowl. Drizzle dressing over lettuce mixture; toss gently to coat. Arrange 2 cups salad on each of 4 plates; top each serving with 1 fillet. Yield: 4 servings.

CALORIES 340 (36% from fat); FAT 13.6g (sat 3.8g, mono 5.2g, poly 3g); PROTEIN 34.3g; CARB 20.9g; FIBER 4.4g; CHOL 73mg; IRON 2.4mg; SODIUM 752mg; CALC 163mg

Escarole-Arugula Salad with Roasted Peppers and Marinated Onions

Onions add potential cancer-fighting compounds that may also protect against diabetes and heart disease.

- 1 red bell pepper
- 1 yellow bell pepper
- 3 tablespoons balsamic vinegar, divided
- 2 teaspoons honey, divided
- 1 cup vertically sliced red onion
- 1 teaspoon fresh thyme leaves
- 1 teaspoon whole-grain Dijon mustard
- ½ teaspoon salt
- ¼ teaspoon freshly ground black pepper
- 1 tablespoon extravirgin olive oil
- 4 cups chopped escarole
- 2 cups baby arugula leaves

❶ Preheat broiler.
❷ Cut bell peppers in half lengthwise; discard seeds and membranes. Place pepper halves, skin sides up, on a foil-lined baking sheet; flatten with hand. Broil 15 minutes or until blackened. Place in a zip-top plastic bag; seal. Let stand 10 minutes. Peel and cut bell peppers into thin strips.
❸ Combine 1 tablespoon balsamic vinegar and 1 teaspoon honey in a medium bowl, stirring with a whisk. Add onion and thyme; toss well to coat. Let stand 15 minutes.
❹ Combine remaining 2 tablespoons vinegar, remaining 1 teaspoon honey, mustard, salt, and black pepper in a small bowl. Gradually add oil, stirring with a whisk. Combine escarole, arugula, bell pepper strips, and onion mixture in a large bowl. Drizzle vinegar mixture over escarole mixture, and toss gently to combine. Yield: 6 servings (serving size: 1 cup).

CALORIES 59 (38% from fat); FAT 2.5g (sat 0.4g, mono 1.7g, poly 0.3g); PROTEIN 1.2g; CARB 8.7g; FIBER 2.2g; CHOL 0mg; IRON 0.7mg; SODIUM 221mg; CALC 39mg

Mixed Greens with Blueberry Vinaigrette

Blueberries in the salad and in the infused vinegar contribute antioxidants.

- 3 tablespoons Blueberry Vinegar
- 1 teaspoon honey
- ½ teaspoon country-style Dijon mustard
- ¼ teaspoon salt
- ⅛ teaspoon freshly ground black pepper
- 1½ tablespoons extravirgin olive oil
- 4 cups baby arugula leaves
- 1 cup chopped frisée
- 1 cup blueberries
- ½ cup thinly sliced red onion

❶ Combine first 5 ingredients in a small bowl. Gradually add oil, stirring with a whisk. Combine arugula and remaining ingredients in a large bowl. Arrange 1 cup salad on each of 6 plates; drizzle 1 tablespoon vinegar mixture on each serving. Yield: 6 servings.

CALORIES 60 (54% from fat); FAT 3.6g (sat 0.5g, mono 2.5g, poly 0.4g); PROTEIN 0.8g; CARB 7.3g; FIBER 1.3g; CHOL 0mg; IRON 0.4mg; SODIUM 115mg; CALC 30mg

MAKE AHEAD
BLUEBERRY VINEGAR:

- 1 cup blueberries
- ¾ cup white wine vinegar
- 2 tablespoons sugar
- ½ small bay leaf

❶ Place blueberries in a small saucepan, and mash with a potato masher. Add vinegar, sugar, and bay leaf to pan, and bring to a boil. Cover, reduce heat, and simmer 10 minutes. Remove from heat; cover and let stand 4 hours. Strain mixture through a fine sieve into a bowl, and discard solids. Cover and chill. Yield: 1 cup (serving size: 1 tablespoon).

CALORIES 7 (0% from fat); FAT 0g; PROTEIN 0g; CARB 1.9g; FIBER 0.1g; CHOL 0mg; IRON 0mg; SODIUM 0mg; CALC 0mg

QUICK & EASY
Mixed Herb Salad

Adding tomatoes, fresh herbs, and pea shoots to a simple bowl of tossed greens boosts its nutrient content. Dressing it with monounsaturated-rich olive oil supplies even more. Pea shoots are the small leaves and tendrils from pea plants, most often snow peas. They're a good source of vitamin A. Substitute mâche if your local market doesn't stock pea shoots. To save time, use ⅓ cup chopped herb salad mix in place of the chive, thyme, and tarragon; look for it near the other packages of fresh herbs.

- 4 cups gourmet salad greens
- 1½ cups fresh pea shoots (about half of a [3-ounce] container)
- 1 cup red cherry tomatoes, halved
- 1 cup yellow cherry tomatoes, halved
- ¼ cup finely chopped fresh chives
- 2 tablespoons finely chopped fresh thyme
- 1 tablespoon finely chopped fresh tarragon
- 3 tablespoons sherry vinegar
- 2 teaspoons honey
- ½ teaspoon Dijon mustard
- ¼ teaspoon salt
- ¼ teaspoon freshly ground black pepper
- 1 tablespoon extravirgin olive oil

❶ Place first 7 ingredients in a large bowl; toss gently to combine.
❷ Combine vinegar and next 4 ingredients in a small bowl. Gradually add oil, stirring with a whisk. Drizzle vinegar mixture over greens mixture; toss gently to coat. Yield: 6 servings (serving size: about 1 cup).

CALORIES 55 (43% from fat); FAT 2.6g (sat 0.4g, mono 1.7g, poly 0.3g); PROTEIN 2.2g; CARB 7g; FIBER 2.3g; CHOL 0mg; IRON 1.5mg; SODIUM 130mg; CALC 54mg

Stovetop Steaming

Learn how this gentle, moist-heat cooking method enhances fish, chicken, vegetables, and more.

STEAMING IS A NATURAL FIT for fresher, lighter springtime fare because this simple technique leaves the ingredients' bright essential flavors and texture intact.

A staple preparation for a number of international cuisines, stovetop steaming offers a healthful way to cook. Many Asian dishes, in particular, use the cooking method—for example, steamed dumplings or pork-filled buns, or fish steamed atop aromatic vegetables. But other foods also benefit from steaming, dishes such as everyday steamed broccoli or green beans. This technique is easy to master, and even if you don't have a designated steamer, you can improvise with equipment you probably already have in your kitchen.

STAFF FAVORITE
MAKE AHEAD • FREEZABLE
Steamed Pork Buns (*Char Siu Bao*)

These buns are a grab-and-go street food in China. They were also popular in our Test Kitchens, where they earned our highest rating. Use a multitray bamboo steamer so you can cook all the buns at one time. To make them up to two months ahead, fill the dough, and freeze unsteamed buns on a tray in the freezer before placing them in a freezer-safe zip-top plastic bag. Steam directly from the freezer for an additional five minutes.

FILLING:

½ teaspoon five-spice powder
1 pound pork tenderloin, trimmed
Cooking spray
1 cup thinly sliced green onions
3 tablespoons hoisin sauce
2 tablespoons rice vinegar
1 tablespoon low-sodium soy sauce
1½ teaspoons honey
1 teaspoon minced peeled fresh ginger
1 teaspoon minced garlic
¼ teaspoon salt

DOUGH:

1 cup warm water (100° to 110°)
3 tablespoons sugar
1 package dry yeast (about 2¼ teaspoons)
3¼ cups all-purpose flour (about 14⅔ ounces)
3 tablespoons canola oil
¼ teaspoon salt
1½ teaspoons baking powder

❶ To prepare filling, rub five-spice powder evenly over pork. Heat a grill pan over medium-high heat. Coat pan with cooking spray. Add pork to pan; cook 18 minutes or until a thermometer registers 155°, turning pork occasionally. Remove pork from pan, and let stand 15 minutes.
❷ Cut pork crosswise into thin slices; cut slices into thin strips. Place pork in a medium bowl. Add onions and next 7 ingredients; stir well. Cover and refrigerate.
❸ To prepare dough, combine 1 cup warm water, sugar, and yeast in a large bowl; let stand 5 minutes.
❹ Lightly spoon flour into dry measuring cups; level with a knife. Add flour, oil, and ¼ teaspoon salt to yeast mixture; stir until a soft dough forms. Turn dough out onto a lightly floured surface. Knead until smooth and elastic (about 10 minutes). Place dough in a large bowl coated with cooking spray, turning to coat top. Cover and let rise in a warm place (85°), free from drafts, 1 hour or until doubled in size. (Gently press two fingers into dough. If indentation remains, dough has risen enough.)
❺ Punch dough down; let rest 5 minutes. Turn dough out onto a clean surface; knead in baking powder. Let dough rest 5 minutes.
❻ Divide dough into 10 equal portions, forming each into a ball. Working with one dough ball at a time (cover remaining dough balls to keep from drying), roll ball into a 5-inch circle. Place ¼ cup filling in center of dough circle. Bring up sides to cover filling and meet on top. (A) Pinch and seal closed with a twist. Repeat procedure with remaining dough balls and filling.
❼ Arrange 5 buns, seam sides down, 1 inch apart, in each tier of a 2-tiered bamboo steamer. Stack tiers; cover with lid.
❽ Add water to a large skillet to a depth of 1 inch; bring to a boil over medium-high heat. Place steamer in pan; steam 15 minutes or until buns are puffed and set. Cool 10 minutes before serving. Yield: 10 servings (serving size: 1 bun).

CALORIES 259 (21% from fat); FAT 6.1g (sat 0.9g, mono 3.2g, poly 1.5g); PROTEIN 14.3g; CARB 35.7g; FIBER 1.6g; CHOL 27mg; IRON 2.9mg; SODIUM 343mg; CALC 54mg

A After adding the filling to the dough, bring up the sides to cover filling and meet on top. Pinch and seal closed with a twist.

Steamed Mussels and Clams with Two Sauces

A large collapsible metal vegetable steamer set inside a Dutch oven works best for this recipe, as that setup can accommodate a large volume of shellfish. Littleneck clams are more tender and succulent than larger varieties. The steaming liquid is discarded, so it adds fragrance but no sodium.

COCKTAIL SAUCE:
- ¼ cup bottled chili sauce
- 1 tablespoon fresh lemon juice
- 1½ teaspoons minced fresh dill
- 1½ teaspoons prepared horseradish

CHIVE BUTTER:
- 2 tablespoons butter, melted
- 2 tablespoons minced fresh chives

SHELLFISH:
- 2 cups white wine
- 2 tablespoons Old Bay seasoning
- 24 littleneck clams
- 2 pounds mussels, scrubbed and debearded

1 To prepare cocktail sauce, combine first 4 ingredients in a small bowl.
2 To prepare chive butter, combine butter and chives in a small bowl; cover and keep warm.
3 To prepare shellfish, place wine and Old Bay in a large Dutch oven; set a large vegetable steamer in pan. Bring wine mixture to a boil over high heat.
4 Add clams to steamer. Steam clams, covered, 8 minutes. Add mussels to steamer. Steam mussels and clams, covered, 8 minutes or until clam and mussel shells open. Discard any unopened shells, and discard wine mixture. Serve shellfish immediately with sauces. Yield: 6 servings (serving size: about 7 mussels, 4 clams, 2½ teaspoons cocktail sauce, and 1¼ teaspoons chive butter).

CALORIES 196 (32% from fat); FAT 6.9g (sat 2.9g, mono 1.6g, poly 1g); PROTEIN 22.5g; CARB 9.6g; FIBER 0.1g; CHOL 65mg; IRON 14.9mg; SODIUM 699mg; CALC 66mg

Asian Aromatic Chicken

Here's a Chinese version of comfort food, sometimes referred to as soy sauce chicken in restaurants.

- 3 tablespoons low-sodium soy sauce
- 2 tablespoons dry sherry
- 2 tablespoons minced green onions
- 1 tablespoon minced peeled fresh ginger
- 1½ teaspoons hoisin sauce
- 1 teaspoon minced garlic
- ½ teaspoon sambal oelek (ground fresh chile paste) or chile paste with garlic
- 1 (3-inch) cinnamon stick, broken
- 1 star anise
- 4 (8-ounce) bone-in chicken breast halves, skinned
- 1 cup fat-free, less-sodium chicken broth

Cooking spray

1 Combine first 9 ingredients in a large zip-top plastic bag. Add chicken to bag; seal and marinate in refrigerator at least 6 hours or up to 24 hours, turning bag occasionally.
2 Remove chicken from bag, reserving marinade. Pour marinade into a large skillet; stir in broth. Arrange chicken in a bamboo steamer coated with cooking spray; cover with steamer lid.
3 Place steamer in pan; bring marinade mixture to a boil. Steam chicken 18 minutes or until a thermometer inserted in center of breasts registers 165°. Transfer chicken to a platter.
4 Remove steamer from pan. Strain marinade mixture through a fine sieve into a bowl; discard solids. Return marinade mixture to pan; bring to a boil over high heat. Cook until reduced to ½ cup (about 2 minutes). Serve sauce with chicken. Yield: 4 servings (serving size: 1 chicken breast half and 2 tablespoons sauce).

CALORIES 183 (10% from fat); FAT 2g (sat 0.5g, mono 0.5g, poly 0.5g); PROTEIN 35.5g; CARB 2.9g; FIBER 0.5g; CHOL 86mg; IRON 1.5mg; SODIUM 634mg; CALC 26mg

Steamed Wasabi Salmon with Ponzu Sauce

Steamed fish retains a moist, delicate texture. Served with a citrus-soy dipping sauce, it's a quick and delicious main dish. Pair with a salad of chilled cucumbers drizzled with rice wine vinegar and sesame oil.

- 3 tablespoons low-sodium soy sauce
- 1½ tablespoons water
- 1½ tablespoons fresh lemon juice
- 1½ teaspoons sugar
- 1½ teaspoons rice vinegar
- 1½ teaspoons wasabi paste
- 1 (1½-pound) center-cut salmon fillet, skinned
- 4 napa (Chinese) cabbage leaves

Thinly sliced green onions (optional)

1 Combine first 4 ingredients, stirring until sugar dissolves; set aside.
2 Combine vinegar and wasabi in a small bowl, stirring until smooth. Spread wasabi mixture evenly over top of salmon.
3 Line a bamboo steamer with cabbage leaves. Place salmon, wasabi sides up, over cabbage; cover with steamer lid.
4 Add water to a large skillet to a depth of 1 inch; bring to a boil. Place steamer in pan; steam salmon 8 minutes or until fish flakes easily when tested with a fork or until desired degree of doneness. Remove salmon from steamer; discard cabbage. Serve salmon with sauce; sprinkle with onions, if desired. Yield: 4 servings (serving size: about 4 ounces salmon and 1½ tablespoons sauce).

CALORIES 254 (38% from fat); FAT 10.7g (sat 2.5g, mono 4.6g, poly 2.5g); PROTEIN 31.6g; CARB 4.2g; FIBER 0.1g; CHOL 80mg; IRON 0.7mg; SODIUM 504mg; CALC 18mg

All About Steaming

Steaming, Defined

This technique involves cooking food over boiling liquid in a tightly sealed pan. The steam released from the liquid surrounds and permeates the food with moisture and heat.

What Steaming Does

Steaming cooks food more gently than almost any other method. Because the liquid never touches the food, it's less likely to jostle, overcook, or absorb too much water. This means food retains its shape, color, and texture. Steaming is a great light cooking technique because it involves no fat. And unlike boiling, which leaches water-soluble nutrients from food, steaming keeps most of the nutrients—as well as the flavor and color—intact.

Best Foods to Steam

Steaming is ideal for foods that need moisture, and foods that should be soft and silken rather than crunchy or caramelized. For example, steamed Asian dumplings develop an irresistible soft-chewy texture, rather than a firm or crunchy one. Almost all vegetables are good candidates (with a few exceptions, such as spongy vegetables like mushrooms and eggplant or tough ones, such as hearty greens).

When selecting a protein, choose light, delicate ingredients, such as chicken breast and most fish and shellfish. But avoid bold-flavored seafood like bluefish or firm-fleshed fish like tuna. Also, stay away from beef or pork, which fare best by browning.

Equipment

Steaming requires little more than a pan with a well-fitting lid and a rack to support the food over the liquid in the pan. Creating a good seal with the lid is crucial for holding in steam. If the lid doesn't fit tightly, cover the pan with foil, and then top with the lid. Many cookware sets come with steamer inserts, as do woks.

If you don't have these, there are other options.

A collapsible metal vegetable steamer works well for vegetables or certain shellfish—foods that you don't mind touching or being stacked on top of each other as they cook. If you don't have a vegetable steamer, you can improvise by placing a footed metal colander in the pan (make sure the lid will close), or set a round cooling rack on top of two ramekins in the bottom of the pan.

For foods that need to lie flat or shouldn't touch (such as salmon fillets or dumplings), try a bamboo steamer. Available at most Asian markets, these steamers come with two or three tiers that can be stacked, allowing you to cook a lot of food at one time. They also come with a lid that rests atop the uppermost tier. Set this type of steamer in a wok or large skillet with an inch of water.

Steaming Liquid

Consider translucent, thin liquids, such as water, broth, juice, wine, beer, or other spirits. These will bubble and steam to create a hot, moist environment. Forgo cloudy liquids such as dairy milk or coconut milk, which will curdle, or thick liquids like tomato sauce, which might burn.

Add just enough liquid to produce a high volume of steam without intruding through the holes or slats in the steamer or rack. Do not allow the water to touch the food or you'll end up boiling and, most likely, overcooking it.

No matter how firmly you cover the pan, the liquid will eventually boil away. For foods that cook longer than 15 or 20 minutes, check the liquid level occasionally. Have extra liquid boiling on the stovetop in a separate pan or teakettle; carefully add it to the pot or wok, not directly over the food.

Aromatics

Seasonings in the liquid can indeed permeate the food. As it cooks, the food's various cellular layers open up in the heat

and trap flavors in the steam, thereby gently enhancing the overall taste. Hard spices and aromatic roots such as cinnamon sticks, lemongrass stalks, star anise pods, and ginger are good options. They impart a subtle perfume, not an intense flavor.

Finishing Flavors

Because steamed foods lack the rich taste of those roasted, sautéed, or seared, many benefit from a sauce: cheese sauce for broccoli, or herbed butter for shellfish, for example. A simple vinaigrette drizzled over steamed food is also a nice finish. Sometimes, the steaming liquid itself can become the sauce, especially if aromatics and spices have been added, and if the sauce is reduced to a thicker consistency, which concentrates its flavor.

Let the food guide the sauce. Spirits other than wine often become too intense when reduced, thus overpowering the fresh-steamed flavors. Steamed buns, fish, and vegetables are delicate, a bonanza of natural flavors. A too-strong sauce will mask the subtlety of these foods.

Steam Safely

Three tips will ensure success:
1 Open the lid away from you so that the steam is released to the back of the stove away from your face.
2 Use silicone baking mitts to pick up a steaming rack. Because the rack will be damp, scalding water can soak through cloth oven mitts and cause a burn.
3 Use tongs or spatulas to remove food from the steamer. Steamed food often retains heat longer because the hot steam has permeated the food.

The Bottom Line

The most important elements of steaming:
1 Keep the food positioned above the liquid.
2 Make sure the pan is covered tightly.
3 Check the liquid level after 15 minutes; add more boiling liquid, if necessary, so the pan doesn't go dry.

Broccoli with Cheddar Sauce

This classic side dish is quick and easy. Steaming for the appropriate time ensures the broccoli is properly crisp-tender.

- 1 tablespoon all-purpose flour
- 1 cup fat-free milk
- ½ cup (2 ounces) shredded reduced-fat extrasharp Cheddar cheese
- 3 tablespoons grated fresh Parmesan cheese
- ½ teaspoon Dijon mustard
- ¼ teaspoon salt
- ¼ teaspoon freshly ground black pepper
- ¼ teaspoon chopped fresh thyme
- 1½ pounds broccoli florets (about 9 cups)

1 Place flour in a medium saucepan. Gradually add milk, stirring constantly with a whisk until smooth. Cook over medium-high heat 2 minutes or until mixture is bubbly and thickened, stirring constantly. Cook 1 minute, stirring constantly. Remove from heat. Add Cheddar cheese and next 5 ingredients, stirring with a whisk until smooth. Keep warm.
2 Add water to a large saucepan to a depth of 1 inch; set a large vegetable steamer in pan. Bring water to a boil over medium-high heat. Add broccoli to steamer. Steam broccoli, covered, 4 minutes or until crisp-tender. Serve broccoli immediately with sauce. Yield: 8 servings (serving size: about 1 cup broccoli and 2 tablespoons sauce).

CALORIES 69 (30% from fat); FAT 2.3g (sat 1.4g, mono 0.6g, poly 0.2g); PROTEIN 6.2g; CARB 7.1g; FIBER 2.5g; CHOL 7mg; IRON 0.8mg; SODIUM 204mg; CALC 143mg

Shrimp-Stuffed Tofu

Create a satisfying light dinner by pairing this aromatic entrée with sautéed bok choy. You needn't worry if you split the tofu slices at their sides when preparing the packets; you can still stuff them, and the filling will firm up in the steamer.

- 1½ cups sliced shiitake mushroom caps (about 2 ounces)
- 2 tablespoons thinly sliced green onions
- 1 tablespoon low-sodium soy sauce
- 1½ teaspoons rice vinegar
- 1 teaspoon minced peeled fresh ginger
- ½ teaspoon dark sesame oil
- ½ teaspoon sambal oelek (ground fresh chile paste) or chile paste with garlic
- 4 ounces peeled and deveined medium shrimp
- 1 garlic clove, thinly sliced
- 1 (14-ounce) block water-packed extrafirm tofu, drained
- Cooking spray
- 4 teaspoons low-sodium soy sauce
- 4 teaspoons rice vinegar
- 2 cups hot cooked short-grain rice
- Thinly sliced green onions (optional)

1 Place first 9 ingredients in a food processor; process until smooth, scraping sides of bowl occasionally.
2 (A) Split tofu block in half horizontally. (B) Cut each half in half diagonally to form 4 triangles. Make a pocket in each tofu triangle by inserting tip of a small knife into center of longest edge. Slice gently back and forth almost to (but not through) outside edges to form a pocket. Gently stuff each pocket with about ¼ cup shrimp mixture. Arrange tofu in a bamboo steamer coated with cooking spray; cover with steamer lid.
3 Add water to a large skillet to a depth of 1 inch; bring to a boil over medium-high heat. Place steamer in pan; steam 15 minutes or until filling is set.
4 Combine 4 teaspoons soy sauce and 4 teaspoons rice vinegar in a small bowl. Place ½ cup rice on each of 4 plates. Top each serving with 1 stuffed tofu triangle. Drizzle each serving with 2 teaspoons soy sauce mixture; garnish with green onions, if desired. Yield: 4 servings.

CALORIES 267 (21% from fat); FAT 6.3g (sat 0.9g, mono 3.5g, poly 1.7g); PROTEIN 18.7g; CARB 31.3g; FIBER 2.5g; CHOL 43mg; IRON 4.2mg; SODIUM 365mg; CALC 97mg

A Using a sharp knife, cut tofu block in half horizontally.

B Cut each half in half diagonally to form 4 triangles.

Shrimp and Mushroom Sui Mei

These open-faced dumplings are a staple of Hong Kong dim sum. Round gyoza skins work best here. If you can't find them, cut square wonton wrappers into circles using a three-inch biscuit cutter. Lining the bamboo steamer with cabbage leaves ensures the dumplings won't stick. To vary the texture and taste, top each dumpling with lump crabmeat or a small piece of scallop instead of shrimp, and dot with hoisin sauce instead of hot sauce.

  Cooking spray
3½ cups thinly sliced cremini mushrooms (about 6 ounces)
1¾ cups thinly sliced shiitake mushroom caps (about 4 ounces)
1 cup thinly sliced green onions
2 tablespoons low-sodium soy sauce
1 tablespoon dry sherry
2½ teaspoons minced peeled ginger
2 teaspoons dark sesame oil
4 ounces peeled and deveined medium shrimp
24 gyoza skins (round wonton wrappers)
6 peeled and deveined medium shrimp, each cut crosswise into 4 pieces
4 large napa (Chinese) cabbage leaves
1 tablespoon sambal oelek (ground fresh chile paste) or Sriracha (hot chile sauce)

❶ Heat a large nonstick skillet over medium-high heat. Coat pan with cooking spray. Add mushrooms to pan; sauté 8 minutes or until liquid evaporates. Spoon mushrooms into a food processor. Add onions and next 5 ingredients; process 10 seconds or until finely chopped.
❷ Working with 1 gyoza skin at a time (cover remaining skins to prevent drying), spoon about 1 tablespoon shrimp mixture into center of skin. Moisten edges of skin with water. (A) Gather up and crimp edges of skin around filling; lightly squeeze skin to adhere to filling, leaving top of dumpling open. Place 1 shrimp piece on top of filling, pressing gently into filling. Place dumpling on a baking sheet; cover loosely with a damp towel to prevent drying. Repeat procedure with remaining skins, filling, and shrimp.
❸ Line each tier of a 2-tiered bamboo steamer with 2 cabbage leaves. Arrange 12 dumplings, 1 inch apart, over cabbage in each steamer basket. Stack tiers, and cover with steamer lid.
❹ Add water to skillet to a depth of 1 inch, and bring to a boil. Place steamer in pan, and steam dumplings 15 minutes or until done. Remove dumplings from steamer, and spoon ⅛ teaspoon sambal oelek onto each dumpling. Discard cabbage. Yield: 8 servings (serving size: 3 dumplings).

CALORIES 120 (14% from fat); FAT 1.9g (sat 0.3g, mono 0.6g, poly 0.8g); PROTEIN 7.2g; CARB 17.6g; FIBER 1.3g; CHOL 31mg; IRON 1.8mg; SODIUM 357mg; CALC 36mg

A After adding the filling to the gyoza skin, moisten edges of skin with water. Gather up and crimp edges of skin around filling; lightly squeeze skin to adhere to filling, leaving top of dumpling open.

> ## Stovetop steaming leaves the ingredients' bright essential flavors and texture intact.

Whole Grain and Italian Sausage–Stuffed Cabbage

Steaming the cabbage leaves before filling them makes them pliable enough to roll up.

2 cups water
½ cup dried porcini mushrooms, crushed (about ½ ounce)
1¼ cups uncooked bulgur
2 teaspoons butter
1 teaspoon olive oil
1 cup finely chopped onion
⅔ cup finely chopped celery
⅔ cup finely chopped carrot
2 garlic cloves, minced
½ teaspoon salt
¼ teaspoon freshly ground black pepper
1 pound hot turkey Italian sausage
12 large Savoy cabbage leaves
2 cups canned crushed tomatoes
1½ tablespoons red wine vinegar
2 teaspoons brown sugar
2 tablespoons chopped fresh parsley

❶ Bring 2 cups water to a boil in a saucepan. Stir in mushrooms; cover, remove from heat, and let stand 10 minutes.
❷ Uncover pan; bring mushroom mixture to a boil. Stir in bulgur; cover, remove from heat, and let stand 30 minutes or until liquid is absorbed. Spoon bulgur mixture into a large bowl.

③ Heat butter and oil in a large nonstick skillet over medium-high heat. Add onion and next 3 ingredients to pan; sauté 7 minutes or until tender and lightly browned. Add vegetables to bulgur mixture; cool slightly. Stir in salt and pepper. Remove casings from sausage. Crumble sausage into bulgur mixture; stir well.

④ Add water to a large Dutch oven to a depth of 2 inches; set a large vegetable steamer in pan. Bring water to a boil over medium-high heat. Add cabbage leaves to steamer. Steam cabbage, covered, 6 minutes or until tender and pliable. Remove cabbage from steamer (do not drain water). Rinse cabbage with cold water; drain and pat dry.

⑤ Working with one cabbage leaf at a time, place ½ cup bulgur mixture in center of leaf. Fold in edges of leaf; roll up. Repeat procedure with remaining cabbage leaves and bulgur mixture to form 12 cabbage rolls. Stack rolls evenly in steamer.

⑥ Return Dutch oven to medium-high heat; bring water to a boil. Steam rolls, covered, 30 minutes, adding more water if necessary.

⑦ Combine tomatoes, vinegar, and sugar in saucepan; cook over medium heat 5 minutes or until thoroughly heated, stirring occasionally. Remove from heat; stir in parsley. Serve sauce with rolls. Yield: 6 servings (serving size: 2 cabbage rolls and about ⅓ cup sauce).

CALORIES 322 (30% from fat); FAT 10.9g (sat 3.3g, mono 4.1g, poly 2.3g); PROTEIN 19.6g; CARB 40.2g; FIBER 10.3g; CHOL 48mg; IRON 4.1mg; SODIUM 839mg; CALC 86mg

IN SEASON
Rhubarb

Fruit or vegetable, either way, it adds zest to sweet and savory dishes.

Those who have rhubarb in their gardens no doubt find its emergence both a welcome harbinger of spring and a bit of an intrigue. And, although we think of rhubarb as red, it can be either red or green (red is usually sweeter). Victoria is an heirloom variety that produces mostly green stalks and only the occasional red one. Cooked, the green stalks break down into a subtle pea-green puree.

Technically, rhubarb is a vegetable, even though we habitually refer to it as "the first fruit of the season." At one point, the United States Customs Court ruled that rhubarb was a fruit, as if government can overrule the laws of nature. That's pretty much how we think of rhubarb, so long as there's plenty of sugar around. Without a sweetener, rhubarb is bracingly sour. Add to that the fact that the leaves are mildly toxic and you might wonder how people first came to eat such a thing. Before sugar became widely available (and cheaper) worldwide, rhubarb was cooked in soups and sauces, especially in the chilly northern parts of the world like Siberia and the Himalayas, where it grows prolifically.

Rhubarb's sourness is flattered by a constellation of other fruits and flavors. Fragrant orange is a constant, and grapefruit's bittersweet flavor is appealing, as well. Blood oranges are even better, given their acidity, deep color, and more complex flavor. Sweet spices like cinnamon, cardamom, nutmeg, and ginger complement rhubarb's tang, as does vanilla. Maple syrup and maple sugar are good alternatives to white sugar, having a nutty flavor with more depth.

However, rhubarb figures well in a variety of desserts. In fact, rhubarb is widely known by its nickname, "pie plant." It can be diced and added to a coffee cake, where it offers a tart little jolt, or cooked into a sweet-sticky jam. Regardless of how it's stewed, rhubarb eventually disintegrates into a puree, so be prepared for a mushy or, at best, irregular consistency in rhubarb dishes. This might be one reason for the frequent pairing of rhubarb with strawberries and apples—aside from sweetness, they provide volume and texture.

Rhubarb-Strawberry Crisp

Be sure to serve shortly after taking the dish out of the oven for superior texture and flavor.

FILLING:
- 6 cups (½-inch) slices rhubarb (about 2 pounds)
- 2½ cups halved strawberries
- ¾ cup granulated sugar
- 3 tablespoons cornstarch
- 1 teaspoon grated orange rind
- ½ teaspoon ground cinnamon
- Cooking spray

TOPPING:
- ⅔ cup all-purpose flour (about 3 ounces)
- ½ cup packed brown sugar
- ½ cup regular oats
- ¼ teaspoon ground cinnamon
- Dash of salt
- 6 tablespoons chilled butter, cut into small pieces

① Preheat oven to 375°.

② To prepare filling, combine first 6 ingredients. Spoon into a 13 x 9–inch baking dish coated with cooking spray.

③ To prepare topping, lightly spoon flour into dry measuring cups. Combine flour and next 4 ingredients in a medium bowl; cut in butter with a pastry blender or 2 knives until mixture is crumbly. Sprinkle topping over filling. Bake at 375° for 30 minutes or until bubbly. Let stand 10 minutes. Yield: 8 servings.

CALORIES 303 (28% from fat); FAT 9.3g (sat 5.5g, mono 2.4g, poly 0.6g); PROTEIN 3.1g; CARB 54.3g; FIBER 3.5g; CHOL 23mg; IRON 1.5mg; SODIUM 89mg; CALC 108mg

How To Clean and Freeze Rhubarb

Because of its short growing season (the bulk of the crop arrives in April and May), rhubarb is a much-sought-after spring commodity—so much so, our Test Kitchens often prep and freeze it for year-round use. When buying, look for deep red, crisp stalks, free of blemishes and cuts, then follow these instructions for prepping and freezing. You'll have plenty of its tart-sweetness on hand for pies, jams, and other desserts year-round.

1 Trim leaves from the top of the stalk, and cut about an inch from the bottom; discard.

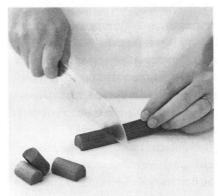

2 After rinsing, pat stalks dry with a towel and cut into one-inch sections. Use now, or read on for freezing directions.

3 Lay cut pieces on a lined baking sheet, and freeze for about an hour (this prevents rhubarb from sticking together).

4 Transfer pieces to a zip-top plastic bag, and store in the freezer for up to six months. Defrost overnight in the refrigerator when ready to use.

Rhubarb-Maple Fool in Phyllo Stacks

The fluffy rhubarb mixture is based on fool, a traditional English dessert of cooked, pureed fruit folded into whipped cream. Here it's spread between crisp layers of maple-flavored phyllo dough. For the prettiest color, use bright red stalks of rhubarb. The intense nutty sweetness of maple sugar affords the best flavor, but you can substitute brown sugar in a pinch. The phyllo crisps can be made ahead and stored in an airtight container for up to three days. Assemble desserts just before serving so you get the benefit of crisp pastry contrasting with the soft rhubarb fool.

CRISPS:
- 2 tablespoons butter
- 10 (14 x 9-inch) sheets frozen phyllo dough, thawed
- 5 tablespoons maple sugar

FOOL:
- 4 cups chopped rhubarb (about 1¼ pounds)
- ½ cup maple sugar
- ½ cup maple syrup
- 2 teaspoons grated orange rind
- ⅓ cup fresh orange juice
- ½ teaspoon ground cinnamon
- ⅛ teaspoon ground nutmeg
- Dash of ground cloves
- Dash of salt
- ⅓ cup whipping cream, chilled
- 2 teaspoons maple sugar
- ½ teaspoon vanilla extract
- ½ cup fat-free sour cream

1 Preheat oven to 350°.

2 To prepare crisps, melt butter in a small skillet over medium heat; cook 3 minutes or until lightly browned, stirring occasionally. Remove from heat.

3 Lightly dab 5 phyllo sheets with half of browned butter; sprinkle each sheet with 1½ teaspoons sugar. Stack layers, and press gently. Cut phyllo stack into 9 (4⅔ x 3-inch) rectangles. Repeat procedure with remaining phyllo, browned butter, and 2½ tablespoons sugar. Place rectangles on baking sheets. Bake at 350° for 5 minutes or until crisp. Remove from pans; cool completely on a wire rack.

④ To prepare fool, combine rhubarb and next 8 ingredients in a large saucepan; bring to boil. Reduce heat, and simmer until reduced to 2½ cups (about 30 minutes), stirring occasionally. Place half of rhubarb mixture in a blender. Remove center piece of blender lid (to allow steam to escape); secure blender lid on blender. Place a clean towel over opening in blender lid (to avoid splatters). Blend until smooth. Pour into a medium bowl. Repeat procedure with remaining rhubarb mixture. Cover and chill completely.

⑤ Place whipping cream, 2 teaspoons sugar, and vanilla in a small bowl; beat with a mixer at high speed until stiff peaks form. Gently fold in sour cream. Fold whipped cream mixture into chilled rhubarb mixture.

⑥ Place 1 phyllo crisp on a dessert plate. Layer crisp with ¼ cup rhubarb mixture, 1 phyllo crisp, ¼ cup rhubarb mixture, and 1 phyllo crisp. Repeat procedure with remaining phyllo crisps and rhubarb mixture. Serve immediately. Yield: 6 servings (serving size: 1 stack).

CALORIES 314 (29% from fat); FAT 10.2g (sat 5.9g, mono 3g, poly 0.6g); PROTEIN 3.3g; CARB 54.1g; FIBER 2.1g; CHOL 30mg; IRON 1.5mg; SODIUM 157mg; CALC 155mg

MAKE AHEAD
Rhubarb and Raspberry Jam with Ricotta Toasts

> 2 cups fresh raspberries
> 3½ cups chopped rhubarb (about 1 pound)
> ½ cup sugar
> ½ teaspoon vanilla extract
> 10 (1½-ounce) slices sturdy rustic bread, toasted
> 1¼ cups fresh whole milk ricotta cheese

① Place raspberries in a blender or food processor; process until smooth. Strain raspberries through a sieve into a bowl, pressing with a spatula; discard seeds. Combine raspberry puree, rhubarb, and sugar in a medium saucepan; bring to a boil. Cover, reduce heat, and simmer 20 minutes. Uncover and cook until reduced to 2½ cups (about 30 minutes), stirring occasionally. Remove from heat; stir in vanilla. Spoon into a bowl; cover and chill. Serve with toast and cheese. Yield: 10 servings (serving size: ¼ cup jam, 1 toast piece, and 2 tablespoons cheese).

CALORIES 227 (25% from fat); FAT 6.2g (sat 3.6g, mono 1.2g, poly 0.2g); PROTEIN 7g; CARB 36.1g; FIBER 2.6g; CHOL 19mg; IRON 3mg; SODIUM 245mg; CALC 401mg

MAKE AHEAD
Gingered Rhubarb Chutney

This sharp, spicy-sweet chutney is good with duck, lamb, and pork—rich meats complemented by the punch of a sour, fruity condiment. You can also serve atop vegetable curry or with cream cheese and crackers as an appetizer. If you prefer a milder chutney, remove the seeds from the jalapeño.

> 1 cup packed brown sugar
> 3 cups finely chopped rhubarb (about 1 pound)
> 1 cup finely chopped onion
> ½ cup cider vinegar
> ¼ cup balsamic vinegar
> ¼ cup dried currants
> 1 tablespoon minced peeled fresh ginger
> 1 teaspoon paprika
> ½ teaspoon salt
> ⅛ teaspoon ground cardamom (optional)
> ½ jalapeño pepper, minced

① Combine all ingredients in a medium saucepan over medium-high heat; bring to a boil. Reduce heat, and simmer 35 minutes or until thick. Serve warm or at room temperature. Yield: 2 cups (serving size: 2 tablespoons).

CALORIES 71 (1% from fat); FAT 0.4g (sat 0g, mono 0g, poly 0.4g); PROTEIN 0.4g; CARB 17.8g; FIBER 0.8g; CHOL 0mg; IRON 0.5mg; SODIUM 83mg; CALC 37mg

Rhubarb 101

Seasonality
Though hothouse rhubarb can be found year-round in some parts of the country, field-grown rhubarb peaks in the spring. Many favor the field-grown plant's more assertive flavor and deeper color.

Selection
Choose thick, firm stalks with no wrinkling or other signs of drying. If there are leaves on the stalks, they should be fresh and unwilted (leaves must be discarded).

Storage
Refrigerate fresh rhubarb in a plastic bag for up to three days. You can also chop rhubarb, place in a heavy-duty zip-top plastic bag, and freeze for up to eight months. (See page 136 for more details.)

Preparation
Trim and discard any leaves. Wash stalks just before using. Rhubarb is almost always cooked—usually with a good amount of sugar to tame its sour taste, similar to the way cranberries are prepared.

Rhubarb–Sour Cream Snack Cake with Walnut Streusel

CAKE:

3½ cups finely chopped rhubarb (about 1 pound)
2 tablespoons all-purpose flour
1½ cups packed brown sugar
5 tablespoons butter, softened
2 large eggs
1 cup fat-free sour cream
1 teaspoon grated orange rind
2 teaspoons vanilla extract
1½ cups all-purpose flour (about 6¾ ounces)
1 cup whole wheat flour (about 4¾ ounces)
1 teaspoon baking soda
1 teaspoon ground cinnamon
½ teaspoon salt
Cooking spray

STREUSEL:

¼ cup turbinado sugar
½ teaspoon ground cinnamon
2 tablespoons chilled butter, cut into small pieces
¼ cup chopped walnuts

❶ Preheat oven to 375°.
❷ To prepare cake, combine rhubarb and 2 tablespoons all-purpose flour in a medium bowl; toss well to coat.
❸ Place brown sugar and 5 tablespoons butter in a large bowl; beat with a mixer at medium speed until light and fluffy. Add eggs, 1 at a time, beating well after each addition. Add sour cream, rind, and vanilla; beat until well combined.
❹ Lightly spoon 1½ cups all-purpose flour and whole wheat flour into dry measuring cups; level with a knife. Combine flours and next 3 ingredients, stirring with a whisk. Gradually add flour mixture to butter mixture, beating at low speed just until combined. Fold in rhubarb mixture. Spread batter into a 9-inch square baking pan coated with cooking spray.
❺ To prepare streusel, combine turbinado sugar and ½ teaspoon cinnamon in a small bowl. Cut in 2 tablespoons butter with a pastry blender or 2 knives until mixture is crumbly; stir in nuts. Sprinkle streusel evenly over batter. Bake at 375° for 50 minutes or until a wooden pick inserted in center comes out clean. Yield: 12 servings (serving size: 1 piece).

CALORIES 326 (27% from fat); FAT 9.8g (sat 4.9g, mono 2.3g, poly 1.7g); PROTEIN 5.9g; CARB 55.6g; FIBER 2.7g; CHOL 55mg; IRON 2.1mg; SODIUM 291mg; CALC 103mg

Rhubarb-Lentil Soup with Crème Fraîche

Soaking the lentils in hot water helps them cook a bit more quickly when they're added to the soup. Because of rhubarb's likeness to the tangy herb sorrel, this dish plays off classic lentil-sorrel soup.

1½ cups boiling water
¾ cup dried petite green lentils
Cooking spray
2 cups finely chopped carrot
1¾ cups finely chopped celery
1½ cups finely chopped red onion
¼ cup chopped fresh parsley
2 cups chopped rhubarb (about 12 ounces)
4 cups fat-free, less-sodium chicken broth
½ teaspoon salt
¼ teaspoon freshly ground black pepper
1 tablespoon chopped fresh dill
6 tablespoons crème fraîche
Dill sprigs (optional)

❶ Pour 1½ cups boiling water over lentils in a small bowl; let stand 10 minutes.
❷ Heat a Dutch oven over medium-high heat. Coat pan with cooking spray. Add carrot and next 3 ingredients to pan; sauté 4 minutes. Add rhubarb, and sauté 3 minutes. Drain lentils, and add lentils to pan. Stir in broth and salt; bring to a boil. Cover, reduce heat, and simmer 35 minutes or until lentils are tender.
❸ Remove from heat; cool 5 minutes. Place 3 cups lentil mixture in a blender or food processor. Remove center piece of blender lid (to allow steam to escape); secure blender lid on blender. Place a clean towel over opening in blender lid (to avoid splatters). Blend until smooth. Return pureed mixture to pan; stir in pepper.
❹ Combine chopped dill and crème fraîche in a small bowl. Serve crème fraîche mixture on top of soup; garnish with dill sprigs, if desired. Yield: 6 servings (serving size: about 1⅓ cups soup and 1 tablespoon crème fraîche mixture).

CALORIES 187 (29% from fat); FAT 6.1g (sat 3.3g, mono 1.4g, poly 0.4g); PROTEIN 8.5g; CARB 25.4g; FIBER 7.3g; CHOL 14mg; IRON 2.2mg; SODIUM 523mg; CALC 96mg

Citrusy Rhubarb Sorbet

You can vary this simple dessert by using tangerine juice in place of the orange juice.

4 cups chopped rhubarb (about 1¼ pounds)
1 cup water
⅔ cup sugar
½ cup fresh orange juice (about 2 large oranges)
Mint sprigs (optional)
Orange rind strips (optional)

❶ Combine first 4 ingredients in a medium saucepan; bring to a boil. Reduce heat, and simmer 20 minutes or until rhubarb is tender. Cool slightly. Place rhubarb mixture in a blender, and process until smooth. Pour into a bowl, and refrigerate 2 hours or until thoroughly chilled. Pour mixture into freezer can of an ice-cream freezer; freeze according to manufacturer's instructions. Place a freezer-safe bowl in a freezer for 10 minutes. Spoon sorbet into bowl; cover and freeze 4 hours or until firm. Garnish with mint and rind, if desired. Yield: 5 servings (serving size: about ⅔ cup).

CALORIES 135 (1% from fat); FAT 0.2g (sat 0.1g, mono 0g, poly 0.1g); PROTEIN 1.1g; CARB 33.7g; FIBER 1.8g; CHOL 0mg; IRON 0.3mg; SODIUM 4mg; CALC 87mg

Lessons From Mom

Some of our favorite cooks share tips and recipes inherited from their mothers and grandmothers.

WE ASKED FOUR FOOD PROS to share memories of cooking with their mothers and other family members. Some learned by watching. Others relished the opportunity to arrange apples in a piecrust or fill steamed rice dumplings. They offered evocative descriptions of meat loaf slathered with ketchup, *dosas* topped with fresh coconut chutney, garlic noodles, and tarte tatin. The common ingredient: motherly love—a feeling of well-being and self-confidence Mom imparted along with every recipe.

Ratatouille with Tofu

This dish epitomizes the fusion of French and Asian cuisine that is the hallmark of Helene An's cooking inheritance: Ratatouille is French, and tofu decidedly Asian. Serve with rice noodles. Offer the extra Pesto Coulis as a dipping sauce with crusty French bread; it's also nice tossed with hot rice or pasta.

Cooking spray
- 1 cup finely chopped carrot
- ½ cup finely chopped onion
- ¼ cup chopped fresh basil
- 2 teaspoons chopped fresh thyme
- 2 teaspoons minced garlic (about 4 cloves)
- 2 cups finely chopped reduced-fat firm tofu, drained (about 11 ounces)
- 2 cups diced eggplant
- 1 cup diced zucchini
- 1 cup chopped plum tomato
- 4 teaspoons Pesto Coulis
- 2 (14-ounce) cans no-salt-added tomato sauce
- 1 teaspoon ground cumin
- ½ teaspoon salt
- ⅛ teaspoon freshly ground black pepper

1 Heat a large Dutch oven over medium-high heat. Coat pan with cooking spray. Add carrot to pan; sauté 6 minutes. Add onion and next 3 ingredients; sauté 4 minutes. Add tofu, eggplant, and zucchini; sauté 4 minutes or until tender. Add tomato, Pesto Coulis, and tomato sauce; bring to a boil. Reduce heat, and simmer 30 minutes, stirring occasionally. Remove from heat; stir in cumin, salt, and pepper. Yield: 4 servings (serving size: 1½ cups).

CALORIES 201 (25% from fat); FAT 5.6g (sat 0.6g, mono 3.4g, poly 0.7g); PROTEIN 12.4g; CARB 28.5g; FIBER 7.7g; CHOL 0mg; IRON 4.3mg; SODIUM 379mg; CALC 235mg

QUICK & EASY • MAKE AHEAD
PESTO COULIS:

- 1 cup parsley leaves (about 1 bunch)
- 1 cup basil leaves (about 1 bunch)
- ½ cup chopped green onion
- ½ cup extravirgin olive oil

1 Combine all ingredients in a food processor. Pulse until smooth. Yield: ¾ cup (serving size: 1 teaspoon).

CALORIES 28 (97% from fat); FAT 3g (sat 0.4g, mono 2.2g, poly 0.3g); PROTEIN 0.1g; CARB 0.3g; FIBER 0.1g; CHOL 0mg; IRON 0.2mg; SODIUM 1mg; CALC 5mg

Hospitality As Art

Helene An's mother never cooked a thing in her life. As the wife of the Vice Consul to the Emperor of Vietnam in Hanoi, she didn't need to, says Helene. "But she had to learn all the basics in order to direct her three chefs. She had to entertain, please guests, and tailor dinner menus to them."

Today, Helene credits her successful family restaurant empire, which includes three restaurants and a line of bottled sauces, to those motherly lessons in the art of hospitality. And she works hard to impart those values along with practical cooking lessons to her daughters.

Forced to flee Saigon in 1975, Helene settled with her husband and three young daughters in San Francisco, where her mother-in-law, Diana, had purchased a small Italian deli. (Helene's mother remained in Vietnam, where she died in 1978.) "I had to jump in and work," she says. That meant cooking in the deli every evening after working eight hours as an accountant. The deli began offering Vietnamese items. Soon, Sam's Deli became Thanh Long, and the city had its first Vietnamese restaurant.

Helene and one of her daughters opened Crustacean in 1991. The menu's unique blend of Chinese, French, and Vietnamese cuisine resulted in Helene being called the "mother of fusion cuisine" in a *San Francisco Chronicle* review. In 1997, the women opened Crustacean Beverly Hills. Today, Helene's 14-year-old granddaughter, "Bobo," spends afternoons in that kitchen soaking up the hands-on and philosophical lessons from her ancestors.

> "The girls were in the kitchen with me all the time. I taught them to sauté, to make noodles, to fill spring rolls, but also the importance of hard work and teamwork."
> —Helene An

Chicken Sauté with Caramelized Ginger Sauce

This recipe from Helene An uses simple ingredients with Asian flair. Serve over rice with steamed bok choy.

- 1 tablespoon canola oil
- 2 tablespoons sugar
- 1½ tablespoons low-sodium soy sauce
- 1 teaspoon chile paste with garlic (such as sambal oelek)
- 1 teaspoon grated fresh ginger
- ¾ cup fat-free, less-sodium chicken broth
- 1 teaspoon sesame oil
- 4 (6-ounce) skinless, boneless chicken breast halves, thinly sliced
- ¼ teaspoon freshly ground black pepper
- ⅛ teaspoon salt

❶ Heat canola oil in a large nonstick skillet over medium heat. Add sugar to pan; cook 1 minute or until sugar dissolves and is lightly browned. Combine soy sauce, chile paste, and ginger in a small bowl; add to pan. Add chicken broth, sesame oil, and chicken to pan; cook 5 minutes or until chicken is done, stirring occasionally. Remove chicken from pan with a slotted spoon. Simmer sauce 10 minutes or until slightly thickened. Return chicken to pan; toss to coat. Sprinkle evenly with pepper and salt. Yield: 4 servings (serving size: 1 cup).

CALORIES 351 (20% from fat); FAT 7.8g (sat 1.3g, mono 3.3g, poly 2.2g); PROTEIN 59.4g; CARB 7.2g; FIBER 0.1g; CHOL 148mg; IRON 2mg; SODIUM 557mg; CALC 30mg

His First Cooking Teacher

When they were kids, David Bonom's older brother tried to teach him how to fix cars. "But I had no interest in learning," says the man who now creates many recipes for *Cooking Light*. (He developed the ones for this chapter's Superfast column, page 158.) "My mother was in the kitchen cooking, and that's where I wanted to be."

Although his mother wasn't a professional, David says, she taught him all the basic techniques he uses today. "We never called it 'braising'; rather it was 'roasting and the liquid goes up to here.'" David's mom explained that putting an inexpensive cut of meat in bottled salad dressing before cooking would make it tender and juicy. Dry rubs? "Well, she told me to sprinkle pork spareribs with powdered garlic and broil them," he remembers.

She also gave David room to experiment. "Basically, whatever I wanted to do in the kitchen was fine with her, as long as I cleaned up," he says. A graduate of Peter Kump's New York Cooking School (now the Institute of Culinary Education), David worked in restaurant kitchens for several years before turning to catering, food writing, and recipe development. When creating recipes, David says he receives inspiration from friends, restaurants, and his mother's family favorites. "Lots of times, I'll prepare a dish and say, 'Man, this is my childhood. It tastes just like I'm in my mother's kitchen.'"

Rubbed Pork Loin with Apricot Glaze and Sauerkraut

"My mother was part German, and this dish represented her heritage," says David Bonom. The recipe taught him three important lessons: Rubbing spices on meat adds great flavor; fruit and pork are a delicious combination; and cooking the sauerkraut in the pan with the pork offers a flavor contrast. Serve with green beans and a glass of riesling or a bottle of beer.

- 1 teaspoon garlic powder
- 1 teaspoon ground cumin
- ¾ teaspoon salt
- ¼ teaspoon freshly ground black pepper
- 1 (2-pound) boneless pork loin, trimmed
- 1 teaspoon olive oil
- Cooking spray
- 1 cup sliced onion
- 2 teaspoons sugar
- 2 cups sauerkraut, drained
- ½ cup apricot preserves, divided
- ½ cup water

❶ Preheat oven to 425°.

❷ Combine first 4 ingredients in a small bowl; rub spice mixture evenly over pork. Heat oil in a large nonstick skillet over medium-high heat. Add pork to pan; cook 5 minutes, browning on all sides. Transfer pork to an 11 x 7–inch baking dish coated with cooking spray. Add onion and sugar to pan; sauté 3 minutes or until onion is lightly browned. Add sauerkraut to pan; sauté 1 minute. Arrange sauerkraut mixture around pork in baking dish. Brush pork with one-third of apricot preserves. Pour ½ cup water over sauerkraut mixture.

❸ Bake at 425° for 15 minutes. Brush pork with one-third of apricot preserves; bake 10 minutes. Brush pork with remaining apricot preserves; bake 10 minutes or until a thermometer inserted in center of pork registers 160° (slightly pink). Remove from oven, and let stand 10 minutes. Cut into slices, and serve with sauerkraut mixture. Yield: 8 servings (serving size: 3 ounces pork and 3 tablespoons sauerkraut mixture).

CALORIES 236 (27% from fat); FAT 7.1g (sat 2.4g, mono 3.3g, poly 0.6g); PROTEIN 24.5g; CARB 17.8g; FIBER 1.4g; CHOL 65mg; IRON 1.3mg; SODIUM 505mg; CALC 42mg

Peach and Blackberry Cobbler

David Bonom's mother made a speedy dessert using frozen fruit and a simple batter. We like it with fresh fruit.

¼ cup butter, melted and divided
Cooking spray
3 cups sliced fresh peaches (about 1 pound)
2 cups fresh blackberries
1 cup plus 1 tablespoon all-purpose flour, divided (about 4½ ounces)
1 cup sugar, divided
¼ teaspoon ground ginger
1 tablespoon baking powder
¼ teaspoon salt
1 cup 1% low-fat milk

❶ Preheat oven to 350°.
❷ Pour 2 tablespoons melted butter into a 2-quart dish coated with cooking spray.
❸ Combine peaches, blackberries, and 1 tablespoon flour in a large bowl; toss gently. Add ¼ cup sugar and ginger; toss gently to combine. Pour peach mixture into prepared baking dish. Lightly spoon remaining 1 cup flour into a dry measuring cup; level with a knife. Combine 1 cup flour, remaining ¾ cup sugar, baking powder, and salt in a large bowl, stirring with a whisk. Add remaining 2 tablespoons melted butter and milk, stirring with a whisk. Pour batter evenly over fruit mixture.
❹ Bake at 350° for 1 hour and 10 minutes or until golden brown. Yield: 8 servings (serving size: ½ cup).

CALORIES 254 (22% from fat); FAT 6.2g (sat 3.8g, mono 1.6g, poly 0.3g); PROTEIN 3.7g; CARB 48.1g; FIBER 3.3g; CHOL 16mg; IRON 1.4mg; SODIUM 313mg; CALC 151mg

"Lots of times, I'll prepare a dish and say, 'Man, this is my childhood. It tastes just like I'm in my mother's kitchen.'"
—David Bonom

Blue-Plate Classic Menu
serves 8

If you're serving a smaller group, halve the pea recipe, but prepare all of the steak because leftovers make good sandwiches.

Marinated London Broil

Peas with shallots and bacon
Cook 2 chopped bacon slices in a large nonstick skillet over medium heat until crisp. Remove bacon from pan with a slotted spoon, reserving drippings in pan. Add ½ cup minced shallots to drippings in pan; cook 3 minutes or until tender, stirring occasionally. Add 6 cups thawed frozen green peas and ½ cup fat-free, less-sodium chicken broth; bring to a boil. Cover, reduce heat, and cook 3 minutes or until peas are tender. Remove from heat; stir in 2 tablespoons chopped fresh parsley, ½ teaspoon salt, and ¼ teaspoon freshly ground black pepper. Sprinkle with bacon.

Mashed potatoes

Marinated London Broil

"I think every mom in the 1950s, '60s, and '70s had some version of this dish, but it taught me how to take a less-expensive, tougher cut of meat and make it delicious," says David Bonom.

½ cup chopped shallots
¼ cup low-sodium soy sauce
3 tablespoons fresh lemon juice
3 tablespoons balsamic vinegar
1 tablespoon olive oil
2 teaspoons fresh thyme
1 teaspoon dried oregano
4 garlic cloves, minced
1 (2-pound) boneless top round steak, trimmed
Cooking spray
½ teaspoon salt
¼ teaspoon freshly ground black pepper

❶ Combine first 8 ingredients in a large zip-top plastic bag. Pierce steak with a fork. Add steak to bag; seal. Marinate in refrigerator 2 hours, turning every 30 minutes.
❷ Preheat broiler.
❸ Remove steak from bag; discard marinade. Scrape shallots and garlic from steak; discard shallots and garlic. Place steak on a broiler pan coated with cooking spray. Sprinkle steak evenly with salt and pepper. Broil 4 inches from heat 6 minutes on each side or until desired degree of doneness. Let stand 10 minutes before cutting against grain. Yield: 8 servings (serving size: 3 ounces).

CALORIES 228 (30% from fat); FAT 7.5g (sat 2.5g, mono 3.3g, poly 0.4g); PROTEIN 36.6g; CARB 1.2g; FIBER 0.1g; CHOL 93mg; IRON 3.4mg; SODIUM 263mg; CALC 12mg

Long-Distance Lessons

When Ganga Iyer was 75 years old, she made her only trip from India to the United States to see her son. She spent her visit preparing dumplings.

"I wanted to learn how to make her steamed rice dumplings," says Ganga's son, Raghavan Iyer, author of *The Turmeric Trail: Recipes and Memories from an Indian Childhood* and winner of the 2004 Cooking Teacher of the Year award from the International Association of Culinary Professionals. "There were so many steps to create the texture she had mastered."

Raghavan credits his petite, soft-spoken mother for the dumplings that dazzle his students and dinner guests. But, more importantly, he is thankful for how she shaped his love of Indian food and ability to share it with others. The youngest of seven children, he grew up in Mumbai (formerly Bombay), savoring the flavorful vegetarian fare his mother served each day.

It was only when he returned to the family home after cooking for himself at college that he comprehended his mother's contribution to the family's well-being. "I had a new appreciation of all the effort it required," Raghavan says. "She was in the kitchen all day long. When I was growing up, I'd wonder, 'What in God's name is she *doing* in there?' Now, of course, I know."

Ganga died in 2006 at the age of 84. Her cooking continues to nourish not only her son and his family, but also those he teaches through cooking classes, magazine articles, and books.

> "When I was growing up, my mother was in the kitchen all day long." —Raghavan Iyer

Reduced Milk with Cardamom and Mango (*Maangai Pal Paysam*)

Raghavan Iyer enjoys this comforting dessert with chopped mango.

- 6 cups whole milk
- 1/3 cup uncooked basmati rice
- 1/2 cup nonfat sweetened condensed milk
- 1/2 teaspoon ground cardamom
- 1/4 teaspoon salt
- 2 cups chopped peeled mango (about 2 large)

1 Combine whole milk and rice in a large saucepan over medium-high heat. Bring to a boil, stirring constantly. Reduce heat to medium, and gently boil 40 minutes or until mixture thickens. (Mixture will be a chowderlike consistency.) Stir in condensed milk, cardamom, and salt; cook 5 minutes, stirring constantly. Spoon 1/2 cup rice mixture into each of 8 dessert bowls. Top each serving with 1/4 cup chopped mango. Yield: 8 servings.

CALORIES 212 (26% from fat); FAT 6.1g (sat 3.5g, mono 1.5g, poly 0.4g); PROTEIN 7.9g; CARB 32.2g; FIBER 1g; CHOL 21mg; IRON 0.2mg; SODIUM 168mg; CALC 262mg

---

Indian Matchmaking Menu

serves 4

A sweet fruit salad offers a cooling counterpoint to the entrée's spice.

Shrimp with Shallots and Curry Leaves

Mango salad

Combine 2 cups chopped peeled ripe mango, 1/3 cup thinly vertically sliced red onion, and 2 tablespoons chopped fresh cilantro. Drizzle with 1 tablespoon fresh lime juice, and sprinkle with 1/8 teaspoon salt; toss to combine.

Coconut sorbet

QUICK & EASY
Shrimp with Shallots and Curry Leaves (*Chochin Jhinga*)

Here, Raghavan Iyer combines shrimp, abundant in India, with a vibrant sauce over rice.

- 1 tablespoon canola oil
- 1/2 cup finely chopped shallots
- 8 large fresh curry leaves
- 2 serrano chiles, stems removed and cut in half lengthwise
- 1 1/2 cups finely chopped tomato (about 1 large)
- 1/2 cup light coconut milk
- 2 tablespoons white vinegar
- 1 teaspoon kosher salt
- 3/4 teaspoon sweet paprika
- 1/4 teaspoon ground red pepper
- 1/4 teaspoon ground turmeric
- 1 1/2 pounds large shrimp, peeled and deveined
- 1/4 ounce (2-inch) julienne-cut fresh peeled ginger
- 2 cups hot cooked rice

1 Heat oil in a large nonstick skillet over medium-high heat. Add shallots, curry leaves, and chiles to pan; sauté 2 minutes or until shallots are lightly browned. Stir in tomato and next 6 ingredients; bring to a boil. Add shrimp to pan. Cover, reduce heat to medium, and cook 3 minutes or until shrimp are done. Remove shrimp from pan with a slotted spoon. Increase heat to medium-high, and cook sauce 2 minutes or until thickened, stirring occasionally. Spoon sauce over shrimp; sprinkle with ginger. Serve with rice. Yield: 4 servings (serving size: 1 cup shrimp mixture and 1/2 cup rice).

CALORIES 360 (21% from fat); FAT 8.4g (sat 2.3g, mono 2.5g, poly 2.3g); PROTEIN 38.3g; CARB 31.2g; FIBER 1.3g; CHOL 259mg; IRON 5.8mg; SODIUM 735mg; CALC 118mg

Rice and Lentils with Curry Leaves and Ginger (*Ven Pongal*)

¼ teaspoon canola oil
2 teaspoons cumin seeds
1 teaspoon black peppercorns
½ cup dried small red lentils
4 cups water
1 cup long-grain rice
¾ teaspoon kosher salt
½ teaspoon ground turmeric
¼ cup finely chopped fresh cilantro
2 tablespoons (1-inch) julienne-sliced peeled fresh ginger
1 tablespoon clarified butter
12 medium-sized fresh curry leaves

1 Heat oil in a small saucepan over medium-high heat. Add cumin seeds and peppercorns to pan. Cook 30 seconds or until cumin turns reddish brown, stirring constantly. Transfer to a mortar; let cool. Crush cumin mixture with a pestle until coarsely ground.

2 Rinse lentils in a sieve with cold running water until water runs clear. Combine lentils, 4 cups water, and rice in a large saucepan; bring to a boil. Stir in cumin mixture, salt, and turmeric; cook 5 minutes, stirring occasionally. Cover, reduce heat to low, and cook 10 minutes, stirring once. Remove from heat, and let stand, covered, 10 minutes. Stir in cilantro and remaining ingredients. Serve immediately. Yield: 8 servings (serving size: ½ cup).

CALORIES 121 (17% from fat); FAT 2.3g (sat 1.2g, mono 0.2g, poly 0.1g); PROTEIN 3g; CARB 21.6g; FIBER 1.5g; CHOL 5mg; IRON 0.9mg; SODIUM 183mg; CALC 27mg

---

Culinary Genes

It wasn't on the menu, and it wasn't palatable, but the vegetable soup concocted each day in the kitchen of his family's Belgian Lion restaurant in San Diego was the pride of aspiring young chef Nathan Coulon. "I used all the potato peelings I could find, the zucchini ends, carrot tops," says Nathan. "Then I insisted that everyone in the kitchen try it. Because I was only four or five years old, they did."

Nathan, who now serves refined fare such as crab ravioli as the sous chef at the Quarter Kitchen restaurant in San Diego, learned classic French cooking from his grandparents and parents, who ran the Belgian Lion. Grandmother Arlene Nathan taught him how to emulsify a vinaigrette, beat eggs for turnip soufflés, and caramelize onions for an onion tart.

"If he saw someone doing something in the kitchen, he *had* to do it himself," says his mother, Michele Coulon, who now owns Michele Coulon Dessertiere café in La Jolla. With almost a decade of experience prepping, cooking, and serving at the Belgian Lion under his belt, Nathan helped his mom open her café in 2001. There he won raves for his cassoulet, Belgian endive salad, and braised chicken with apples. He also perfected his baking skills by helping Michele fill profiteroles and layer elaborate Marjolaine cakes.

Today, the 31-year-old chef still gathers with extended family at his grandparents' home for great food and wine and good-natured ribbing about his garbage soup days.

MAKE AHEAD

Nathan's Lemon Cake

(pictured on page 249)

This is a namesake because Nathan Coulon's mom baked it for his birthday every year.

CAKE:

Cooking spray
2 tablespoons all-purpose flour
2 cups all-purpose flour (about 9 ounces)
1 teaspoon baking powder
½ teaspoon baking soda
½ teaspoon salt
1½ cups granulated sugar
½ cup unsalted butter, softened
3 large eggs
1 cup nonfat buttermilk
2 tablespoons finely grated lemon rind
2 tablespoons fresh lemon juice

ICING:

3 cups powdered sugar
¼ cup unsalted butter, melted
1 tablespoon lemon rind
¼ cup fresh lemon juice
Lemon rind strips (optional)

1 Preheat oven to 350°.

2 To prepare cake, coat 2 (8-inch) round cake pans with cooking spray; line bottoms of pans with wax paper. Coat wax paper with cooking spray. Dust pans with 2 tablespoons flour, and set aside.

3 Lightly spoon 2 cups flour into dry measuring cups, and level with a knife. Combine 2 cups flour and next 3 ingredients, stirring with a whisk.

4 Place granulated sugar and ½ cup butter in a large bowl; beat with a mixer at medium speed until well blended (about 5 minutes). Add eggs, one at a time, beating well after each addition. Add flour mixture and buttermilk alternately to sugar mixture, beginning and ending with flour mixture. Beat in 2 tablespoons lemon rind and 2 tablespoons lemon juice.

5 Pour batter into prepared pans; sharply tap pans once on counter to remove air bubbles. Bake at 350° for 32 minutes or until a wooden pick inserted in center comes out clean. Cool in pans 10 minutes on a wire rack; remove from pans. Cool completely on wire rack; remove wax paper from cake layers.

Continued

6 To prepare icing, combine powdered sugar and next 3 ingredients in a large bowl; stir with a whisk until smooth. Place 1 cake layer on a plate; spread half of icing on top of cake. Top with remaining cake layer. Spread remaining icing over top of cake. Garnish with lemon rind strips, if desired. Store cake loosely covered in refrigerator. Yield: 16 servings (serving size: 1 slice).

CALORIES 317 (27% from fat); FAT 9.5g (sat 5.6g, mono 2.6g, poly 0.5g); PROTEIN 3.6g; CARB 55.7g; FIBER 0.6g; CHOL 56mg; IRON 1mg; SODIUM 165mg; CALC 52mg

Braised Short Ribs

This is based on one of Nathan Coulon's family dishes.

- 2 pounds boneless beef short ribs, trimmed and cut into 2-inch pieces
- ¾ teaspoon salt, divided
- ½ teaspoon freshly ground black pepper, divided
  Cooking spray
- ½ cup thinly sliced yellow onion
- ½ cup thinly sliced carrot
- ½ cup thinly sliced leek
- ¼ cup thinly sliced shallots
- ¼ cup thinly sliced celery
- ¼ cup thinly sliced mushrooms
- 1 garlic clove, crushed
- 2 cups cabernet sauvignon or other dry red wine
- 5 whole black peppercorns
- 2 thyme sprigs
- 1 parsley sprig
- 1 bay leaf
- 2 (14-ounce) cans fat-free, less-sodium beef broth
- 4 teaspoons all-purpose flour
- 1 tablespoon butter
- ¼ cup chopped fresh parsley

1 Sprinkle beef with ½ teaspoon salt and ¼ teaspoon pepper. Line a medium bowl with a 16-inch square piece of cheesecloth. Heat a Dutch oven over medium-high heat. Coat pan with cooking spray. Add half of beef to pan; cook 5 minutes, browning on all sides. Transfer beef to cheesecloth-lined bowl. Repeat procedure with remaining beef. Loosely knot edges of cheesecloth to form a bundle. Keep warm.

2 Add onion and next 6 ingredients to pan; stir in remaining ¼ teaspoon salt and remaining ¼ teaspoon pepper. Sauté 5 minutes or until onion is tender. Add wine and next 4 ingredients to pan; bring to a boil. Cook 11 minutes or until wine almost evaporates. Place meat bundle on top of vegetables; add any liquid from bowl to pan. Add broth to pan; bring to a simmer. Cover, reduce heat, and cook 1½ hours or until beef is tender.

3 Transfer meat bundle to a clean bowl using tongs, and keep warm. Strain broth through a colander into a bowl, and discard solids. Place a zip-top plastic bag inside a 4-cup glass measure. Pour broth into bag, and let stand 10 minutes (fat will rise to the top). Seal bag, and carefully snip off 1 bottom corner of bag. Drain drippings into pan, stopping before fat layer reaches opening; discard fat. Add flour to pan, stirring with a whisk, and bring to a boil. Cook until reduced to 1¼ cups (about 10 minutes). Add butter, stirring until butter melts. Serve with beef. Sprinkle with parsley. Yield: 8 servings (serving size: about 3 ounces beef, about 2½ tablespoons gravy, and about 1½ teaspoons parsley).

CALORIES 143 (55% from fat); FAT 8.7g (sat 4g, mono 3.6g, poly 0.3g); PROTEIN 13.5g; CARB 1.7g; FIBER 0.1g; CHOL 41mg; IRON 1.7mg; SODIUM 448mg; CALC 10mg

QUICK & EASY
Spinach and Prosciutto Salad

- 2 tablespoons balsamic vinegar
- 1 teaspoon dark sesame oil
- 1 teaspoon extravirgin olive oil
- 1 (6-ounce) package washed baby spinach
- ¼ teaspoon black pepper
- 2 ounces thinly sliced Parma prosciutto
- ¼ cup (1 ounce) goat cheese, crumbled

1 Combine first 3 ingredients in a small bowl, stirring with a whisk. Place spinach in a large bowl. Drizzle with half of oil mixture. Add pepper; toss well to coat.

2 Arrange prosciutto slices evenly on 6 salad plates. Top each serving with 1 cup spinach mixture. Drizzle evenly with remaining oil mixture. Sprinkle each serving with 2 teaspoons cheese. Serve immediately. Yield: 6 servings (serving size: 1 salad).

CALORIES 81 (58% from fat); FAT 5.2g (sat 2.5g, mono 1.9g, poly 0.6g); PROTEIN 4.9g; CARB 4.2g; FIBER 1.4g; CHOL 13mg; IRON 1.2mg; SODIUM 237mg; CALC 51mg

DINNER TONIGHT
Grilled Sandwiches

These hearty entrées feature an appealing duo: melted cheese and crisp bread.

Sandwiches Menu 1
serves 4

Patty Melts with Grilled Onions
Baked potato chips
Lime-infused fruit
Combine 4 cups mixed chopped fruit, 1 tablespoon brown sugar, ½ teaspoon grated lime rind, and 2 tablespoons fresh lime juice; toss gently to coat. Cover and chill.

Game Plan
1 Prepare fruit and refrigerate.
2 While onion slices cook:
 • Shape beef into patties.
 • Shred cheese.
3 Cook sandwiches.

Quick Tip
Purchase precut fruit from the produce section of your supermarket for this zesty side.

Patty Melts with Grilled Onions

For a sharper onion taste, use white or red onions in place of Vidalias.
Total time: 36 minutes

- 8 (⅛-inch-thick) slices Vidalia or other sweet onion
- 1 tablespoon balsamic vinegar
- Cooking spray
- 1 pound extralean ground beef
- ¼ teaspoon salt
- ¼ teaspoon freshly ground black pepper
- 3 tablespoons creamy mustard blend (such as Dijonnaise)
- 8 (1-ounce) slices rye bread
- 1 cup (4 ounces) shredded reduced-fat Jarlsberg cheese

1 Arrange onion slices on a plate. Drizzle vinegar over onion. Heat a large grill pan over medium heat. Coat pan with cooking spray. Add onion to pan; cover and cook 3 minutes on each side. Remove from pan; cover and keep warm.

2 Heat pan over medium-high heat. Coat pan with cooking spray. Divide beef into 4 equal portions, shaping each into a ½-inch-thick patty. Sprinkle patties evenly with salt and pepper. Add patties to pan; cook 3 minutes on each side or until done.

3 Spread about 1 teaspoon mustard over each of 4 bread slices; top each with 2 tablespoons cheese, 1 patty, 2 onion slices, and 2 tablespoons cheese. Spread about 1 teaspoon mustard over each of remaining bread slices; place, mustard sides down, on top of sandwiches.

4 Heat pan over medium heat. Coat pan with cooking spray. Add sandwiches to pan. Place a heavy skillet on sandwiches; press gently to flatten. Cook 3 minutes on each side or until bread is toasted (leave skillet on sandwiches while they cook). Yield: 4 servings (serving size: 1 sandwich).

CALORIES 341 (25% from fat); FAT 9.6g (sat 4.4g, mono 3.2g, poly 1g); PROTEIN 31.5g; CARB 31.1g; FIBER 3.6g; CHOL 60mg; IRON 3mg; SODIUM 754mg; CALC 350mg

Sandwiches Menu 2
serves 4

Grilled Portobello, Bell Pepper, and Goat Cheese Sandwiches
Cornichons
Grilled tomato wedges with herbs
Cut each of 4 medium tomatoes into 4 wedges. Brush tomato wedges with 1 tablespoon extravirgin olive oil; sprinkle evenly with ⅛ teaspoon salt and ⅛ teaspoon black pepper. Place tomato wedges on grill rack coated with cooking spray; grill 5 minutes or until lightly browned, turning once. Place tomato wedges on a plate; sprinkle with 2 tablespoons chopped fresh parsley, 1 teaspoon fresh thyme leaves, ⅛ teaspoon salt, and ⅛ teaspoon black pepper.

Game Plan

1 While grill preheats:
- Prepare vinegar mixture for sandwiches.
- Prepare bell peppers and mushrooms for sandwiches.

2 While bell peppers and mushrooms cook:
- Chop basil for sandwiches.
- Cut tomatoes into wedges.

3 While sandwiches cook:
- Grill tomato wedges.
- Chop herbs for tomatoes.

Quick Tip
Use bottled roasted red and yellow bell peppers on the sandwiches.

Grilled Portobello, Bell Pepper, and Goat Cheese Sandwiches

Although you can cook the vegetables, sandwiches, and tomato side dish in a grill pan, this recipe comes together quickly on the increased surface area of an outdoor grill.
Total time: 34 minutes

- ¼ cup balsamic vinegar
- 1 tablespoon olive oil
- 1 garlic clove, minced
- 1 red bell pepper, cut in half and seeded
- 1 yellow bell pepper, cut in half and seeded
- 4 (4-inch) portobello mushroom caps
- Cooking spray
- ⅓ cup chopped fresh basil
- ¼ teaspoon salt
- ¼ teaspoon freshly ground black pepper
- 4 (2-ounce) Kaiser rolls
- ½ cup (4 ounces) soft goat cheese

1 Prepare grill to medium-high heat.

2 Combine first 3 ingredients in a large bowl. Add bell peppers and mushrooms; toss gently to coat. Remove vegetables from vinegar mixture, and discard vinegar mixture.

3 Place bell peppers and mushrooms on a grill rack coated with cooking spray; grill 4 minutes on each side. Remove vegetables from grill; cool slightly. Cut bell peppers into thin strips. Combine bell peppers, basil, salt, and black pepper in a small bowl.

4 Cut rolls in half horizontally; spread cheese evenly over cut sides of rolls. Arrange 1 mushroom cap on bottom half of each roll; top each serving with about ⅓ cup bell pepper mixture and top half of roll.

5 Place sandwiches on grill rack coated with cooking spray. Place a cast-iron or other heavy skillet on top of sandwiches; press gently to flatten. Grill 3 minutes on each side or until bread is toasted (leave skillet on sandwiches while they cook). Yield: 4 servings (serving size: 1 sandwich).

CALORIES 317 (30% from fat); FAT 10.5g (sat 4.8g, mono 3.2g, poly 1.4g); PROTEIN 14g; CARB 41.7g; FIBER 4g; CHOL 13mg; IRON 3.2mg; SODIUM 571mg; CALC 118mg

Classic Italian Panini with Prosciutto and Fresh Mozzarella
Arugula salad
Raspberries with mascarpone
Combine 2 tablespoons sugar, 2 tablespoons water, and ½ teaspoon grated lemon rind in a small microwave-safe bowl; microwave at HIGH 30 seconds or until sugar dissolves. Place 2 cups fresh raspberries in a medium bowl. Drizzle sugar mixture over raspberries; toss gently to combine. Let raspberry mixture stand at room temperature 15 minutes. Top each serving with 1 teaspoon mascarpone cheese.

Game Plan

1 While raspberry mixture stands at room temperature:
  • Hollow out bread.
  • Chop basil.
  • Shred cheese.
  • Slice tomato.
2 While sandwiches cook:
  • Prepare salad.

QUICK & EASY
Classic Italian Panini with Prosciutto and Fresh Mozzarella

Use this recipe as a template, and customize it to your liking. Use hollowed out focaccia or ciabatta, or try different herbs and cheese, for example.
Total time: 21 minutes

  1 (12-ounce) loaf French bread, cut in half horizontally
  ¼ cup reduced-fat mayonnaise
  2 tablespoons chopped fresh basil
  1 cup (4 ounces) shredded fresh mozzarella cheese, divided
  2 ounces very thin slices prosciutto
  2 plum tomatoes, thinly sliced
  Cooking spray

1 Hollow out top and bottom halves of bread, leaving ½-inch-thick shells; reserve torn bread for another use. Spread 2 tablespoons mayonnaise over cut side of each bread half. Sprinkle basil and ½ cup cheese on bottom half of loaf. Top evenly with prosciutto, tomato, and remaining ½ cup cheese. Cover with top half of loaf. Cut filled loaf crosswise into 4 equal pieces.
2 Heat a grill pan over medium heat. Coat pan with cooking spray. Add sandwiches to pan. Place a cast-iron or other heavy skillet on top of sandwiches; press gently to flatten sandwiches. Cook 3 minutes on each side or until bread is toasted (leave skillet on sandwiches while they cook). Yield: 4 servings (serving size: 1 sandwich).

CALORIES 316 (30% from fat); FAT 10.6g (sat 4.8g, mono 2.3g, poly 1.9g); PROTEIN 16.1g; CARB 39.9g; FIBER 2g; CHOL 31mg; IRON 2.8mg; SODIUM 799mg; CALC 196mg

INSPIRED VEGETARIAN
Catalonian Cuisine

The fare of northeast Spain spotlights the vivid qualities of smoky seasonings, fresh produce, and an array of chiles.

Vegetables take the spotlight in Catalonia since they are often served as a course by themselves and not typically as side dishes. Spices such as saffron and smoked paprika add depth to dishes without relying on meats and fish for flavor. Fruity extravirgin olive oil adds subtle flavor and is the cooking medium used in most dishes. (We've kept the amount of oil prudent because in Spain, olive oil is used for marinating, grilling, and sautéing, and dishes are often finished with an extra drizzle.)

Garlic Soup (*Sopa de Ajo*)

This simple appetizer soup (SOH-pah day AH-ho) makes the most of everyday ingredients. Serve with a slice of Tomato and Garlic Toast (page 147) and green salad for a light lunch. Use high-quality ingredients; because this basic soup has few elements, each contributes substantially to its success.

  2 teaspoons olive oil
  5 tablespoons minced garlic
  1 teaspoon sweet smoked paprika
  3 cups organic vegetable broth (such as Emeril's)
  1 cup water
  ¼ teaspoon salt
  ¼ teaspoon freshly ground black pepper
  2 (1-ounce) slices rustic bread, cut into 1-inch cubes
  8 large eggs
  2 tablespoons chopped fresh flat-leaf parsley

1 Preheat broiler.
2 Heat oil in a large saucepan over medium heat. Add garlic to pan; cook 5 minutes or until tender (do not brown). Stir in paprika. Add broth, 1 cup water, salt, and pepper; bring to a boil. Reduce heat, and simmer 10 minutes.
3 Arrange bread cubes in a single layer on a baking sheet; broil 4 minutes or until golden, stirring once halfway through cooking. Reduce oven temperature to 350°.
4 Place about ¼ cup bread cubes in each of 8 ovenproof soup bowls. Break one egg into each bowl; ladle about ½ cup broth mixture into each bowl. Arrange bowls on a baking sheet; bake at 350° for 20 minutes or until egg whites are set but yolks are still runny. Sprinkle evenly with parsley. Yield: 8 servings.

CALORIES 114 (41% from fat); FAT 5.2g (sat 1.3g, mono 2.7g, poly 0.9g); PROTEIN 7.3g; CARB 7.6g; FIBER 0.3g; CHOL 180mg; IRON 1.3mg; SODIUM 398mg; CALC 38mg

Catalonian Salad with Greens and Romesco Vinaigrette (*Xato*)

This hearty green salad (pronounced SHA-toh) would be served as a first-course dish in Spain. We love how the rich vinaigrette and mixed greens smooth the endive's bitter edge. If you can't find curly endive, substitute radicchio or escarole.

¼	cup Catalonian Pepper and Nut Sauce (page 148)
2	tablespoons hot water
1	tablespoon red wine vinegar
6	cups torn curly endive
1	(5-ounce) package gourmet salad greens
9	oil-cured ripe olives, pitted and chopped
2	hard-cooked large eggs, chopped

❶ Combine first 3 ingredients in a small bowl, stirring well with a whisk.
❷ Combine endive and salad greens in a large bowl; toss gently. Place about 1¹/₃ cups greens on each of 10 plates. Drizzle each serving with about 2 teaspoons sauce mixture; divide olives and eggs evenly among salads. Serve immediately. Yield: 10 servings.

CALORIES 52 (61% from fat); FAT 3.5g (sat 0.6g, mono 2.2g, poly 0.6g); PROTEIN 2.5g; CARB 3.2g; FIBER 2g; CHOL 36mg; IRON 1.1mg; SODIUM 68mg; CALC 43mg

---

QUICK & EASY
Tomato and Garlic Toast (*Pa amb Tomaquet*)

Even though the appetizers known as tapas are originally from Andalusia in southern Spain, this simple tapa (pronounced pah ahmb toh-MAH-ket) is popular in Catalonian restaurants and homes. If you have the grill fired up, you can grill the hearty bread instead of broiling it.

6	(1-ounce) slices rustic bread
1	tablespoon extravirgin olive oil
2	large garlic cloves, halved
1	ripe, soft tomato, halved
⅛	teaspoon salt
¼	teaspoon freshly ground black pepper

❶ Preheat broiler.
❷ Arrange bread slices on a baking sheet; brush with oil. Broil 2 minutes on each side or until lightly browned. Rub cut sides of garlic over bread slices; discard garlic. Rub cut sides of tomato over bread (tomato pulp will rub off onto bread); discard tomato. Sprinkle evenly with salt and pepper. Yield: 6 servings (serving size: 1 slice).

CALORIES 102 (28% from fat); FAT 3.2g (sat 0.3g, mono 1.8g, poly 0.6g); PROTEIN 2.6g; CARB 15.8g; FIBER 1.2g; CHOL 0mg; IRON 0.9mg; SODIUM 230mg; CALC 20mg

---

Majorcan Vegetable Pizza (*Coca de Verduras*)

Coca is a crust or pastry that may have a sweet or savory topping. This savory coca is an everyday Catalonian dish. We used leftover Samfaina topped with ricotta cheese (which is very similar to the fresh cheeses you would find in Catalonia) and sprinkled with kosher salt.

½	Catalonian Crust (page 148)
1½	teaspoons cornmeal
3	cups Samfaina (page 149)
½	cup (2 ounces) part-skim ricotta cheese
½	teaspoon kosher salt

❶ Preheat oven to 500°.
❷ Place a baking stone in oven; preheat 30 minutes.
❸ Gently stretch Catalonian Crust into a 12-inch circle, and place on back of a baking sheet sprinkled with cornmeal. Carefully slide dough onto preheated stone, using a spatula as a guide. Spread Samfaina evenly over dough, leaving a ¹/₂-inch border; top evenly with cheese. Sprinkle with salt. Bake at 500° for 16 minutes or until crust is golden. Yield: 6 servings (serving size: 1 slice).

CALORIES 287 (27% from fat); FAT 8.5g (sat 2g, mono 4.5g, poly 1g); PROTEIN 8.7g; CARB 45.8g; FIBER 4.9g; CHOL 8mg; IRON 2.9mg; SODIUM 540mg; CALC 69mg

---

Signature Spanish Ingredients

Sherry vinegar: This nutty, slightly sweet, and smooth vinegar imparts just a trace of oak.

Olive oil: Spanish extravirgin olive oils are now available at large supermarkets and in gourmet stores. Catalonian oil tends to be lighter on the palate than other Spanish olive oils.

Saffron: A signature spice of Spain. For maximum flavor, saffron threads should be handled with care—crushed and added to a dish; toasted and then crushed; or steeped in a warm liquid like wine, stock, or water before being added to a dish. Imparts a golden hue to paella.

Piquillo peppers: These deep-red, bittersweet chiles are ideal for stuffing but may also be served drizzled with oil and sherry vinegar as an appetizer.

Pimentón (paprika): This spice is a signature flavor component of Spanish cooking, whether dulce (sweet), agridulce (bittersweet), or picante (hot). Deeper red and coarser than the Hungarian version, pimentón colors stews and soups, and is the most widely used spice in the Spanish kitchen. Pimentón de la Vera is a smoked paprika, which offers robust, round, and meaty flavors to vegetarian dishes.

Romesco: This small dried pepper flavors the classic nut-thickened Catalonian sauce of the same name. Substitute dried ancho chile since the pepper is rarely exported.

Ñoras (pimiento choricero): These small, round dried peppers are common in Spanish cuisine and offer sweet and earthy backnotes to foods. They may be torn or chopped and added to stews, or rehydrated for paella or sofrito. Substitute sweet unsmoked pimentón.

Rice: Typically a short- to medium-grain rice is used. Bomba and Calasparra are two well-known varieties.

CATALONIAN CRUST:

This recipe makes enough dough for two 12-inch pizzas. Shape the extra dough into a ball, and freeze. Place in a zip-top plastic bag coated with cooking spray; seal tightly, and freeze up to one month. Thaw in the refrigerator 12 hours or overnight before use. Then follow recipe instructions.

- ¼ cup warm water (100° to 110°)
- 1 package dry yeast (about 2¼ teaspoons)
- 4 cups all-purpose flour, divided (about 18 ounces)
- ¾ cup water
- 3 tablespoons olive oil
- ½ teaspoon salt
- Cooking spray

1 Combine ¼ cup warm water and yeast in bowl of a stand mixer, stirring until yeast dissolves. Let stand 5 minutes. Lightly spoon ¼ cup flour into a dry measuring cup; level with a knife. Add ¼ cup flour to yeast mixture, stirring until combined. Cover; let stand 30 minutes.

2 Lightly spoon remaining 3¾ cups flour into dry measuring cups; level with a knife. Gradually add 3¾ cups flour and next 3 ingredients to yeast mixture, beating with mixer at low speed 10 minutes or until a soft dough forms. Place dough in a large bowl coated with cooking spray, turning to coat top. Cover and let rise in a warm place (85°), free from drafts, 1 hour or until doubled in size. (Gently press two fingers into dough. If indentation remains, dough has risen enough.) Punch dough down; cover and let rest 5 minutes. Divide dough in half; shape each portion into a ball. Place dough balls on a lightly floured baking sheet. Cover; chill dough 30 minutes. Yield: 2 (12-inch) crusts, 12 servings (serving size: 1 slice).

CALORIES 186 (18% from fat); FAT 3.8g (sat 0.5g, mono 2.5g, poly 0.5g); PROTEIN 4.7g; CARB 32.7g; FIBER 1.3g; CHOL 0mg; IRON 2.1mg; SODIUM 100mg; CALC 7mg

Catalonian Pepper and Nut Sauce (*Salsa Romesco*)

"Romesco" refers to the type of chile used to flavor this rich sauce. Romesco chiles can be difficult to find, so we use smoky ancho chiles. Much of the flavor in this sauce hinges on the sweet smoked paprika (*pimentón de la Vera dulce*); don't substitute regular paprika, which has duller flavor.

- 2 dried ancho chiles
- 2 small red bell peppers
- ½ cup hazelnuts
- ½ cup blanched almonds, toasted
- 4 garlic cloves, chopped
- 1 (1-ounce) slice bread, toasted
- ¼ cup red wine vinegar
- 2 tablespoons tomato paste
- 4 teaspoons sweet smoked paprika
- ¼ teaspoon ground red pepper
- ⅔ cup extravirgin olive oil
- ¼ cup hot water
- ½ teaspoon salt

1 Place chiles in a small saucepan. Cover with water; bring to a boil. Remove from heat; cover and let stand 20 minutes. Drain well. Remove stems, seeds, and membranes from chiles; discard. Place chiles in a medium bowl.

2 Preheat broiler.

3 Cut bell peppers in half lengthwise; discard seeds and membranes. Place pepper halves, skin sides up, on a foil-lined baking sheet; flatten with hand. Broil 10 minutes or until blackened. Place in a zip-top plastic bag; seal. Let stand 15 minutes. Peel and cut into 2-inch pieces. Add bell peppers to chiles.

4 Reduce oven temperature to 350°.

5 Arrange hazelnuts in a single layer on a baking sheet. Bake at 350° for 8 minutes or until toasted. Turn nuts out onto a towel. Roll up towel; rub off skins. Place hazelnuts in a food processor. Add almonds, garlic, and bread to food processor; process 1 minute or until finely ground. Add chile mixture, vinegar, and next 3 ingredients; process 1 minute or until combined. With processor on, slowly pour oil through food chute; process until well blended. Add ¼ cup hot water and salt; process 10 seconds or until combined. Yield: 2½ cups (serving size: 1 tablespoon).

NOTE: Store in an airtight container in the refrigerator for up to two weeks.

CALORIES 59 (87% from fat); FAT 5.7g (sat 0.7g, mono 3.9g, poly 0.9g); PROTEIN 0.9g; CARB 2.1g; FIBER 0.7g; CHOL 0mg; IRON 0.3mg; SODIUM 36mg; CALC 8mg

Grilled Green Onions and Asparagus with Romesco (*Calçots y Esparragos con Romesco*)

- 16 large green onions (about 4 ounces)
- 1 pound asparagus, trimmed
- 1½ teaspoons extravirgin olive oil, divided
- ¼ teaspoon salt
- ⅛ teaspoon black pepper
- 2 tablespoons Catalonian Pepper and Nut Sauce (at left)

1 Trim root ends of onions, keeping bulb heads intact; discard roots. Trim tops, leaving about 4 inches of upper green portion.

2 Cook onions in boiling water 2 minutes or until tender. Drain and rinse with cold water; drain well, and pat dry. Place in a medium bowl.

3 Cook asparagus in boiling water 4 minutes or until crisp-tender. Drain and rinse with cold water; drain well, and pat dry. Place in another bowl.

4 Heat a grill pan over medium-high heat. Drizzle ½ teaspoon oil over onions, tossing to coat. Arrange onions in an even layer in pan, and grill 30 seconds on each side or until grill marks show. Transfer onions to a platter.

5 Drizzle remaining 1 teaspoon oil over asparagus; toss to coat. Arrange asparagus in an even layer in pan, and grill 1 minute on each side or until grill marks show. Transfer asparagus to platter.

Sprinkle vegetables evenly with salt and pepper. Divide evenly among 4 plates; top each serving with about 1½ teaspoons sauce. Yield: 4 servings.

CALORIES 105 (41% from fat); FAT 4.8g (sat 0.7g, mono 3.2g, poly 0.8g); PROTEIN 4.8g; CARB 12.8g; FIBER 5.3g; CHOL 0mg; IRON 4.1mg; SODIUM 184mg; CALC 104mg

MAKE AHEAD
Samfaina

Samfaina (sam-FINE-nah) is a mix of onions, garlic, eggplant, peppers, tomatoes, and zucchini.

  2 tablespoons extravirgin olive oil
  3 cups coarsely chopped onion
  5 cups (1-inch) cubed peeled eggplant (about 1 pound)
  2 cups (½-inch) cubed zucchini (about ½ pound)
  1 cup chopped red bell pepper
1½ tablespoons minced garlic (about 7 cloves)
2½ cups chopped seeded peeled tomato (about 1½ pounds)
  2 tablespoons chopped fresh parsley
  1 teaspoon chopped fresh thyme
  1 teaspoon salt
  1 teaspoon sweet smoked paprika
  ½ teaspoon freshly ground black pepper

① Heat oil in a large nonstick skillet over medium heat. Add onion to pan; cook 10 minutes or until tender, stirring occasionally. Stir in eggplant and next 3 ingredients; cook 5 minutes, stirring frequently. Stir in tomato, parsley, and thyme. Cover, reduce heat, and simmer 5 minutes. Uncover and simmer 10 minutes or until vegetables are tender and liquid evaporates. Stir in salt, paprika, and black pepper; cook 1 minute. Yield: 10 servings (serving size: ½ cup).

CALORIES 74 (38% from fat); FAT 3.1g (sat 0.5g, mono 2g, poly 0.5g); PROTEIN 2g; CARB 11.6g; FIBER 3.6g; CHOL 0mg; IRON 0.7mg; SODIUM 247mg; CALC 27mg

Indian Idyll

Summery fare flourishes in this outdoor buffet. Bring it home to your patio.

THIS INDIAN-INSPIRED MENU, with its vibrant sweet, tart, and spicy flavors and aromas, will fuel a lively party outside.

What's more, the menu is easy on the host because many of the items have make-ahead components, and you can offer it as a buffet, so you can enjoy time with your guests. Just set the food on colorful platters, and assemble a serve-yourself bar in a corner of the patio for guests to help themselves.

Follow our make-ahead guide (see "Party Countdown," page 152) for preparation tips that will help you finesse the time line.

INDIAN IDYLL MENU

(Serves 8)

Tamarind Martinis

Indian-Spiced Roasted Nuts

Curried Rice Noodles in Lettuce Wraps
or
Cumin-Scented Samosas with Mint Raita

Chai-Brined Shrimp Skewers
or
Grilled Tandoori Chicken

Green Beans and Potatoes in Chunky Tomato Sauce

Toasted Eggplant Curry

Lime-Coconut Granita

QUICK & EASY
Tamarind Martinis

Tamarind, a common ingredient in Indian, Thai, and Mexican cuisines, adds an acidic, slightly tart flavor to food. The pulp is sold in cakes at ethnic markets and some large supermarkets. Use a fork or your hands to break up the paste and separate it from the seeds before straining. If you make these martinis ahead, be sure to shake the drink in a martini shaker or stir it with the crushed ice just before serving.

2½ cups boiling water
  4 ounces unsweetened tamarind pulp
  ½ cup sugar
  ½ cup water
  1 cup vodka
  1 cup fresh lime juice
     Crushed ice
     Sugar (optional)
     Lime wedges (optional)

① Combine 2½ cups boiling water and tamarind in a large bowl; let stand 10 minutes. Break tamarind into small pieces; let stand 5 minutes. Strain mixture through a sieve into a bowl; discard solids.
② Combine ½ cup sugar and ½ cup water in a microwave-safe dish; microwave at HIGH 2 minutes or until sugar

Continued

dissolves, stirring once. Cool. Combine tamarind liquid, sugar syrup, vodka, and juice in a pitcher, stirring well. Add crushed ice; stir or shake well. Garnish rims of 8 martini glasses with sugar, if desired. Strain chilled martini mixture into prepared glasses; garnish with lime wedges, if desired. Yield: 8 servings (serving size: about ½ cup).

CALORIES 146 (1% from fat); FAT 0.1g (sat 0.1g, mono 0g, poly 0g); PROTEIN 0.4g; CARB 21.7g; FIBER 0.7g; CHOL 0mg; IRON 0.3mg; SODIUM 4mg; CALC 12mg

QUICK & EASY • MAKE AHEAD
Indian-Spiced Roasted Nuts

This simple recipe makes a tasty party snack. Use your favorite nuts, and add a bit of heat with a dash of ground red pepper, if you like.

1½ teaspoons brown sugar
1½ teaspoons honey
1 teaspoon canola oil
¾ teaspoon ground cinnamon
⅛ teaspoon salt
⅛ teaspoon ground cardamom
⅛ teaspoon ground cloves
Dash of freshly ground black pepper
¼ cup blanched almonds
¼ cup cashews
¼ cup hazelnuts

1 Preheat oven to 350°.
2 Combine first 8 ingredients in a microwave-safe bowl. Microwave at HIGH 30 seconds; stir until blended. Add nuts; toss to coat.
3 Spread nuts evenly on a baking sheet lined with parchment paper. Bake at 350° for 15 minutes or until golden brown. Cool. Yield: 12 servings (serving size: 1 tablespoon).

CALORIES 60 (75% from fat); FAT 5g (sat 0.5g, mono 3.3g, poly 0.9g); PROTEIN 1.5g; CARB 3.4g; FIBER 0.8g; CHOL 0mg; IRON 0.5mg; SODIUM 44mg; CALC 14mg

Curried Rice Noodles in Lettuce Wraps

Madras curry powder works well in this dish because it adds just a bit of spicy flavor.

4 ounces uncooked rice sticks
2½ teaspoons olive oil
1¼ cups thinly vertically sliced onion
1 tablespoon grated peeled fresh ginger
2½ teaspoons Madras curry powder
4 garlic cloves, minced
1 cup grated carrot
1½ cups thinly sliced napa (Chinese) cabbage
1½ tablespoons water
¼ cup chopped fresh cilantro
2½ tablespoons sake (rice wine) or sherry
1½ tablespoons low-sodium soy sauce
½ teaspoon sugar
½ teaspoon salt
¼ teaspoon freshly ground black pepper
1½ cups fresh bean sprouts
8 Boston lettuce leaves

1 Place rice sticks in a large bowl. Cover with boiling water; let stand 20 minutes. Drain and rinse with cold water; drain.
2 Heat oil in a wok or large skillet over medium-high heat. Add onion and next 3 ingredients to pan; stir-fry 3 minutes. Add carrot; stir-fry 1½ minutes. Add cabbage and 1½ tablespoons water; cook 2 minutes, stirring frequently. Remove from heat.
3 Combine cilantro and next 5 ingredients in a bowl, stirring until sugar dissolves. Add rice sticks, cilantro mixture, and bean sprouts to cabbage mixture; toss to combine. Spoon ⅓ cup cabbage mixture on each lettuce leaf; roll up. Yield: 8 servings (serving size: 1 stuffed leaf).

CALORIES 102 (14% from fat); FAT 1.6g (sat 0.2g, mono 1.1g, poly 0.2g); PROTEIN 2.6g; CARB 18.6g; FIBER 2.1g; CHOL 0mg; IRON 1.2mg; SODIUM 263mg; CALC 33mg

QUICK & EASY
Cumin-Scented Samosas with Mint Raita

Samosas, traditional Indian pastries filled with vegetables, meat, or both, are typically made with homemade dough, then fried. Our samosas remain light and crisp because we enclose the filling in phyllo dough and then bake them.

SAMOSAS:
2¼ cups chopped peeled baking potato
1½ cups chopped peeled carrot
1½ tablespoons olive oil
2 cups finely chopped onion
2½ tablespoons minced peeled fresh ginger
1½ tablespoons minced garlic
¾ teaspoon crushed red pepper
1 tablespoon ground cumin
2 teaspoons ground coriander
1 teaspoon ground cinnamon
¾ teaspoon salt
½ teaspoon freshly ground black pepper
¼ teaspoon ground turmeric
1¼ cups frozen green peas, thawed
½ cup chopped fresh cilantro
1 tablespoon fresh lemon juice
16 (18 x 14-inch) sheets frozen phyllo dough, thawed
Cooking spray
RAITA:
1 cup plain low-fat yogurt
⅓ cup chopped fresh mint

1 To prepare samosas, cook potato and carrot in boiling water 8 minutes or until tender; drain.
2 Heat oil in a wok or large skillet over medium heat. Add onion to pan; cook 10 minutes or until lightly browned, stirring frequently. Add ginger, garlic, and red pepper; cook 2 minutes, stirring frequently. Stir in cumin and next 5 ingredients; cook 15 seconds, stirring constantly. Add potato mixture, peas, cilantro, and juice, stirring well; cool slightly. Place half of pea mixture in a food processor; pulse until coarsely chopped. Spoon

chopped mixture into a bowl. Repeat procedure with remaining pea mixture.

❸ Preheat oven to 350°.

❹ Place 1 phyllo sheet on a large cutting board or work surface (cover remaining dough to prevent drying); lightly coat with cooking spray. Fold phyllo sheet in half lengthwise to form an 18 x 7-inch rectangle. Spoon about 3 tablespoons pea mixture onto bottom end of rectangle, leaving a 1-inch border. Fold left bottom corner over mixture, forming a triangle; fold back and forth into triangles to end of phyllo strip. Tuck edges under triangle; lightly coat seam with cooking spray. Repeat procedure with remaining phyllo, cooking spray, and filling to form 16 samosas. Place triangles, seam sides down, 2 inches apart on baking sheets coated with cooking spray.

❺ Bake at 350° for 13 minutes with 1 baking sheet on bottom rack and 1 baking sheet on second rack from top. Rotate baking sheets; bake an additional 12 minutes or until samosas are lightly browned.

❻ To prepare raita, combine yogurt and mint. Serve with samosas. Yield: 8 servings (serving size: 2 samosas and about 2 tablespoons raita).

CALORIES 200 (22% from fat); FAT 4.9g (sat 1g, mono 2.7g, poly 0.6g); PROTEIN 6.2g; CARB 33.5g; FIBER 4.5g; CHOL 2mg; IRON 1.9mg; SODIUM 394mg; CALC 105mg

QUICK & EASY
Chai-Brined Shrimp Skewers

Shrimp brine in a fraction of the time it takes for large, tougher cuts of meat. If using wooden skewers, be sure to soak them in water for about 30 minutes beforehand. Purchase naan at a local Indian restaurant or gourmet market, or substitute pita bread.

    3 cups water
    2 tablespoons sugar
    1 tablespoon kosher salt
    2 tablespoons grated peeled fresh
       ginger
  ½   teaspoon white peppercorns,
       crushed
    8 whole cardamom pods, crushed
    6 whole cloves
    1 bay leaf
    1 (3-inch) cinnamon stick, broken
    2 tablespoons black tea leaves (such
       as Darjeeling)
    1 cup ice cubes
   32 peeled and deveined large shrimp
       (about 1½ pounds)
    2 large peeled ripe mangoes, each cut
       into 8 (2-inch) pieces
       Cooking spray
  ½   cup sliced green onions
    8 Indian flatbreads (naan)

❶ Combine first 9 ingredients in a large saucepan; bring to a boil. Cover, reduce heat, and simmer 15 minutes. Stir in tea leaves; simmer 2 minutes. Strain mixture through a sieve into a large bowl; discard solids. Stir in ice; chill.

❷ Add shrimp to water mixture; chill 20 minutes.

❸ Prepare grill.

❹ Remove shrimp from bowl; discard liquid. Pat shrimp dry with paper towels. Thread 4 shrimp and 2 mango pieces alternately onto each of 8 (12-inch) skewers.

❺ Place skewers on a grill rack coated with cooking spray. Grill 2 minutes on each side or until shrimp are done. Sprinkle with green onions. Serve with flatbread. Yield: 8 servings (serving size: 1 skewer and 1 piece flatbread).

NOTE: You can use smaller skewers. Simply thread two shrimp alternately with two mango chunks, and serve guests two skewers each. You'll need to purchase an extra mango (which minimally increases the calories per serving) if you opt for this presentation.

CALORIES 306 (16% from fat); FAT 5.3g (sat 2.9g, mono 1.3g, poly 0.6g); PROTEIN 20.4g; CARB 45.5g; FIBER 5.1g; CHOL 97mg; IRON 3.5mg; SODIUM 497mg; CALC 63mg

---

Take It Outside

Buffet dining lends itself to a casual party. Consider these ideas when setting up your own.

• When the weather is pleasant, think of your patio or yard as an extension of your indoor living space. Mix and match your indoor and outdoor furniture for a stylish modern touch and hospitable setting.

• Any type of table works for outdoor entertaining. For a chic ultra-casual touch, pull a tall sofa table outdoors; for a more rustic feel, consider using a wooden farm table or, of course, a picnic table.

• Add sunny colors to reflect the exuberance of the season with bright table coverings; place colorful accent pillows in seats.

• Sew small stones into the corners of your tablecloth or clip the inside edges with fishing weights to keep it from taking flight in the wind.

• Serve dinner on casual pottery, or you can just mix and match dinnerware with everyday flatware, glassware, and cloth napkins.

• Create cozy mini-rooms by grouping chairs under trees or near a water feature. If shade's at a premium, consider renting umbrellas for the occasion.

• Since May evenings can be a bit chilly, be sure to keep a supply of stadium blankets handy, or rent heaters to keep guests warm.

• To ensure flow, position the buffet table so guests can walk around its perimeter.

• Choose serving dishes in assorted colors, sizes, and shapes. Place plates at one end of the table and utensils at the other to keep traffic moving.

• Stock a self-service bar with standards like sodas, bottled water, wine, and beer, as well as this menu's Tamarind Martinis. Situate the bar in the shade, away from the buffet.

• Set out snacks and appetizers just before the party starts so guests can enjoy them right after they arrive.

• Make indoor spaces available, too, just in case the weather turns chilly or rainy.

Party Countdown

Up to one week ahead:
• Prepare Indian-Spiced Roasted Nuts; store in an airtight container.
• Prepare Cumin-Scented Samosas with Mint Raita through step 3. Place in a single layer on baking sheets, and cover tightly with plastic wrap; freeze.

Up to two days ahead:
• Prepare Lime-Coconut Granita. Cover tightly with plastic wrap, and freeze.
• Prepare brine for Chai-Brined Shrimp Skewers.

The day before:
• Marinate chicken for Grilled Tandoori Chicken; chill.
• Slice green onions for Chai-Brined Shrimp Skewers; cover and refrigerate.
• Prepare Tamarind Martini mixture; cover and chill.
• Prepare Mint Raita for samosas.
• Grill eggplant for Toasted Eggplant Curry.

The morning of the party:
• Purchase fresh naan.
• Prepare Curried Rice Noodles in Lettuce Wraps. Cover and refrigerate.
• Prepare Green Beans and Potatoes in Chunky Tomato Sauce. Cover; refrigerate.
• Prepare Toasted Eggplant Curry. Cover and refrigerate.
• Scrape granita with a fork.

One hour before guests arrive:
• Prepare grill.
• Bake Cumin-Scented Samosas; arrange on platter. (If samosas are frozen, they'll need to bake a few minutes longer.)
• Brine shrimp.
• Arrange self-service bar.
• Let Curried Rice Noodles in Lettuce Wraps stand at room temperature 15 to 20 minutes.
• Set out Indian-Spiced Roasted Nuts.

As guests arrive:
• Wrap store-bought naan in foil, and warm in oven at low temperature.
• Grill shrimp skewers and/or chicken thighs.

Just before serving:
• Shake martini mixture with ice.
• Reheat Green Beans and Potatoes in Chunky Tomato Sauce and Toasted Eggplant Curry.
• Fluff granita with a fork.

Grilled Tandoori Chicken

This dish is named for "tandoor," the Indian clay oven it's traditionally cooked in.

MARINADE:
  2 teaspoons canola oil
  4 teaspoons Hungarian sweet paprika
  2 teaspoons garam masala
1½ teaspoons ground cumin
1½ teaspoons ground coriander
  1 teaspoon ground turmeric
  1 teaspoon ground red pepper
  2 cups coarsely chopped onion
  ½ cup coarsely chopped peeled fresh ginger
  2 teaspoons finely chopped seeded serrano pepper
  8 garlic cloves, crushed
  ½ cup plain low-fat yogurt
  2 tablepoons fresh lemon juice
1¾ teaspoons salt

REMAINING INGREDIENTS:
 16 skinless, boneless chicken thighs (about 3 pounds)
  2 cups plain low-fat yogurt
  2 tablepoons fresh lemon juice
  ½ teaspoon ground cumin
  ½ teaspoon ground coriander
  ¼ teaspoon salt
     Cooking spray

❶ Heat oil in a small nonstick skillet over medium-high heat. Add paprika and next 5 ingredients to pan; cook 2 minutes or until fragrant, stirring constantly. Remove from pan; cool.
❷ Place onion and next 3 ingredients in a food processor; process until smooth. Add spice mixture, ½ cup yogurt, 2 tablespoons juice, and 1¾ teaspoons salt to onion mixture; process until smooth. Transfer mixture to a large heavy-duty zip-top plastic bag. Cut 3 shallow slits in each chicken thigh. Add chicken to bag; seal. Toss to coat. Marinate in refrigerator 8 hours or overnight, turning occasionally.
❸ Prepare grill.
❹ Combine 2 cups yogurt and next 4 ingredients in a bowl, stirring well. Cover and chill.
❺ Remove chicken from bag; discard marinade. Place chicken on a grill rack coated with cooking spray. Grill 7 minutes on each side or until done. Serve with yogurt mixture. Yield: 8 servings (serving size: 2 chicken thighs and about ¼ cup yogurt mixture).

CALORIES 256 (28% from fat); FAT 8.1g (sat 2.3g, mono 2.7g, poly 1.8g); PROTEIN 32.2g; CARB 12.7g; FIBER 1.7g; CHOL 119mg; IRON 2.2mg; SODIUM 767mg; CALC 181mg

Green Beans and Potatoes in Chunky Tomato Sauce

To peel tomatoes, score the skin by making a small X on the bottom side with a sharp knife. Place tomato in boiling water for 30 seconds. Remove tomato using a slotted spoon; immediately submerge in a bowl of ice water. Let stand for one minute. Skin should pull off easily with a sharp knife.

1½ tablespoons olive oil
  1 garlic clove, minced
1½ cups diced red potato
  ½ cup chopped celery
  ½ teaspoon salt
1¼ pounds green beans, trimmed
  ¼ cup water
  ⅓ cup chopped fresh cilantro
  ¾ pound plum tomatoes, peeled and coarsely chopped
  ¼ teaspoon freshly ground black pepper
  ¼ teaspoon ground red pepper

❶ Heat oil in a large skillet over medium-high heat. Add garlic to pan; sauté 30 seconds, stirring constantly. Add potato and next 3 ingredients; sauté 1 minute. Add ¼ cup water; cover and cook 5 minutes or until beans are crisp-tender. Add cilantro and tomatoes. Cover, reduce heat, and cook 4 minutes or until tomatoes begin to soften, stirring occasionally. Stir in peppers. Yield: 8 servings (serving size: about ¾ cup).

CALORIES 70 (35% from fat); FAT 2.7g (sat 0.4g, mono 1.9g, poly 0.3g); PROTEIN 1.9g; CARB 11.1g; FIBER 3.8g; CHOL 0mg; IRON 0.7mg; SODIUM 159mg; CALC 47mg

Toasted Eggplant Curry

- 8 Japanese eggplants (about 3 pounds)
- 2 tablespoons canola oil
- 3 cups chopped onion
- 8 garlic cloves, minced
- 2 jalapeño peppers, seeded and chopped
- 5 cups chopped peeled tomato (about 2 pounds)
- 4 teaspoons curry powder
- 2 tablespoons chopped fresh cilantro
- 1 teaspoon salt

① Preheat broiler.

② Pierce eggplants several times with a fork; place on a foil-lined baking sheet. Broil 15 minutes or until blackened, turning frequently. Cool slightly; peel and coarsely chop. Keep warm.

③ Heat oil in a large skillet over medium heat. Add onion, garlic, and peppers to pan; cook 10 minutes or until onion is translucent, stirring frequently. Add tomato and curry powder, stirring well; cover and cook 10 minutes, stirring occasionally. Stir in eggplant, cilantro, and salt. Yield: 8 servings (serving size: 1 cup).

CALORIES 124 (29% from fat); FAT 4g (sat 0.3g, mono 2.2g, poly 1.2g); PROTEIN 4g; CARB 21.8g; FIBER 6.9g; CHOL 0mg; IRON 0.8mg; SODIUM 304mg; CALC 36mg

MAKE AHEAD • FREEZABLE
Lime-Coconut Granita

- 2½ cups water
- ¾ cup sugar
- 1 tablespoon grated lime rind
- ½ cup fresh lime juice (about 4 limes)
- ½ cup light coconut milk

① Combine all ingredients in a large saucepan over medium heat. Cook 3 minutes or until sugar dissolves, stirring constantly. Remove from heat, and cool completely.

② Pour mixture into an 11 x 7–inch baking dish. Cover and freeze 8 hours or until firm. Remove mixture from freezer; let stand 10 minutes. Scrape entire mixture with a fork until fluffy. Yield: 8 servings (serving size: ½ cup).

CALORIES 85 (8% from fat); FAT 0.8g (sat 0.7g, mono 0g, poly 0g); PROTEIN 0.3g; CARB 20.7g; FIBER 0.1g; CHOL 0mg; IRON 0.1mg; SODIUM 6mg; CALC 5mg

MENU OF THE MONTH
Ice Cream Social

Celebrate graduation, birthdays, or just the arrival of warm weather with an old-fashioned dessert party.

ICE CREAM SOCIAL MENU

(Serves 12)

Ice Cream:

Honey-Lavender Ricotta Ice Cream

Chocolate Ice Cream

Key Lime Ice Cream

Sauce:

Classic Hot Fudge Sauce

Easy Raspberry Sauce

Cookies:

Oatmeal-Almond Lace Cookies

Shortbread

Lemon-Cornmeal Cookies

Beverage:

Iced tea or lemonade

MAKE AHEAD • FREEZABLE
Honey-Lavender Ricotta Ice Cream

Infusing the syrup with lavender imparts a subtle floral flavor to this ice cream. Look for fresh ricotta cheese at gourmet markets, or you can make your own. It lends the ice cream wonderful richness. Serve with Easy Raspberry Sauce (page 155), and garnish with lavender sprigs.

- 1 cup sugar
- 1 cup water
- 1 teaspoon dried lavender blossoms
- 3 cups fresh ricotta cheese (about 2 pounds)
- 2 tablespoons honey
- ¼ teaspoon salt

① Combine sugar and 1 cup water in a small saucepan; bring to a boil. Cook 45 seconds or until sugar dissolves. Remove from heat; stir in lavender. Let stand 30 minutes. Strain mixture through a fine mesh sieve into a small bowl; discard solids. Cover and chill 1 hour.

② Combine cheese, honey, and salt in a food processor; process until smooth. With processor on, slowly add lavender syrup through food chute. Pour mixture into freezer can of an ice-cream freezer; freeze according to manufacturer's instructions. Spoon ice cream into a freezer-safe container; cover and freeze 4 hours or until firm. Yield: 1½ quarts (serving size: about ½ cup ice cream).

CALORIES 190 (29% from fat); FAT 6.2g (sat 3.8g, mono 1.8g, poly 0.2g); PROTEIN 11.5g; CARB 23g; FIBER 0g; CHOL 23mg; IRON 0mg; SODIUM 240mg; CALC 250mg

Chocolate Ice Cream

For the best flavor, use high-quality chocolate, such as Ghirardelli or Guittard. Gourmet chocolate is available in the baking aisle at specialty food stores and many supermarkets.

- 3 cups 1% low-fat milk, divided
- ¼ cup sugar
- 3 tablespoons cornstarch
- ⅛ teaspoon salt
- 4 ounces semisweet chocolate, finely chopped

❶ Place 2¼ cups milk in a heavy saucepan; bring to a simmer over medium heat. Combine ¼ cup milk, sugar, cornstarch, and salt in a medium bowl, stirring with a whisk until smooth. Slowly add sugar mixture to pan, stirring constantly with a whisk. Cook 4 minutes or until mixture begins to thicken, stirring constantly with a whisk. Remove pan from heat.
❷ Place chocolate in a small bowl. Bring remaining ½ cup milk just to a boil in a small saucepan over medium heat. Pour hot milk over chocolate; let stand 1 minute. Stir chocolate mixture until smooth. Add chocolate mixture to sugar mixture; stir until well blended. Cover and chill 2 hours.
❸ Pour mixture into freezer can of an ice-cream freezer; freeze according to manufacturer's instructions. Spoon ice cream into a freezer-safe container; cover and freeze 1 hour or until firm. Yield: 1½ quarts (serving size: ½ cup).

CALORIES 95 (33% from fat); FAT 3.5g (sat 2.1g, mono 1.1g, poly 0.1g); PROTEIN 2.4g; CARB 14.9g; FIBER 0.6g; CHOL 2mg; IRON 0.3mg; SODIUM 57mg; CALC 78mg

Key Lime Ice Cream

If you can't find bottled Key lime juice (or fresh Key limes to squeeze for juice), just substitute ¾ cup of the more common (and less potent) bottled Persian lime juice.

- 1½ cups 1% low-fat milk
- ⅔ cup bottled Key lime juice
- ½ cup half-and-half
- ⅛ teaspoon salt
- 1 (14-ounce) can fat-free sweetened condensed milk
- Lime wedges (optional)

❶ Combine first 5 ingredients in a medium bowl, stirring with a whisk. Pour mixture into freezer can of an ice-cream freezer; freeze according to manufacturer's instructions. Spoon ice cream into a freezer-safe container; cover and freeze 1 hour or until firm. Garnish with lime wedges, if desired. Yield: 1 quart (serving size: about ⅓ cup).

CALORIES 119 (11% from fat); FAT 1.5g (sat 0.9g, mono 0.4g, poly 0.1g); PROTEIN 3.8g; CARB 22.2g; FIBER 0g; CHOL 9mg; IRON 0mg; SODIUM 78mg; CALC 133mg

Classic Hot Fudge Sauce

Prepare this a day or two ahead and refrigerate; microwave at MEDIUM for two minutes or until thoroughly heated, stirring after one minute.

- 1 cup sugar
- ⅔ cup 1% low-fat milk
- 2 tablespoons unsweetened cocoa
- 2 tablespoons light-colored corn syrup
- 2 teaspoons butter
- Dash of salt
- 3 ounces bittersweet chocolate, finely chopped
- 1 teaspoon vanilla extract

❶ Combine first 6 ingredients in a medium heavy-duty saucepan over medium heat; bring to a simmer, stirring constantly with a whisk. Cook 2 minutes or until smooth, stirring constantly. Remove from heat. Add chocolate and vanilla, stirring until chocolate melts. Serve warm. Yield: 1½ cups (serving size: 2 tablespoons).

CALORIES 124 (28% from fat); FAT 3.9g (sat 2.1g, mono 0.3g, poly 0g); PROTEIN 1.1g; CARB 24g; FIBER 0.8g; CHOL 2mg; IRON 0.3mg; SODIUM 26mg; CALC 19mg

Mix, Match, and Serve

Tailor your menu to suit the size of the party by mixing and matching the ice creams, sauces, and cookies. For a smaller gathering, for instance, you might serve one ice cream, one sauce, and one or two types of cookies.

Make things easy for guests by scooping single portions of ice cream into one large, chilled serving bowl on the buffet (use one serving bowl per type of ice cream, and chill the bowl in the freezer for about an hour to help the ice cream stay cold). That way, guests can help themselves with a large serving spoon rather than awkwardly scooping their own ice cream. Just before serving, reheat the Classic Hot Fudge Sauce (above), and pour it into a small, microwave-safe serving bowl or gravy boat that has been warmed in the microwave for 30 seconds.

Then simply set out dessert spoons, small bowls, glasses, and plates, and let guests serve themselves. Don't worry if everything doesn't match.

Easy Raspberry Sauce

Fresh in-season raspberries are essential to this ruby-hued sauce. It will keep five days tightly covered in the refrigerator. Pour leftover sauce on French toast.

- 4 cups fresh raspberries
- ¼ cup water
- ⅓ cup sugar
- ½ teaspoon fresh lemon juice

❶ Combine first 3 ingredients in a medium saucepan over medium-high heat; bring to a boil. Reduce heat, and simmer 10 minutes or until slightly thickened, crushing raspberries with back of a spoon. Press mixture through a sieve into a bowl. Discard solids. Spoon raspberry sauce into a small bowl; stir in juice. Cover and chill. Yield: 1½ cups (serving size: 2 tablespoons).

CALORIES 43 (6% from fat); FAT 0.3g (sat 0g, mono 0g, poly 0.2g); PROTEIN 0.5g; CARB 10.5g; FIBER 2.7g; CHOL 0mg; IRON 0.3mg; SODIUM 0mg; CALC 10mg

Oatmeal-Almond Lace Cookies

Keep an eye on these cookies while they bake because they can burn quickly.

- 1 cup regular oats, toasted
- ⅓ cup light-colored corn syrup
- 1 tablespoon canola oil
- 2 tablespoons butter
- ⅓ cup sugar
- 1 large egg
- ¼ teaspoon vanilla extract
- 3 tablespoons all-purpose flour
- 1 teaspoon baking powder
- ¼ teaspoon salt
- ¼ cup chopped blanched almonds, toasted

❶ Preheat oven to 400°.
❷ Combine first 3 ingredients in a medium bowl. Melt butter in a small saucepan over low heat. Cook 2 minutes or until butter begins to brown (do not burn). Pour into oat mixture; stir well.
❸ Place sugar and egg in a medium bowl; beat with a mixer at medium speed until light and fluffy (about 2 minutes). Beat in vanilla.
❹ Combine flour, baking powder, and salt, stirring with a whisk. Stir flour mixture into egg mixture. Stir egg mixture into oat mixture. Add almonds, and stir well.
❺ Drop dough by heaping teaspoonfuls 2 inches apart onto 2 baking sheets lined with parchment paper. Bake at 400° for 4 minutes or until golden. Cool on pans 2 minutes. Transfer parchment to cooling rack; cool completely. Yield: 3 dozen (serving size: 1 cookie).

CALORIES 42 (36% from fat); FAT 1.7g (sat 0.5g, mono 0.7g, poly 0.3g); PROTEIN 0.7g; CARB 6.4g; FIBER 0.3g; CHOL 2mg; IRON 0.2mg; SODIUM 38mg; CALC 12mg

Shortbread

This shortbread is rolled and cut into wedges before it's baked.

- 1 cup all-purpose flour (about 4½ ounces)
- ¼ cup sugar
- Dash of salt
- 5 tablespoons butter, softened
- 2 tablespoons fat-free milk
- 1 teaspoon vanilla extract
- Cooking spray

❶ Lightly spoon flour into a measuring cup, and level with a knife. Combine flour, sugar, and salt in a bowl, stirring with a whisk.
❷ Place butter in a medium bowl; beat with a mixer at medium speed until light and fluffy. Add flour mixture, beating at low speed. Add milk and vanilla; beat until blended. Pat dough into a 4-inch circle; wrap in plastic wrap, and chill 30 minutes.
❸ Preheat oven to 350°.
❹ Unwrap and place dough on plastic wrap. Cover dough with an additional sheet of plastic wrap. Roll dough, still covered, into an 8-inch circle. Place dough on a baking sheet coated with cooking spray. Cut dough into 16 wedges, cutting into, but not through, dough. Pierce dough several times with a fork. Bake at 350° for 20 minutes or until lightly browned. Cool on pan 5 minutes. Cut into wedges. Cool completely on a wire rack. Yield: 16 servings (serving size: 1 wedge).

CALORIES 74 (44% from fat); FAT 3.6g (sat 2.3g, mono 0.9g, poly 0.2g); PROTEIN 0.9g; CARB 9.2g; FIBER 0.2g; CHOL 9mg; IRON 0.4mg; SODIUM 1mg; CALC 4mg

Lemon-Cornmeal Cookies

- 1 cup all-purpose flour (about 4½ ounces)
- ⅓ cup yellow cornmeal
- ½ teaspoon baking soda
- ¼ teaspoon salt
- ¼ teaspoon ground ginger
- ¾ cup plus 2 tablespoons sugar
- 6 tablespoons butter, softened
- 1 large egg
- 1 tablespoon grated lemon rind

❶ Preheat oven to 350°.
❷ Lightly spoon flour into a dry measuring cup, and level with a knife. Combine flour and next 4 ingredients; stir with a whisk. Combine sugar and butter in a large bowl, and beat with a mixer at medium speed until light and fluffy (about 5 minutes). Scrape sides of bowl occasionally. Add egg; beat well. Beat in rind. Add flour mixture to butter mixture, and beat at medium-low speed just until blended.
❸ Spoon about 1½ teaspoons batter 2 inches apart onto 2 parchment-lined baking sheets. Bake at 350° for 12 minutes or until lightly browned and almost firm. Remove from oven. Cool on pans 2 minutes or until firm. Remove from pans. Cool completely on a wire rack. Yield: 3 dozen (serving size: 1 cookie).

CALORIES 55 (34% from fat); FAT 2.1g (sat 1.3g, mono 0.6g, poly 0.1g); PROTEIN 0.7g; CARB 8.6g; FIBER 0.2g; CHOL 11mg; IRON 0.2mg; SODIUM 49mg; CALC 2mg

Cool, Creamy, Chocolaty

With our help, this three-layer sweet stays in our Tennessee reader's repertoire.

Fifteen years ago, a colleague of Claudia Smelser brought Cool, Creamy Chocolate Dessert to a luncheon. When Smelser, an executive secretary in Nashville, Tennessee, learned how easy it was to prepare, she wanted the recipe, and has since delighted family and friends with the delicious treat. However, her desire to moderate the fat and calories in the indulgent dessert prompted her to attempt lightening the recipe. She experimented with sugar-free puddings and reduced-fat cream cheese for the filling, which yielded fairly satisfactory results. But the butter-laden, shortbread textured crust still bothered her. Thus, she solicited the help of *Cooking Light* to tame the creamy and chocolaty dessert.

Smelser jokingly refers to the recipe as the "Girdlebuster," and that name says it all. With a whopping 370 calories and 23 grams of fat per serving, the dessert deserves its nickname.

To lighten it, we start with the buttery, nutty crust. Since the butter and pecans add significant calories and fat, we halve the amounts of both, shaving seven grams of fat and 60 calories from each serving. We add powdered sugar to the crust for sweetness and a little starch, which helps preserve the shortbreadlike texture of the pastry. Toasting and finely chopping the nuts boosts flavor, allowing us to use a smaller volume. To maintain a pleasingly creamy mouthfeel in the filling layers, we swap full-fat dairy products for one percent low-fat milk and a combination of fat-free and reduced fat cream cheeses, and we also use reduced calorie whipped topping. This trims 45 calories and another six grams of fat.

serving size: 1 piece		
	before	after
CALORIES PER SERVING	370	268
FAT	23.4g	10.2g
PERCENT OF TOTAL CALORIES	57%	34%

STAFF FAVORITE • MAKE AHEAD
Cool, Creamy Chocolate Dessert

You can make this up to one day ahead, but spread the remaining whipped topping mixture over the chocolate pudding layer right before serving.

CRUST:
- 1¼ cups all-purpose flour (about 5½ ounces)
- ¼ cup powdered sugar
- 6 tablespoons chilled butter, cut into small pieces
- ¼ cup finely chopped pecans, toasted
- Cooking spray

FILLING:
- 1 cup powdered sugar
- ½ cup (4 ounces) ⅓-less-fat cream cheese, softened
- ½ cup (4 ounces) fat-free cream cheese, softened
- 1 (8-ounce) carton frozen reduced-calorie whipped topping, thawed and divided
- 3 cups 1% low-fat milk
- 2 (3.9-ounce) packages chocolate instant pudding mix
- Unsweetened cocoa (optional)

1 Preheat oven to 325°.

2 To prepare crust, lightly spoon flour into dry measuring cups; level with a knife. Combine flour and ¼ cup sugar in a food processor; pulse 2 times or until combined. Add butter; pulse 10 times or until mixture resembles coarse meal. Stir in pecans. Firmly press mixture into bottom of a 13 x 9–inch baking pan coated with cooking spray. Bake at 325° for 20 minutes or until crust is lightly browned. Cool completely.

3 To prepare filling, place 1 cup sugar and cream cheeses in a medium bowl; beat with a mixer at medium speed until fluffy. Fold in half of whipped topping. Spread cream cheese mixture on cooled crust. Cover loosely; refrigerate 1 hour.

4 Combine milk and pudding mix in a large bowl; beat with a mixer at medium speed 2 minutes. Cover and refrigerate 1 hour or until pudding is set. Spread pudding mixture over cream cheese layer. Spread remaining whipped topping over pudding layer. Cover and chill 30 minutes. Sprinkle with cocoa, if desired. Cut into 15 pieces. Yield: 15 servings (serving size: 1 piece).

CALORIES 268 (34% from fat); FAT 10.2g (sat 6.3g, mono 2.2g, poly 0.7g); PROTEIN 5.2g; CARB 39.5g; FIBER 1.1g; CHOL 20mg; IRON 0.9mg; SODIUM 183mg; CALC 92mg

Pass the Pasta

A Georgia schoolteacher creates a rich, tasty casserole using basic items from her pantry.

Risë Minton, a middle-school science teacher, loves to experiment—in the kitchen as well as the classroom. Last summer she and her husband, Eric, bought a new home in Smyrna, Georgia. Before moving from their old home, she wanted to use up what was in the pantry so she could stock her kitchen with new ingredients. Three-Cheese Baked Penne is the result of her efforts.

Minton loves the flavors of her Italian heritage, such as pungent cheeses; her husband prefers the comfort food of his Southern upbringing, and Three-Cheese Baked Penne was a tasteful compromise. "This dish has the traditional Italian ingredients of foods I grew up with, and macaroni and cheese for my husband." Served with a small green salad and light vinaigrette, Three-Cheese Baked Penne is now a regular standby at the Mintons' new home.

Three-Cheese Baked Penne

"My secret is to cook the penne al dente so it retains its texture after baking."
—Risë Minton, Smyrna, Georgia

2½ cups uncooked whole wheat penne (about 8 ounces tube-shaped pasta)
Cooking spray
2 (4-ounce) links sweet turkey Italian sausage
1 cup finely chopped green bell pepper
1½ teaspoons dried Italian seasoning
1 teaspoon crushed red pepper
⅛ teaspoon black pepper
Dash of salt
10 grape or cherry tomatoes, halved
1 garlic clove, minced
1 (8-ounce) can garlic-and-herb tomato sauce
¾ cup (3 ounces) shredded part-skim mozzarella cheese
½ cup (2 ounces) crumbled goat cheese
¼ cup (1 ounce) grated fresh Parmesan cheese

❶ Preheat oven to 350°.
❷ Cook pasta according to package directions, omitting salt and fat. Drain and keep warm.
❸ Heat a large nonstick skillet over medium-high heat. Coat pan with cooking spray. Remove casings from sausage. Add sausage to pan; cook 2 minutes, stirring to crumble. Add bell pepper and next 6 ingredients to pan; sauté 6 minutes or until bell pepper is tender. Stir in tomato sauce. Reduce heat, and simmer 5 minutes. Add pasta to pan, tossing gently to coat. Spoon pasta mixture into an 8-inch square baking dish coated with cooking spray. Stir in mozzarella and goat cheese; sprinkle with Parmesan. Bake at 350° for 7 minutes or until bubbly and top is browned. Yield: 6 servings (serving size: 1¼ cups).

CALORIES 326 (30% from fat); FAT 10.9g (sat 5.8g, mono 2.9g, poly 1g); PROTEIN 20.8g; CARB 38.9g; FIBER 4.9g; CHOL 47mg; IRON 3mg; SODIUM 641mg; CALC 211mg

World-Class Flavor Menu
serves 4

Asian-inspired side dishes spice up simple pork chops.

Asian Caramelized Pineapple
Sesame noodles
Place 4 ounces uncooked wide rice sticks (rice-flour noodles) in boiling water to cover; let stand 5 minutes. Drain; place noodles in a bowl. Combine 2 tablespoons minced shallots, 3 tablespoons rice vinegar, 2 tablespoons low-sodium soy sauce, 1 tablespoon dark sesame oil, 1 tablespoon canola oil, and ½ teaspoon chile paste with garlic. Drizzle vinegar mixture over noodles; toss well. Sprinkle with 3 tablespoons chopped fresh cilantro and 2 tablespoons chopped peanuts.
Grilled pork chops

Asian Caramelized Pineapple

"I like to grill fish and am always looking for interesting side dishes to serve with it. This is also good with pork chops. It can be served warm or at room temperature."
—Victoria Johnson, Gilbert, Arizona

1½ teaspoons canola oil
1½ tablespoons minced red onion
1 large garlic clove, minced
2 cups diced fresh pineapple
1 tablespoon low-sodium soy sauce
1½ teaspoons chopped seeded red jalapeño pepper
1½ teaspoons fresh lime juice
1 teaspoon chopped peeled fresh ginger
1½ teaspoons chopped fresh cilantro

❶ Heat oil in a large nonstick skillet over medium heat. Add onion and garlic to pan; cook 2 minutes. Add pineapple; cook 5 minutes or until lightly browned. Add soy sauce and next 3 ingredients;

cook 2 minutes. Remove from heat; stir in cilantro. Yield: 4 servings (serving size: about ½ cup).

CALORIES 61 (28% from fat); FAT 1.9g (sat 0.1g, mono 1.1g, poly 0.6g); PROTEIN 0.9g; CARB 11.6g; FIBER 1.3g; CHOL 0mg; IRON 0.4mg; SODIUM 135mg; CALC 15mg

Beef and Gorgonzola Toasts with Herb-Garlic Cream

"This appetizer works for so many occasions because the beef and the herb cream can be prepared ahead."
—Teresa Ralston, New Albany, Ohio

1 (1¼ -pound) beef tenderloin, trimmed
Cooking spray
1 teaspoon kosher salt
½ teaspoon freshly ground black pepper
30 (¼-inch-thick) slices diagonally cut French bread baguette, toasted
10 tablespoons Herb-Garlic Cream (page 158)
30 baby spinach leaves
5 tablespoons (1¼ ounces) crumbled Gorgonzola cheese

❶ Preheat oven to 475°.
❷ Place tenderloin on a broiler pan coated with cooking spray. Sprinkle with salt and pepper. Bake at 475° for 10 minutes. Reduce oven temperature to 425° (do not remove tenderloin from oven); bake an additional 20 minutes or until thermometer registers 145° (medium-rare) to 160° (medium) or until desired degree of doneness. Cover tenderloin with foil; let stand 10 minutes. Cut tenderloin across grain into very thin slices.
❸ Spread each baguette slice with 1 teaspoon Herb-Garlic Cream; top each with 1 spinach leaf. Divide beef evenly among bread slices; sprinkle each with ½ teaspoon cheese. Yield: 30 appetizers (serving size: 1 toast).

CALORIES 97 (38% from fat); FAT 4.1g (sat 1.7g, mono 1.5g, poly 0.3g); PROTEIN 5.8g; CARB 9g; FIBER 0.5g; CHOL 14mg; IRON 0.9mg; SODIUM 194mg; CALC 21mg

HERB-GARLIC CREAM:

The leftover cream can be used as a sandwich spread, on baked potatoes, or with grilled chicken.

- ⅔ cup fat-free sour cream
- 2 tablespoons minced fresh chives
- 2 tablespoons low-fat mayonnaise
- 1½ tablespoons chopped fresh thyme
- 1½ teaspoons Worcestershire sauce
- ¼ teaspoon freshly ground black pepper
- 1 garlic clove, minced

① Combine all ingredients in a small bowl; cover and chill. Yield: 1 cup (serving size: 1 teaspoon).

CALORIES 4 (27% from fat); FAT 0.1g (sat 0g, mono 0g, poly 0.1g); PROTEIN 0.2g; CARB 0.7g; FIBER 0g; CHOL 0mg; IRON 0mg; SODIUM 10mg; CALC 6mg

Turmeric Ginger Chicken Sauté

"I came up with this recipe one night when I was in the mood for ethnic food. This dish combines Indian and Mediterranean cuisines."

—Yvonne Maffei, Lombard, Illinois

- 1 tablespoon olive oil
- ¼ cup chopped red bell pepper
- ¼ cup chopped green bell pepper
- 1 tablespoon finely chopped red onion
- ½ cup thinly sliced red cabbage
- 2 teaspoons grated peeled fresh ginger
- 2 garlic cloves, minced
- 2 pounds skinless, boneless chicken breast halves, cut into 1-inch pieces
- 2 tablespoons chopped fresh parsley
- 2 teaspoons ground turmeric
- 1 teaspoon salt
- ¼ teaspoon paprika
- ½ (10-ounce) package frozen chopped spinach, thawed, drained, and squeezed dry

① Heat oil in a large nonstick skillet over medium-high heat. Add bell peppers to pan; sauté 1 minute, stirring constantly. Add onion; sauté 1 minute. Reduce heat to medium; stir in cabbage, ginger, and garlic. Cook 3 minutes, stirring frequently. Add chicken and next 4 ingredients; cook 5 minutes, stirring frequently. Stir in spinach, and reduce heat to low. Cook 10 minutes or until chicken is done. Yield: 4 servings (serving size: 1½ cups).

CALORIES 321 (26% from fat); FAT 9.1g (sat 2g, mono 4.3g, poly 1.7g); PROTEIN 52.6g; CARB 5.2g; FIBER 2.3g; CHOL 134mg; IRON 3mg; SODIUM 739mg; CALC 91mg

Robin's Rice

"This is one of my favorite side dish recipes because it is quite versatile: Brown rice can be substituted for white rice, leeks or celery for the onion, walnuts for almonds, and beef for chicken broth to suit your taste or what you happen to have on hand."

—Robin Heflin, Camano, Washington

- 1½ teaspoons olive oil
- ⅓ cup chopped onion
- 2 garlic cloves, minced
- ¾ cup uncooked basmati rice
- 2 tablespoons slivered almonds
- ¼ teaspoon salt
- ¼ teaspoon freshly ground black pepper
- 1 (14-ounce) can fat-free, less-sodium chicken broth

① Heat oil in a medium saucepan over medium-high heat. Add onion to pan; sauté 3 minutes. Add garlic; sauté 1 minute. Add rice and almonds; sauté 2 minutes. Add salt, pepper, and broth; bring to a boil. Cover, reduce heat, and simmer about 15 minutes or until liquid is absorbed and rice is tender. Yield: 4 servings (serving size: about ⅔ cup).

CALORIES 181 (19% from fat); FAT 3.9g (sat 0.4g, mono 2.6g, poly 0.7g); PROTEIN 4.4g; CARB 32.4g; FIBER 1.9g; CHOL 0mg; IRON 0.7mg; SODIUM 305mg; CALC 37mg

20 Minute Dishes

From lamb to clams, poultry to pasta, here are simple, fresh, and easy meals you can make superfast.

QUICK & EASY
Sautéed Bass with Shiitake Mushroom Sauce

Serve with a spinach and mandarin orange salad. You can substitute snapper or rainbow trout for the bass, if you wish.

- 2 teaspoons canola oil
- ⅛ teaspoon salt
- ⅛ teaspoon black pepper
- 4 (6-ounce) skinned bass fillets
- 2 cups sliced shiitake mushroom caps
- 1 teaspoon dark sesame oil
- 2 teaspoons bottled ground fresh ginger (such as Spice World)
- 1 teaspoon bottled minced garlic
- 1 cup chopped green onions
- ¼ cup water
- ¼ cup low-sodium soy sauce
- 1 tablespoon lemon juice

① Heat canola oil in a large nonstick skillet over medium-high heat. Sprinkle salt and pepper over fish. Add fish to pan; cook 2½ minutes on each side or until fish flakes easily when tested with a fork or until desired degree of doneness. Remove fish from pan; cover and keep warm.

② Add mushrooms and sesame oil to pan; sauté 2 minutes. Add ginger and garlic; sauté 1 minute. Add green onions and remaining ingredients to pan; sauté 2 minutes. Serve with fish. Yield: 4 servings (serving size: 1 fillet and ¼ cup sauce).

CALORIES 247 (28% from fat); FAT 7.6g (sat 1.2g, mono 3.2g, poly 2.4g); PROTEIN 33.2g; CARB 6.9g; FIBER 1.7g; CHOL 140mg; IRON 2.9mg; SODIUM 629mg; CALC 49mg

Sweet and Sour Shrimp

Add steamed sugar snap peas.

- 1 (3½-ounce) bag boil-in-bag rice
- 8 ounces firm light tofu
- 2 tablespoons cornstarch, divided
- 8 ounces peeled large shrimp
- ¼ cup fat-free, less-sodium chicken broth
- ¼ cup low-sodium soy sauce
- 2 tablespoons sugar
- 3 tablespoons rice vinegar
- 1 tablespoon chile paste with garlic
- 2 teaspoons dark sesame oil
- 2 teaspoons canola oil
- 1 cup prechopped onion
- ½ cup prechopped green bell pepper
- 1 tablespoon ground fresh ginger
- 1 (8-ounce) can pineapple chunks in juice, drained

❶ Cook rice according to package directions, omitting salt and fat; set aside.
❷ Place tofu between paper towels until barely moist; cut into ½-inch cubes. Combine tofu, 1 tablespoon cornstarch, and shrimp. Combine remaining 1 tablespoon cornstarch, broth, and next 4 ingredients; set aside.
❸ Heat sesame oil in a large nonstick skillet over medium-high heat. Add shrimp mixture to pan; sauté 3 minutes. Place shrimp mixture in a bowl. Heat canola oil in pan over medium-high heat. Add onion and next 3 ingredients; sauté 2 minutes. Add shrimp mixture; cook 1 minute. Add broth mixture to pan; cook 1 minute. Serve over rice. Yield: 4 servings (serving size: 1 cup shrimp and ½ cup rice).

CALORIES 318 (19% from fat); FAT 6.8g (sat 1g, mono 2.7g, poly 1.3g); PROTEIN 19.8g; CARB 45.4g; FIBER 2.7g; CHOL 86mg; IRON 2.7mg; SODIUM 681mg; CALC 89mg

Chicken and Mushroom Tacos

Add a side of fat-free refried beans topped with your favorite salsa.

- Cooking spray
- 1¾ cups thinly vertically sliced onion
- 1 jalapeño pepper, seeded and minced
- ¼ teaspoon sugar
- 2 cups presliced mushrooms
- 1 tablespoon bottled minced garlic
- ¼ cup Madeira wine or dry sherry
- 2 cups chopped cooked chicken breast (about 8 ounces)
- 8 (6-inch) corn tortillas
- 1 cup (4 ounces) shredded reduced-fat sharp Cheddar cheese
- ¼ cup light sour cream

❶ Heat a large nonstick skillet over medium-high heat. Coat pan with cooking spray. Add onion; sauté 2 minutes. Add jalapeño; sauté 2 minutes. Sprinkle sugar over onion mixture; sauté 1 minute. Remove onion mixture from pan.
❷ Return pan to heat; recoat with cooking spray. Add mushrooms and garlic to pan; sauté 1 minute. Add Madeira; cover, reduce heat, and simmer 2 minutes. Uncover; cook 2 minutes or until liquid evaporates, stirring frequently. Stir in onion mixture and chicken; cook 3 minutes or until thoroughly heated.
❸ Warm tortillas according to package instructions. Spoon about ⅓ cup chicken mixture onto each tortilla. Top each tortilla with 2 tablespoons cheese; fold in half. Serve with sour cream. Yield: 4 servings (serving size: 2 tacos and 1 tablespoon sour cream).

CALORIES 383 (26% from fat); FAT 11g (sat 5.6g, mono 2.8g, poly 1.3g); PROTEIN 29.9g; CARB 36.3g; FIBER 4g; CHOL 73mg; IRON 1.7mg; SODIUM 389mg; CALC 316mg

Five-Spice Lamb Chops with Citrus-Raisin Couscous

Five-spice powder is a pungent blend of cinnamon, cloves, fennel seed, star anise, and Szechuan peppercorns. Add a side of steamed green beans.

- ¾ cup orange juice
- ½ cup fat-free, less-sodium chicken broth
- ⅓ cup golden raisins
- 1 cup uncooked couscous
- ¼ cup hoisin sauce
- 2 tablespoons honey
- 1 tablespoon seasoned rice vinegar
- 1 teaspoon chili garlic sauce (such as Lee Kum Kee)
- ¼ teaspoon five-spice powder
- Cooking spray
- ¼ teaspoon black pepper
- ⅛ teaspoon salt
- 8 (4-ounce) lamb loin chops, trimmed

❶ Combine first 3 ingredients in a medium saucepan; bring to a boil. Add couscous. Remove from heat; cover and let stand 5 minutes. Fluff with a fork.
❷ Combine hoisin and next 4 ingredients in a small bowl. Heat a large nonstick skillet over medium-high heat. Coat pan with cooking spray. Sprinkle pepper and salt over lamb. Add lamb to pan; cook 5 minutes on each side or until desired degree of doneness. Add hoisin mixture to pan; cook 1 minute or until thoroughly heated, turning to coat lamb. Spoon sauce over lamb; serve with couscous. Yield: 4 servings (serving size: 2 chops, ¾ cup couscous, and about 1½ tablespoons sauce).

CALORIES 428 (14% from fat); FAT 6.5g (sat 2.1g, mono 2.4g, poly 0.9g); PROTEIN 26.2g; CARB 66.1g; FIBER 3.3g; CHOL 61mg; IRON 2.9mg; SODIUM 549mg; CALC 41mg

Steamed Clams and Tomatoes with Angel Hair Pasta

(pictured on page 251)

Add some crusty bread and a simple green salad to round out your supper.

1 (9-ounce) package fresh angel hair pasta
1 tablespoon olive oil
1 cup chopped tomato
1 tablespoon bottled minced garlic
¼ teaspoon crushed red pepper
⅓ cup dry white wine
1 (8-ounce) bottle clam juice
2 dozen littleneck clams, scrubbed
1 tablespoon butter
4 teaspoons chopped fresh flat-leaf parsley

① Cook pasta according to package directions, omitting salt and fat. Drain and keep warm.
② Heat oil in a large nonstick skillet over medium-high heat. Add tomato, garlic, and pepper to pan; sauté 1 minute. Stir in wine and juice; bring to a boil. Add clams. Cover and cook 7 minutes or until shells open. Discard any unopened shells. Remove clams from pan with a slotted spoon; add butter to pan, stirring until butter melts. Place 1 cup pasta in each of 4 shallow bowls; top each serving with 6 clams, ½ cup broth, and 1 teaspoon parsley. Yield: 4 servings.

CALORIES 302 (28% from fat); FAT 9.4g (sat 3.2g, mono 3.3g, poly 0.8g); PROTEIN 15.6g; CARB 39g; FIBER 2.2g; CHOL 63mg; IRON 9.5mg; SODIUM 194mg; CALC 54mg

Jamaican-Spiced Chicken Thighs

Complete the menu with mashed sweet potatoes and a mixed green salad. For more heat, leave the seeds in the jalapeño.

¼ cup minced red onion
1 tablespoon sugar
1 tablespoon finely chopped seeded jalapeño pepper
2 teaspoons cider vinegar
2 teaspoons low-sodium soy sauce
½ teaspoon salt
½ teaspoon ground allspice
½ teaspoon dried thyme
½ teaspoon black pepper
¼ teaspoon ground red pepper
8 skinless, boneless chicken thighs (about 1½ pounds)
Cooking spray

① Combine first 10 ingredients in a large bowl; add chicken, tossing to coat. Heat a grill pan over medium-high heat. Coat pan with cooking spray. Add chicken to pan; cook 4 minutes. Turn chicken over; cook 6 minutes or until done. Yield: 4 servings (serving size: 2 chicken thighs).

CALORIES 187 (27% from fat); FAT 5.7g (sat 1.4g, mono 1.7g, poly 1.4g); PROTEIN 27.5g; CARB 5g; FIBER 0.5g; CHOL 115mg; IRON 1.6mg; SODIUM 503mg; CALC 21mg

ONE MORE TASTE

Blueberry Coffee Cake

This moist, tender cake scored high in our Test Kitchens, where tasters unanimously considered it a delicious way to use fresh blueberries. Studded with plump, juicy pockets of berries, the cake also features a sprinkling of turbinado sugar on top that adds another dimension of texture. Ideal for breakfast, brunch, dessert, or as a snack to savor with coffee, it's a recipe you'll make more than once.

Blueberry Coffee Cake

(pictured on page 250)

1½ cups all-purpose flour (about 6¾ ounces)
1 teaspoon baking powder
¼ teaspoon baking soda
¼ teaspoon salt
¾ cup granulated sugar
6 tablespoons butter, softened
1 teaspoon vanilla extract
1 large egg
1 large egg white
1⅓ cups low-fat buttermilk
Cooking spray
2 cups fresh blueberries, divided
1 tablespoon turbinado sugar

① Preheat oven to 350°.
② Lightly spoon flour into dry measuring cups; level with a knife. Combine flour and next 3 ingredients stirring with a whisk.
③ Place granulated sugar and butter in a large bowl; beat with a mixer at medium speed until well blended (about 2 minutes). Add vanilla, egg, and egg white; beat well. Add flour mixture and buttermilk alternately to sugar mixture, beginning and ending with flour mixture; mix after each addition.
④ Spoon half of batter into a 9-inch round baking pan coated with cooking spray. Sprinkle evenly with 1 cup blueberries. Spoon remaining batter over blueberries; sprinkle evenly with remaining 1 cup blueberries. Sprinkle top evenly with 1 tablespoon turbinado sugar. Bake at 350° for 50 minutes or until a wooden pick inserted in center comes out clean. Cool in pan 10 minutes on a wire rack; remove from pan. Cool completely on wire rack. Yield: 8 servings (serving size: 1 wedge).

CALORIES 287 (31% from fat); FAT 9.9g (sat 5.9g, mono 2.6g, poly 0.6g); PROTEIN 5.4g; CARB 45.4g; FIBER 1.5g; CHOL 51mg; IRON 1.4mg; SODIUM 294mg; CALC 93mg

Summer Cookbook

These winning recipes for everything from starters to sweets showcase the bounty of market-fresh fruit, vegetables, seafood, poultry, pork, and beef.

Appetizers and Drinks

Offer a tempting prelude with these beverages, salads, and dips.

Heirloom Tomato and Avocado Stack

For the prettiest presentation, choose purple, orange, green, and red heirloom tomatoes. Cilantro lends the dressing peppery flavor and a subtle green hue. Vary the taste of the dressing by using basil and lemon rind.

DRESSING:
- ⅓ cup low-fat buttermilk
- ¼ cup chopped fresh cilantro
- 2 tablespoons reduced-fat sour cream
- 1 tablespoon reduced-fat mayonnaise
- ½ teaspoon grated lime rind
- ¼ teaspoon minced fresh garlic
- ¼ teaspoon salt
- ⅛ teaspoon ground cumin
- Dash of ground red pepper

SALAD:
- 4 heirloom tomatoes (about 2 pounds)
- ¼ teaspoon salt
- ¼ cup very thinly vertically sliced red onion
- 1 cup diced peeled avocado (about 1 small)
- Coarsely ground black pepper (optional)

1 To prepare dressing, combine first 9 ingredients in a small food processor or blender; process 30 seconds or until pureed, scraping sides of bowl occasionally. Cover and chill.

2 To prepare salad, slice each tomato crosswise into 4 equal slices (about ½ inch thick). Place 1 tomato slice on each of 4 salad plates; sprinkle slices evenly with ¼ teaspoon salt. Top each serving with a few onion pieces and about 1 tablespoon avocado. Repeat layers 3 times, ending with avocado. Drizzle 2 tablespoons dressing over each serving; sprinkle with black pepper, if desired. Yield: 4 servings.

CALORIES 115 (59% from fat); FAT 7.6g (sat 1.8g, mono 4g, poly 0.9g); PROTEIN 3g; CARB 11.1g; FIBER 3.5g; CHOL 4mg; IRON 0.9mg; SODIUM 366mg; CALC 53mg

Sparkling Sangria
(pictured on page 253)

Cava is a Spanish sparkling wine with less acidity than Champagne; you may substitute another sparkling wine, such as prosecco, if you prefer.

- 1 cup cherries, pitted and halved
- 1 cup blueberries
- 1 cup raspberries
- 1 cup quartered small strawberries
- ½ cup chopped nectarine (about 1)
- ⅓ cup brandy
- 1 cup apricot nectar, chilled
- 1 (750-milliliter) bottle cava, chilled

1 Combine first 6 ingredients in a large pitcher; chill at least 2 hours. Stir in nectar and wine. Serve immediately. Yield: 8 servings (serving size: 1 cup).

CALORIES 153 (3% from fat); FAT 0.5g (sat 0.1g, mono 0.1g, poly 0.2g); PROTEIN 0.9g; CARB 17g; FIBER 2.7g; CHOL 0mg; IRON 0.5mg; SODIUM 2mg; CALC 13mg

Choice Ingredient: Cilantro

Cilantro has a distinctive, pungent, peppery taste featured extensively in Latin and Asian dishes. And because cilantro loses much of its flavor when dehydrated, always try to use fresh leaves.

One serving (approximately nine sprigs of cilantro) contains a relatively high amount of vitamin A and lutein, which is essential for good vision and may help prevent atherosclerosis.

Enjoy chopped cilantro in salsas, salads, and vinaigrettes, or add it to marinades for a fresh flavor. The herb makes a great pesto, too, especially paired with Manchego cheese and pecans. Or try it in place of parsley in a chimichurri sauce to serve with a grilled steak.

Choose plants with bright, even color and no signs of wilting. You can refrigerate cilantro, wrapped in slightly damp paper towels in a plastic bag, for up to a week. Wash and pat dry just before use. If you have a bumper crop of cilantro in the garden, store the extra in a well-sealed plastic zip-top bag in the freezer for up to two months. Simply add the frozen leaves to a recipe—no need to thaw.

Choice Ingredient: Salad Greens

When the weather's hot, foregoing the stove for a dinner of crisp salad greens is more than practical, it's delicious. With a plate of lettuces like arugula, mâche, and romaine, you're in for something at once peppery and nutty, with just a pleasant touch of bitterness or subtly sweet notes. Any assemblage of lettuces offered in your market will result in a similar flavor bouquet. The leafy greens also offer nutritional benefits because they are rich in calcium, iron, and vitamins A and C.

Use the characteristics of a particular lettuce to determine how to pair it. Joanne Weir, host of PBS's *Weir Cooking in the Wine Country*, likes peppery arugula with sweet corn and smoky roasted red peppers or delicate butter lettuce with creamy avocado. She suggests adding stone fruits like apricots, cherries, peaches, or plums to salad greens, as we do with our Grilled Peaches over Arugula with Goat Cheese and Prosciutto (at right).

Look for salad greens that are crisp yet tender. "There is nothing worse than either wilted greens or greens that are tough," Weir says. And if you're buying greens at an outdoor farmers' market, skip those that have been sitting too long in the sun. Wash all salad greens well, as some lettuces can be gritty. Store in an airtight container or plastic bag in the refrigerator crisper drawer for no more than five days.

Grilled Peaches over Arugula with Goat Cheese and Prosciutto

For a bit of crunch, sauté the prosciutto in a nonstick skillet over medium-high heat for two minutes or until crisp.

- ¼ cup balsamic vinegar
- 2 tablespoons honey
- 3 peaches, pitted and each cut into 6 wedges
- Cooking spray
- 1 tablespoon extravirgin olive oil
- ⅛ teaspoon freshly ground black pepper
- Dash of kosher salt
- 10 cups trimmed arugula (about 10 ounces)
- 2 ounces thinly sliced prosciutto, cut into ¼-inch strips
- 2 tablespoons crumbled goat cheese

① Bring vinegar to a boil in a small saucepan over medium-high heat. Reduce heat, and simmer until vinegar is reduced to 2 tablespoons (about 2 minutes). Remove from heat; stir in honey. Cool to room temperature.

② Prepare grill to high heat.

③ Place peach wedges on grill rack coated with cooking spray; grill 30 seconds on each side or until grill marks appear but peaches are still firm. Remove from grill; set aside.

④ Combine oil, pepper, and salt in a large bowl, stirring with a whisk. Add arugula, tossing gently to coat. Arrange arugula mixture on a platter. Top with peach wedges and prosciutto. Drizzle with balsamic syrup; sprinkle with cheese. Yield: 6 servings (serving size: about 1⅓ cups arugula mixture, 3 peach wedges, about ⅓ ounce prosciutto, 1½ teaspoons balsamic syrup, and 1 teaspoon cheese).

CALORIES 100 (36% from fat); FAT 4g (sat 1g, mono 2.4g, poly 0.5g); PROTEIN 3.9g; CARB 13.1g; FIBER 1.3g; CHOL 7mg; IRON 0.8mg; SODIUM 183mg; CALC 61mg

Stone Fruit–Cucumber Salad with Raspberry Vinaigrette

Cooking the fruit over medium heat enhances its sweetness without rendering it too soft. Thin-skinned pickling cucumbers require no peeling. Raspberry jam provides body and sweetness to the vinaigrette. If it's too thick to whisk, microwave at HIGH for five to 10 seconds.

- Cooking spray
- 2 peaches, pitted and each cut into 8 slices
- 2 plums, pitted and each cut into 8 slices
- 2 tablespoons seedless raspberry jam
- 2 tablespoons balsamic vinegar
- 1½ tablespoons extravirgin olive oil
- ¼ teaspoon salt
- 4 cups gourmet salad greens
- 4 cups torn romaine
- 1¼ cups thinly sliced pickling cucumber (about 2)
- Freshly ground black pepper (optional)

① Heat a nonstick skillet over medium heat. Coat pan with cooking spray. Add peach and plum slices to pan; cook 3 minutes on each side or until browned.

② Combine jam and next 3 ingredients; stir with a whisk until smooth. Combine ¼ cup jam mixture, salad greens, and romaine in a large bowl; toss well to coat. Place 2 cups greens mixture on each of 4 plates. Arrange 4 peach slices, 4 plum slices, and about ⅓ cup cucumber on each serving. Drizzle remaining vinaigrette evenly over salads; sprinkle with pepper, if desired. Serve immediately. Yield: 4 servings.

CALORIES 142 (37% from fat); FAT 5.9g (sat 0.8g, mono 3.9g, poly 1g); PROTEIN 3.4g; CARB 22.1g; FIBER 4.2g; CHOL 0mg; IRON 1.5mg; SODIUM 160mg; CALC 85mg

Garlicky Lima Bean Spread

Roasted garlic paste comes in a tube, which makes it easy to squeeze out just the amount you need. Look for it in the spice section of the supermarket. Use a 10-ounce package of frozen baby lima beans if you can't find fresh ones. Serve with summer vegetable crudités such as whole radishes, baby carrots, endive leaves, zucchini, and yellow squash strips.

    2   cups fresh lima beans
    ⅓   cup fresh parsley leaves
    ⅓   cup water
    1   tablespoon fresh lemon juice
    1   tablespoon olive oil
    2   teaspoons roasted garlic paste
    ½   teaspoon salt
    ¼   teaspoon freshly ground black
        pepper
    ¼   teaspoon hot sauce

❶ Sort and wash beans; drain and place in a medium saucepan. Cover with water to 2 inches above beans; bring to a boil. Cover, reduce heat, and simmer 20 minutes or until tender. Drain.
❷ Place beans and remaining ingredients in a food processor; process until smooth. Yield: 8 servings (serving size: 3 tablespoons).

CALORIES 67 (24% from fat); FAT 1.8g (sat 0.3g, mono 1.2g, poly 0.3g); PROTEIN 2.9g; CARB 10.2g; FIBER 2.3g; CHOL 0mg; IRON 1.2mg; SODIUM 157mg; CALC 18mg

Raspberry-Lemon Prosecco Cocktail

You can use any sparkling white wine, but we enjoy the crispness of Italian prosecco. Make the lemon syrup a day ahead, but stir in the wine just before serving.

    ¼   cup sugar
    ¼   cup fresh lemon juice
    1   tablespoon grated lemon rind
    2   (750-milliliter) bottles prosecco,
        chilled
    36 fresh raspberries (about 1 cup)

❶ Combine sugar and juice in a small saucepan; bring to a boil. Reduce heat, and simmer 1 minute, stirring until sugar dissolves. Remove from heat. Stir in rind. Cover and refrigerate overnight. Strain mixture through a fine sieve into a bowl; discard solids.
❷ Combine lemon syrup and prosecco in a pitcher. Pour about ½ cup prosecco mixture into each of 12 Champagne flutes; garnish each serving with 3 raspberries. Serve immediately. Yield: 12 servings.

CALORIES 124 (0% from fat); FAT 0g; PROTEIN 0.2g; CARB 8.5g; FIBER 0.4g; CHOL 0mg; IRON 0.4mg; SODIUM 6mg; CALC 13mg

Strawberry Daiquiris

The Simple Syrup recipe makes enough for three batches of strawberry daiquiris or two batches of the blueberry or raspberry variation. The syrup is also handy for sweetening iced tea.

    1   cup halved strawberries
    ½   cup Simple Syrup
    1   tablespoon fresh lemon juice
    3   cups crushed ice
    ½   cup rum
    3   tablespoons fresh lime juice

❶ Combine first 3 ingredients in a blender, and process until smooth. Strain mixture through a sieve into a bowl, and discard solids. Combine strawberry mixture, crushed ice, rum, and lime juice in blender, and process until smooth. Yield: 6 servings (serving size: ⅔ cup).

CALORIES 107 (1% from fat); FAT 0.1g (sat 0g, mono 0g, poly 0g); PROTEIN 0.2g; CARB 16.7g; FIBER 0.6g; CHOL 0mg; IRON 0.1mg; SODIUM 1mg; CALC 6mg

SIMPLE SYRUP:

    1¼ cups sugar
    1   cup water

❶ Combine sugar and 1 cup water in a small saucepan; bring to a boil. Cook 1½ minutes or until sugar dissolves,

stirring occasionally. Refrigerate until chilled. Yield: 1½ cups (serving size: 3 tablespoons).

CALORIES 121 (0% from fat); FAT 0g; PROTEIN 0g; CARB 31.3g; FIBER 0g; CHOL 0mg; IRON 0mg; SODIUM 1mg; CALC 1mg

BLUEBERRY DAIQUIRI VARIATION:

Substitute 1 cup blueberries for strawberries. Increase Simple Syrup to ¾ cup. Yield: 6 servings (serving size: ⅔ cup).

CALORIES 140 (1% from fat); FAT 0.1g (sat 0g, mono 0g, poly 0g); PROTEIN 0.2g; CARB 25.3g; FIBER 0.6g; CHOL 0mg; IRON 0.1mg; SODIUM 1mg; CALC 4mg

RASPBERRY DAIQUIRI VARIATION:

Substitute 1 (6-ounce) container raspberries for strawberries. Increase Simple Syrup to ¾ cup. Yield: 6 servings (serving size: ⅔ cup).

CALORIES 141 (1% from fat); FAT 0.2g (sat 0g, mono 0g, poly 0.1g); PROTEIN 0.4g; CARB 25.1g; FIBER 0.6g; CHOL 0mg; IRON 0.2mg; SODIUM 1mg; CALC 9mg

Tzatziki

Prepare this traditional Greek dip within an hour of serving time to prevent it from becoming watery. Greek yogurt is thicker and creamier than other yogurt, and we find it superior in this recipe. Serve with pita wedges.

    1   cup grated peeled English cucumber
        (about 1 medium)
    1   cup plain fat-free Greek yogurt
        (such as Fage)
    1   tablespoon chopped fresh mint
    ¼   teaspoon salt
    ¼   teaspoon freshly ground black
        pepper
    1   garlic clove, minced

❶ Pat cucumber dry with paper towels. Combine cucumber and remaining ingredients in a small bowl; cover and chill 1 hour. Yield: 10 servings (serving size: about 2 tablespoons).

CALORIES 17 (5% from fat); FAT 0.1g (sat 0g, mono 0g, poly 0g); PROTEIN 1.6g; CARB 2.5g; FIBER 0.2g; CHOL 0mg; IRON 0.1mg; SODIUM 78mg; CALC 53mg

Tomato and Basil–Topped Garlic Bruschetta

Briefly cook the garlic, onion, and tomato to mellow and meld the flavors. If you have your grill going, toast the bread on it for a smoky finish.

- 6 (1-ounce) slices Italian bread or peasant bread
- 1 garlic clove, halved and divided
- 4 teaspoons olive oil
- 3 cups finely chopped seeded tomato (about 2 pounds)
- ¼ cup finely chopped red onion
- 1 tablespoon balsamic vinegar
- 2 teaspoons capers
- 3 tablespoons thinly sliced fresh basil
- ¼ teaspoon salt
- ⅛ teaspoon freshly ground black pepper

① Preheat oven to 425°.
② Arrange bread slices in a single layer on a baking sheet. Bake at 425° for 8 minutes, turning after 4 minutes. Rub one side of toast with cut side of 1 garlic clove half; set toast aside. Discard garlic clove half. Mince remaining garlic clove half.
③ Heat oil in a medium nonstick skillet over medium heat. Add minced garlic to pan; cook 30 seconds, stirring constantly. Add tomato and onion to pan; cook 30 seconds, stirring constantly. Remove pan from heat. Stir in vinegar and capers. Cool completely. Stir in basil, salt, and pepper. Spoon ⅓ cup tomato mixture onto each toast slice. Serve immediately. Yield: 6 servings (serving size: 1 bruschetta).

CALORIES 128 (30% from fat); FAT 4.2g (sat 0.6g, mono 2.6g, poly 0.6g); PROTEIN 3.4g; CARB 20g; FIBER 2g; CHOL 0mg; IRON 1.2mg; SODIUM 308mg; CALC 31mg

Cucumber Mojitos

The classic Cuban cocktail receives a refreshing update with the addition of cucumber. For another tasty twist on the beverage, see our Peach Mojitos recipe on page 190.

- 2 cups cold water
- 1 cup coarsely chopped cucumber
- ¼ cup sugar
- ¼ cup fresh lime juice (about 2 large)
- 12 mint leaves
- ¾ cup rum
- 1 cup sparkling water, chilled
- 1 cup crushed ice
- 4 mint sprigs
- 4 cucumber slices
- 4 lime wedges

① Place 2 cups water and chopped cucumber in a blender; process until smooth. Strain cucumber mixture through a sieve into a medium bowl; discard solids.
② Place 1 tablespoon sugar, 1 tablespoon lime juice, and 3 mint leaves in a 2-cup glass measure; crush with a wooden spoon. Add 3 tablespoons rum and about ½ cup cucumber mixture; stir until sugar dissolves. Stir in ¼ cup sparkling water. Place ¼ cup ice in a 12-ounce glass; pour cucumber mixture over ice. Garnish with 1 mint sprig, 1 cucumber slice, and 1 lime wedge. Repeat procedure with remaining ingredients. Serve immediately. Yield: 4 servings (serving size: 1 mojito).

CALORIES 166 (1% from fat); FAT 0.1g (sat 0g, mono 0g, poly 0g); PROTEIN 0.3g; CARB 14.5g; FIBER 0.3g; CHOL 0mg; IRON 0.1mg; SODIUM 14mg; CALC 10mg

Entrées

From basic to refined, our main dish recipes showcase summer's best produce.

Chipotle Salmon Burgers

Shape the patties up to eight hours in advance, and cook just before serving. Use a grill pan or nonstick skillet to cook them since they may not hold up on a standard grill. If you have a mini food processor, use it to prepare the mayonnaise mixture. You can use regular hamburger buns instead of English muffins.

MAYONNAISE:
- 3 tablespoons light mayonnaise
- 2 tablespoons finely chopped fresh mango
- 1 tablespoon finely chopped fresh pineapple
- 1 tablespoon chopped fresh cilantro
- ⅛ teaspoon finely grated lime rind

BURGERS:
- ⅓ cup chopped green onions
- ¼ cup chopped fresh cilantro
- 1 tablespoon finely chopped chipotle chile, canned in adobo sauce
- 2 teaspoons fresh lime juice
- ¼ teaspoon salt
- 1 (1¼-pound) salmon fillet, skinned and cut into 1-inch pieces
- Cooking spray
- 4 English muffins
- 4 butter lettuce leaves

① To prepare mayonnaise, combine first 5 ingredients in a food processor or blender; process until smooth. Transfer to a bowl; cover and chill.
② To prepare burgers, place onions and next 3 ingredients in a food processor; process until finely chopped. Add salt and salmon; pulse 4 times or until salmon is coarsely ground and mixture is well blended.
③ Divide salmon mixture into 4 equal portions; shape each portion into a

1-inch-thick patty. Cover and chill 30 minutes.

4 Heat a grill pan over medium-high heat. Coat pan with cooking spray. Add patties to pan; cook 6 minutes on each side or until desired degree of doneness.

5 Wipe skillet with paper towels; recoat with cooking spray. Place 2 muffins, cut sides down, in pan; cook 2 minutes or until lightly toasted. Repeat procedure with cooking spray and remaining muffins.

6 Place 1 muffin bottom on each of 4 plates; top each serving with 1 lettuce leaf and 1 patty. Spread about 1 tablespoon mayonnaise mixture over each patty; place 1 muffin top on each serving. Yield: 4 servings (serving size: 1 burger).

CALORIES 408 (33% from fat); FAT 15g (sat 2.6g, mono 4.5g, poly 6.6g); PROTEIN 37.4g; CARB 28.9g; FIBER 2.9g; CHOL 94mg; IRON 3.8mg; SODIUM 595mg; CALC 124mg

---

Choice Ingredient: Onions

With more than 300 known species of onions, it is no wonder Julia Child once commented, "It's hard to imagine civilization without onions." Indeed, onions have been cultivated for more than 5,000 years and play a prominent role in culinary traditions around the globe. Because onions are high in antioxidants and vitamin C, researchers are investigating the effects of their sulfuric compounds on cancer prevention.

Green onions are harvested before full bulb development, and their mild, slightly spicy flavor enlivens stir-fries and salads. Look for green onions with crisp, bright green tops and a firm white base. Store, refrigerated in a plastic bag, in the crisper bin for up to five days.

Dry (or mature) onions with a mild, sweet flavor, such as Vidalia, can be eaten raw on salads or sandwiches. They are also excellent grilled, roasted, or pickled. Mature onions should have dry, papery skins and no signs of spotting, sprouting, or softness. Store in a cool, dry, and well-ventilated area for up to two months. Once you've cut them, you can refrigerate onions in an airtight container for up to four days.

QUICK & EASY

Crab, Corn, and Tomato Salad with Lemon-Basil Dressing

(pictured on page 253)

The tart dressing contrasts with the sweet corn, tomatoes, and crab. Serve with a lemon wedge, if desired. Pair it with cucumber soup or a grilled sandwich.

- 1 tablespoon grated lemon rind
- 5 tablespoons fresh lemon juice, divided
- 1 tablespoon extravirgin olive oil
- 1 teaspoon honey
- ½ teaspoon Dijon mustard
- ¼ teaspoon salt
- ⅛ teaspoon freshly ground black pepper
- 1 cup fresh corn kernels (about 2 ears)
- ¼ cup thinly sliced basil leaves
- ¼ cup chopped red bell pepper
- 2 tablespoons finely chopped red onion
- 1 pound lump crabmeat, shell pieces removed
- 8 (¼-inch-thick) slices ripe beefsteak tomato
- 2 cups cherry tomatoes, halved

1 Combine rind, 3 tablespoons juice, and next 5 ingredients in a large bowl, stirring well with a whisk. Reserve 1½ tablespoons juice mixture. Add remaining 2 tablespoons juice, corn, and next 4 ingredients to remaining juice mixture; toss gently to coat.

2 Arrange 2 tomato slices and ½ cup cherry tomatoes on each of 4 plates. Drizzle about 1 teaspoon reserved juice mixture over each serving. Top each serving with 1 cup crab mixture. Yield: 4 servings.

CALORIES 242 (21% from fat); FAT 5.6g (sat 0.6g, mono 2.7g, poly 0.7g); PROTEIN 30g; CARB 17.7g; FIBER 3.6g; CHOL 128mg; IRON 1.8mg; SODIUM 613mg; CALC 161mg

---

STAFF FAVORITE

Beef Tenderloin with Mustard and Herbs

(pictured on page 252)

Grill the meat first, and then coat it in the mustard and herb mixture for bright, fresh flavors. Spread the chopped fresh herbs on a sheet of plastic wrap so you can evenly coat the beef with minimal mess. Serve the tenderloin with grilled polenta and a simple salad.

- 1 (2½-pound) beef tenderloin, trimmed
- Cooking spray
- 1 teaspoon salt
- 1 teaspoon freshly ground black pepper
- ⅓ cup finely chopped fresh parsley
- 2 tablespoon chopped fresh thyme
- 1½ tablespoons finely chopped fresh rosemary
- 3 tablespoons Dijon mustard

1 Prepare grill.

2 Lightly coat beef with cooking spray; sprinkle evenly with salt and pepper. Place beef on grill rack coated with cooking spray. Reduce heat to medium. Grill 30 minutes or until a thermometer registers 145° or desired degree of doneness, turning to brown on all sides. Let beef stand 10 minutes.

3 Sprinkle parsley, thyme, and rosemary in an even layer on an 18 x 15–inch sheet of plastic wrap. Brush mustard evenly over beef. Place beef in herb mixture on plastic wrap; roll beef over herbs, pressing gently. Cut beef into slices. Yield: 10 servings (serving size: 3 ounces).

CALORIES 191 (44% from fat); FAT 9.4g (sat 3.7g, mono 3.9g, poly 0.4g); PROTEIN 23.4g; CARB 1.4g; FIBER 0.2g; CHOL 71mg; IRON 1.7mg; SODIUM 393mg; CALC 23mg

Choice Ingredient: Beefsteak Tomatoes

Nothing signals summer like a juicy tomato fresh from the vine. Known as the workhorse of the tomato world, this variety is among the most commonly available in stores and home gardens. Sweet and slightly acidic, beefsteak tomatoes are prized for their size—they can grow up to 2½ pounds.

Try beefsteaks in salads and BLTs or simply adorned with extravirgin olive oil, salt, and pepper. Joanne Weir, host of PBS's *Weir Cooking in the Wine Country* and a frequent *Cooking Light* contributor, sprinkles crumbled ricotta salata cheese, mint, oregano, and chives over tomato slices and drizzles them with balsamic vinaigrette. She also recommends pairing beefsteaks with blue cheese, fresh lemon juice, basil, and roasted bell peppers.

Look for fruit that is firm, richly hued, and free of blemishes. And use your nose: Choose tomatoes that smell like they just came from the garden. Beefsteaks will keep for a few days but, like most tomatoes, are best enjoyed right away. Store at room temperature and never in the refrigerator, Weir says. Cold can make the flesh mealy and diminish the flavor.

QUICK & EASY

Grilled Chicken Thighs with Roasted Grape Tomatoes

You can use this same preparation with tuna steaks.

CHICKEN:

- 1 tablespoon grated lemon rind
- 2 tablespoons fresh lemon juice
- 1 teaspoon olive oil
- 2 garlic cloves, minced
- 8 skinless, boneless chicken thighs (about 1½ pounds)
- ½ teaspoon salt
- ¼ teaspoon freshly ground black pepper
  Cooking spray

TOMATOES:

- 2 cups grape tomatoes
- 2 teaspoons olive oil
- 2 tablespoons chopped fresh parsley
- 1 teaspoon grated lemon rind
- 1 tablespoon fresh lemon juice
- 1 tablespoon capers
- ⅛ teaspoon salt
- ⅛ teaspoon freshly ground black pepper

① Prepare grill.

② To prepare chicken, combine first 4 ingredients in a large zip-top plastic bag. Add chicken to bag; seal. Marinate in refrigerator 15 minutes, turning bag occasionally.

③ Remove chicken from bag; discard marinade. Sprinkle chicken evenly with ½ teaspoon salt and ¼ teaspoon pepper. Place chicken on grill rack coated with cooking spray; grill 5 minutes on each side or until done.

④ Preheat oven to 425°.

⑤ To prepare tomatoes, combine tomatoes and 2 teaspoons oil in an 8-inch square baking dish; toss gently. Bake at 425° for 18 minutes or until tomatoes are tender. Combine tomato mixture, parsley, and remaining ingredients, stirring gently. Serve with chicken. Yield: 4 servings (serving size: 2 chicken thighs and ¼ cup tomato mixture).

CALORIES 194 (36% from fat); FAT 7.8g (sat 1.7g, mono 3.4g, poly 1.6g); PROTEIN 25.9g; CARB 4.5g; FIBER 1.1g; CHOL 106mg; IRON 1.9mg; SODIUM 329mg; CALC 23mg

WINE NOTE: Chicken on its own is a flexible partner for wine, but the capers, lemon, and parsley in this dish call for a varietal that can handle the briny, tart, and herbal qualities of these ingredients: sauvignon blanc. Try Dry Creek Vineyard Fumé Blanc 2006 from Sonoma County, California ($14.50).

Grilled Chicken Salad with Sweet and Spicy Dressing

CHICKEN:

- 2 tablespoons fresh lime juice
- 1 teaspoon ground cumin
- 1 teaspoon olive oil
- ½ teaspoon salt
- 2 garlic cloves, minced
- 4 (6-ounce) skinless, boneless chicken breast halves
  Cooking spray

DRESSING:

- 2 tablespoons chopped fresh cilantro
- 2 tablespoons fresh lime juice
- 2 tablespoons honey
- 1 tablespoon extravirgin olive oil
- 1 teaspoon finely chopped chipotle chile, canned in adobo sauce
- ½ teaspoon Dijon mustard
- ¼ teaspoon salt
- ¼ teaspoon ground cumin

SALAD:

- 8 cups mixed salad greens
- 1 cup thinly sliced peeled cucumber
- ¼ cup thinly sliced red onion
- 2 plum tomatoes, quartered

① To prepare chicken, combine first 5 ingredients in a large zip-top plastic bag. Add chicken to bag; seal. Marinate in refrigerator 1 hour, turning bag occasionally.

② Prepare grill.

③ Remove chicken from bag; discard marinade. Place chicken on grill rack coated with cooking spray; grill 5 minutes on each side or until chicken is done. Let chicken stand 10 minutes; cut across grain into 1-inch-thick slices.

④ To prepare dressing, combine cilantro and next 7 ingredients in a small bowl, stirring well with a whisk.

⑤ To prepare salad, arrange 2 cups greens, ¼ cup cucumber, 1 tablespoon onion, and 2 tomato wedges on each of 4 plates; top each serving with 1 chicken breast half. Drizzle 2 tablespoons dressing over each serving. Yield: 4 servings.

CALORIES 297 (28% from fat); FAT 9.1g (sat 1.8g, mono 4.7g, poly 1.5g); PROTEIN 36.9g; CARB 17.2g; FIBER 3.5g; CHOL 94mg; IRON 3.2mg; SODIUM 587mg; CALC 96mg

QUICK & EASY

Spice-Rubbed Pork Tenderloin with Mustard Barbecue Sauce

(pictured on page 254)

Bacon's savor is key to this sweet-tart sauce.

SAUCE:

2 bacon slices, finely chopped
1 cup chopped onion
½ cup prepared yellow mustard
5 tablespoons honey
3 tablespoons ketchup
2 tablespoons cider vinegar
¼ teaspoon chili powder
¼ teaspoon ground cumin

PORK:

1 tablespoon light brown sugar
1 tablespoon smoked paprika
2 teaspoons chili powder
1 teaspoon garlic powder
1 teaspoon ground cumin
¾ teaspoon salt
½ teaspoon freshly ground black pepper
⅛ teaspoon ground red pepper
2 (1-pound) pork tenderloins, trimmed
Cooking spray

1 Prepare grill.

2 To prepare sauce, cook bacon in a medium saucepan over medium-high heat 4 minutes or until almost crisp, stirring occasionally. Add onion to pan; cook 4 minutes, stirring frequently. Add mustard and next 5 ingredients to pan, and bring to a boil. Reduce heat, and simmer 4 minutes or until slightly thick, stirring occasionally.

3 To prepare pork, combine brown sugar and next 7 ingredients in a small bowl, stirring well; rub mixture evenly over pork. Place pork on grill rack coated with cooking spray. Grill 20 minutes or until a thermometer registers 155° (slightly pink), turning once. Let pork stand 10 minutes. Cut pork crosswise into ½-inch-thick slices. Serve with sauce. Yield: 8 servings (serving size: 3 ounces pork and about 2½ tablespoons sauce).

CALORIES 235 (25% from fat); FAT 6.5g (sat 2.1g, mono 2.8g, poly 0.7g); PROTEIN 26.2g; CARB 17.6g; FIBER 1.3g; CHOL 77mg; IRON 1.8mg; SODIUM 569mg; CALC 26mg

Halibut en Papillote with Potatoes, Green Beans, and Sweet Onions

The olive oil is infused with lemon flavor during cooking, which is then used in the dressing for the veggies. Cook the potatoes and green beans while the fish bakes.

8 thin (¼-inch) slices lemon
4 fresh bay leaves (optional)
4 (6-ounce) halibut fillets
¾ teaspoon salt, divided
½ teaspoon freshly ground black pepper, divided
2 tablespoons extravirgin olive oil, divided
12 ounces small new potatoes, quartered
6 ounces green beans, trimmed
2 tablespoons white wine vinegar
1 tablespoon fresh lemon juice
1 teaspoon Dijon mustard
1 garlic clove, minced
1 cup thinly sliced Vidalia or other sweet onion

1 Preheat oven to 450°.

2 Cut 4 (15 x 24-inch) pieces of parchment paper, and fold in half like a book. Draw a large heart half on each piece with fold being center of heart. Cut out hearts, and lay open.

3 Lay 2 slices of lemon in center of 1 side of each piece of parchment; top each with 1 bay leaf, if desired, and 1 halibut fillet. Sprinkle fillets evenly with ½ teaspoon salt and ¼ teaspoon pepper. Drizzle each fillet with ¾ teaspoon oil. Fold hearts over. Starting at tops of hearts, fold edges of parchment together, overlapping folds as you move along. Twist end tips to secure tightly.

4 Place parchment packets on an ungreased baking sheet. Bake at 450° for 12 minutes. Remove from oven; let rest 5 minutes.

5 Cook potatoes in boiling water 8 minutes or until potatoes are almost tender. Add beans to pan; cook 4 minutes or until crisp-tender. Drain well; keep potatoes and beans warm.

6 Working with one packet at a time, carefully open fish packets and pour liquid from packets into a large bowl. Add remaining 1 tablespoon oil, vinegar, juice, mustard, garlic, remaining ¼ teaspoon salt, and remaining ¼ teaspoon pepper; stir well with a whisk. Add potatoes, beans, and onion to oil mixture; toss well to coat. Arrange vegetable mixture evenly on 4 plates. Top each serving with 1 fillet. Yield: 4 servings.

CALORIES 335 (30% from fat); FAT 11.1g (sat 1.6g, mono 6.3g, poly 2.3g); PROTEIN 38.2g; CARB 20.2g; FIBER 3.5g; CHOL 54mg; IRON 2.6mg; SODIUM 573mg; CALC 114mg

Thai-Coconut Bouillabaisse

- 1 pound jumbo shrimp, unpeeled
- Cooking spray
- 1 cup chopped celery, divided
- 1 cup chopped carrot, divided
- 1 cup chopped onion, divided
- 2 1/2 cups cold water
- 3 black peppercorns
- 1 bay leaf
- 1 teaspoon olive oil
- 1 cup chopped red bell pepper
- 1/2 cup chopped tomato
- 1 tablespoon minced fresh garlic
- 1 teaspoon red curry paste
- 4 (2 x 1/2-inch) lime rind strips
- 1 (13.5-ounce) can light coconut milk
- 12 littleneck clams, scrubbed
- 12 mussels, scrubbed and debearded
- 1/4 cup chopped fresh basil
- 1/4 cup chopped fresh cilantro
- 1 teaspoon salt
- 1/4 teaspoon black pepper
- 1 (6-ounce) skinned halibut fillet or other lean white fish fillet, cut into 1-inch pieces
- Lime wedges (optional)

1 Peel and devein shrimp, reserving shells.

2 Heat a medium saucepan over medium heat. Coat pan with cooking spray. Add shrimp shells to pan; cook 3 minutes, stirring frequently. Add 1/2 cup celery, 1/2 cup carrot, and 1/2 cup onion to pan; cook 1 minute, stirring occasionally. Stir in 2 1/2 cups water, peppercorns, and bay leaf; bring to a boil. Reduce heat, and simmer 30 minutes, stirring occasionally. Strain mixture through a sieve into a bowl; discard solids.

3 Heat oil in a large saucepan over medium heat. Add remaining 1/2 cup celery, remaining 1/2 cup carrot, and remaining 1/2 cup onion to pan; cook 3 minutes, stirring occasionally. Add bell pepper; cook 1 minute, stirring occasionally. Stir in tomato and next 3 ingredients; cook 2 minutes, stirring frequently. Stir in broth mixture and coconut milk; bring to a boil. Add clams and mussels. Cover, reduce heat, and cook 2 minutes or until clams and mussels open. Remove from heat; discard any unopened shells. Stir in shrimp, basil, and next 4 ingredients. Cover and let stand 5 minutes or until shrimp and halibut are done. Discard lime rind. Place 2 clams and 2 mussels in each of 6 bowls. Divide shrimp and fish evenly among bowls. Ladle 2/3 cup broth mixture over each serving. Serve with lime wedges, if desired. Yield: 6 servings.

CALORIES 226 (27% from fat); FAT 6.9g (sat 3.5g, mono 1.2g, poly 1.2g); PROTEIN 30.4g; CARB 10.4g; FIBER 1.4g; CHOL 143mg; IRON 8mg; SODIUM 599mg; CALC 96mg

WINE NOTE: In the south of France, bouillabaisse is traditionally served with a dry rosé. And dry rosé is the best choice even with this not-so-traditional version. The kick of the red curry paste and cilantro, plus the exotic thick creaminess of the coconut milk, need a refreshing wine that has more weight and power than a white. Try any number of rosés from California such as Saxon Brown Flora Ranch Rosé 2006 from Chalk Hill ($20).

Grilled Chicken Caesar on a Skewer

Avoid overcrowding the skewers by spacing chicken and onion wedges about 1/4 inch apart. It's best to cook bread cubes by themselves so the bread doesn't come in contact with raw chicken.

- 3/4 cup fat-free bottled Caesar dressing, divided
- 1 1/4 pounds skinless, boneless chicken breast halves, cut into 1-inch cubes
- 4 ounces country bread, crust trimmed and cut into 1-inch cubes
- Cooking spray
- 1 red onion, cut into 1-inch-thick wedges
- 6 cups torn romaine lettuce
- 1/2 cup (2 ounces) shaved fresh Parmigiano-Reggiano cheese
- Cracked black pepper

1 Combine 2 tablespoons dressing and chicken in a zip-top plastic bag; seal. Marinate in refrigerator 45 minutes, turning bag occasionally.

2 Preheat grill.

3 Thread bread cubes onto 2 (12-inch) skewers; coat with cooking spray. Place skewers on a grill rack. Grill 1 minute on each side or until browned.

4 Remove chicken from bag; discard marinade. Thread chicken and onion alternately onto 6 (12-inch) skewers. Place on a grill rack coated with cooking spray; grill 10 minutes or until chicken is done, turning occasionally. Remove from grill; drizzle each chicken skewer with 2 teaspoons dressing.

5 Combine remaining 6 tablespoons dressing and lettuce in a bowl; toss well to coat. Place about 1 cup lettuce mixture on each of 6 plates; divide bread cubes evenly among plates. Place 1 chicken skewer on each plate. Top each serving with about 1 tablespoon cheese; sprinkle with pepper. Yield: 6 servings.

CALORIES 259 (21% from fat); FAT 6g (sat 2.7g, mono 1.6g, poly 0.7g); PROTEIN 26g; CARB 25.3g; FIBER 3.1g; CHOL 62mg; IRON 2.5mg; SODIUM 652mg; CALC 270mg

Herb-Stuffed Red Snapper

Be careful when testing for doneness, as steam will escape from the foil when you open it. A whole fish makes a dramatic entrée, best served family-style so guests can help themselves to this succulent dish. If you have extra fresh herbs on hand, garnish the platter with them.

- 1 (4-pound) cleaned whole red snapper
- Cooking spray
- 1 teaspoon extravirgin olive oil
- 1 teaspoon salt, divided
- 4 lemon slices
- 4 large fresh basil leaves
- 3 parsley sprigs
- 3 mint sprigs
- 2 thyme sprigs
- 4 lemon wedges

① Prepare grill.
② Score fish by making 3 diagonal cuts on each side. Lay 1 (18 x 12–inch) sheet of foil flat on a work surface, and coat with cooking spray. Place fish in center of sheet; rub oil in fish cavity. Sprinkle ½ teaspoon salt in fish cavity; sprinkle remaining ½ teaspoon salt evenly on both sides of fish. Place lemon slices and next 4 ingredients in fish cavity. Wrap fish in foil, twisting ends to seal; place fish on grill rack. Grill 10 minutes or until fish flakes easily when tested with a fork or until desired degree of doneness. Discard lemon slices and herbs. Serve fish with lemon wedges. Yield: 4 servings (serving size: about 4 ounces fish and 1 lemon wedge).

CALORIES 241 (19% from fat); FAT 5.2g (sat 0.9g, mono 2.2g, poly 1.3g); PROTEIN 44.9g; CARB 1.7g; FIBER 0.5g; CHOL 80mg; IRON 0.5mg; SODIUM 687mg; CALC 75mg

Simple Clambake

This dish combines all the flavors of a traditional New England clambake without much fuss.

- 5 quarts plus 1 cup water, divided
- 2 (1½-pound) live lobsters
- 1 pound small red potatoes, quartered
- ¼ cup fresh lemon juice
- 32 mussels, scrubbed and debearded
- 24 littleneck clams, scrubbed
- 8 parsley sprigs
- 6 ounces turkey kielbasa, cut into ½-inch slices
- 4 thyme sprigs
- 2 ears corn, each cut crosswise into 2-inch pieces
- 2 Vidalia or other sweet onions, peeled and each cut into 8 wedges
- ¼ teaspoon reduced-sodium Old Bay seasoning
- 4 lemon wedges

① Prepare grill.
② Bring 5 quarts water to a boil in an 8-quart stockpot; plunge lobsters head-first, 1 at a time, into water. Return to a boil. Cover, reduce heat, and simmer 2 minutes; drain well.
③ Place potatoes in a saucepan; cover with cold water. Bring to a boil. Reduce heat, and simmer 10 minutes or until almost tender; drain. Place potatoes in a large roasting pan; add remaining 1 cup water, lemon juice, and next 7 ingredients to pan; arrange lobsters over potato mixture. Sprinkle evenly with seasoning; cover with foil.
④ Place pan on grill rack; cook 18 minutes or until clams and mussels open. Discard any unopened shells. Serve with lemon wedges. Yield: 4 servings (serving size: ½ cup potatoes, ¼ cup sausage, 8 mussels, 6 clams, 4 onion wedges, ½ lobster, and 1 lemon wedge).

CALORIES 464 (13% from fat); FAT 6.7g (sat 1.8g, mono 1.4g, poly 1.6g); PROTEIN 53.8g; CARB 48.7g; FIBER 4.9g; CHOL 136mg; IRON 21.7mg; SODIUM 904mg; CALC 237mg

Striped Bass with Lemon-Caper Salt

As you peel the lemon, take care to remove only the yellow rind. The white pith tastes bitter. Roasting the caper mixture heightens its flavor.

- 1 large lemon
- ¼ cup capers, rinsed and drained
- ½ teaspoon kosher salt
- ¼ teaspoon freshly ground black pepper
- 1 tablespoon extravirgin olive oil
- 6 (6-ounce) striped bass or other lean white fish fillets
- Lemon wedges (optional)
- Chopped fresh flat-leaf parsley (optional)

① Preheat oven to 300°.
② Carefully remove rind from lemon using a vegetable peeler; reserve lemon for another use. Coarsely chop rind. Place rind and capers on a baking sheet; bake at 300° for 15 minutes. Let caper mixture stand 10 minutes; finely chop. Stir in salt and pepper.
③ Heat oil in a large nonstick skillet over medium-high heat. Add fish to pan; cook 2 minutes on each side or until fish flakes easily when tested with a fork or until desired degree of doneness. Serve with caper mixture. Garnish with lemon wedges and parsley, if desired. Yield: 6 servings (serving size: 1 fillet and 2 teaspoons caper mixture).

CALORIES 191 (30% from fat); FAT 6.4g (sat 1.2g, mono 2.8g, poly 1.6g); PROTEIN 31.1g; CARB 0.7g; FIBER 0.5g; CHOL 140mg; IRON 1.6mg; SODIUM 447mg; CALC 31mg

Pork Tacos with Corn-Jicama Salsa and Guacamole

Avocado is a source of healthful monounsaturated fat. Crunchy vegetables, fresh herbs, and lime juice boost the flavor of canned beans.

SALSA:
- ½ cup fresh corn kernels
- ½ cup finely diced peeled jicama
- ½ cup canned black beans, rinsed and drained
- 2 tablespoons chopped fresh cilantro
- 1 tablespoon fresh lime juice
- ¼ teaspoon ground cumin
- ¼ teaspoon salt

GUACAMOLE:
- 1 cup cubed peeled avocado
- 1½ tablespoons fresh lime juice
- ¼ teaspoon salt
- ¼ cup finely chopped seeded tomato

TACOS:
- 2 teaspoons chili powder
- 1 teaspoon dried oregano
- 1 teaspoon ground cumin
- ¼ teaspoon salt
- 1 pound pork tenderloin, cut into 2 x ⅛-inch strips
- Cooking spray
- 8 (6-inch) corn tortillas

1 To prepare salsa, combine first 7 ingredients in a small bowl; toss gently. Cover and chill.

2 To prepare guacamole, combine avocado, 1½ tablespoons juice, and ¼ teaspoon salt in a small bowl; mash with a fork until well blended. Stir in tomato. Place a sheet of plastic wrap directly on avocado mixture; set aside.

3 To prepare tacos, combine chili powder and next 3 ingredients in a shallow dish. Add pork to spice mixture; toss to coat.

4 Heat a large nonstick skillet over medium-high heat. Coat pan with cooking spray. Add pork mixture to pan; sauté 4 minutes or until done, turning occasionally. Remove pork from pan; keep warm.

5 Wipe pan clean with paper towels; recoat with cooking spray. Add 2 tortillas to pan; cook 30 seconds on each side or until soft. Remove from pan; keep warm. Repeat procedure with remaining tortillas and cooking spray.

6 Spread about 1½ tablespoons guacamole onto each tortilla; top each tortilla with about ¼ cup pork and about 2 tablespoons salsa. Fold tortillas in half. Yield: 4 servings (serving size: 2 tacos).

CALORIES 361 (29% from fat); FAT 11.6g (sat 2.5g, mono 5.8g, poly 1.9g); PROTEIN 29.8g; CARB 38.9g; FIBER 8.2g; CHOL 74mg; IRON 3.5mg; SODIUM 790mg; CALC 127mg

Sides and Extras

Round out meals with these vibrant and simple accompaniments.

Choice Ingredient: Apricots

Apricots are among the first fruits of summer. With delicate flavor and creamy texture, they're a quintessential treat to usher in the season.

Apricots were first grown in China more than 4,000 years ago. Today, California produces 90 percent of America's crop. Smaller Chinese apricots are one of the most common types available, but you might find other varieties like Riland, Tilton, and Royal in specialty stores and farmers' markets. Many aficionados favor Blenheim apricots, a yellow and green-skinned variety with especially sweet, succulent flesh.

Select apricots that are plump, reasonably firm, and evenly colored, but don't expect perfection. Often the fruit ripens unevenly, with the side that faces the sun as soft as jam and the other still hard. Baking apricots in a crisp or tart or using them in preserves or chutney can help even out texture and flavor. You can store apricots in a plastic bag in the fridge for up to five days.

Fresh Apricot Chutney

- 3½ cups cubed pitted apricots (about 1¼ pounds)
- ½ cup packed light brown sugar
- ½ cup chopped red onion
- ⅓ cup cider vinegar
- ¼ cup golden raisins
- 2 tablespoons honey
- 1 tablespoon minced seeded serrano chile (1 small)
- ½ teaspoon salt
- ½ teaspoon mustard seeds
- ½ teaspoon ground coriander
- ½ teaspoon ground cumin
- ½ teaspoon freshly ground black pepper

1 Combine all ingredients in a medium saucepan over medium-high heat; bring to a simmer, stirring constantly. Reduce heat, and simmer 15 minutes or until thick, stirring occasionally. Serve warm or at room temperature. Yield: 2 cups (serving size: 2 tablespoons).

CALORIES 63 (3% from fat); FAT 0.2g (sat 0g, mono 0.1g, poly 0g); PROTEIN 0.7g; CARB 15.6g; FIBER 1g; CHOL 0mg; IRON 0.4mg; SODIUM 78mg; CALC 15mg

Indian-Spiced Grilled Baby Squash

Grilling enhances the nuttiness of this summer squash. Use white, orange, or yellow pattypan squash for the most colorful skewers.

- 1 tablespoon olive oil
- 1 teaspoon grated peeled fresh ginger
- ½ teaspoon salt
- ½ teaspoon ground coriander
- ¼ teaspoon ground cumin
- 1 pound baby pattypan squash, cut in half crosswise
- 1 red onion, cut into 1-inch pieces
- Cooking spray
- 1 tablespoon fresh lemon juice
- 1 tablespoon thinly sliced fresh mint leaves

❶ Preheat grill.

❷ Combine first 7 ingredients in a large bowl; toss well. Thread squash and onion alternately onto 8 (10-inch) skewers. Place skewers on grill rack coated with cooking spray; grill 10 minutes or until tender, turning frequently. Drizzle with juice. Sprinkle with mint. Yield: 4 servings (serving size: 2 skewers).

CALORIES 61 (53% from fat); FAT 3.6g (sat 0.5g, mono 2.5g, poly 0.5g); PROTEIN 1.7g; CARB 6.9g; FIBER 1.8g; CHOL 0mg; IRON 0.6mg; SODIUM 299mg; CALC 26mg

---

Choice Ingredient: Baby Squash

As with their full-grown counterparts, baby summer squash are best enjoyed during their peak season of early to late summer. Baby squash varieties include miniature versions of the popular yellow and zucchini squashes, as well as the more exotic-looking pattypan and scallopini, which resemble flattened, scallop-shaped saucers.

Baby squash are outsized when it comes to nutritional value. The baby zucchini variety is an excellent source of vitamin C, and its high potassium content may help lower high blood pressure.

Baby squash boast a mildly sweet, nutty flavor and tender flesh. Enjoy them raw in salads or as part of a vegetable tray with your favorite dip. Petite pattypan or scallopini squash are also good in stir-fries, and they fare well on the grill. Or showcase squash alongside other summer vegetables in a quick ratatouille by sautéing squash, onions, garlic, bell peppers, eggplant, and tomatoes, and then simmering the mixture to a thick sauce.

Choose baby squash with shiny, bright-colored skin, avoiding those with spots, bruises, or cracks, and handle gently. Store in a perforated plastic bag in the refrigerator for no more than five days.

QUICK & EASY
Corn on the Cob with Smoked Butter
(pictured on page 254)

Instead of boiling, you can cook the corn on the grill for 10 minutes or until lightly browned; turn frequently.

- 1 tablespoon butter, melted
- 1 teaspoon grated lemon rind
- 1 teaspoon minced shallots
- 1 teaspoon honey
- ½ teaspoon salt
- ½ teaspoon ground cumin
- ¼ teaspoon smoked paprika
- 6 ears shucked corn

❶ Combine first 7 ingredients in a small bowl.

❷ Cook corn in boiling water 5 minutes or until crisp-tender; drain. Brush butter mixture evenly over corn; serve immediately. Yield: 6 servings (serving size: 1 ear of corn).

CALORIES 99 (27% from fat); FAT 3g (sat 1.4g, mono 0.8g, poly 0.6g); PROTEIN 3g; CARB 18.4g; FIBER 2.6g; CHOL 5mg; IRON 0.6mg; SODIUM 224mg; CALC 5mg

---

MAKE AHEAD • FREEZABLE
Fresh Herb Sauce

Serve over fresh beans or peas, or halibut or grouper. Use within one week. Or you can freeze this pesto-like sauce in ice cube trays, transfer cubes to a zip-top plastic bag, and keep frozen for up to two months.

- ½ cup loosely packed fresh parsley
- ½ cup loosely packed fresh basil leaves
- 3 tablespoons loosely packed mint leaves
- 2 tablespoons chopped shallots
- 2 tablespoons cold water
- 1 tablespoon capers
- 1 tablespoon fresh lemon juice
- ⅛ teaspoon kosher salt
- Dash of crushed red pepper
- 2 tablespoons extravirgin olive oil

---

❶ Combine first 9 ingredients in a food processor, and process until herbs are finely minced. With processor on, slowly pour oil through food chute; process until well blended. Yield: ½ cup (serving size: 1 tablespoon).

CALORIES 35 (93% from fat); FAT 3.6g (sat 0.5g, mono 2.5g, poly 0.5g); PROTEIN 0.3g; CARB 1.1g; FIBER 0.3g; CHOL 0mg; IRON 0.4mg; SODIUM 64mg; CALC 12mg

---

QUICK & EASY
Tangy Mustard Coleslaw
(pictured on page 254)

This crisp, creamy salad is good with burgers or fish sandwiches. Add a dash of hot sauce to mustard mixture for extra spiciness.

- 7 cups finely shredded green cabbage (about ½ head)
- 1 cup thinly vertically sliced red onion
- 1 cup grated carrot
- ¼ cup white wine vinegar
- 2 tablespoons sugar
- 2 tablespoons whole-grain mustard
- 2 tablespoons reduced-fat mayonnaise
- ⅛ teaspoon salt
- ⅛ teaspoon black pepper
- ⅛ teaspoon ground red pepper

❶ Combine first 3 ingredients in a large bowl. Combine vinegar and remaining ingredients in a small bowl; stir well with a whisk. Add mustard mixture to cabbage mixture, and toss well to coat. Cover and chill 20 minutes. Stir before serving. Yield: 7 servings (serving size: about 1 cup).

CALORIES 58 (12% from fat); FAT 0.8g (sat 0.1g, mono 0.1g, poly 0.3g); PROTEIN 1.5g; CARB 12.3g; FIBER 3g; CHOL 0mg; IRON 0.5mg; SODIUM 172mg; CALC 43mg

Two-Corn Polenta with Tomatoes, Basil, and Cheese

Corn kernels and polenta layer texture and flavor in this dish. Serve with green beans and grilled pork.

 2 teaspoons olive oil
 2 cups chopped onion (2 medium)
 4 cups fat-free, less-sodium chicken broth
 2 cups fresh corn kernels (about 2 ears)
 2 garlic cloves, chopped
 1 cup instant dry polenta
 ½ cup (2 ounces) grated fresh Parmesan cheese
 ½ teaspoon salt
 ⅛ teaspoon freshly ground black pepper
 1 cup chopped tomato
 ½ cup chopped fresh basil

❶ Heat oil in a Dutch oven over medium heat. Add onion to pan; cook 8 minutes or until tender, stirring occasionally. Stir in broth, corn, and garlic; bring to a boil. Cover, reduce heat, and simmer 5 minutes. Slowly add polenta, stirring with a whisk until thick (about 5 minutes). Add cheese, stirring to melt. Stir in salt and pepper. Remove from heat; sprinkle with tomato and basil. Serve immediately. Yield: 7 servings (serving size: about 1 cup).

CALORIES 194 (20% from fat); FAT 4.3g (sat 1.5g, mono 1.8g, poly 0.4g); PROTEIN 8.9g; CARB 31.6g; FIBER 4.6g; CHOL 6mg; IRON 1.1mg; SODIUM 457mg; CALC 134mg

Stewed Okra with Tomatoes and Bacon

This Creole favorite makes the most of summer produce. Stewing okra with tomatoes produces a saucy side that highlights okra's unique flavor and texture. The dish is tasty as is or ladled over white rice.

 2 bacon slices
 1 cup chopped Vidalia or other sweet onion
 1 cup chopped green bell pepper
 1 garlic clove, minced
 4 cups sliced fresh okra (about 1 pound)
 2 cups chopped tomato
 ½ cup water
 1 to 2 teaspoons hot sauce
 1 teaspoon cider vinegar
 ¾ teaspoon salt
 ½ teaspoon dried thyme
 ½ teaspoon freshly ground black pepper

❶ Cook bacon in a Dutch oven over medium-high heat until crisp. Remove from pan, reserving 2 teaspoons drippings in pan. Crumble bacon.
❷ Add onion, bell pepper, and garlic to drippings in pan, and sauté 5 minutes or until tender. Add okra and remaining ingredients; bring to a boil. Cover, reduce heat, and simmer 20 minutes or until okra is tender. Sprinkle with bacon. Yield: 8 servings (serving size: ½ cup).

CALORIES 59 (32% from fat); FAT 2.1g (sat 0.7g, mono 0.9g, poly 0.3g); PROTEIN 2.7g; CARB 8.8g; FIBER 3.1g; CHOL 3mg; IRON 0.8mg; SODIUM 285mg; CALC 59mg

Desserts

Brimming with the season's sweetest fruits, these treats offer a satisfying finale—and many of the recipes can be prepared in advance.

MAKE AHEAD ▪ FREEZABLE
Lemonade Iced Tea Sorbet

Full-flavored English Breakfast tea is usually made from a blend that includes black tea leaves. But consider substituting your favorite tea to make this refreshing sorbet.

 2 cups boiling water
 4 regular-sized English Breakfast tea bags
 ¾ cup sugar
 ¾ cup fresh lemon juice (about 4 lemons)
 1 cup ice water
 Mint sprigs (optional)

❶ Combine 2 cups boiling water and tea bags in a large bowl; steep 5 minutes. Discard tea bags. Add sugar to tea mixture, stirring until sugar dissolves. Cool completely. Stir in juice and 1 cup ice water; chill 1 hour.
❷ Pour tea mixture into freezer can of an ice-cream freezer; freeze according to manufacturer's instructions. Spoon sorbet into a freezer-safe container. Cover and freeze 1 hour or until firm. Garnish with mint sprigs, if desired. Yield: 8 servings (serving size: ½ cup).

CALORIES 78 (0% from fat); FAT 0g; PROTEIN 0.1g; CARB 20.7g; FIBER 0.1g; CHOL 0mg; IRON 0mg; SODIUM 0mg; CALC 2mg

Choice Ingredients: Lemons and Limes

Available year-round, their peak is in summer. That's good news, since many sweet and savory summertime dishes brighten with just a touch of citrus juice. As two of the most acidic members of the citrus family, lemons and limes impart a refreshing tartness. You can use their juice to add tang to salad dressings and salsas, or squeeze fresh lemon or lime wedges over your favorite grilled vegetables, fish, or seafood. Citrus juice is a key component in marinades for beef, pork, or chicken. Citrus can be a star ingredient, as in our Lemonade Iced Tea Sorbet (page 172), or an accent, as in our Peach-Berry Upside-Down Cake (page 176). Add peeled or grated rind to baked goods, jellies, or jams for a subtle infusion of flavor.

Persian limes are the most commonly available variety and work well in mixed drinks such as margaritas and daiquiris. Smaller yellowish-green Key limes, made famous by Key lime pie, have a more pronounced tartness than other varieties. Buy them when you're lucky enough to find them in grocery stores, or check in specialty or gourmet markets. If a recipe calls for Key lime juice, you can substitute milder Persian lime juice by using an extra tablespoon or two.

When selecting lemons or limes, look for fruit that yields to gentle pressure—a sign there's plenty of juice—with a glossy, bright color and unblemished skin. For the juiciest specimens, choose those heavy for their size with a thin skin. Store at room temperature away from sunlight for up to a week. The citrus will also keep in the refrigerator for up to three weeks. Extra juice may be stored in a well-sealed container in the refrigerator and used within five days or frozen in easy-to-use portions in an ice cube tray.

STAFF FAVORITE • MAKE AHEAD
Guava-Swirled Cheesecake

Guava paste is found in Latin markets and gourmet stores, often in slabs larger than 12 ounces. Slice leftover paste, and serve it with cream cheese or Manchego and crackers as a simple appetizer. Garnish the cheesecake with mint sprigs, if desired.

1⅔ cups sugar, divided
1 cup graham cracker crumbs (about 6 cookie sheets)
1 tablespoon butter, melted
Cooking spray
½ cup water
½ cup fresh lime juice
12 ounces guava paste, cut into small pieces
1 large egg white, lightly beaten
½ cup reduced-fat sour cream
2 (8-ounce) packages ⅓-less-fat cream cheese, softened
1½ teaspoons vanilla extract
⅛ teaspoon salt
4 large egg whites

① Preheat oven to 400°.
② Combine ⅓ cup sugar, crumbs, and butter. Press mixture into bottom and ½ inch up sides of a 9-inch springform pan coated with cooking spray. Bake at 400° for 7 minutes. Cool on a wire rack.
③ Reduce oven temperature to 325°.
④ Combine ⅓ cup sugar, ½ cup water, juice, and guava paste in a small saucepan; bring to a boil. Reduce heat, and simmer 5 minutes, stirring occasionally. Cool slightly. Pour mixture into a blender, and process until smooth. Cool completely. Stir in 1 egg white.
⑤ Combine remaining 1 cup sugar, sour cream, and cheese in a medium bowl; beat with a mixer at low speed until smooth. Beat in vanilla and salt. Gradually add 4 egg whites, 1 at a time, beating well after each addition. Pour cheese mixture into prepared pan. Drizzle guava mixture over cheese mixture; swirl mixtures using tip of a knife. Bake at 325° for 45 minutes or until cheesecake center barely moves when touched.
⑥ Turn oven off; cool cheesecake in closed oven 30 minutes. Remove cheesecake from oven. Run a knife around outside edge. Cool to room temperature. Cover and chill at least 8 hours before serving. Yield: 14 servings (serving size: 1 wedge).

CALORIES 295 (29% from fat); FAT 9.4g (sat 5.6g, mono 2.9g, poly 0.5g); PROTEIN 5.5g; CARB 48.5g; FIBER 0.5g; CHOL 29mg; IRON 0.3mg; SODIUM 87mg; CALC 37mg

MAKE AHEAD
Pound Cake with Lemon-Basil Glaze

Make the cake ahead, and freeze it for up to two weeks. Thaw in the refrigerator, and bring to room temperature before glazing. Follow the directions for applying the glaze in two steps to allow it to permeate the cake more thoroughly. A sprinkle of grated lemon rind and a fresh basil sprig are a lovely garnish.

CAKE:
10 tablespoons butter, softened and divided
1¾ cups plus 2 tablespoons granulated sugar, divided
2¼ cups all-purpose flour (about 10 ounces)
1 teaspoon baking powder
¼ teaspoon baking soda
¼ teaspoon salt
2 teaspoons grated lemon rind
2 teaspoons vanilla extract
3 large eggs
½ cup low-fat buttermilk
2 tablespoons fresh lemon juice
3 large egg whites
GLAZE:
¼ cup half-and-half
3 tablespoons chopped fresh basil
1½ cups powdered sugar, sifted
2 tablespoons fresh lemon juice
Dash of salt

Continued

① Preheat oven to 325°.

② To prepare cake, coat a 12-cup Bundt pan with 1 tablespoon butter, and dust with 2 tablespoons granulated sugar.

③ Lightly spoon flour into dry measuring cups; level with a knife. Combine flour and next 3 ingredients in a bowl, stirring well with a whisk. Combine 1½ cups granulated sugar and remaining 9 tablespoons butter in a large bowl; beat with a mixer at medium-high speed until light and fluffy. Beat in rind and extract. Add eggs, 1 at a time, beating well after each addition. Combine buttermilk and 2 tablespoons juice. Add flour mixture and buttermilk mixture alternately to sugar mixture, beginning and ending with flour mixture.

④ Place egg whites in a large bowl; beat with a mixer at high speed until soft peaks form, using clean, dry beaters. Add remaining ¼ cup granulated sugar, 1 tablespoon at a time, beating until stiff peaks form. Gently fold one-third of egg white mixture into batter; fold in remaining egg white mixture. Spoon batter into prepared pan. Bake at 325° for 55 minutes or until a wooden pick inserted in center comes out clean. Cool cake in pan on a wire rack 10 minutes. Remove cake from pan; cool completely on wire rack.

⑤ To prepare glaze, combine half-and-half and basil in a small microwave-safe bowl; microwave at HIGH 45 seconds. Let stand 5 minutes. Strain mixture through a sieve into a bowl; discard basil. Combine half-and-half mixture, powdered sugar, 2 tablespoons juice, and dash of salt; stir with a whisk until smooth. Drizzle half of glaze over cake; let stand 5 minutes or until set. Repeat procedure with remaining glaze. Yield: 16 servings (serving size: 1 slice).

CALORIES 284 (28% from fat); FAT 8.9g (sat 5.3g, mono 2.4g, poly 0.5g); PROTEIN 4.2g; CARB 47.3g; FIBER 0.5g; CHOL 61mg; IRON 1mg; SODIUM 173mg; CALC 42mg

Orange-Buttermilk Cake with Summer Fruit

This poppy seed cake comes into its own served with fresh fruit macerated in orange syrup.

FRUIT:

1½ cups cherries, pitted and halved
1 cup sliced peaches
1 cup sliced nectarines
1 cup sliced strawberries
¼ cup fresh orange juice
3 tablespoons sugar
1 tablespoon Grand Marnier or other orange liqueur

CAKE:

Cooking spray
3 cups plus 2 tablespoons all-purpose flour, divided (about 13½ ounces)
4 teaspoons poppy seeds
1½ teaspoons baking soda
¼ teaspoon salt
1¾ cups sugar
½ cup butter, softened
3 large eggs
1 cup fat-free buttermilk
¼ cup fresh orange juice

① Preheat oven to 350°.

② To prepare fruit, combine first 7 ingredients in a large bowl; toss gently. Cover and chill.

③ To prepare cake, coat a 12-cup tube pan with cooking spray, and dust with 2 tablespoons flour.

④ Lightly spoon remaining 3 cups flour into dry measuring cups; level with a knife. Combine 3 cups flour and next 3 ingredients in a medium bowl, stirring with a whisk. Place 1¾ cups sugar and butter in a large bowl; beat with a mixer at medium speed until well blended. Add eggs, 1 at a time, beating well after each addition. Combine buttermilk and ¼ cup juice. Add flour mixture to sugar mixture alternately with buttermilk mixture, beginning and ending with flour mixture. Spoon batter into prepared pan. Bake at 350° for 43 minutes or until a wooden pick inserted in center comes out clean. Cool

in pan 10 minutes on a wire rack; remove from pan. Cool completely on wire rack. Serve with fruit mixture. Yield: 16 servings (serving size: 1 slice cake and about ¼ cup fruit mixture).

CALORIES 283 (24% from fat); FAT 7.4g (sat 4g, mono 2g, poly 0.7g); PROTEIN 4.9g; CARB 50g; FIBER 1.6g; CHOL 55mg; IRON 1.5mg; SODIUM 224mg; CALC 45mg

MAKE AHEAD
Coconut-Almond Macaroons

Look for canned almond paste alongside other baking ingredients at your market.

3 tablespoons almond paste
1 teaspoon vanilla extract
4 large egg whites, divided
1⅓ cups powdered sugar
1¼ teaspoons baking powder
¼ teaspoon salt
3½ cups flaked sweetened coconut
½ cup granulated sugar

① Preheat oven to 350°.

② Combine almond paste, vanilla, and 2 egg whites in a large bowl; beat with a mixer until well blended. Combine powdered sugar, baking powder, and salt. Add powdered sugar mixture to almond paste mixture, beating until blended. Stir in coconut.

③ Place remaining 2 egg whites in a medium bowl; beat with a mixer at high speed until soft peaks form using clean, dry beaters. Gradually add granulated sugar, 1 tablespoon at a time, beating until stiff peaks form. Gently fold egg white mixture into coconut mixture.

④ Drop dough by level tablespoons 2 inches apart onto a baking sheet lined with parchment paper. Bake at 350° for 20 minutes or until firm. Cool in pan 2 to 3 minutes on a wire rack. Remove cookies from pan, and cool completely on wire rack. Yield: 32 macaroons (serving size: 1 macaroon).

CALORIES 80 (36% from fat); FAT 3.2g (sat 2.5g, mono 0.4g, poly 0.1g); PROTEIN 0.9g; CARB 12.6g; FIBER 0.4g; CHOL 0mg; IRON 0.2mg; SODIUM 69mg; CALC 15mg

Blueberry Bread Pudding

While this dessert would be a delicious ending to a summer meal, you might serve it as the main dish for brunch. Assemble it ahead, and simply bake and serve when you're ready.

- 1 cup packed brown sugar
- ¼ cup butter
- 2 tablespoons light-colored corn syrup
- Cooking spray
- 2 cups blueberries
- 1 (16-ounce) loaf Italian bread
- 1½ cups whole milk
- 1 teaspoon vanilla extract
- ¼ teaspoon salt
- 5 large eggs, lightly beaten
- 1 teaspoon Grand Marnier or other orange-flavored liqueur (optional)
- 2 teaspoons powdered sugar

1 Combine first 3 ingredients in a small saucepan over medium-high heat; cook 2 minutes or until butter melts and sugar dissolves, stirring frequently. Pour sugar mixture into a 13 x 9-inch baking pan coated with cooking spray; sprinkle evenly with blueberries.

2 Remove crust from bread; reserve crust for another use. Cut bread into 1-inch-thick slices. Arrange bread slices over blueberries.

3 Combine milk and next 3 ingredients in a large bowl, stirring with a whisk until frothy; stir in liqueur, if desired. Pour milk mixture over bread. Cover and chill 8 hours or overnight.

4 Uncover pan; let stand at room temperature 30 minutes.

5 Preheat oven to 350°.

6 Bake at 350° for 40 minutes or until browned. Place a large platter or jelly-roll pan upside down over baking pan; carefully invert onto platter. Sprinkle evenly with powdered sugar. Yield: 9 servings (serving size: 1 piece).

CALORIES 324 (29% from fat); FAT 10.3g (sat 5.1g, mono 3.4g, poly 0.9g); PROTEIN 7.9g; CARB 51g; FIBER 1.8g; CHOL 137mg; IRON 1.8mg; SODIUM 380mg; CALC 110mg

Pistachio Biscotti

The lemon–milk mixture—a potent version of sour milk—will curdle when ready for use in this dish. The mixture "tenderizes" the flour and helps give these cookies a crumbly texture.

- 2 tablespoons fresh lemon juice
- 2 tablespoons whole milk
- 1½ cups all-purpose flour (about 6¾ ounces)
- ¾ cup packed brown sugar
- ½ cup dry-roasted pistachios, chopped
- ⅓ cup stone-ground yellow cornmeal
- ½ teaspoon ground nutmeg
- ¼ teaspoon salt
- 2 tablespoons plus 1 teaspoon butter, divided
- 2 teaspoons grated orange rind
- 1 large egg, lightly beaten
- Cooking spray
- 1 ounce bittersweet chocolate, coarsely chopped

1 Combine juice and milk; let stand 10 minutes.

2 Preheat oven to 350°.

3 Lightly spoon flour into dry measuring cups; level with a knife. Combine flour and next 5 ingredients, stirring well with a whisk. Melt 2 tablespoons butter. Combine melted butter, milk mixture, rind, and egg in a large bowl, stirring well with a whisk. Add flour mixture, stirring until well blended (dough will be crumbly). Turn dough out onto a lightly floured surface; knead lightly 7 times. Shape dough into a 4 x 12–inch log on a baking sheet coated with cooking spray.

4 Bake at 350° for 20 minutes or until golden brown. Reduce oven temperature to 325°. Remove log from baking sheet; cool 10 minutes on a wire rack. Using a serrated knife, cut log diagonally into 24 (½-inch) slices. Place slices upright on baking sheet; bake at 325° for 20 minutes or until crisp. Remove from baking sheet; cool completely on wire rack.

5 Combine remaining 1 teaspoon butter and chocolate in a microwave-safe dish; microwave at HIGH 30 seconds or until chocolate melts, stirring once. Pour chocolate mixture into a small zip-top plastic bag; seal. Snip a tiny hole in 1 corner of bag; drizzle chocolate mixture over cooled biscotti. Let stand 30 minutes. Yield: 2 dozen biscotti (serving size: 1 biscotto).

CALORIES 96 (30% from fat); FAT 3.2g (sat 1.2g, mono 1.1g, poly 0.5g); PROTEIN 1.9g; CARB 15.5g; FIBER 0.7g; CHOL 12mg; IRON 0.7mg; SODIUM 76mg; CALC 13mg

Mango-Lime Parfaits

Mango and lime are a classic Caribbean combination. For convenience, prepare the components of this dish in advance. Store the syrup and mango separately in the refrigerator, and keep the crushed cookies in an airtight container. Assemble just before serving.

- ½ cup sugar
- 2 tablespoons water
- 1 tablespoon light-colored corn syrup
- ¼ cup fresh lime juice
- 3 cups vanilla low-fat ice cream
- 1½ cups chopped peeled mango (about 2)
- 10 gingersnap cookies, crushed

1 Combine first 3 ingredients in a microwave-safe bowl; microwave at HIGH 1 minute or until sugar melts. Cool completely. Add juice to syrup mixture; stir well.

2 Spoon ¼ cup ice cream into each of 6 parfait glasses; top each serving with about 2 tablespoons mango. Drizzle 1 tablespoon syrup mixture over each serving; top each serving with 1½ teaspoons cookie crumbs. Repeat layers with remaining ice cream, mango, syrup mixture, and crumbs. Serve immediately. Yield: 6 servings (serving size: 1 parfait).

CALORIES 301 (17% from fat); FAT 5.8g (sat 2.8g, mono 1.9g, poly 0.4g); PROTEIN 4.1g; CARB 59g; FIBER 1.5g; CHOL 35mg; IRON 0.8mg; SODIUM 127mg; CALC 117mg

Peach-Berry Upside-Down Cake

Use a mixture of summer fruit for a seasonal spin on traditional upside-down cake. For best results, start with a slightly firm peach.

 5 tablespoons butter, softened and divided
 3 tablespoons brown sugar
 1 peach, peeled, pitted, and thinly sliced
 ½ cup blueberries
 ¼ cup raspberries
 ¾ cup granulated sugar
 1 teaspoon grated lemon rind
 1 tablespoon fresh lemon juice
 2 large egg whites
 1 large egg
 1⅓ cups all-purpose flour (about 6 ounces)
 ¾ teaspoon baking powder
 ½ teaspoon baking soda
 ⅛ teaspoon salt
 ⅔ cup low-fat buttermilk

❶ Preheat oven to 350°.
❷ Melt 1 tablespoon butter in a 10-inch cast-iron skillet over medium heat; sprinkle brown sugar evenly in pan. Remove from heat. Arrange peach slices in a circle in center of pan; scatter blueberries and raspberries evenly around peach slices. Set aside.
❸ Place remaining ¼ cup butter and granulated sugar in a large bowl; beat with a mixer at medium speed until well blended. Add rind and next 3 ingredients; beat well. Lightly spoon flour into dry measuring cups; level with a knife. Combine flour and next 3 ingredients, stirring well with a whisk. Add flour mixture and buttermilk alternately to granulated sugar mixture, beginning and ending with flour mixture.
❹ Carefully spoon batter over fruit mixture. Bake at 350° for 35 minutes or until a wooden pick inserted in center comes out clean. Run a knife around edges of pan. Cool cake completely in pan on a wire rack. Place a plate upside down over pan; carefully invert onto plate. Yield: 8 servings (serving size: 1 wedge).

CALORIES 272 (28% from fat); FAT 8.5g (sat 5g, mono 2.2g, poly 0.5g); PROTEIN 5.1g; CARB 45g; FIBER 1.4g; CHOL 47mg; IRON 1.4mg; SODIUM 254mg; CALC 72mg

Sautéed Grape Napoleons with Port Reduction

Use a fine mesh strainer to sift two tablespoons powdered sugar judiciously over the phyllo as you make the layers. Just a bit of sugar along with the cooking spray helps them adhere to one another. Don't worry if they're loosely stacked; the crisp texture provides a nice contrast to the sautéed grapes and creamy cheese.

 9 (14 x 9–inch) sheets frozen phyllo dough, thawed
 Cooking spray
 2 tablespoons plus 2 teaspoons powdered sugar, divided
 ¾ cup tawny port
 1 tablespoon honey
 ¼ teaspoon salt, divided
 2 teaspoons butter
 2 cups seedless green grapes
 1 cup seedless red grapes
 2 teaspoons granulated sugar
 2 teaspoons fresh lemon juice
 1 ounce goat cheese, softened
 1 (3-ounce) package ⅓-less-fat cream cheese, softened
 2 tablespoons chopped walnuts, toasted

❶ Preheat oven to 350°.
❷ Place 1 phyllo sheet on a large cutting board or work surface (cover remaining dough to keep from drying). Lightly coat dough with cooking spray. Place 2 tablespoons powdered sugar in a small sieve; dust phyllo lightly with powdered sugar. Repeat procedure with 2 phyllo sheets, cooking spray, and powdered sugar, ending with powdered sugar; press layers gently to adhere. Cut phyllo stack lengthwise into 3 (3 x 14–inch) rectangles. Cut each rectangle crosswise into 4 (3 x 3½–inch) rectangles to form 12 rectangles. Carefully stack 1 rectangle on top of another to form 6 stacks; press layers gently. Place stacks on a baking sheet lined with parchment paper. Repeat procedure with remaining phyllo, cooking spray, and powdered sugar to form 18 stacks.
❸ Cover phyllo stacks with parchment paper; place another baking sheet on parchment. Bake at 350° for 10 minutes or until stacks are golden and crisp. Carefully remove top baking sheet and parchment. Cool phyllo stacks completely on baking sheet.
❹ Bring port to a boil in a small saucepan over medium-high heat. Cook 10 minutes or until reduced to 1½ tablespoons. Remove from heat; stir in honey and ⅛ teaspoon salt.
❺ Melt butter in a nonstick skillet over medium-high heat. Add remaining ⅛ teaspoon salt, grapes, granulated sugar, and juice. Sauté 10 minutes or until grapes are tender, stirring occasionally. Remove from heat, and cool to room temperature.
❻ Combine cheeses in a small bowl, stirring well.
❼ Place 1 phyllo stack on each of 6 plates, and top with 1 teaspoon cheese mixture and 1 tablespoon grape mixture. Repeat layers once, and top with a phyllo stack. Drizzle 1 teaspoon port mixture onto each plate. Sprinkle each serving with 1 teaspoon walnuts, and dust evenly with remaining 2 teaspoons powdered sugar. Yield: 6 servings (serving size: 1 napoleon).

CALORIES 297 (26% from fat); FAT 8.6g (sat 4.1g, mono 1.7g, poly 1.5g); PROTEIN 4.9g; CARB 43g; FIBER 1.4g; CHOL 16mg; IRON 1.2mg; SODIUM 339mg; CALC 39mg

Choice Ingredient: Grapes

This member of the berry family can be just as versatile as its cousins. Deborah Madison, author of *Local Flavors: Cooking and Eating from America's Farmers' Markets*, combines halved grapes with a bit of crème fraîche, walnuts, and cinnamon or nutmeg for an easy fruit salad. Grapes can also appear in a sorbet or pie—Madison bakes one with Concord grapes every summer. The berries are nice in salads (including chicken salad) and salsas. And, of course, they're delicious in jam.

When it comes to selection, "go for grapes with character," Madison advises. The most flavorful ones often have seeds. Muscat grapes deliver sweet, musky flavor. Thompson seedless, found in many grocery stores, are best when allowed to ripen until they're yellow-green. You can use red and green seedless grapes interchangeably in recipes. You may find other varieties, such as Champagne, Flame, or Crimson, at farmers' markets.

Look for grapes that are plump, richly colored, and fully attached to their stems. Grapes will keep unwashed in a plastic bag in the refrigerator for up to a week, but they're best eaten sooner. Be sure to rinse grapes thoroughly before eating or using them in a recipe, as dust may cling to the clusters.

MAKE AHEAD • FREEZABLE
Strawberry Ice Cream

- 3½ cups 2% reduced-fat milk
- 1 cup sugar
- 6 egg yolks
- 2 cups fresh strawberries, pureed
- 1 teaspoon vanilla extract

1 Heat milk in a heavy saucepan over medium heat to 180° or until tiny bubbles form around edge (do not boil).
2 Combine sugar and egg yolks in a bowl. Beat with a mixer at high speed until thick and pale. Gradually add half of hot milk to egg yolk mixture, stirring constantly. Return milk mixture to pan. Cook over medium-low heat 6 minutes or until a thermometer registers 160°, stirring constantly. Remove from heat. Place pan in a large ice-filled bowl; cool completely, stirring occasionally.
3 Stir in strawberries and vanilla. Pour mixture into freezer can of an ice-cream freezer; freeze according to manufacturer's instructions. Spoon ice cream into a freezer-safe container; cover and freeze 1 hour or until firm. Yield: 8 servings (serving size: 1 cup).

CALORIES 205 (24% from fat); FAT 5.5g (sat 2.5g, mono 2.1g, poly 0.7g); PROTEIN 5.8g; CARB 33.8g; FIBER 0.8g; CHOL 162mg; IRON 0.6mg; SODIUM 60mg; CALC 153mg

MAKE AHEAD • FREEZABLE
Honeydew-Jalapeño Granita

This frozen dessert would make a bracing finish to a Latin-inspired meal. To suit a festive mood, drizzle tequila over the granita and serve with lime wedges.

- 1¼ cups sugar
- 1 cup water
- 2 tablespoons chopped jalapeño pepper
- 4 cups cubed honeydew melon (about ½ large melon)
- 2 tablespoons fresh lime juice
- ⅛ teaspoon salt

1 Combine first 3 ingredients in a saucepan; bring to a boil over medium-high heat. Cook 2 minutes, stirring frequently. Remove from heat, and cool to room temperature.
2 Place sugar mixture in a blender or food processor. Add melon, juice, and salt. Process until smooth. Pour melon mixture into a 13 x 9–inch baking dish. Cover and freeze 8 hours or until firm. Scrape entire mixture with a fork until fluffy. Store in an airtight container in freezer. Yield: 6 servings (serving size: about 1 cup).

CALORIES 203 (0% from fat); FAT 0.1g (sat 0g, mono 0g, poly 0.1g); PROTEIN 0.6g; CARB 52.6g; FIBER 0.8g; CHOL 0mg; IRON 0.1mg; SODIUM 62mg; CALC 9mg

INSPIRED VEGETARIAN
Viva Venezuela

Corn, cheeses, and vegetable salsa deliver the culinary cues in this South American country.

Spanish colonists influenced Venezuela's cuisine, as they did the food of many South American countries. Yet the country's geographic diversity sets its food apart from that of the rest of the continent. Its proximity to the Caribbean, for example, results in many tropical ingredients being incorporated with the corn, peppers, tomatoes, and other produce used by local cooks. This blend of cultural influences and ingredients makes Venezuelan fare unique.

QUICK & EASY
Sautéed Plantains (*Plátanos Fritos*)

The pintón type of plantain, yellow with a few black spots, is used here (see "Very Venezuelan Ingredients," page 178) because it holds its shape when cooked. If only green plantains are available, ripen them at room temperature for a few days.

- 2 plantains, yellow with some black spots (about 1 pound)
- 1 tablespoon canola oil
- ¼ teaspoon kosher salt

1 Peel plantains; cut each crosswise into 3 pieces. Cut each piece lengthwise into 4 slices.
2 Heat oil in a large nonstick skillet over medium heat. Add plantains to pan; cook 3 minutes on each side or until lightly browned. Transfer plantains to a plate; sprinkle with salt. Yield: 4 servings (serving size: 6 plantain slices).

CALORIES 140 (24% from fat); FAT 3.8g (sat 0.4g, mono 2.1g, poly 1.1g); PROTEIN 1.2g; CARB 28.5g; FIBER 2.1g; CHOL 0mg; IRON 0.5mg; SODIUM 121mg; CALC 3mg

Very Venezuelan Ingredients

Here are some ingredients you'll need to make our Venezuelan dishes.

Plantains: Latin American recipes use plantains at three different levels of ripeness: *Verde*, or green, are firm and starchy and used to make dumplings; *pintón* are sweet and yellow with some black spots and work perfectly for sautéing; and *pasado* are black, very soft and sweet, and are roasted or mashed in desserts.

Arepa flour: Also called *masarepa*, *harina precocida*, or *masa al instante*, this is made from finely ground, precooked corn and used to prepare dumplings and fritters in addition to arepas. You can find it in most Hispanic markets and on the Latin/ethnic-food aisle of some supermarkets. Be sure not to substitute the easier-to-find masa harina, a Mexican product used to make tortillas and tamales—your arepas won't taste quite right.

Chayote: Also known as the mirliton or vegetable pear, this wrinkled, pear-shaped vegetable is used raw in salads or cooked a variety of ways throughout Latin and South America. It can be found at many supermarkets, often near the mangoes and other tropical produce. Look for heavy chayotes that are uniformly bright green, with no brown spots or blemishes; store up to one week in a zip-top plastic bag in the refrigerator.

Cheese: Venezuelan cooks commonly use European cheeses like Edam, Gouda, and Parmesan, which you can find in any supermarket. While we use many of the more common European and American cheeses in our recipes, we find the Latin versions worth procuring for more authentic results. Mexican Oaxaca cheese has a texture and stringiness like mozzarella, and *queso fresco*, "fresh cheese" in Spanish, is a mild crumbling cheese. You'll likely find both in Latin groceries or large supermarkets.

QUICK & EASY
Venezuelan White Rice (*Arroz Blanco Venezolano*)

Introduced by the Spanish, rice is a common starch in South America and the Caribbean.

- 1 tablespoon canola oil
- ½ cup finely chopped onion
- ½ cup finely chopped red bell pepper
- 1 garlic clove, minced
- 4 cups water
- ½ teaspoon salt
- 2 cups uncooked long-grain white rice

1 Heat oil in a large saucepan over medium heat. Add onion and pepper to pan; cook 5 minutes or until tender, stirring occasionally. Add garlic; cook 30 seconds, stirring constantly. Add 4 cups water and salt; bring to a boil. Stir in rice. Cover, reduce heat, and simmer 18 minutes or until liquid is absorbed. Remove from heat; let stand 5 minutes before serving. Yield: 6 servings (serving size: about ¾ cup).

CALORIES 232 (9% from fat); FAT 2.4g (sat 0.2g, mono 1.4g, poly 0.7g); PROTEIN 4.3g; CARB 48.7g; FIBER 0.5g; CHOL 0mg; IRON 2mg; SODIUM 202mg; CALC 10mg

Simple Black Beans (*Caraotas Negras*)

Frijoles is the generic Spanish term for beans, but *caraotas* refers specifically to black beans, the most common variety on South American and Caribbean tables.

- 1½ tablespoons canola oil
- 1 cup chopped onion
- ¾ cup finely chopped red bell pepper
- 1½ teaspoons minced garlic
- ½ teaspoon brown sugar
- ¼ teaspoon freshly ground black pepper
- ¼ teaspoon ground cumin
- 1 cup water
- 2 (15-ounce) cans 50%-less-sodium black beans, undrained
- 1 teaspoon white wine vinegar

1 Heat oil in a large Dutch oven over medium heat. Add onion and bell pepper to pan; cook 5 minutes or until tender, stirring occasionally. Stir in garlic and next 3 ingredients; cook 1 minute, stirring constantly. Stir in 1 cup water and beans; bring to a boil. Partially cover, reduce heat, and simmer 30 minutes or until slightly thick, stirring frequently. Remove from heat, and stir in vinegar. Yield: 6 servings (serving size: ⅔ cup).

CALORIES 128 (25% from fat); FAT 3.6g (sat 0.3g, mono 2.1g, poly 1.1g); PROTEIN 6.2g; CARB 23.3g; FIBER 7.6g; CHOL 0mg; IRON 2.2mg; SODIUM 294mg; CALC 58mg

MAKE AHEAD
Avocado Salsa (*Guasacaca*)

Every Latin American country has its own salsa variation; this mixture of avocado, tomato, onion, and jalapeño is popular in Venezuela. Some recipes mash the ingredients into a guacamole-like paste, and others, like ours, are chunky, more like a relish. This version includes a little tangy Dijon mustard and white wine vinegar, which lend a European touch. Serve with Sautéed Plantains (page 177) or baked corn chips. Allow sufficient time (three hours) to let flavors marry before adding the final ingredients and serving.

- 2 cups finely chopped onion
- ¾ cup finely chopped red bell pepper (1 small)
- 3 tablespoons finely chopped seeded jalapeño pepper
- 3 tablespoons extravirgin olive oil
- 3 tablespoons white wine vinegar
- 1 teaspoon Dijon mustard
- ¾ teaspoon sea salt
- ¼ teaspoon freshly ground black pepper
- 1 large garlic clove, minced
- 1½ cups chopped peeled avocado (about 2)
- 1½ cups chopped seeded plum tomato (about 1 pound)
- 2 tablespoons chopped fresh cilantro
- ¼ teaspoon hot pepper sauce

❶ Combine first 9 ingredients in a large bowl; toss gently. Cover and refrigerate 3 hours. Stir in avocado and remaining ingredients just before serving. Yield: 6 cups (serving size: ¼ cup).

CALORIES 46 (72% from fat); FAT 3.7g (sat 0.5g, mono 2.5g, poly 0.5g); PROTEIN 0.8g; CARB 3.5g; FIBER 1g; CHOL 0mg; IRON 0.3mg; SODIUM 77mg; CALC 6mg

Chayote and Hearts of Palm Cebiche Salad

Sometimes referred to as *seviche* or *ceviche,* this dish traditionally uses an acidic marinade to partially "cook" seafood. Here we substitute chayote that's boiled until slightly soft. The brightly flavored dressing and crunchy onion and pepper provide a nice counterpoint to the tender texture and barely sweet flavor of the chayote, hearts of palm, and corn—all Venezuelan favorites. Allow at least three hours for the flavors to marry in the refrigerator before serving. Soaking the onion softens its pungency.

1   chayote (about 9 ounces)
1   cup ice water
¾   cup vertically sliced red onion (1 small)
¾   cup (1½-inch) strips orange bell pepper
½   cup fresh corn kernels (about 1 small ear)
2   tablespoons finely chopped fresh cilantro
1½   tablespoons finely chopped seeded jalapeño pepper
1   (14-ounce) can hearts of palm, rinsed, drained, and cut crosswise into ½-inch slices
¼   cup fresh lemon juice
¼   cup fresh orange juice
2   tablespoons ketchup
1   tablespoon extravirgin olive oil
¼   teaspoon kosher salt
¼   teaspoon hot pepper sauce
     Dash of sugar
6   Boston lettuce leaves
¼   cup chopped pitted ripe olives

❶ Cut chayote in half lengthwise. Cook chayote in boiling water 3 minutes; drain. Rinse with cold water; drain well. Peel chayote; discard seeds and membranes. Cut chayote into ½-inch cubes. Place in a large bowl.
❷ Combine 1 cup ice water and onion in a small bowl. Cover and refrigerate.
❸ Add bell pepper and next 4 ingredients to chayote.
❹ Combine lemon juice and next 6 ingredients in a small bowl; stir well with a whisk. Add juice mixture to chayote mixture; toss gently. Cover and refrigerate at least 3 hours.
❺ Drain onions well. Place 1 lettuce leaf on each of 6 plates; top each serving with ⅔ cup pepper mixture. Top evenly with onion and olives. Yield: 6 servings.

CALORIES 80 (41% from fat); FAT 3.6g (sat 0.5g, mono 2.2g, poly 0.6g); PROTEIN 2.6g; CARB 12.2g; FIBER 3.1g; CHOL 0mg; IRON 2mg; SODIUM 363mg; CALC 48mg

BEER NOTE: This salad is soaked in citrus juices, making a German hefeweizen the perfect choice. Paulaner Hefe-Weizen ($9/six-pack) offers a distinctive banana aroma, while a refreshing tartness from the use of 60 percent wheat helps it to stand up to the high acidity.

STAFF FAVORITE • MAKE AHEAD
Arepas

In Venezuela, these can be baked as we do here, pan-fried, or grilled, all using the same basic dough. Some arepas are thicker and can be split open; our recipe yields a thinner, slightly crisp arepa that serves as a base for toppings. Even though both arepa flour and Mexican masa harina are precooked corn flours, arepa flour is essential to achieve the correct texture for the corn cakes. Look for arepa flour in Latin markets. Since arepa dough is slightly sticky and wet, plastic wrap makes shaping easier.

1   cup yellow arepa flour (harina precocida)
½   teaspoon salt
1½   cups boiling water
     Cooking spray

❶ Lightly spoon flour into a dry measuring cup; level with a knife. Combine flour and salt in a large bowl. Add 1½ cups boiling water; stir with a wooden spoon until well combined and smooth (about 1 minute). Cover and let stand 5 minutes.
❷ Scrape dough out onto a sheet of plastic wrap. Shape dough into a 2-inch-thick disk. Cut dough into 6 equal portions. Working with one dough portion at a time, place dough portion between two sheets of plastic wrap; shape into a ball, and flatten with palm of hand into a 3-inch circle (about ½-inch thick); shape edges to smooth.
❸ Preheat oven to 350°.
❹ Heat a large nonstick skillet over medium heat. Coat pan with cooking spray. Add arepas to pan; cook 5 minutes on each side or until arepas begin to brown and crusts form. Transfer arepas to a baking sheet coated with cooking spray. Bake at 350° for 20 minutes or until arepas sound hollow when lightly tapped. Yield: 6 arepas (serving size: 1 arepa).

CALORIES 69 (9% from fat); FAT 0.7g (sat 0.1g, mono 0.2g, poly 0.3g); PROTEIN 1.8g; CARB 14.5g; FIBER 1.8g; CHOL 0mg; IRON 1.4mg; SODIUM 200mg; CALC 29mg

Arepas with Savory Topping

Venezuelan street vendors stuff thick arepas with rice or eggs. Our recipe creates thin arepas, which are best topped with beans, salsa, and cheese.

- 6 Arepas (page 179)
- 1½ cups Simple Black Beans (page 178), reheated
- 6 tablespoons Avocado Salsa (page 178)
- 9 tablespoons crumbled queso fresco

1 Arrange arepas on a platter. Spoon ¼ cup Simple Black Beans onto each arepa. Top each serving with 1 tablespoon Avocado Salsa and 1½ tablespoons queso fresco. Yield: 6 servings (serving size: 1 topped arepa).

CALORIES 163 (27% from fat); FAT 4.9g (sat 1.5g, mono 1.9g, poly 0.9g); PROTEIN 7.1g; CARB 25.6g; FIBER 5g; CHOL 7mg; IRON 2.4mg; SODIUM 362mg; CALC 118mg

Arepas with Cheese and Fresh Tomatoes

- 6 Arepas (page 179)
- 3 ounces fresh mozzarella cheese, cut into 6 slices
- 2 large plum tomatoes, thinly sliced (about 12 ounces)
- ¼ teaspoon freshly ground black pepper
- ⅛ teaspoon salt
- 2 teaspoons extravirgin olive oil
- 6 large fresh basil leaves

1 Arrange arepas on a platter. Layer each arepa with 1 mozzarella slice and about ⅓ cup tomatoes. Sprinkle tomato layer evenly with pepper and salt. Drizzle with oil, and top with basil. Yield: 6 servings (serving size: 1 topped arepa).

CALORIES 130 (38% from fat); FAT 5.5g (sat 2.2g, mono 2.2g, poly 0.7g); PROTEIN 5.1g; CARB 15.7g; FIBER 2.1g; CHOL 11mg; IRON 1.5mg; SODIUM 339mg; CALC 103mg

Grilling

Whether you cook over charcoal or gas, here are strategies that will ensure your success with a variety of foods.

CONSIDER YOUR OUTDOOR grill an outdoor kitchen. A host of possibilities awaits, from salads with colorful grilled summer vegetables to robust entrées of grilled chicken or fish, even grilled fruit desserts. Best of all, anyone can be a gourmet griller once they master the basics.

STAFF FAVORITE • QUICK & EASY
Sliders with Shallot-Dijon Relish

- ½ teaspoon kosher salt
- ¼ teaspoon freshly ground black pepper
- 1 pound ground sirloin
- Cooking spray
- 3 tablespoons finely chopped shallots
- 1 tablespoon Worcestershire sauce
- 1 tablespoon Dijon mustard
- 2 teaspoons butter, softened
- 8 (1-ounce) Parker House rolls
- 16 dill pickle chips

1 Prepare grill to medium-high heat.
2 Combine first 3 ingredients. Divide meat mixture into 8 equal portions, shaping each into a ¼-inch-thick patty. Lightly coat both sides of patties with cooking spray. Place patties on grill rack; grill 3 minutes on each side or until done.
3 Combine shallots and next 3 ingredients in a small bowl, stirring well. Cut rolls in half horizontally. Spread shallot mixture evenly over cut sides of rolls. Layer 1 patty and 2 pickle chips on bottom half of each roll; top with top halves of rolls. Yield: 8 servings (serving size: 1 slider).

CALORIES 167 (37% from fat); FAT 6.8g (sat 2.6g, mono 2.7g, poly 0.8g); PROTEIN 10.8g; CARB 14.2g; FIBER 1g; CHOL 23mg; IRON 1.8mg; SODIUM 404mg; CALC 7mg

Grilled Chicken with Sriracha Glaze

Dense, bone-in chicken leg quarters benefit from long, slow cooking over indirect heat.

- ⅔ cup mango jam
- 2 tablespoons finely chopped fresh chives
- 2 tablespoons rice vinegar
- 2 tablespoons Sriracha (hot chile sauce, such as Huy Fong)
- 1 tablespoon olive oil
- 4 (12-ounce) bone-in chicken leg-thigh quarters, skinned
- ½ teaspoon kosher salt
- ¼ teaspoon freshly ground black pepper

1 Prepare grill for indirect grilling. If using a gas grill, heat one side to medium-high and leave one side with no heat. If using a charcoal grill, arrange hot coals on either side of charcoal grate, leaving an empty space in middle.
2 Combine first 4 ingredients, stirring until smooth. Reserve ¼ cup mango mixture; set aside.
3 Brush oil evenly over chicken. Sprinkle chicken with salt and pepper.
4 Carefully remove grill rack. Place a disposable aluminum foil pan on unheated part of grill. Carefully return grill rack to grill. Place chicken on grill rack over

unheated part. Brush chicken with about 2 tablespoons remaining mango mixture. Close lid; grill 90 minutes or until a thermometer inserted into meaty part of thigh registers 165°, turning chicken and brushing with about 2 tablespoons mango mixture every 20 minutes. Transfer chicken to a platter. Drizzle chicken with reserved ¼ cup mango mixture. Yield: 4 servings (serving size: 1 leg-thigh quarter and 1 tablespoon mango mixture).

CALORIES 326 (29% from fat); FAT 10.4g (sat 2.3g, mono 4.7g, poly 2.1g); PROTEIN 38.7g; CARB 18.2g; FIBER 2.7g; CHOL 154mg; IRON 4.5mg; SODIUM 515mg; CALC 102mg

QUICK & EASY
Grilled Romaine with Blue Cheese Dressing

3 tablespoons crumbled blue cheese
2 tablespoons reduced-fat mayonnaise
1½ tablespoons fresh lemon juice
1 tablespoon finely chopped shallots
1½ teaspoons water
1 garlic clove, minced
2 romaine lettuce hearts, cut in half lengthwise (about 12 ounces)
Cooking spray
¼ teaspoon kosher salt
¼ teaspoon freshly ground black pepper
1 cup cherry tomatoes, halved

1 Prepare grill to medium-high heat.
2 Combine first 6 ingredients, stirring with a whisk. Cover and chill.
3 Coat lettuce on all sides with cooking spray; sprinkle with salt and pepper. Place lettuce, cut sides down, on grill rack; grill 2 minutes. Remove lettuce from grill; let stand 5 minutes.
4 Place 1 lettuce half on each of 4 salad plates. Top each serving with ¼ cup tomatoes. Drizzle each serving with 1 tablespoon dressing. Serve immediately. Yield: 4 servings.

CALORIES 58 (45% from fat); FAT 2.9g (sat 1.2g, mono 0.5g, poly 0.6g); PROTEIN 2.8g; CARB 6.5g; FIBER 1.5g; CHOL 5mg; IRON 1.3mg; SODIUM 278mg; CALC 80mg

Brown Sugar and Mustard Salmon

Indirect grilling cooks larger fish fillets more slowly and delicately than direct grilling; individual fillets are fine for direct heat. Use a center-cut piece so the fish is an even thickness; it will cook more evenly than a tapered tail end. Leave the skin on, as the fish lifts off the skin easily once cooked. Scrape off the skin remaining on the grill once it has cooled.

2 tablespoons dark brown sugar
2 tablespoons whole-grain Dijon mustard
1 teaspoon freshly ground black pepper
¼ teaspoon kosher salt
¼ teaspoon ground ginger
¼ teaspoon ground coriander
1 garlic clove, minced
1 (1½-pound) center-cut salmon fillet

1 Prepare grill for indirect grilling. If using a gas grill, heat one side to medium-high and leave one side with no heat. If using a charcoal grill, arrange hot coals on either side of charcoal grate, leaving an empty space in the middle.
2 Combine first 7 ingredients, stirring until well blended. Spread mustard mixture over fish; let stand 15 minutes.
3 Carefully remove grill rack. Place a disposable aluminum foil pan on unheated part of grill. Carefully return grill rack to grill. Place fish, skin sides down, on grill rack over unheated part. Close lid; grill 30 minutes or until fish flakes easily when tested with a fork or until desired degree of doneness. Remove fish from grill by inserting a spatula between skin and fish. Discard skin. Yield: 4 servings (serving size: about 5 ounces).

CALORIES 267 (37% from fat); FAT 11.1g (sat 2.5g, mono 4.6g, poly 2.5g); PROTEIN 31.6g; CARB 8.7g; FIBER 0.5g; CHOL 80mg; IRON 0.9mg; SODIUM 340mg; CALC 31mg

Spiedini of Chicken and Zucchini with Almond Salsa Verde

Spiedini is Italian for "little skewers." These grilled kebabs are paired with a zesty sauce of herbs, nuts, citrus, and capers.

SALSA:
1 cup chopped fresh parsley
3 tablespoons capers, chopped
½ teaspoon grated lemon rind
3 tablespoons fresh lemon juice
2 tablespoons chopped almonds, toasted
2 tablespoons chopped fresh chives
1 tablespoon extravirgin olive oil
½ teaspoon chopped fresh thyme
½ teaspoon chopped fresh oregano
¼ teaspoon kosher salt
⅛ teaspoon freshly ground black pepper
1 garlic clove, minced
SPIEDINI:
1½ pounds skinless, boneless chicken breasts, cut into 1-inch pieces
6 small zucchini, cut into 1-inch slices (about 1¼ pounds)
Cooking spray
¼ teaspoon kosher salt
⅛ teaspoon freshly ground black pepper

1 Soak 12 (10-inch) wooden skewers in water 30 minutes to prevent burning.
2 Prepare grill to medium-high heat.
3 To prepare salsa, combine first 12 ingredients; set aside.
4 To prepare spiedini, thread chicken and zucchini alternately onto 12 (10-inch) skewers. Coat spiedini with cooking spray; sprinkle evenly with ¼ teaspoon salt and ⅛ teaspoon pepper. Place on grill rack; grill 6 minutes or until done, turning once. Serve with salsa. Yield: 6 servings (serving size: 2 spiedini and 2½ tablespoons salsa).

CALORIES 187 (26% from fat); FAT 5.5g (sat 0.9g, mono 2.9g, poly 1.1g); PROTEIN 28.7g; CARB 6.3g; FIBER 2.2g; CHOL 66mg; IRON 2.1mg; SODIUM 376mg; CALC 56mg

All About Grilling

Grilling, Defined

Grilling involves cooking food on a rack over a heat source, usually a charcoal fire or ceramic briquettes heated by gas flames. Direct heat quickly sears the outside of food, producing distinctive robust, roasted—and sometimes pleasantly charred—flavors and a nice crust. If food is cooked over moderate heat, it gains a crust as well as a smokier taste.

Equipment

Choosing between a gas or charcoal grill is a lifestyle choice; they perform comparably, if not equally. For the most versatility, choose a grill with a large cooking surface and a lid.

Here are a few other useful tools: a chimney starter for charcoal, long-handled tongs, basting brush, spatula, oven mitts, a wire brush for cleaning, disposable foil pans, and a meat thermometer.

Direct Versus Indirect Heat

Direct grilling involves cooking food squarely over the heat source, usually with the lid off. This method cooks food quickly with intense heat and works best for thin cuts of meat (burgers and several kinds of steaks and chops, for example) and most vegetables. It is not ideal for larger cuts of meat because the high heat will overcook them on the outside before they're done inside.

For food that needs to cook longer (pork shoulder or whole chickens), use **indirect** grilling, with which a fire is built on one or both sides of the food and the hot air circulates around it. Indirect grilling requires a covered grill, which creates convected heat. It's a gentler cooking method than direct grilling, allowing larger cuts to cook completely through without overbrowning. Follow this rule of thumb: If it takes less than 20 to 25 minutes to cook, use direct heat; otherwise, use indirect heat. The exception is large fish fillets, which yield better results over indirect heat even though they can typically be cooked in 15 minutes or less over direct heat. Fish is so delicate that direct grilling can cook it too quickly and render it dry. (Or it can burn oils in the skin, resulting in a fishy odor.) If you use indirect heat, fish will cook perfectly and remain moist.

Keep It Clean

Preheat the rack with all burners on high for 10 to 15 minutes (whether you're using direct or indirect heat). Doing so will incinerate any remaining residue from the last cookout, making it easy to clean off. Then, brush the cooking grates with a brass-bristle grill brush; steel bristles can damage the enamel finish of some grates. (In a pinch, if you don't have a brass-bristle cleaning brush, use a ball of crumpled heavy-duty aluminum foil between a pair of tongs to clean the grates.) Clean the grates vigorously so that they are smooth and free from food that may have adhered from previous grilling. Brush the preheated grill racks each time you grill.

At the start of grilling season, preheat the grill with all burners on high or with an even layer of preheated charcoal for an hour before brushing the cooking grates. You should only need to do this once to get your grates ready for the season; it's the grill version of the principle behind a self-cleaning oven—burning everything off.

Light Up

If you have a gas grill, simply ignite the burners and place them on high to preheat. If using indirect heat, turn off one side of the grill once it's preheated.

If you have a charcoal grill, the easiest way to light charcoal, briquettes or lump hardwood, is in a chimney starter. It's best to choose a high-capacity chimney starter, or you're likely to discover that you need two starters to light enough charcoal for your grill. (A traditional kettle grill works most efficiently with 50 briquettes.) Use an odorless, tasteless fuel starter or crumpled newspaper to initiate the fire. Let the charcoal burn until it is covered with white-gray ash, which indicates it is at the perfect cooking temperature.

If you use the direct heat method, scatter the briquettes evenly across the charcoal grate. If you are using the indirect cooking method, equally divide the briquettes on either side of the grate and place an inexpensive disposable aluminum pan in the empty spot. The food is placed over the drip pan, which catches drips and reflects some heat back to the food. Many cooks place charcoal on one side of the grill and leave the other empty. But distributing the briquettes to each side of the food (if space allows) creates consistent heat that envelops it.

Control the Heat

Maintaining a specific temperature on a gas grill is simply a matter of turning a dial to the appropriate setting. On a charcoal grill, air vents control the heat. To allow airflow, do not cover the bottom air vents with briquettes. Also, leave the vent on the top of the grill at least partially open. The more open the vents, the hotter your grill will cook. If you want medium heat, cover the vents about halfway.

Oil the Food

Whenever possible, coat the food (not the grill rack) with oil or cooking spray to promote caramelization and those telltale grill marks, and to help prevent sticking. If you don't coat the food, its natural juices may evaporate as it grills, leaving the food dry and papery—this is especially true when grilling vegetable slices.

The Bottom Line

The three most important elements about grilling:

1 Use direct heat for thin cuts of meat and other foods that cook quickly. Indirect heat is best for larger cuts.

2 Keep the grill rack clean.

3 Place oiled food on a hot grill rack.

QUICK & EASY

Grilled Asparagus and Arugula Salad with Lemon-Truffle Dressing

Grilling the asparagus creates robust flavor, which stands up well to the earthiness of truffle oil and the peppery bite of arugula. Both the cooking method and the quality of the ingredients create a stellar first course.

- 1 pound asparagus, trimmed
- Cooking spray
- ⅛ teaspoon kosher salt
- ½ teaspoon grated lemon rind
- 1½ tablespoons fresh lemon juice
- 1½ teaspoons truffle oil
- ⅛ teaspoon freshly ground black pepper
- 4 cups trimmed arugula
- ¼ cup (1 ounce) shaved fresh Parmesan cheese

1 Prepare grill to medium-high heat.
2 Place asparagus on a jelly-roll pan. Coat asparagus with cooking spray, and sprinkle with salt; toss gently to coat. Place asparagus on grill rack; grill 3 minutes or until crisp-tender, turning occasionally. Remove asparagus from grill; cut into 2-inch pieces.
3 Combine rind and next 3 ingredients in a large bowl, stirring with a whisk. Add asparagus and arugula; toss gently. Divide asparagus mixture evenly among 4 salad plates. Top each serving with 1 tablespoon cheese. Yield: 4 servings.

CALORIES 80 (45% from fat); FAT 4g (sat 1.3g, mono 1.7g, poly 0.4g); PROTEIN 6.1g; CARB 5.7g; FIBER 2.7g; CHOL 5mg; IRON 2.7mg; SODIUM 193mg; CALC 161mg

Grilled Vegetable Salad

Tailor the types of vegetables to the bounty of your garden or that of farmers' market vendors. Thin asparagus spears may need to cook only four minutes.

VINAIGRETTE:
- 2 tablespoons sherry vinegar
- 1 tablespoon extravirgin olive oil
- 1½ teaspoons honey
- ½ teaspoon Dijon mustard
- ½ teaspoon kosher salt
- ¼ teaspoon freshly ground black pepper

SALAD:
- 8 ounces asparagus, trimmed
- 2 (4-inch) portobello mushroom caps (about 6 ounces)
- 1 zucchini, cut lengthwise into ¼-inch-thick slices
- 1 yellow squash, cut lengthwise into ¼-inch-thick slices
- 1 small red onion, cut into ¼-inch-thick slices
- 1 red bell pepper, halved and seeded
- Cooking spray
- 2 tablespoons chopped fresh basil
- 1 tablespoon chopped fresh chives
- 1 tablespoon chopped fresh parsley
- 6 tablespoons crumbled queso fresco

1 Prepare grill to medium-high heat.
2 To prepare vinaigrette, combine first 6 ingredients in a large bowl; set aside.
3 To prepare salad, coat asparagus, mushrooms, zucchini, squash, onion, and bell pepper with cooking spray. Place vegetables on grill rack; grill 4 minutes on each side or until slightly blackened. Remove vegetables from grill; cool slightly. Cut vegetables into 1-inch pieces.
4 Add vegetables, basil, chives, and parsley to vinaigrette; toss gently to coat. Sprinkle with cheese. Yield: 6 servings (serving size: about ¾ cup salad and 1 tablespoon cheese).

CALORIES 77 (36% from fat); FAT 3.1g (sat 0.7g, mono 1.8g, poly 0.4g); PROTEIN 3.6g; CARB 9.7g; FIBER 2.6g; CHOL 2mg; IRON 1.4mg; SODIUM 184mg; CALC 48mg

Grilled Whole Red Snapper with Citrus-Ginger Hot Sauce

Although fish is often grilled over indirect heat, we prefer cooking whole snapper over moderate direct heat.

SAUCE:
- ⅓ cup fresh orange juice
- 2 tablespoons water
- 1½ tablespoons fresh lime juice
- 1 tablespoon fish sauce
- 1½ teaspoons honey
- 1 teaspoon grated peeled fresh ginger
- 1 teaspoon grated garlic
- ½ teaspoon minced seeded serrano chile
- ½ teaspoon Sriracha (hot chile sauce, such as Huy Fong)
- 1 dried hot red chile, seeded and crushed

FISH:
- 2 (2-pound) cleaned whole red snappers
- 1 tablespoon olive oil
- ½ teaspoon kosher salt
- ½ teaspoon freshly ground black pepper
- 2 lemons, thinly sliced
- 2 garlic cloves, thinly sliced
- Cooking spray

Continued

1 Prepare grill to medium heat.

2 To prepare sauce, combine first 10 ingredients; set aside.

3 To prepare fish, score each fish with 3 diagonal cuts on both sides. Brush outside of fish evenly with oil. Sprinkle with salt and pepper. Stuff lemon and garlic slices into cuts. Place any remaining lemon slices into fish cavities. Coat outside of fish with cooking spray.

4 Place fish on grill rack; grill 40 minutes or until fish flakes easily when tested with a fork. (Fish does not need to be turned.) Serve fish with sauce. Yield: 4 servings (serving size: about 5 ounces fish and about 2½ tablespoons sauce).

CALORIES 237 (22% from fat); FAT 5.9g (sat 1g, mono 2.9g, poly 1.2g); PROTEIN 37.9g; CARB 6.2g; FIBER 0.3g; CHOL 67mg; IRON 0.6mg; SODIUM 673mg; CALC 67mg

ENLIGHTENED COOK
Honor System

Owners of an innovative restaurant invite patrons to pay what they can or volunteer their time for food.

A menu with no prices typically means only the rich can afford it. At Denver's SAME (So All May Eat) Café, no prices—and no cash register—means you pay what you can, even if the currency is a little elbow grease. That's exactly what restaurateurs Brad and Libby Birky have in mind: to make healthful fare available to all.

About 65 percent of diners pay for their meals, while the rest trade work for food. That helps the Birkys stay afloat. And, for now, it's enough. "We know Denver isn't the only town with needs like this. Every city has the working poor," says Brad. "We're just out to quietly change the world, one meal at a time."

QUICK & EASY
Watermelon Salad

½   cup chopped red onion
3   tablespoons fresh lime juice (about 2 limes)
4   cups cubed seeded watermelon
¼   cup pitted kalamata olives
¼   cup finely chopped fresh parsley
¼   cup finely chopped fresh mint
½   cup (2 ounces) feta cheese, crumbled

1 Combine onion and juice in a medium bowl; let stand 10 minutes. Add watermelon and next 3 ingredients. Cover and chill 1 hour. Sprinkle with cheese. Yield: 12 servings (serving size: about ½ cup salad and about 1½ teaspoons cheese).

CALORIES 46 (47% from fat); FAT 2.4g (sat 0.9g, mono 1.3g, poly 0.2g); PROTEIN 1.2g; CARB 5.5g; FIBER 0.5g; CHOL 4mg; IRON 0.3mg; SODIUM 136mg; CALC 34mg

QUICK & EASY • MAKE AHEAD
Southwestern Salsa

¼   cup fresh lime juice (about 2 limes)
3   tablespoons extravirgin olive oil
¼   teaspoon freshly ground black pepper
⅛   teaspoon salt
1½ cups fresh corn kernels (about 3 ears corn)
1   cup grape tomatoes, halved
½   cup chopped fresh cilantro
½   cup chopped red onion
½   cup canned diced tomatoes and green chiles, drained
1   (15-ounce) can black beans, rinsed and drained

1 Combine first 4 ingredients in a medium bowl; stir with a whisk. Add corn and remaining ingredients; toss well. Cover and chill 1 hour. Yield: 12 servings (serving size: about ⅓ cup).

CALORIES 78 (47% from fat); FAT 4.1g (sat 0.6g, mono 2.8g, poly 0.5g); PROTEIN 2.1g; CARB 11.2g; FIBER 2.4g; CHOL 0mg; IRON 0.5mg; SODIUM 186mg; CALC 14mg

QUICK & EASY • MAKE AHEAD
Cool Couscous with Fruit and Nuts

Vary this side salad with whatever type of dried fruit and nuts you have on hand—dried apricots and toasted hazelnuts, for example, or dried cherries and pecans. Serve with grilled jerk-style chicken or pork.

1   cup uncooked couscous
¾   teaspoon kosher salt
1½ cups boiling water
¼   cup orange juice
1   tablespoon canola oil
½   cup dried mixed fruit
2   tablespoons dry-roasted cashews, chopped

1 Combine couscous and salt in a medium bowl; add 1½ cups boiling water. Cover and let stand 8 minutes or until liquid is absorbed. Combine juice and oil; stir into couscous. Cover and chill 30 minutes. Stir in fruit and cashews. Yield: 6 servings (serving size: about ½ cup).

CALORIES 197 (19% from fat); FAT 4.2g (sat 0.8g, mono 2.2g, poly 1g); PROTEIN 4.2g; CARB 35g; FIBER 2.2g; CHOL 0mg; IRON 0.6mg; SODIUM 258mg; CALC 24mg

---

Everybody Eats

Restaurants without set prices or that barter food for work are a rarity. But Denise Cerreta, founder of One World Everybody Eats in Salt Lake City, believes so strongly in the concept that she's crafted a how-to manual. Her five-year-old community kitchen dishes out 120 meals a day to professionals, students, and street people, all paying what they can.

Cerreta is consulting with potential One World restaurateurs in San Francisco; Durham, North Carolina; and Moab, Utah. "It's our vision to help people create a similar restaurant in every city," says Cerreta.

Rice Is Nice

A staple enjoyed around the globe inspires these three satisfying suppers.

Global Rice Menu 1
serves 4

Greek Lamb Pilaf

Green beans with pine nuts and feta

Cook 1 pound trimmed green beans in boiling water 3 minutes or until crisp-tender; drain. Heat 2 teaspoons olive oil over medium-high heat in a large nonstick skillet. Add 4 teaspoons pine nuts to pan; sauté 2 minutes or until lightly browned, stirring constantly. Add beans, ¼ teaspoon salt, and ⅛ teaspoon black pepper; toss to combine. Sprinkle with 4 teaspoons crumbled feta cheese.

Warm pita bread

Game Plan

1 While lamb mixture cooks:
- Trim green beans.

2 While rice cooks:
- Boil green beans.
- Chop tomato, parsley, and mint.

3 While pilaf stands:
- Toast pine nuts, and finish green beans.

Ingredient Tip
Not a fan of lamb? Substitute lean ground beef.

Greek Lamb Pilaf

Lamb, mint, and rice are a classic Greek combination.

Time: 38 minutes

- 2½ cups chopped onion (about 1 large onion)
- ¾ cup chopped carrot (about 1 carrot)
- 3 garlic cloves, minced
- ¾ pound lean ground lamb
- 1 cup uncooked long-grain rice
- ¼ teaspoon ground cinnamon
- 1 (14-ounce) can fat-free, less-sodium chicken broth
- 1 cup chopped plum tomato (about 1 tomato)
- ¼ cup chopped fresh flat-leaf parsley, divided
- 2 tablespoons chopped fresh mint
- 3 tablespoons fresh lemon juice
- ¾ teaspoon salt

1 Heat a large nonstick skillet over medium-high heat. Add first 4 ingredients to pan; cook 5 minutes, stirring to crumble lamb. Stir in rice and cinnamon; sauté 2 minutes. Stir in broth; bring to a boil. Cover, reduce heat, and simmer 20 minutes or until liquid is absorbed. Remove from heat; stir in tomato, 3 tablespoons parsley, and next 3 ingredients. Cover and let stand 5 minutes. Sprinkle with remaining 1 tablespoon parsley. Yield: 4 servings (serving size: 1⅔ cups).

CALORIES 446 (35% from fat); FAT 17.2g (sat 7g, mono 7.2g, poly 1.4g); PROTEIN 26g; CARB 45g; FIBER 2.4g; CHOL 83mg; IRON 2.5mg; SODIUM 748mg; CALC 61mg

---

Global Rice Menu 2
serves 4

Ham Risotto with Sugar Snap Peas

Romaine salad with Parmesan-balsamic dressing

Combine 1 tablespoon extravirgin olive oil, 2 teaspoons balsamic vinegar, 2 teaspoons fresh lemon juice, ⅛ teaspoon salt, ⅛ teaspoon black pepper, and 1 minced garlic clove in a large bowl; stir with a whisk. Stir in 2 tablespoons grated Parmesan cheese. Add 4 cups torn romaine lettuce, 1 cup halved cherry tomatoes, and 1 thinly sliced small yellow bell pepper; toss gently to coat.

Biscotti

Game Plan

1 While broth heats:
- Cook peas.
- Chop ham.
- Prepare vegetables for salad.

2 Cook risotto.

3 While ham heats:
- Prepare salad.

Ham Risotto with Sugar Snap Peas

Time: 43 minutes

- 4 cups fat-free, less-sodium chicken broth
- 8 ounces sugar snap peas, trimmed and cut into 1-inch pieces
- 2 teaspoons olive oil
- 1½ cups thinly sliced leek (about 2 medium leeks)
- 2 garlic cloves, minced
- 1 cup uncooked Arborio rice or other medium-grain rice
- ½ cup dry white wine
- 3 ounces diced cooked ham (about ¾ cup)
- ½ cup freshly grated Parmesan cheese
- ⅛ teaspoon black pepper

Continued

❶ Bring broth to a simmer in a medium saucepan (do not boil). Keep warm.
❷ Cook peas in boiling water 2 minutes or until crisp-tender. Drain and rinse with cold water; drain.
❸ Heat oil in a large saucepan over medium heat. Add leek; cook 5 minutes or until tender, stirring frequently. Add garlic; cook 30 seconds. Stir in rice; cook 1 minute. Add wine; cook 2 minutes or until liquid is nearly absorbed, stirring constantly. Add broth, ½ cup at a time, stirring constantly until each portion of broth is absorbed before adding next (about 20 minutes total). Add ham; cook 3 minutes or until thoroughly heated. Stir in peas, cheese, and pepper. Yield: 4 servings (serving size: 1¼ cups).

CALORIES 334 (21% from fat); FAT 7.7g (sat 2.8g, mono 3.4g, poly 0.6g); PROTEIN 17.1g; CARB 48.8g; FIBER 4g; CHOL 29mg; IRON 2.1mg; SODIUM 632mg; CALC 177mg

Global Rice Menu 3
serves 4

Speedy Paella

Grilled tomato toast

Heat a grill pan over medium-high heat. Add 4 (2-ounce) slices sourdough bread to pan; grill 2 minutes on each side or until lightly browned. Rub 1 side of each bread slice with cut sides of 1 halved garlic clove; discard garlic. Rub bread with cut sides of 1 small halved tomato; discard tomato. Drizzle evenly with 2 teaspoons extravirgin olive oil; sprinkle evenly with ⅛ teaspoon kosher salt.

Chilled cava

Game Plan
1 While saffron steeps in wine:
  • Chop chorizo, onion, bell pepper, and garlic.
  • Cook chorizo.
2 While rice mixture cooks:
  • Prepare toast.

Speedy Paella

Spanish chorizo is made with smoked pork, as opposed to Mexican chorizo, which uses fresh pork. If you can't find the Spanish version, substitute kielbasa.
Time: 45 minutes

- ½ cup dry white wine
- ¼ teaspoon saffron threads, crushed
- 3 ounces Spanish chorizo sausage, cut into ¼-inch-thick slices
- 1 cup coarsely chopped onion (about 1 medium onion)
- ⅔ cup coarsely chopped red bell pepper (about 1 small bell pepper)
- ½ teaspoon hot paprika
- ¼ teaspoon salt
- 2 garlic cloves, minced
- 1 cup uncooked short-grain rice
- 1 cup fat-free, less-sodium chicken broth
- 1 (8-ounce) bottle clam juice
- 1 cup chopped plum tomato (about 1 tomato)
- ½ cup frozen green peas
- 12 littleneck clams
- ½ pound medium shrimp, peeled and deveined

❶ Combine wine and saffron threads in a small bowl; let stand 15 minutes.
❷ Heat a large nonstick skillet over medium-high heat. Add chorizo; cook 3 minutes, stirring occasionally. Remove chorizo from pan. Add onion and pepper to pan; cook 5 minutes, stirring occasionally. Stir in paprika, salt, and garlic; cook 1 minute. Return chorizo to pan. Add wine mixture, rice, broth, and clam juice; bring to a boil. Cover, reduce heat, and cook 15 minutes or until most of liquid is absorbed. Stir in tomato and next 3 ingredients. Cover and cook 5 minutes or until clams open; discard any unopened shells. Yield: 4 servings (serving size: 1¼ cups rice mixture and 3 clams).

CALORIES 394 (23% from fat); FAT 10.2g (sat 3.3g, mono 4.1g, poly 1.3g); PROTEIN 26.9g; CARB 48.6g; FIBER 4.4g; CHOL 116mg; IRON 6.7mg; SODIUM 786mg; CALC 71mg

20 Minute Dishes

From stir-fry to salad, tuna to tenderloin, here are simple, fresh, and easy meals you can make superfast.

Szechuan Pork

Fresh sliced pineapple makes a nice companion for this one-dish meal.

- 6 ounces soba (buckwheat) noodles, uncooked
- 2 teaspoons dark sesame oil
- 1 (1-pound) pork tenderloin, trimmed and cut into 2-inch strips
- 1 tablespoon chili garlic sauce (such as Lee Kum Kee)
- 1 teaspoon bottled ground fresh ginger (such as Spice World)
- ¾ cup red bell pepper strips (about 1 small pepper)
- ¼ cup fat-free, less-sodium chicken broth
- 1½ tablespoons low-sodium soy sauce
- 1 tablespoon peanut butter
- ¾ cup (2-inch) diagonally cut green onions (about 4 green onions)

❶ Cook noodles according to package directions. Drain and rinse with cold water; drain.
❷ Heat oil in a large nonstick skillet over medium-high heat. Add pork, chili garlic sauce, and ginger to pan; stir-fry 2 minutes. Add pepper; stir-fry 2 minutes. Add broth, soy sauce, and peanut butter. Reduce heat to low; cook 1 minute or until sauce is slightly thick. Stir in onions. Serve over noodles. Yield: 4 servings (serving size: 1 cup pork mixture and ½ cup noodles).

CALORIES 338 (23% from fat); FAT 8.6g (sat 2.2g, mono 3.5g, poly 1.9g); PROTEIN 30.4g; CARB 36.8g; FIBER 1.7g; CHOL 63mg; IRON 2.9mg; SODIUM 693mg; CALC 40mg

Pork Medallions with Balsamic-Shallot Sauce

Complement this entrée with Parmesan cheese stirred into quick-cooking polenta and an iceberg wedge drizzled with buttermilk dressing.

- 1 (1-pound) pork tenderloin, trimmed
- ½ teaspoon salt
- ½ teaspoon dried thyme
- ⅛ teaspoon black pepper
- ⅛ teaspoon ground allspice
  Cooking spray
- ¼ cup finely chopped shallots
- 1 teaspoon butter
- 1 tablespoon brown sugar
- 3 tablespoons balsamic vinegar

❶ Cut tenderloin crosswise into 8 pieces. Place each piece between 2 sheets of heavy-duty plastic wrap; pound each piece to ½-inch thickness using a meat mallet or small heavy skillet. Combine salt and next 3 ingredients; rub over both sides of pork.
❷ Heat a large nonstick skillet over medium-high heat. Coat pan with cooking spray. Add pork, and cook 2 minutes on each side or until done. Remove pork from pan; keep warm.
❸ Reduce heat to medium. Add shallots and butter to pan; cook 2 minutes, stirring occasionally. Add sugar and vinegar; cook 30 seconds or until sugar melts, stirring constantly. Spoon sauce over pork. Yield: 4 servings (serving size: 2 medallions and about 1 tablespoon sauce).

CALORIES 226 (25% from fat); FAT 6.4g (sat 2.5g, mono 2.4g, poly 0.5g); PROTEIN 32.3g; CARB 7.3g; FIBER 0.2g; CHOL 92mg; IRON 2mg; SODIUM 371mg; CALC 19mg

Spicy Lemon Trout

Serve with a spinach-mushroom salad and French bread.

- 2 teaspoons fresh lemon juice
- 2 teaspoons olive oil
- 4 (6-ounce) dressed trout
- 1 teaspoon dried thyme
- ½ teaspoon salt
- ½ teaspoon Spanish smoked paprika
- ¼ teaspoon ground red pepper
- 12 thin lemon slices (about 2 lemons)
  Cooking spray

❶ Preheat broiler.
❷ Combine juice and oil; brush inside of fish. Combine thyme and next 3 ingredients; sprinkle evenly inside cavity of each fish. Place 3 lemon slices into cavity of each fish. Place fish on broiler pan coated with cooking spray; broil 4 minutes on each side or until fish flakes easily when tested with a fork or until desired degree of doneness. Yield: 4 servings (serving size: 5 ounces fish).

CALORIES 374 (38% from fat); FAT 15.7g (sat 4g, mono 5.6g, poly 4.5g); PROTEIN 52.7g; CARB 6.4g; FIBER 2.8g; CHOL 156mg; IRON 1.8mg; SODIUM 424mg; CALC 235mg

WINE NOTE: Chardonnay comes in a wide variety of styles, and Tormaresca Chardonnay 2006 ($11) from Italy's Puglia region is well-balanced, fresh, and lean. This wine's modest amount of oak tones helps it remain bright and fruity. Its fresh mineral qualities complement the delicate flavors of the fish, while the zippy acidity resonates with the lemon and smoky paprika.

Tenderloin Steaks with Red Onion Marmalade

Serve this company-worthy entrée with garlic mashed potatoes and sautéed green beans, and pour a bottle of cabernet sauvignon.

  Cooking spray
- 1 large red onion, sliced and separated into rings (about 2 cups)
- 2 tablespoons red wine vinegar
- 2 tablespoons honey
- ½ teaspoon salt, divided
- 1 teaspoon dried thyme
- ¼ teaspoon freshly ground black pepper
- 4 (4-ounce) beef tenderloin steaks, trimmed (1 inch thick)

❶ Preheat broiler.
❷ Heat a large nonstick skillet over medium-high heat. Coat pan with cooking spray. Add onion to pan. Cover and cook 3 minutes. Add vinegar, honey, and ¼ teaspoon salt to pan. Reduce heat, and simmer, uncovered, 8 minutes or until slightly thick, stirring occasionally.
❸ Sprinkle remaining ¼ teaspoon salt, thyme, and pepper evenly over beef. Place beef on a broiler pan coated with cooking spray; broil 4 minutes on each side or until desired degree of doneness. Serve with onion mixture. Yield: 4 servings (serving size: 1 steak and ⅓ cup marmalade).

CALORIES 289 (36% from fat); FAT 11.4g (sat 4.3g, mono 4.3g, poly 0.4g); PROTEIN 32.5g; CARB 12.6g; FIBER 0.8g; CHOL 95mg; IRON 4.7mg; SODIUM 369mg; CALC 25mg

Asian Chicken Salad

- 2 tablespoons seasoned rice vinegar
- 1 tablespoon low-sodium soy sauce
- 1 tablespoon dark sesame oil
- 1 teaspoon bottled ground fresh ginger (such as Spice World)
- 1 teaspoon honey
- 6 cups gourmet salad greens
- 2 cups chopped cooked chicken
- 1 cup matchstick-cut carrots
- 1 cup snow peas, trimmed and cut lengthwise into thin strips
- 2 tablespoons sliced almonds, toasted

❶ Combine first 5 ingredients in a large bowl, stirring well with a whisk. Add salad greens and next 3 ingredients; toss gently to coat. Sprinkle with almonds. Yield: 4 servings (serving size: 1³/₄ cups).

CALORIES 172 (31% from fat); FAT 6g (sat 0.9g, mono 2.7g, poly 2g); PROTEIN 19.6g; CARB 10.9g; FIBER 3.5g; CHOL 38mg; IRON 1.6mg; SODIUM 538mg; CALC 73mg

Tuna Steaks with Wasabi-Ginger Glaze

- 2 tablespoons low-sodium soy sauce, divided
- 4 (6-ounce) tuna steaks (1 inch thick)
- 2 tablespoons ginger marmalade (such as Dundee)
- 2 teaspoons wasabi paste
- Cooking spray
- 2 tablespoons chopped fresh cilantro

❶ Spoon 1 tablespoon soy sauce over fish; let stand 5 minutes.
❷ Combine remaining 1 tablespoon soy sauce, marmalade, and wasabi paste in a small bowl, stirring with a whisk.
❸ Heat a grill pan over medium-high heat. Coat pan with cooking spray. Add fish to pan; cook 2 minutes on each side. Spoon marmalade mixture over tuna; cook 1 minute or until medium-rare or desired degree of doneness. Remove tuna from pan; sprinkle with cilantro. Yield: 4 servings (serving size: 1 steak and 1¹/₂ teaspoons cilantro).

CALORIES 281 (7% from fat); FAT 2.3g (sat 0.5g, mono 0.3g, poly 0.6g); PROTEIN 51.4g; CARB 7.7g; FIBER 0.1g; CHOL 98mg; IRON 1.8mg; SODIUM 397mg; CALC 37mg

A Specialty Between Friends

A Colorado teacher uses on-hand components to create a delicious crustless quiche for a friend.

Crustless Smoked Turkey and Spinach Quiche

"Sprinkle some of the Swiss cheese in the pie plate first before adding the ham and egg mixture.

—Wendy McMillan, Longmont, Colorado

- Cooking spray
- ³/₄ cup (4 ounces) cubed smoked turkey ham (such as Jennie-O)
- ¹/₂ cup chopped onion
- ¹/₈ teaspoon freshly ground black pepper
- ³/₄ cup (3 ounces) shredded Swiss cheese, divided
- 1 cup fresh baby spinach leaves
- 1 cup fat-free cottage cheese
- ¹/₂ cup evaporated fat-free milk
- ¹/₄ cup (1 ounce) shredded reduced-fat Cheddar cheese
- 2 large eggs, lightly beaten
- 2 large egg whites, lightly beaten
- ¹/₂ cup all-purpose flour (about 2¹/₄ ounces)
- 1 teaspoon baking powder

❶ Preheat oven to 350°.
❷ Heat a large nonstick skillet over medium-high heat. Coat pan with cooking spray. Add ham, onion, and pepper to pan; sauté 4 minutes or until ham is lightly browned.
❸ Sprinkle ¹/₄ cup Swiss cheese in a 9-inch pie plate coated with cooking spray. Top with ham mixture.
❹ Combine remaining ¹/₂ cup Swiss cheese, spinach, and next 5 ingredients in a large bowl; stir with a whisk.
❺ Lightly spoon flour into a dry measuring cup; level with a knife. Combine flour and baking powder in a small bowl, stirring with a whisk. Add flour mixture to egg mixture, stirring with a whisk until blended. Pour egg mixture over ham mixture. Bake at 350° for 45 minutes or until a knife inserted in center of quiche comes out clean. Yield: 8 servings (serving size: 1 wedge).

CALORIES 152 (30% from fat); FAT 5.1g (sat 2.8g, mono 1.3g, poly 0.5g); PROTEIN 14.2g; CARB 11.2g; FIBER 0.5g; CHOL 68mg; IRON 1mg; SODIUM 427mg; CALC 225mg

Crab Cakes

"Fresh lump crabmeat makes all the difference in this recipe. In addition to lemon wedges, you can top the crab cakes with a mixture of light sour cream, horseradish, and chives."

—Nancee Melin, Tucson, Arizona

- 1 pound lump crabmeat, drained and shell pieces removed
- ¹/₂ cup crushed whole wheat crackers (about 12 crackers)
- ¹/₃ cup finely chopped red bell pepper
- ¹/₃ cup finely chopped green bell pepper
- ¹/₄ cup light mayonnaise
- 1 tablespoon chopped fresh parsley
- 1 teaspoon garlic powder
- 1 teaspoon prepared mustard
- 2 teaspoons Worcestershire sauce
- ¹/₄ teaspoon Hungarian hot paprika
- ¹/₈ teaspoon freshly ground black pepper
- 3 large egg whites, lightly beaten
- Cooking spray
- 4 lemon wedges

❶ Preheat broiler.

❷ Combine first 12 ingredients in a medium bowl. Divide mixture into 4 equal portions, shaping each into a 1-inch-thick patty. Place patties on a baking sheet coated with cooking spray. Broil 3 inches from heat 10 minutes or until browned. Serve with lemon wedges. Yield: 4 servings (serving size: 1 crab cake and 1 wedge).

CALORIES 280 (32% from fat); FAT 10.3g (sat 1.7g, mono 2.9g, poly 4.6g); PROTEIN 25.2g; CARB 21.9g; FIBER 3.4g; CHOL 72mg; IRON 1.6mg; SODIUM 699mg; CALC 75mg

MAKE AHEAD
Roasted Vegetable and Quinoa Salad

"Quinoa [KEEN-wah] is a tiny, bead-shaped, ivory-colored grain, with a delicate flavor. This salad is really refreshing on a hot day. I like to pair it with chicken."

—Gretchen Hofing, Clinton, Michigan

    1   red bell pepper
    3   cups water
 1½   cups uncooked quinoa
    ¼   cup balsamic blend seasoned rice vinegar (such as Nakano)
    2   teaspoons olive oil
    ¼   teaspoon black pepper
    2   cups chopped carrot
        Cooking spray
 3½   cups chopped zucchini
 1¾   cups chopped yellow squash
    1   cup (4 ounces) crumbled reduced-fat feta cheese
    1   garlic clove, minced

❶ Preheat broiler.

❷ Cut bell pepper in half lengthwise; discard seeds and membranes. Place pepper halves, skin sides up, on a foil-lined baking sheet; flatten with hand. Broil 15 minutes or until blackened. Place in a zip-top plastic bag; seal. Let stand 15 minutes. Peel and cut pepper into strips.

❸ Reduce oven temperature to 500°.

❹ Bring 3 cups water to a boil in a medium saucepan; stir in quinoa. Cover, reduce heat, and cook 15 minutes or until liquid is absorbed. Remove pan from heat, and set aside.

❺ Combine vinegar, oil, and black pepper in a medium bowl, stirring with a whisk. Add carrot; toss to coat. Drain carrot in a fine sieve over a bowl, reserving carrot and vinegar mixture. Place carrot on a baking sheet coated with cooking spray. Bake at 500° for 10 minutes. Add zucchini and squash to reserved vinegar mixture in bowl; toss well to coat. Drain zucchini mixture in a fine sieve over a bowl, reserving zucchini and vinegar mixtures. Add zucchini mixture to carrot on baking sheet in a single layer. Bake an additional 20 minutes or until vegetables are browned. Remove from oven; cool completely.

❻ Combine quinoa, roasted vegetables, reserved vinegar mixture, cheese, and garlic in a large bowl; stir well. Cover and chill. Yield: 8 servings (serving size: 1 cup).

CALORIES 196 (23% from fat); FAT 4.9g (sat 1.4g, mono 1.6g, poly 1g); PROTEIN 8.2g; CARB 30g; FIBER 4.7g; CHOL 5mg; IRON 2.5mg; SODIUM 379mg; CALC 78mg

MAKE AHEAD
Raas Malaai (*Baked Pudding*)

"I lightened my original version of this Indian pudding because it used full-fat ricotta cheese, heavy cream, and lots of nuts and sugar."

—Rupa Kothandapani, Birmingham, Alabama

 1½   cups sugar
    1   teaspoon vanilla extract
    ⅛   teaspoon salt
    1   (15-ounce) carton part-skim ricotta cheese
        Cooking spray
    ⅔   cup whole milk
    ⅛   teaspoon ground cardamom or ground cinnamon
    ¼   cup chopped pistachios

❶ Preheat oven to 350°.

❷ Combine first 4 ingredients in a medium bowl. Spread evenly in an 8-inch square baking dish coated with cooking spray. Bake at 350° for 30 minutes or until edges are lightly browned and center is almost set. Cool on a wire rack.

❸ Cut pudding into 12 equal portions. Pour milk over pudding. Cover and refrigerate 8 hours or overnight. Sprinkle cardamom over pudding. Spoon 1 serving pudding and about 2 teaspoons milk into each of 12 small bowls, and top each serving with 1 teaspoon pistachios. Yield: 12 servings.

CALORIES 167 (24% from fat); FAT 4.4g (sat 2.1g, mono 1.6g, poly 0.5g); PROTEIN 5g; CARB 28.2g; FIBER 0.3g; CHOL 12mg; IRON 0.3mg; SODIUM 74mg; CALC 115mg

Chicken and Rice with Cilantro-Poblano Sauce

"I like to serve this with a green salad and crusty bread."

—Charlene Chambers, Ormond Beach, Florida

    ¼   cup chopped green onions
    ¼   cup fresh cilantro leaves
    ¼   teaspoon sea salt
    ⅛   teaspoon black pepper
    1   poblano chile, seeded and chopped
    1   garlic clove, minced
    1   (14-ounce) can fat-free, less-sodium chicken broth, divided
    2   tablespoons olive oil, divided
    ½   cup chopped green onions, divided
    1   (8-ounce) package sliced cremini mushrooms
    1   garlic clove, minced
    1   cup uncooked long-grain rice
    ½   cup water
    1   teaspoon ground cumin
    2   tablespoons chopped fresh flat-leaf parsley
    1   tablespoon butter
    4   (6-ounce) skinless, boneless chicken breast halves
    ¼   teaspoon sea salt
    ⅛   teaspoon black pepper
    1   teaspoon olive oil
    ¾   cup grape or cherry tomatoes, halved
        Cilantro sprigs (optional)

Continued

① Combine first 6 ingredients and ½ cup broth in a food processor; process until blended.

② Heat 1 tablespoon oil in a large skillet over medium-high heat. Add ¼ cup onions, mushrooms, and garlic clove to pan; sauté 2 minutes. Add cilantro mixture, remaining broth, rice, ½ cup water, and cumin to pan; bring to a boil. Cover, reduce heat, and simmer 25 minutes or until liquid is absorbed. Remove from heat; cover and let stand 5 minutes. Add parsley to rice mixture; fluff with a fork.

③ Heat remaining 1 tablespoon oil and butter in a large skillet over medium-high heat. Sprinkle chicken with ¼ teaspoon salt and ⅛ teaspoon pepper. Add chicken to pan; cook 5 minutes on each side or until done. Remove chicken from pan; cut each chicken piece crosswise into ½-inch slices.

④ Heat 1 teaspoon oil in a small saucepan over medium-high heat. Add remaining ¼ cup onions and tomatoes; sauté 2 minutes. Arrange 1 cup rice mixture on each of 4 plates; top each serving with 1 breast half and 2 tablespoons tomato mixture. Garnish with cilantro sprigs, if desired. Yield: 4 servings.

CALORIES 501 (28% from fat); FAT 15.7g (sat 4.2g, mono 8.1g, poly 2.1g); PROTEIN 42.1g; CARB 45.7g; FIBER 3.8g; CHOL 102mg; IRON 5mg; SODIUM 609mg; CALC 94mg

LIGHTEN UP
Quick Bread

This Montana reader's family favorite is trimmed down in time to enjoy with seasonal squash.

serving size: 1 slice		
	before	after
CALORIES PER SERVING	207	167
FAT	11.1g	5.9g
PERCENT OF TOTAL CALORIES	48%	32%

MAKE AHEAD • FREEZABLE
Zucchini-Pineapple Quick Bread

This recipe, by Martha Kitchens Parks of Missoula, Montana, makes two loaves. Freeze the extra loaf, tightly wrapped in plastic wrap and heavy-duty aluminum foil, for up to one month. Thaw at room temperature.

 3   cups sifted all-purpose flour (about 13½ ounces)
1½   teaspoons ground cinnamon
 1   teaspoon salt
 1   teaspoon baking soda
 ½   teaspoon baking powder
 2   large eggs
 2   cups sugar
 2   cups grated zucchini (about 1½ medium zucchini)
⅔   cup canola oil
 ½   cup egg substitute
 2   teaspoons vanilla extract
 2   (8-ounce) cans crushed pineapple in juice, drained
Baking spray with flour

① Preheat oven to 325°.

② Lightly spoon flour into dry measuring cups, and level with a knife. Combine flour and next 4 ingredients in a large bowl, stirring well with a whisk.

③ Beat eggs with a mixer at medium speed until foamy. Add sugar and next 4 ingredients, beating until well blended. Add zucchini mixture to flour mixture, stirring just until moist. Fold in pineapple. Spoon batter into 2 (9 x 5-inch) loaf pans coated with baking spray. Bake at 325° for 1 hour or until a wooden pick inserted in center comes out clean. Cool 10 minutes in pans on a wire rack; remove from pans. Cool completely on wire rack. Yield: 2 loaves, 14 servings per loaf (serving size: 1 slice).

CALORIES 167 (32% from fat); FAT 5.9g (sat 0.5g, mono 3.3g, poly 1.7g); PROTEIN 2.4g; CARB 26.5g; FIBER 0.7g; CHOL 15mg; IRON 0.9mg; SODIUM 151mg; CALC 16mg

ONE MORE TASTE
Peach Mojitos

Few drinks help beat the heat like the mojito. Fizzy, sweet-tart, and minty, the classic Cuban cocktail refreshes from the very first sip. With these Peach Mojitos, we've kept the traditional recipe mostly intact but added sweet, juicy fruit. We still muddle mint with lime and sugar, still use rum, and top it off with crisp club soda. But fresh peach puree forms the base of this version. The stone fruit makes an irresistible partner for the citrus and mint.

QUICK & EASY
Peach Mojitos

Use a wooden muddler to crush the mint mixture in the pitcher, if available.

 3   cups coarsely chopped peeled ripe peaches (about 1 pound)
 1   teaspoon grated lime rind
 1   cup fresh lime juice (about 4 large limes)
¾   cup sugar
 ½   cup packed mint leaves
 2   cups white rum
 4   cups club soda, chilled
Crushed ice
Mint sprigs (optional)

① Place peaches in a blender or food processor; process until smooth. Press peach puree through a fine sieve into a bowl; discard solids.

② Combine rind and next 3 ingredients in a large pitcher; crush juice mixture with back of a long spoon. Add peach puree and rum to pitcher, stirring until sugar dissolves. Stir in club soda. Serve over crushed ice. Garnish with mint sprigs, if desired. Yield: 10 servings (serving size: about ⅔ cup).

CALORIES 186 (1% from fat); FAT 0.1g (sat 0g, mono 0g, poly 0.1g); PROTEIN 0.6g; CARB 21.6g; FIBER 0.9g; CHOL 0mg; IRON 0.3mg; SODIUM 21mg; CALC 14mg

Three Cheers for the Red, White, and Blue

Fourth of July festivities are as diverse as the nation itself. Our regionally inspired menus offer three feasts for Independence Day.

AT LEAST ONE OF America's founding fathers had a premonition the nation would observe Independence Day with patriotic passion for centuries to come. In a letter to his wife, Abigail, John Adams foretold that the occasion would be marked with "pomp and parade, with shows, games, sports, guns, bells, bonfires, and illuminations from one end of this continent to the other."

While fun and fireworks are both common, our national birthday parties reflect the diversity of the American spirit, and the food is as varied as the people who call the USA home. The menus we share here feature that regional character. Three different parts of the country—New England, the Midwest, and the Southwest—represent the whole country in the way their regional dishes figures into their celebrations (for West Coast specialties, see this chapter's Inspired Vegetarian column, page 206).

Littleneck Clams with Sausage

Grilled clams pop open from the heat, letting you know they're done and eliminating the need for shucking.

- 1 cup dry white wine
- 2 teaspoons grated lemon rind
- ¼ teaspoon crushed red pepper
- ⅛ teaspoon kosher salt
- 3 garlic cloves, thinly sliced
- 4 ounces hot chicken Italian sausage
- Cooking spray
- 36 littleneck clams
- 1 cup grape tomatoes, halved
- 2 tablespoons finely chopped fresh parsley
- 6 lemon wedges

1 Prepare grill.
2 Combine first 5 ingredients in a small saucepan; bring to a boil. Reduce heat, and simmer until reduced to ½ cup (about 5 minutes). Keep warm.
3 Place sausage on a grill rack coated with cooking spray, and grill 10 minutes or until done, turning occasionally. Cool. Cut in half lengthwise, and cut each half crosswise into thin slices.
4 Place clams in a disposable aluminum foil pan. Place pan on grill rack; cover and grill 5 minutes. Uncover and grill 5 minutes or until shells open. Discard any unopened shells. Combine clams, juice from clams, wine mixture, sausage, tomatoes, and parsley in a large bowl. Divide clam mixture evenly among 6 shallow bowls. Serve with lemon wedges. Yield: 6 servings (serving size: 6 clams, about 3 tablespoons sausage, about 2 tablespoons sauce, and 1 lemon wedge).

CALORIES 78 (23% from fat); FAT 2g (sat 0.6g, mono 0.6g, poly 0.5g); PROTEIN 10.4g; CARB 4.8g; FIBER 0.6g; CHOL 39mg; IRON 8.4mg; SODIUM 177mg; CALC 57mg

NEW ENGLAND FOURTH MENU

(Serves 6)

Littleneck Clams with Sausage

Peas and Pods

Steamed new potatoes with parsley

Grilled Salmon with Tangy Cucumber Sauce

Blueberry and Blackberry Galette with Cornmeal Crust

BEER NOTE: Reach for an English-style pale ale, like Cisco Brewers Whale's Tale Pale Ale from Nantucket ($8/4-pack), to serve with this menu. English-style pale ales are less hoppy and bitter than their American counterparts. The earthy English hops and caramel malt in this beer complement the fuller flavors of sausage and salmon, but the beer remains refreshing and balanced.

Peas and Pods

New Englanders accompany their holiday salmon with fresh peas, part of the region's summer bounty. Mint adds bright flavor and accents the natural sweetness of the peas.

- ¾ pound sugar snap peas, trimmed
- 2 cups fresh or frozen petite green peas, thawed
- 1½ tablespoons butter, softened
- ¼ teaspoon kosher salt
- 2 tablespoons finely chopped fresh mint

Continued

❶ Steam snap peas, covered, 2 minutes. Add green peas to pan; steam 2 minutes. ❷ Combine peas, butter, and salt in a large bowl; toss gently to coat. Sprinkle with mint. Yield: 6 servings (serving size: 2/3 cup).

CALORIES 87 (29% from fat); FAT 2.8g (sat 1.8g, mono 0.7g, poly 0.1g); PROTEIN 3.4g; CARB 10.7g; FIBER 3.4g; CHOL 8mg; IRON 1.3mg; SODIUM 105mg; CALC 42mg

Grilled Salmon with Tangy Cucumber Sauce

This recipe showcases the classic combination of salmon, cucumber, and horseradish. Use two spatulas to make handling the salmon easier. Garnish with lemon wedges, if desired.

- 1½ cups fat-free sour cream
- 1 cup cubed seeded peeled cucumber
- 2 tablespoons chopped green onions
- 2 tablespoons chopped fresh dill
- 1½ teaspoons fresh lemon juice
- 1 teaspoon prepared horseradish
- ¾ teaspoon kosher salt, divided
- 1 (3-pound) salmon fillet (about ¾-inch thick)
- ¼ teaspoon freshly ground black pepper
  Cooking spray
  Dill sprigs (optional)

❶ Combine first 6 ingredients in a medium bowl. Add ¼ teaspoon salt; stir well. Cover and chill 30 minutes. ❷ Prepare grill. ❸ Sprinkle fish with remaining ½ teaspoon salt and pepper. Place fish, skin sides up, on grill rack coated with cooking spray; grill 3 minutes. Rotate fish one quarter-turn (45 degrees) for diamond-shaped crosshatches. Grill 3 minutes. Turn fish over; grill 4 minutes or until desired degree of doneness. Serve with sauce and dill sprigs, if desired. Yield: 6 servings (serving size: 6 ounces salmon and ⅓ cup sauce).

CALORIES 340 (33% from fat); FAT 12.4g (sat 1.9g, mono 4.1g, poly 4.9g); PROTEIN 42.7g; CARB 10.9g; FIBER 0.3g; CHOL 117mg; IRON 1.7mg; SODIUM 374mg; CALC 149mg

STAFF FAVORITE

Blueberry and Blackberry Galette with Cornmeal Crust

The rich, buttery pastry dough is easy and forgiving. Simply roll it out onto parchment paper with a lightly floured rolling pin, and then use the parchment to transfer it to a baking sheet. If you're lucky enough to find wild blueberries like the ones that grow in Maine, use them in this rustic summer tart.

PASTRY:
- 1¾ cups all-purpose flour (about 7¾ ounces)
- ⅓ cup granulated sugar
- ¼ cup cornmeal
- ¼ teaspoon salt
- ½ cup chilled butter, cut into small pieces
- ⅓ cup fat-free buttermilk

FILLING:
- 4 cups blueberries
- 2 cups blackberries
- ½ cup granulated sugar
- 3 tablespoons all-purpose flour
- 2 tablespoons lemon juice
- 2 tablespoons fat-free milk
- 1 large egg white, lightly beaten
- 1½ tablespoons turbinado sugar

❶ To prepare pastry, lightly spoon flour into dry measuring cups, and level with a knife. Combine flour and next 3 ingredients in a food processor; pulse 2 times. Add butter to flour mixture; pulse 4 or 5 times or until mixture resembles coarse meal. With processor on, slowly add buttermilk through food chute; process just until dough forms a ball. Gently press dough into a 4-inch circle on plastic wrap; cover. Chill 30 minutes. ❷ Preheat oven to 350°. ❸ Unwrap and place dough on a sheet of parchment paper. Roll dough into a 15-inch circle. Place dough on parchment on a baking sheet. ❹ To prepare filling, combine blueberries and next 4 ingredients in a medium

bowl; toss gently to coat. Arrange berry mixture in center of dough, leaving a 2-inch border. Fold edges of dough toward center, pressing gently to seal (dough will only partially cover berry mixture). ❺ Combine milk and egg white in a small bowl, stirring well with a whisk. Brush dough with milk mixture; sprinkle turbinado sugar evenly over dough. Bake at 350° for 1 hour or until pastry is golden brown. Let stand 30 minutes; cut into wedges. Yield: 10 servings (serving size: 1 wedge).

CALORIES 306 (28% from fat); FAT 9.7g (sat 5.8g, mono 2.4g, poly 0.6g); PROTEIN 4.3g; CARB 52.2g; FIBER 3.7g; CHOL 24mg; IRON 1.7mg; SODIUM 138mg; CALC 33mg

New England

As you might expect of a city with a football team called the Patriots, Boston proudly promotes "America's biggest Independence Day party." Almost a million people attend the multiday event, which includes Chowderfest on the Boston City Hall Plaza, a pageant of fighter jets dashing through the skies, patriotic music from the Boston Pops orchestra, and nine tons of fireworks launched from river barges.

Just 60 miles to the south, tiny Bristol, Rhode Island, lays claim to the oldest continuing Independence Day celebration in the country, observed without fail since 1785. The town's gala parade still follows a route lined with stately 18th-century homes, and its main street flaunts a red, white, and blue stripe down its center year-round.

MAKE AHEAD
Marinated Green Bean and Potato Salad

¾ pound green beans, trimmed
½ pound wax beans, trimmed
½ pound fingerling potatoes, halved
      lengthwise
¼ cup white wine vinegar, divided
1 tablespoon extravirgin olive oil
½ teaspoon kosher salt, divided
½ teaspoon freshly ground black
      pepper
1 tablespoon minced fresh parsley
2 center-cut bacon slices, cooked
      and crumbled

❶ Cook beans in boiling water 5 minutes or until crisp-tender. Drain and plunge beans into ice water; drain.
❷ Place potatoes in a saucepan; cover with water. Bring to a boil. Reduce heat, and simmer 5 minutes or until tender; drain. Return potatoes to pan over medium heat. Add 2 tablespoons vinegar to pan; bring to a boil. Remove from heat.
❸ Combine remaining 2 tablespoons vinegar, oil, ¼ teaspoon salt, and pepper in a small bowl, stirring with a whisk. Drizzle beans with vinegar mixture; toss well to coat. Place beans on a serving platter; arrange potatoes over beans. Sprinkle with remaining ¼ teaspoon

salt, parsley, and bacon. Serve at room temperature. Yield: 6 servings (serving size: about 1 cup salad).

CALORIES 86 (34% from fat); FAT 3.2g (sat 0.6g, mono 2g, poly 0.4g); PROTEIN 3.2g; CARB 13g; FIBER 3.9g; CHOL 2mg; IRON 1.4mg; SODIUM 208mg; CALC 41mg

High Plains Steaks

Grilled steak is a Fourth of July staple throughout the country, and the Midwest is renowned for its beef.

1 tablespoon prepared yellow
      mustard
1 teaspoon kosher salt
1 teaspoon freshly ground black
      pepper
2 teaspoons Worcestershire sauce
3 (8-ounce) sirloin strip steaks
Cooking spray

❶ Prepare grill.
❷ Combine first 4 ingredients in a small bowl. Rub mustard mixture over both sides of steaks. Cover with plastic wrap; let stand 30 minutes.
❸ Place steaks on a grill rack coated with cooking spray; grill 3 minutes on each side or until desired degree of doneness. Let stand 10 minutes before slicing. Yield: 6 servings (serving size: 3 ounces).

CALORIES 155 (30% from fat); FAT 5.2g (sat 2g, mono 2.2g, poly 0.2g); PROTEIN 24.6g; CARB 0.7g; FIBER 0.2g; CHOL 67mg; IRON 2.2mg; SODIUM 427mg; CALC 10mg

---

The Midwest

South Dakota likes to celebrate with cowboy festivities, including the Fourth of July Rodeo in Fort Pierre and the Bull Stampede in Mobridge. If you attend the Black Hills Roundup in Belle Fourche, you cap off the day with fireworks over Mount Rushmore.

Indianapolis offers an ice cream social at the historic home of President Benjamin Harrison. Meanwhile, the Living History Farms of Urbandale, Iowa, present a vintage-style baseball game, with rules dating to 1875, along with pie-eating and watermelon-seed-spitting contests.

Cherry Crisp

The bountiful cherry crop in Wisconsin and Michigan provides the inspiration for this fruit dessert with all-American appeal.

FILLING:
6 cups (about 2 pounds) sweet
      cherries, pitted
⅓ cup granulated sugar
¼ cup cornstarch
1 tablespoon fresh lemon juice
¼ teaspoon almond extract
⅛ teaspoon salt
Cooking spray
TOPPING:
½ cup all-purpose flour (about
      2¼ ounces)
½ cup old-fashioned rolled oats
½ cup packed light brown sugar
⅛ teaspoon salt
6 tablespoons chilled butter, cut into
      small pieces
⅓ cup sliced almonds

❶ Preheat oven to 375°.
❷ To prepare filling, combine first 6 ingredients in a large bowl; toss gently. Spoon cherry mixture into an 11 x 7-inch baking dish coated with cooking spray.
❸ To prepare topping, lightly spoon flour into a dry measuring cup; level with a knife. Combine flour and next 3 ingredients in a medium bowl, stirring with a whisk. Cut in butter with a pastry blender or 2 knives until mixture resembles coarse meal. Stir in almonds. Sprinkle oat mixture evenly over cherry mixture. Bake at 375° for 45 minutes or until filling is bubbly and topping is crisp. Let stand 5 minutes; serve warm. Yield: 8 servings.

CALORIES 311 (33% from fat); FAT 11.2g (sat 5.6g, mono 3.5g, poly 0.8g); PROTEIN 4.1g; CARB 51.4g; FIBER 3.4g; CHOL 23mg; IRON 1.1mg; SODIUM 140mg; CALC 43mg

The Southwest

In New Mexico, Santa Feans observe Independence Day on their beloved historic plaza, where they gather in the morning for a festive pancake breakfast followed by hours of mariachi music.

Much of Arizona sizzles on the Fourth with temperatures above 100 degrees. The town of Oatman puts the intense heat and sunshine to work. The "hot enough to fry an egg on a sidewalk" saying inspired the wacky "Sidewalk Egg Fry." Participants are given two eggs each that can be cracked directly onto the sidewalk or into a skillet or other contraption. The sun does the cooking, aided by magnifiers, and the best fried egg wins the prize.

The former mining town of Telluride, Colorado, hosts one of the country's most delightful small-town parades. Virtually every adult, child, and dog in the vicinity gathers on the few short blocks of Main Street, where not a single traffic light detracts, to participate in the parade or cheer it on from the sidelines. As the event winds down, a fire engine leads the residents to a rib cookout in a local park, and at the end of the day everyone gathers in a natural amphitheater, gazing at fireworks exploding against what are truly "purple mountain majesties."

MAKE AHEAD

Chickpea Salad with Cilantro Dressing

Chickpeas are a popular component of Southwestern cooking, as is the herb cilantro. To allow time for the flavors to develop, let this salad stand an hour before spooning it over the lettuce leaves.

- 2 cups chopped fresh cilantro
- 2 tablespoons extravirgin olive oil
- ½ teaspoon grated lime rind
- 2 tablespoons fresh lime juice
- ⅛ teaspoon salt
- 2 garlic cloves
- 2 pickled jalapeño pepper slices
- ¼ cup fat-free, less-sodium chicken broth
- ½ cup chopped seeded peeled cucumber
- ½ cup thinly sliced radishes
- ¼ cup chopped celery
- 2 (15½-ounce) cans chickpeas (garbanzo beans), rinsed and drained
- 12 Boston lettuce leaves

❶ Combine first 7 ingredients in a food processor or blender; process until well blended. Add broth; pulse until combined.
❷ Combine cucumber and next 3 ingredients in a large bowl. Drizzle with cilantro mixture; toss to coat. Arrange lettuce leaves on a platter; spoon chickpea mixture over lettuce. Yield: 6 servings (serving size: about ⅔ cup chickpea mixture and 2 lettuce leaves).

CALORIES 161 (33% from fat); FAT 5.9g (sat 0.8g, mono 3.6g, poly 1.2g); PROTEIN 5.4g; CARB 23.2g; FIBER 5g; CHOL 0mg; IRON 1.8mg; SODIUM 382mg; CALC 57mg

MAKE AHEAD

Charred Corn Relish

The corn will blacken slightly as it grills, giving the dish a pleasant smoky quality.

- 4 ears shucked corn
- Cooking spray
- ½ cup diced red bell pepper
- ½ cup halved grape tomatoes
- 2 tablespoons finely chopped red onion
- 2 tablespoons thinly sliced green onions
- ½ to 1 chipotle chile, canned in adobo sauce, minced
- 1 tablespoon fresh lime juice
- 2 teaspoons canola oil
- ¼ teaspoon sugar
- ¼ teaspoon kosher salt
- ¼ teaspoon ground cumin

❶ Prepare grill.
❷ Lightly coat corn with cooking spray. Place corn on grill rack; grill 20 minutes, turning occasionally. Cool completely. Cut kernels from ears of corn; place in a medium bowl. Discard cobs.
❸ Add bell pepper and next 4 ingredients to bowl; toss well. Combine juice and remaining ingredients in a small bowl, stirring with a whisk. Drizzle juice mixture over corn mixture; toss well. Cover and chill at least 30 minutes. Yield: 6 servings (serving size: ½ cup).

CALORIES 76 (29% from fat); FAT 2.4g (sat 0.3g, mono 0.9g, poly 1g); PROTEIN 2.3g; CARB 14g; FIBER 2.4g; CHOL 0mg; IRON 0.6mg; SODIUM 117mg; CALC 6mg

Chickpeas are a popular component of Southwestern cooking, as is the herb cilantro.

Grilled Chicken Tostadas

This dish gives a Southwestern accent to the American summertime classic, grilled chicken. For more intensity, pickle the onions overnight. Achiote paste is made in part from ground annatto seed. It is a deep red, mildly spicy seasoning; you can find it at large supermarkets or Latin grocery stores.

PICKLED ONIONS:

- 4 cups thinly sliced red onion (about 1 large)
- 2 cups boiling water
- ½ cup fresh orange juice (about 1 medium orange)
- ½ cup red wine vinegar
- ⅛ teaspoon kosher salt

CHICKEN:

- 2 garlic cloves, unpeeled
- ½ cup fresh orange juice (about 1 medium orange)
- ½ cup red wine vinegar
- 2 tablespoons achiote paste, crumbled
- 2 tablespoons fresh lime juice
- 2 teaspoons olive oil
- ½ teaspoon kosher salt
- ¼ teaspoon ground allspice
- ¼ teaspoon freshly ground black pepper
- 1½ pounds skinless, boneless chicken breasts

REMAINING INGREDIENTS:

- Cooking spray
- 12 (6-inch) corn tortillas
- 2 cups shredded leaf lettuce
- ¾ cup chopped peeled avocado
- ¾ cup crumbled queso fresco cheese
- Pickled jalapeño pepper slices (optional)
- Reduced-fat sour cream (optional)
- Cilantro leaves (optional)

1 To prepare pickled onions, combine onion and 2 cups boiling water in a large bowl. Cover and let stand 15 minutes; drain. Add ½ cup juice, ½ cup vinegar, and ⅛ teaspoon salt to onions. Cover and chill at least 2 hours.

2 To prepare chicken, heat a small nonstick skillet over medium heat. Add garlic to pan; cook 7 minutes or until tender, stirring occasionally. Remove from pan; peel and mash. Combine garlic, ½ cup juice, and next 7 ingredients in a large zip-top plastic bag. Seal bag, and shake vigorously to dissolve achiote paste. Place each chicken breast half between 2 sheets of heavy-duty plastic wrap, and pound to ½-inch thickness using a meat mallet or small heavy skillet. Add chicken to bag; seal and marinate in refrigerator 30 minutes, turning bag occasionally.

3 Prepare grill.

4 Remove chicken from bag; discard marinade. Place chicken on grill rack coated with cooking spray; grill 5 minutes on each side or until done. Let stand 15 minutes. Shred with 2 forks.

5 Lightly coat tortillas on each side with cooking spray. Place tortillas on grill rack; grill 2 minutes on each side or until lightly browned.

6 Arrange 2 tortillas, overlapping halfway, on each of 6 plates. Top each serving with about ½ cup chicken and about ½ cup pickled onions. Drizzle evenly with vinegar mixture. Top each serving with ⅓ cup lettuce, 2 tablespoons avocado, and 2 tablespoons cheese. Garnish with jalapeños, sour cream, and cilantro, if desired. Yield: 6 servings.

CALORIES 314 (24% from fat); FAT 8.3g (sat 2.5g, mono 3.2g, poly 1.3g); PROTEIN 33g; CARB 27g; FIBER 3.7g; CHOL 76mg; IRON 1.6mg; SODIUM 213mg; CALC 141mg

MAKE AHEAD
Frozen Mint Margaritas

We use silver, or clear, tequila in this recipe. For an appealing presentation, rub the rims of the margarita glasses with lime wedges and dip the rims in a half-and-half mixture of kosher salt and sugar. Serve with fresh lime wedges as a garnish, if desired.

- 1 cup sugar
- 1 cup packed fresh mint leaves
- 2 cups water
- ¾ cup tequila, divided
- ½ cup fresh lime juice (about 4 limes)
- 2 tablespoons Grand Marnier (orange-flavored liqueur)
- 3 to 4 dashes Angostura bitters (optional)

1 Combine first 3 ingredients and ½ cup tequila in a medium saucepan over medium heat; cook 3 minutes or until tiny bubbles form around edge of pan. Remove tequila mixture from heat; steep 15 minutes. Strain through a sieve into a bowl; discard mint. Stir in juice, Grand Marnier, and remaining ¼ cup tequila. Cool to room temperature. Add bitters, if desired.

2 Place mixture in a zip-top plastic bag; seal and freeze 2 hours (alcohol will separate). Knead bag to combine mixture. Pour ⅔ cup margarita into each of 6 margarita glasses. Yield: 6 servings.

CALORIES 222 (0% from fat); FAT 0g; PROTEIN 0.1g; CARB 36.9g; FIBER 0.2g; CHOL 0mg; IRON 0.1mg; SODIUM 1mg; CALC 6mg

Bring Out Their Best

Coax more flavor and nutrition from your produce with these secrets to proper care and handling.

FRESH FRUITS AND vegetables are among the most nutritious foods you can choose. They're low in calories yet rich in vitamins, minerals, fiber, and antioxidants. That's why produce, along with whole grains, forms the basis of a healthful diet. What's more, the way you store, prepare, and cook these foods can magnify (or preserve) their already healthful properties.

Soba Salad with Soy-Wasabi Vinaigrette

In addition to their satisfying textures, steamed vegetables retain more water-soluble nutrients than their boiled counterparts. Curly soba noodles, found in the international or ethnic aisle of your grocery store, impart a neutral flavor that works well in this Asian-inspired entrée.

 1 garlic clove
 6 ounces Japanese curly noodles
    (chucka soba), uncooked
 1 cup frozen shelled edamame
    (green soybeans)
 4 ounces snow peas, trimmed and
    halved crosswise (about 1½ cups)
 4 ounces whole baby carrots,
    quartered lengthwise
 3 tablespoons rice vinegar
 3 tablespoons low-sodium soy sauce
 1 tablespoon sesame oil
 1 tablespoon prepared wasabi paste
 ½ cup thinly sliced radishes

❶ Mince garlic; let stand 10 minutes.
❷ Cook pasta according to package directions, omitting salt and fat. Drain and rinse with cold water; drain well.
❸ Steam edamame, peas, and carrots 4 minutes or until crisp-tender. Drain and plunge vegetables into ice water; drain.
❹ Combine garlic, vinegar, and next 3 ingredients in a large bowl; stir with a whisk. Add pasta, vegetable mixture, and radishes; toss gently to coat. Serve immediately. Yield: 4 servings (serving size: about 1½ cups).

CALORIES 274 (20% from fat); FAT 6g (sat 0.7g, mono 1.6g, poly 2.2g); PROTEIN 9.2g; CARB 41.6g; FIBER 4g; CHOL 0mg; IRON 2mg; SODIUM 740mg; CALC 47mg

QUICK & EASY
Grilled Ginger-Lime Shrimp

Since the chopped garlic is part of the marinade, which adheres well to the shrimp, it has plenty of time to develop its potent nutritional compounds. Serve over rice.

 ½ cup fresh cilantro leaves
 ¼ cup thinly sliced green onions
 2 tablespoons chopped peeled fresh
    ginger
 1 tablespoon fresh lime juice
 1 tablespoon canola oil
 ½ teaspoon salt
 ½ teaspoon dark sesame oil
 4 garlic cloves, chopped
 1 jalapeño pepper, seeded and
    chopped
 1½ pounds large shrimp, peeled and
    deveined (about 32 shrimp)
    Cooking spray

❶ Combine first 9 ingredients in a food processor, and process until coarsely chopped.
❷ Combine cilantro mixture and shrimp in a large zip-top plastic bag; seal and shake well. Refrigerate 30 minutes.
❸ Prepare grill.
❹ Remove shrimp from bag; discard marinade. Thread 4 shrimp on each of 8 (8-inch) skewers. Place shrimp skewers on a grill rack coated with cooking spray; grill 5 minutes or until done, turning once. Yield: 4 servings (serving size: 2 skewers).

CALORIES 204 (22% from fat); FAT 5g (sat 0.7g, mono 1.6g, poly 1.8g); PROTEIN 34.7g; CARB 2.9g; FIBER 0.3g; CHOL 259mg; IRON 4.2mg; SODIUM 401mg; CALC 95mg

QUICK & EASY
Steamed Carrots with Garlic-Ginger Butter

(pictured on page 254)

Be sure to use true baby carrots with tops. So-called baby carrots sold in bags are often whittled-down mature vegetables; their texture will be too tough for this recipe.

 2 garlic cloves
 1 pound baby carrots with tops,
    peeled
 1 tablespoon butter
 1 teaspoon minced peeled fresh ginger
 1 tablespoon chopped fresh cilantro
 ½ teaspoon grated lime rind
 1 tablespoon fresh lime juice
 ¼ teaspoon salt

❶ Mince garlic; let stand 10 minutes.
❷ Steam carrots, covered, 10 minutes or until tender.
❸ Heat butter in large nonstick skillet over medium heat. Add garlic and ginger to pan; cook 1 minute, stirring constantly. Remove from heat; stir in carrots, cilantro, and remaining ingredients. Yield: 4 servings.

CALORIES 69 (39% from fat); FAT 3g (sat 1.8g, mono 0.8g, poly 0.2g); PROTEIN 0.9g; CARB 10.3g; FIBER 3.4g; CHOL 8mg; IRON 1.1mg; SODIUM 257mg; CALC 41mg

Fingerling Potato Salad with Gremolata Dressing

Great for salads because they hold their shape once cooked, these fingerlings are steamed, which enables them to retain more nutrients than boiled.

- ½ pound white fingerling potatoes
- ½ pound red fingerling potatoes
- 2 tablespoons fresh lemon juice
- ½ teaspoon salt
- ¼ teaspoon freshly ground black pepper
- 1 tablespoon extravirgin olive oil
- 1 teaspoon grated lemon rind
- 1 garlic clove, crushed and minced
- 1 tablespoon chopped fresh flat-leaf parsley
- 1 tablespoon capers, drained

❶ Steam potatoes, covered, 12 minutes or until tender. Cover and chill.
❷ Combine juice, salt, and pepper in a large bowl; slowly add oil, stirring well with a whisk. Stir in rind and garlic; let stand 10 minutes. Stir in parsley and capers.
❸ Cut potatoes into quarters; add potatoes to juice mixture, tossing to coat. Yield: 4 servings (serving size: ³/₄ cup).

CALORIES 125 (26% from fat); FAT 3.6g (sat 0.5g, mono 2.5g, poly 0.4g); PROTEIN 2.6g; CARB 21.4g; FIBER 2.2g; CHOL 0mg; IRON 1mg SODIUM 370mg; CALC 16mg

QUICK & EASY
Clams in Tomato-Basil Broth

Cooking tomato in oil renders lycopene more easily absorbed by the body.

- 4 garlic cloves
- 1 tablespoon olive oil
- 1 cup finely chopped onion (1 small)
- 3 cups coarsely chopped tomato (2 large)
- ½ cup white wine
- ½ cup clam juice
- ¼ teaspoon crushed red pepper
- 4 dozen littleneck clams (about 2¼ pounds)
- ¼ cup chopped fresh basil

❶ Mince garlic; let stand 10 minutes.
❷ Heat oil in a large Dutch oven over medium heat. Add onion to pan, and cook 3 minutes or until tender, stirring occasionally. Add garlic, and cook 1 minute, stirring constantly.
❸ Add tomato and next 3 ingredients to pan; bring to a boil. Add clams; cover and cook 8 minutes or until clams open. Discard any unopened shells. Stir in basil. Yield: 4 servings (serving size: 2 cups).

CALORIES 141 (30% from fat); FAT 4.7g (sat 0.6g, mono 2.6g, poly 0.8g); PROTEIN 15.2g; CARB 9.6g; FIBER 1.6g; CHOL 38mg; IRON 16mg; SODIUM 132mg; CALC 79mg

Chile-Spiced Fruit Salad with Queso Fresco

Watermelon develops more of the antioxidant lycopene when stored at room temperature. Serve this dish as a side, or as a sweet-spicy dessert.

- ¼ cup sugar
- ¼ cup water
- 1 large jalapeño pepper, cut in half lengthwise
- 2 cups cubed seedless watermelon
- 1 cup fresh blueberries
- 1 large peach, peeled and sliced
- 2 tablespoons fresh lime juice
- 7½ teaspoons crumbled queso fresco

❶ Combine sugar and ¼ cup water in a medium heavy saucepan; bring to a boil. Cook 15 seconds or until sugar dissolves. Remove from heat; add jalapeño to sugar mixture. Cover and let stand 1 hour or until cooled to room temperature. Strain sugar mixture through a fine mesh sieve into a bowl; discard solids.
❷ Combine watermelon, blueberries, and peach in a large bowl. Stir in sugar mixture and juice, tossing gently to coat. Sprinkle with cheese. Yield: 5 servings (serving size: about ²/₃ cup salad and about 1 teaspoon cheese).

CALORIES 105 (9% from fat); FAT 0.4g (sat 0.3g, mono 0.1g, poly 0.1g); PROTEIN 2g; CARB 24.2g; FIBER 1.7g; CHOL 2mg; IRON 0.4mg; SODIUM 12mg; CALC 32mg

Slice It Right

Clinical trials have shown that eating about two cloves of garlic per day may help prevent platelets in blood from clumping, which may help keep your arteries unobstructed and reduce your risk of heart attack. Lab studies have linked those benefits to thiosulfinates, compounds that also give garlic and onions their pungent smell.

To test how different preparation and cooking methods affected thiosulfinates, plant geneticist Philipp Simon, PhD, of the University of Wisconsin, Madison, and a group of researchers at Cuyo University in Argentina gathered four pounds of garlic and crushed half with a garlic press. They let all the garlic sit at room temperature for 10 minutes and then cooked batches of each sample in a 400° oven, in a microwave, or in boiling water for up to 20 minutes. Next, they tested whether each batch of garlic could alter how well blood platelets clumped. Garlic cooked whole had no anti-clumping ability, but crushed, lightly cooked garlic had a significant effect in reducing platelet clumping.

The reason: Thiosulfinates don't form until the clove is crushed or cut. "At the moment of cutting, thiosulfinates are formed," Simon explains. "The more cells you break, the more of the compound is released, so chop garlic as best you can into little pieces." Let chopped garlic sit for 10 minutes to allow time for thiosulfinates to develop, then cook briefly, or not at all. When preparing a meal, chop the amount you need and set it aside while you complete other tasks, such as preheating the oven.

Cook It Carefully

Vitamins come in two forms: fat-soluble, which includes vitamins A, D, E, and K; and water-soluble, such as vitamin C and B vitamins (like thiamin, niacin, riboflavin, and folate). As the name suggests, water-soluble vitamins dissolve in water—either inside your body or on your stovetop. (Fat-soluble vitamins employ different absorption mechanisms.)

"Fruits and vegetables are 80 to 90 percent water," says food biochemist Diane Barrett, PhD, of the Department of Food Science and Technology at the University of California, Davis. "You lose the structure of the cells with heat from cooking, and water-soluble nutrients leach into the cooking water." Last year in a review of 56 studies that examined the effects of cooking on nutrient retention, researchers from Barrett's group found that boiled fresh produce, on average, loses up to 55 percent of its vitamin C and 66 percent of its thiamin in cooking water. If you don't consume the cooking water, you don't fully benefit from the vitamins in it.

Steaming helps fruits and vegetables retain water-soluble vitamins. More nutrients remain inside a steamed vegetable since little water is used and there is minimal contact between the food and water. A study from Denmark's Royal Veterinary and Agricultural University found that boiled broccoli retained only 45 to 64 percent of vitamin C after five minutes, whereas steamed broccoli maintained levels of 83 to 100 percent.

Besides the nutritional benefit, steamed vegetables have a pleasing texture. "Steam vegetables until they are crisp-tender," Neville says. "Then you'll get brighter colors and fresher flavors."

Limiting the amount of time you cook a fruit or vegetable also can help preserve its nutrients. "If you heat foods in boiling water or a hot oven, the heat has to penetrate from the outside in," Barrett says. During that time, cell walls are broken down, releasing nutrients. Microwaving quickly and uniformly applies heat throughout the produce, cooking in less time so fewer nutrients are lost.

Heirloom Tomato Ketchup

Both store-bought and homemade ketchup contain lycopene, an antioxidant associated with decreased risk of chronic diseases. We found this rendition well worth making because it has about half the sodium of regular ketchup.

- 2 garlic cloves
- ½ teaspoon yellow mustard seeds
- ½ teaspoon celery seeds
- ¼ teaspoon whole allspice
- ¼ teaspoon black peppercorns
- 3 pounds heirloom tomatoes, cut into chunks (about 4½ cups)
- 2 cups chopped onion (1 medium)
- 1 cup chopped red bell pepper (1 small)
- ⅓ cup cider vinegar
- 1 tablespoon sugar
- ½ teaspoon salt

1 Chop garlic; let stand 10 minutes.
2 Place mustard seeds and next 3 ingredients on a double layer of cheesecloth. Gather edges of cheesecloth together; tie securely.
3 Combine cheesecloth bag, garlic, tomatoes, and next 3 ingredients in a large Dutch oven; bring to a boil. Cover, reduce heat, and simmer 20 minutes. Remove cheesecloth bag, and set aside.
4 Place half of tomato mixture in a blender. Remove center piece of blender lid (to allow steam to escape); secure blender lid on blender. Place a clean towel over opening in blender lid (to avoid splatters). Blend until smooth. Strain smooth mixture through a fine mesh sieve into a bowl; discard solids. Repeat procedure with remaining tomato mixture. Return mixture to pan. Add cheesecloth bag, sugar, and salt to pan, and bring to a boil. Reduce heat, and simmer, uncovered, until reduced to 1 cup (about 45 minutes). Yield: 1 cup (serving size: 1 tablespoon).

CALORIES 23 (8% from fat); FAT 0.2g (sat 0g, mono 0g, poly 0.1g); PROTEIN 0.9g; CARB 5g; FIBER 1.2g; CHOL 0mg; IRON 0.3mg; SODIUM 79mg; CALC 11mg

Grilled Grouper with Basil-Lime Pistou

Pistou (pees-TOO) is a southern French interpretation of pesto, the Italian herb and nut paste. Resting the chopped garlic allows heart-healthful compounds to develop. You can also prepare the fish in a grill pan, cooking it about four minutes on each side.

PISTOU:
- 1 cup fresh basil leaves
- ¼ cup (1 ounce) grated fresh Parmesan cheese
- ½ teaspoon grated lime rind
- 2 tablespoons fresh lime juice
- 1½ tablespoons extravirgin olive oil
- ⅛ teaspoon salt
- 3 garlic cloves

GROUPER:
- 4 (6-ounce) grouper fillets (about ½ inch thick)
- ½ teaspoon salt
- ¼ teaspoon freshly ground black pepper
- Cooking spray

1 To prepare pistou, combine first 7 ingredients in a food processor; pulse until finely chopped. Let stand 10 minutes.
2 Prepare grill.
3 To prepare grouper, sprinkle fish evenly with ½ teaspoon salt and pepper. Place fish on grill rack coated with cooking spray; grill 4 minutes on each side or until fish flakes easily when tested with a fork. Serve with pistou. Yield: 4 servings (serving size: 1 fillet and about 1 tablespoon pistou).

CALORIES 226 (33% from fat); FAT 8.2g (sat 2g, mono 4.5g, poly 1.2g); PROTEIN 34.1g; CARB 2.2g; FIBER 0.6g; CHOL 64mg; IRON 1.9mg; SODIUM 514mg; CALC 105mg

WINE NOTE: Soellner Wogenrain Grüner Veltliner 2006 ($16) from Austria boasts herbal and green pea aromas that pair well with the fresh, green flavors of this dish. The wine's bright, mouthwatering acidity slices through the olive oil and brings out the lime zest.

Steamed Green Beans with Tomato-Garlic Vinaigrette

The heady, tangy vinaigrette complements the crisp, sweet green beans. Use a garlic press, if you have one, to crush the garlic for this summery dressing; a press crushes garlic into small pieces, encouraging good-for-you compounds to develop.

- 1 tablespoon white wine vinegar
- ½ teaspoon Dijon mustard
- ¼ teaspoon salt
- ⅛ teaspoon freshly ground black pepper
- 2 garlic cloves, crushed and minced
- 1 tablespoon extravirgin olive oil
- ½ cup seeded chopped tomato
- 2 teaspoons chopped fresh thyme
- 1 pound green beans, trimmed

① Combine first 5 ingredients in a medium bowl; slowly add oil, stirring with a whisk to combine. Stir in tomato and thyme; let stand 10 minutes.
② Steam beans, covered, 7 minutes or until crisp-tender. Cut into 2-inch pieces; add to tomato mixture, tossing gently to coat. Yield: 4 servings (serving size: ¾ cup).

CALORIES 73 (44% from fat); FAT 3.6g (sat 0.5g, mono 2.5g, poly 0.5g); PROTEIN 2.4g; CARB 9.8g; FIBER 4.2g; CHOL 0mg; IRON 1.4mg; SODIUM 162mg; CALC 48mg

Watermelon-Ginger Punch

Loosely based on a Korean watermelon and ginger beverage, this refreshingly sweet drink will maximize lycopene if you allow the whole fruit to ripen at room temperature instead of putting it in the fridge right after purchase. You can chill the punch (and any leftover melon) for up to two days without significantly reducing the amount of antioxidant in the fruit.

- 8 cups seedless watermelon cubes, divided
- ½ cup sugar
- ½ cup fresh lime juice
- 2 tablespoons grated peeled fresh ginger
- 18 (1-inch) seedless watermelon balls
- 1 cup sparkling water, chilled
  Cracked ice (optional)

① Place 4 cups watermelon in a blender; process until smooth. Strain through a sieve into a pitcher; discard solids. Repeat procedure with remaining watermelon. Combine sugar, juice, and ginger in a bowl; stir with a whisk until sugar dissolves. Add juice mixture and watermelon balls to pitcher; stir in sparkling water just before serving. Serve over cracked ice, if desired. Yield: 6 servings (serving size: 1 cup).

CALORIES 143 (3% from fat); FAT 0.3g (sat 0g, mono 0.1g, poly 0.1g); PROTEIN 1.6g; CARB 36.8g; FIBER 1.1g; CHOL 0mg; IRON 0.6mg; SODIUM 11mg; CALC 22mg

Harvest Lycopene

In the case of lycopene, temperature affects its development and availability. Lycopene is an antioxidant that gives tomatoes, watermelon, guavas, and red-fleshed grapefruits their rich red color.

In 2006, a team from the USDA Agricultural Research Service in Lane, Oklahoma tested lycopene levels by gathering watermelons and storing them at 41° (roughly the temperature inside a refrigerator), 55° (the temperature of a cooler), or 70° (room temperature). After two weeks, they found that melons stored at room temperature developed a richer rouge and gained as much as 40 percent more lycopene (14 milligrams per 1½-cup serving), depending on the variety, than melons stored in the refrigerator. That's nearly half of an acceptable daily intake of 30 milligrams of lycopene.

"Fruits and vegetables are alive after they're harvested," says Penelope Perkins-Veazie, PhD, the plant physiologist who conducted the watermelon study. "The normal biological processes in watermelon that produce lycopene are strong at room temperature, while cooler temperatures slow them down."

Perkins-Veazie recommends letting a whole melon sit on the counter for up to five days to fully ripen and develop lycopene. Then place it in the fridge to chill before enjoying (unless the melon has been cut, in which case it should be refrigerated immediately). "It will taste sweeter and crisper if it's cold, and if stored for two days or less you will not lose any of the lycopene gained while the melon sat out," Perkins-Veazie says.

Tomatoes' supply of lycopene also is affected by temperature, but in a different way. "With the lycopene from tomatoes, the benefits are actually better when they're processed," says Neville. "Lycopene is inside cells, and when the cell walls are broken during processing, it's released and can be absorbed," says Steven J. Schwartz, PhD, professor of food science at Ohio State University in Columbus. Heat alters lycopene's molecular structure, making it two to three times easier for our bodies to absorb than raw.

Allow whole watermelons to sit on the counter for up to five days to fully ripen and develop lycopene.

Summer Squash

Here are some quick and easy ways to prepare the most popular varieties.

Zucchini and other summer squash are abundant and inexpensive at markets during the summer.

While zucchini and yellow crookneck squash are among the most familiar varieties, you'll also find yellow squash (which look like a golden version of zucchini); small, scallop-shaped green, yellow, and white pattypan squash; and scallopini (shaped like pattypan but larger and speckled green). And you'll occasionally see the round green Eight Ball and elongated green tatuma.

Select firm, unblemished squash. Smaller ones are tender and have bright flavor, while larger ones tend to be watery and seedy (use larger squash in baked goods, which benefit from their moisture). Store squash in a perforated plastic bag in the refrigerator crisper drawer for up to three days. The skin and seeds are edible, so you needn't worry about peeling and seeding it. And unlike its cool-weather cousins, summer squash cooks quickly.

Summer squash are mild-flavored, so you can use them interchangeably in most recipes. They're delicious raw. But cooking, especially sautéing or grilling, enhances their flavor and softens their texture.

Parmesan Zucchini Sticks with Smoky Roasted Romesco Sauce

Crunchy breaded zucchini spears are delicious dipped in a summery sauce of roasted red peppers. The sauce is a zesty embellishment for grilled meats, too.

SAUCE:

- 3 red bell peppers
- 2 plum tomatoes, halved lengthwise
- ½ cup (½-inch) cubed French bread baguette, crusts removed
- 1½ tablespoons smoked almonds
- 1 tablespoon extravirgin olive oil
- 1 tablespoon sherry vinegar or red wine vinegar
- ¼ teaspoon Spanish smoked paprika
- ¼ teaspoon kosher salt
- ⅛ teaspoon ground red pepper
- 1 large garlic clove

ZUCCHINI:

- 3 large zucchini (about 1½ pounds)
- 1 cup dry breadcrumbs
- ½ cup panko (Japanese breadcrumbs)
- ¼ cup (1 ounce) grated fresh Parmesan cheese
- ½ teaspoon salt
- ½ teaspoon freshly ground black pepper
- ½ cup egg substitute
- Cooking spray

1 Preheat broiler.

2 To prepare sauce, cut bell peppers in half lengthwise; discard seeds and membranes. Place bell pepper halves and tomatoes, skin sides up, on a foil-lined baking sheet; flatten bell peppers with hand. Broil 10 minutes or until blackened. Place in a zip-top plastic bag; seal. Let stand 15 minutes. Peel and coarsely chop, reserving any liquid.

3 Combine bell peppers, tomatoes, reserved liquid, cubed bread, and next 7 ingredients in a blender or food processor; process until smooth.

4 Preheat oven to 400°.

5 To prepare zucchini, cut each zucchini in half crosswise; cut each half length-wise into 8 wedges. Combine breadcrumbs and next 4 ingredients in a shallow dish, and place egg substitute in another. Dip zucchini in egg substitute; dredge in breadcrumb mixture. Place zucchini on a wire rack coated with cooking spray. Lightly coat zucchini with cooking spray. Bake at 400° for 25 minutes or until golden brown. Serve immediately with sauce. Yield: 8 servings (serving size: 6 zucchini sticks and ¼ cup sauce).

CALORIES 170 (30% from fat); FAT 5.6g (sat 1.3g, mono 2.5g, poly 1.3g); PROTEIN 8.4g; CARB 23.4g; FIBER 3.9g; CHOL 3mg; IRON 1.9mg; SODIUM 434mg; CALC 107mg

MAKE AHEAD
Squash and Rice Salad with Shrimp and Herbs

Prepare the salad up to a day ahead so the flavors fully develop.

- 3 tablespoons seasoned rice vinegar
- 1 teaspoon finely grated lime rind
- 2 tablespoons freshly squeezed lime juice
- 2 tablespoons minced shallots
- ½ teaspoon salt
- ½ teaspoon crushed red pepper
- 3 tablespoons peanut oil
- 3 cups cooked white rice
- 2 cups diced zucchini (about ¾ pound)
- ¼ cup finely chopped red onion
- ¼ cup chopped fresh basil
- 3 tablespoons chopped fresh mint
- 1 pound cooked and peeled medium shrimp

1 Combine first 6 ingredients; let stand 10 minutes. Add oil; stir with a whisk.

2 Combine vinegar mixture, rice, and remaining ingredients in a large bowl; toss well. Cover and refrigerate at least 2 hours. Yield: 4 servings (serving size: 1½ cups).

CALORIES 387 (30% from fat); FAT 13g (sat 2.3g, mono 5.5g, poly 4.6g); PROTEIN 27.4g; CARB 39.5g; FIBER 1.7g; CHOL 172mg; IRON 4.7mg; SODIUM 474mg; CALC 94mg

Summer Squash Pizza

(pictured on page 255)

You can use all zucchini or yellow squash for this grilled pie. Serve one slice as an appetizer or two with a salad for a simple supper.

- 1 teaspoon olive oil
- 1 teaspoon balsamic vinegar
- ⅛ teaspoon salt
- ⅛ teaspoon freshly ground black pepper
- 1 zucchini, cut lengthwise into ¼-inch-thick slices
- 1 yellow squash, cut lengthwise into ¼-inch-thick slices
- Cooking spray
- 1 (12-inch) packaged pizza crust (such as Mama Mary's)
- 2 plum tomatoes, cut into ⅛-inch-thick slices
- ¼ cup (1 ounce) finely grated pecorino Romano cheese
- 2 tablespoons thinly sliced fresh basil
- ½ teaspoon finely chopped fresh oregano

1 Prepare grill.
2 Combine first 6 ingredients in a large bowl, tossing gently to coat. Place squash mixture on grill rack coated with cooking spray; grill 2 minutes on each side or until tender.
3 Reduce grill temperature to medium.
4 Lightly coat pizza crust with cooking spray; grill 1 minute on each side or until lightly toasted. Arrange zucchini and squash over crust. Arrange tomatoes over squash; sprinkle with cheese. Grill 5 minutes or until thoroughly heated. Remove from grill; sprinkle with basil and oregano. Yield: 8 servings (serving size: 1 slice).

CALORIES 165 (33% from fat); FAT 6.1g (sat 1.5g, mono 0.7g, poly 0.1g); PROTEIN 5.6g; CARB 23.5g; FIBER 1.5g; CHOL 4mg; IRON 1.6mg; SODIUM 225mg; CALC 92mg

Zucchini-Orange Bread

Using grated zucchini in baked goods is a classic way to use surplus squash.

BREAD:
- 3 cups all-purpose flour (about 13½ ounces)
- 1 teaspoon salt
- 1 teaspoon baking powder
- ¼ teaspoon baking soda
- 1 cup granulated sugar
- ½ cup egg substitute
- ⅓ cup canola oil
- 1 tablespoon grated orange rind
- 1 tablespoon fresh orange juice
- 2 cups shredded zucchini (about 1 large)
- ½ cup coarsely chopped walnuts
- Cooking spray

GLAZE:
- ½ cup powdered sugar
- 2 tablespoons fresh orange juice

1 Preheat oven to 350°.
2 To prepare bread, lightly spoon flour into dry measuring cups; level with a knife. Combine flour and next 3 ingredients in a large bowl, stirring with a whisk; make a well in center of mixture. Combine granulated sugar and next 4 ingredients. Add sugar mixture to flour mixture, stirring just until moist. Fold in zucchini and walnuts. Divide batter between 2 (8 x 4–inch) loaf pans coated with cooking spray. Bake at 350° for 50 minutes or until a wooden pick inserted in center comes out clean. Cool 10 minutes in pans on a wire rack; remove from pans.
3 To prepare glaze, combine powdered sugar and 2 tablespoons juice, stirring with a whisk. Drizzle evenly over warm loaves. Cool completely on wire rack. Yield: 2 loaves, 12 slices each (serving size: 1 slice).

CALORIES 145 (32% from fat); FAT 5.1g (sat 0.4g, mono 2.1g, poly 2.3g); PROTEIN 2.8g; CARB 22.5g; FIBER 0.7g; CHOL 0mg; IRON 1mg; SODIUM 142mg; CALC 21mg

Sweet and Sour Pattypan Squash and Green Beans

Serve these pickles with cocktails or with grilled poultry or fish. This recipe makes four (one-pint) jars—enough to keep and give away to friends and neighbors.

- ½ pound green beans, trimmed
- 2 cups seasoned rice vinegar
- 2 cups white vinegar
- ⅔ cup sugar
- 1 teaspoon salt
- 5 cups halved yellow baby pattypan squash (about 1½ pounds)
- 3 tablespoons thinly sliced shallots
- 1 tablespoon sesame seeds
- ½ teaspoon crushed red pepper
- 12 black peppercorns
- 12 cilantro sprigs
- 4 garlic cloves, crushed
- 4 (¼-inch-thick) slices peeled fresh ginger

1 Cook beans in boiling water 1 minute. Drain and plunge beans into ice water; drain.
2 Combine rice vinegar and next 3 ingredients in a medium saucepan; bring to a boil. Cook until sugar dissolves.
3 Combine beans, squash, and remaining ingredients in a large bowl. Pour hot vinegar mixture over squash mixture. Toss well. Cover and refrigerate 8 hours, stirring occasionally. Yield: 8 cups (serving size: ¼ cup).
NOTE: Squash mixture can be evenly divided among 4 (1-pint) jars. Store in refrigerator up to 1 week.

CALORIES 86 (2% from fat); FAT 0.2g (sat 0g, mono 0g, poly 0.1g); PROTEIN 0.5g; CARB 21.1g; FIBER 0.4g; CHOL 0mg; IRON 0.4mg; SODIUM 385mg; CALC 13mg

Cucuzza-Tomato Sauce over Spaghetti

Cooking Light Associate Art Director Shay McNamee's grandfather grows cucuzza (a squash similar to zucchini), and her Sicilian-born grandmother uses it to prepare this garlicky recipe. You can substitute zucchini or yellow squash.

- 2 tablespoons olive oil
- ½ cup chopped onion (about 1 small)
- 6 garlic cloves, minced
- 1 teaspoon salt
- ½ teaspoon freshly ground black pepper
- 2 (26-ounce) jars fat-free tomato-basil pasta sauce
- 1 (1¼-pound) cucuzza, peeled and cut crosswise into ¼-inch-thick slices (about 5 cups)
- 8 cups hot cooked spaghetti (1 pound uncooked)
- ½ cup (2 ounces) grated Parmesan cheese
- ½ cup thinly sliced fresh basil

❶ Heat oil in a Dutch oven over medium-high heat. Add onion to pan, and sauté 4 minutes or until tender. Add garlic, and sauté 30 seconds. Add salt and next 3 ingredients to pan. Reduce heat, and simmer 55 minutes or until squash is tender. Serve over pasta. Sprinkle with cheese and basil. Yield: 8 servings (serving size: 1 cup pasta, ¾ cup squash mixture, 1 tablespoon cheese, and 1 tablespoon basil).

CALORIES 355 (15% from fat); FAT 5.9g (sat 1.4g, mono 2.9g, poly 0.5g); PROTEIN 13g; CARB 60.3g; FIBER 5.1g; CHOL 4mg; IRON 1.2mg; SODIUM 238mg; CALC 235mg

Marinating

Whether it's a short dip or a long soak, this method enhances a variety of foods.

MARINATING IS A versatile and indispensable technique. It boosts the flavor of lean cuts of meat and also works wonders with vegetables and fruits. It doesn't require special equipment and involves simple steps to produce unfussy—but delicious—food.

STAFF FAVORITE
Maple Grilled Salmon

The sweet-sour marinade is cooked down to a syrupy glaze that's brushed on the fish as it cooks. The citrus and maple flavors would also be tasty with pork.

- ¼ cup rice wine vinegar
- 3 tablespoons maple syrup
- 2 tablespoons fresh orange juice
- 4 (6-ounce) salmon fillets, skinned
- Cooking spray
- ¼ teaspoon salt
- ¼ teaspoon freshly ground black pepper

❶ Combine first 3 ingredients in a large zip-top plastic bag; add fish. Seal and marinate in refrigerator 3 hours.
❷ Preheat grill or grill pan to medium-high heat.
❸ Remove fish from bag, reserving marinade. Pour marinade into a small saucepan; bring to a boil. Cook until reduced to 2 tablespoons (about 5 minutes).
❹ Place fish on grill rack or pan coated with cooking spray; grill 4 minutes on each side or until fish flakes easily when tested with a fork or until desired degree of doneness, basting occasionally with marinade. Remove fish from grill; sprinkle with salt and pepper. Yield: 4 servings (serving size: 1 fillet).

CALORIES 270 (35% from fat); FAT 10.6g (sat 2.5g, mono 4.6g, poly 2.5g); PROTEIN 31.1g; CARB 11g; FIBER 0.1g; CHOL 80mg; IRON 0.7mg; SODIUM 216mg; CALC 27mg

MAKE AHEAD
Red Wine–Marinated Beef Stew

- 5 parsley sprigs
- 5 thyme sprigs
- 1 bay leaf
- 3 cups dry red wine
- 1½ cups vertically sliced onion (about 1 medium)
- ½ cup thinly sliced carrot
- 2 garlic cloves, minced
- 1 (2-pound) boneless chuck roast, trimmed and cut into 1-inch cubes
- Cooking spray
- 1 pound cremini mushrooms, halved
- ¼ cup all-purpose flour (about 1 ounce)
- 1 teaspoon salt, divided
- ½ teaspoon freshly ground black pepper, divided
- 2 cups less-sodium beef broth
- ¼ cup chopped fresh parsley

❶ Place first 3 ingredients on a double layer of cheesecloth. Gather edges of cheesecloth together; tie securely. Combine cheesecloth bag, wine, and next 4 ingredients in a large zip-top plastic bag; seal. Marinate in refrigerator 4 hours or up to 24 hours. Drain beef mixture in a colander over a bowl, reserving marinade. Set cheesecloth bag aside.
❷ Heat a large Dutch oven over medium-high heat. Coat pan with cooking spray. Add beef mixture to pan; sauté 6 minutes

or until browned, stirring occasionally. Remove beef mixture from pan. Add mushrooms to pan; sauté 3 minutes or until lightly browned, stirring occasionally. Return beef mixture to pan. Lightly spoon flour into a dry measuring cup; level with a knife. Add flour, ½ teaspoon salt, and ¼ teaspoon pepper to pan; cook 1 minute, stirring constantly. Add reserved marinade, cheesecloth bag, and broth; bring to a boil. Cover, reduce heat, and simmer 1½ hours or until beef is tender. Stir in remaining ½ teaspoon salt and remaining ¼ teaspoon pepper. Sprinkle with chopped parsley. Discard cheesecloth bag. Yield: 6 servings (serving size: 1 cup).

CALORIES 311 (28% from fat); FAT 9.7g (sat 2.8g, mono 5g, poly 0.4g); PROTEIN 40.7g; CARB 13.1g; FIBER 1.5g; CHOL 91mg; IRON 5.9mg; SODIUM 665mg; CALC 49mg

Teriyaki Pork and Pineapple

This sweet-salty marinade is excellent for almost any tender cut of meat that's cubed and skewered—chicken breasts or thighs, or beef tenderloin or sirloin. Reducing the marinade concentrates its flavor and helps it stick to the kebabs. Although we usually marinate in zip-top plastic bags, we recommend using a bowl for this recipe so it's easier to scoop out the pork with a slotted spoon. Serve over white and wild rice pilaf.

  ½ cup mirin (sweet rice wine)
  ½ cup sake (rice wine)
  ¼ cup low-sodium soy sauce
  1 pound pork tenderloin, trimmed and cut into 24 pieces
  24 (1-inch) pieces red onion (about 1 medium)
  24 (1-inch) cubes pineapple (about 12 ounces)
    Cooking spray

❶ Combine first 3 ingredients in a small saucepan; bring to a boil over medium-high heat. Cook until reduced to ⅔ cup (about 10 minutes). Remove from heat; cool completely.

❷ Combine cooled marinade and pork in a medium bowl. Cover and marinate in refrigerator 2 hours.
❸ Prepare grill to medium-high heat.
❹ Remove pork from bowl with a slotted spoon, reserving marinade. Place marinade in a small saucepan; bring to a boil. Reduce heat, and simmer 5 minutes. Cool slightly.
❺ Thread 2 pork cubes, 2 red onion pieces, and 2 pineapple cubes alternately onto each of 12 (8-inch) skewers. Lightly coat kebabs with cooking spray. Place kebabs on a grill rack coated with cooking spray; grill 3 minutes on each side or until done, basting frequently with marinade. Yield: 4 servings (serving size: 3 kebabs).

CALORIES 289 (17% from fat); FAT 5.4g (sat 1.8g, mono 2g, poly 0.5g); PROTEIN 24.4g; CARB 24.6g; FIBER 1.1g; CHOL 65mg; IRON 1.9mg; SODIUM 580mg; CALC 23mg

Chicken Baked in White Wine Marinade

Baking the chicken with the marinade infuses it with more flavor. Bone-in, skin-on chicken breasts stay moist and succulent; the skin is discarded after baking. For the prettiest presentation, remove meat from the bones, and slice thinly across the grain.

  1 cup dry white wine
  1 cup vertically sliced onion
  1 teaspoon chopped fresh thyme
  4 (8-ounce) bone-in chicken breast halves
  2 garlic cloves, minced
  1 bay leaf
  ½ teaspoon salt
  ¼ teaspoon freshly ground black pepper

❶ Combine first 6 ingredients in a large zip-top plastic bag; seal. Marinate in refrigerator 4 hours or up to 24 hours, turning occasionally.
❷ Preheat oven to 375°.
❸ Place chicken, skin sides up, in an 11 x 7–inch baking dish. Pour marinade over chicken. Cover and bake at 375° for 20 minutes. Uncover and bake an additional 40 minutes or until done. Transfer chicken to a platter. Discard skin, bay leaf, and marinade. Sprinkle chicken evenly with salt and pepper. Yield: 4 servings (serving size: 1 breast half).

CALORIES 184 (19% from fat); FAT 3.8g (sat 1.1g, mono 1.3g, poly 0.8g); PROTEIN 33.2g; CARB 2.1g; FIBER 0.3g; CHOL 90mg; IRON 1.3mg; SODIUM 377mg; CALC 24mg

Escabèche-Style Scallops

Escabèche is a Spanish dish in which cooked seafood is marinated and served cold as an appetizer. Though it's traditionally made with sardines, escabèche is also good with other seafood, including scallops and shrimp.

  1 pound medium sea scallops (18 to 24 count)
  2 tablespoons balsamic vinegar
  1 tablespoon extravirgin olive oil
  1 teaspoon finely chopped fresh thyme
  ¼ teaspoon salt
  ¼ teaspoon freshly ground black pepper
  3 cups trimmed watercress

❶ Heat a large cast-iron skillet over high heat. Add scallops to pan; cook 1 minute or until browned. Turn over, and cook 30 seconds. Place scallops in a bowl.
❷ Combine vinegar and next 4 ingredients, stirring with a whisk. Pour vinegar mixture over scallops. Cover and refrigerate 30 minutes, stirring occasionally. Arrange ½ cup watercress on each of 6 salad plates. Remove scallops from marinade with a slotted spoon, reserving marinade. Divide scallops evenly among plates. Drizzle each serving with about 1 tablespoon marinade. Yield: 6 servings.

CALORIES 93 (28% from fat); FAT 2.9g (sat 0.4g, mono 1.7g, poly 0.4g); PROTEIN 13.1g; CARB 3g; FIBER 0.1g; CHOL 25mg; IRON 0.4mg; SODIUM 228mg; CALC 41mg

All About Marinating

Marinating, Defined

It refers to soaking food (usually meat) in a flavorful liquid called a marinade. Marinating is a technique that's been around at least since the Renaissance, when acidic mixtures were commonly used to help preserve foods.

What Marinating Does

Ideally a marinade flavors, not tenderizes, foods. Though marinades are often purported to have tenderizing effects, the ingredients only permeate the surface of food and have little effect on the interior.

Best Bets for Marinating

Small or thin cuts of meat and poultry are generally good candidates. Larger cuts, such as roasts, may not benefit since they offer less surface area. Tender vegetables, such as mushrooms, zucchini, yellow squash, and eggplant, absorb flavor from marinades and taste especially good grilled. A brief stint works well for fish and shellfish (see "Soak Time" at right), and it's beneficial, too, for some tender fruits, such as berries, orange sections, and melons. (When it's fruit that is being marinated, the technique is called "macerating.")

Equipment

Because many marinades are acidic, it's best to soak food in a nonreactive container like those made of glass, ceramic, plastic, or stainless steel. Reactive metals such as aluminum or copper will respond to acids by discoloring the food and giving it a metallic taste. For easy cleanup, a zip-top plastic bag works well.

Marinade Ingredients

Many marinades include an acidic element, such as citrus juice or vinegar, which boosts flavor and may tenderize the surface proteins of meat. Oil is another common constituent, as it coats food, carries flavor, and helps food stay moist. Robust ingredients such as garlic, soy sauce, and Asian fish sauce enhance the savory qualities of meats and fish.

Types of Marinades

Perhaps the most common is the kind used to flavor fish or meat that is to be grilled or sautéed. Because these cooking methods only heat the meat to about 135 to 165°, well below the boiling point of alcohol, these marinades should not contain wine, or the meat will taste of alcohol.

Wine is fine, however, for a second kind of marinade, one used for stews and braises, because these dishes are cooked for a prolonged period at a temperature that boils off the alcohol and eliminates any harsh flavor.

A third kind of marinade includes those that "cook" raw foods, usually seafood (as in the popular Latin dish seviche). Lime and/or lemon juice turns the flesh opaque and firm so it appears "cooked," but the food is actually still raw.

A fourth category of marinade is used to marinate cooked fish in a vinegar-based mixture to impart more subtle flavors. (This type of dish is called *escabèche*.)

Safety Concerns

Always marinate meat and fish in the refrigerator. You can use some of the marinade for basting after removing the meat or fish from it only if you bring the marinade to a boil and cook for five minutes to kill any bacteria.

Although the acid in a marinade appears to "cook" raw fish in seviche, it doesn't eliminate bacteria the same way cooking with heat does. When marinating fish that won't be cooked, make sure the fish is sushi-grade, or frozen-at-sea (FAS) fish; both are safe for healthy adults to consume raw.

Soak Time

The length of time you marinate food depends on both the food and the marinade. Delicate fish, shellfish, and fruit usually soak for a shorter period of time (from 20 minutes to a few hours), while meats can go longer (up to a day or two). If, however, meat is soaking in a highly acidic marinade, its texture may turn grainy if soaked too long (more than a couple of hours, in most cases).

Season Last

For our recipes that include added salt, we sprinkle it on after food is cooked instead of including salt in the marinade. That way, none of the salt is lost when the marinade is discarded. Seasoning after the food is cooked also allows the small amount of salt we use to have a bigger impact on the overall taste.

The Bottom Line

The three most important elements to remember about marinating:
1 Marinate in a nonreactive container.
2 Soak food for only the time specified in the recipe.
3 Salt the food after it's cooked.

Soy-Marinated Chicken Thighs

Soy sauce is great in marinades for grilled meats, as it stands up to charred flavors. The simple solution would also be tasty with steaks, pork tenderloin, or pork chops.

- 3 tablespoons low-sodium soy sauce
- 2 tablespoons extravirgin olive oil
- 2 teaspoons chopped fresh thyme
- 8 (2-ounce) skinless, boneless chicken thighs
- 2 garlic cloves, minced
- Cooking spray

❶ Combine first 5 ingredients in a large zip-top plastic bag; seal. Marinate in refrigerator 4 hours or up to 24 hours, turning occasionally.
❷ Prepare grill to medium-high heat.
❸ Remove chicken from bag; discard marinade. Place chicken on grill rack coated with cooking spray; grill 3 minutes on each side or until done. Yield: 4 servings (serving size: 2 thighs).

CALORIES 136 (44% from fat); FAT 6.7g (sat 1.3g, mono 3.5g, poly 1.2g); PROTEIN 17.1g; CARB 0.8g; FIBER 0.1g; CHOL 71mg; IRON 1.1mg; SODIUM 273mg; CALC 12mg

Thai-Style Marinated Raw Fish

A pungent mixture of lime juice, fish sauce, and ginger infuses raw halibut with intense flavor for a unique first course. Don't marinate any longer than 30 minutes, as the citrus will begin to alter the texture of the fish. For food safety purposes, use thawed frozen-at-sea (FAS) halibut. (See "Safety Concerns" on page 204.)

- 1 pound halibut, skinned and cut into ⅛-inch-thick slices
- 3 tablespoons fresh lime juice
- 1 tablespoon fish sauce
- 1 teaspoon sugar
- 1 teaspoon grated peeled fresh ginger

❶ Divide fish slices evenly among 6 plates. Combine juice and remaining ingredients; brush evenly over fish. Cover and chill 30 minutes. Serve immediately. Yield: 6 servings.

CALORIES 89 (17% from fat); FAT 1.7g (sat 0.3g, mono 0.6g, poly 0.6g); PROTEIN 15.9g; CARB 1.5g; FIBER 0g; CHOL 24mg; IRON 0.7mg; SODIUM 260mg; CALC 38mg

Southeast Asian Grilled Flank Steak

Open-grained flank steak absorbs lots of flavor from this spicy marinade. Serve this dish with a salad of rice stick noodles, radishes, carrots, and snow peas.

- 3 tablespoons fresh lime juice
- 1 tablespoon sugar
- 1 tablespoon fish sauce
- 2 teaspoons Sriracha (hot chile sauce, such as Huy Fong)
- ½ teaspoon ground coriander
- 2 garlic cloves, minced
- 1 pound flank steak, trimmed
- Cooking spray
- ¼ teaspoon salt

❶ Combine first 6 ingredients in a large zip-top plastic bag. Add steak; seal and marinate in refrigerator 24 hours, turning occasionally.
❷ Prepare grill to medium-high heat.
❸ Remove steak from marinade; discard marinade.
❹ Place steak on grill rack coated with cooking spray; grill 4 minutes on each side or until desired degree of doneness. Remove steak from grill; sprinkle with salt. Let stand 5 minutes. Cut across grain into thin slices. Yield: 4 servings (serving size: 3 ounces).

CALORIES 180 (40% from fat); FAT 7.9g (sat 3.2g, mono 3.2g, poly 0.3g); PROTEIN 23.5g; CARB 2.5g; FIBER 0g; CHOL 43mg; IRON 1.6mg; SODIUM 374mg; CALC 18mg

Strawberries Romanoff

Marinating fruit in liquid is also called "macerating." Orange-flavored liqueur complements fresh berries in this classic dessert. Macerate for only the length of time specified so the strawberries retain their texture.

- 4 cups sliced strawberries (about 1½ pounds)
- 3 tablespoons powdered sugar
- ¼ cup Cointreau or Grand Marnier (orange-flavored liqueur)
- ⅓ cup whipping cream, chilled
- 3 tablespoons powdered sugar
- ¼ teaspoon vanilla extract
- Mint sprigs (optional)

❶ Combine first 3 ingredients in a bowl. Cover and chill 3½ hours.
❷ Place cream, 3 tablespoons sugar, and vanilla in a small bowl; beat with a mixer at high speed until stiff peaks form. Spoon over strawberry mixture. Garnish with mint, if desired. Serve immediately. Yield: 4 servings (serving size: about ¾ cup strawberry mixture and 3 tablespoons whipped cream mixture).

CALORIES 207 (29% from fat); FAT 6.7g (sat 3.9g, mono 1.9g, poly 0.5g); PROTEIN 1.6g; CARB 31.2g; FIBER 3.4g; CHOL 22mg; IRON 0.7mg; SODIUM 10mg; CALC 41mg

California Wine Country Cuisine

With its Mediterranean influences and quality local produce, this region's food showcases the season's best ingredients.

Northern California's wine country, including Napa and Sonoma counties, has a hospitable climate for cultivating diverse produce, in addition to the grapes that made the area famous. This intersection of produce, wine, and terrain inspires some of the country's most inventive chefs and lively vegetarian fare.

Although it's prized for innovation, the region's cuisine is true to its roots. Early settlers from Spain and Italy brought their cuisines and shaped the area's decidedly Mediterranean palate. Spanish missionaries planted some of the first olive trees centuries ago, and now olive orchards grow varieties like Spanish Manzanillo and Sevillano. These olives add zest and robust, fruity notes to vegetarian grilled pizzas and risottos or make a briny tapenade for sandwich spreads and dips. Italian immigrants brought grape varieties like sangiovese and nebbiolo, as well as pastas, breads, and fresh vegetable sauces flecked with herbs.

The region is known for its artisanal cheeses. Goat cheeses, sometimes ripened with vegetable ash, add creaminess to pastas or pizzas. The complex flavors and creamy or crumbly textures of blue cheese enhance simple salads or dips. From buttery soft to grating cheeses, cow's milk varieties add heft to sandwiches and pastas.

You can use the region's signature herbs, such as rosemary or thyme, to embellish fresh produce. California wine country's old-world culinary roots are a natural fit for the following summertime dishes.

Goat Cheese and Greens Piadine

A *piadina*, a thin, chewy flatbread cooked over coals, is an ideal vehicle to showcase fresh produce.

- 1 tablespoon minced shallots
- 2 tablespoons balsamic vinegar
- 2 teaspoons extravirgin olive oil
- ¼ teaspoon kosher salt
- ¼ teaspoon freshly ground black pepper
- 1 recipe Flatbread Dough (page 208)
- 2 tablespoons cornmeal
- 2 teaspoons extravirgin olive oil
- 3 cups trimmed arugula (about 2 ounces)
- 1½ cups thinly sliced ripe plums (about 2)
- 2½ tablespoons chopped unsalted almonds, toasted
- ½ cup (about 2 ounces) crumbled goat cheese

1 Preheat oven to 350°.
2 Combine first 5 ingredients in a large bowl; stir with a whisk. Set aside.
3 Punch Flatbread Dough down; cover and let rest 5 minutes. Divide dough into 2 equal portions. Working with one portion at a time (cover remaining dough), roll each half into a 12-inch circle on a floured surface. Place each dough circle on a baking sheet sprinkled with 1 tablespoon cornmeal. Brush each portion with 1 teaspoon oil, leaving ½-inch borders. Pierce entire surface liberally with a fork. Bake at 350° for 10 minutes or until crisp.
4 Add arugula, plums, and almonds to vinegar mixture; toss gently to coat.
5 Remove flatbreads to cutting board; top each with half of arugula mixture and ¼ cup goat cheese. Cut each piadina in half. Yield: 4 servings (serving size: ½ piadina).

CALORIES 421 (26% from fat); FAT 12g (sat 3.1g, mono 6.4g, poly 1.7g); PROTEIN 13.2g; CARB 65.6g; FIBER 4.2g; CHOL 7mg; IRON 4.6mg; SODIUM 476mg; CALC 75mg

Soup and Sandwich Menu
serves 6

This vegetarian plate is a fresh choice for a casual dinner with friends. You can prepare the soup up to a day ahead.

Sweet Corn and Squash Soup

Tomato-goat cheese sandwich
Lightly toast 12 sourdough bread slices. Rub the cut side of a halved garlic clove over one side of each of 6 bread slices. Spread 1 tablespoon soft goat cheese over each of remaining 6 bread slices. Combine 1 tablespoon balsamic vinegar, 2 teaspoons extravirgin olive oil, ¼ teaspoon kosher salt, and ¼ teaspoon freshly ground black pepper; drizzle evenly over 6 (½-inch) beefsteak tomato slices. Layer 1 bread slice, garlic side up; 1 beefsteak tomato slice; 4 basil leaves; and 1 bread slice, goat cheese side down; repeat procedure with remaining ingredients.

Lemon sorbet

MAKE AHEAD
Sweet Corn and Squash Soup

This delicately flavored dish is a choice opener for a meal featuring seasonal vegetables. Chopped chives are a nice garnish if squash blossoms aren't available. Make this up to one day ahead; cover and refrigerate. Gently reheat before serving.

- 1 tablespoon butter
- 2 cups chopped onion (about 1 large)
- 4 cups fresh corn kernels (about 7 ears)
- 3 cups water
- 2 cups chopped yellow squash
- ¼ teaspoon salt
- ¼ teaspoon freshly ground black pepper
- 6 fresh squash blossoms, thinly sliced (optional)

1 Melt butter in a Dutch oven over medium-low heat. Add onion to pan; cover and cook 10 minutes or until tender, stirring occasionally. Add corn and next 4 ingredients; bring to a boil. Reduce heat, and simmer 15 minutes. Cool slightly. Place half of corn mixture in a blender. Remove center piece of blender lid (to allow steam to escape); secure blender lid on blender. Place a clean towel over opening in blender lid (to avoid splatters). Blend until smooth. Strain corn mixture through a sieve into a large bowl; discard solids. Repeat procedure with remaining corn mixture. Garnish with squash blossom slices, if desired. Yield: 6 servings (serving size: about 3/4 cup soup).

CALORIES 177 (20% from fat); FAT 4g (sat 1.5g, mono 1.1g, poly 1.1g); PROTEIN 6g; CARB 35.5g; FIBER 5.4g; CHOL 5mg; IRON 1mg; SODIUM 143mg; CALC 22mg

QUICK & EASY
Summer Squash Ribbons with Oregano, Basil, and Lemon

You can also toss the ribbons with wide flat pasta, such as pappardelle, for a delicious entrée. While we recommend basil and oregano, use whatever fresh herbs you have on hand. Serve with a crisp sauvignon blanc and crusty bread.

- 3 small zucchini (about 1 pound)
- 3 small yellow squash (about 1 pound)
- 1 tablespoon extravirgin olive oil
- 1/4 teaspoon grated lemon rind
- 1 tablespoon fresh lemon juice
- 1/2 teaspoon salt
- 1/8 teaspoon freshly ground black pepper
- 1 garlic clove, minced
- 1/3 cup thinly sliced fresh basil
- 1 tablespoon chopped fresh oregano
- 1/4 cup (1 ounce) shaved fresh Parmesan cheese

1 Shave zucchini and squash into ribbons using a vegetable peeler, stopping at seeds; place ribbons in a large bowl. Discard seed cores.
2 Combine oil and next 5 ingredients in a small bowl; stir with a whisk. Drizzle oil mixture over vegetable ribbons; sprinkle with basil and oregano. Toss gently. Sprinkle with cheese. Serve immediately. Yield: 8 servings (serving size: 1/2 cup vegetable mixture and 1 1/2 teaspoons cheese).

CALORIES 50 (52% from fat); FAT 2.9g (sat 0.9g, mono 1.6g, poly 0.3g); PROTEIN 2.8g; CARB 4.4g; FIBER 1.3g; CHOL 3mg; IRON 0.5mg; SODIUM 207mg; CALC 62mg

STAFF FAVORITE
Parmesan Flans with Tomatoes and Basil

Use a variety of colorful tomatoes, including red, yellow, orange, and green, to make this elegant dish more visually appealing. Pair it with a chilled soup, salad, and wine for a light meal.

- Cooking spray
- 3 tablespoons all-purpose flour
- 1 cup 1% low-fat milk
- 4 large egg whites, lightly beaten
- 2 large eggs, lightly beaten
- 3/4 cup (3 ounces) finely grated Parmigiano-Reggiano cheese
- 1/8 teaspoon salt
- 1/8 teaspoon freshly ground black pepper
- 2 cups chopped seeded tomato
- Dash of salt
- Dash of freshly ground black pepper
- 1/4 cup thinly sliced fresh basil

1 Preheat oven to 375°.
2 Coat 4 (6-ounce) custard cups or ramekins with cooking spray. Place flour in a medium bowl. Gradually add milk to bowl, stirring constantly with a whisk until blended. Add egg whites and eggs; stir well. Add cheese, 1/8 teaspoon salt, and 1/8 teaspoon pepper; stir well. Divide mixture evenly among prepared custard cups. Place custard cups in a 9-inch square baking pan; add hot water to pan to a depth of 1 inch. Bake at 375° for 25 minutes or until puffy and set.
3 Combine tomato, dash of salt, and dash of pepper in a medium bowl. Loosen edges of flans with a knife or rubber spatula. Place a plate, upside down, on top of each cup; invert onto plates. Spoon 1/2 cup tomato mixture over each flan. Top each serving with 1 tablespoon basil. Yield: 4 servings.

CALORIES 192 (34% from fat); FAT 7.3g (sat 3.7g, mono 2.5g, poly 0.7g); PROTEIN 16.7g; CARB 14.2g; FIBER 1.3g; CHOL 106mg; IRON 1.5mg; SODIUM 478mg; CALC 286mg

Roasted Bell Pepper, Olive, and Caper Crostini

Inspired by classic Mediterranean tapenade, this tangy spread is a good source of beneficial monounsaturated fat.

- 2 yellow bell peppers
- 2 red bell peppers
- 1/4 cup pitted kalamata olives, chopped
- 3 tablespoons capers, chopped
- 2 tablespoons chopped fresh flat-leaf parsley
- 4 teaspoons extravirgin olive oil
- 1 tablespoon fresh lemon juice
- 1/8 teaspoon crushed red pepper
- 1/8 teaspoon salt
- 1/8 teaspoon freshly ground black pepper
- 1 garlic clove, minced
- 24 (1/2-inch-thick) slices diagonally cut French bread baguette, toasted

1 Preheat broiler.
2 Cut bell peppers in half lengthwise; discard seeds and membranes. Place pepper halves, skin sides up, on a foil-lined baking sheet; flatten with hand. Broil 15 minutes or until blackened. Place in a zip-top plastic bag; seal. Let stand 20 minutes. Peel and chop.
3 Combine bell peppers, olives, and next 8 ingredients in a medium bowl. Serve with bread. Yield: 12 servings (serving size: 2 bread slices and 2 tablespoons bell pepper mixture).

CALORIES 115 (21% from fat); FAT 2.7g (sat 0.4g, mono 1.8g, poly 0.4g); PROTEIN 3.2g; CARB 21.2g; FIBER 1.5g; CHOL 0mg; IRON 1.3mg; SODIUM 332mg; CALC 9mg

Farro, Avocado, Cucumber, and Cherry Tomato Salad

Farro is a whole grain with a pleasantly chewy texture. Look for it at specialty markets and gourmet grocers or health food stores. With crunchy cucumber, sweet cherry tomatoes, and buttery avocado, this dish makes a refreshing lunch. Pair it with a simple starter soup and whole-grain crackers for dinner.

- 1 cup uncooked farro or spelt
- 4 teaspoons extravirgin olive oil
- ¼ teaspoon fresh grated lime rind
- 1 tablespoon fresh lime juice
- 1 tablespoon white wine vinegar
- ¾ teaspoon salt
- ½ teaspoon black pepper
- 2 cups red, orange, and yellow cherry tomatoes, halved
- 1¾ cups chopped seeded English cucumber (about 1 small)
- ¼ cup fresh cilantro leaves
- ¾ cup sliced peeled avocado (about 1 small)

1 Place farro in a large saucepan; cover with water to 2 inches above farro. Bring to a boil. Cover, reduce heat, and simmer 30 minutes. Drain and rinse with cold water; drain well.
2 Combine oil and next 5 ingredients in a large bowl; stir with a whisk. Add farro, tomatoes, cucumber, and cilantro; toss gently to coat. Place about 1 cup farro mixture on each of 5 plates; garnish evenly with avocado. Serve immediately. Yield: 5 servings.

CALORIES 208 (36% from fat); FAT 8.3g (sat 1.1g, mono 4.8g, poly 1g); PROTEIN 5.6g; CARB 33.4g; FIBER 6.1g; CHOL 0mg; IRON 2.1mg; SODIUM 363mg; CALC 16mg

Flatbread with Asparagus, Fontina, and Pickled Onions

Make the roasted garlic, pickled onions, and blanched asparagus ahead, then top and bake the pizza. If you don't have a pizza stone, preheat a rimless baking sheet while you prepare the pizza.

- 1 large whole garlic head
- Cooking spray
- 1 tablespoon extravirgin olive oil
- 2½ cups vertically sliced red onion
- 1 cup red wine vinegar
- 2¼ teaspoons kosher salt, divided
- 1½ cups (½-inch) slices asparagus (about 8 ounces)
- 1 recipe Flatbread Dough (at right)
- 2 tablespoons cornmeal, divided
- ¾ cup (3 ounces) shredded fontina cheese, divided

1 Preheat oven to 400°.
2 Remove white papery skin from garlic head (do not peel or separate cloves). Coat garlic with cooking spray. Wrap garlic head in foil. Bake at 400° for 45 minutes or until tender; cool 10 minutes. Separate cloves; squeeze to extract garlic pulp. Discard skins. Combine garlic pulp and oil in a small bowl, stirring until smooth.
3 Preheat oven to 500°.
4 Place a pizza stone on bottom oven rack. Preheat pizza stone 30 minutes.
5 Combine onion, vinegar, and 2 teaspoons salt in a bowl; let stand 20 minutes. Remove 1 cup onion mixture with a slotted spoon; set aside. Reserve remaining onion mixture for another use.
6 Cook asparagus in boiling water 2 minutes or until crisp-tender. Drain and rinse with cold running water; drain. Pat dry with paper towels.
7 Divide dough in half. Working with 1 portion at a time (cover remaining dough to keep from drying), roll dough into an 11-inch circle on a lightly floured surface. Place dough on a baking sheet (or jelly-roll pan) sprinkled with 1 tablespoon cornmeal. Spread half of garlic mixture over dough. Top with ½ cup onion mixture and ¾ cup asparagus, leaving a 1-inch border. Sprinkle with 6 tablespoons cheese. Slide topped dough onto preheated pizza stone, using a spatula as a guide. Bake at 500° for 8 minutes or until cheese melts and crust is golden brown. Remove from pizza stone using pizza peel. Place pizza on a cutting board; sprinkle with ⅛ teaspoon salt. Cut into 6 wedges. Repeat procedure with remaining dough, 1 tablespoon cornmeal, garlic mixture, ½ cup onion mixture, ¾ cup asparagus, 6 tablespoons cheese, and ⅛ teaspoon salt. Yield: 2 flatbreads, 12 servings (serving size: 1 wedge).

CALORIES 283 (23% from fat); FAT 7.3g (sat 3.2g, mono 3g, poly 0.7g); PROTEIN 10.7g; CARB 43.2g; FIBER 2.9g; CHOL 16mg; IRON 3.5mg; SODIUM 425mg; CALC 118mg

MAKE AHEAD
Flatbread Dough

This versatile dough is used to make the Flatbread with Asparagus, Fontina, and Pickled Onions (at left), as well as the Goat Cheese and Greens Piadine (page 206).

- 2¼ cups all-purpose flour, divided (about 10 ounces)
- Dash of sugar
- 1 package dry yeast (about 2¼ teaspoons)
- 6 tablespoons warm water (100° to 110°)
- ½ cup warm water (100° to 110°)
- ½ teaspoon salt
- Cooking spray

1 Lightly spoon flour into dry measuring cups; level with a knife.
2 Dissolve sugar and yeast in 6 tablespoons warm water in a large bowl; stir in ¼ cup flour. Let stand 30 minutes or until bubbly. Add 1¾ cups flour, ½ cup warm water, and salt to yeast mixture; stir until a soft dough forms. Turn dough out onto a lightly floured surface. Knead

until smooth and elastic (about 8 minutes); add enough of remaining flour, 1 tablespoon at a time, to prevent dough from sticking to hands. Place dough in a large bowl coated with cooking spray, turning to coat top. Cover and let rise in a warm place (85°), free from drafts, 1 hour or until doubled in size. (Gently press two fingers into dough. If indentation remains, dough has risen enough.) Punch dough down; cover and let rest 5 minutes. Yield: 2 (11-inch) pizza crusts, 12 servings.

CALORIES 88 (3% from fat); FAT 0.3g (sat 0g, mono 0g, poly 0.1g); PROTEIN 2.7g; CARB 18.2g; FIBER 0.8g; CHOL 0mg; IRON 1.2mg; SODIUM 99mg; CALC 4mg

Fresh Cherries with Riesling Zabaglione

Zabaglione is an Italian dessert sauce traditionally flavored with Marsala wine. We use a fruity California riesling for a fresh twist. For an even richer and thicker sauce, you could use a late-harvest sémillon or sauvignon blanc.

  4   cups pitted sweet cherries
      (about 1½ pounds)
  3   tablespoons sugar
  1   tablespoon water
  3   large egg yolks
  ¼   cup riesling or other slightly
      sweet white wine

1 Divide cherries evenly among 6 small dessert bowls.
2 Combine sugar, 1 tablespoon water, and egg yolks in top of a double boiler, stirring well with a whisk. Stir in wine. Cook over simmering water until thick and mixture reaches 160° (about 8 minutes), stirring constantly with a whisk. Serve warm over cherries. Yield: 6 servings (serving size: about ⅔ cup cherries and about 3 tablespoons zabaglione).

CALORIES 128 (23% from fat); FAT 3.2g (sat 1g, mono 1.2g, poly 0.6g); PROTEIN 2.5g; CARB 23.6g; FIBER 2.3g; CHOL 102mg; IRON 0.6mg; SODIUM 4mg; CALC 26mg

Urban Orchard

In a trend that's gaining popularity across the country, the nonprofit group EarthWorks helps Bostonians reclaim green space and enjoy the fruitful results.

GROWING UP IN Hyde Park, an inner-city Boston neighborhood, Brian Judge never tasted an apricot. In fact, before joining EarthWorks Boston, a nonprofit group dedicated to reclaiming neglected urban space, he'd never even seen one. Now, three years later, apricots have become at-work perks for the high school junior. "They're definitely the best part of the job," says Judge, 16. "The first one I had came off a tree, and I've still never had one from the store."

He picked his first apricot at the Shirley Eustis orchard in nearby Roxbury in 2005, after discovering EarthWorks (www.earthworksboston.org) through an outdoor education program at his local YMCA.

Founded in 1989 by Bill Taylor, then a physics graduate student and environmental activist, EarthWorks started out with the simple goal of raising environmental awareness and preserving the city's green space. But Taylor and other volunteers quickly realized that if they provided tangible incentives, they could get the local community involved and yield better results. The solution was the Urban Orchards Project. By reclaiming public parks and schoolyards in Boston's low-income neighborhoods with volunteer-planted fruit and nut trees, they could offer community members the pleasure of picking and eating fresh fruit free of charge, no membership required.

STAFF FAVORITE • MAKE AHEAD
FREEZABLE
Spiked Peach Limeade Granita

If you prefer to serve this as a beverage, skip the freezing and scraping steps.

  4   cups water
  3   cups peach slices (about 3
        medium)
  1⅓   cups sugar
  6   mint leaves
  1⅓   cups fresh lime juice
  ¾   cup rum
        Peach slices (optional)
        Fresh mint sprigs (optional)

1 Combine first 4 ingredients in a medium saucepan; bring to a boil. Reduce heat; simmer 5 minutes. Cool; discard mint.

2 Place half of peach mixture in a blender; process until smooth. Pour pureed peach mixture into a 13 x 9-inch baking dish. Combine remaining peach mixture, juice, and rum in blender; process until smooth. Add to baking dish.
3 Freeze 8 hours or until firm. Remove mixture from freezer; scrape entire mixture with a fork until fluffy. Serve immediately. Garnish with peach slices and mint sprigs, if desired. Yield: 8 servings (serving size: about 1 cup).

CALORIES 202 (less than 1% from fat); FAT 0.1g (sat 0g, mono 0.1g, poly 0g); PROTEIN 0.5g; CARB 40.3g; FIBER 0.7g; CHOL 0mg; IRON 0.2mg; SODIUM 5mg; CALC 12mg

Peppered Pork Tenderloin with Blue Cheese Plums

Grill the plums for intense flavor.

- 2 tablespoons chopped fresh rosemary
- 2 teaspoons fennel seeds
- 2 teaspoons coriander seeds
- 1 teaspoon kosher salt
- 1 teaspoon freshly ground black pepper
- 2 (1-pound) pork tenderloins, trimmed
- 2½ teaspoons olive oil, divided
- Cooking spray
- 8 plums, halved and pitted
- ¾ cup (3 ounces) crumbled blue cheese
- Rosemary sprigs (optional)

1 Place first 3 ingredients in a spice or coffee grinder; process until finely ground. Combine spice mixture with salt and pepper in a small bowl. Rub pork with 1 teaspoon oil. Sprinkle spice mixture evenly over pork; wrap with plastic wrap. Refrigerate 2 hours.
2 Prepare grill.
3 Place pork on a grill rack coated with cooking spray; grill 16 minutes or until a thermometer inserted in thickest portion registers 155°, turning once. Let stand 10 minutes; cut pork crosswise into ¼-inch-thick slices.
4 Place plum halves in a shallow dish. Drizzle with remaining 1½ teaspoons oil; toss gently to coat. Place plums, cut sides down, on a grill rack coated with cooking spray. Grill 3 minutes or until golden. Serve with cheese and pork. Garnish with rosemary sprigs, if desired. Yield: 8 servings (serving size: 3 ounces pork, 2 plum halves, and 1½ tablespoons cheese).

CALORIES 222 (35% from fat); FAT 8.5g (sat 3.5g, mono 3.5g, poly 0.6g); PROTEIN 25.5g; CARB 10.6g; FIBER 1.6g; CHOL 71mg; IRON 1.6mg; SODIUM 429mg; CALC 73mg

---

MAKE AHEAD
Cherry Ripple Sour Cream Coffee Cake

STREUSEL:
- ½ cup whole wheat flour (about 2¼ ounces)
- ½ cup regular oats
- ½ cup packed brown sugar
- 3 tablespoons chopped pecans
- 1 teaspoon ground cinnamon
- 2 tablespoons frozen orange juice concentrate, thawed
- 1 tablespoon canola oil

CAKE:
- Cooking spray
- ¼ cup canola oil
- 2 tablespoons butter, melted
- 1 cup granulated sugar
- 2 teaspoons vanilla extract
- 1 large egg
- 1 large egg white
- 2 cups all-purpose flour (about 9 ounces)
- 1 teaspoon baking soda
- 1 teaspoon baking powder
- ½ teaspoon salt
- 1 cup fat-free sour cream
- 2 cups pitted fresh cherries, coarsely chopped (about 10 ounces)

1 To prepare streusel, lightly spoon whole wheat flour into a dry measuring cup; level with a knife. Combine whole wheat flour and next 4 ingredients. Add concentrate and 1 tablespoon oil; stir until crumbly.
2 Preheat oven to 350°.
3 To prepare cake, coat a 9-inch tube pan with cooking spray. Combine ¼ cup oil and butter in a medium bowl. Add granulated sugar and next 3 ingredients; beat with a mixer at medium speed until smooth.
4 Lightly spoon all-purpose flour into dry measuring cups; level with a knife. Combine all-purpose flour and next 3 ingredients in a large bowl. Add flour mixture and sour cream alternately to egg mixture, beginning and ending with flour mixture. Stir in cherries.

5 Spoon half of batter into prepared pan; sprinkle with half of streusel. Spoon in remaining batter; top with remaining streusel. Bake at 350° for 55 minutes or until a wooden pick inserted in center comes out clean. Cool in pan 10 minutes on a wire rack; run a knife around outside edge. Cool completely in pan. Yield: 16 servings (serving size: 1 piece).

CALORIES 246 (28% from fat); FAT 7.6g (sat 1.5g, mono 3.8g, poly 1.9g); PROTEIN 4g; CARB 41.5g; FIBER 1.8g; CHOL 18mg; IRON 1.4mg; SODIUM 227mg; CALC 53mg

---

MAKE AHEAD
Cherry-Berry Jam

Homemade jam is a luxurious splurge for morning toast or plain yogurt. Minimal sugar is added to this recipe, so the flavor of the fruit shines. Use a bit of this jam to sweeten marinades for grilled pork or chicken. This recipe yields enough jam to keep some and share some with friends. It should stay fresh for up to three weeks in the refrigerator.

- 2 cups pitted fresh cherries (about 12 ounces)
- 1½ cups blackberries
- 1½ cups raspberries
- ¾ cup sugar
- 1½ teaspoons fresh lemon juice

1 Combine all ingredients in a medium, heavy saucepan over medium-high heat; bring to a boil. Reduce heat, and simmer until reduced to 2 cups (about 1½ hours), stirring occasionally. Spoon into a bowl. Cover and chill. Yield: 3 cups (serving size: 2 tablespoons).

CALORIES 41 (4% from fat); FAT 0.2g (sat 0g, mono 0g, poly 0.1g); PROTEIN 0.4g; CARB 10.1g; FIBER 1.2g; CHOL 0mg; IRON 0.2mg; SODIUM 0mg; CALC 6mg

Nectarine Cheesecake with Pistachio Brittle

Once you add the eggs to the cheesecake batter, pulse just until combined. Incorporating too much air at that stage can cause the cheesecake to puff up as it bakes and sink as it cools, leaving a cracked or sunken appearance.

CRUST:

Cooking spray

6 graham cracker sheets

2 tablespoons shelled dry-roasted unsalted pistachios

1 tablespoon canola oil

FILLING:

2 cups pitted, peeled, diced nectarine (about 2 nectarines)

1 cup plus 1 tablespoon sugar, divided

1 (16-ounce) container 2% low-fat cottage cheese

1½ cups (12 ounces) ⅓-less-fat cream cheese, softened

¼ cup cornstarch

1 cup reduced-fat sour cream

1½ teaspoons vanilla extract

2 large egg whites, lightly beaten

1 large egg, lightly beaten

BRITTLE:

½ cup sugar

⅓ cup water

¼ cup coarsely chopped shelled dry-roasted unsalted pistachios

SAUCE:

2 cups pitted, peeled chopped nectarine (about 2 nectarines)

2 tablespoons sugar

1 teaspoon fresh lemon juice

1 Preheat oven to 325°.

2 To prepare crust, wrap heavy-duty aluminum foil around bottom and sides of a 10-inch springform pan. Lightly coat pan with cooking spray.

3 Place graham crackers and 2 tablespoons pistachios in a food processor; process until finely ground. Add oil; process until moist. Firmly press crumb mixture into bottom and 1 inch up sides of prepared pan.

4 To prepare filling, combine 2 cups diced nectarine and 1 tablespoon sugar in a small saucepan. Cover and cook over low heat 5 minutes or until sugar dissolves. Uncover and cook 5 minutes or until mixture thickens. Cool.

5 Place cottage cheese in food processor; process until smooth. Add nectarine mixture, remaining 1 cup sugar, cream cheese, and cornstarch; process until smooth. Add sour cream and next 3 ingredients; pulse just until combined. Pour cheese mixture into prepared pan. Place pan in a shallow roasting pan; add enough boiling water to come halfway up sides of pan.

6 Bake at 325° for 50 minutes or until center barely moves when pan is touched. Turn oven off, and open oven door; cool cheesecake in oven 1 hour. Remove cheesecake from roasting pan; run a knife around outside edge. Discard foil. Cool completely on a wire rack. Cover and chill at least 8 hours.

7 To prepare brittle, coat a baking sheet with cooking spray. Combine ½ cup sugar and ⅓ cup water in a small saucepan over medium-high heat; bring to a boil. Cook 1 minute or until sugar dissolves. Continue cooking 4 minutes or until golden (do not stir). Remove from heat; carefully stir in ¼ cup pistachios. Quickly spread mixture in a thin layer onto prepared baking sheet. Cool completely; break into small pieces. Sprinkle brittle around edge of cheesecake.

8 To prepare sauce, combine 2 cups nectarine, 2 tablespoons sugar, and juice in a blender; process until smooth. Serve with cheesecake. Yield: 16 servings (serving size: 1 cheesecake wedge and 1 tablespoon sauce).

CALORIES 263 (35% from fat); FAT 10.3g (sat 5g, mono 2.3g, poly 1g); PROTEIN 9.3g; CARB 34.4g; FIBER 1g; CHOL 36mg; IRON 0.5mg; SODIUM 263mg; CALC 61mg

---

Grow Your Own Community Orchard

Research successful projects.
Community programs similar to Earth-Works have sprung up in Austin, Texas; Birmingham, Alabama; Philadelphia; Chicago; and Los Angeles. If you're considering pursuing an urban farm in your town, first check out these other exciting urban green space efforts:
• Austin, Texas: TreeFolks (www.treefolks.org)
• Birmingham, Alabama: Jones Valley Urban Farm (www.jvuf.org)
• Chicago: Openlands (www.openlands.org)
• Los Angeles: Tree People (www.treepeople.org)
• Philadelphia: Philly Orchard Project (www.phillyorchards.org)
• Southern California: Common Vision (www.commonvision.org)

Consider the most appropriate site.
"Before we look at the physical characteristics of a potential location, we look at the characteristics of the community," says Edwin Marty, director of Jones Valley Urban Farms in Birmingham, Alabama. "We try to identify people who would be interested in getting involved in various aspects of the farm, from financial sponsorship to gardening volunteers." Support from members of the community ensures a garden's success.

There are many different ways to acquire access to the land once an appropriate site is targeted. Marty says the most common scenarios involve accessing privately owned unused land by way of a contract or easement, or many community gardens are established on public lands, like the EarthWorks Orchards.

Query the experts. Your local arboretum or cooperative extension can offer guidance as to which plants will thrive, optimum growing seasons, and options for organic farming.

Curried Chicken Salad with Nectarines

It's worth seeking out Madras curry powder, which balances fiery heat with earthy cumin and coriander, for this dish.

- 3 cups shredded cooked chicken breast (about 1 pound)
- 2 cups (1-inch) cubed nectarine (about 2 large)
- ½ cup diced celery
- ⅓ cup chopped green onions
- ¼ cup reduced-fat mayonnaise
- 2 tablespoons fat-free buttermilk
- 1 tablespoon fresh lemon juice
- ½ teaspoon salt
- ½ teaspoon curry powder
- ¼ teaspoon freshly ground black pepper
- 3 tablespoons sliced almonds, toasted

❶ Combine first 4 ingredients in a large bowl. Combine mayonnaise and next 5 ingredients in a small bowl, stirring well with a whisk. Drizzle mayonnaise mixture over chicken mixture; toss gently to coat. Sprinkle with almonds. Yield: 6 servings (serving size: about ¾ cup).

CALORIES 194 (30% from fat); FAT 6.5g (sat 1g, mono 2.4g, poly 1.8g); PROTEIN 25.4g; CARB 9.5g; FIBER 1.9g; CHOL 64mg; IRON 1.4mg; SODIUM 355mg; CALC 46mg

Up from the Grassroots

EarthWorks is one of an increasing number of urban agriculture projects across the country. According to Amy DeShon, MPA, executive director of the American Community Gardening Association (ACGA), urban farms are becoming critical suppliers for food banks and other groups fighting hunger. Rising food and energy costs have created a greater demand for fresh local produce, and traditional grocery stores—previously the main supplier for these groups—have become more efficient in purchasing, so there is little surplus food to donate. Urban agriculture helps fill the void.

Spinach Salad with Stone Fruits and Maple-Spiced Pecans

Serve with sautéed chicken or duck breast.

- 6 tablespoons chopped pecans
- ⅓ cup plus 1 tablespoon maple syrup
- ¼ teaspoon salt, divided
- ¼ teaspoon ground red pepper, divided
- Cooking spray
- ½ cup rice wine vinegar
- 1 teaspoon Dijon mustard
- ½ teaspoon grated peeled fresh ginger
- ½ cup thinly sliced red onion
- 2 ripe peeled, sliced peaches
- 2 ripe peeled, sliced plums
- 6 cups baby spinach leaves

❶ Preheat oven to 325°.
❷ Combine pecans, 1 tablespoon syrup, ⅛ teaspoon salt, and ⅛ teaspoon pepper in a medium bowl, tossing well to coat. Spread pecan mixture evenly on a baking sheet coated with cooking spray. Bake at 325° for 15 minutes, stirring after 5 minutes. Cool completely on baking sheet on a wire rack. Break nut mixture into small pieces.
❸ Combine remaining ⅓ cup syrup, remaining ⅛ teaspoon salt, remaining ⅛ teaspoon pepper, vinegar, mustard, and ginger in a small bowl, stirring well with a whisk.
❹ Heat a large nonstick skillet over medium heat. Coat pan with cooking spray. Add vinegar mixture to pan; cook 1 minute or until hot. Add onion, peaches, and plums to pan; cook 1 minute or until warm.
❺ Arrange 1 cup spinach on each of 6 plates; top each serving with about ⅓ cup fruit mixture and 1 tablespoon nut mixture. Serve immediately. Yield: 6 servings.

CALORIES 121 (28% from fat); FAT 3.8g (sat 0.4g, mono 2.2g, poly 1.2g); PROTEIN 1.3g; CARB 22.6g; FIBER 1.9g; CHOL 0mg; IRON 1mg; SODIUM 253mg; CALC 26mg

Summer Fruit Chutney

Pair this chutney with grilled chicken or pork, or serve with flatbread such as naan. The flavor complements the Curried Chicken Salad with Nectarines (at left). Refrigerated, it will keep for up to three weeks.

- ½ cup cider vinegar
- ¼ cup granulated sugar
- ¼ cup packed brown sugar
- 4 whole cloves
- 1 (3-inch) cinnamon stick
- ½ cup golden raisins
- 2 tablespoons thinly sliced peeled ginger
- ½ teaspoon yellow mustard seeds
- ½ teaspoon crushed red pepper
- 1½ pounds firm ripe nectarines, peeled, pitted, and chopped
- 1 pound firm ripe peaches, peeled, pitted, and chopped

❶ Combine first 3 ingredients in a large saucepan; bring to a boil. Place cloves and cinnamon stick on a double layer of cheesecloth. Gather edges; tie securely. Add cheesecloth bag, raisins, and next 3 ingredients to pan. Reduce heat, and simmer 8 minutes. Add nectarines and peaches; bring to a boil. Reduce heat, and simmer until reduced to 4 cups (about 45 minutes), stirring occasionally. Discard bundle. Spoon into a bowl. Cover and chill at least 2 hours. Yield: 8 servings (serving size: ½ cup).

CALORIES 146 (4% from fat); FAT 0.7g (sat 0g, mono 0.2g, poly 0.1g); PROTEIN 1.6g; CARB 35.9g; FIBER 2.7g; CHOL 0mg; IRON 0.9mg; SODIUM 8mg; CALC 19mg

Seafood Special

An East Coast accountant combines a variety of fresh shellfish and pantry staples for a delicious warm-weather dish.

Gordon Katz, a certified public accountant and history writer from Ellicott City, Maryland, enjoys creating new dishes with fresh seafood. As the principal cook in the household, Katz wants his dishes to be healthful for his family. He adopted a more healthful approach to cooking after his wife, Cindy, overcame a serious illness seven years ago. "Unfortunately, it often takes that type of event to provide the catalyst for change," he says.

And yet it's the fresh seafood from nearby markets that truly inspires his cooking. Katz created Shellfish with Chipotle and Tequila three summers ago. "Cindy and I love shellfish, so I wanted to combine several varieties."

Returning from the market with clams, scallops, and shrimp, Katz went through his pantry for spices, herbs, and broths. "I love the fire of chipotle, but a little goes a long way, so I needed something to temper the heat," he says. "I discovered a bottle of tequila and a few limes in the fridge, and thought they would work perfectly." Tomato paste and diced tomatoes help balance the spice, while turmeric, cumin, and oregano also punch up the flavor.

The result of his creative tinkering is a colorful and delicious dish that is an appealing complement to a beautiful summer evening.

Shellfish with Chipotle and Tequila

"Before cooking, soak the clams thoroughly to enhance their sweetness. I place them in a container, cover with water, add a touch of cornmeal, and keep them cool in the fridge for about an hour."

—Gordon Katz, Ellicott City, Maryland

 1 teaspoon olive oil
 Cooking spray
 1½ cups chopped yellow onion (about 1 large)
 ½ cup chopped red bell pepper
 ½ teaspoon freshly ground black pepper
 ¼ teaspoon kosher salt
 4 garlic cloves, minced
 1¾ cups water
 ¼ cup tequila
 2 tablespoons fresh lime juice (about 1 lime)
 2 teaspoons tomato paste
 1½ teaspoons chopped seeded chipotle chile, canned in adobo sauce
 1 teaspoon ground cumin
 ½ teaspoon dried thyme
 ½ teaspoon dried oregano
 ½ teaspoon ground turmeric
 1 (14.5-ounce) can no-salt-added diced tomatoes, undrained
 1 (14-ounce) can fat-free, less-sodium chicken broth
 24 littleneck clams
 ½ pound sea scallops
 ½ pound peeled and deveined medium shrimp
 ¼ cup chopped fresh cilantro
 ¼ cup chopped green onions

❶ Heat oil in a Dutch oven coated with cooking spray over medium-high heat. Add yellow onion and next 3 ingredients to pan; sauté 5 minutes or until tender. Add garlic; sauté 2 minutes. Add 1¾ cups water and next 10 ingredients to pan. Reduce heat to low, and simmer 12 minutes, stirring occasionally.
❷ Arrange clams in a steamer. Cover and steam over boiling water 8 minutes or until shells open. Discard any unopened shells; set aside.
❸ Add scallops and shrimp to tomato mixture; cook 7 minutes or just until done. Ladle 2 cups soup into each of 4 large shallow bowls; top each serving with 6 clams, 1 tablespoon cilantro, and 1 tablespoon green onions. Yield: 4 servings.

CALORIES 288 (13% from fat); FAT 4g (sat 0.5g, mono 1.1g, poly 1g); PROTEIN 38.1g; CARB 17.2g; FIBER 3.5g; CHOL 143mg; IRON 18.6mg; SODIUM 661mg; CALC 142mg

QUICK & EASY
Tex-Mex Beef and Bean Dip

"I was playing around one day trying to update the ground beef topping for a taco salad and came up with a great-tasting dip. I replaced the packaged taco seasoning with a combination of chipotle chile powder and ground cumin, substituted some of the ground beef with a can of pinto beans to lower the fat, and used crumbled queso fresco cheese in place of shredded sharp Cheddar for a more authentic Mexican flavor. When I was satisfied with the results, I served it to friends, who said it would be a great party dip served with baked tortilla chips. It has been a hit ever since."

—Germaine Perambo, St. Simon's Island, Georgia

 ½ pound ground sirloin
 2 tablespoons no-salt-added tomato paste
 1 to 2 teaspoons chipotle chile powder
 ¾ teaspoon ground cumin
 1 (15-ounce) can pinto beans, rinsed and drained
 1 (14.5-ounce) can diced tomatoes, undrained
 ¾ cup (3 ounces) crumbled queso fresco
 ¼ cup thinly sliced green onions
 3 ounces bite-size baked tortilla chips (about 60, such as Tostitos Scoops)

Continued

❶ Cook beef in a large nonstick skillet over medium-high heat until browned, stirring to crumble. Drain well; return beef to pan. Add tomato paste and next 4 ingredients, and bring to a boil. Reduce heat, and simmer 5 minutes or until thick, stirring occasionally.

❷ Spoon meat mixture into a serving bowl; top with cheese and onions. Serve with tortilla chips. Yield: 12 servings (serving size: ¼ cup dip and 5 chips).

CALORIES 99 (23% from fat); FAT 2.5g (sat 1.1g, mono 0.7g, poly 0.1g); PROTEIN 7.3g; CARB 11.7g; FIBER 1.9g; CHOL 15mg; IRON 1.2mg; SODIUM 216mg; CALC 53mg

MAKE AHEAD • FREEZABLE
Carrot Bread

"I lightened my mother-in-law's quick bread recipe that she shared with me because my husband enjoyed the original when he was growing up. He was thrilled with the results of my version but prefers it without nuts. Because our children love nuts, I usually double the recipe and add walnuts to half the batter to make a loaf for them. Then everyone's happy."

—Sarah Brinkley,
Endeavor, Wisconsin

¾ cup sliced carrot (about 4 ounces)
1½ cups whole wheat flour (about 7 ounces)
1 teaspoon ground cinnamon
¾ teaspoon salt
½ teaspoon baking soda
½ teaspoon baking powder
¼ teaspoon ground ginger
¼ teaspoon ground cloves
⅔ cup sugar
¼ cup canola oil
¼ cup vanilla fat-free yogurt
1 large egg, lightly beaten
1 large egg white, lightly beaten
Cooking spray

❶ Preheat oven to 350°.
❷ Cook carrot in boiling water 15 minutes or until tender; drain. Place carrot in a food processor; process until smooth.

❸ Lightly spoon flour into dry measuring cups; level with a knife. Combine flour and next 6 ingredients in a large bowl. Combine carrot, sugar, and next 4 ingredients in a small bowl, stirring with a whisk. Add carrot mixture to flour mixture, stirring just until combined.

❹ Pour batter into an 8-inch loaf pan coated with cooking spray. Bake at 350° for 50 minutes or until a wooden pick inserted in center comes out clean. Cool bread in pan 10 minutes on a wire rack; remove from pan. Cool completely on a wire rack. Cut bread into 12 slices. Yield: 1 loaf; 12 servings (serving size: 1 slice).

CALORIES 151 (32% from fat); FAT 5.3g (sat 0.5g, mono 3g, poly 1.6g); PROTEIN 3.2g; CARB 24g; FIBER 2.1g; CHOL 15mg; IRON 0.9mg; SODIUM 240mg; CALC 34mg

Chocolate Sandwich Cookies with Marshmallow Cream Filling

"I'm originally from the South, and Moon Pies were a special treat. I started looking for a recipe to make my own when I moved to New York, but the closest I could come to them was a recipe in a New England cookbook. My lightened adaptation can be made ahead of time and frozen for up to a month if the cookies are tightly wrapped. Make sure to have the cookies ready when the marshmallow filling is made—the filling firms up quickly as it cools."

—Susan Kwun, New York City

COOKIES:
1 cup sugar
5 tablespoons butter, softened
1 teaspoon vanilla extract
2 large eggs
2 cups all-purpose flour (about 9 ounces)
5 tablespoons unsweetened cocoa
1 teaspoon salt
1 teaspoon baking powder
1 teaspoon baking soda
1 cup fat-free buttermilk
Cooking spray

FILLING:
1 envelope unflavored gelatin (about 2½ teaspoons)
¾ cup cold water, divided
½ cup sugar
¼ cup light-colored corn syrup
⅛ teaspoon salt
½ teaspoon vanilla extract

❶ Preheat oven to 375°.
❷ To prepare cookies, combine 1 cup sugar and butter in a large bowl. Beat with a mixer at medium speed until well blended (about 2 minutes). Add 1 teaspoon vanilla and eggs; beat until combined. Lightly spoon flour into dry measuring cups; level with a knife. Combine flour and next 4 ingredients; stir well with a whisk. Add flour mixture and buttermilk alternately to sugar mixture, beginning and ending with flour mixture; mix after each addition.

❸ Drop dough by rounded tablespoons 2 inches apart onto baking sheets coated with cooking spray. Bake at 375° for 10 minutes or until set. Cool on pans 5 minutes. Remove from pans; cool completely on wire racks.

❹ To prepare filling, sprinkle gelatin over ½ cup cold water in a large bowl; set aside. Combine remaining ¼ cup water, ½ cup sugar, syrup, and ⅛ teaspoon salt in a medium saucepan over medium-high heat. Cook, without stirring, until a candy thermometer registers 244°. Remove from heat. Gradually pour hot sugar syrup into softened gelatin mixture, beating with a mixer at low speed, then at high speed until thick (about 6 minutes), scraping sides of bowl occasionally. Add ½ teaspoon vanilla; beat until well blended.

❺ Quickly spread about 2 tablespoons filling over bottom side of 1 cookie; top with another cookie. Repeat procedure with remaining filling and cookies. Yield: 16 servings (serving size: 1 cookie sandwich).

CALORIES 197 (21% from fat); FAT 4.6g (sat 2.6g, mono 1.3g, poly 0.3g); PROTEIN 3.7g; CARB 36.6g; FIBER 1g; CHOL 36mg; IRON 1.1mg; SODIUM 329mg; CALC 46mg

Summer Supper Menu
serves 6

Make tacos with any leftover rice and steak.

Southwestern Confetti Salad

Spice-rubbed flank steak

Prepare grill to medium-high heat. Combine 1 tablespoon brown sugar, 1½ teaspoons paprika, 1 teaspoon ground cumin, 1 teaspoon ancho chile powder, ½ teaspoon kosher salt, and ½ teaspoon garlic powder. Rub 1 teaspoon canola oil over 1 (1½-pound) trimmed flank steak. Rub spice mixture evenly over steak. Place steak on grill rack; grill 5 minutes on each side or until desired degree of doneness. Remove steak from grill; let stand 10 minutes. Cut across grain into thin slices.

Margaritas

MAKE AHEAD
Southwestern Confetti Salad

"This recipe was one of my husband's staple meals during college. I've made it fresher and healthier by using fresh vegetables and substituting brown rice for white rice."

—Karen Waldman,
Brookfield, Connecticut

1 cup cooked brown rice
1 cup fresh corn kernels (about 2 ears)
1 cup coarsely chopped zucchini
1 cup grated carrot
½ cup diced plum tomato
⅓ cup diced red bell pepper
¼ cup chopped green onions
2 tablespoons diced red onion
2 tablespoons chopped fresh cilantro
1 tablespoon fresh lime juice
1 tablespoon canola oil
1 tablespoon minced seeded pickled jalapeño peppers
½ teaspoon kosher salt
½ teaspoon chili powder
¼ teaspoon freshly ground black pepper
1 (15-ounce) can black beans, rinsed and drained

❶ Combine all ingredients in a large bowl, stirring well to combine. Cover and chill at least 1 hour. Yield: 6 servings (serving size: about 1 cup).

CALORIES 122 (23% from fat); FAT 3.1g (sat 0.3g, mono 1.6g, poly 1g); PROTEIN 4.1g; CARB 22.7g; FIBER 4.5g; CHOL 0mg; IRON 1.3mg; SODIUM 359mg; CALC 32mg

LIGHTEN UP
Super Shrimp Étouffée

A spicy shrimp stew is sensibly adapted for a young couple with a healthful goal.

Katharine O'Hara McIntyre, an attorney in Washington, D.C., began dating her Louisiana-native husband, Charles Aaron, while attending law school in New Orleans. He introduced her to "some wonderful foods," including a shrimp étouffée, a spicy Cajun classic made with a rich, nutty roux. After much trial and error, Katharine perfected a recipe for the dish that easily adjusts to accommodate a dinner for two or a hungry crowd of 10. Unfortunately, the expansion of her culinary repertoire with such indulgent dishes, combined with the stresses of a recent move to Maryland and intense study for the bar exam, began to stretch the couple's waistlines, as well. They have since adopted more healthful cooking habits, but Katharine would like to treat Charles to his beloved Louisiana fare on a more regular basis. She requested our help revising the recipe so they can enjoy it without compromising their commitment to living well.

serving size: about 1¼ cups étouffée and ⅔ cup rice		
	before	after
CALORIES PER SERVING	623	395
FAT	32.5g	12.2g
PERCENT OF TOTAL CALORIES	47%	28%

STAFF FAVORITE
Shrimp Étouffée

This spicy Cajun classic is traditionally served over white rice.

4 cups fat-free, less-sodium chicken broth
1 teaspoon dried thyme
1 teaspoon dried basil
1 bay leaf
⅓ cup butter, divided
½ cup all-purpose flour (about 2¼ ounces)
Cooking spray
1½ cups chopped onion
⅔ cup diced celery
½ cup chopped red bell pepper
½ cup chopped green bell pepper
¾ cup water
¼ cup tomato paste
1 tablespoon salt-free Cajun seasoning
1½ teaspoons minced garlic
¼ teaspoon salt
¼ teaspoon black pepper
¼ teaspoon ground red pepper
1 teaspoon Worcestershire sauce
½ cup chopped green onions
½ cup chopped fresh flat-leaf parsley, divided
1 pound medium shrimp, peeled and deveined (about 30 shrimp)
4 cups hot cooked long-grain rice

❶ Combine first 4 ingredients in a small saucepan over medium heat; bring to a simmer. Cover and remove from heat.

❷ Melt ¼ cup butter in a medium saucepan over medium heat. Lightly spoon flour into a dry measuring cup; level with a knife. Add flour to pan; cook 8 minutes or until very brown, stirring constantly with a whisk. Remove from heat. Add 1 cup broth mixture to pan; stir with a whisk until smooth. Add remaining 3 cups broth mixture, stirring with a whisk until smooth; set aside.

Continued

3 Melt remaining 4 teaspoons butter in a large Dutch oven coated with cooking spray over medium-high heat. Add onion and next 3 ingredients to pan; cook 10 minutes or until vegetables are tender and onion is golden brown, stirring occasionally. Stir in 3/4 cup water, scraping pan to loosen browned bits. Add tomato paste and next 5 ingredients to onion mixture; cook 1 minute, stirring constantly. Add reserved broth mixture and Worcestershire sauce to pan, stirring well; bring to a simmer. Cook 10 minutes, stirring occasionally. Add green onions, 1/4 cup parsley, and shrimp; cook 3 minutes or until shrimp are done. Discard bay leaf. Serve over rice. Sprinkle each serving with 2 teaspoons remaining parsley. Yield: 6 servings (serving size: about 1 1/4 cups étouffée and 2/3 cup rice).

CALORIES 395 (28% from fat); FAT 12.2g (sat 6.9g, mono 3g, poly 1.1g); PROTEIN 22.6g; CARB 47.9g; FIBER 3.6g; CHOL 142mg; IRON 4.9mg; SODIUM 655mg; CALC 102mg

WINE NOTE: A traditional shrimp étouffée is fabulous with something cold and bold that can refreshingly stand up to the spices. A great choice is a dry rosé from Spain; these wines are a fabulous foil for Cajun dishes. Try El Coto Rosado from Rioja. The 2006 is $13.

Creative Kebabs

Supper goes international with this selection of worldly skewered entrées from the grill.

Kebab Menu 1
serves 4

Hoisin-Glazed Beef Kebabs

Grilled baby bok choy
Cut 4 baby bok choy in half lengthwise; place in a large bowl. Drizzle with 1 tablespoon low-sodium soy sauce and 2 teaspoons dark sesame oil; toss to coat. Arrange bok choy on a grill rack coated with cooking spray; grill 2 minutes on each side or until leaves begin to brown. Return bok choy to bowl; cover with plastic wrap. Let stand 3 minutes or until tender. Sprinkle evenly with 1/4 teaspoon salt.

Rice stick noodles

Game Plan
1 While grill preheats:
  • Marinate beef.
  • Combine bok choy with seasonings.
2 While kebabs grill:
  • Cook noodles.
  • Grill bok choy.

Prep Tip
If you don't have enough room to grill the kebabs and bok choy at the same time, steam the vegetables in two tablespoons chicken broth, then toss with seasonings.

Hoisin-Glazed Beef Kebabs

Soybean-based hoisin sauce is a spicy-sweet Chinese condiment. Spiked here with honey, seasoned rice vinegar, ginger, and chile paste with garlic, it makes a tasty base for a barbecue sauce.
Total time: 45 minutes

  2 tablespoons hoisin sauce
  1½ teaspoons honey
  ½ teaspoon seasoned rice vinegar
  ½ teaspoon grated peeled fresh ginger
  ½ teaspoon chile paste with garlic
  1 pound beef tenderloin filets, cut into 16 cubes
  16 (2-inch) pieces green onions (about 4 onions)
  16 grape tomatoes
  Cooking spray

1 Preheat grill to medium-high heat.
2 Combine first 5 ingredients in a medium bowl. Add beef to bowl; toss well to coat. Let stand at room temperature 20 minutes.
3 Thread 4 beef cubes, 4 onion pieces, and 4 tomatoes alternately onto each of 4 (12-inch) skewers. Place kebabs on a grill rack coated with cooking spray; grill 5 minutes on each side or until desired degree of doneness. Yield: 4 servings (serving size: 1 kebab).

CALORIES 227 (36% from fat); FAT 9.1g (sat 3.3g, mono 3.4g, poly 0.5g); PROTEIN 25.4g; CARB 10.4g; FIBER 1.7g; CHOL 72mg; IRON 3.7mg; SODIUM 212mg; CALC 34mg

Kebab Menu 2

serves 4

Italian Herbed Shrimp Kebabs

Tomato bruschetta

Grill 4 (1½-ounce) slices country-style sourdough bread 1 minute on each side or until lightly toasted. Remove bread from grill; rub one side of each bread slice with cut sides of a halved garlic clove. Combine ¾ cup chopped tomato, 2 tablespoons chopped fresh basil, 1 tablespoon balsamic vinegar, 2 teaspoons extravirgin olive oil, and ¼ teaspoon salt. Top each bread slice with about 3 tablespoons tomato mixture.

Grilled asparagus

Game Plan

1 While grill preheats:
  - Marinate shrimp.
  - Prepare tomato topping.
  - Trim asparagus.

2 While kebabs grill:
  - Grill bread.
  - Grill asparagus.

Italian Herbed Shrimp Kebabs

The pestolike marinade would also work well on chicken breasts or scallops.

Total time: 43 minutes

- ½ cup packed fresh basil leaves
- ½ cup fresh cilantro leaves
- ¼ cup fresh parsley leaves
- 2 tablespoons fresh lemon juice
- 2 tablespoons water
- 1 garlic clove
- 4 teaspoons extravirgin olive oil, divided
- 24 peeled and deveined jumbo shrimp (about 1½ pounds)
- 1 zucchini, cut into 20 (½-inch-thick) slices
  Cooking spray
- ½ teaspoon salt
- ¼ teaspoon black pepper

1 Prepare grill to medium-high heat.

2 Place first 6 ingredients in a blender or small food processor; add 2 teaspoons oil. Process until smooth. Transfer basil mixture to a medium bowl. Add shrimp; toss well to coat. Let stand at room temperature 15 minutes.

3 Thread 6 shrimp and 5 zucchini slices alternately onto each of 4 (12-inch) skewers. Drizzle kebabs evenly with remaining 2 teaspoons oil. Place kebabs on grill rack coated with cooking spray; grill 3 minutes on each side or until done. Sprinkle evenly with salt and pepper. Yield: 4 servings (serving size: 1 kebab).

CALORIES 235 (30% from fat); FAT 7.8g (sat 1.3g, mono 3.8g, poly 1.9g); PROTEIN 35.5g; CARB 4.7g; FIBER 1g; CHOL 259mg; IRON 4.7mg; SODIUM 555mg; CALC 113mg

Kebab Menu 3

serves 4

Pork Saté with Peanut-Mirin Sauce

Gingered sugar snap peas

Heat 1 tablespoon canola oil in a large nonstick skillet over medium-high heat. Add 1 tablespoon grated peeled fresh ginger and 2 minced garlic cloves to pan; cook 30 seconds or until fragrant, stirring constantly. Add 8 ounces trimmed sugar snap peas; sauté 2 minutes. Stir in ¼ cup water; cook 1 minute or until most of water evaporates. Stir in ¼ teaspoon salt and ⅛ teaspoon freshly ground black pepper; cook 30 seconds or until peas are crisp-tender.

Steamed basmati rice

Game Plan

1 While grill preheats:
  - Marinate pork.
  - Prepare sauce.
  - Bring water to a boil for rice.

2 While rice cooks:
  - Cook peas.
  - Grill skewers.

Pork Saté with Peanut-Mirin Sauce

Total time: 45 minutes

PORK:
- 2 teaspoons grated lime rind
- 2 tablespoons fresh lime juice
- 1 tablespoon peanut butter
- 2 teaspoons sugar
- 2 teaspoons fish sauce
- ½ teaspoon curry powder
- ¼ teaspoon salt
- ¼ teaspoon ground coriander
- 2 garlic cloves, minced
- 1 pound pork tenderloin, trimmed and cut into 16 (4-inch-long) strips

SAUCE:
- 1½ tablespoons sugar
- 2 tablespoons seasoned rice vinegar
- 2 tablespoons fresh lime juice
- 2 tablespoons mirin (sweet rice wine)
- 1 tablespoon chopped fresh cilantro
- 1 teaspoon fish sauce
- 1 serrano chile, seeded and finely chopped
- 1 tablespoon dry-roasted peanuts, chopped

REMAINING INGREDIENT:
  Cooking spray

1 Prepare grill to medium-high heat.

2 To prepare pork, combine first 9 ingredients in a medium bowl, stirring until smooth. Add pork; toss well to coat. Let stand at room temperature 15 minutes.

3 To prepare sauce, combine 1½ tablespoons sugar and next 6 ingredients, stirring with a whisk. Stir in peanuts.

4 Thread 2 pork pieces lengthwise onto each of 8 (12-inch) skewers. Place skewers on a grill rack coated with cooking spray; grill 3 minutes on each side or until done. Serve with sauce. Yield: 4 servings (serving size: 2 skewers and about 4 teaspoons sauce).

CALORIES 232 (30% from fat); FAT 7.7g (sat 2g, mono 3.4g, poly 1.5g); PROTEIN 24.9g; CARB 14g; FIBER 0.9g; CHOL 63mg; IRON 1.6mg; SODIUM 589mg; CALC 19mg

Chicken Shawarma

Chopped vegetable salad

Combine 2 cups chopped cucumber, 1 cup chopped red bell pepper, 1 cup chopped tomato, ½ cup chopped green bell pepper, ½ cup chopped red onion, ½ cup chopped fresh parsley, 2 tablespoons red wine vinegar, 1 tablespoon extravirgin olive oil, ½ teaspoon salt, and ¼ teaspoon pepper.

Greek yogurt with honey and walnuts

Game Plan

1 While grill preheats:
- Marinate chicken.
- Prepare salad, and let stand at room temperature.

2 While chicken grills:
- Prepare yogurt sauce.
- Toast pitas.

QUICK & EASY
Chicken Shawarma

Total time: 45 minutes

CHICKEN:
- 2 tablespoons fresh lemon juice
- 1 teaspoon curry powder
- 2 teaspoons extravirgin olive oil
- ¾ teaspoon salt
- ½ teaspoon ground cumin
- 3 garlic cloves, minced
- 1 pound skinless, boneless chicken breast, cut into 16 (3-inch) strips

SAUCE:
- ½ cup plain 2% reduced-fat Greek yogurt (such as Fage)
- 2 tablespoons tahini
- 2 teaspoons fresh lemon juice
- ¼ teaspoon salt
- 1 garlic clove, minced

REMAINING INGREDIENTS:
- Cooking spray
- 4 (6-inch) pitas
- 1 cup chopped romaine lettuce
- 8 (¼-inch-thick) tomato slices

① Preheat grill to medium-high heat.
② To prepare chicken, combine first 6 ingredients in a medium bowl. Add chicken; toss well to coat. Let stand at room temperature 20 minutes.
③ To prepare sauce, combine yogurt and next 4 ingredients, stirring with a whisk.
④ Thread 2 chicken strips onto each of 8 (12-inch) skewers. Place kebabs on a grill rack coated with cooking spray; grill 4 minutes on each side or until done.
⑤ Place pitas on grill rack; grill 1 minute on each side or until lightly toasted. Place 1 pita on each of 4 plates; top each serving with ¼ cup lettuce and 2 tomato slices. Top each serving with 4 chicken pieces; drizzle each serving with 2 tablespoons sauce. Yield: 4 servings.

CALORIES 384 (23% from fat); FAT 9.8g (sat 2.1g, mono 4.1g, poly 2.7g); PROTEIN 34.4g; CARB 40g; FIBER 2.5g; CHOL 64mg; IRON 4.3mg; SODIUM 821mg; CALC 106mg

SUPERFAST
20 Minute Dishes

From steak to soup, fish to chicken, here are simple, fresh, and easy meals you can make superfast.

QUICK & EASY
Thai-Style Roasted Trout

Fresh lime juice complements the sweet taste of trout. Steamed asparagus and jasmine rice make good sides.

- 2 tablespoons fresh lime juice
- 1 tablespoon fish sauce
- 2 teaspoons dark sesame oil
- ½ teaspoon crushed red pepper
- 4 (6-ounce) trout
- Cooking spray
- ¼ cup coarsely chopped fresh cilantro
- Lime slices (optional)
- Cilantro sprigs (optional)

① Preheat oven to 450°.
② Combine first 4 ingredients in a small bowl; stir well.
③ Arrange trout on a jelly-roll pan coated with cooking spray. Brush half of juice mixture inside of fish. Bake at 450° for 5 minutes. Brush remaining juice mixture over fish. Bake an additional 5 minutes or until fish flakes easily when tested with a fork or until desired degree of doneness. Sprinkle with cilantro; garnish with lime slices and cilantro sprigs, if desired. Yield: 4 servings (serving size: 1 fish and 1 tablespoon cilantro).

CALORIES 280 (39% from fat); FAT 12.2g (sat 3.1g, mono 3.9g, poly 4.1g); PROTEIN 39.3g; CARB 1g; FIBER 0.1g; CHOL 117mg; IRON 0.7mg; SODIUM 443mg; CALC 150mg

QUICK & EASY
Filet Mignon with Fresh Herb and Garlic Rub

The filet mignon comes from the small end of the tenderloin. Serve with roasted red potato wedges and steamed broccoli florets. Place florets in a microwave-safe bowl with a little water. Cover with wax paper and microwave at HIGH 3 minutes or until crisp-tender.

- 2 teaspoons bottled minced garlic
- 1½ teaspoons minced fresh basil
- 1½ teaspoons minced fresh thyme
- 1½ teaspoons minced fresh rosemary
- ½ teaspoon salt
- ¼ teaspoon black pepper
- 4 (4-ounce) beef tenderloin steaks, trimmed (1 inch thick)
- Cooking spray

① Combine first 6 ingredients in a small bowl; rub evenly over steaks.
② Heat a large nonstick skillet over medium-high heat. Coat pan with cooking spray. Add steaks to pan, and cook 4 minutes on each side or until desired degree of doneness. Yield: 4 servings (serving size: 1 steak).

CALORIES 189 (42% from fat); FAT 8.8g (sat 3.2, mono 3.2g, poly 0.3g); PROTEIN 24.1g; CARB 0.8g; FIBER 0.2g; CHOL 71mg; IRON 3.1mg; SODIUM 349mg; CALC 9mg

Avocado Soup with Citrus-Shrimp Relish

This lovely no-cook soup makes a refreshing entrée with a green salad.

RELISH:

- 2 tablespoons chopped fresh cilantro
- 1 teaspoon grated lemon rind
- 1 teaspoon finely chopped red onion
- 1 teaspoon extravirgin olive oil
- 8 ounces peeled and deveined medium shrimp, steamed and coarsely chopped

SOUP:

- 2 cups fat-free, less-sodium chicken broth
- 1¾ cups chopped avocado (about 2)
- 1 cup water
- 1 cup rinsed and drained canned navy beans
- ½ cup fat-free plain yogurt
- 1½ tablespoons fresh lemon juice
- ¼ teaspoon salt
- ¼ teaspoon black pepper
- ¼ teaspoon hot pepper sauce (such as Tabasco)
- 1 small jalapeño pepper, seeded and chopped
- ¼ cup (1 ounce) crumbled queso fresco

1 To prepare relish, combine first 5 ingredients in a small bowl, tossing gently.
2 To prepare soup, combine broth and next 9 ingredients in a blender; process until smooth, scraping sides. Ladle 1¼ cups avocado mixture into each of 4 bowls; top each serving with ¼ cup shrimp mixture and 1 tablespoon cheese. Yield: 4 servings.

CALORIES 292 (41% from fat); FAT 13.2g (sat 2.2g, mono 7.8g, poly 2.6g); PROTEIN 23.9g; CARB 22.5g; FIBER 7.3g; CHOL 118mg; IRON 3.4mg; SODIUM 832mg; CALC 146mg

Mediterranean Chicken Salad Pitas

Greek yogurt has a thick, rich consistency similar to sour cream. Add honeydew melon and cantaloupe slices on the side.

- 1 cup plain whole-milk Greek yogurt (such as Fage Total Classic)
- 2 tablespoons lemon juice
- ½ teaspoon ground cumin
- ¼ teaspoon crushed red pepper
- 3 cups chopped cooked chicken
- 1 cup chopped red bell pepper (about 1 large)
- ½ cup chopped pitted green olives (about 20 small)
- ½ cup diced red onion
- ¼ cup chopped fresh cilantro
- 1 (15-ounce) can no-salt-added chickpeas (garbanzo beans), rinsed and drained
- 6 (6-inch) whole wheat pitas, cut in half
- 12 Bibb lettuce leaves
- 6 (⅛-inch-thick) slices tomato, cut in half

1 Combine first 4 ingredients in a small bowl; set aside. Combine chicken and next 5 ingredients in a large bowl. Add yogurt mixture to chicken mixture; toss gently to coat. Line each pita half with 1 lettuce leaf and 1 tomato piece; add ½ cup chicken mixture to each pita half. Yield: 6 servings (serving size: 2 stuffed pita halves).

CALORIES 404 (23% from fat); FAT 10.2g (sat 3.8g, mono 4g, poly 1.5g); PROTEIN 33.6g; CARB 46.4g; FIBER 6g; CHOL 66mg; IRON 3.4mg; SODIUM 575mg; CALC 110mg

Spicy Mustard Shrimp

Serve with sautéed sliced zucchini and orzo tossed with chopped fresh flat-leaf parsley.

- 2 teaspoons canola oil
- 1 pound peeled and deveined large shrimp
- 1 tablespoon whole-grain Dijon mustard
- 1½ teaspoons chipotle hot pepper sauce (such as Tabasco)
- ⅔ cup (3-inch) diagonally cut green onions
- 1 cup diced peeled mango (about 1 medium)
- ¼ cup chopped fresh cilantro
- 4 lime wedges

1 Heat oil in a large nonstick skillet over medium-high heat. Add shrimp to pan; sauté 1 minute. Add mustard and pepper sauce; sauté 2 minutes, stirring frequently. Stir in onions; cook 1 minute. Remove from heat; stir in mango. Sprinkle with cilantro. Serve with lime wedges. Yield: 4 servings (serving size: about 1 cup shrimp mixture, 1 tablespoon cilantro, and 1 lime wedge).

CALORIES 181 (22% from fat); FAT 4.5g (sat 0.6g, mono 1.7g, poly 1.5g); PROTEIN 23.5g; CARB 10.3g; FIBER 1.9g; CHOL 172mg; IRON 3.1mg; SODIUM 247mg; CALC 82mg

Fresh Cherry Pie

Fresh-baked cherry pie is a classic, and an ideal way to end a summertime meal. We enthusiastically recommend this version; it earned our Test Kitchens' top marks for deliciously showcasing ripe, juicy cherries combined with a flaky, golden crust.

STAFF FAVORITE • MAKE AHEAD

Fresh Cherry Pie

(pictured on page 256)

Some pie connoisseurs prefer sour cherries; we love the way sweet ones worked in this filling. A cherry pitter makes quick work of preparing them. We like the OXO Good Grips Cherry Pitter ($12).

2 tablespoons uncooked quick-cooking tapioca
6 cups pitted sweet cherries
¾ cup granulated sugar
¼ cup cornstarch
1 tablespoon fresh lemon juice
¼ teaspoon almond extract
⅛ teaspoon salt
1 (15-ounce) package refrigerated pie dough (such as Pillsbury)
Cooking spray
2 tablespoons water
1 large egg white, lightly beaten
2 tablespoons turbinado sugar

1 Place tapioca in a spice or coffee grinder; process until finely ground. Combine tapioca, cherries, and next 5 ingredients in a large bowl; toss well. Let cherry mixture stand 30 minutes; stir to combine.

2 Preheat oven to 400°.

3 Roll 1 (9-inch) dough portion into an 11-inch circle. Fit dough into a 9-inch pie plate coated with cooking spray, allowing dough to extend over edge of plate. Spoon cherry mixture and any remaining liquid into dough. Roll remaining (9-inch) dough portion into a 12-inch circle. Cut dough into 12 (1-inch-wide) strips; arrange in a lattice pattern over cherry mixture. Fold edges under; crimp.

4 Combine 2 tablespoons water and egg white in a small bowl. Brush egg white mixture over dough on top of pie, and sprinkle dough evenly with 2 tablespoons turbinado sugar. Bake at 400° for 20 minutes. Shield edges of piecrust with foil, and bake an additional 40 minutes or until crust is golden brown and filling is thick and bubbly. Cool pie in pan 45 minutes on a wire rack. Yield: 12 servings (serving size: 1 wedge).

CALORIES 282 (32% from fat); FAT 9.9g (sat 4.1g, mono 4.3g, poly 1.2g); PROTEIN 2.5g; CARB 47.3g; FIBER 1.7g; CHOL 7mg; IRON 0.3mg; SODIUM 161mg; CALC 11mg

How To Make a Decorative Piecrust

There's more than one way to prepare a piecrust. In the demonstration, we flute the edge before filling, then lay the lattice in, pressing it gently into the side. The Fresh Cherry Pie (above) suggests latticing the top, then crimping. After testing each technique, we're happy to say both work, and the results will delight the eyes as much as the palate. You'll need enough dough (homemade or refrigerated pie dough) for two crusts: one for the pie plate, the other to create the lattice.

1 Press one piecrust into pie plate, making sure there are no air bubbles, then tuck extra dough under edges.

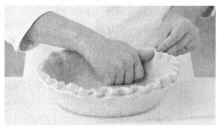

2 Pinch dough with thumb and index finger of one hand, while pressing inward with thumb of other hand.

3 Return to reserved piecrust, and use a pastry cutter to cut 10 (½-inch-wide) strips to cover top of pie.

4 Pour filling into pie. Then work from center outward laying one strip horizontally, then one vertically.

5 Continue alternating strips, leaving about ½ inch between each, as you weave them over and under.

6 Be sure each strip is long enough to reach the edge of the pie, then push them into the side to seal in place.

Tomato Parade

An avid home gardener and cook shares favorite heirloom varieties and delicious dishes to show-case them.

SUMMER IS TOMATO TIME. For many, the excitement begins when the first of the summer's crop arrives at the farmers' market, where you may find an array of shapes, sizes, textures, and flavors for just a few short months.

One tasty version is the heirloom variety. *Heirloom* is a term used to describe any tomato plant that's openly pollinated (by wind and bees) and has been cultivated for more than 50 years. Seeds from the best plants are saved at the end of the growing season for future use. Years ago these prized seeds became family heirlooms passed from one generation to the next. Today they're sometimes called heritage seeds.

Hybrid tomatoes, which include the standard supermarket varieties, are man-made crosses of different lines bred to achieve certain characteristics like standard size or hardiness. By contrast, most heirloom tomatoes don't grow in uniform shapes or sizes. Heirloom fruit ripen sporadically, and they're not as disease-resistant or hardy for transport, making them less practical for large-scale production. They typically are cultivated by small-scale farmers and home gardeners.

There's nothing quite like the flavor of a ripe tomato, fresh from the vine, but the array of choices can be mind-boggling. Here are 12 varieties of heirloom tomatoes (see page 222) along with recipes that make fine use of them.

QUICK & EASY

Halibut with Persimmon Tomato and Dill Relish

You can substitute another orange tomato variety, such as Valencia.

- 2 cups diced Persimmon tomato (about 3 medium)
- 3 tablespoons finely chopped red onion
- 1 tablespoon finely chopped seeded jalapeño pepper
- 2 teaspoons fresh lemon juice
- 1 teaspoon chopped fresh dill
- ½ teaspoon salt, divided
- ½ teaspoon freshly ground black pepper, divided
- 6 (6-ounce) halibut fillets
- 1 tablespoon extravirgin olive oil
- Cooking spray
- Dill sprigs (optional)

1. Prepare grill.
2. Combine first 5 ingredients in a medium bowl; stir in ¼ teaspoon salt and ¼ teaspoon black pepper. Toss gently.
3. Brush fish with oil; sprinkle evenly with remaining ¼ teaspoon salt and remaining ¼ teaspoon black pepper. Place fish on grill rack coated with cooking spray; grill 2 minutes on each side or until fish flakes easily when tested with a fork or until desired degree of doneness. Serve with tomato mixture; garnish with dill sprigs, if desired. Yield: 6 servings (serving size: 1 fillet and ⅓ cup tomato mixture).

CALORIES 211 (26% from fat); FAT 6.2g (sat 0.9g, mono 2.9g, poly 1.6g); PROTEIN 34.8g; CARB 2.6g; FIBER 0.7g; CHOL 52mg; IRON 1.7mg; SODIUM 308mg; CALC 81mg

QUICK & EASY

Mr. Stripey Tomato, Arugula, and Pancetta Sandwiches

These sandwiches are a new interpretation of the classic BLT. Pancetta is Italian cured bacon; substitute domestic cured bacon, if necessary. You can prepare the mayonnaise mixture and cook the pancetta up to one day ahead.

- 2 tablespoons light mayonnaise
- 1 tablespoon minced shallots
- 2 teaspoons Dijon mustard
- ½ teaspoon minced fresh sage
- 2 ounces pancetta, cut into 8 thin slices
- Cooking spray
- 8 (1-ounce) slices rustic sourdough bread, toasted
- 4 Mr. Stripey tomatoes, each cut into 4 (½-inch-thick) slices (about 1¾ pounds)
- 1 cup arugula

1. Preheat oven to 400°.
2. Combine first 4 ingredients in a bowl, stirring well.
3. Arrange pancetta in a single layer on a baking sheet coated with cooking spray. Bake at 400° for 8 minutes or until crisp. Drain on paper towels.
4. Spread mayonnaise mixture evenly over bread slices. Top each of 4 bread slices with 2 pancetta slices, 4 tomato slices, and ¼ cup arugula. Top sandwiches with remaining 4 bread slices. Yield: 4 servings (serving size: 1 sandwich).

CALORIES 282 (28% from fat); FAT 8.7g (sat 2.8g, mono 1.7g, poly 4.1g); PROTEIN 10.5g; CARB 41.9g; FIBER 3.5g; CHOL 13mg; IRON 3mg; SODIUM 699mg; CALC 44mg

Heirloom Tomato Roundup

Brandywine: This tomato is an excellent multipurpose beefsteak variety. Although it's difficult to verify exact origin, some experts speculate that it was first cultivated by the Amish more than a century ago. This fruit is grown in yellow, red, pink, and purple-fleshed varieties. With a classic tomato taste, the classic red Brandywine is full-flavored with a pleasant acidity, a floral aroma similar to roses, and a supple buttery texture.

Persimmon: A prolific rose-orange beefsteak, some say this creamy, meaty, gorgeous tomato was cultivated by Thomas Jefferson. It has a near perfect acid-to-sugar balance.

Limmony (also spelled Lemony): A Russian variety, this pale yellow beefsteak tomato has a strong, zesty, sweet citrusy flavor.

Mr. Stripey: A pale yellow tomato with pinkish-orange blush, and occasionally, green stripes, Mr. Stripey is a delicate beefsteak with low acid content that allows its sweetness to shine. The flavor boasts notes of melon, and the firm skin provides a nice contrast to the tender flesh when eaten raw.

Cherokee Purple: As the name implies, this meaty beefsteak variety has a deep purple color that tends toward brown or black. The firm, juicy, sweet-tart flesh, along with its jammy hue, often leads people to find the flavor evocative of a spicy zinfandel wine. Indeed, it has similar vegetal undertones that are balanced with a natural sweetness.

Mortgage Lifter: This pink-fleshed beefsteak was originally bred by a radiator repairman from West Virginia in the 1930s. Seedlings of the tomato were sold for $1 each, paying off his $6,000 mortgage in six years. This tomato can tip the scale at two pounds. It's also known for its mild, sweet flavor.

Sungold: These little prolific orange cherry tomatoes grow in pretty, long clusters. The flavor is a nice balance of citrusy tartness, with hints of grape, orange, and floral flavors and a pleasant sweetness.

Abraham Lincoln: This dark red globe tomato is juicy and meaty with a robust flavor similar to ketchup, but slightly less sweet.

Green Zebra: At full maturity, this is a yellowish-green tomato with dark green striations. Although it's a beefsteak variety, the fruit is typically smaller than its kin, about the size of a baseball. The flavor is mildly spicy and slightly tart.

Old Ivory Egg: A mild-flavored yellow plum, this tomato earned its name because it is the size and shape of a chicken's egg. It's a creamy ivory color that turns yellow as it ripens. Enjoy the mild, sweet flavor of this variety either cooked or raw. It's a great garden selection, as it produces fruit up until frost.

Green Grape: This delicious little fruit looks like a big Muscat grape. The mild flavor has a nice sweetness balanced by bright acidity, and it's deliciously juicy.

Yellow Pear: Sometimes called Beam's yellow pear, these are firm, tart, tiny, pear-shaped tomatoes with citruslike acidity.

QUICK & EASY

Roasted Brandywine Tomato, Fennel, and Shrimp with Feta

Roasting the tomatoes heightens their natural flavor and sweetness. Serve this dish over hot cooked rice or pasta.

- 4 cups thinly sliced fennel bulb (about 2 small)
- 1 cup red bell pepper strips
- Cooking spray
- 1 tablespoon extravirgin olive oil, divided
- ½ teaspoon salt, divided
- 3 red Brandywine tomatoes, peeled and each cut into ¾-inch-thick wedges (about 2 pounds)
- 6 garlic cloves, minced
- 1½ pounds peeled and deveined medium shrimp
- ½ cup (2 ounces) crumbled feta cheese
- 1 tablespoon chopped fresh basil

1. Preheat broiler.
2. Combine fennel and bell pepper on a baking sheet coated with cooking spray. Drizzle vegetable mixture with 1½ teaspoons oil; sprinkle with ¼ teaspoon salt. Toss to coat. Broil 10 minutes. Add tomatoes to pan; toss gently. Broil 10 minutes.
3. Combine remaining 1½ teaspoons oil, garlic, and shrimp in a bowl; toss to coat. Add shrimp mixture to pan. Broil 6 minutes or until shrimp are done and vegetables are charred and tender. Transfer shrimp mixture to a large bowl. Add remaining ¼ teaspoon salt; toss gently. Sprinkle mixture with cheese and basil. Yield: 5 servings (serving size: about 1¼ cups and about 1 tablespoon cheese).

CALORIES 266 (28% from fat); FAT 8.2g (sat 2.6g, mono 2.9g, poly 1.6g); PROTEIN 32.3g; CARB 17.1g; FIBER 5.1g; CHOL 217mg; IRON 4.6mg; SODIUM 611mg; CALC 189mg

---

QUICK & EASY

Old Ivory Egg Tomato, Watermelon, and Mint Salad

The sweetness of the watermelon brings out the flavor of the yellow plum tomatoes, the feta adds a touch of salt, and the mint finishes the salad with a refreshing note. Cut the watermelon into wedges that are similar in size to the tomato slices.

- 3 cups (½-inch-thick) slices Old Ivory Egg tomato (about 1 pound)
- 3 cups (½-inch thick) seedless watermelon wedges (about 12 ounces)
- ¼ teaspoon sea salt
- ¼ teaspoon freshly ground black pepper
- 2 tablespoons small mint leaves
- 1 tablespoon fresh lime juice
- 1 teaspoon extravirgin olive oil
- ¼ cup (1 ounce) crumbled feta cheese

① Arrange tomato and watermelon alternately on a platter; sprinkle evenly with salt and pepper. Scatter mint over tomato mixture. Drizzle with juice and oil; top with cheese. Yield: 4 servings (serving size: about 1½ cups).

CALORIES 80 (36% from fat); FAT 3.2g (sat 1.3g, mono 1.3g, poly 0.4g); PROTEIN 2.6g; CARB 12.5g; FIBER 1.7g; CHOL 6mg; IRON 0.8mg; SODIUM 234mg; CALC 50mg

QUICK & EASY
Sungold Tomato Salsa Cruda with Orzo

Sungold tomatoes are little orange-gold cherry tomatoes with a delicious sweet flavor. The salsa *cruda,* an uncooked sauce, would be a tasty and pretty addition to your next backyard barbecue.

```
8   ounces uncooked orzo (rice-shaped
    pasta)
4   cups Sungold tomatoes, halved
    (about 2 pounds)
½   cup chopped fresh basil
⅓   cup thinly sliced green onions
2   tablespoons finely chopped fresh
    oregano
1½  tablespoons extravirgin olive oil
1   tablespoon white balsamic vinegar
¾   teaspoon salt
½   teaspoon freshly ground black
    pepper
2   garlic cloves, minced
½   cup (2 ounces) shaved Parmesan
    cheese
```

① Cook pasta according to package directions, omitting salt and fat. Rinse with cold water; drain well.
② Combine pasta, tomatoes, and next 8 ingredients in a bowl; toss to coat. Top with cheese. Yield: 8 servings (serving size: 1 cup pasta mixture and 1 tablespoon cheese).

CALORIES 161 (28% from fat); FAT 4.9g (sat 1.3g, mono 2.3g, poly 0.6g); PROTEIN 6.4g; CARB 23.6g; FIBER 1.9g; CHOL 4mg; IRON 0.8mg; SODIUM 325mg; CALC 81mg

STAFF FAVORITE • QUICK & EASY
Ham and Cheese Tartines with Cherokee Purple Tomato Salad

A tartine is an open-faced sandwich. Manchego, a sheep's-milk cheese, and serrano ham give this salad a Spanish flair.

TARTINES:
```
4   (1½-ounce) slices ciabatta bread,
    toasted
1   ounce serrano ham, cut into 4 thin
    slices
3   ounces Manchego cheese, cut
    into 4 thin slices
1   teaspoon chopped fresh oregano
```
SALAD:
```
1   tablespoon finely chopped fresh
    oregano
1   tablespoon finely chopped shallots
1   tablespoon sherry vinegar
2   teaspoons extravirgin olive oil
1   garlic clove, minced
4   cups torn Boston lettuce
3   cups thinly sliced honeydew
    melon
3   Cherokee Purple tomatoes, halved
    lengthwise and thinly sliced (about
    2 pounds)
```

① Preheat broiler.
② To prepare tartines, place bread slices in a single layer on a baking sheet. Arrange 1 ham slice and 1 cheese slice on each bread slice. Broil 3 minutes or until cheese melts. Sprinkle evenly with 1 teaspoon oregano.
③ To prepare salad, combine 1 tablespoon oregano and next 4 ingredients in a bowl, stirring well with a whisk. Arrange 1 cup lettuce on each of 4 plates. Top each serving with ¾ cup honeydew and ½ cup tomato slices. Drizzle each serving with about 1 tablespoon dressing. Place 1 tartine on each plate. Yield: 4 servings.

CALORIES 269 (34% from fat); FAT 10.3g (sat 3.9g, mono 4.5g, poly 0.8g); PROTEIN 11.2g; CARB 34.4g; FIBER 2.2g; CHOL 19mg; IRON 2.4mg; SODIUM 730mg; CALC 135mg

What's That Name Again?

Specific heirloom tomato names can be confusing because they differ from one region to the next. For example, the Mortgage Lifter is also sometimes called Radiator Charlie. A Brandywine grown for generations in one part of the country may not resemble a Brandywine grown elsewhere, as each plant adapts to its environment, creating slightly different fruit. The flavor of each tomato is influenced by weather, the soil it grows in, as well as the other crops planted in close proximity.

There are thousands of varieties of heirloom tomatoes, all from different seed sources. This can make it tricky to distinguish one variety from another, especially if you're comparing one pale yellow, small, globe tomato that boasts vivid citrus flavor with another that has similar characteristics.

Moreover, most farmers' markets and specialty foods stores simply label the array of multicolored tomatoes *heirloom tomatoes*. When you can't be sure of a tomato's true name or origin, simply find the best-quality tomatoes grown in your area.

Regardless of variety, though, heirloom tomatoes benefit from simple treatment in the kitchen to best allow their flavors to shine. Most heirloom tomatoes are best enjoyed uncooked or minimally cooked, ideal for the warm-weather season in which they thrive.

Selection and Storage

When shopping for tomatoes, look for bright, shiny skin and firm flesh that yields slightly to gentle pressure. Although tomatoes are best eaten as soon after harvest as possible, they'll keep up to four days, stored at room temperature and out of direct sunlight. Arrange the fruit in a single layer, stem sides up, with plenty of space in between to allow air to circulate. Never refrigerate tomatoes, as chilling causes sugars to convert to starch, diminishing the flavor and leaving the flesh mealy.

Gorgonzola and Mortgage Lifter Tomato Pizza

Mortgage Lifter tomatoes, a pink-fleshed beefsteak variety, are also often labeled "Radiator Charlie." Vital wheat gluten strengthens the dough. Look for it at health-food stores and large supermarkets.

- 1 package active dry yeast (about 2¼ teaspoons)
- ⅓ cup warm water (100° to 110°)
- ½ cup whole wheat flour (about 2.5 ounces)
- ½ cup all-purpose flour (about 2.25 ounces)
- 1 tablespoon vital wheat gluten
- 1 teaspoon extravirgin olive oil
- ½ teaspoon kosher salt
  Cooking spray
- 1 tablespoon cornmeal
- ¾ cup (3 ounces) shredded part-skim mozzarella cheese
- ½ cup (2 ounces) crumbled Gorgonzola cheese
- 2 Mortgage Lifter tomatoes, cut into ¼-inch-thick slices (about 1 pound)
- 2 tablespoons chopped fresh basil
- 1 garlic clove, minced
- ¼ teaspoon salt
- ¼ teaspoon crushed red pepper

❶ Dissolve yeast in ⅓ cup warm water in a large bowl; let stand 5 minutes. Lightly spoon flours into dry measuring cups, and level with a knife. Add flours, wheat gluten, oil, and kosher salt; stir until a soft dough forms.
❷ Turn dough out onto a lightly floured surface. Knead until smooth and elastic (about 3 minutes). Place dough in a bowl coated with cooking spray, turning to coat top. Cover and let rise in a warm place (85°), free from drafts, 1 hour or until doubled in size. (Press two fingers into dough. If indentation remains, dough has risen enough.)
❸ Preheat oven to 450°.
❹ Punch dough down. Roll dough into a 10 x 14–inch rectangle on a lightly floured surface. Place dough on a baking sheet coated with cooking spray and sprinkled with cornmeal. Cover and let rise in a warm place (85°), free from drafts, 20 minutes.
❺ Sprinkle cheeses evenly over dough. Arrange tomato slices in a single layer over cheese. Combine basil and remaining ingredients in a bowl; sprinkle evenly over tomatoes.
❻ Bake at 450° for 12 minutes or until crust is golden brown. Cut pizza into 8 (5 x 3½-inch) rectangles. Yield: 4 servings (serving size: 2 rectangles).

CALORIES 261 (32% from fat); FAT 9.2g (sat 5.4g, mono 1.9g, poly 0.5g); PROTEIN 16.3g; CARB 29.5g; FIBER 4.5g; CHOL 25mg; IRON 2.2mg; SODIUM 680mg; CALC 237mg

Green Zebra Tomato and Crab Stacks

Serve two stacks over a bed of mixed greens, and top with a little chopped avocado for a refreshing main dish salad.

- 2½ tablespoons white balsamic vinegar
- 1 tablespoon minced shallots
- 1 tablespoon minced fresh tarragon
- 2 teaspoons extravirgin olive oil
- 1 pound Dungeness crabmeat
- 12 (½-inch-thick) slices Green Zebra tomato (about 1 pound)
- ¼ teaspoon fine sea salt, divided
- ¼ teaspoon freshly ground black pepper, divided
- 6 tarragon sprigs (optional)

❶ Combine first 4 ingredients in a bowl, stirring well with a whisk. Add crabmeat; toss gently to coat.
❷ Place one tomato slice on each of 6 plates; sprinkle evenly with ⅛ teaspoon salt and ⅛ teaspoon pepper. Divide crab mixture evenly over tomatoes. Arrange remaining tomato slices over crab mixture; sprinkle evenly with remaining ⅛ teaspoon salt and remaining ⅛ teaspoon pepper. Garnish with tarragon springs, if desired. Yield: 6 servings.

CALORIES 89 (30% from fat); FAT 3g (sat 0.2g, mono 1.4g, poly 0.7g); PROTEIN 11.7g; CARB 4.7g; FIBER 0.7g; CHOL 68mg; IRON 0.9mg; SODIUM 513mg; CALC 39mg

Heirloom Tomato Salad with Herbs and Capers

Use a combination of your favorite varieties. We like a mix of red Brandywine, Green Zebra, and Persimmon for the beefsteak tomatoes, and Sungold, Yellow Pear, and Green Grape for the cherry tomatoes.

- 2 cups assorted heirloom cherry tomatoes, halved
- ½ cup (2 ounces) crumbled reduced-fat feta cheese
- ¼ cup thinly sliced fresh basil
- 3 tablespoons chopped fresh flat-leaf parsley
- 2 tablespoons chopped fresh mint
- 1 tablespoon drained capers, chopped
- 1 tablespoon balsamic vinegar
- 1 tablespoon extravirgin olive oil
- 2 pounds assorted beefsteak heirloom tomatoes, each cut into 6 wedges
- ½ teaspoon salt
- ¼ teaspoon freshly ground black pepper
- 6 (½-ounce) slices sourdough bread, toasted or grilled

❶ Combine first 9 ingredients in a bowl. Sprinkle tomato mixture with salt and pepper; toss gently. Serve with bread. Yield: 6 servings (serving size: about 1¼ cups tomato mixture and 1 bread slice).

CALORIES 112 (34% from fat); FAT 4.2g (sat 1.2g, mono 1.7g, poly 0.5g); PROTEIN 5.6g; CARB 14.9g; FIBER 2.6g; CHOL 3mg; IRON 1.5mg; SODIUM 519mg; CALC 47mg

Thai Beef and Green Grape Tomato Salad

Bright, citrusy Green Grape tomatoes are worth seeking out for this salad because their flavor plays into the hot, sour, salty, sweet combination in most Thai dishes. Although this variety is increasingly available, look for the assorted small heirloom cherry tomatoes sold in quart containers if you can't find Green Grapes.

DRESSING:

- 2 tablespoons fresh lime juice
- 2 tablespoons low-sodium soy sauce
- 1 tablespoon brown sugar
- 2 teaspoons peanut oil
- 2 teaspoons chile paste with garlic (such as sambal oelek)
- 2 teaspoons grated peeled fresh ginger
- 2 teaspoons Thai fish sauce (such as Three Crabs)

SALAD:

- 3 tablespoons brown sugar
- 1 tablespoon grated peeled fresh ginger
- 1 tablespoon low-sodium soy sauce
- 1 tablespoon Thai fish sauce (such as Three Crabs)
- 2 garlic cloves, minced
- 1 (1¼-pound) flank steak
- Cooking spray
- 4 cups chopped romaine lettuce
- 2¾ cups halved Green Grape tomatoes (about 12 ounces)
- ¾ cup thinly sliced radishes
- ½ cup thinly sliced seeded peeled cucumber
- ¼ cup vertically sliced red onion
- 1 tablespoon chopped fresh cilantro
- 1 tablespoon chopped fresh basil
- 1 tablespoon chopped fresh mint

1 To prepare dressing, combine first 7 ingredients in a bowl, stirring well; set aside.

2 To prepare salad, combine 3 tablespoons brown sugar and next 4 ingredients in a large zip-top plastic bag. Add steak to bag; seal. Marinate in refrigerator 4 to 6 hours, turning bag occasionally.

3 Prepare grill.

4 Remove steak from bag, and discard marinade. Place steak on grill rack coated with cooking spray; grill 7 minutes on each side or until desired degree of doneness. Let steak stand 10 minutes; cut steak diagonally across grain into thin slices.

5 Combine lettuce and remaining ingredients in a large bowl. Add dressing; toss gently to coat. Arrange about 1½ cups lettuce mixture on each of 5 plates; top each serving with about 3 ounces steak. Yield: 5 servings.

CALORIES 275 (33% from fat); FAT 10.2g (sat 3.6g, mono 4.1g, poly 1.1g); PROTEIN 26.1g; CARB 19.9g; FIBER 2.6g; CHOL 43mg; IRON 3mg; SODIUM 884mg; CALC 65mg

---

Fish for Dinner Menu
serves 8

To get a jump start on the meal, prepare the farro mixture up to a day ahead, and bring to room temperature before plating over tomato slices.

Farro, Green Bean, Corn, and Abraham Lincoln Tomato Salad

Lemon grilled trout

Prepare grill. Open each of 8 (8-ounce) dressed whole rainbow trout as you would a book. Sprinkle 1 teaspoon kosher salt and ½ teaspoon freshly ground black pepper evenly over fish. Arrange 3 (¼-inch) lemon slices and 1 thyme sprig on bottom half of each fish; fold over to cover with top half of fish. Place on a grill rack coated with cooking spray; grill 2 minutes on each side or until fish flakes easily when tested with a fork or until desired degree of doneness. Garnish with additional thyme sprigs, if desired.

Flatbread

Farro, Green Bean, Corn, and Abraham Lincoln Tomato Salad

Farro is an old-world, nutty-flavored wheat grain from Italy. Serve this fresh salad with any grilled meat, poultry, or fish. Substitute another red globe or beefsteak tomato if you can't find Abraham Lincoln.

- ⅓ cup farro or spelt berries (about 5 ounces)
- 1 cup (1-inch) cut green beans
- 2 tablespoons finely chopped shallots
- 1 tablespoon extravirgin olive oil
- 1 tablespoon fresh lemon juice
- 1½ teaspoons white wine vinegar
- ½ teaspoon Dijon mustard
- 1 garlic clove, minced
- ½ cup fresh corn kernels
- 1 tablespoon chopped fresh oregano
- ¾ teaspoon salt, divided
- ½ teaspoon freshly ground black pepper, divided
- 4 Abraham Lincoln tomatoes, each cut into 6 slices (about 1½ pounds)

1 Place farro in a large saucepan; cover with water 2 inches above farro. Bring to a boil. Cover, reduce heat, and simmer 28 minutes. Add beans to pan; cook 2 minutes or until crisp-tender. Drain and rinse with cold water; drain.

2 Combine shallots and next 5 ingredients in a medium bowl, stirring well with a whisk. Add farro mixture, corn, and oregano; toss gently to coat. Stir in ¼ teaspoon salt and ¼ teaspoon pepper.

3 Arrange 3 tomato slices on each of 8 plates; sprinkle evenly with remaining ½ teaspoon salt and remaining ¼ teaspoon pepper. Top each serving with about ¼ cup farro mixture. Yield: 8 servings.

CALORIES 104 (23% from fat); FAT 2.7g (sat 0.3g, mono 1.3g, poly 0.2g); PROTEIN 3.5g; CARB 20g; FIBER 1.4g; CHOL 0mg; IRON 1.1mg; SODIUM 230mg; CALC 18mg

Heirloom Tomato Salad with Tomato Granita

Yellow-red Mr. Stripey tomatoes give this ice a light hue. Use red or purple tomatoes for a darker granita, if you prefer. Mixing purple basil with deep-green Italian basil yields a nuanced flavor and a lovely garnish.

This refreshingly simple dish puts tomatoes to use in two ways. Icy tomato granita atop succulent room-temperature tomatoes offers a pleasing contrast of textures and temperatures. Include an assortment of tomatoes in the salad to boost eye appeal; doing so will also make the taste vary from slice to slice.

Heirloom Tomato Salad with Tomato Granita

GRANITA:
- 1 tablespoon red wine vinegar
- 2 teaspoons extravirgin olive oil
- ¼ teaspoon kosher salt
- 8 ounces seeded peeled heirloom tomato

SALAD:
- 4 assorted heirloom tomatoes, cut into ¼-inch-thick slices (about 2 pounds)
- ½ teaspoon freshly ground black pepper
- ¼ teaspoon kosher salt
- 1 tablespoon thinly sliced fresh basil

① To prepare granita, place first 4 ingredients in a blender or food processor; process until smooth. Place tomato mixture in an 8-inch square baking dish; cover and freeze until firm, stirring twice during first 2 hours. Remove mixture from freezer; scrape entire mixture with a fork until fluffy.

② To prepare salad, arrange tomato slices on a platter. Sprinkle tomatoes with pepper and ¼ teaspoon salt. Top with granita. Sprinkle with basil. Yield: 6 servings (serving size: about 3 tomato slices and 2 tablespoons granita).

CALORIES 54 (37% from fat); FAT 2.2g (sat 0.3g, mono 1.2g, poly 0.5g); PROTEIN 1.6g; CARB 8.9g; FIBER 2.1g; CHOL 0mg; IRON 0.9mg; SODIUM 174mg; CALC 11mg

Farm in the City

Abby Mandel launched Chicago's Green City Market and made it one of the country's leading purveyors of local food.

For Abby Mandel, the desire for readily available, quality foods was a great motivator. In the mid-1990s, the Chicago-based cookbook author and former syndicated food columnist surveyed the city's markets and found them, despite their proximity to America's farming heartland, lacking local and organically grown foods. Back then, even at neighborhood farmers' markets, some of the goods looked like they came off a middleman's truck rather than from a nearby grower's fields.

Mandel's solution: Start a new market—the Green City Market—in 1999. "Its mission is to make local, quality, sustainable foods more accessible to Chicagoans," says Mandel. Now in its 10th season, the nonprofit greenmarket showcases regional agriculture, helps sustain small farms, and educates the public about local foods.

German Apple Pancake

Local apples begin to appear at farmers' markets in late August. We love the dramatic presentation of this large pancake—it puffs up gloriously—as well as its rich, custardlike texture. Use any type of firm, tart apple—Granny Smith, pippin, Northern Spy, or Sierra Beauty, for example.

BATTER:
- ½ cup all-purpose flour (about 2.25 ounces)
- 1 tablespoon granulated sugar
- ½ teaspoon baking powder
- ⅛ teaspoon salt
- ⅛ teaspoon grated whole nutmeg
- 1 cup egg substitute
- 1 cup fat-free milk
- 2 tablespoons butter, melted
- 1 teaspoon vanilla extract

APPLE MIXTURE:
- Cooking spray
- ½ cup granulated sugar, divided
- ½ teaspoon ground cinnamon
- ½ teaspoon grated whole nutmeg
- 1 cup thinly sliced Granny Smith apple

REMAINING INGREDIENT:
- 1 tablespoon powdered sugar

① To prepare batter, lightly spoon flour into a dry measuring cup; level with a knife. Combine flour and next 4 ingredients in a medium bowl, stirring with a whisk. Combine egg substitute and next 3 ingredients in a small bowl, stirring with a whisk. Add egg substitute mixture to flour mixture, stirring with a whisk. Let stand 30 minutes.

② Preheat oven to 425°.

③ To prepare apple mixture, coat bottom and sides of a 10-inch ovenproof skillet with cooking spray. Combine ¼ cup granulated sugar, cinnamon, and ½ teaspoon nutmeg; sprinkle evenly over bottom and sides of pan. Arrange apple in an even spokelike layer in pan. Sprinkle apple with remaining ¼ cup granulated sugar. Cook over medium heat 8 minutes or until mixture bubbles. Slowly pour batter over apple mixture.

④ Bake at 425° for 15 minutes. Reduce oven temperature to 375° (do not remove pancake from oven); bake an additional 13 minutes or until center is set. Carefully loosen pancake with a spatula. Gently slide pancake onto a serving platter. Sift powdered sugar over top. Cut into 6 wedges; serve immediately. Yield: 6 servings (serving size: 1 wedge).

CALORIES 173 (28% from fat); FAT 5.4g (sat 2.8g, mono 1.4g, poly 0.9g); PROTEIN 7.7g; CARB 23.2g; FIBER 0.9g; CHOL 11mg; IRON 1.5mg; SODIUM 213mg; CALC 101mg

QUICK & EASY
Albuquerque Corn Salad

Farmers' markets overflow with corn this time of year; this Southwestern-accented salad is a delicious way to use the bounty. Because the corn is so fresh, all it needs is a quick sauté. Serve warm or at room temperature, garnished with cilantro sprigs.

- 1 tablespoon olive oil
- ⅔ cup chopped jicama
- 1 tablespoon minced jalapeño pepper
- 2 cups fresh corn kernels (about 4 ears)
- 1¾ cups thinly sliced green onions (about 8 onions)
- ⅔ cup chopped red bell pepper
- ½ teaspoon ground cumin
- ¼ teaspoon salt

❶ Heat oil in a large nonstick skillet over medium-high heat. Add jicama and jalapeño to pan; sauté 2 minutes, stirring frequently. Add corn and remaining ingredients; sauté 2 minutes, stirring frequently. Yield: 4 servings (serving size: about ½ cup).

CALORIES 151 (36% from fat); FAT 6.1g (sat 0.5g, mono 2.5g, poly 0.5g); PROTEIN 5.3g; CARB 24.9g; FIBER 4.9g; CHOL 0mg; IRON 1.4mg; SODIUM 157mg; CALC 38mg

QUICK & EASY
Macaroni Salad with Summer Tomatoes

White balsamic vinegar helps this side dish maintain its fresh appeal. Serve with grilled chicken. Or, for a meatless entrée, add mozzarella, feta, or goat cheese.

- 8 ounces uncooked medium elbow macaroni
- 3 tablespoons white balsamic vinegar
- 1 tablespoon minced fresh basil
- ¾ teaspoon salt
- ½ teaspoon sugar
- ¼ teaspoon crushed red pepper
- 3 tablespoons extravirgin olive oil, divided
- 2 teaspoons minced garlic, divided
- 4 cups chopped seeded tomato (about 6 tomatoes)
- 1 (1-ounce) slice white bread
- ⅛ teaspoon salt
- 2 tablespoons thinly sliced fresh basil

❶ Cook pasta according to package directions, omitting salt and fat. Drain and rinse with cold water; drain. Cover and chill.
❷ Combine vinegar and next 4 ingredients in a large bowl. Add 2 tablespoons oil and 1½ teaspoons garlic, stirring with a whisk. Add pasta and tomato; toss well to coat.
❸ Place bread in a food processor; pulse 5 times or until coarse crumbs measure ½ cup. Heat remaining 1 tablespoon oil in a nonstick skillet over medium-high heat. Add breadcrumbs and remaining ½ teaspoon garlic to pan; sauté 2 minutes or until browned and crisp, stirring frequently. Remove from heat; stir in ⅛ teaspoon salt. Cool. Serve pasta with breadcrumb mixture and sliced basil. Yield: 8 servings (serving size: about ¾ cup salad, about 1 tablespoon breadcrumbs, and ¾ teaspoon basil).

CALORIES 187 (29% from fat); FAT 6.1g (sat 0.9g, mono 4.2g, poly 0.8g); PROTEIN 4.8g; CARB 28.4g; FIBER 2g; CHOL 0mg; IRON 1.5mg; SODIUM 285mg; CALC 19mg

Hot Hit

A Texas musician creates a delectable chicken entrée harmonized with spices, peanut butter, and tomatoes.

For Mary Cutrufello, a professional musician in Austin, Texas, eating healthfully can be a challenge. As a songwriter, vocalist, and guitar player, Cutrufello spends extended periods on the road traveling to gigs with her band. "After I turned 30, I could no longer get away with eating too much 'road food' from a weight standpoint," she says. "So when I return home, it feels great to cook and eat healthfully."

When she's not writing and performing, Cutrufello enjoys experimenting with recipe development in the kitchen. She created this delectable, fiery dish about four years ago and often prepares it and freezes leftovers. "It's nice to have a dish I can thaw and serve over rice for a quick meal," she says.

Cutrufello's Spicy Peanut Chicken over Rice was created one day when she made her own peanut butter in the blender, which inspired her to tinker with flavor combinations. "In this dish, you can definitely taste the curry powder; the heat comes from the crushed red pepper. The peanut butter is subtle and similar to the flavor of an Asian saté. Plum tomatoes and tomato paste balance the heat of the spices." She adds, "I like to serve it over brown rice for its texture and whole-grain benefits.

"I love creating food that's healthful yet tasty," she says. "It's like a puzzle to solve when I'm in the kitchen." Whether she's experimenting with musical styles or flavor combinations, Cutrufello has found the perfect harmony.

Spicy Peanut Chicken over Rice

"This makes enough to freeze leftovers, which keep for up to a month. Spoon single servings into airtight containers; thaw overnight in the refrigerator, and reheat in a saucepan. You can increase the crushed red pepper, if you like; a dollop of yogurt on top balances the spiciness."

—Mary Cutrufello, Austin, Texas

- 1 tablespoon peanut oil
- 1 cup chopped onion (about 1 medium)
- 1½ tablespoons minced garlic (about 4 cloves)
- 2½ pounds skinless, boneless chicken breast halves, cut into 1-inch pieces
- ⅓ cup chunky peanut butter
- 1½ teaspoons curry powder
- 1 teaspoon salt
- 1 teaspoon crushed red pepper
- ½ teaspoon freshly ground black pepper
- 1 (6-ounce) can tomato paste
- 3 cups chopped plum tomato (about 6 tomatoes)
- 2 (14-ounce) cans fat-free, less-sodium chicken broth
- 8 cups hot cooked brown rice
- ¾ cup 2% Greek-style yogurt (such as Fage)

1 Heat oil in a Dutch oven over medium heat. Add onion and garlic to pan; cook 5 minutes or until tender, stirring frequently. Add chicken to pan; cook 4 minutes or until chicken is done, stirring frequently. Stir in peanut butter and next 5 ingredients; cook 1 minute. Add tomato and broth to pan; bring to a boil. Reduce heat, and simmer 30 minutes or until slightly thickened, stirring occasionally. Serve chicken mixture over rice; top each serving with yogurt. Yield: 12 servings (serving size: ¾ cup chicken mixture, ⅔ cup brown rice, and 1 tablespoon yogurt).

CALORIES 340 (20% from fat); FAT 7.6g (sat 1.6g, mono 3.1g, poly 2.2g); PROTEIN 30g; CARB 38g; FIBER 4.6g; CHOL 56mg; IRON 2.1mg; SODIUM 523mg; CALC 59mg

Eggplant Marinara Pasta Casserole

"Now that I am retired, I have more time to cook. My husband and I love to travel, and this dish was inspired by a trip to Italy. Pancetta is Italian bacon and comes in a sausagelike roll; it lends a salty bite to the marinara."

—Glenda Mann, Longview, Texas

- 6 cups (½-inch) cubed eggplant (about 1 pound)
- 1½ teaspoons kosher salt, divided Cooking spray
- 1 ounce pancetta, chopped
- 2 cups thinly sliced onion
- 1 tablespoon extravirgin olive oil
- 2 garlic cloves, minced
- ¼ cup dry white wine
- 1 tablespoon chopped fresh basil
- 1 teaspoon chopped fresh oregano
- ½ teaspoon crushed red pepper
- 1 (28-ounce) can diced tomatoes, undrained
- 16 ounces uncooked penne (tube-shaped pasta)
- 1 cup (4 ounces) shredded fontina cheese
- 1 (3-inch) piece French bread baguette (2 ounces)
- ½ cup (2 ounces) grated fresh Parmesan cheese

1 Arrange eggplant on several layers of heavy-duty paper towels. Sprinkle eggplant with 1 teaspoon salt; let stand 15 minutes. Pat dry with additional paper towels.

2 Preheat oven to 450°.

3 Arrange eggplant in a single layer on a baking sheet coated with cooking spray. Bake at 450° for 30 minutes or until lightly browned, stirring after 15 minutes. Remove from baking sheet; cool.

4 Cook pancetta in a Dutch oven over medium heat until crisp. Add onion, oil, and garlic to pan; cook 6 minutes or until onion is lightly browned, stirring frequently. Add wine to pan; cook until liquid evaporates, scraping pan to loosen browned bits. Stir in remaining ½ teaspoon salt, basil, and next 3 ingredients. Bring to a simmer over medium heat; partially cover, and cook 20 minutes, stirring occasionally. Remove from heat; stir in eggplant.

5 Cook pasta according to package directions, omitting salt and fat. Drain pasta in a colander over a bowl, reserving ¼ cup cooking water. Add pasta and reserved ¼ cup cooking water to tomato mixture; stir well. Spoon pasta mixture into a 13 x 9-inch baking dish coated with cooking spray. Sprinkle evenly with fontina.

6 Place baguette in a food processor; pulse 10 times or until coarse crumbs measure 1½ cups. Add Parmesan to processor; pulse 5 times. Sprinkle breadcrumb mixture evenly over fontina.

7 Bake at 450° for 12 minutes or until cheese melts and begins to brown. Yield: 8 servings (serving size: about 2 cups).

CALORIES 401 (24% from fat); FAT 10.6g (sat 4.8g, mono 3.7g, poly 0.6g); PROTEIN 16.6g; CARB 58.5g; FIBER 5.4g; CHOL 26mg; IRON 1.7mg; SODIUM 768mg; CALC 183mg

WINE NOTE: With an American take on an Italian dish, why not try an American take on a red Italian wine, like Tamás Estates Sangiovese 2005 ($14), an American wine made from the same grape as Italian Chianti. With its medium body and plentiful acidity, sangiovese is a classic choice with all tomato dishes, and offers tart cherry and sweet vanilla flavors that nicely balance each other.

Whole Wheat Banana Bread

"Whole wheat and soy flours boost the nutrition in this loaf."

—Barry Wise, Visalia, California

- 1 cup warm water (100° to 110°)
- 1 package dry yeast (about 2¼ teaspoons)
- 1 cup mashed ripe banana
- 2¼ cups bread flour (about 10.5 ounces), divided
- 1 cup whole wheat flour (about 4.75 ounces)
- ½ cup soy flour (about 2 ounces)
- 1¼ teaspoons salt
- Cooking spray
- 1 teaspoon butter, melted

❶ Combine 1 cup warm water and yeast; let stand 5 minutes. Stir in banana.
❷ Lightly spoon flours into dry measuring cups; level with a knife. Add 2 cups bread flour, wheat flour, soy flour, and salt to yeast mixture; stir until a soft dough forms. Turn dough out onto a floured surface. Knead until smooth and elastic (about 8 minutes); add enough of remaining ¼ cup bread flour, 1 tablespoon at a time, to prevent dough from sticking to hands (dough will feel sticky).
❸ Place dough in a large bowl coated with cooking spray; turn to coat top. Cover; let rise in a warm place (85°), free from drafts, 45 minutes or until doubled in size. (Press two fingers into dough. If indentation remains, dough has risen enough.) Punch dough down; cover and let rest 5 minutes. Roll dough into a 14 x 7–inch rectangle on a floured surface. Roll up tightly, starting with a short edge, pressing firmly to eliminate air pockets; pinch seam and ends to seal. Place roll, seam side down, in a 9 x 5–inch loaf pan coated with cooking spray. Coat top with cooking spray. Cover; let rise in a warm place 30 minutes or until doubled in size. (Press two fingers into dough. If indentation remains, dough has risen enough.)
❹ Preheat oven to 400°.
❺ Bake at 400° for 1 hour or until lightly browned on bottom and sounds hollow when tapped. Remove from pan; brush with butter. Cool completely. Yield: 12 servings (serving size: 1 slice).

CALORIES 153 (9% from fat); FAT 1.5g (sat 0.4g, mono 0.5g, poly 0.2g); PROTEIN 6.3g; CARB 29.8g; FIBER 3.2g; CHOL 1mg; IRON 2mg; SODIUM 249mg; CALC 8mg

Fresh Lemon Rice

"My family prefers rice for weeknight meals, so I'm always looking for ways to vary the flavor without using a lot of ingredients or effort."

—Maggie Brain, The Woodlands, Texas

- 3 cups water
- 2 cups uncooked basmati rice
- ¾ teaspoon salt
- 1 tablespoon extravirgin olive oil
- 1 tablespoon butter
- 1 teaspoon brown mustard seeds
- 3 tablespoons chopped fresh cilantro
- 2 teaspoons grated lemon rind
- 2 teaspoons fresh lemon juice
- Cilantro sprigs (optional)

❶ Combine first 3 ingredients in a large saucepan over medium-high heat; bring to a boil. Cover, reduce heat, and simmer 15 minutes or until liquid is absorbed and rice is tender. Remove pan from heat; let stand 5 minutes. Fluff with a fork.
❷ Heat oil and butter in a small skillet over medium-high heat until butter melts. Add mustard seeds to pan; cook 2 minutes or until seeds begin to pop. Scrape seed mixture into rice mixture using a rubber spatula. Add chopped cilantro, rind, and juice to rice mixture; stir well. Garnish with cilantro sprigs, if desired. Yield: 6 servings (serving size: 1 cup).

CALORIES 146 (27% from fat); FAT 4.3g (sat 1.5g, mono 2.1g, poly 0.3g); PROTEIN 2.2g; CARB 24.5g; FIBER 0.6g; CHOL 5mg; IRON 0.3mg; SODIUM 309mg; CALC 4mg

French Martini Sorbet

"We live in the Napa Valley, where we developed our passion for great food and wine. This is a twist on one of my favorite cocktails. The red food coloring gives the sorbet a light rose color, but it is optional. Three small scoops in a martini glass make an elegant presentation."

—Lynnsey Elshere, American Canyon, California

- 1¼ cups granulated sugar
- ¾ cup water
- 3 cups unsweetened pineapple juice
- ¼ cup fresh lemon juice
- ¼ cup Chambord (raspberry-flavored liqueur)
- 2 tablespoons vodka
- 3 drops red food coloring (optional)

❶ Combine sugar and ¾ cup water in a small saucepan over medium-high heat. Cook 2 minutes or until sugar dissolves, stirring constantly. Remove from heat; cool completely.
❷ Combine sugar mixture, juices, Chambord, vodka, and food coloring, if desired, in a large bowl; stir well. Pour mixture into freezer can of an ice-cream freezer; freeze according to manufacturer's instructions. Spoon sorbet into a freezer-safe container; cover and freeze 8 hours or overnight. Yield: 8 servings (serving size: ½ cup).

CALORIES 207 (0% from fat); FAT 0.1g (sat 0g, mono 0g, poly 0.1g); PROTEIN 0.4g; CARB 46.4g; FIBER 0.2g; CHOL 0mg; IRON 0.3mg; SODIUM 3mg; CALC 14mg

Grill Once, Eat Twice

Cook extra portions tonight to jump-start dinner tomorrow.

YOU'RE PROBABLY ENJOYING the benefits of grilling this summer. But think twice about it. You can fire up the grill once and cook enough to eat two times—dinner for tonight, plus extra food that can be turned into a second, different meal for another night. Following are ideas for beautifully crafted makeovers. Salmon takes on sweet-smoky barbecue flavor one night, for example, then transforms into Latin-inspired tacos later.

Grilling extra food puts you steps ahead for a second weeknight meal. The robust flavors from food that was cooked over a flame means less work in the kitchen. A simple marinade, spice rub, or easy sauce turns meat, fish, or vegetables into a great grilled entrée. And that bold caramelized taste holds up until the next day (or even a couple of days). For instance, when our Lemon-Grilled Chicken Breasts are chilled and then sliced a day or two later to top a zesty main-course Caesar salad, the rich, smoky flavor still shines.

LAMB MENU ONE

Lamb Steaks with Herbes de Provence and Grilled Sweet Onions

Orzo with grape tomatoes and sautéed zucchini

Focaccia

QUICK & EASY

Lamb Steaks with Herbes de Provence and Grilled Sweet Onions

To make our Greek Lamb Pizza (at right) the next night, set aside one steak and two onion slices.

- 3 (9-ounce) lamb leg steaks, trimmed (about 1 inch thick)
- Cooking spray
- 1 tablespoon dried herbes de Provence, crushed
- 1 teaspoon kosher salt, divided
- ¾ teaspoon freshly ground black pepper, divided
- 6 (½-inch-thick) slices Vidalia or other sweet onion (about 1 large)

1 Prepare grill.
2 Coat both sides of steaks with cooking spray. Sprinkle both sides of steaks evenly with herbes de Provence, ¾ teaspoon salt, and ½ teaspoon pepper.
3 Coat both sides of onion slices with cooking spray. Sprinkle onion with remaining ¼ teaspoon salt and remaining ¼ teaspoon pepper.
4 Place steaks and onion on grill rack coated with cooking spray; grill 4 minutes on each side or until steaks are desired degree of doneness and onion is tender. Remove from grill; cover and let stand 5 minutes. Cut steaks diagonally across grain into thin slices; discard bones. Serve steak with onion. Yield: 6 servings (serving size: 3 ounces steak and 1 onion slice).

CALORIES 139 (34% from fat); FAT 5.3g (sat 1.9g, mono 2.3g, poly 0.4g); PROTEIN 16.5g; CARB 5.9g; FIBER 1.3g; CHOL 51mg; IRON 1.6mg; SODIUM 356mg; CALC 26mg

---

Safe Storage

Take precautions to ensure leftovers stay fresh and safe.

- Refrigerate leftover food within two hours of cooking, or within one hour if the ambient temperature of the leftovers is above 90°.

- Store leftovers in wide, shallow containers. Deep containers may allow food to trap heat and not cool quickly enough .
- Use most cooked leftovers within three to four days. Cooked fish is best used within two days.

LAMB MENU TWO

Greek Lamb Pizza

Romaine salad with cucumbers, kalamata olives, and tomatoes

Honey-drizzled Greek yogurt with almond cookies

Greek Lamb Pizza

- 1 (10-ounce) Italian cheese-flavored thin pizza crust (such as Boboli)
- ¾ cup fat-free marinara sauce
- 2 servings Lamb Steaks with Herbes de Provence and Grilled Sweet Onions (at left), cut into 1-inch pieces
- ½ cup (2 ounces) crumbled feta cheese
- ⅔ cup (about 2½ ounces) shredded part-skim mozzarella cheese
- ¼ cup sliced pepperoncini peppers

1 Preheat oven to 450°.
2 Place pizza crust on a baking sheet. Spread marinara sauce over crust, leaving a ½-inch border. Top evenly with Lamb Steaks with Herbes de Provence and Grilled Sweet Onions. Sprinkle with cheeses. Bake pizza at 450° for 12 minutes or until cheeses melt. Remove pizza from oven; sprinkle with peppers. Cut pizza into 8 wedges. Yield: 4 servings (serving size: 2 wedges).

CALORIES 392 (31% from fat); FAT 13.4g (sat 6.8g, mono 4g, poly 0.7g); PROTEIN 23.1g; CARB 43.7g; FIBER 2.8g; CHOL 49mg; IRON 3.7mg; SODIUM 969mg; CALC 312mg

QUICK & EASY

Grilled Vegetable Pitas with Goat Cheese and Pesto Mayo

(pictured on page 257)

¼ cup reduced-fat mayonnaise
1 tablespoon commercial pesto
2 whole wheat pitas, cut in half
4 leaf lettuce leaves
4 servings Simple Grilled Vegetables
½ cup (2 ounces) crumbled goat cheese

① Combine mayonnaise and pesto.
② Spread 1 tablespoon mayonnaise mixture into each pita half. Stuff each pita half with 1 lettuce leaf, 1 serving Simple Grilled Vegetables, and 2 tablespoons cheese. Serve immediately. Yield: 4 servings (servings size: 1 stuffed pita half).

CALORIES 220 (30% from fat); FAT 7.3g (sat 2.5g, mono 1.6g, poly 1.6g); PROTEIN 8.9g; CARB 33.7g; FIBER 5.8g; CHOL 7mg; IRON 2.1mg; SODIUM 505mg; CALC 62mg

QUICK & EASY

SIMPLE GRILLED VEGETABLES:

8 (4-inch) portobello mushroom caps (about 1 pound)
4 red bell peppers, quartered
2 Vidalia or other sweet onions, each cut into 4 slices (about 1¼ pounds)
Cooking spray
½ teaspoon kosher salt
¼ teaspoon freshly ground black pepper
1½ tablespoons balsamic vinegar

① Prepare grill to medium-high heat.
② Arrange mushrooms, gill sides up; bell pepper; and onion on a baking sheet. Coat vegetables with cooking spray. Sprinkle evenly with salt and pepper. Drizzle vinegar over mushrooms. Place vegetables on grill rack; grill 5 minutes on each side or until tender. Yield: 8 servings (serving size: 1 mushroom, 2 bell pepper pieces, and 1 onion slice).

CALORIES 65 (4% from fat); FAT 0.3g (sat 0.1g, mono 0g, poly 0.1g); PROTEIN 2.8g; CARB 13.7g; FIBER 3.3g; CHOL 0mg; IRON 0.8mg; SODIUM 127mg; CALC 26mg

VEGETABLE MENU
TWO

*Herbed Penne with
Simple Grilled Vegetables*

Green salad with pear tomatoes

Baguette

Herbed Penne with Simple Grilled Vegetables

Leftover charred vegetables and fresh herbs create a simple and satisfying vegetarian entrée. For a heartier version, stir in two cups chopped chicken.

2 tablespoons olive oil, divided
4 servings Simple Grilled Vegetables (at left), cut into ¾-inch pieces
¾ teaspoon kosher salt, divided
½ teaspoon freshly ground black pepper, divided
¼ teaspoon crushed red pepper
4 cups hot cooked penne (about 8 ounces uncooked tube-shaped pasta)
¼ cup coarsely chopped fresh flat-leaf parsley
¼ cup coarsely chopped fresh basil
½ cup (2 ounces) shaved Parmigiano-Reggiano cheese

① Heat 1 tablespoon oil in a large nonstick skillet over medium heat. Add Simple Grilled Vegetables to pan; cook 4 minutes or until thoroughly heated, stirring occasionally. Stir in ¼ teaspoon salt, ¼ teaspoon black pepper, and red pepper. Remove from heat.
② Combine pasta, parsley, basil, remaining 1 tablespoon oil, remaining ½ teaspoon salt, and remaining ¼ teaspoon black pepper in a large bowl; toss well. Add Simple Grilled Vegetables; toss well. Sprinkle with cheese. Yield: 4 servings (serving size: 2 cups pasta mixture and 2 tablespoons cheese).

CALORIES 392 (27% from fat); FAT 11.8g (sat 3.3g, mono 6g, poly 0.9g); PROTEIN 15g; CARB 55.5g; FIBER 4.6g; CHOL 10mg; IRON 2.1mg; SODIUM 710mg; CALC 205mg

QUICK & EASY

Lemon-Grilled Chicken Breasts

Save three breast halves to make our Hearts of Romaine Caesar Salad with Grilled Chicken (page 232). Garnish the plate with grilled lemon slices.

3 tablespoons fresh lemon juice
2 tablespoons extravirgin olive oil
2 garlic cloves, minced
7 (6-ounce) skinless, boneless chicken breast halves
½ teaspoon kosher salt
½ teaspoon freshly ground black pepper
Cooking spray

① Prepare grill to medium-high heat.
② Combine first 4 ingredients in a large zip-top plastic bag; seal. Marinate in refrigerator 30 minutes, turning occasionally. Remove chicken from bag; discard

Continued

marinade. Sprinkle chicken evenly with salt and pepper.

❸ Place chicken on grill rack coated with cooking spray; grill 6 minutes on each side or until done. Yield: 7 servings (serving size: 1 breast half).

CALORIES 159 (20% from fat); FAT 3.5g (sat 0.7g, mono 1.8g, poly 0.6g); PROTEIN 29.5g; CARB 0.5g; FIBER 0.1g; CHOL 74mg; IRON 1mg; SODIUM 218mg; CALC 16mg

CHICKEN MENU TWO

Hearts of Romaine Caesar Salad with Grilled Chicken

Soft breadsticks

Cubed cantaloupe with cracked black pepper

Hearts of Romaine Caesar Salad with Grilled Chicken

Coddling the egg makes it creamy but does not heat it to 160°, the temperature required to kill bacteria. Use a pasteurized whole egg if you have safety concerns.

- 1 large egg
- 2 canned anchovy fillets
- 2 garlic cloves
- ½ teaspoon freshly ground black pepper
- ¼ teaspoon kosher salt
- 1 tablespoon fresh lemon juice
- 1 tablespoon extravirgin olive oil
- 1 tablespoon water
- 1⅓ cups plain croutons
- 2 heads hearts of romaine lettuce, leaves separated (about 14 ounces)
- 3 servings Lemon-Grilled Chicken Breasts (page 231), thinly sliced
- ¼ cup (1 ounce) grated Parmigiano-Reggiano cheese

❶ Place egg in a small bowl or coffee mug; cover with boiling water. Let stand 1 minute. Rinse egg with cold water; break egg into a small bowl.

❷ Combine anchovy and next 3 ingredients in a mini food processor; process until minced. Add egg and juice; process 1 minute or until thick. Gradually add oil and 1 tablespoon water, processing until blended.

❸ Combine croutons, lettuce, Lemon-Grilled Chicken Breasts, and egg mixture in a bowl; toss gently. Divide salad evenly among 4 plates. Sprinkle each with 1 tablespoon cheese. Yield: 4 servings.

CALORIES 261 (35% from fat); FAT 10.1g (sat 2.8g, mono 5.2g, poly 1.3g); PROTEIN 29.3g; CARB 12.5g; FIBER 1.8g; CHOL 115mg; IRON 2.9mg; SODIUM 561mg; CALC 165mg

SALMON MENU ONE

Cedar-Planked Salmon with Barbecue Spice Rub

Roasted new potato wedges

Spinach salad with peaches, red onions, and commercial raspberry vinaigrette

STAFF FAVORITE
Cedar-Planked Salmon with Barbecue Spice Rub

An assertive spice blend gives salmon a robust taste that works well on its own and in tacos. Reserve half of the fish for Grilled Salmon Tacos with Chipotle Sauce (at right). Look for cedar planks in gourmet markets or large supermarkets.

- 1 (15 x 6½ x ⅜-inch) cedar grilling plank
- 1½ teaspoons kosher salt
- 1½ teaspoons dark brown sugar
- 1 teaspoon ground cumin
- 1 teaspoon dried thyme, crushed
- ¾ teaspoon coarsely ground black pepper
- ¾ teaspoon Hungarian sweet paprika
- ¾ teaspoon chili powder
- ¼ teaspoon ground cinnamon
- 1 (3-pound) center-cut salmon fillet, skinned

❶ Immerse and soak plank in water 1 hour; drain.

❷ Prepare grill to medium-high heat.

❸ Combine salt and next 7 ingredients; rub salt mixture over fish.

❹ Place plank on grill rack; grill 3 minutes or until lightly charred. Carefully turn plank over; place fish on charred side of plank. Cover and grill 25 minutes or until fish flakes easily when tested with a fork or until desired degree of doneness. Cut fish crosswise into 8 (4½-ounce) pieces. Yield: 8 servings (serving size: 1 piece).

CALORIES 233 (41% from fat); FAT 10.6g (sat 2.5g, mono 4.6g, poly 2.5g); PROTEIN 31.1g; CARB 1.4g; FIBER 0.4g; CHOL 80mg; IRON 0.8mg; SODIUM 420mg; CALC 22mg

SALMON MENU TWO

Grilled Salmon Tacos with Chipotle Sauce

Corn on the cob

Summer fruit salad

Grilled Salmon Tacos with Chipotle Sauce

Just a few embellishments turn Cedar-Planked Salmon (at left) into a new meal.

SAUCE:
- ½ cup fat-free mayonnaise
- 2 tablespoons minced fresh cilantro
- 2 tablespoons fat-free buttermilk
- 2 teaspoons minced chipotle chile, canned in adobo sauce (about 1 chile)

TACOS:
- 4 servings Cedar-Planked Salmon with Barbecue Spice Rub (at left), coarsely chopped
- 8 (6-inch) white corn tortillas
- 4 cups shredded green cabbage
- ⅓ cup chopped green onions
- 3 tablespoons fresh lime juice
- 1 cup diced seeded tomato (about 2 tomatoes)

1. Preheat oven to 250°.
2. To prepare sauce, combine first 4 ingredients in a small bowl.
3. To prepare tacos, place Cedar-Planked Salmon with Barbecue Spice Rub in a baking dish. Cover with foil. Wrap tortillas tightly in foil. Bake fish and tortillas at 250° for 15 minutes or until thoroughly heated.
4. Combine cabbage, onions, and juice; toss well.
5. Spread about 4 teaspoons sauce down center of each tortilla. Top each tortilla with about 2 ounces Cedar-Planked Salmon with Barbecue Spice Rub, ½ cup cabbage mixture, and 2 tablespoons tomato; fold in half. Serve immediately. Yield: 4 servings (serving size: 2 tacos).

CALORIES 408 (29% from fat); FAT 13g (sat 2.9g, mono 5g, poly 3.1g); PROTEIN 35.8g; CARB 37.8g; FIBER 6.6g; CHOL 84mg; IRON 2.2mg; SODIUM 798mg; CALC 166mg

---

FLANK STEAK MENU ONE

Garlic-Rubbed Flank Steak with Chimichurri Sauce

Black beans

Yellow rice

QUICK & EASY
Garlic-Rubbed Flank Steak with Chimichurri Sauce

Set aside half of the flank steak for Steak Panzanella (at right) another night.

½ cup packed fresh flat-leaf parsley leaves
2 tablespoons fresh lemon juice
½ teaspoon crushed red pepper
¼ teaspoon kosher salt
¼ teaspoon sugar
¼ teaspoon ground cumin
1 large garlic clove
2 tablespoons extravirgin olive oil
1 tablespoon water
4 servings Garlic-Rubbed Flank Steak

1. Place first 7 ingredients in a food processor; process until finely minced. With processor on, slowly pour oil and 1 tablespoon water through food chute; process until well blended. Serve sauce with Garlic-Rubbed Flank Steak. Yield: 4 servings (serving size: 3 ounces steak and 1 tablespoon sauce).

CALORIES 221 (50% from fat); FAT 12.4g (sat 3.2g, mono 7.1g, poly 1g); PROTEIN 24.2g; CARB 2.2g; FIBER 0.5g; CHOL 37mg; IRON 2.1mg; SODIUM 349mg; CALC 33mg

QUICK & EASY
GARLIC-RUBBED FLANK STEAK:

1 (2-pound) flank steak, trimmed
¾ teaspoon kosher salt
½ teaspoon freshly ground black pepper
2 garlic cloves, minced
Cooking spray

1. Prepare grill to medium-high heat.
2. Rub steak evenly with salt, pepper, and garlic. Place steak on grill rack coated with cooking spray; cover and grill 6 minutes. Turn steak over; cover and grill 4 minutes or until desired degree of doneness. Remove steak from grill; cover and let stand 5 minutes. Cut steak diagonally across grain into thin slices. Yield: 8 servings (serving size: 3 ounces).

CALORIES 153 (32% from fat); FAT 5.5g (sat 2.3g, mono 2.2g, poly 0.2g); PROTEIN 23.8g; CARB 0.3g; FIBER 0.1g; CHOL 37mg; IRON 1.5mg; SODIUM 227mg; CALC 19mg

---

FLANK STEAK MENU TWO

Steak Panzanella

Lemon sorbet with fresh summer berries

Steak Panzanella

Leftover steak adds substance to classic Italian bread salad. Toss vegetables with vinaigrette, and let stand at room temperature to draw out flavorful juices. With bread, vegetables, and meat, this dish doesn't need any accompaniments other than a glass of wine (try pinot noir).

½ pound day-old ciabatta bread, cut into 1-inch cubes (about 4 cups)
2½ cups coarsely chopped tomato (about 1 pound)
1 cup coarsely chopped English cucumber
½ cup coarsely chopped fresh basil
½ cup vertically sliced red onion
½ cup julienne-cut bottled roasted red bell peppers
1½ tablespoons capers
1 garlic clove, minced
3 tablespoons sherry vinegar
1 tablespoon extravirgin olive oil
¾ teaspoon sugar
½ teaspoon freshly ground black pepper
¼ teaspoon kosher salt
1½ cups loosely packed arugula
4 servings Garlic-Rubbed Flank Steak (at left), cut into 1-inch pieces

1. Preheat oven to 400°.
2. Arrange bread cubes in a single layer on a baking sheet. Bake at 400° for 8 minutes or until toasted; cool.
3. Combine tomato and next 6 ingredients in a large bowl. Combine vinegar and next 4 ingredients. Add vinegar mixture to tomato mixture; toss well. Cover and let stand 1 hour.
4. Add bread cubes, arugula, and Garlic-Rubbed Flank Steak to tomato mixture; toss gently to coat. Serve immediately. Yield: 4 servings (serving size: 2 cups).

CALORIES 387 (28% from fat); FAT 11.9g (sat 3.1g, mono 6.6g, poly 1.1g); PROTEIN 30.8g; CARB 40.3g; FIBER 3.5g; CHOL 37mg; IRON 4.3mg; SODIUM 890mg; CALC 63mg

Eat Up, Drink Up

Factor in food when considering your hydration needs.

IF YOUR WATER BOTTLE travels with you everywhere, sip on this thought: Drinking water isn't the only way to stay hydrated. Food can significantly affect your daily fluid needs. In fact, you can obtain much of the liquid you need from the food and beverages (other than water) you eat and drink every day.

Vietnamese Summer Rolls

This refreshing no-cook summer roll recipe offers menu flexibility: Serving two rolls constitutes an entrée, or you can serve one as an appetizer.
Water tally: 3 ounces

ROLLS:
- 1 cup thinly sliced Bibb lettuce
- ½ cup bean sprouts
- ½ cup cooked bean threads (cellophane noodles, about 1 ounce uncooked)
- ½ cup shredded carrot
- ¼ cup chopped green onions (about 2)
- ¼ cup thinly sliced basil
- ¼ cup chopped mint
- 6 ounces cooked peeled and deveined shrimp, coarsely chopped
- 8 (8-inch) round sheets rice paper

DIPPING SAUCE:
- 2 tablespoons rice wine vinegar
- 2 tablespoons fresh lime juice (about 1 lime)
- 1 tablespoon sugar
- 1 teaspoon chile paste with garlic (such as sambal oelek)
- 1 teaspoon low-sodium soy sauce

❶ To prepare rolls, combine first 8 ingredients in a bowl.
❷ Add hot water to a large, shallow dish to a depth of 1 inch. Place 1 rice paper sheet in dish; let stand 30 seconds or just until soft. Place sheet on a flat surface. Arrange ⅓ cup shrimp mixture over half of sheet, leaving a ½-inch border.

Folding sides of sheet over filling and starting with filled side, roll up jelly-roll fashion. Gently press seam to seal. Place roll, seam side down, on a serving platter (cover to keep from drying). Repeat procedure with remaining shrimp mixture and rice paper sheets.
❸ To prepare dipping sauce, combine vinegar and remaining ingredients; stir with a whisk. Serve with summer rolls. Yield: 4 servings (serving size: 2 rolls and about 1½ tablespoons dipping sauce).

CALORIES 164 (5% from fat); FAT 0.9g (sat 0.2g, mono 0.1g, poly 0.3g); PROTEIN 12.3g; CARB 27.1g; FIBER 1.2g; CHOL 83mg; IRON 2.2mg; SODIUM 206mg; CALC 43mg

Cucumber, Asian Pear, and Watermelon Salad with Ricotta Salata

If you can't find ricotta salata, you can use feta, which is more pungent but just as tasty.
Water tally: 5.3 ounces

- 2 cups (1-inch) cubed peeled seedless cucumber
- 2 cups (1-inch) cubed seedless watermelon
- 2 cups halved red grapes
- ¾ cup peeled, cubed Asian pear (about 1 pear)
- ½ cup reduced-fat sour cream
- 1½ teaspoons grated lime rind
- 2 tablespoons fresh lime juice
- 1 tablespoon honey
- ⅛ teaspoon ground red pepper
- ⅓ cup (3 ounces) crumbled ricotta salata cheese

❶ Combine first 4 ingredients in a large bowl. Combine sour cream and next 4 ingredients in a small bowl, stirring with a whisk. Pour sour cream mixture over fruit mixture; toss well to coat. Sprinkle with cheese. Yield: 8 servings (serving size: about 1 cup salad and 2 teaspoons cheese).

CALORIES 118 (34% from fat); FAT 4.4g (sat 2.8g, mono 0.5g, poly 0.1g); PROTEIN 3.1g; CARB 18.5g; FIBER 2.1g; CHOL 17mg; IRON 0.4mg; SODIUM 130mg; CALC 91mg

QUICK & EASY
Spicy Shrimp Tacos with Grilled Tomatillo Salsa

If you want to make the salsa a day ahead but don't want to fire up the grill, you can char the tomatillos over a gas cooktop burner. Use a pair of tongs to hold the tomatillo over the flame, turning the fruit occasionally to blacken its skin evenly. Use a grill basket, if you have one, to cook the shrimp instead of threading them on skewers. Serve with black beans, sour cream, and sliced cantaloupe.
Water tally: 7.8 ounces

SALSA:
- ½ pound tomatillos
- Cooking spray
- ⅔ cup chopped green onions (about 4 green onions)
- ¼ cup chopped fresh cilantro
- 3 tablespoons lime juice (about 1 lime)
- ¼ teaspoon salt
- ½ jalapeño pepper, seeds removed and chopped
- 1 garlic clove

TACOS:
- 1 pound medium peeled and deveined shrimp
- 1 tablespoon hot pepper sauce (such as Tabasco)
- ½ teaspoon ancho chili powder
- ½ teaspoon ground cumin
- ¼ teaspoon salt
- 8 (6-inch) corn tortillas
- 2 cups shredded cabbage
- 1 cup shredded carrot

① Prepare grill.

② To prepare salsa, remove husks and stems from tomatillos. Place tomatillos on a grill rack coated with cooking spray. Grill 10 minutes or until slightly blackened on each side, turning occasionally. Cool completely; coarsely chop. Place tomatillos, onions, and next 5 ingredients in food processor. Pulse 7 times or until coarsely chopped.

③ To prepare tacos, thread shrimp evenly on 6 (10-inch) skewers. Place skewers on a grill rack coated with cooking spray. Grill 2 minutes or until shrimp are done, turning once. Remove shrimp from skewers, and place in a medium bowl. Add hot pepper sauce and next 3 ingredients; toss to coat.

④ Heat tortillas on grill 1 minute on each side. Top each tortilla with ¼ cup cabbage and 2 tablespoons carrot. Divide shrimp mixture evenly among tortillas; top each with 2 tablespoons salsa. Yield: 4 servings (serving size: 2 tacos).

CALORIES 252 (14% from fat); FAT 3.9g (sat 0.5g, mono 0.4g, poly 1.6g); PROTEIN 26.9g; CARB 30.2g; FIBER 5.5g; CHOL 172mg; IRON 3.8mg; SODIUM 507mg; CALC 125mg

Veggie Plate Menu
serves 8

Capitalize on the bounty of late-summer produce.

Fava Beans with Pesto and Cavatappi

Garden salad

Combine 4 cups torn romaine lettuce, 1 bunch trimmed watercress, ½ cup thinly sliced radishes, ½ cup julienne-cut carrot, ½ cup thinly sliced red onion, and ½ cup thinly sliced English cucumber. Combine 3 tablespoons extravirgin olive oil, 3 tablespoons sherry vinegar, 1 tablespoon minced shallots, ½ teaspoon kosher salt, and ¼ teaspoon freshly ground black pepper. Drizzle dressing over salad; toss to coat.

Ciabatta slices

Fava Beans with Pesto and Cavatappi

This vegetarian main dish shows off summer-fresh fava beans. If you can't find them, substitute fresh lima beans or even thawed frozen edamame.
Water tally: 3.9 ounces

- 2 pounds unshelled fava beans (about 3 cups shelled)
- 1 cup fresh basil leaves (about 1 ounce)
- ¼ cup chopped fresh mint
- 2 tablespoons fresh lemon juice
- 1 teaspoon salt
- ¼ teaspoon freshly ground black pepper
- 1 garlic clove, minced
- 3 tablespoons extravirgin olive oil
- 1 pound uncooked cavatappi pasta
- ½ cup grape tomatoes, halved
- ½ cup (2 ounces) grated fresh Parmesan cheese

① Remove beans from pods; discard pods. Cook beans in boiling water 1 minute. Drain and rinse with cold water; drain. Remove outer skins from beans; discard skins.

② Combine basil and next 5 ingredients in a food processor; process until smooth. With processor on, slowly pour oil through food chute, and process until well blended.

③ Cook pasta according to package directions, omitting salt and fat; drain. Combine pasta and basil mixture in a large bowl, tossing to coat. Add beans and tomatoes, tossing to combine. Sprinkle with cheese. Yield: 8 servings (serving size: about 1¼ cups pasta and 1 tablespoon cheese).

CALORIES 335 (24% from fat); FAT 8.9g (sat 1.9g, mono 4.7g, poly 1.5g); PROTEIN 17.3g; CARB 51.9g; FIBER 2.7g; CHOL 46mg; IRON 4.1mg; SODIUM 411mg; CALC 116mg

In the Kitchen

Obviously, cooking affects a food's moisture content. "Water can be a vital part of a dish simply because it provides a medium for food to cook in without searing or burning," says food scientist Shirley Corriher, author of *CookWise: The Secrets of Cooking Revealed*. Just think about water's critical role in preparing grains and starches like pasta, rice, and hot cereals. When we cook these foods in boiling water, their starch granules soak up water, causing them to swell and soften. This increases their fluid content as much as sixfold.

Cooking can make other foods lose small amounts of fluid. "Meat is packed with water, and that water is retained in a network of proteins," says Harold McGee, PhD, author of *On Food and Cooking: The Science and Lore of the Kitchen*. "But when you heat those proteins, they coagulate. That's the equivalent of squeezing a sponge, so you force moisture out of the food." Cooking meat causes it to release about 20 to 30 percent of its original water content. But because foods like meat, poultry, and fish are inherently rich in water, they still contribute to our overall fluid needs, even when cooked.

Caffeine Considerations

You may have heard about the dehydrating effects of caffeine. But leading health authorities like the Institute of Medicine and the American College of Sports Medicine say that's a myth. While caffeine does signal our kidneys to get rid of excess water, it does so for only a short time, so we still retain more fluid than we lose after sipping a caffeinated beverage.

The Institute of Medicine reports caffeinated beverages contribute to our daily water needs as much as noncaffeinated drinks. In a study published in 2007 in the *International Journal of Sport Nutrition and Exercise Metabolism,* when researchers asked cyclists to bike for two-plus hours under hot, humid conditions, they found a caffeine-infused sports drink was as hydrating as a traditional sports drink.

What You Really Need

Water is an important nutrient that comprises 50 to 60 percent of your body weight, and it also helps transport other nutrients within the body. Yet because the body doesn't store water, you have to replenish the supply.

How much do you need? For years, we've been told to drink eight glasses of water a day for optimal health. But that one-size-fits-all prescription has given way to a more flexible approach. Health experts have found that fluid requirements vary from person to person, and for many of us, the best way to stay adequately hydrated is to use thirst as a guide.

Several factors influence your need for water, including climate, muscle mass, physical activity, and diet. (People who have more muscle need more water—that's why men generally have higher fluid requirements than women.)

Food, often overlooked as a water source, can be a rich supply of fluid. On average, it provides 20 percent of the fluid we need—and far more if you choose water-rich fare. That translates to about two cups for the typical female and three cups for most men each day; most people require a total of roughly 11 to 15 cups of water daily, according to the Institute of Medicine.

Food aids hydration in other ways, too. Since sipping a beverage helps moisten and wash down food, eating encourages us to drink more liquid. That's why we consume most of our beverages with meals. Food also provides minerals, like sodium and potassium, that help our bodies hold on to water, so the liquids we consume with—or in the form of—food are better retained than those we drink between meals.

QUICK & EASY

Sake-Poached Salmon with Wilted Greens and Shallot Vinaigrette

The salmon and mixed greens contribute most of the water to this simple yet tasty entrée.

Water tally: 9.2 ounces

VINAIGRETTE:
- 2½ tablespoons minced shallots
- 2 tablespoons lemon juice
- 1 tablespoon rice wine vinegar
- 2 teaspoons honey
- 2 teaspoons low-sodium soy sauce
- 1 tablespoon extravirgin olive oil

SALMON:
- 1 cup water
- ½ cup sake (rice wine)
- 1 (½-inch) piece of peeled fresh ginger, thinly sliced
- 4 (6-ounce) salmon fillets (1 inch thick)
- 6 cups chopped trimmed Swiss chard (about 8 ounces)
- 5 cups spinach leaves (about 3 ounces)
- ½ teaspoon salt
- ¼ teaspoon freshly ground black pepper

❶ To prepare vinaigrette, combine first 5 ingredients in a small bowl. Slowly add oil, stirring constantly with a whisk. Set aside.

❷ To prepare salmon, combine 1 cup water, sake, and ginger in a large sauté pan over medium-high heat; bring to a boil. Reduce heat, and add salmon to pan. Cover and simmer 6 minutes. Remove salmon and ginger from pan. Discard ginger.

❸ Add Swiss chard and spinach to pan; cook 2 minutes or until wilted. Stir in salt and pepper. Divide spinach mixture evenly among 4 plates. Top each serving with 1 salmon fillet; drizzle each serving with 2 tablespoons vinaigrette. Yield: 4 servings.

CALORIES 385 (38% from fat); FAT 16.1g (sat 2.5g, mono 6.6g, poly 5.5g); PROTEIN 41.1g; CARB 10.3g; FIBER 1.9g; CHOL 107mg; IRON 3.8mg; SODIUM 617mg; CALC 95mg

---

QUICK & EASY

Pink Peppercorn Mahimahi with Tropical Salsa

Pink peppercorns lend this entrée pretty color and impart a sweet note to the salsa.

Water tally: 7.1 ounces

- 1¼ cups chopped pineapple
- ½ cup chopped red onion
- ¼ cup chopped fresh cilantro
- 2 tablespoons flaked sweetened coconut
- 2 tablespoons fresh lime juice
- 1 jalapeño pepper, finely chopped
- 2 teaspoons pink peppercorns, crushed and divided
- ½ cup panko (Japanese breadcrumbs)
- 3 tablespoons finely chopped macadamia nuts
- ½ teaspoon sea salt, divided
- ½ cup light coconut milk
- 2 tablespoons low-sodium soy sauce
- 4 (6-ounce) mahimahi or other firm white fish fillets
- 1½ tablespoons olive oil
- Cooking spray

❶ Preheat oven to 400°.

❷ Combine first 6 ingredients and 1 teaspoon peppercorns in a bowl; set aside.

❸ Combine panko, nuts, remaining 1 teaspoon peppercorns, and ¼ teaspoon salt in a shallow dish. Combine milk and soy sauce in another shallow dish. Sprinkle fish with remaining ¼ teaspoon salt. Dip one side of fish in milk mixture; dredge dipped side in panko mixture.

❹ Heat oil in a large ovenproof skillet coated with cooking spray over medium-high heat. Add fish to pan, crust sides down; cook 3 minutes. Turn fish over, and bake at 400° for 10 minutes or until fish flakes easily when tested with a fork or until desired degree of doneness. Serve with salsa. Yield: 4 servings (serving size: 1 fillet and ½ cup salsa).

CALORIES 331 (37% from fat); FAT 13.6g (sat 3.8g, mono 7.6g, poly 1g); PROTEIN 34.5g; CARB 18.3g; FIBER 2.5g; CHOL 124mg; IRON 2.8mg; SODIUM 743mg; CALC 49mg

Zucchini Eggplant Lasagna

This recipe makes use of summer-fresh produce in a meatless entrée.
Water tally: 5.8 ounces

- 1 large eggplant, cut crosswise into ¼-inch-thick slices
- ¾ teaspoon salt, divided
- 2 teaspoons olive oil
- ¾ cup chopped onion (about 1 medium onion)
- 3 garlic cloves, chopped
- ¾ teaspoon freshly ground black pepper, divided
- ½ teaspoon chopped fresh oregano
- ⅛ teaspoon ground red pepper
- 1 (28-ounce) can crushed tomatoes
- 1 cup fresh basil leaves, chopped
- 1 cup (8 ounces) part-skim ricotta cheese
- Cooking spray
- 1 (8-ounce) package precooked lasagna noodles
- 2 zucchini, cut into ¼-inch-thick slices
- 2½ cups (10 ounces) shredded part-skim mozzarella cheese

❶ Preheat oven to 350°.
❷ Arrange eggplant slices in a single layer on several layers of paper towels. Sprinkle evenly with ½ teaspoon salt; let stand 15 minutes.
❸ Heat oil in a large skillet over medium-high heat. Add onion and garlic to pan; sauté 2 minutes, stirring frequently. Add remaining ¼ teaspoon salt, ¼ teaspoon black pepper, and next 3 ingredients; bring to a boil. Reduce heat, and simmer 10 minutes, stirring occasionally.
❹ Combine basil, ricotta, and remaining ½ teaspoon black pepper in a small bowl. Spread ½ cup tomato mixture in a 13 x 9–inch baking dish coated with cooking spray. Arrange 4 noodles over tomato mixture; top with half of eggplant and half of zucchini. Spread ricotta mixture over vegetables; cover with 4 noodles. Spread 1 cup tomato mixture over noodles; layer with remaining eggplant and

zucchini slices. Arrange remaining 4 noodles over vegetables, and spread remaining tomato mixture over noodles. Top evenly with mozzarella. Cover with foil coated with cooking spray. Bake at 350° for 35 minutes. Uncover and bake an additional 25 minutes or until browned. Cool for 5 minutes. Yield: 12 servings.

CALORIES 216 (32% from fat); FAT 7.7g (sat 4.2g, mono 2g, poly 0.4g); PROTEIN 12.7g; CARB 25.7g; FIBER 4.2g; CHOL 21mg; IRON 1.3mg; SODIUM 393mg; CALC 247mg

MAKE AHEAD • FREEZABLE
Cucumber Granita

Leave the peel on the cucumbers—it enhances the granita's emerald hue. Allowing the pureed cucumber mixture to sit in a cheesecloth-lined sieve over a bowl overnight infuses the granita with color and flavor. For extra zip, add a teaspoon of cracked black pepper when pureeing cucumbers.
Water tally: 3.3 ounces

- 4 cucumbers (about 3 pounds)
- 1 tablespoon honey
- Lemon wedges (optional)
- Cucumber slices (optional)

❶ Cut cucumbers into 3-inch chunks. Place half of cucumber chunks and honey in a blender or food processor; process until smooth. Strain pureed cucumber mixture through a large cheesecloth-lined sieve into a bowl. Repeat procedure with remaining cucumbers. Cover and chill cucumber mixture 8 hours or overnight.
❷ Press chilled cucumber mixture lightly with a wooden spoon or rubber spatula to squeeze out juice; discard solids. Pour juice into a 13 x 9-inch baking dish. Cover and freeze at least 8 hours or until firm.
❸ Remove mixture from freezer; scrape entire mixture with a fork until fluffy. Garnish with lemon wedges and cucumber slices, if desired. Yield: 12 servings (serving size: ½ cup).
NOTE: Freeze for up to 1 month.

CALORIES 16 (0% from fat); FAT 0g; PROTEIN 1g; CARB 3.5g; FIBER 1g; CHOL 0mg; IRON 0.4mg; SODIUM 0mg; CALC 20mg

1 Day, 11½ Cups of Water

Food can provide much of the water you need if you choose fluid-rich fare. All foods contain some water, but the amount varies considerably.

Breakfast:
- 1 cup low-fat Greek yogurt with 2 tablespoons raspberry jam: 7.3 ounces
- 1 slice whole-grain toast: 0.3 ounces
- 1 cup coffee with 2 tablespoons fat-free milk: 9.3 ounces
- 1 (8-ounce) glass fresh orange juice: 7.7 ounces

Morning snack:
- 1 hard-cooked large egg: 1.3 ounces
- 1 (8-ounce) glass water: 8 ounces

Lunch:
- Turkey wrap (2 ounces sliced turkey breast, 1 romaine lettuce leaf, 2 tomato slices, 1 tablespoon reduced-fat mayonnaise, 1 [8-inch] fat-free flour tortilla): 3.5 ounces
- Cucumber, Asian Pear, and Watermelon Salad with Ricotta Salata (page 234): 5.3 ounces
- 1 (8-ounce) glass water: 8 ounces

Afternoon snack:
- ½ cup 1% low-fat cottage cheese with 6 red grapes: 3.9 ounces
- 1 (8-ounce) glass water: 8 ounces

Dinner:
- Sake-Poached Salmon with Wilted Greens and Shallot Vinaigrette (page 236): 9.6 ounces
- 1 cup cooked brown rice: 5 ounces
- ½ cup stir-fried snow peas: 2.6 ounces
- 1 (5-ounce) glass sauvignon blanc: 4.5 ounces
- 1 (8-ounce) glass water: 8 ounces

Total: 92.3 ounces (about 11½ cups)

Curing & Pickling

Enhance meats and fish and preserve seasonal produce that you can enjoy weeks later with these time-honored methods.

ORIGINATING AS A MEANS TO PREVENT food from spoiling in prerefrigeration days, curing and pickling techniques create distinctive characteristics in all manner of produce and meats. Consider classic bread-and-butter pickles, which gain a sweet-savory-tangy taste from soaking in a vinegar brine, or Swedish gravlax, a dish where a salt-sugar cure creates buttery, melt-in-your-mouth paper-thin slices of fish.

While traditional canning for pickled foods requires sterilized jars and steam pots, here we offer a simpler refrigerator method that doesn't use any special equipment. Nor do our cured fish and poultry recipes, which involve only salt and time. With our streamlined techniques, you can preserve brilliant summer produce and create classic cured meats.

MAKE AHEAD
Gingered Watermelon Rind

Watermelon rind is cured in salt, then pickled. A Southern tradition, this relish is customarily served at picnics and barbecues. Since this recipe only uses the rind, you can use the flesh to prepare Cucumber, Asian Pear, and Watermelon Salad with Ricotta Salata (page 234).

- 1 (5-pound) watermelon
- 3 tablespoons kosher salt
- 1½ cups sugar
- ½ cup white vinegar
- ½ cup cider vinegar
- 1 teaspoon pickling spice
- 1 (1-inch) piece peeled fresh ginger, thinly sliced

❶ Cut watermelon in half. Scoop out watermelon pulp; reserve for another use. Carefully remove outer green layer from watermelon rind using a vegetable peeler. Cut peeled rind into 1½-inch cubes to measure about 4 cups.
❷ Combine rind and salt in a large zip-top plastic bag. Seal and refrigerate 24 hours, turning bag occasionally.

❸ Remove rind from bag; drain. Rinse rind thoroughly with cold water; drain. Place rind in a large saucepan. Cover with water to 2 inches above rind; bring to a boil. Cover, reduce heat, and simmer 15 minutes or until crisp-tender. Drain and rinse with cold water; drain well. Place rind in a large bowl.
❹ Combine sugar and remaining ingredients in a large saucepan; bring to a boil, stirring until sugar dissolves. Pour hot sugar mixture over rind; let stand at room temperature 2 hours. Cover and refrigerate 5 days. Store in an airtight container in refrigerator up to 3 weeks. Yield: 12 servings (serving size: about ¼ cup drained rind).

CALORIES 13 (0% from fat); FAT 0g; PROTEIN 0.3g; CARB 3.1g; FIBER 0.6g; CHOL 0mg; IRON 0.1mg; SODIUM 156mg; CALC 10mg

MAKE AHEAD
Duck "Prosciutto"

Classic prosciutto is salt-cured ham; we use a similar curing method for duck breasts. Hang the duck from a rack in the refrigerator as it cures so air can circulate around it. For the tastiest results, do not trim the fat from the breasts. We tried this recipe with several brands of kosher salt and found Morton coarse kosher salt best preserved the duck's distinctive flavor. Serve with Parmigiano-Reggiano cheese and cantaloupe.

- 4 cups kosher salt, divided
- 2 (8-ounce) boneless duck breast halves
- ½ teaspoon freshly ground black pepper

❶ Spread 1¼ cups salt in an 8-inch square baking dish; arrange duck breast halves, skin sides up, in a single layer over salt. Top duck with remaining 2¾ cups salt, pressing down to pack. Cover and refrigerate 24 hours. Remove duck from salt; discard salt. Rinse duck thoroughly with cold water; drain. Pat duck dry; sprinkle evenly with pepper.
❷ Place each breast half on a double layer of cheesecloth. Gather edges of cheesecloth together; tie securely. Hang duck in refrigerator for 2 weeks. Unwrap; cut prosciutto into very thin slices. Store in an airtight container in refrigerator up to 5 days. Yield: 10 ounces (serving size: ½ ounce).

CALORIES 46 (49% from fat); FAT 2.5g (sat 0.7g, mono 1.2g, poly 0.4g); PROTEIN 5.6g; CARB 0g; FIBER 0g; CHOL 31mg; IRON 0.8mg; SODIUM 301mg; CALC 2mg

> Refrigerator pickling is simple to do and requires no special equipment.

All About Curing & Pickling

Curing, Defined

Curing is a method of preserving food (usually meat or fish) to prevent spoilage. Food can be cured by brining (soaking food in a saltwater solution), smoking, or salting (packing food in salt)—we focus on salting here, which is easy to do at home. Curing has long been a way to make perishable, protein-rich foods last from barn to market, as in the case of bacon and prosciutto, or from shore to home, as in the case of salt cod or kippered herring.

What Salt-Curing Does

The salt works on at least three fronts. First, it inhibits bacterial growth, thereby preserving foods like duck breasts or salmon for moderate lengths of time. That said, the salt doesn't inhibit all bacterial growth. Instead it allows for a moderate amount of fermentation—and thus the meat ends up with a mild, somewhat sweet twang, usually no more than a hint in the overall taste. Second, salt breaks down protein in muscle fibers so the meat or fish is more tender—as is evidenced in gravlax, corned beef brisket, or kosher chickens. Finally, salt can be used as a dehydrating agent, which creates dense and chewy but nonetheless tender meat or fish—the signature texture of ham, lox, or bacon.

Curing Time

Fish like salmon or halibut is cured for 24 to 48 hours, depending on how firm the flesh is. Meats like brisket or duck breasts are cured for longer periods; their muscular structures are more resilient to the salt's action. With meat, the larger the cut, the longer the cure. But timing is crucial. Too little time in the salt, and the fish or meat will not be adequately tenderized; too long, and the whole thing will turn unappealingly soft and mushy. So it's important to use the times specified in the recipes.

Shelf life

Because our home-cured meat and fish recipes use lower salt concentrations for a shorter time, and because they don't use nitrates (preservative chemical compounds used in many commercial products), they have a shorter shelf life than commercially cured foods. Nitrate-free cured meat or fish will last three to five days tightly covered in the refrigerator.

Best Bets for Curing

In general, meat and fish are the best options, particularly those cuts and varieties that are relatively high in fat, such as brisket, duck, ham, and salmon. Already-tender cuts or fillets like tenderloin or shrimp would gain little from the salt cure, no more than a strange aftertaste.

Most vegetables benefit little from a salt cure—except for those with very high water concentrations like cabbage, cucumber, and eggplant. Once these foods are salted, they release much of their liquid and are then suitable for sauces, relishes, and the like. If not presalted, they would release liquid into the dish and water down the taste.

Pickling, Defined

To pickle food is to preserve it by immersing it in a seasoned vinegar-based solution (often referred to as a brine). Flavors can be salty, sweet, or hot.

What Pickling Does

This technique encourages certain naturally occurring and harmless microbes to feed on the sugars produced as the food's proteins break down in the presence of salt. These microbes produce lactic acid, carbon dioxide, and even alcohol—compounds which in turn help preserve the food. Also, these helpful microbes leave most of the beneficial vitamins and minerals intact and further enhance the taste of the food preserved. In other words, the food is still nutritious and tasty weeks later.

Best Bets For Pickling

Sturdy vegetables work best—cabbage, cucumbers, olives, radishes, carrots, green beans, onions, and asparagus. Most fruits and many leafy greens simply wilt and break down too far.

Pickling Time

Depending on the ingredients in the pickling liquid, food can be pickled in a few hours or can take a week or more.

Shelf Life

Keep pickled vegetables in the refrigerator for a couple of weeks (or possibly longer). Store in a nonreactive container—glass or plastic works well—to prevent discoloration and "off" flavor. To ensure freshness, make sure all the vegetables are fully submerged in the liquid and that the head space in the storage container does not allow for much air. As you consume pickles from the jar, change to progressively smaller containers, always tightly sealed for cold storage. If some of the pickling solution has been lost over time, add a little water so everything is well covered.

A Few Words About Salt

Salt is essential to cured and pickled foods—to wilt the vegetables, inhibit bacterial growth, or create the characteristic texture—so these items are naturally high in sodium. The sodium content of our pickles and cured foods is comparable to or lower than their commercial counterparts. Balance these higher-sodium foods with minimally seasoned ones.

The Bottom Line

The three most important elements to remember about curing and pickling:
1 Salt is essential to the process; use the amount specified.
2 Choose fatty meat or fish for curing.
3 Sturdy vegetables are your best bet for pickling.

Japanese-Style Daikon and Carrot Pickles

Lime-spiked vegetables work well as a relish with grilled tuna or salmon. Daikons are long, white, tubular Asian radishes with a pungent smell and a mild flavor. Look for them in gourmet markets and Asian groceries.

1½	pounds daikon radishes, peeled
1¼	pounds carrots, peeled
½	cup rice vinegar
¼	cup mirin (sweet rice wine)
2	tablespoons sesame seeds, toasted
2	tablespoons fresh lime juice
2	teaspoons kosher salt
2	teaspoons grated orange rind

1 Hold each radish by the tip end. Shave radishes into ribbons with a vegetable peeler to measure 4½ cups. Repeat procedure with carrots, shaving to measure 6 cups. Combine radishes, carrots, vinegar, and remaining ingredients in a large bowl, tossing to coat. Cover and refrigerate 4 hours or overnight. Store in an airtight container in refrigerator up to 3 days. Yield: 10 servings (serving size: about ½ cup drained pickles).

CALORIES 53 (17% from fat); FAT 1g (sat 0.2g, mono 0.3g, poly 0.4g); PROTEIN 1.2g; CARB 10.1g; FIBER 3g; CHOL 0mg; IRON 0.5mg; SODIUM 193mg; CALC 38mg

Pickled vegetables are a hallmark of Asian cuisine, especially Japanese and Korean fare.

Every Night Korean Menu
serves 4

The cabbage pairs well with grilled meats.

Kimchi-Style Cabbage
Spice-rubbed flank steak

Prepare grill. Rub a 1-pound trimmed flank steak with 2 teaspoons dark sesame oil; sprinkle evenly with 2 teaspoons brown sugar, ½ teaspoon kosher salt, ¼ teaspoon garlic powder, ¼ teaspoon ground red pepper, ¼ teaspoon freshly ground black pepper, and ⅛ teaspoon ground ginger. Place steak on grill rack coated with cooking spray; grill 5 minutes on each side or until desired degree of doneness. Let stand 5 minutes. Cut across grain into thin slices. Sprinkle with 1 teaspoon toasted sesame seeds.

Steamed white rice

Kimchi-Style Cabbage

Kimchi is a spicy Korean condiment that's often fermented and aged (sometimes for months) to develop a pungent flavor. It's traditionally served with steamed white rice and pairs well with stir-fries.

½	cup kosher salt, divided
2¾	pounds napa (Chinese) cabbage, quartered lengthwise
2	cups thinly sliced green onions (about 2 bunches)
2	cups finely grated peeled daikon radish (about 1 medium)
1½	cups water
½	cup rice vinegar
3	tablespoons sambal oelek (ground fresh chile paste)
2	tablespoons sugar
2	tablespoons minced fresh garlic
1½	tablespoons grated peeled fresh ginger

1 Reserve ½ teaspoon salt; set aside. Place cabbage in a large bowl; sprinkle remaining salt over cabbage, sprinkling between leaves. Weigh down cabbage with a smaller bowl filled with cans. Let stand at room temperature 2 hours; drain. Rinse cabbage thoroughly with cold water; drain. Remove cabbage leaves from core; discard core.

2 Combine reserved ½ teaspoon salt, onions, and remaining ingredients in a medium bowl. Spread radish mixture onto cabbage leaves; arrange leaves in layers in a 1-quart airtight container, pressing leaves to compress mixture. Top leaves with any remaining radish mixture. Cover and refrigerate 1 week. Store in an airtight container in refrigerator up to 2 weeks. Yield: 32 servings (serving size: about 1½ ounces).

CALORIES 16 (0% from fat); FAT 0g; PROTEIN 0.5g; CARB 3.4g; FIBER 0.8g; CHOL 0mg; IRON 0.1mg; SODIUM 179mg; CALC 35mg

Refrigerator Pickling

Before the days of refrigeration, pickling was hot work—a huge pot of boiling water billowing clouds of steam through the kitchen. Refrigerator pickling takes away the need for kettle steamers, special jars, and vacuum-tight lids. The chilly environment of the refrigerator impedes bacterial growth without your having to boil out excess air in vacuum-sealed jars. In other words, simply follow the recipe and let the cool refrigerator stand in for the boiling vat.

Golden Winter Soup, page 24

Cardamom-Lime Sweet Rolls,
page 40

Spanish Daube, page 36

Peanut-Crusted Chicken
with Pineapple Salsa,
page 79

Ginger-Shrimp Pot Stickers with Spicy Peanut Dipping Sauce, page 63

Spiced Pork Tenderloin with Maple-Chipotle Sauce, page 84

Mango and Black Bean Salad, page 58

**Light and Fresh Potato Salad,
page 119**

**Crab Cakes with Roasted Vegetables and
Tangy Butter Sauce, page 96**

Whole Wheat Tagliolini with Fresh Cherry Tomato Sauce, page 109

Chicken-Orzo Salad with Goat Cheese,
page 122

Nathan's Lemon Cake,
page 143

Blueberry Coffee Cake, page 160

Sautéed Tuna and Green Onion Stalks
on Romaine, page 125

Steamed Clams and Tomatoes with
Angel Hair Pasta, page 160

Beef Tenderloin with Mustard and Herbs,
page 165

Sparkling Sangria, page 161

Crab, Corn, and Tomato Salad with Lemon-Basil Dressing, page 165

Steamed Carrots with Garlic-Ginger Butter,
page 196

Spice-Rubbed Pork Tenderloin with Mustard
Barbecue Sauce, page 167; Corn on the Cob with
Smoked Butter, page 171; and Tangy Mustard
Coleslaw, page 171

Summer Squash Pizza, page 201

Bread-and-Butter Pickles,
page 273

Fresh Cherry Pie, page 220

Grilled Vegetable Pitas with Goat
Cheese and Pesto Mayo, page 231

Beet and Walnut Salad,
page 297

Cheddar-Bacon Drop Biscuits, page 323

Venison, Sausage, and Black Bean Chili, page 286

Dark Chocolate and Cherry
Brownies, page 280

**Black Lentil and Couscous Salad,
page 314**

**Pan-Roasted Chicken, Squash, and Chard Salad
with Bacon Vinaigrette, page 307**

Walnut-Crusted Pork Chops with
Autumn Vegetable Wild Rice, page 308

Steak Frites with Shallot Pan Reduction, page 280

Flounder with Cilantro-Curry Topping and Toasted Coconut, page 373

Classic Cranberry Sauce, page 361

Egg and Cheese Breakfast Tacos
with Homemade Salsa, page 325

(Left to Right): Flaky Buttermilk Biscuits, page 359;
Spiced Pumpkin Biscuits, page 360; Parmesan-Pepper Biscuits,
page 360; Pistachio-Cranberry Scones, page 360

Cranberry-Oatmeal Bars, page 355

Pork Vindaloo, page 374

Oat-Crusted Pecan Pie with Fresh Cranberry Sauce, page 376

Chicken Tamale Casserole, page 371

Brussels Sprouts with Currants and Pine Nuts, page 351

California Ambrosia, page 390

Mulled Wine Sangria, page 415

Satsuma Cloud Tart, page 418

Red Wine Pear Crisp with Spiced Streusel, page 416

Fennel-Cured Halibut Gravlax

Like salmon, the usual choice for this Swedish delicacy, cured halibut is delicious. For food safety, it's best to use thawed frozen-at-sea (FAS) halibut. Depending on the size of the fillets, you may use two to five pieces. Don't use one large fillet, as the salt cure will not seep evenly throughout the fish. Slice the gravlax into paper-thin strips with a thin, sharp knife, angling the blade for wider slices. Serve as an appetizer with rye or pumpernickel toasts and cream cheese. Garnish with dill sprigs.

- ⅓ cup coarse sea salt
- ⅓ cup sugar
- ⅓ cup chopped fennel fronds
- ¼ cup olive oil
- 1 teaspoon freshly ground black pepper
- 2 pounds halibut fillets, skinned
- 3 tablespoons finely chopped fresh dill

1 Combine first 5 ingredients in a food processor, and process until finely ground.
2 Arrange fish in a single layer in a 13 x 9-inch baking dish. Rub salt mixture evenly over fish. Cover and refrigerate fish 24 hours.
3 Rinse fish thoroughly with cold water; pat dry. Pat dill onto fish. Cut fish into ¹⁄₁₆–inch slices. Store in an airtight container in refrigerator up to 3 days. Yield: 12 servings (serving size: about 2¹⁄₂ ounces).

CALORIES 95 (22% from fat); FAT 2.3g (sat 0.3g, mono 1.1g, poly 0.6g); PROTEIN 14.8g; CARB 2.8g; FIBER 0g; CHOL 23mg; IRON 0.6mg; SODIUM 631mg; CALC 34mg

WINE NOTE: Gravlax is fantastic with a wine that's beginning to make a big splash in the States—*grüner veltliner*. The most famous white wine of Austria, grüner veltliner is fresh, clean, crisp, and slightly peppery, giving it the right "bite" to balance cured fish. A terrific choice is the 2007 Nigl Grünuer Veltliner Kremser Freiheit from the Wachau region of Austria ($20).

Bread-and-Butter Pickles
(pictured on page 256)

This recipe yields lots of cucumber pickles. Try them on sandwiches or burgers, as a complement to field peas, or as a snack with whole-grain mustard, Cheddar cheese, and crackers. Thin-skinned pickling cucumbers are essential.

- 5½ cups thinly sliced pickling cucumbers (about 1½ pounds)
- 1½ tablespoons kosher salt
- 1 cup thinly sliced onion
- 1 cup sugar
- 1 cup white vinegar
- ½ cup cider vinegar
- ¼ cup packed brown sugar
- 1½ teaspoons mustard seeds
- ½ teaspoon celery seeds
- ⅛ teaspoon turmeric

1 Combine cucumbers and salt in a large bowl; cover and chill 1½ hours. Drain; rinse cucumbers with cold water. Drain; return cucumbers to bowl. Add onion.
2 Combine sugar and remaining ingredients in a medium saucepan; bring to a simmer over medium heat, stirring until sugar dissolves. Pour hot vinegar mixture over cucumber mixture; let stand at room temperature 1 hour. Cover and refrigerate 24 hours. Store in an airtight container in refrigerator up to 2 weeks. Yield: 16 servings (serving size: about ¼ cup drained pickles).

CALORIES 18 (5% from fat); FAT 0.1g (sat 0g, mono 0g, poly 0g); PROTEIN 0.4g; CARB 4.4g; FIBER 0.5g; CHOL 0mg; IRON 0.1mg; SODIUM 168mg; CALC 8mg

Spicy Pickled Vegetables

This Tex-Mex favorite is enjoyed with nachos, tacos, or chili. The carrots and green beans would also make good stirrers for a Bloody Mary. Drop onions into boiling water for 15 to 30 seconds to make them easier to peel.

- 6 cups water
- 4 teaspoons kosher salt
- 1 teaspoon ground cumin
- 1 pound baby carrots
- 2 cups pearl onions, peeled (about 10 ounces)
- ⅓ cup sliced jalapeño peppers (about 2 large)
- 8 ounces haricots verts, trimmed
- 4 cups white vinegar

1 Bring first 3 ingredients to a boil in a large nonreactive saucepan. Add carrots to pan; cook 2 minutes. Add onions; cook 1 minute. Add jalapeños; cook 1 minute. Add beans; cook 1 minute. Remove from heat; stir in vinegar. Let stand at room temperature 1 hour. Pour into a large bowl; cover and refrigerate 24 hours. Store in an airtight container in refrigerator up to 2 weeks. Yield: 20 servings (serving size: about ⅓ cup drained vegetables).

CALORIES 17 (5% from fat); FAT 0.1g (sat 0g, mono 0g, poly 0g); PROTEIN 0.4g; CARB 3.7g; FIBER 1.3g; CHOL 0mg; IRON 0.4mg; SODIUM 208mg; CALC 12mg

Red Sauerkraut

This simplified version requires little of the labor of traditional kraut. For a more robust result, cut cored cabbage into quarters and slice crosswise into thin strips instead of shredding it.

  7 cups shredded red cabbage
    (about 1 [2-pound] cabbage)
  1 cup shredded carrot
2½ tablespoons kosher salt
1¾ cups white vinegar
  2 teaspoons caraway seeds
1½ teaspoons mustard seeds
1½ teaspoons black peppercorns
  ½ teaspoon whole allspice
  1 cup water
  1 teaspoon sugar

❶ Combine first 3 ingredients in a large bowl. Weigh down cabbage with a smaller bowl filled with cans. Let stand at room temperature 24 hours, tossing occasionally.
❷ Bring vinegar and next 4 ingredients to a boil in a large nonreactive saucepan; reduce heat, and simmer 5 minutes. Cover and let stand at room temperature 24 hours.
❸ Rinse cabbage mixture thoroughly with cold water. Drain and squeeze dry. Place cabbage mixture in large bowl.
❹ Strain vinegar mixture through a colander into a bowl; discard solids. Stir 1 cup water and sugar into vinegar; pour over cabbage mixture, pressing down to immerse. Cover and refrigerate 5 days. Store in an airtight container in refrigerator up to 1 week. Yield: 9 servings (serving size: about ½ cup drained sauerkraut).

CALORIES 22 (4% from fat); FAT 0.1g (sat 0g, mono 0g, poly 0.1g); PROTEIN 0.9g; CARB 5.2g; FIBER 1.5g; CHOL 0mg; IRON 0.5mg; SODIUM 180mg; CALC 29mg

Cool Pasta Plates

These internationally inspired supper salads require minimal cooking.

Pasta Menu 1
serves 4

Fusilli with Pistachio Pesto
Garlic bread
Combine 1½ teaspoons minced fresh garlic and 1 tablespoon melted butter, stirring well with a fork. Brush 4 (½-inch-thick) slices ciabatta or other crusty Italian bread with about 1 teaspoon garlic mixture. Place bread slices on a baking sheet coated with cooking spray. Bake at 375° for 5 minutes or until lightly browned.

Melon slices

Game Plan
1 While pasta water comes to a boil:
  • Preheat oven.
  • Prepare pesto mixture.
  • Cut lemon wedges, if desired.
2 While pasta cooks:
  • Prepare garlic bread.
  • Slice melon.
3 Toss pasta.

Quick Tip
At the supermarket, look for pistachios that have been roasted and shelled, and this dish will come together in a flash.

Fusilli with Pistachio Pesto

Classic Italian pesto usually contains pine nuts. This adaptation substitutes pistachios for a tasty twist. The pesto mixture is also a nice companion for grilled chicken or shrimp.
Total time: 25 minutes

  8 ounces uncooked fusilli pasta
  2 cups fresh basil leaves
  ¼ cup shelled, roasted pistachios, divided
1½ tablespoons extravirgin olive oil
  ½ teaspoon salt
  2 garlic cloves, coarsely chopped
  ¼ cup (1 ounce) grated fresh Parmesan cheese
  1 cup grape tomatoes, halved
Lemon wedges (optional)

❶ Cook pasta according to package directions, omitting salt and fat. Drain pasta in a sieve over a bowl, reserving ¼ cup pasta water. Rinse pasta with cold water; drain.
❷ Combine basil, 3 tablespoons pistachios, and next 3 ingredients in a food processor. Process until smooth, scraping sides. Transfer basil mixture to a large bowl; stir cheese and reserved ¼ cup pasta water into basil mixture. Add pasta and tomatoes to basil mixture; toss gently to coat. Sprinkle with remaining 1 tablespoon pistachios. Serve with lemon wedges, if desired. Yield: 4 servings (serving size: 1¼ cups pasta and ¾ teaspoon pistachios).

CALORIES 334 (31% from fat); FAT 11.4g (sat 2.3g, mono 6.1g, poly 2.1g); PROTEIN 12.3g; CARB 47.7g; FIBER 3.9g; CHOL 4mg; IRON 3.1mg; SODIUM 407mg; CALC 112mg

Pasta Menu 2

serves 4

Cold Soba Noodles with Vietnamese Pork

Snow pea and carrot slaw

Combine 2 cups thinly vertically sliced snow peas, 1 cup shredded carrot, ¼ cup thinly vertically sliced red onion, and ¼ teaspoon salt. Combine 2 tablespoons rice vinegar, 2 teaspoons sesame oil, and 2 teaspoons tamari; stir well. Drizzle vinegar mixture over pea mixture; toss to coat.

Coffee with sweetened condensed milk

Game Plan

1 While pork marinates:
  • Bring pasta water to a boil.
  • Prepare ingredients for pasta.
  • Prepare slaw.
2 Cook pasta.
3 Cook pork.

QUICK & EASY
Cold Soba Noodles with Vietnamese Pork

Total time: 37 minutes

- 3 tablespoons chopped green onions, divided
- 2 tablespoons dark sesame oil, divided
- 4 teaspoons fish sauce, divided
- 1 tablespoon reduced-sodium tamari
- 2 teaspoons brown sugar
- ¼ teaspoon ground black pepper
- ½ pound boneless pork cutlets, trimmed and cut into ½-inch-thick strips
- 8 ounces uncooked organic soba noodles
- 2 tablespoons rice wine vinegar
- 1 teaspoon chile paste with garlic
- 3 cups chopped napa (Chinese) cabbage
- ½ cup finely chopped red bell pepper
- Cooking spray

1 Combine 1 tablespoon onions, 1 tablespoon oil, 1 teaspoon fish sauce, and next 4 ingredients in a large zip-top plastic bag; seal. Marinate in refrigerator 20 minutes.
2 Cook noodles according to package directions, omitting salt and fat. Drain.
3 Combine remaining 1 tablespoon oil, remaining 1 tablespoon fish sauce, vinegar, and chile paste in a large bowl, stirring well. Add noodles, cabbage, and bell pepper; toss to coat.
4 Heat a skillet over medium-high heat. Coat pan with cooking spray. Remove pork from marinade, discarding marinade. Add pork to pan; cook 1½ minutes or until done. Arrange pork over noodle mixture. Sprinkle with remaining 2 tablespoons onions. Yield: 4 servings (serving size: 2¼ cups noodle mixture, ½ cup pork, and 1½ teaspoons green onions).

CALORIES 384 (31% from fat); FAT 13.4g (sat 2.8g, mono 4.9g, poly 3.3g); PROTEIN 18.7g; CARB 45.8g; FIBER 3.4g; CHOL 30mg; IRON 3.1mg; SODIUM 765mg; CALC 82mg

Pasta Menu 3

serves 4

Cavatappi Niçoise

Herbed goat cheese toasts

Preheat broiler. Combine ¼ cup soft goat cheese, 2 teaspoons chopped fresh parsley, ½ teaspoon chopped fresh thyme, and ½ teaspoon minced fresh shallot, stirring well. Spread about 1 tablespoon cheese mixture over each of 4 (1-ounce) baguette slices. Broil 2 minutes or until lightly browned.

Fresh berries

Game Plan

1 While pasta water comes to a boil:
  • Preheat broiler.
  • Prepare goat cheese mixture.
  • Prepare ingredients for pasta.
2 While pasta cooks:
  • Assemble toasts.
  • Wash berries.
3 While toasts broil:
  • Toss pasta.

QUICK & EASY
Cavatappi Niçoise

Look for Mediterranean white tuna at specialty markets. This premium product makes a difference in this salad.
Total time: 32 minutes

- 8 ounces haricots verts, trimmed and halved
- 8 ounces uncooked cavatappi pasta
- 1 (7.76-ounce) can solid white tuna, packed in oil
- 1 cup grape tomatoes, halved
- ⅓ cup niçoise olives, pitted
- 2 tablespoons minced shallots
- 2 tablespoons capers, drained
- 2 tablespoons extravirgin olive oil
- 1 tablespoon red wine vinegar
- 1 tablespoon balsamic vinegar
- ¼ teaspoon freshly ground black pepper
- ⅛ teaspoon salt
- 4 anchovy fillets, drained

1 Cook beans in boiling water 3 minutes; remove with a slotted spoon. Rinse with cold water; drain. Place beans in a large bowl. Add pasta to boiling water, and cook according to package directions, omitting salt and fat. Drain and rinse with cold water; drain. Add pasta to beans.
2 Drain tuna in a sieve over a bowl, reserving oil. Flake tuna with a fork. Add tuna and next 4 ingredients to bowl; toss. Combine reserved oil, olive oil, and remaining ingredients in a blender; process until smooth. Pour oil mixture over pasta mixture; toss to coat. Yield: 4 servings (serving size: 2¼ cups).

CALORIES 431 (27% from fat); FAT 12.8g (sat 1.6g, mono 7.7g, poly 1.6g); PROTEIN 26.5g; CARB 50.4g; FIBER 3.9g; CHOL 23mg; IRON 2.8mg; SODIUM 852mg; CALC 59mg

20 Minute Dishes

From scallops to salmon, chicken to lamb, here are simple, fresh, and easy meals you can make superfast.

STAFF FAVORITE • QUICK & EASY
Thai Chicken in Cabbage Leaves

The ground chicken filling has seasonings similar to those in *larb*, a popular Thai appetizer. Add sticky rice and sautéed fresh snow peas with chopped red bell pepper to complete the meal. Squeeze a lime wedge over the chicken for extra zip.

- 1 cup water
- ¾ cup vertically sliced red onion
- 1 pound ground chicken breast
- 3 tablespoons fresh lime juice
- 3 tablespoons finely chopped fresh mint
- 2 tablespoons finely chopped fresh cilantro
- 4 teaspoons Thai fish sauce
- ¼ to ½ teaspoon crushed red pepper
- 16 napa (Chinese) cabbage leaves (about 1 head)
-     Lime wedges (optional)

❶ Heat a nonstick skillet over medium-high heat. Add first 3 ingredients to pan. Cook 5 minutes or until chicken is done, stirring to crumble. Drain. Return chicken mixture to pan; stir in juice and next 4 ingredients.

❷ Spoon about 3 tablespoons chicken mixture onto each cabbage leaf. Serve with lime wedges, if desired. Yield: 4 servings (serving size: 4 stuffed leaves).

CALORIES 147 (4% from fat); FAT 0.6g (sat 0.2g, mono 0.1g, poly 0.1g); PROTEIN 26.7g; CARB 8.5g; FIBER 2.4g; CHOL 66mg; IRON 0.2mg; SODIUM 557mg; CALC 77mg

QUICK & EASY
Seared Scallops with Fresh Linguine and Romano Cheese

The key to obtaining the perfect sear on the scallops is to cook them in a very hot pan. Fresh linguine has a silky texture that provides a nice contrast to the browned crust on the scallops. Add mixed greens tossed with a balsamic vinaigrette.

- 1 (9-ounce) package refrigerated linguine
- ¼ cup plus 2 tablespoons (about 1½ ounces) finely grated fresh Romano cheese, divided
- 2 tablespoons olive oil, divided
- 2 tablespoons chopped fresh basil
- ½ teaspoon black pepper
- ⅛ teaspoon salt
- 1½ pounds sea scallops
- 4 lemon wedges

❶ Cook pasta according to package directions, omitting salt and fat. Drain pasta in a colander over a bowl, reserving 2 tablespoons pasta water. Combine pasta, reserved 2 tablespoons pasta water, ¼ cup cheese, 1 tablespoon oil, basil, and pepper in a large bowl; toss well.

❷ Heat remaining 1 tablespoon oil in a large cast-iron skillet over high heat. Sprinkle salt evenly over scallops; add scallops to pan. Cook 1 minute on each side or until golden.

❸ Place 1 cup pasta mixture on each of 4 plates; top each serving with about 3 scallops and 1½ teaspoons remaining cheese. Serve with lemon wedges. Yield: 4 servings.

CALORIES 495 (23% from fat); FAT 12.5g (sat 3g, mono 5.8g, poly 1.5g); PROTEIN 51.7g; CARB 42.4g; FIBER 1.9g; CHOL 110mg; IRON 5.6mg; SODIUM 872mg; CALC 177mg

QUICK & EASY
Salmon with Spicy Cucumber Salad and Peanuts

The spicy-sweet vinegar dressing in the salad complements the salmon seasoned with just salt and pepper. To easily seed the cucumber, peel, cut in half lengthwise, and scrape the seeds out with a spoon.

- 4 cups sliced seeded peeled cucumber (about 2 large)
- ¼ cup seasoned rice vinegar
- 2 tablespoons chopped fresh parsley
- 2 teaspoons sugar
- ½ teaspoon crushed red pepper
- ½ teaspoon salt, divided
-     Cooking spray
- ¼ teaspoon black pepper
- 4 (6-ounce) salmon fillets
- 4 teaspoons chopped unsalted, dry-roasted peanuts

❶ Combine first 5 ingredients in a medium bowl; stir in ¼ teaspoon salt.
❷ Heat a large nonstick skillet over medium-high heat. Coat pan with cooking spray. Sprinkle remaining ¼ teaspoon salt and black pepper over fish. Add fish to pan; cook 4 minutes on each side or until fish flakes easily when tested with a fork or until desired degree of doneness. Place 1 fillet in each of 4 shallow bowls, and top each serving with 1 cup cucumber salad and 1 teaspoon peanuts. Yield: 4 servings.

CALORIES 262 (38% from fat); FAT 11g (sat 1.7g, mono 3.8g, poly 4.2g); PROTEIN 30.5g; CARB 8.9g; FIBER 1.3g; CHOL 81mg; IRON 1.7mg; SODIUM 666mg; CALC 41mg

Lamb Chops with Herb Vinaigrette

Add garlic mashed potatoes and steamed broccoli florets. If you have bottled roasted red bell peppers in your refrigerator, you can substitute them for the pimiento.

½ teaspoon salt, divided
½ teaspoon black pepper
8 (4-ounce) lamb loin chops
2 tablespoons finely chopped shallots
1½ tablespoons water
1 tablespoon red wine vinegar
1½ teaspoons lemon juice
1½ teaspoons extravirgin olive oil
1 teaspoon Dijon mustard
1½ tablespoons finely chopped fresh flat-leaf parsley
1½ tablespoons finely chopped fresh tarragon
1 tablespoon finely chopped fresh mint
1 tablespoon finely chopped pimiento

❶ Preheat broiler.
❷ Sprinkle ¼ teaspoon salt and pepper over lamb. Place lamb on the rack of a broiler pan or roasting pan; place rack in pan. Broil 5 minutes on each side or until desired degree of doneness.
❸ Combine shallots, 1½ tablespoons water, and vinegar in a small microwave-safe bowl; microwave at HIGH 30 seconds. Stir in remaining ¼ teaspoon salt, juice, oil, and mustard, stirring with a whisk. Add parsley and remaining ingredients, stirring well. Serve vinaigrette over lamb. Yield: 4 servings (serving size: 2 chops and 1 tablespoon vinaigrette).

CALORIES 349 (39% from fat); FAT 15.2g (sat 5.1g, mono 6.7g, poly 1.4g); PROTEIN 47.7g; CARB 1.9g; FIBER 0.2g; CHOL 150mg; IRON 4.6mg; SODIUM 482mg; CALC 37mg

Onion-Smothered Italian Burgers

Serve corn on the cob as a quick and easy side dish and low-fat strawberry ice cream for dessert.

1 teaspoon olive oil
2 cups thinly sliced Vidalia or other sweet onion
2 teaspoons sugar
¼ teaspoon salt
⅛ teaspoon black pepper
1 tablespoon balsamic vinegar
3 tablespoons preshredded fresh Parmesan cheese
2 tablespoons tomato paste
1 teaspoon dried oregano
½ teaspoon garlic powder
¼ teaspoon dried basil
1 pound extra lean ground beef
Cooking spray
4 (1½-ounce) hamburger buns

❶ Heat oil in a large nonstick skillet over medium-high heat. Add onion and next 3 ingredients to pan. Cook 6 minutes or until lightly browned, stirring occasionally. Add vinegar to pan; cook 30 seconds, stirring constantly.
❷ Combine cheese and next 5 ingredients in a medium bowl; shape meat mixture into 4 (3-inch) patties. Heat a grill pan over medium-high heat. Coat pan with cooking spray. Add patties to pan. Cook 5 minutes on each side or until desired degree of doneness. Place 1 patty on bottom half of each bun; top each patty with ¼ cup onion mixture and top half of a bun. Yield: 4 servings (serving size: 1 burger).

CALORIES 330 (24% from fat); FAT 8.9g (sat 3g, mono 3.7g, poly 1.5g); PROTEIN 28.9g; CARB 33.7g; FIBER 2.9g; CHOL 65mg; IRON 4mg; SODIUM 541mg; CALC 142mg

Chicken Breasts with Avocado, Tomato, and Cucumber Salsa

Baked tortilla chips make a crunchy companion for this simple summer supper. Try the salsa another night on grilled fish or shrimp.

Cooking spray
¾ teaspoon salt, divided
¼ teaspoon chipotle chile powder
4 (6-ounce) skinless, boneless chicken breast halves
1¼ cups coarsely chopped seeded peeled cucumber (about 1 large)
1 cup grape tomatoes, halved
½ cup prechopped red onion
½ cup chopped peeled avocado
2 tablespoons chopped fresh cilantro
2 tablespoons fresh lime juice
1 jalapeño pepper, seeded and finely chopped

❶ Heat a grill pan over medium-high heat. Coat pan with cooking spray. Sprinkle ½ teaspoon salt and chile powder evenly over chicken; add chicken to pan. Cook 6 minutes on each side or until done, and remove from heat.
❷ Combine remaining ¼ teaspoon salt, cucumber, and remaining ingredients in a medium bowl, tossing well. Serve with chicken. Yield: 4 servings (serving size: 1 chicken breast half and ¾ cup salsa).

CALORIES 243 (28% from fat); FAT 7.6g (sat 1.6g, mono 3.5g, poly 1.3g); PROTEIN 35.6g; CARB 7.3g; FIBER 2.7g; CHOL 94mg; IRON 1.7mg; SODIUM 533mg; CALC 34mg

Wedding Cookie Conundrum

We solve a Connecticut banker's baking problems with ingredient modifications and a change in technique.

After sampling this luscious take on a traditional wedding cookie—a short-breadlike sweet studded with crunchy nuts and chewy dried cherries, and then blanketed in powdered sugar—Scott Javor, a corporate finance banker from Stamford, Connecticut, was hooked. However, he strives to maintain a healthy weight and knew this butter-rich recipe needed a major overhaul so he could enjoy the cookies for more than special occasions.

With one cup of creamy butter, one-half cup pistachios, and plenty of powdered sugar, the original version of each bite-sized cookie was packed with 118 calories and seven grams of fat, nearly 60 percent of which were the saturated type. As Javor can attest, it is hard to stop at one cookie, so fat and calories add up quickly.

The butter, which helps give this dessert its characteristic crumbly texture, is also its main fat and calorie contributor. To start, we halved the butter amount, cutting 25 calories and about 2.8 grams of fat per cookie. To maintain a shortbreadlike texture, we used a food processor to incorporate air when combining the flour and butter while handling the delicate dough as little as possible to ensure tender results. And since we reduced the butter (the key source of moisture in the original recipe), we added a little water to moisten the dough, plus cornstarch to maintain the cookie's texture. To manage calories, we halved the amount of pistachios, finely chopping them for better distribution among the cookies.

Reducing these elements trimmed another few calories per cookie.

Javor likes the revamped cookies and finds them easier to make. Even with fewer chopped pistachios, Javor says he still enjoys the slight sweetness they contribute. "These cookies are good," he says. "They are just sweet enough, and the delicate, crumbly texture was what I wanted." The cookies can be made up to four days ahead and stored in an airtight container. Now he can have his cookie and eat it, too.

STAFF FAVORITE • MAKE AHEAD
Cherry-Pistachio Wedding Cookies

The combination of tender cake flour and sturdy all-purpose flour produces delicate cookies. The dough will be crumbly after you've combined all the ingredients but will hold its shape once molded in a tablespoon measure and turned onto a baking sheet. You may need to add one to two additional teaspoons of ice water to the dough to achieve the crumbly consistency.

- 1½ cups cake flour (about 6 ounces)
- ⅔ cup all-purpose flour (about 3 ounces)
- 1¼ cups powdered sugar, divided
- 2 teaspoons cornstarch
- ¼ teaspoon salt
- ½ cup chilled butter, cut into small pieces
- 3 teaspoons ice water
- 1½ teaspoons vanilla extract
- ½ cup dried tart cherries
- ¼ cup finely chopped salted dry-roasted pistachios
- Cooking spray

1 Preheat oven to 350°.
2 Lightly spoon flours into dry measuring cups; level with a knife. Combine flours, ¾ cup powdered sugar, cornstarch, and salt in a food processor; pulse to combine. With food processor on, add butter through food chute a few pieces at a time; process 1 minute or until mixture is the texture of sand.
3 Combine 3 teaspoons ice water and vanilla in a small bowl. With food processor on, slowly add ice water mixture through food chute; process 1 minute or until very well combined. (Mixture will remain crumbly.) Add cherries and pistachios; pulse 10 times or just until combined. Transfer mixture to a bowl. (Mixture will be crumbly.) Gently press mixture into a tablespoon; level and pack lightly with heel of your hand. Turn out onto a baking sheet coated with cooking spray. Repeat with remaining dough to form 32 cookies.
4 Bake at 350° for 15 minutes or just until bottoms are golden. Remove from oven; cool 10 minutes on baking sheet.
5 Place remaining ½ cup powdered sugar in a large bowl. Add cooled cookies; toss gently to coat. Transfer cookies to wax paper to cool completely. Yield: 32 servings (serving size: 1 cookie).

CALORIES 86 (36% from fat); FAT 3.4g (sat 1.9g, mono 1g, poly 0.3g); PROTEIN 1g; CARB 12.9g; FIBER 0.8g; CHOL 8mg; IRON 0.6mg; SODIUM 43mg; CALC 4mg

serving size: 1 cookie		
	before	after
CALORIES PER SERVING	118	86
FAT	7g	3.4g
PERCENT OF TOTAL CALORIES	53%	36%

Go Ahead, Give In

Cravings are common. Here are clever ways to satisfy them without going overboard.

IT'S BEEN ANOTHER one of those days: places to go, deadlines to meet, meals to cook. You find yourself daydreaming about crisp, salty potato chips. Pretty soon it's an insistent, must-have-it-now craving, and before you know it, your hand is deep in the bag.

Rather than berate your lack of willpower, once in a while indulge yourself. In a 2007 Tufts University study of healthy women, 91 percent reported having food cravings (which the researchers define as an intense desire to eat a specific food). In other words, cravings are common, and the key to successful weight management, experts say, is learning to address cravings rather than always denying them. "You first have to accept that having cravings is normal, but you don't have to give in to every one," says Tufts study coauthor Susan Roberts, PhD. "The people in our research who manage their weight the best are not those who crave foods less often but those who give in some of the time."

Ethnic-Spicy-Crunchy

MAKE AHEAD

Bahn Mi

- ½ cup shredded carrot
- ½ cup grated peeled daikon radish
- 1 tablespoon cider vinegar
- 2 teaspoons sugar
- ¼ teaspoon kosher salt
- 3 tablespoons chili garlic sauce
- 1½ teaspoons sugar
- 1 (1-pound) pork tenderloin, trimmed
- Cooking spray
- ½ teaspoon salt
- 3 tablespoons fat-free mayonnaise
- 2 (20-inch) baguettes (about 8½ ounces each)
- 16 thin cucumber slices (about 1 cucumber)
- 16 cilantro sprigs
- ¼ cup thinly sliced green onions
- 1 jalapeño pepper, seeded and thinly sliced

❶ Combine first 5 ingredients; cover and let stand 15 minutes to 1 hour. Drain.
❷ Preheat oven to 400°.

❸ Combine chili garlic sauce and 1½ teaspoons sugar; stir well. Place pork on rack of a small roasting pan or broiler pan coated with cooking spray. Spread 2 tablespoons chili garlic sauce mixture evenly over pork; sprinkle pork with ½ teaspoon salt. Bake at 400° for 20 minutes or until a thermometer registers 155° (slightly pink). Cool; cover pork, and refrigerate.
❹ Combine mayonnaise and remaining chili garlic sauce mixture; cover and refrigerate.
❺ Cut each baguette horizontally, cutting to, but not through, other side using a serrated knife. Spread mayonnaise mixture evenly on cut sides of baguettes. Cut pork into thin slices; divide evenly between baguettes. Top evenly with carrot mixture. Arrange 8 cucumber slices and 8 cilantro sprigs on each baguette. Top evenly with onions and jalapeño. Press top gently to close; cut each baguette into 4 equal servings. Yield: 8 servings (serving size: 1 sandwich).

CALORIES 343 (22% from fat); FAT 8.3g (sat 1.8g, mono 2.7g, poly 3.2g); PROTEIN 17.5g; CARB 50.2g; FIBER 4.2g; CHOL 37mg; IRON 2.1mg; SODIUM 721mg; CALC 20mg

Trigger Happy

Brian Wansink, PhD, director of Cornell University's Food and Brand Lab and author of *Mindless Eating: Why We Eat More Than We Think*, has made a career of studying people's behavior relating to food. He says cravings fall into two basic categories: snacks (with potato chips, ice cream, cookies, and chocolate leading the list) and meal foods (pizza, pasta, burgers, casseroles, and the like). Which comfort food you choose can be affected by age and gender. "Women tend to crave sweet stuff, men salty stuff," Roberts says. "And premenstrual women's cravings are more likely to be insistent."

What triggers a food longing? Hormonal fluctuations are thought to be the cause in premenstrual women, though no one knows for sure, says Roberts. Other theories include a physical need for calories and emotional cues. "If you haven't eaten for hours and you're really hungry, that is a physical craving, and you should eat," says Bonnie Taub-Dix, MA, RD, CDN, spokesperson for the American Dietetic Association. Emotional yens, on the other hand, may be set off by almost anything: a song, a person, a feeling, a situation that's associated with a particular food—any reminder can kick a hankering into gear, "even if you're not hungry," Taub-Dix says.

Although stress is a commonly cited culprit, research shows that positive events trigger cravings even more than negative feelings, says Wansink. "In one of our studies, we rigged games so that people would either succeed or lose, and we found that they ended up having a stronger craving when they won."

Creamy-Cheesy

QUICK & EASY

Hot Artichoke-Cheese Dip

This warm dip is just the thing when you hanker for a creamy, cheesy snack. And because you are likely to have the ingredients on hand in the fridge and freezer, it's also great for impromptu entertaining.

- 2 garlic cloves
- 1 green onion, cut into pieces
- 1/3 cup (1 1/2 ounces) grated Parmigiano-Reggiano cheese, divided
- 1/3 cup reduced-fat mayonnaise
- 1/4 cup (2 ounces) 1/3-less-fat cream cheese
- 1 tablespoon fresh lemon juice
- 1/4 teaspoon crushed red pepper
- 12 ounces frozen artichoke hearts, thawed and drained
  Cooking spray
- 24 (1/2-ounce) slices baguette, toasted

1 Preheat oven to 400°.
2 Place garlic and onion in a food processor; process until finely chopped. Add 1/4 cup Parmigiano-Reggiano and next 4 ingredients; process until almost smooth. Add artichoke hearts; pulse until artichoke hearts are coarsely chopped. Spoon mixture into a 3-cup gratin dish coated with cooking spray; sprinkle evenly with remaining Parmigiano-Reggiano. Bake at 400° for 15 minutes or until thoroughly heated and bubbly. Serve hot with baguette slices. Yield: 12 servings (serving size: 2 1/2 tablespoons dip and 2 baguette slices).

CALORIES 126 (24% from fat); FAT 3.4g (sat 1.3g, mono 0.6g, poly 0.5g); PROTEIN 5.1g; CARB 20.8g; FIBER 2.3g; CHOL 7mg; IRON 1.1mg; SODIUM 334mg; CALC 59mg

Meaty-Salty

Steak Frites with Shallot Pan Reduction

(pictured on page 263)

Many CookingLight.com users crave hearty meals, and our take on the classic French bistro dish satisfies. You can add a side of sautéed spinach to round out the plate for a company-worthy supper.

- 1 3/4 pounds baking potatoes (about 2 large potatoes), peeled and cut into 1/2-inch sticks
  Cooking spray
- 3/4 teaspoon kosher salt, divided
- 2 teaspoons chopped fresh thyme, divided
- 1 pound boneless sirloin steak, trimmed
- 1/2 teaspoon freshly ground black pepper, divided
- 2 tablespoons finely chopped shallots
- 2 tablespoons brandy
- 3/4 cup less-sodium beef broth
- 1 tablespoon Dijon mustard
- 1 1/2 teaspoons butter

1 Position 1 oven rack on highest setting. Position another rack on lowest setting.
2 Preheat oven to 450°.
3 Arrange potatoes in a single layer on 2 baking sheets. Coat with cooking spray; sprinkle with 1/4 teaspoon salt. Place pans on top and bottom racks. Bake at 450° for 40 minutes or until golden brown, stirring potatoes and rotating pans halfway through. Toss potatoes with 1 teaspoon thyme.
4 Heat a 12-inch heavy nonstick skillet over medium-high heat. Coat pan with cooking spray. Sprinkle both sides of steak with 1/4 teaspoon salt and 1/4 teaspoon pepper. Add steak to pan; sauté 3 minutes on each side or until desired degree of doneness. Remove from pan; keep warm.
5 Add shallots to pan; sauté 2 minutes. Add brandy; bring to a boil, scraping pan to loosen browned bits. Add broth, mustard, and remaining 1 teaspoon thyme;

bring to a boil. Cook until reduced to 2/3 cup (about 3 minutes). Add remaining 1/4 teaspoon salt and remaining 1/4 teaspoon pepper. Add butter, stirring with a whisk.
6 Cut steak into slices. Serve with shallot sauce and potatoes. Yield: 4 servings (serving size: 3 ounces steak, about 3 tablespoons sauce, and about 8 frites).

CALORIES 347 (18% from fat); FAT 6.8g (sat 2.7g, mono 2.4g, poly 0.4g); PROTEIN 28.9g; CARB 37.7g; FIBER 2.7g; CHOL 73mg; IRON 4.9mg; SODIUM 612mg; CALC 39mg

Sweet-Chocolate

MAKE AHEAD

Dark Chocolate and Cherry Brownies

(pictured on page 260)

CookingLight.com users agree: Sweets are a top craving, and chocolate is in a class by itself. These rich brownies are just the ticket. Lining the pan with parchment paper helps prevent the moist brownies from sticking.

  Cooking spray
- 3/4 cup all-purpose flour (about 3.4 ounces)
- 1 cup sugar
- 3/4 cup unsweetened cocoa
- 1 teaspoon baking powder
- 3/4 teaspoon salt
- 1/3 cup cherry preserves
- 1/3 cup water
- 5 tablespoons butter
- 1 large egg, lightly beaten
- 1 large egg white, lightly beaten
- 1/3 cup semisweet chocolate chips
  Powdered sugar (optional)

1 Preheat oven to 350°.
2 Line a 9-inch square baking pan with parchment paper; coat with cooking spray.
3 Lightly spoon flour into dry measuring cups; level with a knife. Combine flour and next 4 ingredients in a large bowl; stir with a whisk. Combine preserves, 1/3 cup water, and butter in a small saucepan; bring to a boil. Add preserves

mixture to flour mixture; stir well. Add egg and egg white; stir until smooth. Stir in chocolate chips. Scrape batter into prepared pan. Bake at 350° for 25 minutes or until a wooden pick inserted in center comes out with a few moist crumbs. Cool in pan on a wire rack. Garnish with powdered sugar, if desired. Yield: 16 servings.

CALORIES 155 (31% from fat); FAT 5.4g (sat 3g, mono 1.4g, poly 0.2g); PROTEIN 2.2g; CARB 25.8g; FIBER 1.1g; CHOL 23mg; IRON 1mg; SODIUM 168mg; CALC 10mg

Sweet-Chocolate

MAKE AHEAD

Chocolate Sauce

Homemade chocolate sauce has a lovely silkiness, and we offer three variations in addition to this basic recipe. It's wonderful drizzled over low-fat vanilla ice cream or angel food cake, or use it as a dipper with fresh fruit. Be sure to use high-quality chocolate for the best results.

½ cup 2% reduced-fat milk
3 tablespoons sugar
1 tablespoon unsweetened cocoa
Dash of salt
¼ cup 60% cacao chocolate chips (such as Ghirardelli)
¼ teaspoon vanilla extract

❶ Combine first 4 ingredients in a small saucepan; bring to a boil, stirring constantly with a whisk. Remove from heat. Stir in chocolate chips; let stand 1 minute.
❷ Cook over medium heat 1 minute or until sauce is smooth and slightly thickened, stirring constantly. Remove from heat; stir in vanilla. Yield: 8 servings (serving size: about 1 tablespoon).

CALORIES 69 (34% from fat); FAT 2.6g (sat 1.4g, mono 0.1g, poly 0g); PROTEIN 0.9g; CARB 10.3g; FIBER 0.1g; CHOL 1mg; IRON 0.1mg; SODIUM 26mg; CALC 19mg

MEXICAN CHOCOLATE VARIATION:
Add ¼ teaspoon ground cinnamon to milk mixture. Add 1 teaspoon instant espresso granules with chocolate chips.

Strategies That Work

Given cravings' universal nature, experts agree that if you rarely enjoy a food you crave, you're more likely to go overboard when you finally do give in. Indeed, according to the Tufts study, people who *occasionally* give in to hankerings manage their weight most successfully. These healthful strategies can help, too.

Eat regularly. Waiting too long between meals can turn normal hunger pangs into an out-of-control craving. "It's hard to make a good choice when you're starving," says Taub-Dix. Her suggestion: Keep healthful options—energy bars, skim milk, even an almond butter and jelly sandwich—on hand to keep hunger in check.

Delay gratification. When a craving hits, slip your mind into rational gear by saying, "not now, maybe tomorrow," suggests Roberts. Saying "later" rather than "never" may help decrease the frequency of cravings, she adds.

Keep it real. Eating an apple isn't likely to satisfy a yen for chocolate. Instead, enjoy what you really want—in moderation. Wansink's research shows that "each subsequent taste of a food is rated as less enjoyable than the previous taste. The first bite is always the best; the second bite, second best." If you eat half of what you'd normally want, Wansink says, "your satisfaction rating [will still be] very, very high."

Practice portion control. It's easy to overeat if you munch straight from a box of cereal, for instance, or a bag of pretzels. Taub-Dix suggests portioning one-cup servings into zip-top plastic bags. "This way you won't eat to excess."

In fact, snacks are fine. The USDA Dietary Guidelines allow 100 to 300 "

discretionary" calories daily (to calculate your daily discretionary calories, visit MyPyramid.gov). An ounce of dark chocolate (142 calories), for example, or 1.25 ounces of baked potato chips (166 calories) fall well within that range.

Choose high-quality foods with nutritional benefits. Tapenade spread on a fresh baguette will offer salty-meaty flavor from the olives (as well as heart-healthy fatty acids) and tasty carbs from the bread. If chocolate is your weakness, go for gourmet dark chocolate, which offers beneficial antioxidants along with great flavor. If you want something creamy, try thick Greek yogurt drizzled with honey (you'll gain some calcium as well as the rich creaminess you really want).

Keep a food diary. This can help if cravings are frequent and often lead to overeating. "I suggest my patients write down what they're feeling" when they have a craving, says Taub-Dix. "It helps to transfer your feelings onto that piece of paper, and you may find you don't have to eat." Also note the types of food and even the times you eat; look for patterns so you're not caught off guard. Addressing underlying issues like physical hunger or boredom or stress may help people minimize cravings, says Roberts. "The idea is to live with your cravings and not let them control you."

Simply anticipating what triggers a craving may help you be better prepared with a healthful option. We developed these recipes based on an informal survey on the CookingLight.com bulletin boards. Overall, our readers tend to crave salty, sweet, creamy, and ethnic flavors. And chocolate is in a category by itself.

ORANGE-CHOCOLATE VARIATION:
Combine 2 (5 x 1-inch) strips orange rind, milk, sugar, and salt; bring to a boil, stirring constantly with a whisk. Remove pan from heat; cover and let stand 10 minutes. Strain milk mixture through a fine sieve into a bowl. Discard solids. Return milk mixture to pan. Add cocoa; proceed with recipe with step 2.

MINT-CHOCOLATE VARIATION:
Combine 8 sliced mint leaves, milk, sugar, and salt; bring to a boil, stirring constantly with a whisk. Remove pan from heat; cover and let stand 10 minutes. Strain milk mixture through a fine sieve into a bowl. Discard solids. Add cocoa; proceed with recipe with step 2.

Ethnic-Crunchy

MAKE AHEAD

Chipotle Black Bean Dip with Corn Chips

A common craving among CookingLight. com users is chips; our homemade tortilla chips keep fat and sodium in check. This snack quells an oft-cited yen for Mexican fare and has protein, complex carbs, and fiber.

6 (6-inch) corn tortillas
Cooking spray
⅛ teaspoon salt
1 teaspoon olive oil
1 cup chopped onion
1 teaspoon cumin seeds
1 garlic clove, minced
¼ teaspoon dried oregano
1 (15-ounce) can black beans, undrained
¼ cup (about 1 ounce) shredded part-skim mozzarella cheese
2 tablespoons crumbled queso fresco
⅓ cup canned no-salt-added diced tomatoes, undrained
1 chipotle chile, canned in adobo sauce
2 tablespoons chopped fresh cilantro

❶ Preheat oven to 400°.
❷ Cut each tortilla into 6 wedges. Arrange wedges in a single layer on a large baking sheet coated with cooking spray. Sprinkle with salt. Bake at 400° for 10 minutes or until golden brown and crisp, stirring occasionally.
❸ Heat oil in a medium saucepan over medium heat. Add onion to pan; cook 8 minutes or until tender, stirring occasionally. Add cumin and garlic; cook 1 minute. Add oregano and beans; bring to a boil. Mash with a potato masher. Reduce heat, and simmer 10 minutes or until thickened, stirring occasionally.
❹ Spoon bean mixture into a 3-cup gratin dish coated with cooking spray. Top with cheeses. Bake at 400° for 12 minutes or until hot and bubbly.

❺ Combine tomatoes and chile in a mini food processor; process until smooth. Spoon tomato mixture over bean mixture. Sprinkle with cilantro. Yield: 6 servings (serving size: about ¼ cup bean mixture and 6 tortilla chips).

CALORIES 142 (22% from fat); FAT 3.5g (sat 1g, mono 1.1g, poly 0.5g); PROTEIN 6.6g; CARB 27.7g; FIBER 6g; CHOL 4mg; IRON 1.6mg; SODIUM 502mg; CALC 128mg

Ethnic-Spicy

Whole Spice Chicken Curry and Fragrant Rice Pilaf with Peas

Find kaffir lime leaves in Asian markets and some health-food stores, or substitute ¼ teaspoon grated lime rind for each kaffir lime leaf used in the recipe.

CHICKEN:
½ teaspoon cumin seeds
4 whole cloves
3 green cardamom pods, lightly crushed
2 teaspoons canola oil
2 cups finely chopped onion
1 tablespoon finely grated peeled fresh ginger
4 garlic cloves, minced
1 tablespoon all-purpose flour
½ teaspoon ground turmeric
¼ teaspoon crushed red pepper
½ cup light coconut milk
¾ teaspoon salt
¼ teaspoon black pepper
1 (14-ounce) can fat-free, less-sodium chicken broth
1 fresh bay leaf
1 fresh kaffir lime leaf
1 (3-inch) cinnamon stick
2½ pounds bone-in chicken breasts, skinned

RICE:
2¼ cups water
1½ cups uncooked long-grain white rice
1 teaspoon cumin seeds
¼ teaspoon salt
1 fresh bay leaf
1 fresh kaffir lime leaf
1 cup frozen peas, thawed

REMAINING INGREDIENTS:
3 tablespoons dry-roasted cashews, salted and chopped
2 tablespoons chopped fresh cilantro

❶ To prepare chicken, place first 3 ingredients on a double layer of cheesecloth. Gather edges of cheesecloth together, and tie securely.
❷ Heat oil in a heavy Dutch oven over medium heat. Add onion to pan; cook 8 minutes or until tender, stirring occasionally. Add ginger and garlic; cook 1 minute. Add flour, turmeric, and red pepper; cook 2 minutes, stirring constantly. Add cheesecloth bag, coconut milk, and next 6 ingredients; bring to a boil. Add chicken. Cover, reduce heat, and simmer 20 minutes or until chicken is done, turning once. Remove chicken from pan with a slotted spoon; cool slightly. Cook liquid in pan, uncovered, 10 minutes or until slightly thickened. Discard bay leaf, lime leaf, cinnamon stick, and cheesecloth bag. Remove meat from bones; shred with 2 forks, and return to pan. Cook 10 minutes.
❸ To prepare rice, combine 2¼ cups water and next 5 ingredients in a medium saucepan; bring to a boil. Cover, reduce heat, and simmer 20 minutes. Sprinkle peas over rice; cover and simmer 10 minutes or until peas are heated through, rice is tender, and liquid is absorbed. Discard bay leaf and lime leaf. Place ¾ cup rice mixture on each of 6 plates; top each serving with ¾ cup chicken mixture, 1½ teaspoons cashews, and 1 teaspoon cilantro. Yield: 6 servings.

CALORIES 444 (14% from fat); FAT 7g (sat 2.1g, mono 2.7g, poly 1.4g); PROTEIN 42.4g; CARB 50.5g; FIBER 3.4g; CHOL 88mg; IRON 4.7mg; SODIUM 710mg; CALC 69mg

Cheesy-Carbs
Three-Cheese Macaroni and Cheese

For a weeknight supper, bake the macaroni in an 8-inch square baking dish for 35 minutes.

- 1 teaspoon olive oil
- 1 cup finely chopped onion (about 1 medium)
- 2 tablespoons all-purpose flour
- 1 garlic clove, minced
- 1½ cups 1% low-fat milk
- 1 bay leaf
- ½ cup (2 ounces) crumbled Gorgonzola cheese
- ¾ cup (3 ounces) grated Parmigiano-Reggiano cheese, divided
- ¼ teaspoon salt
- 2 cups uncooked elbow macaroni (about 8 ounces)
- Cooking spray
- ⅔ cup (about 2½ ounces) shredded part-skim mozzarella cheese
- ⅔ cup panko (Japanese breadcrumbs)
- ⅛ teaspoon freshly ground black pepper

❶ Heat oil in a medium saucepan over medium heat. Add onion to pan; cook 8 minutes or until tender, stirring occasionally. Add flour and garlic; cook 1 minute, stirring constantly. Stir in milk and bay leaf; bring to a boil. Cook 2 minutes or until thick, stirring constantly with a whisk. Add Gorgonzola, ½ cup Parmigiano-Reggiano, and salt; stir until cheeses melt. Discard bay leaf.
❷ Preheat oven to 375°.
❸ Cook pasta in boiling water 5 minutes or until almost tender, omitting salt and fat; drain well. Add pasta to cheese mixture, stirring well. Place about ½ cup pasta mixture into each of 6 (1-cup) ramekins coated with cooking spray. Sprinkle evenly with mozzarella. Top evenly with remaining pasta mixture. Combine remaining ¼ cup Parmigiano-Reggiano and panko; sprinkle evenly over pasta mixture. Spray lightly with cooking spray; sprinkle with pepper. Bake at 375° for 25 minutes or until heated. Yield: 6 servings (serving size: 1 ramekin).

CALORIES 321 (28% from fat); FAT 9.9g (sat 5.6g, mono 2.3g, poly 0.9g); PROTEIN 17.4g; CARB 40.8g; FIBER 2.4g; CHOL 26mg; IRON 1.5mg; SODIUM 487mg; CALC 332mg

Salty-Cheesy
QUICK & EASY • MAKE AHEAD
Pecorino and Romaine Salad with Garlicky Lemon Dressing

Shaved pecorino Romano stars in this salad, which will satisfy a longing for cheese and salty flavors. Prepare the croutons a day or two ahead (step 2); store at room temperature in a zip-top plastic bag. Make the dressing (step 3) the night before, and refrigerate in an airtight container.

- 8 (¼-inch-thick) slices ciabatta bread (about 4 ounces)
- 1 garlic clove, peeled and halved
- Cooking spray
- 1 tablespoon fresh lemon juice
- 1 tablespoon extravirgin olive oil
- 1 teaspoon Dijon mustard
- 1 teaspoon Worcestershire sauce
- ¼ teaspoon anchovy paste
- 1 garlic clove, crushed
- 6 cups torn romaine lettuce
- Cracked black pepper
- ¼ cup (1 ounce) shaved pecorino Romano cheese

❶ Preheat oven to 400°.
❷ Place bread on a baking sheet; bake at 400° for 5 minutes or until toasted. Rub toasted bread slices with cut sides of garlic clove; discard garlic clove halves. Cut bread into ½-inch cubes. Place bread cubes on pan; coat with cooking spray. Bake 5 minutes or until golden. Cool.
❸ Combine juice and next 5 ingredients in a small bowl; stir with a whisk.
❹ Place lettuce in a large bowl. Pour juice mixture over lettuce; toss gently to coat. Sprinkle with pepper. Top with croutons and cheese. Yield: 6 servings (serving size: 1 cup lettuce mixture, ½ cup croutons, and 2 teaspoons cheese).

CALORIES 118 (39% from fat); FAT 5.1g (sat 1.2g, mono 2.3g, poly 0.4g); PROTEIN 4.4g; CARB 14.7g; FIBER 1.5g; CHOL 4mg; IRON 1.1mg; SODIUM 254mg; CALC 69mg

---

Choice Ingredient: Kosher Salt

Learn: Kosher salt is so named because its large crystals are ideal for making meats kosher. (Jewish dietary law stipulates the blood must be removed from meat before eating.) This is often accomplished by "koshering," sprinkling coarse salt on the surface of the meat to draw out and absorb the fluid. Kosher salt contains no additives, such as iodine or starch. Because of its pure flavor, kosher salt is a favorite of chefs and many home cooks.

Purchase: Look for kosher salt in the spice and baking aisle of your local market. It's usually sold in one- to three-pound boxes with a pour spout.

Store: No matter what type of salt you purchase, keep it free from excessive humidity or moisture, as this can cause the crystals to clump. Otherwise, kosher salt will keep—literally—forever.

Use: Granule size varies among brands. Also, be aware that a teaspoon of table salt can be equivalent to 1½ to 2 teaspoons of kosher salt. (Check the back of the box for appropriate conversion ratios.) It's often used to line the rims of margarita glasses. You can also sprinkle kosher salt atop rolls and other baked goods just before baking for a sparkly, crunchy topping.

Serving a Crowd

Problem: A Maine reader frets about preparing supper for a large group. Strategy: Save time and reduce stress with uncomplicated dishes that feature make-ahead components.

When Bob and Cindy Gurry left their fast-paced, 70-hour-a-week city jobs in Massachusetts a year ago and moved their family of four to the small seaside town of Scarborough, Maine, it meant they'd finally have time for entertaining. Bob says he envisioned hosting dinner parties and inviting eight or 10 of his new neighbors. But there's one hurdle. "Cooking for a big crowd is a little intimidating," he admits. Cindy is willing to share cooking duties, but the couple needs advice about how to manage meals for large groups.

To ensure the Gurrys' success, we offer a few key strategies: Choose straightforward recipes, prep the ingredients in advance, and divide cooking duties. This efficient, no-fuss approach allows the couple to throw dinner parties they'll be sure to enjoy as much as their guests.

EARLY-FALL DINNER PARTY MENU

(Serves 10)

Fig and Goat Cheese Bruschetta

Grilled Chicken and Pesto Farfalle

Chardonnay

Caramel-Apple Cheesecake

Coffee, tea

MAKE AHEAD
Fig and Goat Cheese Bruschetta

Prepare the fig jam up to three days in advance, and store in the refrigerator. Bring to room temperature, and assemble bruschetta just before serving. For smaller groups, use half the amount of bread. Leftover jam is great on toast at breakfast.

1¼ cups chopped dried Mission figs (about 9 ounces)
⅓ cup sugar
⅓ cup coarsely chopped orange sections
1 teaspoon grated orange rind
⅓ cup fresh orange juice (about 1 orange)
½ teaspoon chopped fresh rosemary
¼ teaspoon freshly ground black pepper
40 (½-inch-thick) slices French bread baguette, toasted (about 8 ounces)
1¼ cups (10 ounces) crumbled goat cheese
5 teaspoons finely chopped walnuts

❶ Combine first 7 ingredients in a small saucepan; bring to a boil. Cover, reduce heat, and simmer 10 minutes or until figs are tender. Uncover and cook 5 minutes or until mixture thickens. Remove from heat; cool to room temperature.
❷ Preheat broiler.
❸ Top each bread slice with 1½ teaspoons fig mixture and 1½ teaspoons goat cheese. Arrange bruschetta on a baking sheet; sprinkle evenly with walnuts. Broil 2 minutes or until nuts begin to brown. Serve warm. Yield: 20 servings (serving size: 2 bruschetta).

CALORIES 138 (31% from fat); FAT 4.7g (sat 2.3g, mono 1.1g, poly 1g); PROTEIN 4.2g; CARB 21g; FIBER 2.1g; CHOL 7mg; IRON 0.8mg; SODIUM 121mg; CALC 45mg

---

Grilled Chicken and Pesto Farfalle

This dish comes together quickly if one person grills chicken while another cooks the pasta and sauce. Garnish with basil sprigs, if desired. If you serve wine, a chardonnay complements the creamy sauce.

1¾ pounds skinless, boneless chicken breast halves
1 teaspoon salt, divided
¾ teaspoon freshly ground black pepper, divided
Cooking spray
20 ounces uncooked farfalle (bow tie pasta)
1 tablespoon butter
3 garlic cloves, minced
1½ cups 1% low-fat milk, divided
2 tablespoons all-purpose flour
1 (3.5-ounce) jar commercial pesto (about ⅓ cup)
¾ cup half-and-half
2 cups (8 ounces) shredded fresh Parmesan cheese, divided
4 cups halved grape tomatoes (about 2 pints)
½ cup chopped fresh basil

❶ Prepare grill to medium-high heat.
❷ Sprinkle chicken evenly with ¼ teaspoon salt and ¼ teaspoon pepper. Place chicken on grill rack coated with cooking spray; grill 10 minutes or until done, turning after 6 minutes. Remove from grill; let stand 5 minutes. Cut chicken into ½-inch pieces; keep warm.
❸ Cook pasta according to package directions, omitting salt and fat. Drain in a colander over a bowl, reserving ¼ cup cooking liquid. Place pasta in a large bowl.
❹ Heat butter in a medium saucepan over medium heat. Add garlic to pan; cook 1 minute, stirring occasionally. Combine ½ cup milk and flour in a small bowl, stirring with a whisk. Add milk mixture to pan, stirring constantly with a whisk. Stir in pesto. Gradually add remaining 1 cup milk and half-and-half, stirring constantly with a whisk. Cook 8 minutes or

until sauce thickens, stirring frequently. Add ¼ cup reserved cooking liquid, remaining ¾ teaspoon salt, remaining ½ teaspoon pepper, and 1 cup cheese; stir until cheese melts.

5 Add chicken and sauce to pasta, tossing well to coat. Add tomatoes and basil; toss gently. Sprinkle with remaining 1 cup cheese. Serve immediately. Yield: 10 servings (serving size: 2 cups pasta and about 1½ tablespoons cheese).

CALORIES 508 (30% from fat); FAT 16.7g (sat 7.7g, mono 6.5g, poly 1.1g); PROTEIN 38.3g; CARB 50.7g; FIBER 2.9g; CHOL 81mg; IRON 3.5mg; SODIUM 781mg; CALC 397mg

---

Crowd Control

Keep it simple. Elaborate dishes are impressive, but they often require lots of prep time, particularly when you're cooking for 10 or more. Stick to recipes with relatively few components or streamlined preparations you can handle easily.

Opt for one-dish meals like casseroles, stews, or main-dish salads. Eliminating side dishes wherever possible reduces your workload.

Showcase a few high-quality ingredients. You don't need to spend lavishly or prepare fancy recipes to impress guests if your components are stellar. Buy fresh wild salmon for plank-grilled fillets, for instance, or ripe farmers' market produce for a simple mixed vegetable salad.

Work in advance, preparing a salad, dessert, or components of the main course. The goal is to minimize active cooking time after guests arrive. In colder months, offer braised dishes and slow-roasted meats, which you can put in the oven earlier in the day, then simply serve when ready.

Divvy up the duties. When some foods are grilled and others are cooked on the stovetop, a couple can share the cooking responsibilities (see Grilled Chicken and Pesto Farfalle on page 284). This way, food prep is faster and neither partner is overwhelmed.

Let guests help. Consider compose-it-yourself dishes like tostadas or chili with various toppings so guests serve themselves.

MAKE AHEAD
Caramel-Apple Cheesecake

This creamy cheesecake showcases fall flavors. Granny Smith apples lend a pleasant tartness, but you can substitute Rome, Braeburn, or your favorite apple variety. Make this cake the night before your gathering.

CRUST:
- 1 cup graham cracker crumbs (about 8 cookie sheets)
- 1 tablespoon egg white
- 1 tablespoon water
- Cooking spray

CHEESECAKE:
- 1¾ cups sugar
- ½ cup light sour cream
- 3 tablespoons all-purpose flour
- 1½ teaspoons vanilla extract
- ½ teaspoon ground cinnamon
- ¼ teaspoon ground nutmeg
- 2 (8-ounce) blocks ⅓-less-fat cream cheese, softened
- 1 (8-ounce) block fat-free cream cheese, softened
- 4 large eggs

TOPPING:
- ⅓ cup sugar
- 3 tablespoons water
- ½ teaspoon fresh lemon juice
- 1 tablespoon butter
- 2 tablespoons half-and-half
- 1¾ cups thinly sliced peeled Granny Smith apple (about 8 ounces)
- Dash of nutmeg

1 Preheat oven to 400°.

2 To prepare crust, combine first 3 ingredients in a bowl; toss with a fork until moist. Press mixture lightly into bottom of a 9-inch springform pan coated with cooking spray. Bake at 400° for 6 minutes. Remove from oven; cool on a wire rack. Wrap outside of pan with a double layer of foil. Reduce oven temperature to 325°.

3 To prepare cheesecake, place 1¾ cups sugar and next 7 ingredients in food processor; process until smooth. Add eggs, 1 at a time; process until blended. Pour cheese mixture into prepared pan. Place pan in a large roasting pan; add hot water to larger pan to a depth of 1 inch.

4 Bake at 325° for 1 hour or until cheesecake center barely moves when pan is touched. Remove from oven; let stand in water bath 10 minutes. Run a knife around outside edge of cheesecake. Remove pan from water bath; cool on a wire rack to room temperature. Cover and chill at least 8 hours.

5 To prepare topping, combine ⅓ cup sugar, 3 tablespoons water, and lemon juice in a small, heavy saucepan; cook over medium-high heat until sugar dissolves, stirring frequently. Cook 4 minutes or until golden (do not stir). Remove from heat. Add butter to pan; stir gently until butter melts. Stir in half-and-half. Cool slightly.

6 Heat a large nonstick skillet over medium-high heat. Coat pan with cooking spray. Add apple to pan; sauté 5 minutes or until lightly browned. Stir in sugar mixture and nutmeg. Serve topping with cheesecake. Yield: 16 servings (serving size: 1 cheesecake wedge and 1 tablespoon topping).

CALORIES 256 (33% from fat); FAT 9.5g (sat 5.6g, mono 2.7g, poly 0.7g); PROTEIN 7.6g; CARB 35.8g; FIBER 0.4g; CHOL 79mg; IRON 0.6mg; SODIUM 268mg; CALC 59mg

Hot Competition

At an annual Atlanta chili contest, competitors share their secrets for award-winning chili.

"I'M A PURIST," explains Jeanette Hall, a competitor at Atlanta's largest annual cook-off, a rollicking fall festival that draws more than 12,000 tasters to Stone Mountain Park, near the city.

Hall points to the beef bobbing in the russet-colored stew, and explains that she spent most of the previous night hand-cubing 40 pounds of lean eye of round. "It may have given me carpal tunnel syndrome," she says with a laugh, "but it was worth it."

By this point her husband, Peter, has ventured forth with his entry—a thin, ground-meat chili that pops with spice. "My mother's from India," he explains. "She taught me how to blend spices, so I use eight or nine different chiles."

Chili may be as common as any food in America, but it invariably reflects the personality of the cook. Always familiar, always different. That's why crowds—from the thousands milling about Stone Mountain Park to the dozens crammed in a family room for a kickoff party—love it.

MAKE AHEAD

Venison, Sausage, and Black Bean Chili

(pictured on page 259)

Use jalapeño-flavored or andouille chicken sausage to lend fire to the dish, or blunt the spice with mild goat cheese or sour cream.

- ¼ pound spicy chicken sausage
- Cooking spray
- 2 cups chopped onion (about 2 medium)
- 3 garlic cloves, minced
- 1 pound boneless venison loin, trimmed and cut into ½-inch pieces
- 2 tablespoons tomato paste
- 2 cups fat-free, less-sodium chicken broth
- 1 cup chopped plum tomato (about 2 medium)
- 1 cup water
- 2 tablespoons ancho chile powder
- ½ teaspoon kosher salt
- ½ teaspoon ground cumin
- 1 (15-ounce) can no-salt-added black beans, rinsed and drained
- ¼ cup (1 ounce) crumbled goat cheese
- Jalapeño pepper slices (optional)

➊ Remove casings from sausage. Heat a large Dutch oven over medium-high heat. Coat pan with cooking spray. Add sausage, onion, and garlic to pan; sauté 5 minutes or until onion is tender, stirring to crumble sausage. Add venison; cook 4 minutes or until venison is browned. Stir in tomato paste; cook 3 minutes, stirring occasionally. Add broth and next 5 ingredients, scraping pan to loosen browned bits; bring to a boil. Cover, reduce heat, and simmer 1 hour and 15 minutes or until venison is tender. Stir in beans; cook 10 minutes or until thoroughly heated. Top each serving with goat cheese. Serve with jalapeño slices, if desired. Yield: 4 servings (serving size: 1 cup chili and 1 tablespoon crumbled goat cheese).

CALORIES 291 (22% from fat); FAT 7.1g (sat 3.3g, mono 2.1g, poly 1g); PROTEIN 36.8g; CARB 20.7g; FIBER 5.5g; CHOL 132mg; IRON 5.9mg; SODIUM 928mg; CALC 105mg

MAKE AHEAD

White Chili

This dish uses hot pepper sauce made from jalapeños; it's milder than the red hot pepper varieties. Stirring frequently toward the end of cooking time prevents the bean-thickened broth from sticking to the bottom and scorching.

- 2 teaspoons canola oil
- 1½ cups chopped onion (about 1 large)
- 3 garlic cloves, minced
- 2 cups fat-free, less-sodium chicken broth
- 5 teaspoons green hot pepper sauce
- ½ teaspoon kosher salt
- 1¼ pounds skinless, boneless chicken breast halves
- 2 tablespoons stone-ground cornmeal
- 1 (19-ounce) can cannellini beans or other white beans, rinsed and drained
- ½ cup plain fat-free yogurt
- 2 tablespoons thinly sliced green onions (about 1)
- Lime wedges (optional)

➊ Heat oil in a Dutch oven over medium heat. Add chopped onion and garlic to pan; cook 5 minutes or until onion is tender, stirring occasionally. Add broth and next 3 ingredients to pan; bring to a boil. Cover, reduce heat to low, and simmer 15 minutes. Remove chicken from broth mixture; cool.

➋ Add cornmeal and beans to broth mixture, stirring with a whisk; simmer 15 minutes. Mash about ¼ cup beans against side of pan. Cut chicken into bite-sized pieces. Add chicken to pan; simmer 5 minutes or until mixture thickens, stirring frequently. Top each serving with yogurt; sprinkle with green onions. Serve with lime wedges, if desired. Yield: 6 servings (serving size: about ¾ cup chili, 4 teaspoons yogurt, and 1 teaspoon green onions).

CALORIES 198 (19% from fat); FAT 4.1g (sat 0.8g, mono 1.7g, poly 1.2g); PROTEIN 24.8g; CARB 14.3g; FIBER 3g; CHOL 56mg; IRON 1.6mg; SODIUM 456mg; CALC 63mg

STAFF FAVORITE • MAKE AHEAD
New Mexican Chile Verde

12   Anaheim chiles, halved and seeded
      (about 1½ pounds)
Cooking spray
2   cups chopped onion (about
      2 medium)
1¼   pounds boneless pork loin, cut into
      ¾-inch pieces
1   garlic clove, minced
2   cups fat-free, less-sodium chicken
      broth
1   teaspoon dried oregano
¾   teaspoon kosher salt
1   (15.5-ounce) can white hominy,
      drained

① Preheat broiler.
② Place chiles on a foil-lined baking sheet; broil 8 minutes or until blackened, turning after 4 minutes. Peel and chop.
③ Heat a large Dutch oven over medium-high heat. Coat pan with cooking spray. Add onion, pork, and garlic to pan; sauté 4 minutes or until pork is browned. Add chopped chiles, broth, oregano, and salt; bring to a boil. Cover, reduce heat, and simmer 1 hour or until pork is tender. Stir in hominy; cook 10 minutes or until thoroughly heated. Yield: 6 servings (serving size: about 1 cup).

CALORIES 243 (28% from fat); FAT 7.5g (sat 2.6g, mono 3.3g, poly 0.9g); PROTEIN 24.8g; CARB 20g; FIBER 3.3g; CHOL 56mg; IRON 2.4mg; SODIUM 389mg; CALC 51mg

MAKE AHEAD
Spicy Jalapeño Corn Bread

Corn bread is a classic side for chili. This dish provides ample servings; seal extra portions in plastic wrap, and store at room temperature for up to one day.

Cooking spray
1¼   cups stone-ground cornmeal
1   cup fresh corn kernels (about 2
     ears)
¾   teaspoon kosher salt
½   teaspoon baking soda
1   cup nonfat buttermilk
½   cup (2 ounces) shredded reduced-
     fat Cheddar cheese
2   tablespoons minced pickled
     jalapeño peppers
1½   tablespoons butter, melted
1½   tablespoons honey
1   tablespoon canola oil
2   large eggs, lightly beaten

① Preheat oven to 375°.
② Place a 9-inch cast-iron skillet coated with cooking spray in oven 5 minutes or until heated.
③ Combine cornmeal and next 3 ingredients in a large bowl, stirring with a whisk; make a well in center of mixture. Combine buttermilk and remaining ingredients in a small bowl; add to cornmeal mixture. Stir just until combined. Spoon mixture into preheated pan. Bake at 375° for 30 minutes or until a wooden pick inserted in center comes out clean. Cool in pan 10 minutes on a wire rack. Cut into 12 wedges. Yield: 12 servings (serving size: 1 wedge).

CALORIES 138 (33% from fat); FAT 5.1g (sat 1.9g, mono 1.4g, poly 0.6g); PROTEIN 4.7g; CARB 19.5g; FIBER 2.9g; CHOL 43mg; IRON 0.8mg; SODIUM 263mg; CALC 68mg

---

Popular Peppers

Chiles make the chili. Here are favored hot pepper varieties cited by contestants in the Great Miller Lite Chili Cook-Off. Scoville units measure each chile's heat level; the higher the number, the hotter the chile. For perspective, a bell pepper registers 0 Scoville units.

Pasilla: Most often dried, this pepper gives chili a deep reddish-black color and smoky flavor.
Scoville units: 4,000

New Mexican chiles: Many cultivars of this pod—often found dried— are used in chile verde.
Scoville units: 4,500–5,000

Jalapeño: The most widely used hot pepper adds a bright, forward heat. Pickled jalapeño rings can show up among chili toppings.
Scoville units: 5,500

Chile de arbol: This hot, slender, bright red pepper is related to cayenne. In powdered form, it can crank up the fire in a chili powder mix.
Scoville units: 23,000

Serrano: This small, hot chile is prized for its "back heat" that registers at the back of the throat.
Scoville units: 25,000

Habanero: Some chili cooks cautiously add habanero—the hottest chile around—or a habanero hot sauce to their recipes. This pepper has distinct sweetness but intensely hot spice. Tip: Orange habaneros are hotter than red ones.
Scoville units: 150,000–210,000+

Springfield Chilli

The Illinois version of chili is typically spelled with an extra "l" and features coarse-grind beef, which we augment here with ground turkey breast. Regular ground meat will work just fine.

- 1 bacon slice, finely chopped
- 2¼ cups finely chopped onion, divided (about 2 medium)
- 2 garlic cloves, minced
- 1 pound coarsely ground turkey breast
- ½ pound coarsely ground sirloin
- 1 (12-ounce) can beer (such as Budweiser)
- 3 tablespoons chili powder
- 1 teaspoon Worcestershire sauce
- ½ teaspoon kosher salt
- ¼ teaspoon ground cumin
- 1 (14½-ounce) can diced tomatoes, undrained
- 1 (8-ounce) can no-salt-added tomato sauce
- 1 (15-ounce) can pinto beans, rinsed and drained
- ½ cup (2 ounces) reduced-fat shredded Cheddar cheese

1 Cook bacon in a large Dutch oven over medium heat 5 minutes or until browned. Stir in 2 cups onion; cover and cook until onion is tender (about 5 minutes). Uncover and stir in garlic; cook 1 minute. **2** Increase heat to medium-high; add turkey and sirloin to pan. Cook 5 minutes or until browned, stirring to crumble. Add beer; cook until liquid is reduced to ⅓ cup (about 7 minutes). Stir in chili powder and next 5 ingredients. Cover, reduce heat, and simmer 30 minutes or until mixture thickens. Stir in beans; cook 10 minutes or until thoroughly heated. Ladle 1 cup chili into each of 6 bowls. Top each with 4 teaspoons cheese and 2 teaspoons remaining onion. Yield: 6 servings.

CALORIES 278 (25% from fat); FAT 7.7g (sat 3.4g, mono 2.2g, poly 0.6g); PROTEIN 33.1g; CARB 20.3g; FIBER 4.5g; CHOL 52mg; IRON 3.2mg; SODIUM 623mg; CALC 123mg

Cincinnati Five-Way Chili

The phrase "five-way" refers to the number of accompaniments Queen City natives serve with their uniquely spiced chili.

- Cooking spray
- 1 pound ground turkey
- ½ pound ground sirloin
- 2½ cups chopped onion (about 2 medium), divided
- 2 garlic cloves, minced
- 1 cup water
- 3 tablespoons spicy barbecue sauce
- 2 tablespoons brown sugar
- 2 tablespoons chili powder
- 4 teaspoons white vinegar
- ¾ teaspoon ground cumin
- ¾ teaspoon ground cinnamon
- ½ teaspoon kosher salt
- ½ teaspoon ground allspice
- ½ teaspoon freshly ground black pepper
- ¼ teaspoon ground coriander
- ½ ounce unsweetened chocolate, chopped
- 1 (10¾-ounce) can tomato puree
- 3½ cups hot cooked spaghetti (about 8 ounces uncooked pasta)
- ¾ cup (3 ounces) reduced-fat shredded Cheddar cheese
- 1 (15-ounce) can kidney beans, rinsed, drained, and warmed (about 1½ cups)
- Oyster crackers (optional)

1 Heat a large Dutch oven over medium-high heat. Coat pan with cooking spray. Add turkey and sirloin to pan; cook 5 minutes or until browned, stirring to crumble. Add 2 cups onion and garlic; cook 5 minutes or until onion is tender, stirring occasionally. Stir in 1 cup water and next 12 ingredients; bring to a boil. Cover, reduce heat, and simmer 45 minutes. Place about ½ cup spaghetti into each of 6 bowls. Ladle 1 cup chili into each bowl. Top each serving with 4 teaspoons remaining onion, 2 tablespoons cheese, and 2½ tablespoons beans. Serve with crackers, if desired. Yield: 6 servings.

CALORIES 464 (29% from fat); FAT 14.9g (sat 6g, mono 5.1g, poly 2.1g); PROTEIN 34.5g; CARB 48.8g; FIBER 7.2g; CHOL 88mg; IRON 5.4mg; SODIUM 870mg; CALC 189mg

High Plains Buffalo Chili

Similar in flavor to beef and with less saturated fat, buffalo makes an excellent choice for chili. Stirring in the cornmeal at the end yields a distinct taste and texture.

- 1 teaspoon canola oil
- 1½ cups chopped onion (about 1 large)
- 2 garlic cloves, minced
- 1½ pounds lean ground buffalo
- 2 tablespoons New Mexican chile powder
- ½ teaspoon ground red pepper
- 3½ cups water
- 2 cups diced peeled baking potato (about 8 ounces)
- 2 tablespoons tomato paste
- 1½ teaspoons kosher salt
- 1 teaspoon dried oregano
- 1 teaspoon Worcestershire sauce
- ½ teaspoon dried rubbed sage
- 1 tablespoon stone-ground cornmeal

1 Heat oil in a Dutch oven over medium-high heat. Add onion and garlic to pan; sauté 5 minutes or until tender. Add buffalo; cook 5 minutes or until browned, stirring to crumble. Stir in chile powder and pepper. **2** Add 3½ cups water and next 6 ingredients to pan; bring to a boil. Reduce heat, and simmer 50 minutes or until potato is very tender. Stir in cornmeal; cook 5 minutes, stirring occasionally. Yield: 6 servings (serving size: 1 cup).

CALORIES 216 (23% from fat); FAT 5.4g (sat 1.7g, mono 2g, poly 0.7g); PROTEIN 25.9g; CARB 15.6g; FIBER 2.9g; CHOL 55mg; IRON 3.7mg; SODIUM 603mg; CALC 31mg

Vegetarian Chili

Chipotle lends subtle yet deep smoky spice to this substantial meat-free dish. We use a light-bodied lager beer along with vegetable broth to deglaze the pan. Serve with baked tortilla chips.

- 2 teaspoons canola oil
- 2 cups chopped onion (about 1)
- 1½ cups chopped green bell pepper (about 1)
- 1½ cups chopped red bell pepper (about 1)
- 1 tablespoon chili powder
- 2 garlic cloves, minced
- 2 cups organic vegetable broth (such as Emeril's)
- 1 cup beer
- 1 tablespoon chopped chipotle chile, canned in adobo sauce
- 1 (15½-ounce) can small red beans, rinsed and drained
- 1 (15½-ounce) can chickpeas (garbanzo beans), rinsed and drained
- 1 (15-ounce) can cannellini beans, rinsed and drained
- 1 (14½-ounce) can fire-roasted diced tomatoes, undrained
- ½ teaspoon kosher salt
- ½ cup preshredded reduced-fat Mexican blend cheese

① Heat oil in a large Dutch oven over medium-high heat. Add onion and bell peppers to pan; sauté 10 minutes or until vegetables are tender. Add chili powder and garlic to pan; cook 1 minute, stirring constantly. Add broth and beer, scraping pan to loosen browned bits. Add chipotle and next 4 ingredients to pan; simmer 40 minutes or until thick. Stir in salt. Sprinkle each serving with cheese. Yield: 6 servings (serving size: about 1½ cups chili and 4 teaspoons cheese).

CALORIES 216 (19% from fat); FAT 4.5g (sat 1.4g, mono 1.1g, poly 1g); PROTEIN 10.1g; CARB 35.1g; FIBER 8.8g; CHOL 5mg; IRON 2.4mg; SODIUM 711mg; CALC 193mg

Stir-frying

Turn up the heat for this sizzling method.

STIR-FRYING IS a fast and fresh way to cook. Simply toss and turn bite-sized pieces of food in a little hot oil in a wok over high heat, and in five minutes or less, the work is done. Vegetables emerge crisp and bright. Meats are flavorful, tender, and well seared.

Stir-frying fits hectic lifestyles and health-conscious tastes. It works wonders with fresh ingredients like bell peppers, zucchini, and corn, and because foods cook in a flash, vegetables retain their color and texture. It's a versatile technique you can use every day.

Pepper Beef

This quick entrée is equally tasty with just one type of bell pepper.

- ¾ pound flank steak, trimmed
- 2 tablespoons low-sodium soy sauce
- 1 tablespoon Shaoxing (Chinese rice wine), dry sherry, or sake
- 1 teaspoon sugar
- ½ teaspoon freshly ground black pepper
- 2 tablespoons canola oil, divided
- 1 cup vertically sliced yellow onion
- 1½ tablespoons minced garlic
- 1 cup thinly sliced red bell pepper strips (about 1 medium)
- 1 cup thinly sliced green bell pepper strips (about 1 medium)
- ½ teaspoon salt
- 3 cups hot cooked short-grain rice

① Cut steak across grain into ¼-inch slices; cut slices into ½-inch-wide strips. Cut strips into 3-inch-long pieces. Combine steak pieces, soy sauce, and next 3 ingredients.
② Heat a 14-inch wok over high heat. Add 1 tablespoon oil to wok, swirling to coat. Add onion and garlic; stir-fry 30 seconds or until onion begins to brown. Add bell peppers; stir-fry 2 minutes or until crisp-tender. Spoon bell pepper mixture into a large bowl.

③ Add 1½ teaspoons oil to wok, swirling to coat. Add half of steak mixture; stir-fry 1 minute or until browned. Add cooked steak mixture to bell pepper mixture. Repeat procedure with remaining 1½ teaspoons oil and remaining steak mixture. Return steak mixture to wok; sprinkle with salt. Stir-fry 1 minute or just until heated. Serve over rice. Yield: 4 servings (serving size: 1 cup beef mixture and ¾ cup rice).

CALORIES 422 (27% from fat); FAT 12.5g (sat 2.4g, mono 5.9g, poly 2.4g); PROTEIN 23.2g; CARB 50.6g; FIBER 3.6g; CHOL 28mg; IRON 3.9mg; SODIUM 613mg; CALC 40mg

WINE NOTE: When it comes to wine, this simple beef recipe needs care because green bell peppers can make many red wines taste green and weedy, while soy sauce can make reds taste hollow. So choose a wine with a lot of fruitiness and berry flavors. A great choice is traditional Beaujolais—especially one of the cru Beaujolais such as Moulin-à-Vent. The Georges duBoeuf Beaujolais Moulin-à-Vent (Flower Label) 2006 from Burgundy, France, is $14.

Ham and Egg Fried Rice

Fried rice has the best texture when prepared with cold cooked rice, making it an ideal use for leftovers. Tiny rounds of thinly sliced green beans add flecks of color and crunch.

- 4 cups cold cooked long-grain rice
- 1½ tablespoons canola oil
- 1½ cups chopped onion
- 1 tablespoon minced garlic
- 1 cup thinly horizontally sliced green beans
- ¾ cup diced ham (about 4 ounces)
- ¼ cup low-sodium soy sauce
- 2½ teaspoons dark sesame oil
- ¼ teaspoon freshly ground black pepper
- 2 large eggs, lightly beaten
- ¼ cup (1-inch) slices green onions

1 Break up rice with hands to remove large clumps, if necessary.

2 Heat a 14-inch wok over high heat. Add canola oil to wok, swirling to coat. Add chopped onion and garlic; stir-fry 1 minute or until onion begins to brown. Add beans and ham; stir-fry 2 minutes or until ham begins to brown.

3 Reduce heat to medium-high. Add cold rice to wok; stir-fry 2 minutes. Stir in soy sauce, sesame oil, and pepper. Push rice mixture up sides of wok. Pour eggs in open space in center of wok; cook 30 seconds or until set, stirring to scramble. Gently stir scrambled eggs into rice mixture. Sprinkle with green onions. Yield: 4 servings (serving size: about 1¼ cups).

CALORIES 397 (29% from fat); FAT 12.8g (sat 2.3g, mono 5.4g, poly 3.2g); PROTEIN 14.5g; CARB 54.5g; FIBER 2.8g; CHOL 121mg; IRON 3.3mg; SODIUM 868mg; CALC 57mg

Black Bean Pork and Zucchini

Many Chinese recipes rely on a robust sauce of crushed fermented black beans and garlic to add a deep, savory flavor to meat, vegetable, and seafood dishes. Look for the sauce in jars on the Asian foods aisle of your supermarket.

PORK:
- ¾ pound pork tenderloin, trimmed
- 1 tablespoon Shaoxing (Chinese rice wine), dry sherry, or sake
- 1 tablespoon low-sodium soy sauce
- 1 teaspoon cornstarch

SAUCE:
- ½ cup water
- 2 tablespoons Shaoxing (Chinese rice wine), dry sherry, or sake
- 1 tablespoon black bean and garlic sauce (such as Lee Kum Kee)
- 2 teaspoons cornstarch
- ¼ teaspoon salt

REMAINING INGREDIENTS:
- 1 pound zucchini
- 2 tablespoons canola oil, divided
- 1 tablespoon minced peeled fresh ginger
- ¼ cup thinly sliced green onions
- 3 cups hot cooked short-grain rice

1 To prepare pork, cut pork crosswise into 3-inch pieces. Cut each piece lengthwise into ¼-inch slices; cut slices into ½-inch-wide strips. Combine pork and next 3 ingredients; cover and refrigerate 20 minutes.

2 To prepare sauce, combine ½ cup water and next 4 ingredients; set aside.

3 Cut zucchini crosswise into 2-inch pieces. Cut each piece lengthwise into ¼-inch slices; cut slices into ½-inch-wide strips.

4 Heat a 14-inch wok over high heat. Add 2 teaspoons oil to wok, swirling to coat. Add zucchini and ginger to wok; stir-fry 1 minute or just until crisp-tender. Spoon into a bowl.

5 Add 2 teaspoons oil to wok, swirling to coat. Add half of pork mixture to wok; stir-fry 2 minutes or until browned. Add cooked pork mixture to zucchini mixture. Repeat procedure with remaining 2 teaspoons oil and remaining pork mixture. Return zucchini mixture to wok. Stir sauce; add sauce to wok. Stir-fry 1 minute or until thickened. Spoon into a serving dish. Sprinkle with onions. Serve over rice. Yield: 4 servings (serving size: about ¾ cup pork mixture and ¾ cup rice).

CALORIES 398 (24% from fat); FAT 10.6g (sat 1.7g, mono 5.6g, poly 2.7g); PROTEIN 23.1g; CARB 48.1g; FIBER 3.1g; CHOL 55mg; IRON 4.1mg; SODIUM 654mg; CALC 29mg

QUICK & EASY
Sizzling Shrimp with Corn Relish

Serve over rice for a hearty dinner or over a bed of baby spinach for a lighter meal.

- 1½ tablespoons fresh lime juice
- 1 tablespoon fish sauce
- ½ teaspoon sugar
- 2 tablespoons canola oil
- ½ cup chopped shallots
- 1 tablespoon minced garlic
- 1 tablespoon minced jalapeño pepper (about 1 small)
- 1½ pounds peeled and deveined medium shrimp
- 1½ cups fresh corn kernels (about 3 ears)
- ⅓ cup chopped fresh cilantro

1 Combine first 3 ingredients; set aside.

2 Heat a 14-inch wok over high heat. Add oil to wok, swirling to coat. Add shallots, garlic, and jalapeño to wok; stir-fry 30 seconds or just until shallots begin to brown. Add shrimp; stir-fry 3 minutes or until shrimp are done. Add corn; stir-fry 1 minute or just until corn is heated. Stir in juice mixture; sprinkle with cilantro. Yield: 4 servings (serving size: 1 cup).

CALORIES 332 (30% from fat); FAT 11.2g (sat 1.2g, mono 4.8g, poly 3.6g); PROTEIN 37.6g; CARB 19.9g; FIBER 2.1g; CHOL 259mg; IRON 4.8mg; SODIUM 612mg; CALC 101mg

All About Stir-Frying

Origins

Stir-frying was first developed in China as a cooking method that worked efficiently on simple brick stoves. The typical stovetop had a hole over the fire chamber. A round-bottomed wok fit over the lipped hole, capturing the heat efficiently. All it took was a small, hot fire to make the wok very hot. Oil and chopped food were stirred and tossed in the pan, cooking in minutes and making efficient use of precious fuel.

What Stir-frying Does

The high temperature required for stir-frying sears food quickly and preserves the natural juices. It takes only minutes (two to five, usually), so vegetables stay bright and crisp, meat browned and succulent. When the heat is high and the cooking quick, the Cantonese describe the result as *wok hay*—loosely translated "the breath of a wok." It's a difficult quality to define, but you can experience it in the first few moments after food is removed from the wok. The food tastes vibrant and fresh, characterized by concentrated, harmonious flavors with a hint of smokiness. To appreciate wok hay, serve food immediately.

Best Bets for Stir-frying

Most vegetables cut into thin, bite-sized pieces are ideal, especially those with high moisture content, such as summer squash and bell peppers. Denser vegetables like broccoli work well, too, but may need to either be blanched first or allowed to steam briefly with a little liquid after the initial stir-frying to become tender. Leafy greens such as spinach cook in seconds once they hit the hot oil.

Tender cuts of meat—such as chicken breasts, flank steak, or pork tenderloin—stir-fry beautifully when cut into thin, bite-sized strips. Avoid large or tough chunks of meat from items such as pork shoulder or beef stew meat, which require long, slow cooking to become tender. Shrimp, scallops, and firm-fleshed fish such as halibut work well, but delicate, flaky fish such as flounder or tilapia may fall apart.

Equipment

All you need for stir-frying are a wok and a broad, curved spatula. A wok, which is shaped like a big, wide bowl with high sloping sides, is designed for stir-frying. The curve of the pan makes it easy for a spatula to scrape down the sides and toss the food without accidentally turning it out of the pan.

The best choice for the typical home cooktop is a rolled carbon steel or enamel-clad cast-iron wok, 14 inches across, with a flat bottom. Carbon steel woks often cost less than $20 at retail stores or online sources, while enamel-clad cast-iron woks are pricier at about $160 or more. (Round-bottom woks may work on gas burners but will not sit steadily on electric ranges.) Over time and with frequent use, carbon steel and cast-iron woks darken and develop a patina that creates a natural nonstick finish. Avoid pans that come with a nonstick finish, as they can't be used over high heat and the finish deters browning.

In place of a wok, a 12-inch stainless-steel sauté pan with sloped sides can be used. Choose one that conducts heat well. Since these pans don't develop a nonstick patina, they often require more oil for cooking, and food may stick more readily. With the flatter shape and shallow sides of the pan, it's also a bit harder to move the food.

You'll also need a wide spatula. Wok spatulas, shaped like wide shovels, are slightly curved so they can easily slide down the sides of the pan. A lid is helpful for dense vegetables that may need to be briefly steamed at the end of cooking.

Size Wise

When stir-frying, foods must be cut into thin, bite-sized pieces so they'll cook quickly. Generally, they should be of similar shape and size. If the sizes vary widely, foods will cook unevenly.

Mise en Place

Stir-frying proceeds at a fast pace and takes attention. The total cooking time may only be five or so minutes, which doesn't allow time to prepare ingredients midstream. Read the recipe through, then cut, measure, and mix ingredients, and set them near the wok. Get out the serving dish. Then turn on the heat.

Make Room

Stir-fry thinly sliced meat in small batches of six ounces or less, so the pan is not overcrowded—otherwise, you risk a soggy result. With less juicy foods, cornstarch-coated pieces, or thicker pieces such as shrimp, you can sometimes cook up to one pound at a time.

Limit vegetables to about four to six cups at a time (or eight to 10 cups for leafy greens). If you use more than one vegetable, add the thickest, densest pieces first, followed by smaller, thinner pieces so everything is done at the same time.

Keep Moving

Once the food is in the pan, it needs to be constantly flipped to prevent burning. Use your spatula to efficiently scoop the food.

The Bottom Line

The three most important elements to remember about stir-frying:

1 Ready the wok over high heat at least a couple of minutes before adding oil.

2 Load the wok with a workable amount of food.

3 Keep moving the food with a wide wok spatula once it's in the pan.

Korean Sesame Beef with Lettuce Wraps

Based on the classic Korean barbecue dish *bulgogi*, this recipe offers savory-sweet-garlicky beef wrapped in lettuce leaves with rice and kimchi. Kimchi is a traditional Korean condiment of fiery fermented cabbage. Look for it at Asian markets or in the supermarket's produce section.

- ¾ pound flank steak, trimmed
- ⅓ cup thinly sliced green onions, divided
- 2 tablespoons low-sodium soy sauce
- 1 tablespoon sugar
- 1 tablespoon minced garlic
- 1 teaspoon dark sesame oil
- 2 tablespoons canola oil, divided
- 1 tablespoon toasted sesame seeds
- 4 cups hot cooked short-grain rice
- 1 cup kimchi
- 16 red leaf lettuce leaves

❶ Cut steak across grain into ¼-inch slices; cut slices into ½-inch-wide strips. Cut strips into 3-inch-long pieces. Combine steak pieces, ¼ cup onions, and next 4 ingredients.

❷ Heat a 14-inch wok over high heat. Add 1 tablespoon canola oil to wok, swirling to coat. Add half of steak mixture to wok; stir-fry 2 minutes or until lightly browned. Spoon cooked steak mixture into a bowl. Repeat procedure with remaining 1 tablespoon canola oil and remaining steak mixture. Sprinkle with remaining onions and sesame seeds. Spoon ¼ cup rice, about 2 tablespoons steak mixture, and 1 tablespoon kimchi onto each lettuce leaf; roll up. Serve immediately. Yield: 4 servings (serving size: 4 filled lettuce leaves).

CALORIES 498 (27% from fat); FAT 14.8g (sat 2.7g, mono 6.8g, poly 3.3g); PROTEIN 25.2g; CARB 62.2g; FIBER 3.2g; CHOL 28mg; IRON 8.7mg; SODIUM 581mg; CALC 88mg

Speedy Stir-fry Menu
serves 4

Kung Pao Shrimp

Bok choy with five-spice sauce

Combine 1 cup fat-free, less-sodium chicken broth and ¼ teaspoon five-spice powder in a large skillet; bring to a boil. Place 4 halved baby bok choy in a single layer in pan. Cover and cook 3 minutes or until crisp-tender. Remove bok choy. Stir in 1 tablespoon low-sodium soy sauce, 2 teaspoons rice vinegar, and ¼ teaspoon crushed red pepper; cook until reduced to ¼ cup. Serve with bok choy.

Fortune cookies and orange wedges

Kung Pao Shrimp

For a spicier kick to the pungent glaze, leave the seeds in the chiles.

SHRIMP:
- 1 tablespoon Shaoxing (Chinese rice wine), dry sherry, or sake
- 1 teaspoon cornstarch
- ½ teaspoon salt
- 1 pound peeled and deveined medium shrimp

SAUCE:
- 2 tablespoons water
- 1 tablespoon Chinese black vinegar or balsamic vinegar
- 1 tablespoon low-sodium soy sauce
- 1 tablespoon sugar
- ¾ teaspoon cornstarch
- ½ teaspoon dark sesame oil

REMAINING INGREDIENTS:
- 2 tablespoons canola oil
- 1⅓ cups thinly sliced green bell pepper strips (about 1 large)
- 1 tablespoon minced garlic
- 1 tablespoon minced peeled fresh ginger
- 3 to 4 small dried hot red chiles, broken in half and seeded
- ¼ cup chopped unsalted, dry-roasted peanuts
- 3 cups hot cooked short-grain rice

❶ To prepare shrimp, combine first 4 ingredients; cover and chill 10 minutes.

❷ To prepare sauce, combine 2 tablespoons water and next 5 ingredients.

❸ Heat a 14-inch wok over high heat. Add canola oil to wok, swirling to coat. Add bell pepper and next 3 ingredients; stir-fry 1 minute or just until chiles begin to lightly brown (do not burn). Add shrimp mixture to wok; stir-fry 2 minutes or until shrimp are done. Stir sauce; add sauce to wok. Stir-fry 30 seconds or until sauce thickens. Sprinkle with peanuts. Serve over rice. Yield: 4 servings (serving size: ¾ cup shrimp mixture and ¾ cup rice).

CALORIES 485 (28% from fat); FAT 15g (sat 1.7g, mono 7g, poly 4.7g); PROTEIN 29.9g; CARB 54.8g; FIBER 3.4g; CHOL 172mg; IRON 5.7mg; SODIUM 603mg; CALC 77mg

Sichuan Green Beans

In restaurants, these green beans are typically deep-fried in oil. This simplified home version stir-fries the beans until browned and blistered, then combines them with lively seasonings for a robust side dish.

- 1 pound green beans, trimmed and cut into 2-inch pieces
- 1 tablespoon canola oil, divided
- ¼ cup chopped shallots
- 1½ tablespoons minced garlic
- 1 tablespoon minced peeled fresh ginger
- ½ teaspoon crushed red pepper
- 1 tablespoon Chinese black vinegar or balsamic vinegar
- 1 tablespoon low-sodium soy sauce
- ½ teaspoon salt

❶ Cook beans in boiling water 2 minutes or until crisp-tender. Drain and rinse with cold running water; drain. Pat beans completely dry with paper towels.

❷ Heat a 14-inch wok over high heat. Add 1½ teaspoons oil to wok, swirling to coat. Add beans; stir-fry 3 minutes or until browned. Spoon beans into a bowl.

❸ Add remaining 1½ teaspoons oil to wok, swirling to coat. Add shallots and next 3 ingredients; stir-fry 15 seconds or just until garlic begins to brown. Return beans to wok. Add vinegar, soy sauce, and salt to wok; toss to combine. Yield: 6 servings (serving size: about ½ cup).

CALORIES 60 (42% from fat); FAT 2.8g (sat 0.2g, mono 1.4g, poly 0.7g); PROTEIN 1.3g; CARB 7.4g; FIBER 2.9g; CHOL 0mg; IRON 0.5mg; SODIUM 287mg; CALC 40mg

Curried Chicken and Cashews

Madras curry powder delivers more intensity than regular curry powder. For less heat, leave the chiles whole.

SAUCE:

⅓ cup fat-free, less-sodium chicken broth
3 tablespoons water
1½ tablespoons fish sauce
1 teaspoon sugar
1 teaspoon rice vinegar

REMAINING INGREDIENTS:

¾ pound skinless, boneless chicken breast halves
2 tablespoons canola oil, divided
1½ cups vertically sliced onion
1 tablespoon minced peeled fresh ginger
1 tablespoon minced garlic
1 teaspoon Madras curry powder
3 small dried hot red chiles, broken in half
⅓ cup chopped fresh cilantro
¼ cup dry-roasted salted cashews, chopped
3 cups hot cooked short-grain rice

❶ To prepare sauce, combine first 5 ingredients; set aside.
❷ Cut chicken across grain into ¼-inch slices; cut slices into ½-inch-wide strips. Cut strips into 3-inch-long pieces.
❸ Heat a 14-inch wok over high heat. Add 1 tablespoon oil to wok, swirling to coat. Add half of chicken to wok; stir-fry 2 minutes. Spoon cooked chicken into a

bowl. Repeat procedure with 2 teaspoons oil and remaining chicken.
❹ Add remaining 1 teaspoon oil to wok, swirling to coat. Add onion, ginger, and garlic to wok; stir-fry 1 minute or until lightly browned. Add curry powder and chiles; stir-fry 30 seconds. Add sauce and chicken to wok; stir-fry 1 minute. Spoon into a serving dish. Sprinkle with cilantro and cashews. Serve over rice. Yield: 4 servings (serving size: 1 cup chicken mixture and ¾ cup rice).

CALORIES 439 (27% from fat); FAT 13g (sat 1.7g, mono 6.9g, poly 3.2g); PROTEIN 26g; CARB 52.6g; FIBER 3.2g; CHOL 49mg; IRON 3.9mg; SODIUM 669mg; CALC 37mg`

ONE MORE TASTE
Baja-Style Grilled Rock Lobster Tails

Rock lobster, also called spiny lobster, lacks the large front claws of the American or Maine variety, but it is prized by lobster lovers for its most important attribute: a meaty tail, which is utterly delectable. The warm-water crustacean is often enjoyed at shore dives along the coast in Mexico and Southern California, seasoned with citrus juice and hot sauce and served taco-style. Use fresh tails, if you can find them; on the West Coast, rock lobster season opens in the fall. Otherwise, frozen will work just fine. Sweet, tangy, spicy, and succulent, this dish proves that rock lobster rocks.

Baja-Style Grilled Rock Lobster Tails

Use kitchen shears or a cleaver to cut the tails in half. Lightly char green onions alongside the tails on the grill. We like dousing the tails in Mexican hot sauce, such as Cholula, for authentic flavor. Serve with ice-cold Mexican beer.

LOBSTER:

6 (8-ounce) rock or spiny lobster tails
12 green onions
Cooking spray

SAUCE:

1 tablespoon grated orange rind
2 tablespoons fresh orange juice
1 tablespoon fresh lime juice
1 tablespoon olive oil
½ teaspoon dried oregano
¼ teaspoon salt
Dash of hot sauce
1 garlic clove, minced
2 tablespoons butter, melted

REMAINING INGREDIENTS:

6 (6-inch) flour tortillas
Lime wedges (optional)

❶ Preheat grill.
❷ To prepare lobster, cut each lobster tail in half lengthwise. Coat lobster tails and onions with cooking spray. Place lobster tails, cut sides down, on grill rack coated with cooking spray; grill 3 minutes. Turn lobster; grill 5 minutes. Place onions on grill rack; grill 3 minutes or until tender.
❸ To prepare sauce, combine rind and next 7 ingredients in a medium bowl, stirring well with a whisk. Gradually add butter, stirring constantly with a whisk. Drizzle sauce over cut sides of lobster tails.
❹ Warm tortillas according to package directions. Serve with lobster and lime wedges, if desired. Yield: 6 servings (serving size: 1 lobster tail, 2 green onions, and 1 tortilla).

CALORIES 358 (28% from fat); FAT 11.2g (sat 3.7g, mono 4.4g, poly 1.9g); PROTEIN 38.4g; CARB 24g; FIBER 2g; CHOL 129mg; IRON 3.7mg; SODIUM 616mg; CALC 152mg

Dinner in the Grove

The annual walnut harvest is cause for celebration for this California family.

MATTHIEU KOHLMEYER APPEARS to have a charmed life, especially as he relaxes with friends and family in early fall in a walnut orchard in Woodland, California, where a bounty of ripe nuts hangs heavy on the trees. As the founder of La Tourangelle, which produces artisanal nut oils, Kohlmeyer celebrates the start of another harvest with a menu spotlighting the ingredient in dishes redolent with crisp, toasty flavor. It is Kohlmeyer's sixth harvest in California since arriving from France to produce the first French-style walnut oil in the States.

His family owns Les Huileries de la Croix Verte et la Tourangelle, a 150-year-old mill near Saumur in the Loire Valley of France where they make toasted nut oils using time-honored methods. When they decided to expand to the United States, instead of exporting the French oil, they exported Matthieu, then 24 and fresh out of business school. It's a strategy similar to the one French Champagne producers employed when they set up shop in Northern California (Moet and Chandon opened Domain Chandon; Louis Roederer and Tattinger followed suit). French production methods were combined with an American crop to produce products that were equal or superior to other domestic offerings.

WALNUT HARVEST MENU

(Serves 6)

Savory Walnut Wafers

Mushroom Walnut Turnovers

Roast Chicken with Pears, Shallots, and Walnuts
or
Fruit and Walnut–Stuffed Pork Loin

Classic Walnut Boule

Walnut Rice

Haricots verts

Beet and Walnut Salad

Walnut Cake with Praline Frosting

MAKE AHEAD
Savory Walnut Wafers

These savory wafers are a tasty make-ahead prelude to any fall meal. They make a wonderful addition to a fresh fruit and cheese plate for dessert, as well.

- ½ cup all-purpose flour (about 2.25 ounces)
- 2 tablespoons chopped walnuts, toasted
- 1 tablespoon cornstarch
- 1 teaspoon brown sugar
- ¼ teaspoon chopped fresh rosemary
- ¼ teaspoon salt
- 4 teaspoons chilled butter, cut into small pieces
- 2 tablespoons ice water
- Cooking spray

❶ Lightly spoon flour into a dry measuring cup; level with a knife. Combine flour and next 5 ingredients in a food processor; pulse until walnuts are finely ground. Add butter; pulse just until mixture resembles coarse meal. Add 2 tablespoons ice water; pulse until dough is moist. Scrape mixture onto a work surface; knead briefly, just until dough comes together (mixture will seem crumbly). Press dough into a 12-inch log on a sheet of plastic wrap. Cover and place in freezer 1 hour or until firm.

❷ Preheat oven to 350°.

❸ Cut dough crosswise into 16 equal portions; roll each portion into a ball. Place 1 ball on a baking sheet coated with cooking spray (cover remaining balls to prevent drying). Using bottom of a glass, flatten ball to form a 2-inch round. Repeat procedure with remaining balls, leaving approximately 1 inch between flattened rounds on baking sheet. Bake at 350° for 10 minutes or until lightly browned. Cool on a wire rack. Yield: 16 servings (serving size: 1 wafer).

CALORIES 32 (45% from fat); FAT 1.6g (sat 0.7g, mono 0.3g, poly 0.5g); PROTEIN 0.6g; CARB 3.9g; FIBER 0.2g; CHOL 3mg; IRON 0.2mg; SODIUM 44mg; CALC 2mg

---

Mushroom Walnut Turnovers

With a mushroom filling encased in walnut pastry, these turnovers taste like fall.

FILLING:
- Cooking spray
- 2 tablespoons finely chopped shallots
- 8 ounces mixed wild mushrooms, chopped
- ⅓ cup dry white wine
- 1 tablespoon fat-free cream cheese
- 2 teaspoons chopped fresh thyme
- ½ teaspoon salt

PASTRY:
- 3 tablespoons chopped walnuts, toasted
- 1¼ cups all-purpose flour (about 5.25 ounces)
- ½ teaspoon salt
- 1½ tablespoons chilled butter, cut into small pieces
- ¼ cup ice water
- 2 large egg whites, lightly beaten and divided
- 1 tablespoon fat-free milk

1 To prepare filling, heat a skillet over medium-high heat. Coat pan with cooking spray. Add shallots and mushrooms to pan; sauté 6 minutes, stirring frequently. Add wine to pan; cook 5 minutes or until liquid almost evaporates. Remove from heat. Stir in cheese, thyme, and ¹⁄₂ teaspoon salt. Cool to room temperature.

2 Preheat oven to 350°.

3 To prepare pastry, place walnuts in food processor; process until smooth, scraping sides of bowl. Lightly spoon flour into dry measuring cups; level with a knife. Add flour, ¹⁄₂ teaspoon salt, and butter to food processor; pulse to combine. Place flour mixture in a medium bowl. Add ice water and 1 egg white to bowl; stir until moist. Turn dough out onto a lightly floured surface. Divide dough into 18 equal portions; roll each portion into a ball. Roll 1 ball into a 3-inch circle (cover remaining dough to prevent drying). Spoon about 2 teaspoons mushroom mixture in center of circle. Fold dough over filling; crimp edges with a fork to seal. Place on a baking sheet lined with parchment paper. Repeat procedure with remaining dough balls and filling, placing turnovers about 1 inch apart on baking sheet. Combine remaining egg white and milk in a bowl. Lightly brush turnovers with milk mixture.

4 Bake at 350° for 16 minutes. Cool on a wire rack. Yield: 9 servings (serving size: 2 turnovers).

CALORIES 110 (31% from fat); FAT 3.8g (sat 1.4g, mono 0.7g, poly 1.3g); PROTEIN 4.1g; CARB 15.2g; FIBER 0.9g; CHOL 5mg; IRON 1.1mg; SODIUM 300mg; CALC 14mg

Fall Classics Menu
serves 6

Seasonal flavors are incorporated into this simple roast chicken, so a slightly peppery salad dressed with oil and vinegar makes a choice companion.

Roast Chicken with Pears, Shallots, and Walnuts

Arugula and spinach salad

Combine 6 cups arugula and 2 cups fresh baby spinach in a large bowl. Combine 3 tablespoons extravirgin olive oil and 1¹⁄₂ tablespoons Champagne vinegar, stirring well. Drizzle oil mixture over salad; sprinkle with ¹⁄₂ teaspoon salt and ¹⁄₄ teaspoon freshly ground black pepper. Toss gently. Shave 2 ounces Parmigiano-Reggiano cheese over salad.

Crusty French bread

Roast Chicken with Pears, Shallots, and Walnuts

Heat can diminish the flavor of delicate walnut oil, so we add it to the sauce after the pan is removed from the burner. For the best results, start with firm pears.

 1 (4-pound) whole roasting chicken
 2 garlic cloves, peeled and crushed
 2 fresh rosemary sprigs
 1 lemon, quartered
 2 teaspoons chopped fresh rosemary
 1 teaspoon salt, divided
 1 teaspoon olive oil
 6 shallots, peeled and quartered
 3 firm pears, peeled, cored, and each cut into 8 wedges
 ¹⁄₂ cup fat-free, less-sodium chicken broth
 ¹⁄₄ cup walnut halves
 ¹⁄₂ cup water
 3 tablespoons Champagne vinegar
 2 tablespoons honey
 1 tablespoon fresh lemon juice
 1 garlic clove, minced
 2 teaspoons toasted walnut oil

1 Preheat oven to 425°.

2 Remove and discard giblets and neck from chicken. Place crushed garlic, rosemary sprigs, and lemon in body cavity. Combine chopped rosemary, ³⁄₄ teaspoon salt, and olive oil. Starting at neck cavity, loosen skin from breast and drumsticks by inserting fingers, gently pushing between skin and meat. Rub oil mixture under skin. Lift wing tips up and over back; tuck under chicken. Tie legs together with twine. Place chicken, breast side up, in a roasting pan.

3 Bake at 425° for 25 minutes. Arrange shallots and pears around chicken. Add broth to pan; baste chicken. Bake 30 minutes. Stir pears and shallots; baste chicken. Add walnuts to pan. Bake an additional 10 minutes or until a thermometer inserted in meaty part of thigh registers 165°. Let stand 20 minutes.

4 Place a zip-top plastic bag inside a 2-cup glass measure. Pour drippings from pan into bag; add ¹⁄₂ cup water. Let stand 2 minutes (fat will rise to top). Seal bag; carefully snip off 1 bottom corner of bag. Drain drippings into measuring cup, stopping before fat layer reaches opening; discard fat. Return drippings to pan, and cook over medium heat, scraping pan to loosen browned bits. Add remaining ¹⁄₄ teaspoon salt, vinegar, and next 3 ingredients; cook until reduced to ¹⁄₂ cup (about 4 minutes). Remove from heat; stir in walnut oil.

5 Remove skin from chicken; discard skin. Carve chicken; arrange chicken and pear mixture on a platter. Serve with sauce. Yield: 6 servings (serving size: 3 ounces chicken, about ¹⁄₄ cup pear mixture, and 4 teaspoons sauce).

CALORIES 313 (36% from fat); FAT 12.4g (sat 2.4g, mono 3.9g, poly 4.9g); PROTEIN 27.9g; CARB 22.7g; FIBER 3.8g; CHOL 78mg; IRON 1.7mg; SODIUM 506mg; CALC 37mg

Fruit and Walnut–Stuffed Pork Loin

Dried fruits are rehydrated in a blend of orange-flavored liqueur and red wine. Use a combination of orange juice and chicken broth for a nonalcoholic alternative. The pork loin is coated in a breadcrumb mixture to form a crisp crust.

½ cup dry red wine
¼ cup dried sour cherries
¼ cup chopped dried apricots
¼ cup chopped dried plums
2 tablespoons Triple Sec (orange-flavored liqueur)
⅓ cup finely chopped walnuts
2 tablespoons chopped shallots
1¼ teaspoons salt, divided
½ teaspoon grated lemon rind
2 (1-ounce) slices French bread
1 teaspoon chopped fresh thyme
¼ teaspoon freshly ground black pepper
2 garlic cloves, minced
1 (2½-pound) boneless center-cut pork loin roast, trimmed
2 tablespoons Dijon mustard
Cooking spray
Parsley sprigs (optional)

❶ Preheat oven to 400°.
❷ Combine first 5 ingredients in a medium microwave-safe bowl; microwave at HIGH 2 minutes. Let stand 10 minutes or until fruit is plump. Drain mixture in a sieve. Combine fruit mixture, walnuts, shallots, ¼ teaspoon salt, and rind.
❸ Combine ¾ teaspoon salt, bread, and next 3 ingredients in a food processor; process until fine crumbs form.
❹ Cut pork in half lengthwise, cutting to, but not through, other side; open halves, laying pork flat. Starting from center, cut each half lengthwise, cutting to, but not through, other side; open halves, laying pork flat. Cover with plastic wrap; pound to an even thickness. Discard plastic wrap. Spread fruit mixture over pork, leaving a ½-inch border.

Roll up pork, jelly-roll fashion, starting with one long side. Secure with wooden picks. Sprinkle outside of pork evenly with remaining ¼ teaspoon salt; brush evenly with mustard. Sprinkle breadcrumb mixture over pork; press gently to adhere. Place pork on a broiler pan coated with cooking spray. Bake at 400° for 55 minutes or until a meat thermometer inserted in thickest part registers 155°. Let pork stand 10 minutes. Remove wooden picks. Cut into 16 (½-inch-thick) slices. Garnish with parsley sprigs, if desired. Yield: 8 servings (serving size: 2 slices).

CALORIES 323 (35% from fat); FAT 12.4g (sat 3.7g, mono 4.5g, poly 3.1g); PROTEIN 29.7g; CARB 18.9g; FIBER 1.4g; CHOL 79mg; IRON 1.9mg; SODIUM 573mg; CALC 41mg

MAKE AHEAD
Classic Walnut Boule

Boule, the French word for "ball," often refers to round loaves of crusty bread. You can use any leftovers to make sandwiches for lunch, or simply toast a slice, slather it with butter or jam, and enjoy it for breakfast.

3 tablespoons sugar
1 package dry yeast (2¼ teaspoons)
1 cup warm water (100° to 110°)
1 tablespoon toasted walnut oil
2¼ cups bread flour, divided (about 10.7 ounces)
1 cup whole wheat flour (about 4.75 ounces)
1½ teaspoons salt
Cooking spray
½ cup coarsely chopped walnuts, toasted
2 tablespoons yellow cornmeal
1 tablespoon fat-free milk
1 large egg white, lightly beaten

❶ Dissolve sugar and yeast in 1 cup warm water in a large bowl; let stand 5 minutes. Stir in oil. Lightly spoon flours into dry measuring cups; level with a knife. Add 2 cups bread flour, whole wheat flour, and salt to yeast mixture; stir until a soft dough forms. Turn dough out onto a lightly floured surface. Knead until dough is smooth and elastic (about 5 minutes); add enough of remaining bread flour, 1 tablespoon at a time, to prevent dough from sticking to hands (dough will feel sticky).
❷ Place dough in a large bowl coated with cooking spray, turning to coat top. Cover and let rise in a warm place (85°), free from drafts, 1 hour or until doubled in size. (Gently press two fingers into dough. If indentation remains, dough has risen enough.) Punch dough down; knead in walnuts. Shape dough into a 9-inch round on a lightly floured surface. Place dough on a large baking sheet sprinkled with cornmeal. Cover and let rise 1 hour or until doubled in size.
❸ Preheat oven to 350°.
❹ Uncover dough. Combine milk and egg white; brush over dough. Score dough by making two diagonal slits with a sharp knife; make two diagonal slits in opposite direction to create a crosshatch pattern. Bake at 350° for 30 minutes or until bread is browned on bottom and sounds hollow when tapped. Cool on a wire rack. Yield: 16 servings (serving size: 1 slice).

CALORIES 122 (25% from fat); FAT 3.4g (sat 0.3g, mono 0.6g, poly 2.3g); PROTEIN 4.1g; CARB 20.3g; FIBER 1.7g; CHOL 0mg; IRON 1.2mg; SODIUM 226mg; CALC 8mg

Walnut Rice

2¾ cups water
¼ cup dry white wine
¾ teaspoon salt
1½ cups uncooked long-grain rice
¼ cup finely chopped fresh flat-leaf parsley
¼ cup walnuts, toasted and chopped
2 tablespoons toasted walnut oil
¼ teaspoon freshly ground black pepper

❶ Bring first 3 ingredients to a boil in a medium saucepan; add rice. Cover, reduce heat, and simmer 20 minutes or until liquid is absorbed. Remove from heat. Stir in parsley and remaining ingredients. Yield: 8 servings (serving size: ²/₃ cup).

CALORIES 243 (30% from fat); FAT 8g (sat 0.8g, mono 1.6g, poly 5.3g); PROTEIN 4.1g; CARB 38g; FIBER 1g; CHOL 0mg; IRON 2.3mg; SODIUM 300mg; CALC 22mg

---

Handful of Health Benefits

Walnuts are packed with nutrients—protein, phosphorous, magnesium, antioxidants, and polyunsaturated fat. They also are a great source of heart-healthy alpha-linolenic acid (ALA), an essential omega-3 fatty acid; walnuts have the highest levels of omega-3 content of any nuts. The National Academy of Sciences recommends a daily omega-3 intake of 1.1 grams for women and 1.6 grams for men; a one-ounce serving of walnuts contains 2.6 grams of omega-3s.

The nuts have been found to help the heart in a variety of ways. Researchers at Pennsylvania State University found that walnuts may help reduce the risk of heart disease by lowering cholesterol, reducing inflammation, and improving artery function. And the U.S. Physicians' Health Study at Harvard, following 21,545 men, showed that participants who ate at least one ounce of nuts twice a week had a significantly reduced risk of sudden cardiac death.

Beet and Walnut Salad

(pictured on page 258)

For an impressive presentation, use a combination of golden and ruby beets.

DRESSING:

⅓ cup fresh lemon juice
3 tablespoons sugar
2 tablespoons finely chopped shallots
2 teaspoons extravirgin olive oil
¼ teaspoon salt

SALAD:

16 baby beets (about 1 pound)
½ cup water
10 cups mixed salad greens
¼ teaspoon salt
3 tablespoons coarsely chopped walnuts, toasted
3 tablespoons crumbled blue cheese
1 tablespoon chopped fresh chives

❶ To prepare dressing, combine first 5 ingredients, stirring with a whisk.
❷ Preheat oven to 375°.
❸ To prepare salad, leave root and 1 inch of stem on beets; scrub with a brush. Place beets in an 11 x 7-inch baking dish; add ½ cup water. Cover and bake at 375° for 35 minutes or until tender. Drain and cool. Trim off beet roots; rub off skins. Cut each beet into quarters. Place beets in a small bowl; drizzle with 1 tablespoon dressing.
❹ Place salad greens on a large platter; sprinkle evenly with ¼ teaspoon salt. Drizzle remaining dressing over greens. Top with beets, walnuts, cheese, and chives. Yield: 8 servings (serving size: about 1½ cups).

CALORIES 98 (38% from fat); FAT 4.1g (sat 1g, mono 1.3g, poly 1.6g); PROTEIN 3.2g; CARB 13.9g; FIBER 3.3g; CHOL 2mg; IRON 1.5mg; SODIUM 254mg; CALC 69mg

---

The pleasantly bitter flavor of walnuts is a welcome addition to savory and sweet recipes.

Walnut Cake with Praline Frosting

This easy sheet cake is rich enough for adults to enjoy after dinner with coffee, yet just sweet enough to be a treat for children, too.

CAKE:

2 cups all-purpose flour (about 9 ounces)
½ teaspoon baking soda
½ teaspoon salt
7 tablespoons butter, softened
1 cup granulated sugar
¼ cup packed brown sugar
2 large eggs
1 large egg white
1 teaspoon vanilla extract
1 cup 1% low-fat buttermilk
6 tablespoons chopped walnuts, toasted
Cooking spray

FROSTING:

½ cup packed brown sugar
6 tablespoons 1% low-fat milk, divided
2 tablespoons butter
1 tablespoon light corn syrup
Dash of salt
2 cups powdered sugar
½ teaspoon vanilla extract
2 tablespoons chopped walnuts, toasted

Continued

① Preheat oven to 350°.

② To prepare cake, lightly spoon flour into dry measuring cups; level with a knife. Combine flour, baking soda, and ½ teaspoon salt, stirring well with a whisk.

③ Place 7 tablespoons butter, 1 cup granulated sugar, and ¼ cup brown sugar in a mixing bowl; beat with a mixer at medium-high speed until light and fluffy (about 3 minutes). Add eggs, 1 at a time, beating well after each addition. Beat in egg white. Beat in 1 teaspoon vanilla. Add flour mixture alternately with buttermilk, beginning and ending with flour mixture. Fold in 6 tablespoons walnuts. Scrape batter into a 13 x 9–inch pan coated with cooking spray.

④ Bake at 350° for 28 minutes or until a wooden pick inserted in center comes out clean. Cool in pan on a wire rack.

⑤ To prepare frosting, place ½ cup brown sugar, ¼ cup milk, 2 tablespoons butter, corn syrup, and dash of salt in a saucepan over medium-high heat; bring to a boil, stirring occasionally. Cook 2 minutes. Scrape brown sugar mixture into a bowl. Add remaining 2 tablespoons milk and powdered sugar; beat with a mixer at high speed 2 minutes or until slightly cooled and thick. Beat in ½ teaspoon vanilla. Spread frosting in an even layer over cooled cake; sprinkle with 2 tablespoons walnuts. Let cake stand until frosting sets; cut into squares. Yield: 16 servings (serving size: 1 square).

CALORIES 306 (29% from fat); FAT 9.8g (sat 4.6g, mono 2.3g, poly 2.1g); PROTEIN 4g; CARB 52g; FIBER 0.7g; CHOL 44mg; IRON 1.2mg; SODIUM 204mg; CALC 51mg

Game Night, Pizza Night

Gather everyone for a night of board games and our mix-and-match lineup of pizzas.

GAME NIGHT PIZZA MENU

(Serves 8)

Lima Bean Dip

Arugula Salad

Pizza Margherita

Sausage Pizza

Roasted Beet Pizza

Venezia Bianco

Chianti

Cinnamon-Ginger Cookies

Coffee, tea

WINE NOTE: The variety of tastes and toppings in this menu means these pizzas can go with red or white wine. A bold Italian Chianti, like Melini Chianti San Lorenzo 2006 ($15), has the acidity to stand up to tomato sauce, while the wine's rustic, dried-cherry flavors are great with more intense toppings like spicy chicken sausage. With more delicate toppings, such as roasted beets, and the salad, try Masi Modello della Venezia Bianco ($10), a refreshing Italian white blend that comes with pear and floral aromas.

Lima Bean Dip
(Salsa di Fagioli)

Fava beans are traditional in this hummus-like dip. Use them, if you find them, in place of the lima beans.

- 1 pound frozen baby lima beans
- 3 tablespoons sesame seeds, toasted
- ¼ cup fresh lemon juice
- 1 tablespoon extravirgin olive oil
- ¾ teaspoon kosher salt
- 1 garlic clove

① Cook beans in boiling water 10 minutes or until very tender. Drain, reserving ½ cup cooking liquid.

② Place sesame seeds in a blender; process until finely ground. Add juice and remaining ingredients; process until blended. Add beans and ½ cup reserved liquid; process until almost smooth, scraping sides of blender occasionally. Yield: 8 servings (serving size: about ¼ cup).

CALORIES 95 (32% from fat); FAT 3.4g (sat 0.3g, mono 1.4g, poly 0.2g); PROTEIN 4.7g; CARB 13g; FIBER 3.6g; CHOL 0mg; IRON 1.4mg; SODIUM 195mg; CALC 21mg

---

Make-Ahead Time Line

2 days ahead:
- Bake Cinnamon-Ginger Cookies; cool to room temperature, and store in an airtight container.

The night before:
- Prepare Lima Bean Dip, and refrigerate; let stand at room temperature for 30 minutes before serving.
- Clean and cut up vegetables to serve with dip; refrigerate.
- Make sausage mixture (step 3) for Sausage Pizza; refrigerate.
- Roast beets (step 2) for Roasted Beet Pizza; refrigerate.
- Wash arugula for salad; refrigerate.

1 hour before guests arrive:
- Prepare Basic Pizza Dough.
- Combine dressing ingredients and shave cheese for Arugula Salad.

Arugula Salad
(*Insalata di Rucola*)

This salad is delicious for entertaining, yet simple enough to become part of your weeknight repertoire.

- 7 cups trimmed arugula (about 5 ounces)
- ¼ cup thinly sliced shallots
- 2 tablespoons fresh lemon juice
- 4 teaspoons extravirgin olive oil
- 1 tablespoon water
- ¼ teaspoon kosher salt
- ¼ teaspoon freshly ground black pepper
- ¼ cup (1 ounce) shaved fresh Parmigiano-Reggiano cheese

① Place arugula in a large bowl. Combine shallots and next 5 ingredients; stir with a whisk. Pour over arugula; toss. Sprinkle with cheese. Yield: 8 servings (serving size: about ¾ cup salad and 1½ teaspoons cheese).

CALORIES 38 (76% from fat); FAT 3.2g (sat 0.8g, mono 2g, poly 0.3g); PROTEIN 1.5g; CARB 1.3g; FIBER 0.3g; CHOL 2mg; IRON 0.3mg; SODIUM 102mg; CALC 57mg

Basic Pizza Dough

This recipe yields enough dough for one pizza; increase the batches according to the number of pizzas you want to prepare.

- ½ teaspoon dry yeast
- 6 to 7 tablespoons warm water (100° to 110°), divided
- 1 cup all-purpose flour (about 4.5 ounces)
- ½ teaspoon salt
  Cooking spray
- 1 tablespoon cornmeal

① Dissolve yeast in ¼ cup warm water in a small bowl; let stand 5 minutes.
② Lightly spoon flour into a dry measuring cup; level with a knife. Place flour and salt in a food processor; pulse 2 times or until blended. With processor on, slowly add yeast mixture through food chute. Add enough of remaining warm water, 1 tablespoon at a time, until dough forms a ball; process 30 seconds. Turn dough out onto a floured surface; knead lightly 4 or 5 times. Place dough in a bowl coated with cooking spray, turning to coat top. Cover and let rise in a warm place (85°), free from drafts, 1 hour or until doubled in size. (Gently press two fingers into dough. If indentation remains, dough has risen enough.)
③ Punch dough down; cover and let rest 5 minutes.
④ Roll dough into a 10-inch circle on a lightly floured surface. Place dough on an inverted baking sheet sprinkled with cornmeal. Top and bake according to recipe. Yield: 1 (10-inch) crust; 8 servings.

CALORIES 62 (3% from fat); FAT 0.2g (sat 0g, mono 0g, poly 0.1g); PROTEIN 1.8g; CARB 12.9g; FIBER 0.6g; CHOL 0mg; IRON 0.8mg; SODIUM 146mg; CALC 3mg

Pizza Margherita

This is our take on the traditional Neapolitan pizza resplendent with the red, white, and green of the Italian flag. Gently patting the tomato slices with a paper towel prevents the pizza from becoming soggy.

- 1 teaspoon extravirgin olive oil, divided
- 1 (10-inch) Basic Pizza Dough (at left)
- 6 very thin tomato slices
- 3 ounces buffalo mozzarella, cut into small pieces
- 3 tablespoons torn fresh basil
- ¼ teaspoon kosher salt
- ⅛ teaspoon freshly ground black pepper

① Position an oven rack in lowest setting. Place a pizza stone on rack.
② Preheat oven to 500°. Preheat pizza stone 30 minutes.
③ Gently brush ½ teaspoon oil over Basic Pizza Dough. Pat tomato slices with a paper towel. Arrange cheese over dough, leaving a ½-inch border. Top with tomato slices. Slide dough onto preheated pizza stone, using a spatula as a guide.
④ Bake at 500° for 9 minutes or until crust is golden. Remove from pizza stone. Drizzle with remaining ½ teaspoon oil. Sprinkle with basil, salt, and pepper. Cut into 8 wedges. Yield: 8 servings (serving size: 1 wedge).

CALORIES 99 (28% from fat); FAT 3.1g (sat 1.6g, mono 0.5g, poly 0.1g); PROTEIN 3.8g; CARB 13.6g; FIBER 0.7g; CHOL 8mg; IRON 0.9mg; SODIUM 220mg; CALC 65mg

Sausage Pizza
(*Pizza alla Salsiccia*)

The combination of Italian sausage, fennel, and red onion combines pleasant spicy heat with intriguing anise flavor for a complex-tasting pizza.

- 1½ teaspoons olive oil
- ¼ to ½ teaspoon crushed red pepper
- 1 (4-ounce) link sweet turkey Italian sausage
- ½ cup vertically sliced fennel bulb
- ½ cup thinly vertically sliced red onion (about 1 small onion)
- ¼ teaspoon kosher salt
- ⅔ cup chopped seeded tomato (about 2 tomatoes)
- 1 (10-inch) Basic Pizza Dough (at left)
- ¼ cup (1 ounce) grated fresh Parmigiano-Reggiano cheese

① Position an oven rack in lowest setting. Place a pizza stone on rack.
② Preheat oven to 500°. Preheat pizza stone 30 minutes.
③ Heat oil in a large nonstick skillet over medium-high heat. Add pepper to pan; cook 10 seconds. Remove casings from sausage. Add sausage, fennel, and onion to pan; sauté 4 minutes or until browned, stirring to crumble sausage. Stir in salt. Add tomato; sauté 2 minutes or until tender. Remove from heat.
④ Spread sausage mixture over Basic Pizza Dough, leaving a ½-inch border.

Continued

Slide dough onto preheated pizza stone, using a spatula as a guide.

⑤ Bake at 500° for 8 minutes or until crust is golden. Remove from pizza stone. Sprinkle with cheese. Cut pizza into 8 wedges. Yield: 8 servings (serving size: 1 wedge).

CALORIES 123 (25% from fat); FAT 3.4g (sat 1g, mono 0.9g, poly 0.2g); PROTEIN 6.4g; CARB 16.7g; FIBER 1.6g; CHOL 15mg; IRON 1.4mg; SODIUM 365mg; CALC 43mg

Roasted Beet Pizza
(Pizza alla Barbabietola Arrostito)

"People who think they don't like beets often become converts after sampling this tasty pizza," says Senior Food Editor Alison Ashton. Roast several golden beets at once, and enjoy the extras with salads, on sandwiches, or as a snack with crusty bread and goat cheese.

　1　(4-ounce) golden beet
　1　teaspoon olive oil
　1　(10-inch) Basic Pizza Dough
　　　(page 299)
　½　cup (2 ounces) crumbled feta
　　　cheese
　¼　cup vertically sliced shallots
　¼　teaspoon kosher salt
　1　teaspoon honey

① Preheat oven to 450°.
② Leave root and 1 inch of stem on beet; scrub with a brush. Wrap beet in foil. Bake at 450° for 40 minutes or until tender. Remove from oven; cool. Trim off beet root; rub off skin. Cut beet in half crosswise; thinly slice halves.
③ Position an oven rack in lowest setting. Place a pizza stone on rack.
④ Increase oven temperature to 500°. Preheat pizza stone 30 minutes.
⑤ Gently brush oil over Basic Pizza Dough. Arrange cheese, beets, and shallots evenly over dough, leaving a ½-inch border. Slide dough onto preheated pizza stone, using a spatula as a guide.

⑥ Bake at 500° for 8 minutes or until crust is golden. Remove from pizza stone. Sprinkle with salt, and drizzle with honey. Cut into 8 wedges. Yield: 8 servings (serving size: 1 wedge).

CALORIES 104 (20% from fat); FAT 2.3g (sat 1.2g, mono 0.8g, poly 0.2g); PROTEIN 3.5g; CARB 17.7g; FIBER 1g; CHOL 6mg; IRON 1.2mg; SODIUM 295mg; CALC 40mg

Cinnamon-Ginger Cookies
(Biscotti dello Canella-Zenzero)

These drop cookies are terrific with a cup of coffee or tea—and easy for guests to eat while they play games. For the best flavor, make sure your spices are fresh; if they smell strong, they are good to use.

　1½　cups all-purpose flour (about
　　　6.75 ounces)
　1½　teaspoons ground cinnamon
　¾　teaspoon baking soda
　¼　teaspoon ground ginger
　⅛　teaspoon ground cloves
　⅛　teaspoon grated nutmeg
　　　Dash of salt
　6　tablespoons butter, softened
　¾　cup sugar, divided
　3　tablespoons fat-free milk
　3　tablespoons molasses
　1　teaspoon vanilla extract
　　　Cooking spray

① Preheat oven to 350°.
② Lightly spoon flour into dry measuring cups; level with a knife. Combine flour and next 6 ingredients, stirring with a whisk.
③ Combine butter and ¼ cup sugar in a medium bowl, and beat with a mixer at medium speed until light and fluffy (about 3 minutes). Beat in milk, molasses, and vanilla. Add flour mixture to butter mixture, and beat at low speed until blended. Shape dough into a 6-inch disk. Cover and chill 30 minutes.
④ Lightly coat hands with cooking spray. Shape dough into 30 balls (about 2 teaspoons each). Place remaining ½ cup sugar in a shallow bowl. Roll dough balls

in sugar; place 2 inches apart on baking sheets coated with cooking spray. Flatten balls slightly with bottom of a glass. Bake at 350° for 12 minutes or until lightly browned. Cool on pans 4 minutes. Remove cookies from pans; cool completely on wire racks. Yield: 30 cookies (serving size: 1 cookie).

CALORIES 69 (31% from fat); FAT 2.4g (sat 1.5g, mono 0.6g, poly 0.1g); PROTEIN 0.7g; CARB 11.5g; FIBER 0.2g; CHOL 6mg; IRON 0.4mg; SODIUM 54mg; CALC 9mg

Mom's Moussaka

A Nevada writer captures her mother's love for Greek and Armenian cuisine in this hearty specialty.

　　Christine Datian, a copywriter and technical writer from Las Vegas, often prepares this delicious twist on a Greek classic for her husband, John. During Datian's childhood, her mother, Alice, often served global fare at dinner. "This recipe is based on a Greek moussaka recipe," Datian says. "My mother prepared the dish with lamb, layering it with potatoes or rice, rather than eggplant, to please my picky brother. She put an Armenian spin on it, adding tomato sauce and sometimes dried or fresh mint."

　　American, Greek, Armenian, Italian, and Turkish dishes were mainstays on the dinner table during Datian's childhood. Her parents, both first-generation Armenian Americans, were introduced to one another by the owner of Dan's Café, a Greek restaurant in Fresno, California. "They ate there often since Dan made Greek and Armenian dishes, like lamb shanks, meatballs, pilaf, soups, and desserts," Datian recalls. Her mother used the same classic ingredients in her cooking, passing an appreciation of the foodways to her children.

　　She enjoys preparing her mother's adaptation of this dish. And, like her mother, improvises when necessary. "This dish is versatile," she says. "If you don't have lamb, use beef, or try fresh chopped tomatoes instead of canned tomato sauce."

MAKE AHEAD • FREEZABLE
Potato and Lamb Moussaka

"Sometimes I change up the recipe and top this casserole with crumbled feta cheese. I like serving it with a simple Greek salad, pita bread, and a great red wine."

—Christine Datian, Las Vegas, Nevada

Cooking spray
2 pounds peeled baking potato, cut into ¼-inch-thick slices
1 cup chopped onion (about 1 medium)
2 garlic cloves, chopped
1 pound ground lamb
1 cup no-salt-added tomato sauce
½ cup chopped green bell pepper
½ cup chopped red bell pepper
½ cup finely chopped fresh flat-leaf parsley
1 teaspoon salt
1 teaspoon ground cumin
½ teaspoon freshly ground black pepper
¼ teaspoon ground cinnamon
1 cup 1% low-fat milk
2 large eggs, lightly beaten

❶ Heat a large nonstick skillet over medium heat. Coat pan with cooking spray. Add one-third of potato slices to pan; cook 3 minutes on each side or until lightly browned. Transfer potato to a bowl. Repeat procedure with cooking spray and remaining potato slices.
❷ Preheat oven to 350°.
❸ Recoat pan with cooking spray. Add onion, garlic, and lamb to pan; cook 3 minutes or until lamb begins to brown. Add tomato sauce and next 7 ingredients; cook 10 minutes.
❹ Arrange half of potato slices in a 13 x 9–inch baking dish coated with

cooking spray. Arrange lamb mixture over potatoes; top with remaining potato slices. Combine milk and eggs in a small bowl; pour over potato mixture. Bake at 350° for 30 minutes or until top is golden and set. Remove from oven; let stand 10 minutes before serving. Yield: 6 servings (serving size: 1 piece).

CALORIES 369 (33% from fat); FAT 13.7g (sat 5.5g, mono 5.5g, poly 1.2g); PROTEIN 21.4g; CARB 40.3g; FIBER 4.7g; CHOL 127mg; IRON 2.8mg; SODIUM 501mg; CALC 111mg

Shiitake and Cabbage Noodles with Tofu

"Trying the instant Asian-style noodle bowls from the grocery store inspired me to come up with this dish, as I wanted more vegetables, less sodium, and the addition of tofu."

—Barb Combs, Fort Collins, Colorado

2 tablespoons seasoned rice vinegar
1 tablespoon low-sodium soy sauce
1 teaspoon minced garlic
1 teaspoon dark sesame oil
1 teaspoon Sriracha (hot chile sauce, such as Huy Fong)
½ teaspoon minced peeled fresh ginger
1 (14-ounce) package firm tofu, drained and cut into ½-inch cubes
2 cups boiling water
½ ounce dried shiitake mushrooms (about ½ cup)
Cooking spray
½ teaspoon dark sesame oil
1 tablespoon low-sodium soy sauce
4 cups angel hair slaw
½ cup sliced green onions
1 (14-ounce) can fat-free, less-sodium chicken broth
3 cups hot cooked udon noodles (thick, round fresh Japanese wheat noodles)

❶ Combine first 6 ingredients in a bowl. Add tofu; toss gently to coat. Cover and chill 30 minutes.
❷ Combine 2 cups boiling water and mushrooms in a bowl; cover and let

stand 20 minutes. Drain mushrooms in a colander over a bowl, reserving liquid. Rinse and slice mushrooms; set aside. Strain reserved liquid through a paper towel–lined colander into a bowl; discard solids.
❸ Heat a Dutch oven over medium-high heat. Coat pan with cooking spray. Add tofu mixture to pan; sauté 7 minutes or until liquid evaporates, stirring occasionally. Remove tofu from pan. Heat ½ teaspoon oil in pan. Add 1 tablespoon soy sauce, slaw, onions, and mushrooms to pan; sauté 2 minutes or until slaw wilts. Add reserved mushroom liquid, tofu mixture, and broth to pan; bring to a boil. Cover, reduce heat, and simmer 5 minutes. Place ¾ cup noodles in each of 4 bowls. Pour 1¾ cups slaw mixture over each serving. Yield: 4 servings.

CALORIES 341 (30% from fat); FAT 11.3g (sat 1.6g, mono 2.7g, poly 5.7g); PROTEIN 21.9g; CARB 41.8g; FIBER 5.8g; CHOL 0mg; IRON 11.7mg; SODIUM 898mg; CALC 742mg

MAKE AHEAD
Chocolate Coconut Oatmeal Cookies

"I don't do a lot of cooking, but I like baking and having healthful sweets on hand. A little coconut and dark chocolate make great additions to a cookie. I like to have one with coffee."

—Marilyn McRae, Anniston, Alabama

1 cup all-purpose flour (about 4.5 ounces)
1 cup quick-cooking oats
½ teaspoon baking powder
¼ teaspoon baking soda
¼ teaspoon salt
½ cup packed brown sugar
6 tablespoons granulated sugar
¼ cup butter, softened
1 large egg
¾ teaspoon vanilla extract
¼ cup flaked sweetened coconut
¼ cup finely chopped dark chocolate
Cooking spray

Continued

① Preheat oven to 350°.

② Lightly spoon flour into a dry measuring cup; level with a knife. Combine flour and next 4 ingredients; stir with a whisk.

③ Place sugars and butter in a large bowl; beat with a mixer at medium speed until well blended (about 2 minutes). Add egg, beating well. Beat in vanilla. Add flour mixture to butter mixture; stir just until combined. Stir in coconut and chocolate.

④ Scrape dough onto a lightly floured surface, and divide into 24 portions. Roll each portion into a ball. Place 12 balls on each of 2 baking sheets coated with cooking spray; flatten slightly with heel of your hand. Bake, 1 sheet at a time, at 350° for 15 minutes or until tops are set and cookies are lightly browned on bottoms. Remove cookies from pan; cool on wire racks. Yield: 2 dozen (serving size: 1 cookie).

CALORIES 99 (32% from fat); FAT 3.5g (sat 2g, mono 0.7g, poly 0.2g); PROTEIN 1.4g; CARB 16g; FIBER 0.5g; CHOL 14mg; IRON 0.6mg; SODIUM 66mg; CALC 15mg

Simple Mexican Supper Menu
serves 4

Substitute grilled pork tenderloin in place of chicken, or use your favorite cheese for the quesadillas.

Black Bean–Tomato Soup with Cilantro-Lime Cream

Grilled chicken and cheese quesadillas

Place ½ cup shredded Monterey Jack cheese with jalapeño peppers on each of 2 (8-inch) flour tortillas; top each with ½ cup shredded cooked chicken. Place 1 (8-inch) flour tortilla over each serving. Heat a large skillet over medium-high heat. Coat pan with cooking spray. Working with 1 quesadilla at a time, cook 2 minutes on each side or until browned. Cut each quesadilla into quarters. Serve with salsa.

Margarita on the rocks

Black Bean–Tomato Soup with Cilantro-Lime Cream

"This soup is easy to prepare and has plenty of flavor."

—Gloria Bradley, Naperville, Illinois

2 center-cut bacon slices, chopped
½ cup chopped onion (about 1 small)
¼ cup chopped celery
1 teaspoon ground cumin, divided
½ teaspoon chipotle chile powder
1 garlic clove, minced
¼ teaspoon ground black pepper
1 (15-ounce) can black beans, rinsed and drained
1 (14.5-ounce) can no-salt-added organic diced tomatoes, undrained
1 (14-ounce) can fat-free, less-sodium chicken broth
¼ cup reduced-fat sour cream
1 tablespoon minced fresh cilantro
½ teaspoon grated lime rind
1 tablespoon fresh lime juice

① Cook bacon in a large saucepan over medium heat until crisp. Remove bacon with a slotted spoon, reserving 1 teaspoon drippings in pan; set bacon aside. Add onion and celery to pan; cook 5 minutes or until celery is tender. Stir in ¾ teaspoon cumin, chile powder, and garlic; cook 1 minute. Stir in bacon, pepper, and next 3 ingredients; bring to a boil. Cover, reduce heat, and simmer 10 minutes. Place half of bean mixture in a blender. Remove center piece of blender lid (to allow steam to escape); secure blender lid on blender. Place a clean towel over opening in blender lid (to avoid splatters). Process until smooth. Pour into a large bowl. Repeat procedure with remaining bean mixture. Keep warm.

② Combine sour cream, remaining ¼ teaspoon cumin, cilantro, rind, and juice in a small bowl. Drizzle over soup. Yield: 4 servings (serving size: 1 cup soup and 1½ tablespoons cream).

CALORIES 123 (31% from fat); FAT 4.3g (sat 2g, mono 1.6g, poly 0.4g); PROTEIN 6.4g; CARB 16.3g; FIBER 5.1g; CHOL 10mg; IRON 2.1mg; SODIUM 488mg; CALC 58mg

These right-sized menus allow you to comfortably feed two with no leftovers.

Dinner for Two Menu 1
serves 2

Thai Coconut Curry Shrimp

Sautéed snow peas

Heat ½ teaspoon canola oil in a large nonstick skillet over medium-high heat. Add 2 cups trimmed fresh snow peas, ¼ teaspoon salt, and ¼ teaspoon crushed red pepper to pan; sauté 2 minutes or until crisp-tender, tossing frequently with tongs.

Hot cooked long-grain rice

Game Plan
1 While rice cooks:
   • Trim snow peas.
   • Prepare shrimp.
2 Prepare snow peas.

QUICK & EASY
Thai Coconut Curry Shrimp

Red curry paste conveys plenty of spicy heat, so a little goes a long way. Total time: 19 minutes

1 teaspoon canola oil
½ cup chopped onion
¼ teaspoon red curry paste (such as Thai Kitchen)
1 teaspoon sugar
12 ounces large shrimp, peeled and deveined
⅓ cup light coconut milk
2 teaspoons fish sauce
¼ cup chopped green onions
1 tablespoon chopped fresh basil

1 Heat oil in a large nonstick skillet over medium-high heat. Add onion and curry paste to pan, and sauté 1 minute, stirring occasionally. Stir in sugar; sauté 15 seconds. Add shrimp; sauté 3 minutes or until shrimp are done, stirring frequently. Stir in coconut milk and fish sauce; cook 30 seconds or until thoroughly heated. Remove from heat; stir in green onions and basil. Yield: 2 servings (serving size: 1 cup).

CALORIES 255 (26% from fat); FAT 7.4g (sat 2.6g, mono 1.8g, poly 1.9g); PROTEIN 36.1g; CARB 10.2g; FIBER 1.1g; CHOL 259mg; IRON 4.6mg; SODIUM 740mg; CALC 111mg

Dinner for Two Menu 2

serves 2

Ziti with Spinach, Cherry Tomatoes, and Gorgonzola Sauce

Garlic breadsticks

Combine 1 tablespoon melted butter and 1½ teaspoons minced garlic, stirring well. Brush refrigerated breadstick dough with garlic mixture. Separate dough into individual breadsticks. Place on a baking sheet coated with cooking spray, twisting each portion as you place it on the baking sheet. Bake at 375° for 13 minutes or until the breadsticks are lightly golden brown.

Green salad

Game Plan

1 While pasta water comes to a boil:
• Preheat oven.
• Prepare tomato mixture for pasta.
2 While pasta cooks:
• Prepare breadsticks.
• Toss salad.
3 Toss pasta with tomato mixture and spinach.

Quick Tip

Purchasing prewashed bagged baby spinach saves time since there are no tough stems to remove.

QUICK & EASY
Ziti with Spinach, Cherry Tomatoes, and Gorgonzola Sauce

Gorgonzola, an Italian blue cheese, gives this grown-up mac and cheese dish pungent flavor. If you'd like to make it more family-friendly, substitute your favorite blue or other creamy cheese. You can also substitute penne or rigatoni for ziti.
Total time: 40 minutes

    4   ounces uncooked ziti
    ½   teaspoon extravirgin olive oil
    1   cup cherry tomatoes, halved
    ¼   teaspoon salt
    ⅛   teaspoon crushed red pepper
    1   garlic clove, minced
    6   tablespoons half-and-half
    3   tablespoons Gorgonzola cheese, crumbled
    1   cup fresh spinach

1 Cook pasta according to package directions, omitting salt and fat; drain.
2 Heat oil in a large nonstick skillet over medium heat. Add tomatoes and next 3 ingredients to pan; cook 1 minute, stirring occasionally. Stir in half-and-half and cheese; cook 2 minutes or until slightly thick, stirring constantly. Stir in spinach and pasta; cook 1 minute or until spinach wilts, tossing occasionally. Yield: 2 servings (serving size: 1¼ cups).

CALORIES 335 (28% from fat); FAT 10.4g (sat 5.9g, mono 2.4g, poly 0.4g); PROTEIN 12.3g; CARB 49.9g; FIBER 3.6g; CHOL 26mg; IRON 2.6mg; SODIUM 485mg; CALC 129mg

Dinner for Two Menu 3

serves 2

Quick Barbecue Chicken

Spicy corn on the cob

Combine 2 teaspoons butter, ¼ teaspoon salt, ¼ teaspoon sugar, ⅛ teaspoon chipotle chile powder, and ⅛ teaspoon ground cumin in a small bowl, stirring until smooth. Place 2 ears of corn on a grill rack coated with cooking spray. Grill 15 minutes, turning occasionally. Spread butter mixture evenly over hot corn until melted.

Coleslaw

Game Plan

1 While the grill preheats:
• Season chicken.
2 While chicken cooks:
• Prepare butter mixture for corn.
• Grill corn.
• Prepare coleslaw.

QUICK & EASY
Quick Barbecue Chicken

Rub the spice paste under the skin of the chicken breast, and grill for a simple, delicious late-summer dinner. Leave the skin on the chicken as it cooks so the breasts will remain juicy, and discard skin just before serving.
Total time: 45 minutes

    2   teaspoons olive oil
    1   teaspoon sugar
    1   teaspoon chili powder
    ½   teaspoon salt
    ¼   teaspoon garlic powder
    ¼   teaspoon ground cumin
    ⅛   teaspoon ground ginger
    ⅛   teaspoon ground cinnamon
    ⅛   teaspoon freshly ground black pepper
    2   (8-ounce) bone-in chicken breast halves
        Cooking spray

Continued

❶ Prepare grill.

❷ Combine first 9 ingredients in a bowl, stirring well. Loosen skin from chicken by inserting fingers, gently pushing between skin and meat; rub spice mixture evenly under skin over meat. Lightly coat skin with cooking spray. Place chicken, breast sides down, on a grill rack coated with cooking spray; grill 30 minutes or until a thermometer inserted in thickest part registers 165°, turning twice. Let stand 10 minutes. Remove skin; discard. Yield: 2 servings (serving size: 1 chicken breast half).

CALORIES 308 (28% from fat); FAT 9.7g (sat 2.1g, mono 5g, poly 1.6g); PROTEIN 49.4g; CARB 2.7g; FIBER 0.3g; CHOL 131mg; IRON 1.7mg; SODIUM 738mg; CALC 27mg

SUPERFAST
20 Minute Dishes

From shrimp to salmon, chicken to lamb, here are simple, fresh, and easy meals you can make superfast.

QUICK & EASY
Black-Eyed Pea Cakes with Adobo Cream

Serve with rice dusted with salt-free Creole seasoning and a simple tomato salad.

- ¼ cup fat-free sour cream
- 1 teaspoon adobo sauce
- 1 (15.8-ounce) can no-salt-added black-eyed peas, rinsed and drained
- ¼ cup dry breadcrumbs
- 1 tablespoon finely chopped onion
- ½ teaspoon bottled minced garlic
- ½ teaspoon ground cumin
- ½ teaspoon salt
- ¼ teaspoon black pepper
- 1 large egg, lightly beaten
- 1 large egg white, lightly beaten
- 1½ teaspoons olive oil
- ¼ cup (about 1 ounce) shredded Monterey Jack cheese

❶ Combine sour cream and adobo sauce in a small bowl.

❷ Place peas in a medium bowl; partially mash with a fork. Stir in breadcrumbs and next 7 ingredients. With floured hands, divide pea mixture into 4 equal portions, shaping each portion into a ½-inch-thick patty.

❸ Heat oil in a large nonstick skillet over medium-high heat. Add patties to pan; cook 2 minutes on each side or until golden and thoroughly heated. Remove from pan; top each cake with 1 tablespoon cheese. Serve with sour cream mixture. Yield: 4 servings (serving size: 1 patty and about 1 tablespoon sauce).

CALORIES 173 (33% from fat); FAT 6.3g (sat 2.1g, mono 2.4g, poly 0.9g); PROTEIN 10.2g; CARB 19.3g; FIBER 3.6g; CHOL 59mg; IRON 2mg; SODIUM 462mg; CALC 118mg

QUICK & EASY
Open-Faced Chicken and Muenster Sandwiches with Apricot-Dijon Spread

Inspired by French bistro fare, this sandwich is good with simple baked chips or a fruit salad.

- 4 teaspoons apricot preserves
- 4 teaspoons Dijon mustard
- 4 (2-ounce) slices country bread
- Cooking spray
- 1 cup thinly sliced peeled Ambrosia or Fuji apple (about ⅓ pound)
- ¼ cup prechopped onion
- 2½ cups bagged prewashed spinach
- 2 cups shredded skinless, boneless rotisserie chicken breast (about 12 ounces)
- 4 (1-ounce) Muenster cheese slices

❶ Preheat broiler.

❷ Combine preserves and mustard in a small bowl; stir with a whisk. Spread 1 side of each bread slice with 2 teaspoons mustard mixture. Place bread slices, mustard mixture sides up, on a baking sheet coated with cooking spray.

❸ Heat a large skillet over medium-high heat. Coat pan with cooking spray. Add apple and onion to pan; cook 3 minutes or until tender, stirring occasionally. Add spinach; cook 1 minute or until spinach begins to wilt. Layer each of 4 bread slices with ¼ cup spinach mixture, ½ cup chicken, and 1 cheese slice. Broil sandwiches 1½ minutes or until cheese is bubbly. Remove from heat, and serve immediately. Yield: 4 servings (serving size: 1 sandwich).

CALORIES 440 (27% from fat); FAT 13.2g (sat 6.3g, mono 3.8g, poly 1.4g); PROTEIN 38.7g; CARB 40g; FIBER 2.4g; CHOL 100mg; IRON 3.6mg; SODIUM 750mg; CALC 286mg

QUICK & EASY
Herbes de Provence Lamb Chops with Orzo

Garnish each plate with a lemon wedge and thyme sprig, and pair with a glass of fruity red wine to create a Provençal menu.

- 1 cup uncooked orzo
- ⅔ cup torn spinach
- ½ cup chopped red bell pepper
- ⅓ cup sliced green onions
- 2 teaspoons grated lemon rind
- 2 teaspoons chopped fresh parsley
- 2 teaspoons olive oil
- ½ teaspoon salt, divided
- 1 tablespoon dried herbes de Provence
- 1 tablespoon Dijon mustard
- ¼ teaspoon freshly ground black pepper
- 8 (3-ounce) lamb loin chops
- Cooking spray

❶ Preheat broiler.

❷ Prepare pasta according to package directions, omitting salt and fat. Drain. Combine pasta, spinach, and next 5 ingredients in a medium bowl. Stir in ¼ teaspoon salt.

❸ Combine remaining ¼ teaspoon salt, herbes de Provence, mustard, and pepper in a small bowl. Rub lamb evenly with herb mixture. Place on a broiler pan coated with cooking spray; broil 6 minutes or until desired degree of doneness,

turning once halfway through cooking.
Serve with pasta mixture. Yield: 4 servings (serving size: 2 lamb chops and ½
cup pasta mixture).

CALORIES 471 (30% from fat); FAT 15.6g (sat 4.8g, mono 7.1g,
poly 1.1g); PROTEIN 44.1g; CARB 35.3g; FIBER 2.9g;
CHOL 121mg; IRON 4.4mg; SODIUM 499mg; CALC 48mg

Smoky Shrimp and Parmesan-Polenta Cakes

Smoked paprika, available in supermarkets, is nice to spice up sour cream, eggs,
or rice. Its pungency offsets the shrimp's
sweetness.

 1 tablespoon olive oil
 1 pound peeled and deveined medium
    shrimp
 ¼ cup dry white wine
 1 tablespoon chopped fresh chives
 1 tablespoon fresh lemon juice
 ¼ teaspoon Spanish smoked paprika
 1 (17-ounce) tube polenta, cut into
    8 (½-inch) slices
 Cooking spray
 8 teaspoons marinara sauce
 8 teaspoons grated fresh Parmesan
    cheese
 1 tablespoon chopped fresh flat-leaf
    parsley

❶ Preheat broiler.
❷ Heat oil in a large skillet over medium-high heat. Add shrimp to pan; sauté 3
minutes or until done, stirring frequently. Remove from heat; stir in wine
and next 3 ingredients, tossing to coat.
Keep warm.
❸ Place polenta slices on a baking sheet
coated with cooking spray. Top each slice
with 1 teaspoon sauce and 1 teaspoon
cheese; broil 3 minutes or until cheese
melts. Place 2 polenta slices on each of 4
plates; top each serving evenly with
shrimp mixture. Sprinkle with parsley.
Yield: 4 servings.

CALORIES 231 (21% from fat); FAT 5.4g (sat 1.3g, mono 2.9g,
poly 0.8g); PROTEIN 21.7g; CARB 18.8g; FIBER 2.4g;
CHOL 171mg; IRON 3.7mg; SODIUM 386mg; CALC 75mg

Sirloin Steaks with Mushroom Sauce and Chive-Garlic Potatoes

Serve with sautéed haricots verts.

 4 (4-ounce) boneless sirloin steaks,
    trimmed (about 1 inch thick)
 ⅜ teaspoon black pepper, divided
 ¼ teaspoon salt, divided
 1 tablespoon olive oil
 1 (8-ounce) package sliced cremini
    mushrooms
 ½ cup dry red wine
 ½ cup water
 2 teaspoons all-purpose flour
 1 (24-ounce) package refrigerated
    mashed potatoes
 ⅓ cup chopped chives
 ½ teaspoon garlic powder

❶ Sprinkle steaks evenly with ¼ teaspoon
pepper and ⅛ teaspoon salt. Heat oil in a
large nonstick skillet over medium-high
heat. Reduce heat to medium. Add steaks
to pan; cook 2 minutes on each side or until desired degree of doneness. Remove
from pan; keep warm.
❷ Add mushrooms to pan; cook 5 minutes or until tender and beginning to
brown, stirring frequently. Combine
wine, ½ cup water, flour, remaining
⅛ teaspoon pepper, and remaining
⅛ teaspoon salt; stir well with a whisk.
Add wine mixture to pan; bring to a boil.
Cook 2 minutes or until thick; stir constantly. Remove from heat.
❸ Prepare potatoes according to package
directions. Stir in chives and garlic
powder. Place ¾ cup potatoes on each of
4 plates. Top each with 1 steak and about
¼ cup mushroom sauce. Yield: 4 servings.

CALORIES 326 (29% from fat); FAT 10.4g (sat 3.4g, mono 4.9g,
poly 0.7g); PROTEIN 28.4g; CARB 29.8g; FIBER 3.6g;
CHOL 69mg; IRON 4.1mg; SODIUM 682mg; CALC 46mg

Mediterranean Salmon Salad

Shorter pastas like orzo generally cook
faster than the longer varieties. In a pinch,
use canned drained wild sockeye
salmon—and flake with two forks—in
place of the sautéed fillets.

 ½ cup uncooked orzo
 2 (6-ounce) salmon fillets (about
    1 inch thick)
 ¼ teaspoon salt
 ¼ teaspoon dried oregano
 ⅛ teaspoon black pepper
 Cooking spray
 2 cups torn spinach
 ½ cup chopped red bell pepper
 ¼ cup chopped green onions
 3 tablespoons fresh lemon juice
 2 tablespoons crumbled feta cheese
 4 kalamata olives, pitted and chopped

❶ Preheat broiler.
❷ Cook pasta according to package
directions, omitting salt and fat.
❸ Sprinkle fillets evenly with salt, oregano, and black pepper. Place on a broiler
pan coated with cooking spray. Broil 10
minutes or until fish flakes easily when
tested with a fork or until desired degree
of doneness. Let stand 5 minutes; break
into bite-sized pieces with 2 forks.
❹ Combine pasta, fish, spinach, and
remaining ingredients in a medium
bowl; toss well. Yield: 4 servings (serving
size: 1 cup).

CALORIES 231 (30% from fat); FAT 7.7g (sat 1.6g, mono 2.7g,
poly 2.3g); PROTEIN 20.3g; CARB 19.3g; FIBER 1.8g;
CHOL 49mg; IRON 1.3mg; SODIUM 310mg; CALC 56mg

Better Breakfast Rolls

An Ohio reader seeks a nutritional overhaul of her grandmother's sweet favorite.

For more than 50 years, Philomena Olivo, the grandmother of Angela Thompson of Cleveland, Ohio, has delighted friends and family with her irresistible Pecan Sticky Rolls. These yeast-raised cinnamon buns are extravagant: The butter- and egg-enriched dough is formed into oversized bakery-style rolls smothered in a gooey brown sugar–butter sauce and topped with pecans. Thompson recently had a private baking lesson with her grandmother during which Olivo divulged the secrets of this treasured family recipe. However, with the knowledge of just how much butter, sugar, and eggs go into the sweet pastry, Thompson decided she needed an updated version to enjoy these special treats while adhering to a healthful lifestyle.

Portion size was an issue here, so our first step was to increase the recipe's yield from six servings to 15 still generously sized rolls. Then we used skim milk instead of whole and ½ cup egg substitute in place of the egg to shave a few calories while maintaining the dough's richness. The filling and rich sauce are the high-fat and calorie culprits, so we halved the butter in both components to trim 30 calories and five grams of fat (three grams saturated) per roll. To curb calories, we reduced the granulated sugar in the filling by one-third and the brown sugar in the sauce by one-fourth to drop another 20 calories per portion. Using dark brown sugar—which has a higher moisture content and stronger molasses flavor than light brown sugar—offers richness and preserves the stickiness of the sauce. We also used fewer high-calorie pecans (and toasted them to intensify their flavor), cutting another 10 calories per serving.

serving size: 1 roll		
	before	after
CALORIES PER SERVING	835	275
FAT	35.6g	7.6g
PERCENT OF TOTAL CALORIES	38%	25%

STAFF FAVORITE
Pecan Sticky Rolls

DOUGH:
- ¾ cup warm skim milk (100° to 110°)
- ¼ cup granulated sugar
- ½ teaspoon salt
- 1 package dry yeast (about 2¼ teaspoons)
- ¼ cup warm water (100° to 110°)
- ½ cup egg substitute
- 3 tablespoons butter, melted and cooled
- 4 cups all-purpose flour (about 18 ounces), divided
- Cooking spray

SAUCE:
- ¾ cup packed dark brown sugar
- 3 tablespoons butter, melted
- 2 tablespoons hot water
- ⅓ cup finely chopped pecans, toasted

FILLING:
- ⅔ cup granulated sugar
- 1 tablespoon ground cinnamon
- 1½ tablespoons butter, melted

1. To prepare dough, combine first 3 ingredients in a large bowl.
2. Dissolve yeast in ¼ cup warm water in a small bowl; let stand 5 minutes. Stir yeast mixture into milk mixture. Add egg substitute and 3 tablespoons melted butter; stir until well combined.
3. Lightly spoon flour into dry measuring cups; level with a knife. Add 3¾ cups flour to yeast mixture; stir until smooth. Turn dough out onto a lightly floured surface. Knead until smooth and elastic (about 8 minutes); add enough of remaining ¼ cup flour, 1 tablespoon at a time, to prevent dough from sticking to hands (dough will feel slightly soft and tacky).
4. Place dough in a large bowl coated with cooking spray; turn to coat top. Cover and let rise in a warm place (85°), free from drafts, 45 minutes. Punch dough down and turn over in bowl; lightly coat with cooking spray. Cover and let rise 45 minutes. Punch dough down; cover and let rest 5 minutes.
5. To prepare sauce, combine brown sugar, 3 tablespoons butter, and 2 tablespoons hot water in a small bowl; stir with a whisk until smooth. Scrape brown sugar mixture into a 13 x 9–inch baking pan coated with cooking spray, spreading evenly with a spatula. Sprinkle brown sugar mixture evenly with pecans, and set aside.
6. To prepare filling, combine ⅔ cup granulated sugar and cinnamon in a small bowl. Turn dough out onto a lightly floured surface; pat dough into a 16 x 12–inch rectangle. Brush surface of dough with 1½ tablespoons melted butter. Sprinkle granulated sugar mixture evenly over dough, leaving a ½-inch border. Beginning with a long side, roll up jelly-roll fashion; pinch seam to seal (do not seal ends of roll). Cut roll into 15 slices (approximately 1 inch wide). Arrange slices, cut sides up, in prepared pan. Lightly coat rolls with cooking spray; cover and let rise in a warm place (85°), free from drafts, 30 minutes or until doubled in size.
7. Preheat oven to 350°.
8. Uncover rolls, and bake at 350° for 20 minutes or until lightly browned. Let stand 1 minute; carefully invert onto serving platter. Yield: 15 servings (serving size: 1 roll).

CALORIES 275 (25% from fat); FAT 7.6g (sat 3.8g, mono 2.6g, poly 0.8g); PROTEIN 4.9g; CARB 47g; FIBER 1.4g; CHOL 15mg; IRON 2.2mg; SODIUM 146mg; CALC 37mg

Market Basket Challenge

We asked some of our favorite cooks to prepare a recipe using the same items. The result: seven deliciously different innovations.

AT PARIS'S RENOWNED cooking school Le Cordon Bleu, the test known as *le panier* (French for "basket") strikes fear in the hearts of aspiring professional chefs. The challenge begins with a "basket"—not an actual woven container, but rather a short list of ingredients the students must transform into a cohesive recipe. They hope for harmonious items, such as basil, cheese, and tomatoes, but prepare for any possible combination, knowing a good cook has to think on his or her feet.

It's a common way to test the inventiveness of chefs in training and professionals alike. According to John Kinsella, certified master chef and president of the American Culinary Federation, professional chefs in Germany's Kuchenmeister, England's Master Craftsman, and France's Compagnon de France are put through similar paces. It has also been a requirement in America's Certified Master Chef exam since 1980.

We thought it would be interesting to create a *Cooking Light* challenge for some of our favorite chefs, cookbook authors, and teachers. We chose cooks from far-ranging backgrounds, knowing that each would bring particular tastes and talents to the table. Next we devised an autumn market basket, filled with some of our favorite and most versatile seasonal ingredients (see "Rules of Engagement" below). As is standard with basket challenges, we gave them a list of required ingredients, as well as a list of optional items. Some (butternut squash, apples) would likely find easy harmonies, while others (mushrooms, hot peppers) would take some finesse.

It was no problem for these cooks. One was inspired by *soupe au pistou* (a classic French summer vegetable soup), and with the addition of chicken and fall ingredients, it took on American flair and tastes like Thanksgiving in New England. Another brought Chinese flavor principles into the mix. A third saw the ingredients and created the season's first braise. All their recipes demonstrate that the same ingredients can yield a variety of dishes.

Rules of Engagement

We asked each of our challenge cooks to prepare a healthful, balanced, and tasty meal following these guidelines:
• Base the dish on either a whole chicken or pork chops.
• Use at least six of the following seven ingredients: butternut squash, apples, mushrooms, walnuts, bacon, Swiss chard, and hot peppers.

• Freely add any common cold storage or pantry staples, such as broth, canned tomatoes, salt and pepper, onions, garlic, carrots, or citrus fruits.
• Add one optional ingredient of your choice.
• Pair the dish with an appropriate starch to round out the meal.

Four-Star Home Cooking

What separates a four-star chef from the rest of us? We might see a basket of ingredients in search of a recipe, while **Eric Ripert** finds a cornucopia of "infinite possibilities." Our basket offered "all the great products you could find in your greenmarket in the fall," says the chef and co-owner of New York's Le Bernardin. Working with three principles—comfort, elegance, and healthfulness—he fashioned a pan-roasted chicken with a hearty, unexpected, and simply assembled autumn salad. It's a four-star dish anyone can prepare.

STAFF FAVORITE
Pan-Roasted Chicken, Squash, and Chard Salad with Bacon Vinaigrette
(pictured on page 261)

Ripert starts with one whole roasting chicken and quarters it; you can purchase the parts separately as the recipe directs.

CHICKEN:
- 2 bone-in chicken breast halves
- 2 chicken leg quarters
- ½ teaspoon salt
- ¼ teaspoon freshly ground black pepper
- 2 teaspoons canola oil

SALAD:
- 1⅔ cups sliced Fuji apple
- 1 tablespoon fresh lemon juice
- 8 ounces Swiss chard leaves, thinly sliced
- 1 tablespoon butter
- 4¼ cups (¼-inch) cubed peeled butternut squash (about 1½ pounds)
- ¼ teaspoon salt
- ¼ teaspoon freshly ground black pepper, divided
- 3 tablespoons maple syrup

Continued

2 bacon slices, cut crosswise into
   ½-inch pieces
8 ounces wild mushrooms, halved
2 garlic cloves, minced
3 tablespoons apple cider vinegar
¼ cup fat-free, less-sodium chicken
   broth

REMAINING INGREDIENT:

3 tablespoons walnuts, toasted and
   coarsely chopped

❶ Preheat oven to 400°.

❷ To prepare chicken, loosen skin from breast halves and leg quarters by inserting fingers, gently pushing between skin and meat. Combine ½ teaspoon salt and ¼ teaspoon pepper; rub salt mixture evenly under loosened skin. Heat oil in a large ovenproof skillet over medium-high heat. Add chicken, skin side down, to pan; cook 5 minutes or until brown. Bake at 400° for 28 minutes or until a thermometer registers 165°. Remove chicken from pan; let stand 10 minutes. Discard skin. Place a zip-top plastic bag inside a 2-cup glass measure. Pour drippings into bag; let stand 10 minutes (fat will rise to top). Seal bag; carefully snip off 1 bottom corner of bag. Drain drippings into a bowl, stopping before fat layer reaches opening. Reserve drippings and 2 tablespoons fat; discard remaining fat.

❸ To prepare salad, combine apple, juice, and chard in a large bowl; toss to coat. Melt butter in a large skillet over medium-high heat. Add squash to pan; sprinkle with ¼ teaspoon salt and ⅛ teaspoon pepper. Cook 10 minutes or until tender, turning to brown on all sides. Remove from heat; stir in syrup. Add squash mixture to apple mixture. Sprinkle salad with remaining ⅛ teaspoon pepper; toss.

❹ To prepare vinaigrette, heat reserved 2 tablespoons chicken fat in pan over medium heat. Add bacon to pan; cook 4 minutes or until crisp, stirring occasionally. Add mushrooms and garlic to bacon mixture; cook 3 minutes, stirring frequently. Stir in vinegar, scraping pan to

loosen browned bits; cook 1 minute or until liquid evaporates. Stir in reserved chicken drippings and broth; bring to a boil. Remove from heat. Arrange 2 cups apple mixture on each of 4 plates; drizzle each serving with ¼ cup vinaigrette. Top each serving with 1 chicken breast half or 1 leg quarter, and sprinkle each serving with 2¼ teaspoons walnuts. Yield: 4 servings.

CALORIES 488 (35% from fat); FAT 19.2g (sat 5.2g, mono 6.4g, poly 5.3g); PROTEIN 41.5g; CARB 40.8g; FIBER 6g; CHOL 128mg; IRON 5.1mg; SODIUM 845mg; CALC 143mg

---

Southwest Touch

They may have four James Beard Awards to their credit, but cookbook authors **Cheryl Alters Jamison** and **Bill Jamison** know that not every culinary experiment is a success. "We started out with a smothered pork chop, but the butternut squash just overwhelmed the pork," recalls Cheryl. However, a walnut-crusted chop paired well with wild rice into which they tossed the remaining market basket ingredients. Did the jalapeño find a home? That goes without saying for a couple who make their home near Santa Fe, New Mexico. "We always enjoy a little of that picante touch," Cheryl says.

Walnut-Crusted Pork Chops with Autumn Vegetable Wild Rice

(pictured on page 262)

Apples, mushrooms, and Swiss chard make a nice contrast to the wild rice's crunchy texture.

PORK:

4 (4-ounce) boneless center-cut pork
   chops, trimmed
1½ teaspoons Worcestershire sauce
¾ teaspoon kosher salt
½ teaspoon dried sage
¼ teaspoon black pepper
⅓ cup walnuts, finely ground
1 bacon slice
¼ cup fat-free, less-sodium chicken
   broth

RICE:

   Cooking spray
1 cup finely chopped onion
½ cup diced carrot
2 teaspoons diced seeded jalapeño
   pepper
1 garlic clove, minced
1½ cups finely trimmed chopped Swiss
   chard
1 cup sliced cremini mushrooms
1 cup chopped peeled Granny Smith
   apple
2 cups cooked wild rice
½ cup fat-free, less-sodium chicken
   broth
¼ cup chopped fresh flat-leaf parsley

❶ To prepare pork, place chops in a shallow dish; drizzle evenly with Worcestershire. Combine salt, sage, and black pepper in a small bowl. Reserve ¾ teaspoon salt mixture. Add walnuts to remaining salt mixture; toss well. Press walnut mixture onto both sides of pork. Cover and refrigerate 30 minutes.

❷ Cook bacon in a large nonstick skillet over medium heat until crisp. Remove bacon from pan; crumble. Add pork to drippings in pan; cook 1½ minutes on each side or until lightly browned. Add ¼ cup broth to pan. Cover, reduce heat, and cook 6 minutes or until desired degree of doneness. Remove pork from pan.

❸ To prepare rice, heat a large saucepan over medium heat. Coat pan with cooking spray. Add onion and next 3 ingredients; cover and cook 5 minutes or until onion is tender. Stir in reserved ¾ teaspoon salt mixture, chard, mushrooms, and apple. Cover and cook 5 minutes or until carrot is tender. Stir in rice and ½ cup broth. Bring to a simmer; cook, uncovered, 5 minutes or until liquid is absorbed. Stir in bacon. Place 1 cup rice mixture on each of 4 plates; top each serving with 1 pork chop. Drizzle each serving with pan drippings; sprinkle each with 1 tablespoon parsley. Yield: 4 servings.

CALORIES 379 (35% from fat); FAT 14.7g (sat 3.5g, mono 4.4g, poly 5.5g); PROTEIN 29.1g; CARB 34.6g; FIBER 5g; CHOL 69mg; IRON 2.6mg; SODIUM 600mg; CALC 65mg

Franco-American Creation

The culinary brains behind the rapidly expanding BLT group of restaurants in New York City, and across the country in Washington D.C., Los Angeles, Las Vegas, Puerto Rico, and White Plains, New York, **Laurent Tourondel** earned fame by reinterpreting simple American favorites, such as steaks and hamburgers, from a French perspective. For example, his BLT Steak restaurants offer American steak house–style dishes prepared using French techniques. For this challenge, he says, "I was inspired by the French classic soupe au pistou, but used decidedly American fall ingredients for the soup. The walnut pesto adds flavor, color, and body."

Chicken Barley Soup with Walnut Pesto

Habanero peppers are fiery hot, so handle them carefully. In this dish, you simply pierce the chile with a fork and float it in the broth as the soup cooks. Remove it with a slotted spoon before serving.

SOUP:

- 5 bacon slices, chopped
- 1½ cups chopped onion
- 2 tablespoons minced fresh garlic
- 2 (4-inch) portobello mushroom caps, chopped
- 1 (3-pound) whole chicken, skinned
- 1 thyme sprig
- 4½ quarts cold water
- 8 ounces Swiss chard
- 1 cup uncooked pearl barley, rinsed and drained
- 1 cup (½-inch) cubed peeled butternut squash
- ½ cup finely chopped carrot
- ½ cup finely chopped celery
- ¼ cup finely chopped Granny Smith apple
- 1 habanero pepper
- ¾ teaspoon salt
- ¼ teaspoon black pepper

PESTO:

- ¼ cup walnuts, toasted
- ¼ cup (1 ounce) freshly grated Parmigiano-Reggiano cheese
- 2 tablespoons extravirgin olive oil
- 1 tablespoon minced fresh garlic
- ¼ teaspoon salt

① Cook bacon in a large skillet over medium heat until crisp. Add onion, garlic, and mushrooms to pan; cook 5 minutes, stirring frequently. Set aside.

② Remove and discard giblets and neck from chicken. Place chicken and thyme in a large Dutch oven over medium heat. Cover with 4½ quarts water; bring to a simmer. Skim fat from surface; discard. Remove stems and center ribs from Swiss chard. Coarsely chop stems and ribs; reserve leaves. Add stems, ribs, barley, and next 4 ingredients to pan; bring to a simmer. Pierce habanero with a fork; add to pan. Cook 35 minutes or until chicken is done.

③ Remove chicken from pan; cool slightly. Remove meat from bones; chop meat. Discard bones, thyme sprig, and habanero. Drain barley mixture in a sieve over a bowl. Reserve 4 cups broth for another use. Return remaining 6 cups broth to pan; bring to a boil. Cook 10 minutes. Return chicken and barley mixture to pan; bring to a simmer. Add mushroom mixture. Cook 2 minutes or until thoroughly heated. Stir in ¾ teaspoon salt and black pepper.

④ To prepare pesto, cook Swiss chard leaves in boiling water 2 minutes. Drain and rinse with cold water; drain. Place leaves, walnuts, and remaining ingredients in a food processor; process until smooth. Serve with soup. Yield: 8 servings (serving size: 1¾ cups soup and 2 tablespoons pesto).

CALORIES 416 (30% from fat); FAT 13.7g (sat 3.1g, mono 5.6g, poly 3.7g); PROTEIN 41.8g; CARB 31.7g; FIBER 6.6g; CHOL 117mg; IRON 3.5mg; SODIUM 641mg; CALC 78mg

Big Easy Flavor

New Orleanian **John Besh** likes to draw on the rich culinary heritage of his hometown while using local ingredients produced in a sustainable manner. He raises heritage-breed Berkshire hogs on his farm and prefers their superior flavor. He met our challenge with stuffed pork chops—a dish sure to appeal to his four young sons. The chef may source Kobe beef and Maine lobster for the menu at his downtown restaurant August, but he says it's a different story at home. "My wife does all the shopping," he says. "It's not uncommon for me to just open up the fridge and start cooking based on whatever she bought."

Stuffed Heritage Pork Chops with Creamy Grits

The inspiration for this dish is a Creole classic, grillades and grits. Look for Berkshire, Duroc, and other heritage pork at specialty markets.

PORK:

- 4 cups water
- 4 cups fresh orange juice
- ½ cup coarsely chopped jalapeño pepper (about 2 peppers)
- ¼ cup packed brown sugar
- 2½ tablespoons fine sea salt
- 4 (8-ounce) bone-in center-cut heritage pork chops (such as Berkshire)
- 2 slices bacon
- ½ cup finely diced onion
- ¼ cup finely diced apple
- ¼ cup thinly sliced mushrooms
- ¼ cup finely chopped peeled butternut squash
- ¼ cup finely chopped Swiss chard
- 1 garlic clove, minced
- ¼ teaspoon salt
- ¼ teaspoon freshly ground black pepper
- 1 tablespoon olive oil

Continued

SAUCE:

- 1½ cups finely chopped onion
- ¼ cup finely chopped celery
- 1 teaspoon minced jalapeño pepper
- 1 garlic clove, minced
- 2 tablespoons all-purpose flour
- ½ cup fat-free, less-sodium beef broth
- ½ cup water
- ½ cup no-salt-added canned whole tomatoes, coarsely chopped

GRITS:

- 2½ cups water
- ⅛ teaspoon salt
- ½ cup stone-ground grits
- 1 tablespoon butter
- 2 tablespoons fat-free, less-sodium beef broth

❶ To prepare pork, combine first 5 ingredients in an airtight container, stirring until sugar dissolves. Add pork; seal and refrigerate 8 hours or overnight. Remove pork from brine; pat dry. Discard brine.
❷ Cook bacon in a nonstick skillet over medium heat until crisp. Remove bacon from pan; crumble. Add ½ cup onion and next 5 ingredients to drippings in pan; cook 8 minutes or until squash is tender and liquid evaporates, stirring frequently. Stir in bacon.
❸ Cut 1 (1-inch) horizontal slit through thickest portion of each pork chop to form pockets. Stuff about 3 tablespoons vegetable mixture into each chop. Sprinkle both sides of chops evenly with ¼ teaspoon salt and ¼ teaspoon black pepper. Heat oil in a large cast-iron skillet over high heat. Add pork to pan; cook 3 minutes on each side or until browned. Remove pork from pan; reduce heat to medium-low.
❹ To prepare sauce, add 1½ cups onion to pan; cook 4 minutes or until browned, stirring frequently. Add celery, jalapeño, and garlic to pan; cook 3 minutes, stirring constantly. Stir in flour; cook 1 minute. Add ½ cup broth and ½ cup water, stirring until flour dissolves. Add tomatoes; increase heat to medium-high. Return pork to pan; simmer 10 minutes or until desired degree of doneness.

❺ To prepare grits, bring 2½ cups water and ⅛ teaspoon salt to a boil in a saucepan. Slowly add grits, stirring constantly. Reduce heat, and simmer 20 minutes or until liquid is absorbed, stirring frequently. Remove from heat; stir in butter and 2 tablespoons broth. Serve with pork and sauce. Yield: 4 servings (serving size: ½ cup grits, 1 pork chop, and ⅓ cup sauce).

CALORIES 475 (35% from fat); FAT 18.5g (sat 6.8g, mono 8.7g, poly 1.6g); PROTEIN 40.6g; CARB 35.5g; FIBER 3.2g; CHOL 111mg; IRON 2.9mg; SODIUM 954mg; CALC 73mg

---

A Moment of Panic

Bay Area cooking teacher, cookbook author, and PBS television host **Joanne Weir** welcomed the challenge because she teaches her students to improvise. "See what looks freshest in the market and go from there," she always advises. But when she saw our particular market basket, she had a moment of panic. "Jalapeños and mushrooms? I almost bowed out." Then she went through the list ingredient by ingredient. The walnuts and bacon combined with butter to moisten the pork chop, while the greens could be wilted and layered with the apples and vegetables into a pretty tian. When she remembered how well a bit of hot pepper perks up wilted greens, she had her jalapeño.

Cider-Brined Pork Chops with Walnut-Bacon Butter and Apple and Butternut Squash Tian

Brining yields wonderfully moist chops. *Tian,* a French word that refers to shallow earthen casserole dishes, also refers to the layered vegetables that are often cooked in them.

PORK:

- 5 cups apple cider
- 2 cups water
- ⅓ cup kosher salt
- 6 (8-ounce) bone-in center-cut pork chops, trimmed

TIAN:

- 1 teaspoon extravirgin olive oil
- 3 cups coarsely chopped Swiss chard
- 1 teaspoon minced seeded jalapeño pepper
- 2 garlic cloves, minced
- 8 ounces butternut squash, peeled and cut into ⅛-inch-thick slices
- 1 large Rome apple, peeled, cored, and cut into ⅛-inch-thick slices (about 6½ ounces)
- 1 pound Yukon gold potatoes, peeled and cut into ⅛-inch-thick slices
- Cooking spray
- ½ teaspoon salt
- ½ teaspoon freshly ground black pepper
- ½ cup apple cider
- ¼ cup fat-free, less-sodium chicken broth
- 1 (1-ounce) slice white bread
- ¼ cup (1 ounce) shredded Gruyère cheese

WALNUT BUTTER:

- 2 tablespoons finely chopped walnuts, toasted
- 2 tablespoons unsalted butter, softened
- ½ teaspoon grated orange rind
- ¼ teaspoon freshly ground black pepper
- Dash of ground nutmeg
- 1 slice applewood-smoked bacon, cooked and finely crumbled

REMAINING INGREDIENT:

- ¼ teaspoon freshly ground black pepper

❶ To prepare pork, combine first 3 ingredients in a large bowl; stir until salt dissolves. Add pork chops to cider mixture; cover and refrigerate 2 hours.
❷ Preheat oven to 425°.
❸ To prepare tian, heat oil in a large nonstick skillet over medium-high heat. Add chard, jalapeño, and garlic to pan; sauté 3 minutes or until chard wilts, stirring occasionally. Layer half of squash, apple, potatoes, and chard mixture in a shallow 2-quart broiler-safe baking dish coated with cooking spray. Sprinkle vegetables

with ¼ teaspoon salt and ¼ teaspoon black pepper. Repeat layers with remaining squash, apple, potato, chard mixture, ¼ teaspoon salt, and ¼ teaspoon black pepper. Combine ½ cup cider and broth; pour mixture into baking dish. Cover dish with foil. Bake at 425° for 50 minutes or until vegetables are tender.

❹ Preheat broiler.

❺ Place bread in a food processor; pulse 10 times or until coarse crumbs measure 1 cup. Combine breadcrumbs and cheese; sprinkle over vegetable mixture. Broil 2 minutes or until breadcrumbs are browned. Remove from broiler, and keep warm.

❻ To prepare walnut butter, combine walnuts and next 5 ingredients in a bowl, stirring well.

❼ Remove pork from brine mixture; discard brine mixture. Pat pork dry with paper towels. Sprinkle pork with ¼ teaspoon black pepper. Heat a large nonstick skillet over medium-high heat. Coat pan with cooking spray. Add pork to pan; cook 5 minutes on each side or until a thermometer registers 155° or until desired degree of doneness. Place about 1 cup tian on each of 6 plates; top each serving with 1 pork chop. Divide walnut butter evenly among pork chops. Yield: 6 servings.

CALORIES 369 (35% from fat); FAT 14.5g (sat 5.9g, mono 5.2g, poly 2g); PROTEIN 28.1g; CARB 32.8g; FIBER 3.2g; CHOL 77mg; IRON 2.1mg; SODIUM 840mg; CALC 120mg

---

East Meets West

Cookbook author and teacher **Corinne Trang** wanted to fashion an Asian dish with butternut squash and apples, and admits her first idea—stuffed apples—was a "disaster." But once she started pondering an Eastern answer to Thanksgiving dinner, her chicken with veggie-and-bacon-flecked brown rice stuffing came into focus. The key for her was to hit the five flavor notes of Chinese cooking—sweet, sour, bitter, salty, and spicy—for balance.

Roast Chicken with Sticky Rice Skillet Stuffing

Look for brown sticky rice at Asian markets, or use white sticky rice if you prefer. To make this meal as healthful as possible, Trang did not use any fat other than what comes naturally from the chicken and bacon.

CHICKEN:
- ½ cup cilantro leaves
- 1 teaspoon grated lemon rind
- 1 tablespoon fresh lemon juice
- ¼ teaspoon kosher salt
- ½ serrano chile
- 4 garlic cloves, peeled and divided
- 1 (3-pound) whole chicken

SAUCE:
- ½ cup fat-free, less-sodium chicken broth
- 1 teaspoon all-purpose flour
- 1 teaspoon maple syrup
- ⅛ teaspoon freshly ground black pepper

STUFFING:
- 1 slice applewood-smoked bacon
- ¼ cup minced onion
- 1 tablespoon minced peeled fresh ginger
- 2 garlic cloves, minced
- 3½ cups trimmed, chopped Swiss chard leaves
- 1 cup shiitake mushrooms caps, thinly sliced (about 2 ounces)
- 1 cup brown short-grain sticky sweet rice
- 2¾ cups fat-free, less-sodium chicken broth
- ½ cup diced butternut squash
- 1 tablespoon maple syrup
- ¼ teaspoon freshly ground black pepper
- ⅓ cup chopped walnuts, toasted

❶ Preheat oven to 375°.

❷ To prepare chicken, combine first 5 ingredients in a food processor. Add 2 garlic cloves; pulse until finely chopped. Remove and discard giblets and neck from chicken. Starting at neck cavity, loosen skin from breast and drumsticks by inserting fingers, gently pushing between skin and meat. Pierce skin and flesh several times with a fork. Lift wing tips up and over back; tuck under chicken. Rub cilantro mixture under loosened skin and over breast and drumsticks. Place chicken, breast side up, on a roasting rack; place rack in a roasting pan. Place remaining 2 garlic cloves on pan under chicken. Bake at 375° for 45 minutes or until a thermometer inserted in meaty part of thigh registers 165°. Let stand 10 minutes. Discard skin.

❸ To prepare sauce, place roasting pan on stovetop over medium-low heat. Add ½ cup broth to pan; bring to a boil, scraping pan to loosen browned bits. Squeeze 2 roasted garlic cloves to extract pulp; discard skins. Strain broth mixture through a sieve into a small saucepan; discard solids. Add flour, stirring well with a whisk; bring to boil. Cook 1 minute, stirring constantly. Remove from heat. Stir in 1 teaspoon syrup and ⅛ teaspoon pepper.

❹ To prepare stuffing, cook bacon in a large nonstick skillet over medium heat until crisp. Remove bacon from pan; crumble. Add onion, ginger, and minced garlic to drippings in pan; cook 3 minutes or until lightly browned, stirring frequently. Stir in chard and mushrooms; cook 5 minutes or until chard wilts. Add crumbled bacon and rice; cook 30 seconds, stirring constantly. Stir in 2¾ cups broth; bring to a boil. Cover, reduce heat, and cook 45 minutes or until rice is just tender and liquid is nearly absorbed. Add squash and 1 tablespoon syrup to pan; cover and cook 10 minutes or until squash is tender. Stir in ¼ teaspoon black pepper. Sprinkle with walnuts. Yield: 4 servings (serving size: 3 ounces chicken, about 1½ teaspoons sauce, and ¾ cup stuffing.)

CALORIES 515 (23% from fat); FAT 13.4g (sat 2.3g, mono 3.4g, poly 5.6g); PROTEIN 46.1g; CARB 52g; FIBER 4.7g; CHOL 115mg; IRON 4.5mg; SODIUM 725mg; CALC 95mg

For the Love of Lentils

Braised Chicken with Mushrooms and Chard

Fresh cherry peppers have a slightly sweet note, and the heat level ranges from mild to moderate. For more spice, substitute jalapeño pepper.

- 2 tablespoons all-purpose flour
- 2 teaspoons ground cumin
- 1/8 teaspoon freshly ground black pepper
- 1/2 teaspoon salt, divided
- 2 bone-in chicken breast halves
- 2 bone-in chicken thighs
- 2 chicken drumsticks
- 4 bacon slices
- 1 cup chopped onion
- 1 cup (1/2-inch) cubed peeled butternut squash
- 1 (8-ounce) package sliced mushrooms
- 1 cup chopped Golden Delicious apple
- 1 1/2 teaspoons minced fresh garlic
- 1/4 cup dry sherry
- 4 cups chopped Swiss chard
- 1 tablespoon sliced cherry pepper
- 1 cup fat-free, less-sodium chicken broth

❶ Combine first 3 ingredients and 1/4 teaspoon salt in a shallow dish. Dredge chicken in flour mixture. Cook bacon in a large skillet over medium heat until crisp. Remove bacon from pan; crumble.

Add chicken to drippings in pan; cook 4 minutes on each side or until browned. Remove chicken from pan.
❷ Add onion, squash, and mushrooms to pan; cook 5 minutes, stirring frequently. Add apple and garlic; cook 1 minute. Stir in sherry; cook 1 minute or until liquid evaporates. Add chard; cook 2 minutes or until wilted, stirring constantly. Add cherry pepper; cook 30 seconds. Return chicken to pan; add broth. Bring mixture to a boil. Cover, reduce heat, and simmer 15 minutes or until a thermometer inserted into thickest part of chicken thigh registers 165°. Stir in remaining 1/4 teaspoon salt. Sprinkle with crumbled bacon. Yield: 4 servings (serving size: 1 chicken breast half or 1 thigh and 1 drumstick and about 1 1/4 cups vegetable mixture).

CALORIES 409 (25% from fat); FAT 11.2g (sat 3.4g, mono 4.1g, poly 2.1g); PROTEIN 52.1g; CARB 22.6g; FIBER 3.7g; CHOL 151mg; IRON 4.2mg; SODIUM 823mg; CALC 82mg

WINE NOTE: A supple red, like merlot, is a good choice for this recipe. While we normally think of white wine with chicken, this dish's smoky bacon and earthy mushrooms, along with braising, give it the rich flavors to match red. A basic Blackstone Merlot ($12), with plummy fruit, a medium body, and very soft tannins, won't overpower the dish or clash with the sweet heat of cherry peppers.

With a bag in the pantry, you'll have the start of a comforting meal or side dish.

Lentils are one of the oldest cultivated legumes and are always sold dried. They have an advantage over other dried legumes with convenience. Dried beans and peas need to be presoaked before cooking and often take more than an hour of simmering to become tender. But because lentils are small and flat, the cooking liquid doesn't have far to penetrate—so they cook relatively quickly (usually 40 minutes or less) with no need for presoaking. This makes them an ideal pantry item for weeknight suppers.

Lentils are notably high in protein (about 25 percent), so they're a great choice for vegetarians. They are also a good source of folate, iron, and fiber, and contribute some B vitamins and zinc.

They're a widely adaptable, nutritious staple that serves as the basis of many comforting, satisfying, cool-weather dishes. Their versatility easily takes them from dips to soups to salads—and cuisines from France to India to the Middle East.

Red Lentil–Rice Cakes with Simple Tomato Salsa

Crisp on the outside and creamy on the inside, these salsa-topped cakes make a lovely vegetarian entrée. They offer a great way to use leftover basmati rice; if you're starting with cooked rice, use about 1 1/2 cups.

SALSA:
- 3 cups finely chopped plum tomato (about 6 tomatoes)
- 1/4 cup chopped fresh basil
- 1 tablespoon balsamic vinegar
- 2 teaspoons capers
- 1/4 teaspoon salt

CAKES:

- 5 cups water, divided
- 1 cup dried small red lentils
- ½ cup uncooked basmati rice
- 2 tablespoons olive oil, divided
- ½ cup finely chopped red bell pepper
- ½ cup finely chopped red onion
- ½ teaspoon fennel seeds, crushed
- 2 garlic cloves, minced
- ¾ cup (3 ounces) shredded part-skim mozzarella cheese
- ¼ cup dry breadcrumbs
- 1 tablespoon chopped fresh basil
- 1 teaspoon salt
- ¼ teaspoon black pepper
- 2 large egg whites, lightly beaten

1 To prepare salsa, combine first 5 ingredients; set aside.

2 To prepare cakes, bring 4 cups water and lentils to a boil in a medium saucepan. Reduce heat; simmer 20 minutes or until tender. Drain and rinse with cold water; drain. Place lentils in a large bowl.

3 Combine remaining 1 cup water and rice in pan; bring to a boil. Cover, reduce heat, and simmer 18 minutes or until liquid is absorbed. Cool 10 minutes. Add rice to lentils.

4 Heat 1 teaspoon oil in a large nonstick skillet over medium-high heat. Add bell pepper and next 3 ingredients to pan; sauté 2 minutes or until tender. Cool 10 minutes. Add to rice mixture. Add cheese and remaining ingredients, stirring well. Let stand 10 minutes.

5 Wipe skillet clean with paper towels. Heat 2 teaspoons oil in skillet over medium heat. Spoon half of rice mixture by ⅓-cupfuls into pan, spreading to form 6 (3-inch) circles; cook 5 minutes or until lightly browned. Carefully turn cakes over; cook 5 minutes. Remove cakes from pan. Repeat procedure with remaining 1 tablespoon oil and remaining rice mixture. Serve with salsa. Yield: 6 servings (serving size: 2 cakes and ½ cup salsa).

CALORIES 279 (28% from fat); FAT 8.7g (sat 2.5g, mono 4.2g, poly 0.8g); PROTEIN 15.9g; CARB 35.8g; FIBER 6.6g; CHOL 8mg; IRON 2.8mg; SODIUM 660mg; CALC 142mg

QUICK & EASY

Bacon, Onion, and Brown Lentil Skillet

Humble brown lentils are fitting for this homey main dish. Pair with corn bread and sautéed Swiss chard or braised collard greens.

- 6 center-cut bacon slices
- 1 cup chopped onion
- 1 cup chopped carrot
- 1 cup chopped celery
- 1 teaspoon chopped fresh thyme
- 6 garlic cloves, minced
- 3 cups fat-free, less-sodium chicken broth
- 1 cup dried brown lentils
- 1 cup water
- 2 tablespoons chopped fresh parsley
- ¼ teaspoon freshly ground black pepper

1 Cook bacon in a large nonstick skillet over medium-high heat until crisp. Remove bacon from pan, reserving 2 teaspoons drippings in pan. Crumble bacon; set aside. Add onion to drippings in pan; sauté 5 minutes or until lightly browned. Add carrot and next 3 ingredients; cook 5 minutes or until crisp-tender. Add broth, lentils, and 1 cup water; bring to a boil. Cover, reduce heat, and simmer 15 minutes or until lentils are just tender. Uncover and increase heat to medium-high; cook 6 minutes or until liquid almost evaporates. Remove from heat; stir in parsley and pepper. Sprinkle with bacon. Yield: 4 servings (serving size: about 1⅓ cups).

CALORIES 278 (21% from fat); FAT 6.4g (sat 2.3g, mono 2.9g, poly 1g); PROTEIN 18.6g; CARB 38.5g; FIBER 13.8g; CHOL 11mg; IRON 5.5mg; SODIUM 534mg; CALC 80mg

Lentil Glossary

Brown: Also called regular or continental, these are the most readily available and most commonly used in the United States. They have a slightly nutty, earthy taste and can turn mushy if overcooked. Use them in homey dishes with herbs like bay leaf, thyme, and sage, as well as sausage and bacon.

Red: These have a neutral quality and break down to become somewhat creamy when cooked. Try them in assertively spiced Indian soups and purees (such as dal), or other dishes where lentils don't have to retain their shape.

Small Green: Also called French or Puy, this variety tends to cook more slowly than other types and retains a firm al dente texture when cooked. Their slightly peppery flavor works in salads, risotto, and unpureed soups—dishes where their firm texture stands out.

Black: These lentils (also called beluga) sparkle when cooked so that they resemble beluga caviar. They have an earthy flavor and hold their small round shape well when cooked. Use them in salads and unpureed soups, so their color, shape, and texture shine.

Pantry Basics

Store lentils in an airtight container in a cool, dark place for up to one year. Older lentils may take longer to cook, so be sure to taste them for doneness.

Lentil Look-Alikes

Indian markets sometimes use the term "lentil," or "dal" (which refers to both the legume and the pureed dish featuring lentils), loosely. Packages labeled "yellow lentils" may actually contain yellow split peas, a variety of chickpeas, or pigeon peas. Because of this inconsistency, we do not include recipes calling for yellow lentils.

Brown Lentil Hummus with Toasted Pita Crisps

Lentils stand in for chickpeas in this variation on the Middle Eastern dip.

- 5 cups water
- ⅔ cup dried brown lentils
- 3 (6-inch) whole wheat pitas, each cut into 8 wedges
  Cooking spray
- ¼ teaspoon ground coriander
- ¾ teaspoon salt, divided
- 1½ tablespoons fresh lemon juice
- 1½ tablespoons tahini (sesame seed paste)
- ¼ teaspoon hot pepper sauce (such as Tabasco)
- 2 garlic cloves
- 1 tablespoon chopped fresh cilantro

1 Preheat oven to 425°.
2 Bring 5 cups water and lentils to a boil in a medium saucepan. Cover, reduce heat, and simmer 20 minutes or until tender. Drain and rinse with cold water; drain.
3 Arrange pita wedges in a single layer on a baking sheet; coat pita wedges with cooking spray. Sprinkle evenly with coriander and ¼ teaspoon salt. Bake at 425° for 10 minutes or until golden brown.
4 Combine cooked lentils, remaining ½ teaspoon salt, juice, and next 3 ingredients in a food processor; process until smooth. Spoon mixture into a bowl; cover and chill. Sprinkle lentil mixture with cilantro. Serve with pita crisps. Yield: 12 servings (serving size: about 2½ tablespoons lentil mixture and 2 pita crisps).

CALORIES 91 (15% from fat); FAT 1.5g (sat 0.2g, mono 0.5g, poly 0.7g); PROTEIN 4.7g; CARB 15.7g; FIBER 3.7g; CHOL 0mg; IRON 1.6mg; SODIUM 235mg; CALC 12mg

Pancetta, French Lentil, and Spinach Risotto

A quartet of alliums—onion, leek, shallot, and garlic—imbues savory flavor to this entrée dotted with green lentils. For a peppery finish, use arugula in place of spinach.

- 4 cups water
- ½ cup dried petite green lentils
- 4 cups fat-free, less-sodium chicken broth
  Cooking spray
- 2 ounces pancetta, chopped
- 1 cup chopped onion
- 1 cup chopped leek
- ¼ cup chopped shallots
- 4 garlic cloves, minced
- 1 cup uncooked Arborio rice
- ½ cup dry white wine
- 2 cups fresh baby spinach (about 2 ounces)
- ½ cup (2 ounces) grated fresh Parmigiano-Reggiano cheese

1 Combine 4 cups water and lentils in a medium saucepan; bring to a boil. Reduce heat, and simmer 25 minutes or until just tender. Drain and rinse with cold water; drain.
2 Bring broth to a simmer in a small saucepan (do not boil). Keep warm over low heat.
3 Heat a large saucepan over medium heat. Coat pan with cooking spray. Add pancetta to pan; cook 5 minutes or until crisp, stirring occasionally. Stir in onion and next 3 ingredients; cook 5 minutes or until tender, stirring occasionally. Add rice; cook 1 minute, stirring constantly. Stir in wine, and cook until liquid evaporates (about 1 minute), stirring constantly. Stir in 1 cup broth; cook 5 minutes or until liquid is nearly absorbed, stirring constantly. Add remaining broth, ½ cup at a time, stirring constantly until each portion of broth is absorbed before adding next (about 22 minutes total). Stir in spinach; cook 1 minute or until spinach wilts. Stir in lentils; cook 1 minute or until thoroughly heated. Remove from heat; stir in cheese. Serve immediately. Yield: 6 servings (serving size: 1 cup).

CALORIES 282 (21% from fat); FAT 6.7g (sat 2.8g, mono 2g, poly 0.5g); PROTEIN 14g; CARB 42.7g; FIBER 5.4g; CHOL 14mg; IRON 2.2mg; SODIUM 603mg; CALC 179mg

Black Lentil and Couscous Salad
(pictured on page 261)

This zesty side is modeled after tabbouleh, the Middle Eastern salad of bulgur wheat, tomatoes, cucumbers, herbs, lemon juice, and olive oil. Here, we use couscous instead of bulgur and add black lentils for color and texture. Serve chilled or at room temperature.

- ½ cup dried black lentils
- 5 cups water, divided
- ¾ cup uncooked couscous
- ¾ teaspoon salt, divided
- 1 cup cherry tomatoes, quartered
- ⅓ cup golden raisins
- ⅓ cup finely chopped red onion
- ⅓ cup finely chopped cucumber
- ¼ cup chopped fresh parsley
- 3 tablespoons chopped fresh mint
- 1 teaspoon grated lemon rind
- 3 tablespoons fresh lemon juice
- 2 tablespoons extravirgin olive oil

1 Rinse lentils with cold water; drain. Place lentils and 4 cups water in a large saucepan; bring to a boil. Reduce heat, and simmer 20 minutes or until tender. Drain and rinse with cold water; drain.
2 Bring remaining 1 cup water to a boil in a saucepan; gradually stir in couscous and ¼ teaspoon salt. Remove from heat; cover and let stand 5 minutes. Fluff with a fork. Combine lentils, couscous, remaining ½ teaspoon salt, tomatoes, and remaining ingredients in a large bowl. Yield: 6 servings (serving size: 1 cup).

CALORIES 175 (25% from fat); FAT 4.8g (sat 0.7g, mono 3.3g, poly 0.6g); PROTEIN 4.5g; CARB 28.8g; FIBER 2.8g; CHOL 0mg; IRON 1mg; SODIUM 322mg; CALC 31mg

Spiced Coconut–Red Lentil Soup

A handheld immersion blender makes quick work of pureeing this yellow-hued soup in the pot.

- 2 teaspoons olive oil
- 2 cups chopped onion
- 1 tablespoon minced peeled fresh ginger
- 1 teaspoon ground cumin
- ½ teaspoon ground coriander
- ⅛ teaspoon ground cinnamon
- 5 garlic cloves, minced
- 3 cups fat-free, less-sodium chicken broth
- 1 cup dried small red lentils
- ½ cup water
- 1 cup light coconut milk
- 3 tablespoons chopped fresh basil
- 2 tablespoons fresh lime juice
- ¼ teaspoon salt

❶ Heat oil in a large saucepan over medium heat. Add onion; cook 12 minutes or until golden. Stir in ginger and next 4 ingredients; cook 1 minute, stirring constantly. Add broth, lentils, and ½ cup water; bring to a boil. Cover, reduce heat, and simmer 25 minutes or until lentils are tender.

❷ Remove from heat; let stand 5 minutes. Place half of lentil mixture in a blender. Remove center piece of blender lid (to allow steam to escape); secure blender lid on blender. Place a clean towel over opening in blender lid (to avoid splatters). Blend until smooth. Pour pureed mixture into a large bowl. Repeat procedure with remaining lentil mixture. Return pureed mixture to pan. Stir in milk and remaining ingredients; cook over medium heat 2 minutes. Yield: 4 servings (serving size: about 1⅓ cups).

CALORIES 282 (21% from fat); FAT 6.7g (sat 3.2g, mono 1.8g, poly 0.3g); PROTEIN 16.8g; CARB 41.6g; FIBER 9.3g; CHOL 0mg; IRON 3.9mg; SODIUM 463mg; CALC 65mg

Curried Dal with Basmati-Raisin Pilaf

Here, red lentils cook until they start to break down in the classic dish *dal*.

PILAF:
- 3 cups water
- 1½ cups uncooked basmati rice
- ⅓ cup golden raisins
- ½ teaspoon salt
- ½ teaspoon fennel seeds
- 2 (3-inch) cinnamon sticks
- 2 cardamom pods
- 1 bay leaf

DAL:
- 1 tablespoon olive oil
- 1½ cups chopped onion
- 1 tablespoon minced peeled fresh ginger
- 1 teaspoon curry powder
- ½ teaspoon ground cumin
- 3 garlic cloves, minced
- 4 cups water
- 1½ cups dried small red lentils
- 1 cup chopped plum tomato
- ¾ teaspoon salt
- 1 serrano chile, minced
- ¼ cup chopped fresh cilantro

❶ To prepare pilaf, combine first 8 ingredients in a medium saucepan over medium-high heat. Bring to a boil; stir once. Reduce heat to medium-low; simmer, uncovered, 15 minutes or until water is absorbed and rice is tender. Discard cinnamon, cardamom, and bay leaf.

❷ To prepare dal, heat oil in a large saucepan over medium-high heat. Add onion to pan; sauté 5 minutes or until lightly browned. Stir in ginger and next 3 ingredients; cook 30 seconds, stirring constantly. Add 4 cups water and next 4 ingredients; bring to boil. Cover, reduce heat, and simmer 15 minutes or until lentils are tender. Stir in cilantro. Serve over pilaf. Yield: 6 servings (serving size: ¾ cup dal and about ⅔ cup pilaf).

CALORIES 328 (10% from fat); FAT 3.6g (sat 0.4g, mono 1.7g, poly 0.3g); PROTEIN 15.8g; CARB 60.2g; FIBER 9.5g; CHOL 0mg; IRON 4.1mg; SODIUM 509mg; CALC 59mg

MAKE AHEAD
Lentil Soup
(*Potage de Lentille*)

Small French green lentils (also called Puy lentils) are great for soups because they hold their shape well.

- 2 tablespoons olive oil
- 2½ cups chopped Rio or other sweet onion
- 1 cup chopped celery
- 1 cup chopped carrot
- ½ teaspoon dried thyme
- 4 garlic cloves, minced
- 1 bay leaf
- 1½ cups dried petite green lentils
- 4 cups fat-free, less-sodium chicken broth
- 1 cup water
- 1 (14.5-ounce) can petite-cut diced tomatoes, drained
- 2 tablespoons fresh lemon juice
- ½ teaspoon salt
- ¾ teaspoon freshly ground black pepper, divided

❶ Heat oil in a large saucepan over medium-high heat. Add onion and next 5 ingredients to pan; sauté 12 minutes. Add lentils; cook 2 minutes, stirring constantly. Stir in broth, 1 cup water, and tomatoes; bring to a boil. Cover, reduce heat, and simmer 40 minutes or until lentils are very tender. Remove from heat; let stand 5 minutes. Discard bay leaf.

❷ Place 3 cups lentil mixture in a blender. Remove center piece of blender lid (to allow steam to escape); secure blender lid on blender. Place a clean towel over opening in blender lid (to avoid splatters). Blend until smooth. Return pureed mixture to pan; stir in juice, salt, and ¼ teaspoon pepper. Sprinkle with remaining ½ teaspoon pepper. Yield: 8 servings (serving size: 1 cup).

CALORIES 192 (21% from fat); FAT 4.4g (sat 0.5g, mono 2.5g, poly 0.4g); PROTEIN 9.9g; CARB 30.4g; FIBER 7.8g; CHOL 0mg; IRON 2.7mg; SODIUM 414mg; CALC 56mg

In the Shaker Kitchen

What's old is new again: This unique American religious group's use of seasonal ingredients and unfussy fare appeals to today's cooks.

WHEN MOST PEOPLE think of the Shakers, they envision elegantly simple furniture. But the Shakers, who were arguably the most successful communal religious group in American history, strove for perfection in all aspects of their lives as part of their goal to create heaven on earth. They paid as careful attention to the quality of their diet as they did to building a table or chair.

In our pursuit of healthy living, we can learn a great deal from them. Much as Shaker craftsmen used quality wood to build furniture, Shaker cooks believed that the way to a good meal and health was to start with fresh ingredients.

The Shakers are often described as simple folk, but they were shrewd observers of changing markets in America. (See "Who Were the Shakers?" on page 319.) At their peak of nearly 6,000 members and 19 communities in the mid-1800s, they were renowned for the level of detail they brought to most everything they did, from designing a building for one of their communities to preparing a meal. They were eager to adopt new methods to increase efficiency, whether it was designing a tool for woodworking or building a special oven to accommodate baking dozens of pies at once.

(See "Who Were the Shakers?" on page 319.)

SIMPLE SHAKER SUPPER MENU

(Serves 6)

Tomato-Based White Wine Fish Soup

Steamed Brown Bread

Chardonnay

Lemon Pie

Coffee and tea

Tomato-Based White Wine Fish Soup

1½	tablespoons olive oil
1	cup chopped onion
2	garlic cloves, minced
5	tablespoons tomato paste
1	cup chopped fennel bulb
1	cup thinly sliced carrot
1	cup chopped red bell pepper
1	cup dry white wine
2	(8-ounce) bottles clam juice
½	pound peeled and deveined shrimp, chopped
½	pound sea scallops
½	pound skinless halibut fillets, cut into 1-inch pieces
1½	teaspoons chopped fresh tarragon
½	teaspoon chopped fresh thyme
½	teaspoon freshly ground black pepper
	Thyme sprigs (optional)

❶ Heat oil in a large Dutch oven over medium-high heat. Add onion to pan; sauté 2 minutes, stirring occasionally. Add garlic; sauté 1 minute, stirring constantly. Reduce heat to medium. Add tomato paste to pan; cook 7 minutes or until paste begins to brown, stirring occasionally. Add fennel and next 4 ingredients; bring to a boil. Reduce heat, and simmer 15 minutes or until vegetables are just tender. Stir in shrimp, scallops, and fish. Cover and cook 5 minutes or until fish is done. Gently stir in tarragon, chopped thyme, and pepper. Garnish with thyme sprigs, if desired. Yield: 6 servings (serving size: 1 cup).

CALORIES 191 (27% from fat); FAT 5.7g (sat 0.9g, mono 3g, poly 1.1g); PROTEIN 23.7g; CARB 11.8g; FIBER 2.4g; CHOL 99mg; IRON 2.3mg; SODIUM 451mg; CALC 80mg

---

MAKE AHEAD
Steamed Brown Bread

Steaming the bread creates moist, dense loaves. For an afternoon snack with tea, spread slices with marmalade.

1	cup whole wheat flour (about 4.75 ounces)
1	cup rye flour (about 4 ounces)
1	cup cornmeal
1	cup raisins
2	teaspoons baking soda
½	teaspoon salt
2	cups buttermilk
¾	cup molasses
2	tablespoons butter, melted
1	tablespoon grated orange rind
	Cooking spray

❶ Preheat oven to 350°.
❷ Lightly spoon flours into dry measuring cups; level with a knife. Combine flours and next 4 ingredients in a large bowl; stir with a whisk. Combine buttermilk and next 3 ingredients. Add to dry ingredients; stir just until moistened. Divide batter evenly between 2 (8-inch) loaf pans coated with cooking spray. Tightly cover each pan with foil. Place

pans in a 13 x 9–inch baking pan. Add boiling water to a depth of 1 inch. Cover larger pan with foil.

3 Bake at 350° for 1 hour and 10 minutes or until a knife inserted in center comes out clean. (Top of bread will feel slightly sticky.) Remove pans from water. Cool 10 minutes on a wire rack. Remove from pans; cool completely. Yield: 2 loaves, 12 servings each (serving size: 1 slice).

CALORIES 124 (14% from fat); FAT 1.9g (sat 1.1g, mono 0.3g, poly 1.2g); PROTEIN 2.5g; CARB 25.4g; FIBER 1.9g; CHOL 5mg; IRON 1.1mg; SODIUM 190mg; CALC 28mg

GRACIOUS PLENTY MENU

(Serves 8)

Shaker Split Pea Soup

Herbed Roast Pork

Shaker Corn Bread

Green Beans with Savory

Easy Pickled Beets

Eldress Bertha's Applesauce

Autumn Apple Cake

Apple cider

QUICK & EASY
Green Beans with Savory

Try the same crisp-tender preparation with asparagus, sugar snap peas, or broccoli florets. Garnish with lemon slices.

- 2 pounds green beans, trimmed
- 2 tablespoons butter
- 1 teaspoon fresh lemon juice
- ¼ teaspoon dried savory
- ¾ teaspoon salt
- ¼ teaspoon black pepper

1 Cook beans in boiling water 5 minutes or until crisp-tender. Drain and rinse with cold water; drain.

2 Melt butter in a large nonstick skillet over medium-high heat. Cook 1 minute or until lightly browned. Add beans, juice, and savory to pan, tossing to coat. Sprinkle with salt and pepper. Yield: 8 servings (serving size: 1 cup).

CALORIES 61 (44% from fat); FAT 3g (sat 1.8g, mono 0.7g, poly 0.2g); PROTEIN 2.1g; CARB 8.2g; FIBER 3.9g; CHOL 8mg; IRON 1.2mg; SODIUM 245mg; CALC 43mg

Shaker Corn Bread

- ¼ cup all-purpose flour (about 1.1 ounces)
- 1 cup yellow cornmeal
- 1 cup fresh corn kernels (about 2 ears)
- 2 tablespoons chopped fresh dill
- 1 tablespoon baking powder
- 1 teaspoon salt
- ½ cup egg substitute
- 1½ cups 2% reduced-fat milk
- 3 tablespoons melted butter
- 2 tablespoons honey
- Cooking spray

1 Preheat oven to 375°.

2 Lightly spoon flour into a dry measuring cup; level with a knife. Combine flour and next 5 ingredients in a large bowl. Combine egg substitute and next 3 ingredients; stir with a whisk. Make a well in center of dry ingredients; add milk mixture. Stir just until combined. Spoon into a 9-inch baking pan coated with cooking spray.

3 Bake at 375° for 35 minutes or until a wooden pick inserted in center comes out clean. Cool in pan. Cut into squares. Yield: 9 servings (serving size: 1 square).

CALORIES 163 (30% from fat); FAT 5.5g (sat 3g, mono 1.5g, poly 0.6g); PROTEIN 5.3g; CARB 23.9g; FIBER 1.7g; CHOL 13mg; IRON 1.4mg; SODIUM 500mg; CALC 150mg

MAKE AHEAD
Easy Pickled Beets

The Shakers often pickled produce to preserve it. Just six ingredients go into a sweet-and-sour side. Use a mix of red and golden beets, if you like. You'll need to double this recipe for the "Gracious Plenty" menu (at left).

- 1 pound small beets (about 7 beets)
- ½ cup white vinegar
- ¼ cup sugar
- ¼ teaspoon salt
- ½ teaspoon black peppercorns
- 2 bay leaves

1 Leave root and 1-inch stem on beets; scrub with a brush. Place in a medium saucepan; cover with water. Bring to a boil. Cover, reduce heat, and simmer 45 minutes or until tender. Drain and rinse with cold water; drain. Cool slightly. Trim off beet roots; rub off skins. Cut beets into thin slices; place in a large bowl.

2 Combine vinegar and sugar in a small saucepan. Bring to a boil; cook 5 minutes. Remove from heat; stir in salt, peppercorns, and bay leaves. Pour vinegar mixture over beets; cover and chill. Discard bay leaves. Yield: 4 servings (serving size: about ½ cup).

CALORIES 81 (1% from fat); FAT 0.1g (sat 0g, mono 0g, poly 0.1g); PROTEIN 1.2g; CARB 19.8g; FIBER 2.1g; CHOL 0mg; IRON 0.6mg; SODIUM 207mg; CALC 13mg

Autumn Apple Cake

Apples were a popular crop at Shaker communities in New England, and residents used them in pies and cakes like this one. Use a sweet, crisp apple such as Pink Lady, Braeburn, or Sundowner.

Cooking spray
1 tablespoon all-purpose flour
1½ cups all-purpose flour (about 6.75 ounces)
2 teaspoons baking powder
¼ teaspoon salt
¼ teaspoon ground cinnamon
¾ cup granulated sugar
5 tablespoons butter, softened
1 teaspoon vanilla extract
1 large egg
½ cup 2% reduced-fat milk
1 cup finely chopped peeled Pink Lady apple (about 1 medium)
½ cup golden raisins
¼ cup finely chopped walnuts
1 teaspoon powdered sugar

❶ Preheat oven to 350°.
❷ Coat a 9-inch round cake pan with cooking spray, and dust with 1 tablespoon flour.
❸ Lightly spoon 1½ cups flour into dry measuring cups; level with a knife. Combine flour and next 3 ingredients in a small bowl, stirring with a whisk. Place granulated sugar and butter in a large bowl; beat with a mixer until blended. Beat in vanilla and egg. Beat in flour mixture alternately with milk, beginning and ending with flour mixture. Fold in apple, raisins, and walnuts. Scrape batter into prepared pan. Bake at 350° for 30 minutes or until a wooden pick inserted in center comes out clean. Cool 10 minutes in pan on a wire rack. Remove from pan; cool completely on wire rack. Sift powdered sugar over cake. Cut into wedges. Yield: 8 servings (serving size: 1 wedge).

CALORIES 304 (31% from fat); FAT 10.6g (sat 5.1g, mono 2.5g, poly 2.2g); PROTEIN 4.8g; CARB 48.9g; FIBER 1.7g; CHOL 42mg; IRON 1.7mg; SODIUM 263mg; CALC 106mg

Hearty Homecoming Menu
serves 8

This meal is a perfect, easy Columbus Day weekend supper. Substitute fontina if you can't find raclette.

Shaker Split Pea Soup

Grilled raclette sandwiches
Combine ¼ cup whole-grain Dijon mustard and 1 tablespoon chopped fresh chives. Spread mustard mixture evenly over 4 (1-ounce) slices sourdough bread. Top each serving with 1 ounce thinly sliced raclette and 1 bread slice. Heat a large nonstick skillet over medium heat. Coat both sides of sandwiches with cooking spray. Place 4 sandwiches in pan; cook 3 minutes on each side or until toasted. Repeat procedure with remaining sandwiches.

Green salad

Shaker Split Pea Soup

Dried savory is an herb the Shakers used often. If you can't find it, substitute a pinch of dried sage or increase the amount of dried thyme to ½ teaspoon. For a smoother texture, puree the soup in a blender or in the pot with an immersion blender.

3 slices center-cut bacon, chopped
1½ cups finely chopped onion
5 cups water
1½ cups green split peas
¼ teaspoon dried thyme
¼ teaspoon dried savory
¼ teaspoon freshly ground black pepper
1 teaspoon kosher salt
Thyme sprigs (optional)

❶ Cook bacon in a Dutch oven over medium heat 5 minutes. Add onion to pan; cook 5 minutes or until onion is tender and lightly browned, stirring occasionally. Add 5 cups water, scraping pan to loosen browned bits. Add peas and

next 3 ingredients to pan; bring to a boil. Cover, reduce heat, and simmer 1 hour and 20 minutes. Mash with a potato masher to desired consistency. Stir in salt. Garnish with thyme sprigs, if desired. Yield: 8 servings (serving size: about ½ cup).

CALORIES 149 (8% from fat); FAT 1.3g (sat 0.4g, mono 0.5g, poly 0.3g); PROTEIN 10.2g; CARB 25.3g; FIBER 10g; CHOL 2mg; IRON 1.8mg; SODIUM 294mg; CALC 32mg

Herbed Roast Pork

A similar version of this recipe was occasionally prepared at Sabbathday Lake Shaker Community.

1½ tablespoons butter, softened
1¼ teaspoons kosher salt
½ teaspoon dried sage
½ teaspoon dried thyme
¼ teaspoon dried oregano
2 (1-pound) pork tenderloins, trimmed
Cooking spray

❶ Preheat oven to 475°.
❷ Combine first 5 ingredients in a small bowl. Rub butter mixture over pork. Place pork on a broiler pan coated with cooking spray. Bake at 475° for 17 minutes or until a thermometer registers 155° (slightly pink). Let stand 5 minutes. Cut into thin slices. Yield: 8 servings (serving size: about 3 ounces).

CALORIES 156 (35% from fat); FAT 6g (sat 2.7g, mono 2.3g, poly 0.5g); PROTEIN 23.8g; CARB 0.2g; FIBER 0.1g; CHOL 79mg; IRON 1.5mg; SODIUM 435mg; CALC 10mg

Historic Sites

There are 15 Shaker communities listed on the National Park Service's National Register of Historic Places. Many, including Canterbury Shaker Village, serve Shaker-inspired meals. You can learn more about these and other Shaker historic sites at the National Park Service's Web site at www.nps.gov/history/nr/travel/shaker.

Eldress Bertha's Applesauce

Eldress Bertha Lindsay was one of the last surviving residents at Canterbury Shaker Village. She liked to make this sauce with Baldwin apples. We tested it with Pink Lady apples, which are easier to find.

- 5½ cups chopped peeled Pink Lady apple (about 4)
- ½ cup water
- ¼ cup sugar
- 1½ tablespoons fresh lemon juice
- 1 (2-inch) cinnamon stick
- ¼ teaspoon salt
- Dash of almond extract

1 Combine first 5 ingredients in a large saucepan; bring to a boil. Cover, reduce heat, and simmer 35 minutes or until soft. Discard cinnamon stick. Mash with a potato masher to desired consistency. Stir in salt and extract. Yield: 2¼ cups (serving size: about ¼ cup).

CALORIES 91 (0% from fat); FAT 0g; PROTEIN 0.5g; CARB 23.4g; FIBER 2.5g; CHOL 0mg; IRON 0.2mg; SODIUM 36mg; CALC 10mg

---

Who Were the Shakers?

The first Shakers were radical religious enthusiasts in Manchester, England, led by Mother Ann Lee (1736–1784). They eventually became known as the "United Society of Believers in Christ's Second Appearing," but their common name came from their early ecstatic form of worship. To escape religious persecution, they sailed to New York in 1774. Their British heritage and beliefs in celibacy and pacifism did not make them popular in early revolutionary America. As a result, they formed largely self-reliant communities so they could work and worship in peace, and established settlements in Maine, New Hampshire, Massachusetts, Connecticut, New York, Indiana, Ohio, Kentucky, and Florida.

Lemon Pie

Shaker lemon pie is an iconic American dessert that traditionally features thinly sliced whole lemons macerated in sugar overnight, which results in a filling that is chewy, bitter, sour, and sweet all at the same time. We've updated this pie with grated lemon rind for a smoother filling.

- 3 lemons
- 2 cups granulated sugar
- ½ (15-ounce) package refrigerated pie dough (such as Pillsbury)
- Cooking spray
- 3 tablespoons all-purpose flour
- ¼ teaspoon salt
- 4 large eggs, lightly beaten
- ½ cup heavy whipping cream
- 2 tablespoons powdered sugar

1 Grate ½ cup rind from lemons. Remove white pithy part of rind; discard. Chop lemons; discard seeds. Combine rind, chopped lemon, and granulated sugar in a large bowl; toss well. Cover and let stand at room temperature 24 hours, stirring occasionally.
2 Preheat oven to 450°.
3 Roll dough into an 11-inch circle; fit into a 9-inch pie plate coated with cooking spray. Fold edges under, and flute. Add flour, salt, and eggs to lemon mixture, stirring with a whisk until combined. Pour lemon mixture into crust. Bake at 450° for 15 minutes.
4 Reduce oven temperature to 375°. Shield edges of piecrust with foil; bake at 375° for 25 minutes or until filling is set. Cool completely on a wire rack.
5 Combine cream and powdered sugar. Beat with a mixer at high speed until stiff peaks form. Serve with pie. Yield: 12 servings (serving size: 1 wedge and 1½ tablespoons whipped cream).

CALORIES 282 (32% from fat); FAT 9.9g (sat 4.4g, mono 1.7g, poly 0.4g); PROTEIN 2.8g; CARB 46.3g; FIBER 0.6g; CHOL 86mg; IRON 0.4mg; SODIUM 149mg; CALC 21mg

---

Just Right

These smart-sized renditions of comfort food are perfect for a pair.

When you cook for two, you may find yourself preparing a recipe that serves four or six, and then enjoying the leftovers for another day or two. That strategy is smart for dishes that store well and aren't compromised when reheated—most soups and stews, for example.

But some recipes fare best when they're eaten fresh. Pasta carbonara is rich and creamy when first prepared, but the noodles soak up the luscious sauce as it stands. The corn bread topping for a tamale pie may become gummy if you keep it in the fridge for a couple of days, and you wouldn't even consider storing leftover nachos, which become soggy. Following is a collection of fresh-is-best recipes that are appropriately fitted for two—with no leftovers.

Herbed Chicken and Dumplings

Fluffy herb-flecked dumplings, tender vegetables, and rich dark-meat chicken combine in this soul-satisfying classic.

- Cooking spray
- 8 ounces skinless, boneless chicken thighs, cut into bite-sized pieces
- ¾ cup (¼-inch) diagonally cut celery
- ½ cup (¼-inch) diagonally cut carrot
- ½ cup chopped onion
- ⅛ teaspoon dried thyme
- 3 parsley sprigs
- 1 bay leaf
- 3 cups fat-free, less-sodium chicken broth
- ½ cup all-purpose flour (about 2.25 ounces)
- 1 tablespoon chopped fresh parsley
- ¼ teaspoon baking powder
- ¼ teaspoon salt
- ¼ cup 1% low-fat milk   *Continued*

1 Heat a large saucepan over medium-high heat. Coat pan with cooking spray. Add chicken to pan; cook 4 minutes, browning on all sides. Remove chicken from pan; keep warm. Add celery and next 5 ingredients to pan; sauté 5 minutes or until onion is tender. Return chicken to pan; cook 1 minute. Add broth to pan; bring mixture to a boil. Cover, reduce heat, and simmer 30 minutes. **2** Lightly spoon flour into a dry measuring cup; level with a knife. Combine flour and next 3 ingredients in a medium bowl. Add milk, stirring just until moist. Spoon by heaping teaspoonfuls into broth mixture; cover and simmer 10 minutes or until dumplings are done. Discard parsley sprigs and bay leaf. Yield: 2 servings (serving size: 2 cups).

CALORIES 285 (16% from fat); FAT 5.2g (sat 1.5g, mono 1.9g, poly 1.2g); PROTEIN 25g; CARB 35.2g; FIBER 3.1g; CHOL 55mg; IRON 3.4mg; SODIUM 596mg; CALC 133mg

If you need to serve a larger group, these recipes can be doubled easily—just use a larger pan to cook them in.

Linguine Carbonara

The luxurious, velvety texture of a good pasta carbonara is ephemeral at best, so you must enjoy it right away. Tempering the egg with hot pasta water keeps the sauce creamy by preventing it from curdling. For a smoky taste, use bacon in place of pancetta.

- 4 ounces uncooked linguine
- ½ cup 1% low-fat milk
- 3 tablespoons grated fresh Parmesan cheese
- 1 tablespoon chopped fresh parsley
- ⅛ teaspoon salt
- ⅛ teaspoon freshly ground black pepper
- Cooking spray
- ⅓ cup chopped pancetta (about 1½ ounces)
- ¼ cup finely chopped onion
- 1 garlic clove, minced
- 1 large egg

1 Cook pasta according to package directions, omitting salt and fat. Drain pasta in a colander over a bowl, reserving ¼ cup cooking liquid. Keep warm. **2** Combine milk and next 4 ingredients in a small bowl; set aside. **3** Heat a medium nonstick skillet over medium-high heat. Coat pan with cooking spray. Add pancetta to pan; sauté 3 minutes or until lightly browned. Add onion and garlic to pan; sauté 3 minutes or until onion is lightly browned. Reduce heat to medium-low. Add milk mixture and pasta to pan; toss gently to coat. **4** Place egg in a small bowl; stir with a whisk. Gradually add ¼ cup reserved hot cooking liquid, stirring constantly with a whisk. Gradually add egg mixture to pan, stirring constantly; cook 4 minutes or until sauce is thick and creamy. Yield: 2 servings (serving size: about 1¼ cups).

CALORIES 387 (30% from fat); FAT 13g (sat 5.8g, mono 4.5g, poly 1.3g); PROTEIN 19.2g; CARB 48.2g; FIBER 2.3g; CHOL 130mg; IRON 2.6mg; SODIUM 682mg; CALC 192mg

Seafood Risotto

Risotto must be served immediately so you can best savor its rich creaminess. With this version, there's just enough for two healthful portions. Complete the meal with a salad, bread, and crisp white wine.

- 2 cups fat-free, less-sodium chicken broth
- 1 (8-ounce) bottle clam juice
- 2 teaspoons butter
- ¼ cup chopped shallots
- ½ cup uncooked Arborio rice
- ⅛ teaspoon saffron threads, crushed
- 1 tablespoon fresh lemon juice
- ½ cup grape tomatoes, halved
- 4 ounces medium shrimp, peeled and deveined
- 4 ounces bay scallops
- 2 tablespoons whipping cream
- Chopped fresh parsley (optional)

1 Bring broth and clam juice to a simmer in a medium saucepan (do not boil). Keep warm over low heat. **2** Melt butter in a large saucepan over medium heat. Add shallots to pan; cook 2 minutes or until tender, stirring frequently. Add rice and saffron to pan; cook 30 seconds, stirring constantly. Add lemon juice to pan; cook 15 seconds, stirring constantly. Stir in ½ cup hot broth mixture; cook 2 minutes or until liquid is nearly absorbed, stirring constantly. Add remaining broth mixture, ½ cup at a time, stirring constantly until each portion of broth is absorbed before adding next (about 18 minutes total). **3** Stir in tomatoes; cook 1 minute. Stir in shrimp and scallops; cook 4 minutes or until shrimp and scallops are done, stirring occasionally. Remove from heat; stir in cream. Sprinkle with parsley, if desired. Yield: 2 servings (serving size: about 1¼ cups).

CALORIES 400 (23% from fat); FAT 10.1g (sat 4.9g, mono 2.6g, poly 1.1g); PROTEIN 30.2g; CARB 49.1g; FIBER 2.6g; CHOL 118mg; IRON 2.8mg; SODIUM 520mg; CALC 89mg

Panko-Crusted Pork Chops with Creamy Herb Dressing

PORK:

  2 teaspoons all-purpose flour
 ¼ teaspoon salt
 ¼ teaspoon onion powder
 ¼ teaspoon ground cumin
 ¼ teaspoon chili powder
 ⅛ teaspoon ground red pepper
  1 teaspoon low-sodium soy sauce
  1 large egg white
 ⅓ cup panko (Japanese breadcrumbs)
  2 (4-ounce) boneless center-cut loin pork chops (about ½ inch thick)
  1 teaspoon canola oil
     Cooking spray

DRESSING:

  2 tablespoons fat-free sour cream
  1 tablespoon fat-free milk
  1 tablespoon reduced-fat mayonnaise
  1 tablespoon chopped green onions
  1 tablespoon chopped fresh flat-leaf parsley
  1 teaspoon cider vinegar
 ¼ teaspoon garlic powder

❶ Preheat oven to 450°.
❷ To prepare pork, combine first 6 ingredients in a shallow dish. Combine soy sauce and egg white in a medium bowl, stirring with a whisk. Place panko in a shallow dish.
❸ Dredge pork in flour mixture; dip in egg mixture. Dredge in panko. Heat oil in a large nonstick skillet over medium-high heat. Add pork to pan; cook 1 minute on each side. Place pork on a baking sheet coated with cooking spray. Bake at 450° for 6 minutes or until done.
❹ To prepare dressing, combine sour cream and remaining ingredients. Serve dressing with pork. Yield: 2 servings (serving size: 1 pork chop and about 2 tablespoons dressing).

CALORIES 268 (32% from fat); FAT 9.5g (sat 2.2g, mono 4g, poly 1.8g); PROTEIN 30g; CARB 13.6g; FIBER 0.7g; CHOL 74mg; IRON 1.3mg; SODIUM 608mg; CALC 72mg

Smoky-Spicy Tamale Pies

While ground chipotle chile offers smoky notes, you can also use ⅛ teaspoon ground red pepper for pure fiery flavor.

  4 ounces ground turkey
 ½ cup chopped onion
 ½ cup frozen whole-kernel corn, thawed
  2 garlic cloves, minced
  1 teaspoon chili powder
 ½ teaspoon ground cumin
 ¼ teaspoon ground chipotle chile pepper
  1 cup canned organic red kidney beans, rinsed and drained
  1 (14.5-ounce) can fire-roasted tomatoes with green chiles, undrained (such as Muir Glen)
     Cooking spray
 ¼ cup all-purpose flour (about 1.1 ounces)
 ¼ cup yellow cornmeal
 ½ teaspoon baking powder
 ⅛ teaspoon salt
 ¼ cup fat-free milk
  1 large egg white

❶ Preheat oven to 375°.
❷ Cook turkey in a large nonstick skillet over medium-high heat until browned, stirring to crumble. Add onion, corn, and garlic to pan; sauté 2 minutes. Stir in chili powder, cumin, and chipotle; cook 30 seconds. Add beans and tomatoes to pan; cook 1 minute. Divide turkey mixture evenly between 2 (1½-cup) ramekins coated with cooking spray.
❸ Lightly spoon flour into a dry measuring cup; level with a knife. Combine flour and next 3 ingredients, stirring with a whisk. Combine milk and egg white, stirring with a whisk. Add milk mixture to flour mixture; stir just until moist. Spoon batter evenly over turkey mixture. Place ramekins on a baking sheet. Bake at 375° for 25 minutes or until crust is browned. Yield: 2 servings (serving size: 1 pie).

CALORIES 431 (11% from fat); FAT 5.2g (sat 1.4g, mono 1.9g, poly 1.3g); PROTEIN 25.9g; CARB 68.7g; FIBER 9.4g; CHOL 45mg; IRON 5.5mg; SODIUM 964mg; CALC 186mg

Steak and Bean Nachos

 ¼ teaspoon sugar
 ¼ teaspoon ground ancho chile pepper
 ¼ teaspoon ground coriander
 ⅛ teaspoon salt
 ⅛ teaspoon ground red pepper
  6 ounces flank steak, trimmed
  4 (6-inch) corn tortillas, each cut into 8 wedges
     Cooking spray
  1 small onion, cut into ¼-inch-thick slices (about 6 ounces)
 ½ cup organic refried pinto beans
 ½ cup (2 ounces) shredded reduced-fat sharp Cheddar cheese
  2 tablespoons pickled jalapeño pepper slices
 ⅓ cup bottled black bean and corn salsa

❶ Preheat oven to 400°.
❷ Combine first 5 ingredients; rub over both sides of steak. Let stand 10 minutes.
❸ Arrange tortilla wedges in a single layer on a large baking sheet coated with cooking spray. Bake at 400° for 8 minutes or until lightly browned.
❹ Heat a grill pan over medium-high heat. Coat pan with cooking spray. Add steak to pan; cook 4 minutes on each side or until desired degree of doneness. Place steak on a cutting board; let stand 5 minutes. Cut steak into ½-inch pieces. Coat onion slices with cooking spray. Add onion to pan; cook 4 minutes on each side or until tender. Coarsely chop onion.
❺ Arrange tortilla chips in two small piles on baking sheet. Top each evenly with steak, onion, beans, cheese, and jalapeño. Bake at 400° for 5 minutes or until cheese melts. Top each serving with about 2½ tablespoons salsa. Yield: 2 servings.

CALORIES 412 (29% from fat); FAT 13.2g (sat 6.4g, mono 3.7g, poly 1g); PROTEIN 37.9g; CARB 38.2g; FIBER 6.8g; CHOL 57mg; IRON 2.9mg; SODIUM 832mg; CALC 274mg

Sodium Savvy

This mineral is found naturally in some foods and, in the form of salt, seasons recipes. Learn how to maximize flavor with sensible amounts.

SODIUM CHLORIDE—SALT—is an important ingredient in many recipes. Both professional and home cooks equate salt with flavor. However, the more we use, the more our palates desire.

"Sodium has benefits, like helping to maintain the body's right balance of fluids," says cardiologist Richard Katz, MD, director of the cardiology division of George Washington University. "But ingesting too much salt is a prime cause of increased blood pressure. Higher blood pressure is a major cause of heart attacks and strokes, both of which can be reduced by minimizing salt intake." Even among healthy adults there is usually room for improvement. "If blood pressure is 125/70, it's better at 120/70," Katz says. (The American Heart Association [AHA] notes that low blood pressure is relative for each person and is a concern when it drops suddenly. Your doctor can help you reach a blood pressure goal that best enhances your health.)

Various organizations, including the USDA, AHA, and *Cooking Light*, recommend less than 2,300 milligrams sodium daily (the amount in one teaspoon of table salt) for healthy people. Most Americans consume closer to 4,000 milligrams a day.

"Only a quarter of sodium intake actually comes from salting our food," says AHA President Dan Jones, MD. "More than 75 percent of sodium in our diets comes from processed foods." Salt is a natural preservative and it enhances flavor, so it's no surprise that salt and other forms of sodium are included in packaged foods (see "Ubiquitous Mineral," page 324).

Because salt is so pervasive in our food supply, "One has to be sodium-conscious at every step: at purchase, at preparation, and at consumption," says Jones. The most effective overall strategy to control sodium intake is to cook food at home as often as possible using fresh fruits and vegetables, grains, low-fat dairy products, fresh meat, poultry, and fish.

QUICK & EASY
Spicy Garlic Broccoli Rabe

Finishing salt (fleur de sel), quality oil, and heat subdue broccoli rabe's bitter edge. Serve with pork chops and potatoes.

- 1 bunch broccoli rabe (rapini), trimmed and cut into 2-inch pieces (about 6 cups)
- 4 teaspoons extravirgin olive oil, divided
- 3 garlic cloves, sliced
- 1 tablespoon fresh lemon juice
- 1 teaspoon crushed red pepper
- ¼ teaspoon fleur de sel

❶ Cook broccoli rabe in boiling water 2 minutes or until crisp-tender. Drain and plunge into ice water; drain. Squeeze dry. ❷ Heat 2 teaspoons oil in a large nonstick skillet over medium heat. Add garlic to pan; cook 1 minute. Add broccoli rabe, juice, and pepper to pan; cook 3 minutes, stirring occasionally. Remove from heat. Drizzle with remaining 2 teaspoons oil, and sprinkle with fleur de sel. Yield: 4 servings (serving size: ½ cup).

CALORIES 64 (65% from fat); FAT 4.6g (sat 0.6g, mono 3.3g, poly 0.5g); PROTEIN 2.5g; CARB 4.3g; FIBER 0.2g; CHOL 0mg; IRON 0.6mg; SODIUM 139mg; CALC 35mg

Open-Faced Beef Sandwiches with Greens and Horseradish Cream

Texas toast—sometimes labeled grill, griddle, or French toast bread—is the thick-sliced fresh bread available in many supermarkets. You can substitute a 1.4-ounce slice of Italian or French bread. Since bread is typically high in sodium, serving a sandwich open-faced cuts down on the mineral. Salting the beef a bit before broiling adds a little flavor; we save the rest of the salt to season the meat after it's sliced.

HORSERADISH CREAM:
- 2½ tablespoons drained prepared horseradish
- 2 tablespoons light sour cream
- 2 tablespoons crème fraîche

SANDWICH:
- Cooking spray
- 3½ cups vertically sliced onion (about 2 large)
- ½ teaspoon kosher salt, divided
- 1 (1-pound) flank steak, trimmed
- ¼ teaspoon freshly ground black pepper
- 2 cups trimmed arugula
- 2 teaspoons extravirgin olive oil
- 1 teaspoon balsamic vinegar
- 4 (1½-ounce) slices Texas toast, lightly toasted

❶ To prepare cream, combine first 3 ingredients in a small bowl; cover and chill. ❷ Preheat broiler. ❸ To prepare sandwiches, heat a large nonstick skillet over medium heat. Coat pan with cooking spray. Add onion and ⅛ teaspoon salt to pan; cover and cook 10 minutes, stirring frequently. Uncover and cook 10 minutes or until onion is golden brown. ❹ Sprinkle steak with ⅛ teaspoon salt and pepper. Place steak on a broiler pan coated with cooking spray; broil 5 minutes on each side or until desired degree of doneness. Let stand 5 minutes. Cut steak diagonally across grain into thin slices. Combine steak and remaining ¼ teaspoon salt in a bowl, and toss to coat.

⑤ Combine arugula, oil, and vinegar in a medium bowl; toss gently. Spread 2 tablespoons horseradish cream over each bread slice; top each with about ⅓ cup onion, ½ cup arugula mixture, and 3 ounces of steak. Yield: 4 servings (serving size: 1 open-faced sandwich).

CALORIES 383 (30% from fat); FAT 12.8g (sat 5.8g, mono 4.6g, poly 0.7g); PROTEIN 29.5g; CARB 36.5g; FIBER 4g; CHOL 47mg; IRON 3.1mg; SODIUM 543mg; CALC 186mg

MAKE AHEAD
Focaccia with Garlic and Olives

Salt tames the fermenting action of yeast dough, so it guards against bland, tough breads. Here, we use a little salt in the dough and boost the flavor with a finishing sprinkle of chunky *fleur de sel* (flower of salt).

     1 teaspoon sugar
     1 package active dry yeast (about
        2¼ teaspoons)
    ⅔ cup warm water (100° to 110°)
     2 cups all-purpose flour (about
        9 ounces), divided
    ¼ teaspoon salt
    2½ tablespoons olive oil, divided
     3 tablespoons finely chopped
        kalamata olives
        Cooking spray
     4 garlic cloves, thinly sliced
    ¼ teaspoon fleur de sel

❶ Dissolve sugar and yeast in ⅔ cup warm water in a large bowl, and let stand 5 minutes.

❷ Lightly spoon flour into dry measuring cups; level with a knife. Combine 1¾ cups flour (about 8 ounces) and ¼ teaspoon salt; stir with a whisk. Add flour mixture and 1 tablespoon oil to yeast mixture, stirring to combine; fold in olives. Turn dough out onto a floured surface. Knead until smooth and elastic (about 5 minutes); add enough of remaining ¼ cup flour, 1 tablespoon at a time, to

prevent dough from sticking to hands (dough will feel sticky). Place dough in a large bowl coated with cooking spray, turning to coat top. Cover and let rise in a warm place (85°), free from drafts, 1 hour or until doubled in size. (Gently press two fingers into dough. If indentation remains, dough has risen enough.) Press dough into a 13 x 8-inch rectangle on a jelly-roll pan coated with cooking spray. Cover and let rise 30 minutes.

❸ Preheat oven to 475°.

❹ Brush remaining 1½ tablespoons oil over dough. Sprinkle evenly with garlic and fleur de sel. Bake at 475° for 12 minutes or until golden. Transfer to a wire rack, and cool completely. Cut into 10 equal portions. Yield: 10 servings (serving size: 1 piece).

CALORIES 124 (31% from fat); FAT 4.3g (sat 0.6g, mono 3.1g, poly 0.5g); PROTEIN 2.8g; CARB 18.2g; FIBER 0.8g; CHOL 0mg; IRON 1.3mg; SODIUM 160mg; CALC 4mg

QUICK & EASY
Rise and Shine Oatmeal

Some breakfast cereals harbor surprising amounts of sodium. One serving of this oatmeal fits comfortably into the 2,300 milligrams daily recommendation.

     2 cups 1% low-fat milk
     2 cups regular oats
    ½ cup golden raisins
     2 tablespoons honey
    ½ teaspoon kosher salt
    ½ teaspoon vanilla extract
    ½ teaspoon ground cinnamon
     6 tablespoons sliced almonds, toasted
     2 tablespoons brown sugar

❶ Bring milk to a boil over medium heat. Stir in oats; cook 5 minutes. Remove from heat; stir in raisins and next 4 ingredients. Serve with nuts and sugar. Yield: 4 servings (serving size: 1 cup oatmeal mixture, 1½ tablespoons almonds, and 1½ teaspoons sugar).

CALORIES 380 (20% from fat); FAT 8.4g (sat 1.6g, mono 4g, poly 2.1g); PROTEIN 13g; CARB 66.3g; FIBER 6.1g; CHOL 5mg; IRON 2.4mg; SODIUM 304mg; CALC 216mg

QUICK & EASY
Cheddar-Bacon Drop Biscuits

(pictured on page 259)

A few slices of applewood-smoked bacon and sharp Cheddar cheese boost the savory character of this quick bread. Serve warm to best harness the salty notes.

     2 cups all-purpose flour (about
        9 ounces)
    ½ teaspoon baking soda
    ¼ teaspoon kosher salt
    3½ tablespoons chilled butter, cut into
        small pieces
    ⅓ cup (1½ ounces) finely shredded
        sharp Cheddar cheese
     2 applewood-smoked bacon slices,
        cooked and crumbled
    ¾ cup nonfat buttermilk
    ¼ cup water
        Cooking spray

❶ Preheat oven to 400°.

❷ Lightly spoon flour into dry measuring cups; level with a knife. Combine flour, baking soda, and salt in a large bowl; stir with a whisk. Cut in butter with a pastry blender or 2 knives until mixture resembles coarse meal. Stir in cheese and bacon. Add buttermilk and ¼ cup water, stirring just until moist. Drop dough by 2 level tablespoonfuls 1 inch apart onto a baking sheet coated with cooking spray. Bake at 400° for 11 minutes or until golden brown. Serve warm. Yield: 18 biscuits (serving size: 1 biscuit).

CALORIES 91 (37% from fat); FAT 3.7g (sat 2.2g, mono 0.8g, poly 0.1g); PROTEIN 2.8g; CARB 11.5g; FIBER 0.4g; CHOL 10mg; IRON 0.7mg; SODIUM 127mg; CALC 32mg

White Bean and Kale Stew

Steeping a savory cheese rind in a soup's broth infuses cheesy, salty accents throughout. Cooking your own beans is simple if you've planned ahead, though you can rinse and drain canned ones for a higher-sodium result.

1	pound dried Great Northern beans
2	applewood-smoked bacon slices
2	cups chopped onion (2 medium)
6	garlic cloves, minced
6	cups fat-free, less-sodium chicken broth
2	cups water
1½	tablespoons minced fresh thyme
1	tablespoon minced fresh rosemary
1	bunch kale, stemmed and cut into 2-inch pieces (about 5 cups)
1	(2-ounce) piece Parmigiano-Reggiano rind
2	tablespoons fresh lemon juice

1 Sort and wash beans; place in a large bowl. Cover with water to 2 inches above beans; cover and let stand 8 hours. Drain.
2 Cook bacon in a large Dutch oven over medium heat until crisp. Remove bacon from pan with a slotted spoon, reserving 2 teaspoons drippings in pan. Crumble bacon. Add onion to drippings in pan; cook 6 minutes or until tender, stirring occasionally. Add garlic; cook 30 seconds.
3 Add beans, broth, and next 4 ingredients to pan; bring to a boil. Add rind to pan. Cover, reduce heat, and simmer 1 hour and 15 minutes or until beans are tender. Remove from heat; discard rind. Stir in juice. Garnish each serving with about ¾ teaspoon bacon. Yield: 8 servings (serving size: about 1½ cups).

CALORIES 307 (19% from fat); FAT 6.6g (sat 2.6g, mono 2.6g, poly 1g); PROTEIN 20.5g; CARB 44.2g; FIBER 10.9g; CHOL 11mg; IRON 6.3mg; SODIUM 505mg; CALC 216mg

Coconut-Crusted Salmon with Tamarind Barbecue Sauce

SAUCE:

1	teaspoon canola oil
½	cup chopped shallots
1	tablespoon grated peeled fresh ginger
2	garlic cloves, minced
1	tablespoon tomato paste
1	cup hot water
3	tablespoons Tamarind Extract
½	teaspoon brown sugar
¼	teaspoon ground red pepper
1	tablespoon sweet soy sauce
½	teaspoon dark sesame oil

SALMON:

3	tablespoons panko (Japanese breadcrumbs)
3	tablespoons flaked sweetened coconut
⅛	teaspoon ground turmeric
4	(6-ounce) salmon fillets (about 1 inch thick)
½	teaspoon kosher salt
¼	teaspoon ground coriander
¼	teaspoon freshly ground black pepper
	Cooking spray

1 To prepare sauce, heat canola oil in a medium saucepan over medium-high heat. Add shallots to pan; sauté 2 minutes, stirring frequently. Add ginger and garlic; sauté 1 minute, stirring constantly. Add tomato paste; cook 1 minute, stirring constantly. Add 1 cup hot water and next 3 ingredients; bring to a boil. Reduce heat, and simmer 10 minutes, stirring occasionally. Remove from heat; stir in soy sauce and sesame oil.
2 Preheat oven to 400°.
3 To prepare salmon, combine panko, coconut, and turmeric in a shallow bowl. Sprinkle fillets evenly with salt, coriander, and black pepper. Dredge fillets in panko mixture.
4 Heat a large ovenproof skillet over medium heat. Coat pan with cooking spray. Add fillets to pan, skin sides up; cook 2 minutes. Carefully turn fillets over; place skillet in oven. Bake at 400° for 6 minutes or until fish flakes easily when tested with a fork or until desired degree of doneness. Yield: 4 servings (serving size: 1 fillet and 2 tablespoons sauce).

CALORIES 281 (40% from fat); FAT 12.5g (sat 3.5g, mono 5.1g, poly 2.8g); PROTEIN 32.1g; CARB 8.3g; FIBER 0.9g; CHOL 80mg; IRON 0.9mg; SODIUM 409mg; CALC 25mg

MAKE AHEAD

TAMARIND EXTRACT:

Asian grocery stores carry concentrated tamarind pulp (complete with seeds) in small square packages from Thailand and India. Refrigerate leftover extract for up to two weeks.

1½	cups boiling water, divided
4	ounces tamarind pulp

1 Combine 1 cup boiling water and tamarind pulp in a small saucepan. Let stand, covered, 1 hour, stirring to combine. Drain tamarind mixture in a sieve over a bowl, reserving liquid. Return solids to pan. Add remaining ½ cup boiling water, stirring to combine. Press tamarind mixture through sieve over bowl, reserving liquid; discard solids. Yield: 1¼ cups (serving size: 1 tablespoon).

CALORIES 15 (0% from fat); FAT 0g; PROTEIN 0.2g; CARB 3.9g; FIBER 0.3g; CHOL 0mg; IRON 0.2mg; SODIUM 2mg; CALC 5mg

Egg and Cheese Breakfast Tacos with Homemade Salsa

(pictured on page 264)

Fresh-made salsa tastes more vibrant than bottled, and you control the added sodium. Corn tortillas have a fraction of the sodium in flour ones.

- 1 cup chopped tomato
- ¼ cup chopped red onion
- 2 tablespoons chopped fresh cilantro
- 1 teaspoon minced jalapeño pepper
- ¼ teaspoon kosher salt
- 4 teaspoons fresh lime juice, divided
- 1 teaspoon minced garlic, divided
- 1 cup organic refried beans
- ¼ teaspoon ground cumin
- 1 tablespoon 1% low-fat milk
- 6 large eggs, lightly beaten
  Cooking spray
- ¼ cup chopped green onions
- 8 (6-inch) corn tortillas
- ½ cup (2 ounces) shredded Monterey Jack cheese with jalapeño peppers
- 8 teaspoons reduced-fat sour cream

1 Combine first 5 ingredients in a small bowl. Stir in 2 teaspoons juice and ½ teaspoon garlic. Combine beans, cumin, remaining 2 teaspoons juice, and remaining ½ teaspoon garlic in another bowl.

2 Combine milk and eggs in a medium bowl; stir with a whisk. Heat a large nonstick skillet over medium-high heat. Coat pan with cooking spray. Add green onions to pan; sauté 1 minute, stirring frequently. Stir in egg mixture; cook 3 minutes or until soft-scrambled, stirring constantly. Remove from heat.

3 Warm tortillas according to package directions. Spread 1 tablespoon bean mixture on each tortilla. Spoon about 2 tablespoons egg mixture down center of each tortilla. Top each serving with 1 tablespoon tomato mixture, 1 tablespoon cheese, and 1 teaspoon sour cream. Yield: 4 servings (serving size: 2 tacos).

CALORIES 334 (36% from fat); FAT 13.3g (sat 5.5g, mono 4.2g, poly 2.3g); PROTEIN 19g; CARB 34g; FIBER 6.5g; CHOL 289mg; IRON 2.9mg; SODIUM 407mg; CALC 201mg

All in a Day

We used MyPyramid.gov to create a menu for an average American adult (using some of our featured recipes), incorporating whole grains, fruits, vegetables, dairy, and lean protein—all in the context of a daily 2,000-calorie, sodium-prudent diet.

Food/serving	Calories	Sodium (mg)
BREAKFAST:		
Rise and Shine Oatmeal (page 323)	380	304
Medium banana	110	Trace
1 cup skim milk	83	103
SNACK:		
1 small apple	55	1
1 ounce Swiss cheese	107	74
5 whole wheat crackers	177	264
LUNCH:		
Chicken with Tomato-Ginger Chutney (page 326)	243	352
½ cup cooked brown rice (dash of salt)	109	148
1 cup steamed broccoli florets (1 teaspoon oil, dash each of crushed red pepper and salt)	62	167
Salad (1 cup greens, ¼ cup carrot, ¼ cup tomato, 1 tablespoon oil and vinegar)	89	26
SNACK:		
3 cups reduced-fat microwave popcorn	44	144
DINNER:		
White Bean and Kale Stew (page 324)	307	505
1-ounce slice whole wheat bread	66	137
⅔ cup reduced-fat yogurt	111	55
2 tablespoons granola	56	5
Total:	**1,999**	**2,285**

Low- and fat-free foods may be a bit higher in sodium than their full-fat counterparts. When fat, a major vehicle for flavor, is removed, ingredients like sodium may be added to compensate.

Chicken with Tomato-Ginger Chutney

We sprinkle the salt directly on the poultry before cooking so it's not lost in the flour used for dredging. A little salt heightens flavors in the spicy-sweet chutney.

CHICKEN:

- 2 tablespoons all-purpose flour
- 4 (6-ounce) skinless, boneless chicken breast halves
- ¼ teaspoon kosher salt
- 1 tablespoon olive oil

CHUTNEY:

- 1 teaspoon olive oil
- 1 cup chopped onion (about 1 medium)
- 1 teaspoon minced peeled fresh ginger
- 2 garlic cloves, minced
- 1½ cups chopped seeded plum tomato
- ½ cup fat-free, less-sodium chicken broth
- 1 tablespoon chopped jalapeño pepper
- 1½ teaspoons sugar
- 1½ teaspoons fresh lemon juice
- 1 teaspoon ground mustard
- ¾ teaspoon ground cumin
- ¾ teaspoon ground fenugreek seeds (1½ teaspoons whole)
- ¼ teaspoon kosher salt

① To prepare chicken, place flour in a shallow dish. Sprinkle chicken evenly with ¼ teaspoon kosher salt; dredge chicken in flour. Heat 1 tablespoon oil in a large nonstick skillet over medium-high heat. Add chicken to pan; cook 6 minutes on each side or until chicken is done and lightly browned. Remove from pan; keep warm. Wipe pan with a paper towel.

② To prepare chutney, heat 1 teaspoon oil in pan over medium-high heat; add onion, ginger, and garlic to pan. Cook 4 minutes or just until tender. Add tomato and remaining ingredients; bring to a boil. Cover, reduce heat, and simmer 20 minutes. Uncover and cook 6 minutes or until slightly thickened. Serve chutney with chicken. Yield: 4 servings (serving size: 1 chicken breast half and about ⅓ cup chutney).

CALORIES 243 (30% from fat); FAT 8.1g (sat 1.5g, mono 4.3g, poly 1.2g); PROTEIN 30.6g; CARB 11g; FIBER 2.3g; CHOL 76mg; IRON 1.9mg; SODIUM 352mg; CALC 41mg

MAKE AHEAD
Green Papaya and Mango Salad

This is a streamlined version of a favorite Thai salad. Even though fish sauce is a high-sodium ingredient, a tablespoon adds ample body and flavor to the dressing. Serve the salad as a refreshing accompaniment to spicy grilled pork or chicken.

- 2 cups shredded green papaya (about ½ pound)
- 2 cups cherry tomatoes, halved
- 1½ cups (½-inch) cubed peeled ripe mango (about 1)
- 1 cup bean sprouts
- 2 tablespoons chopped green onions
- 3 tablespoons fresh lime juice
- 1 tablespoon fish sauce
- 2 teaspoons honey
- 1 small jalapeño pepper, chopped
- Fresh cilantro sprigs (optional)
- Fresh mint sprigs (optional)

① Combine first 5 ingredients in a large bowl. Combine juice and next 3 ingredients in a small bowl; pour juice mixture over papaya mixture. Toss gently to combine. Cover and let stand 30 minutes. Garnish with cilantro and mint, if desired. Yield: 6 servings (serving size: 1 cup).

CALORIES 64 (6% from fat); FAT 0.4g (sat 0.1g, mono 0.1g, poly 0.1g); PROTEIN 1.6g; CARB 15.9g; FIBER 2.3g; CHOL 0mg; IRON 0.6mg; SODIUM 240mg; CALC 22mg

Grilled Jerk-Marinated Pork Kebabs

A little low-sodium soy sauce perks up the marinade to flavor the meat. Sprinkling salt on the meat at the end of grilling helps balance the sweet and fiery spices in the Jerk seasoning and enlivens the grilled vegetables.

- 2 tablespoons minced jalapeño pepper (about 1)
- 1 tablespoon apple cider vinegar
- 1 tablespoon low-sodium soy sauce
- 1 teaspoon dried thyme
- ½ teaspoon ground cinnamon
- ½ teaspoon ground red pepper
- ½ teaspoon freshly ground black pepper
- ¼ teaspoon ground allspice
- 1 (1-pound) pork tenderloin, trimmed and cut into 1-inch cubes
- 2 cups cherry tomatoes
- 1 cup (1-inch) pineapple pieces
- 1 green bell pepper, cut into 1-inch pieces
- 1 small red onion, cut into ½-inch pieces
- Cooking spray
- ¼ teaspoon kosher salt

① Combine first 9 ingredients in a large zip-top plastic bag. Seal; marinate in refrigerator 1½ hours, turning bag occasionally.

② Prepare grill.

③ Remove pork from bag; discard marinade. Thread pork, tomatoes, pineapple, bell pepper, and onion alternately onto 8 (12-inch) wooden skewers. Place on a grill rack coated with cooking spray, and grill 10 minutes, turning once. Sprinkle with salt. Yield: 4 servings (serving size: 2 kebabs).

CALORIES 189 (20% from fat); FAT 4.3g (sat 1.4g, mono 1.8g, poly 0.6g); PROTEIN 25.4g; CARB 12.5g; FIBER 2.7g; CHOL 74mg; IRON 2.3mg; SODIUM 296mg; CALC 29mg

Caramelizing

Relish the nutty, rich taste of cooked sugar in sweet and savory applications.

CARAMELIZING NOT ONLY makes foods rich and dark in color but also enhances and concentrates the taste. Golden-hued, hearty desserts like Tarte Tatin (page 331) and savories such as caramelized onion soup warm appetites as the weather cools.

STAFF FAVORITE • MAKE AHEAD
Classic Crème Caramel

Nutty caramel coats delicate baked custard in this rich dessert, also referred to as "flan" in Spain. Although we specify cooking the caramel until golden, you can cook it longer for a deep amber color; the bitter notes of the darker caramel add a nice contrast to the sweet custard. The custards chill overnight, so they're a great make-ahead option for a dinner party. Baking at a low temperature means there's no need for a water bath. Since the seeds are not scraped from the vanilla bean, you can allow it to dry after steeping in the milk and reserve it for another use.

    4   cups 2% reduced-fat milk
    1   vanilla bean, split lengthwise
    Cooking spray
    1⅔ cups sugar, divided
    ¼   cup water
    ¼   teaspoon kosher salt
    6   large eggs
    3   tablespoons heavy whipping
        cream

❶ Preheat oven to 225°.
❷ Heat milk and vanilla bean over medium-high heat in a medium, heavy saucepan to 180° or until tiny bubbles form around edge (do not boil); remove pan from heat. Cover and set aside.
❸ Coat 10 (6-ounce) custard cups with cooking spray; arrange cups on a jelly-roll pan.

❹ Combine 1 cup sugar and ¼ cup water in a small, heavy saucepan; cook over medium-high heat until sugar dissolves, stirring frequently. Cook 7 minutes or until golden (do not stir). Immediately pour into prepared custard cups, tipping quickly until caramelized sugar coats bottom of cups.
❺ Combine remaining ⅔ cup sugar, salt, and eggs in a large bowl, stirring with a whisk. Remove vanilla bean from milk mixture; reserve bean for another use. Gradually pour warm milk mixture into egg mixture, stirring constantly with a whisk; stir in cream. Strain egg mixture through a sieve into a large bowl; pour about ½ cup egg mixture over caramelized sugar in each custard cup. Bake at 225° for 2 hours or until custards are just set. Remove from oven; cool to room temperature. Place plastic wrap on surface of custards; chill overnight.
❻ Loosen edges of custards with a knife or rubber spatula. Place a dessert plate, upside down, on top of each cup; invert onto plates. Drizzle any remaining caramelized syrup over custards. Yield: 10 servings (serving size: 1 custard).

CALORIES 236 (25% from fat); FAT 6.5g (sat 3.1g, mono 2.2g, poly 0.5g); PROTEIN 7.1g; CARB 38.4g; FIBER 0g; CHOL 140mg; IRON 0.6mg; SODIUM 139mg; CALC 138mg

MAKE AHEAD
Oranges with Caramel and Cardamom Syrup

Deep amber caramel possesses faint bitter notes that pair well with the sweet-tangy oranges. Orange-flower water infuses this simple dessert with Moroccan flair; look for it in gourmet markets or Middle Eastern grocery stores.

    ½   cup water
    2   cardamom pods, crushed
    6   tablespoons sugar
    5   navel oranges (about 2¼ pounds)
    1   cup whole-milk Greek yogurt
    2   tablespoons honey
    ⅛   teaspoon orange-flower water
    Mint sprigs (optional)

❶ Combine ½ cup water and cardamom in a small, heavy saucepan; bring to a boil. Remove from heat; cover and let stand 20 minutes. Strain through a fine sieve into a small bowl; discard solids.
❷ Combine 1 tablespoon cardamom water and sugar in pan over medium heat, and cook 9 minutes or until sugar dissolves and is barely golden (do not stir). Increase heat to medium-high, and cook 1 minute or until mixture darkens to a deep amber. Remove from heat; carefully pour remaining cardamom water down side of pan. Return pan to medium-high heat; stir until well blended. Remove pan from heat.
❸ Peel oranges. Cut each orange crosswise into 6 slices. Arrange slices on a rimmed platter; pour hot syrup over oranges. Cover and chill overnight.
❹ Combine yogurt, honey, and orange-flower water in a small bowl. Serve yogurt mixture with oranges. Garnish with mint sprigs, if desired. Yield: 6 servings (serving size: 5 orange slices and 3 tablespoons yogurt mixture).

CALORIES 170 (21% from fat); FAT 3.9g (sat 3g, mono 0.6g, poly 0g); PROTEIN 3.7g; CARB 32.3g; FIBER 2.6g; CHOL 7mg; IRON 0.1mg; SODIUM 12mg; CALC 73mg

Duck Breasts with Pinot Noir and Cherry Sauce

This recipe starts with a *gastrique,* a classic combination of caramelized sugar, vinegar, and fruit. Whipping cream finishes the sauce, adding velvety richness that underscores the robust flavor of duck. Serve with green and wax beans.

       3   tablespoons sugar
       2   tablespoons water
     ½   cup dried tart cherries
       3   tablespoons red wine vinegar
       1   tablespoon olive oil, divided
     ¼   teaspoon salt, divided
     ⅛   teaspoon freshly ground black
            pepper
       4   (6-ounce) boneless duck breast
            halves, skinned
     ¼   cup chopped shallots
       1   garlic clove, minced
     1½   cups pinot noir or other spicy dry red
            wine
     ½   cup fat-free, less-sodium chicken
            broth
     ¼   cup whipping cream

❶ Combine sugar and 2 tablespoons water in a small, heavy saucepan over medium-high heat; cook until sugar dissolves, stirring gently as needed to dissolve sugar evenly (about 1 minute). Cook 5 minutes or until golden (do not stir). Remove from heat; carefully stir in cherries and vinegar (caramelized sugar will harden and stick to spoon). Place pan over low heat until caramelized sugar melts.
❷ Heat 2 teaspoons oil in a large nonstick skillet over medium-high heat. Sprinkle ⅛ teaspoon salt and pepper over duck. Add duck to pan; cook 5 minutes. Turn duck over; cook 4 minutes or until desired degree of doneness. Remove from pan; let stand 5 minutes. Cut duck across grain into thin slices.
❸ Return skillet to medium heat. Add remaining 1 teaspoon oil, shallots, and garlic to pan; cook 1 minute or until tender, stirring frequently. Add wine to pan;

increase heat to medium-high. Bring mixture to a boil; cook until reduced to ¾ cup (about 6 minutes). Add broth; bring to a boil. Cook until reduced to ½ cup (about 6 minutes). Strain wine mixture through a fine sieve into cherry mixture; discard solids. Bring cherry mixture to a simmer over medium heat. Stir in cream; simmer 3 minutes. Remove from heat; stir in remaining ⅛ teaspoon salt. Serve sauce over duck. Yield: 4 servings (serving size: 1 duck breast half and ¼ cup sauce).

CALORIES 416 (29% from fat); FAT 13.2g (sat 4.9g, mono 5.6g, poly 1.2g); PROTEIN 48.1g; CARB 23.7g; FIBER 4.3g; CHOL 264mg; IRON 8.5mg; SODIUM 387mg; CALC 42mg

Caramelized Onion and Shiitake Soup with Gruyère–Blue Cheese Toasts

Earthy shiitake mushrooms and pungent cheese toasts give this soup more heartiness than classic French onion soup.

SOUP:

       1   tablespoon olive oil
       8   cups vertically sliced yellow onion
            (about 2 pounds)
       5   cups sliced shiitake mushroom caps
            (about 10 ounces whole
            mushrooms)
       4   garlic cloves, minced
       2   thyme sprigs
     ½   cup dry white wine
       1   (14-ounce) can fat-free, less-sodium
            chicken broth
       1   (14-ounce) can fat-free, less-sodium
            beef broth
     ½   teaspoon salt
     ½   teaspoon freshly ground black
            pepper

TOASTS:

     12   (½-inch-thick) slices French
            bread baguette, toasted (about
            6 ounces)
     ¼   cup (1 ounce) grated Gruyère
            cheese
     ¼   cup (1 ounce) crumbled Gorgonzola
     ½   teaspoon finely chopped fresh
            thyme

❶ To prepare soup, heat oil in a large Dutch oven over medium-high heat. Add onion to pan; sauté 15 minutes or until almost tender, stirring frequently. Reduce heat to medium-low; cook until deep golden brown (about 40 minutes), stirring occasionally.
❷ Increase heat to medium. Add mushrooms to pan; cook 10 minutes or until mushrooms are tender, stirring frequently. Stir in garlic and thyme sprigs; cook 2 minutes, stirring frequently. Increase heat to medium-high. Add wine to pan; cook 2 minutes or until most of liquid evaporates. Add broths to pan; bring to a simmer. Reduce heat, and simmer 45 minutes. Stir in salt and pepper. Discard thyme sprigs.
❸ To prepare toasts, preheat broiler.
❹ Arrange bread in a single layer on a baking sheet. Top each bread slice with 1 teaspoon Gruyère and 1 teaspoon Gorgonzola. Broil 2 minutes or until cheese melts. Sprinkle chopped thyme over cheese. Ladle about 1 cup soup into each of 6 bowls; top each serving with 2 toasts. Yield: 6 servings.

CALORIES 208 (23% from fat); FAT 5.4g (sat 2.3g, mono 2.2g, poly 0.4g); PROTEIN 8.9g; CARB 33.4g; FIBER 3.9g; CHOL 9mg; IRON 2.1mg; SODIUM 694mg; CALC 115mg

All About Caramelizing

Caramelizing, Defined

Caramelizing is the process of cooking sugar until it browns. When table sugar is heated to high temperatures (about 340°), it melts and darkens. As it turns from clear to dark amber, the sugar undergoes chemical changes. The sugars break apart and reform new compounds—as many as 128 different compounds have been identified during the caramel-making process—adding buttery, nutty, acidic, and bitter notes. Cooking can also "caramelize" the natural sugars in fruits and vegetables (see "Other 'Caramelized' Foods," at right).

Equipment

High-quality heavy saucepans ensure that even browning occurs. Thin or uneven pans tend to have hot spots that can burn rather than brown the sugar. It also helps to use pans with light metal interiors, such as stainless steel. Dark metal makes it difficult to see if the caramel is browning properly.

Two Methods

The most common techniques for caramelizing sugar are the dry method and the wet method. The former involves melting and browning sugar (by itself) in a pan. This is a tricky strategy often used by candy makers.

We prefer the wet method, which involves dissolving sugar in water, then cooking until the water evaporates and the melted sugar browns. This technique is best for home cooks because it helps prevent the sugar from burning. The addition of water also lengthens the time required for the sugar to caramelize, so more chemical reactions occur and produce more complex flavor.

No Stirring

Using the wet technique, add specified amounts of sugar and water to a heavy saucepan over medium-high heat, and stir only until the sugar dissolves. Once it does, cook—without stirring—until the caramel reaches the desired color. As the water evaporates, the mixture will begin to darken. This darkening will occur unevenly, but do not stir the caramel, as stirring incorporates air, lowers the temperature, and inhibits proper browning. If you stir before the water evaporates, the syrup may crystallize. Plus, the caramel will adhere to the spoon, creating a mess.

Keep an Eye on Color

As the caramel darkens, the flavor intensifies. Pale golden caramel is mild, while deep amber caramel tastes rich with a hint of bitterness. As the mixture begins to darken, it's important to watch it carefully—it takes only seconds to go from perfect dark amber to overdone. If it cooks too long, it will appear almost black and have a bitter, burned smell and flavor. If that happens, you'll need to start over.

Work Quickly

When caramel deepens to the desired shade of brown, remove it from the heat immediately and quickly continue with specific recipe instructions. If caramel is left in the pan too long, it can cool and begin to harden. If the caramel becomes too thick to pour, simply reheat it over low heat, swirling the pan occasionally until the mixture becomes liquid again.

Caramelizing vs. Maillard Reactions

Although baked goods and meat develop a nutty, slightly sweet richness when browned, they're technically not caramelized, but undergo what is called "Maillard reactions." Named after the French chemist who identified the process in the early 1900s, Maillard reactions refer to the process of caramel-like flavor developing in foods as they brown. These reactions are similar to classic sugar caramelizing except they involve a series of complex reactions between proteins and sugars (rather than just sugar). Also, Maillard reactions occur at much lower heat than true sugar caramelization.

Hot Stuff

When your caramel reaches the perfect golden amber hue with a wisp of nutty aroma, you may be tempted to taste it. Don't. The molten caramel, which has been heated to about 340°, is too hot to touch or taste.

Other "Caramelized" Foods

Caramelizing is about more than just sugar. "Caramelized" is also a catchall culinary term for cooking foods other than sugar—most notably onions, but other vegetables and fruits, too—to a rich brown color and an intensified sweetness. Caramelized onions can be cooked to a sweet, caramel-brown, jamlike mixture. As onions sauté, their strong sulfur compounds dissolve and new compounds develop that are as sweet as sugar. Brussels sprouts also become sweeter as they brown, as cooking breaks down the cell structure and makes existing sugars more pronounced. In general, most vegetables that are naturally rich in sugars and low in acid—such as carrots, onions, and members of the cabbage family—lend themselves best to caramelizing.

The Bottom Line

The three most important elements to remember about caramelizing:

1 Use a heavy, preferably light-colored, pan.
2 Once the sugar dissolves into the water, do not stir.
3 Remove pan from heat immediately after caramel reaches the desired color.

Vietnamese Caramelized Pork with Coriander Rice

Caramelized sugar creates a sweet-salty glaze for marinated pork strips. Served with spinach and rice, it's a satisfying one-dish meal.

MARINADE:

- 1 pound thin-cut boneless center-cut pork loin chops, trimmed
- ¼ cup chopped green onions
- 1 tablespoon brown sugar
- 1 tablespoon fresh lime juice
- 1 tablespoon fish sauce
- ½ teaspoon crushed red pepper
- 4 garlic cloves, minced

RICE:

- ¼ teaspoon coriander seeds, crushed
- 2 cups water
- ¼ teaspoon salt
- 1 cup uncooked long-grain white rice
- 1 tablespoon chopped fresh cilantro

REMAINING INGREDIENTS:

- Cooking spray
- 3 tablespoons granulated sugar
- 1 tablespoon water
- 2 teaspoons peanut oil
- 1 teaspoon grated peeled fresh ginger
- 1 teaspoon minced garlic
- 6 cups packed baby spinach leaves (about 4 ounces)
- ¼ teaspoon salt
- ¼ cup chopped green onions
- 2 tablespoons coarsely chopped fresh mint leaves

❶ To prepare marinade, cut pork across grain into ¼-inch-thick slices. Combine pork and next 6 ingredients in a large zip-top plastic bag; seal. Marinate in refrigerator 30 minutes, turning occasionally.
❷ While pork marinates, cook coriander in a medium saucepan over medium-high heat 1 minute or until lightly toasted, stirring frequently. Add 2 cups water and ¼ teaspoon salt to pan; bring to a boil. Stir in rice; cover, reduce heat, and simmer 16 minutes or until liquid is absorbed. Stir in cilantro.
❸ Remove pork from bag; discard marinade. Heat a large nonstick skillet over medium-high heat. Coat pan with cooking spray. Add pork to pan; sauté 1 minute or until lightly browned. Remove pork from pan; wipe pan clean with paper towels.
❹ Add granulated sugar and 1 tablespoon water to pan; cook over medium-high heat 1 minute or until sugar dissolves, stirring constantly. Cook 4 minutes or until golden (do not stir). Return pork to pan; cook 1 minute, tossing to coat. Transfer pork mixture to a bowl.
❺ Heat oil in pan over medium heat. Add ginger and 1 teaspoon garlic to pan; cook 30 seconds, stirring constantly. Add half of spinach to pan; cover and cook 1 minute or until spinach wilts. Remove from heat. Add remaining spinach and ¼ teaspoon salt to pan; toss to combine. Transfer spinach to a platter; top with pork mixture. Sprinkle with ¼ cup green onions and mint. Serve with rice. Yield: 4 servings (serving size: ½ cup pork mixture, ½ cup spinach, and ½ cup rice).

CALORIES 440 (17% from fat); FAT 8.5g (sat 2.5g, mono 3.8g, poly 1.5g); PROTEIN 30.1g; CARB 59g; FIBER 2.7g; CHOL 71mg; IRON 4mg; SODIUM 772mg; CALC 84mg

WINE NOTE: With the vibrant flavors of this dish, reach for a full-bodied yet refreshing white, like Nobilo Pinot Gris ($13) from New Zealand. This wine has a touch of sweetness that complements the sweet pork and caramelized glaze while balancing the ginger and red pepper heat. Bright acid and citrus flavors ready your palate for another bite.

Dinner with Friends Menu

serves 6

This menu capitalizes on the robust tastes of autumn.

Caramelized Shallots and Brussels Sprouts with Pancetta

Peppered filet mignon

Combine 1 tablespoon cracked black pepper, 2 teaspoons chopped fresh thyme, 1 teaspoon kosher salt, and 2 minced garlic cloves; rub evenly over both sides of 6 (4-ounce) beef tenderloin steaks (1 inch thick). Heat a large, heavy skillet over medium-high heat. Add 1 tablespoon butter to pan, swirling until butter melts. Add steaks to pan; cook 3 minutes on each side or until desired degree of doneness.

Mashed Yukon gold potatoes

QUICK & EASY

Caramelized Shallots and Brussels Sprouts with Pancetta

- 1½ pounds Brussels sprouts, halved
- Cooking spray
- 1 tablespoon olive oil
- ⅔ cup thinly sliced shallots
- ½ teaspoon black pepper
- ¼ teaspoon salt
- 1 ounce finely chopped pancetta
- 4 teaspoons brown sugar
- 2 teaspoon vermouth

❶ Preheat oven to 400°.
❷ Arrange Brussels sprouts on a jelly-roll pan coated with cooking spray. Drizzle with oil; toss to coat. Bake at 400° for 15 minutes. Add shallots and next 3 ingredients to pan; toss well. Bake at 400° for 10 minutes. Add sugar and vermouth; toss to coat. Bake an additional 10 minutes or until caramelized. Yield: 6 servings (serving size: about ⅔ cup).

CALORIES 117 (32% from fat); FAT 4.2g (sat 1.1g, mono 2.3g, poly 0.5g); PROTEIN 5.3g; CARB 16.9g; FIBER 4.9g; CHOL 3mg; IRON 2mg; SODIUM 209mg; CALC 61mg

Tarte Tatin

This iconic dessert was allegedly created by the Tatin sisters of France's Loire Valley. Legend is that while trying to repair a baking error, they ended up with this upside-down dessert of flaky pastry and apples bathed in caramel.

CRUST:

- 1 cup all-purpose flour (about 4.5 ounces)
- 1 tablespoon sugar
- ½ teaspoon salt
- 6 tablespoons unsalted butter, chilled and cut into small pieces
- 2 tablespoons ice water

FILLING:

- 3½ pounds small Gala apples (about 9), peeled, cored, and each cut into 8 wedges
- tablespoon fresh lemon juice
- ¼ teaspoon salt
- 2 tablespoons unsalted butter
- ¾ cup sugar

1 To prepare crust, lightly spoon flour into a dry measuring cup; level with a knife. Combine flour, 1 tablespoon sugar, and ½ teaspoon salt in a food processor; pulse until combined. Add 6 tablespoons chilled butter; pulse until mixture resembles coarse meal. Add 2 tablespoons ice water, and pulse until mixture forms clumps. Gently press dough into a 6-inch circle on heavy-duty plastic wrap; cover and freeze 30 minutes.

2 To prepare filling, combine apples, juice, and ¼ teaspoon salt in a large bowl, tossing to coat. Melt 2 tablespoons butter in a 9½-inch cast-iron skillet over medium-high heat. Add ¾ cup sugar to pan; cook 4 minutes or until golden brown, stirring constantly. Remove pan from heat. Arrange half of apples, rounded side down, in a circular pattern over sugar mixture in pan. Top with remaining apples, rounded side up. Cook over medium heat 15 minutes. Remove from heat; let stand 15 minutes.

3 Preheat oven to 400°.

4 Working quickly, roll dough into an 11-inch circle on a heavily floured surface. Place dough over apples; fold edges under. Cut 4 (1-inch) slits into top of pastry using a sharp knife. Bake at 400° for 40 minutes or until crust is lightly browned. Remove from oven; let stand 5 minutes. Place a plate upside down on top of pan. Carefully invert tart onto plate. Serve warm. Yield: 8 servings (serving size: 1 wedge).

CALORIES 318 (33% from fat); FAT 11.7g (sat 7.3g, mono 3g, poly 0.6g); PROTEIN 2.2g; CARB 54.2g; FIBER 2.6g; CHOL 30mg; IRON 0.9mg; SODIUM 223mg; CALC 15mg

Cashew Chicken Conundrum

A Canadian reader sends in a nutty curry entrée for one of our most challenging makeovers.

While living in Kenya with her husband, Abby Huck, a stay-at-home mom from Ottawa, Ontario, was introduced to Indian Cashew Chicken—a dish of chicken thighs marinated in a nut-yogurt mixture and cooked with tomatoes and cream. The friend who prepared the meal shared the recipe, but when Huck read the ingredient list, she saw why the dish was so sumptuous. Among its elements were the aforementioned chicken thighs, along with plenty of heavy cream and butter—all sources of saturated fat. Huck tries to avoid such foods, and she knew the delicately spiced Indian dish would not fit into her meal plans.

With one cup each of heavy cream and cashews, one-third cup butter, and two pounds of chicken thighs, the original recipe tips the scales at 712 calories and 51 grams of fat per serving. Besides the high total fat and calorie counts, one serving also contains 22 grams of saturated fat—more than the maximum 16 grams recommended daily by the American Heart Association (AHA) for a 2,000-calorie diet. The chicken thighs, cream, and butter also contribute most of the dish's 200 milligrams of cholesterol per portion, or two-thirds the maximum daily recommended amount, according to the AHA.

We focused on the high-fat ingredients, which also helped cut calories. First, we eliminated the butter for sautéing the onion, reducing 11 grams total fat (about seven grams saturated) and 100 calories per serving, and instead caramelized the onions in cooking spray. We finished the sauce with 3 tablespoons of half-and-half, in place of heavy cream, to preserve the dish's signature richness, while shaving nearly 130 calories and 14 grams of fat (nearly nine grams saturated). We replaced half the dark-meat chicken thighs with breast meat, which trimmed another 80 calories and seven grams of fat per serving. Lowering the amount of cashews to two-thirds cup dropped another 65 calories and five grams of fat. Thick, tangy fat-free Greek-style yogurt stood in for whole yogurt. Because the lightened recipe has substantially less fat (and fat smooths the taste of pungent ingredients), we reduced the amounts of garlic and spices to maintain the subtle balance of flavors in the original recipe.

serving size: 1 cup	before	after
CALORIES PER SERVING	712	340
FAT	51.3g	13.6g
PERCENT OF TOTAL CALORIES	65%	36%

Continued

Indian Cashew Chicken

A take on the Indian dish *murgh makhani*, this entrée recipe varies but typically has a thick sauce punctuated with Indian spices. To mimic the full-bodied sauce, we caramelize onions and later simmer the mixture to a thick, marinara-like consistency. Serve over brown basmati rice or with naan flatbread.

- ⅔ cup cashews, toasted
- ⅔ cup fat-free Greek-style yogurt
- ¼ cup tomato paste
- 2 tablespoons white vinegar
- 1¼ teaspoons garam masala
- 1 teaspoon ground coriander
- 1 teaspoon grated peeled fresh ginger
- ¼ teaspoon ground red pepper
- 2 garlic cloves, chopped
- 4 skinless, boneless chicken thighs, cut into bite-sized pieces (about 14 ounces)
- 2 (8-ounce) skinless, boneless chicken breasts, cut into bite-sized pieces
- Cooking spray
- 2¾ cups finely chopped onion (2 large)
- 2 green cardamom pods, lightly crushed
- 1 (2-inch) cinnamon stick
- 2 cups fat-free, less-sodium chicken broth
- 1 cup organic tomato puree (such as Muir Glen Organic)
- 1 teaspoon Hungarian sweet paprika
- ¼ teaspoon salt
- 3 tablespoons half-and-half
- Chopped fresh cilantro (optional)

① Combine first 9 ingredients in a blender or food processor; process until smooth. Combine nut mixture and chicken in a large bowl; cover and refrigerate 3 hours or overnight.
② Heat a large Dutch oven over medium-low heat. Coat pan with cooking spray. Add onion, cardamom, and cinnamon stick to pan; cover and cook 10 minutes or until onion is golden, stirring frequently.
③ Add chicken mixture to pan; cook 10 minutes, stirring frequently. Stir in broth and next 3 ingredients, scraping pan to loosen browned bits. Cook 1 hour or until thick. Stir in half-and-half; cook 1 minute, stirring occasionally. Remove from heat. Discard cinnamon stick. Garnish with cilantro, if desired. Yield: 6 servings (serving size: about 1 cup).

CALORIES 340 (36% from fat); FAT 13.6g (sat 3.4g, mono 5.8g, poly 2.6g); PROTEIN 36.7g; CARB 18.7g; FIBER 3.8g; CHOL 91mg; IRON 3.2mg; SODIUM 435mg; CALC 83mg

READER RECIPES
Spice It Up

An Alabama financial advisor accents tacos with toasted spiced pumpkin seeds for a new fall favorite.

Linda Croley loves the bold, smoky flavor of tacos she's enjoyed in the Southwest. But she could do without the typical high calorie and fat content from the meat, cheese, and fried tortillas. So when Croley, a financial advisor from Birmingham, Alabama, began lightening her favorite recipes last year, she created a delicious, light taco without sacrificing flavor: Pork Tacos with Slaw and Spicy Pepitas.

Pork Tacos with Slaw and Spicy Pepitas

"This is a very easy dish that can be prepped in advance. After that, it's a snap. Be sure to slice the pork thinly; it does not take long to cook. Pepitas (pumpkinseed kernels) are popular in Mexican cooking; keep an eye on them while toasting so they don't burn. I like to serve this dish with salsa and baked chips."

—Linda Croley,
Birmingham, Alabama

- 1 teaspoon ground cumin
- 1 teaspoon chili powder
- ½ teaspoon salt
- ½ teaspoon garlic powder
- ½ teaspoon ground ancho or chipotle chile pepper
- ½ teaspoon black pepper
- 1 pound boneless center-cut loin pork chops (about ½ inch thick)
- Cooking spray
- ¼ cup fresh lime juice, divided
- ½ cup sliced red bell pepper
- 2 tablespoons thinly sliced green onions
- 1 tablespoon minced jalapeño pepper
- ½ (16-ounce) package coleslaw (about 3 cups)
- 12 (6-inch) white or yellow corn tortillas
- 6 tablespoons light sour cream
- 6 tablespoons Spicy Pepitas

① Combine first 6 ingredients in a small bowl. Lightly coat pork with cooking spray; rub spice mixture over both sides of pork. Cover and refrigerate 1 hour.
② Preheat grill.
③ Place pork on a grill rack coated with cooking spray; grill 1 minute on each side or until done. Cut pork into ¼-inch slices. Combine pork and 2 tablespoons juice in a medium bowl, tossing to coat.
④ Combine remaining 2 tablespoons juice, bell pepper, and next 3 ingredients in a large bowl, tossing well.
⑤ Heat a nonstick griddle over medium heat. Coat griddle with cooking spray. Arrange 6 tortillas in a single layer; cook 1 minute on each side or until lightly browned. Repeat procedure with cooking spray and remaining 6 tortillas. Divide pork mixture evenly among tortillas; top each tortilla with 2 tablespoons coleslaw mixture, 1½ teaspoons sour cream, and 1½ teaspoons Spicy Pepitas. Yield: 6 servings (serving size: 2 filled tacos).

CALORIES 271 (35% from fat); FAT 10.2g (sat 2.9g, mono 3.3g, poly 2.2g); PROTEIN 20.7g; CARB 25.9g; FIBER 4.2g; CHOL 48mg; IRON 1.3mg; SODIUM 322mg; CALC 72mg

SPICY PEPITAS:

Store the leftover pepitas in a zip-top plastic bag; sprinkle them over a salad, or enjoy as a snack.

- 1 cup unsalted pumpkinseed kernels
- 1 tablespoon canola oil
- ½ teaspoon ground cumin
- ½ teaspoon chili powder
- ¼ teaspoon salt
- ¼ teaspoon garlic powder
- ¼ teaspoon ground ancho or chipotle chile pepper
- ¼ teaspoon black pepper

❶ Combine all ingredients in a small bowl. Heat a medium nonstick skillet over medium heat. Add mixture to pan; cook 10 minutes or until browned, stirring frequently. Remove from pan; cool completely. Yield: 1 cup (serving size: 1 tablespoon).

CALORIES 47 (69% from fat); FAT 3.6g (sat 0.6g, mono 1.3g, poly 1.3g); PROTEIN 1.5g; CARB 1.8g; FIBER 0.8g; CHOL 0mg; IRON 0.4mg; SODIUM 41mg; CALC 8mg

Island Fresh Menu
serves 4

Tropical flavors add warmth to a chilly fall night.

Grilled Chicken with Mango-Pineapple Salsa

Green rice
Prepare 1 cup uncooked long-grain basmati rice according to package directions, omitting salt and fat. Place 1 cup loosely packed fresh cilantro leaves; ¼ cup fat-free, less-sodium chicken broth; 2 tablespoons chopped green onions; ½ teaspoon salt; ¼ teaspoon freshly ground black pepper; and 1 garlic clove in a blender. Process until smooth. Add sauce to rice; toss gently to combine.

Plantain chips

Grilled Chicken with Mango-Pineapple Salsa

"Prepare the salsa while the chicken marinates. Add steamed brown rice."
—Lauren Katz, Ashburn, Virginia

SALSA:
- ⅔ cup diced peeled ripe mango (1 medium)
- ⅔ cup diced fresh pineapple
- 2 tablespoons minced red onion
- 1 tablespoon minced seeded jalapeño pepper
- 1½ teaspoons chopped fresh cilantro
- 1½ teaspoons fresh lime juice
- ⅛ teaspoon salt
- ⅛ teaspoon freshly ground black pepper

CHICKEN:
- 4 (6-ounce) skinless, boneless chicken breast halves
- ¼ cup pineapple juice
- 3 tablespoons chopped fresh cilantro
- 3 tablespoons low-sodium soy sauce
- 2 tablespoons honey
- 1 teaspoon fresh lime juice
- Dash of crushed red pepper
- Cooking spray

❶ To prepare salsa, combine first 8 ingredients. Cover; refrigerate 30 minutes.
❷ To prepare chicken, place each chicken breast half between 2 sheets of heavy-duty plastic wrap; pound to ½-inch thickness using a meat mallet or small heavy skillet. Combine pineapple juice and next 5 ingredients in a large zip-top plastic bag. Add chicken to bag; seal. Marinate in refrigerator 30 minutes.
❸ Prepare grill.
❹ Remove chicken from bag, reserving marinade. Place chicken on a grill rack coated with cooking spray; grill 3 minutes on each side or until done.
❺ Place reserved marinade in a small saucepan; bring to a boil. Reduce heat, and cook until reduced to ¼ cup (about

5 minutes). Drizzle over chicken. Serve salsa with chicken. Yield: 4 servings (serving size: 1 chicken breast half, 1 tablespoon sauce, and ¼ cup salsa).

CALORIES 222 (14% from fat); FAT 3.4g (sat 0.9, mono 1.1g, poly 0.7g); PROTEIN 26.9g; CARB 21.1g; FIBER 1.3g; CHOL 70mg; IRON 1.4mg; SODIUM 537mg; CALC 27mg

Fresh Tomato Soup

"I love tomato soup and have found a way to enjoy it when the weather gets cooler by using plum tomatoes. They're flavorful year-round."
—Danese Blackwell, Farmington, Utah

- 2 cups fat-free, less-sodium chicken broth
- 1 cup chopped onion
- ¾ cup chopped celery
- 1 tablespoon thinly sliced fresh basil
- 1 tablespoon tomato paste
- 2 pounds plum tomatoes, cut into wedges
- ½ teaspoon salt
- ¼ teaspoon freshly ground black pepper
- 6 tablespoons plain low-fat yogurt
- 3 tablespoons thinly sliced fresh basil

❶ Combine first 6 ingredients in a large saucepan; bring to a boil. Reduce heat, and simmer 30 minutes. Place half of tomato mixture in a blender. Remove center piece of blender lid (to allow steam to escape); secure blender lid on blender. Place a clean towel over opening in blender lid (to avoid splatters). Blend until smooth. Pour into a large bowl. Repeat procedure with remaining tomato mixture. Stir in salt and pepper. Ladle ¾ cup soup into each of 6 bowls; top each serving with 1 tablespoon yogurt and 1½ teaspoons basil. Yield: 6 servings.

CALORIES 58 (12% from fat); FAT 0.8g (sat 0.3g, mono 0.1g, poly 0.2g); PROTEIN 3.1g; CARB 11.3g; FIBER 2.8g; CHOL 1mg; IRON 1.1mg; SODIUM 382mg; CALC 49mg

Frizzled Ham and Fig Salad

"This is a nice change of pace for a small dinner salad."

—Julie DeMatteo,
Clementon, New Jersey

Cooking spray
5 ounces ham, cut into 1-inch strips
3 tablespoons red wine vinegar
1 tablespoon extravirgin olive oil
1 tablespoon honey
1 teaspoon Dijon mustard
⅛ teaspoon salt
8 cups mixed salad greens
1 cup chopped dried Calimyrna figs
(about 6)
1 tablespoon slivered almonds,
toasted
¼ cup (1 ounce) shaved reduced-fat
Cheddar cheese

❶ Heat a large nonstick skillet over medium-high heat. Coat pan with cooking spray. Add ham to pan; cook 2 minutes or until lightly browned. Remove from heat; set aside.
❷ Combine vinegar and next 4 ingredients in a large bowl; stir with a whisk. Add ham, greens, figs, and almonds to bowl; toss well. Arrange 1 cup salad on each of 8 plates; top each serving with about 1½ teaspoons cheese. Yield: 8 servings.

CALORIES 143 (37% from fat); FAT 5.8g (sat 1.5g, mono 2.9g, poly 0.6g); PROTEIN 5.1g; CARB 20.5g; FIBER 3.7g; CHOL 10mg; IRON 1.4mg; SODIUM 264mg; CALC 98mg

20 Minute Dishes

From steak to lamb, pork to pasta, here are simple, fresh, and easy meals you can make superfast.

Pasta with Prosciutto and Spinach

Add watermelon, cantaloupe, and honeydew melon wedges as a side dish to complete the menu.

1 (9-ounce) package fresh cheese
tortellini (such as DiGiorno)
1 tablespoon pine nuts
1 teaspoon olive oil
6 large garlic cloves, finely chopped
1 (6-ounce) package fresh baby
spinach
¼ cup (1 ounce) preshredded
Parmesan cheese
¼ teaspoon black pepper
2 ounces prosciutto, thinly sliced

❶ Cook pasta according to package directions, omitting salt and fat; drain. Transfer pasta to a large bowl.
❷ Heat a large nonstick skillet over medium heat. Add nuts to pan; cook 1½ minutes or until toasted, stirring occasionally. Add nuts to bowl.
❸ Heat oil in pan over medium heat. Add garlic to pan; cook 2 minutes, stirring occasionally. Add spinach to pan; cook 2 minutes or until spinach wilts, stirring constantly. Add spinach mixture, cheese, pepper, and prosciutto to bowl; toss well. Yield: 4 servings (serving size: 1 cup).

CALORIES 292 (28% from fat); FAT 9.2g (sat 3.2g, mono 2.3g, poly 1.1g); PROTEIN 14.6g; CARB 38.8g; FIBER 3.8g; CHOL 32mg; IRON 1.8mg; SODIUM 618mg; CALC 103mg

Beef Tenderloin Steaks with Port Reduction and Blue Cheese

Add Brussels sprouts and wild rice to this entertaining-worthy dish. Use a large skillet to accommodate cooking the four steaks at once. If they're crowded in a small pan, the steaks will "steam," affecting the meat's texture.

4 (4-ounce) filet mignon steaks,
trimmed
¼ teaspoon salt
¼ teaspoon black pepper
Cooking spray
¾ cup port or other sweet red wine
2 tablespoons jellied cranberry sauce
2 tablespoons fat-free, less-sodium
beef broth
⅛ teaspoon salt
⅛ teaspoon black pepper
1 garlic clove, minced
2 tablespoons crumbled blue cheese

❶ Heat a large cast-iron skillet over medium-high heat. Sprinkle steaks with ¼ teaspoon salt and ¼ teaspoon pepper; coat steaks with cooking spray. Add steaks to pan; cook 4 minutes on each side or until desired degree of doneness. Remove steaks from pan; keep warm.
❷ Add port and next 5 ingredients to pan, scraping pan to loosen browned bits. Reduce heat, and cook until liquid is reduced to ¼ cup (about 4 minutes). Serve steaks with sauce; top with cheese. Yield: 4 servings (serving size: 1 steak, 1 tablespoon sauce, and 1½ teaspoons cheese).

CALORIES 282 (33% from fat); FAT 10.2g (sat 4.1g, mono 3.8g, poly 0.4g); PROTEIN 24.7g; CARB 9.8g; FIBER 0.2g; CHOL 73mg; IRON 3.3mg; SODIUM 361mg; CALC 35mg

Spinach Salad with Spiced Pork and Ginger Dressing

Crisp flatbread can round out this satisfying salad supper. You can also serve the seasoned pork as an entrée without the salad, if you wish.

- 1 (1-pound) pork tenderloin, trimmed
- 1 tablespoon Sriracha (hot chile sauce, such as Huy Fong)
- 2 tablespoons brown sugar
- ½ teaspoon garlic powder
- ¼ teaspoon salt
- Cooking spray
- 3 cups baby spinach leaves
- 2 cups thinly sliced Napa cabbage
- 1 cup red bell pepper strips
- ¼ cup low-fat sesame ginger dressing (such as Newman's Own)

1 Cut pork crosswise into ½-inch slices; flatten each slice slightly with hand. Combine pork and Sriracha in a bowl, tossing to coat. Add sugar, garlic powder, and salt; toss well.

2 Heat a large nonstick skillet over medium-high heat. Coat pan with cooking spray. Add pork mixture to pan, and cook 3 minutes on each side or until done. Remove from heat; keep warm.

3 Combine spinach, cabbage, and bell pepper in a large bowl. Add dressing; toss well. Arrange 1½ cups spinach mixture in each of 4 shallow bowls; top each serving with 3 ounces pork. Yield: 4 servings.

CALORIES 202 (21% from fat); FAT 4.7g (sat 1.4g, mono 1.8g, poly 0.5g); PROTEIN 25g; CARB 14.7g; FIBER 1.9g; CHOL 74mg; IRON 2.2mg; SODIUM 490mg; CALC 56mg

Pork with Lemon-Caper Sauce

Serve with orzo and green beans.

- ⅓ cup all-purpose flour
- ⅛ teaspoon salt
- 3 tablespoons Italian-seasoned breadcrumbs
- 3 tablespoons preshredded fresh Parmesan cheese
- ¼ teaspoon black pepper
- 1 large egg white, lightly beaten
- 4 (4-ounce) boneless center-cut pork chops (about ½ inch thick)
- Cooking spray
- 2 teaspoons olive oil
- ½ cup fat-free, less-sodium chicken broth
- 1 tablespoon dry white wine
- ¼ teaspoon grated lemon rind
- 1 tablespoon fresh lemon juice
- 2 teaspoons capers, rinsed and drained

1 Combine flour and salt in a shallow dish. Place breadcrumbs, cheese, and pepper in a shallow dish; place egg white in another shallow dish. Dredge pork in flour mixture, dip in egg white, and dredge in breadcrumb mixture. Coat pork with cooking spray.

2 Heat oil in a large nonstick skillet over medium-high heat. Add pork to pan; cook 4 minutes on each side or until done. Remove from pan; keep warm. Add broth and remaining ingredients to pan, scraping pan to loosen browned bits. Cook 2 minutes or until reduced to ¼ cup (about 2 minutes). Serve with pork. Yield: 4 servings (serving size: 1 chop and 1 tablespoon sauce).

CALORIES 256 (35% from fat); FAT 10.1g (sat 3.3g, mono 4.9g, poly 0.8g); PROTEIN 28.2g; CARB 11.5g; FIBER 0.7g; CHOL 68mg; IRON 1.5mg; SODIUM 419mg; CALC 82mg

Indian-Spiced Chicken Burgers

Garam masala is a blend of ground spices including cinnamon, cumin, dried chiles, and coriander. Wear plastic gloves to keep the chicken mixture from sticking to your hands. Serve with cucumber spears.

PATTIES:
- ¼ cup presliced green onions
- 1 tablespoon lemon juice
- 2 teaspoons garam masala
- 1 teaspoon bottled ground fresh ginger (such as Spice World)
- ¼ teaspoon salt
- ¼ teaspoon ground red pepper
- 1 pound ground chicken
- Cooking spray

REMAINING INGREDIENTS:
- ¼ cup 2% low-fat Greek yogurt
- 1½ teaspoons chopped fresh mint
- ⅛ teaspoon salt
- ¼ cup hot mango chutney
- 4 (1½-ounce) hamburger buns
- 1 cup fresh spinach leaves

1 To prepare patties, combine first 7 ingredients in a large bowl. Divide mixture into 4 equal portions, shaping each into a ½-inch-thick patty. Heat a large nonstick skillet over medium-high heat. Coat pan with cooking spray. Add patties to pan; cook 7 minutes on each side or until done.

2 Combine yogurt, mint, and ⅛ teaspoon salt. Spread 1 tablespoon chutney on bottom half of each of 4 buns; top each with 1 patty, 1 tablespoon yogurt mixture, ¼ cup spinach, and a bun top. Yield: 4 servings (serving size: 1 burger).

CALORIES 364 (36% from fat); FAT 14.5g (sat 4.8g, mono 4g, poly 3.8g); PROTEIN 25g; CARB 34.4g; FIBER 1.6g; CHOL 137mg; IRON 3.3mg; SODIUM 766mg; CALC 130mg

Lamb Chops with Mint-Fig Sauce

Serve with mashed sweet potatoes and steamed broccoli spears.

- 8 (4-ounce) lamb loin chops, trimmed
- ½ teaspoon salt
- ½ teaspoon black pepper
- Cooking spray
- 2 tablespoons fig preserves (such as Braswell's)
- 2 tablespoons fat-free, less-sodium beef broth
- 1 tablespoon fresh lemon juice
- ½ teaspoon bottled minced garlic
- 4 teaspoons chopped fresh mint

1 Preheat broiler.

2 Sprinkle lamb with salt and pepper. Place lamb on a broiler pan coated with cooking spray; broil 4 minutes on each side or until desired degree of doneness. Keep warm.

3 Combine preserves and next 3 ingredients in a small microwave-safe bowl. Microwave at HIGH 20 seconds; stir in mint. Serve with lamb. Yield: 4 servings (serving size: 2 chops and about 1 tablespoon sauce).

CALORIES 213 (33% from fat); FAT 7.8g (sat 2.8g, mono 3.1g, poly 0.7g); PROTEIN 27.3g; CARB 6.2g; FIBER 0.1g; CHOL 86mg; IRON 2.5mg; SODIUM 397mg; CALC 18mg

Saucy Suppers

These hearty meals feature meat, poultry, shellfish, and vegetables in deeply flavored broths and reductions.

Saucy Supper Menu 1
serves 4

Weeknight Coq au Vin

Egg noodles

Caramelized pears over vanilla ice cream

Melt 1 tablespoon butter in a large non-stick skillet over medium heat. Add 2 tablespoons brown sugar and 1 tablespoon Grand Marnier (orange-flavored liqueur) to pan; cook 30 seconds. Add 4 cups sliced peeled Bosc pear, ⅛ teaspoon ground cinnamon, and a dash of nutmeg; cook 10 minutes or until pear is tender, stirring occasionally. Remove from heat. Stir in 1 tablespoon Grand Marnier and 1 teaspoon fresh lemon juice. Serve over vanilla low-fat ice cream.

Game Plan
1 Cook bacon, and brown chicken.
2 While chicken cooks:
- Prepare pears.
3 While sauce reduces:
- Cook and drain egg noodles.

Weeknight Coq au Vin

Total time: 45 minutes

- 2 bacon slices, chopped
- 4 (4-ounce) bone-in chicken thighs, skinned
- 4 (4-ounce) chicken drumsticks, skinned
- ½ teaspoon salt
- ½ teaspoon freshly ground black pepper
- ¼ cup finely chopped fresh flat-leaf parsley, divided
- 1½ cups sliced cremini mushrooms
- 1½ cups dry red wine
- 1 cup chopped carrot
- ½ cup chopped shallots
- ½ cup fat-free, less-sodium chicken broth
- 1 tablespoon brandy
- 2 teaspoons tomato paste
- 1 teaspoon minced fresh thyme
- 1 garlic clove, minced

1 Cook bacon in a large Dutch oven over medium-high heat 2 minutes. Sprinkle chicken with salt and pepper. Add chicken to pan; cook 2 minutes. Stir in 3 tablespoons parsley, mushrooms, and remaining ingredients; bring to a boil. Cover, reduce heat, and simmer 25 minutes or until chicken is done.

2 Remove chicken with a slotted spoon; keep warm. Bring cooking liquid to a boil; cook until reduced to 3 cups (about 6 minutes). Return chicken to pan; cook 1 minute or until thoroughly heated. Sprinkle with remaining 1 tablespoon parsley. Yield: 4 servings (serving size: 1 thigh, 1 drumstick, and ¾ cup sauce).

CALORIES 345 (33% from fat); FAT 12.7g (sat 3.7g, mono 4.7g, poly 2.7g); PROTEIN 43.7g; CARB 11g; FIBER 1.6g; CHOL 150mg; IRON 3.3mg; SODIUM 595mg; CALC 60mg

Saucy Supper Menu 2

serves 4

Lemongrass Pork

Soba noodles

Ginger-macadamia frozen yogurt

Stir 2 tablespoons toasted macadamia nuts and 4 teaspoons chopped crystallized ginger into 2 cups softened vanilla frozen yogurt. Freeze yogurt mixture.

Game Plan

1 Prepare yogurt mixture, and freeze.

2 Cook pork.

3 While vegetables for pork cook:
  • Prepare noodles.

QUICK & EASY

Lemongrass Pork

A Southeast Asian–accented broth adds zest to pork and vegetables in this flavorful dish, while soba noodles provide an earthy base.

Total time: 42 minutes

Cooking spray

4 (4-ounce) boneless center-cut loin pork chops (about 1/2 inch thick)

1/4 teaspoon freshly ground black pepper

1/8 teaspoon salt

2 tablespoons chopped green onions

1 tablespoon finely chopped peeled fresh lemongrass

1 tablespoon finely chopped peeled fresh ginger

1 tablespoon low-sodium soy sauce

8 ounces carrot, halved lengthwise and cut into 3-inch pieces

1 (14-ounce) can fat-free, less-sodium chicken broth

1 garlic clove, sliced

4 baby bok choy, halved

1 tablespoon chopped fresh cilantro

1 tablespoon fresh lime juice

❶ Heat a large nonstick skillet over medium-high heat. Coat pan with cooking spray. Sprinkle pork with pepper and salt. Add pork to pan; cook 3 1/2 minutes on each side or until pork is done. Remove from pan; keep warm.

❷ Add onions and next 6 ingredients to pan. Bring to a simmer. Cook 6 minutes. Arrange bok choy in a single layer over carrot mixture. Cover, reduce heat to medium, and cook 4 minutes or until bok choy is tender. Stir in cilantro and juice. Cut each pork chop into 1/2-inch-thick slices. Spoon 1/2 cup vegetable mixture into each of 4 shallow bowls; top each serving with 3 ounces pork. Yield: 4 servings.

CALORIES 210 (32% from fat); FAT 7.4g (sat 2.6g, mono 3.2g, poly 0.8g); PROTEIN 27.1g; CARB 8.9g; FIBER 2.2g; CHOL 67mg; IRON 1.9mg; SODIUM 357mg; CALC 104mg

Saucy Supper Menu 3

serves 4

Sausage and Clams with Chickpeas

Fideos

Heat a large skillet over medium heat. Coat pan with cooking spray. Add 1 cup (4 ounces) angel hair pasta broken into 1-inch pieces to pan; cook 3 minutes or until pasta begins to brown, stirring frequently. Stir in 1/2 cup chopped onion and 1 minced garlic clove; cook 2 minutes, stirring occasionally. Add 1/4 teaspoon freshly ground black pepper, 1/8 teaspoon salt, and 1 (14-ounce) can fat-free, less-sodium chicken broth; cover, reduce heat, and simmer 5 minutes. Uncover and cook 10 minutes or until noodles are tender.

Reduced-fat pound cake

Game Plan

1 While sausage mixture simmers:
  • Start fideos.

2 While fideos cook uncovered:
  • Add clams and chickpeas to sausage mixture.

QUICK & EASY

Sausage and Clams with Chickpeas

This recipe features the Portuguese-inspired combination of sausage, kale, and clams. Use sweet turkey Italian sausage if you prefer less spice.

Total time: 35 minutes

Cooking spray

12 ounces hot turkey Italian sausage

1/2 cup chopped onion

3 garlic cloves, chopped

2 tablespoons Madeira wine or dry sherry

8 cups chopped kale (about 10 ounces)

1/8 teaspoon salt

1 (14-ounce) can fat-free, less-sodium chicken broth

16 littleneck clams

1 (15 1/2-ounce) can chickpeas (garbanzo beans), rinsed and drained

❶ Heat a Dutch oven over high heat. Coat pan with cooking spray. Remove casings from sausage. Add sausage to pan; cook 4 minutes or until browned, stirring to crumble. Reduce heat to medium. Stir in onion and garlic; cook 1 minute, stirring occasionally. Add Madeira; cook 1 minute or until liquid evaporates. Add kale, salt, and broth; cover, reduce heat, and simmer 15 minutes. Stir in clams and chickpeas; cook, covered, 10 minutes or until shells open. Discard any unopened shells. Yield: 4 servings (serving size: 2 cups).

CALORIES 349 (33% from fat); FAT 12.6g (sat 3g, mono 4.8g, poly 3.4g); PROTEIN 31.1g; CARB 30.8g; FIBER 5.7g; CHOL 70mg; IRON 13.1mg; SODIUM 842mg; CALC 242mg

Quick Beef Boliche

Romaine salad with mango vinaigrette

Combine 6 cups sliced romaine lettuce and ¾ cup cubed peeled ripe mango in a large bowl. Place another ¾ cup cubed peeled ripe mango, 1 tablespoon white wine vinegar, and a dash of salt in a blender; process until smooth. Drizzle dressing over lettuce mixture. Top each serving with 2 teaspoons chopped pistachios.

Black beans

Game Plan

1 Sauté beef, sausage, and vegetables.

2 While beef mixture simmers:
  • Prepare salad and dressing.
  • Heat and season beans.

QUICK & EASY
Quick Beef Boliche

This Cuban dish traditionally cooks for a long time. In this twist, we offer similar tastes with a faster preparation.
Total time: 45 minutes

  Cooking spray
  1 (1-pound) top sirloin, cut into (1-inch) pieces
  ½ teaspoon salt
  ¼ teaspoon freshly ground black pepper
  3 ounces hot chicken Italian sausage
  ¾ cup prechopped green bell pepper
  ½ cup prechopped onion
  ½ cup prechopped celery
  3 garlic cloves, minced
  2 cups refrigerated diced potatoes with onions (such as Simply Potatoes)
  ¼ cup sliced pimiento-stuffed olives, divided
  1 bay leaf
  1 (14½-ounce) can no-salt-added diced tomatoes, undrained
  1 tablespoon fresh lime juice
  Lime wedges (optional)

① Heat a large Dutch oven over high heat. Coat pan with cooking spray. Sprinkle beef with salt and black pepper. Add beef to pan; sauté 3 minutes or until browned. Remove casings from sausage. Add sausage to pan; sauté 1 minute or until browned, stirring to crumble. Stir in bell pepper and next 3 ingredients; sauté 2 minutes or until tender. Add potatoes, 2 tablespoons olives, and bay leaf to pan. Pour tomatoes evenly over beef mixture. Cover, reduce heat, and simmer 35 minutes or until beef is tender. Discard bay leaf. Stir in remaining 2 tablespoons olives and lime juice. Serve with lime wedges, if desired. Yield: 4 servings (serving size: 1¼ cups).

CALORIES 281 (23% from fat); FAT 7g (sat 2.4g, mono 2.9g, poly 0.7g); PROTEIN 29.8g; CARB 24.6g; FIBER 4.9g; CHOL 62mg; IRON 2.6mg; SODIUM 684mg; CALC 52mg

---

ONE MORE TASTE
Peanut Butter and Chocolate Cookies

Chocolate and peanut butter is an enduringly irresistible combination. A fresh batch of these nutty cookies is sure to provide rich, sweet comfort.

MAKE AHEAD
Peanut Butter and Chocolate Cookies

COOKIES:
  1½ cups all-purpose flour (about 6.75 ounces)
  1½ teaspoons baking powder
  ½ teaspoon salt
  1 cup granulated sugar
  ¼ cup creamy peanut butter
  2 tablespoons butter, softened
  ¼ cup 1% low-fat milk
  2 large eggs
  ½ teaspoon vanilla extract
  Cooking spray

ICING:
  1½ cups powdered sugar, divided
  3½ tablespoons 1% low-fat milk, divided
  2 tablespoons whipping cream, divided
  3 tablespoons creamy peanut butter
  1 ounce bittersweet chocolate chips
  1 teaspoon unsweetened cocoa

① Preheat oven to 375°.

② To prepare cookies, lightly spoon flour into dry measuring cups; level with a knife. Combine flour, baking powder, and salt, stirring well with a whisk. Combine granulated sugar, ¼ cup peanut butter, and butter in a large bowl; beat with a mixer at medium speed until well blended (about 2 minutes). Beat in ¼ cup milk. Add eggs, 1 at a time, beating well after each addition. Beat in vanilla. Add flour mixture to sugar mixture; beat at low speed until well blended.

③ Spoon dough mixture into a pastry bag fitted with ½-inch round tip. Pipe 36 (1½-inch-round) mounds onto 2 baking sheets coated with cooking spray. Bake at 375° for 11 minutes. Cool 1 minute on pans. Remove from pans; cool completely on wire racks.

④ To prepare icing, combine ¾ cup powdered sugar, 2 tablespoons milk, 1 tablespoon cream, and 3 tablespoons peanut butter in a medium bowl; stir well. Spoon peanut butter mixture into a small zip-top plastic bag; set aside. Place chips in a glass bowl; microwave at HIGH 30 seconds or until almost melted, stirring until smooth. Add remaining ¾ cup powdered sugar, remaining 1½ tablespoons milk, remaining 1 tablespoon cream, and cocoa to melted chocolate, stirring well with a whisk. Spoon chocolate mixture into a small zip-top plastic bag. Starting with peanut butter mixture, snip a tiny hole in corner of bag; drizzle icing on half of each cookie. Repeat procedure with chocolate frosting on other half of each cookie. Let stand 10 minutes or until icing is set. Yield: 36 cookies (serving size: 1 cookie).

CALORIES 96 (29% from fat); FAT 3.1g (sat 1.1g, mono 1.1g, poly 0.5g); PROTEIN 1.8g; CARB 16g; FIBER 0.4g; CHOL 15mg; IRON 0.4mg; SODIUM 78mg; CALC 19mg

The *Cooking Light* Holiday Cookbook

Every recipe you need for stunning celebrations, from libations and hors d'oeuvres to roasts, side dishes, desserts, and delectable gifts.

Starters & Drinks

Launch the festivities with spirited cocktails, no-fuss dips, creative salads, and hearty soups.

QUICK & EASY • MAKE AHEAD
Spinach Salad with Gorgonzola, Pistachios, and Pepper Jelly Vinaigrette

Red pepper jelly adds a snappy note to the vinaigrette. You can prepare the vinaigrette (step 1) earlier in the day and refrigerate; let it come to room temperature before tossing it with the spinach.

- ¼ cup red pepper jelly
- 2 tablespoons cider vinegar
- 1 tablespoon extravirgin olive oil
- ⅛ teaspoon kosher salt
- ⅛ teaspoon freshly ground black pepper
- 8 cups fresh baby spinach
- ¼ cup (1 ounce) crumbled Gorgonzola cheese
- ¼ cup dry-roasted pistachios

1 Place jelly in a 1-cup glass measure. Microwave at HIGH 30 seconds. Add vinegar and next 3 ingredients, stirring with a whisk until blended. Cool to room temperature.
2 Combine spinach and cheese in a large bowl. Drizzle vinegar mixture over spinach mixture; toss well. Sprinkle with nuts. Serve immediately. Yield: 6 servings (serving size: 1 cup spinach mixture and 2 teaspoons nuts).

CALORIES 101 (54% from fat); FAT 6.1g (sat 1.6g, mono 3g, poly 1.1g); PROTEIN 2.9g; CARB 10.4g; FIBER 2.3g; CHOL 4mg; IRON 1.3mg; SODIUM 187mg; CALC 54mg

Roasted Cauliflower Soup with Hazelnut Oil

Roasted hazelnut oil, available in gourmet stores and many supermarkets, lends a wonderful toasty character to this soup. Or try truffle oil instead. You also could serve smaller portions in demitasse cups as part of a cocktail buffet.

- 1 whole garlic head
- 12 cups cauliflower florets (about 2 pounds)
- Cooking spray
- 1 tablespoon olive oil
- 2 cups thinly sliced onion
- 4 cups fat-free milk
- 1 (14-ounce) can fat-free, less-sodium chicken broth
- 2 fresh thyme sprigs
- 1½ tablespoons roasted hazelnut oil
- ½ teaspoon salt
- ¼ teaspoon freshly ground black pepper
- ½ cup chopped fresh parsley

1 Preheat oven to 425°.
2 Remove white papery skin from garlic head (do not peel or separate cloves). Wrap in foil. Arrange cauliflower in a single layer on a baking sheet coated with cooking spray. Add garlic to pan. Bake garlic and cauliflower at 425° for 35 minutes or until golden brown, turning cauliflower after 20 minutes. Cool

Continued

10 minutes. Separate garlic cloves; squeeze to extract garlic pulp. Discard skins.

❸ Heat olive oil in a large Dutch oven over medium-high heat. Add onion to pan; sauté 8 minutes or until tender, stirring frequently. Add milk, broth, and thyme sprigs; bring to a simmer. Cook 10 minutes, stirring occasionally.

❹ Discard thyme sprigs. Stir in reserved garlic pulp and cauliflower. Place half of milk mixture in a blender. Remove center piece of blender lid (to allow steam to escape); secure blender lid on blender. Place a clean towel over opening in blender lid (to avoid splatters). Blend until smooth. Pour into a large bowl. Repeat procedure with remaining milk mixture. Stir in hazelnut oil, salt, and pepper. Ladle 1 cup soup into each of 12 bowls; top each serving with 2 teaspoons parsley. Yield: 12 servings.

CALORIES 87 (31% from fat); FAT 3g (sat 0.3g, mono 2.2g, poly 0.4g); PROTEIN 5.1g; CARB 11.1g; FIBER 2.4g; CHOL 1mg; IRON 0.6mg; SODIUM 233mg; CALC 113mg

---

COCKTAIL PARTY MENU

(Serves 10)*

Pink Grapefruit and Lychee Cocktail

Gingered Pear and Brandy Cocktail

Orange Chipotle-Spiced Pecan Mix

Traditional Hummus or variation

Spicy Baked Pita Chips

Shrimp Skewers with Coconut, Jalapeño, and Cilantro Dipping Sauce

*Double recipes as needed to complete this cocktail menu.

QUICK & EASY
Pink Grapefruit and Lychee Cocktail

Pink grapefruit stars in this pretty beverage. Look for canned lychee fruit in the ethnic foods aisle at the supermarket or at Asian groceries. If you're preparing our Cocktail Party Menu (at left), you'll want to double this recipe.

  1 (20-ounce) can lychees in syrup, undrained
  Crushed ice
  1 cup unsweetened pink grapefruit juice
  ½ cup vodka
  5 pink grapefruit sections

❶ Drain lychees in a colander over a bowl, reserving 1 cup syrup. Discard remaining liquid. Drop 1 lychee in bottom of each of 5 glasses; fill each glass halfway with crushed ice. Reserve remaining lychees for another use.

❷ Combine reserved 1 cup lychee syrup, juice, and vodka in a large martini shaker filled halfway with ice; shake until well chilled. Strain ½ cup syrup mixture into each prepared glass; garnish each serving with 1 grapefruit section. Serve immediately. Yield: 5 servings.

CALORIES 131 (0% from fat); FAT 0g; PROTEIN 0.6g; CARB 16.8g; FIBER 0.5g; CHOL 0mg; IRON 0.6mg; SODIUM 2mg; CALC 8mg

---

MAKE AHEAD
Gingered Pear and Brandy Cocktail

Simply prepare the gingered sugar syrup (step 1), and refrigerate it until you're ready to shake and serve the cocktails.

  ¼ cup water
  3 tablespoons sugar
  ¼ cup chopped peeled fresh ginger
  3 cups pear juice
  1 cup cognac
  10 lemon rind twists

❶ Combine ¼ cup water and sugar in a small saucepan over medium-high heat; cook until sugar dissolves. Remove from heat. Add ginger. Cover and let stand 15 minutes. Strain sugar mixture through a fine sieve. Discard solids. Chill sugar mixture 30 minutes or until ready to use.

❷ Fill a large martini shaker halfway with ice. Add sugar mixture, juice, and cognac; shake until chilled. Strain ½ cup mixture into each of 10 martini glasses. Garnish each serving with 1 lemon rind twist. Yield: 10 servings.

CALORIES 111 (0% from fat); FAT 0g; PROTEIN 0.1g; CARB 15.4g; FIBER 0.5g; CHOL 0mg; IRON 0.4mg; SODIUM 3mg; CALC 5mg

---

MAKE AHEAD
Orange Chipotle-Spiced Pecan Mix

Prepare a batch of this smoky-sweet mix to have on hand when visitors drop by.

  1 tablespoon grated orange rind
  1 tablespoon fresh orange juice
  1 large egg white
  2 cups pecan halves
  1 tablespoon dark brown sugar
  1 teaspoon kosher salt
  ½ teaspoon ground chipotle chile pepper
  Cooking spray
  ½ cup sweetened dried cranberries

❶ Preheat oven to 225°.

❷ Combine first 3 ingredients in a medium bowl; stir with a whisk. Stir in pecans. Combine sugar, salt, and pepper. Add to pecan mixture; toss well. Spread mixture in a single layer on a jelly-roll pan coated with cooking spray. Bake at 225° for 1 hour, stirring occasionally. Remove from oven; cool completely. Stir in cranberries. Yield: 2½ cups (serving size: 2 tablespoons).

NOTE: Store in an airtight container for up to one week.

CALORIES 91 (76% from fat); FAT 7.7g (sat 0.7g, mono 4.6g, poly 2.4g); PROTEIN 1.2g; CARB 4.8g; FIBER 0.8g; CHOL 0mg; IRON 0.3mg; SODIUM 98mg; CALC 1mg

Traditional Hummus

This Middle Eastern dip is traditionally made with chickpeas, tahini, lemon juice, and olive oil; it lends itself to several variations. Prepare and refrigerate it a day ahead; let it stand at room temperature for 30 minutes before serving. Garnish with a lemon wedge and fresh parsley sprig, and serve with Spicy Baked Pita Chips (at right).

2   (15.5-ounce) cans no-salt-added chickpeas (garbanzo beans), rinsed and drained
2   garlic cloves, crushed
½   cup water
¼   cup tahini (sesame seed paste)
3   tablespoons fresh lemon juice
2   tablespoons extravirgin olive oil
¾   teaspoon salt
¼   teaspoon black pepper

❶ Place beans and garlic in a food processor; pulse 5 times or until chopped. Add ½ cup water and remaining ingredients; pulse until smooth, scraping down sides as needed. Yield: 3¼ cups (serving size: 2 tablespoons).

CALORIES 44 (51% from fat); FAT 2.5g (sat 0.3g, mono 1.2g, poly 0.7g); PROTEIN 1.5g; CARB 4.4g; FIBER 0.9g; CHOL 0mg; IRON 0.3mg; SODIUM 74mg; CALC 12mg

FETA-BAKED HUMMUS VARIATION:
Combine Traditional Hummus, ½ cup (2 ounces) crumbled reduced-fat feta cheese, ¼ cup chopped fresh parsley, and ½ teaspoon ground cumin. Transfer mixture to an 8-inch square baking dish coated with cooking spray. Sprinkle with ½ cup (2 ounces) crumbled reduced-fat feta cheese. Bake at 400° for 25 minutes or until lightly browned. Garnish with parsley sprigs. Yield: 4 cups (serving size: about 2 tablespoons).

CALORIES 44 (51% from fat); FAT 2.5g (sat 0.6g, mono 1g, poly 0.6g); PROTEIN 2g; CARB 3.8g; FIBER 0.8g; CHOL 1mg; IRON 0.3mg; SODIUM 109mg; CALC 21mg

WHITE BEAN AND ROASTED GARLIC HUMMUS VARIATION:
Since this variation calls for roasted garlic, you can just omit the raw crushed garlic cloves from Traditional Hummus.

Remove white papery skin from 2 whole garlic heads (do not peel or separate cloves). Wrap each head separately in foil. Bake at 350° for 1 hour; cool 10 minutes. Separate cloves; squeeze to extract garlic pulp. Discard skins. Place garlic pulp, Traditional Hummus, and 1 (15-ounce) can rinsed and drained cannellini beans (or other white beans) in a food processor; pulse 5 times or until chopped. Add ¼ cup water; process until smooth, scraping down sides as needed. Stir in ¾ teaspoon chopped fresh rosemary. Yield: 5 cups (serving size: about 2 tablespoons).

CALORIES 36 (40% from fat); FAT 1.6g (sat 0.2g, mono 0.8g, poly 0.5g); PROTEIN 1.4g; CARB 4.2g; FIBER 1g; CHOL 0mg; IRON 0.3mg; SODIUM 65mg; CALC 13mg

SPICY RED PEPPER HUMMUS VARIATION:
Cut 2 red bell peppers in half lengthwise; discard seeds and membranes. Place pepper halves, skin sides up, on a foil-lined baking sheet; flatten with hand. Broil 15 minutes or until blackened. Place in a zip-top plastic bag; seal. Let stand 10 minutes. Peel and cut into strips. Combine bell peppers, 2 teaspoons chile paste with garlic (such as sambal oelek), ½ teaspoon paprika, and ⅛ teaspoon ground red pepper in a food processor; pulse until smooth. Transfer pepper mixture to a serving bowl; stir in Traditional Hummus. Yield: 4 cups (serving size: about 2 tablespoons).

CALORIES 39 (46% from fat); FAT 2g (sat 0.3g, mono 1g, poly 0.6g); PROTEIN 1.4g; CARB 4.3g; FIBER 1g; CHOL 0mg; IRON 0.3mg; SODIUM 74mg; CALC 11mg

Spicy Baked Pita Chips

6   (6-inch) pitas
Cooking spray
½   teaspoon kosher salt
¼   teaspoon garlic powder
⅛   teaspoon ground red pepper
⅛   teaspoon freshly ground black pepper

❶ Preheat oven to 350°.
❷ Cut each pita into 8 wedges; separate each wedge into 2 pieces. Arrange wedges in a single layer on 2 jelly-roll pans coated with cooking spray. Lightly coat wedges with cooking spray. Combine salt and remaining ingredients in a small bowl; sprinkle wedges evenly with spice mixture. Bake at 350° for 13 minutes or until crisp and golden brown. Yield: 32 servings (serving size: 3 chips).

CALORIES 30 (0% from fat); FAT 0g; PROTEIN 1.3g; CARB 6.2g; FIBER 0.2g; CHOL 0mg; IRON 0.5mg; SODIUM 59mg; CALC 8mg

The Holiday Liquor Cabinet

To make our cocktail recipes and other mixed drinks, here are helpful items to have on hand:
- Brandy (such as cognac or Armagnac)
- Orange-flavored liqueur (such as Grand Marnier)
- Bourbon or Tennessee whiskey
- Gin
- Vodka
- Sparkling wine (Spanish cava and Italian prosecco are most affordable)
- Assorted fruit juices (pink grapefruit, orange, cranberry, and such)
- Mixers (club soda, tonic water, ginger ale)
- Seasonal garnishes (star anise, cinnamon sticks)

Suggested tools to mix your drinks: martini shaker, strainer, bar knife, stirrer, ice tongs or spoon, double-jigger measure, bottle opener, and corkscrew. Basic bar tool sets start at about $20.

Shrimp Skewers with Coconut, Jalapeño, and Cilantro Dipping Sauce

Purchase the best fresh shrimp you can find, and ask the fishmonger to peel and devein them for you.

DIPPING SAUCE:

- 3 tablespoons light coconut milk
- ¼ cup chopped fresh cilantro leaves
- ¼ cup chopped seeded jalapeño pepper (about 2)
- 1 tablespoon fresh lime juice
- ¼ teaspoon salt

SKEWERS:

- 2 tablespoons fresh pineapple juice
- 1 tablespoon extravirgin olive oil
- 1 teaspoon grated lime rind
- 1 teaspoon minced garlic
- ¼ teaspoon salt
- ⅛ teaspoon ground red pepper
- 20 jumbo shrimp, peeled and deveined (about ½ pound)
- 20 (1-inch) cubes fresh pineapple (about ½ pound)
- Cooking spray

① To prepare dipping sauce, combine first 4 ingredients in a blender; process until smooth. Stir in ¼ teaspoon salt; cover and chill 30 minutes.

② To prepare skewers, combine pineapple juice and next 5 ingredients in a large bowl. Add shrimp; toss to coat. Let stand 10 minutes.

③ Thread 2 shrimp and 2 pineapple cubes alternately onto each of 10 (6-inch) skewers. Brush skewers with pineapple juice mixture. Heat a heavy grill pan over medium-high heat. Coat pan with cooking spray. Add skewers to pan; cook 4 minutes on each side or until shrimp are done. Serve with dipping sauce. Yield: 10 servings (serving size: 1 skewer and about 1 tablespoon sauce).

CALORIES 49 (35% from fat); FAT 1.9g (sat 0.5g, mono 1g, poly 0.3g); PROTEIN 3.2g; CARB 5.4g; FIBER 0.6g; CHOL 21mg; IRON 0.5mg; SODIUM 141mg; CALC 14mg

QUICK & EASY • MAKE AHEAD

Arugula Salad with Goat Cheese, Bacon, and Balsamic-Fig Dressing

Mix the tangy-sweet dressing up to three days ahead, and refrigerate.

DRESSING:

- 3 tablespoons balsamic vinegar
- 3 dried Black Mission figs, chopped
- 3 tablespoons water
- 2 tablespoons fat-free, less-sodium chicken broth
- 2 tablespoons extravirgin olive oil
- 1½ teaspoons honey
- ½ teaspoon minced shallots
- ¼ teaspoon chopped fresh thyme

SALAD:

- 8 cups trimmed arugula (about 4 ounces)
- ¼ cup thinly sliced red onion
- ¼ teaspoon freshly ground black pepper
- ⅛ teaspoon salt
- 3 center-cut bacon slices, cooked and crumbled
- 2 tablespoons crumbled goat cheese

① To prepare dressing, combine balsamic vinegar and figs in a small saucepan over medium-high heat; bring to a boil. Cover, remove from heat, and let stand 15 minutes. Combine vinegar mixture, 3 tablespoons water, and next 5 ingredients in a blender; process until smooth.

② To prepare salad, place 1⅓ cups arugula on each of 6 plates. Divide onion evenly among plates. Drizzle about 3 tablespoons dressing over each serving; sprinkle evenly with pepper and salt. Sprinkle evenly with bacon. Top each serving with 1 teaspoon goat cheese. Serve immediately. Yield: 6 servings.

CALORIES 91 (45% from fat); FAT 4.5g (sat 1.3g, mono 2.4g, poly 0.6g); PROTEIN 3g; CARB 10.9g; FIBER 1.7g; CHOL 5mg; IRON 0.9mg; SODIUM 147mg; CALC 88mg

MAKE AHEAD

Caramelized Sweet Onion Dip

If time is tight, you can caramelize the onions (step 2) earlier in the day; combine with the other ingredients, and bake just before guests arrive. Serve with a crunchy dipper like melba toast.

- 1 tablespoon butter, divided
- 3 cups diced Rio or other sweet onion (about 2 large)
- ¼ teaspoon kosher salt, divided
- ½ teaspoon minced garlic
- 1 cup reduced-fat mayonnaise
- ½ cup light sour cream
- ½ teaspoon garlic powder
- ¼ teaspoon freshly ground black pepper
- ¼ teaspoon Worcestershire sauce
- Cooking spray
- ⅓ cup whole wheat panko (Japanese breadcrumbs)
- 1 tablespoon chopped fresh parsley

① Preheat oven to 350°.

② Melt 1½ teaspoons butter in a large skillet over medium-high heat. Add onion and ⅛ teaspoon salt to pan; cook 15 minutes or until tender, stirring occasionally. Add garlic; cook 10 minutes or until onion is golden brown and very tender, stirring occasionally. Remove from heat; cool 5 minutes.

③ Combine remaining ⅛ teaspoon salt, mayonnaise, and next 4 ingredients in a medium bowl, stirring until smooth. Stir in onion mixture. Transfer mixture to a 1-quart baking dish coated with cooking spray.

④ Melt remaining 1½ teaspoons butter. Combine melted butter and panko. Sprinkle panko mixture evenly over onion mixture. Bake at 350° for 15 minutes or until thoroughly heated and bubbly. Sprinkle with parsley. Serve hot. Yield: 10 servings (serving size: about ¼ cup).

CALORIES 86 (55% from fat); FAT 5.3g (sat 1.3g, mono 0.3g, poly 1.6g); PROTEIN 1.3g; CARB 11.4g; FIBER 0.7g; CHOL 7mg; IRON 0.2mg; SODIUM 288mg; CALC 15mg

Spiked Spiced Russian Tea

Scale back to ½ cup bourbon if you prefer a less spirited beverage. This brew smells wonderful as it simmers.

- 6 cups water
- 2 large tea bags
- 2 cups fresh orange juice (about 4 oranges)
- 6 tablespoons honey
- 4 whole cloves
- 2 (3-inch) cinnamon sticks
- 2 (2-inch) strips lemon rind
- ¾ cup bourbon

1 Bring 6 cups water to a boil in a large saucepan, and remove from heat. Add tea bags to pan; cover and steep 5 minutes. Discard tea bags. Add juice and next 4 ingredients; bring to a simmer. Cook 10 minutes, stirring occasionally. Strain tea mixture through a fine sieve into a bowl, and discard solids. Stir in bourbon. Yield: 8 servings (serving size: 1 cup).

CALORIES 124 (0% from fat); FAT 0g; PROTEIN 0.5g; CARB 19.5g; FIBER 0.2g; CHOL 0mg; IRON 0.2mg; SODIUM 1mg; CALC 8mg

White Hot Spiced Chocolate

This drink is best made with fine ingredients like fresh nutmeg and top-quality white chocolate (we tested with Ghirardelli white chocolate chips). You can find both at a gourmet grocery or large supermarket.

- 3 cups 1% low-fat milk
- ⅛ teaspoon grated whole nutmeg
- 1 (3-inch) cinnamon stick
- ½ cup premium white chocolate chips
- ½ teaspoon vanilla extract
- ½ cup frozen fat-free whipped topping, thawed
  Grated whole nutmeg (optional)

1 Combine first 3 ingredients in a medium saucepan over medium heat; bring to a simmer, stirring constantly. Add white chocolate chips, stirring until chips melt. Remove from heat; stir in vanilla. Discard cinnamon stick. Serve with whipped topping. Sprinkle with additional nutmeg, if desired. Yield: 8 servings (serving size: about ½ cup hot chocolate and 1 tablespoon whipped topping).

CALORIES 117 (38% from fat); FAT 5g (sat 4.1g, mono 0.3g, poly 0g); PROTEIN 3g; CARB 14.4g; FIBER 0g; CHOL 4mg; IRON 0.1mg; SODIUM 64mg; CALC 113mg

Roasted Garlic Pizza

Roast the garlic a day ahead; cool, extract the pulp, and refrigerate until you're ready to assemble the pizza. A slice of this pizza makes a tasty hors d'oeuvre, or serve two slices with a tossed salad for supper.

- 1 whole garlic head
- ½ teaspoon active dry yeast
- ⅓ cup warm water (100° to 110°)
- ½ cup all-purpose flour (about 2.25 ounces)
- ½ cup bread flour (about 2.38 ounces)
- ½ teaspoon kosher salt
- 1 teaspoon olive oil
  Cooking spray
- 1 tablespoon cornmeal
- 1 cup (4 ounces) shredded part-skim mozzarella cheese
- ¼ cup (1 ounce) grated Parmigiano-Reggiano cheese
- 2 teaspoons chopped fresh oregano
- ¼ teaspoon crushed red pepper

1 Preheat oven to 375°.
2 Remove white papery skin from garlic head (do not peel or separate cloves). Wrap head in foil. Bake at 375° for 45 minutes; cool 10 minutes. Separate cloves; squeeze to extract garlic pulp. Discard skins.
3 Dissolve yeast in ⅓ cup warm water in a small bowl, and let stand 5 minutes. Lightly spoon flours into dry measuring cups; level with a knife. Place flours and salt in a food processor; pulse 2 times or until blended. Add oil to yeast mixture, stirring with a whisk. With processor on, slowly add yeast mixture through food chute; process until dough forms a ball. Process 1 additional minute. Turn dough out onto a floured surface; knead lightly 4 to 5 times. Place dough in a large bowl coated with cooking spray, turning to coat top. Cover and let rise in a warm place (85°), free from drafts, 1 hour or until doubled in size. (Gently press two fingers into dough. If indentation remains, dough has risen enough.)
4 Preheat oven to 400°.
5 Punch dough down; cover and let rest 5 minutes. Roll dough into a 10-inch circle on a floured surface. Place dough on pizza pan or baking sheet sprinkled with cornmeal. Spread roasted garlic evenly over dough, leaving a ½-inch border; top with cheeses, oregano, and pepper. Bake at 400° for 12 minutes or until crust is golden brown. Cut into 8 wedges. Yield: 8 servings (serving size: 1 wedge).

CALORIES 127 (27% from fat); FAT 3.9g (sat 2g, mono 1.3g, poly 0.3g); PROTEIN 6.7g; CARB 16.2g; FIBER 0.7g; CHOL 10mg; IRON 1mg; SODIUM 2mg; CALC 137mg

Oysters on the Half Shell with Cucumber-Sake Mignonette

- ½ cup minced peeled English cucumber
- ¼ cup rice wine vinegar
- 2 tablespoons sake (rice wine)
- ½ teaspoon minced shallots
- ¼ teaspoon freshly ground black pepper
- ⅛ teaspoon sea salt
- 16 shucked oysters

1 Combine first 6 ingredients in a small bowl; stir gently. Chill 15 minutes. Spoon 1½ teaspoons cucumber mixture over each oyster. Yield: 8 servings (serving size: 2 oysters).

CALORIES 29 (22% from fat); FAT 0.7g (sat 0.2g, mono 0.1g, poly 0.3g); PROTEIN 2.1g; CARB 2.5g; FIBER 0.1g; CHOL 15mg; IRON 2mg; SODIUM 96mg; CALC 14mg

Roast Butternut Squash Soup with Apples and Garam Masala

With butternut squash, apples, and maple syrup, this soup is rich with cool-weather flavors. If you prepare a batch of our Garam Masala (page 364), use it in this recipe.

    8   cups (1-inch) cubed peeled
        butternut squash (about
        2 medium)
    3   tablespoons canola oil, divided
    2   tablespoons maple syrup
  1¼   teaspoons garam masala
    1   teaspoon kosher salt
    ⅛   teaspoon freshly ground black
        pepper
        Cooking spray
    ¼   cup finely chopped shallots
    4   cups chopped Braeburn apple
        (about 1 pound)
    ¼   cup dry white wine
    3   cups water
    1   (14-ounce) can fat-free,
        less-sodium chicken broth
    2   tablespoons half-and-half

1 Preheat oven to 400°.
2 Combine squash, 2 tablespoons oil, syrup, and next 3 ingredients. Arrange squash mixture in a single layer on a jelly-roll pan coated with cooking spray. Bake at 400° for 45 minutes or until squash is tender.
3 Heat remaining 1 tablespoon oil in a large skillet over medium-high heat. Add shallots to pan; sauté 2 minutes or until tender. Stir in apple; sauté 4 minutes or until tender. Stir in wine; cook 1 minute. Stir in squash mixture, 3 cups water, and broth. Bring to a simmer; cook 3 minutes. Place half of squash mixture in a blender. Remove center piece of blender lid (to allow steam to escape); secure blender lid on blender. Place a clean towel over opening in blender lid (to avoid splatters). Blend until smooth. Strain squash mixture through a sieve into a bowl; discard solids. Repeat procedure with remaining squash mixture. Stir in half-and-half. Yield: 10 servings (serving size: about ¾ cup).

CALORIES 165 (26% from fat); FAT 4.7g (sat 0.8g, mono 3g, poly 0.5g); PROTEIN 2.7g; CARB 32g; FIBER 4.7g; CHOL 1mg; IRON 1.7mg; SODIUM 263mg; CALC 108mg

Entrées

These main dishes suit a variety of occasions this season, from a quick and casual weeknight supper to a dressy feast for guests.

THANKSGIVING DINNER MENU
(Serves 12)*

Arugula Salad with Goat Cheese, Bacon, and Balsamic-Fig Dressing (page 342)

Roast Turkey with Onion and Cranberry Chutney (at right)

Wild Rice Pilaf with Sausage, Shiitake Mushrooms, and Celery (page 353)

Brussels Sprouts with Currants and Pine Nuts (page 351)

Gratin of Cauliflower with Gruyère (page 351)

Bakery Dinner Rolls (page 358)

Pear Pie with Streusel Topping and Caramel Sauce (page 354)

Beaujolais nouveau

Coffee

*Double recipes for side dishes as needed to complete this holiday feast.

Roast Turkey with Onion and Cranberry Chutney

    1   (12-pound) fresh or frozen turkey,
        thawed
    ¼   cup butter, softened
  1¼   teaspoons salt, divided
    2   teaspoons chopped fresh thyme,
        divided
    1   teaspoon freshly ground black
        pepper, divided
    5   cups chopped onion (about 3 large)
    ⅔   cup dry red wine
    ½   cup sugar
    ½   cup dried cranberries
    ⅓   cup red wine vinegar

1 Preheat oven to 450°.
2 Remove and discard giblets and neck from turkey, or reserve for another use. Trim excess fat. Tie ends of legs together with twine. Starting at neck cavity, loosen skin from breast and drumsticks by inserting fingers, gently pushing between skin and meat. Combine butter, 1 teaspoon salt, 1 teaspoon thyme, and ½ teaspoon pepper. Rub butter mixture under loosened skin over breast and drumsticks. Lift wing tips up and over back; tuck under turkey. Place turkey, breast side up, in a roasting pan. Bake at 450° for 30 minutes.
3 Reduce oven temperature to 350° (do not remove turkey from oven). Bake turkey at 350° for 1½ hours or until a thermometer inserted into meaty part of thigh registers 165°. Remove turkey from oven; let stand 30 minutes. Discard skin.
4 Combine remaining ¼ teaspoon salt, remaining ½ teaspoon pepper, onion, and remaining ingredients in a medium saucepan; bring to a boil. Reduce heat, and simmer 1 hour and 15 minutes or until thick, stirring occasionally. Remove from heat; stir in remaining 1 teaspoon thyme. Cool. Yield: 12 servings (serving size: about 6 ounces turkey and about ¼ cup chutney).

CALORIES 438 (20% from fat); FAT 9.9g (sat 4.4g, mono 2.3g, poly 1.9g); PROTEIN 67.4g; CARB 15.9g; FIBER 1g; CHOL 232mg; IRON 4.7mg; SODIUM 427mg; CALC 58mg

TURKEY WITH SMOKED PAPRIKA AND GLAZED CARROTS VARIATION: Prepare recipe through loosening turkey skin. Substitute 2 tablespoons finely chopped shallots, 1 tablespoon smoked paprika, and 3 minced garlic cloves for thyme; combine butter, shallots, paprika, garlic, $3/4$ teaspoon salt, and $1/4$ teaspoon freshly ground black pepper for turkey rub. Substitute 6 cups coarsely chopped carrot, 1 cup fat-free, less-sodium chicken broth, 2 tablespoons sherry vinegar, and 1 tablespoon honey for onion and remaining ingredients. Combine carrot, broth, vinegar, and honey in a large skillet; bring to a boil. Reduce heat, and simmer 55 minutes or until liquid evaporates and carrot is tender. Remove from heat; stir in 1 tablespoon chopped chives, 1 tablespoon butter, $1/4$ teaspoon salt, and $1/4$ teaspoon pepper. Yield: 12 servings (serving size: about 6 ounces turkey and about $1/3$ cup carrots).

CALORIES 416 (24% from fat); FAT 10.9g (sat 5g, mono 2.5g, poly 2g); PROTEIN 67.8g; CARB 8.2g; FIBER 1.9g; CHOL 234mg; IRON 4.7mg; SODIUM 464mg; CALC 70mg

QUICK & EASY
Turkey Cutlets with Pancetta-Sage Sauce

Enjoy a turkey dinner on a weeknight or for a smaller Thanksgiving party with this simple dish. Serve with mashed potatoes or egg noodles.

- $1^1/2$ pounds turkey breast cutlets (about 8 cutlets)
- $1/2$ teaspoon salt
- $1/8$ teaspoon freshly ground black pepper
- Cooking spray
- $1/3$ cup thinly sliced pancetta (about 1 ounce)
- 2 tablespoons thinly sliced fresh sage
- $3/4$ cup white wine
- $1/2$ cup fat-free, less-sodium chicken broth
- 2 tablespoons butter, cut into small pieces

❶ Sprinkle turkey evenly with salt and pepper. Heat a large nonstick skillet over medium heat. Coat pan with cooking spray. Add half of cutlets to pan; cook 1 minute on each side or until browned and done. Repeat procedure with remaining cutlets; keep warm.
❷ Add pancetta and sage to pan; cook 3 minutes or until pancetta is browned, stirring occasionally. Add wine; bring to a boil. Cook until reduced to $1/2$ cup (about 3 minutes). Add broth; bring to a boil. Cook until reduced to about $2/3$ cup (about 2 minutes). Remove pan from heat; stir in butter. Serve with turkey. Yield: 4 servings (serving size: about 4 ounces turkey and about $2^1/2$ tablespoons sauce).

CALORIES 269 (31% from fat); FAT 9.1g (sat 5g, mono 2.7g, poly 0.8g); PROTEIN 43.1g; CARB 0.8g; FIBER 0g; CHOL 126mg; IRON 2.2mg; SODIUM 595mg; CALC 28mg

Red Currant–Glazed Cornish Hens and Pearl Onions

A sweet, sticky glaze makes these hens irresistible. Use white, red, or gold pearl onions in this dish.

- $1/2$ cup red currant jelly
- $1/3$ cup apple juice
- 1 tablespoon finely chopped shallots
- 2 teaspoons fresh lemon juice
- $1/2$ teaspoon grated peeled fresh ginger
- $1/4$ teaspoon chopped fresh thyme
- 1 teaspoon salt, divided
- 2 ($1^1/2$-pound) Cornish hens
- Cooking spray
- $1/4$ teaspoon freshly ground black pepper, divided
- 2 quarts water
- 1 pound pearl onions
- 1 tablespoon butter
- 1 tablespoon sugar
- 1 tablespoon fresh lemon juice

❶ Preheat oven to 425°.
❷ Combine first 6 ingredients in a small saucepan. Stir in $1/4$ teaspoon salt; bring to a boil. Reduce heat to medium, and simmer 10 minutes, stirring occasionally.
❸ Remove and discard giblets and necks from hens. Remove skin; trim excess fat. Split hens in half lengthwise. Place hen halves, meaty sides up, in a roasting pan coated with cooking spray. Sprinkle with $1/2$ teaspoon salt and $1/8$ teaspoon pepper. Bake at 425° for 10 minutes. Remove from oven, and brush hens with half of jelly mixture. Reduce oven temperature to 400°. Bake at 400° for 8 minutes. Remove from oven, and brush hens with remaining half of jelly mixture. Bake at 400° for 7 minutes or until a thermometer registers 165°.
❹ Bring 2 quarts water to a boil in a large saucepan. Add onions to pan; cook 2 minutes. Remove onions with a slotted spoon. Drain and rinse under cold running water; drain. Pinch stem end of each onion; discard peels. Melt butter in a large nonstick skillet over medium heat. Add onions, sugar, 1 tablespoon lemon juice, remaining $1/4$ teaspoon salt, and remaining $1/8$ teaspoon pepper to pan; cook 12 minutes or until golden brown, stirring frequently. Serve with hens. Yield: 4 servings (serving size: 1 hen half and $1/3$ cup onion mixture).

CALORIES 402 (18% from fat); FAT 8.2g (sat 3.2g, mono 2.5g, poly 1.4g); PROTEIN 33.6g; CARB 48.7g; FIBER 0.1g; CHOL 154mg; IRON 1.6mg; SODIUM 718mg; CALC 49mg

Turkey: Fresh vs. Frozen

The basic turkey question for most of us this time of year is whether to buy fresh or frozen. Each has its advantages; the answer depends on your priorities. Frozen turkey is cheapest and most widely available. But it will occupy some valuable real estate in the refrigerator as it thaws—about five hours per pound, or almost three days for a 12-pound bird.

Fresh turkey costs slightly more, and you need to order it in advance. But because the meat has not undergone the freezing/thawing process, the flavor and texture of fresh turkey are generally considered superior.

Shallot and Sage–Roasted Turkey with Shallot Gravy

This dish uses sage—one of the key flavorings of the season—rubbed onto the turkey and placed inside its cavity. The gravy echoes the sage and shallot theme. Prepare giblet broth while the turkey roasts. Do not use the liver in the broth—it will turn the mixture bitter.

- 1 (12-pound) fresh or frozen turkey, thawed
- ¼ cup finely chopped shallots (about 1)
- ¼ cup butter, softened
- 2 tablespoons finely chopped sage, divided
- 1¼ teaspoons salt, divided
- 1¼ teaspoons freshly ground black pepper, divided
- 1 cup chopped onion (about 1 medium), divided
- 1 cup chopped carrot (about 3 medium), divided
- 1 cup chopped celery (about 2 stalks), divided
- 4 fresh sage sprigs, divided
- 6 cups cold water, divided
- 1 (14-ounce) can fat-free, less-sodium chicken broth
- ¼ cup all-purpose flour (about 1.1 ounces)
- 1 tablespoon olive oil
- 1 cup thinly sliced shallots (about 4)

❶ Preheat oven to 450°.
❷ Remove and reserve giblets and neck from turkey. Trim excess fat. Tie ends of legs together with twine. Starting at neck cavity, loosen skin from breast and drumsticks by inserting fingers, gently pushing between skin and meat. Combine ¼ cup chopped shallots, butter, 1 tablespoon chopped sage, 1 teaspoon salt, and 1 teaspoon pepper. Rub butter mixture under loosened skin over breast and drumsticks. Stuff ½ cup onion, ½ cup carrot, ½ cup celery, and 3 sage sprigs into body cavity. Lift wing tips up and over back; tuck under turkey. Place turkey, breast side up, on a roasting pan. Pour 1 cup water and broth into pan. Bake at 450° for 30 minutes.
❸ Reduce oven temperature to 350° (do not remove turkey from oven). Bake turkey at 350° for 1½ hours or until thermometer inserted into meaty part of thigh registers 165°. Remove turkey from oven; let stand 30 minutes. Discard skin.
❹ Combine reserved giblets, neck, remaining ½ cup onion, remaining ½ cup carrot, remaining ½ cup celery, remaining 1 sage sprig, and remaining 5 cups water in a large saucepan; bring to a boil. Reduce heat, and simmer until liquid is reduced to 2 cups (about 1½ hours). Strain mixture through a sieve, reserving stock. Discard solids.
❺ Place a zip-top plastic bag inside a 2-cup glass measure. Pour turkey drippings into bag; let stand 10 minutes (fat will rise to top). Seal bag; carefully snip off 1 bottom corner of bag. Drain drippings into a measuring cup, stopping before fat layer reaches opening.
❻ Place giblet stock in a small bowl. Add enough drippings to measure 4 cups. Discard remaining drippings. Lightly spoon flour into a dry measuring cup; level with a knife. Add flour to drippings mixture, stirring well with a whisk.
❼ Heat oil in a medium saucepan over medium heat. Add 1 cup sliced shallots to pan; cook 5 minutes or until lightly browned. Stir in giblet mixture and remaining ¼ teaspoon salt; bring to a boil. Cook 2 minutes or until thickened, stirring constantly. Stir in remaining 1 tablespoon chopped sage and remaining ¼ teaspoon pepper. Yield 12 servings (serving size: about 6 ounces turkey and ¼ cup gravy).

CALORIES 407 (24% from fat); FAT 10.9g (sat 4.5g, mono 3.1g, poly 2g); PROTEIN 67.9g; CARB 5.1g; FIBER 0.3g; CHOL 232mg; IRON 4.8mg; SODIUM 494mg; CALC 57mg

Spice-Brined Turkey with Cider Pan Gravy

You can use a double layer of turkey brining bags, then keep the bagged turkey in a stockpot in the refrigerator to guard against punctures. Garnish the turkey with fresh herbs and apples, if desired.

- 5 quarts water
- ¾ cup plus 2 tablespoons kosher salt
- 1½ cups thinly sliced peeled fresh ginger (about 6 ounces)
- 2 tablespoons coarsely crushed cloves
- 2 tablespoons coarsely crushed cardamom pods
- 2 tablespoons coarsely crushed whole allspice
- 2 tablespoons coarsely crushed black peppercorns
- 1 (12-pound) fresh or frozen turkey, thawed
- 1 (14-ounce) can fat-free, less-sodium chicken broth, divided
- 1½ cups apple cider
- ¼ cup all-purpose flour (about 1.1 ounces)
- ¼ teaspoon freshly ground black pepper

❶ Combine first 7 ingredients in a large stockpot over medium-high heat. Cook until salt dissolves. Remove pan from heat; cool completely.
❷ Remove and discard giblets and neck from turkey, or reserve for another use. Trim excess fat. Tie ends of legs together with kitchen twine. Lift wing tips up and over back; tuck under turkey. Add turkey to pan, turning to coat. Cover and refrigerate 24 hours, turning occasionally.
❸ Preheat oven to 450°.
❹ Remove turkey from brine; discard brine. Rinse turkey with cold water; pat dry. Place turkey, breast side up, in a roasting pan. Pour 1 cup broth into pan. Bake at 450° for 30 minutes.

⑤ Reduce oven temperature to 350°
(do not remove turkey from oven). Bake
turkey at 350° for 1½ hours or until thermometer inserted into meaty part of
thigh registers 165°. Remove turkey from
oven; let stand 30 minutes. Discard skin.
⑥ Place a zip-top plastic bag inside a
2-cup glass measure. Pour drippings into
bag; let stand 10 minutes (fat will rise to
top). Seal bag; carefully snip off 1 bottom
corner of bag. Drain drippings into a
measuring cup, stopping before fat layer
reaches opening (reserve 1 tablespoon
fat). Combine drippings, remaining
broth, and cider in a small bowl. Place
roasting pan on stove top over medium
heat, scraping to loosen browned bits.
Lightly spoon flour into a dry measuring
cup; level with a knife. Add flour and reserved fat to pan; cook 1 minute, stirring
frequently. Slowly add broth mixture,
stirring with a whisk; cook 4 minutes or
until thickened, stirring occasionally.
Stir in pepper. Yield 12 servings (serving
size: about 6 ounces turkey and about
¼ cup sauce).

CALORIES 379 (17% from fat); FAT 7.1g (sat 2.4g, mono 1.8g,
poly 1.9g); PROTEIN 67.5g; CARB 6.9g; FIBER 0.2g;
CHOL 223mg; IRON 4.6mg; SODIUM 878mg; CALC 48mg

Beef Tenderloin with Roasted Tomato Salsa

For vibrant tomato flavor this time of
year, roasting plum tomatoes is your
best bet. The process maximizes their
sweetness and makes the flesh supple
and silken.

SALSA:

- 6 plum tomatoes, cut in half
  lengthwise (about 1½ pounds)
- 1 sweet onion, cut into ¼-inch-thick
  slices (about ¾ pound)
- 1 teaspoon extravirgin olive oil
  Cooking spray
- 3 garlic cloves, peeled
- 2 tablespoons chopped fresh basil
- 1 teaspoon balsamic vinegar
- ¼ teaspoon salt

BEEF:

- 1 (2-pound) beef tenderloin, trimmed
- 1 teaspoon salt
- 1 teaspoon ground coriander
- ¼ teaspoon freshly ground black
  pepper

① Preheat oven to 350°.
② To prepare salsa, brush tomatoes and
onion with oil; place on a baking sheet
coated with cooking spray. Bake at 350°
for 15 minutes. Wrap garlic in foil; add to
baking sheet. Bake at 350° for 45 minutes
or until vegetables are tender. Remove
from oven; cool 10 minutes.
③ Coarsely chop tomatoes and onion;
place in a large bowl. Mash garlic with a
fork; add to tomato mixture. Stir in basil,
vinegar, and ¼ teaspoon salt.
④ Increase oven temperature to 450°.
⑤ To prepare beef, sprinkle beef with
1 teaspoon salt, coriander, and pepper.
Place on a broiler pan coated with cooking
spray. Bake at 450° for 33 minutes or until
a thermometer registers 135° or until
desired degree of doneness. Remove from
oven; let stand 10 minutes before slicing.
Serve with salsa. Yield: 8 servings (serving
size: 3 ounces beef and ¼ cup salsa).

CALORIES 171 (31% from fat); FAT 5.9g (sat 2.1g, mono 2.5g,
poly 0.3g); PROTEIN 23.1g; CARB 5.5g; FIBER 1g; CHOL 52mg;
IRON 1.7mg; SODIUM 422mg; CALC 32mg

STAFF FAVORITE
Mixed Peppercorn Beef Tenderloin with Shallot-Port Reduction

A variety of black, white, pink, and green
peppercorns updates the standard *au
poivre* coating. The deeply flavored,
slightly sweet sauce balances the spice of
the pepper. Serve with haricots verts and
mashed potatoes.

BEEF:

- 1 (2-pound) beef tenderloin, trimmed
- 1 teaspoon salt
- 1½ tablespoons cracked mixed
  peppercorns
  Cooking spray

REDUCTION:

- 2 cups ruby port or other sweet red
  wine
- 1½ cups fat-free, less-sodium beef
  broth
- ¼ cup finely chopped shallots
- ⅛ teaspoon salt
- 2 fresh parsley sprigs
- 1 fresh thyme sprig
- 1½ tablespoons all-purpose flour
- 3 tablespoons water
- 1 tablespoon butter
- ½ teaspoon balsamic vinegar

① Preheat oven to 450°.
② To prepare beef, sprinkle beef evenly
with 1 teaspoon salt and peppercorns,
pressing firmly to adhere. Place beef
in a shallow roasting pan coated with
cooking spray. Bake at 450° for 33 minutes or until a thermometer registers
135° or until desired degree of doneness.
Let stand 10 minutes before slicing.
③ To prepare reduction, combine port
and next 5 ingredients in a medium
saucepan; bring to a boil. Cook until
reduced to 1¼ cups (about 15 minutes).
Strain port mixture through a sieve over
a bowl; discard solids. Combine flour and
3 tablespoons water. Return port mixture
to pan; add flour mixture to pan, stirring
with a whisk. Bring to a boil; cook 1 minute or until thickened, stirring constantly
with a whisk. Remove from heat; stir in
butter and vinegar. Yield: 8 servings
(serving size: about 3 ounces beef and
2 tablespoons reduction).

CALORIES 173 (35% from fat); FAT 6.7g (sat 2.9g, mono 2.5g,
poly 0.3g); PROTEIN 23.2g; CARB 3.7g; FIBER 0.4g;
CHOL 56mg; IRON 1.9mg; SODIUM 477mg; CALC 28mg

Marinated Beef Tenderloin with Caramelized Onion and Mushroom Ragout

Onions and mushrooms naturally complement rich beef. Use cremini mushrooms in the ragout for a more robust flavor.

BEEF:

- ¼ cup finely chopped shallots
- 2 tablespoons balsamic vinegar
- 2 tablespoons low-sodium soy sauce
- 1 tablespoon Dijon mustard
- 1 tablespoon honey
- 2 garlic cloves, minced
- 1 (2-pound) beef tenderloin, trimmed
- ½ teaspoon salt
- ¼ teaspoon freshly ground black pepper
  Cooking spray

RAGOUT:

- 1 teaspoon olive oil
- 2 cups thinly sliced sweet onion
- 2 garlic cloves, minced
- 8 cups sliced mushrooms (about 1 pound)
- 1 tablespoon low-sodium soy sauce
- 1 teaspoon chopped fresh thyme
- ¼ cup Madeira wine or dry sherry
- ⅓ cup fat-free, less-sodium beef broth
- 1 tablespoon balsamic vinegar
- ⅛ teaspoon salt
- ⅛ teaspoon freshly ground black pepper

1 To prepare beef, combine first 6 ingredients in a large zip-top plastic bag. Add beef to bag; seal. Marinate in refrigerator 4 hours, turning occasionally.

2 Preheat oven to 450°.

3 Remove beef from bag; discard marinade. Sprinkle beef with ½ teaspoon salt and ¼ teaspoon pepper. Place beef on a broiler pan coated with cooking spray. Bake at 450° for 35 minutes or until a thermometer registers 135° or until desired degree of doneness. Place tenderloin on a platter; let stand 10 minutes before slicing.

4 To prepare ragout, heat oil in a large nonstick skillet over medium heat. Add onion to pan; cook 15 minutes or until lightly browned, stirring occasionally. Add garlic; cook 1 minute, stirring occasionally. Increase heat to medium-high. Add mushrooms, 1 tablespoon soy sauce, and thyme; sauté 8 minutes. Stir in wine; cook 2 minutes or until liquid almost evaporates. Add broth; cook 2 minutes or until liquid almost evaporates. Remove from heat; stir in 1 tablespoon vinegar, ⅛ teaspoon salt, and ⅛ teaspoon pepper. Yield: 8 servings (serving size: 3 ounces beef and about ⅓ cup ragout).

CALORIES 212 (26% from fat); FAT 6g (sat 2.1g, mono 2.5g, poly 0.4g); PROTEIN 25.1g; CARB 12.1g; FIBER 1.4g; CHOL 52mg; IRON 2.1mg; SODIUM 502mg; CALC 35mg

Seared Beef Tenderloin with Dijon and Herbs

An herb-mustard coating is a classic preparation for beef tenderloin. Add one teaspoon chopped fresh tarragon to the herb mixture, if desired. Serve with roasted potatoes and Brussels sprouts for an easy yet special dinner for guests.

- 1 (2-pound) beef tenderloin, trimmed
- ¾ teaspoon salt
- ¼ teaspoon freshly ground black pepper
  Cooking spray
- 3 tablespoons Dijon mustard
- 1 garlic clove, minced
- 2 tablespoons chopped fresh parsley
- 1 tablespoon chopped fresh rosemary
- 1 teaspoon chopped fresh thyme

1 Preheat oven to 425°.

2 Sprinkle beef with salt and pepper. Heat a large nonstick skillet over medium-high heat. Coat pan with cooking spray. Add beef to pan; cook 2 minutes on each side or until browned.

3 Combine mustard and garlic in a small bowl. Rub mustard mixture evenly over beef. Combine parsley, rosemary, and thyme in a small bowl. Sprinkle beef evenly with parsley mixture. Place beef on a broiler pan coated with cooking spray. Bake at 425° for 26 minutes or until a thermometer registers 135° or until desired degree of doneness. Place tenderloin on a platter; let stand 10 minutes before slicing. Yield: 8 servings (serving size: about 3 ounces).

CALORIES 149 (32% from fat); FAT 5.3g (sat 2g, mono 2.1g, poly 0.2g); PROTEIN 22.3g; CARB 1.4g; FIBER 0.1g; CHOL 52mg; IRON 1.5mg; SODIUM 404mg; CALC 19mg

Classic Bouillabaisse with Rouille-Topped Croutons

We use red snapper in this dish, but cod, haddock, halibut, or other fresh white fillets will work.

ROUILLE:

- ⅔ cup chopped bottled roasted red bell peppers
- 3 tablespoons reduced-fat mayonnaise

CROUTONS:

- 4 ounces sourdough bread baguette, cut diagonally into 6 slices
- 1 garlic clove, halved

BOUILLABAISSE:

- 1 tablespoon olive oil
- 1 cup chopped onion (about 1 medium)
- 2 garlic cloves, minced
- ¾ cup chopped plum tomato (about 2)
- ½ teaspoon saffron threads, lightly crushed
- 3½ cups (¾-inch) cubed red potato (about 1 pound)
- 2½ cups thinly sliced fennel bulb (about 8 ounces)
- 3 cups clam juice
- 1 (14-ounce) can fat-free, less-sodium chicken broth
- 24 littleneck clams
- 24 mussels, scrubbed and debearded
- 12 ounces large shrimp, peeled and deveined
- 1 (1-pound) red snapper fillet, cut into 12 (2-inch) pieces
- 6 tablespoons fresh chopped parsley

1 Preheat oven to 400°.

2 To prepare rouille, combine bell peppers and mayonnaise in a blender or food processor; process until smooth. Set aside.

3 To prepare croutons, arrange baguette slices in a single layer on a baking sheet; bake at 400° for 8 minutes or until toasted. Rub one side of each crouton with cut sides of garlic clove halves; discard garlic clove halves. Set aside croutons.

4 To prepare bouillabaisse, heat oil in a large Dutch oven over medium heat. Add onion and garlic to pan; cook 8 minutes or until tender. Add tomato; cook 3 minutes. Add saffron; cook 30 seconds. Add potato and next 3 ingredients; bring to a boil. Cover, reduce heat, and simmer 10 minutes or until potato is almost done. Increase heat to medium. Add clams; cover and simmer 5 minutes. Add mussels; cover and simmer 3 minutes. Add shrimp and fish; cover and simmer 5 minutes or until shells open, shrimp is done, and fish flakes easily when tested with a fork or until desired degree of doneness. Discard any unopened shells.

5 Ladle 2 cups seafood mixture into each of 6 shallow bowls. Spread each crouton with about 1 tablespoon rouille. Place 1 crouton on top of each bowl; sprinkle each serving with 1 tablespoon parsley. Yield: 6 servings.

CALORIES 341 (17% from fat); FAT 6.5g (sat 0.9g, mono 2.2g, poly 1.8g); PROTEIN 37.8g; CARB 32.6g; FIBER 3.7g; CHOL 142mg; IRON 10.4mg; SODIUM 882mg; CALC 121mg

Braised Lamb Shanks with Parsley-Mint Gremolata

Mint, a favored partner for lamb, fits nicely into the gremolata. Serve these tender shanks with polenta, mashed potatoes, or risotto and broccoli rabe.

LAMB:

- 1 tablespoon minced fresh thyme
- 1 teaspoon salt
- 1 teaspoon minced fresh rosemary
- ½ teaspoon freshly ground black pepper
- 4 (12-ounce) lamb shanks
- 1 tablespoon olive oil
- 2 cups chopped onion (about 1 large)
- 1 cup chopped carrot (about 2 large)
- 3 garlic cloves, minced
- 2 cups dry red wine
- ¾ cup fat-free, less-sodium chicken broth
- ¾ cup fat-free, less-sodium beef broth

GREMOLATA:

- ¼ cup finely chopped fresh flat-leaf parsley
- 2 tablespoons finely chopped fresh mint
- 1 tablespoon grated lemon rind
- 1 tablespoon minced garlic

1 To prepare lamb, combine first 4 ingredients; set aside 1 teaspoon herb mixture. Rub lamb evenly with remaining herb mixture. Heat oil in a large Dutch oven over medium heat. Add lamb to pan; cook 2 minutes on each side or until browned. Remove lamb from pan; keep warm. Add onion, carrot, and garlic to pan; cook 5 minutes or until lightly browned and tender, stirring occasionally. Add wine and reserved 1 teaspoon herb mixture; bring to a boil. Cook until liquid is reduced to 2 cups (about 6 minutes). Add broths; bring to a boil. Cook until liquid is reduced to 1¾ cups (about 5 minutes). Return lamb to pan; cover, reduce heat, and simmer 2½ hours or until lamb is tender, turning shanks occasionally.

2 To prepare gremolata, combine parsley and remaining ingredients.

3 Remove lamb and vegetables from pan with a slotted spoon; keep warm. Place a large zip-top plastic bag inside an 8-cup glass measure or bowl. Pour broth mixture into bag; let stand 10 minutes (fat will rise to top). Seal bag, and carefully snip off 1 bottom corner of bag. Drain drippings into pan, stopping before fat layer reaches opening; discard fat. Bring broth mixture to a boil; cook until reduced to 2 cups and thickened (about 12 minutes). Spoon sauce over lamb and vegetables; top with gremolata. Yield: 4 servings (serving size: 1 shank, about ½ cup sauce, and 2 tablespoons gremolata).

CALORIES 257 (30% from fat); FAT 8.5g (sat 2.6g, mono 4.4g, poly 0.7g); PROTEIN 33.2g; CARB 11.1g; FIBER 2.3g; CHOL 100mg; IRON 3.6mg; SODIUM 870mg; CALC 61mg

Maple-Sage Roasted Pork Tenderloin

Only four ingredients give pork tenderloin outstanding flavor in this dish. Serve with sweet potatoes and sautéed spinach for a dinner that's ready in less than an hour.

- 1 tablespoon maple syrup
- 1 teaspoon chopped fresh sage
- ½ teaspoon salt
- ¼ teaspoon freshly ground black pepper
- 1 (1-pound) pork tenderloin, trimmed
  Cooking spray

1 Combine first 5 ingredients in a large zip-top plastic bag; seal and turn to coat. Marinate in refrigerator 30 minutes.

2 Preheat oven to 400°.

3 Remove pork from bag. Place pork on a foil-lined baking sheet coated with cooking spray. Bake at 400° for 25 minutes or until a thermometer registers 155°. Cover loosely with foil. Let stand 10 minutes before slicing. Yield: 4 servings (serving size: 3 ounces).

CALORIES 153 (24% from fat); FAT 4.1g (sat 1.4g, mono 1.6g, poly 0.4g); PROTEIN 24g; CARB 3.5g; FIBER 0g; CHOL 67mg; IRON 1.3mg; SODIUM 343mg; CALC 10mg

Pasta Party Menu

serves 10

Parmesan and Root Vegetable Lasagna

Winter greens salad

Combine 6 cups torn Boston lettuce, 2 cups torn radicchio, and 2 cups thinly sliced endive in a large bowl. Combine 1½ tablespoons red wine vinegar, ½ teaspoon sugar, ½ teaspoon salt, ½ teaspoon Dijon mustard, and ¼ teaspoon freshly ground black pepper in a medium bowl, stirring with a whisk. Gradually add in ¼ cup extravirgin olive oil, stirring with a whisk. Drizzle vinaigrette over salad; toss gently to coat.

Garlic bread

Parmesan and Root Vegetable Lasagna

Wash the pan well before using it again to cook the strained milk mixture—that ensures a silken sauce.

- 6 cups (½-inch) cubed peeled butternut squash (about 2½ pounds)
- 2¼ cups (½-inch) cubed peeled sweet potato (about 1 pound)
- 2 cups coarsely chopped onion, divided
- 1 tablespoon olive oil
  Cooking spray
- 4 cups 1% low-fat milk
- ⅛ teaspoon ground nutmeg
- ⅛ teaspoon ground cinnamon
- 1 bay leaf
- ⅓ cup all-purpose flour (about 1.5 ounces)
- ½ teaspoon salt
- ¼ teaspoon freshly ground black pepper
- 1¼ cups (5 ounces) grated Parmigiano-Reggiano cheese
- 9 packaged no-boil lasagna noodles
- 1½ cups (6 ounces) shredded part-skim mozzarella cheese

① Preheat oven to 450°.

② Combine squash, potato, 1 cup onion, and oil in a roasting pan coated with cooking spray, tossing to coat vegetables. Bake at 450° for 30 minutes or until vegetables are tender, stirring once; set aside.

③ Combine remaining 1 cup onion, milk, and next 3 ingredients in a medium saucepan over medium-high heat; bring to a simmer. Remove from heat; let stand 15 minutes. Strain milk mixture through a fine sieve over a bowl; discard solids. Return milk mixture to pan. Lightly spoon flour into a dry measuring cup; level with a knife. Add flour, salt, and pepper to milk mixture, stirring with a whisk. Cook over medium heat 10 minutes or until thick, stirring frequently with a whisk. Remove from heat; stir in Parmigiano-Reggiano.

④ Reduce oven temperature to 375°.

⑤ Spread ½ cup milk mixture in bottom of a 13 x 9–inch baking dish coated with cooking spray. Arrange 3 noodles over milk mixture; top with half of squash mixture, ½ cup mozzarella, and 1 cup milk mixture. Repeat layers with noodles, squash mixture, mozzarella, and milk mixture. Top with remaining 3 noodles. Spread remaining 1 cup milk mixture over noodles; sprinkle with remaining ½ cup mozzarella. Cover with foil coated with cooking spray. Bake at 375° for 30 minutes. Uncover; bake an additional 20 minutes. Let stand 10 minutes. Yield: 10 servings.

CALORIES 322 (24% from fat); FAT 8.4g (sat 3.9g, mono 2.2g, poly 0.5g); PROTEIN 16.6g; CARB 45.8g; FIBER 4.6g; CHOL 19mg; IRON 2.1mg; SODIUM 471mg; CALC 422mg

Sides

These accompaniments transform an ordinary plate into something special.

Green Beans with Toasted Walnuts and Breadcrumbs

Toast fresh breadcrumbs in flavorful olive oil, and combine them with chopped toasted walnuts to add texture to this heart-healthy side dish.

- 1 cup sliced shallots
- 2 pounds green beans, trimmed
  Cooking spray
- 2 tablespoons extravirgin olive oil, divided
- ½ teaspoon salt
- ½ teaspoon sugar
- 3 (1-ounce) slices French bread baguette
- ¼ cup (1 ounce) freshly grated Parmigiano-Reggiano cheese
- 3 tablespoons chopped walnuts, toasted
- 1 teaspoon grated lemon rind

1 Preheat oven to 425°.

2 Place shallots and beans in a small roasting pan coated with cooking spray. Drizzle with 1 tablespoon oil; toss. Sprinkle mixture evenly with salt and sugar; toss to combine. Bake at 425° for 20 minutes or until beans are crisp-tender. Transfer mixture to a serving bowl.

3 Place bread in a food processor; pulse 10 times or until coarse crumbs measure 1½ cups. Heat remaining 1 tablespoon oil in a large skillet over medium heat. Add breadcrumbs to pan; cook 5 minutes or until golden, stirring frequently. Remove from heat; stir in cheese, walnuts, and rind. Add breadcrumb mixture to beans; toss to combine. Yield: 8 servings (serving size: about 1 cup).

CALORIES 159 (35% from fat); FAT 6.1g (sat 1.3g, mono 3g, poly 1.6g); PROTEIN 6.3g; CARB 23.6g; FIBER 5g; CHOL 2.6mg; IRON 1.7mg; SODIUM 277mg; CALC 106mg

Brussels Sprouts with Currants and Pine Nuts
(pictured on page 269)

Peel away the outer leaves from trimmed fresh Brussels sprouts, reserving the leaves and centers. This technique shortens the cook time and makes a nice presentation.

1½ pounds Brussels sprouts, trimmed
1 tablespoon pine nuts
1 tablespoon butter
¼ cup finely chopped shallots
2 tablespoons dried currants
1 teaspoon chopped fresh thyme
¼ teaspoon salt
¼ teaspoon freshly ground black pepper
½ cup fat-free, less-sodium chicken broth

1 Separate sprouts into leaves, leaving just the centers intact. Set aside.

2 Heat a large nonstick skillet over medium-high heat. Add nuts to pan; cook 2 minutes or until toasted, stirring constantly. Coarsely chop nuts.

3 Melt butter in pan over medium-high heat. Add shallots to pan; sauté 1 minute or until golden, stirring frequently. Stir in Brussels sprouts centers and leaves, currants, and next 3 ingredients; toss to combine. Add broth. Cover, reduce heat, and cook 7 minutes. Increase heat to medium-high. Uncover; cook 4 minutes or until liquid evaporates and sprout centers are tender, stirring frequently. Remove from heat; sprinkle with nuts. Yield: 6 servings (serving size: about ½ cup).

CALORIES 90 (32% from fat); FAT 3.2g (sat 1.4g; mono 0.8g; poly 0.7g); PROTEIN 4.5g; CARB 13.9g; FIBER 4.7g; CHOL 5mg; IRON 1.9mg; SODIUM 173mg; CALC 56mg

Gratin of Cauliflower with Gruyère

Gruyère's nutty, earthy flavor is a nice match for subtle cauliflower, and crisp breadcrumbs add texture. Substitute broccoli for the cauliflower, if you prefer. You can prepare all the elements for the dish a day ahead, if necessary. Refrigerate the sauce, the cauliflower, and the breadcrumb mixture separately, and simply assemble before baking.

1 medium head cauliflower, trimmed and cut into florets (about 2 pounds)
Cooking spray
½ teaspoon kosher salt, divided
2 teaspoons butter
⅓ cup panko (Japanese breadcrumbs)
½ cup (2 ounces) shredded Gruyère cheese, divided
2 tablespoons finely chopped fresh chives
½ cup finely chopped onion
1 garlic clove, minced
3 tablespoons all-purpose flour
2 cups 2% reduced-fat milk
3 tablespoons chopped fresh flat-leaf parsley
¼ teaspoon freshly ground black pepper

1 Preheat oven to 400°.

2 Place cauliflower in a 2-quart broiler-safe baking dish lightly coated with cooking spray; coat cauliflower with cooking spray. Sprinkle with ¼ teaspoon salt; toss. Bake at 400° for 30 minutes or until almost tender. Cool 5 minutes.

3 Preheat broiler.

4 Melt butter in a saucepan over medium heat. Remove from heat. Stir in panko. Stir in ¼ cup cheese and chives.

5 Heat a medium saucepan over medium-high heat. Coat pan with cooking spray. Add onion to pan; sauté 4 minutes or until almost tender, stirring frequently. Add garlic; sauté 1 minute, stirring constantly. Add flour; cook 1 minute, stirring constantly. Gradually add milk, stirring with a whisk; bring to a boil. Cook 3 minutes or until thick, stirring constantly. Remove from heat; stir in remaining ¼ cup cheese, remaining ¼ teaspoon salt, parsley, and pepper. Pour milk mixture over cauliflower mixture; toss. Top evenly with cheese mixture. Broil 3 minutes or until golden brown and thoroughly heated. Yield: 6 servings (serving size: ⅔ cup).

CALORIES 161 (34% from fat); FAT 6g (sat 3.6g, mono 1.7g, poly 0.3g); PROTEIN 9.7g; CARB 18g; FIBER 3.6g; CHOL 20mg; IRON 1mg; SODIUM 295mg; CALC 233mg

Soft Polenta with Wild Mushroom Sauté

This is an easy and versatile side dish. The polenta is topped with a quick sauté of wild mushrooms (or use exotics, like shiitake and oyster, if wild are not available). If you replace the chicken broth with vegetable broth, this side dish can serve four as a vegetarian entrée. Garnish with sage sprigs.

    2 tablespoons butter
  1½ cups thinly sliced leek
   12 ounces wild mushrooms, sliced
    2 tablespoons finely chopped fresh
       flat-leaf parsley
    3 tablespoons dry sherry
    1 teaspoon finely chopped fresh sage
   ¼ teaspoon salt, divided
   ¼ teaspoon freshly ground black
       pepper, divided
    2 cups water
    2 bay leaves
    1 (14-ounce) can fat-free, less-sodium
       chicken broth
    1 cup quick-cooking polenta
    2 tablespoons shredded fresh
       pecorino Romano cheese
    2 tablespoons shaved fresh pecorino
       Romano cheese

① Melt butter in a large nonstick skillet over medium heat. Add leek to pan; cook 2 minutes or until tender, stirring occasionally. Add mushrooms; cook 7 minutes or until moisture evaporates, stirring occasionally. Stir in parsley, sherry, sage, ⅛ teaspoon salt, and ⅛ teaspoon pepper; cook 1 minute.
② Combine 2 cups water, bay leaves, and broth in a medium saucepan; bring to a boil. Gradually add polenta to pan, stirring constantly with a whisk. Reduce heat, and simmer 5 minutes or until thick, stirring frequently with a whisk. Remove from heat; discard bay leaves. Stir in remaining ⅛ teaspoon salt, remaining ⅛ teaspoon pepper, and shredded cheese. Spoon ⅔ cup polenta onto each of 6 plates; top each serving with ½ cup mushroom mixture and 1 teaspoon shaved cheese. Yield: 6 servings.

CALORIES 179 (28% from fat); FAT 5.5g (sat 3.2g, mono 1.4g, poly 0.2g); PROTEIN 5.7g; CARB 20.3g; FIBER 3.4g; CHOL 14mg; IRON 1.3mg; SODIUM 350mg; CALC 72mg

Smashed Potatoes with Goat Cheese and Chives

If you want to make the potatoes ahead, chill them and reheat just before serving, adding extra liquid to desired consistency. Stir in the chives just before serving. For a nice presentation, sprinkle additional chives over the top.

    3 pounds peeled baking potatoes,
       cut into 1-inch pieces
  1¼ teaspoons salt, divided
    2 tablespoons butter
   ¾ cup (6 ounces) goat cheese
   ¼ teaspoon freshly ground black
       pepper
    1 cup 2% reduced-fat milk
    3 tablespoons finely chopped fresh
       chives

① Place potatoes in a saucepan, and cover with cold water to 2 inches above potatoes. Add ¼ teaspoon salt; bring to a boil. Reduce heat, and simmer 15 minutes or until tender; drain. Return potatoes to pan over low heat; add remaining 1 teaspoon salt and butter to pan. Mash potatoes with a potato masher to desired consistency.
② Add cheese and pepper to potato mixture; stir until cheese melts. Stir in milk; cook 1 minute or until thoroughly heated, stirring frequently. Remove from heat; stir in chives. Yield: 12 servings (serving size: about ⅔ cup).

CALORIES 155 (29% from fat); FAT 5.4g (sat 3.5g, mono 1.3g, poly 0.2g); PROTEIN 5.8g; CARB 21.7g; FIBER 1.5g; CHOL 13mg; IRON 1.3mg; SODIUM 283mg; CALC 61mg

SPICY SOUTHWEST SMASHED POTATOES WITH CHEDDAR VARIATION: Prepare recipe through step 1. Substitute ¾ cup (3 ounces) shredded extrasharp Cheddar cheese for goat cheese; omit black pepper, milk, and chives. Stir in ½ teaspoon ground cumin and ¼ teaspoon ancho chile powder. Combine ⅓ cup half-and-half, 5 crushed garlic cloves, and 3 coarsely chopped serrano chiles in a small saucepan; cook over medium-high heat to 180° or until tiny bubbles form around edge (do not boil). Remove from heat; let stand 10 minutes. Strain mixture through a sieve over bowl; discard solids. Stir half-and-half into potato mixture; cook over low heat 30 seconds or until thoroughly heated, stirring frequently. Remove from heat; stir in 1 (8-ounce) container reduced-fat sour cream. Yield: 12 servings (serving size: ⅔ cup).

CALORIES 192 (35% from fat); FAT 7.5g (sat 4.8g, mono 1.4g, poly 0.2g); PROTEIN 5.3g; CARB 25.4g; FIBER 2.7g; CHOL 23mg; IRON 1.3mg; SODIUM 287mg; CALC 100mg

PARMESAN AND BLACK PEPPER SMASHED POTATOES VARIATION: Prepare the recipe through step 1. Substitute 1½ cups (6 ounces) freshly grated Parmigiano-Reggiano cheese for goat cheese. Increase to ¾ teaspoon freshly ground black pepper and 1½ cups 2% reduced-fat milk; omit chives. Stir in ¼ cup chopped fresh flat-leaf parsley. Yield: 12 servings (serving size: ⅔ cup).

CALORIES 181 (32% from fat); FAT 6.5g (sat 4.1g, mono 1.9g, poly 0.2g); PROTEIN 8.9g; CARB 22.6g; FIBER 1.6g; CHOL 18mg; IRON 1.2mg; SODIUM 428mg; CALC 232mg

Spinach with Raisins and Pine Nuts

A classic Catalonian preparation, this dish would round out a dinner of roast beef and potatoes.

- ¼ cup raisins
- 1 teaspoon olive oil
- 1 cup chopped onion
- 2 pounds bagged prewashed spinach
- ¼ cup pine nuts, toasted
- ½ teaspoon salt
- ¼ teaspoon freshly ground black pepper

① Place raisins in a small bowl; cover with hot water. Let stand 5 minutes or until plump; drain.

② Heat oil in a Dutch oven over medium heat. Add onion to pan; cook 10 minutes or until tender, stirring occasionally. Add about one-fourth of spinach to pan; cook 3 minutes or until spinach wilts, stirring occasionally. Repeat procedure 3 times with remaining spinach. Stir in raisins, nuts, salt, and pepper. Yield: 10 servings (serving size: ½ cup).

CALORIES 68 (40% from fat); FAT 3g (sat 0.6g, mono 1g, poly 1.2g); PROTEIN 3.5g; CARB 8.4g; FIBER 2.8g; CHOL 0mg; IRON 2.8mg; SODIUM 193mg; CALC 96mg

Orange-Balsamic Caramelized Fennel

This tasty side dish is perfect for busy cooks since it's mostly hands-free. The flavors pair well with roast pork or poultry.

- 4 (1-pound) fennel bulbs with stalks, trimmed
- Cooking spray
- 1 teaspoon sugar, divided
- 1 cup fat-free, less-sodium chicken broth
- ¼ cup orange juice
- 1 tablespoon balsamic vinegar
- ½ teaspoon fennel seeds, crushed
- ½ teaspoon kosher salt
- 2 garlic cloves, sliced

① Cut each fennel bulb in half through root end; cut each half into quarters to form 16 total pieces. Chop 1 tablespoon fronds; reserve.

② Heat a large nonstick skillet over medium-high heat. Coat pan with cooking spray. Place 8 fennel pieces in a single layer in pan; sprinkle evenly with ½ teaspoon sugar. Cook 3 minutes on each side or until lightly browned. Remove fennel from pan; recoat pan with cooking spray. Repeat procedure with remaining fennel and sugar.

③ Return fennel to pan. Stir in broth and remaining ingredients; bring to a boil. Reduce heat, and simmer 38 minutes or until fennel is crisp-tender and liquid is almost evaporated, turning occasionally. Top with reserved fennel fronds. Yield: 8 servings (serving size: ½ cup).

CALORIES 47 (8% from fat); FAT 0.4g (sat 0g, mono 0.1g, poly 0.1g); PROTEIN 1.7g; CARB 10.5g; FIBER 3.7g; CHOL 0mg; IRON 0.9mg; SODIUM 238mg; CALC 62mg

Acorn Squash Wedges with Maple-Harissa Glaze

Winter squash gets a little pizzazz with the addition of the piquant Moroccan chile paste, harissa. Brands can have differing spice intensities; taste before deciding how much to add. For a variation, replace the harissa with a couple of teaspoons minced canned chipotle chiles in adobo and about one teaspoon of the adobo sauce from the can.

- 2 medium acorn squash, each cut into 3 wedges and seeded
- Cooking spray
- ½ teaspoon kosher salt
- 3 tablespoons maple syrup
- 1 tablespoon unsalted butter, melted
- 1 tablespoon water
- 1½ teaspoons harissa paste
- 4 teaspoons sesame seeds

① Preheat oven to 400°.

② Arrange squash, cut sides up, on a baking sheet lined with parchment paper. Coat squash lightly with cooking spray; sprinkle evenly with salt. Combine syrup and next 3 ingredients in a bowl, stirring well; drizzle evenly into each squash cavity. Bake at 400° for 30 minutes. Sprinkle squash evenly with sesame seeds; bake 20 minutes or until seeds are toasted and squash is tender. Yield: 6 servings (serving size: 1 squash wedge).

CALORIES 113 (25% from fat); FAT 3.1g (sat 1.4g, mono 0.9g, poly 0.6g); PROTEIN 1.5g; CARB 22.3g; FIBER 2.4g; CHOL 5mg; IRON 1.5mg; SODIUM 167mg; CALC 75mg

Wild Rice Pilaf with Sausage, Shiitake Mushrooms, and Celery

- 1 cup uncooked wild rice
- 2 cups fat-free, less-sodium chicken broth
- 1 cup water
- ½ teaspoon kosher salt
- 1 bay leaf
- 2 ounces reduced-fat pork sausage (such as Jimmy Dean)
- 2 cups thinly sliced shiitake mushrooms caps (about 4 ounces)
- 1 cup chopped shallots (about 3 large)
- ½ cup chopped celery
- 2 tablespoons dry white wine
- ¼ teaspoon rubbed sage
- 2 tablespoons chopped fresh parsley

① Combine first 5 ingredients in a medium saucepan; bring to a boil. Cover, reduce heat, and simmer 45 minutes or until rice is tender. Discard bay leaf; do not drain.

② Heat a large nonstick skillet over medium heat. Add sausage to pan; cook 5 minutes, stirring to crumble. Add mushrooms, shallots, and celery. Cover, reduce heat, and cook 8 minutes. Stir in wild rice mixture, wine, and sage. Cook 8 minutes or until almost all liquid is absorbed. Sprinkle with parsley. Yield: 8 servings (serving size: about ½ cup).

CALORIES 114 (13% from fat); FAT 1.6g (sat 0.5g, mono 0g, poly 0.2g); PROTEIN 5.3g; CARB 19.6g; FIBER 1.7g; CHOL 5mg; IRON 1mg; SODIUM 292mg; CALC 17mg

Indian-Spiced Roast Potatoes and Parsnips

Toasting brown mustard seeds in chili oil enhances their characteristic sharpness. Be sure to cover the pan because the seeds will pop as they cook. Use yellow mustard seeds for a tamer heat.

- 1 tablespoon chili oil
- 2 teaspoons brown mustard seeds
- 1 teaspoon coriander seeds
- ½ teaspoon ground cumin
- ¼ teaspoon garam masala
- 1 tablespoon olive oil
- ½ teaspoon salt
- ¼ teaspoon sugar
- 1½ pounds Yukon gold potatoes, cut into ½-inch-thick slices
- ½ pound parsnips, cut into ½-inch-thick diagonal slices
  Cooking spray
- 2 tablespoons chopped fresh cilantro

1 Preheat oven to 450°.
2 Combine chili oil, mustard seeds, and coriander seeds in a small nonstick skillet over medium-high heat. Cover and cook 2 minutes or until seeds begin to pop, shaking pan occasionally. Remove from heat; let stand, covered, 1 minute. Stir in cumin and garam masala.
3 Combine spice mixture, olive oil, and next 4 ingredients in a roasting pan coated with cooking spray; toss to coat. Bake at 450° for 20 minutes or until vegetables are tender, turning vegetables after 10 minutes. Sprinkle vegetable mixture with cilantro; toss. Yield: 6 servings (serving size: about ¾ cup).

CALORIES 168 (26% from fat); FAT 4.9g (sat 0.6g, mono 3.3g, poly 0.5g); PROTEIN 3.5g; CARB 27.7g; FIBER 2.6g; CHOL 0mg; IRON 1.4mg; SODIUM 208mg; CALC 21mg

Desserts

End every meal on a high note with one of these sweet treats.

MAKE AHEAD
Double-Ginger Pumpkin Flans

If you don't have individual ramekins, use custard cups or a 1½-quart baking dish, which will require an additional 15 to 20 minutes in the oven.

CARAMEL:
  Cooking spray
- ½ cup sugar
- ¼ cup water

FLAN:
- ⅓ cup sugar
- 6 large egg yolks
- 1 cup canned unsweetened pumpkin
- 1 teaspoon vanilla extract
- ½ teaspoon ground ginger
- ½ teaspoon ground cinnamon
- 1 cup 2% reduced-fat milk
- ½ cup half-and-half
- 1 teaspoon grated peeled fresh ginger

1 Preheat oven to 325°.
2 To prepare caramel, lightly coat 6 (6-ounce) ramekins with cooking spray. Combine ½ cup sugar and ¼ cup water in a small, heavy saucepan over medium heat. Cook 4 minutes or until sugar dissolves, stirring occasionally. Increase heat to medium-high. Cook, without stirring, 6 minutes or until mixture turns golden around outside edges. Divide evenly into prepared ramekins. Set aside.
3 To prepare flan, combine ⅓ cup sugar and egg yolks in a medium bowl, stirring well with a whisk. Stir in pumpkin and next 3 ingredients. Combine milk, half-and-half, and fresh ginger. Heat milk mixture over medium-high heat in a heavy saucepan to 180° or until tiny bubbles form around edge (do not boil). Gradually add half of hot milk mixture to egg

mixture, stirring constantly with a whisk. Return milk mixture to pan. Reduce heat, and cook to 160°, stirring constantly with a whisk. Remove from heat. Strain through a sieve over a large bowl; discard solids.
4 Divide milk mixture evenly among prepared ramekins. Place cups in a 13 x 9–inch baking pan; add hot water to pan to a depth of 1-inch. Bake at 325° for 50 minutes or until a knife inserted in center comes out clean. Remove cups from pan; cool completely on a wire rack. Chill at least 8 hours.
5 Carefully loosen edges of custards with a knife. Invert ramekins onto plates. Drizzle any remaining caramel over custards. Yield: 6 servings (serving size: 1 flan).

CALORIES 224 (31% from fat); FAT 7.6g (sat 3.6g, mono 2.9g, poly 0.8g); PROTEIN 5.1g; CARB 34.9g; FIBER 1.3g; CHOL 215mg; IRON 1.2mg; SODIUM 39mg; CALC 106mg

Pear Pie with Streusel Topping and Caramel Sauce

Bartlett or Anjou pears work best in this pie. Be sure to purchase firm, slightly under-ripe fruit for this pie since the pears soften and give off juice as they cook.

PIE:
- ⅔ cup all-purpose flour (about 3 ounces), divided
- ½ cup granulated sugar
- ½ teaspoon ground cinnamon
- ⅛ teaspoon salt
- 3 tablespoons fresh lemon juice
- 6 firm pears, peeled, cored, and cut lengthwise into ½-inch-thick wedges
- ½ (15-ounce) package refrigerated pie dough (such as Pillsbury)
  Cooking spray
- ⅓ cup packed brown sugar
- 3 tablespoons chilled butter, cut into small pieces

SAUCE:
- ⅓ cup packed brown sugar
- 3 tablespoons heavy whipping cream
- 2 tablespoons butter, softened
- 2 teaspoons water

① Preheat oven to 375°.

② To prepare pie, lightly spoon flour into dry measuring cups; level with a knife. Combine ⅓ cup flour and next 3 ingredients in a large bowl. Add juice and pears to flour mixture; toss gently to coat. Roll dough into an 11-inch circle; fit dough into a 9-inch pie plate coated with cooking spray. Fold edges under and flute. Arrange pear mixture in a layer in prepared crust.

③ Combine remaining ⅓ cup flour and ⅓ cup brown sugar in a bowl. Cut in 3 tablespoons cold butter with a pastry blender or 2 knives until mixture resembles coarse meal. Sprinkle butter mixture evenly over pears. Bake at 375° for 1 hour or until lightly browned. Cool on a wire rack 10 minutes.

④ To prepare sauce, combine ⅓ cup brown sugar, cream, and 2 tablespoons softened butter in a small heavy saucepan over medium-high heat; bring to a boil. Cook 1 minute or until thickened. Remove from heat; stir in 2 teaspoons water. Serve at room temperature or slightly warmed with pie. Yield: 12 servings (serving size: 1 wedge pie and about 1½ teaspoons sauce).

CALORIES 287 (35% from fat); FAT 11g (sat 5.5g, mono 1.7g, poly 0.3g); PROTEIN 1.5g; CARB 47.5g; FIBER 2.8g; CHOL 20mg; IRON 0.7mg; SODIUM 139mg; CALC 24mg

MAKE AHEAD

Cranberry-Oatmeal Bars

(pictured on page 266)

These bar cookies strike a nice flavor balance: not too sweet and not too tart.

CRUST:

- 1 cup all-purpose flour (about 4.5 ounces)
- 1 cup quick-cooking oats
- ½ cup packed brown sugar
- ¼ teaspoon salt
- ¼ teaspoon baking soda
- ¼ teaspoon ground cinnamon
- 6 tablespoons butter, melted
- 3 tablespoons fresh orange juice
- Cooking spray

FILLING:

- 1⅓ cups dried cranberries (about 6 ounces)
- ¾ cup sour cream
- ½ cup granulated sugar
- 2 tablespoons all-purpose flour
- 1 teaspoon vanilla extract
- ½ teaspoon grated orange rind
- 1 large egg white, lightly beaten

① Preheat oven to 325°.

② To prepare crust, lightly spoon flour into a dry measuring cup; level with a knife. Combine flour and next 5 ingredients in a medium bowl, stirring well with a whisk. Drizzle butter and juice over flour mixture, stirring until moistened (mixture will be crumbly). Reserve ½ cup oat mixture. Press remaining oat mixture into bottom of an 11 x 7–inch baking dish coated with cooking spray.

③ To prepare filling, combine cranberries and remaining ingredients in a medium bowl, stirring well. Spread cranberry mixture over prepared crust; sprinkle reserved oat mixture evenly over filling. Bake at 325° for 40 minutes or until edges are golden. Cool completely in pan on a wire rack. Yield: 24 servings (serving size: 1 square).

CALORIES 133 (31% from fat); FAT 4.6g (sat 2.6g, mono 0.8g, poly 0.2g); PROTEIN 1.5g; CARB 21.9g; FIBER 0.9g; CHOL 13mg; IRON 0.6mg; SODIUM 67mg; CALC 20mg

MAKE AHEAD

CHERRY-OATMEAL BARS VARIATION: Substitute dried cherries for the dried cranberries and lemon rind for the orange rind in filling. Yield: 24 servings.

CALORIES 135 (31% from fat); FAT 4.6g (sat 2.6g, mono 0.8g, poly 0.2g); PROTEIN 1.7g; CARB 21.5g; FIBER 1.3g; CHOL 13mg; IRON 0.7mg; SODIUM 68mg; CALC 27mg

MAKE AHEAD

MAPLE-DATE-OATMEAL BARS VARIATION: Substitute chopped pitted dates for dried cranberries. Omit sugar from filling; add 2 tablespoons maple syrup and 2 tablespoons brown sugar. Yield: 24 servings.

CALORIES 124 (33% from fat); FAT 4.6g (sat 2.6g, mono 0.8g, poly 0.2g); PROTEIN 1.7g; CARB 19.8g; FIBER 1.1g; CHOL 13mg; IRON 0.7mg; SODIUM 68mg; CALC 26mg

MAKE AHEAD • FREEZABLE

Old-Fashioned Gingerbread

To garnish, sift powdered sugar over the top or dollop squares with whipped cream.

- 2½ cups all-purpose flour (about 11.25 ounces)
- 2 teaspoons baking soda
- 1½ teaspoons ground ginger
- 1 teaspoon ground cinnamon
- ½ teaspoon salt
- ¼ teaspoon ground cloves
- ½ cup packed brown sugar
- ¼ cup canola oil
- 1 large egg
- ⅔ cup molasses
- 1 (4-ounce) container unsweetened applesauce
- ½ cup fat-free buttermilk
- Cooking spray

① Preheat oven to 350°.

② Lightly spoon flour into dry measuring cups; level with a knife. Combine flour and next 5 ingredients in a bowl, stirring well.

③ Combine sugar, oil, and egg in a large bowl; beat with a mixer at medium speed until combined. Stir in molasses and applesauce.

④ Add flour mixture and buttermilk alternately to egg mixture, beginning and ending with flour mixture. Spoon batter into a 9-inch square baking pan coated with cooking spray. Bake at 350° for 35 minutes or until a wooden pick inserted into center comes out clean.

⑤ Cool in pan on a wire rack for 15 minutes. Cut into squares. Yield: 16 servings (serving size: 1 square).

CALORIES 173 (21% from fat); FAT 4g (sat 0.4g, mono 2.2g, poly 1.2g); PROTEIN 2.7g; CARB 32.5g; FIBER 0.7g; CHOL 13mg; IRON 3mg; SODIUM 253mg; CALC 89mg

Chocolate Roulade

Dutch process cocoa is treated with alkali to neutralize its acid, so it gives baked goods a dramatic dark appearance but imparts milder chocolate flavor than natural cocoa. For the best of both types, we used Hershey's Special Dark (a blend of natural and Dutched cocoas) for a pleasant balance of duskiness and chocolaty taste.

Cooking spray
2 tablespoons dry breadcrumbs
2/3 cup unsweetened cocoa
5 tablespoons cake flour
1/2 teaspoon baking powder
1/4 teaspoon baking soda
1/4 teaspoon salt
2 large egg yolks
3/4 cup granulated sugar, divided
1 teaspoon vanilla extract
5 large egg whites
3 tablespoons powdered sugar, divided
2 cups frozen reduced-calorie whipped topping, thawed
1/4 teaspoon ground cinnamon
Dash of ground ginger
Dash of ground cloves

❶ Preheat oven to 375°.
❷ Lightly coat a 15 x 10–inch jelly-roll pan with cooking spray; line bottom with parchment paper. Coat paper with cooking spray; dust with breadcrumbs. Set aside.
❸ Sift together cocoa and next 4 ingredients into a medium bowl. Set aside.
❹ Place egg yolks in a medium mixing bowl; beat with a mixer at high speed 2 minutes. Gradually add 1/4 cup granulated sugar and vanilla, beating until thick and pale (about 2 minutes). Using clean, dry beaters, beat egg whites in a medium bowl at high speed until foamy. Gradually add remaining 1/2 cup granulated sugar, 1 tablespoon at a time, beating until stiff peaks form.
❺ Gently stir one-third of egg white mixture into yolk mixture; gently fold in one-third of cocoa mixture. Repeat procedure twice.
❻ Pour batter into prepared pan, spreading evenly. Bake at 375° for 13 minutes or until cake springs back when touched lightly in center. Loosen cake from sides of pan, and turn out onto a dish towel dusted with 2 tablespoons of powdered sugar. Carefully peel off parchment paper, and cool for 1 minute. Starting at narrow end, roll up cake and towel together. Place, seam side down, on a wire rack, and cool.
❼ Unroll cake carefully, and remove towel. Combine whipped topping and next 3 ingredients in a bowl, stirring well. Spread whipped topping mixture evenly over cake, leaving a 1/2-inch border around edges. Reroll cake, and place seam side down on a platter. Cover and chill for 1 hour. Dust cake with remaining 1 tablespoon powdered sugar. Yield: 8 servings (serving size: 1 slice).

CALORIES 187 (23% from fat); FAT 4.7g (sat 3.1g, mono 1g, poly 0.3g); PROTEIN 5.3g; CARB 34.6g; FIBER 2.3g; CHOL 52mg; IRON 1.7mg; SODIUM 208mg; CALC 50mg

For Good Measure

We list flour amounts in most of our ingredient lists by cup measure and also provide a weight for those with a kitchen scale. Because precision is crucial in lightened baked goods (too much flour will yield a dry product), it's preferable to measure by weight, which is more accurate and ensures the same great results we achieve in our Test Kitchens. If you use measuring cups, though, make sure to:
• Use dry measuring cups (without spouts).
• Stir the flour in the canister before spooning it out.
• Lightly spoon the flour into the measuring cup, and then level off the excess flour with the flat side of a knife.

If you measure flour in other ways (scooping it out of the canister, for example), you may end up with more flour than we intend for the recipe.

Yellow Butter Cake with Vanilla Meringue Frosting

CAKE:
Cooking spray
1 1/2 cups all-purpose flour (about 6.75 ounces)
1/3 cup potato starch (about 2 ounces)
1 1/2 teaspoons baking powder
1 teaspoon salt
1 3/4 cups sugar
10 tablespoons butter, softened
3 large eggs
3/4 cup whole milk
1/4 cup half-and-half
2 tablespoons bourbon
1 tablespoon vanilla extract

FROSTING:
1 cup sugar
1/4 cup water
5 large egg whites
1/2 teaspoon cream of tartar
Dash of salt
1/4 cup butter, softened
1/2 teaspoon vanilla extract

❶ Preheat oven to 350°.
❷ To prepare cake, line bottoms of 2 (9-inch) cake pans with parchment paper; coat pans lightly with cooking spray. Lightly spoon flour into dry measuring cups; level with a knife. Lightly spoon potato starch into a dry measuring cup; level with a knife. Combine flour, potato starch, baking powder, and 1 teaspoon salt, stirring well with a whisk.
❸ Place 1 3/4 cups sugar and 10 tablespoons butter in a large bowl; beat with a mixer at medium speed until light and fluffy. Add eggs, 1 at a time, beating well after each addition. Combine milk and half-and-half. Add flour mixture and milk mixture alternately to butter mixture, beginning and ending with flour mixture. Beat just until combined. Fold in bourbon and 1 tablespoon vanilla. Divide batter evenly between prepared pans. Bake at 350° for 28 minutes or until a wooden pick inserted in center comes out clean. Cool in pans 25 minutes on

wire racks; remove from pans. Cool completely on wire racks.

④ To prepare frosting, combine 1 cup sugar and ¼ cup water in a saucepan; bring to a boil. Cook 3 minutes, without stirring, or until candy thermometer registers 250°. Combine egg whites, cream of tartar, and dash of salt in a large bowl. Using clean, dry beaters, beat with a mixer at high speed until foamy. Pour hot sugar syrup in a thin stream over egg white mixture, beating at high speed until stiff peaks form, about 3 minutes. Reduce mixer speed to low; continue beating until egg white mixture cools (about 12 minutes). Beat ¼ cup butter until light and fluffy; stir in ½ teaspoon vanilla. Fold in 1 cup egg white mixture. Fold butter mixture into remaining egg white mixture, stirring until smooth.

⑤ Place 1 cake layer on a plate; spread with 1 cup frosting. Top with remaining cake layer. Spread remaining frosting over top and sides of cake. Yield: 16 servings (serving size: 1 slice).

CALORIES 312 (34% from fat); FAT 11.8g (sat 7.1g, mono 3.2g, poly 0.6g); PROTEIN 4.1g; CARB 46.8g; FIBER 0.3g; CHOL 69mg; IRON 0.8mg; SODIUM 298mg; CALC 60mg

BUTTERY YELLOW CUPCAKES WITH CHOCOLATE MERINGUE FROSTING VARIATION:

① Lightly coat 24 muffin cups with cooking spray. Divide batter evenly among prepared muffins cups; bake at 350° for 18 minutes or until a wooden pick inserted in center comes out clean. Cool in pans 5 minutes. Remove cupcakes from pans; cool completely on wire racks.

② Cut frosting recipe in half, using 3 egg whites and omitting butter and vanilla. Fold ¼ cup unsweetened cocoa into cooled meringue mixture, and top each cupcake with about 2 tablespoons frosting. Sprinkle 1 tablespoon unsweetened cocoa evenly over cupcakes, if desired. Yield: 24 servings (serving size: 1 cupcake).

CALORIES 177 (31% from fat); FAT 6.1g (sat 3.6g, mono 1.7g, poly 0.3g); PROTEIN 2.6g; CARB 27.8g; FIBER 0.5g; CHOL 41mg; IRON 0.7mg; SODIUM 148mg; CALC 40mg

MAKE AHEAD
Chocolate Butter Cake with Creamy Coconut Frosting

Chilling the pastry cream in step 4 makes it easier to combine with the meringue.

CAKE:

   Cooking spray
1½   cups all-purpose flour (about 6.75 ounces)
 ½   cup unsweetened cocoa, sifted
1½   teaspoons baking powder
 ½   teaspoon salt
1¾   cups sugar
 ½   cup unsalted butter, softened
 3   large eggs
 1   cup whole milk
 1   tablespoon vanilla extract

FROSTING:

 1   cup 2% reduced-fat milk
 ½   cup flaked unsweetened coconut, toasted and divided
 ¾   cup sugar, divided
 1   tablespoon cornstarch
 1   large egg
 2   tablespoons unsalted butter
 2   tablespoons water
 3   large egg whites
 ¼   teaspoon cream of tartar
   Dash of salt

① Preheat oven to 350°.

② To prepare cake, line bottoms of 2 (9-inch) round cake pans with parchment paper. Coat pans lightly with cooking spray. Lightly spoon flour into dry measuring cups; level with a knife. Combine flour and next 3 ingredients in a bowl, stirring well with a whisk. Place 1¾ cups sugar and ½ cup butter in a large bowl; beat with a mixer at medium speed until light and fluffy (about 2 minutes). Add 3 eggs, 1 at a time, beating well after each addition. Add flour mixture and whole milk alternately to butter mixture, beginning and ending with flour mixture; beat just until combined. Fold in vanilla.

③ Divide batter evenly into prepared pans. Bake at 350° for 27 minutes or

until a wooden pick inserted in center comes out clean. Cool 25 minutes in pans on wire racks. Remove cakes from pans; cool completely on wire racks.

④ To prepare frosting, combine reduced-fat milk and ¼ cup coconut in a small saucepan; bring to a boil. Remove from heat; let stand 15 minutes. Strain milk mixture through a sieve over a bowl; discard solids. Return milk to pan over medium heat. Combine ¼ cup sugar, cornstarch, and 1 egg in a small bowl, stirring well with a whisk. Gradually add egg mixture to pan; bring to a boil, stirring constantly. Reduce heat, and cook 1 minute, stirring constantly with a whisk. Remove from heat; add 2 tablespoons butter, stirring until butter melts. Place pan in a large ice-filled bowl; let stand 15 minutes or until pastry cream cools to room temperature, stirring occasionally. Remove pan from ice. Spoon mixture into a bowl. Place plastic wrap on surface; chill.

⑤ Combine remaining ½ cup sugar and 2 tablespoons water in a saucepan; bring to a boil. Cook 3 minutes, without stirring, or until a candy thermometer registers 250°. Combine egg whites, cream of tartar, and dash of salt in a large bowl; beat with a mixer at high speed until foamy. Pour hot sugar syrup in a thin stream over egg whites; beat until stiff peaks form. Gently stir one-fourth of egg white mixture into chilled pastry cream; gently fold in remaining egg white mixture.

⑥ Place 1 cake layer on a plate; spread about 2 cups frosting over cake, leaving a (½-inch) border around edges. Top with remaining cake layer. Spread remaining frosting over top of cake. Sprinkle remaining ¼ cup coconut evenly over top of cake. Yield: 16 servings (serving size: 1 slice).

CALORIES 283 (33% from fat); FAT 10.4g (sat 6.3g, mono 2.7g, poly 0.6g); PROTEIN 5.2g; CARB 44.2g; FIBER 1.4g; CHOL 74mg; IRON 1.3mg; SODIUM 161mg; CALC 83mg

Saffron Rice Pudding with Cranberries, Almonds, and Pistachios

This dish is inspired by *shole zard,* a traditional Persian dessert. Our version features cranberries, which lend a sweet-tart note.

- ²/₃ cup uncooked basmati rice
- 4 cups 1% low-fat milk, divided
- ⅛ teaspoon saffron threads, crushed
- ²/₃ cup sugar
- ½ cup sweetened dried cranberries
- 3 tablespoons sliced almonds, toasted
- ⅛ teaspoon vanilla extract
- 1 teaspoon grated orange rind
- 3 tablespoons shelled dry-roasted pistachios, finely chopped

❶ Rinse rice with cold water; place in a small bowl. Cover with water to 1 inch above rice; soak 1 hour. Drain well. Combine 2 tablespoons milk and saffron in a small bowl; let stand 30 minutes.
❷ Place remaining milk in a medium saucepan; bring to a simmer over medium heat. Stir in rice, saffron mixture, and sugar; cook 30 minutes or until rice is tender, stirring occasionally.
❸ Stir in cranberries, almonds, and vanilla; cook 2 minutes. Remove from heat; stir in rind. Spoon about ½ cup rice mixture into each of 6 small bowls. Sprinkle each serving with 1½ teaspoons nuts. Yield: 6 servings.

CALORIES 261 (18% from fat); FAT 5.2g (sat 1.4g, mono 2.4g, poly 1.1g); PROTEIN 7.5g; CARB 48.1g; FIBER 1g; CHOL 6.5mg; IRON 0.5mg; SODIUM 83mg; CALC 214mg

Extras

Enjoy top-rated traditional breads and condiments with delicious variations.

MAKE AHEAD • FREEZABLE
Bakery Dinner Rolls

Brushing the dough with egg yolk creates a shiny golden glaze on these standard yeast rolls. Though we bake them in muffin tins for uniformity, you can also bake them directly on a baking sheet.

- 2 tablespoons sugar
- 1 package dry yeast (about 2¼ teaspoons)
- ²/₃ cup warm water (100° to 110°)
- 3 tablespoons butter, melted
- 1¾ cups all-purpose flour (about 7.9 ounces), divided
- ½ teaspoon salt
- Cooking spray
- 1 large egg yolk, lightly beaten

❶ Dissolve sugar and yeast in ²/₃ cup warm water in a small bowl; let stand 5 minutes. Stir in butter.
❷ Lightly spoon flour into dry measuring cups; level with a knife. Combine 1½ cups (about 6.75 ounces) flour and salt in a large bowl, stirring with a whisk. Add yeast mixture to flour mixture; stir until a soft dough forms. Turn dough out onto a lightly floured surface. Knead until smooth and elastic (about 4 minutes); add enough of remaining ¼ cup flour, 1 tablespoon at a time, to prevent dough from sticking to hands. Place dough in a large bowl coated with cooking spray, turning to coat. Cover and let rise in a warm place (85°), free from drafts, 1 hour or until doubled in size. (Press two fingers into dough. If indentation remains, dough has risen enough.) Punch dough down; cover and let rest 5 minutes.
❸ Divide dough into 12 equal portions, shaping each into a ball. Place 1 dough ball in each of 12 muffin cups coated with cooking spray. Cover and let rise 20 minutes or until doubled in size.
❹ Preheat oven to 400°.
❺ Gently brush dough with egg yolk. Bake at 400° for 13 minutes or until browned. Cool in pan on a wire rack for 2 minutes. Remove rolls from pan. Serve warm, or cool completely on wire rack. Yield: 12 servings (serving size: 1 roll).

CALORIES 98 (29% from fat); FAT 3.2g (sat 1.9g, mono 0.9g, poly 0.2g); PROTEIN 2.3g; CARB 14.7g; FIBER 0.6g; CHOL 25mg; IRON 1mg; SODIUM 120mg; CALC 4mg

MAKE AHEAD • FREEZABLE
ORANGE-FENNEL ROLLS VARIATION:
Add 1½ teaspoons grated orange rind and 1 teaspoon crushed fennel seeds to flour mixture. Omit egg yolk glaze. Arrange 12 dough balls, 2 inches apart, on a baking sheet lined with parchment paper. Bake at 400° for 10 minutes or until browned. Yield: 12 servings (serving size: 1 roll).

CALORIES 95 (27% from fat); FAT 2.9g (sat 1.8g, mono 0.8g, poly 0.1g); PROTEIN 2.1g; CARB 14.8g; FIBER 0.7g; CHOL 8mg; IRON 1mg; SODIUM 119mg; CALC 4mg

Make-Ahead Breads

Most of our bread recipes lend themselves to freezing, which is a smart option for the busy holiday season. If you choose to prepare one in advance, follow a few rules for success. After baking, allow the bread to cool completely. Wrap it in heavy-duty foil, then place in a zip-top plastic bag. Freeze for up to two months. Thaw bread at room temperature, and reheat (still wrapped in foil) at 325° for 10 to 30 minutes, depending on the size of the bread—dinner rolls will reheat quickly, whereas a whole loaf will take a bit longer.

Not all of our breads, however, take well to freezing. Any bread with a glaze or sugary topping, such as our Fig-Walnut Sticky Buns (page 360), loses its gooey appeal after being frozen and thawed. And because our biscuits are lower in fat than traditional versions, they suffer from being made ahead, so they're best enjoyed warm from the oven.

Basic Beer-Cheese Bread

This savory quick bread pairs well with soup or chili and is ideal for an open house or casual get-together.

- 1 tablespoon olive oil
- ½ cup finely chopped yellow onion
- ¼ teaspoon freshly ground black pepper
- 1 garlic clove, minced
- 3 cups all-purpose flour (about 13.5 ounces)
- 3 tablespoons sugar
- 2 teaspoons baking powder
- 1 teaspoon salt
- 1 cup (4 ounces) shredded Monterey Jack cheese
- 1 (12-ounce) bottle lager-style beer (such as Budweiser)
- Cooking spray
- 2 tablespoons melted butter, divided

❶ Preheat oven to 375°.
❷ Heat oil in a small skillet over medium-low heat. Add onion to pan; cook 10 minutes or until browned, stirring occasionally. Stir in pepper and garlic; cook 1 minute.
❸ Lightly spoon flour into dry measuring cups; level with a knife. Combine flour and next 3 ingredients in a large bowl, stirring with a whisk; make a well in center of mixture. Add onion mixture, cheese, and beer to flour mixture, stirring just until moist.
❹ Spoon batter into a 9 x 5-inch loaf pan coated with cooking spray. Drizzle 1 tablespoon butter over batter. Bake at 375° for 35 minutes. Drizzle remaining 1 tablespoon butter over batter. Bake an additional 25 minutes or until deep golden brown and a wooden pick inserted into center comes out clean. Cool in pan 5 minutes on a wire rack; remove from pan. Cool completely on wire rack. Yield: 16 servings (serving size: 1 slice).

CALORIES 144 (28% from fat); FAT 4.4g (sat 2.4g, mono 1.6g, poly 0.2g); PROTEIN 4.3g; CARB 20.6g; FIBER 0.7g; CHOL 10mg; IRON 1.3mg; SODIUM 257mg; CALC 89mg

APPLE-CHEDDAR BEER BREAD VARIATION: Substitute ½ cup minced shallots for onion. Place ½ cup shredded peeled Gala apple in paper towels; squeeze until barely moist. Cook shallots and apple in oil over medium heat for 7 minutes. Substitute 1 cup shredded extrasharp white Cheddar cheese for Monterey Jack. Substitute 1 (12-ounce) bottle hard cider for lager. Yield: 16 servings (serving size: 1 slice).

CALORIES 151 (27% from fat); FAT 4.6g (sat 2.5g, mono 1.6g, poly 0.3g); PROTEIN 4.4g; CARB 21.9g; FIBER 0.8g; CHOL 11mg; IRON 1.3mg; SODIUM 265mg; CALC 87mg

MANCHEGO-JALAPEÑO BEER BREAD VARIATION: Substitute ¼ cup thinly sliced green onions and ¼ cup finely chopped jalapeño pepper for onion; cook over medium heat for 3 minutes. Substitute 1 cup (4 ounces) shredded Manchego cheese for Monterey Jack cheese. Substitute 1 (12-ounce) bottle Mexican beer (such as Dos Equis) for lager-style beer. Yield: 16 servings (serving size: 1 slice).

CALORIES 148 (28% from fat); FAT 4.6g (sat 2.4g, mono 1.7g, poly 0.3g); PROTEIN 4.7g; CARB 20.6g; FIBER 0.7g; CHOL 12mg; IRON 1.3mg; SODIUM 244mg; CALC 108mg

SOPRESSATA-ASIAGO BEER BREAD VARIATION: Substitute ½ cup minced shallots and 2 tablespoons chopped green onions for onion. Substitute ¾ cup (3 ounces) grated Asiago cheese for Monterey Jack cheese. Substitute 1 (12-ounce) bottle Italian lager beer (such as Peroni) for lager-style beer. Stir 2 ounces finely chopped Sopressata salami into batter. Yield: 16 servings (serving size: 1 slice).

CALORIES 154 (29% from fat); FAT 5g (sat 2.4g, mono 2g, poly 0.3g); PROTEIN 5g; CARB 21.2g; FIBER 0.7g; CHOL 11mg; IRON 1.4mg; SODIUM 301mg; CALC 89mg

Flaky Buttermilk Biscuits
(pictured on page 265)

Using a light hand with the dough will help to ensure tender biscuits. This method of folding the dough creates irresistible flaky layers.

- 2 cups all-purpose flour (about 9 ounces)
- 2½ teaspoons baking powder
- ½ teaspoon salt
- 5 tablespoons chilled butter, cut into small pieces
- ¾ cup fat-free buttermilk
- 3 tablespoons honey

❶ Preheat oven to 400°.
❷ Lightly spoon flour into dry measuring cups; level with a knife. Combine flour, baking powder, and salt in a large bowl; cut in butter with a pastry blender or 2 knives until mixture resembles coarse meal. Chill 10 minutes.
❸ Combine buttermilk and honey, stirring with a whisk until well blended. Add buttermilk mixture to flour mixture; stir just until moist.
❹ Turn dough out onto a lightly floured surface; knead lightly 4 times. Roll dough into a (½-inch-thick) 9 x 5–inch rectangle; dust top of dough with flour. Fold dough crosswise into thirds (as if folding a piece of paper to fit into an envelope). Reroll dough into a (½-inch-thick) 9 x 5–inch rectangle; dust top of dough with flour. Fold dough crosswise into thirds; gently roll or pat to a ¾-inch thickness. Cut dough with a 1¾-inch biscuit cutter to form 14 dough rounds. Place dough rounds, 1 inch apart, on a baking sheet lined with parchment paper. Bake at 400° for 12 minutes or until golden. Remove from pan; cool 2 minutes on wire racks. Serve warm. Yield: 14 servings (serving size: 1 biscuit).

CALORIES 121 (31% from fat); FAT 4.2g (sat 2.6g, mono 1.1g, poly 0.2g); PROTEIN 2.4g; CARB 18.4g; FIBER 0.5g; CHOL 11mg; IRON 0.9mg; SODIUM 198mg; CALC 63mg

Continued

SPICED PUMPKIN BISCUITS VARIATION:
(pictured on page 265)

Add 1¼ teaspoons pumpkin pie spice to flour mixture. Decrease buttermilk to ⅓ cup; add ¾ cup canned pumpkin to buttermilk mixture. Bake at 400° for 14 minutes. Yield: 14 servings (serving size: 1 biscuit).

CALORIES 122 (32% from fat); FAT 4.3g (sat 2.6g, mono 1.1g, poly 0.2g); PROTEIN 2.3g; CARB 18.9g; FIBER 0.9g; CHOL 11mg; IRON 1.1mg; SODIUM 192mg; CALC 59mg

PARMESAN-PEPPER BISCUITS VARIATION:
(pictured on page 265)

Add 1 teaspoon freshly ground black pepper to flour mixture. Decrease butter to ¼ cup. Add ½ cup (2 ounces) grated fresh Parmesan cheese to buttermilk mixture. Bake at 400° for 13 minutes. Yield: 14 servings (serving size: 1 biscuit).

CALORIES 131 (32% from fat); FAT 4.7g (sat 2.9g, mono 0.9g, poly 0.2g); PROTEIN 4.2g; CARB 18.5g; FIBER 0.5g; CHOL 13mg; IRON 0.9mg; SODIUM 239mg; CALC 98mg

MAKE AHEAD
Pistachio-Cranberry Scones
(pictured on page 265)

Our basic biscuit dough (page 359) is enriched with sugar, egg, fruit, and nuts to make a sweet breakfast scone that's equally tasty served warm or at room temperature.

- 2 cups all-purpose flour (about 9 ounces)
- 2½ teaspoons baking powder
- ¼ teaspoon salt
- 5 tablespoons chilled butter, cut into small pieces
- ⅓ cup fat-free buttermilk
- ¼ cup granulated sugar
- 3 tablespoons honey
- 2 teaspoons grated lemon rind
- 1 large egg, lightly beaten
- ⅓ cup sweetened dried cranberries
- ¼ cup chopped pistachios, toasted
- 1 large egg white
- 2 tablespoons turbinado sugar

1 Preheat oven to 400°.

2 Lightly spoon flour into dry measuring cups; level with a knife. Combine flour, baking powder, and salt in a bowl; cut in butter with a pastry blender or 2 knives until mixture resembles coarse meal. Cover and chill flour mixture 10 minutes.

3 Combine buttermilk and next 4 ingredients, stirring with a whisk until well blended. Stir in cranberries and nuts. Add buttermilk mixture to flour mixture; stir just until dough is moist.

4 Turn dough out onto a lightly floured surface. Pat dough into an 8-inch circle on a baking sheet lined with parchment paper. Cut dough into 12 wedges (do not separate wedges). Brush egg white over dough; sprinkle evenly with turbinado sugar. Bake at 400° for 13 minutes or until golden. Remove from pan; cool 2 minutes on wire racks. Serve warm or at room temperature. Yield: 12 servings (serving size: 1 scone).

CALORIES 191 (30% from fat); FAT 6.4g (sat 3.3g, mono 2g, poly 0.6g); PROTEIN 3.9g; CARB 29.9g; FIBER 1g; CHOL 30mg; IRON 1.3mg; SODIUM 184mg; CALC 66mg

STAFF FAVORITE
Fig-Walnut Sticky Buns

These sweet rolls are delicious enough to garner our highest rating for taste.

- 2 tablespoons granulated sugar
- 1 package dry yeast (about 2¼ teaspoons)
- ⅔ cup warm water (100° to 110°)
- 5 tablespoons butter, melted and divided
- 1¾ cups all-purpose flour (about 7.9 ounces), divided
- ¼ teaspoon salt
- ¼ teaspoon ground nutmeg
- Cooking spray
- ¾ cup packed brown sugar, divided
- 2 tablespoons dark corn syrup
- 2 tablespoons 1% low-fat milk
- ½ cup finely chopped dried Black Mission figs
- ¼ cup finely chopped walnuts
- 1½ teaspoons ground cinnamon

1 Dissolve granulated sugar and yeast in ⅔ cup warm water in a small bowl; let mixture stand 5 minutes. Stir in 3 tablespoons melted butter.

2 Lightly spoon flour into dry measuring cups; level with a knife. Combine 1½ cups flour, salt, and nutmeg in a large bowl, stirring with a whisk. Add yeast mixture to flour mixture; stir until a soft dough forms. Turn dough out onto a lightly floured surface. Knead until smooth and elastic (about 4 minutes); add enough of remaining ¼ cup flour, 1 tablespoon at a time, to prevent the dough from sticking to hands. Place dough in a large bowl coated with cooking spray, turning to coat top. Cover and let rise in a warm place (85°), free from drafts, 1 hour or until doubled in size.

3 Combine ½ cup brown sugar, syrup, and milk in a small saucepan; bring mixture to a boil. Remove pan from heat; stir in figs. Sprinkle walnuts evenly into a 13 x 9–inch baking pan coated with cooking spray; spoon fig mixture evenly over nuts in pan.

4 Combine remaining ¼ cup brown sugar and cinnamon in a small bowl; set aside.

5 Preheat oven to 375°.

6 Punch dough down; let rest 5 minutes. Roll dough into a 12 x 10–inch rectangle on a lightly floured surface. Brush remaining 2 tablespoons butter over dough, leaving a 1-inch border. Sprinkle dough with cinnamon mixture. Roll up rectangle tightly, starting with long edge, pressing firmly to eliminate air pockets; pinch seam to seal (do not seal ends). Cut into 12 (1-inch-wide) slices. Place slices, cut sides up, into pan. (Slices do not fill pan but will once dough rises.) Cover pan with a damp towel; let rise in a warm place (85°), free from drafts, 15 minutes or until doubled in size.

7 Bake at 375° for 15 minutes or until buns are lightly browned. Cool buns in pan on a wire rack for 5 minutes. Place a serving platter upside down on top of pan; invert buns onto platter. Serve warm. Yield: 12 servings (serving size: 1 bun).

CALORIES 211 (28% from fat); FAT 6.5g (sat 3.2g, mono 1.5g, poly 1.4g); PROTEIN 2.8g; CARB 36.7g; FIBER 1.7g; CHOL 13mg; IRON 1.6mg; SODIUM 96mg; CALC 37mg

QUICK & EASY • MAKE AHEAD
Apricot Mustard Sauce

Prepare the sauce up to two days in advance, and reheat in a saucepan over medium-low heat before serving. This sauce is delicious with ham, roast chicken, or pork.

- 1 tablespoon extravirgin olive oil
- 3 tablespoons minced red onion
- 1 cup apricot nectar
- 2/3 cup finely chopped dried apricots
- 3 tablespoons apricot preserves
- 2 tablespoons Dijon mustard
- 1 teaspoon minced fresh sage

❶ Heat oil in a medium nonstick skillet over medium heat. Add onion to pan; cook 5 minutes or until tender, stirring occasionally. Add nectar and apricots to pan; cook until liquid is reduced to 1/2 cup (about 8 minutes). Stir in preserves and mustard; cook 1 1/2 minutes. Stir in sage; cook 30 seconds. Serve warm. Yield: 1 1/2 cups (serving size: 2 tablespoons).

CALORIES 61 (18% from fat); FAT 1.2g (sat 0.2g, mono 0.8g, poly 0.2g); PROTEIN 0.5g; CARB 12.6g; FIBER 0.7g; CHOL 0mg; IRON 0.5mg; SODIUM 63mg; CALC 8mg

MAKE AHEAD
Saffron Aioli

Saffron adds earthy flavor and a golden hue to the classic French condiment. Serve on fish, over steamed vegetables, as a sandwich spread, or as an appetizer on crostini.

- 1 tablespoon warm water
- Dash of saffron threads, crushed
- 1 cup canola mayonnaise (such as Hellmann's)
- 1 1/2 teaspoons balsamic vinegar
- 1/4 teaspoon salt
- 1 large garlic clove, minced
- 1 tablespoon extravirgin olive oil

❶ Combine 1 tablespoon warm water and saffron in a medium bowl, and let stand 30 minutes.
❷ Add mayonnaise and next 3 ingredients to saffron mixture, stirring well with a whisk. Gradually add oil, stirring with a whisk until smooth. Yield: about 1 1/4 cups (serving size: 1 tablespoon).

CALORIES 34 (93% from fat); FAT 3.5g (sat 0.1g, mono 2.5g, poly 0.9g); PROTEIN 0g; CARB 0.1g; FIBER 0g; CHOL 0mg; IRON 0mg; SODIUM 118mg; CALC 0mg

MAKE AHEAD
Chunky Chai Applesauce

- 1/2 cup apple cider
- 2 pounds Granny Smith apples, peeled, cored, and chopped
- 1 cup packed brown sugar
- 1 1/2 tablespoons fresh lemon juice
- 1/2 teaspoon ground cinnamon
- 1/8 teaspoon ground ginger
- 1/8 teaspoon ground nutmeg
- 1/8 teaspoon ground cardamom
- Dash of ground cloves
- Dash of freshly ground black pepper

❶ Combine cider and apples in a large saucepan; bring to a boil over medium-high heat. Cover, reduce heat, and simmer 20 minutes or until apples are tender, stirring occasionally. Stir in sugar and remaining ingredients; simmer 12 minutes, stirring occasionally until mixture is thick. Cover and chill. Yield: 3 2/3 cups (serving size: about 1/4 cup).

CALORIES 88 (0% from fat); FAT 0g; PROTEIN 0.2g; CARB 23.2g; FIBER 1.2g; CHOL 0mg; IRON 0.4mg; SODIUM 6mg; CALC 17mg

MAKE AHEAD
Classic Cranberry Sauce
(pictured on page 264)

Cinnamon, ginger, and cloves boost the taste of this traditional whole-berry cranberry sauce. Vary the character by adding toasted nuts or other fruits. Use leftover sauce in our Dinner Tonight recipes (page 375) in this chapter.

- 1 1/2 cups sugar
- 3/4 cup fresh orange juice (about 3 oranges)
- 1/2 teaspoon ground cinnamon
- 1/4 teaspoon ground ginger
- Dash of ground cloves
- 1 (12-ounce) package fresh cranberries
- 1 tablespoon grated orange rind

❶ Combine first 6 ingredients in a medium saucepan; bring to a boil over medium-high heat. Reduce heat to medium; cook 12 minutes or until cranberries pop. Remove from heat; stir in rind. Cool completely. Serve chilled or at room temperature. Yield: 3 cups (serving size: 2 tablespoons).

CALORIES 59 (0% from fat); FAT 0g; PROTEIN 0.1g; CARB 15g; FIBER 0.7g; CHOL 0mg; IRON 0.1mg; SODIUM 0mg; CALC 3mg

Gifts from the Kitchen

Show your love with presents that have a homemade touch.

Porcini Mushroom Risotto

To give as a gift, pour rice in a jar, and top with dried mushrooms. Bundle the thyme and bay leaf in a cheesecloth sachet, and place in jar. Along with a copy of this recipe, you could also give a bottle of red wine like Barbera or pinot noir or a wedge of Parmigiano-Reggiano.

 5 ounces dried porcini mushrooms
 2 cups boiling water
 7 cups fat-free, less-sodium chicken broth
 2 tablespoons butter
 2 tablespoons olive oil
 1 cup chopped onion
 4 garlic cloves, minced
 2 cups uncooked Arborio rice or other medium-grain rice
 1 cup dry white wine
 1 teaspoon dried thyme
 1 bay leaf
 1 cup (4 ounces) grated fresh Parmigiano-Reggiano cheese
 ¼ teaspoon salt
 ¼ teaspoon freshly ground black pepper

❶ Combine mushrooms and 2 cups boiling water in a bowl. Cover and let stand 30 minutes or until tender. Drain and rinse in a colander; drain. Chop mushrooms.
❷ Bring broth to a simmer (do not boil). Keep warm over low heat.
❸ Heat butter and oil in a large saucepan over medium heat. Add onion and garlic to pan; cook 8 minutes or until tender, stirring frequently. Add rice; cook 1 minute, stirring constantly. Add wine; cook 2 minutes or until absorbed, stirring constantly. Stir in mushrooms, thyme, and bay leaf. Add broth, ½ cup at a time,

stirring constantly until each portion of broth is absorbed before adding next (about 25 minutes total). Discard bay leaf. Stir in cheese, salt, and pepper. Yield: 8 servings (serving size: 1 cup).

CALORIES 362 (24% from fat); FAT 9.8g (sat 4.1g, mono 4.1g, poly 0.6g); PROTEIN 14.8g; CARB 51g; FIBER 7.8g; CHOL 16mg; IRON 4.2mg; SODIUM 569mg; CALC 137mg

MAKE AHEAD • FREEZABLE
Vanilla Buttermilk Pound Cakes

You can also prepare these cakes in two (8 x 4-inch) loaf pans. Bake at 350° for one hour or until done.

 3 cups all-purpose flour (about 13.5 ounces)
 1 teaspoon baking powder
 ½ teaspoon baking soda
 ½ teaspoon salt
 2 cups sugar
 ¾ cup butter, softened
 1 teaspoon vanilla extract
 3 large eggs
 1⅓ cups low-fat buttermilk
    Cooking spray

❶ Preheat oven to 350°.
❷ Lightly spoon flour into dry measuring cups, and level with a knife. Combine flour and next 3 ingredients; stir with a whisk. Place sugar, butter, and vanilla in a large bowl; beat with a mixer at medium speed until light and fluffy. Add eggs, 1 at a time, beating well after each addition. Add flour mixture and buttermilk to sugar mixture, beginning and ending with flour mixture.
❸ Spoon batter into 5 (5¾ x 3¾-inch) loaf pans coated with cooking spray. Bake at 350° for 40 minutes or until a wooden pick inserted in center comes out clean. Cool in pans 10 minutes on a wire rack. Remove from pans. Cool completely on a wire rack. Yield: 5 loaves, 6 servings per loaf (serving size: 1 slice).

CALORIES 144 (32% from fat); FAT 5.1g (sat 3.1g, mono 1.4g, poly 0.2g); PROTEIN 2.2g; CARB 22.3g; FIBER 0.3g; CHOL 34mg; IRON 0.7mg; SODIUM 95mg; CALC 25mg

MAKE AHEAD
Limoncello

This Italian liqueur is good ice cold on its own, in a lemon drop martini, mixed with sparkling wine, or splashed over a bowl of fresh fruit. Since it takes two weeks to infuse the bracing citrusy flavor into the vodka, start this gift early, and decant it into pretty sterilized glass bottles.

 4 cups vodka
 ½ cup lemon rind strips (about 7 lemons)
 3 cups water
 1½ cups sugar

❶ Combine vodka and rind in a bowl. Cover and let stand at room temperature for 2 weeks. Strain through a sieve into a bowl; discard solids.
❷ Combine 3 cups water and sugar in a large saucepan. Cook over medium heat until sugar dissolves, stirring occasionally. Remove from heat, and cool to room temperature. Add to vodka mixture.
❸ Divide limoncello evenly among 3 sterilized (750-milliliter) bottles, and seal. Yield: 7 cups (serving size: about ¼ cup).
NOTE: Store in refrigerator up to one year.

CALORIES 125 (0% from fat); FAT 0g; PROTEIN 0g; CARB 10.7g; FIBER 0g; CHOL 0mg; IRON 0mg; SODIUM 1mg; CALC 1mg

For Longer Storage

The U.S. Department of Agriculture says foods that are stored in sterilized containers can last at least 18 months. To sterilize clean, clear glass bottles, jars, and accompanying lids, place both vessels and tops in a large saucepan or stockpot. Fill the pan to cover contents with hot (not boiling) water, and boil for 15 minutes. Use tongs to carefully remove bottles and lids, and fill and seal containers while still hot. Visit the National Center for Home Food Preservation (www.uga.edu/nchfp/index.html) for more information on sterilization.

MAKE AHEAD
Cinnamon Caramel Sauce

Drizzle this smooth, sweet sauce on chocolate cake, apple pie, pound cake, or low-fat vanilla ice cream. Store refrigerated in an airtight container for up to five days, and bring to room temperature before using. Omit the cinnamon, if you prefer.

 2 cups sugar
 ½ cup water
 ¼ cup hot water
 6 tablespoons half-and-half
 ½ teaspoon kosher salt
 1 (3-inch) cinnamon stick

❶ Combine sugar and ½ cup water in a small, heavy saucepan over high heat; cook until sugar dissolves, stirring as needed to dissolve sugar evenly (about 2 minutes). Cook another 8 minutes or until golden (do not stir). Remove from heat; cool slightly. Carefully stir in ¼ cup hot water, half-and-half, and salt. Add cinnamon stick; cool to room temperature. Discard cinnamon stick. Divide sugar mixture between two sterilized (8-ounce) glass jars. Cover and refrigerate. Serve at room temperature or slightly warmed. Yield: 1⅓ cups (serving size: 1 tablespoon).

CALORIES 83 (5% from fat); FAT 0.5g (sat 0.3g, mono 0g, poly 0g); PROTEIN 0.1g; CARB 20.2g; FIBER 0g; CHOL 2mg; IRON 0mg; SODIUM 49mg; CALC 5mg

MAKE AHEAD
Indian-Spiced Cocktail Nuts

Redolent with cinnamon, coriander, cumin, and the fire of cayenne, these nuts make a delicious accompaniment to cocktails. Garam masala, the Indian spice blend, is located on the spice aisle of large supermarkets or at Indian grocery stores, but you can use our fresh Garam Masala (page 364) and give extra with these nuts. Package in a jar with a homemade tag. Reheat nuts by placing on a baking sheet and toasting for five minutes in a preheated 350° oven.

 1 (11.5-ounce) container lightly salted mixed nuts (such as Planters)
 1¼ teaspoons garam masala
 ½ teaspoon ground ginger
 ½ teaspoon ground cumin
 ½ teaspoon olive oil
 ¼ teaspoon ground red pepper

❶ Preheat oven to 325°.
❷ Combine all ingredients in a medium bowl, and toss well to coat. Spread nut mixture in a single layer on a jelly-roll pan lined with parchment paper. Bake at 325° for 25 minutes or until lightly toasted, stirring twice during cooking time. Cool. Yield: 2¼ cups (serving size: 2 tablespoons).

NOTE: Store nuts, tightly covered, up to one week.

CALORIES 104 (78% from fat); FAT 9g (sat 1.2g, mono 5.5g, poly 1.9g); PROTEIN 3g; CARB 4.5g; FIBER 1.6g; CHOL 0mg; IRON 0.7mg; SODIUM 39mg; CALC 14mg

MAKE AHEAD
Chocolate, Cherry, and Hazelnut Biscotti

Package a dozen of these cookies in decorative plastic bags or cellophane from a craft store, and present with high-quality coffee beans. Use a heavy-duty stand mixer for this recipe's very stiff dough.

 ½ cup hazelnuts
 ½ cup port or other sweet red wine
 ½ cup dried cherries
 ½ cup packed brown sugar
 3 ounces bittersweet chocolate, coarsely chopped
 1½ teaspoons vanilla extract
 1 large egg
 1 large egg yolk
 1 cup all-purpose flour (about 4.5 ounces)
 ½ cup unsweetened cocoa
 1 tablespoon instant espresso granules
 1½ teaspoons baking powder
 ¼ teaspoon salt

❶ Preheat oven to 350°.
❷ Place hazelnuts on a baking sheet. Bake at 350° for 10 minutes, stirring once. Turn nuts out onto a towel. Roll up towel; rub off skins. Chop nuts.
❸ Pour wine in a small microwave-safe bowl. Microwave at HIGH 1 minute. Add cherries, and let stand for 30 minutes. Drain well.
❹ Place sugar and chocolate in a food processor; process until chocolate is finely ground.
❺ Place vanilla, egg, and egg yolk in a large bowl; beat with a mixer at medium speed until blended (about 1 minute). Add sugar mixture; beat 1 minute.
❻ Lightly spoon flour into a dry measuring cup, and level with a knife. Combine flour and remaining ingredients, and stir with a whisk. Gradually add flour mixture to egg mixture, beating until blended. Add hazelnuts and cherries; beat just until blended. (Dough will be very stiff.) Turn dough out onto a lightly floured surface, and knead lightly several times. Divide dough in half; shape each portion into an 8-inch-long roll. Place rolls on a baking sheet lined with parchment paper; pat each roll to a 1-inch thickness. Bake at 350° for 20 minutes. Remove from oven, and cool on a baking sheet for 10 minutes.
❼ Reduce oven temperature to 325°.
❽ Cut each roll diagonally into 12 slices. Place, cut sides down, on baking sheet. Bake at 325° for 10 minutes. Turn cookies over; bake an additional 10 minutes (cookies will be slightly soft in center but will harden as they cool). Cool completely on wire rack. Yield: 2 dozen (serving size: 1 biscotto).

CALORIES 94 (34% from fat); FAT 3.5g (sat 1g, mono 1.3g, poly 0.3g); PROTEIN 1.9g; CARB 14.2g; FIBER 1.3g; CHOL 17mg; IRON 0.9mg; SODIUM 61mg; CALC 29mg

Chocolate Shortbread

Rich shortbread is easy to prepare and keeps for several days in an airtight container. Softened butter should be pliable but not easily spreadable. Because this mixture is already dark, it's hard to tell when the shortbread browns. Check your oven temperature using an oven thermometer, and bake just until the shortbread is set.

> 1 cup all-purpose flour (about 4.5 ounces)
> 3 tablespoons unsweetened premium dark cocoa
> ¼ teaspoon salt
> ½ cup powdered sugar
> 5 tablespoons butter, softened
> ¼ cup canola oil
> Cooking spray

1 Lightly spoon flour into a dry measuring cup; level with a knife. Combine flour, cocoa, and salt in a small bowl; stir with a whisk.
2 Place sugar, butter, and oil in a medium bowl; mix with hands until combined. Add flour mixture, mixing with hands until combined; wrap in plastic wrap. Refrigerate 30 minutes.
3 Preheat oven to 325°.
4 Place dough on a baking sheet coated with cooking spray; press dough into an 8 x 5-inch rectangle about ³/₈-inch thick. Pierce entire surface liberally with a fork. Bake at 325° for 30 minutes or just until set. Cut shortbread into 24 pieces. Cool completely. Yield: 2 dozen (serving size: 1 cookie).

CALORIES 72 (60% from fat); FAT 4.8g (sat 1.7g, mono 2.1g, poly 0.8g); PROTEIN 0.7g; CARB 7g; FIBER 0.3g; CHOL 6mg; IRON 0.3mg; SODIUM 42mg; CALC 2mg

LEMON SHORTBREAD VARIATION:
Substitute 3 tablespoons cornstarch for the unsweetened cocoa. Add ½ teaspoon grated lemon rind to flour mixture. Knead dough lightly 4 times or just until smooth before chilling. Bake 30 minutes or just until set and edges are golden. Yield: 2 dozen (serving size: 1 cookie).

CALORIES 74 (58% from fat); FAT 4.8g (sat 1.7g, mono 2g, poly 0.8g); PROTEIN 0.6g; CARB 7.5g; FIBER 0.2g; CHOL 6mg; IRON 0.3mg; SODIUM 42mg; CALC 2mg

BROWN SUGAR SHORTBREAD VARIATION:
These double easily; just bake each batch separately for the best results.

Use a total of 1¼ cups all-purpose flour (about 5.5 ounces), and substitute 3 tablespoons cornstarch for the cocoa. Omit powdered sugar and oil, and use ½ cup packed light brown sugar and 7 tablespoons butter (total), softened. Sprinkle dough with 1½ teaspoons ice water; knead dough lightly 4 times or just until smooth. Bake for 25 minutes or just until set and edges are golden. Yield: 2 dozen (serving size: 1 cookie).

CALORIES 74 (41% from fat); FAT 3.4g (sat 2.1g, mono 0.9g, poly 0.2g); PROTEIN 0.7g; CARB 10.4g; FIBER 0.2g; CHOL 9mg; IRON 0.4mg; SODIUM 50mg; CALC 6mg

Za'atar

Mix ¼ cup of Za'atar with ½ cup olive oil for a zesty dipping sauce for breads.

> ¼ cup ground sumac
> 2 tablespoons dried thyme
> 2 tablespoons dried oregano
> 1 tablespoon toasted sesame seeds
> 1 teaspoon kosher salt

1 Combine all ingredients in a small bowl. Store in an airtight container. Yield: ½ cup (serving size: ¼ teaspoon).

CALORIES 6 (15% from fat); FAT 0.1g (sat 0g, mono 0.1g, poly 0g); PROTEIN 0.1g; CARB 1g; FIBER 0.3g; CHOL 0mg; IRON 0.4mg; SODIUM 61mg; CALC 8mg

Garam Masala

Literally translated as "warm mixture," garam masala, an aromatic North Indian spice blend, is used in everything from flatbreads to soups.

> 2 tablespoons cumin seeds
> 2 tablespoons coriander seeds
> 2 tablespoons cardamom seeds
> 2 tablespoons black peppercorns
> 1 teaspoon whole cloves
> 1 teaspoon grated whole nutmeg
> 1 (2-inch) cinnamon stick, broken

1 Combine all ingredients in a spice or coffee grinder; process until finely ground. Store in an airtight container. Yield: ¾ cup (serving size: ¼ teaspoon).
NOTE: Freeze Garam Masala in an airtight container for up to six months.

CALORIES 2 (45% from fat); FAT 0.1g (sat 0g, mono 0.1g, poly 0g); PROTEIN 0.1g; CARB 0.4g; FIBER 0.2g; CHOL 0mg; IRON 0.2mg; SODIUM 1mg; CALC 5mg

Herbes de Provence

This version of southern France's seasoning blend uses dried herbs. Mix with olive oil and brush on fish before baking, rub on a turkey before roasting, or whisk into homemade salad dressing. Double the recipe to make two gifts.

> 1 tablespoon dried thyme
> 1 tablespoon dried basil
> 1 tablespoon dried rosemary, crushed
> 1 tablespoon dried tarragon
> 1 tablespoon dried savory
> 1 teaspoon dried marjoram
> 1 teaspoon dried oregano
> 1 teaspoon dried lavender (optional)
> 1 bay leaf, crushed

1 Combine all ingredients. Store in an airtight container. Yield: about ⅓ cup (serving size: ¼ teaspoon).

CALORIES 4 (23% from fat); FAT 0.1g (sat 0g, mono 0g, poly 0g); PROTEIN 0.1g; CARB 0.7g; FIBER 0.4g; CHOL 0mg; IRON 0.4mg; SODIUM 1mg; CALC 17mg

Revamped Holiday Dishes

We've improved the dietary profiles of three readers' favorites.

serving size: 1 slice		
	before	after
CALORIES PER SERVING	241	194
FAT	10.2g	6.5g
PERCENT OF TOTAL CALORIES	38%	30%

MAKE AHEAD • FREEZABLE

Pumpkin–Honey Beer Quick Bread

Give the second loaf away, or wrap in plastic wrap and freeze for up to two months. Ground flaxseed and water add moisture to the batter for a smooth-textured bread.

3¼ cups all-purpose flour (about 14.6 ounces)
2 teaspoons salt
2 teaspoons baking soda
1 teaspoon baking powder
1 teaspoon ground cinnamon
1 teaspoon pumpkin pie spice
½ cup water
⅓ cup ground flaxseed
2½ cups sugar
⅔ cup canola oil
⅔ cup honey beer (at room temperature)
½ cup egg substitute
2 large eggs
1 (15-ounce) can pumpkin
Cooking spray

❶ Preheat oven to 350°.
❷ Lightly spoon flour into dry measuring cups; level with a knife. Combine flour and next 5 ingredients in a medium bowl; stir with a whisk.
❸ Combine ½ cup water and flaxseed.
❹ Place sugar and next 4 ingredients in a large bowl; beat with a mixer at medium-high speed until well blended. Add flax-seed mixture and pumpkin; beat at low speed just until blended. Add flour mixture; beat just until combined. Divide batter between 2 (9 x 5-inch) loaf pans coated with cooking spray. Bake at 350° for 1 hour and 10 minutes or until a wooden pick inserted in center comes out clean. Cool 10 minutes in pans on a wire rack; remove from pans. Cool completely on wire rack. Yield: 2 loaves, 14 servings per loaf (serving size: 1 slice).

CALORIES 194 (30% from fat); FAT 6.5g (sat 0.6g, mono 3.4g, poly 2.1g); PROTEIN 2.9g; CARB 31.3g; FIBER 1.3g; CHOL 15mg; IRON 1.2mg; SODIUM 287mg; CALC 27mg

serving size: ⅔ cup		
	before	after
CALORIES PER SERVING	227	146
FAT	15.6g	6.4g
PERCENT OF TOTAL CALORIES	61%	39%

Oyster and Wild Rice Casserole

This side dish would be a fine accompaniment to roast turkey or pork any time.

2½ cups water
1¾ cups fat-free, less-sodium beef broth, divided
1 (5-ounce) package uncooked long-grain and wild rice mix (such as Mahatma)
3 tablespoons butter, divided
1 to 4 dashes hot sauce
2 quarts shucked oysters, well drained
Cooking spray
½ teaspoon fine sea salt
½ teaspoon freshly ground black pepper
2½ tablespoons minced shallots
1 garlic clove, minced
1 (10¾-ounce) can condensed reduced-fat, reduced-sodium cream of mushroom soup
½ cup half-and-half
Chopped fresh parsley (optional)
Crushed red pepper (optional)

❶ Preheat oven to 350°.
❷ Bring 2½ cups water and 1¼ cups broth to a boil in a medium saucepan; add rice mix. Cover, reduce heat, and simmer 25 minutes or until rice is tender. Drain well. Stir in 2 tablespoons butter and hot sauce; fluff with a fork.
❸ Melt remaining 1 tablespoon butter in a large skillet over medium-high heat. Add oysters to pan; sauté 3 minutes or until edges curl. Remove oysters with a slotted spoon; discard remaining cooking liquid.
❹ Place half of rice mixture in a 13 x 9-inch baking dish coated with cooking spray. Arrange oysters evenly over rice; sprinkle with salt and pepper. Top oysters with remaining rice mixture.
❺ Heat a small saucepan over medium heat. Coat pan with cooking spray. Add shallots and garlic to pan; cook 1 minute, stirring occasionally. Stir in remaining ½ cup broth and mushroom soup; cook 2 minutes or until thoroughly heated. Remove from heat; stir in half-and-half. Pour broth mixture evenly over rice mixture. Bake at 350° for 40 minutes or until golden brown and bubbly. Garnish with parsley and crushed red pepper, if desired. Yield: 12 servings (serving size: about ⅔ cup).

CALORIES 146 (39% from fat); FAT 6.4g (sat 3.2g, mono 1.4g, poly 0.9g); PROTEIN 7.1g; CARB 14.6g; FIBER 0.6g; CHOL 51mg; IRON 5.3mg; SODIUM 496mg; CALC 76mg

serving size: ⅔ cup		
	before	after
CALORIES PER SERVING	289	258
FAT	14.2g	9.2g
PERCENT OF TOTAL CALORIES	44%	32%

Continued

Sweet Potato Casserole

Make sure to use a metal baking pan or broiler-safe ceramic dish.

POTATOES:

- 2 pounds sweet potatoes, peeled and chopped
- ¾ cup granulated sugar
- ¼ cup evaporated low-fat milk
- 3 tablespoons butter, melted
- 1 teaspoon vanilla extract
- ½ teaspoon salt
- 2 large eggs
- Cooking spray

TOPPING:

- ⅓ cup all-purpose flour (about 1.5 ounces)
- ⅔ cup packed brown sugar
- ⅛ teaspoon salt
- 2 tablespoons melted butter
- ½ cup chopped pecans

1 Preheat oven to 350°.

2 To prepare potatoes, place potatoes in a Dutch oven; cover with water. Bring to a boil. Reduce heat, and simmer 20 minutes or until tender; drain. Cool 5 minutes.

3 Place potatoes in a large bowl; add granulated sugar and next 4 ingredients. Beat with a mixer at medium speed until smooth. Add eggs; beat well. Pour potato mixture into a 13 x 9-inch baking pan coated with cooking spray.

4 To prepare topping, lightly spoon flour into a dry measuring cup; level with a knife. Combine flour, brown sugar, and ⅛ teaspoon salt; stir with a whisk. Stir in 2 tablespoons melted butter. Sprinkle flour mixture evenly over potato mixture; arrange pecans evenly over top. Bake at 350° for 25 minutes or just until golden.

5 Preheat broiler (remove casserole from oven).

6 Broil casserole 45 seconds or until topping is bubbly. Let stand 10 minutes before serving. Yield: 12 servings (serving size: about ⅔ cup).

CALORIES 258 (32% from fat); FAT 9.2g (sat 3.6g, mono 3.6g, poly 1.5g); PROTEIN 3.3g; CARB 42g; FIBER 2.5g; CHOL 43mg; IRON 1.2mg; SODIUM 199mg; CALC 54mg

Roasting

Use this classic oven method for succulent meat and richly browned vegetables.

ROASTING MAY BE one of the easiest cooking techniques. Your oven does most of the work while you spend time with family, friends, or a good book—all of which make it particularly appealing during the busy holidays. Your effort comes primarily before the actual cooking begins. Foods are simply prepared—chickens trussed, tenderloins and hams rubbed with seasonings, vegetables cut up—and then they cook, mostly hands-free, until they emerge with browned, hearty flavors.

Classic "Prime" Rib

This holiday classic is all about the technique—roast at a low temperature to ensure gently cooked meat with a medium-rare center. Although called "prime" rib, there are few prime-grade beef rib roasts sold to consumers; most go to restaurants. The two grades just below prime, choice and select, are leaner than prime and still quite tasty.

- 1 (6½-pound) rib-eye roast, French-cut and trimmed
- 1 tablespoon kosher salt
- 1½ teaspoons freshly ground black pepper

1 Preheat oven to 325°.

2 Rub roast on all sides with salt and pepper. Place roast, bone side down, in a roasting pan. Loop and tie twine between each of the bones (to help the roast hold its shape as it cooks). Bake at 325° for 2 hours or until a thermometer inserted into thickest portion of roast registers 130° or until desired degree of doneness. Remove from oven. Place roast on a cutting board. Let stand 10 minutes before serving. Yield: 17 servings (serving size: about 3 ounces beef).

CALORIES 186 (52% from fat); FAT 10.7g (sat 4.3g, mono 4.5g, poly 0.3g); PROTEIN 20.9g; CARB 0.1g; FIBER 0.1g; CHOL 61mg; IRON 2.2mg; SODIUM 394mg; CALC 8mg

New Potatoes with Roasted Garlic Vinaigrette

While raw garlic is pungent, roasted garlic is sweet and mild with a buttery texture.

- 3 tablespoons olive oil, divided
- 1¼ teaspoons kosher salt, divided
- ½ teaspoon black pepper, divided
- 7 garlic cloves, unpeeled
- 3 pounds small red potatoes, quartered
- 3 tablespoons minced chives
- 2 tablespoons white wine vinegar
- 2 teaspoons Dijon mustard

1 Preheat oven to 400°.

2 Combine 1½ tablespoons oil, ½ teaspoon salt, ¼ teaspoon pepper, garlic, and potatoes in a roasting pan or jelly-roll pan; toss well to coat. Bake at 400° for 1 hour and 10 minutes or until tender, stirring after 35 minutes. Cool 10 minutes.

3 Squeeze garlic cloves to extract pulp. Discard skins. Combine garlic pulp, remaining 1½ tablespoons oil, remaining ¾ teaspoon salt, remaining ¼ teaspoon pepper, chives, vinegar, and mustard in a large bowl; stir well with a whisk. Add potatoes to bowl; toss well to coat. Yield: 8 servings (serving size: about ¾ cup).

CALORIES 170 (28% from fat); FAT 5.3g (sat 0.8g, mono 3.7g, poly 0.6g); PROTEIN 3.4g; CARB 28.3g; FIBER 3g; CHOL 0mg; IRON 1.3mg; SODIUM 335mg; CALC 23mg

Bistro Roast Chicken

Fresh herbs, butter, and Dijon mustard provide big flavor in this simple roast chicken. It first cooks breast side down, then is turned over to finish cooking. This method ensures moist breast meat. Look for a bird labeled "roasting chicken" or "roaster"—these usually have more meat and are more tender than broiler-fryers.

- 2 tablespoons minced fresh tarragon
- 1 tablespoon minced fresh thyme
- 4 teaspoons butter, melted
- 1 teaspoon salt
- 1 teaspoon Dijon mustard
- 1/2 teaspoon freshly ground black pepper
- 1 (4 1/2-pound) roasting chicken
  Cooking spray

1 Preheat oven to 375°.
2 Combine first 6 ingredients in a small bowl.
3 Remove and discard giblets and neck from chicken. Trim excess fat. Starting at neck cavity, loosen skin from breast and drumsticks by inserting fingers, gently pushing between skin and meat. Rub herb mixture under loosened skin and over breast and drumsticks. Tie legs together with kitchen twine. Lift wing tips up and over back; tuck under chicken. Place chicken, breast side down, on rack of a broiler pan or shallow roasting pan coated with cooking spray; place rack in pan.
4 Bake chicken at 375° for 40 minutes. Carefully turn chicken over (breast side up). Bake an additional 40 minutes or until a thermometer inserted in meaty part of thigh registers 165°. Place chicken on a cutting board; let stand 10 minutes before carving. Discard skin. Yield: 5 servings (serving size: about 4 ounces chicken).

CALORIES 262 (30% from fat); FAT 8.7g (sat 3.3g, mono 2.5g, poly 1.5g); PROTEIN 42.5g; CARB 0.6g; FIBER 0.1g; CHOL 143mg; IRON 2.2mg; SODIUM 674mg; CALC 32mg

Ham with Bourbon-Peach Glaze

For a pretty presentation, garnish the platter with orange slices, cranberries, fresh bay leaves, and parsley.

- 2/3 cup peach preserves
- 1/4 cup bourbon
- 1 teaspoon ground cumin
- 1/2 teaspoon ground ginger
- 1/2 teaspoon ground coriander
- 1/2 teaspoon freshly ground black pepper
- 1 (7 1/2-pound) 33%-less-sodium smoked, fully cooked ham half
- 20 whole cloves
  Cooking spray
- 1 cup water

1 Preheat oven to 325°.
2 Combine preserves and bourbon in a small saucepan. Bring to a boil; remove from heat. Stir in cumin and next 3 ingredients. Cool slightly.
3 Trim fat and rind from ham. Score outside of ham in a diamond pattern; stud with cloves. Place ham on rack of a broiler pan or roasting pan coated with cooking spray. Pour 1 cup water into pan; place rack in pan. Brush ham with 1/4 cup preserves mixture. Bake at 325° for 2 hours or until a thermometer registers 140°, basting ham with remaining preserves mixture every 30 minutes. Transfer ham to a platter; let stand 15 minutes. Discard cloves before serving. Yield: 28 servings (serving size: about 3 ounces ham).

CALORIES 143 (38% from fat); FAT 6.1g (sat 2g, mono 2.9g, poly 0.7g); PROTEIN 14.2g; CARB 7.1g; FIBER 0g; CHOL 51mg; IRON 0.8mg; SODIUM 871mg; CALC 1mg

Tuscan Pork Tenderloin

Roasting a small cut, such as pork tenderloin, at high heat—500°—creates a browned exterior and moist interior. (Cooking at lower temperatures will still produce fine results, but the pork won't develop a crust by the time it reaches the desired internal temperature.) The endive and shallots form an edible rack for the meat to rest on as it cooks.

- 4 teaspoons olive oil, divided
- 2 teaspoons white balsamic vinegar
- 1 teaspoon kosher salt, divided
- 5 large shallots, halved
- 3 heads Belgian endive, quartered lengthwise (about 1 pound)
- 1 1/2 teaspoons finely chopped fresh rosemary
- 1 teaspoon grated lemon rind
- 1 teaspoon fresh lemon juice
- 1/2 teaspoon fennel seeds, crushed
- 1/2 teaspoon freshly ground black pepper
- 2 garlic cloves, minced
- 1 (1-pound) pork tenderloin

1 Preheat oven to 500°.
2 Combine 1 tablespoon oil, vinegar, 1/2 teaspoon salt, shallots, and endive in a roasting pan; toss well to coat. Arrange vegetables evenly down center of pan.
3 Combine remaining 1 teaspoon oil, remaining 1/2 teaspoon salt, rosemary, and next 5 ingredients in a small bowl. Rub rosemary mixture onto pork. Arrange pork on top of vegetables. Bake at 500° for 17 minutes or until a thermometer registers 155°. Let vegetables and pork stand 10 minutes. Cut pork crosswise into 12 slices. Yield: 4 servings (serving size: 3 slices pork and about 1/4 cup vegetables).

CALORIES 238 (33% from fat); FAT 8.6g (sat 2g, mono 5.1g, poly 1g); PROTEIN 26.3g; CARB 14.4g; FIBER 4.2g; CHOL 74mg; IRON 2.4mg; SODIUM 537mg; CALC 55mg

All About Roasting

What Roasting Does

Roasting involves cooking food in an uncovered pan in the oven. It is a dry cooking technique, as opposed to wet techniques like braising, stewing, or steaming. Dry, hot air surrounds the food, cooking it evenly on all sides.

Depending on the food you're preparing, you can roast at low, moderate, or high temperatures.

Best Bets for Roasting

Large cuts of meat work well: ham, whole turkeys or chickens, or tenderloins. Smaller cuts like boneless chicken breasts or fish fillets may dry out in the oven (they're usually better sautéed). Roasting is also ideal for dense vegetables such as potatoes, beets, and winter squash, as it concentrates their natural sugars and intensifies their flavor.

Oven Temperature

Choose the temperature according to the type of food you're roasting. Vegetables usually need a moderate temperature near 375° so that internal water evaporates quickly to concentrate the flavor without the food browning too deeply or becoming too soft.

In general, use low (250°) to moderate (375°) heat for large roasts so they'll cook evenly and slowly (high heat would burn the outside of the roast before it's done on the inside). High-heat (above 400°) roasting works well for small, tender cuts such as tenderloins because it quickly produces a browned crust, and the meat cooks adequately in a short time.

Equipment

A **heavy roasting pan** with a rack is a good investment for your kitchen. A roasting pan has low sides, allowing more of the oven's heat to make contact with the food. Choose a heavy pan, as it will distribute heat evenly and isn't as likely to burn pan drippings. A rack is helpful to suspend food that produces a lot of drippings (whole poultry or fatty roasts, for example) out of the liquid. If you don't have a rack, place a wire cooling rack in the pan. You can also use a broiler pan for roasting, but these pans are shallow, so be careful not to spill hot drippings out of the pan.

You'll need **butchers' twine** to truss (tie) chickens, turkeys, and some roasts so they hold their shape as they cook. Look for food-safe butchers' twine at cookware stores, some hardware stores, and many large supermarkets. Or ask your butcher to include some twine with your purchase.

A **meat thermometer** is essential since the key to perfectly roasted meats is to not overcook them. Choose an instant-read or a remote digital model.

Basting

Whether you should baste meat or leave it alone as it cooks depends on various factors. A standing rib roast, for example, should not be basted because one of its best features is the salty crust that forms over the meat as it roasts; you wouldn't want to wash that away. And whole chickens and turkeys have enough fat under the skin (which we discard after cooking) that they self-baste as the fat slowly melts and coats the meat.

Frequent basting also means you're opening the oven door and letting the heat escape, which could lengthen the cooking time or prevent the meat from properly browning. Understand that basting isn't necessary to keep food moist. If, however, you want to add more flavor in the form of a glaze, basting is a worthwhile endeavor.

Let It Rest

All meat should rest for 10 to 20 minutes after it's removed from the oven. Larger cuts—a standing rib roast, for example—retain enough internal heat so that they continue to cook after they come out of the oven, up to an added 10 degrees or so. Smaller cuts like pork tenderloins do not have enough mass to continue cooking by more than a couple of degrees.

But the main reason meat should rest is to allow the juices to redistribute. If you sliced into a roast chicken or beef roast immediately upon pulling it out of the oven, all the juices would pour out onto the platter, and the resulting meat would be dry.

About Doneness

We follow the U.S. Department of Agriculture's guidelines for cooking poultry to an internal temperature of 165° and for reheating fully cooked ham to 140°. For some beef, lamb, pork, and game cuts, however, we prefer cooking to lower temperatures than the USDA recommends because it produces juicier results. If you are pregnant, older, have a compromised immune system, or are serving to children, follow the USDA's recommendation to cook beef or lamb to a minimum of 145°, and pork and game to 160°.

The Bottom Line

The three most important elements to remember about roasting:

1 Generally, choose lower oven temperatures for larger cuts of meat and higher oven temperatures for smaller cuts.
2 Use a heavy roasting pan.
3 Allow the meat to rest for 10 to 20 minutes before slicing.

Orange-Scented Beets

     8 cups (1-inch) cubed peeled beets
        (about 3½ pounds with tops)
   1½ tablespoons grated orange rind
   1½ tablespoons canola oil
     ½ teaspoon freshly ground black
        pepper
     2 teaspoons balsamic vinegar
     ¾ teaspoon kosher salt

❶ Preheat oven to 375°.
❷ Combine first 4 ingredients in a roasting pan or jelly-roll pan; toss well to coat. Bake at 375° for 45 minutes or until tender, stirring occasionally. Stir in vinegar and salt. Yield: 6 servings (serving size: about ¾ cup).

CALORIES 113 (30% from fat); FAT 3.8g (sat 0.3g, mono 2.1g, poly 1.2g); PROTEIN 3g; CARB 18.1g; FIBER 5.3g; CHOL 0mg; IRON 1.5mg; SODIUM 377mg; CALC 33mg

Roasted Fennel with Dill and Lemon

Keep the fennel bulbs' cores partially intact to prevent the wedges from falling apart.

     2 large fennel bulbs (about 2 pounds)
   1½ tablespoons extravirgin olive oil,
        divided
     ½ teaspoon kosher salt, divided
     ½ teaspoon chopped fresh dill, divided
     ¼ teaspoon black pepper
     2 teaspoons fresh lemon juice

❶ Preheat oven to 375°.
❷ Cut each fennel bulb in half lengthwise. Remove most of core using a sharp knife. Cut each bulb half lengthwise into quarters. Combine fennel, 1 tablespoon oil, ¼ teaspoon salt, ¼ teaspoon dill, and pepper in a small roasting pan; toss well to coat. Cover and bake at 375° for 20 minutes or until almost tender.
❸ Uncover fennel; bake an additional 20 minutes or until lightly browned and tender, turning occasionally. Place fennel in a large bowl. Add remaining 1½ teaspoons oil, remaining ¼ teaspoon salt,

remaining ¼ teaspoon dill, and juice; toss gently to combine. Yield: 4 servings (serving size: 4 wedges).

CALORIES 116 (43% from fat); FAT 5.5g (sat 0.7g, mono 3.7g, poly 0.5g); PROTEIN 2.8g; CARB 16.8g; FIBER 7.1g; CHOL 0mg; IRON 1.7mg; SODIUM 353mg; CALC 112mg

MAKE AHEAD
Roasted Butternut Squash and Shallot Soup

Spicy fresh ginger complements the sweet roasted winter squash and shallots in this easy recipe. Serve with a grilled cheese sandwich for a simple supper.

     4 cups (1-inch) cubed peeled
        butternut squash (about
        1½ pounds)
     1 tablespoon olive oil
     ¼ teaspoon salt
     4 large shallots, peeled and halved
     1 (½-inch) piece peeled fresh ginger,
        thinly sliced
   2½ cups fat-free, less-sodium chicken
        broth
     2 tablespoons (1-inch) slices fresh
        chives
        Cracked black pepper (optional)

❶ Preheat oven to 375°.
❷ Combine first 5 ingredients in a roasting pan or jelly-roll pan; toss well. Bake at 375° for 50 minutes or until tender, stirring occasionally. Cool 10 minutes.
❸ Place half of squash mixture and half of broth in a blender. Remove center piece of blender lid (to allow steam to escape); secure blender lid on blender. Place a clean towel over opening in blender lid (to avoid splatters). Blend until smooth. Pour into a large saucepan. Repeat procedure with remaining squash mixture and broth. Cook over medium heat 5 minutes or until thoroughly heated. Top with chives and pepper, if desired. Yield: 6 servings (serving size: ⅔ cup soup and 1 teaspoon chives).

CALORIES 112 (20% from fat); FAT 2.5g (sat 0.4g, mono 1.7g, poly 0.3g); PROTEIN 3.3g; CARB 22.4g; FIBER 3.6g; CHOL 0mg; IRON 1.6mg; SODIUM 266mg; CALC 84mg

Southwestern Spice-Rubbed Bison Tenderloin

Bison (sometimes labeled buffalo) tenderloin is a lean cut, so cook it quickly at moderately high heat to ensure it stays juicy and tender. We prefer it rare, but adjust the cook time to suit your preference. Chateaubriand-cut refers to the center-cut portion of the tenderloin, so the roast is a uniform thickness throughout. If your local butchers don't stock bison meat, try online sources like www.buffalohillsbisonmeat.com or www.highplainsbison.com—or substitute beef tenderloin.

     1 tablespoon canola oil
   1½ teaspoons ancho chile powder
     1 teaspoon ground cumin
     1 teaspoon dark brown sugar
     ½ teaspoon salt
     ½ teaspoon dried oregano
     ½ teaspoon freshly ground black
        pepper
     ¼ teaspoon garlic powder
     ¼ teaspoon celery seeds
     1 (2-pound) chateaubriand-cut
        bison tenderloin
     1 tablespoon fresh lime juice
        Cooking spray

❶ Combine first 9 ingredients in a small bowl. Place bison in a dish; drizzle with juice. Rub spice mixture over bison. Cover and refrigerate 1 hour.
❷ Preheat oven to 425°.
❸ Let bison stand at room temperature 15 minutes. Secure bison at 2-inch intervals with twine.
❹ Place bison in a small roasting pan coated with cooking spray. Bake at 425° for 25 minutes or until a thermometer registers 115° or until desired degree of doneness (temperature will continue to rise as roast stands). Remove from oven; let stand 20 minutes before slicing. Yield: 8 servings (serving size: 3 ounces).

CALORIES 144 (25% from fat); FAT 4g (sat 0.9g, mono 1.9g, poly 0.8g); PROTEIN 24.4g; CARB 1.3g; FIBER 0.4g; CHOL 70mg; IRON 3.2mg; SODIUM 202mg; CALC 14mg

Network of Care

Members of an Atlanta church develop an online community to deliver nourishing meals to congregants in need.

Soon after Mary Jo Bryan gave birth to her son, James, she learned that her husband, Clay, had advanced metastatic cancer. Three months later, Clay was gone and Mary Jo found herself alone with an infant. "I had no time to cook and no energy," she recalls of those first surreal weeks afterward. But friends stocked her freezer with meals for weeks, including four dozen blueberry muffins. "I was amazed at how useful those muffins were," Mary Jo says. Some days they were all she could think to eat. Fifteen seconds in the microwave gave her a taste of something homemade.

From those muffins came the idea for E-Care Meal Delivery. E-Care is the e-mail list Mary Jo, Reverend Chris Epperson, and church members Fifi Guest and Sue Mobley at All Saints Episcopal Church in Atlanta established to create an electronic community among the 3,000 or so congregants on All Saints' rolls. Subscribers receive regular e-mails soliciting prayers for church members and friends. Mary Jo recognized that the E-Care network could also identify members in need of meals and organize deliveries of heat-and-eat dinners from the church's kitchen.

Working with friends at All Saints, she set up the program seven years ago and has kept it going since. Whenever a church member welcomes a new baby, suffers an illness, or deals with a tragedy, the clergy alert E-Care administrators. They send a volunteer to the church kitchen to pick up the appropriate number of servings of a main course, side dish, and dessert from the freezer. The food arrives beautifully wrapped with cooking instructions, a list of ingredients, and a thoughtful card.

E-Care also periodically enlists members to restock the freezer. Volunteers prepare foil pans of chicken spaghetti casserole and broccoli with Swiss cheese sauce. (We share lightened versions of these favorites here.)

QUICK & EASY • MAKE AHEAD
FREEZABLE

Swiss Broccoli Casserole

The E-Care group prepares up to a dozen batches at a time of a similar side dish to freeze and deliver to church members. We added cooked rice to make it more substantial, plus a sprinkling of breadcrumbs for a little crunch.

- ⅔ cup 2% reduced-fat milk
- ¾ teaspoon salt
- ¼ teaspoon freshly ground black pepper
- 1 (10.75-ounce) can condensed 30% reduced-sodium 98% fat-free cream of mushroom soup, undiluted
- ½ cup (2 ounces) shredded Swiss cheese
- 1 cup cooked rice
- 2 (10-ounce) packages frozen chopped broccoli, thawed
- Cooking spray
- 1 (1-ounce) slice white bread

❶ Preheat oven to 350°.
❷ Combine first 4 ingredients in a large saucepan over medium-high heat; bring to a simmer. Add cheese; stir until melted. Remove from heat; stir in cooked rice and broccoli. Transfer broccoli mixture to an 11 x 7–inch baking dish coated with cooking spray.
❸ Place bread in a food processor; pulse 10 times or until coarse crumbs measure ½ cup. Sprinkle broccoli mixture with breadcrumbs. Cover and bake at 350° for 15 minutes. Uncover and bake an additional 15 minutes. Yield: 8 servings (serving size: about ¾ cup).

CALORIES 111 (28% from fat); FAT 3.5g (sat 1.8g, mono 0.8g, poly 0.6g); PROTEIN 5.7g; CARB 14.9g; FIBER 2.6g; CHOL 9mg; IRON 1.1mg; SODIUM 439mg; CALC 163mg

QUICK & EASY • MAKE AHEAD
FREEZABLE

Aunt Liz's Chicken Spaghetti Casserole

Bake a frozen casserole covered for 55 minutes at 350°; uncover and bake an additional 10 minutes or until it's hot and bubbly.

- 2 cups chopped cooked chicken breast
- 2 cups uncooked spaghetti noodles, broken into 2-inch pieces (about 7 ounces)
- 1 cup (¼-inch-thick) sliced celery
- 1 cup chopped red bell pepper
- 1 cup chopped onion
- 1 cup fat-free, less-sodium chicken broth
- ½ teaspoon salt
- ¼ teaspoon freshly ground black pepper
- 2 (10.75-ounce) cans condensed 30% reduced-sodium 98% fat-free cream of mushroom soup, undiluted
- Cooking spray
- 1 cup (4 ounces) shredded Cheddar cheese, divided

❶ Preheat oven to 350°.
❷ Combine first 5 ingredients in a large bowl. Combine broth and next 3 ingredients in a medium bowl, stirring with a whisk. Add soup mixture to chicken mixture; toss. Divide mixture evenly between 2 (8-inch) square or 2-quart baking dishes coated with cooking spray. Sprinkle ½ cup cheese over each casserole. Cover with foil coated with cooking spray. Bake for 35 minutes at 350°. Uncover and bake an additional 10 minutes. Yield: 2 casseroles; 4 servings each (serving size: about 1 cup).

CALORIES 261 (27% from fat); FAT 7.8g (sat 3.9g, mono 2.2g, poly 1.1g); PROTEIN 19g; CARB 28g; FIBER 2.1g; CHOL 47mg; IRON 1.8mg; SODIUM 652mg; CALC 134mg

Simple Stir-Fry

A Vancouver journalist's quick and easy dish is inspired by the Asian food of her childhood.

Charlene Dy, a journalist from Vancouver, British Columbia, grew up in Manila, Philippines. She credits her travels across Asia for influencing her cooking today. When her friend, who is Chinese, had a baby, Dy jumped at the opportunity to cook a light dish with Asian accents. "In Chinese culture, many believe ginger helps purify and strengthen a woman after she gives birth," Dy says. "I created a fresh meal based on this principle."

Dy called upon a variety of Asian culinary influences and ingredients, such as ginger, sesame oil, and soy sauce. "I based my recipe on a popular Chinese dish, which traditionally highlights a white-fleshed fish, but opted for shrimp instead," she says. "Rice wine helps eliminate a saline or 'oceany' flavor from some types of seafood and leaves the dish with the fresh flavor I had in mind."

Dy uses a standard stir-fry technique to cook this quick and easy meal. She thinks the celery is particularly crisp and savory in this dish. "Cooking it so briefly at moderately high heat retains a lot of celery's delightful crunch, and Asian ingredients like ginger, garlic, and sesame oil really highlight celery's bracing aroma. In this dish, it's almost like it's been given a new identity."

Dy loves the simple method, but stresses the importance of prepping the ingredients first. "Chop before you start the stir-fry," she says, "so you don't overcook the celery and seafood."

QUICK & EASY
Stir-Fried Ginger Shrimp

Serve with jasmine rice and melon slices.

  1   pound medium shrimp, peeled and deveined
  1   teaspoon chopped peeled fresh ginger
  ½   teaspoon salt
      Dash of white pepper
  ½   cup water
  1   tablespoon mirin (sweet rice wine)
  2   teaspoons low-sodium soy sauce
  1½ teaspoons cornstarch
  1   teaspoon sugar
  1   teaspoon dark sesame oil
  ½   teaspoon chile paste with garlic (such as sambal oelek)
  1   tablespoon canola oil, divided
  1   cup thinly vertically sliced onion
  4   garlic cloves, minced
  1   cup diagonally cut celery

1 Place shrimp in a medium bowl. Sprinkle with ginger, salt, and pepper; toss well. Let stand 5 minutes.
2 Combine ½ cup water and next 6 ingredients in a small bowl, stirring with a whisk.
3 Heat 1 teaspoon canola oil in a large nonstick skillet over medium-high heat. Add shrimp mixture to pan; stir-fry 2 minutes. Remove shrimp mixture from pan; set aside. Wipe pan dry with a paper towel. Heat remaining 2 teaspoons canola oil in pan over medium-high heat. Add onion and garlic; stir-fry 1 minute. Add celery; stir-fry 1 minute. Return shrimp mixture to pan; stir-fry 1 minute or until shrimp are done.
4 Add water mixture to pan. Bring to a boil; cook 1 minute or until thick, stirring constantly with a whisk. Serve immediately. Yield: 4 servings (serving size: about 1 cup).

CALORIES 192 (31% from fat); FAT 6.7g (sat 0.8g, mono 2.9g, poly 2.3g); PROTEIN 23.8g; CARB 7.2g; FIBER 0.8g; CHOL 172mg; IRON 3mg; SODIUM 594mg; CALC 82mg

FREEZABLE
Chicken Tamale Casserole
(pictured on page 269)

"I came up with this dish to satisfy my cravings for the tamales I had at Mexican restaurants when I was growing up in Houston. Homemade tamales are too time-consuming to prepare for weeknight meals, but I discovered a corn bread mix approximates the flavor."
—Risë Minton, Smyrna, Georgia

  1   cup (4 ounces) preshredded 4-cheese Mexican blend cheese, divided
  ⅓   cup fat-free milk
  ¼   cup egg substitute
  1   teaspoon ground cumin
  ⅛   teaspoon ground red pepper
  1   (14¾-ounce) can cream-style corn
  1   (8.5-ounce) package corn muffin mix (such as Martha White)
  1   (4-ounce) can chopped green chiles, drained
      Cooking spray
  1   (10-ounce) can red enchilada sauce (such as Old El Paso)
  2   cups shredded cooked chicken breast
  ½   cup fat-free sour cream

1 Preheat oven to 400°.
2 Combine ¼ cup cheese and next 7 ingredients in a large bowl, stirring just until moist. Pour mixture into a 13 x 9–inch baking dish coated with cooking spray.
3 Bake at 400° for 15 minutes or until set. Pierce entire surface liberally with a fork; pour enchilada sauce over top. Top with chicken; sprinkle with remaining ¾ cup cheese. Bake at 400° for 15 minutes or until cheese melts. Remove from oven; let stand 5 minutes. Cut into 8 pieces; top each serving with 1 tablespoon sour cream. Yield: 8 servings.

CALORIES 354 (36% from fat); FAT 14.1g (sat 7.1g, mono 3.3g, poly 1.2g); PROTEIN 18.9g; CARB 36.3g; FIBER 2.5g; CHOL 58mg; IRON 1.7mg; SODIUM 620mg; CALC 179mg

Roasted Butternut Bisque

"I am a student in culinary school and also a volunteer at the local farmers' market. I enjoy creating dishes such as this soup using fresh seasonal vegetables when they first appear at the market."

—Katy McNulty,
Sewickley, Pennsylvania

    4   cups cubed peeled butternut squash
        (about 1 pound)
Cooking spray
    ¼   teaspoon salt
    ¼   teaspoon freshly ground black
        pepper
    1   tablespoon butter
    2   tablespoons finely chopped shallots
    1   garlic clove, finely chopped
  2½   cups organic vegetable broth (such
        as Swanson Certified Organic)
  1½   cups fat-free buttermilk
    1   tablespoon chopped fresh flat-leaf
        parsley

1 Preheat oven to 375°.
2 Place squash in a 2-quart baking dish coated with cooking spray. Lightly coat squash with cooking spray. Sprinkle squash with salt and pepper; toss well. Bake at 375° for 30 minutes or until tender.
3 Melt butter in a Dutch oven over medium heat. Add shallots and garlic to pan; cook 3 minutes, stirring occasionally. Add squash and broth to pan; bring to a boil, and cook 2 minutes. Stir in buttermilk. Reduce heat, and cook 2 minutes, stirring constantly. Place one-third of squash mixture in a blender. Remove center piece of blender lid (to allow steam to escape); secure blender lid on blender. Place a clean towel over opening in blender lid (to avoid splatters). Blend until smooth. Pour into a large bowl. Repeat procedure with remaining squash mixture. Sprinkle with parsley. Yield: 4 servings (serving size: 1⅓ cups).

CALORIES 104 (26% from fat); FAT 3g (sat 1.9g, mono 0.8g, poly 0.1g); PROTEIN 4.8g; CARB 15.9g; FIBER 0.7g; CHOL 8mg; IRON 1.1mg; SODIUM 616mg; CALC 143mg

---

Easy Weeknight Meal Menu
serves 4

Pork Tenderloin with Paprika Spice Rub

Spinach sauté
Melt 1 tablespoon butter in a large Dutch oven over medium heat. Add 2 tablespoons minced shallots and 1 minced garlic clove; cook 2 minutes, stirring occasionally. Increase heat to medium-high. Add 1 (10-ounce) package fresh spinach; cook 1 minute or until spinach starts to wilt, stirring frequently. Add a second package of spinach; cook 2 to 3 minutes or until spinach wilts, stirring frequently. Stir in ⅛ teaspoon ground nutmeg.

Egg noodles tossed with butter and chives

Pork Tenderloin with Paprika Spice Rub

"The spice blend makes enough for several recipes."
    —Jane Panza, Woodbury, Connecticut

    1   tablespoon Paprika Spice Blend
    1   (1-pound) pork tenderloin, trimmed
Cooking spray

1 Preheat oven to 500°.
2 Rub Paprika Spice Blend over pork. Place pork in a roasting pan coated with cooking spray. Bake at 500° for 20 minutes or until a thermometer registers 155°. Yield: 4 servings (serving size: 3 ounces).

CALORIES 191 (26% from fat); FAT 5.6g (sat 1.9g, mono 2.2g, poly 0.5g); PROTEIN 32.1g; CARB 0.9g; FIBER 0.3g; CHOL 90mg; IRON 1.8mg; SODIUM 284mg; CALC 10mg

PAPRIKA SPICE BLEND:

    ¼   cup paprika
    2   tablespoons salt
    2   tablespoons ground cumin
    2   tablespoons brown sugar
    2   tablespoons chili powder
    2   tablespoons black pepper
    1   tablespoon garlic powder

---

1 Combine all ingredients; store in an airtight container. Yield: about 1 cup (serving size: 1 tablespoon).

CALORIES 19 (19% from fat); FAT 0.4g (sat 0g, mono 0g, poly 0g); PROTEIN 0.7g; CARB 3.5g; FIBER 1.1g; CHOL 0mg; IRON 0.6mg; SODIUM 882mg; CALC 14mg

---

Hearty Stew Supper Menu
serves 4

Sweet and Spicy Chicken and White Bean Stew

Pineapple-mango salad
Combine 1½ cups cubed ripe peeled mango, 1½ cups cubed fresh pineapple, ¼ cup finely chopped red onion, and ½ teaspoon sambal oelek; toss well to combine.

Indian beer (such as Kingfisher)

Sweet and Spicy Chicken and White Bean Stew

"Lemongrass lends a delicate hint of citrus to this stew. "
    —Lindsay Weiss, Overland Park, Kansas

    2   tablespoons canola oil
    ½   teaspoon ground cardamom
    ⅛   teaspoon ground cloves
    3   garlic cloves, minced
    2   cups finely chopped onion
    ½   teaspoon chili powder
    ¼   teaspoon ground turmeric
    ½   teaspoon ground coriander
    1   (15.5-ounce) can cannellini beans
        or other white beans, undrained
    ¾   pound skinless, boneless chicken
        breast halves, cut into bite-sized
        pieces
    1   cup light coconut milk
    ½   cup water
    1   tablespoon chopped peeled fresh
        lemongrass (about 1 stalk)
    1   (14.5-ounce) can fire-roasted diced
        tomatoes, undrained
    1   (8-ounce) baking potato, cut into
        ½-inch cubes
    ¼   cup chopped fresh cilantro

① Heat oil in a Dutch oven over medium-high heat. Add cardamom, cloves, and garlic to pan; cook 30 seconds, stirring constantly. Add onion; sauté 8 minutes or until tender. Add chili powder, turmeric, and coriander; cook 30 seconds. Add beans and chicken; stir to coat. Add milk and next 4 ingredients to pan. Cover, reduce heat, and simmer 30 minutes or until potato is tender. Serve with cilantro. Yield: 4 servings (serving size: 1¾ cups stew and 1 tablespoon cilantro).

CALORIES 364 (29% from fat); FAT 11.7g (sat 3.7g, mono 4.4g, poly 2.8g); PROTEIN 27.3g; CARB 37.5g; FIBER 6.7g; CHOL 49mg; IRON 3.8mg; SODIUM 544mg; CALC 82mg

20 Minute Dishes

From shrimp to chicken, flounder to pork, here are simple, fresh, and easy meals you can prepare superfast.

QUICK & EASY
Flounder with Cilantro-Curry Topping and Toasted Coconut
(pictured on page 263)

You can substitute tilapia or snapper for flounder. Serve this fish with brown basmati rice and sautéed sliced carrots.

- ½ teaspoon salt, divided
- 4 (6-ounce) flounder fillets
- Cooking spray
- 2 tablespoons flaked sweetened coconut
- 1 cup cilantro sprigs
- 2 tablespoons fresh lemon juice
- 2 tablespoons extravirgin olive oil
- 1 teaspoon curry powder
- 3 garlic cloves, peeled
- 1 jalapeño pepper, halved and seeded
- Lemon wedges (optional)

① Preheat broiler.
② Sprinkle ¼ teaspoon salt over fish. Heat a large nonstick skillet over medium-high heat. Coat pan with cooking spray. Add fish to pan; cook 4 minutes on each side or until fish flakes easily when tested with a fork or until desired degree of doneness.
③ Place coconut on a baking sheet; broil for 2 minutes or until toasted, stirring occasionally.
④ Combine remaining ¼ teaspoon salt, cilantro, and next 5 ingredients in a food processor; process until finely chopped. Spoon 2 tablespoons cilantro mixture over each fillet; sprinkle each serving with 1½ teaspoons coconut. Garnish with lemon wedges, if desired. Yield: 4 servings.

CALORIES 234 (37% from fat); FAT 9.5g (sat 2g, mono 5.4g, poly 1.3g); PROTEIN 32.5g; CARB 3.3g; FIBER 0.7g; CHOL 82mg; IRON 1mg; SODIUM 442mg; CALC 41mg

QUICK & EASY
Wild Rice and Mushroom Soup with Chicken

Add sliced whole wheat French bread and mixed salad greens to complete the menu.

- 4 cups fat-free, less-sodium chicken broth, divided
- 1 (2.75-ounce) package quick-cooking wild rice (such as Gourmet House)
- 1 tablespoon olive oil
- ½ cup prechopped onion
- ½ cup chopped red bell pepper
- ⅓ cup matchstick-cut carrots
- 1 teaspoon bottled minced garlic
- ½ teaspoon dried thyme
- 1 teaspoon butter
- 2 (4-ounce) packages presliced exotic mushroom blend (such as shiitake, cremini, and oyster)
- 2 cups shredded cooked chicken breast
- ⅛ teaspoon salt
- ⅛ teaspoon black pepper

① Bring 1⅓ cups broth to a boil in a medium saucepan; add rice to pan.

Cover, reduce heat, and simmer 5 minutes or until liquid is absorbed. Set aside.
② Heat oil in a Dutch oven over medium-high heat. Add onion and next 4 ingredients to pan; sauté 3 minutes, stirring occasionally. Stir in butter and mushrooms; sauté 3 minutes or until lightly browned. Add remaining 2⅔ cups broth, rice, chicken, salt, and pepper to pan; cook 3 minutes or until thoroughly heated, stirring occasionally. Yield: 4 servings (serving size: 1½ cups).

CALORIES 281 (24% from fat); FAT 7.5g (sat 1.9g, mono 3.8g, poly 1.3g); PROTEIN 28.9g; CARB 23g; FIBER 4g; CHOL 62mg; IRON 2.8mg; SODIUM 541mg; CALC 42mg

QUICK & EASY
Chipotle Shrimp Tacos

- 2 teaspoons chili powder
- 1 teaspoon sugar
- ½ teaspoon salt
- ½ teaspoon ground cumin
- ¼ teaspoon ground chipotle chile powder
- 32 peeled and deveined large shrimp (about 1½ pounds)
- 1 teaspoon olive oil
- 8 (6-inch) white corn tortillas
- 2 cups shredded iceberg lettuce
- 1 ripe avocado, peeled and cut into 16 slices
- ¾ cup salsa verde

① Combine first 5 ingredients in a large bowl; add shrimp, tossing to coat.
② Heat oil in a large nonstick skillet over medium-high heat. Add shrimp mixture to pan; cook 1½ minutes on each side or until done. Remove from heat.
③ Heat tortillas in microwave according to package directions. Place 2 tortillas on each of 4 plates; arrange 4 shrimp on each tortilla. Top each tortilla with ¼ cup lettuce, 2 avocado slices, and 1½ tablespoons salsa. Yield: 4 servings (serving size: 2 filled tacos).

CALORIES 366 (29% from fat); FAT 11.8g (sat 1.6g, mono 5.5g, poly 2.6g); PROTEIN 37.7g; CARB 28.2g; FIBER 5.4g; CHOL 259mg; IRON 4.6mg; SODIUM 747mg; CALC 121mg

Hamburger Stroganoff

Add a tossed green salad and sautéed red and green bell pepper strips for a satisfying fall meal.

- 8 ounces uncooked medium egg noodles
- 1 teaspoon olive oil
- 1 pound extra lean ground beef
- 1 cup prechopped onion
- 1 teaspoon bottled minced garlic
- 1 (8-ounce) package presliced cremini mushrooms
- 2 tablespoons all-purpose flour
- 1 cup fat-free, less-sodium beef broth
- 1¼ teaspoons kosher salt
- ⅛ teaspoon black pepper
- ¾ cup reduced-fat sour cream
- 1 tablespoon dry sherry
- 3 tablespoons chopped fresh parsley

❶ Cook pasta according to package directions, omitting salt and fat. Drain and rinse under cold water; drain.
❷ Heat oil in a large nonstick skillet over medium-high heat. Add beef to pan; cook 4 minutes or until browned, stirring to crumble. Add onion, garlic, and mushrooms to pan; cook 4 minutes or until most of liquid evaporates, stirring frequently. Sprinkle with flour; cook 1 minute, stirring constantly. Stir in broth; bring to a boil. Reduce heat, and simmer 1 minute or until slightly thick. Stir in salt and pepper.
❸ Remove from heat. Stir in sour cream and sherry. Serve over pasta. Sprinkle with parsley. Yield: 6 servings (serving size: about ½ cup stroganoff, ⅔ cup pasta, and 1½ teaspoons parsley).

CALORIES 322 (27% from fat); FAT 9.8g (sat 4.4g, mono 3.5g, poly 1.1g); PROTEIN 23.9g; CARB 35.1g; FIBER 2.1g; CHOL 82mg; IRON 3.2mg; SODIUM 541mg; CALC 70mg

Pork Vindaloo

(pictured on page 267)

Garam masala is a spice blend. Serve with okra, which complements the stew's curry flavor.

- 2 (3½-ounce) bags boil-in-bag brown rice
- 2 teaspoons canola oil
- 1 (8-ounce) container prechopped onion
- 1 (1-pound) pork tenderloin, trimmed and cut into 1-inch pieces
- 1¼ teaspoons garam masala
- 1 teaspoon garlic powder
- 1 teaspoon mustard seeds
- 2 teaspoons bottled ground fresh ginger (such as Spice World)
- ¼ to ½ teaspoon ground red pepper
- ¼ cup fat-free, less-sodium chicken broth
- 1 (14.5-ounce) can petite diced tomatoes, undrained
- 1 (8-ounce) can tomato sauce
- 2 tablespoons chopped fresh cilantro
- 1 tablespoon red wine vinegar

❶ Prepare rice according to package directions, omitting salt and fat; set aside.
❷ Heat oil in a large nonstick skillet over medium-high heat. Add onion to pan; sauté 2 minutes. Combine pork and next 5 ingredients; toss well. Add pork mixture to pan; sauté for 5 minutes or until lightly browned.
❸ Add broth to pan, scraping bottom of pan to loosen browned bits. Add tomatoes and tomato sauce; cook 3 minutes, stirring occasionally. Remove from heat; stir in cilantro and vinegar. Serve over rice. Yield: 4 servings (serving size: 1 cup pork mixture and about ¾ cup rice).

CALORIES 392 (18% from fat); FAT 7.8g (sat 1.6g, mono 3.3g, poly 1.2g); PROTEIN 31.2g; CARB 51.8g; FIBER 4.4g; CHOL 74mg; IRON 3.1mg; SODIUM 678mg; CALC 107mg

Peanutty Baked Chicken Cutlets

A quick spritz of cooking spray on the cutlets before they hit the hot oven enhances the crispness and color of the crust. Serve chicken with baked sweet potatoes and broccoli spears.

- 2 tablespoons honey
- 2 tablespoons Dijon mustard
- ⅓ cup peanuts
- 1 cup panko (Japanese breadcrumbs)
- 4 (½-inch-thick) chicken breast cutlets (about 1 pound)
- Cooking spray
- ¼ cup peach chutney

❶ Preheat oven to 500°.
❷ Combine honey and mustard in a small bowl; stir well. Place peanuts in a food processor; pulse until finely chopped. Combine peanuts and panko in a shallow bowl.
❸ Brush each cutlet with honey mixture; dredge cutlets in panko mixture. Place cutlets on a baking sheet coated with cooking spray; lightly coat cutlets with cooking spray. Bake at 500° for 8 minutes or until done. Serve with chutney. Yield: 4 servings (serving size: 1 cutlet and 1 tablespoon chutney).

CALORIES 282 (25% from fat); FAT 7.8g (sat 1.5g, mono 3.3g, poly 2g); PROTEIN 27.2g; CARB 25.6g; FIBER 1.6g; CHOL 63mg; IRON 1.1mg; SODIUM 299mg; CALC 22mg

Better the Next Day

Use leftover Thanksgiving turkey, mashed potatoes, and cranberry sauce to create speedy, satisfying suppers.

Leftovers Menu 1

serves 4

Turkey and Wild Mushroom Hash Cakes

Broccolini with garlic and red pepper

Heat 1 tablespoon canola oil in a large nonstick skillet over medium-high heat. Add ¼ teaspoon crushed red pepper and 2 minced garlic cloves; sauté 30 seconds. Add ½ cup water and 1 pound trimmed Broccolini; sauté 2 minutes. Cover, reduce heat to low, and cook 10 minutes or until tender.

Cranberry sauce

Game Plan

1 Combine ingredients for hash cakes.
2 While hash cakes chill:
   • Prepare ingredients for Broccolini.
   • Sauté crushed red pepper and garlic for Broccolini.
3 While Broccolini simmers:
   • Cook hash cakes.

QUICK & EASY

Turkey and Wild Mushroom Hash Cakes

Total time: 45 minutes

   Cooking spray
2 cups chopped shiitake mushroom caps (about 4 ounces)
1 garlic clove, minced
2 cups chopped cooked turkey breast (about 10 ounces)
2 cups mashed cooked baking potatoes
¾ cups panko (Japanese breadcrumbs), divided
½ cup (2 ounces) shredded Cheddar cheese
⅓ cup thinly sliced green onions
1½ tablespoons finely chopped fresh thyme
¼ teaspoon salt
¼ teaspoon black pepper
1 tablespoon canola oil, divided

① Heat a large nonstick skillet over medium-high heat. Coat pan with cooking spray. Add mushrooms and garlic to pan; sauté 5 minutes or until tender, stirring frequently. Combine mushroom mixture, turkey, potatoes, ¼ cup panko, and next 5 ingredients in a large bowl. Divide mixture into 8 equal portions, shaping each into a ½-inch-thick patty. Refrigerate 10 minutes. Dredge patties in remaining ½ cup panko.
② Heat 1½ teaspoons oil in a large nonstick skillet over medium-high heat. Add 4 patties; cook 2 minutes on each side. Repeat procedure with remaining 1½ teaspoons oil and remaining 4 patties. Yield: 4 servings (serving size: 2 patties).

CALORIES 263 (33% from fat); FAT 10g (sat 3.8g, mono 3.6g, poly 1.2g); PROTEIN 25.1g; CARB 18.2g; FIBER 2.2g; CHOL 68mg; IRON 2mg; SODIUM 556mg; CALC 134mg

---

Leftovers Menu 2

serves 4

Turkey Curry

Cranberry-mango chutney

Combine ¾ cup mango chutney, ¼ cup whole-berry cranberry sauce, and ¼ cup finely chopped Granny Smith apple in a small bowl.

Boil-in-bag brown rice

Game Plan

1 While water for rice comes to a boil:
   • Chop ingredients for curry.
   • Sauté onion for curry.
2 While curry simmers:
   • Prepare cranberry-mango chutney.
3 Cook rice.

QUICK & EASY

Turkey Curry

Try cooked chicken or shrimp in this dish instead of turkey.

Total time: 38 minutes

2 tablespoons canola oil
1½ cups chopped onion (about 1 large onion)
2 tablespoons all-purpose flour
1½ teaspoons curry powder
1 (14-ounce) can fat-free, less-sodium chicken broth
3 cups chopped cooked turkey (about 1 pound)
½ teaspoon salt
2 tablespoons chopped fresh cilantro

① Heat oil in a large nonstick skillet over medium-high heat. Add onion to pan; sauté 4 minutes. Add flour and curry powder; sauté 1 minute. Stir in broth; bring to a boil. Stir in turkey and salt. Reduce heat, and simmer 5 minutes or until thickened. Sprinkle with cilantro. Yield: 4 servings (serving size: ¾ cup turkey mixture and 1½ teaspoons cilantro).

CALORIES 229 (31% from fat); FAT 7.9g (sat 0.8g, mono 4.3g, poly 2.3g); PROTEIN 29.5g; CARB 8.7g; FIBER 1.4g; CHOL 70mg; IRON 1.9mg; SODIUM 550mg; CALC 29mg

Leftovers Menu 3
serves 4

Turkey and Potato Soup with Canadian Bacon

Arugula and grape tomato salad

Cranberry-Cointreau sundaes

Combine 1 cup whole-berry cranberry sauce and 2 tablespoons Cointreau (orange-flavored liqueur) in a small saucepan over medium-high heat; bring to a simmer, stirring constantly with a whisk. Cook 2 minutes, stirring occasionally. Serve warm over vanilla low-fat frozen yogurt.

Game Plan
1 Chop ingredients for soup.
2 Sauté ingredients for soup.
3 While soup simmers:
  • Prepare salad.
  • Prepare sauce for sundaes.

QUICK & EASY
Turkey and Potato Soup with Canadian Bacon

Total time: 40 minutes

- 1 tablespoon canola oil
- 1½ cups chopped onion (about 1 large onion)
- 1 cup chopped celery
- 2 carrots, halved lengthwise and thinly sliced (about 1 cup)
- 1 ounce Canadian bacon, chopped
- 3 cups fat-free, less-sodium chicken broth
- 3 cups chopped cooked turkey (about 1 pound)
- 2½ cups mashed cooked peeled baking potatoes
- 1 tablespoon chopped fresh sage
- ¼ teaspoon freshly ground black pepper
  Sage sprigs (optional)

❶ Heat oil in a Dutch oven over medium heat. Add onion and next 3 ingredients; cook 6 minutes, stirring occasionally. Add broth and next 3 ingredients, stirring

with a whisk until blended; bring to a boil. Reduce heat, and simmer 10 minutes. Stir in pepper. Garnish with sage sprigs, if desired. Yield: 4 servings (serving size: 2 cups).

CALORIES 300 (22% from fat); FAT 7.3g (sat 1g, mono 2.7g, poly 1.7g); PROTEIN 29g; CARB 28.7g; FIBER 4.3g; CHOL 81mg; IRON 2.2mg; SODIUM 897mg; CALC 75mg

ONE MORE TASTE
Oat-Crusted Pecan Pie with Fresh Cranberry Sauce

Pecan pie is a holiday standard, particularly in the South. This version offers a fresh way to enjoy the classic dessert.

MAKE AHEAD
Oat-Crusted Pecan Pie with Fresh Cranberry Sauce
(pictured on page 268)

CRUST:
- 1¾ cups old-fashioned rolled oats
- 3 tablespoons granulated sugar
- ¼ teaspoon salt
- 3½ tablespoons cold butter, cut into small pieces
- 1 tablespoon ice water
  Cooking spray

FILLING:
- ¾ cup packed brown sugar
- ⅔ cup light-colored corn syrup
- 3 tablespoons all-purpose flour
- 3 tablespoons molasses
- 1 tablespoon melted butter
- ½ teaspoon vanilla extract
- ¼ teaspoon salt
- 2 large eggs
- 1 large egg white
- ⅔ cup pecan halves

SAUCE:
- 1½ cups fresh cranberries
- ⅔ cup granulated sugar
- ½ cup fresh orange juice
- ¼ cup water
- ½ teaspoon cornstarch

❶ Preheat oven to 400°.
❷ To prepare crust, place first 3 ingredients in a food processor; process until finely ground. Add butter; pulse 5 times or until combined. Add 1 tablespoon ice water; pulse just until combined (mixture will be crumbly). Press oat mixture into bottom and up sides of a 9-inch deep-dish pie plate coated with cooking spray. Bake at 400° for 15 minutes or until lightly browned. Cool 5 minutes on a wire rack.
❸ Reduce oven temperature to 350°.
❹ To prepare filling, combine brown sugar and next 8 ingredients in a medium bowl, stirring well. Stir in pecan halves. Spoon filling into prepared crust. Bake at 350° for 48 minutes or until center is set. Cool to room temperature on a wire rack.
❺ To prepare sauce, combine cranberries, ⅔ cup granulated sugar, and juice in a small saucepan over medium-high heat; bring to a boil. Reduce heat, and simmer until cranberries begin to pop, about 3 minutes, stirring occasionally.
❻ Combine ¼ cup water and cornstarch in a small bowl, stirring with a whisk. Stir cornstarch mixture into cranberry mixture; bring to a boil. Cook 1 minute, stirring often; remove from heat. Cool completely. Serve pie with sauce. Yield: 12 servings (serving size: 1 wedge pie and about 1½ tablespoons sauce).

CALORIES 329 (28% from fat); FAT 10.3g (sat 3.5g, mono 4.1g, poly 1.9g); PROTEIN 46.5g; CARB 58.4g; FIBER 2g; CHOL 47mg; IRON 1.4mg; SODIUM 164mg; CALC 43mg

Good Nutrition is Always in Season

Eating well is key to staying in top health during the busy winter months.

IT'S NO SECRET that cold and flu season peaks in winter. And if you're looking for ways to stay well, one priority, say experts, is simple: Follow a wholesome diet, just as you should any time of year. But that can be a tall order during the busy holiday season, when hectic social schedules and family commitments often interfere with regular meals.

Food alone can't protect against the common cold or influenza, and the science isn't yet clear on which or how much of some nutrients may help bolster immunity to reduce your risk of getting sick. But experts agree that a diet rich in a variety of produce, whole grains, lean proteins, and low-fat dairy products—along with adequate sleep, moderate exercise, and minimal stress—contributes to a well-functioning immune system and may promote a faster recovery if you do come down with a cold or flu.

Cauliflower-Apple Soup with Apple Cider Reduction

Soothing soups provide nutrients like vitamins and fluids.

1 cup apple cider
2 teaspoons olive oil
2 cups chopped onion
2 teaspoons Madras curry powder
1 teaspoon chopped garlic
6 cups cauliflower florets (about 1½ pounds)
5 cups fat-free, less-sodium chicken broth
1 Gala apple, peeled, cored and chopped
⅓ cup half-and-half
2 teaspoons fresh lemon juice
¾ teaspoon kosher salt
⅛ teaspoon freshly ground black pepper
Coarsely ground black pepper (optional)

❶ Bring cider to a boil in a small saucepan. Cook until cider is reduced to ¼ cup (about 5 minutes). Remove from heat, and cool to room temperature.
❷ Heat oil in a large Dutch oven over medium-high heat. Add onion to pan; sauté 3 minutes. Add curry powder and garlic to pan; sauté 1 minute, stirring constantly. Add cauliflower, broth, and apple; bring to a boil. Cover, reduce heat, and simmer 15 minutes or until cauliflower is very tender.
❸ Remove pan from heat; cool 5 minutes. Place half of cauliflower mixture in a blender. Remove center piece of blender lid (to allow steam to escape); secure blender lid on blender. Place a clean towel over opening in blender lid (to avoid splatters). Blend until smooth. Pour into a large bowl. Repeat procedure with remaining cauliflower mixture. Return to pan. Stir in half-and-half; cook over medium heat 5 minutes or until thoroughly heated (do not boil). Remove from heat; stir in juice, salt, and ⅛ teaspoon pepper. Ladle about 1 cup soup into each of 8 bowls; drizzle each serving with 1½ teaspoons cider reduction. Garnish with coarsely ground pepper, if desired. Yield: 8 servings.

CALORIES 98 (24% from fat); FAT 2.6g (sat 1g, mono 1.3g, poly 0.3g); PROTEIN 4.2g; CARB 16.1g; FIBER 3.8g; CHOL 4mg; IRON 1mg; SODIUM 450mg; CALC 52mg

QUICK & EASY • MAKE AHEAD
Pomegranate–Apple Cider Toddy

A hot beverage is often just what we want in cold weather or at the onset of a bout of cold or flu. This hot drink offers warm spice with cloves and sweet cinnamon. Substitute ⅓ cup rum for the apple cider if you'd like an alcoholic version.

8 whole cloves
2 (3-inch) cinnamon sticks
3 cups pomegranate juice
½ cup apple cider
⅓ cup honey
Thin tangerine slices (optional)
Cinnamon sticks (optional)

❶ Place cloves and 2 cinnamon sticks on a double layer of cheesecloth. Gather edges of cheesecloth together; tie securely. Combine cheesecloth bag, juice, apple cider, and honey in a medium saucepan; bring to a simmer. Cover, reduce heat, and cook 30 minutes. Remove from heat; discard cheesecloth bag. Garnish with tangerine slices and cinnamon sticks, if desired. Serve warm. Yield: 7 servings (serving size: ½ cup).

CALORIES 119 (0% from fat); FAT 0g; PROTEIN 0.5g; CARB 30.8g; FIBER 0g; CHOL 0mg; IRON 0.2mg; SODIUM 14mg; CALC 18mg

Roasted Oysters with Lemon-Anise Stuffing

Oysters are a good source of zinc, a mineral identified with healthy immune systems. A serving of this tasty appetizer offers all the zinc you need in a day, about 13 milligrams.

 1 (1½-ounce) slice white bread
 2 teaspoons butter
1½ cups finely chopped fennel
 1 garlic clove, minced
 ¼ cup fat-free, less-sodium chicken broth
 ¼ teaspoon kosher salt
 2 tablespoons anise liqueur (such as ouzo)
 ⅓ cup (1½ ounces) grated fresh Parmigiano-Reggiano cheese
 1 tablespoon chopped fennel fronds
 ½ teaspoon grated lemon rind
 2 teaspoons fresh lemon juice
    Dash of ground red pepper
12 shucked oysters

❶ Preheat oven to 350°.
❷ Place bread in a food processor; pulse 10 times or until coarse crumbs measure about 1 cup. Spread on a baking sheet. Bake at 350° for 8 minutes or until toasted. Transfer to a plate; cool.
❸ Position oven rack to top one-third of oven. Increase oven temperature to 425°.
❹ Melt butter in a large nonstick skillet over medium heat. Add fennel and garlic to pan; cook 2 minutes, stirring frequently. Add broth and salt; cover and cook 5 minutes or until fennel is tender. Uncover and cook 2 minutes or until liquid evaporates. Stir in liqueur; cook 1 minute or until liqueur evaporates. Transfer fennel mixture to a bowl; add breadcrumbs, cheese, and next 4 ingredients. Toss to combine.
❺ Arrange oysters in a single layer on a large baking pan. Top each oyster with about 1 tablespoon fennel mixture. Bake at 425° for 10 minutes or until edges of oysters begin to curl and stuffing is lightly browned. Serve immediately. Yield: 4 servings (serving size: 3 oysters).

CALORIES 125 (36% from fat); FAT 5g (sat 2.8g, mono 1.2g, poly 0.3g); PROTEIN 6.2g; CARB 12.4g; FIBER 1.4g; CHOL 21mg; IRON 2.9mg; SODIUM 395mg; CALC 143mg

WINE NOTE: Contrast the rich texture of these oysters with a cold, crisp chablis. A classic partner for oysters, chablis brings out the mineral quality of these prized shellfish while its palate-cleansing acidity nicely slices the butter- and cheese-laced stuffing. William Fevre Chablis Champs Royaux 2007 ($24) is a good entry-level chablis, with its orchard fruit and floral aromas, lively citrus flavor, and steely finish.

Lemon Chicken Orzo Soup

Chicken noodle soup is probably the top comfort food of all time. You'll need to start a day ahead to prepare the soup's tasty broth. A serving of soup provides about 200 micrograms vitamin A, just shy of one-third of the RDA.

 1 (4-pound) whole chicken
 2 carrots, peeled, cut in 1-inch pieces
 2 celery stalks, cut in 1-inch pieces
 1 onion, peeled and sliced
 6 garlic cloves, crushed
 4 sprigs fresh flat-leaf parsley
 2 teaspoons whole black peppercorns
 2 bay leaves
 6 cups water
1⅓ cups chopped carrot
1¼ cups chopped onion
 1 cup chopped celery
 2 teaspoons salt
 8 ounces uncooked orzo (rice-shaped pasta)
 ¼ cup chopped fresh flat-leaf parsley
2½ teaspoons grated lemon rind
 ¼ cup fresh lemon juice
    Lemon wedges (optional)
    Coarsely cracked black pepper (optional)

❶ Remove and discard giblets and neck from chicken. Place chicken in a large Dutch oven. Add 2 chopped carrots and next 6 ingredients to pan. Add 6 cups water; bring to a simmer. Reduce heat, and simmer 45 minutes.
❷ Remove chicken from pan; place chicken in a bowl. Chill 15 minutes. Discard skin; remove meat from bones, discarding bones. Chop chicken into bite-sized pieces; cover and chill. Strain broth mixture through a sieve into a large bowl; discard solids. Cool broth mixture to room temperature. Cover and chill 8 to 24 hours. Skim fat from surface; discard.
❸ Add enough water to broth to equal 9 cups; place broth mixture in a large Dutch oven. Add 1⅓ cups carrot and next 3 ingredients to pan; bring to a boil. Cover, reduce heat, and simmer 15 minutes or until vegetables are tender. Add chopped chicken, and simmer 3 minutes or until thoroughly heated. Keep warm.
❹ Cook pasta according to package directions, omitting salt and fat. Add pasta to pan; stir in parsley, rind, and juice. Garnish each serving with lemon wedges and cracked black pepper, if desired. Yield: 8 servings (serving size: about 1¾ cups soup).

CALORIES 235 (20% from fat); FAT 5.2g (sat 1.3g, mono 1.8g, poly 1.1g); PROTEIN 21.3g; CARB 24.6g; FIBER 2.3g; CHOL 53mg; IRON 1.1mg; SODIUM 679mg; CALC 39mg

Tropical Citrus Compote

This fruit combo is refreshing by itself, and a serving offers about a day's worth of vitamin C. Garnished with thinly sliced lime rind, it can also top waffles or pound cake.

- ½ cup water
- ½ cup sugar
- 1 teaspoon grated lime rind
- 1 teaspoon grated orange rind
- 1½ cups orange sections (about 3 oranges)
- 1½ cups chopped peeled mango (about 1 mango)
- 1½ cups chopped peeled papaya (about 1 papaya)
- 1 cup red grapefruit sections (about 2 grapefruit)

1 Combine ½ cup water and sugar in a small saucepan; bring to a boil, stirring until sugar dissolves. Remove from heat; stir in rinds. Cool to room temperature. Strain sugar mixture through a fine sieve into a bowl; discard solids.

2 Combine orange sections and remaining ingredients in a bowl. Add sugar mixture; toss gently. Yield: 4 servings (serving size: 1 cup).

CALORIES 139 (2% from fat); FAT 0.3g (sat 0.1g, mono 0.1g, poly 0.1g); PROTEIN 1.1g; CARB 35.6g; FIBER 2.9g; CHOL 0mg; IRON 0.2mg; SODIUM 3mg; CALC 37mg

Seared Cod with Swiss Chard and Almonds

Winter greens make a pretty plated entrée and are nutritious, too. The greens provide more than half the recommended vitamins A and C, and the fish and greens supply a little zinc. Serve with couscous or orzo.

- 4 teaspoons olive oil, divided
- 3 tablespoons slivered almonds
- 1¼ teaspoons sweet Hungarian paprika, divided
- 2 garlic cloves, thinly sliced
- 10 cups thinly sliced trimmed Swiss chard (about 2 bunches trimmed)
- ¾ teaspoon salt, divided
- ¼ teaspoon sherry vinegar
- 4 (6-ounce) cod fillets

1 Heat 2 teaspoons oil in a large nonstick skillet over medium heat. Add almonds to pan; cook 2 minutes or until lightly browned, stirring constantly. Transfer to a small bowl using a slotted spoon. Sprinkle almonds with ¼ teaspoon paprika, stirring to coat. Set aside.

2 Add garlic to pan; cook 1 minute or until golden, stirring constantly. Add 3⅓ cups chard to pan; cook 1½ minutes or until wilted, stirring constantly. Repeat procedure 2 times with remaining chard. Stir in ½ teaspoon salt; cover and cook 5 minutes or until tender. Stir in vinegar. Remove from pan; wipe skillet with paper towels.

3 Sprinkle fish evenly with remaining 1 teaspoon paprika and remaining ¼ teaspoon salt. Heat remaining 2 teaspoons oil in pan over medium-high heat. Add fish to pan; cook 2 minutes on each side or until fish flakes easily when tested with a fork or until desired degree of doneness. Serve fish with chard; top evenly with almonds. Yield: 4 servings (serving size: 1 fillet, ½ cup chard, and 2¼ teaspoons almonds).

CALORIES 243 (33% from fat); FAT 8.6g (sat 1.1g, mono 5.1g, poly 1.6g); PROTEIN 34.5g; CARB 7.9g; FIBER 3.4g; CHOL 73mg; IRON 4mg; SODIUM 897mg; CALC 129mg

Butternut Squash Gratin with Blue Cheese and Sage

Besides being a great side for simple roast chicken or beef tenderloin, seasonal squash provides more than a day's worth of vitamin A and about half the daily recommended vitamin C.

- 5 cups (¾-inch) cubed peeled butternut squash (about 2 pounds)
- 1 (1½-ounce) slice white bread
- 4 teaspoons olive oil, divided
- 2 cups thinly sliced onion
- 1 tablespoon chopped fresh sage
- ½ teaspoon salt
- ¼ teaspoon freshly ground pepper
  Cooking spray
- ½ cup (2 ounces) crumbled blue cheese

1 Preheat oven to 400°.

2 Steam squash, covered, 10 minutes or until tender.

3 Place bread in a food processor; pulse 12 times or until coarse crumbs measure ½ cup. Transfer to a small bowl; add 2 teaspoons oil, and toss with a fork to combine.

4 Heat remaining 2 teaspoons oil in a large nonstick skillet over medium-high heat. Add onion to pan; sauté 5 minutes or until tender, stirring occasionally. Transfer onion to a large bowl. Add squash, sage, salt, and pepper to bowl; toss gently to combine. Spoon squash mixture into an 11 x 7–inch baking dish coated with cooking spray. Bake at 400° for 20 minutes. Sprinkle cheese evenly over squash mixture; sprinkle evenly with breadcrumb mixture. Bake an additional 10 minutes or until cheese melts and crumbs are browned. Yield: 6 servings (serving size: about 1 cup).

CALORIES 186 (31% from fat); FAT 6.4g (sat 2.4g, mono 2.9g, poly 0.5g); PROTEIN 5.1g; CARB 30.9g; FIBER 4.8g; CHOL 7mg; IRON 1.7mg; SODIUM 379mg; CALC 173mg

Tomato-Poblano Soup

The tomatoes and chiles contribute a day's worth of vitamin C in a serving of the soup. You can chop the canned whole tomatoes on a cutting board with a knife, but using kitchen shears to cut the fruit in the can makes for quick cleanup. Use low-sodium or organic vegetable broth for a vegetarian appetizer.

- 4 poblano chiles
- 2 teaspoons olive oil
- 2½ cups chopped onion
- 1 teaspoon ground cumin
- ½ teaspoon ground coriander
- 2 garlic cloves, chopped
- 1 (28-ounce) can no-salt-added whole peeled plum tomatoes, undrained
- 4 cups fat-free, less-sodium chicken broth
- 2 tablespoons fresh lime juice
- ¼ teaspoon kosher salt
- 6 tablespoons chopped fresh cilantro
- 6 teaspoons sour cream
- Lime wedges (optional)

❶ Preheat broiler.
❷ Cut chiles in half lengthwise; discard seeds and membranes. Place pepper halves, skin sides up, on a foil-lined baking sheet; flatten with hand. Broil 18 minutes or until blackened. Place in a zip-top plastic bag; seal. Let stand 10 minutes. Peel and coarsely chop.
❸ Heat oil in a large Dutch oven over medium-high heat. Add onion to pan; sauté 3 minutes. Add cumin, coriander, and garlic to pan; sauté 1 minute.
❹ Using kitchen shears, coarsely chop tomatoes in can. Add tomatoes, chiles, and broth to pan, stirring to combine; bring to a boil. Reduce heat, and simmer 30 minutes. Remove from heat; cool 5 minutes.
❺ Place half of tomato mixture in a blender. Remove center piece of blender lid (to allow steam to escape); secure blender lid on blender. Place a clean towel over opening in blender lid (to avoid splatters). Blend until almost smooth. Pour into a large bowl. Repeat procedure with remaining tomato mixture. Stir in juice and salt. Ladle about 1 cup soup into each of 6 bowls; top each serving with 1 tablespoon cilantro and 1 teaspoon sour cream. Serve with lime wedges, if desired. Yield: 6 servings.

CALORIES 102 (26% from fat); FAT 3g (sat 0.9g, mono 1.5g, poly 0.3g); PROTEIN 3.7g; CARB 13.3g; FIBER 3.3g; CHOL 2mg; IRON 1.9mg; SODIUM 362mg; CALC 78mg

Smoky Meatballs in Serrano Ham–Tomato Sauce

This one-dish meal combines beef, a great source of zinc, with vitamin C–rich tomatoes. To prepare ahead, cook prepared meatballs, cool, and freeze in a zip-top plastic bag for up to one month. When you're ready to serve, defrost the meatballs in the refrigerator and sauté the ham. Add the thawed meatballs along with the tomatoes to the cooked onion mixture.

- 1 (1½-ounce) slice white bread
- 1 pound 92% lean ground beef
- ¼ cup finely chopped onion
- 2 tablespoons chopped fresh flat-leaf parsley
- 1½ teaspoons minced garlic
- ½ teaspoon kosher salt
- ½ teaspoon smoked paprika
- ¼ teaspoon black pepper
- 1 large egg, lightly beaten
- 2 teaspoons olive oil, divided
- 2 ounces Serrano ham, finely chopped
- Cooking spray
- 2 cups chopped onion
- 1¼ cups chopped red bell pepper
- 1½ teaspoons minced fresh garlic
- ½ cup dry sherry
- 1 (28-ounce) can no-salt-added whole peeled tomatoes, undrained and chopped
- 4 cups hot cooked fettuccine (about 8 ounces uncooked pasta)
- ¼ cup finely shredded aged Manchego cheese
- Chopped fresh flat-leaf parsley (optional)

❶ Place bread in a food processor; pulse 12 times or until coarse crumbs measure ½ cup. Combine breadcrumbs, beef, and next 7 ingredients in a bowl. Using wet hands, shape mixture into 20 (about 2 tablespoons each) meatballs. Set aside.
❷ Heat 1 teaspoon oil in a large Dutch oven over medium heat. Add ham to pan; cook 3 minutes or until well browned, stirring frequently. Transfer to a large bowl. Add remaining 1 teaspoon oil to pan. Add meatballs; cook 5 minutes or until browned, turning frequently. Add meatballs to ham in bowl. Coat pan with cooking spray. Add onion, bell pepper, and garlic to pan; cook 5 minutes or until tender, stirring frequently. Add sherry; cook 3 minutes or until liquid almost evaporates, scraping pan to loosen browned bits. Add tomatoes and meatball mixture; bring to a boil. Cover, reduce heat, and simmer 30 minutes or until sauce is slightly thickened. Remove from heat, and keep warm.
❸ Place 1 cup pasta in each of 4 shallow bowls; top with 5 meatballs, ¾ cup sauce, and 1 tablespoon cheese. Garnish with parsley, if desired. Yield: 4 servings.

CALORIES 559 (28% from fat); FAT 17.6g (sat 6.6g, mono 7.2g, poly 1.2g); PROTEIN 38.5g; CARB 61.3g; FIBER 4.7g; CHOL 128mg; IRON 6mg; SODIUM 704mg; CALC 180mg

Southeast Asian Roast Chicken with Coconut Rice

Chicken offers the iron and zinc healthy immune systems need. One serving of the chicken contains about 25 percent of the daily zinc requirements.

CHICKEN:
- ½ cup whole fresh cilantro leaves
- 2 tablespoons chopped peeled fresh ginger
- 1 tablespoon thinly sliced lemongrass
- 1 tablespoon water
- 2 garlic cloves, peeled
- ½ Thai bird chile , seeded and chopped
- ½ teaspoon salt
- 1 (3¾-pound) roasting chicken
- Cooking spray

RICE:

- 1 cup uncooked jasmine or basmati rice
- 1 cup water
- ½ teaspoon salt
- 4 (2 x ½-inch) julienne slices peeled fresh ginger
- 1 (3-inch) cinnamon stick
- 1 (14-ounce) can light coconut milk

1 Preheat oven to 375°.

2 To prepare chicken, place first 7 ingredients in a food processor; process until finely minced.

3 Discard giblets and neck from chicken. Pat dry. Trim excess fat. Starting at neck cavity, loosen skin from breast and drumsticks by inserting fingers, gently pushing between skin and meat. Spread cilantro mixture under loosened skin. Lift wing tips up and over back, and tuck under chicken.

4 Place chicken, breast side up, on a broiler pan coated with cooking spray. Bake 1¼ hours or until an instant-read thermometer inserted into thickest part of thigh registers 165°. Cover chicken loosely with foil; let stand 10 minutes. Discard skin.

5 To prepare rice, combine rice and remaining ingredients in a medium saucepan; bring to a boil. Cover, reduce heat, and simmer 15 minutes or until liquid is absorbed and rice is tender. Let stand, covered, 5 minutes. Fluff with a fork. Remove and discard ginger slices and cinnamon stick. Serve with chicken. Yield: 4 servings (serving size: about 5 ounces chicken and 1 cup rice).

CALORIES 376 (34% from fat); FAT 14.1g (sat 7g, mono 3.6g, poly 2.2g); PROTEIN 38.3g; CARB 22.9g; FIBER 0.4g; CHOL 106mg; IRON 2.5mg; SODIUM 723mg; CALC 24mg

Twelve Days of Cookies

Fresh-baked cookies are a Christmas essential. Serve them with hot cocoa, coffee, and mulled cider, wrap them for gifts, or enjoy them for dessert.

Day 1: Dinner Party Dessert

Grown-up treats suitable for the end of a lavish meal, anise cookies are traditional in various international cuisines, including Italian, German, and Mexican.

MAKE AHEAD • FREEZABLE

Anise Tea Crescents

Rolling the cookies in powdered sugar while they're still warm results in a deliciously sweet, snowy coating.

- 1½ cups all-purpose flour (about 6.75 ounces)
- ¼ cup cornstarch
- ½ teaspoon salt
- 1¼ cups powdered sugar, divided
- 5 tablespoons butter, softened
- 2 tablespoons canola oil
- 2 tablespoons 2% reduced-fat milk
- 1½ teaspoons vanilla extract
- 1 teaspoon aniseed, crushed

1 Preheat oven to 350°.

2 Lightly spoon flour into dry measuring cups; level with a knife. Combine flour, cornstarch, and salt in a medium bowl, stirring with a whisk.

3 Beat ¾ cup sugar, butter, and oil with a mixer at medium speed until light and fluffy. Add milk and vanilla; beat until well blended. Add flour mixture and aniseed; beat at low speed until blended. Shape dough into 32 (2-inch) logs; bend logs to form crescent shapes. Arrange 16 crescents 1 inch apart on a baking sheet. Bake at 350° for 14 minutes or until edges are golden. Remove from oven; cool on pan 3 minutes. Repeat procedure with remaining 16 crescents.

4 Sift remaining ½ cup sugar into a medium bowl; toss warm cookies in sugar to coat. Cool completely on a wire rack. Yield: 32 cookies (serving size: 2 cookies).

CALORIES 131 (37% from fat); FAT 5.4g (sat 2.4g, mono 2g, poly 0.7g); PROTEIN 1.3g; CARB 19.2g; FIBER 0.3g; CHOL 10mg; IRON 0.6mg; SODIUM 100mg; CALC 4mg

Lively Leaveners

Fresh and effective baking powder and baking soda are essential to the quality of your baked goods. Both items will keep for six months to a year if stored tightly sealed at room temperature. Check expiration dates on the containers before using. To double-check the freshness of baking powder, mix 1 teaspoon powder with ⅓ cup hot water. For baking soda, mix ½ teaspoon soda with a few drops of vinegar. In both cases, vigorous bubbles indicate the leavener is fresh.

Crisp versions of the traditional German spiced Christmas cookies make getting bows on boxes a more enjoyable pursuit.

MAKE AHEAD • FREEZABLE

Lebkuchen

Letting the dough rest at least 24 hours before baking allows the spices to meld.

COOKIES:

- ¾   cup packed brown sugar
- ½   cup honey
- ¼   cup butter
- ¼   cup dark molasses
- 2   teaspoons instant coffee granules
- 1   large egg, lightly beaten
- ¾   cup finely ground almonds
- ½   cup chopped candied orange peel
- 3½ cups all-purpose flour (about 15.75 ounces)
- 1   teaspoon ground cinnamon
- ½   teaspoon baking soda
- ½   teaspoon ground cardamom
- ½   teaspoon ground cloves
- ¼   teaspoon ground ginger
- ⅛   teaspoon salt

GLAZE:

- ¾   cup powdered sugar
- 2   teaspoons lemon juice
- 1½ teaspoons water

❶ To prepare cookies, combine first 4 ingredients in a medium saucepan over medium heat; cook 3 minutes or until sugar dissolves, stirring constantly (do not boil). Pour sugar mixture into a large bowl; cool to room temperature. Add coffee and egg to sugar mixture, stirring with a whisk. Stir in almonds and orange peel.

❷ Lightly spoon flour into dry measuring cups; level with a knife. Combine flour and next 6 ingredients in a medium bowl. Add flour mixture to sugar mixture, stirring to form a stiff dough. Turn dough out onto a lightly floured surface; knead 1 minute or until well combined. Wrap dough in plastic wrap; refrigerate at least 24 hours.

❸ Preheat oven to 325°.

❹ Cover two large baking sheets with parchment paper. Divide dough into 4 equal portions. Working with 1 portion of dough at a time, roll dough into an 8 x 6–inch rectangle. Cut each rectangle into 16 (3 x 1–inch) bars; place bars 1 inch apart on prepared baking sheets. Bake at 325° for 20 minutes or until firm. Remove from pans; cool on wire racks.

❺ To prepare glaze, combine powdered sugar, lemon juice, and 1½ teaspoons water in a small bowl, stirring until smooth. Drizzle glaze over warm cookies. Yield: 64 cookies (serving size: 2 cookies).

CALORIES 133 (18% from fat); FAT 2.7g (sat 1g, mono 1.2g, poly 0.4g); PROTEIN 2g; CARB 25.9g; FIBER 0.8g; CHOL 10mg; IRON 1mg; SODIUM 47mg; CALC 22mg

Day 3: Holiday Celebration Star

These moist, flavorful bars feature the seasonal pairing of peppermint and chocolate. They're sure to be a hit with everyone—children included—at your holiday party.

MAKE AHEAD

Peppermint Cheesecake Brownies

Tint the cheesecake batter with two or three drops of red food coloring to give it a pink tinge, if you like. When swirling the cheesecake and brownie batters in step 4, don't disturb the bottom brownie layer. Cool these bars completely before serving.

CHEESECAKE BATTER:

- 1   (8-ounce) block ⅓-less-fat cream cheese
- ⅓   cup granulated sugar
- ¼   teaspoon peppermint extract
- 1   large egg
- 1   large egg white
- 1   tablespoon all-purpose flour

BROWNIE BATTER:

- 1   cup all-purpose flour (about 4.5 ounces)
- ½   cup unsweetened cocoa
- ½   teaspoon salt
- 1½ cups packed brown sugar
- ¼   cup canola oil
- ¼   cup buttermilk
- 2   teaspoons vanilla extract
- 2   large egg whites
- 1   large egg
- Cooking spray

❶ Preheat oven to 350°.

❷ To prepare cheesecake batter, place cheese in a medium bowl; beat with a mixer at medium speed until smooth. Add granulated sugar and peppermint extract; beat well. Add 1 egg and 1 egg white; beat well. Add 1 tablespoon flour; beat just until blended.

❸ To prepare brownie batter, lightly spoon 1 cup flour into a dry measuring cup; level with a knife. Combine 1 cup flour, cocoa, and salt in a medium bowl, stirring with a whisk. Combine brown sugar and next 5 ingredients in a large bowl; beat with a mixer at medium-high speed until well blended. Add flour mixture to brown sugar mixture; beat at low speed just until blended.

❹ Reserve ½ cup of brownie batter. Pour remaining batter into a 9-inch square baking pan coated with cooking spray. Carefully pour cheesecake batter over top; spread evenly to edges. Dot cheesecake batter with reserved brownie batter. Swirl top two layers of batters together using tip of a knife. Bake at 350° for 26 minutes or until top is set. Cool completely in pan on a wire rack. Yield: 16 servings (serving size: 1 bar).

CALORIES 213 (32% from fat); FAT 7.5g (sat 2.6g, mono 2.3g, poly 1.1g); PROTEIN 4.4g; CARB 32.3g; FIBER 0.7g; CHOL 37mg; IRON 1.3mg; SODIUM 169mg; CALC 32mg

MAKE AHEAD • FREEZABLE

Swedish Almond Cardamom Stars

Don't substitute marzipan for the almond paste, which is sold in tubes or cans—it's too sweet for this buttery cookie. Look for the paste in tubes, such as Odense brand, or in cans, like King Arthur brand.

COOKIES:

- 2 cups all-purpose flour (about 9 ounces)
- 1 cup powdered sugar
- ½ teaspoon baking soda
- ½ teaspoon ground cardamom
- ¼ teaspoon salt
- ¼ cup almond paste, crumbled
- 1 tablespoon butter, chilled and cut into small pieces
- ⅓ cup fresh orange juice
- 3 tablespoons canola oil

ICING:

- 2 cups powdered sugar
- 3 tablespoons 2% reduced-fat milk

❶ To prepare cookies, lightly spoon flour into dry measuring cups; level with a knife. Combine flour and next 4 ingredients in a food processor; process until blended. Add almond paste and butter; process until blended. Combine juice and oil. With processor on, slowly pour juice mixture through food chute; process until dough forms a ball.

❷ Divide dough in half. Working with 1 portion at a time, gently press dough 4-inch squares on heavy-duty plastic wrap. Cover with additional plastic wrap. Roll each half of dough, still covered, to a ¼-inch thickness. Chill 1 hour.

❸ Preheat oven to 375°.

❹ Working with 1 portion of dough at a time, remove top sheet of plastic wrap; turn dough over. Remove remaining plastic wrap. Cut with a 2½-inch star-shaped cookie cutter into 24 stars; place stars 2 inches apart on 2 baking sheets lined with parchment paper. Bake at 375° for 8 minutes or until lightly browned. Cool on pans 5 minutes. Remove from pans; cool on wire racks. Repeat procedure with remaining half of dough.

❺ To prepare icing, combine 2 cups sugar and milk, stirring with a whisk until smooth. Spread about 1 teaspoon icing over each warm cookie; chill 1 hour. Yield: 4 dozen (serving size: 2 cookies).

CALORIES 124 (21% from fat); FAT 2.9g (sat 0.5g, mono 1.6g, poly 0.7g); PROTEIN 1.3g; CARB 23.5g; FIBER 0.4g; CHOL 1mg; IRON 0.5mg; SODIUM 55mg; CALC 6mg

MAKE AHEAD • FREEZABLE

Double-Chocolate Biscotti

Vanilla extract enhances the dusky mix of cocoa and minichips in these cookies.

- 1½ cups all-purpose flour (about 6.75 ounces)
- 1 cup sugar
- ½ cup unsweetened cocoa
- ½ cup semisweet chocolate minichips
- ½ teaspoon baking powder
- ½ teaspoon baking soda
- ½ teaspoon salt
- 1 teaspoon vanilla extract
- 2 large eggs, lightly beaten
- 1 large egg white, lightly beaten
- Cooking spray

❶ Preheat oven to 350°.

❷ Lightly spoon flour into dry measuring cups; level with a knife. Combine flour and next 6 ingredients in a medium bowl, stirring with a whisk. Combine vanilla, eggs, and egg white in a large bowl, stirring with a whisk. Add flour mixture to egg mixture; stir until well blended. Divide dough in half. Turn dough out onto a baking sheet coated with cooking spray. Shape each dough half into a 12-inch-long roll using floured hands; pat to ½-inch thickness.

❸ Bake at 350° for 22 minutes. Remove rolls from baking sheet; cool 10 minutes on a wire rack. Cut each roll diagonally into 18 (½-inch) slices. Carefully stand slices upright on baking sheet. Bake biscotti an additional 15 minutes or until almost firm (biscotti will be slightly soft in center but will harden as they cool). Remove from baking sheet; cool completely on wire rack. Yield: 3 dozen (serving size: 2 biscotti).

CALORIES 117 (17% from fat); FAT 2.2g (sat 1g, mono 0.7g, poly 0.1g); PROTEIN 2.5g; CARB 22.5g; FIBER 1g; CHOL 24mg; IRON 1.1mg; SODIUM 125mg; CALC 12mg

MAKE AHEAD • FREEZABLE

Chocolate Peanut Butter Cookies

This simple mix-and-drop dough comes together in minutes.

- 1 cup granulated sugar
- 1 cup packed brown sugar
- ½ cup creamy peanut butter
- ¼ cup water
- ¼ cup canola oil
- 2 teaspoons vanilla extract
- 2 large egg whites
- 1 large egg
- 2⅔ cups all-purpose flour (about 12 ounces)
- 1 teaspoon baking powder
- 1 teaspoon baking soda
- ½ teaspoon salt
- ⅔ cup semisweet chocolate minichips

Continued

1 Preheat oven to 350°.

2 Combine first 8 ingredients in a large bowl; beat with a mixer at medium speed until smooth.

3 Lightly spoon flour into dry measuring cups; level with a knife. Combine flour and next 3 ingredients in a small bowl; stir with a whisk. Add flour mixture to peanut butter mixture, stirring just until combined. Stir in minichips. Drop dough by tablespoonfuls 2 inches apart on 2 baking sheets. Bake at 350° for 12 minutes or until golden. Cool on a wire rack. Yield: 3 dozen (serving size: 1 cookie).

CALORIES 128 (32% from fat); FAT 4.5g (sat 1.1g, mono 2.2g, poly 1g); PROTEIN 2.3g; CARB 20.5g; FIBER 0.6g; CHOL 6mg; IRON 0.8mg; SODIUM 106mg; CALC 16mg

Day 7: Christmastime Brunch

These java-tinged cookies are a natural for a Sunday morning sendoff for weekend company.

MAKE AHEAD • FREEZABLE

Espresso Crinkles

Lightly coat your hands with flour to make rolling the dough into balls easier. The dough freezes well. Freeze the dough after step 1, thaw in the refrigerator, then proceed with step 3. The powdered sugar coating gives these cookies an appealing cracked finish. Serve with coffee.

- 1 cup all-purpose flour (about 4.5 ounces)
- 1¼ cups powdered sugar, divided
- ¼ cup unsweetened cocoa
- 1¼ teaspoons baking powder
- ⅛ teaspoon salt
- 5¼ teaspoons canola oil
- 1½ ounces unsweetened chocolate, chopped
- 1 teaspoon instant espresso granules
- ¾ cup packed brown sugar
- 3 tablespoons light-colored corn syrup
- 1½ teaspoons vanilla extract
- 2 large egg whites, lightly beaten

1 Lightly spoon flour into a dry measuring cup; level with a knife. Combine flour, ¾ cup powdered sugar, cocoa, baking powder, and salt in a medium bowl; stir with a whisk. Combine oil and chocolate in a small saucepan over low heat; cook until chocolate melts, stirring constantly. Add espresso granules to pan; stir until blended. Remove from heat. Pour chocolate mixture into a large bowl; cool 5 minutes. Stir in brown sugar, syrup, and vanilla. Add egg whites, stirring with a whisk. Add flour mixture to egg mixture, stirring gently just until combined. Cover; chill at least 2 hours or overnight.

2 Preheat oven to 350°.

3 Roll dough into 1-inch balls. Dredge balls in remaining ½ cup powdered sugar; place balls 2 inches apart on 2 baking sheets. Bake at 350° for 10 minutes or until tops are cracked and almost set. Cool cookies on pans 2 minutes or until set; remove from pans. Cool on a wire rack. Yield: 2 dozen (serving size: 1 cookie).

CALORIES 98 (18% from fat); FAT 2g (sat 0.6g, mono 0.6g, poly 0.3g); PROTEIN 1.2g; CARB 19.5g; FIBER 0.6g; CHOL 0mg; IRON 0.7mg; SODIUM 47mg; CALC 21mg

Day 8: Tokens for Carolers

This big batch of crisp meringues is ideal for a large gathering. Hot cocoa makes a fine accompaniment.

MAKE AHEAD

Chocolate-Hazelnut Meringue Kisses

These meringues can also be made into drop cookies. Just drop them by level tablespoonfuls onto prepared baking sheets.

- ¼ cup finely chopped hazelnuts, toasted
- ¼ cup unsweetened cocoa
- 1 ounce bittersweet chocolate, coarsely chopped
- ¼ cup sifted powdered sugar
- 1½ tablespoons cornstarch
- 3 large egg whites
- ¼ teaspoon cream of tartar
- Dash of salt
- ⅔ cup granulated sugar
- 1 teaspoon vanilla extract

1 Preheat oven to 325°.

2 Combine first 3 ingredients in a food processor; process until finely ground. Combine hazelnut mixture, powdered sugar, and cornstarch in a medium bowl, stirring with a whisk.

3 Place egg whites, cream of tartar, and salt in a large bowl; beat with a mixer at high speed until soft peaks form. Add granulated sugar, 1 tablespoon at a time, beating until stiff peaks form. Gently fold hazelnut mixture and vanilla into egg mixture.

4 Cover a baking sheet with parchment paper. Spoon egg mixture into a pastry bag fitted with a ½-inch round tip. Pipe 24 (1½-inch-round) mounds onto prepared baking sheet. Bake at 325° for 30 minutes or until dry to touch. (Meringues are done when surface is dry and meringues can be removed from paper without sticking to fingers.) Turn oven off; partially open oven door. Cool meringues in oven 30 minutes. Remove from oven; carefully remove meringues from paper. Repeat procedure twice with remaining egg mixture. Yield: 6 dozen (serving size: 6 kisses).

CALORIES 94 (26% from fat); FAT 2.7g (sat 0.6g, mono 1.1g, poly 0.2g); PROTEIN 1.8g; CARB 16.8g; FIBER 0.7g; CHOL 0mg; IRON 0.4mg; SODIUM 26mg; CALC 4mg

Day 9: Afternoon Treat

Sweet goodies boast Southern flair in this cornmeal-based recipe. Serve with hot tea and toddies to warm up after enjoying outdoor activities in brisk weather.

MAKE AHEAD

Lemon Cornmeal Cookies

Cornmeal lends chewiness and an appealing texture. For variety, substitute orange or lime rind for the lemon.

1¼ cups all-purpose flour (about 5.6 ounces)
½ cup cornmeal
2 teaspoons baking powder
¼ teaspoon salt
½ cup sugar
¼ cup butter, softened
¼ cup canola oil
¼ cup light-colored corn syrup
2 teaspoons grated lemon rind
2 large egg whites
Cooking spray

1 Preheat oven to 350°.
2 Lightly spoon flour into dry measuring cups; level with a knife. Combine flour and next 3 ingredients in a medium bowl, stirring with a whisk.
3 Place sugar and butter in a large bowl; beat with a mixer at medium speed until well blended (about 5 minutes). Add oil and next 3 ingredients, beating until blended. Gradually add flour mixture to sugar mixture; beat well. Drop dough by level tablespoonfuls 1 inch apart on 2 baking sheets coated with cooking spray. Bake at 350° for 10 minutes or until edges are golden. Place baking sheets on wire racks; cool completely. Yield: 2 dozen (serving size: 1 cookie).

CALORIES 96 (40% from fat); FAT 4.3g (sat 1.4g, mono 1.9g, poly 0.8g); PROTEIN 1.2g; CARB 13.6g; FIBER 0.4g; CHOL 5mg; IRON 0.5mg; SODIUM 85mg; CALC 24mg

Day 10: Give Some, Enjoy Some

Cinnamon, nutmeg, and vanilla bring spicy sweetness to these thin rounds, which can be packaged as gifts.

MAKE AHEAD • FREEZABLE

Spiced Vanilla Cookies

In step 2, you'll get best results if you keep dough portions chilled and work on only one portion at a time.

2¼ cups all-purpose flour (about 10.1 ounces)
1 tablespoon ground cinnamon
½ teaspoon grated nutmeg
¼ teaspoon baking soda
¼ teaspoon salt
½ cup sugar
3 tablespoons butter, softened
2 tablespoons canola oil
¼ cup light-colored corn syrup
1 tablespoon vanilla extract
1 large egg white

1 Lightly spoon flour into dry measuring cups; level with a knife. Combine flour and next 4 ingredients in a medium bowl, stirring with a whisk. Combine sugar, butter, and oil in a large bowl; beat with a mixer at medium speed until smooth. Add syrup, vanilla, and egg white to sugar mixture, beating until well blended. Gradually add flour mixture to sugar mixture; beat at low speed just until combined. Divide dough in half; roll each half into a ball. Cover with plastic wrap; chill 1 hour.
2 Working with 1 portion at a time, gently press dough into a 4-inch square on heavy-duty plastic wrap. Cover with additional plastic wrap. Roll dough, still covered, to a ¼-inch thickness. Repeat procedure with remaining dough; chill 30 minutes.
3 Preheat oven to 375°.
4 Working with 1 portion at a time, remove top sheet of plastic wrap. Turn dough over; remove remaining plastic wrap. Cut with a 2-inch round cutter into 18 cookies; place cookies 2 inches apart on a baking sheet lined with parchment paper. Repeat procedure with remaining dough portion. Bake at 375° for 8 minutes or until lightly browned. Cool on pans 5 minutes. Remove from pans; cool on wire racks. Yield: 3 dozen (serving size: 2 cookies).

CALORIES 119 (27% from fat); FAT 3.5g (sat 1.3g, mono 1.4g, poly 0.5g); PROTEIN 1.7g; CARB 20g; FIBER 0.6g; CHOL 5mg; IRON 0.9mg; SODIUM 70mg; CALC 6mg

Day 11: After Shopping

Ground pecans stand in for almonds in this macaroon and complement the figs. They're a fine reward for finishing off your gift list.

MAKE AHEAD

Fig-Pecan Macaroons

1 cup chopped pecans
1 teaspoon ground cinnamon
2 teaspoons grated lemon rind
¼ teaspoon cream of tartar
Dash of salt
2 large egg whites
1¾ cups powdered sugar, divided
¾ cup finely chopped dried Black Mission figs (about 8)

1 Preheat oven to 300°.
2 Combine pecans and cinnamon in a food processor; process until finely ground. Add rind; process until blended.
3 Place cream of tartar, salt, and egg whites in a large bowl; beat with a mixer at medium speed until foamy. Increase speed to high, and beat until stiff peaks form. Place 2 tablespoons sugar in a small bowl. Gradually add remaining sugar to egg mixture; beat at low speed until blended. Fold in pecan mixture. Add figs to reserved sugar, tossing to coat; fold fig mixture into egg mixture.
4 Cover 2 baking sheets with parchment paper. Drop egg mixture by rounded

Continued

teaspoonfuls 1 inch apart on prepared baking sheets. Bake at 300° for 20 minutes or until edges are lightly browned. Place pans on wire racks; cool completely. Yield: 4 dozen (serving size: 2 macaroons).

CALORIES 86 (38% from fat); FAT 3.6g (sat 0.3g, mono 2g, poly 1.1g); PROTEIN 1g; CARB 13.6g; FIBER 1.2g; CHOL 0mg; IRON 0.3mg; SODIUM 12mg; CALC 15mg

Day 12: Snacks with the Show

These chewy treats use toffee bits for a crunchy twist on the classic oatmeal cookie. Make a batch and have friends over to watch your favorite holiday DVD.

MAKE AHEAD • FREEZABLE
Oatmeal Toffee Cookies

- ¾ cup all-purpose flour
- 1 cup old-fashioned rolled oats
- ½ teaspoon baking soda
- ¼ teaspoon salt
- ¾ cup packed brown sugar
- ¼ cup butter, softened
- 1 teaspoon vanilla extract
- 1 large egg
- ⅓ cup almond toffee bits
- Cooking spray

1 Preheat oven to 350°.
2 Lightly spoon flour into dry measuring cups; level with a knife. Combine flour and next 3 ingredients in a medium bowl; stir with a whisk. Place sugar and butter in a large bowl; beat with a mixer at medium speed until well blended (about 5 minutes). Add vanilla and egg; beat well. Add flour mixture; beat just until combined. Stir in toffee bits.
3 Drop dough by tablespoonfuls 2 inches apart on 2 baking sheets coated with cooking spray. Bake at 350° for 11 minutes or until lightly browned. Cool on pans 1 minute. Remove cookies from pans; cool completely on wire racks. Yield: 2 dozen (serving size: 1 cookie).

CALORIES 90 (34% from fat); FAT 3.4g (sat 1.6g, mono 0.6g, poly 0.1g); PROTEIN 1.2g; CARB 13.6g; FIBER 0.4g; CHOL 15mg; IRON 0.5mg; SODIUM 88mg; CALC 9mg

Réveillon Revival

How the Brennan family, among the Crescent City's most successful restaurateurs, breathed new life into an old French tradition.

BY THE TIME the very merry divorcée Adelaide Brennan—a glamorous redhead reputed to be the most beautiful woman in all of New Orleans—descended the winding stairway of the Greek Revival home she shared with her sister, Ella, their annual Christmas Eve bash was in full swing. Many close friends and most of the large Brennan clan gathered for the strictly black-tie, Uptown affair, which the sisters hosted from the mid-1960s until the '80s.

The soirees were a nod to a nearly extinct Crescent City holiday tradition, known as the *Réveillon*, which translates loosely to "awakening" in French. In the 1800s, the New Orleans Creoles, a multicultural group of Catholics that included French immigrants, adopted the French tradition. As in the old country, celebrants fasted all day before taking communion at Midnight Mass on Christmas Eve and New Year's Eve, and then they rewarded their piety with luxurious, prolonged feasts in the wee hours after mass.

The Brennans—whose various second- and third-generation representatives own and operate beloved New Orleans institutions such as Commander's Palace and Brennan's—have kept the Réveillon going and made it something everyone can enjoy. Ella Brennan's Commander's Palace is among the dozens of Big Easy restaurants that began in recent years serving prix-fixe Réveillon menus throughout the holidays. It's a way to keep alive the storied tradition, which hasn't been celebrated widely in family homes for years and is now more of a dining-out phenomenon.

RÉVEILLON MENU
(Serves 8)

Roasted Pheasant and Oyster Gumbo

Réveillon Salad

Lacquered Flounder
or
Duck and Black-Eyed Pea Cassoulet

Toasted Pecan Wild Rice

Louisiana Citrus Crepes
or
Eggnog Ice Cream

QUICK & EASY
Réveillon Salad

- 1½ cups (1-inch) cubed peeled fresh pumpkin (about 12 ounces)
- Cooking spray
- ¾ teaspoon kosher salt, divided
- ½ teaspoon freshly ground black pepper, divided
- 14 cups lightly packed gourmet salad greens
- ¾ cup golden raisins
- ¼ cup hard cider
- 3 tablespoons fresh lemon juice
- 3 tablespoons canola oil
- 2 tablespoons Dijon mustard
- 1 tablespoon sugar
- 8 gingersnaps, crushed (about 2 ounces)

1 Preheat oven to 400°.
2 Place pumpkin in a single layer on a jelly-roll pan coated with cooking spray.

Coat pumpkin lightly with cooking spray; toss. Sprinkle with ¼ teaspoon salt and ¼ teaspoon pepper; toss. Bake at 400° for 18 minutes or until tender, stirring occasionally. Cool completely.

❸ Combine pumpkin, greens, raisins, and ¼ teaspoon salt in a large bowl; toss gently. Combine remaining ¼ teaspoon salt, remaining ¼ teaspoon pepper, cider, and next 4 ingredients in a blender; process until blended. Drizzle cider mixture over salad mixture; toss gently. Sprinkle with crushed cookies. Serve immediately. Yield: 8 servings (serving size: about 1½ cups).

CALORIES 151 (38% from fat); FAT 6.3g (sat 0.6g, mono 3.5g, poly 1.8g); PROTEIN 2.7g; CARB 23.2g; FIBER 2.9g; CHOL 0mg; IRON 2.1mg; SODIUM 282mg; CALC 71mg

Roasted Pheasant and Oyster Gumbo

Filé powder (ground sassafras leaves) adds a mild flavor, similar to eucalyptus, and is often added to gumbo for its thickening properties.

```
1   (2¾-pound) pheasant
    Cooking spray
½   teaspoon kosher salt
½   teaspoon black pepper
2   tablespoons butter
3   tablespoons all-purpose flour
2   teaspoons canola oil
1½  cups chopped yellow onion
1½  cups chopped green bell pepper
1½  cups chopped celery
1   teaspoon herbes de Provence
5   garlic cloves, minced
2   bay leaves
4   ounces andouille sausage, diced
6   cups fat-free, less-sodium
    chicken broth
1½  teaspoons Creole seasoning
1½  teaspoons Worcestershire sauce
1½  teaspoons hot pepper sauce
    (such as Tabasco)
1   cup shucked oysters, undrained
1   teaspoon filé powder
4   cups hot cooked rice
¾   cup thinly sliced green onions
```

❶ Preheat oven to 425°.

❷ Remove neck and giblets from pheasant; discard. Place pheasant in a small roasting pan coated with cooking spray. Starting at neck cavity, loosen skin from breast and drumsticks by inserting fingers, gently pushing between skin and meat. Rub salt and pepper under loosened skin and over breast and drumsticks. Bake at 425° for 10 minutes. Cover legs with foil.

❸ Reduce oven temperature to 350°. (Do not remove pheasant from oven.) Bake pheasant 30 minutes or until juices run clear. Cool. Remove and discard skin. Remove meat from bones; shred meat. Discard bones.

❹ Melt butter in a small saucepan over medium-high heat; stir in flour. Cook 7 minutes or until dark brown, stirring constantly. Remove from heat.

❺ Heat oil in a Dutch oven over medium-high heat. Add yellow onion, bell pepper, and celery to pan; sauté 6 minutes, stirring occasionally. Add herbes de Provence, garlic, and bay leaves; sauté 3 minutes. Add shredded pheasant and sausage to pan; sauté 5 minutes. Add flour mixture; cook 30 seconds, stirring well. Stir in broth; bring to a boil. Reduce heat, and simmer 30 minutes (skim foam from surface, if necessary). Stir in Creole seasoning, Worcestershire, and hot pepper sauce; cook 30 minutes, stirring occasionally. Add oysters; cook 2 minutes or until edges begin to curl. Remove from heat. Stir in filé powder. Discard bay leaves. Serve over rice; sprinkle with green onions. Yield: 16 servings (serving size: ¼ cup rice, ½ cup gumbo, and about 2 teaspoons green onions).

CALORIES 180 (36% from fat); FAT 7.1g (sat 2.5g, mono 2.9g, poly 1g); PROTEIN 11.7g; CARB 16.5g; FIBER 1.4g; CHOL 36mg; IRON 2.4mg; SODIUM 362mg; CALC 37mg

Lacquered Flounder

Cane vinegar is made from sugar cane syrup. Look for Steen's vinegar, made in Louisiana, or substitute Champagne vinegar. Turbinado sugar gives the glaze a golden color and imparts a hint of molasses to the flavor. Substitute granulated sugar, if necessary.

```
1   dried cascabel chile
4   cups fresh satsuma orange or
    tangerine juice (about 16 satsumas)
¼   cup turbinado sugar
½   teaspoon cane vinegar
8   (6-ounce) flounder fillets, skinned
1½  teaspoons Creole seasoning
2   tablespoons canola oil, divided
```

❶ Pierce chile with a knife. Combine chile and next 3 ingredients in a Dutch oven; bring to a boil over medium-high heat. Cook until reduced to 1 cup (about 20 minutes), stirring occasionally. Reduce heat, and simmer until reduced to ¾ cup (about 10 minutes), stirring occasionally. Discard chile.

❷ Preheat oven to 350°.

❸ Sprinkle both sides of fish with Creole seasoning. Heat 1 tablespoon oil in a nonstick skillet over medium-high heat. Add 4 fillets to pan; sauté 2 minutes on each side or until browned. Place fish on a baking sheet; spread about 1 tablespoon juice mixture over each fillet. Repeat procedure with remaining oil, fish, and juice mixture.

❹ Bake at 350° for 5 minutes or until fish flakes easily when tested with a fork or until desired degree of doneness. Yield: 8 servings (serving size: 1 fillet).

CALORIES 258 (20% from fat); FAT 5.8g (sat 0.8g, mono 2.5g, poly 1.9g); PROTEIN 31.8g; CARB 18.5g; FIBER 0.3g; CHOL 87mg; IRON 0.8mg; SODIUM 250mg; CALC 41mg

Duck and Black-Eyed Pea Cassoulet

Black-eyed peas stand in for the white beans used in the traditional French dish.

- 6 slices applewood-smoked bacon, chopped
- 6 (10-ounce) duck leg quarters, skinned
- 1 teaspoon salt, divided
- 1 teaspoon freshly ground black pepper, divided
- 1 cup finely chopped yellow onion
- ¼ cup chopped garlic (about 7 cloves)
- 1½ cups chopped cremini mushrooms
- 1 cup finely chopped celery
- ½ cup finely chopped carrot
- 6 cups fat-free, less-sodium chicken broth
- 6 cups frozen black-eyed peas, thawed
- 2 tablespoons chopped fresh thyme, divided
- 2 tablespoons chopped fresh flat-leaf parsley, divided

❶ Cook bacon in a large, deep Dutch oven over medium heat until crisp. Remove bacon, reserving 3 tablespoons drippings in pan; set bacon aside. Increase heat to medium-high.
❷ Sprinkle duck with ½ teaspoon salt and ½ teaspoon pepper. Add half of duck legs to drippings in pan; cook 3 minutes on each side or until browned. Remove from pan. Repeat procedure with re-maining duck. Add onion and garlic to pan; sauté 3 minutes, stirring fre-quently. Add remaining ½ teaspoon salt, remaining ½ teaspoon pepper, mush-rooms, celery, and carrot. Cover, reduce heat to low, and cook 20 minutes or until very tender, stirring occasionally.
❸ Stir in broth, peas, 1 tablespoon thyme, and 1 tablespoon parsley. Return duck and accumulated juices to pan; bring to a boil. Reduce heat, and simmer 1 hour and 20 minutes or until duck is tender, slightly mashing beans

occasionally with a fork or potato masher. Remove duck from pan; cool slightly. Remove meat from bones; shred. Discard bones. Return meat to pan. Simmer 20 minutes or until mixture is thick, stirring occasionally. Stir in remaining 1 tablespoon thyme and remaining 1 tablespoon parsley. Sprinkle with bacon. Yield: 8 servings (serving size: about 1¼ cups).

CALORIES 307 (32% from fat); FAT 10.9g (sat 3.5g, mono 4.7g, poly 1.5g); PROTEIN 24.4g; CARB 27g; FIBER 7.6g; CHOL 69mg; IRON 3.4mg; SODIUM 795mg; CALC 185mg

Toasted Pecan Wild Rice

If the rice doesn't absorb all of the broth as it cooks, drain off the excess liquid before stirring in the remaining ingredients.

- 2 teaspoons olive oil
- ½ cup chopped pecans
- 4½ cups fat-free, less-sodium chicken broth
- 2 cups uncooked wild rice
- 3 tablespoons chopped fresh flat-leaf parsley
- 1½ tablespoons butter
- ¾ teaspoon salt
- ¼ teaspoon freshly ground black pepper

❶ Heat oil in a medium saucepan over medium-high heat. Add pecans to pan; cook 1 minute or until lightly toasted. Remove pecans from pan.
❷ Add broth and rice to pan; bring to a boil. Cover, reduce heat, and simmer 1 hour or until tender. Drain, if necessary. Place rice in a serving bowl; stir in pars-ley and remaining ingredients. Sprinkle with pecans. Yield: 8 servings (serving size: about ⅔ cup rice mixture and 1 tablespoon pecans).

CALORIES 251 (33% from fat); FAT 9.3g (sat 2.1g, mono 4.6g, poly 2.2g); PROTEIN 8.5g; CARB 35.6g; FIBER 4.2g; CHOL 6mg; IRON 1.5mg; SODIUM 460mg; CALC 21mg

Louisiana Citrus Crepes

Although Tory McPhail uses Louisiana citrus, you can prepare these crepes with your favorite varieties of oranges and grapefruits. You can prepare the filling up to two days ahead. Cook the crepes up to two weeks ahead, and freeze them. Thaw frozen crepes in the refrigerator for 24 hours, and let them come to room temperature before serving.

FILLING:
- 2 cups fat-free milk
- 1 (5-inch) vanilla bean, split lengthwise
- ½ cup granulated sugar
- 2 tablespoons cornstarch
- Dash of salt
- 3 large egg yolks, lightly beaten
- ½ cup reduced-fat sour cream

CREPES:
- ½ cup fat-free milk
- 5 tablespoons water
- 2 tablespoons butter, melted
- ½ teaspoon vanilla extract
- 1 large egg, lightly beaten
- ⅔ cup all-purpose flour (about 3 ounces)
- ½ teaspoon granulated sugar
- ¼ teaspoon salt
- Cooking spray

REMAINING INGREDIENTS:
- 1 cup navel orange sections (about 2 medium)
- 1 cup red grapefruit sections (about 2 medium)
- ¼ cup granulated sugar
- 2 tablespoons chopped fresh mint
- 1 tablespoon powdered sugar
- 8 mint sprigs (optional)

❶ To prepare filling, pour 2 cups milk into a medium heavy saucepan. Scrape seeds from vanilla bean; add seeds and bean to pan. Cook milk over medium-high heat to 180° or until tiny bubbles form around edge (do not boil). Remove from heat.
❷ Combine ½ cup granulated sugar, cornstarch, dash of salt, and egg yolks,

stirring with a whisk. Gradually add 1 cup hot milk mixture to egg mixture, stirring with a whisk. Return milk mixture to pan; bring to a boil over medium heat, stirring constantly with a whisk. Cook 1 minute; remove from heat. Spoon into a bowl; discard vanilla bean. Stir in sour cream. Place plastic wrap on surface of custard. Chill thoroughly.

③ To prepare crepes, combine ½ cup milk and next 4 ingredients in a blender. Lightly spoon flour into a dry measuring cup; level with a knife. Add flour, ½ teaspoon granulated sugar, and ¼ teaspoon salt to blender. Process until smooth. Chill 1 hour.

④ Heat an 8-inch nonstick crepe pan or skillet over medium heat. Coat pan lightly with cooking spray. Pour about 3 tablespoons batter into pan; quickly tilt pan in all directions so batter covers pan with a thin film. Cook about 2 minutes. Carefully lift edge of crepe with a spatula to test for doneness. Turn crepe when it can be shaken loose from pan and underside is lightly browned; cook 1 minute or until center is set.

⑤ Place crepe on a towel; cool completely. Repeat procedure until all of batter is used. Stack crêpes between single layers of wax paper to prevent sticking.

⑥ To prepare remaining ingredients, combine orange sections and next 3 ingredients; toss gently to dissolve sugar.

⑦ Place 1 crepe on each of 8 dessert plates; spread about ⅓ cup chilled filling over each crepe. Fold each into a triangle. Top each serving with ¼ cup fruit mixture. Sprinkle crepes evenly with powdered sugar. Garnish with mint sprigs, if desired. Yield: 8 servings.

CALORIES 266 (21% from fat); FAT 6.3g (sat 3.4g, mono 1.8g, poly 0.5g); PROTEIN 6.9g; CARB 46.5g; FIBER 2g; CHOL 113mg; IRON 1mg; SODIUM 181mg; CALC 145mg

---

STAFF FAVORITE • MAKE AHEAD
FREEZABLE

Eggnog Ice Cream

Because the alcohol in the bourbon doesn't fully cook off, the ice cream doesn't freeze hard in the churn. Freeze a dish for one hour, and spoon the soft-serve mixture into it for the best texture.

    1¾ cups half-and-half
    2¼ cups 2% reduced-fat milk
      1 (2-inch) cinnamon stick
      1 (5-inch) vanilla bean, split
         lengthwise
      1 cup sugar
      ⅓ cup bourbon
      ½ teaspoon ground nutmeg
      5 large egg yolks, lightly beaten
    Freshly grated nutmeg (optional)

① Combine first 3 ingredients in a heavy saucepan over medium-high heat. Scrape seeds from vanilla bean; add seeds and bean to milk mixture. Heat milk mixture to 180° or until tiny bubbles form around edge (do not boil). Remove from heat.

② Combine sugar and next 3 ingredients in a bowl, stirring with a whisk. Gradually add half of hot milk mixture to egg mixture, stirring constantly with a whisk. Return milk mixture to pan. Reduce heat to medium. Heat mixture to 160°, stirring constantly. Discard vanilla bean and cinnamon stick. Pour mixture into a bowl; place plastic wrap on surface of custard. Chill thoroughly.

③ Pour mixture into freezer can of an ice-cream freezer; freeze according to manufacturer's instructions. Spoon ice cream into a freezer-safe container; cover and freeze 8 hours or until firm. Garnish with freshly grated nutmeg, if desired. Yield: 8 servings (serving size: ⅔ cup).

CALORIES 260 (35% from fat); FAT 10.2g (sat 5.6g, mono 3.4g, poly 0.7g); PROTEIN 5.5g; CARB 31g; FIBER 0g; CHOL 153mg; IRON 0.4mg; SODIUM 61mg; CALC 152mg

---

Creole vs. Cajun

In New Orleans, the Réveillon is all about Creole food, which is distinct from Cajun food in Louisiana. Sophisticated Creole cooking combines the many influences of early New Orleans—and the wide array of ingredients and spices that have historically been available in the international port city. French and Spanish settlers, along with slaves brought from Africa and free people of color from the Caribbean, helped build Louisiana's biggest city, and Creole food is, quite literally, their melting pot.

In contrast, rustic Cajun food is Creole's "country cousin," says Chef John Besh. Fishermen and trappers who made their way to rural southern Louisiana from France, by way of Canada's eastern coast, developed the cuisine, which includes hearty interpretations of regional classics like gumbo and jambalaya.

Modern Réveillon

For New Orleans chefs, Christmas is a time to honor old customs that have migrated from homes to restaurants. "The Réveillon has evolved," says Chef John Besh, whose upcoming book *My New Orleans* will include a chapter on the tradition, and whose Restaurant August is among local eateries that prepare prix-fixe menus throughout December. "This is a chance to really showcase our culture."

Like his counterpart Tory McPhail at Commander's Palace, Besh looks to antique cookbooks and old restaurant menus for direction. The result is a seven-course menu of elaborate comfort food, including the likes of shellfish étouffée or daube beef stew—"slow-cooked, complex, [with] lots of love," he says—and desserts such as a white cake layered with bananas Foster and frosted with Creole cream cheese (Louisiana's unique clabbered cream, similar to sour cream). For his part, McPhail's prix-fixe menu combines his zeal for locally sourced ingredients with years of tradition in a robust feast likely to feature smoked goose gumbo, glazed quail, and bread pudding soufflé with whiskey sauce.

Christmas Reminisced

Four noted authors gracefully recall how food shaped a special holiday memory.

A Wintertime Miracle in Southern California

By Betty Fussell

First off, was there a big, round lump in the toe? What I looked for Christmas morning when I ran toward my stocking, hung by a nail in the wall next to the heater that kept us warm during winter, was the toe. As I unhooked the stocking, felt the weight and roundness of the lump, I thanked God and Santa. They knew I was the Good Girl, my brother the Bad Boy. Bad boys got a potato in the toe of their stockings. Good girls got an orange.

For my family, who had moved in the late 1920s from the blizzards of Kansas to the sunshine of Riverside, California—in the desert of the state's Inland Empire—oranges in wintertime were a sign of God's miracles, like that of Christ's birth in a desert like ours, only without the oranges. At least not the navel orange, which had been transplanted to Southern California from Brazil to take root and produce a flourishing industry. I was, in fact, born in an orange grove, and the scent of orange blossoms in December compensated for the smudge pots (oil-burning devices used in the groves to protect against chilly nights) that darkened our curtains and walls and nostrils with thick smoke when the frost came on.

Because navels were so abundant, we snacked on them like candy, or rammed a stick of porous peppermint down through the top of the orange and sucked up juice through the peppermint-flavored straw. No matter that oranges were common as winter sunshine; they remained special because it was winter, as my grandparents reminded me with a fierceness that implied, "Get down on your knees, child, and thank the Lord." My grandfather thanked the Lord at every meal but at Christmas gave special thanks for the food of angels. That was his Calvinist triumph over pagan gods and his translation of their favorite food into ours: California Ambrosia.

It was a dish so easy a child could make it, and I did, eagerly. There was even a recipe for it in *A Child's First Cook Book*. Peel the oranges, slice them, put them in a bowl, and add grated coconut, which, as I remember, came in a can. Cover the bowl with wax paper held in place by a rubber band, and chill it in the icebox. That was it. And after our big noontime dinner of roast turkey and mashed potatoes and canned green beans, ambrosia was as refreshing as it was special. Only later did I learn that people in other parts of the country added stuff like canned pineapple, canned mandarin oranges, miniature marshmallows, or maraschino cherries. Unthinkable. If you had the miracle of sweet, juicy orange flesh without seeds, why would you swaddle it in anything but grated coconut? Unless, of course, you were a grown-up, your teetotaling ancestors were long gone, and you were happy to gild the lily with another of God's gifts, Grand Marnier.

Betty Fussell is a James Beard Award–winning food writer and cookbook author who specializes in American cuisine. Her latest book is Raising Steaks: The Life and Times of American Beef.

MAKE AHEAD
California Ambrosia
(pictured on page 270)

Three ingredients combine to yield a deliciously juicy fruit salad. A hint of orange liqueur enhances the taste of the fruit.

- 4 large navel oranges
- 2/3 cup flaked sweetened coconut
- 1 tablespoon Grand Marnier or other orange-flavored liqueur

1 Peel and section oranges over a bowl, reserving juice. Place orange sections in bowl with juice. Add coconut and liqueur; stir gently. Cover and refrigerate 3 hours. Yield: 4 servings (serving size: 2/3 cup).

CALORIES 137 (24% from fat); FAT 3.7g (sat 3.3g, mono 0.2g, poly 0.1g); PROTEIN 1.7g; CARB 25.5g; FIBER 4.3g; CHOL 0mg; IRON 0.4mg; SODIUM 37mg; CALC 62mg

> "It was a dish so easy a child could make it, and I did, eagerly."
>
> —Betty Fussell

Santa's Special Cake

By Jim Harrison

As the chill of early December sets in, television commercials depict the delightful sight of a one-horse sleigh with bells ringing and children singing as they make their way through the snow to their brightly lit home.

Everyone yearns for the greeting-card Christmas. Yet, for most of us, it is not the snow, nor the sleigh bells, nor the singing that build in our memories year after year. We pull from the past to enjoy the present, and so it is that the Christmases of childhood become the Christmases of adulthood. We strive to re-create the traditions, the foods, and the atmosphere of the way we were and the way we long to be again.

Family togetherness is the order of the day, and it was no different in Michigan at the Harrison house of the 1940s and '50s. Our annual fruitcake ritual began long before the Yuletide season with the gathering and shelling of pecans from our trees in the yard. All of us—my parents, two brothers, and I—were involved, as we were making fruitcakes for our teachers' gifts, some for us, and most importantly a cake for Santa Claus. Together, the family worked our way toward Christmas. As the final month of the year approached, my mother would bring out the mixing bowls and pull out a recipe card that actually came from my grandmother's kitchen. The batter was placed in a variety of whatever-size baking tins we had, and on top of some cakes we made designs using pieces of pecans.

A very special small cake was for Santa, and handled with extreme care. Several red cherries and pieces of green fruit were saved out of the mixture to be placed on top as part of the decoration. My daddy had a real knack for precision and neatness, while my mama had somewhat of an artistic touch. Santa's cake was different, and the making of it stirred our childish excitement.

The process of wrapping the cooked cakes in cheesecloth soaked with rum always fascinated me. The finished wrapped products were put away in clean lard cans to be stored on the upper shelves of the dark kitchen closet. Crude signs were posted, strongly admonishing not to be disturbed until Christmas, as the kitchen closet was the symbol of good times to come. On Christmas Eve, Santa's cake was carefully unwrapped and neatly sliced into a few pieces. The same small plate was used every year, and the cake, with a glass of fresh milk, was placed on the mantel with a note from Jimmy, Phil, and Wendel explaining how good we had been that year.

Christmas morning the milk and two pieces of cake were always gone, replaced by a note thanking us and signed "Santa Claus." Some time afterward I recognized how closely Santa's note resembled my daddy's neat handwriting, but only these many years later have I realized and appreciated the extra joy the Harrison fruitcake ritual brought us.

Try hard as we can, we do not return to that past, but my Christmases now always include a gathering of me and my two brothers' families. The three Harrison boys do indeed happily speak of those times and things of the past as we now eat the fruitcake of this day.

Jim Harrison is a novelist, poet, and food writer whose work includes Legends of the Fall *and* The Raw and the Cooked.

MAKE AHEAD
Christmas Fruitcake

Cooking spray
- 2 teaspoons all-purpose flour
- 1 cup raisins
- $\frac{2}{3}$ cup dried currants
- $\frac{1}{2}$ cup chopped pistachios
- $\frac{1}{2}$ cup finely chopped dried apricots
- $\frac{1}{2}$ cup finely chopped dried figs
- $1\frac{1}{2}$ tablespoons all-purpose flour
- 1 cup all-purpose flour
- $\frac{1}{2}$ teaspoon baking soda
- $\frac{1}{2}$ teaspoon ground cinnamon
- $\frac{1}{4}$ teaspoon salt
- $\frac{1}{8}$ teaspoon ground nutmeg
- $\frac{1}{2}$ cup butter
- $\frac{2}{3}$ cup packed brown sugar
- $\frac{1}{2}$ cup egg substitute
- $\frac{1}{2}$ cup dark rum, divided
- 1 teaspoon grated orange rind

1 Preheat oven to 325°.

2 Coat an 8 x 4–inch loaf pan with cooking spray; dust pan with 2 teaspoons flour. Set aside.

3 Combine raisins and next 5 ingredients in a medium bowl; toss well to coat.

4 Lightly spoon 1 cup flour into a dry measuring cup; level with a knife. Combine 1 cup flour and next 4 ingredients in a small bowl, stirring with a whisk.

5 Melt butter in a saucepan over medium heat. Remove from heat. Stir in sugar, egg substitute, $\frac{1}{4}$ cup rum, and rind. Add flour mixture, stirring until smooth. Gradually fold in fruit mixture. Spoon batter into prepared pan. Cover with foil.

6 Bake at 325° for 1 hour or until a wooden pick inserted in center comes out with a few moist crumbs. Pierce top of cake several times with a wooden pick; brush remaining $\frac{1}{4}$ cup rum over top of warm cake. Cool completely in pan on a wire rack. Remove cake from pan. Wrap cake in plastic wrap, then wrap in foil. Refrigerate 24 hours before serving. Yield: 12 servings (serving size: 1 slice).

CALORIES 306 (30% from fat); FAT 10.3g (sat 5.2g, mono 3.2g, poly 1.1g); PROTEIN 4.5g; CARB 48.4g; FIBER 3.6g; CHOL 20mg; IRON 2.2mg; SODIUM 190mg; CALC 54mg

Sweet and Sour Braised Cabbage (*Rotkohl*)

This colorful combination is a tasty accompaniment for roast meats or poultry. Although traditional versions don't use bacon, we love the smoky flavor it adds. For a more classic rendition, omit the bacon and use one tablespoon butter or schmaltz (rendered fat).

- 4 slices applewood-smoked bacon (such as Neuske's), chopped
- 2 cups thinly vertically sliced onion (about 1 large)
- 3 cups chopped peeled Granny Smith apple (about 2 medium)
- 10 cups thinly sliced red cabbage (about 2 pounds)
- 1 cup apple cider
- ¼ cup red wine vinegar
- 2 tablespoons sugar
- 1 teaspoon kosher salt
- 3 whole cloves
- 1 bay leaf

1 Cook bacon in a Dutch oven over medium-high heat until crisp. Remove bacon from pan, reserving 1 tablespoon drippings in pan; set bacon aside. Add onion to drippings in pan; sauté 3 minutes. Add apple to pan; sauté 2 minutes. Add cabbage to pan; sauté 2 minutes. Add cider and remaining ingredients; bring to a boil. Cover, reduce heat, and simmer 1 hour and 15 minutes or until cabbage is tender, stirring occasionally. Discard cloves and bay leaf. Sprinkle with bacon. Yield: 8 servings (serving size: about ¾ cup).

CALORIES 139 (25% from fat); FAT 3.9g (sat 1.7g, mono 1.4g, poly 0.4g); PROTEIN 3.1g; CARB 24.4g; FIBER 3.4g; CHOL 7mg; IRON 1.1mg; SODIUM 399mg; CALC 61mg

A Christmas Latecomer

By Corby Kummer

"He comes to the table with wet hair!" That was the scandalized cry of several of the nine grown children in a large German family with whom I spent wonderful Christmases in my 20s, when I was eager to experience what my conservative Jewish upbringing had denied me.

By great good fortune, I came to be friendly with a family as generous and hospitable as they were strict Catholics, of Austrian and Croatian heritage though they lived outside Frankfurt. One became a priest, one a monk, and one grandmother had retired to a nunnery. They patiently taught me how to invest folkloric traditions with spiritual depth. And those traditions were what I and every child grew up seeing or celebrating. The hand-blown glass ornaments, the magical Advent calendars with their opening doors, decorated evergreens, which is sometimes attributed to Martin Luther, founder of the Reformation— almost everything we think of as meaning Christmas started in Germany.

And more. Over the bough-draped front door someone drew in beautiful chalk letters the mysterious legend "C+M+B," which my friends explained meant the three kings, Caspar, Melchior, and Balthazar. In the crisp air we would walk across the courtyard for Christmas Eve services in the family chapel, to which most members of the small town belonged, everyone at the service singing carols, balancing hymnals in one hand and lit candles in gold paper holders in the other. Afterward, in the huge salon, the children would sing around the piano as their father played, and after midnight each sibling would go to her or his own white linen–covered table and open gifts one by one. The evening went well into the small hours of Christmas morning.

The centerpiece of each table was a *Bunte Teller,* a plate covered with molded marzipan and chocolates, oranges, and *Kipferl,* the heavenly Austrian vanilla and nut half-moons dusted with powdered sugar that closely resemble Mexican wedding cookies or Russian tea cakes.

The tradition that stained itself into my memory was *Rotkohl,* the sweet-and-sour red cabbage that was the indispensable accompaniment to roast goose. In truth, the goose itself was always something of an annual question mark, depending on who cooked it and how much fat she had been able to melt out; sometimes it was too tough to cut or eat with any decorum. But the cabbage never failed, with its sweet apples made tart with vinegar, cloves, bay, and the secret ingredient—*Schmaltz,* which, as with most every German cook, meant lard rather than chicken fat.

Now I'm lucky to be part of an extended German-American family that gives each (grown) child a *Bunte Teller* on Christmas morning—and serves *Rotkohl* with whatever the main course happens to be. I always politely wait for everyone to take seconds, and then do what I wanted with my old-World family in the Old World, polish off every last red shred.

The wet hair? I've tried to mend my ways. My German friends dressed for Christmas Eve dinner, meaning black tie. The most festive and yet serious evening of the year demanded long preparations, not racing down to the table from the shower. But festivity, even if accompanied by formality, really meant understanding the spirit of giving and gratitude—and, as they impressed upon me for life, that had nothing to do with lovely gifts or even dry hair.

Corby Kummer is a James Beard Award–winning food writer for The Atlantic. *His books include* The Joy of Coffee *and* The Pleasures of Slow Food.

Whispery Eggs with Crabmeat and Herbs

"My grandfather in New Orleans used to toss fresh lump crabmeat into everything from seafood casseroles to stuffed mirlitons; it's also great with eggs for an easy, sophisticated breakfast. Whisking the eggs vigorously (even with an immersion blender) yields fluffy, whispery results."

—Kim Sunée

- 4 large eggs, lightly beaten
- 2 large egg whites, lightly beaten
- 1 tablespoon crème fraîche
- ¼ teaspoon fine sea salt
- ¼ teaspoon black pepper
- 1 teaspoon butter
- 1 teaspoon olive oil
- 1 shallot, thinly sliced
- 4 teaspoons chopped fresh parsley
- 1 teaspoon chopped fresh tarragon
- 1 teaspoon chopped fresh thyme
- 1 cup lump crabmeat, drained and shell pieces removed
- 16 (½-inch-thick) slices diagonally cut French bread baguette, toasted

Louisiana hot sauce (optional)

1 Combine eggs and egg whites in a large bowl; beat vigorously with a whisk 1 minute. Add crème fraîche, salt, and pepper; beat vigorously with a whisk 1 minute.

2 Heat butter and oil in a large nonstick skillet over medium-high heat. Add shallot to pan; sauté 2 minutes, stirring frequently. Stir in parsley, tarragon, and thyme. Reduce heat to medium-low. Stir egg mixture with a whisk. Add egg mixture to pan; cook 1 minute, stirring occasionally. Fold in crabmeat; cook 1 minute or until eggs reach desired consistency, stirring gently. Arrange 4 baguette slices on each of 4 plates; spoon about 1 cup egg mixture onto each serving. Serve with hot sauce, if desired. Yield: 4 servings.

CALORIES 222 (36% from fat); FAT 8.9g (sat 3.2g, mono 3.5g, poly 1.1g); PROTEIN 16.9g; CARB 18.9g; FIBER 0.7g; CHOL 247mg; IRON 2.3mg; SODIUM 517mg; CALC 65mg

A Touch of Louisiana in France

By Kim Sunée

I was raised in Louisiana, sucking spicy crawfish heads and eating bayou-colored gumbos, so I thought I could handle any culinary extravagance I might encounter during my 10 years in Europe. I did well in Sweden and Spain, but I met my match during Christmas in Provence.

My first holiday celebrations in Haute-Provence—about an hour from Marseille—were a rich blur of excess: potted goose sautéed with thinly sliced potatoes; dozens of cold, briny oysters; and Texas toast–sized slices of *foie gras en torchon*—all shared with a houseful of guests.

Christmas morning was the only time I really had to myself. I would slip out of the house in the stinging cold predawn and go for a run in the woods behind our property. Accompanied by my yellow Lab, Gribouille, we would greet the hunters, who rose even earlier. I find it's always smart to make friends with strapping men carrying guns. I liked the hunters best when they had black winter truffles bulging out of their pockets.

After my run, I'd return to sleepy houseguests with grumbling stomachs. The evening before, we had indulged in the traditional *Gros Souper*—a meatless dinner served before Midnight Mass, followed by another more elaborate meal, *Le Réveillon* (see page 386). How the guests could be hungry again, I could only understand having been raised in New Orleans.

No one I knew in Provence was particularly religious, but they were fervent about their meals. *The Gros Souper* included about seven courses of regional specialties, including *l'aigo boulido,* a peasant soup of boiled garlic and herbs; cauliflower; snails; fish; and vegetables with *anchoïade* (a thick garlic sauce of crushed anchovies and olive oil). The meal continued with local cheeses, and then, because the menu is meat-free and therefore "light," one must taste all of the Thirteen Desserts—traditionally to represent Jesus and the apostles at the Last Supper.

Olivier, my companion at the time, was raised in Provence, and his mother insisted on the Thirteen Desserts. These often included everything from dried figs, nuts, raisins, and almonds to winter apples, pears, dates, plums, quince jelly, homemade white and black nougat, and my favorite, the traditional *pompe à l'huile*—a brioche made with olive oil and flavored with orange blossom water. These were all served with sweet wine. For my poor liver, it did feel like the Last Supper, but then there was Le Réveillon—the feast after Midnight Mass. This often included more vegetables, roasted game birds, and the traditional *bûche de Noël*—a chocolate Yule log.

After that kind of excess, I preferred to start Christmas Day with a simple herb-and-honey infusion. But for my Provençal friends and family I'd set out a platter of dates, thick orange slices, honeycomb, *fromage blanc,* and some leftover roasted chestnuts and croissants. And, as a hostess raised in the American South, I channeled my grandfather, who taught me the love of cooking and sharing, and whipped up soft scrambles of yard eggs from the farmer across the way. The children loved to call these cloudlike eggs "whispery." Of course, when eggs are ultra fresh and the yolks so yellow and luscious, they hardly need embellishment, but in Louisiana, we love to toss fresh lump crabmeat into everything. Sometimes, during my morning run, the Provençal hunters would slip me one of those small black truffles, and I would shave it on top of the eggs with a pat of salted butter—a perfect "Last Supper."

Kim Sunée lived in Europe for more than 10 years. She is the author of Trail of Crumbs: Hunger, Love, and the Search for Home, *and is the food editor of* Cottage Living *magazine. She is currently at work on her second book. Visit her Web site at www.kimsunee.com.*

Nantucket Noel

From a seafaring Santa to a boatload of decorated trees, Nantucket goes overboard for its Christmas season celebration. We offer an island-inspired feast worthy of the occasion.

THIRTY MILES OFF THE COAST of Massachusetts, Nantucket is among New England's loveliest and most exclusive summer hideaways. Yet Nantucket Town may be at its most beautiful during the cold off-season, particularly for the festival known as "Nantucket Noel," running from Thanksgiving to New Year's.

The highlight of Nantucket Noel is the Christmas Stroll, always on the first weekend of December. Some 10,000 visitors join the merriment, complete with a visit from Santa Claus, who arrives by sea on a Coast Guard cutter.

The end of the evening is a great time to relish a local holiday feast. Opening courses in our menu offer renditions of island bounty, such as its famed seafood. Inspired by Nantucket's rich history and colorful customs, these dishes will help you create a Christmas celebration to remember.

FESTIVE REPAST MENU
(Serves 8)

Champagne

Lobster-Tarragon Toasts

Oyster and Wild Rice Bisque

Nantucket Bay Scallops with Bay-Scented Butter

Beef Tenderloin with Port-Beach Plum Reduction

Colonial Corn Pudding

Eastham Turnip-Potato Gratin

Roasted Brussels Sprouts and Chestnuts

Fresh Thyme Popovers

Pinot noir

Ginger Pumpkin Cheesecake

Stone Fence

MAKE AHEAD
Lobster-Tarragon Toasts

16 (½-inch thick) slices French bread baguette (about 4½ ounces)
Cooking spray
1 cup chopped cooked lobster tail (about 5 ounces)
2 tablespoons minced onion
2 tablespoons minced celery
1 tablespoon plus 1 teaspoon reduced-fat mayonnaise
2 to 3 teaspoons chopped fresh tarragon
2 teaspoons plain fat-free Greek yogurt
⅛ teaspoon salt

❶ Preheat oven to 375°.
❷ Place bread on a baking sheet. Lightly coat tops with cooking spray. Bake at 375° for 8 minutes or until toasted. Cool.
❸ Combine lobster and remaining ingredients in a bowl. Spoon 1 rounded tablespoon lobster mixture onto each toast. Yield: 8 servings (serving size: 2 toasts).

CALORIES 91 (21% from fat); FAT 2.1g (sat 0.3g, mono 0.5g, poly 1g); PROTEIN 5.2g; CARB 12.9g; FIBER 1g; CHOL 13mg; IRON 0.4mg; SODIUM 223mg; CALC 17mg

---

Oyster and Wild Rice Bisque

Use Wellfleet oysters from Cape Cod, if possible. Reminiscent of chowder, this bisque is a touch lighter, filled out with wild rice rather than the more common potatoes. Substitute salt pork—an old New England favorite—for bacon, if you prefer.

1½ bacon slices, chopped
2 cups chopped onion (about 2 medium)
2 cups shucked oysters, undrained
1 cup clam juice
1 tablespoon all-purpose flour
1 cup fat-free, less-sodium chicken broth
1 bay leaf
1½ cups cooked wild rice
1¼ cups whole milk
3 tablespoons half-and-half
½ teaspoon kosher salt
¼ teaspoon freshly ground black pepper
Chopped fresh flat-leaf parsley (optional)

❶ Cook bacon in a large heavy saucepan over medium-low heat 6 minutes or until crisp. Stir in onion; cover and cook 8 minutes or until onion is tender, stirring occasionally.
❷ Drain oysters in a sieve over a bowl. Reserve oysters; add oyster liquid to pan. Combine clam juice and flour in a small bowl; stir with a whisk until smooth. Add clam juice mixture, broth, and bay leaf to pan. Increase heat to medium-high. Bring mixture to a boil; cook until reduced to 2 cups (about 6 minutes).
❸ Reduce heat to low. Discard bay leaf. Stir in rice and next 4 ingredients. Cover and simmer 10 minutes. Stir in reserved oysters; cook 5 minutes or until edges of oysters curl. Sprinkle with parsley, if desired. Yield: 8 servings (serving size: about ¾ cup).

CALORIES 141 (33% from fat); FAT 5.2g (sat 2.1g, mono 1.4g, poly 0.8g); PROTEIN 8.2g; CARB 15.5g; FIBER 1.3g; CHOL 43mg; IRON 4.6mg; SODIUM 357mg; CALC 91mg

Nantucket Bay Scallops with Bay-Scented Butter

Small bay scallops are often sweeter and more tender than larger sea scallops. Pat them dry before coating with cooking spray so they will sear rather than steam in the pan. Bay-scented butter tinged with a hint of lemon flavors the scallops, while panko provides crunchy texture. Serve in scallop shells for a handsome presentation.

2 tablespoons butter
2 bay leaves
1½ pounds bay scallops
   Cooking spray
½ teaspoon kosher salt
1½ teaspoons fresh lemon juice
¼ cup panko (Japanese breadcrumbs)
1 teaspoon grated lemon rind
   Chopped fresh chives (optional)

❶ Place butter and bay leaves in a small saucepan over medium-low heat; cook 5 minutes or until butter melts. Remove from heat; let stand 30 minutes. Skim solids off top; discard solids and bay leaves.
❷ Lightly coat scallops with cooking spray. Heat a large, heavy skillet over high heat. Add half of scallops to pan; sauté 1 minute or until browned on both sides, turning once. Place in a bowl. Repeat procedure with remaining scallops. Sprinkle scallops with salt. Add juice and half of butter to scallops, tossing to coat.
❸ Combine panko and remaining butter. Heat pan over medium-low heat. Add panko mixture to pan; cook 2 minutes or until panko is golden brown, stirring occasionally. Remove panko from pan.
❹ Place ⅓ cup scallops into each of 8 ramekins. Top each serving with 1½ teaspoons panko and ⅛ teaspoon lemon rind. Sprinkle with chives, if desired. Yield: 8 servings (servings size: ⅓ cup scallops).

CALORIES 107 (30% from fat); FAT 3.6g (sat 1.9g, mono 0.8g, poly 0.3g); PROTEIN 14.6g; CARB 3.4g; FIBER 0.1g; CHOL 36mg; IRON 0.3mg; SODIUM 280mg; CALC 22mg

Beef Tenderloin with Port-Beach Plum Reduction

Beef tenderloin serves as the dinner's grand centerpiece. A reduction sauce of port and a Nantucket favorite, beach plum jelly, enhances the meat. Tiny wild beach plums are too sour to eat out of hand, so they are often made into jelly. Red currant jelly is a readily available substitute.

1 (1¾-pound) beef tenderloin, trimmed
   Cooking spray
1 tablespoon coarsely ground black pepper
1¾ teaspoons kosher salt, divided
1½ cups thinly sliced shallots (about 4 large)
1 tablespoon butter
1½ cups fat-free, less-sodium chicken broth
1 cup ruby port
½ cup beach plum jelly
2 tablespoons balsamic vinegar
2 teaspoons fresh thyme
1 teaspoon chopped fresh rosemary

❶ Lightly coat beef with cooking spray; sprinkle evenly on all sides with pepper and 1½ teaspoons salt. Loosely cover beef with plastic wrap; let stand at room temperature 30 minutes.
❷ Preheat oven to 450°.
❸ Heat a large, heavy skillet over medium-high heat. Coat pan with cooking spray. Add beef to pan; cook 2 minutes on all sides or until browned. Place beef on a broiler pan coated with cooking spray. Bake at 450° for 20 minutes or until desired degree of doneness. Remove from oven; let stand 15 minutes.
❹ Return skillet to medium-high heat; add shallots and butter to pan, scraping pan to loosen browned bits. Cook 1 minute, stirring constantly. Stir in broth and remaining ingredients; bring to a boil. Cook until reduced to 1½ cups (about 17 minutes). Remove from heat; stir in remaining ¼ teaspoon salt.
❺ Cut beef crosswise into 16 slices. Serve with sauce. Yield: 8 servings (serving size: 2 beef slices and 3 tablespoons sauce).

CALORIES 227 (25% from fat); FAT 6.4g (sat 2.8g, mono 2.3g, poly 0.3g); PROTEIN 22g; CARB 19.7g; FIBER 0.5g; CHOL 53mg; IRON 1.9mg; SODIUM 557mg; CALC 34mg

MAKE AHEAD
Colonial Corn Pudding

Corn pudding evolved from the popular colonial Indian pudding, which was itself a cornmeal adaptation of flour-based English porridge. Nantucket farmers raise fabulous summer sweet corn, which savvy local cooks freeze for a holiday pudding or chowder. You can substitute store-bought frozen corn in this custardy baked side dish. When it's done, the edges should be a little crusty, and the center still slightly soft. If time is an issue, make the dish ahead, refrigerate, and then reheat before serving.

3 cups frozen whole-kernel corn kernels, thawed and divided
¾ cup evaporated fat-free milk, divided
2 tablespoons half-and-half
½ teaspoon salt
⅛ teaspoon white pepper
   Dash of freshly ground nutmeg
1 large egg, lightly beaten
1 large egg white, lightly beaten
6 tablespoons oyster crackers, crushed and divided
3 tablespoons stone-ground cornmeal
   Cooking spray
½ cup (2 ounces) shredded sharp Cheddar cheese
2 teaspoons butter, melted

❶ Preheat oven to 350°.
❷ Combine 1 cup corn, ¼ cup evaporated milk, and half-and-half in a blender; process until smooth. Combine remaining ½ cup evaporated milk, salt, and next 4 ingredients in a large bowl. Stir in pureed corn mixture, remaining 2 cups corn, 3 tablespoons crackers, and cornmeal.

Continued

❸ Spoon mixture into an 8-inch square baking dish coated with cooking spray. Sprinkle evenly with cheese. Combine remaining 3 tablespoons crackers and butter in a small bowl; sprinkle cracker mixture evenly over cheese. Bake at 350° for 30 minutes or until golden brown. Serve warm. Yield: 8 servings (serving size: about ½ cup).

CALORIES 145 (32% from fat); FAT 5.2g (sat 2.7g, mono 1.6g, poly 0.6g); PROTEIN 6.9g; CARB 19g; FIBER 1.7g; CHOL 34mg; IRON 0.7mg; SODIUM 277mg; CALC 122mg

STAFF FAVORITE
Eastham Turnip-Potato Gratin

The Cape Cod town of Eastham is noted for its extra-sweet turnips, though other varieties will work in this dish. While many gratins are rich with cream, chicken broth serves as the liquid here, to delicious effect. While a mandoline makes quick and even vegetable slices, though a sharp knife will do just fine. If you have a double oven, preheat the broiler while the casserole finishes baking at 350°.

- 1¼   pounds turnips, peeled and cut into ⅛-inch-thick slices
- Cooking spray
- ½   teaspoon kosher salt
- ½   teaspoon freshly ground black pepper
- ¾   pound baking potato, peeled and cut into (⅛-inch-thick) slices
- ¾   cup (3 ounces) grated Gruyère cheese, divided
- ¾   cup fat-free, less-sodium chicken broth

❶ Place turnips in a medium saucepan; cover with water. Bring to a boil. Reduce heat, and simmer 15 minutes or until tender. Drain and pat dry.
❷ Preheat oven to 350°.
❸ Arrange one-third of turnips in a 2-quart baking dish coated with cooking spray; sprinkle with one-third of salt and one-third of pepper. Arrange half of potato over turnip. Sprinkle 6 tablespoons cheese evenly over potato. Arrange one-third of turnips over cheese; sprinkle with one-third of salt and one-third of pepper. Arrange remaining potato over turnip. Arrange remaining turnips over potato; sprinkle with remaining salt and remaining pepper. Pour broth over vegetables. Cover with foil, pressing foil down onto turnip slices. Bake at 350° for 1 hour.
❹ Preheat broiler.
❺ Uncover vegetables; sprinkle with remaining 6 tablespoons cheese. Broil 8 minutes or until lightly browned. Yield: 8 servings (serving size: ¾ cup).

CALORIES 96 (32% from fat); FAT 3.4g (sat 1.9g, mono 1g, poly 0.2g); PROTEIN 4.7g; CARB 12.4g; FIBER 1.9g; CHOL 11mg; IRON 0.6mg; SODIUM 243mg; CALC 130mg

Roasted Brussels Sprouts and Chestnuts

Brussels sprouts are finest in winter. Trim and cut the sprouts up to a day ahead, then keep refrigerated in a zip-top plastic bag.

- 4   cups trimmed and quartered Brussels sprouts (about 1½ pounds)
- 1¼   cups halved bottled chestnuts
- 4   teaspoons olive oil
- ½   teaspoon kosher salt
- ¼   teaspoon coarsely ground black pepper
- Dash of ground red pepper
- 1   tablespoon butter

❶ Preheat oven to 400°.
❷ Combine sprouts and chestnuts in a large bowl. Add oil and next 3 ingredients; toss well to coat. Spread in a single layer on a jelly-roll pan.
❸ Bake at 400° for 25 minutes or until sprouts are tender, stirring after 15 minutes. Remove from oven. Add butter to sprout mixture, tossing until butter melts. Yield: 8 servings (serving size: about ½ cup).

CALORIES 124 (32% from fat); FAT 4.4g (sat 1.4g, mono 2.2g, poly 0.6g); PROTEIN 3.6g; CARB 19.5g; FIBER 4.4g; CHOL 4mg; IRON 1.4mg; SODIUM 149mg; CALC 43mg

Fresh Thyme Popovers

Based on the old English Yorkshire pudding, popovers are a quick bread classically paired with beef dishes. Make the popover batter up to two hours ahead and refrigerate until 15 minutes before you plan to bake them. Popover cups are tall and narrow so the batter "pops over" the top as it bakes; you can find a popover pan at any kitchenware shop. Muffin cups will also do (with 5 minutes less time in the oven), though they won't puff quite as dramatically.

- 1   cup all-purpose flour (about 4.5 ounces)
- 2   teaspoons minced fresh thyme
- ½   teaspoon salt
- 1   cup 1% low-fat milk
- 2   large eggs, lightly beaten
- 1   tablespoon butter, melted
- Cooking spray
- 1   tablespoon finely grated Parmigiano-Reggiano cheese

❶ Preheat oven to 375°.
❷ Lightly spoon flour into a dry measuring cup; level with a knife. Combine flour, thyme, and salt, stirring with a whisk. Combine milk and eggs in a medium bowl, stirring with a whisk until blended; let stand 30 minutes. Gradually add flour mixture to milk mixture, stirring well with a whisk. Stir in butter.
❸ Coat 8 popover cups with cooking spray; sprinkle cheese evenly among cups. Place cups in oven at 375° for 5 minutes. Divide batter evenly into prepared cups. Bake at 375° for 40 minutes or until golden. Serve immediately. Yield: 8 servings (serving size: 1 popover).

CALORIES 97 (27% from fat); FAT 2.9g (sat 1.5g, mono 1g, poly 0.3g); PROTEIN 4.3g; CARB 12.4g; FIBER 0.4g; CHOL 51mg; IRON 1mg; SODIUM 200mg; CALC 52mg

Ginger Pumpkin Cheesecake

Large crystals of raw brown Demerara sugar look and taste lovely, but the cake is still delicious without it.

CRUST:

- 1 cup graham cracker crumbs (about 7 cookie sheets)
- 3 tablespoons granulated sugar
- ½ teaspoon ground ginger
- 1 large egg white, lightly beaten
  Cooking spray

FILLING:

- 1 (8-ounce) block fat-free cream cheese, softened
- 1 (8-ounce) block ⅓-less-fat cream cheese, softened
- ¾ cup granulated sugar
- 1 tablespoon vanilla extract
- 2 teaspoons fresh lemon juice
- ½ teaspoon ground ginger
- 1 (15-ounce) can pumpkin
- 3 large eggs
- 1 tablespoon Demerara sugar

❶ Preheat oven to 350°.
❷ To prepare crust, combine first 4 ingredients in a bowl; toss with a fork until well blended. Press crumb mixture into bottom of a 9-inch springform pan coated with cooking spray. Bake at 350° for 8 minutes. Cool on a wire rack.
❸ Reduce oven temperature to 300°.
❹ To prepare filling, place cream cheeses in a food processor; process until smooth. Add ¾ cup granulated sugar and next 4 ingredients; process until smooth. Add eggs, 1 at a time; process well after each addition. Pour cheese mixture into prepared pan. Bake at 300° for 50 minutes or until almost set. Turn oven off; partially open oven door. Cool cheesecake in oven 30 minutes. Remove from oven; cool on a wire rack. Cover and chill 8 hours. Sprinkle with Demerara sugar just before serving. Yield: 12 servings (serving size: 1 wedge).

CALORIES 194 (28% from fat); FAT 6.1g (sat 3.3g, mono 2g, poly 0.6g); PROTEIN 7.5g; CARB 27.1g; FIBER 1.3g; CHOL 60mg; IRON 1mg; SODIUM 254mg; CALC 67mg

Stone Fence

This take on the old New England drink features apple brandy rather than the usual rum.

- 3 cups apple cider
- ¾ cup Calvados (apple brandy)
- ⅛ teaspoon Angostura bitters
- 1 (25.4-ounce) bottle sparkling apple juice
  Ice
- 8 slices unpeeled Rome apple (optional)
- 8 (3-inch) cinnamon sticks (optional)

❶ Combine first 4 ingredients in a pitcher. Serve over ice. Garnish with apple slices and cinnamon sticks, if desired. Yield: 8 servings (serving size: about ¾ cup).

CALORIES 147 (1% from fat); FAT 0.1g (sat 0g, mono 0g, poly 0.1g); PROTEIN 0.4g; CARB 24.7g; FIBER 0.1g; CHOL 0mg; IRON 0.4mg; SODIUM 3mg; CALC 7mg

Baked Cranberries with Rum

- 1 (12-ounce) bag fresh or frozen cranberries, thawed
- ¾ cup sugar
- ¼ teaspoon ground cinnamon
  Dash freshly grated nutmeg
  Cooking spray
- 2 tablespoons light rum

❶ Preheat oven to 350°.
❷ Combine first 4 ingredients in an 8-inch square baking dish coated with cooking spray; cover tightly with foil. Bake at 350° for 30 minutes; uncover and stir gently. Bake, uncovered, an additional 15 minutes or until cranberries are tender and sauce is syrupy. Remove from oven; stir in rum. Cool to room temperature. Chill at least 1 hour before serving. Yield: 8 servings (serving size: ¼ cup).

CALORIES 100 (1% from fat); FAT 0.1g (sat 0g, mono 0g, poly 0g); PROTEIN 0.2g; CARB 24g; FIBER 2g; CHOL 0mg; IRON 0.1mg; SODIUM 1mg; CALC 5mg

Israeli Hanukkah

Sit down to a commemorative dinner that gathers culinary traditions from Morocco to Middle Europe.

ISRAELI HANUKKAH MENU
(Serves 8)

Hummus with Preserved Lemon and Sun-Dried Tomatoes

Potato-Cilantro Tunisian Brik with Harissa

Winter Salad

Za'atar-Crusted Chicken Schnitzel

Riesling

Orange, Date, and Nut Cake

Coffee, tea

Continued

Hummus with Preserved Lemon and Sun-Dried Tomatoes

You can pick up jars of preserved lemon at Middle Eastern markets, or prepare our Simple Preserved Lemons (page 91). Be sure to use tahini made with toasted sesame seeds for the best flavor. You can soak and cook the chickpeas (steps 1 and 2) up to 3 days ahead and refrigerate; combine with the remaining ingredients an hour or so before serving. Serve as a dip with pita bread.

- 1 cup dried chickpeas (garbanzo beans)
- 6 cups water
- ½ cup sun-dried tomatoes, chopped
- ¼ cup tahini (sesame seed paste)
- ¼ cup fresh lemon juice
- ½ teaspoon salt
- ½ teaspoon ground cumin
- ¼ teaspoon freshly ground black pepper
- 2 garlic cloves, minced
- 2 tablespoons diced preserved lemon, divided
- 1 tablespoon chopped fresh parsley
- 1 tablespoon extravirgin olive oil

1 Sort and wash chickpeas; place in a bowl. Cover with water to 2 inches above chickpeas; cover and let stand 8 hours. Drain.

2 Combine chickpeas and 6 cups water in a large saucepan; bring to a boil. Reduce heat, and simmer 2 hours or until very tender. Drain chickpeas in a colander over a bowl; reserve ⅔ cup cooking liquid.

3 Place tomatoes in a bowl; cover with boiling water. Cover and let stand 20 minutes or until tender; drain.

4 Combine chickpeas, reserved ⅔ cup cooking liquid, tahini, and next 5 ingredients in a food processor; process until smooth.

5 Reserve 1 tablespoon tomatoes. Stir remaining tomatoes and 1 tablespoon preserved lemon into chickpea mixture. Spoon mixture onto a serving plate; spread to a ¾-inch thickness. Sprinkle with reserved 1 tablespoon tomatoes, remaining 1 tablespoon preserved lemon, and parsley. Drizzle with oil. Yield: 12 servings (serving size: ¼ cup).

CALORIES 105 (41% from fat); FAT 5g (sat 0.6g, mono 2.1g, poly 1.8g); PROTEIN 4.3g; CARB 12.5g; FIBER 3.2g; CHOL 0mg; IRON 1.5mg; SODIUM 229mg; CALC 29mg

Potato-Cilantro Tunisian Brik with Harissa

Tunisian brik is a popular savory pastry traditionally filled with tuna and hard-cooked egg. We fill this version with potato in a North African play on latkes.

- 1 cup chopped peeled baking potato
- ¼ cup finely chopped onion
- 2 tablespoons chopped fresh cilantro
- 2 teaspoons extravirgin olive oil
- ½ teaspoon hot paprika
- ¼ teaspoon salt
- ¼ teaspoon freshly ground black pepper
- 16 wonton wrappers
  Cooking spray
- ½ cup Harissa

1 Preheat oven to 375°.

2 Cook potato in boiling water 8 minutes or until tender; drain. Mash with a fork. Combine potato and next 6 ingredients. Spoon about 2 teaspoons potato mixture into center of each wonton wrapper. Moisten edges of each wrapper with water; bring 2 opposite corners together. Press edges together to seal, forming triangles. Place brik on a large baking sheet coated with cooking spray. Lightly coat tops of brik with cooking spray.

3 Bake at 375° for 12 minutes or until golden. Serve with Harissa. Yield: 8 servings (serving size: 2 brik and 1 tablespoon Harissa).

CALORIES 165 (19% from fat); FAT 3.6g (sat 0.5g, mono 2.4g, poly 0.4g); PROTEIN 5.2g; CARB 32.7g; FIBER 1.1g; CHOL 7mg; IRON 1.3mg; SODIUM 416mg; CALC 18mg

HARISSA:

- ¼ pound dried New Mexican chile peppers (about 15)
- ½ cup water
- ¼ cup extravirgin olive oil
- 1 teaspoon ground cumin
- 1 teaspoon ground coriander
- 1 teaspoon kosher salt
- 7 garlic cloves

1 Remove stems and seeds from chiles. Place chiles in a bowl; cover with boiling water. Cover and let stand 30 minutes or until tender. Drain chiles, pressing to remove excess water. Place chiles and remaining ingredients in a blender; process until smooth, scraping sides of container occasionally. Store in an airtight container in refrigerator up to 2 weeks. Yield: 1¾ cups (serving size: 1 tablespoon).

CALORIES 19 (95% from fat); FAT 2g (sat 0.3g, mono 1.5g, poly 0.2g); PROTEIN 0.1g; CARB 4.3g; FIBER 0g; CHOL 0mg; IRON 0mg; SODIUM 67mg; CALC 2mg

Winter Salad

Israeli cuisine encompasses a number of Mediterranean influences. This salad is based on a Moroccan dish with lemon juice and fennel. The addition of grapefruit, pomegranate, and avocado represents the bounty of Israel.

- ¼ cup fresh lemon juice
- ½ teaspoon salt
- ¼ teaspoon freshly ground black pepper
- 1 garlic clove, minced
- 2 tablespoons extravirgin olive oil
- 2 cups thinly sliced fennel
- ½ cup diagonally sliced celery
- 4 cups torn romaine lettuce
- 2 cups grapefruit sections (about 2 grapefruit)
- 1 cup pomegranate seeds
- ½ cup chopped peeled avocado
- 2 tablespoons pine nuts, toasted

1 Combine first 4 ingredients in a small bowl. Gradually add oil, stirring with a whisk.

② Combine 1 tablespoon juice mixture, fennel, and celery in a bowl; cover and refrigerate 2 hours. Set aside remaining juice mixture.

③ Place lettuce on a large serving platter; top with celery mixture, grapefruit, and remaining ingredients. Drizzle with remaining juice mixture. Yield: 8 servings (serving size: ½ cup lettuce, about ⅓ cup fennel mixture, ¼ cup grapefruit, 2 tablespoons pomegranate seeds, 1 tablespoon avocado, ¾ teaspoon pine nuts, and about 2¼ teaspoons dressing).

CALORIES 105 (57% from fat); FAT 6.6g (sat 0.9g, mono 3.8g, poly 1.5g); PROTEIN 1.7g; CARB 12.2g; FIBER 2.7g; CHOL 0mg; IRON 0.8mg; SODIUM 169mg; CALC 33mg

QUICK & EASY
Za'atar-Crusted Chicken Schnitzel

Schnitzel is a beloved main dish brought to Israel by Austrian immigrants, and the addition of za'atar (a popular Middle Eastern spice blend of sesame seeds mixed with powdered sumac and dried thyme) lends it Mediterranean flair. Buy za'atar at ethnic markets or specialty spice stores, or make your own using our recipe for Za'atar (page 364).

1½ cups panko (Japanese breadcrumbs)
¼ cup za'atar
1 tablespoon toasted sesame seeds
1 teaspoon salt, divided
½ teaspoon freshly ground black pepper, divided
2 large eggs
1 large egg white
8 (6-ounce) skinless, boneless chicken breast halves
2 tablespoons olive oil, divided
   Cooking spray
1 lemon, cut into 8 wedges

① Preheat oven to 400°.
② Combine panko, za'atar, sesame seeds, ½ teaspoon salt, and ¼ teaspoon pepper in a shallow dish. Place eggs and egg white in another shallow dish; lightly beat with a fork. Sprinkle chicken

with remaining ½ teaspoon salt and remaining ¼ teaspoon pepper. Dredge 4 breast halves in panko mixture, then egg mixture. Dredge again in panko mixture.

③ Heat 1 tablespoon oil in a large nonstick skillet over medium-high heat. Add 4 coated chicken breast halves to pan. Cook 3 minutes on each side or until lightly browned, turning carefully with a spatula. Place on a baking sheet coated with cooking spray. Repeat procedure with remaining chicken, panko mixture, egg mixture, and oil.

④ Bake at 400° for 10 minutes or until done. Serve with lemon wedges. Yield: 8 servings (serving size: 1 chicken breast half and 1 lemon wedge).

CALORIES 286 (30% from fat); FAT 9.5g (sat 2g, mono 4.5g, poly 1.6g); PROTEIN 38.2g; CARB 9.5g; FIBER 1.5g; CHOL 147mg; IRON 2.6mg; SODIUM 434mg; CALC 47mg

MAKE AHEAD
Baked Soufganiyot

Israelis enjoy jelly-filled donuts, called *soufganiyot* (soof-GHAHN-ee-yote), during Hanukkah. The donuts traditionally are fried, but we bake them to trim calories. We found using a plastic condiment bottle (available at supermarkets and kitchen supply stores) is the easiest way to fill the donuts with jelly. Serve this as a snack during Hanukkah. It's not part of our menu because it contains milk; kosher law prohibits serving milk and meat at the same meal. Store at room temperature up to two days.

1½ teaspoons dry yeast
¾ cup warm 1% low-fat milk, divided
6 tablespoons granulated sugar
1 tablespoon butter
1 teaspoon grated orange rind
½ teaspoon vanilla extract
½ teaspoon kosher salt
1 large egg
3¼ cups all-purpose flour, divided (about 14.5 ounces)
   Cooking spray
¾ cup strawberry jam
1 tablespoon powdered sugar

① Dissolve yeast in ½ cup warm milk in a large bowl; let stand 5 minutes or until foamy. Add remaining ¼ cup warm milk, granulated sugar, and next 5 ingredients; beat with a mixer at medium speed until blended (butter will not be completely melted). Lightly spoon flour into dry measuring cups; level with a knife. Add 2 cups flour to yeast mixture; beat at medium speed until smooth. Stir in 1 cup flour to form a soft dough. Turn dough out onto a floured surface. Knead until smooth and elastic (about 8 minutes); add enough of remaining ¼ cup flour, 1 tablespoon at a time, to prevent dough from sticking to hands (dough will feel sticky).

② Place dough in a large bowl coated with cooking spray, turning to coat top. Cover and let rise in a warm place (85°), free from drafts, 1 hour or until doubled in size. (Gently press two fingers into dough. If indentation remains, dough has risen enough.) Punch dough down; cover and let rest 5 minutes. Divide dough into 16 portions, rolling each portion into a ball.

③ Place balls on a large baking sheet lined with parchment paper. Cover and let rise 45 minutes or until doubled in size.

④ Preheat oven to 375°.

⑤ Uncover balls. Bake at 375° for 14 minutes or until browned. Remove from pan; cool completely on a wire rack.

⑥ Make a pocket in each roll using the handle of a wooden spoon, pushing to but not through opposite end. Fill with about 2 teaspoons jam, using a plastic condiment bottle or piping bag. Sprinkle rolls with powdered sugar. Yield: 8 servings (serving size: 2 rolls).

CALORIES 316 (7% from fat); FAT 2.5g (sat 1.4g, mono 0.8g, poly 0.2g); PROTEIN 6.8g; CARB 66g; FIBER 1.4g; CHOL 32mg; IRON 2.6mg; SODIUM 148mg; CALC 33mg

Orange, Date, and Nut Cake

GLAZE:
- ¼ cup sugar
- ¼ cup water
- 1½ tablespoons Grand Marnier (orange-flavored liqueur)

CAKE:
- 1¼ cups sugar, divided
- 3 large eggs
- 1 cup water
- 1 teaspoon grated orange rind
- 1 cup fresh orange juice
- ½ cup canola oil
- 2 cups dry breadcrumbs
- 1 cup ground walnuts
- ¾ cup whole pitted dates, chopped
- ¼ teaspoon salt
- 3 large egg whites
- Cooking spray

❶ To prepare glaze, combine ¼ cup sugar and ¼ cup water in a small saucepan; bring to a boil. Cook until reduced to ⅓ cup (about 1½ minutes). Remove from heat; stir in liqueur. Cool.

❷ Preheat oven to 350°.

❸ To prepare cake, combine 1 cup sugar and eggs in a large bowl; beat with a mixer at high speed until thick and pale. Beat in 1 cup water and next 3 ingredients. Stir in breadcrumbs and next 3 ingredients; let stand 3 minutes.

❹ Beat egg whites with a mixer at high speed until soft peaks form using clean, dry beaters. Gradually add remaining ¼ cup sugar, 1 tablespoon at a time, beating until stiff peaks form. Stir one-fourth of egg white mixture into batter. Gently fold remaining egg white mixture into batter. Gently spoon mixture into a 13 x 9–inch baking pan coated with cooking spray.

❺ Bake at 350° for 45 minutes or until golden brown. Remove from oven. Pierce top of cake with a wooden pick. Lightly brush glaze over warm cake. Cool on a wire rack 2 hours. Yield: 16 servings.

CALORIES 272 (40% from fat); FAT 12g (sat 1.3g, mono 5.1g, poly 4.8g); PROTEIN 4.7g; CARB 37.4g; FIBER 1.6g; CHOL 40mg; IRON 1.1mg; SODIUM 160mg; CALC 41mg

Height of the Holidays

A hearty menu by a roaring fire is a welcome offering for a snowy Wyoming Christmas.

JACKSON HOLE YULETIDE DINNER MENU

(Serves 10)

Goat Cheese-Stuffed Jalapeños with Ranchero Sauce

Whiskey-Marinated Tenderloins
or
Chorizo-Stuffed Trout

Sweet Onion Relish

Beans with Beef Jerky

Bacon-Chipotle Twice-Baked Potatoes
or
Hominy Spoonbread

Pinot noir

Cast-Iron Apple Cobbler

Cowboy Coffee Bar

Goat Cheese–Stuffed Jalapeños with Ranchero Sauce

Prepare the sauce up to two days ahead and refrigerate. Grill the jalapeños a day ahead and refrigerate. Stuff and bake them just before serving.

RANCHERO SAUCE:
- 1 teaspoon canola oil
- 2 cups vertically sliced onion
- 3 garlic cloves, minced
- ½ cup water
- 1 teaspoon cumin seeds
- ½ teaspoon salt
- ½ teaspoon Mexican oregano
- 1 (15-ounce) can fire-roasted diced tomatoes
- 1 (8-ounce) can no-salt-added tomato sauce

JALAPEÑOS:
- Cooking spray
- 10 large jalapeño peppers (about 4 inches long)
- ¼ cup (2 ounces) block-style fat-free cream cheese, softened
- ¼ teaspoon salt
- 1 (4-ounce) package goat cheese, softened
- 1 garlic clove, minced

REMAINING INGREDIENT:
- 10 corn tortillas, warmed according to package directions

❶ To prepare ranchero sauce, heat oil in a large nonstick skillet over medium-high heat. Add onion to pan; sauté

3 minutes. Add garlic; sauté 1 minute. Add ½ cup water and next 5 ingredients. Cover and simmer 20 minutes. Uncover and simmer 5 minutes.

❷ Preheat oven to 400°.

❸ Heat a grill pan over medium-high heat. Coat pan with cooking spray. Add jalapeños to pan; cook 9 minutes or until tender and blackened, turning occasionally. Cut a lengthwise slit in each jalapeño; discard stems, seeds, and membranes.

❹ Combine cream cheese and next 3 ingredients. Fill each jalapeño with about 1 tablespoon cheese mixture. Place jalapeños on a baking sheet coated with cooking spray. Bake at 400° for 7 minutes or until thoroughly heated. Serve with tortillas and ranchero sauce. Yield: 10 servings (serving size: 1 stuffed jalapeño, ⅓ cup sauce, and 1 tortilla).

CALORIES 126 (34% from fat); FAT 4.7g (sat 2.4g, mono 1.1g, poly 0.6g); PROTEIN 5.3g; CARB 17.2g; FIBER 2.7g; CHOL 10mg; IRON 0.9mg; SODIUM 283mg; CALC 75mg

Whiskey-Marinated Tenderloins

Jackson Hole residents might use venison; we use the more readily available beef. Call ahead to order tenderloins from the butcher, who can trim the steaks to your specifications. Serve with Sweet Onion Relish (at right). Depending on the size of your grill pan, you may need to cook the steaks in batches. If you live in a warmer climate, grill them outdoors.

- ¼ cup bourbon
- 2 tablespoons dark brown sugar
- 1 tablespoon Worcestershire sauce
- ½ teaspoon ground cumin
- 3 garlic cloves, minced
- 10 (4-ounce) beef tenderloin steaks, trimmed (1¼ inch thick)
- 1 teaspoon kosher salt
- ½ teaspoon freshly ground black pepper
  Cooking spray

❶ Combine first 5 ingredients in a large zip-top plastic bag. Add beef to bag; seal.

Shake to coat beef evenly with bourbon mixture. Marinate in refrigerator at least 2 hours, turning bag occasionally.

❷ Remove beef from bag; discard marinade. Sprinkle beef evenly with salt and pepper. Heat a large cast-iron grill pan over medium-high heat. Coat pan with cooking spray. Add beef to pan; cook 4 minutes on each side or until desired degree of doneness. Yield: 10 servings (serving size: 1 steak).

CALORIES 270 (38% from fat); FAT 11.4g (sat 4.2g, mono 4.3g, poly 0.4g); PROTEIN 32.1g; CARB 3.5g; FIBER 0.1g; CHOL 95mg; IRON 4.3mg; SODIUM 278mg; CALC 15mg

Chorizo-Stuffed Trout

When shopping for this dish, be sure to pick up Mexican chorizo, which is made from fresh pork (as opposed to Spanish chorizo, which uses smoked pork).

- 4 (1-ounce) slices white bread
- 1 teaspoon canola oil
- 2½ cups finely chopped mushrooms (about 8 ounces)
- ¾ cup finely chopped shallots
- 4 garlic cloves, minced
- 2½ ounces Mexican chorizo
- ⅓ cup finely chopped cilantro
- 1 teaspoon salt, divided
- ½ teaspoon freshly ground black pepper
- 10 (6-ounce) dressed whole trout
  Cooking spray
- 10 lemon wedges

❶ Position one oven rack in middle of oven and one oven rack on bottom level of oven. Preheat oven to 450°.

❷ Place bread in a food processor; pulse 10 times or until coarse crumbs measure 2 cups.

❸ Heat oil in a large nonstick skillet over medium-high heat. Add mushrooms and next 3 ingredients to pan; sauté 5 minutes or until mushrooms are tender. Remove from heat. Stir in breadcrumbs, cilantro, and ½ teaspoon salt.

❹ Sprinkle remaining ½ teaspoon salt and pepper evenly inside fish. Spoon

¼ cup mushroom mixture inside each fish. Place fish on 2 jelly-roll pans coated with cooking spray. Place pans on middle and bottom oven racks. Bake at 450° for 15 minutes. Rotate pans on racks; bake an additional 10 minutes or until fish flakes easily when tested with a fork or desired degree of doneness. Serve with lemon wedges. Yield: 10 servings (serving size: 1 whole trout and 1 lemon wedge).

CALORIES 201 (35% from fat); FAT 7.8g (sat 2.3g, mono 2.7g, poly 1.4g); PROTEIN 23.5g; CARB 8.5g; FIBER 0.8g; CHOL 105mg; IRON 1.1mg; SODIUM 459mg; CALC 44mg

MAKE AHEAD
Sweet Onion Relish

This tangy-sweet relish pairs nicely with the Whiskey-Marinated Tenderloins (at left), or serve it as an appetizer atop toasted baguette slices. You can make the relish a day or two ahead and refrigerate; bring it to room temperature before serving. Prepare an extra batch or two for holiday giving.

- 1 tablespoon butter
- 4 cups chopped sweet onion (about 2 large)
- ½ cup apple cider vinegar
- ½ cup fat-free, low-sodium chicken broth
- 1 tablespoon brown sugar
- ½ teaspoon kosher salt
- ½ teaspoon freshly ground black pepper

❶ Melt butter in a large skillet over medium heat. Add onion to pan; cook 15 minutes or until golden brown, stirring occasionally. Add vinegar and remaining ingredients; simmer 15 minutes or until liquid evaporates. Yield: 10 servings (serving size: about ⅓ cup).

CALORIES 43 (25% from fat); FAT 1.2g (sat 0.7g, mono 0.3g, poly 0g); PROTEIN 0.6g; CARB 8g; FIBER 0.6g; CHOL 3mg; IRON 0.2mg; SODIUM 130mg; CALC 15mg

Beans with Beef Jerky

Smoky jerky lends earthy flavor to this side. For spicy heat, add a diced jalapeño.

2 teaspoons olive oil
3 cups chopped onion (about 1 large)
1 cup chopped green bell pepper (about 1 medium)
5 garlic cloves, minced
1½ cups fat-free, less-sodium chicken broth
½ cup (2 ounces) pepper beef jerky, minced
2 tablespoons molasses
2 teaspoons ground cumin
3 (15-ounce) cans pinto beans, rinsed and drained

1. Heat oil in a Dutch oven over medium heat. Add onion, bell pepper, and garlic to pan; cook 5 minutes, stirring occasionally. Add broth and remaining ingredients; bring to a boil. Cover, reduce heat, and simmer 1 hour, stirring occasionally. Uncover and cook until liquid is reduced to about half (about 15 minutes). Yield: 10 servings (serving size: about ½ cup).

CALORIES 156 (13% from fat); FAT 2.2g (sat 0.3g, mono 0.8g, poly 0.4g); PROTEIN 8.9g; CARB 25.9g; FIBER 6.2g; CHOL 6mg; IRON 2.6mg; SODIUM 487mg; CALC 77mg

Bacon-Chipotle Twice-Baked Potatoes

If you don't care for the spicy chipotle chiles, omit them—these simple potatoes are good either way.

6 baking potatoes (about 3 pounds)
1¼ cups low-fat buttermilk
1¼ cups (5 ounces) shredded extrasharp Cheddar cheese, divided
⅓ cup thinly sliced green onions
2 tablespoons finely chopped chipotle chile, canned in adobo sauce
1 teaspoon salt
4 bacon slices, cooked and crumbled

1. Preheat oven to 450°.
2. Pierce potatoes with a fork. Bake potatoes at 450° for 50 minutes or until done; cool slightly. Cut each potato in half lengthwise; scoop out pulp, leaving ¼-inch-thick shells. Combine potato pulp, buttermilk, ¾ cup cheese, and remaining ingredients in a large bowl.
3. Spoon potato mixture evenly into 10 shells; discard remaining 2 shells. Sprinkle remaining ½ cup cheese evenly over potatoes. Bake at 450° for 15 minutes or until thoroughly heated. Yield 10 servings (serving size: 1 stuffed shell).

CALORIES 241 (22% from fat); FAT 6g (sat 3.1g, mono 2g, poly 0.3g); PROTEIN 9.6g; CARB 37g; FIBER 4.1g; CHOL 19mg; IRON 1.9mg; SODIUM 464mg; CALC 168mg

Hominy Spoonbread

A combination of fat-free and full-fat ingredients lightens this spoonbread's caloric load while maintaining its traditional richness.

Cooking spray
1½ cups diced onion (about 1 large)
4 garlic cloves, minced
3 (15.5-ounce) cans golden hominy, rinsed and drained
¼ cup (2 ounces) ⅓-less-fat cream cheese, softened
¼ cup (2 ounces) fat-free cream cheese, softened
3 cups 1% low-fat milk
½ cup egg substitute
2 large eggs
1 tablespoon sugar
½ teaspoon hot sauce
¼ teaspoon salt
¼ teaspoon freshly ground black pepper

1. Preheat oven to 350°.
2. Heat a large nonstick skillet over medium-high heat. Coat pan with cooking spray. Add onion and garlic to pan; sauté 5 minutes or until golden. Set aside.
3. Place hominy in a food processor; process 1 minute or until finely ground. Set aside.
4. Combine cheeses in a large bowl; beat with a mixer at medium speed until smooth. Add milk, egg substitute, and eggs; beat well. Add hominy, sugar, and remaining ingredients; stir well. Stir in onion mixture. Pour mixture into a 13 x 9–inch baking dish coated with cooking spray. Bake at 350° for 1 hour or until set. Yield: 10 servings (serving size: about ½ cup).

CALORIES 119 (26% from fat); FAT 3.5g (sat 1.7g, mono 0.7g, poly 0.4g); PROTEIN 7.4g; CARB 13.9g; FIBER 1.8g; CHOL 50mg; IRON 0.7mg; SODIUM 477mg; CALC 133mg

Cast-Iron Apple Cobbler

For a smaller gathering, halve the recipe and bake it in a 12-inch cast-iron skillet.

1½ cups all-purpose flour (about 6.75 ounces), divided
12 cups thinly sliced peeled Fuji apple (about 4 pounds)
⅔ cup sugar, divided
2 tablespoons butter, melted
2 teaspoons vanilla extract
¾ teaspoon salt, divided
½ teaspoon ground cinnamon
¼ teaspoon ground nutmeg
½ cup water
2 teaspoons baking powder
¼ cup chilled butter, cut into small pieces
1 cup low-fat buttermilk

1. Preheat oven to 375°.
2. Lightly spoon flour into dry measuring cups; level with a knife. Combine ½ cup flour, apple, ⅓ cup sugar, 2 tablespoons butter, vanilla, ½ teaspoon salt, cinnamon, and nutmeg in a large bowl, tossing well. Place apple mixture in a large cast-iron Dutch oven. Add ½ cup water.
3. Combine remaining 1 cup flour, remaining ⅓ cup sugar, remaining ¼ teaspoon salt, and baking powder in a medium bowl; cut in ¼ cup butter with a pastry blender or 2 knives until mixture resembles coarse meal. Add buttermilk, stirring until just moist. Drop batter by heaping tablespoons over apple mixture.

Bake at 375° for 1 hour or until bubbly and browned. Serve warm. Yield: 10 servings (serving size: about 3/4 cup).

CALORIES 257 (26% from fat); FAT 7.4g (sat 4.5g, mono 1.9g, poly 0.4g); PROTEIN 3.2g; CARB 46.1g; FIBER 2.3g; CHOL 19mg; IRON 1.1mg; SODIUM 349mg; CALC 96mg

QUICK & EASY
Cowboy Coffee Bar

Preparing the coffee in a large pan and allowing it to sit for 15 minutes before straining the grounds mimics the way cowboys once made coffee over an open fire. Pour the brew into a carafe and set it out with the bourbon and whipped cream for guests to help themselves.

    12 cups water
     2 cups dark roast coffee, coarsely
         ground
    1/2 cup powdered nondairy creamer
    1/3 cup cocoa powder
    1/4 cup sugar
     1 teaspoon ground cinnamon
    1/8 teaspoon ground red pepper
    10 tablespoons bourbon
    10 tablespoons fat-free commercial
         whipped cream (such as Reddi-Wip)

❶ Bring 12 cups water to a boil in a large saucepan. Add coffee grounds to pan. Remove from heat; let stand 15 minutes, or until coffee grounds sink to bottom of pan. Pour through a fine mesh strainer into a large saucepan.
❷ Combine creamer and next 4 ingredients. Add to pan, stirring with a whisk. Pour coffee mixture into a carafe. Serve with bourbon and whipped cream. Yield: 10 servings (serving size: about 3/4 cup coffee, 1 tablespoon bourbon, and 1 tablespoon whipped cream).

CALORIES 81 (10% from fat); FAT 0.9g (sat 0.4g, mono 0.3g, poly 0.1g); PROTEIN 0.7g; CARB 9g; FIBER 1.1g; CHOL 0mg; IRON 0.5mg; SODIUM 18mg; CALC 18mg

INSPIRED VEGETARIAN
Ethiopian Tastes

For enjoyable spicy and zesty fare, try this African cooking.

The landlocked African nation of Ethiopia is known for dishes that employ local herbs and spices—fenugreek, cumin, cardamom, coriander, saffron, mustard, ginger, basil—and reflect a rich history of vegetarian cooking.

Religious traditions practiced by Muslims, Jews, and Catholics have also shaped the country's cooking to accommodate many dietary restrictions. Approximately half of Ethiopians are Muslim, so there are a lot of Arabic influences in food (especially in Eastern Ethiopia), like abstaining from pork and the use of many spices and nuts to flavor dishes. Another Arab influence is one of hospitality: Ethiopia is a country where families open their doors to travelers, so homemakers keep food on hand to accommodate religious fasting as well as the dietary restrictions of holidays such as Lent or Ramadan.

But these same religious restrictions have also fostered the country's creative vegetarian fare. Since meat is not always readily available, Ethiopian cooks have learned to use a variety of seasonings and aromatics to create spice blends that coax vivid flavor from familiar vegetables and fruits. Corn, for example, is combined with mashed potatoes and coconut milk for a sweet-spicy side dish. And corn is also paired with sharp mustard greens and tomatoes in a thick side dish perfect with local *injera* bread made from the whole grain called teff.

In fact, teff, which grows abundantly in the expansive Ethiopian highlands, is the foundation of the local diet. It's used to make injera, a sour, tangy, spongy, round, crepelike bread. At meals, one large round of injera is topped with a variety of stews and dips. Diners will have several additional rounds of injera within reach and tear off pieces to use as an edible utensil to scoop up food.

An Ethiopian meal of a meatless stew, vegetable sides, salads, injera, and cheese balances flavors and textures. Injera offers sour tanginess that offsets spicy, saucy sides. Crunchy peanuts contrast with mild cucumber in a salad that is a cool reprieve from the fiery entrées, while fresh cheese with herbs is a creamy, refreshing accompaniment. With injera, some dips and salads, a stew (or pasta), and fresh cheese, you'll have an ideal Ethiopian-inspired meal. Just make sure to leave room for dessert, which typically is sweetened Ethiopian coffee—probably the country's best-known export—and a slice of fresh fruit. It's a meal that would do any Ethiopian host proud.

STAFF FAVORITE
Teff Injera Bread with Carrot-Ginger Chutney

You can use the same amount of whole wheat flour in place of the teff flour, but you'll need to add 1/2 cup water to the batter, and the characteristic tangy flavor may be subdued.

CHUTNEY:

     2 tablespoons olive oil
     4 cups (1/2-inch) cubed peeled
         carrot (4 medium)
    3/4 cup finely chopped shallots
         (about 3 large)
     4 garlic cloves, minced
     2 (3 x 1/2-inch) julienne-cut strips
         peeled fresh ginger
     2 tablespoons sugar
     2 tablespoons honey
     1 tablespoon butter
     4 cardamom pods, bruised
     2 thyme sprigs
     2 cups organic vegetable broth
         (such as Emeril's)
    1/2 teaspoon salt

Continued

INJERA:

- 2 cups teff whole-grain flour (about 9 ounces)
- 1 cup all-purpose flour (about 4.5 ounces)
- 1½ teaspoons baking soda
- 1 teaspoon salt
- 2½ cups club soda
- ¾ cup plain yogurt
- Cooking spray

❶ To prepare chutney, heat oil in a large nonstick skillet over medium-high heat. Add carrot and next 3 ingredients to pan. Reduce heat to low, and cook 10 minutes, stirring occasionally. Add sugar and next 4 ingredients; cook 1 minute, stirring constantly. Stir in broth; bring to a boil. Reduce heat, and simmer 45 minutes or until carrot is tender and liquid almost evaporates. Discard thyme and ginger. Stir in ½ teaspoon salt; cool.

❷ To prepare injera, lightly spoon flours into dry measuring cups; level with a knife. Combine flours, baking soda, and 1 teaspoon salt in a large bowl; stir with a whisk. Combine club soda and yogurt in a small bowl, stirring with a whisk until smooth. Add yogurt mixture to flour mixture; stir with a whisk until smooth.

❸ Heat a large nonstick skillet over medium-high heat. Coat pan with cooking spray. Pour about ⅓ cup batter onto pan in a spiral, starting at center; cook 20 seconds. Cover pan; cook 40 seconds or just until set. Transfer flatbread to a plate, and cover with a cloth to keep warm. Repeat procedure with cooking spray and remaining batter, wiping pan dry with a paper towel between flatbreads. Serve flatbreads with chutney. Yield: 14 servings (serving size: 1 flatbread and about 2 tablespoons chutney).

CALORIES 171 (20% from fat); FAT 3.8g (sat 1.1g, mono 1.8g, poly 0.3g); PROTEIN 4.2g; CARB 30.5g; FIBER 3.8g; CHOL 4mg; IRON 2mg; SODIUM 520mg; CALC 70mg

Red Whole Wheat Penne

Probably the main foreign influence on Ethiopian cuisine is Italian. Pasta saltata is a common dish, cooked with rich butter, olive oil, pasta, berbere spice blend, and fiery chiles. This healthful version with whole wheat pasta uses almonds to create a pestolike sauce, and the red color comes from the hot harissa condiment. And just like the traditional Genovese version of the dish, this pasta is served with potatoes.

- 1 pound peeled Yukon gold potatoes (about 2)
- ¼ cup extravirgin olive oil, divided
- ½ cup blanched whole almonds
- ¼ cup thinly sliced shallots (about 1 large)
- 2 garlic cloves, minced
- ¼ cup fresh lemon juice
- 2 tablespoons grated fresh Parmesan cheese
- 2 tablespoons harissa
- 1 teaspoon salt
- 6 cups hot cooked whole wheat penne (about 12 ounces uncooked tubeshaped pasta)
- ¼ cup chopped arugula
- ¼ cup chopped basil

❶ Place potatoes in a saucepan; cover with water. Bring to a boil. Reduce heat, and simmer 15 minutes or until tender. Drain potatoes in a colander over a bowl, reserving 1½ cups liquid. Cool potatoes slightly; cut into ½-inch pieces.

❷ Heat 1 tablespoon oil in a small skillet over low heat. Add almonds, shallots, and garlic to pan; cook 8 minutes or until almonds are golden, stirring often. Remove from heat; cool.

❸ Place almond mixture in a food processor; add remaining 3 tablespoons oil, juice, and next 3 ingredients; process 1 minute or until well blended and almost smooth. With processor on, slowly pour 1½ cups reserved cooking liquid through food chute; process 1 minute or until smooth.

❹ Combine pasta, potatoes, and almond mixture in a large bowl, tossing gently. Fold in arugula; sprinkle with basil. Yield: 4 servings (serving size: about 2 cups).

CALORIES 318 (38% from fat); FAT 13.6g (sat 1.6g, mono 8g, poly 3.3g); PROTEIN 9.3g; CARB 47.6g; FIBER 6.7g; CHOL 1mg; IRON 2.3mg; SODIUM 325mg; CALC 71mg

Lentil-Edamame Stew

Fava beans are traditional in this stew, which we updated with edamame.

- 1 cup dried lentils
- ¾ cup frozen shelled edamame (green soybeans)
- 2 tablespoons olive oil
- 1½ cups minced red onion
- 3 garlic cloves, minced
- 1 (14.5-ounce) can diced tomatoes, undrained
- 6 tablespoons fresh lemon juice
- 1 tablespoon chopped fresh parsley
- 1 tablespoon chopped fresh mint
- ½ teaspoon salt
- ½ teaspoon ground cumin
- ⅛ teaspoon ground red pepper
- ⅛ teaspoon ground cinnamon
- Dash of ground cloves

❶ Place lentils in a large saucepan; cover with water to 2 inches above lentils. Bring to a boil; cover, reduce heat, and simmer 20 minutes or until tender. Drain well, and set aside.

❷ Place edamame in a small saucepan; cover with water to 2 inches above edamame. Bring to a boil; cook 2 minutes or until edamame are tender. Remove from heat; drain well.

❸ Heat oil in a Dutch oven over medium-high heat. Add onion, garlic, and tomatoes to pan; sauté 6 minutes or until onion is translucent, stirring often. Stir in lentils, edamame, juice, and remaining ingredients. Cook 2 minutes or until thoroughly heated, stirring often. Yield: 4 servings (serving size: about 1 cup).

CALORIES 320 (23% from fat); FAT 8g (sat 1.1g, mono 5.2g, poly 1.4g); PROTEIN 18.6g; CARB 48.4g; FIBER 10.7g; CHOL 0mg; IRON 5.7mg; SODIUM 432mg; CALC 59mg

Ethiopian Essentials

Some of the common ingredients in Ethiopian cuisine are available at large supermarkets or ethnic grocery stores.

Teff flour: The word *teff* in Amharic means "lost" because the grains are the smallest of all whole grains. Due to the popularity of whole grains (and gluten-free options), teff is available in grain and flour forms from Bob's Red Mill (www.bobsredmill.com) or health food stores. Unlike other whole grains, since teff is so tiny, you need to buy the flour form for our recipe (or any requiring teff flour) because a spice grinder won't be able to break down the grains. You're more likely to find a mild-flavored, lighter-colored variety of the grain; the darker teff grains have a stronger tangy flavor. Kept in an airtight container in a cool, dry place, the flour should last for up to one year.

Coffee: Ethiopia has been called the home of coffee. The robust arabica bean grows well in the hilly forests and highlands, and the country exports premium varieties from different regions. Depending on where they're grown, coffee beans have varying notes, from fruity to sharp and acidic. The beverage, usually served after a meal, is such a part of the culture that a coffee ceremony exists to extend hospitality and friendship. Beans are roasted at the host's home, then ground by hand, and the resulting coffee is strained several times before being poured into cups from a dramatic height.

Berbere spice: Like *ras el hanout* of Morocco or *herbes de Provence* in France, this Ethiopian chile and spice blend varies with each cook. You can have a *berbere* made solely of dried spices and chiles, or wet blends including garlic, fresh chiles, and onion. Typically, the dried blend contains smoky cumin; oniony fenugreek; toasted and ground pepper—either paprika, ground red pepper, or dried chiles; pungent ground ginger; citrusy coriander; and cardamom. Since few blends are commercially available (though you can find one at www.flavorbank.com), we've added a few of the main berbere spices to some recipes.

Fresh Cheese with Herbs

A thermometer is essential for the success of this easy condiment. Stir the milk mixture gently and only occasionally up to 170°. Stirring too vigorously or frequently (more than every few minutes) will inhibit curd formation. After the juice has been added and the milk mixture reaches 170°, do not stir or the curds won't separate from the whey, and you'll have a grainy and thin mixture. This herby, tangy cheese is the cooling counterpoint to zesty sauces and incendiary chiles in Ethiopian cuisine. Store in an airtight container in the refrigerator for up to one week.

- 8 cups low-fat buttermilk
- ½ cup fresh lemon juice (about 3 large)
- 1 tablespoon chopped fresh chives
- 1½ teaspoons chopped fresh cilantro
- 1½ teaspoons chopped fresh parsley
- ¼ teaspoon salt
- ¼ teaspoon black pepper

❶ Line a large colander or sieve with 5 layers of dampened cheesecloth, allowing cheesecloth to extend over edges of colander; place colander in a large bowl.
❷ Heat buttermilk in a large, heavy saucepan over medium-high heat. Attach a candy thermometer to edge of pan so thermometer extends at least 2 inches into buttermilk. Cook until candy thermometer registers 170° (about 20 minutes), gently stirring occasionally. Stir in juice. As soon as buttermilk mixture reaches 170° again, stop stirring (whey and curds will begin separating at this point). Continue to cook, without stirring, until thermometer registers 190°. (Do not stir, or curds that have formed will break apart.) Immediately remove pan from heat. (Bottom of pan may be slightly scorched.) Using a slotted spoon, gently spoon curds into cheesecloth-lined colander; discard whey, or reserve for another use. Return colander to bowl; cover with plastic wrap. Refrigerate 8 hours or overnight.
❸ Scrape cheese into a bowl. Add chives and remaining ingredients; toss gently with a fork to combine. Yield: 10 servings (serving size: about 3 tablespoons).

CALORIES 91 (20% from fat); FAT 2g (sat 1.2g, mono 0g, poly 0g); PROTEIN 7.3g; CARB 11.5g; FIBER 0.1g; CHOL 12mg; IRON 0mg; SODIUM 275mg; CALC 202mg

Corn Mashed Potatoes

This basic side dish incorporates a quartet of Ethiopian tastes: coconut, corn, potatoes, and earthy spice.

- 2¼ cups diced peeled baking potatoes
- 1¾ cups diced peeled sweet potatoes
- 1 cup frozen whole-kernel corn, thawed and drained
- ¾ cup light coconut milk
- 1 tablespoon olive oil
- 1 tablespoon butter
- 1 teaspoon curry powder
- ½ teaspoon salt
- ¼ teaspoon ground turmeric

❶ Place potatoes in a saucepan; cover with water. Bring to a boil. Reduce heat, and simmer 10 minutes or until potatoes are almost tender. Add corn to pan; cook 5 minutes or until potatoes are tender. Drain well. Place potato mixture in a large bowl, and mash potato mixture with a potato masher.
❷ Combine coconut milk, oil, and butter in a small saucepan; bring to a boil. Stir milk mixture, curry, salt, and turmeric into potato mixture. Yield: 8 servings (serving size: ½ cup).

CALORIES 140 (29% from fat); FAT 4.5g (sat 2.3g, mono 1.7g, poly 0.4g); PROTEIN 2.6g; CARB 24.1g; FIBER 2.3g; CHOL 4mg; IRON 0.8mg; SODIUM 324mg; CALC 13mg

Cucumber-Mango Salad

The blend of sweet, fiery, and smoky qualities common to Ethiopian fare is exemplified in this simple salad. Serve with Teff Injera Bread (page 403). Since red jalapeños are sometimes hard to find, you can always double up on the milder green variety.

2 cups thinly sliced peeled English cucumber (about 1)
1½ cups finely chopped red onion
½ teaspoon salt
1 garlic clove, minced
1 teaspoon peanut oil
2 cups chopped seeded tomato (about 1 pound)
3 tablespoons chopped unsalted, dry-roasted peanuts
1 tablespoon finely chopped seeded red jalapeño pepper (about 1)
1 tablespoon finely chopped seeded green jalapeño pepper (about 1)
¼ teaspoon coriander seeds, crushed
¼ teaspoon ground cumin
⅛ teaspoon ground red pepper
Dash of ground cinnamon
Dash of ground cloves
1¾ cups diced peeled ripe mango (about 1)
1 tablespoon chopped fresh cilantro
3 tablespoons fresh lime juice

❶ Combine first 4 ingredients in a colander; toss gently to coat. Let stand at least 20 minutes.
❷ Heat oil in a large skillet over medium-high heat. Add tomato and next 8 ingredients to pan; sauté 5 minutes or until tomato is tender. Remove from heat; cool to room temperature (about 20 minutes).
❸ Combine drained cucumber mixture, tomato mixture, mango, cilantro, and juice in a medium bowl; toss gently to combine. Yield: 6 servings (serving size: ⅔ cup).

CALORIES 95 (32% from fat); FAT 3.4g (sat 0.5g, mono 1.5g, poly 1.1g); PROTEIN 2.8g; CARB 15.9g; FIBER 2.9g; CHOL 0mg; IRON 0.7mg; SODIUM 204mg; CALC 31mg

Curry-Spiced Samosas with Plum-Tomato Marmalade

Samosas have long been present throughout Eastern Africa due to the Indian trading routes. This sautéed version of the Indian snack is best served with the marmalade to temper the curry paste's heat. Plums from South America will work fine in this recipe.

MARMALADE:
2 tablespoons pine nuts
2 cups coarsely chopped plum (about 3)
2 tablespoons chopped shallots
1½ teaspoons olive oil
1½ teaspoons butter
2 tomatoes, quartered (about 1 pound)
1 garlic clove, chopped
1 tablespoon sugar
½ teaspoon harissa
1 thyme sprig
1 (2-inch) piece vanilla bean
½ teaspoon chopped fresh basil
¼ teaspoon salt

FILLING:
Cooking spray
½ cup thinly sliced yellow onion
1 pound Yukon gold potatoes, peeled and cut into ¼-inch cubes (about 3 cups)
½ cup chopped carrot
2½ teaspoons red curry paste
1 garlic clove, minced
1 cup water
⅓ cup light coconut milk
2 teaspoons fresh lime juice
¼ teaspoon salt

DOUGH:
1 teaspoon ground turmeric
½ teaspoon ground ginger
½ teaspoon ground cinnamon
1½ cups all-purpose flour (about 6.75 ounces)
½ teaspoon salt
¼ teaspoon baking soda
¼ cup hot water
6 tablespoons fresh lemon juice
7 teaspoons peanut oil, divided

❶ To prepare marmalade, place pine nuts in a large saucepan over medium heat; cook 2 minutes or until fragrant and golden brown, stirring often. Add plum and next 5 ingredients to pan; bring to a simmer, and cook 30 minutes, stirring often. Stir in sugar and next 3 ingredients. Simmer 20 minutes or until very thick. Remove from heat; cover and let stand 30 minutes. Discard thyme sprig and vanilla bean; stir in basil and ¼ teaspoon salt.
❷ To prepare filling, heat a large non-stick skillet over medium-high heat. Coat pan with cooking spray. Add onion and potato to pan; sauté 5 minutes or until onion is tender. Reduce heat to low. Add carrot, curry paste, and minced garlic to pan; cook 5 minutes, stirring occasionally. Add 1 cup water and coconut milk; bring to a simmer. Cook 15 minutes or until liquid almost evaporates and potatoes are tender. Stir in lime juice and ¼ teaspoon salt. Transfer to a bowl; cool. Partially mash potato mixture with a fork.
❸ To prepare dough, combine turmeric, ginger, and cinnamon in a small skillet over medium-high heat. Cook 30 seconds or until fragrant, stirring constantly. Transfer to a plate; cool.
❹ Lightly spoon flour into dry measuring cups; level with a knife. Place flour, toasted spices, salt, and baking soda in a food processor; pulse to combine. Combine ¼ cup hot water, lemon juice, and 1 tablespoon oil in a bowl. Pour hot water mixture through food chute with food processor on; process until dough forms a ball. Place dough in a bowl coated with cooking spray, turning to coat top. Cover and let rest 15 minutes.
❺ Divide dough into 12 equal portions. Working with 1 portion at a time (cover remaining dough to prevent drying), roll out on a lightly floured surface to a 4-inch circle. Place 2 tablespoons filling in center of dough circle. Moisten edges of dough with water; fold dough over filling to make a half moon. Crimp edges with a fork to seal. Repeat with

remaining 11 dough portions and filling to form 12 samosas.

⑥ Heat 2 teaspoons peanut oil in a large skillet over medium-high heat. Add 6 samosas to pan; cook 3 minutes or until golden brown. Turn and cook 3 minutes or until golden brown. Transfer to a paper towel–lined plate. Repeat procedure with remaining 2 teaspoons peanut oil and remaining 6 samosas. Serve with marmalade. Yield: 12 servings (serving size: 1 samosa and about 2 tablespoons marmalade).

CALORIES 161 (29% from fat); FAT 5.2g (sat 1.3g, mono 2.1g, poly 1.5g); PROTEIN 3.2g; CARB 26.3g; FIBER 2.1g; CHOL 1mg; IRON 1.3mg; SODIUM 255mg; CALC 14mg

TECHNIQUE
Tamale Time

Make your own version of this traditional Christmastime specialty and unwrap a delicious present.

Depending upon your vantage point, tamales are either an ancient Hispanic food or the newest culinary trend. The cylinders of ground corn, bound with lard, piped with savory or sweet filling, rolled in cornhusks, and steamed, have been around in one form or another for more than 5,000 years. The Aztecs prepared tamales for ceremonies and festivals, and tamales are a staple in Mexican-American communities during the holidays.

Tamales are, at heart, a handmade, home-cooked specialty. Every Christmas season, Mexican-American families gather to form convivial assembly lines to prepare dozens of tamales in several varieties to serve during the holidays, give as gifts, and freeze to enjoy in the new year. Tamales aren't difficult to prepare, and the fillings are limited only by your imagination and preference. Our recipes reflect the gamut of flavors, from the traditional Pork and Ancho Chile Tamales with Mexican Red Sauce (page 408) to newer combinations like Shrimp and Cilantro Pesto Tamales (page 408) or Goat Cheese Tamales with Olives and Raisins (page 409).

MAKE AHEAD
Basic Masa Dough

Prepare this dough up to three days ahead and refrigerate in an airtight container.

    2   cups fat-free, less-sodium chicken
        broth
    2   ancho chiles
  1½   cups fresh corn kernels (about
        3 ears)
  3¾   cups masa harina
  1½   teaspoons salt
  1½   teaspoons baking powder
    ¼   cup chilled lard

① Combine broth and chiles in a microwave-safe bowl. Microwave at HIGH 2 minutes or until chiles are tender. Combine broth mixture and corn in a blender; process until smooth.

② Lightly spoon masa into dry measuring cups; level with a knife. Combine masa, salt, and baking powder, stirring well with a whisk. Cut in lard with a pastry blender or two knives until mixture resembles coarse meal. Add broth mixture to masa mixture; stir until a soft dough forms. Cover and chill until ready to use. Yield: 26 servings (serving size: about 3 tablespoons).

CALORIES 97 (28% from fat); FAT 3g (sat 0.9g, mono 1.1g, poly 0.8g); PROTEIN 2.2g; CARB 16.2g; FIBER 2.1g; CHOL 2mg; IRON 0.8mg; SODIUM 233mg; CALC 51mg

Make Your Own Tamales

Born and raised in Texas, *Cooking Light* Associate Food Editor Julianna Grimes knows her tamales. She's often prepared batches to give as gifts during the holidays. You can follow her lead and that of many Mexican-American families, gather a few friends to set up an assembly line, and prepare several varieties. You'll need a few specific ingredients, which you can find at many large supermarkets and any Latin grocery. You also can find them, as well as tamale-making kits, at MexGrocer.com:

Masa harina: flour made from sun-dried corn kernels cooked in limewater and then ground

Lard: traditionally used to bind the dough. Made from rendered pork fat, you'll find lard sold in tubs in the grocery meat section. Our recipe for Basic Masa Dough (at left) uses just a touch of lard to bind the dough; you also could use an equal amount of vegetable shortening.

Dried corn husks: These are used to wrap the tamales for cooking and are not eaten. Other traditional wrappers include banana and plantain leaves.

Traditionally, tamales are cooked in a *tamalera,* a huge metal pot with a steamer tray that can accommodate up to six dozen tamales at a time. Test Kitchens Professional Tiffany Vickers found you can achieve similar results in the oven by placing tamales on a broiler rack with a damp towel, covering the tamales with another damp towel, and placing the rack in a broiler pan filled with a couple of cups of hot water. (Old dish towels are best as they may discolor.) This method allows you to cook two dozen tamales at a time without the need for a special pot.

Tamales are an ideal make-ahead treat. Simply cool cooked tamales to room temperature, wrap individually in heavy-duty plastic wrap, and store in zip-top plastic freezer bags. They'll keep in the freezer for up to two months. To reheat, wrap frozen tamales in a damp towel and microwave at HIGH for 2 minutes.

Pork and Ancho Chile Tamales with Mexican Red Sauce

The pork mixture can be made a day or two ahead.

- 24 dried corn husks
- ½ cup fat-free, less-sodium chicken broth
- ⅓ cup dried cherries
- 1 poblano chile pepper
- 1 cup chopped onion
- 3 tablespoons fresh lime juice
- 2 tablespoons brown sugar
- 1 teaspoon ground cumin
- ½ teaspoon salt
- 5 garlic cloves
- 1 (1-pound) pork tenderloin
- Cooking spray
- 4½ cups Basic Masa Dough (page 407)
- 2 cups hot water
- 1¼ cups Mexican hot-style tomato sauce
- Lime wedges (optional)

① Place corn husks in a large bowl; cover with water. Weight husks down with a can; soak 30 minutes. Drain husks.
② Combine broth, cherries, and poblano in a microwave-safe dish. Microwave at high 2 minutes or until cherries and poblano are tender. Combine broth mixture, onion, and next 5 ingredients in a blender; process until smooth. Reserve ½ cup broth mixture; cover and chill. Place remaining broth mixture in a zip-top plastic bag. Add pork; seal and marinate in refrigerator 1 hour, turning bag occasionally.
③ Preheat oven to 450°.
④ Remove pork from bag; discard marinade. Place pork on a broiler pan coated with cooking spray. Bake at 450° for 30 minutes or until a thermometer registers 160° (slightly pink). Let pork stand 20 minutes; shred pork with 2 forks. Toss shredded pork with reserved ½ cup broth mixture.
⑤ Working with one husk at a time, place about 3 tablespoons Basic Masa Dough in the center of husk, about ½ inch from top of husk; press dough into a 4 x 3-inch-wide rectangle. Spoon about 1 heaping tablespoon pork mixture down one side of dough. Using corn husk as your guide, fold husk over tamale, being sure to cover filling with dough; fold over 1 more time. Fold bottom end of husk under. Place tamale, seam side down, on a damp towel-lined rack of a broiler pan. Repeat procedure with remaining husks, Basic Masa Dough, and filling. Cover filled tamales with another damp kitchen towel. Pour 2 cups hot water in bottom of a broiler pan; place rack in pan. Steam tamales at 450° for 55 minutes, adding water frequently to maintain towel dampness. Let tamales stand 10 minutes. Serve with sauce. Serve with lime wedges, if desired. Yield: 12 servings (serving size: 2 tamales and about 5 teaspoons sauce).

CALORIES 283 (24% from fat); FAT 7.6g (sat 2.3g, mono 2.8g, poly 1.8g); PROTEIN 13.3g; CARB 42g; FIBER 5.3g; CHOL 28mg; IRON 3.3mg; SODIUM 720mg; CALC 122mg

Shrimp and Cilantro Pesto Tamales

The shrimp cook as the tamales steam, so they're tender and perfectly done.

- 24 dried corn husks
- 1 cup fresh cilantro leaves
- ½ cup sliced green onions
- 2 tablespoons fresh lime juice
- 1 tablespoon extravirgin olive oil
- ¼ teaspoon salt
- 3 garlic cloves
- 1 cup fresh corn kernels (about 2 ears)
- 1 pound medium shrimp, peeled, deveined, and chopped
- 4½ cups Basic Masa Dough (page 407)
- 2 cups hot water
- Lime wedges (optional)

① Place corn husks in a large bowl; cover with water. Weight husks down with a can; soak 30 minutes. Drain husks.
② Preheat oven to 450°.
③ Combine cilantro and next 5 ingredients in a food processor; process until finely chopped. Combine cilantro mixture, corn, and shrimp; tossing well to coat.
④ Working with one husk at a time, place about 3 tablespoons Basic Masa Dough in center of husk about ½ inch from top of husk; press dough into a 4 x 3-inch-wide rectangle. Spoon about 1 heaping tablespoon shrimp mixture down one side of dough. Using corn husk as your guide, fold husk over tamale, being sure to cover filling with dough; fold over 1 more time. Fold bottom end of husk under. Place tamale, seam side down, on a towel-lined rack of a broiler pan. Repeat procedure with remaining husks, Basic Masa Dough, and filling. Cover filled tamales with another damp kitchen towel. Pour 2 cups hot water in bottom of a broiler pan; place rack in pan.
⑤ Steam tamales at 450° for 55 minutes, adding water frequently to maintain towel dampness. Let tamales stand 10 minutes. Serve with lime wedges, if desired. Yield: 12 servings (serving size: 2 tamales).

CALORIES 263 (27% from fat); FAT 8g (sat 2.2g, mono 3.2g, poly 2g); PROTEIN 12.6g; CARB 36.9g; FIBER 4.7g; CHOL 61mg; IRON 2.6mg; SODIUM 574mg; CALC 128mg

Chipotle Beef Tamales

- 24 dried corn husks
- Cooking spray
- 1 cup chopped onion
- 3 garlic cloves, minced
- 1 teaspoon dried oregano
- ¼ teaspoon salt
- 1 pound ground sirloin
- 1 (7-ounce) can chipotle sauce
- 4½ cups Basic Masa Dough (page 407)
- 2 cups hot water

① Place corn husks in a large bowl; cover with water. Weight husks down with a can; soak 30 minutes. Drain husks.
② Heat a large nonstick skillet over medium-high heat. Coat pan with cooking spray. Add onion to pan; sauté

3 minutes. Add garlic; sauté 1 minute. Add oregano, salt, and beef; cook 8 minutes or until beef is browned, stirring to crumble. Add chipotle sauce; cook 2 minutes, stirring often.

③ Preheat oven to 450°.

④ Working with one husk at a time, place about 3 tablespoons Basic Masa Dough in center of husk about ½ inch from top of husk; press dough into a 4 x 3-inch-wide rectangle. Spoon about 1 heaping tablespoon beef mixture down one side of dough. Using corn husk as your guide, fold husk over tamale, being sure to cover filling with dough; fold over 1 more time. Fold bottom end of husk under. Place tamale, seam side down, on a damp towel-lined rack of a broiler pan. Repeat procedure with remaining husks, Basic Masa Dough, and filling. Cover filled tamales with another damp kitchen towel. Pour 2 cups hot water in bottom of a broiler pan; place rack in pan.

⑤ Steam tamales at 450° for 55 minutes, adding water frequently to maintain towel dampness. Let tamales stand 10 minutes. Yield: 12 servings (serving size: 2 tamales).

CALORIES 278 (25% from fat); FAT 7.7g (sat 2.5g, mono 2.8g, poly 1.7g); PROTEIN 11.9g; CARB 42.3g; FIBER 4.4g; CHOL 24mg; IRON 2.2mg; SODIUM 586mg; CALC 108mg

MAKE AHEAD • FREEZABLE

Goat Cheese Tamales with Olives and Raisins

To make these tamales vegetarian, prepare the Basic Masa Dough with vegetable shortening instead of lard.

16 dried corn husks
 1 cup golden raisins
 ½ cup sliced green onions
 ¼ cup fat-free sour cream
 ¼ teaspoon salt
 6 Spanish olives, coarsely chopped
 2 egg whites, lightly beaten
 1 (3-ounce) log goat cheese
 3 ounces block fat-free cream cheese
 2 cups Basic Masa Dough (page 407)
 2 cups hot water

① Place corn husks in a large bowl; cover with water. Weight husks down with a can; soak 30 minutes. Drain husks.

② Preheat oven to 450°.

③ Combine raisins and next 7 ingredients, stirring well to combine. Working with one husk at a time, place 3 tablespoons Basic Masa Dough in center of husk about ½ inch from top of husk; press dough into a 4 x 3-inch-wide rectangle. Spoon about 1 tablespoon cheese mixture down one side of dough. Using corn husk as your guide, fold husk over tamale, being sure to cover filling with dough; fold over 1 more time. Fold bottom end of husk under. Place tamale, seam side down, on a towel-lined rack of a broiler pan. Repeat procedure with remaining husks, Basic Masa Dough, and filling. Cover filled tamales with another damp kitchen towel. Pour 2 cups hot water in bottom of a broiler pan; place rack in pan.

④ Steam tamales at 450° for 55 minutes, adding water frequently to maintain towel dampness. Let tamales stand 10 minutes. Yield: 8 servings (serving size: 2 tamales).

CALORIES 314 (28% from fat); FAT 9.8g (sat 4.2g, mono 3.2g, poly 1.7g); PROTEIN 10g; CARB 49.6g; FIBER 5.2g; CHOL 14mg; IRON 2.2mg; SODIUM 709mg; CALC 181mg

MAKE AHEAD • FREEZABLE

Saffron Chicken and Sausage Tamales with Cilantro Cream

24 dried corn husks
FILLING:
    Cooking spray
 ½ cup diced smoked pork sausage (about 3 ounces)
 2 cups chopped onion
 4 garlic cloves, minced
 ½ cup fat-free, less-sodium chicken broth
 ¼ teaspoon saffron threads
2¼ cups shredded roasted chicken breast
4½ cups Basic Masa Dough (page 407)
 2 cups hot water

CREAM:
 ¾ cup fat-free sour cream
 ½ cup finely chopped fresh cilantro
 1 tablespoon fresh lemon juice
 ¾ teaspoon hot sauce

① Place corn husks in a large bowl; cover with water. Weight husks down with a can; soak 30 minutes. Drain husks.

② To prepare filling, heat a large nonstick skillet over medium-high heat. Coat pan with cooking spray. Add sausage to pan; sauté 2 minutes or until browned. Add onion; sauté 2 minutes. Add garlic; sauté 1 minute. Stir in broth and saffron; bring to a boil. Reduce heat and simmer 2 minutes. Stir in chicken; remove from heat.

③ Preheat oven to 450°.

④ Working with one husk at a time, place about 3 tablespoons Basic Masa Dough in center of husk about ½ inch from top of husk; press dough into a 4 x 3-inch-wide rectangle. Spoon about 1 heaping tablespoon chicken mixture down one side of dough. Using corn husk as your guide, fold husk over tamale, being sure to cover filling with dough; fold over 1 more time. Fold bottom end of husk under. Place tamale, seam side down, on a towel-lined rack of a broiler pan. Repeat procedure with remaining husks, Basic Masa Dough, and filling. Cover filled tamales with another damp kitchen towel. Pour 2 cups hot water in bottom of a broiler pan; place rack in pan.

⑤ Steam tamales at 450° for 55 minutes, adding water frequently to maintain towel dampness. Let tamales stand 10 minutes.

⑥ To prepare cream, combine sour cream and remaining ingredients, stirring well. Serve with tamales. Yield: 12 servings (serving size: 2 tamales and about 1 tablespoon cream).

CALORIES 293 (29% from fat); FAT 9.5g (sat 3g, mono 3.5g, poly 2g); PROTEIN 15.3g; CARB 38.1g; FIBER 4.5g; CHOL 32mg; IRON 2mg; SODIUM 621mg; CALC 139mg

Pan-frying

Learn to cook covetously crispy, crunchy entrées and sides.

PAN-FRIED FOODS embody some thoroughly appealing qualities—crisp coatings, browned surfaces, and tender interiors. Think of the satisfying texture and taste of breaded chicken cutlets or browned potato latkes. This technique involves less oil than deep-frying, so it's less messy and more spatter-proof. It's easy to master once you learn a few tips.

Prosciutto and Fontina–Stuffed Chicken Breasts

Finely ground cracker crumbs create a golden crust. You can save the step of making your own crumbs if your supermarket stocks cracker meal; if so, start with about 1½ cups. Serve with a crisp green salad to contrast the creamy, melted cheese filling.

  Cooking spray
1 ounce chopped prosciutto
1½ teaspoons minced, fresh rosemary
2 garlic cloves, minced
¼ cup (1 ounce) shredded fontina cheese
4 (6-ounce) skinless, boneless chicken breast halves
¼ teaspoon freshly ground black pepper
42 saltine crackers (about 1 sleeve)
½ cup all-purpose flour
2 large egg whites, lightly beaten
1 tablespoon Dijon mustard
2 tablespoons canola oil

❶ Heat a large nonstick skillet over medium-high heat. Coat pan with cooking spray. Add prosciutto to pan; sauté 2 minutes or until browned. Add rosemary and garlic to pan; sauté 1 minute. Spoon prosciutto mixture into a bowl; cool to room temperature. Stir in cheese; set aside.

❷ Cut a horizontal slit through thickest portion of each chicken breast half to form a pocket. Stuff about 2 tablespoons prosciutto mixture into each pocket; press lightly to flatten. Sprinkle chicken evenly with pepper.

❸ Place crackers in a food processor; process 2 minutes or until finely ground. Place cracker crumbs in a shallow dish. Place flour in another shallow dish. Combine egg whites and mustard in another shallow dish, stirring with a whisk.

❹ Working with one chicken breast half at a time, dredge chicken in flour, shaking off excess. Dip chicken into egg white mixture, allowing excess to drip off. Coat chicken completely with cracker crumbs. Set aside. Repeat procedure with remaining chicken, flour, egg white mixture, and cracker crumbs.

❺ Heat pan over medium-high heat. Add oil to pan, swirling to coat. Add chicken to pan; reduce heat to medium, and cook 10 minutes on each side or until browned and done. Yield: 4 servings (serving size: 1 stuffed breast half).

CALORIES 381 (33% from fat); FAT 14g (sat 3g, mono 6.4g, poly 2.9g); PROTEIN 46.6g; CARB 14.1g; FIBER 0.6g; CHOL 113mg; IRON 2.4mg; SODIUM 591mg; CALC 74mg

Pan-Fried Halibut with Rémoulade

Panko has recently become widely available, so you should find it in your grocery store.

SAUCE:
2 tablespoons reduced-fat mayonnaise
1 tablespoon chopped fresh parsley
1 teaspoon chopped capers
1 teaspoon whole-grain Dijon mustard
½ teaspoon minced fresh garlic
½ teaspoon fresh lemon juice

FISH:
¼ cup all-purpose flour
½ cup panko (Japanese breadcrumbs)
1 large egg white, lightly beaten
2 (6-ounce) skinless halibut fillets
¼ teaspoon salt
¼ teaspoon garlic powder
1 tablespoon canola oil
2 lemon wedges

❶ To prepare sauce, combine first 6 ingredients.

❷ Place flour in a shallow dish. Place panko in another shallow dish. Place egg white in another shallow dish.

❸ Sprinkle fish evenly with salt and garlic powder. Working with 1 fillet at a time, dredge fish in flour, shaking off excess. Dip fish into egg white, allowing excess to drip off. Coat fish completely with panko, pressing lightly to adhere. Set aside. Repeat procedure with remaining fish, flour, egg white, and panko.

❹ Heat a large nonstick skillet over medium-high heat. Add oil to pan, swirling to coat. Add fish to pan; reduce heat to medium, and cook 4 minutes on each side or until browned and fish flakes easily when tested with a fork or until desired degree of doneness. Serve with sauce and lemon wedges. Yield: 2 servings (serving size: 1 fillet, about 1 tablespoon sauce, and 1 lemon wedge).

CALORIES 347 (35% from fat); FAT 13.5g (sat 1.1g, mono 5.4g, poly 4.3g); PROTEIN 39.7g; CARB 15.2g; FIBER 0.7g; CHOL 54mg; IRON 1.7mg; SODIUM 691mg; CALC 86mg

All About Pan-frying

Pan-frying, Defined

This method entails cooking food in an uncovered pan in a moderate amount of fat. It's similar to sautéing but requires more fat and often lower temperatures.

Best Bets for Pan-frying

Fish fillets; thin, tender cuts such as pork chops or boneless, skinless chicken breast halves; and sturdy vegetables such as potatoes, green tomato slices, and onions are good choices. Juicy foods such as ripe tomatoes will be rendered mushy, and tougher cuts like brisket or pork shoulder won't cook long enough to become tender.

Equipment

Use a skillet or sauté pan—wide, with sloped or straight sides. Choose a heavy-bottomed pan for evenly distributed heat with no hot spots. We use nonstick skillets to help ensure the coatings stay on the food. These pans also allow you to use less oil than traditional pan-fried recipes.

Coatings

Many pan-fried dishes benefit from a coating of flour, breadcrumbs, cracker meal, or cornmeal. These coatings help to both create the desired crisp crust and insulate the food to prevent it from over-cooking. Place each of the coating ingredients in a separate shallow dish, such as a pie plate, so there's enough room for the food to lie flat.

Most of our breaded recipes use a three-step approach: The food is first dusted in flour to help all the other coatings cling, then dipped into an egg wash to help the main coating adhere, and finally dredged in the main/heavier coating of panko or breadcrumbs, for example. You'll find it helpful to designate one hand as the dry hand (for handling the food as it goes into the dry ingredients) and the other as the wet hand (for dipping food into the egg wash). If you use the same hand or both hands for every step, you'll end up with a mess of flour-egg-breadcrumbs stuck to your skin. Don't let the food sit too long after it's breaded or it may become gummy.

Breading Amounts

As you prepare these recipes, you'll notice we call for more breading ingredients than will actually stick to the food. (You'll discard whatever is left over.) Having more than you need makes it easier to coat the food. Plus, it's hard—and messy—to add additional breadcrumbs or flour once you've started the process.

Although it has become our standard recipe style to call for flour as exact weight measurements, these recipes are an exception. For a cake recipe, using a little more or less flour than specified can mean a dry, tough result or a cake that doesn't rise. For breading, though, the exact amount matters less.

Fats for Frying

Choose a neutral-flavored oil—such as canola oil, regular olive oil, or peanut oil—that can withstand moderately high heat. Flavorful oils such as extravirgin olive oil or dark sesame oil may burn or create harsh flavors in the food. Butter may also burn at high temperatures but can work over medium-high heat for shorter cook times, or over medium heat for longer periods. To prevent food from sticking, heat the pan first and then add the oil or butter.

Temperature

For the crunchiest texture, it helps to start many foods on medium-high heat to initiate browning, then reduce the heat to medium to allow it to finish cooking more slowly. Other recipes will be successful using medium-high or medium heat for the entire cook time; follow the recipe's specific instructions for best results.

Allow Some Breathing Room

Take care not to overcrowd the pan, as doing so lowers the temperature and may cause food to stick. It may also hinder evaporation as the food cooks, creating steam in the bottom of the pan and ultimately a soggy crust.

Do Not Disturb

Be aware that the side you put down in the pan first will look the best, so place the food in the pan presentation-side-down. For chicken breasts, this means the rounded side; for fish fillets, it's the rounded rib side (not the skin side). To make sure the coatings stay on the food, turn it only once as it cooks. Disturbing it too soon may cause the breading to fall off or stick to the pan.

Serve Immediately

Pan-fried offerings are best just after they are cooked, when they're hot and crunchy.

The Bottom Line

The three most important elements to remember about pan-frying:
1 Don't overcrowd the pan.
2 Cook the food shortly after applying coatings.
3 Turn the food only once as it cooks.

For the best texture, serve pan-fried foods immediately.

Weeknight Italian Menu

serves 4

Creamy polenta is a fitting complement to crisp, milanese-style pork chops. In place of chard, you can also serve sautéed broccolini or broccoli rabe.

Parmesan and Sage–Crusted Pork Chops

Creamy mascarpone polenta

Combine 2 cups water, ¾ cup 2% reduced-fat milk, and ½ teaspoon salt in a medium saucepan; bring to a boil. Gradually add ¾ cup instant dry polenta, stirring constantly with a whisk; reduce heat, and cook 2 minutes or until thick, stirring constantly. Remove from heat. Add ⅓ cup mascarpone cheese, stirring until cheese melts.

Sautéed Swiss chard

Parmesan and Sage–Crusted Pork Chops

High-quality Parmigiano-Reggiano cheese and fresh sage add robust flavors to lean pork chops. Serve with sautéed Swiss chard and creamy polenta for a quick weeknight dinner.

- 1 (1¼-ounce) slice white bread, torn into pieces
- ¼ cup (1 ounce) grated Parmigiano-Reggiano cheese
- 1 tablespoon chopped fresh sage
- ¼ teaspoon salt
- ¼ teaspoon freshly ground black pepper
- ¼ cup all-purpose flour
- 1 tablespoon prepared mustard
- 2 large egg whites, lightly beaten
- 4 (4-ounce) boneless thin-cut pork loin chops, trimmed
- 1½ tablespoons canola oil

❶ Place bread in a food processor; pulse 10 times or until coarse crumbs measure about 1 cup. Combine breadcrumbs, cheese, and next 3 ingredients in a shallow dish. Place flour in another shallow dish. Combine mustard and egg whites in another shallow dish, stirring with a whisk.
❷ Working with one pork chop at a time, dredge pork in flour, shaking off excess. Dip pork into egg white mixture, allowing excess to drip off. Coat pork completely with breadcrumb mixture. Set aside. Repeat procedure with remaining pork, flour, egg white mixture, and breadcrumb mixture.
❸ Heat a large nonstick skillet over medium heat. Add oil to pan, swirling to coat. Add pork to pan; cook 3 minutes on each side or until browned and done. Yield: 4 servings (serving size: 1 pork chop).

CALORIES 272 (45% from fat); FAT 13.6g (sat 3.7g, mono 6.6g, poly 2.2g); PROTEIN 28.8g; CARB 7g; FIBER 0.4g; CHOL 69mg; IRON 1.3mg; SODIUM 409mg; CALC 102mg

Striped Bass Meunière

Meunière refers to a classic preparation of lightly seasoned fish dredged in flour and cooked in butter. Any firm-fleshed white fish will work well in this recipe; try halibut or mahimahi. Serve with rice.

- ½ cup all-purpose flour
- ½ cup 2% reduced-fat milk
- 4 (6-ounce) striped bass fillets
- ½ teaspoon salt, divided
- ½ teaspoon freshly ground black pepper, divided
- 2 tablespoons butter, divided
- ¼ cup minced shallots
- ¼ cup white balsamic vinegar
- ¼ cup fat-free, less-sodium chicken broth
- 2 tablespoons chopped fresh parsley

❶ Place flour in a shallow dish. Place milk in another shallow dish. Sprinkle fish evenly with ¼ teaspoon salt and ¼ teaspoon pepper. Working with one fillet at a time, dredge fish in flour, shaking off excess. Dip fish into milk, allowing excess to drip off; dredge again in flour. Set aside. Repeat procedure with remaining fish, flour, and milk.
❷ Heat a large nonstick skillet over medium-high heat. Add 1 tablespoon butter to pan, swirling until butter melts. Add 2 fillets to pan; reduce heat to medium, and cook 4 minutes on each side or until golden brown and fish flakes easily when tested with a fork or until desired degree of doneness. Remove fish from pan; keep warm. Repeat procedure with remaining 1 tablespoon butter and 2 fillets.
❸ Increase heat to medium-high. Add shallots and remaining ¼ teaspoon salt to pan; sauté 1 minute. Add vinegar and broth; simmer 1 minute. Add parsley and remaining ¼ teaspoon pepper. Spoon sauce over fish. Yield: 4 servings (serving size: 1 fillet and 2 tablespoons sauce).

CALORIES 258 (35% from fat); FAT 9.9g (sat 4.6g, mono 2.7g, poly 1.6g); PROTEIN 32.1g; CARB 7.7g; FIBER 0.3g; CHOL 156mg; IRON 2mg; SODIUM 493mg; CALC 48mg

WINE NOTE: This delicate preparation with its savory butter flavors needs a light, crisp, unoaked white wine that will act as the "lemon" to balance the flavors of the fish. Patient Cottat Sauvignon Blanc 2006 Vin de Pays du Jardin de la France is a standout and a steal at $13.

Southwestern-Style Mashed Potato Cakes

These cheese, corn, and chile–stuffed cakes are a welcome accompaniment to seared steak or chicken. Or you can serve two cakes per person for a vegetarian main dish. As you form the patties, it may seem as though there is too much filling—but you'll find that the mashed potatoes mold around the filling to seal it in.

- 2 baking potatoes (about 1 pound), peeled and diced
- 2 tablespoons all-purpose flour
- ¼ teaspoon salt
- 1 garlic clove, minced
- ½ cup (2 ounces) finely diced reduced-fat extra-sharp Cheddar cheese
- ¼ cup frozen whole-kernel corn, thawed
- 1 tablespoon chopped pickled jalapeño peppers
- ½ cup all-purpose flour
- 2 large egg whites, lightly beaten
- 1 cup panko (Japanese breadcrumbs)
- 2 tablespoons butter

1 Place potatoes in a medium saucepan; cover with water. Bring to a boil. Reduce heat, and simmer 8 minutes or until just tender; drain well in a colander. Cool to room temperature.

2 Place potatoes in a large bowl. Add 2 tablespoons flour, salt, and garlic; mash with a fork or potato masher until smooth. Cover and chill 20 minutes.

3 Combine cheese, corn, and jalapeños.

4 Place ½ cup flour in a shallow dish.

5 Divide potato mixture into 16 equal portions. Flatten each portion into a 2-inch round patty. Top 1 potato patty with about 1½ tablespoons cheese mixture. Top with 1 potato patty; press gently to seal edges. Carefully dredge in ½ cup flour, brushing off excess. Place potato cake on a plate. Repeat procedure with remaining potato patties, cheese mixture, and flour to form 8 potato cakes.

6 Place egg whites in a shallow dish. Place panko in another shallow dish. Dip 1 potato cake in egg whites, allowing excess to drip off. Coat potato cake completely with panko, pressing gently to adhere. Set aside. Repeat procedure with remaining potato cakes, egg whites, and panko.

7 Heat a large nonstick skillet over medium-high heat. Add butter to pan, swirling until butter melts. Add potato cakes to pan; reduce to medium, and cook 3 minutes on each side or until browned. Yield: 8 servings (serving size: 1 cake).

CALORIES 137 (30% from fat); FAT 4.6g (sat 2.8g, mono 0.8g, poly 0.2g); PROTEIN 4.9g; CARB 19.1g; FIBER 1.2g; CHOL 13mg; IRON 0.4mg; SODIUM 197mg; CALC 56mg

Spicy Chicken Sandwiches with Cilantro-Lime Mayo

Chicken cutlets are encrusted with tortilla chip crumbs, which yield a satisfying crunch.

MAYO:
- ¼ cup reduced-fat mayonnaise
- 2 tablespoons chopped fresh cilantro
- 1 teaspoon fresh lime juice
- 1 garlic clove, minced

CHICKEN:
- ¼ cup egg substitute
- 3 tablespoons hot sauce (such as Tabasco)
- 1 teaspoon dried oregano
- ½ teaspoon salt
- 2 (6-ounce) skinless, boneless chicken breast halves
- 4½ ounces baked tortilla chips (about 6 cups)
- 2 tablespoons olive oil

REMAINING INGREDIENTS:
- 4 (2-ounce) Kaiser rolls, split
- 4 lettuce leaves
- 4 (⅛-inch-thick) red onion slices

1 To prepare mayo, combine first 4 ingredients.

2 To prepare chicken, combine egg substitute and next 3 ingredients in a large zip-top plastic bag. Cut chicken breast halves in half horizontally to form 4 cutlets. Add chicken to bag; seal. Marinate in refrigerator 2 hours or up to 8 hours, turning bag occasionally.

3 Place tortilla chips in a food processor; process 1 minute or until ground. Place ground chips in a shallow dish.

4 Working with one cutlet at a time, remove chicken from marinade, allowing excess to drip off. Coat chicken completely in chips. Set aside. Repeat procedure with remaining chicken and chips.

5 Heat a large nonstick skillet over medium heat. Add oil to pan, swirling to coat. Add chicken to pan; cook 3 minutes on each side or until browned and done. Spread mayo evenly over cut sides of rolls. Layer bottom half of each roll with 1 chicken cutlet, 1 lettuce leaf, and 1 onion slice; top with top halves of rolls. Yield: 4 servings (serving size: 1 sandwich).

CALORIES 419 (28% from fat); FAT 13.2g (sat 1.7g, mono 6.1g, poly 3.4g); PROTEIN 28.1g; CARB 46.8g; FIBER 2.6g; CHOL 49mg; IRON 3.2mg; SODIUM 759mg; CALC 101mg

Tofu Steaks with Red Pepper-Walnut Sauce

The herb-flecked marinade also serves as the base of a Mediterranean-style dipping sauce. Serve with couscous or toasted bread to enjoy all of the sauce.

 1 (14-ounce) package water-packed reduced-fat extra-firm tofu
 ¼ cup finely chopped fresh basil
 ¼ cup water
 2 tablespoons chopped fresh parsley
 2 tablespoons white wine vinegar
 1 tablespoon chopped fresh thyme
 1 tablespoon Dijon mustard
 ½ teaspoon salt
 ½ teaspoon crushed red pepper
 8 garlic cloves, minced
 ½ cup all-purpose flour
 ½ cup egg substitute
 2 cups panko (Japanese breadcrumbs)
 2 tablespoons olive oil
 3 tablespoons chopped walnuts, toasted
 1 (12-ounce) bottle roasted red peppers, drained

❶ Cut tofu crosswise into 4 slices. Place tofu slices on several layers of heavy-duty paper towels; cover with additional paper towels. Let stand 30 minutes, pressing down occasionally.

❷ Combine basil and next 8 ingredients in a large zip-top plastic bag. Add tofu to bag; seal. Marinate in refrigerator 1 hour, turning bag occasionally.

❸ Place flour in a shallow dish. Place egg substitute in another shallow dish. Place panko in another shallow dish.

❹ Remove tofu from marinade, reserving marinade. Working with one tofu piece at a time, dredge tofu in flour, shaking off excess. Dip tofu in egg substitute, allowing excess to drip off. Coat tofu completely with panko, pressing lightly to adhere. Set aside. Repeat procedure with remaining tofu, flour, egg substitute, and panko.

❺ Heat a large nonstick skillet over medium-high heat. Add oil to pan, swirling to coat. Add tofu to pan; reduce heat to medium, and cook 4 minutes on each side or until browned. Remove from pan; keep warm.

❻ Combine reserved marinade, walnuts, and bell peppers in a blender; process until smooth (about 2 minutes). Pour bell pepper mixture into pan; cook over medium-high heat 2 minutes or until thoroughly heated. Serve with tofu. Yield: 4 servings (serving size: 1 tofu piece and about ⅓ cup sauce).

CALORIES 291 (47% from fat); FAT 15.1g (sat 1.3g, mono 6.4g, poly 5.9g); PROTEIN 15.9g; CARB 23g; FIBER 3.5g; CHOL 0mg; IRON 2.8mg; SODIUM 661mg; CALC 74mg

Vegetable Pakoras

These Indian fritters get their intensity from Madras curry powder. A hit of chutney cools the palate.

 ⅔ cup all-purpose flour (about 3 ounces)
 2 teaspoons Madras curry powder
 1 teaspoon cumin seeds
 ½ teaspoon salt
 ⅓ cup water
 1 large egg, lightly beaten
 ¾ cup (¼-inch) diced peeled sweet potato
 1 cup (¼-inch) pieces cauliflower
 ½ cup finely diced onion
 2 tablespoons finely chopped fresh cilantro
 1 garlic clove, minced
 ½ jalapeño pepper, finely diced
 3 tablespoons peanut oil, divided
 6 tablespoons mango chutney

❶ Lightly spoon flour into dry measuring cups; level with a knife. Combine flour and next 3 ingredients in a large bowl, stirring with a whisk. Combine ⅓ cup water and egg in a small bowl, stirring with a whisk. Add egg mixture to flour mixture, stirring with a whisk until smooth. Cover and let stand 10 minutes.

❷ Place potato in a small saucepan; cover with water. Bring to a boil; reduce heat, and simmer 5 minutes or until just tender. Drain and cool to room temperature. Add potato and next 5 ingredients to flour mixture; stir until well combined (batter will be very thick).

❸ Heat a large nonstick skillet over medium-high heat. Add 1½ tablespoons oil to pan, swirling to coat. Drop 2 tablespoons batter into pan, and flatten slightly with back of a spoon. Repeat procedure to make 6 pakoras. Reduce heat to medium, and cook 4 minutes on each side or until browned. Remove from pan; drain on paper towels. Repeat procedure with remaining 1½ tablespoons oil and batter. Serve with chutney. Yield: 6 servings (serving size: 2 pakoras and 1 tablespoon chutney).

CALORIES 198 (30% from fat); FAT 6.5g (sat 1.2g, mono 2.9g, poly 1.9g); PROTEIN 3.5g; CARB 30.9g; FIBER 1.9g; CHOL 35mg; IRON 1.5mg; SODIUM 393mg; CALC 26mg

Breading Amounts

As you prepare these recipes, you'll notice we call for more breading ingredients than will actually stick to the food. (You'll discard whatever is left over.) Having more than you need makes it easier to coat the food. Plus, it's hard—and messy—to add additional breadcrumbs or flour once you've started the process.

Although it has become our standard recipe style to call for flour as exact weight measurements, these recipes are an exception. For a cake recipe, using a little more or less flour than specified can mean a dry, tough result or a cake that doesn't rise. For breading, though, the exact amount matters less.

Basic Potato Latkes

The reserved potato starch helps bind the potato-onion mixture, and adds heft to this traditional Hanukkah treat. Use the shredding blade of a food processor for the quickest prep and the fluffiest texture. Thoroughly combine the potato and onion, as the onion helps prevent discoloration. Serve latkes with applesauce and sour cream.

    2   pounds baking potato, peeled
    1   small onion (about 6 ounces), peeled
   ¼   cup egg substitute
    2   tablespoons all-purpose flour
    1   teaspoon kosher salt
   ¼   teaspoon freshly ground black
        pepper
   ¼   cup chopped fresh flat-leaf parsley
    3   tablespoons canola oil, divided

1 Shred potato and onion using shredding blade of a food processor. Combine shredded potato and onion in a colander over a large bowl; toss well to combine. Let stand 15 minutes, pressing occasionally with back of a spoon until most of liquid drains off. Remove colander from bowl. Carefully pour off potato liquid, reserving thick white layer of potato starch in bottom of bowl.
2 Combine egg substitute and next 3 ingredients in a small bowl, stirring with a whisk. Add egg mixture to potato starch in large bowl, stirring well with a whisk. Add potato mixture and parsley to bowl, tossing well.
3 Heat a 12-inch nonstick skillet over medium-high heat. Add 1½ tablespoons oil to pan, swirling to coat. Add potato mixture in ¼-cupfuls to pan to form 6 latkes; flatten slightly. Cook 4 minutes on each side or until golden brown. Remove latkes from pan; keep warm. Repeat procedure with remaining 1½ tablespoons oil and remaining potato mixture. Yield: 6 servings (serving size: 2 latkes).

CALORIES 208 (31% from fat); FAT 7.2g (sat 0.6g, mono 4.1g, poly 2.1g); PROTEIN 4.9g; CARB 32.3g; FIBER 2.6g; CHOL 0mg; IRON 1.8mg; SODIUM 345mg; CALC 34mg

---

ON HAND
Spiced Wine and Beyond

Enjoy the delicious versatility of the cinnamon, allspice, clove, and orange mixture known as mulling spices.

QUICK & EASY
Mulling Spice Blend

One of the advantages of making your own spice blend is that you can tailor the flavors to your taste. Because these spices are steeped in liquid and then discarded, they add no calories to recipes.

    2   teaspoons whole allspice
   ¼   teaspoon whole cloves
    1   (3-inch) cinnamon stick, broken in
        half
    1   (3 x 1-inch) strip orange rind

1 Combine all ingredients on a double layer of cheesecloth. Gather edges of cheesecloth together; tie securely. Yield: 1 sachet.

QUICK & EASY
Hot Mulled Wine

   ⅓   cup sugar
   ¼   cup bourbon
    1   (750-milliliter) bottle cabernet
        sauvignon or other dry red wine
    1   sachet Mulling Spice Blend
        (above)
        Cinnamon sticks (optional)

1 Combine first 4 ingredients in a large saucepan. Bring to a simmer; cook 20 minutes. Remove sachet; discard. Serve warm. Garnish with cinnamon sticks, if desired. Yield: 6 servings (serving size: ½ cup).

CALORIES 170 (0% from fat); FAT 0g; PROTEIN 0.1g; CARB 14.4g; FIBER 0g; CHOL 0mg; IRON 0.6mg; SODIUM 5mg; CALC 10mg

---

Commercial Blends

We found that our homemade Mulling Spice Blend made more intensely flavored recipes, but you can also use a commercial blend. The ingredients vary from brand to brand but probably include cinnamon, allspice, and cloves. Some supermarkets carry mulling spices, especially around the holidays. You can also get them online from sources such as www.penzeys.com or www.thespicehouse.com.

MAKE AHEAD
Mulled Wine Sangria
(pictured on page 270)

You'll love the heady flavors in this version of the classic Spanish drink. It's a good make-ahead option for entertaining; add the club soda just before serving.

    1   (750-milliliter) bottle merlot or
        other red wine, chilled and divided
   ⅓   cup sugar
    1   sachet Mulling Spice Blend
        (at left)
   ½   cup fresh orange juice (about
        1 large orange)
    1   (16-ounce) bag frozen unsweetened
        strawberries
   ½   orange, thinly sliced and cut
        in half
    1   (12-ounce) can club soda

1 Combine 1 cup wine, sugar, and sachet in a small saucepan; bring to a simmer. Cook 5 minutes. Remove from heat; cool. Discard sachet. Pour wine mixture into a pitcher; add remaining 3 cups wine. Chill thoroughly. Add juice and remaining ingredients. Yield: 8 servings (serving size: 1 cup).

CALORIES 143 (1% from fat); FAT 0.1g (sat 0g, mono 0g, poly 0.1g); PROTEIN 0.5g; CARB 18.7g; FIBER 1.4g; CHOL 0mg; IRON 0.9mg; SODIUM 14mg; CALC 24mg

Red Wine Pear Crisp with Spiced Streusel

(pictured on page 272)

Pears and red wine combine beautifully in this version of an old-fashioned crisp. Dried spices are easier to use in the streusel and filling than our Mulling Spice Blend sachet, and we've varied the flavor by using lemon rind instead of orange rind. Make sure that the pears are firm and not too ripe, or they will become mushy when cooked with the wine. Bosc and Anjou pears work well.

STREUSEL:

- ½ cup all-purpose flour (about 2.25 ounces)
- ½ cup regular oats
- ¼ cup packed brown sugar
- ½ teaspoon ground cinnamon
- ¼ teaspoon ground allspice
- ⅛ teaspoon salt
- 3 tablespoons butter, melted

FILLING:

- ⅔ cup cabernet sauvignon or other dry red wine
- ½ cup granulated sugar
- 1 tablespoon grated lemon rind
- ½ teaspoon ground cinnamon
- ½ teaspoon ground allspice
- 4 peeled Bosc pears, cored and thinly sliced (about 1½ pounds)
  Cooking spray

REMAINING INGREDIENTS:

- ¾ cup frozen reduced-calorie whipped topping, thawed
- ⅛ teaspoon ground cinnamon (optional)

1 Preheat oven to 350°.

2 To prepare streusel, lightly spoon flour into a dry measuring cup; level with a knife. Combine flour and next 5 ingredients in a medium bowl. Add butter, stirring with a fork until crumbly. Set aside.

3 To prepare filling, combine wine and granulated sugar in a large nonstick skillet over medium-high heat; bring to a simmer, stirring until sugar dissolves. Reduce heat to medium. Add rind and next 3 ingredients to pan, stirring to coat; simmer 15 minutes or until pears are tender.

4 Spoon pear mixture into an 8-inch square baking dish coated with cooking spray. Sprinkle streusel evenly over pear mixture. Bake at 350° for 30 minutes or until bubbly and lightly browned. Serve with whipped topping. Sprinkle with ⅛ teaspoon cinnamon, if desired. Yield: 6 servings (serving size: about ¾ cup crisp and 2 tablespoons whipped topping).

CALORIES 311 (21% from fat); FAT 7.4g (sat 4.7g, mono 1.6g, poly 0.4g); PROTEIN 2.5g; CARB 56.8g; FIBER 4.2g; CHOL 15mg; IRON 1.3mg; SODIUM 96mg; CALC 32mg

QUICK & EASY • MAKE AHEAD

Spiced Red Wine–Cranberry Sauce

Instead of cooking the cranberries with our Mulling Spice Blend, we used orange juice and ground spices to deliver more intense flavors.

- 1 cup sugar
- ¾ cup cabernet sauvignon or other dry red wine
- ¼ cup fresh orange juice
- ¾ teaspoon ground cinnamon
- ½ teaspoon ground allspice
- 1 (12-ounce) package fresh cranberries

1 Combine first 5 ingredients in a medium saucepan; bring to a boil. Reduce heat, and simmer 3 minutes or until sugar dissolves. Add cranberries; simmer 12 minutes or until cranberries pop and mixture thickens slightly. Remove from heat; cool to room temperature. Cover and chill (mixture will thicken as it chills). Yield: 10 servings (serving size: ¼ cup).

CALORIES 112 (1% from fat); FAT 0.1g (sat 0g, mono 0g, poly 0.1g); PROTEIN 0.2g; CARB 25.5g; FIBER 1.7g; CHOL 0mg; IRON 0.3mg; SODIUM 2mg; CALC 8mg

Creamy Rice Pudding with Mulling Spices

- 2 cups water
- 1 sachet Mulling Spice Blend (page 415)
- 1 cup uncooked medium-grain rice
- 2 cups 2% reduced-fat milk
- ⅓ cup sugar
- 1 teaspoon vanilla extract
- ⅛ teaspoon salt

1 Combine 2 cups water and sachet in a medium saucepan; bring to a simmer. Cook 5 minutes. Discard sachet. Stir in rice; bring to a boil. Cover, reduce heat, and simmer 15 minutes. Add milk and sugar. Cook over medium heat 15 minutes or until thick and rice is tender, stirring constantly. Remove from heat. Stir in vanilla and salt. Serve warm. Yield: 6 servings (serving size: ⅔ cup).

CALORIES 202 (8% from fat); FAT 1.8g (sat 1g, mono 0.5g, poly 0.1g); PROTEIN 4.9g; CARB 40.9g; FIBER 0.5g; CHOL 6mg; IRON 1.5mg; SODIUM 92mg; CALC 104mg

MAKE AHEAD

Dark Chocolate Mulled Wine Sauce

- 1 cup cabernet sauvignon or other dry red wine
- ½ cup sugar
- 1 sachet Mulling Spice Blend (page 415)
- ½ cup Dutch process cocoa
- ½ cup light-colored corn syrup
- 1 ounce semisweet chocolate, chopped

1 Combine first 3 ingredients in a small saucepan; bring to a simmer. Cook 5 minutes. Discard sachet. Add cocoa and corn syrup, stirring with a whisk until smooth. Simmer 2 minutes; remove from heat. Add chocolate, stirring until chocolate melts. Cool to room temperature. Yield: 2 cups (serving size: 2 tablespoons).

CALORIES 80 (12% from fat); FAT 1.1g (sat 0.6g, mono 0.4g, poly 0g); PROTEIN 0.7g; CARB 16.8g; FIBER 1g; CHOL 0mg; IRON 0.5mg; SODIUM 8mg; CALC 7mg

Sensational Citrus

Prized for sweet, tender, and juicy flesh, satsuma oranges show their potential in a wide range of dishes.

Among the sunny-colored citrus fruits that brighten produce aisles during winter, satsumas hit peak season in December. Part of the mandarin orange family, which also includes tangerines and clementines, satsumas are one of the sweetest citrus varieties, with a meltingly tender texture. Their moderately thick skin peels off readily, and with easy-to-separate segments, they make convenient and healthful out-of-hand snacks.

Typically classed with mandarin oranges in the family of *Citrus reticulata* (a name that references the netlike, or reticulated, white pith beneath the rind), satsumas are sometimes considered a separate species, *Citrus unshiu*. "To me, the satsuma belongs in its own category," says Aliza Green, chef and author of *Starting With Ingredients*. "The mandarin is the big category, which contains all the zipper-skinned [easy-peel] fruits. They probably originated in northeast India but like most citrus fruits were cultivated in China and then brought to the west." Hence the name mandarin. Satsumas, a Japanese variety named for a former province of that country, were developed in the 16th century and introduced to Florida in 1876. Today, most American satsumas are grown in California, followed by coastal Louisiana and Alabama, where mild winters allow the fruit to flourish.

"Satsumas have that perfect balance of sweet and tart, with a rounded flavor and a great acid edge," Green says. "And they just melt in your mouth."

We offer both sweet and savory recipes to showcase this winter delicacy, demonstrating how satsumas enhance beverages, baked goods, sauces, and more.

Roasted Endive with Satsuma Vinaigrette

Satsuma juice, reduced and intensified, coats and complements the pleasantly bitter roasted endive in this side dish.

- 1 cup fresh satsuma orange juice (about 4 satsumas)
- 12 large heads Belgian endive, trimmed (about 2½ pounds)
- 1½ tablespoons extravirgin olive oil, divided
- ¾ teaspoon salt, divided
- ½ teaspoon freshly ground black pepper, divided
- 4 teaspoons fresh lemon juice
- 1 tablespoon chopped fresh chives
- 2 teaspoons grated satsuma orange rind
- 1 teaspoon honey
- ¼ teaspoon ground coriander
- 3 satsuma oranges, peeled and sectioned

1 Preheat oven to 450°.
2 Place juice in a small saucepan over medium-high heat; bring to a boil. Cook until reduced to ⅓ cup (about 14 minutes). Set aside 4 teaspoons reduced juice.
3 Cut endive in half lengthwise. Arrange endive halves in a single layer on a jelly-roll pan coated with 1½ teaspoons oil. Brush endive with ¼ cup reduced juice; sprinkle with ¼ teaspoon salt and ¼ teaspoon pepper. Bake at 450° for 10 minutes or until golden.
4 Combine remaining 1 tablespoon oil, remaining ½ teaspoon salt, remaining ¼ teaspoon pepper, reserved 4 teaspoons reduced juice, lemon juice, and next 4 ingredients in a bowl; stir well with a whisk.
5 Place endive on a platter; top with satsuma sections. Drizzle with vinaigrette. Yield: 6 servings (serving size: 4 endive halves, 2 teaspoons vinaigrette, and about 2 tablespoons satsuma sections).

CALORIES 108 (32% from fat); FAT 3.8g (sat 0.5g, mono 2.5g, poly 0.5g); PROTEIN 2.3g; CARB 18.9g; FIBER 6.9g; CHOL 0mg; IRON 0.7mg; SODIUM 300mg; CALC 62mg

MAKE AHEAD • FREEZABLE
Satsuma Granita

- ¾ cup sugar
- ¾ cup water
- 1½ cups fresh satsuma orange juice (about 6 satsumas)
- 2 tablespoons grated satsuma orange rind

1 Place sugar and ¾ cup water in a medium saucepan over high heat; cook 1 minute or until sugar dissolves, stirring constantly. Stir in juice and rind; remove from heat. Pour juice mixture into a 13 x 9–inch baking pan. Cool to room temperature. Cover and freeze at least 8 hours or until firm.
2 Remove mixture from freezer; scrape entire mixture with a fork until fluffy. Yield: 6 servings (serving size: ⅔ cup).

CALORIES 125 (1% from fat); FAT 0.1g (sat 0g, mono 0g, poly 0.1g); PROTEIN 0.3g; CARB 31.7g; FIBER 0.3g; CHOL 0mg; IRON 0.1mg; SODIUM 1mg; CALC 15mg

All in the Family

Because of their relatively similar size and appearance, satsumas are often confused with tangerines and clementines, all members of the mandarin orange family. The main difference, says Aliza Green, is what lies inside the satsuma: particularly thin membranes filled to capacity with liquid, which mean less pulp and more of the prized juice.

Oven-Roasted Chicken Breasts with Satsuma Tapenade

Satsuma flavor brightens a classic olive-and-caper mixture in this dinner dish.

½ cup fresh satsuma orange juice (about 2 satsumas)
1 cup pitted kalamata olives
1 tablespoon capers
2 teaspoons grated satsuma orange rind
2 garlic cloves, minced
2 anchovy fillets, drained
2 tablespoons extravirgin olive oil, divided
6 (8-ounce) bone-in chicken breast halves, skinned
¼ teaspoon salt
¼ teaspoon freshly ground black pepper
Satsuma orange wedges (optional)
Flat-leaf parsley sprigs (optional)

1 Place juice in a small saucepan. Bring to a simmer over medium heat; cook until reduced to ¼ cup (about 3 minutes). Place juice, olives, and next 4 ingredients in a food processor. Add 1 tablespoon oil; process until well blended.
2 Preheat oven to 425°.
3 Sprinkle chicken evenly with salt and pepper. Heat 1½ teaspoons oil in a large nonstick skillet over medium heat. Add 3 breast halves to pan, meat sides down; cook 5 minutes or until lightly browned. Place chicken on a jelly-roll pan. Repeat procedure with remaining 1½ teaspoons oil and remaining 3 breast halves. Bake at 425° for 15 minutes or until chicken is done. Serve with tapenade. Garnish with satsuma wedges and parsley, if desired. Yield: 6 servings (serving size: 1 chicken breast half and 2 tablespoons tapenade).

CALORIES 279 (30% from fat); FAT 9.3g (sat 1.6g, mono 5.7g, poly 1.2g); PROTEIN 42.8g; CARB 4.1g; FIBER 0.9g; CHOL 106mg; IRON 2.2mg; SODIUM 514mg; CALC 51mg

Seared Sea Scallops with Satsuma, Parsley, and Shallot Salsa

Cook scallops in two batches if needed to prevent crowding the pan.

½ cup minced shallots (about 2 shallots)
3 tablespoons chopped fresh parsley
1 tablespoon grated satsuma orange rind
3 tablespoons fresh satsuma orange juice
2 tablespoons extravirgin olive oil
1 tablespoon white wine vinegar
½ teaspoon salt, divided
½ teaspoon freshly ground black pepper, divided
2 satsuma oranges, peeled and sectioned
Cooking spray
18 large sea scallops (about 1¾ pounds)
2 cups trimmed watercress (about 1 bunch)
Satsuma orange wedges (optional)

1 Combine first 6 ingredients in a small bowl. Add ¼ teaspoon salt and ¼ teaspoon pepper; stir well with a whisk. Add satsuma sections. Let stand 30 minutes.
2 Heat a cast-iron skillet over medium-high heat. Coat pan with cooking spray. Add scallops to pan; cook 2 minutes or until browned. Turn scallops over. Sprinkle with remaining ¼ teaspoon salt and remaining ¼ teaspoon pepper; cook 2 minutes or until done.
3 Place ⅓ cup watercress on each of 6 plates. Arrange 3 scallops on each serving; top each serving with 2 tablespoons salsa. Garnish with orange wedges, if desired. Yield: 6 servings.

CALORIES 187 (28% from fat); FAT 5.7g (sat 0.8g, mono 3.4g, poly 0.9g); PROTEIN 23.2g; CARB 10.5g; FIBER 0.9g; CHOL 44mg; IRON 0.8mg; SODIUM 418mg; CALC 67mg

Satsuma Cloud Tart

(pictured on page 271)

Satsuma rind is more subtle than orange rind, so if you want pronounced flavor, use three tablespoons in the filling.

CRUST:
1½ cups all-purpose flour (about 6.75 ounces)
1½ tablespoons sugar
⅛ teaspoon salt
6 tablespoons chilled butter, cut into small pieces
5 tablespoons ice water
FILLING:
½ cup sugar
3 large egg yolks
¼ cup all-purpose flour (about 1.1 ounces)
2 tablespoons grated satsuma orange rind
6 tablespoons satsuma orange juice
2 tablespoons lemon juice
1 tablespoon butter, melted
MERINGUE:
3 large egg whites
½ cup sugar
½ teaspoon vanilla extract

1 To prepare crust, lightly spoon 1½ cups flour into dry measuring cups; level with a knife. Combine 1½ cups flour, 1½ tablespoons sugar, and salt in a food processor; process until blended. Add 6 tablespoons butter; pulse until mixture resembles coarse meal. With processor on, slowly pour 5 tablespoons ice water through food chute; process until dough forms a ball. Shape dough into a 6-inch circle. Wrap in plastic wrap; chill 30 minutes.
2 Preheat oven to 400°.
3 Roll dough out to a 10-inch circle on a lightly floured surface. Place dough in a 9-inch round removable-bottom tart pan. Fold edges under; press dough against sides of pan. Line bottom of dough with a piece of foil; arrange pie weights or dried beans on foil. Bake at 400° for 10 minutes or until edge is lightly browned. Remove pie weights and foil; reduce oven

temperature to 375°. Bake an additional 15 minutes or until crust is golden. Cool 10 minutes.

④ To prepare filling, combine ½ cup sugar and egg yolks in a large bowl; beat with a mixer at medium-high speed 3 minutes or until thick. Lightly spoon ¼ cup flour into a dry measuring cup; level with a knife. Add ¼ cup flour and next 4 ingredients; stir just until combined. Pour mixture into cooled crust. Bake at 375° for 20 minutes or until filling is set. Remove from oven; cool completely. Reduce oven temperature to 325°.

⑤ To prepare meringue, beat egg whites with a mixer at high speed until soft peaks form using clean, dry beaters. Gradually add ½ cup sugar, 1 tablespoon at a time, beating until stiff peaks form. Gently fold in vanilla. Spread meringue evenly over filling, sealing to edge of crust. Bake at 325° for 25 minutes; cool 1 hour on a wire rack. Yield: 10 servings (serving size: 1 wedge).

CALORIES 262 (33% from fat); FAT 9.5g (sat 5.6g, mono 2.7g, poly 0.6g); PROTEIN 4.3g; CARB 40.4g; FIBER 0.8g; CHOL 83mg; IRON 1.2mg; SODIUM 106mg; CALC 17mg

MAKE AHEAD
Satsuma Cocktail

Frozen satsuma sections serve both to decorate the glass and keep the drink chilled.

- 1 satsuma orange, peeled and sectioned
- Crushed ice
- ½ cup dry gin
- ½ cup fresh satsuma orange juice (about 2 satsumas)
- 1 tablespoon Grand Marnier (orange-flavored liqueur)
- Satsuma orange rind (optional)

① Rinse satsuma sections in cold water. Drain; freeze 30 minutes or until firm.
② Place crushed ice in a martini shaker. Add gin, juice, and Grand Marnier to shaker; shake well. Strain ½ cup gin mixture into each of 2 martini glasses. Add 4 frozen satsuma sections to each glass. Garnish with rind, if desired. Yield: 2 servings.

CALORIES 213 (1% from fat); FAT 0.3g (sat 0g, mono 0.1g, poly 0.1g); PROTEIN 0.6g; CARB 14.5g; FIBER 0.9g; CHOL 0mg; IRON 0.2mg; SODIUM 2mg; CALC 26mg

MAKE AHEAD
Candied Satsuma Peel

Use as a garnish for Satsuma Cloud Tart (page 418) or Satsuma Chocolate Cupcakes (page 417), or serve along with cookies, petits fours, and chocolates when entertaining. Store sugar and peel in an airtight container between layers of wax paper for up to a month.

- 12 satsuma oranges
- 2½ cups sugar, divided
- ¾ cup water

① Peel satsumas; scrape white pith from rind. Reserve orange sections for another use. Cut rind into ¼-inch-wide strips.
② Combine 1½ cups sugar and ¾ cup water in a medium saucepan over medium heat; cook 2 minutes or until sugar dissolves, stirring constantly. Stir in rind; cover, reduce heat, and simmer 3 minutes. Remove from heat; cool completely. Drain rind mixture in a sieve into a bowl. Discard liquid. Pat rind dry with paper towels. Place remaining 1 cup sugar and rind in a medium bowl, tossing well to coat. Yield: 1½ cups (serving size: about 1 tablespoon).

CALORIES 48 (0% from fat); FAT 0g; PROTEIN 0.1g; CARB 12.4g; FIBER 0.4g; CHOL 0mg; IRON 0mg; SODIUM 0mg; CALC 6mg

HAPPY ENDINGS
Gingerly Sweet

That pungent, peppery taste makes these desserts irresistibly welcome.

MAKE AHEAD • FREEZABLE
Moravian Wafers

- 1¼ cups all-purpose flour (about 5.5 ounces)
- ¾ teaspoon ground cinnamon
- ¾ teaspoon ground ginger
- ½ teaspoon white pepper
- ½ teaspoon ground cloves
- ½ teaspoon dry mustard
- ¼ teaspoon salt
- ¼ teaspoon baking soda
- ¼ teaspoon ground allspice
- 3 tablespoons butter, softened
- 2 tablespoons brown sugar
- ⅓ cup molasses
- Cooking spray

① Preheat oven to 350°.
② Lightly spoon flour into dry measuring cups; level with a knife. Combine flour and next 8 ingredients, stirring with a whisk.
③ Place butter, sugar, and molasses in a large bowl; beat with a mixer at high speed 2 minutes. Add flour mixture; beat just until blended (dough will be crumbly). Divide dough into 4 equal portions.
④ Place each portion on a sheet of wax paper; cover with plastic wrap. Roll each portion to a ⅛-inch thickness. Freeze 10 minutes; remove plastic wrap. Cut with a 2½-inch round cutter. Place cookies on baking sheets coated with cooking spray. Bake at 350° for 6 minutes or until edges of cookies are browned. Cool 5 minutes on baking sheets. Remove from baking sheets; cool completely on wire racks. Repeat procedure with remaining dough. Yield: 3 dozen (serving size: 1 cookie).

CALORIES 37 (24% from fat); FAT 1g (sat 0.6g, mono 0.3g, poly 0.1g); PROTEIN 0.5g; CARB 6.5g; FIBER 0.2g; CHOL 3mg; IRON 0.4mg; SODIUM 27mg; CALC 9mg

Ginger Orange Swirl Cake

The orange marmalade mixture is swirled into the mild ginger-orange cake batter to form pockets of gooey, orange-ginger goodness.

Cooking spray
- 1 tablespoon all-purpose flour
- ¾ cup granulated sugar
- ⅓ cup butter, softened
- 1 tablespoon grated orange rind
- 1 tablespoon orange juice concentrate
- 2 large eggs
- 2 cups all-purpose flour (about 9 ounces)
- 1 tablespoon ground ginger
- 1 teaspoon baking powder
- 1 teaspoon baking soda
- ½ teaspoon salt
- 1 (8-ounce) carton reduced-fat sour cream
- ¼ cup packed light brown sugar
- ¼ cup crystallized ginger, minced (about 1 ounce)
- ¼ cup orange marmalade

1 Preheat oven to 325°.

2 Coat an 11 x 7-inch baking dish with cooking spray; dust with 1 tablespoon flour.

3 Place granulated sugar, butter, and orange rind in a bowl; beat with a mixer at medium speed until well blended. Add orange juice concentrate and eggs, 1 at a time, beating well after each addition.

4 Lightly spoon 2 cups flour into dry measuring cups, level with a knife. Combine 2 cups flour and next 4 ingredients, stirring with a whisk. Beating with a mixer at low speed, add flour mixture to butter mixture alternately with sour cream, beginning and ending with flour mixture. Beat just until blended.

5 Combine 3 tablespoons batter, brown sugar, crystallized ginger, and marmalade.

6 Spoon remaining batter into prepared dish. Dollop marmalade mixture over batter; swirl batters together using tip of a knife.

7 Bake at 325° for 38 minutes or until lightly browned. Cool completely on a wire rack. Yield: 12 servings.

CALORIES 254 (30% from fat); FAT 8.4g (sat 4.9g, mono 2.3g, poly 0.5g); PROTEIN 4g; CARB 41.6g; FIBER 0.7g; CHOL 56mg; IRON 1.4mg; SODIUM 271mg; CALC 63mg

Tropical Gingerbread Cake

For taller layers, use 2 (8-inch) pans and bake just until a wooden pick comes out clean. You can also swap the orange marmalade for lime or ginger preserves.

CAKE:
Cooking spray
- 2 cups all-purpose flour (about 9 ounces)
- 1 teaspoon baking powder
- ½ teaspoon ground cinnamon
- ¼ teaspoon salt
- ½ cup butter, softened
- ¾ cup granulated sugar, divided
- ½ cup packed brown sugar
- 2 tablespoons finely chopped peeled fresh ginger
- 2 large egg yolks
- 2 tablespoons molasses
- ¾ cup light coconut milk
- 4 large egg whites

FROSTING:
- 3 large egg whites
- Dash of salt
- ¾ cup granulated sugar
- ¼ cup water
- ½ teaspoon vanilla extract

REMAINING INGREDIENTS:
- ¼ cup orange marmalade
- ¼ cup flaked sweetened coconut, toasted

1 Preheat oven to 350°.

2 To prepare cake, lightly coat 2 (9-inch) cake pans with cooking spray.

3 Lightly spoon flour into dry measuring cups; level with a knife. Combine flour and next 3 ingredients, stirring well with a whisk.

4 Place butter, ½ cup granulated sugar, brown sugar, and ginger in a large bowl; beat with a mixer at medium speed until well blended (about 5 minutes). Add egg yolks, 1 at a time, beating well after each addition. Beat in molasses. Beating at low speed, add flour mixture to butter mixture alternately with coconut milk, beginning and ending with flour mixture.

5 Beat 4 egg whites with a mixer at high speed until soft peaks form using clean, dry beaters. Gradually add remaining ¼ cup granulated sugar, 1 tablespoon at a time, beating until stiff peaks form.

6 Gently stir one-fourth of egg white mixture into batter; gently fold in remaining egg white mixture. Pour batter into prepared pans.

7 Bake at 350° for 25 minutes or until a wooden pick inserted in center comes out clean. Cool in pans 10 minutes on a wire rack. Remove from pans; cool completely on wire racks.

8 To prepare frosting, place 3 egg whites and dash of salt in a large bowl; beat with a mixer at high speed until foamy using clean, dry beaters. Combine ¾ cup granulated sugar and ¼ cup water in a small saucepan; bring to boil. Cook, without stirring, until candy thermometer registers 250°. Pour hot sugar syrup in a thin stream over egg white mixture, beating at high speed until stiff peaks form. Beat in vanilla.

9 Place 1 cake layer on a plate; spread with marmalade and 1 cup frosting. Top with remaining cake layer. Spread remaining frosting over top and sides of cake; sprinkle top of cake with toasted coconut. Store cake loosely covered in refrigerator. Yield: 16 servings (serving size: 1 slice).

CALORIES 253 (26% from fat); FAT 7.4g (sat 4.5g, mono 1.8g, poly 0.4g); PROTEIN 3.7g; CARB 44g; FIBER 0.6g; CHOL 41mg; IRON 1.1mg; SODIUM 117mg; CALC 39mg

Double Ginger Cupcakes with Lemon Glaze

Start with 3 teaspoons lemon juice when making the glaze, and add the extra teaspoon if you want a thinner consistency.

CUPCAKES:

    1   cup all-purpose flour (about
        4.5 ounces)
    1   teaspoon ground ginger
    ½   teaspoon baking powder
    ½   teaspoon baking soda
    ½   teaspoon ground cinnamon
    ¼   teaspoon salt
    ⅛   teaspoon ground allspice
    ½   cup low-fat buttermilk
    ¼   cup molasses
    ½   cup packed light brown sugar
    3   tablespoons butter, softened
    1½ teaspoons grated peeled fresh
        ginger
    1   large egg, lightly beaten

GLAZE:

    ⅔   cup powdered sugar, sifted
    3   to 4 teaspoons fresh lemon juice

① Preheat oven to 350°.

② To prepare cupcakes, line 12 muffin cups with foil liners.

③ Lightly spoon flour into a dry measuring cup; level with a knife. Combine flour and next 6 ingredients, stirring with a whisk.

④ Combine buttermilk and molasses, stirring with a whisk.

⑤ Place brown sugar and butter in a large bowl; beat with a mixer at medium speed until well blended (about 1 minute). Add fresh ginger and egg; beat well. Beating at low speed, add flour mixture to butter mixture alternately with molasses mixture, beginning and ending with flour mixture. Beat just until blended. Divide batter evenly among muffin cups.

⑥ Bake at 350° for 20 minutes or until a wooden pick inserted in center comes out clean. Cool 10 minutes in pan on a wire rack. Remove from pan.

⑦ To prepare glaze, combine powdered sugar and juice, stirring until smooth. Drizzle over warm cupcakes. Yield: 1 dozen (serving size: 1 cupcake).

CALORIES 155 (20% from fat); FAT 3.5g (sat 2g, mono 0.9g, poly 0.2g); PROTEIN 2g; CARB 29.6g; FIBER 0.4g; CHOL 26mg; IRON 1.2mg; SODIUM 145mg; CALC 51mg

Hot and Spicy Gingerbread Loaf

        Cooking spray
    1   tablespoon flour
    2½ cups all-purpose flour (about
        11.25 ounces)
    2   teaspoons baking powder
    2   teaspoons ground ginger
    1   teaspoon ground cinnamon
    ½   teaspoon salt
    ½   teaspoon baking soda
    ½   teaspoon black pepper
    ¼   teaspoon dry mustard
    ¼   teaspoon ground cloves
    ½   cup water
    ½   cup plain low-fat yogurt
    ¼   cup molasses
    1½ teaspoons instant coffee granules
    ¼   cup butter, softened
    ¾   cup packed brown sugar
    2   teaspoons grated peeled fresh ginger
    1   large egg
    1   large egg white

① Preheat oven to 350°.

② Coat a 9 x 5-inch loaf pan with cooking spray; dust with 1 tablespoon flour.

③ Lightly spoon 2½ cups flour into dry measuring cups; level with a knife. Combine 2½ cups flour and next 8 ingredients, stirring with a whisk.

④ Combine ½ cup water and next 3 ingredients in a bowl, stirring with a whisk.

⑤ Place butter in a large bowl; beat with a mixer at medium speed until smooth (about 1 minute). Add sugar and fresh ginger; beat at medium speed until well combined (about 1 minute). Add egg and egg white, 1 at a time, beating well after each addition. Beating at low speed, add

flour mixture to butter mixture alternately with yogurt mixture, beginning and ending with flour mixture.

⑥ Spoon batter into prepared pan. Bake at 350° for 40 minutes or until a wooden pick inserted in center comes out clean. Cool 10 minutes in pan on a wire rack. Remove from pan; cool completely on wire rack. Yield: 14 servings (serving size: 1 slice).

CALORIES 186 (19% from fat); FAT 4g (sat 2.3g, mono 1g, poly 0.3g); PROTEIN 3.6g; CARB 34.3g; FIBER 0.8g; CHOL 24mg; IRON 1.9mg; SODIUM 222mg; CALC 87mg

New England Gingerbread Cake with Maple-Apple Butter Spread

CAKE:

        Cooking spray
    1   tablespoon all-purpose flour
    2¼ cups all-purpose flour
    1½ teaspoons ground cinnamon
    1   teaspoon baking powder
    1   teaspoon baking soda
    1   tablespoon ground ginger
    ½   teaspoon salt
    ¼   teaspoon ground allspice
    ¾   cup low-fat buttermilk
    ½   cup apple butter
    ½   cup maple syrup
    6   tablespoons butter, softened
    1   cup sugar
    1   tablespoon minced peeled fresh
        ginger
    2   large eggs

SPREAD:

    ¼   cup butter, softened
    3   tablespoons maple syrup
    1   tablespoon apple butter

① Preheat oven to 350°.

② To prepare cake, coat a 12-cup tube pan with cooking spray; dust with 1 tablespoon flour.

③ Lightly spoon 2¼ cups flour into dry measuring cups; level with a knife. Combine 2¼ cups flour and next 6 ingredients, stirring with a whisk.

Continued

④ Combine buttermilk, ½ cup apple butter, and ½ cup syrup, stirring with a whisk.

⑤ Place butter in a large bowl; beat with a mixer at medium speed until smooth (about 1 minute). Add sugar and fresh ginger; beat at medium speed until well combined (about 1 minute). Add eggs, 1 at a time, beating well after each addition. Beating at low speed, add flour mixture to sugar mixture alternately with buttermilk mixture, beginning and ending with flour mixture.

⑥ Spoon batter into prepared pan. Bake at 350° for 45 minutes or until a wooden pick inserted in center comes out clean. Cool 10 minutes in pan on a wire rack. Remove from pan; cool completely on wire rack.

⑦ To prepare spread, place ¼ cup butter, 3 tablespoons syrup, and 1 tablespoon apple butter in a bowl; beat with a mixer at high speed 2 minutes or until well blended. Yield: 16 servings (serving size: 1 slice and 1 teaspoon spread).

CALORIES 247 (29% from fat); FAT 8g (sat 4.8g, mono 2.1g, poly 0.5g); PROTEIN 3.2g; CARB 41.1g; FIBER 0.8g; CHOL 46mg; IRON 1.3mg; SODIUM 208mg; CALC 52mg

LIGHTEN UP
Sweet Solution

We tinker with a Pennsylvania travel agent's adored cake to preserve its delectably sticky character with fewer calories.

While sailing in the Caribbean with her husband and friends four years ago, Carolyn Worrall, a travel agent from Pittsburgh, enjoyed Sticky Date and Coconut Cake—a puddinglike cake infused with dates and smothered in a brown sugar and coconut topping. Worrall and her husband, Tom, have since enjoyed this treat at home, though they knew its high-calorie and fat content didn't fit their healthful lifestyle goals. Worrall hoped a lightened version would enable them to enjoy the cake more often.

serving size: 1 wedge		
	before	after
CALORIES PER SERVING	342	268
FAT	11.7g	6.5g
PERCENT OF TOTAL CALORIES	31%	22%

STAFF FAVORITE • MAKE AHEAD
Sticky Date and Coconut Cake

Be sure to coat the bottom and sides of the springform pan with cooking spray so this puddinglike cake doesn't stick.

CAKE:
- 1 cup chopped pitted dates
- 1 cup water
- 3 tablespoons butter
- 1 teaspoon baking soda
- Dash of salt
- 1½ cups all-purpose flour (about 6.75 ounces)
- 1 teaspoon baking powder
- ½ teaspoon salt
- 1 cup granulated sugar
- 1 teaspoon vanilla extract
- 1 large egg, lightly beaten
- Cooking spray

TOPPING:
- ⅔ cup packed light brown sugar
- ½ cup flaked sweetened coconut
- 2½ tablespoons butter
- 2 teaspoons fat-free milk

① Preheat oven to 350°.
② To prepare cake, combine first 5 ingredients in a small saucepan; bring to a boil, stirring occasionally. Remove from heat; let stand 10 minutes or until dates are tender.
③ Lightly spoon flour into dry measuring cups; level with a knife. Combine flour, baking powder, and ½ teaspoon salt in a large bowl. Stir in date mixture, granulated sugar, vanilla, and egg until well combined. Pour batter into a 9-inch springform pan coated with cooking spray. Bake at 350° for 20 minutes.
④ To prepare topping, combine brown sugar and remaining ingredients in a

small saucepan; bring to a boil. Reduce heat, and simmer 1 minute. Pour brown sugar mixture over cake; bake at 350° for an additional 13 minutes or until a wooden pick inserted in center comes out clean. Cool in pan 5 minutes on a wire rack. Run a knife around outside edge. Cool completely on wire rack. Yield: 12 servings (serving size: 1 wedge).

CALORIES 268 (22% from fat); FAT 6.5g (sat 4.2g, mono 1.6g, poly 0.3g); PROTEIN 2.5g; CARB 51.6g; FIBER 1.7g; CHOL 31mg; IRON 1.2mg; SODIUM 313mg; CALC 46mg

READER RECIPES
Winter Warm-up

A personal chef from San Diego creates a spicy, sweet chicken soup inspired by her love of Thai cuisine.

Tina Washburn, a personal chef from San Diego, prefers a bowl of soup—not cereal—for breakfast. "A healthful soup has warm appeal, particularly during flu season," she says. "I heat it up for breakfast to boost my metabolism and keep me going the rest of the day." With this in mind, she created Coconut-Curry Chicken Soup.

Washburn suffered from allergies and other ailments as a child, which inspired her to learn about proper nutrition and diet. "Growing up in Portland, Oregon, I was raised to be physically fit, but my allergies were a concern," she says. "As an adult, I am more aware of food choices and plan meals around dishes that help me feel my best."

Combining an array of spices with a selection of nutritious vegetables, Coconut-Curry Chicken Soup is a hit with Washburn's triathlon clients as part of a healthful meal plan to sustain them during their vigorous workouts.

Coconut-Curry Chicken Soup

"The aroma, color, texture, and combination of flavors make Thai cuisine so delicious. The coconut milk gives the soup a creamy, smooth texture. Cook and shred the chicken before you start the recipe. This soup also reheats well."

—Tina Washburn, San Diego

- 4 cups water
- 3 cups fresh spinach leaves
- ½ pound snow peas, trimmed and cut in half crosswise
- 1 (5¾-ounce) package pad Thai noodles (wide rice stick noodles)
- 1 tablespoon canola oil
- ¼ cup thinly sliced shallots
- 2 teaspoons red curry paste
- 1½ teaspoons curry powder
- ½ teaspoon ground turmeric
- ½ teaspoon ground coriander
- 2 garlic cloves, minced
- 6 cups fat-free, less-sodium chicken broth
- 1 (13.5-ounce) can light coconut milk
- 2½ cups shredded cooked chicken breast (about 1 pound)
- ½ cup chopped green onions
- 2 tablespoons sugar
- 2 tablespoons fish sauce
- ½ cup chopped fresh cilantro
- 4 small hot red chiles, seeded and chopped or ¼ teaspoon crushed red pepper
- 7 lime wedges

❶ Bring 4 cups water to a boil in a large saucepan. Add spinach and peas to pan; cook 30 seconds. Remove vegetables from pan with a slotted spoon; place in a large bowl. Add noodles to pan; cook 3 minutes. Drain; add noodles to spinach mixture.
❷ Heat oil in pan over medium-high heat. Add shallots and next 5 ingredients to pan; sauté 1 minute, stirring constantly. Add broth to pan; bring to a boil. Add milk to pan; reduce heat, and simmer 5 minutes. Add chicken and next

3 ingredients to pan; cook 2 minutes. Pour chicken mixture over noodle mixture in bowl. Stir in cilantro and chiles. Serve with lime wedges. Yield: 7 servings (serving size: 2 cups soup and 1 lime wedge).

CALORIES 315 (22% from fat); FAT 7.8g (sat 3.7g, mono 2.2g, poly 1.3g); PROTEIN 29.3g; CARB 30.9g; FIBER 2.4g; CHOL 62mg; IRON 3.2mg; SODIUM 841mg; CALC 78mg

---

QUICK & EASY • MAKE AHEAD
Quick Black Bean Soup

"Black beans are a huge family favorite. My 19-month-old son eats the beans right out of the can, so I always set some aside for him."

—Vicki Miller, Powell, Ohio

- ¼ cup chopped red onion
- ¼ cup water
- 1 teaspoon ground cumin
- ¼ teaspoon ground red pepper
- 1 (14-ounce) can fat-free, less-sodium chicken broth
- 2 (15-ounce) cans black beans, rinsed, drained, and divided
- 2 teaspoons fresh lime juice
- Cooking spray
- ¼ cup (2 ounces) finely chopped reduced-fat ham (such as Hormel)

❶ Combine first 5 ingredients in a large saucepan. Add 1½ cans beans; bring to a boil. Reduce heat, and simmer 15 minutes. Place bean mixture in a blender. Remove center piece of blender lid (to allow steam to escape); secure blender lid on blender. Place a clean towel over opening in blender lid (to avoid splatters). Blend until smooth. Return soup to pan. Add remaining ½ can of beans to pan; cook 2 minutes. Stir in juice; set aside.
❷ Heat a small nonstick skillet over medium heat. Coat pan with cooking spray. Add ham to pan; cook 2 minutes or until lightly browned. Ladle 1 cup soup into each of 4 bowls; top each serving with 1 tablespoon ham. Yield: 4 servings.

CALORIES 105 (8% from fat); FAT 0.9g (sat 0.3g, mono 0.4g, poly 0.1g); PROTEIN 9g; CARB 20.3g; FIBER 7.1g; CHOL 8mg; IRON 2.4mg; SODIUM 713mg; CALC 56mg

---

QUICK & EASY
Pasta Puttanesca

"This spicy dish has bold flavors using items from my pantry. I learned this trick for pitting olives: Place the back of your hand on the flat side of the knife against the olive, then give it a hard press to lightly smash it."

—Nicolette Manescalchi, Minneapolis

- 1 teaspoon extravirgin olive oil
- 3 canned anchovy fillets, chopped (about ¼ ounce)
- 4 garlic cloves, minced
- ½ teaspoon crushed red pepper
- ⅓ cup vodka
- ½ cup chopped pitted kalamata olives
- 1 (28-ounce) can crushed tomatoes, undrained
- 1 (14.5-ounce) can diced tomatoes, drained
- ¼ cup (1 ounce) grated fresh Parmesan cheese
- ½ teaspoon kosher salt
- ½ teaspoon freshly ground black pepper
- 8 cups hot cooked linguine (about 1 pound uncooked pasta)
- ⅓ cup (1½ ounces) grated fresh Parmesan cheese

❶ Heat oil in a large saucepan over medium heat. Add anchovies to pan; cook 1 minute. Add garlic; cook 30 seconds. Add red pepper; cook 30 seconds. Add vodka; cook 1 minute. Add olives and tomatoes; bring to a boil. Reduce heat, and stir in ¼ cup cheese, salt, and pepper.
❷ Combine tomato mixture and pasta in a large bowl; toss well. Arrange about 1¼ cups pasta mixture on each of 8 plates; sprinkle each serving with 2 teaspoons cheese. Yield: 8 servings.

CALORIES 322 (16% from fat); FAT 5.9g (sat 1.4g, mono 2.7g, poly 0.6g); PROTEIN 11.9g; CARB 52.1g; FIBER 3.8g; CHOL 6mg; IRON 2.4mg; SODIUM 595mg; CALC 116mg

Mocha Crunch Cream Torte

"This coffee-flavored dessert is a special treat after dinner, especially with a cup of coffee. I added almond brickle chips to provide a little crunch between the cake layers and on top of the cake. During the holidays, I serve this cake because the combination of chocolate and mocha flavors is a nice change from traditional desserts."

—Katie Wolosick, Atlanta

CAKE:

Cooking spray
½ cup unsweetened cocoa
½ cup boiling water
1 ounce bittersweet chocolate, chopped
¾ cup granulated sugar
½ cup packed dark brown sugar
¼ cup butter, softened
½ cup egg substitute
2 cups cake flour (about 8 ounces)
1½ teaspoons baking soda
¼ teaspoon salt
1 cup nonfat buttermilk
⅓ cup fat-free sour cream
2 teaspoons vanilla extract

FROSTING:

2 cups powdered sugar
6 tablespoons (3 ounces) ⅓-less-fat cream cheese, softened
1 tablespoon instant coffee granules
1 tablespoon butter, softened
⅔ cup almond brickle chips, divided (such as Heath)

❶ Preheat oven to 350°.
❷ To prepare cake, coat 2 (9-inch) round cake pans with cooking spray; line bottoms with wax paper. Coat wax paper with cooking spray.
❸ Combine cocoa, ½ cup boiling water, and chocolate in a small bowl, stirring until smooth. Cool.
❹ Place granulated sugar, brown sugar, and ¼ cup butter in a large bowl; beat with a mixer at medium speed until well blended (about 2 minutes). Add egg

substitute; beat well. Lightly spoon flour into dry measuring cups; level with a knife. Combine flour, soda, and salt, stirring with a whisk. Combine buttermilk, sour cream, and vanilla. Add flour mixture and buttermilk mixture alternately to sugar mixture, beginning and ending with flour mixture; mix after each addition. Add cocoa mixture; beat well.
❺ Pour batter into prepared pans; sharply tap pans once on counter to remove air bubbles. Bake at 350° for 25 minutes or until a wooden pick inserted in center comes out clean. Cool in pans 10 minutes on a wire rack; remove from pans. Cool completely on wire rack.
❻ To prepare frosting, combine powdered sugar and next 3 ingredients in a bowl. Beat with a mixer at medium speed until smooth.
❼ Place one cake layer on a plate. Spread half of frosting on top; sprinkle with ⅓ cup brickle chips. Top with remaining cake layer. Spread remaining frosting over top layer; sprinkle with remaining brickle chips. Yield: 16 servings (serving size: 1 wedge).

CALORIES 315 (28% from fat); FAT 9.6g (sat 4.7g, mono 2.5g, poly 0.7g); PROTEIN 4.4g; CARB 54.8g; FIBER 1.3g; CHOL 17mg; IRON 2mg; SODIUM 294mg; CALC 48mg

Taste of Germany Menu

serves 6

Caraway seeds add savory anise flavor to the cabbage.

Bavarian Potato-Cucumber Salad

Cabbage sauté with carraway

Heat 1½ tablespoons olive oil in a Dutch oven over medium-high heat. Add 2 cups sliced onion to pan; sauté 3 minutes. Add 6 cups thinly sliced green cabbage; sauté 8 minutes or until cabbage wilts. Stir in ½ cup fat-free, less-sodium chicken broth; ½ teaspoon salt; ½ teaspoon freshly ground black pepper; and ½ teaspoon caraway seeds. Cover, reduce heat, and simmer 5 minutes or until tender.

Grilled turkey bratwurst

Bavarian Potato-Cucumber Salad

"I prefer the flavor of an olive oil vinaigrette rather than a mayonnaise dressing for potato salad. Cucumber slices add a fresh taste, too."

—Michael Ruggeberg, Aspen, Colorado

2 cups thinly sliced peeled seedless cucumber
1 teaspoon kosher salt
1 pound small Yukon gold potatoes, quartered
1 pound small red potatoes, quartered
3 tablespoons less-sodium beef broth
2 tablespoons dry white wine
3 tablespoons Champagne vinegar or white wine vinegar
2 tablespoons extravirgin olive oil
¾ teaspoon freshly ground black pepper
½ teaspoon Dijon mustard
Dash of ground nutmeg
¼ cup minced green onions
2 tablespoons minced fresh flat-leaf parsley
2 tablespoons minced fresh chives

❶ Combine cucumber and salt in a large bowl. Let stand 30 minutes.
❷ Cook potatoes in boiling water 20 minutes or until just tender; drain. Combine potatoes, broth, and wine in a bowl. Let stand 5 minutes. Add potato mixture to cucumber mixture.
❸ Combine vinegar and next 4 ingredients in a small bowl; stir with a whisk until blended. Add vinegar mixture, onions, parsley, and chives to potato mixture; toss well. Yield: 6 servings (serving size: 1 cup).

CALORIES 177 (23% from fat); FAT 4.5g (sat 0.6g, mono 3.3g, poly 0.5g); PROTEIN 4.1g; CARB 28.7g; FIBER 2.3g; CHOL 0mg; IRON 1.6mg; SODIUM 348mg; CALC 7mg

20 Minute Dishes

From steak to salmon, chicken to pork, here are simple, fresh, and easy meals you can make superfast.

Salmon with Sweet Chile Sauce

Serve with soba noodles tossed with low-sodium soy sauce and dark sesame oil. Add steamed broccoli florets on the side.

- 4 (6-ounce) salmon fillets, skinned
- 1 teaspoon ground coriander
- ½ teaspoon salt
- Cooking spray
- 2 tablespoons honey
- 1 tablespoon fresh lime juice
- 2 teaspoons low-sodium soy sauce
- ½ to 1 teaspoon Sriracha (hot chile sauce, such as Huy Fong)
- 4 teaspoons thinly sliced green onions

1 Sprinkle fish evenly with coriander and salt. Heat a large nonstick skillet over medium-high heat. Coat pan with cooking spray. Add fish to pan; cook 4 minutes on each side or until fish flakes easily when tested with a fork or until desired degree of doneness.

2 Combine honey and next 3 ingredients; drizzle over fish. Sprinkle with green onions. Yield: 4 servings (serving size: 1 fillet and 1 tablespoon sauce).

CALORIES 262 (36% from fat); FAT 10.5g (sat 2.5g, mono 4.6g, poly 2.5g); PROTEIN 31.2g; CARB 9.5g; FIBER 0.1g; CHOL 80mg; IRON 0.6; SODIUM 460mg; CALC 18mg

Cornmeal Crusted Tilapia Sandwiches with Lime Butter

Plate with grapes and coleslaw for a weeknight supper.

- 3 tablespoons yellow cornmeal
- 1 tablespoon chili powder
- 1 teaspoon ground cumin
- ½ teaspoon salt
- ½ teaspoon ground coriander
- ⅛ teaspoon ground red pepper
- 4 (6-ounce) tilapia fillets
- Cooking spray
- 2 tablespoons butter, softened
- 1 teaspoon grated lime rind
- ½ teaspoon fresh lime juice
- 4 (1½-ounce) French bread rolls, toasted
- 4 (¼-inch-thick) slices tomato
- 1 cup shredded red leaf lettuce

1 Preheat broiler.

2 Combine first 6 ingredients in a shallow dish. Coat both sides of fish with cooking spray. Dredge fish in cornmeal mixture.

3 Place fish on a broiler pan coated with cooking spray. Broil 10 minutes or until fish flakes easily when tested with a fork or until desired degree of doneness.

4 Combine butter, rind, and juice in a small bowl; stir well.

5 Spread 1½ teaspoons butter mixture over cut side of each of 4 roll tops. Place 1 fillet, 1 tomato slice, and ¼ cup lettuce on each of 4 roll bottoms. Place top halves of rolls on sandwiches. Yield: 4 servings (serving size: 1 sandwich).

CALORIES 345 (26% from fat); FAT 9.9g (sat 4.6g, mono 2.3g, poly 1g); PROTEIN 39.2g; CARB 26.3g; FIBER 2g; CHOL 100mg; IRON 2.6mg; SODIUM 708mg; CALC 68mg

Chicken with Dried Plums and Sage

Add quick-cooking whole wheat couscous and steamed green beans to accompany this dish.

- 4 (6-ounce) skinless, boneless chicken breast halves
- 2 tablespoons chopped fresh sage, divided
- ½ teaspoon salt
- ¼ teaspoon black pepper, divided
- 4 teaspoons olive oil, divided
- 2 cups thinly sliced onion (about 1 large)
- ½ cup dry white wine
- ½ cup fat-free, less-sodium chicken broth
- 12 pitted dried plums, halved (about ½ cup)
- 1½ teaspoons balsamic vinegar

1 Place each chicken breast half between 2 sheets of heavy-duty plastic wrap; pound to ½-inch thickness using a meat mallet or small heavy skillet. Sprinkle chicken with 1 tablespoon sage, salt, and ⅛ teaspoon pepper.

2 Heat 2 teaspoons oil in a large nonstick skillet over medium heat. Add chicken to pan; cook 3 minutes on each side or until done. Remove chicken from pan; keep warm. Heat remaining 2 teaspoons oil in pan. Add onion to pan; cook 3 minutes or until tender. Stir in wine and broth; bring to a boil. Add remaining 1 tablespoon sage and plums to pan; cook 4 minutes or until mixture thickens. Stir in remaining ⅛ teaspoon pepper and vinegar. Yield: 4 servings (serving size: 1 chicken breast half and about ½ cup sauce).

CALORIES 301 (26% from fat); FAT 8.7g (sat 1.8g, mono 4.7g, poly 1.4g); PROTEIN 35.4g; CARB 19.8g; FIBER 2.3g; CHOL 94mg; IRON 1.6mg; SODIUM 438mg; CALC 49mg

Cumin-Pepper Flank Steak with Horseradish Chimichurri

Chimichurri is a thick herb sauce for meat popular in Argentina. Round out the meal with whole wheat flour tortillas and sautéed sliced carrots.

CHIMICHURRI:

- ⅔ cup fresh flat-leaf parsley leaves
- 2 tablespoons chopped green onions
- 2 tablespoons water
- 1 tablespoon prepared horseradish
- 1 tablespoon red wine vinegar
- 1 teaspoon olive oil
- ⅛ teaspoon salt
- 1 garlic clove, peeled

STEAK:

- 1 (1-pound) flank steak, trimmed
- 1 teaspoon ground cumin
- ½ teaspoon salt
- ¼ teaspoon black pepper
- 1 teaspoon olive oil

❶ To prepare chimichurri, combine first 8 ingredients in a food processor; process until smooth.

❷ To prepare steak, rub steak with cumin, ½ teaspoon salt, and pepper. Heat 1 teaspoon oil in a large nonstick skillet over medium-high heat. Add steak to pan; cook 3 minutes on each side or until desired degree of doneness. Remove from pan; let stand 5 minutes. Cut steak diagonally across grain into thin slices. Serve with chimichurri. Yield: 4 servings (serving size: 3 ounces steak and 1½ tablespoons chimichurri).

CALORIES 201 (47% from fat); FAT 10.4g (sat 3.6g, mono 4.9g, poly 0.6g); PROTEIN 23.8g; CARB 1.8g; FIBER 0.8g; CHOL 43mg; IRON 2.4mg; SODIUM 433mg; CALC 40mg

Warm Spinach Salad with Pork and Pears

This main dish salad is a meal in itself; a loaf of whole-grain or sesame seed bread completes the dinner. Savory blue cheese balances the sweetness of the pears and raisins; choose a premium variety such as Maytag for more intensity.

- Cooking spray
- 1 (1-pound) pork tenderloin, trimmed and cut crosswise into 12 slices
- ½ teaspoon salt, divided
- ¼ teaspoon black pepper, divided
- 3 tablespoons water
- 3 tablespoons sherry vinegar or red wine vinegar
- 1 tablespoon extravirgin olive oil
- 2 cups thinly sliced Anjou or Bartlett pears (about 2)
- ¼ cup golden raisins
- 1 (5-ounce) package baby spinach
- 2 tablespoons crumbled blue cheese

❶ Heat a large nonstick skillet over medium-high heat. Coat pan with cooking spray. Sprinkle pork evenly with ¼ teaspoon salt and ⅛ teaspoon pepper. Add pork to pan; cook 4 minutes on each side or until browned.

❷ Combine remaining ¼ teaspoon salt, remaining ⅛ teaspoon pepper, 3 tablespoons water, vinegar, and oil in a small bowl, stirring with a whisk.

❸ Combine pear, raisins, and spinach in a large bowl; toss well. Arrange 2 cups spinach mixture on each of 4 plates; drizzle evenly with vinegar mixture. Top each serving with 3 pork slices and 1½ teaspoons cheese. Yield: 4 servings.

CALORIES 296 (30% from fat); FAT 10.1g (sat 3g, mono 4.8g, poly 0.8g); PROTEIN 25.5g; CARB 27.4g; FIBER 4.5g; CHOL 68mg; IRON 2.8mg; SODIUM 471mg; CALC 117mg

Falafel Pitas

Fresh crudités, such as bell pepper wedges, radishes, and carrot or celery sticks, are a crunchy side.

- ¼ cup plain dry breadcrumbs
- ¼ cup fresh flat-leaf parsley leaves
- 2 tablespoons chopped green onions
- 1 teaspoon ground cumin
- ½ teaspoon ground coriander
- ¼ teaspoon salt
- 1 (15-ounce) can chickpeas (garbanzo beans), drained and rinsed
- 1 large egg
- 1 garlic clove, chopped
- Pinch of ground red pepper
- Cooking spray
- ¼ cup shredded seeded peeled cucumber
- ¼ cup plain 2% low-fat Greek yogurt (such as Fage Total Classic)
- 1 teaspoon fresh lemon juice
- ⅛ teaspoon salt
- 2 (6-inch) whole wheat pitas, halved
- 4 Bibb lettuce leaves
- 8 (¼-inch-thick) tomato slices

❶ Combine first 10 ingredients in a food processor. Process until finely chopped. Divide mixture into 4 equal portions; shape each portion into a ½-inch-thick patty. Heat a large nonstick skillet over medium-high heat. Coat pan with cooking spray. Add patties to pan; cook 3 minutes on each side or until lightly browned.

❷ Combine cucumber and next 3 ingredients in a small bowl. Line each pita half with 1 lettuce leaf and 2 tomato slices. Place 1 patty in each pita half. Top each patty with about 1 tablespoon cucumber mixture. Yield: 4 servings (serving size: 1 stuffed pita half).

CALORIES 220 (18% from fat); FAT 4.4g (sat 0.8g, mono 1.2g, poly 1.5g); PROTEIN 10.4g; CARB 37.2g; FIBER 6.7g; CHOL 54mg; IRON 3.2mg; SODIUM 617mg; CALC 83mg

Prime-time Poultry

From casual weeknight suppers to elegant entertaining, these versatile menus can be on the table in less than 45 minutes.

Quick Poultry Menu 1
serves 4

Chicken and Basil Calzones

Spinach and orange salad

Combine 6 cups prewashed, bagged baby spinach, 1½ cups fresh orange sections, ⅓ cup slivered red onion, and 3 tablespoons toasted coarsely chopped pecans in a large bowl. Combine 2 tablespoons fresh lemon juice, 2 tablespoons honey, 1½ tablespoon extravirgin olive oil, 2 teaspoons Dijon mustard, ⅛ teaspoon salt, and ⅛ teaspoon freshly ground black pepper, stirring with a whisk. Drizzle vinaigrette over salad; toss gently to coat.

Biscotti

Game Plan

1 While oven preheats:
 • Prepare filling for calzones.
2 Assemble calzones.
3 While calzones bake:
 • Prepare ingredients for salad.
4 Toss salad.

Quick Tip

If you're pressed for time, use canned Mandarin oranges packed in light syrup in place of the fresh orange sections in the salad. Be sure to drain them first.

Chicken and Basil Calzones

Ground chicken breast is a lean alternative to ground beef. Substitute ground sirloin if you prefer.
Total time: 40 minutes

 Cooking spray
 2 garlic cloves, minced
 1 pound ground chicken breast
 ¾ cup prepared pizza sauce
 ¼ teaspoon crushed red pepper
 ¼ cup chopped fresh basil
 1 (13.8-ounce) can refrigerated pizza crust dough
 ½ cup (2 ounces) shredded part-skim mozzarella cheese

1 Preheat oven to 425°.
2 Heat a large nonstick skillet over medium-high heat. Coat pan with cooking spray. Add garlic and chicken to pan; sauté 5 minutes or until chicken is no longer pink, stirring to crumble. Stir in pizza sauce and pepper. Reduce heat, and simmer 5 minutes, stirring occasionally. Remove from heat; stir in basil. Let stand 10 minutes.
3 Unroll dough onto a baking sheet coated with cooking spray; cut dough into quarters. Pat each portion into an 8 x 6–inch rectangle. Divide chicken mixture evenly among rectangles; top each serving with 2 tablespoons cheese. Working with one rectangle at a time, fold dough in half over filling, pinching edges to seal. Repeat procedure with remaining rectangles. Bake at 425° for 12 minutes or until golden. Yield: 4 servings (serving size: 1 calzone).

CALORIES 459 (14% from fat); FAT 7.1g (sat 1.8g, mono 1g, poly 0.4g); PROTEIN 39.1g; CARB 56.4g; FIBER 3g; CHOL 74mg; IRON 3.7mg; SODIUM 919mg; CALC 111mg

Quick Poultry Menu 2
serves 4

Farfalle with Cauliflower and Turkey Sausage

Sautéed broccoli rabe

Cook 1 pound trimmed broccoli rabe and 2 teaspoons salt 2 minutes in 6 quarts boiling water. Drain and plunge broccoli rabe into ice water. Drain and squeeze out excess moisture. Pat broccoli rabe dry with paper towels. Heat 1 tablespoon extravirgin olive oil in a large skillet over medium heat. Add 2 thinly sliced garlic cloves to pan; cook 4 minutes or until tender and fragrant, stirring occasionally. Increase heat to medium-high; add broccoli rabe, ¼ teaspoon salt, and ¼ teaspoon crushed red pepper to pan. Cook 1 minute or until thoroughly heated, tossing occasionally.

Garlic bread

Game Plan

1 While oven preheats:
 • Bring water to a boil for pasta and broccoli rabe.
 • Prepare cauliflower and sausage mixture.
2 While sausage mixture cooks:
 • Cook pasta.
 • Heat bread.
 • Cook broccoli rabe.
3 Toss pasta.

Continued

Farfalle with Cauliflower and Turkey Sausage

Pierce sausages with the tip of a sharp knife before combining them with the cauliflower to ensure they retain their uniform shape as they cook. Garnish with chopped parsley.

Total time: 42 minutes

- 2 (4-ounce) links mild Italian turkey sausage
- 3 cups small cauliflower florets
- 2 tablespoons extravirgin olive oil, divided
- ½ teaspoon salt, divided
- 5 garlic cloves, sliced
- 4 cups uncooked farfalle (bow tie pasta)
- ½ teaspoon crushed red pepper
- ½ cup (2 ounces) grated fresh pecorino Romano cheese
- ¼ teaspoon freshly ground black pepper

1 Preheat oven to 450°.

2 Pierce sausage several times with a knife. Combine sausage, cauliflower, and 1 tablespoon oil in a small roasting pan; toss. Sprinkle evenly with ¼ teaspoon salt. Bake at 450° for 15 minutes. Add garlic to pan; toss. Bake an additional 5 minutes or until sausage is done. Let stand 5 minutes. Cut sausage crosswise into ¼-inch-thick slices.

3 Cook pasta according to package directions, omitting salt and fat; drain, reserving 2 tablespoons cooking liquid. Combine pasta, reserved cooking liquid, remaining 1 tablespoon oil, remaining ¼ teaspoon salt, and red pepper in a large bowl; toss. Add cauliflower mixture, sausage, and cheese; toss gently to combine. Sprinkle with black pepper. Yield: 4 servings (serving size: about 1½ cups).

CALORIES 436 (35% from fat); FAT 16.8g (sat 5.2g, mono 7.5g, poly 1.8g); PROTEIN 24.1g; CARB 48.2g; FIBER 3.8g; CHOL 62mg; IRON 2.4mg; SODIUM 830mg; CALC 185mg

Quick Poultry Menu 3
serves 6

Roast Peppered Cornish Hens

Roasted green beans with bacon and almonds

Slice 2 applewood-smoked bacon slices crosswise into ½-inch slices. Combine bacon, 1½ pounds trimmed fresh green beans, ¾ teaspoon salt, and ½ teaspoon freshly ground black pepper; toss. Place bean mixture in a small roasting pan in a single layer; bake at 400° for 20 minutes or until beans are crisp-tender and bacon is done, turning once. Sprinkle with 3 tablespoons toasted sliced almonds.

Couscous

Game Plan

1 While oven preheats:
- Prepare glaze for hens.
- Slice bacon.
- Trim green beans.

2 While hens roast:
- Prepare couscous.
- Put beans in oven with hens during last 10 minutes.

Roast Peppered Cornish Hens

Tangy mustard, sweet jelly, and spicy black pepper combine for a simple glaze for these game hens. If you are planning a small holiday gathering, this recipe is a nice alternative to a large turkey.

Total time: 40 minutes

- 3 (1¼-pound) Cornish hens, trimmed and skinned
  Cooking spray
- ¼ cup spicy brown mustard
- ¼ cup currant jelly
- 1½ teaspoons fresh coarsely ground black pepper
- ½ teaspoon salt

1 Preheat oven to 400°.

2 Remove and discard giblets and necks from hens. Split hens in half lengthwise. Place hen halves, breast sides up, in a shallow roasting pan coated with cooking spray.

3 Combine mustard and jelly. Brush mustard mixture evenly over hens; sprinkle evenly with pepper and salt. Bake at 400° for 30 minutes or until a thermometer inserted in meaty part of thigh registers 165°. Let stand 10 minutes. Yield: 6 servings (serving size: ½ hen).

CALORIES 209 (21% from fat); FAT 4.9g (sat 1.1g, mono 1.4g, poly 1.1g); PROTEIN 27.5g; CARB 11.3g; FIBER 1.4g; CHOL 122mg; IRON 1.1mg; SODIUM 428mg; CALC 29mg

Quick Poultry Menu 4
serves 4

Stuffed Turkey Rolls with Cranberry Glaze

Buttered Brussels sprouts

Combine 1 pound trimmed, quartered Brussels sprouts, 2 teaspoons olive oil, ½ teaspoon salt, and ¼ teaspoon freshly ground black pepper in a small roasting pan; toss. Bake at 425° for 20 minutes or until lightly browned. Melt 2 tablespoons butter in a small saucepan over medium heat; cook 3 minutes or until lightly browned, shaking pan occasionally. Drizzle butter over Brussels sprouts; toss.

Rice pilaf

Game Plan

1 While oven preheats:
- Assemble turkey rolls.

2 While turkey cooks:
- Prepare Brussels sprouts.
- Prepare rice.
- Prepare cranberry glaze.

Stuffed Turkey Rolls with Cranberry Glaze

Impressive enough to serve guests, but simple enough for a weeknight supper, this recipe combines the classic turkey and stuffing in a single dish.
Total time: 30 minutes

- 1 tablespoon butter
- ½ cup diced peeled apple
- ⅓ cup chopped onion
- 1 garlic clove, minced
- ¾ cup fat-free, less-sodium chicken broth
- ¼ teaspoon dried sage
- 1 cup dry seasoned stuffing mix
- 8 (2-ounce) turkey cutlets
- ¼ teaspoon salt
- ¼ teaspoon freshly ground black pepper
- Cooking spray
- 1 cup canned whole cranberry sauce
- ¼ cup orange juice

❶ Heat butter in a large nonstick skillet over medium-high heat. Add apple, onion, and garlic to pan; sauté 5 minutes or until tender, stirring occasionally. Add broth and sage to pan; bring to a boil. Stir in stuffing mix. Remove from heat; set aside.
❷ Place each turkey cutlet between 2 sheets of heavy duty plastic wrap; pound to ¼-inch thickness using a meat mallet or small heavy skillet. Spread ¼ cup stuffing mixture over each cutlet, leaving a ½-inch border around edges. Roll up jelly-roll fashion; secure each roll with wooden picks. Sprinkle rolls evenly with salt and pepper.
❸ Heat a large nonstick skillet over medium-high heat. Coat pan with cooking spray. Add rolls to pan; sauté 3 minutes on each side or until browned. Cover, reduce heat, and cook 10 minutes or until done.
❹ Combine cranberry sauce and juice in a saucepan; bring to a simmer, stirring constantly. Serve with rolls. Yield: 4 servings (serving size: 2 turkey rolls and about ¼ cup sauce).

CALORIES 385 (11% from fat); FAT 4.5g (sat 2.1g, mono 1.2g, poly 0.4g); PROTEIN 32.1g; CARB 54.1g; FIBER 2.7g; CHOL 53mg; IRON 2.8mg; SODIUM 827mg; CALC 41mg

Hot Chocolate Fudge Cakes

High-quality dark chocolate makes this warm dessert shine like the stars on a clear December night. Specifically, a dusky 71 percent cocoa bar lends just the right amount of bitterness to amplify the sultry espresso notes in the cakes. Between their decidedly rich flavor and sumptuous textures that combine a crusty top with a molten interior, these cakes earned our Test Kitchens' highest rating. They'd be a grand finale at a special dinner party, and a luscious way to ring out the year with one more taste.

Hot Chocolate Fudge Cakes

These hot-from-the-oven desserts are ideal for a holiday celebration and can mostly be made in advance—up to two days before the 'do.

- ¾ cup all-purpose flour (about 3.4 ounces)
- ⅔ cup unsweetened cocoa
- 5 teaspoons instant espresso powder
- 1½ teaspoons baking powder
- ¼ teaspoon salt
- ¼ cup unsalted butter, softened
- ⅔ cup granulated sugar
- ⅔ cup packed brown sugar
- 1 cup egg substitute
- 1½ teaspoons vanilla extract
- 1 (2.6-ounce) bar dark (71 percent cocoa) chocolate (such as Valrhona Le Noir Amer), finely chopped
- 2 tablespoons powdered sugar

❶ Lightly spoon flour into dry measuring cups; level with a knife. Sift together flour and next 4 ingredients.
❷ Place butter in a large bowl; beat with a mixer at medium speed 1 minute. Add granulated and brown sugars, beating until well blended (about 5 minutes). Add egg substitute and vanilla, beating until well blended. Fold flour mixture into sugar mixture; fold in chocolate. Divide batter evenly among 10 (4-ounce) ramekins; arrange ramekins on a jelly-roll pan. Cover and refrigerate 4 hours or up to 2 days.
❸ Preheat oven to 350°.
❹ Let ramekins stand at room temperature 10 minutes. Uncover and bake at 350° for 21 minutes or until cakes are puffy and slightly crusty on top. Sprinkle evenly with powdered sugar; serve immediately. Yield: 10 servings (serving size: 1 cake).

CALORIES 260 (28% from fat); FAT 8.2g (sat 4.5g, mono 2.3g, poly 0.2g); PROTEIN 5.1g; CARB 43.9g; FIBER 1.8g; CHOL 12mg; IRON 2.3mg; SODIUM 189mg; CALC 63mg

Menu Index

A topical guide to all the menus that appear in Cooking Light Annual Recipes 2009. *See page 449 for the General Recipe Index.*

Dinner Tonight

Tilapia Menu 1 *(page 49)*
serves 4
Grilled Tilapia with Smoked Paprika and Parmesan Polenta
Sautéed broccoli rabe
Orange sections

Tilapia Menu 2 *(page 49)*
serves 4
Roasted Tilapia with Tomatoes and Olives
Arugula salad
Brown rice

Tilapia Menu 3 *(page 50)*
serves 4
Pan-Seared Tilapia with Citrus Vinaigrette
Couscous pilaf
Roasted Brussels sprouts

Casserole Menu 1 *(page 81)*
serves 8
Ham and Cheese Macaroni Bake with Peas
Spinach salad with poppy seed dressing
Orange sections over low-fat vanilla ice cream

Casserole Menu 2 *(page 82)*
serves 4
Parmesan Chicken and Rice Casserole
Green beans with warm bacon dressing
Broiled plum tomatoes

Casserole Menu 3 *(page 82)*
serves 6
Shrimp and Grits Casserole
Cherry tomato salad
Lima beans

Gnocchi Menu 1 *(page 120)*
serves 4
Gnocchi with Broccoli Rabe, Caramelized Garlic, and Parmesan
Sliced oranges and red onions
Angel food cake with raspberries

Gnocchi Menu 2 *(page 120)*
serves 4
Gnocchi with Asparagus and Pancetta
Mesclun salad with Dijon dressing
Low-fat coffee Ice cream with chocolate sauce

Gnocchi Menu 3 *(page 121)*
serves 4
Gnocchi with Chicken Sausage, Bell Pepper, and Fennel
Creamy tomato soup
Chocolate sorbet

Sandwiches Menu 1 *(page 144)*
serves 4
Patty Melts with Grilled Onions
Baked potato chips
Lime-infused fruit

Sandwiches Menu 2 *(page 145)*
serves 4
Grilled Portobello, Bell Pepper, and Goat Cheese Sandwiches
Cornichons
Grilled tomato wedges with herbs

Sandwiches Menu 3 *(page 146)*
serves 4
Classic Italian Panini with Prosciutto and Fresh Mozzarella
Arugula salad
Raspberries with mascarpone

Global Rice Menu 1 *(page 185)*
serves 4
Greek Lamb Pilaf
Green beans with pine nuts and feta
Warm pita bread

Global Rice Menu 2 *(page 185)*
serves 4
Ham Risotto with Sugar Snap Peas
Romaine salad with Parmesan-balsamic dressing
Biscotti

Global Rice Menu 3 *(page 186)*
serves 4
Speedy Paella
Grilled tomato toast
Chilled cava

Kebab Menu 1 *(page 216)*
serves 4
Hoisin-Glazed Beef Kebabs
Grilled baby bok choy
Rice stick noodles

Kebab Menu 2 *(page 217)*
serves 4
Italian Herbed Shrimp Kebabs
Tomato bruschetta
Grilled asparagus

Kebab Menu 3 *(page 217)*
serves 4
Pork Saté with Peanut-Mirin Sauce
Gingered sugar snap peas
Steamed basmati rice

Kebab Menu 4 *(page 218)*
serves 4
Chicken Shawarma
Chopped vegetable salad
Greek yogurt with honey and walnuts

Pasta Menu 1 *(page 274)*
serves 4
Fusilli with Pistachio Pesto
Garlic bread
Melon slices

Pasta Menu 2 *(page 275)*
serves 4
Cold Soba Noodles with Vietnamese Pork
Snow pea and carrot slaw
Coffee with sweetened condensed milk

Pasta Menu 3 *(page 275)*
serves 4
Cavatappi Niçoise
Herbed goat cheese toasts
Fresh berries

Dinner for Two Menu 1 *(page 302)*
serves 2
Thai Coconut Curry Shrimp
Sautéed snow peas
Hot cooked long-grain rice

Dinner for Two Menu 2 *(page 303)*
serves 2
Ziti with Spinach, Cherry Tomatoes, and Gorgonzola Sauce
Garlic breadsticks
Green salad

Dinner for Two Menu 3 *(page 303)*
serves 2
Quick Barbecue Chicken
Spicy corn on the cob
Coleslaw

Saucy Supper Menu 1 *(page 336)*
serves 4
Weeknight Coq au Vin
Egg noodles
Caramelized pears over vanilla ice cream

Saucy Supper Menu 2 *(page 337)*
serves 4
Lemongrass Pork
Soba noodles
Ginger-macadamia frozen yogurt

Simple Suppers

Hearty Homecoming Menu *(page 318)*
serves 8
Shaker Split Pea Soup
Grilled raclette sandwiches
Green salad

Easy Weeknight Meal Menu *(page 372)*
serves 4
Pork Tenderloin with Paprika Spice Rub
Spinach sauté
Egg noodles tossed with butter and chives

Hearty Stew Supper Menu *(page 372)*
serves 4
Sweet and Spicy Chicken and White Bean Stew
Pineapple-mango salad
Indian beer (such as Kingfisher)

Casual Entertaining

Dinner Day Menu *(page 41)*
serves 6
Edamole with crudités
Winter Minestrone
Bitter Greens Salad
Lemon Chicken with Ginger and Pine Nuts or
    Chile-Brined Roasted Pork Loin
Baked Pommes Frites or **Turnip-Gruyère Gratin**
Chardonnay
Apple Upside-Down Cake or **Butter Rum Pound Cake**
Coffee and tea

Blue-Plate Classic Menu *(page 141)*
serves 8
Marinated London Broil
Peas with shallots and bacon
Mashed potatoes

Ice Cream Social Menu *(page 153)*
serves 12
Honey-Lavender Ricotta Ice Cream
Chocolate Ice Cream
Key Lime Ice Cream
Classic Hot Fudge Sauce
Easy Raspberry Sauce
Oatmeal-Almond Lace Cookies
Shortbread
Lemon-Cornmeal Cookies
Iced tea or lemonade

Backyard Barbecue Menu *(page 167)*
serves 8
Spice-Rubbed Pork Tenderloin with Mustard
    Barbecue Sauce
Creamy coleslaw
16 dinner rolls

Soup and Sandwich Menu *(page 206)*
serves 6
Sweet Corn and Squash Soup
Tomato-goat cheese sandwich
Lemon sorbet

**Early-Fall Dinner Party
Menu** *(page 284)*
serves 10
Fig and Goat Cheese Bruschetta
Grilled Chicken and Pesto Farfalle
Chardonnay
Caramel-Apple Cheesecake
Coffee, tea

Chili Party Menu *(page 287)*
serves 6
Chipotle Black Bean Dip with Corn Chips
Pecorino and Romaine Salad with Garlicky Lemon
    Dressing
New Mexican Chile Verde
Spicy Jalapeño Corn Bread
Vanilla ice cream with **Mexican Chocolate Sauce**
Coffee

Walnut Harvest Menu *(page 294)*
serves 6
Savory Walnut Wafers
Mushroom Walnut Turnovers
Roast Chicken with Pears, Shallots, and Walnuts or
    Fruit and Walnut–Stuffed Pork Loin
Classic Walnut Boule
Walnut Rice
Haricots verts
Beet and Walnut Salad
Walnut Cake with Praline Frosting

Game Night Pizza Menu *(page 298)*
serves 8
Lima Bean Dip
Arugula Salad
Pizza Margherita
Sausage Pizza
Roasted Beet Pizza
Venezia Bianco
Chianti
Cinnamon-Ginger Cookies
Coffee, tea

Gracious Plenty Menu *(page 317)*
serves 8
Shaker Split Pea Soup
Herbed Roast Pork
Shaker Corn Bread
Green Beans with Savory
Easy Pickled Beets
Eldress Bertha's Applesauce
Autumn Apple Cake
Apple cider

Dinner with Friends Menu *(page 330)*
serves 6
Caramelized Shallots and Brussels Sprouts with
    Pancetta
Peppered filet mignon
Mashed Yukon gold potatoes

Cocktail Party Menu *(page 340)*
serves 10
Pink Grapefruit and Lychee Cocktail
Gingered Pear and Brandy Cocktail
Orange Chipotle-Spiced Pecan Mix
Traditional Hummus or variation
Spicy Baked Pita Chips
Shrimp Skewers with Coconut, Jalapeño, and
    Cilantro Dipping Sauce

Pasta Party Menu *(page 350)*
serves 10
Parmesan and Root Vegetable Lasagna
Winter greens salad
Garlic bread

Company's Coming Menu *(page 350)*
serves 4
Spinach Salad with Gorgonzola, Pistachios,
    and Pepper Jelly Vinaigrette
Maple-Sage Roasted Pork Tenderloin
Green Beans with Toasted Walnuts and Breadcrumbs
Couscous
Chocolate Butter Cake with Creamy Coconut Frosting

Special Occasion

Valentine's Dinner Menu *(page 44)*
serves 2
Onion Soup with Cheese Crostini
Spicy Grilled Shrimp over Shaved Fennel Slaw
Fennel and Rosemary–Crusted Roasted Rack of Lamb
Spicy-Sweet Pepper Medley
Truffled Polenta
Cinnamon-Orange Crème Brûlée

Easter Brunch Buffet Menu *(page 73)*
serves 12
White Sangria
Smoked Salmon Dip
Basil-Lime Fruit Salad
Brown Sugar and Spice-Crusted Ham or **Garlic-**
    Studded Rosemary Roast Rack of Lamb
Lemon-Chive Roasted Vegetables
Spotted Puppies
Easter Egg Cookies or **Ginger Angel Food Cake**
    with Coconut Frosting
Coffee or tea

Global Seder Menu *(page 111)*
serves 8
Chicken Soup with Matzo Balls
French Honey-Baked Chicken with Preserved Lemons
    or **Brisket with Olives and Preserved Lemons** or
    Persian Pomegranate-Walnut Chicken
Moroccan Tri-Color Pepper Salad
Quinoa Salad with Asparagus, Dates, and Orange
Sauvignon blanc (with chicken)
Rioja (with brisket)
Lemon-Almond Cake with Lemon Curd Filling or
    Chocolate-Pecan Macaroons
Coffee, tea

New England Fourth Menu (page 191)
serves 6

Littleneck Clams with Sausage
Peas and Pods
Steamed new potatoes with parsley
Grilled Salmon with Tangy Cucumber Sauce
Blueberry and Blackberry Galette with Cornmeal Crust

A Taste of the Midwest Menu (page 193)
serves 6

Marinated Green Bean and Potato Salad
High Plains Steaks
Dinner rolls
Cherry Crisp

Southwestern Celebration Menu (page 194)
serves 6

Chickpea Salad with Cilantro Dressing
Charred Corn Relish
Grilled Chicken Tostadas
Frozen Mint Margaritas

Thanksgiving Dinner Menu (page 344)
serves 12

Arugula Salad with Goat Cheese, Bacon, and Balsamic-Fig Dressing
Roast Turkey with Onion and Cranberry Chutney
Wild Rice Pilaf with Sausage, Shiitake Mushrooms, and Celery
Brussels Sprouts with Currants and Pine Nuts
Gratin of Cauliflower with Gruyère
Bakery Dinner Rolls
Pear Pie with Streusel Topping and Caramel Sauce
Beaujolais nouveau
Coffee

Festive Repast Menu (page 394)
serves 8

Champagne
Lobster-Tarragon Toasts
Oyster and Wild Rice Bisque
Nantucket Bay Scallops with Bay-Scented Butter
Beef Tenderloin with Port-Beach Plum Reduction
Colonial Corn Pudding
Eastham Turnip-Potato Gratin
Roasted Brussels Sprouts and Chestnuts
Fresh Thyme Popovers
Pinot noir
Ginger Pumpkin Cheesecake
Stone Fence

Réveillon Menu (page 386)
serves 8

Roasted Pheasant and Oyster Gumbo
Réveillon Salad
Laquered Flounder or Duck and Black-Eyed Pea Cassoulet
Lemon Chicken with Ginger and Pine Nuts or **Chile-Brined Roasted Pork Loin**
Toasted Pecan Wild Rice
Louisiana Citrus Crepes or **Eggnog Ice Cream**

Israeli Hanukkah Menu (page 397)
serves 8

Hummus with Preserved Lemon and Sun-Dried Tomatoes
Potato-Cilantro Tunisian Brik with Harissa
Winter Salad
Za'atar-Crusted Chicken Schnitzel
Riesling
Orange, Date, and Nut Cake
Coffee, tea

Jackson Hole Yuletide Dinner Menu (page 400)
serves 10

Goat Cheese-Stuffed Jalapeños with Ranchero Sauce
Whiskey-Marinated Tenderloins or **Chorizo-Stuffed Trout**
Sweet Onion Relish
Beans with Beef Jerky
Bacon-Chipotle Twice-Baked Potatoes or **Hominy Spoonbread**
Pinot noir
Cast-Iron Apple Cobbler
Cowboy Coffee Bar

Global Kitchen

Cuban Table Menu (page 36)
serves 8

Ropa Vieja
Grapefruit-avocado salad
Warm tortillas

Inspired by Italy Menu (page 53)
serves 4

Fennel-Rubbed Pork Tenderloin with Shallot-Onion Agrodolce
Pecorino polenta
Sautéed Broccolini

Asian Steak Dinner Menu (page 94)
serves 4

Flank Steak with Hot Peanut Sauce
Glazed baby bok choy
Steamed short-grain rice

Italian Fare Menu (page 102)
serves 6

Sautéed Chard with Pancetta
Gorgonzola polenta
Grilled pork chops

Indian Matchmaking Menu (page 142)
serves 4

Shrimp with Shallots and Curry Leaves
Mango salad
Coconut sorbet

Indian Idyll Menu (page 149)
serves 8

Tamarind Martinis
Indian-Spiced Roasted Nuts
Curried Rice Noodles in Lettuce Wraps or **Cumin-Scented Samosas with Mint Raita**
Chai-Brined Shrimp Skewers or **Grilled Tandoori Chicken**
Green Beans and Potatoes in Chunky Tomato Sauce
Toasted Eggplant Curry
Lime-Coconut Granita

World-Class Flavor Menu (page 157)
serves 4

Asian Caramelized Pineapple
Sesame noodles
Grilled pork chops

Far-Eastern Tastes Menu (page 168)
serves 6

Thai-Coconut Bouillabaisse
Mango and avocado salad
Baguette

Asian Sizzle Menu (page 205)
serves 4

Soy-Marinated Chicken Thighs
Grilled cucumber spears
Udon noodles with green onions

Every Night Korean Menu (page 240)
serves 4

Kimchi-Style Cabbage
Spice-rubbed flank steak
Steamed white rice

Simple Mexican Supper Menu (page 302)
serves 4

Black Bean–Tomato Soup with Cilantro-Lime Cream
Grilled chicken and cheese quesadillas
Margarita on the rocks

Island Fresh Menu (page 333)
serves 4

Grilled Chicken with Mango-Pineapple Salsa
Green rice
Plantain chips

Weeknight Italian Menu (page 412)
serves 4

Parmesan and Sage–Crusted Pork Chops
Creamy mascarpone polenta
Sautéed Swiss chard

Taste of Germany Menu (page 424)
serves 6

Bavarian Potato-Cucumber Salad
Cabbage sauté with carraway
Broiled turkey bratwurst or sausage

Recipe Title Index

An alphabetical listing of every recipe title that appeared in the magazine in 2008.
See page 449 for the General Recipe Index.

Month-by-Month Index

A month-by-month listing of every food story with recipe titles that appeared in the magazine in 2008. See page 449 for the General Recipe Index.

The *Cooking Light* Summer Cookbook

July

General Recipe Index

A listing by major ingredient and food category for every recipe that appeared in Cooking Light magazine in 2008.

449

NUTRITIONAL ANALYSIS

HOW TO USE IT AND WHY Glance at the end of any *Cooking Light* recipe, and you'll see how committed we are to helping you make the best of today's light cooking. With chefs, registered dietitians, home economists, and a computer system that analyzes every ingredient we use, *Cooking Light* gives you authoritative dietary detail like no other magazine. We go to such lengths so you can see how our recipes fit into your healthful eating plan. If you're trying to lose weight, the calorie and fat figures will probably help most. But if you're keeping a close eye on the sodium, cholesterol, and saturated fat in your diet, we provide those numbers, too. And because many women don't get enough iron or calcium, we can also help there, as well. Finally, there's a fiber analysis for those of us who don't get enough roughage.

Here's a helpful guide to put our nutrition analysis numbers into perspective. Remember, one size doesn't fit all, so take your lifestyle, age, and circumstances into consideration when determining your nutrition needs. For example, pregnant or breast-feeding women need more protein, calories, and calcium. And men older than 50 need 1,200mg of calcium daily, 200mg more than the amount recommended for younger men.

IN OUR NUTRITIONAL ANALYSIS, WE USE THESE ABBREVIATIONS:

sat	saturated fat	**CHOL**	cholesterol
mono	monounsaturated fat	**CALC**	calcium
poly	polyunsaturated fat	**g**	gram
CARB	carbohydrates	**mg**	milligram

Daily Nutrition Guide

	WOMEN AGES 25 TO 50	WOMEN OVER 50	MEN OVER 24
Calories	2,000	2,000 or less	2,700
Protein	50g	50g or less	63g
Fat	65g or less	65g or less	88g or less
Saturated Fat	20g or less	20g or less	27g or less
Carbohydrates	304g	304g	410g
Fiber	25g to 35g	25g to 35g	25g to 35g
Cholesterol	300mg or less	300mg or less	300mg or less
Iron	18mg	8mg	8mg
Sodium	2,300mg or less	1,500mg or less	2,300mg or less
Calcium	1,000mg	1,200mg	1,000mg

The nutritional values used in our calculations either come from The Food Processor, Version 7.5 (ESHA Research), or are provided by food manufacturers.

Credits

Contributing Recipe Developers and Writers:
Bruce Aidells
Darina Allen
Helene An
Karen Ansel, MS, RD
Linda Lau Anusasananan
Lidia Bastianich
John Besh
Brad Birky
David Bonom
Elisa Bosley
Mary Boswell
Warren Brown
Maureen Callahan, MS, RD
Penelope Casas
Maureen Clancy
Katherine Cobbs
Nathan Coulon
Laura Daily
Brooke Dojny

John T. Edge
Scott Fagin
Kathy Farrell-Kingsley
Shirley Fong-Torres
Laura Fraser
Betty Fussell
Elaine Glusac
Joyce Goldstein
Rachael Moeller Gorman
Jeff Gremillion
David Hagedorn
James Haller
Jaime Harder, MA, RD
Jim Harrison
Julie Hasson
Alyson Moreland Haynes
Joshua Haynes
Giuliano Hazan
Lia Huber
Lorrie Hulston

Raghavan Iyer
Patsy Jamieson
Bill Jamison
Cheryl Alters Jamison
Barbara Kafka
Wendy Kalen
Elizabeth Karmel
Jeanne Thiel Kelley
John Kessler
Maria Baez Kijac
Corby Kummer
Barbara Lauterbach
Karen Levin
Deborah Madison
Donata Maggipinto
Abby Mandel
Domenica Marchetti
Jennifer Martinkus
Dana McCauley
Kathryn McNulty
Tory McPhail
Jackie Mills, MS, RD
Paulette Mitchell

Diane Morgan
Joan Nathan
Micol Negrin
Kate Nelson
Cynthia Nicholson
Cynthia Nims
Megan Patterson, MS, RD
Marge Perry
James Peterson
Michelle Powers
Maria Ricapito
Victoria Abbott Riccardi
Eric Ripert
Marcus Samuelsson
Sharon Sanders
Suvir Saran
Mark Scarbrough
Andrew Schloss
Nina Simonds
Marcia Whyte Smart

Sally Squires
Lisë Stern
Billy Strynkowski
Kim Sunée
Laurent Tourondel
Corinne Trang
Bruce Weinstein
Joanne Weir
Chuck Williams
Melissa Williams
Mike Wilson
Joy E. Zacharia, RD
Laura Zapalowski

Wine Note Contributors:
Jeffery Lindenmuth
Karen MacNeil

Contributing Photo Stylists:
Melanie J. Clarke
Martha Condra

Lydia Degaris-Pursell
Francine Matalon-Degni
Katie Stoddard

Contributing Photographers:
Bill Bettencourt
Billy Brown
Eric Futran
Beau Gustafson
Lee Harrelson
Andrea Hillebrand
Kindra Clineff
Becky Luigart-Stayner
Douglas Merriam
Laura Moss
Howard L. Puckett
Melissa Springer